Human Development

TENTH EDITION

Thomas L. Crandell and
Corinne Haines Crandell
Broome Community College

James W. Vander Zanden
The Ohio State University

McGraw Hill

Connect
Learn
Succeed™

The McGraw·Hill Companies

Connect
Learn
Succeed™

Published by McGraw-Hill, an imprint of The McGraw-Hill Companies, Inc., 1221 Avenue of the Americas, New York, NY 10020. Copyright © 2012, 2009, 2007, 2003, 2000, 1997, 1993, 1989, 1978. All rights reserved. No part of this publication may be reproduced or distributed in any form or by any means, or stored in a database or retrieval system, without the prior written consent of The McGraw-Hill Companies, Inc., including, but not limited to, in any network or other electronic storage or transmission, or broadcast for distance learning.

This book is printed on acid-free paper.

1 2 3 4 5 6 7 8 9 0 DOW/DOW 1 0 9 8 7 6 5 4 3 2 1

ISBN: 978-0-07-353218-9
MHID: 0-07-353218-5

Sponsoring Editor: *Allison McNamara*
Marketing Manager: *Julia Larkin*
Developmental Editor: *Janice Wiggins-Clarke*
Production Editor: *Holly Irish*
Production Service: *Aaron Downey, Matrix Productions Inc.*
Manuscript Editor: *Connie Day*
Text Designer: *Glenda King*
Cover Designer: *Preston Thomas*
Photo Research: *David Tietz*
Buyer: *Tandra Jorgensen*
Media Project Manager: *Andrea Helmbolt*
Digital Product Manager: *Jay Gubernick*
Composition: *10/12 Stempel Garamond by MPS Limited, a Macmillan Company*
Printing: *45# New Era Matte Plus, R. R. Donnelley & Sons/Willard*

Vice President Editorial: *Michael Ryan*
Publisher: *Mike Sugarman*
Editorial Director: *William Glass*
Director of Development: *Lisa Pinto*

Cover: © David P. Hall/Corbis

Credits: The credits section for this book begins on page 719 and is considered an extension of the copyright page.

Library of Congress Cataloging-in-Publication Data

Crandell, Thomas L.
  Human development / Thomas L. Crandell and Corinne Haines Crandell, James W. Vander Zanden. — 10th ed.
    p. cm.
  ISBN 978-0-07-353218-9 — ISBN 978-0-07-131490-9
1. Developmental psychology—Textbooks. I. Crandell, Corinne Haines. II. Vander Zanden, James Wilfrid. III. Title.
  BF713.V36 2012
  155—dc23

                                                                              2011035420

www.mhhe.com

CONTENTS IN BRIEF

CONTENTS

PREFACE

TO PROVIDE YOU WITH THE MOST recent research findings in human development over the past three years, we have done an exhaustive search of the research literature across many disciplines to provide the most up-to-date, organized, and easy-to-read account of the overall organization and sequence of development across the life span. As with the past nine editions, we strive to continue our legacy as McGraw-Hill's premier multidisciplinary human development textbook by offering our readers a wide array of contexts in which to make sense of the complex nature of the human condition. Changing demographics, new biosocial technologies, increased plasticity within and between stages of development, the implications of fertility decline in Western societies, the lengthening of the life span, and the globalization of cultures require today's students to understand human development through an increasingly multicultural and multidisciplinary lens. In addition, the recent serious challenges posed by global economic decline, geopolitical unrest, and massive natural disasters in various countries contribute to our understanding of the resilience of the human condition.

While remaining committed to covering the subject matter comprehensively, we have shortened this revision by an equivalent of 20 pages. The text was written to hold students' interest and attention, and it can be used in a typical semester (14 to 15 weeks) for traditional classroom instruction, blended-instruction classes (some traditional and some online), and courses offered solely online.

Also, unlike many competing textbooks, the tenth edition of *Human Development* is not cluttered with visual features that undermine the reader's ability to distinguish the most important information, and the key relationships among ideas, from everything else on the page. Too often textbook pages are filled with large, distracting figures, multiple colors, and numerous photos that overwhelm the reader's short-term memory and create cognitive overload. Although they may look appealing in marketing brochures, such graphic devices as large photos, boxed inserts, multiple highlighting techniques, several competing colors, many key terms defined in the margins, and other misplaced pedagogical devices confuse the reader and make it difficult to focus on the information to be learned—*the content of the text itself.* Each page of the Crandell, Crandell, & Vander Zanden tenth edition is organized using in-text learning aids based on sound principles of human learning, information usability, and cognitive psychology.

You, the student, in reading this text, will soon come to realize that human development is emerging as a truly vibrant and relevant field for the twenty-first century—but every text is written from a unique perspective based on the professional backgrounds and life experiences of the authors. So, before you read about human development over the next several months, you may well ask, "What *are* the unique backgrounds of the authors of this text?"

Tom Crandell, an educational psychologist and psychology professor, and Corinne Crandell, an adjunct psychology instructor, continue to build on the foundation of James Vander Zanden's work. We teach developmental psychology classes, conduct research, write about human development, and actively reflect upon the stages of life across the life span. We bring to this text a wealth of knowledge blended with personal experience about the issues facing nuclear families, divorced and single parents, stepfamilies, families with children with special needs, Millennial cohabiting couples, families facing economic uncertainty, families supporting aging relatives, and families coping with the recent loss of a beloved parent and grandparent.

Our third child, Becky, our daughter/stepdaughter with Down syndrome, has particularly enriched our lives, and she and her friends and coworkers have made us more conscious of the complexity of human development. We are pleased to note that since (in the seventh edition of our text) we began providing information about the development of *all* individuals (including those differently abled), some other authors of books about life-span development have followed our lead. In our view, this only makes sense! Many of the clients and patients served in the psychology, education, health care, therapeutic, human services, and social services fields are "atypical" individuals who need professional guidance to achieve their full potential. Thus we continue, in this tenth edition, to include some information about the development of differently abled persons. Our other three adult children have been equally successful and are pursuing careers and/or raising our four grandchildren, who are a joy. At the same time, our mothers are in late adulthood and have needed increasing assistance. One of our mothers recently became seriously ill and passed away very quickly, after living a full, healthy life of nearly 97 years. We are left with countless memories and a deep appreciation for her lifetime of caring and love. The richness of life experience is truly coming full circle for us.

James Vander Zanden, sociologist and professor emeritus at Ohio State University and the author of this text for 20 years, wrote this book from the perspective of a man who endured abuse from an early age and subsequently had a troubled childhood and adolescence. He became intrigued by the study of human behavior, decided to make it his career, and dedicated himself to betterment of the human condition. Prior to writing the first edition of this text, James Vander Zanden lost his wife to illness, and he was left with the awesome responsibility of raising two young sons as a single parent. Leaving the academic environment for a few years, he began researching and writing *Human Development* and assumed the role of full-time parent to his children. His work in the area of human development over the life span helped him immensely in raising his sons. Both young men have earned Ph.D. degrees and are living happy, productive, and rewarding lives.

In U.S. contemporary life, about 5 percent of men in the United States are single parents, balancing the responsibilities of working and raising children. In a poignant revelation, James Vander Zanden admits difficulties "moving ahead" in his professional career during those child-raising years; his challenges were not unlike the obstacles faced by many employed women who, as either single or married mothers, are also devoted to parenting their children. Yet looking back, James Vander Zanden believes the rewards and satisfaction of parenthood were far greater than those found in academia.

Just as the birth of a new child in a family changes the entire family, so too does newer research about human development add to the expanding collection of classic theories about what is "normal" or what can be "expected" along the trajectory of human life stages. Students reading this text will learn that the study of human development has generated a diverse body of knowledge that incorporates a variety of views and theoretical approaches. Some theories address a single aspect of development, whereas others cover changes over the entire life span. Developmental psychologists are reaching out to other disciplines and embracing a multidisciplinary, collaborative approach that draws on concepts and contributions from anthropology, biology, sociology, social psychology, gender studies, medicine, social history, demography, criminology, and many other fields. Our cross-cultural knowledge base is expanding, and the Internet offers nearly instant access to published empirical findings from research conducted around the world. The result is that the field has much to offer humans in their global efforts to cope with serious social problems such as poverty, disease, and an ever-growing aging and ethnically diverse population.

Although developmentalists recognize individual variation due to genetic influences, they also study the environmental (social and ecological) context in which behavior occurs. Developmentalists are especially concerned with the far-reaching environmental effects of poverty on human development. To investigate contemporary concerns, they are placing greater reliance on time-extended research designs and are enlarging the breadth of their research objectives.

We hope that students who read this textbook will find answers to their questions about their own lives, much as we have done in our research and writing of this book. It is our earnest desire that courses in human development and developmental psychology help students move toward Abraham Maslow's ideal of becoming self-actualized men and women. They should acquire a new vision of the human experience, which can help them lead fuller, richer, and more productive lives. For readers who are or will be parents, another of our goals is to help you increase your understanding of the needs of growing children and improve your parenting skills.

We share the belief of many people that education is not the sum of 8, 12, 16, or more years of schooling. Instead, it is a lifelong habit, a striving for growth and wise living. Education is something we retain after we have put away our texts, recycled our lecture notes, and forgotten the minutiae we learned for an exam. Therefore, textbooks must present controversy and unanswered questions. Otherwise, students may come to believe that facts are the stuff of education, and they will derive a false sense of security from cramming their heads full of information rather than expanding their minds with thoughtful analysis. The essence of human development is real people living in a real world, and many of the special features in this tenth edition of *Human Development* offer students an opportunity to think critically about various developmental issues and how these issues are related to their personal lives—and to the lives of those they hope to assist in their professional careers.

To The Instructor

This text is not another human development book about the experience of only the "average" person. And it is not another book that skims the surface of cross-cultural research. Our text enables students to gain a good understanding of the issues surrounding the diverse population in the United States and other societies today so that they can formulate questions and pursue further learning that will enable them to become professionals of the twenty-first century. Thus, the past few editions have been used not only in U.S. colleges and universities but also in England, Canada, and (in translation) China.

Throughout this text, we look at populations at risk and consider how they experience development and why their experience is different. We explain how poverty, race-ethnicity, gender, age, and ability shape development and decision making. These are overarching issues that future service providers in the fields of psychology, education, health care, therapy, and human services need to understand if they are to provide effective interventions and support. We have also taken care to give your students a variety of examples of how developmental theory can be translated into applications useful in both their personal and their professional lives.

ORGANIZATION AND FOCUS OF THE TENTH EDITION

This textbook views human physical, cognitive, moral, emotional, and social growth as blending in an unending, dynamic process. In terms of its approach to the study of the life span, *Human Development* emphasizes development in context. This approach focuses on the development of people within families and the larger ecological-societal contexts implied by this theme. By examining the groundbreaking work of prominent developmentalists such as G. Stanley Hall, Alfred Binet, Lewis Terman, Jean Piaget, Erik Erikson, Urie Bronfenbrenner, Lev Vygotsky, Alfred Adler, Diana Baumrind, Dr. Benjamin Spock, Dr. T. Berry Brazelton, Andrew Meltzoff, K. Warner Schaie, Daniel Levinson, Bernice Neugarten, Paul and Margret Baltes, and Elisabeth Kübler-Ross, students will come to understand the complex network of developmental tasks that shape us as we move through the life span.

Much like the course of human life, this edition reflects both continuity and change. Like previous editions, the tenth edition of *Human Development* features a chronological approach to studying the life span and consists of 19 chapters. The first two chapters orient the student to the central research methods and the wide variety of theories applied in the study of human development. Chapter 3 examines beginnings: reproduction, heredity and genetics, and the prenatal period. Chapter 4 presents birth and the first two years of infant growth. Chapters 5 and 6 address the cognitive, language, emotional, and social development of the infant. From Chapter 7, "Early Childhood," to Chapter 18, "Late Adulthood," each stage of the life span is organized into two chapters: Physical, cognitive, and moral development are examined in the first of these two, and emotional and social development follow in the second chapter of each pair. Chapter 19 deals with end-of-life preparations, dying, death, and coping with grief and loss.

PEDAGOGY AND DESIGN OF THIS TEXT

We have provided readers with carefully prepared learning aids to help them identify, understand, and remember the most important information presented (both for evaluation on tests of the material and for application in the real world). These learning aids include **chapter previews, critical thinking questions,** within-text **review questions,** highlighting of **key terms,** end-of-**chapter summaries** of key concepts, and a **glossary** of terms at the end of the book. The design of the text has been updated for clarity of presentation to enhance student learning.

The **chapter preview** serves as an advance organizer—a cognitive bridge between the concepts learned in the previous chapter and the new concepts to be introduced in the current chapter. The **critical thinking questions** were devised to encourage students to challenge their own beliefs about critical issues of human development related to that chapter. The **in-text review questions** that appear at intervals serve as positive reinforcers and give students an opportunity to assess and review what they have just read.

Updated photo elements and graphics were carefully selected and strategically placed to pique and maintain the interest of learners. The section titled **Segue** at the end of each chapter helps readers review what they have just learned and relate it to the new information to follow in the next chapter. **Topical summary statements** provide an organizational framework to help students remember and integrate what they have learned. These summary statements can also be used by students who are "top-down" learners and prefer to look at an overview of the material before reading the specific content of the chapter. The **key terms** listing provide a concise review of the basic vocabulary to be learned in each chapter. The lists of relevant **Web sites** were carefully selected to enable the reader to follow up on issues of interest, discussion, or further research. The **chapter summaries** and the end-of-text **glossary** list key concepts and definitions for easy referral and serve as excellent review sources for students who are required to take comprehensive finals or state certification exams.

PRACTICAL AND INFORMATIVE BOXED MATERIAL

In an effort to highlight the most current issues in a comprehensive and accessible manner, three different kinds of boxes are carefully woven into the text narrative. The **More Information You Can Use** boxes offer practical information that can help students make better-informed decisions as they encounter real-life situations. **Further Developments** boxes take an in-depth look at specific issues across the life span. **Implications for Practice** boxes provide readers who are exploring careers in human development with helpful information furnished by professionals working in key occupations.

NEW TO THE TENTH EDITION

This edition has been significantly streamlined to make it easier to use as a learning tool for both classroom and online learners. The page count has been reduced by pruning outdated or repetitive information, and new research has been judiciously selected to ensure that students have the most current information on important developmental topics—without unnecessary statistical density.

We had several main objectives in revising the tenth edition:

1. To improve the readability of our textbook by streamlining all chapters. This edition has been reduced by an equivalent of 20 pages. We accomplished this without altering the warm and caring tone or the helpful themes for which our textbook is recognized.

2. To reduce statistical density, in order to promote ease of learning and comprehension of key concepts and facts.

3. To provide additional research on how gender, race-ethnicity, and social-economic circumstances affect development. For example, more studies on gay, lesbian, bisexual, and transgender issues across the life span are included.

4. To present students with the most up-to-date research in many domains of study across the human life span. Overall, this edition contains about 1,000 new references, including important research that examines development from both a multicultural and a multidisciplinary perspective.

5. To add new boxed topics that highlight important and interesting developmental issues. In addition, several **Implications for Practice** boxes provide information for students interested in pursuing some careers related to human development: genetic counselor, licensed certified social worker, speech-language pathologist, special education teacher, family nurse practitioner, occupational/physical therapist, and professor and gerontologist.

6. To introduce students to new information and strategies for managing many experiences and challenges that they will face across the life span—in their personal lives as well as in their professional roles.

THINKING CRITICALLY

As we have said, a course on human development should do more than lay out for students a body of scientific findings. Rote memorization of definitions and facts does not do justice to the dynamic nature of this subject matter. We must encourage students to think critically and creatively about their own development and how it is shaped by the world around them. This text will provide students with a deeper understanding of the human experience and the variety of factors that directly or indirectly mold their life course.

The challenging, real-life topics we discuss include research on the complex effects of immigration (Chapter 1); the emergence of the "young-old" and the "oldest-old" (Chapter 2); the newest assisted reproductive technologies, updated research on the Human Genome Project, and stem-cell research and human cloning (Chapter 3); the effects of poverty on preterm births and infancy by race-ethnicity, as well as various practices in labor and delivery (Chapter 4); differing theories of language acquisition, bilingualism, and effects of infant media viewing on cognitive and language outcomes (Chapter 5); current research on gay and lesbian parenting, child care across cultures, rising rates of autism, the effects of child maltreatment, and parenting practices that promote child well-being (Chapter 6); demographic trends and implications for children's health, (Chapter 7); health beliefs and practices across cultures; Muslim American cultural expectations; the influence of biology, brain, and hormones on gender behaviors; and parenting practices (Chapter 8); the latest statistics on child obesity and its implications, current research on ADHD and learning disabilities, and why Asian children strive for excellence (Chapter 9); children of "choice mothers" (Chapter 10); adolescent health-risk behaviors, including risk for HIV/AIDS; an assessment of how U.S. students compare academically with other students around the globe; and new research on the effects of father absence from the home (Chapter 11); the racial-ethnic socialization of teens, and statistics and outcomes of higher teen school dropout rates (Chapter 12); traits of the Millennial Generation, sexual health issues, and emerging adulthood as a new stage of development (Chapter 13); surviving the early years of marriage; how divorce affects successive generations; and young-adult lifestyle arrangements in Western cultures, including rising rates of cohabitation and decline of marriage (Chapter 14); the benefits and risks of popular diet programs in middle age, and the challenge of maintaining physical and cognitive health into old age (Chapter 15); factors promoting lifelong marriage, and stepfamily adaptations (Chapter 16); longer life expectancy across cultures, faith and well-being in late life, emergence of the oldest cohort as a political and social force in America, rising rates of Alzheimer's disease and latest research, and the debate between generations on Social Security and health care (Chapter 17); research findings on lesbian and gay elderly, cross-cultural approaches to providing for a rapidly increasing number of elders, policy issues in an aging society, faith and adjustment to aging, and grandparenting and great-grandparenting (Chapter 18); the right-to-die and hospice movements, the impact of religious beliefs, rituals that surround dying and death, and cross-cultural perspectives on dying and grief (Chapter 19).

COMMITMENT TO DIVERSITY

Past editions of *Human Development* have been lauded for their sensitivity and coverage of issues of race-ethnicity, class, gender, aging, and ability. The tenth edition continues this legacy by updating and integrating information on cross-cultural, minority, gender, and individual differences wherever possible. The tenth edition of *Human Development* reflects our attitude toward human diversity—this exciting aspect of U.S. culture is integrated into discussions in every chapter of the text, rather than separated out as boxed material. This edition considers the light that recent developmental research has shed on important issues for growing immigrant populations, including Hispanic Americans, Asian Americans, and Muslim Americans. Because more women than ever in Western cultures are bearing children in middle age and using fertility procedures to do so, the known risks are greater for pregnancies with multiple fetuses. Thus, the special needs and mandated services for children born with developmental differences are presented. This edition continues to address the development of lesbian, gay, bisexual, and transgender individuals from adolescence into late adulthood. And it explores the fact that nearly all societies of the world are creating policies to address the rapidly increasing elderly population.

Calling attention to emerging issues in human development is a crucial component of our task as teachers and authors. Specific examples of this approach include research on the complex effects of immigration in the United States (Chapter 1); the range of developmental theories across various domains of the life course (Chapter 2); the Human Genome Project and the trend of childbirth in midlife (Chapter 3); childbirth in America (Chapter 4); boosting babies' brain power (Chapter 5); the rising incidence of autism (Chapter 6); health beliefs and practices across cultures, including the use of video games with health benefits (Chapter 7); preparing children from widely diverse backgrounds for kindergarten (Chapter 8); educating students with differing abilities and cultural backgrounds, genius and giftedness, and bilingualism and ESL instruction (Chapter 9); services for children of veterans (Chapter 10); the rise in cosmetic surgery for teens, the continuing decline in teen pregnancy rates, and the increase in moral relativism among teens (Chapter 11); cultural aspects of adolescent identity formation; racial and ethnic socialization; sexual minority teens and transition to early adulthood; text messaging, "sext" messaging, and teens; and changing employment trends for teens (Chapter 12); emerging adulthood as a new stage of development, and coping with the long-term effects of child sexual abuse (Chapter 13); the increase in cohabitation and decline of marriage in Western cultures, the continuing rise in single parenthood across Western societies, same-sex relationships, lesbian and gay parenthood, and the diversity among the roles that fathers play and among the family structures found in U.S. households (Chapter 14); the impact of the large Baby Boom generation, the risks and benefits of hormone replacement therapy, the latest information for breast cancer survivors in Western countries, and the impact of the *Patient Protection and Affordable Care Act* for retirees (Chapter 15); the diversity of family households in middle age, unemployment and early retirement in middle age, the increasing numbers of elderly who continue working, and the increase of social networking in middle age (Chapter 16); the increasing use of telemedicine and telehealth among seniors, the challenges that women in particular face when they survive their spouse, the increasing rates of Alzheimer's disease, and the presence of ever more centenarians and supercentenarians (Chapter 17); the increasing numbers of minority elderly in the U.S. population; increasing rates of volunteerism among the elderly; older adults and online relationships; the social well-being of lesbian, gay, bisexual, and transgender elderly; the increasing numbers of grandparents raising grandchildren; and how faith contributes to well-being in late adulthood (Chapter 18); expansion of the hospice movement, the "end-of-life choice" (or "right-to-die") movement, who makes end-of-life decisions, and cross-cultural views of an afterlife (Chapter 19).

Expanded Coverage on Crucial Issues

In addition to including coverage of such topics as early intervention services for children born at risk (Chapter 7) and the latest research on results of longitudinal studies of the effects of divorce on future generations (Chapter 14), the tenth edition of *Human Development* is unrivaled in its detailed coverage of numerous critical issues. This unique quality is an outgrowth of our commitment to students' learning and overall breadth of knowledge.

We begin by addressing the changing conception of age and aging, including a focus on how "old age" has been redefined in the Western world (Chapter 1). Student concerns about relevancy are addressed in a box about how to put developmental theory to use in one's own life

(Chapter 2). Information on the Human Genome Project has been updated. Breakthroughs in infertility treatments and information on stem-cell research and human cloning are covered (Chapter 3). We have added information about how the effects of poverty on preterm births and infancy interact with the variable of race-ethnicity. Traditional cultural beliefs and practices in labor and delivery among various ethnic groups are discussed, as is the significance of early caregiver bonding within diverse family structures (Chapter 4). We describe the effects of video viewing on babies' cognitive and language development (Chapter 5). There is expanded coverage of raising a child with a pervasive developmental disorder such as autism or attention-deficit disorder, as well as understanding the needs of an intellectually gifted or talented child (Chapters 8 and 9).

The more recent research we have discussed in this edition of *Human Development* addresses such topics as emotional health and its relationship to cognitive growth and later job and life satisfaction (Chapters 6, 8, 16, and 18); gay and lesbian parenting (Chapter 5); early education practices in different cultures and the range of extensive services needed to educate an increasing number of children from diverse racial and ethnic backgrounds (Chapters 6, 7, and 9); and child-care practices across cultures and cross-cultural expectations for emotional-social development in early childhood. Information on the Individuals with Disabilities Education Act (IDEA) is updated with recent regulations for educating children with a learning disability or attention-deficit hyperactivity disorder (Chapter 9). The family continues to be a special focus, as we consider the influence of mothers and fathers, single parents, same-sex parents, and stepparents on children's emotional-social development (Chapter 10); adolescent substance abuse, sexual orientation and sexual behaviors, and increasing rates of teenage obesity.

Also discussed are the expanding social influence of teen networking sites, such as *Facebook* (Chapters 11 and 12); emerging adulthood as a new stage of development (Chapter 13); demographic differences among the present four generations of adults, lesbian and gay parenthood, and differing work experiences for men and women (Chapter 13). Americans' redefinition of middle age by maximizing physical abilities and staying healthy in midlife, reproduction after menopause, factors promoting lifelong marriage, and the increasing cohabitation rate among older adults are described (Chapters 15, 16, and 17). We also address the oldest American cohort as a political force and the longer lives that millions live, creating generational tensions (including the Social Security and health-care debates); the greater role played by faith and well-being in later life; the role of the elderly across cultures; and the trend of more grandparents raising their grandchildren (Chapters 17 and 18). In Chapter 17 the extension of life by many years (transhumanism) is introduced; personal choice, the right-to-die debate, and the hospice movement are discussed; and cross-cultural and religious views on coping with dying and death are summarized.

Positive Approach to Adulthood and Aging

The text features an extensive, candid discussion of the aging process, from young adulthood through late adulthood. Topics examined include the latest research and theories on biological aging, the longevity of a growing number of centenarians, methods of life extension, memory loss and cognitive functioning, programs for retired middle-aged and older adults, the special needs of lesbian and gay elderly, theories of adjustment to physical decline and loss of social relationships, sexuality in late adulthood, adult day care and various institutional arrangements, psychosocial changes and aging (including the use of online social networking), the role of faith for many who are aging, the psychosocial needs of widows and widowers, and planning for one's own end-of-life care and needs. Many of these issues on aging are presented from cross-cultural perspectives. At the suggestion of reviewers, we added a new section on various views of near-death experiences and an afterlife.

New Photo Program

In looking through this tenth edition, you will undoubtedly note the beauty and creativity of our updated photo program (which is more than 50 percent revised). The photos and illustrations in *Human Development* display our commitment to making concepts as clear as possible *and* to representing humanity in all its diversity. Sensitivity to race-ethnicity, gender, age, and ability (or disability) is significant, and this is reflected in the photos we have chosen for this edition.

New References

The tenth edition of *Human Development* is both a useful teaching tool and a resource of considerable depth for students and instructors. In each chapter, the citations to source material have been streamlined to allow for easier reading of the text. The more than 1,000 new references that have been added to this edition are strategically integrated throughout the text. Additionally, at the conclusion of each chapter, the reader is invited to explore up-to-date research findings and relevant professional organizations by visiting a number of Web sites on the Internet. These Web sites can be hot-linked through the McGraw-Hill Higher Education Online Learning Center at www.mhhe.com/crandell10.

SUPPLEMENTS

The supplements listed here may accompany the tenth edition of *Human Development*. Please contact your local McGraw-Hill representative for details concerning policies, prices, and availability, because some restrictions may apply. You can find your local representative by using the "Rep Locator" option at www.mhhe.com.

For Instructors

Instructor's Manual
Prepared by Craig Vivian
Monmouth College

This collection of resources includes tools to benefit any classroom, such as learning objectives, chapter summaries, lecture topics, classroom activities, student projects, updated and expanded video suggestions, and a list of Internet sites. The Instructor's Manual can be found in the **Instructor's Edition** section of this text's **Online Learning Center**, and instructors can gain access by a simple registration process by contacting your local McGraw-Hill representative.

Online Learning Center
(www.mhhe.com/crandell10)
The **Instructor's Edition** of this text's companion Web site includes the Instructor's Manual, the Test Bank, a full set of PowerPoint presentations, suggested web links to Internet resources from this text, and an Image Gallery of selected images and tables from the book. Access to the Instructor's Edition is password protected.

McGraw-Hill's Visual Assets Database (VAD) for Life-Span Development
Jasna Jovanovic
University of Illinois—Urbana-Champaign

McGraw-Hill's Visual Assets Database is a password-protected online database of hundreds of multimedia resources for use in classroom presentations, including original video clips, audio clips, photographs, and illustrations—all designed to bring concepts in human development to life. For information about this unique resource, contact your McGraw-Hill representative.

McGraw-Hill Contemporary Learning Series
Taking Sides: Clashing Views on Controversial Issues in Life-Span Development
In this debate-style reader, current controversial issues are presented in a format designed to stimulate student interest and develop critical thinking skills. Each issue is thoughtfully framed with an issue summary, an issue introduction, and a postscript. An instructor's manual with testing material is available for each volume. "*Taking Sides in the Classroom*" is also an excellent instructor resource with practical suggestions for incorporating this effective approach in the classroom. Each *Taking Sides* reader features an annotated listing of selected Web sites and is supported by our student Web site, www.mhcls.com.

Annual Editions: Human Development
This annually updated collection of articles covers topics related to the latest research and thinking in human development. These editions contain useful features, including a topic guide, an annotated table of contents, unit overviews, and a topical index. An instructor's guide, containing testing materials, is also available.

Notable Sources in Human Development
This resource is a collection of articles, book excerpts, and research studies that have shaped the study of human development and our contemporary understanding of it. The selections are organized around major areas of study within human development. Each selection is preceded by a headnote that establishes the relevance of the article or study and provides biographical information on the author.

For Students

Online Learning Center
(www.mhhe.com/crandell10)
The companion Web site for *Human Development*, Tenth Edition, offers an array of resources for students, including chapter outlines, learning objectives, links to Internet resources, and multiple-choice practice questions. Web access is easy and it is free for student use.

Text Availability in Digital Auditory Format
Students who need to rely on an oral/auditory version of this text can find the text as a digital file that can be downloaded through **Learning Ally** (formerly *Recording for Blind & Dyslexic*) website for a minimal fee at **www.learningally.org**. "Learning Ally offers Individual Membership for eligible people with visual impairments or dyslexia who experience difficulty in reading print material." Their audiobooks are also accessible for Apple Iphone, Ipad, and Ipod Touch. Our text is one of only a few covering life span development that are available in this important alternative format.

Multimedia Courseware for Child Development and Multimedia Courseware for Adult Development
Charlotte J. Patterson
University of Virginia

These interactive CD-ROMs include video footage of classic and contemporary experiments, detailed viewing guides, challenging previews, follow-up quizzes and interactive feedback, graphics, graduated developmental charts, a variety of hands-on projects, related Web sites, and navigation aids. The CD-ROMs are programmed in a modular format. Their content focuses on integrating digital media to better explain physical, cognitive, social, and emotional development throughout childhood, adolescence, and adulthood. They are compatible with both Macintosh and Windows computers.

ACKNOWLEDGMENTS

In truth, authors play but one part in the production of textbooks. Consider the thousands of researchers who have dedicated themselves to the scholarly investigation of human behavior and life-span development. Consider the labors of countless journal editors and reviewers who assist them in framing clear and accurately formatted reports of their empirical findings. And consider the enormous effort expended by the personnel of research-grant agencies and reviewers who seek to allocate scarce resources to the most promising studies. Indeed, a vast number of scholars across the generations have contributed to our contemporary reservoir of knowledge about human development.

Textbook authors simply seek to extract, from that reservoir, the knowledge most critical for student learners and to present it in a coherent and meaningful manner. A number of reviewers helped us shape the manuscript into its final form. They assessed its clarity of expression, technical accuracy, and thoroughness of coverage. Their help was invaluable, and we are deeply indebted to them. For the *Tenth Edition*, we extend thanks to

Carl Bryan, Central Carolina Community College

Kathryn Markell, Anoka-Ramsey Community College

Patricia Perez, Harold Washington College

William Price, North Country Community College

Julie Ramisch, Michigan State University

Jane Russell, Kentucky Community and Technical College, Hopkinsville

Kenneth Tercyakk, Georgetown University

Joan Thomas-Spiegel, Long Beach City College

Meeshay Williams-Wheeler, North Carolina A&T University

In addition, we have continued to build on the foundation provided by reviewers of the three previous editions. They are

Jerry J. Bigner, Colorado State University

Whitney Ann Brosi, Michigan State University

Stephen Burgess, Southwestern Oklahoma State University

Deborah Campbell, College of the Sequoias

Robin Campbell, Brevard Community College

Deborah M. Cox, Madisonville Community College

Rhoda Cummings, University of Nevada, Reno

Dana H. Davidson, University of Hawaii

Lilli Downes, Polk Community College

Scott R. Freeman, Valencia Community College

Karen L. Freiberg, University of Maryland-Baltimore County

William Fuller, Angelo State University

Jean Gerard, Bowling Green State University

Deborah T. Gold, Duke University Medical Center

Robert J. Griffore, Michigan State University

Patricia E. Guth, Westmoreland County Community College

Harry W. Hoemann, Bowling Green State University

Jean Hunt, Cumberland College

Russell A. Isabella, University of Utah

Jada D. Kearns, Valencia Community College

Michael S. Kelly, Henderson State University

Joyce Splann Krothe, Indiana University

Kathleen LaVoy, Seattle University

Patsy Lawson, Volunteer State University

Robert B. Lee, Fort Valley State University

Timothy Lehmann, Valencia Community College

Elizabeth A. Lemense, Western Kentucky University

Pamela A. Meinert, Kent State University

Linda W. Morse, Mississippi State University

Joyce Munsch, Texas Tech University

Ana Maria Myers, Polk Community College

Gail Overbey, Southeast Missouri State University

Lisa Pescara-Kovach, University of Toledo

James D. Rodgers, Hawkeye Community College

Robert F. Schultz, Fulton Montgomery Community College

George Scollin, Rivier College

Elliot M. Sharpe, Maryville University

Jack P. Shilkret, Anne Arundel Community College

Laurence Simon, Kingsborough Community College

Lynda Szymanski, College of St. Catherine

Joan Thomas-Spiegel, Los Angeles Harbor College

Robert S. Weisskirch, California State University Fullerton

Peggy Williams-Petersen, Germanna Community College

A very special thanks to researchers, authors, and professors of literature and creative writing at Broome Community College, Ellen Brandt, PhD., Mary Seel, PhD, and Christopher Origer, PhD. They contributed their expertise to many of these chapters. We particularly appreciate the up-to-date and relevant information in the fields of sociology, women's studies, and psychology that they brought to this edition. We also give credit to our colleague and friend, George Bieger, PhD, and professor of Educational Studies at Indiana University of Pennsylvania, who helped to update our sections on Research Methods. We are especially grateful for the contributions of a conscientious doctoral student in neuropsychology, Joshua Peck, Queens College, who helped us gather and organize information on prenatal development, brain development, and cognitive functioning across the life span. Ben Andrus, our dedicated research assistant and information resource specialist, was invaluable in providing us current empirical research findings on topics across the entire life span. His persistent efforts helped us secure the most current research articles available through the nation's interlibrary loan system. We are also grateful to Gilda Votra for her dedicated administrative assistance and keen attention to detail in updating the glossary and reorganizing the book's extensive list of nearly 3,000 references. JoAnn Barton, an extremely competent secretary in our Liberal Arts Division, is dependable and always came through with a smile. Our college's Copy Center professionals, Gary Hitchcock, Howard Nickerson, and Sandi Springstead, contributed to our ability to meet many deadlines and reminded us that laughter is still the best medicine.

We are indebted to everyone at McGraw-Hill who helped to produce this book and want to express special thanks to the following professionals in the domain of publishing: to Mike Sugarman, executive editor of Psychology, for supporting our work and our vision to make the tenth edition a human development text that will benefit learners in both their academic and their personal lives; to developmental editor Janice Wiggins-Clarke who provided guidance through the initial revision; to Aaron Downey, production manager at Matrix Productions, who kept the copyediting project on schedule and coordinated various aspects of production; to Holly Irish, project manager, for overseeing the project through the production process and keeping us on schedule; to Connie Day, a highly professional copyeditor who improved the quality of our manuscript; to photo researcher David Tietz who helped us manage an extensive photo revision in this edition; and to permissions editor Marty Moga, for securing the necessary permissions from a wide variety of authors and sources. This project has been a total team undertaking at all times. We sincerely appreciate the encouragement and enthusiasm each person brought to this undertaking and the professional competence each one exhibited in bringing the tenth edition of *Human Development* to completion.

Finally, we wish to acknowledge the many contributions of our parents. They raised us, provided us with a healthy upbringing, and encouraged and supported us— but three have now passed on to their heavenly reward. They had common sense, worked hard, and gave us the foundation to be healthy parents and grandparents to our own four children and four grandchildren. They also taught us, by guidance and example, how to cope with the developmental changes of our own journey through life with faith, humor, and a positive outlook. We lovingly dedicate this book to them.

Thomas L. Crandell, PhD

Corinne H. Crandell, MS

ABOUT THE AUTHORS

We bring an extensive blend of academic, professional, and personal experiences to this text on your behalf. We have been teaching students from the middle school, high school, community college, and graduate levels in a variety of professional capacities for more than 40 years. During this time, we have seen our student population become more diverse, composed of a blend of traditional and nontraditional learners from rural, urban, suburban, and distant cultures. As our student population began to include more adult learners and students with learning disabilities, we prepared ourselves to understand the individual learning needs of our students and improved our instruction.

Thomas L. Crandell   After earning a BA from King's College in Wilkes-Barre and an MA in counseling psychology from Scranton University, Tom taught a variety of undergraduate psychology courses at Broome Community College and worked in college admissions and then as a college counselor for several years. At age 34, he continued his formal education at Cornell University in pursuit of a PhD in psychology and education. While at Cornell, Tom received a research assistantship sponsored by the Office of Naval Research, and he subsequently helped to initiate and develop one of the most productive reading research programs in the country. His experimental findings on learning styles and instructional design have been adopted by researchers and practitioners worldwide. He first won international recognition when his doctoral dissertation was selected as one of the top five in the country by the International Reading Association.

Tom's focus as a college professor and educational psychologist has been on individual differences in learning and atypical development in children and adults. He takes great pride in a course on human exceptionalities that he developed and has taught to over 2,000 undergraduates. His students have become special education teachers, nurses, psychologists, sociologists, social workers, physical therapists, speech therapists, occupational therapists, recreation therapists, members of the clergy, managers of nonprofit agencies, and informed parents. Students often return to tell him that his course changed their entire career plan and how much they enjoy working with individuals in a wide array of jobs that necessitate a broad understanding of human development.

In addition to being a professor, Tom has been a consultant in educational, business, and legal settings for the past 40 years and has authored numerous articles on the design of online educational materials for ease of learning and ease of use. Many of these design strategies have been incorporated into the tenth edition of this text. In 1996 he earned the "Distinguished Article of the Year" award in the Frank R. Smith Competition held by the *Journal for the Society of Technical Communications*. In 2010, Tom was awarded the first *Outstanding Educator Award* from his alma mater, King's College in Wilkes-Barre, Pennsylvania. Tom has also coached youth basketball and soccer. He continues to teach adult religious education and volunteers in a local food pantry. He has maintained a healthy lifestyle, with a passion for basketball and golf, throughout his years of professional growth and development. He especially enjoys spending time with his grandchildren, pictured here.

Corinne Haines Crandell   In addition to earning a BS from the University at Albany and an MS in counseling and psychology from the State University of New York at Oneonta, Corinne has completed graduate studies in reading, special education, and learning disabilities. She has had a variety of instructional experiences at the community college level, teaching psychology classes for more than 20 years, and has also been a college counselor. She also co-authored developmental psychology study guides, instructor's manuals, and computerized study guides for more than 10 years. And in 1997 she developed the first distance-learning course in developmental psychology, which continues to be offered through the State University of New York (SUNY) Learning Network (SLN). She also supervised student interns in Broome Community College's human services program at nearly 40 social service agencies. For five years she taught in a middle school and worked with children with learning disabilities in grades 4 through 8. Additionally, she was coordinator of the gifted and talented program for a private school district comprising 12 schools. Corinne coached and judged in the regional Odyssey of the Mind program for several years, and for five years she was a board member at a local Association for Retarded Citizens, now called ACHIEVE. She continues to be a lector and teaches confirmation classes to high school students, and she especially enjoys being a grandmother.

THE STUDY OF HUMAN DEVELOPMENT

Researching the process of human development across cultures provides us with an opportunity to improve the human condition, as well as to acquire the knowledge we need to optimize life satisfaction. We therefore begin with an overview of how diverse social science and life science researchers (collectively known as developmentalists) approach the monumental task of studying humans over the course of the life span. Our discussion includes the goals of the scientific community, the recognized framework for studying the life span, what aspects of development warrant extensive examination, and what scientific methods are used to conduct research with humans. Chapter 2 discusses the main developmental theories over the past 100 years, when social scientists, biologists, and chemists focused on studying discrete aspects of human development. Earlier introspective methods of investigating subconscious experience and contemporary measurable evidence about microscopic genetic codes, neurons, and hormones all contribute to our understanding of the human condition. Contemporary researchers are focusing on how to integrate scientific findings and theory gleaned from numerous cultures into a more meaningful whole encompassing human development.

1 Introduction

Critical Thinking Questions

1. Developmental change takes place in three fundamental domains: physical, cognitive, and emotional-social. Which domain has been most important for your becoming who you are? Will any one of the domains become more important as you get older?

2. Make a list of three aspects of yourself that have changed over the last 10 years and three that have remained constant. How do you feel about both the "dynamic" and the "static" aspects of yourself?

3. If investigators had researched your personal development over time, where would they have noticed the most change? The least change? If they continued their research, where do you think they would probably see the most change, and where the least change, over the next 10 years?

4. If we could answer most of the important questions about human development by continuously studying 10 individuals who interact with each other from birth until death, would the knowledge gained from that study justify keeping them isolated from the rest of the world for their entire lives?

Outline

Development takes place in three essential areas: physical, cognitive, and emotional-social. In other words, you develop when your body, mind, spirit, and social relationships change. But many factors—institutions, society, family, and each person's nature—affect individuals and can help or hinder their personal development.

Over the last century, research on development has focused on several areas, including sensation, emotion, cognition, the self, behavior, thought, and genetics.

THE MAJOR CONCERNS OF SCIENCE

I believe that the extraordinary should be pursued. But extraordinary claims require extraordinary evidence.

—**Dr. Carl Sagan,** *American astronomer, astrophysicist, professor of critical thinking, and author*

This renowned scientist's thought captures the sense of wonder and inquisitiveness about nature that lies behind much contemporary interest in the study of human development. Human development consists of opposing processes of becoming someone different—while remaining in some respects the same person over an extended period of time.

Research is essential to understanding human development, and there are diverse methods for obtaining analyzable evidence. Expanding the field of study globally and disseminating valid research findings help to improve the quality of life over an ever-increasing human life span. As we strive to live with the highs and lows and the gains and losses that inevitably occur over a lifetime, we hope that, as we accumulate both knowledge and experience, we will be able to lead a more optimal life (Scheibe, Freund, & Baltes, 2007).

Continuity and Change in Development

To live is to change. Indeed, life is never static but always in flux. Nature has no fixed entities, only transition and transformation. According to modern physics—particularly quantum mechanics—the objects we normally see and feel consist of nothing more than patterns of energy that are forever moving and changing. From electrons to galaxies, from amoebas to humans, from families to societies, every phenomenon exists in a state of continual "becoming." The fertilized egg you developed from was smaller than the period at the end of this sentence. All of us undergo dramatic changes as we pass from the embryonic and fetal stages through infancy, childhood, adolescence, adulthood, and old age. We start small, grow up, and grow old, just as countless generations of our forebears have done.

Change occurs across many dimensions—biological, psychological, and emotional-social (Caspi & Shiner, 2006). Life-span perspectives on human development focus on long-term sequences and patterns of change in human behavior. Each perspective is unique in tracing the ways people develop and change across the life span (Scheibe et al., 2007).

Contradictory as it may seem, life also entails continuity. At age 70 we are in many ways the same persons we were at 5 or 25. Many aspects of our biological organism, our gender roles, and our thought processes carry across different life periods. Features of life that are relatively lasting and uninterrupted give us a sense of identity and stability over time. As a consequence of such continuities, most of us experience ourselves not as just so many disjointed bits and pieces but rather as wholes—larger, independent entities that possess a basic oneness—and much of the change in our lives is not accidental or haphazard.

The Study of Human Development

Scientists refer to the elements of change and constancy over the life span as development. **Development** is defined as the orderly and sequential changes that occur with the passage of time as an organism moves from conception to death. Development occurs through processes that are biologically programmed within the organism and processes of interaction with the environment that transform the organism.

Human development over the life span is a process of becoming something different, while remaining in some respects the same. Perhaps what is uniquely human is that we remain in an unending state of development. Life is always an unfinished business, and death is its only cessation.

Traditionally, life-span development has primarily been the province of psychologists. Most commonly the field is called developmental psychology or, if focused primarily on children, child development or child psychology. Psychology itself is often defined as the scientific study of behavior and mental processes. **Developmental psychology** is the branch of psychology that deals with how individuals change with time, while remaining in some respects the same. The field of life-span development has expanded to include not only infant, child, adolescent, and adult psychology but also biology, genetics, women's studies, medicine, sociology, gerontology, anthropology, and cross-cultural psychology. A multidisciplinary approach stimulates fresh perspectives and advances in knowledge.

The Goals of Developmental Psychologists

People actively shape and give direction to their own development (Riediger, Freund, & Baltes, 2005). Within the context of developmental theory across the life span, scientists focus on four major goals related to a continuum of optimization of functioning in the early years and compensation for losses with advancing years (Ebner, Freund, & Baltes, 2006):

1. *To describe changes that typically occur across the life span.* Social scientists describe the paths that young adults (ages 18 to 29) take as they move from parental homes. What percent go to work, enter college or military life, stay single or enter

cohabitation or married life, or withdraw into a subculture or prison?

2. *To explain these changes—to specify the determinants of developmental change.* What factors impact a young person's decision to leave home and establish a "new" life? How do peers, culture, economics, and religious affiliation, for example, influence the decision to follow a path of delay, leave-taking, or return (Arnett, 2007b)?

3. *To predict developmental changes.* What are the expected consequences of delayed leave-taking or frequent return to home on the young adult? And what is its impact on the parent(s) and society (Arnett, 2007b)? College graduates with high student loans and divorced or single young adults with children have higher return rates.

4. *To be able to use their knowledge to intervene in the course of events in order to control them.* Social scientists describe a "boomerang generation" made up of many in their twenties and older who leave home and later return to the support of the parental home—leading to a new stage of life in industrialized societies called "emerging adulthood" (Arnett, 2007b). See more on emerging adulthood in Chapter 14.

But even as scientists strive for knowledge and control, they must continually remind themselves of the ethical dangers described by eminent physicist J. Robert Oppenheimer (1955): "The acquisition of knowledge opens up the terrifying prospects of controlling what people do and how they feel." We return to the matter of ethical standards in scientific research later in this chapter. Be sure to keep in mind the four scientific goals—describing, explaining, predicting, and having the ability to control or manage developmental changes—as you examine the different domains and theories of human development in this book.

Questions

How is development defined? What are the four main goals of the study of human development?

A FRAMEWORK FOR STUDYING DEVELOPMENT

If we are to organize information about human development from a variety of perspectives, we need some sort of framework that is both meaningful and manageable. Studying human development involves considering many details simultaneously. A framework provides us with categories for bringing together bits of information

that we believe are related. *Categories* enable us to simplify and generalize large quantities of information by clustering certain components. A framework helps us find our way in an enormously complex and diverse field. One way to organize information about development is in terms of four basic categories:

- The major domains of development
- The processes of development
- The context of development
- The timing of developmental events

Let's look at each of these categories to see how they fit within a given framework.

The Major Domains of Development

Developmental change takes place in three fundamental domains: physical, cognitive, and emotional-social. Think how much you have changed in the years since you first entered school. Your body, the way you think, and how you interact with others are aspects of "you" that have undergone transformations and will continue to do so.

Physical development involves changes that occur in a person's body, including changes in weight and height; in the brain, heart, and other organ structures and processes; and in skeletal, muscular, and neurological features that affect motor skills. Consider, for instance, the physical changes that take place at adolescence, which together are called *puberty.* At puberty young people undergo revolutionary changes in growth and development. Adolescents catch up with adults in size and strength. Accompanying these changes is the rapid development of the reproductive system and attainment of reproductive capability—the ability to conceive children. Hormonal and brain changes are also occurring.

Historically, women have been valued for their reproductive ability. Some cultures continue to value—or devalue—women for their ability to produce sons as the father's heirs, and in some countries women are still the "property" of the husband (Moreau & Yousafzai, 2004).

Moreover, the concepts "woman" and "man" are social creations that little girls and boys try to fit as they grow up. Our efforts have biological and social consequences—how active we are, what we should weigh, what clothes we wear, what games we play, what and how much we eat, with whom we are allowed to socialize, what kinds of schools we go to (if we are permitted to do so), what work we do (solely in the home or outside of the home), and whether we are forced into marriage and childbearing at early ages. Until quite recently, women's biology has largely been described by physicians and scientists who were, for the most part, educated, economically privileged men; these men have had strong personal and political interests in describing women in ways that make it appear "natural" for women to play roles that are important for men's well-being.

At the turn of the 1900s, when American women tried to enroll in colleges, scientists originally claimed that women could not be educated because their brains were too small. As that claim became indefensible, they claimed that girls needed to devote energy to the proper functioning of their ovaries and womb—and that if they diverted this energy to their brains, their reproductive organs would shrivel, they would become sterile, and the human species would die out. Women who attempted to develop their intellectual capacities encountered obstacles and endured ridicule while paving the way for other women. The notion that women's reproductive organs need nurturing did not spare the working-class, poor, or ethnic-minority women who labored in the factories and homes of the upper class. A century later, American

Mary Whiton Calkins, 1863–1930, Early Developmentalist
Mary Calkins attended Smith College in 1880. In spite of not being permitted to register as a student, she trained at Harvard under the direction of William James, set up an experimental lab, and taught the first experimental psychology course at Wellesley College. Even though she wrote a scholarly thesis and sat for the Ph.D. exam at Harvard and performed brilliantly, she was denied the degree. As an early pioneer in human development, she published a text in introductory psychology, was elected in 1905 as the first female president of the American Psychological Association, and in 1918 became the first woman to be elected president of the American Philosophical Association.

women earn approximately half of all doctorates in psychology, they make up about 50 percent of new students at U.S. medical schools, and two women have recently been leading candidates for the U.S. presidency (Sherrod, 2006). More remarkably, in Afghanistan, after more than 5,000 years of strict patriarchal oppression, women are slowly emerging as legal citizens to exercise their human rights to education, health care, the franchise (the right to vote), and occupational pursuits (Armstrong, 2004).

Cognitive development involves changes that occur in mental activity, including changes in sensation, perception, memory, thought, reasoning, and language (Baltes, Reuter-Lorenz, & Rösler, 2006). Again consider adolescence. Young people gradually acquire several substantial intellectual capacities. Compared with children, for instance, adolescents more ably think about abstract concepts such as democracy, social justice, morality, and environmental sustainability. Young people become capable of dealing with hypothetical situations and achieve the ability to monitor and control their own mental experiences and thought processes. With advancing age, adults may or may not maximize resources to maintain, stabilize, or regain cognitive functioning (Ebner et al., 2006).

Emotional-social development includes changes in an individual's personality, emotions, and relationships with others (Egeland, 2007). All societies distinguish between individuals viewed as children and individuals regarded as adults, and our relationships with children are qualitatively different from the relationships we have with adults. Adolescence is a period of social redefinition in which young people undergo changes in their social roles and status. Contemporary society distinguishes between people who are "underage," or minors, and those who have reached the age of majority, or adults. Adults are permitted to drive cars, drink alcohol, serve in the military, and vote. How each of us becomes a unique adult can be seen as the result of interaction between the personal "self" and our social environment. As we will see in Chapter 11, some societies recognize adolescence or entry into adulthood through a special initiation ceremony—a rite of passage.

Although we differentiate among these domains of development, we do not want to lose sight of the unitary nature of the individual. Physical, cognitive, moral, and emotional-social factors are intertwined in every aspect of development. Scientists are increasingly aware that what happens in any one domain depends largely on what happens in the others (Sroufe, 2007).

Question

Historically, how has American society determined the norms (standards of behavior evident in the majority) for how females and males should behave, what they should do, and what they can become?

The Processes of Development

Development meets us at every turn. Infants are born. The jacket the 2-year-old wears in the spring is outgrown by winter. At puberty, youth exhibit a marked spurt in size and acquire various secondary sexual characteristics. Individuals commonly leave their parents' homes and set out on careers, establish families of their own, see their own children leave home, retire, and so on. The concepts of growth, maturation, and learning are important to our understanding of these events.

Growth takes place through metabolic processes from within. One of the most noticeable features of early development is the increase in size that occurs with age. The organism takes in a variety of substances, breaks them down into their chemical components, and then reassembles them into new materials to sustain life. Most organisms get larger as they become older. For some organisms, including humans, growth levels off as they approach sexual maturity. Others—many plant and fish forms—continue the growth process until they die.

Maturation consists of the more or less automatic unfolding of biological potential in a set, irreversible sequence. Both growth and maturation involve biological change. *Growth* is the increase in the number of an individual's cells, whereas *maturation* entails the development of the individual's organs and limbs in relation to their ability to function and reflects the unfolding of genetically prescribed, or "preprogrammed," patterns of behavior. Such changes are relatively independent of environmental events, as long as environmental conditions remain normal. As we will see in Chapter 4, an infant's motor development after birth follows a regular sequence—grasping, sitting, crawling, standing, and walking. Similarly, at about 10 to 14 years of age, puberty brings many changes, including ovulation in girls and sperm production in boys, providing the potential for reproduction.

Learning is the more or less permanent modification in behavior that results from the individual's experience in the environment. Learning occurs across the entire life span—in the family, among peers, at school, on the job, and in many other spheres. Learning differs from maturation in that maturation typically occurs without any specific experience or practice. Learning, however, depends on both growth and maturation, which underlie a person's readiness for certain kinds of activity, physical and mental. The ability to learn is clearly critical, for it allows each of us to adapt to changing environmental conditions. Hence, learning provides the important element of flexibility in behavior (Baltes et al., 2006).

As we will emphasize in this text, the biological forces of growth and maturation should not be contrasted with the environmental forces of learning. Too often the nature-nurture controversy is presented as a dichotomy—nature *or* nurture. Rather, it is the interaction between heredity and environment that gives an individual her or his unique characteristics (Grusec & Hastings, 2007). As we interact with the world about us—as we act upon, transform, and modify the world—we in turn are shaped and altered by the consequences of our actions (Kegan, 1988; Piaget, 1963; Vygotsky, 1978). We literally change ourselves through our actions.

As we pass through life, our biological organism is altered by dietary practices, activity level, alcohol and drug intake, smoking habits, illness, exposure to X rays and radiation, and so on. Furthermore, as many of us enter school, finish school, seek a job, marry, settle on a career, have children, become grandparents, and retire, we arrive at new conceptions of self. In these and many other ways, we are engaged in a lifelong process in which we are forged and shaped as we interact with our environment (Charles & Pasupathi, 2003). In brief, development occurs throughout our lifetime—in the prenatal period, infancy, childhood, adolescence, adulthood, and old age.

> *Questions*
>
> What should be considered a normal relationship among growth, maturation, and learning? For example, if the learning component develops quickly relative to the growth and maturation components, we would call the child "precocious." What might happen if a child matures too quickly?

Initiation Ceremonies and Religious Rites of Passage
Beginning around age 13, Jewish children are obligated to observe the holy commandments. The bar mitzvah, or bat mitzvah, is an optional initiation ceremony that formally marks that transition. Youths say the blessing in Hebrew or recite from the Torah as an indication that they are ready to assume the rights and responsibilities of an adult.

The Context of Development

To understand human development, we must consider the environmental context in which it occurs (Rathunde & Csikszentmihalyi, 2006). In his **ecological approach** to development, Urie Bronfenbrenner (1917–2005) (1979, 1986, 1997) asserts that the study of developmental influences must include the person's interaction with the environment, the person's changing physical and social settings, the relationship among those settings, and how the entire process is affected by the society in which the settings are embedded (Ceci, 2006). (See the *Further Developments* box, "Researching the Complex Effects of Immigration.")

Bronfenbrenner examines the *mutual* accommodations between the developing person and these changing contexts in terms of four levels of environmental influence: the microsystem, the mesosystem, the exosystem, and the macrosystem (see Figure 2.5 on page 49). Consider, for instance, Maria and Jami. Both are seventh-graders who live in a large U.S. city. In many ways their lives and surroundings seem similar. Yet they live in rather different worlds. Keep important differences in mind as you read their scenarios:

Maria   Maria is the oldest of three children. Her family immigrated to the United States when she was an infant. Both of her parents work outside the home at full-time jobs, but they are usually able to arrange their schedules so that one parent is home when the children return from school. Should the parents be delayed, the children know they are to go to a neighbor—a grandmotherly figure—to spend the afternoon. Maria often helps her mother or father prepare a dinner "just like we used to eat in Nicaragua." The family members who do not cook on a given evening are the ones who later clean up. Homework is taken seriously by Maria and her parents. The children are allowed to watch television each night, but only after they have completed their homework. Her parents encourage the children to speak Spanish at home but insist that they speak English outside the home. Maria is enthusiastic about her butterfly collection, and family members help her hunt butterflies on family outings. She is somewhat of a loner but has one very close friend.

Jami   Jami is 12 and lives with her parents and an older brother. Both of her parents have full-time jobs that require them to commute more than an hour each way. Chaos occurs on weekday mornings as the family members prepare to leave for school and work. Jami is on her own until her parents return home in the evening. Jami's parents have demanding work schedules, and one of them is usually working on the weekends. Her mother assumes responsibility for preparing a traditional evening meal, but fast food is starting to replace home-cooked meals on a regular basis. Jami's father does not do housework; when he is not working, he can be found with friends at a local bar.

Although Jami realizes that getting a good education is important, she has difficulty concentrating in school. She spends a good deal of time with her friends, all of whom enjoy riding the bus downtown to go to the movies. On these occasions they "hang out" and occasionally shoplift or smoke a little marijuana. Her parents disapprove of her friends, so Jami keeps her friends and her parents apart.

In Bronfenbrenner's model, the **microsystem** consists of the network of social relationships and the physical settings in which a person is involved each day. Maria's microsystem consists of her two siblings, mother, father, neighbor, peers, school, and so on. Likewise, Jami's microsystem consists of her parents, brother, friends, school, and so on. The **mesosystem** consists of the interrelationships among the various settings in which the developing person is immersed. Both Maria and Jami come from two-parent families in which both parents work. Yet their home environments have substantially different effects on their schooling. Maria's family setting is supportive of academic achievement. Without necessarily being aware of it, Maria's parents are employing a principle of the Russian educator A. S. Makarenko (1967), who was quite successful in working with wayward adolescents in the 1920s: "The maximum support with the maximum of challenge." Although Jami's parents also stress the importance of doing well at school, Jami is not experiencing the same gentle but firm push that encourages Maria to move on and develop into a capable young adult. Jami's family has dispensed with the amenities of family self-discipline in favor of whatever is easiest. Moreover, Jami is heavily dependent on peers, and such dependence is one of the strongest predictors of problem behavior in adolescence (Tolan, Gorman-Smith, & Henry, 2003).

An environment that is "external" to the developing person is called an exosystem. The **exosystem** consists of social structures that directly or indirectly affect a person's life: school, the world of work, mass media, government agencies, and various social networks. The development of children like Maria and Jami is influenced not only by what happens in their environments but also by what occurs in their parents' settings. Stress in the workplace often carries over to the home, where it has consequences for the parents' marriage. Children who feel rootless or caught in conflict at home find it difficult to pay attention in school. Like Jami, they often look to a group of peers with similar histories, who, having no welcoming place to go and little to do that challenges them, seek excitement on the streets. Despite encountering job stresses somewhat similar to those of Jami's parents, Maria's parents have made a deliberate effort to create arrangements that work against Maria's becoming alienated.

FURTHER DEVELOPMENTS

Researching the Complex Effects of Immigration

Many countries of the world are experiencing unprecedented migration, yet there is little research on migratory effects for either individuals or societies (Suárez-Orozco, 2007). The United States continues to be a nation of immigrants, and daily news reports highlight some aspect of public policy and immigration reform. Those of you who are reading this text and preparing for occupations of the twenty-first century will certainly be serving many students, clients, patients, and customers who were foreign-born.

Since the early 2000s, the number of immigrants living in the United States has risen by at least 16 percent (see Figure 1.1). "One in five children in the U.S. (over 14 million children) is either an immigrant or the child of an immigrant" (Dodge & Putallaz, 2007). Authorized foreign-born people arrive in several programs: (1) most through planned family reunification of immediate family members; (2) temporary worker programs (often as highly skilled engineers, doctors, nurses, and scientists, and some agricultural workers); or (3) humanitarian asylum programs for refugees. The majority of authorized immigrants come from Mexico, India, Taiwan, the Philippines, and Vietnam (Bornstein, Deater-Deckard, & Lansford, 2007). Of special concern are those immigrant families with children that are unauthorized and remain undocumented.

To date, there is little psychological, sociological, or medical research reported on the issues facing immigrant children and their families in modern American society. More social scientists, economists, public policy specialists, and legal and medical practitioners are beginning to use a variety of methods to collect scientific information that will contribute to interventions, policies, and solutions to

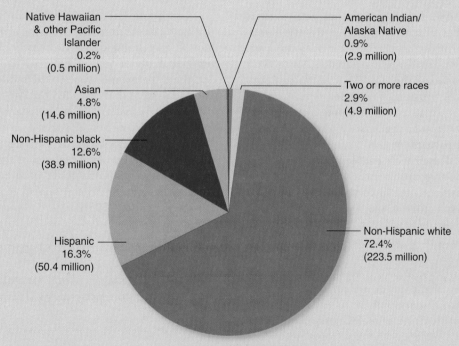

Total = 308.7 million

FIGURE 1.1 Distribution of U.S. Population by Race/Ethnicity: 2010 (by percent)
Numbering about 50 million, or more than 16 percent of the total population of the United States, Hispanics have become the largest U.S. minority group. Yet they emigrate from many countries and cultural subgroups of the Caribbean islands, Mexico, and Central and South America.
Source: U.S. Census Bureau, Population Division. (2011). Population distribution and change: 2000 to 2010. An overview: Race and Hispanic origin and the 2010 Census. Retrieved May 24, 2011, from http://2010.census.gov/2010census/data/

continued

improve the lives of all families. Certainly such migration to a new society leads to many assimilation/acculturation conflicts: using a new language, learning about a new culture while maintaining their own cultural identity, getting employed and earning sufficient income, living with disruption of family ties and roles, and navigating the educational, social service, civil, legal, and health-care systems of society (Bornstein et al., 2007).

Nearly all people who uproot their families and move to other regions of the world are enduring great hardship to improve the lives of their children. Those of you who become social scientists who examine the psychological, social, economic, legal, and religious factors that affect immigrant populations will certainly aid in transforming and improving our country and many others in the twenty-first century.

The **macrosystem** consists of the overarching cultural patterns of a society that are expressed in family, educational, economic, political, and religious institutions. We have seen how the world of work contributes to alienation in Jami's family. When we look to the broader societal context, we note that the United States is beginning to catch up with other industrialized nations in providing child-care services and other benefits designed to promote the well-being of families (see Chapters 6 and 8). But only some American parents enjoy such benefits as maternity and paternity leaves, flex time, job-sharing arrangements, and personal leave to care for sick children or ailing parents. Along with most U.S. families today, the families of Maria and Jami are experiencing the erosion of extended family, neighborhood, and other institutional support systems that in the past were central to the health and well-being of children and their parents.

The ecological approach enables us to view the developing person's environment as a nested arrangement of structures, each contained within the next. The most immediate structure is the setting in which the person currently carries out his or her daily activities; each ensuing structure is progressively more encompassing, until we reach the most inclusive, or societal, level (Shiraev & Levy, 2007). These dynamic interlocking structures challenge us to consider the risks and opportunities for development at each level. For instance, such problems as homelessness, child abuse and neglect, school violence, and psychopathology can be insightfully viewed as products of contextual factors that interact with individual and institutional vulnerabilities, particularly those of the family (Fiese & Spagnola, 2007).

The ecological approach enables us to see people actively immersed in a real world of everyday life. Imagine how much more extensive the information gathered would be if a researcher were allowed to record your day-to-day experiences, rather than just interviewing

you in a clinical setting. However, this seeming advantage is also the ecological approach's major disadvantage: We usually have enormous difficulty studying people in contexts where a great many factors are operating simultaneously. Because so many factors bear on a person, we find it impractical, indeed impossible, to take them all into account. Only when we control a large array of factors can we get a secure "fix" on any one of them.

Critiquing his own model, Bronfenbrenner recognized a need to incorporate an investigation of biological, psychological, and behavioral aspects of the individual under study. Further, he saw the need to add the dimension of time to the model and introduced another system that he called the **chronosystem**, showing that there is change and constancy not only in the individual person but in society as well. As he states, "Not only do persons in the same age group share a life history of common experience, but those of a given age in different generations could have quite diverse experiences, depending on the period in which they live" (Bronfenbrenner, 2005).

Question

Can you give examples of how each of the ecological systems is affecting the growing U.S. immigrant population?

The Timing of Developmental Events

Time plays an important role in development. Traditionally, the passage of time has been treated as synonymous with chronological age, emphasizing changes that occur within individuals as they grow older. More recently, social and behavioral scientists have broadened their focus. They consider changes that occur over time, not only within the person but also in the environment, and examine the dynamic relation between these two processes. Paul Baltes (1939–2006) and Margret Baltes (1939–1999) contributed to our understanding of these changes by identifying three sets of influences that mediate through the individual, acting and interacting to produce development (Baltes & Baltes, 1998; Baltes, Lindenberger, & Staudinger, 2006):

1. **Normative age-graded influences** have a strong relation to chronological age. Among youth in early adolescence, such as Maria and Jami, these influences include the physical, cognitive, and psychosocial changes discussed earlier. Maria and Jami are entering puberty, a condition associated with biological maturation. But they have also encountered age-graded social influences, such as the abrupt transition from a highly structured elementary school setting to a less structured and more complex middle school or junior high environment.

2. **Normative history-graded influences** involve historical factors. Although there is considerable cultural similarity among the members of a society, each age cohort is unique because it is exposed to a unique segment of history. An **age cohort** (also called a *birth cohort*) is a group of persons born in the same time interval. Because society changes over time, the members of different age cohorts age in different ways. Members of each new generation enter and leave childhood, adolescence, adulthood, and old age at a similar point in time, so they experience certain decisive economic, social, political, and military events at similar junctures. As a consequence of the unique events of the era in which they live out their lives—for instance, the Great Depression of the 1930s, World War II, the prosperity of the 1950s, the Vietnam War, the age of telecommunications, and September 11, 2001, and global terrorism— each generation fashions a somewhat unique style of thought and life.

3. **Nonnormative life events** involve unique turning points at which people change some direction in their lives. A person might suffer severe injury in an accident or a combat situation, experience a natural catastrophe, win millions in a lottery, undergo a religious conversion, give birth to multiples of children at one time, secure a divorce, or set out on a new career at midlife or later. Nonnormative influences do not impinge on everyone, nor do they necessarily occur in easily discernible sequences or patterns. Although these determinants have significance for individual life histories, the determinants are not closely associated with either age or history.

Not surprisingly, each age cohort of U.S. youth over the past 80 years has acquired a somewhat different popular image, and each generation confronted an environment different from that faced by earlier generations (Schaie, 2007) (see Table 1.1). Awareness of a person's age cohort can help psychologists, social workers, and other human service workers to assess the worldviews and particular needs of that individual.

History-graded influences do not operate only in one direction. Consider age cohorts. They are not simply acted on by social and historical forces. Because people of different cohorts age in distinct ways, they contribute to changes in society and alter history's course. As society moves through time, statuses and roles change. The flow of new generations results in some loss to the cultural inventory, a reevaluation of its components, and the introduction of new elements.

In particular, although parental generations play a crucial part in predisposing their offspring to specific values and behaviors, new generations are not necessarily bound to replicate their elders' views and perspectives. These observations call our attention to the important part that cultural and historical factors play in development. What is true in the United States and other Western societies is not necessarily true in other parts of the world. And what is true for the first decade of the 2000s might not have been true in the 1960s or the 1770s. Accordingly, if social and behavioral scientists wish to determine whether their findings hold in general for human behavior, they must look to other societies and historical periods to test their ideas. Examining behavior from a cross-cultural perspective is a more common approach in psychological research today (Kağitçibaşi, 2007). Technological developments in the twenty-first century should aid researchers as they continue to explore human development from a worldwide perspective.

Questions

Look at the pictures in Table 1.1, "Generations," and imagine what the members of each age cohort thought about the times they were living in. What impression do you have of each era from witnessing it through media such as movies, music, and literature? Is it difficult to understand the experiences of another age cohort?

TABLE 1.1 Generations

Social demographers suggest that each age cohort consists of people who are born during the same era of history and thus experience the same historical, global, and social events; form similar attitudes and values; share common tastes (as in clothing, hairstyles, music, entertainment), and go through the same defining moments (such as wars or natural disasters).

Age Cohort	History-Graded Event	Demographics	General Traits
b. 1925–1945 Silent Generation		Ages 67 to 87	Lived through the Great Depression years after the stock market crash of 1929 and World War II. Hoboes, soup kitchens, and shelters were common in the U.S. They are hard-working, economically conservative, and have strong values. A college education was considered a privilege, and ensuring that their children could attend college was essential. An increasing percentage are raising their grandchildren or are more involved in their grandchildren's lives.
b. 1946–1964 Baby Boom or Boomers		About 78 million people, ages 48 to 66; by 2030, will surge to 20 percent of the U.S. population	More likely to plan or delay parenting until having achieved their own personal, educational, and professional goals. More women of this generation began to get college degrees. Grew up during the era of "Rock 'n' Roll." Now "sandwiched" between elderly parents and their Millennial children. More involved in the education of their children, and more protective than any other generation. In the late 1960s, this cohort of college students protested against war, curfews, and dress codes, gaining more independence and self-governance. Boomers have redefined each life stage they have passed through and are likely to revise views of aging and retirement.
b. 1965–1980 Generation X, Gen Xers; also called "baby busters"		About 60 million, ages 32 to 47	More likely to be raised in day care and were set aside to allow parents to complete their goals. Often considered to be at risk, neglected, aggressive, complainers, self-oriented, slackers, and alienated. Grew up with fewer societal standards amid political, social, economic, and cultural changes, including the emergence of computer technology and the Internet. Many were likely to return to parental homes after college to get established and pay back college loans. More likely to cohabit and marry later, if at all.
b. Early 1980s– early 2000s Millennials; also called Echo Boomers, and Generation Y		More diverse racial and ethnic groups, ranging from about 78 to 80 million (1/3 of the American population), ages 12 to 31	Likely to be first in their family to go to college; described as sheltered, confident, team-oriented, achieving, pressured, and conventional. Tend to respect elders, follow rules, and create positive changes through community service. The most cared for and protected children in U.S. history who have had highly structured childhoods. Tend to come from small families. Demonstrate more traditional values and a return to strong family attachments. Social problems for teens have declined. Higher rates of high school graduation and college attendance. Have technical savvy using wireless Internet, instant messaging, social networks, Twitter, cell phones, video games, iPods, debit cards, ATMs, online banking, etc.

Source: Adapted from Donovan, J. (2002–2003). Changing demographics and generational shifts: Understanding and working with the families of today's college students. *Student Affairs in Higher Education,* 12. Retrieved October 17, 2004 from http://www.sahe.colostate.edu/journal_archive.asp

Nonnormative Life Events Some people experience a life event that creates a unique turning point or challenge in their lives. What makes these kinds of events so challenging?

PARTITIONING THE LIFE SPAN: CULTURAL AND HISTORICAL PERSPECTIVES

The Age-Old Question: Who Am I?

Because nature bestows on everyone a biological cycle that begins with conception and continues through old age and death, all societies must deal with the *life cycle*. Age is a major dimension of social organization.

For instance, all societies use age to allow or disallow benefits, activities, and endeavors. People are assigned roles in a manner that bears little relation to their unique abilities or qualities. Like one's sex, age is a master status, which governs entry to many other statuses and makes its own distinct imprint on them. Within the United States, for instance, age operates *directly* as a criterion for driving a car without supervision (recently, many states have raised the age at which this privilege is conferred from 16 to 18 years), voting (age 18), becoming president (age 35), and receiving Social Security retirement benefits (age 62). Age also operates *indirectly* as a criterion for certain roles through its linkage with other factors. For example, age linked with reproductive capacity limits entry into the parental role. Age linked with 12 years of elementary and secondary school usually permits entry into college.

Because age is a *master status,* a change in chronological age accompanies most changes in role over a person's life span—entering school, completing school, getting one's first job, marrying, having children, being promoted at work, seeing one's youngest child marry, becoming a grandparent, retiring, and so on. Recent generations have reversed the order of some of these milestones, by having babies before marriage, for example, or by cohabiting and perhaps never marrying at all. Age

is a critical dimension by which individuals locate themselves within society and in turn are located by others (Settersten, Furstenberg, & Rumbaut, 2005).

Age functions as a reference point that enables people to orient themselves in terms of *what* or *where* they are within various social networks, such as the family, the school, the church, and the world of work. It is one ingredient that provides people with the answer to the question "Who am I?" In brief, it helps people establish their identities.

Cultural Variability

The part that *social definitions* play in dividing the life cycle is highlighted when we compare the cultural practices of different societies. **Culture** is the social heritage of a people—those learned patterns of thinking, feeling, and acting that are transmitted from one generation to the next. Upon the organic age grid, societies weave varying social arrangements. A 14-year-old girl might be expecting to be a junior high school student in one culture, a mother of two children in another; a 45-year-old man might be at the peak of a business career, still moving up in a political career, or retired from a career in major league baseball—or dead and worshipped as an ancestor in some other society. All societies divide biological time into socially relevant units; and although birth, puberty, and death are biological facts of life, *society* gives each its distinctive meaning and assigns each its social consequences (Kağitçibaşi, 2007).

Viewed this way, all societies are divided into **age strata**—social layers based on time periods in life. Age strata organize people in society in much the same way that the earth's crust is organized by stratified geological layers. Grouping by age strata has certain similarities to class stratification. Both involve the differentiation and ranking of people as superior or inferior, higher or lower. But unlike movement up or down the class ladder, the mobility of individuals through the age strata is not dependent on motivational and recruitment factors. Mobility from one age stratum to the next is largely biologically determined and irreversible.

People's behavior within various age strata is regulated by **social norms**—expectations that specify what constitutes appropriate and inappropriate behavior for individuals at various periods in the life span. In some cases, an informal consensus provides the standards by which people judge each other's behavior. Hence, the notion that you ought to "act your age" pervades many spheres of life. Within the United States, for instance, it is thought that a child of 6 is "too young" to baby-sit for other youngsters. By the same token, a man of 60 is thought to be "too old" to "party." In other cases, laws set floors and ceilings in various institutional spheres. For instance, there are laws regarding marriage without parental consent, entry into the labor force, and eligibility for Social Security and Medicare benefits. We need only think of such terms as *childish, juvenile, youth culture, adolescence, senior citizen,* and *the generation gap* to be aware of the potency of age in determining expectations about behavior in our own society. Indeed, we even find apartment dwellings reserved exclusively for a particular age group, such as young singles, and communities designed for a particular age group, such as retired people.

Changing Conceptions of Age

In the United States we commonly think of the life span in terms of prenatal development, infancy, childhood, adolescence, adulthood, middle age, and old age. Yet the French historian Philippe Ariès (1962) said that in the Middle Ages, the concept of childhood was not defined as we know it today. Children were regarded as small adults. Child rearing meant little more than allowing children to participate in adult affairs. Only around the year 1600 did a new concept of childhood emerge.

The past 200 years have witnessed still another revolutionary change in children's lives. School enrollments have risen sharply to the highest level of all time (Snyder & Dillow, 2011). School enrollment today is nearly 100 percent of the child population, aged 5 through 16, because of compulsory attendance requirements. In 2010 more than one-fourth of the U.S. population, or 76 million people, were enrolled in an educational setting from elementary school through college (Snyder & Dillow, 2011) (see Figure 1.2). As children have come to spend larger portions of the year in formal educational settings, they have less time at home with their parents and siblings. Additionally, as more mothers have entered the paid labor force, more younger children have come to spend substantial portions of their nonweekend days in day-care centers and preschools (see Figure 1.2). The

motivating force underlying these major social changes has been parents' desire to improve their family's social and economic status (Acs & Nelson, 2002).

The notion of adolescence is even more recent, dating from the nineteenth and early twentieth centuries in the United States as a consequence of compulsory school legislation, child labor laws, and special legal procedures for "juveniles," including additional educational opportunities through high school that made a social fact of adolescence. Now an additional new stage, **emerging adulthood** (see Chapter 13), is evolving between adolescence and adulthood (Arnett, 2000). Recent developments—rising prosperity in the 1990s followed by economic downturn in the early 2000s, the increase in educational level, and the enormously high educational demands of a postindustrial society—have prolonged the transition to adulthood (Settersten et al., 2005).

The notion of "old age" has also undergone change in the Western world. Whereas Renaissance men were already considered "old" in their forties, today many men in their forties are likely to be considered young to middle-age. Currently, another division is emerging, one between "young-old" and "old-old" (Ebner et al., 2006). The young-old are viewed as enjoying a postretirement period of physical vigor, leisure time, and new opportunities for community service and self-fulfillment. And even the old-old are viewed differently: In the past, the old-old were seen as an elderly minority in need of special care and support (Neugarten, 1982a, 1982b). Whereas the first scientific studies looking at aging used subjects aged 60 to 70, today's researchers are increasing our knowledge of aging in persons over 70, because in industrialized countries there is a growing population of seniors living into their eighties and well beyond.

These emerging distinctions tend to blur many of our assumptions regarding people's rights and responsibilities with respect to social age. All across adulthood, age has increasingly become a poor predictor of the timing of major

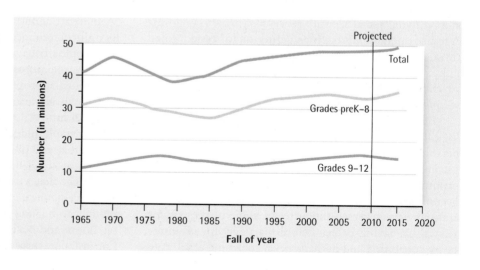

FIGURE 1.2 Public Elementary and Secondary School Enrollment in Prekindergarten Through Grade 12 by Grade Level with Projections: Fall 1965–2019 The recent growth in U.S. school enrollment is driven by the number of babies born during 1981–1994, when births increased to about 4 million annually, and is increased by immigration. What is the projected trend? *Source:* Snyder, T. D., & Dillow, S. A. (2011). *Digest of Education Statistics: 2010.* Washington, D.C.: National Center for Education Statistics. Table 3. Enrollment in educational institutions, by level and control of institution: Selected years, 1969–70 through fall 2019. Retrieved from http://nces.ed.gov/pubs2011/2011015.pdf

TABLE 1.2 The Changing Nature of U.S. Families: 1900–2010

Variable	1900	1950	2010 (unless noted)
Average household size (persons)	4.8	3.4	2.59
Households with 7 or more people (percent)	20.4	4.9	1.8
Living arrangements of children by family status (percent)			
Two-parent farm family	41	17	2 2007
Two-parent nonfarm family	45	79	64 2007
Father breadwinner, mother homemaker	43	56	23
Dual earner	2	13	60 2007
Single parent	9	6	26.5
Median age at first marriage (years)			
Men	26	23	28
Women	22	20	26
Life expectancy at birth (years)			
Males	46	65	75.3 2008
Females	48	71	80.3 2008
Infant mortality rate (deaths per 1,000 births)	100	29	6.5
Age 65 and older (percent)	4	8	12.9 2009
Total fertility rate (children born over woman's lifetime)	3.6	3.1	2.1

Source: Kaya, B. (2010, November 10). U.S. Census Bureau reports men and women wait longer to marry. [Press release.] Retrieved May 23, 2011, from http://www.census.gov/newsroom/releases/archives/families_households/cb10-174.html. U.S. Census Bureau, Housing and Household Economic Statistics Division, Fertility & Family Statistics Branch. (2011). America's Families and Living Arrangements: 2010. Retrieved May 23, 2011, from http://www.census.gov/population/www/socdemo/hh-fam/cps2010.html. Miniño, A. M., Xu, J., & Kochanek, K. D. (2010, December 9). Deaths: Preliminary data for 2008. *National Vital Statistics Reports,* 59(2), 1–72. Retrieved May 23, 2011, from http://www.cdc.gov/nchs/data/nvsr/nvsr59/nvsr59_02.pdf

life events, such as changes in health, work status, family status, interests, and needs (see Table 1.2). As Bernice L. Neugarten and Dail A. Neugarten (1987) observe, "We have conflicting images rather than stereotypes of age: the 70-year-old in a wheelchair, but also the 70-year-old on the tennis court; the 18-year-old who is married and supporting a family, but also the 18-year-old college student who brings his laundry home to his mother each week" (pp. 30–32).

However, even though some timetables are losing their significance, others are becoming more compelling. Many young people may feel like failures if they have not "made it" in corporate life by age 35. A young woman who has delayed marriage because of her career may feel under enormous pressure to marry and bear a child upon approaching her mid- to late thirties—and older. Historical definitions of *social age,* then, influence the standards we use in giving meaning to the life course and in contemplating the time past and the time remaining.

> **Questions**
>
> How does age traditionally factor into the social network of a society? In what way is the notion of becoming an "adult" changing in American culture? What about your idea of what typifies a "senior citizen"?

THE NATURE OF DEVELOPMENTAL RESEARCH

The task of science is to make the world intelligible to us. Albert Einstein once observed that "the whole of science is nothing more than a refinement of everyday thinking." So we do scientific research in much the same way that we ask questions and come to conclusions in our everyday lives. We make guesses and mistakes; we argue our conclusions with one another; we try out our ideas to see what fits, and we get rid of what doesn't. There is one important way in which scientific inquiry differs from ordinary inquiry: It specifies a systematic and formal process for gathering facts and searching for a logical explanation of them (Graziano & Rualin, 2007). This process, called the **scientific method,** is a series of steps that enable us to be clear about what we studied, how we studied it, and what our conclusions were. Sufficient detail must be given to allow others to replicate our research and verify our conclusions. These steps of the scientific method provide a framework for objective inquiry: (1) select a researchable problem; (2) formulate a **hypothesis**—a tentative proposition that can be tested; (3) test the hypothesis; (4) draw conclusions about the hypothesis; and (5) make the findings of the study available to the scientific community.

How do we use this method to help us understand and explain human development? First, let's consider some questions we might ask about development: Are there certain measurable factors in childhood that are predictive of success in different areas of adult life? Which children are more prone to violence, and what can be done to teach these children self-control and conflict resolution techniques? Who is likely to be affected by anorexia, and what steps can we take to save this person's life? Does everyone's memory decline with age? What aspects of personality and social competency are related to longevity? Are there peaks in the frequency of sexual activity for men and women, or does it generally increase or decrease with age? It is easy to choose any one of these questions and come up with a researchable problem. Perhaps through your reading and life experience you could suggest a hypothesis—a proposition that can be tested scientifically—that might answer one of these questions. Next you need to test your hypothesis. To do that requires choosing a *research design* that will provide valid (accurate) and reliable (consistent) information to support or reject your hypothesis.

Research Design

In developmental psychology, research focuses on change that occurs over time or with age. Three basic kinds of designs are used: (1) longitudinal, (2) cross-sectional, and (3) sequential. Each of these designs is of interest for answering scientific questions in the developmental sciences (Schaie, 2007). Experimental designs, although powerful, are seldom used in developmental studies because usually it is not possible to exercise the control necessary for experimental design. Interesting variables such as spatial ability, memory, and physical characteristics cannot be assigned to groups of individuals or manipulated in terms of quantity or quality presented. Other methods used in developmental research include case studies, observational methods, surveys, and cross-cultural studies (see Table 1.3).

Throughout our discussion of various research designs, you will see examples of how a developmental researcher might explore the relationship between lifestyle practices and health and fitness status over time. So what exactly are we studying?

We have known for decades that certain lifestyle choices promote health and fitness, whereas other choices lead to poor health and a tendency toward disease. For example, healthy eating habits that limit fried foods and foods that are high in sugar and fats lead to improved health and lower risk of many diseases. Similarly, regular exercise promotes better health and increases both longevity and quality of life. On the other hand, certain practices (such as smoking and excessive use of alcohol) have been linked to greater risk of many diseases and have been shown to shorten life expectancy and decrease the quality of life of people who engage in those practices. How did scientists come to learn about the developmental effects of lifestyle choices on health and fitness?

There are several research strategies that can be used to study the relationship between lifestyle practices and health. These strategies, or research designs, will be discussed in the following sections. They include the longitudinal design, the cross-sectional design, and the sequential design.

The Longitudinal Design

The **longitudinal design** is used to study the same individuals at different points in their lives. We can then compare the group at these regular intervals and describe their behavior and characteristics of interest. This method allows us to look at change sequentially and offers insight into why people turn out similarly or differently in adulthood.

TABLE 1.3 Research Designs

Type of Research	Advantages	Disadvantages
Longitudinal—*studies the same individual at different points in his or her life*	Enables researchers to describe change sequentially and offers insight into why people turn out similarly or differently in adulthood	Cannot control for nonnormative events Selective attrition Time-consuming and costly Testing and tester consistency
Cross-sectional—*compares different groups of people of different ages at the same point in time*	Less costly and time-consuming than longitudinal studies	Confounding of age and cohort
Sequential—*measures more than one age cohort over time*	Overcomes the problem of confounding age and cohort	Costly and complex to plan and analyze over time
Experimental—*measures whether a variable (X) is one of the factors that causes or does not cause characteristic (Y) to occur*	One of the most rigorously objective research designs	Difficult to control for some variables Human behavior in lab may not reflect real-life behavior Costly and time-consuming

The Terman Life-Cycle Study, a classic longitudinal study—indeed, the grandparent of life-course research—was begun by psychologist Lewis Terman in 1921–1922 (Friedman & Brownell, 1995). Terman followed 1,528 gifted boys and girls from California public schools (who later nicknamed themselves "Termites") and a control group of children of average intelligence from preadolescence through adulthood. These subjects have been studied at 5- to 10-year intervals ever since. The 856 boys and 672 girls were selected on the basis of their intelligence quotients, or IQs (between 135 and 200 on the Stanford-Binet scale), which were said to represent the top 1 percent of the population. Terman found that the gifted youngsters were generally taller, heavier, and stronger than those with average IQs. Moreover, they tended to be more active socially and to mature faster than average children (Terman & Merrill, 1937). One of the effects of the study has been to dispel the belief that the acceleration of bright children in school is harmful.

After Terman's death, other psychologists continued the project, and their research has provided longitudinal data on religion and politics, health, marriage, emotional development, family history and careers, longevity, and cause of death (Holahan & Suzuki, 2004). One notable recent finding is that "Termites" whose parents divorced had a greater risk of early death (the average age of death for men was 76, compared with age 80 for those whose parents remained married; for women, the corresponding ages of death were 82 and 86 years). Researchers speculate that the stress and anxiety associated with their parents' strife took a toll in earlier mortality (Martin & Friedman, 2000).

Limitations of the Longitudinal Design Although the longitudinal design enables us to study development over time, it has a number of disadvantages. Two major problems are selective attrition and dropout. Subjects drop out because they become ill or die, move away and are difficult to locate, or lose interest in continuing the study. **Selective attrition** means simply that the individuals who drop out tend to be different from those who remain in the study. For example, those who remain might come from the most cooperative and stable families or might be more intelligent or successful. These changes can bias the sample of subjects as it becomes smaller over time (surprisingly enough, only 10 percent of the "Termites" were unaccounted for in 1995). Other problems include testing and tester consistency over the length of the study. It is impossible to test every person at every scheduled testing on every test item. They might refuse to comply on some items. And children or their parents occasionally forget appointments (Willett, Singer, & Martin, 1998). Comparable data might not be collected from every subject at every time interval. Likewise, changes (such as turnover or burnout) in the staff

that tests or observes the participants can result in inconsistencies in the measurements taken.

More important, longitudinal studies cannot control for unusual events during this group's life span. Effects of such economic and social events can make it hard to generalize findings from one age cohort to another age cohort born 10 or 20 years later and can distort the amount or direction of the change reported:

> War, depression, changing cultures, and technological advances all make considerable impacts. What are the differential effects on 2-year-olds of depression-caused worries and insecurities, of TV or no TV, of the shifting climate of the baby-experts' advice from strict-diet, let-him-cry, no-pampering schedules to permissive, cuddling, "enriching" loving care? (Bayley, 1965, p. 189)

The time and money required to complete a long-term study can also be prohibitive (Brooks-Gunn, Phelps, & Elder, 1991). For example, 20 national agencies collaborate annually to fund and report research on the well-being of America's children (Federal Interagency Forum, 2007). Finally, there is the problem of finding out tomorrow what relevant factors should have been considered yesterday. Once set in motion, the project is difficult to alter, even when newer techniques might improve the overall design. For example, computerized testing or a survey on a Web page could make it easier for participants to record their data and would be less expensive than bringing individuals into a research lab, but would the data be comparable to the data collected earlier? What would be the effect of having no tester-participant interaction? Would participants' responses be affected by their computer experience or comfort level working electronically?

Despite these limitations, longitudinal studies have direct implications for explaining theories of development and aging (Hofer & Sliwinski, 2006). For example, if our research interest is the relationship between lifestyle practices and health status, we might design the following study: Select a sample of 10-year-olds and observe their lifestyle practices. We could do this by directly observing them, by interviewing them or their parents, or by some kind of survey that they (or their parents) might complete. This observation could result in an overall score for lifestyle practices. Using those scores, we might place the children in one of three groups: Group 1, low scores (referring to children who exhibit unhealthy lifestyle practices); Group 2, medium scores (referring to children who exhibit a mixture of healthy and unhealthy practices); and Group 3, high scores (referring to children who exhibit healthy lifestyle practices).

We might also obtain some measure of the children's health and fitness status. This could be done by interviewing or surveying the children's parents about health issues that they might have, and we might also administer

FIGURE 1.3 Longitudinal Research Study
Showing the Relationship Between Lifestyle
Practices and Health/Fitness Status The bars
are color-coded to indicate the lifestyle practices
of the group, and the height of each bar indicates
the assessed health/fitness status for that group.
The scores shown here are the hypothetical average
scores at each age.

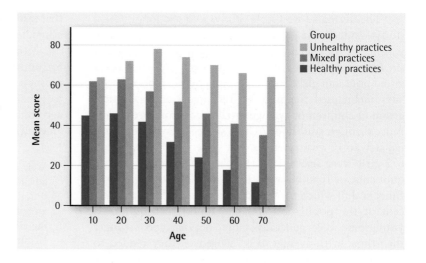

some kind of fitness assessment, such as the Missouri
Assessment Program (Missouri Physical Assessment
Manual, 2000) or the YMCA Fitness Assessment
(Golding, 2005). Using one of these instruments, we
would find each child's fitness score.

We would assess this same group (cohort) every
10 years and repeat these measurements, and we could
then use a chart like the one in Figure 1.3, which shows the
relationship between lifestyle practices and fitness status,
and how that relationship might change over time.

Figure 1.3 describes our hypothetical results on the
relationship between lifestyle practices and health/fitness
status over time, the number of participants tested each
time, and their age at the time of testing.

Question

Based on the "results" shown in Figure 1.3, what can
you say about age and the relationship between
lifestyle practices and fitness status of these participants
over time?

The Cross-Sectional Design

The hallmark of the longitudinal design is taking successive measurements of the same individuals. In contrast,
the **cross-sectional design** investigates development by
simultaneously comparing different age groups. To study,
using a cross-sectional design, the same question from the
previous example—that is, the relationship, over time,
between lifestyle practices and health/fitness status—we
would collect the same kind of data from groups of people. However, unlike in our longitudinal research example, now we would select a group of 10-year-olds, a
group of 20-year-olds, a group of 30-year-olds, and so
on, through our last group, 70-year-olds. We would then
assess the lifestyle practices and the health/fitness status of all seven groups at the same time. What savings in
time and money! You don't have to wait 60 years for the
data collection to be complete, nor do you have to worry
about locating your participants and bringing them back
for retesting. Staff turnover is not an issue, nor in most
cases are there problems with participant cooperation
and testing inconsistencies. Figure 1.4 summarizes the

FIGURE 1.4 Cross-Sectional Study Showing
the Relationship Between Lifestyle Practices
and Health/Fitness Status In this study, different groups of people of various ages were assessed,
at about the same time, on their lifestyle practices
and their health/fitness status. The scores shown
here are the hypothetical average health/fitness
scores for each age group.

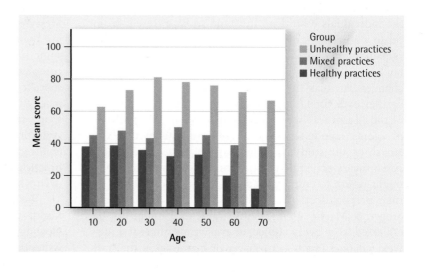

hypothetical results from the cross-sectional study of the relationship, over time, between lifestyle practices and health/fitness status. These findings seem to confirm the hypothesis that health and fitness decline with age more rapidly for those who do not maintain a healthy lifestyle (see Figure 1.4). But can we really say that? Could there be other differences (besides lifestyle practices) among these selected groups that are affecting their health and fitness?

Limitations of the Cross-Sectional Design The confounding of age and cohort is the major disadvantage in cross-sectional research. **Confounding** in research means the elements are mingled and thus cannot be distinguished or separated. We can never be sure that the reported age-related differences between participants are not the product of other differences between the groups. For instance, the groups might differ in social environment, intelligence, or diet. For this reason, the comparability of the groups can be substantiated only through careful sampling and measurement techniques. For example, if you were to investigate how many years of formal schooling your grandparents received, compared with your parents, compared with you yourself, you would probably determine that your generation has the resources to earn a higher level of education, delaying full-time work status and most likely delaying childbearing. We know that the life experiences of a typical 20-year-old today are much different from those of a 20-year-old in the 1930s or the 1950s.

These problems are highlighted by cross-sectional studies of intelligence. Such studies rather consistently show that average scores on intelligence tests begin to decline around 20 years of age and continue to drop throughout adulthood. But as we will see in Chapter 15, cross-sectional studies do not make allowance for *cohort differences* in performance on intelligence tests. Each successive generation of Americans has received more schooling than the preceding generation. Consequently, the overall performance of each generation of Americans on intelligence tests improves. Improvement caused by increasing education creates the erroneous impression that intelligence declines with chronological age (see Chapter 15).

Sequential Design

A **sequential design** involves measuring more than one cohort over time. This combination approach—collecting data over time and across groups—overcomes the age/cohort confounding found in cross-sectional studies, as well as the effect of unique events found in longitudinal designs. If we consider our example of examining changes in health/fitness status over time, this time using a sequential design, we could select a sample

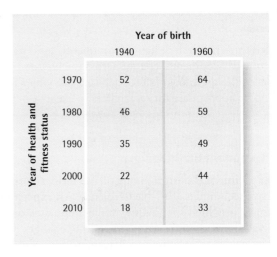

FIGURE 1.5 Results of a Sequential Design Study to Examine Health/Fitness Status over Time Health/fitness status of two cohorts of adults (one cohort born in 1940 and the other born in 1960) was assessed five times at 10-year intervals from 1970 to 2010. The numbers reported are hypothetical average health/fitness status scores for each cohort at each time interval. Data in the same row, between columns, represent cross-sectional comparisons for different participants. Data within a column represent longitudinal comparisons for the same participants.

of 20-year-olds (born in 1950) and a sample of 40-year-olds (born in 1930), assess their health/fitness status, and then bring each cohort back for successive measurements at specific time intervals. Figure 1.5 provides some hypothetical data on the health/fitness measurements, using a sequential design. Health/fitness status was assessed in adults born in 1930 for the ages 40, 50, 60, 70, and 80. For adults born in 1950, measurements were taken at ages 20, 30, 40, 50, and 60. Each health/fitness status score reported in the figure is the group average for a particular time interval. First, study the scores of the 1930 group over time, and then look at the scores for the 1950 group. Finally, compare the scores of the two groups at a particular age—for example, when both groups were measured at age 40.

Limitations of Sequential Designs Sequential designs can be complex and difficult to analyze if the groups measured longitudinally (over time) are found to be very different in the variable under study. For example, if 40-year-olds born in 1940 have significantly lower health and fitness scores than 40-year-olds born in 1960, it is difficult to combine these scores for an overall average measurement. Doing so might distort the sequential changes in health and fitness status throughout the study. The issues of time and money continue to be a limitation, just as they are when any group is followed over a longer period of time.

The Experimental Design

The **experimental design** is one of the most rigorously objective techniques available to science. An **experiment** is a study in which the investigator manipulates one or more variables and measures the resulting changes in the other variables in an effort to determine the cause of a specific behavior. Experiments are "questions put to nature." They are the only effective technique for establishing a cause-and-effect relationship. This is a relationship in which a particular characteristic or occurrence (X) is one of the factors that causes another characteristic or occurrence (Y). Scientists design an experimental study in such a way that it is possible to determine whether X does or does not cause Y. To say that X causes Y is simply to indicate that whenever X occurs, Y follows at some later time.

In an experiment, researchers try to find out whether a causal relationship exists between two variables, X and Y. They systematically vary the first variable (X) and observe the effects on the second variable (Y). Factor X, the factor that is under study and is manipulated in an experiment, is called the **independent variable.** It is independent of what the participant or participants do. The independent variable is assumed to be the causal factor in the behavior being studied. Researchers must also attempt to control for **extraneous variables,** factors that could confound the outcome of the study; these might include the age and gender of the participants, the time of day the study is conducted, the educational attainment of the subjects, and so on (see Figure 1.6).

The study is planned such that the individuals in the **experimental group** are administered the independent variable (some refer to this as the "treatment"). In comparison, the **control group** of participants should be identical to the experimental group except that they will not be administered the independent variable while they perform the same task as the experimental group.

We need to determine whether the independent variable has made any difference in the performance of the experimental group of participants. We call the end result of the experiment—the factor that is affected—the

FIGURE 1.6 Sample Experimental Design
Elements of an experiment to assess the effects of certain lifestyle practices on health/fitness status. This design asks whether engaging in specific practices results in higher levels of health/fitness performance. What is the hypothesis in this example?

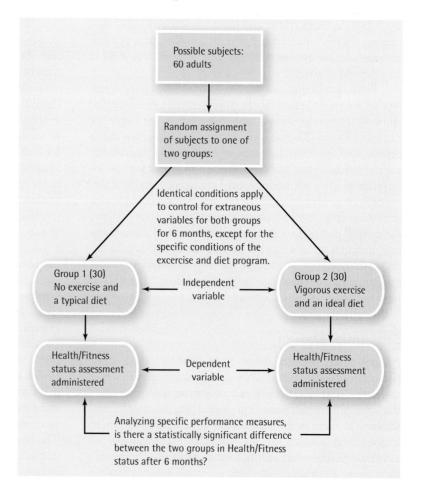

dependent variable, which is some measure of the participants' behavior. For instance, dependent variables are often administered in the form of paper-and-pencil tests or performance tests, because the researcher must quantify data in some measurable way. The researcher then performs various statistical analyses in order to compare results and to look for any significant differences (e.g., How did the performance of the experimental group vary from the performance of the control group?).

Let's think back to the relationship between lifestyle practices and health/fitness status. In a true experiment, we would have to vary lifestyle practices in a systematic manner and then measure the effect of those variations in lifestyle practices on health/fitness status. Suppose, from our review of relevant literature on the topic, we hypothesized that better lifestyle practices lead to better health and fitness. We could design an experiment to test this hypothesis.

We could recruit a large group of volunteers, say 60 people. Then we could randomly assign those people to one of two groups: Group 1 would simply have a sedentary lifestyle with a typical American diet; Group 2 would be put on a program of vigorous exercise six times a week, and they would be given an ideal healthy diet. Then we would run the program described above for an extended period of time, say 6 months, after which we would measure the health/fitness status of the two groups and compare them with each other. In comparing the groups, we would calculate the mean (average) health/fitness status for each group and then compare the group means. This experiment is illustrated in Figure 1.6.

In this example, the lifestyle group would be the independent variable (no exercise/normal diet versus vigorous exercise/ideal diet). At the end of the 6-month period, the scores on the health/fitness status assessment would be the dependent variable. If the average health/fitness scores were significantly higher for the experimental group, our hypothesis would be supported.

Experiments must be replicated by other researchers with different groups of subjects to see whether there is consistency in results before any major theory can be substantiated.

Limitations of the Experimental Design in Developmental Psychology   It is difficult to use an experimental approach in developmental psychology, for several reasons. The first, as indicated earlier, is the inability to assign participants to the variable of interest. Developmental psychologists cannot manipulate many of the variables they study—such as age, gender, abusive family background, or ethnicity. These variables come with the individual, along with many other variables that can confuse us when we try to interpret their effects on the dependent variable. Second, many of the questions we ask

involve the effects of stressful or dangerous experiences, such as tobacco or alcohol use, medical procedures, or the withholding of treatments thought to be beneficial. Manipulations of these variables would be unethical, if not impossible. Third, some argue that how people behave or perform in an experimental lab setting is not how they actually behave in a "real-world" setting. Fourth, planning, designing, conducting, and evaluating a true experimental design is very time-consuming and costly.

> **Questions**
>
> Why is the experimental design considered to be the only one with which it is possible to determine the cause of a specific behavior? Why is the experimental design seldom used in most developmental studies?

The Case-Study Method

The **case-study method** is a longitudinal design that focuses on a single individual rather than on a group of subjects (see Table 1.4 on page 26). Its aim is the same as that of other longitudinal approaches—the accumulation of developmental information. An early form of the case-study method was the "baby biography." Over the past two centuries, a small number of parents have kept detailed observational diaries of their children's behavior. Charles Darwin, for example, wrote a biographical account of his infant son.

A good deal of the early work of Jean Piaget, an influential Swiss developmental psychologist, was based on the case-study approach (Wallace et al., 1994). Piaget (1952) carefully observed the behavior of his three children—Lucienne, Laurent, and Jacqueline—and used this information to formulate hypotheses about cognitive development. Examples and applications of Piaget's theory are discussed further in Chapter 7.

Case studies have also had a prominent place in the clinical treatment of maladjusted and emotionally disturbed individuals. Sigmund Freud and his followers have stressed the part that early experience plays in mental illness. According to this view, the task of the therapist is to help patients reconstruct their own histories so that, in the process, they can resolve their inner conflicts. An example of a classic case study, published in the late 1950s by psychiatrists Thigpen and Cleckley, is *The Three Faces of Eve*, about a woman with multiple personality disorder (now called *dissociative identity disorder*). More recently, the clinical approach has been extended to the study of healthy individuals. Case studies are often used by researchers who study individuals who exhibit behavior that is an exception from the norm, such as a child genius or a serial murderer.

Limitations of the Case-Study Method   The case-study method has a number of drawbacks. The data are recorded on only one individual, and it is difficult to generalize from one case to the whole population of interest. Of course, if the kind of case study is repeated many times, on many individuals, as was the research Piaget did with children, the findings are more valuable. A second problem is the extended interaction between the observer or experimenter and the subject under study. Because case studies normally involve frequent contact between researcher and subject over a long period of time, researchers and subjects become familiar with each other, and the objectivity of the results may be in question. The experimenter might even become a part of the subject's treatment, and the same results would not necessarily be found by a different researcher.

The Social Survey Method

Researchers use the **social survey method** to study the incidence of specific behaviors or attitudes in a large population of people (see Table 1.3). Suppose researchers want to discover the prevalence and characteristics of people who are home-schooling their own children, or the frequency and type of drug use among teenagers, or the impact of a public campaign promoting senior day care. Using the social survey method, researchers ask questions of a sample of individuals who are representative of the population of individuals likely to be affected. These questions can be asked through personal interviews, by phone, by mail, or on the Internet in questionnaire form. When surveys are mailed, the researchers must rely on the people selected to answer the questions and return the document for analysis. For example, in the past several decades in the United States, census takers came to our homes and interviewed us, while filling out a very long questionnaire. The national census in 2010 was not conducted in quite the same way, because that has become far too costly and labor-intensive, and because so many people are working during the daytime hours when the census taker would come. Census researchers also must try to interview homeless and institutionalized Americans, as well as immigrants. Social scientists at the Census Bureau have a tremendous logistical task in such a large-scale survey, and it takes years to analyze and report the data collected.

For survey research to produce useful results, the sample of participants must be *representative*, and the questions must be well designed, easy to answer, and clear. For example, open-ended questions that require long answers might have a lower return rate than a simple check-off list. However, open-ended questions might give the researcher more details about a subject's attitude and practice. A survey that is too lengthy or detailed—no matter how significant or timely the questions might be—is likely to get a very poor response rate.

The representativeness of the sample is based on **random sampling.** There are different methods of random sampling, but the basic idea is that each member of the population sampled has the same probability of being chosen. This enables the researcher to generalize her or his findings from the sample to the population of interest. In other words, if we want to be able to talk about the societal issue of teenage pregnancy, we cannot simply interview 500 students from one high school and report the results as representing the national population of teenagers (for instance, students in an urban high school probably are not representative of students in suburban or rural schools). If we interview 100 students from Tampa, 100 from New York City, 100 from Topeka, 100 from Kokomo, and 100 from San Bernardino, perhaps then we can talk about this issue on a national scale. The design and clarity of the questions are particularly important when a document is to be mailed and respondents will not be able to ask for assistance in understanding the questions. Social scientists interested in conducting surveys usually take advanced courses in psychological statistics to learn how to design a reliable survey and analyze it accurately.

Limitations of the Social Survey Method   The greatest concerns in survey research are response rate and bias. Are the individuals who chose to respond (less than a 50 percent return is common) different from the participants who chose not to fill out the survey or agree to be interviewed? This is similar to the problem of *selective attrition* in longitudinal research. In addition, many people who are surveyed give answers that they think the researcher expects or that they think will make them seem mature or "good," whereas other respondents exaggerate when responding. Many adults are sensitive to questions that touch on matters they consider private (such as sexual practices, income, and political or religious beliefs) and are unable or unwilling to give accurate answers on these subjects. Finally, the survey method has limited use with children and cannot be used at all with infants.

The Naturalistic Observation Method

In **naturalistic observation,** researchers intensively watch behavior as it occurs and record it by means of note pad, videotape, or other method (see Table 1.4). Observers must be careful not to disturb or affect the events under investigation. This method produces more detail and greater depth of insight than the social survey method (Cahill, 1990), but it is effective only for a smaller range of subjects. For example, naturalistic observation has been used extensively to observe young children's interactions in a nursery or preschool setting, but it would be much harder to use this method to study

Participating in a Social Survey A survey participant's attitude can affect a rational response.
Source: Bill Watterson.

adults at work. (See the *More Information You Can Use* box on page 24, "Tips for Observing Children.")

An advantage of naturalistic observation is that it is independent of the participant's ability or willingness to report on given matters. Many people lack sufficient self-insight to tell the researcher about certain aspects of their behavior. Or if their behavior is illegal, socially unacceptable, or deviant, they may be reluctant to talk about it.

Using more systematic techniques through observation can provide greater objectivity in collecting and analyzing the data. One technique, **time sampling,** involves counting the occurrence of a specific behavior for a number of time intervals of the same duration. An example would be to count the number of times two children interact during 30-second intervals. Researchers who do not want to lose the sequential flow of events focus on a class of behaviors, such as fighting on a playground, and record the time lapse for each episode; this approach is termed **event sampling.** Still other researchers use precoded behavior categories. They determine beforehand what behaviors they will observe and then record these behaviors using code symbols. Videotaping in observational studies has given researchers much greater reliability in coding, as well as greater flexibility in choosing the events or behaviors observed.

Limitations of Naturalistic Observation Naturalistic observation can provide a rich source of ideas for more extensive future study. But it is not a particularly strong technique for testing hypotheses. The researcher lacks control over the behavior of the individuals being observed. Furthermore, no independent variable is "manipulated." Consequently, the theorizing associated with naturalistic observation (such as trying to understand why a behavior occurs) tends to be highly speculative. The observer might be biased, have certain expectations, and look for those behaviors to record. Still another problem with this method is that the observer's presence can alter the behavior he or she is observing—all of us tend to act differently when we

know we are under close scrutiny. In spite of these shortcomings, there is support for observing behavior as it takes place spontaneously within its natural context. Indeed, some researchers argue that observing subjects in their natural setting does greater justice to the rich, genuine, and dynamic quality of human life.

Questions

What are the advantages and limitations of each of the following research methods: experiment, case study, social survey, and naturalistic observation? If you were going to observe a child, what might you do to prepare for this observation?

Cross-Cultural Studies

Have you noticed society (and the world) changing at a rather rapid pace? Have such changes affected your life, or do you believe they have little impact on your own personal development, values, or ideologies? For example, when you recently called for computer technical support or ordered merchandise or service, were you speaking with a person from another country? Have you or a loved one recently returned from a tour of duty in Iraq or Afghanistan? Are immigrants moving into your community? Are you planning a semester of study in another country? As a college student, do you have international students as classmates or lab partners?

Since the first publication of this text about 30 years ago, James Vander Zanden, a sociologist, incorporated research findings about human development from various societies. Historically, however, for the past century the majority of developmental researchers narrowly focused their interests on Euro-American subjects across the life span—an approach that does not yield an accurate account of human development (Patterson & Hastings, 2007). Additionally, much of our present understanding

MORE INFORMATION YOU CAN USE

Tips for Observing Children

One of the best ways to learn about children is to observe them. To provide access to the full drama, color, and richness of the world of children, many instructors have their students watch children in the laboratory or in the field. Here are a number of tips that may prove helpful for observing children:

- The minimal aids you will need for observation generally include paper, pen, a timepiece, and a writing board.
- Record the date, time interval, location, and situation, along with the age and sex of the subject or subjects.
- Most observations take place in nursery school settings. Add diversity to your report by observing children in parks, streets, stores, vacant lots, homes, and swimming pools.
- Have the purpose of your research firmly in mind. You should explicitly define and limit in advance the range of situations and behaviors you will observe. Will you watch the entire playground, giving a running account of events? Will you concentrate on one or two individuals? Will you record the activities of an entire group? Or will you focus only on certain types of behavior, such as aggression?
- Once the target behavior is identified, describe both the behavior and the social context in which it occurs. Include not only what a child says and does but also what others say and do to the child. Report spoken words, cries, screams, startle responses, jumping, running away, and related behaviors.
- Describe the relevant body language—the nonverbal communication of meaning through physical movements and gestures. Body language includes smiles, frowns, scowls, menacing gestures, twisting, and other acts that illuminate the intensity and affect of behavior.
- Give descriptions of behavior, not interpretations that generalize about behavior.
- Make notes in improvised shorthand. Immediately after an observation session, transcribe your notes into a full report. The longer the interval between your full recording of observations and the events themselves, the less accurate, the less detailed, and the more biased your report will be.
- Limit your periods of observation to half an hour, which is about as long as a researcher can remain alert enough to perceive and remember the multitude of simultaneous and sequential occurrences.
- At times, children will notice your observing them. If they ask what you are doing, be truthful. Explain it

openly and frankly. According to Wright and Barker (1950), children under the age of 9 generally display little self-consciousness when being observed.
- Keep in mind that one of the greatest sources of unreliability in observation is the researcher's selective perceptions influenced by his or her own needs and values. For example, observers who sharply disapprove of aggressive behaviors tend to overrecord these behaviors. Remember at all times that objectivity is your goal.
- Use time sampling for some observations. Time your field notes at intervals of a minute or even 30 seconds. You may wish to tally the children's behavior in terms of helping, resistance, submission, giving, and other responses.

Use event sampling of behavioral sequences or episodes for some observations. Helen Dawe's 1934 study of the quarrels of preschool children provides a good model. Dawe made "running notes" on prepared forms that provided space for recording (1) the name, age, and sex of every subject, (2) the duration of the quarrel, (3) what the children were doing at the onset of the quarrel, (4) the reason for the quarrel, (5) the role of each subject, (6) specific motor and verbal behavior, (7) the outcome, and (8) the aftereffects. The advantage of event sampling is that it allows you to structure the field of observation into natural units of behavior.

Naturalistic Observation What might you be studying in this setting? Would you use time sampling or event sampling? What are some strengths and limitations of this research method?

of human development flows from decades of analyses and recommendations based on research limited to mainstream members of such Euro-American societies (and mainly to the males of such societies). It has been pointed out that "those with more power within a society have the ability to define what counts as knowledge and to make definitions of knowledge to appear natural rather than artificially constructed" (Gjerde, 2004, p. 145).

At the beginning of the twenty-first century, that power structure is definitely shifting. The collegial consciousness of diversity issues—necessitated by increasing U.S. immigration, corporate and communications globalization, and an ever-changing mix of social, ethnic, and religious groups entering many societies throughout the world—is driving a broader, richer understanding of human development across cultures. Presently, it is exciting to report an acceleration of cross-cultural developmental research, with a broader-based focus on societal, racial, ethnic, gender, education, and religious differences and similarities—and among members of ethnic-minority groups within the United States (Chia & Poe, 2004) (see Table 1.4 on page 26).

Developmentalists use the **cross-cultural method** to discover which theories hold for all societies, which hold for only certain types of societies, and which hold for only one particular society. Societies differ culturally in a good many ways. Consequently, youngsters grow up with different social definitions of the behavior that is and is not appropriate for them as members of particular age groups.

When researchers can compare data from two or more societies and cultures, then culture, rather than individuals, is the subject of analysis. Cross-cultural

New Directions in Development It is believed that this 2004 election marked the first time that an election had occurred in 5,000 years of Afghanistan's history. Remarkably, a 19-year-old woman was the first to cast her ballot. Such a new cultural practice has significantly changed her developmental path into adulthood.

studies might focus on a single issue, such as child-care practices, puberty rites at adolescence, depression across the life span, living conditions of the elderly, or a wide variety of behaviors and customs (Denmark, 2004). A person's cultural orientation is a powerful influence on his or her view of self, social relationships, values, morals, and developmental path. Yet McLeod (2004, p. 188) reminds us that even within cultures, wide variation exists in individual members of a racial or ethnic group, such as in "social class, regional identification, country of origin, generational history, recency of immigration, acculturation status, language preference, etc."

Studies dealing with grandparenthood provide a good illustration of cross-cultural research. According to anthropologist A. R. Radcliffe-Brown (1940), tensions between parents and children tend to draw grandparent and grandchild together. To test this hypothesis, a number of researchers examined cross-cultural data (Apple, 1956; Nauck & Suckow, 2006). They found close and warm relationships between children and their grandparents only in cultures where grandparents do not serve as disciplinarians. Where grandparents have a disciplinary role, grandparents and grandchildren do not have easy, friendly, playful relations. Other investigators have found strong ethnic differences in grandparenting styles (Goodman & Silverstein, 2006). For example, Mexican American grandparents are more likely to live in a three-generational family with their grandchildren, more often have compassionate, supportive relationships with their grandchildren, and provide more help than Anglo grandparents (Kazdin, 2000).

Such empirical research is increasingly being published in psychological, sociological, educational, medical, scientific, and human services journals and will be relevant to how each of you perform your daily work-related tasks with the diverse populations you serve. Division 45 of the APA, the Society for the Psychological Study of Ethnic Minority Issues, the International Association for Cross Cultural Psychology, and the Center for Cross Cultural Research promote the research mission to broaden understanding of diverse cultural and ethnic groups worldwide. This text incorporates research findings from many societies about cultural practices and values pertaining to prenatal care, birthing and neonatal practices, child rearing, educational and health-care practices, gender roles, family structure and work roles, life expectancy and quality of life for the aging, and practices surrounding dying, death, and an afterlife.

Limitations of Cross-Cultural Studies Like other research approaches, the cross-cultural study has limitations. First, the quality of the data varies from casual, unprofessional accounts by explorers and missionaries to the most sophisticated fieldwork by trained anthropologists, sociologists, and psychologists. Second, data for some research problems are lacking for many cultures.

Third, the data tend to focus on the typical behaviors and practices of a people but seldom provide information on individual differences among them. Nonetheless, as distinguished anthropologist George Peter Murdock has written, cross-cultural research has demonstrated that it is "unsafe" for the scientist "to generalize his knowledge of Euro-American societies, however profound, to mankind [humankind] in general" (Murdock, 1957, p. 251).

For example, let us say that a social scientist wants to study the prevalence of the personality trait of "shyness" in young children both in the United States and in Japan. How we define "shyness" in children in the United States (embarrassment at being called upon, being very quiet or meek, and so on) might be a prevalent personality trait of most Japanese children, where modesty, self-discipline, and respect for parents, teachers, and adults are still the norm. To be singled out for the highest grades or the best performance at a task might be an embarrassment or shameful to a Japanese child who has been taught the Confucian philosophy of unity within the group. American society, on the other hand, tends to reward the outspoken, more assertive child, who we say will "get ahead" in life. Cross-cultural researchers must be careful not to impose their own cultural views on the behavior under study.

Question

What are some of the advantages and limitations of using cross-cultural studies?

TABLE 1.4 Research Methods

Type	Limitations
Case study—*a type of longitudinal study that focuses on one individual*	Difficult to generalize data from one individual
	Familiarity of research and subject compromises objectivity
Social survey—*survey of a sample of individuals*	Low response rate
	Bias
Naturalistic—*intensive observation of the behavior of people in their natural setting*	Lack of control
	No independent variable
	Bias
Cross-cultural—*compares data from two or more societies or cultures*	Variability of quality of data
	Research questions may not be applicable
	Seldom provides information on individual differences

RESEARCH ANALYSIS

After the research design has been implemented and the subjects chosen and measured, the data are ready to be analyzed statistically. In studies of development we use two broad categories of analysis. First, we can compare different age groups on the variable of interest by simply calculating an average score for each group. We did this informally when we looked at the data on health and fitness using longitudinal and cross-sectional methodologies. We can report sample means and measures of variability and perform various statistical tests to determine how probable it is that the observed differences could have occurred by chance.

Second, we can look at the relationship between two variables using *correlational analysis*. This type of analysis allows us to quantify the association or relationship in terms of strength and direction.

Correlational Analysis

Sometimes social scientists and medical researchers want to know the degree to which two or more behaviors are associated with each other. **Correlational analysis** does not prove causation, but it can be used for predictive purposes (Aronson, Brewer, & Carlsmith, 1985). For example, in American society over the past decade or so, we have heard through the media that there is an association or relationship between eating a high-fat diet and poor health, such as increased incidence of obesity and diabetes, higher risk of heart attack, and other overall health risks. Likewise, we also have heard that eating fruits and vegetables daily typically can reduce one's level of bad cholesterol, promoting better health. These are examples of relationships. Having a low cholesterol reading by itself is not the cause of excellent health—but it is one of the many factors predictive of better health.

If two conditions occur and rise or fall in value together, then there is some measure of a positive relationship. For example, eating chocolate bars daily is likely to be associated with a higher cholesterol reading. That is, as the first condition (amount of chocolate eaten) increases, the second condition (cholesterol level) also increases. This is an example of a positive correlation. On the other hand, if two conditions tend to occur in opposition to each other, then those conditions have a negative correlation. For instance, when people eat more fruits and vegetables, their cholesterol scores tend to decrease. Medical researchers and social scientists are always searching for these types of associations in an effort to improve our health.

Plotting the data on a graph or through the use of a mathematical formula can help us determine the extent and direction of these relationships. A **correlation coefficient (r)** is the numerical expression of the degree or extent of relationship between two variables or conditions (note that the word explains itself: *co-relation,* meaning "with relation"). A correlation coefficient can range

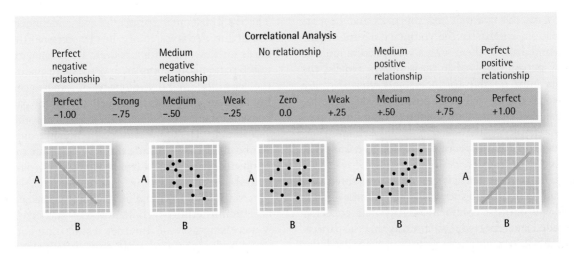

FIGURE 1.7 Degrees of Relationship Using Correlational Analysis The graphs depict a possible range of relationships between two variables. By plotting data on a scatter diagram, we begin to see something about the strength and direction (+) or (−) of the correlation. The graph on the far left is an example of a perfect negative relationship (unlikely in the real world). As one variable increases, the other would have to decrease in the same measure. Eating fruits and vegetables to lower bad cholesterol is an example of a negative correlation. With no relationship, the points scatter all over the graph, which tells us the relationship is closer to 0.0. For example, if one plotted the weather and IQ, the chances are great that one would find no relationship whatsoever.

In a perfect positive relationship, such as that shown on the far right, as one variable goes up in value, the other variable goes up in the same measure. This would be a +1.00 correlation. An example of a perfect positive relationship occurs when you get paid for the hours you work: If you work 1 hour at $6 per hour, you will make $6; if you work 2 hours, you will make $12; if you work 5 hours, you will make $30. Perfect relationships are rare in real life. (As a consequence of tax withholding, even your take-home paycheck is lower than the full amount, and the more you make, the more is taken out). Correlations, even very strong ones, whether positive or negative, do not show causation. Why?

from −1.00 to +1.00. If it is +1.00, then we say there is a perfect positive relationship between two variables (as one variable increases, the other increases). If it is −1.00, then there is a perfect negative relationship between two variables (as one variable increases, the other decreases). A correlation of 0.0 means that there is no relationship between the variables (see Figure 1.7). Remember, however, that correlation does not imply causation.

In social and developmental research, we seldom find perfect correlations, but moderately strong correlations can be found in either a positive or a negative direction and can be helpful in explaining certain relationships. For example, one of the strongest positive correlations examined is that of the IQ scores of identical twins. The IQ score of one identical twin is strongly predictive of the IQ score of the other twin. A well-publicized example of a negative correlation is the relationship between the number of hours children watch television and their grades in school: The more hours of TV children watch per day, the lower their grades.

Questions

How would you begin to examine the hypothesis that students who study more get higher grades? What conditions would you need to examine? What type of correlation is this?

ETHICAL STANDARDS FOR HUMAN DEVELOPMENT RESEARCH

Any research on human development involves some risks and raises some ethical questions, yet research on humans is essential to making progress in understanding the developmental process. How can we learn about how people interact, raise their children, and make decisions about marriage and work, and at the same time safeguard their privacy? Anytime we study humans, we must balance the need to know with the need to protect individuals' personal rights and privacy. The following guidelines and principles established by the American Psychological Association (2003) must be followed any time humans are the participants of our research.

Informed consent: First, the researcher must obtain written consent to participate from each participant. This consent must be voluntary. For example, research often takes place on college campuses, and it is easy to imagine participation being linked to grades, extra credit, or even less tangible rewards such as staying in a professor's good graces or getting a good recommendation for graduate school or a job. At any time before, during, or after the research, an individual can withhold her or his consent. Second, the researchers must tell all individuals the purpose of the research and the risks and benefits of participation, emphasize the voluntary nature of participation, and provide them with a way to communicate with a key person involved in the research. Finally, the participants must be able to understand what they are being asked to do, as well as its purpose, risks, benefits, and results. Participants with cognitive disabilities, participants diagnosed with a mental illness, and children and adolescents should have special safeguards to ensure that their rights are protected.

Right to privacy: Participants must be assured that the information they share and all research records of their behaviors will be kept confidential. Any data collected must be coded and reported in such a way that the participant cannot be identified. Even if names are not used, the data should never be reported individually, unless specific permission to do so is given by the participant.

The American Psychological Association updated the guidelines effective in 2003. The new Ethical Principles of Psychologists and Code of Conduct stipulates that with a written release, clients' test data must be made available to them. This allows them more autonomy regarding health-care decision making. The code also defines "test data" and "test materials" and offers protections for psychology graduate students participating in psychotherapy requirements (Smith, 2003).

The Society for Research in Child Development (SRCD) has also issued a recently updated set of guidelines.

The SRCD lists all the principles and guidelines on its Web site at http://www.srcd.org in the section Ethical Standards for Research with Children. Research with children raises particularly complex and sensitive issues, because the legal and moral legitimacy of experimentation on human beings depends fundamentally on the participant's consent (Stanley & Sieber, 1992). Finally, both the APA and the SRCD state that the experimenter must assume responsibility for detecting and correcting any undesirable results that might follow from an individual's participation in the research.

Along with the rapid increase in the use of the Internet, administering psychological tests and surveys online is increasing as well. Internet testing raises many new issues and concerns. People with little or no access to computers or no prior experience with the Internet may be at a disadvantage when taking an online test. Some ethical issues of Internet testing are related to the lack of control over ensuring a professional context for test administration, appropriate use of the test, qualifications of test assessors, maintaining security, attaining informed consent, interpreting assessment results, proper release of test data, and use of obsolete tests (Naglieri et al., 2004).

Question

How do we protect humans from unethical studies?

SEGUE

As we have seen, the study of human development is dynamic, and researchers from many disciplines and across societies contribute to our understanding of the range and depth of human behavior. The growth, learning, and maturation of individuals and groups are examined across cultures, because each society's interpretation of what is and what is not normal and natural affects the lives of the individuals within each culture. Developmentalists study the domains, processes, context, and timing of events to understand both changes and continuities of human behavior.

All societies divide the life span in terms of age, defining stages that range from the moment of conception to the moment of death—and some cultures promote belief in an afterlife. Societies differ in the prestige they accord various age groupings, particularly young children and the elderly. Also, societies specify expectations for appropriate behavior within each age grouping. The most profound changes in families over the past 200 years in industrialized societies include a shift from rural to urban and suburban life, smaller families, more time spent in formal schooling, more single

parents, more women entering the paid labor force, parents and children spending less time together, and a significant increase in senior citizens who are living much longer. Developmentalists continue to study the role of biology and behavior, how a person's sense of self develops, how and in what ways a person's environment shapes development, maturation in cognitive development, moral maturation, and improvement in the quality of each person's life. Several scientific research methods are used to examine many developmental issues of individuals and groups over the course of the life span.

When we do research with humans, we assume major responsibilities. We must study problems and human behaviors in a rigorous and disciplined way, collect and analyze data objectively, and report our results honestly. At the same time, we have the responsibility to safeguard the rights and privacy of the individuals we are studying and to protect them from harm.

In Chapter 2, we provide an overview of the strengths and weaknesses of major theories of human cognitive, moral, emotional, and social development over a lifetime.

SUMMARY

The Major Concerns of Science

1. The study of human development involves the exploration of both change and continuity.
2. The field of human development has four major goals: (a) to describe the changes that occur across the human life span, (b) to explain these changes, (c) to predict developmental changes, and (d) to intervene in the course of events in order to control them.

A Framework for Studying Development

3. Developmental change takes place in three fundamental domains: physical development, cognitive development, and emotional-social development. Yet each of these factors is intertwined in every aspect of human development.
4. The concepts of growth, maturation, and learning are important to our understanding of human development. The interaction between heredity and environment gives each individual his or her unique characteristics.
5. Bronfenbrenner's ecological approach to development examines the mutual accommodations between the developing person and four levels of expanding environmental influence from the network of social relationships and the physical settings in which a person is involved daily; to the overarching cultural patterns of a society that are expressed in family, educational, economic, political, and religious institutions.
6. The passage of time has been treated as synonymous with chronological age, but social and behavioral scientists have broadened their focus to take into account the changes that occur over time in the environment—and the dynamic relation between change in the person and change in the environment.

Partitioning the Life Span: Cultural and Historical Perspectives

7. All societies divide this cycle into age strata that reflect social definitions, but definitions often vary from one culture to another and from one historical period to another.
8. Age is a master status, so most changes in roles over a person's life span are accompanied by a change in chronological age. Each culture gives distinctive meaning, and assigns social responsibilities, to those in various life stages.
9. All societies are organized into age strata, and people's behavior within various age strata is regulated by the social norms or specific expectations for appropriate and inappropriate behavior.
10. In the United States, we view the life span in terms of prenatal development, infancy, childhood, adolescence, adulthood, and old age. Some developmentalists suggest that there is a newer stage of emerging adulthood, between adolescence and adulthood. Because many Americans are living well into their eighties and well beyond, old age is evolving into young-old and the old-old.

The Nature of Developmental Research

11. Using the scientific method, developmental researchers focus on change that occurs over time or with age. The scientific method incorporates these steps: select a researchable problem, formulate a hypothesis, test that hypothesis, draw conclusions about the hypothesis, and make the findings available to the scientific community.
12. In developmental research, three basic designs are used: (a) the longitudinal design, (b) the cross-sectional design, and (c) the sequential design.
13. The longitudinal design measures the same individuals at regular intervals between birth and death. It allows researchers to describe sequential change, but such studies cannot control for unusual events during the participants' life span, and they are time-consuming and costly.
14. The cross-sectional design compares different groups of people of different ages at the same time.
15. The sequential design involves measuring more than one age cohort over time. Conducting sequential designs can also be costly and complex.
16. The experimental design is one of the most rigorously objective techniques available to science. When conducted with precision, it offers the only effective technique for establishing cause-and-effect relationships. Two groups of individuals are compared: the experimental group and the control group, and the scores of these two groups are analyzed for statistically significant differences to determine whether a causal relationship exists.
17. The case-study method is a longitudinal study that describes one individual's experience and behavior over time and provides rich detail and description, but its findings cannot easily be generalized to other individuals, other settings, or other time periods.
18. The social survey method uses questionnaires, interviews, and surveys to measure attitudes and behaviors of a sample of people who represent a larger group of the population.
19. The naturalistic observation method enables a researcher to study people independently of their ability or willingness to report on themselves.
20. The cross-cultural method allows scientists to specify which theories in human development hold true for all societies, which hold for only certain types of societies, and which hold for only a particular society.

Research Analysis

21. Correlational analysis quantifies the relationship between two or more variables in terms of strength and direction, but it does not prove causation. It can be used for prediction, depending on the strength of the positive or negative relationship.

Ethical Standards for Human Development Research

22. A scientist must conduct research with respect for the integrity of the participants and must secure informed consent, acquaint participants with any risks, and inform participants that their individual performance will be kept confidential. The American Psychological Association and the Society for Research in Child Development have developed strict guidelines that must be followed with research participants.

KEY TERMS

age cohort *(11)*

age strata *(13)*

case-study method *(21)*

chronosystem *(10)*

cognitive development *(6)*

confounding *(19)*

control group *(20)*

correlational analysis *(26)*

correlation coefficient *(r) (26)*

cross-cultural method *(25)*

cross-sectional design *(18)*

culture *(13)*

dependent variable *(21)*

development *(4)*

developmental psychology *(4)*

ecological approach *(8)*

emerging adulthood *(14)*

emotional-social development *(6)*

event sampling *(23)*

exosystem *(8)*

experiment *(20)*

experimental design *(20)*

experimental group *(20)*

extraneous variables *(20)*

growth *(7)*

hypothesis *(15)*

independent variable *(20)*

informed consent *(27)*

learning *(7)*

longitudinal design *(16)*

macrosystem *(10)*

maturation *(7)*

mesosystem *(8)*

microsystem *(8)*

naturalistic observation *(22)*

nonnormative life events *(11)*

normative age-graded influences *(11)*

normative history-graded influences *(11)*

physical development *(5)*

random sampling *(22)*

right to privacy *(28)*

scientific method *(15)*

selective attrition *(17)*

sequential design *(19)*

social norms *(13)*

social survey method *(22)*

time sampling *(23)*

FOLLOWING UP ON THE INTERNET

Web sites for this chapter focus on professional organizations in the field of human development. Please access the text Web site at www.mhhe.com/crandell10 for up-to-date hot-linked Internet addresses for the following organizations and resources:

The American Psychological Association (APA)

http://www.apa.org/

APA Division 7: Developmental Psychology

http://www.apa.org/about/division/div7.aspx

APA Division 45: Society for the Psychological Study of Ethnic Minority Issues

http://www.apa.org/about/division/div45.aspx

Association for Psychological Science

http://www.psychologicalscience.org/

International Association for Cross Cultural Psychology

http://www.iaccp.org/drupal/

Society for Research in Child Development (SRCD)

http://www.srcd.org/

Theories of Development

1. Suppose someone comes up with a new theory of development called the "Food Theory," which states that human development can be explained in terms of the foods we eat. Because no two people eat exactly the same foods, it follows that no two people develop in exactly the same way. Why would you accept or reject this theory?

2. If genetic scientists took one of your cells and cloned you—and then gave the cloned infant to the same caregivers you had—do you think the clone would turn out to be just like you?

3. Do theories of development aid us in understanding by providing a framework, or limit us by forcing connections?

4. In what ways is a theory that tries to explain how humans develop similar to a theory that attempts to explain how the universe developed?

Theories enable us to see the world coherently and to act on the world in a rational way. Over the past century in Western cultures, many theories have evolved that attempt to explain how human personality develops, why we behave as we do, what environmental conditions motivate us to act in certain ways, and how these factors are interrelated. Some of these theories base their explanations on critical physical and social-emotional circumstances in our earliest years of life; some on the impact of environmental influences of our family, community, and culture; some on our distinct learning and thought processes; some on successful completion of specific developmental "tasks" at each stage over the life span; and some on how a healthy—or unhealthy—sense of self shapes our personality and behaviors. Over the past two decades, the universal applicability of traditional theoretical models of development has been challenged. Many of the long-standing theories presented in this chapter were formulated by Western white males about Western white males. Some newer theories seek to explain the development of women, nonwhites, and people who live in non-Western cultures.

Cross-cultural social scientists are putting the older theoretical models to the test on a broader scale in scholarly debates in university settings, in international conferences, and in chat rooms and online discussion groups. This is leading to newer perspectives on individual development in all domains. More recently, the American Psychological Association established a division called International Psychology, and more than 30 cross-cultural associations are listed on the American Psychological Society Web site. These encourage professionals from all disciplines to collaborate and examine human development on a global scale.

THEORY: A DEFINITION

College students often complain, "Why do we have to bother with all these theories? Why not just let the facts speak for themselves!" Unfortunately, facts do not "speak for themselves." Before facts can speak to us in a meaningful way, we must find relationships among them. For example, you might baby-sit, care for younger brothers or sisters, have children of your own, or anticipate having children. What do you do when they misbehave? Do you scold them, threaten them, spank them, forbid them to engage in a favorite activity, reason with them, ignore them, or demonstrate the behavior you expect? The actions you take are based on your theory—whether explicit or not—about how children learn. Perhaps the theory is embedded in a proverb or maxim, such as Spare the Rod and Spoil the Child, You Got to Toughen Kids Up for Life, Just Give Them Loads of Love, Spanking Children Causes Emotional Problems, or Children Are to Be Seen and Not Heard. However, the various functions of theory will become more evident as we define the concept and examine some major types of theories of human development.

A **theory** is a set of interrelated statements that provides an explanation for a class of events. It is "a way of binding together a multitude of facts so that one may comprehend them all at once" (G. A. Kelly, 1955, p. 18). The value of the knowledge yielded by the application of theory lies in the control it gives us over our experience. Theory serves as a guide to action. By formulating a theory, we attempt to make sense of our experiences. We must somehow "catch" fleeting events and find a way to describe and explain them. Only then can we predict and influence the world around us. Theory is the "fabric" we weave to accomplish these ends, just as a fine garment is crafted from pieces of fabric and thread, carefully sewn together, and worn for a particular purpose.

More specifically, a theory performs a number of functions. First, it allows us to organize our observations and to deal meaningfully with information that would otherwise be chaotic and useless. As French mathematician Jules-Henri Poincaré (1854–1912) observed, "Science is built up with facts, as a house is with stones, but a collection of facts is no more a science than a heap of stones is a house." Second, theory enables us to see relationships among facts and uncover implications that would not otherwise be evident in isolated bits of data. Third, it stimulates inquiry as we search for knowledge about many different and often puzzling aspects of behavior. A theory, then, inspires research that can be used to verify, disprove, or modify that theory. So research continually challenges us to craft new and better theories (see Figure 2.1). In human development, as in other social and behavioral sciences, it is often difficult

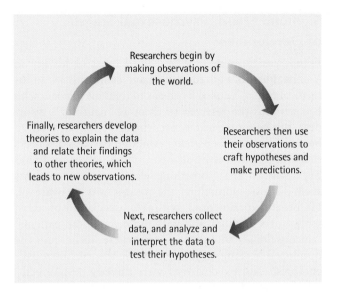

to determine how conclusively the evidence supports a theory, let alone to choose among competing theories. It is a considerably easier task to decide whether the evidence is harmonious with a theory (Lieberson, 1992).

FIGURE 2.1 The Relationships Among Theory, Scientific Method, and Observations of the World

Questions

What is the purpose of a good theory? In what ways is a good theory useful to our lives?

PSYCHOANALYTIC THEORIES

The history of psychology—like the history of the twentieth century—could not be written without discussing the contributions of Sigmund Freud (1856–1939). Both supporters and critics of his theory of personality regard it as a revolutionary milestone in the history of human thought (Robinson, 1993). His notions of how behavior is motivated have influenced the work of a multitude of philosophers, social scientists, psychiatrists, and other mental-health practitioners. And characters in countless plays and novels have been built on Freud's view of the individual.

Central to **psychoanalytic theory** is the view that personality is fashioned progressively as the individual passes through various psychosexual stages. Freud proposed that people operate from three states of being: the *id*, which seeks self-gratification; the *superego*, which seeks to do what is morally proper; and the *ego*, the rational mediator between the id and superego. Now let us consider psychoanalytic theory.

Sigmund Freud: Psychosexual Stages of Development

Freud was born in 1856 and lived most of his life in Vienna. He was a gifted student and scholar. Early in his medical career, he used hypnosis to treat his patients who had nervous (he referred to them as "neurotic") disorders. But he soon became disenchanted with this method because some of his patients exhibited nervous disorders that could not be attributed to anything physical. Freud hypothesized that something else caused his patients such distress—something the patient was unaware of. He began experimenting with free association of ideas, with dream analysis, and with hypnosis to tap patients' "unconscious" thoughts. Using these techniques he developed his famous psychoanalytic theory. Many psychologists and psychiatrists were directly or indirectly influenced by Freud's teachings (Fromm, 1980).

The Role of the Unconscious   Freud stressed the role in our behavior of *unconscious motivation*—stemming from impulses buried below the level of awareness. According to Freud, human behavior arises from a struggle between societal prohibitions and instinctual drives associated with sex and aggression. Those drives, or impulses, lead to self-preservation and seeking pleasure. Because certain behaviors are forbidden and punishable, many instinctual impulses are driven out of our conscious awareness early in our lives into the realm of the unconscious. Nonetheless, they affect our behavior later in our lives. They find new expression in slips of the tongue ("Freudian slips"), dreams, bizarre symptoms of mental disorder, religion, the arts, literature, and myth. For Freud, the early years of childhood are critically important; what happens to an individual later in life is merely a ripple on the surface of a personality structure that was firmly established during the child's first five to six years.

Sigmund Freud In the early 1900s Sigmund Freud, an Austrian psychiatrist, founded psychoanalytic theory. He is famous for formulating psychosexual stages and therapeutic techniques to bring unconscious thoughts and feelings to conscious experience.

Psychosexual Stages   Freud said that all human beings, starting in infancy, pass through a series of **psychosexual stages.** Freud proposed three key psychosexual stages of development—oral, anal, and phallic (see Figure 2.2). Each stage is dominated by the development of sensitivity in a particular erogenous, or pleasure-giving, zone of the body; and each stage poses a unique conflict that must be resolved before passing on to the next stage. If a person is unsuccessful in resolving the conflict, the resulting frustration becomes chronic and remains a central feature of that person's psychological makeup. This is known as a *complex.* According to Freud's theory, the sources of conflict during the phallic stage result in the

Characteristic	Oral	Anal	Phallic
Time period	Birth to approximately 18 months	Approximately 18 months to 3 years	Approximately the third to seventh year
Pleasurable body zones	Mouth, lips, and tongue	Anus, rectum, and bladder	The genitals
Most pleasurable activity	Sucking during the early phase; biting during the later phase	In the early phase, expelling feces and urine; in the later phase, retaining feces and urine	Masturbation
Sources of conflict	Terminating breast-feeding	Toilet training	In boys, the Oedipal complex In girls, the Electra complex

FIGURE 2.2 Freud's Key to Psychosexual Stages

Oedipal complex for boys and the *Electra* complex for girls. At this stage a boy feels sexual love for his mother and hostile rivalry toward his father, which causes him to fear punishment by the father through castration. A girl feels sexual love for her father and hostile rivalry toward her mother, which leads her to conclude that she and her mother have been castrated (because they lack penises). This leads to "penis envy" and a feeling of inferiority (Patterson & Hastings, 2007).

On the other hand, individuals who do not develop a complex may become so addicted to the pleasures of a given stage that they are not willing to move on to later stages and instead become fixated. **Fixation** is the tendency to stay at a particular stage. An individual who is troubled by a conflict at any stage seeks to reduce tension by engaging in the behavior characteristic of that stage.

For Freud, the stages from birth to age 7 were more important to the development of the basic personality structure. He identified two later, less important stages that he referred to as *periods:* the *latency* period and the *genital* period. The latency period corresponds to the middle childhood years. During this phase, Freud thought children suppress most of their sexual feelings and become interested in games, sports, and friendships—boys associate with boys, girls with girls. Sexual reawakening occurs at puberty, launching the *genital* period. In this stage the equilibrium of the latency period is upset. Young people begin experiencing romantic infatuations, emotional upheavals, and the desire to have a satisfactory sexual relationship.

Appraisal of Freud's Work   For decades Freud's ideas dominated much clinical therapy. To many people Freud opened an entirely new psychological world. His emphasis on environment, not biology or heredity, as the primary factor in mental health and illness was particularly hopeful. In fact, people were so fascinated with the novelty of Freud's insights that few questioned their truth. Nonetheless, scientists have come to recognize that Freudian theory is difficult to evaluate because it makes few predictions that can be scientifically tested (Roazen, 1992). Freudians say that only a personal psychoanalysis can reveal the truth of the theory's assertions. Unconscious motivation is, by definition, not in the conscious mind. Consequently, scientists lack the means to observe and study such motivation objectively (Shiraev & Levy, 2007).

Freud constructed his developmental stages almost entirely on the basis of inferences from adult patients. Recent historical research has depicted Freud as occasionally claiming cures when there were none and as suppressing or distorting the facts of cases to prove his theoretical points (Crews, 1998). Also, despite stressing the importance of the early years, Freud rarely worked with children. However, other child psychoanalysts,

such as his daughter Anna, did apply his theories to the treatment of children.

Freudian theorists tended not only to ignore women's experience but also to blame them for the psychological difficulties of others. For example, as recently as the 1950s, Bruno Bettleheim (1903–1990), a Freudian psychoanalyst, claimed that autism resulted from children being raised by mothers devoid of warmth and love, whom he termed "refrigerator mothers" (1950). This conceptualization put a heavy burden on mothers at that time who were attempting to understand a child with such a complex disorder.

In contrast to Freud's views, psychiatrist Jean Baker Miller thought that relationships are the central need in human life and that problems that develop are caused by relational disconnections. She states that personality growth occurs within relationships and that infants respond to the emotions of caregivers. The goal is to continue to form intimate relationships, not to strive for autonomy and individuation (Fletcher, Jordan, & Miller, 2000). Finally, critics charge that Freudian theory is a poor guide to healthy personality development because his patients were suffering from emotional difficulties (Torrey, 1992).

By the early 1970s, a new generation of U.S. psychiatrists was turning to psychobiology and considering defects of nature, not nurture, to be the primary factors in mental illness. These psychiatrists claimed that neurochemical factors, not childhood traumas, best explain mental illness and addictions—hence they looked to genes and the biochemistry of the brain, not to bad parenting, to explain how mental illness is transmitted from one generation to another. The shift away from Freudian theory in no way detracts from the revolutionary significance of Freud's work. He deserves considerable credit for directing attention to the importance of early social experience in human development and to the impact those experiences have in the later stages of life.

Questions

What are the distinct features of Freud's psychoanalytic theory? What are the strengths and weaknesses of this theory? How is Freud's theory viewed by many contemporary psychologists?

Erik Erikson: Psychosocial Stages of Development

One of Freud's major contributions was to stimulate the work of other theorists and researchers. Erik Erikson was one of the most talented and imaginative of these theorists. A neo-Freudian psychoanalyst from Denmark, Erikson (1902–1994) came to the United States in 1933. While acknowledging Freud's genius and contributions, Erikson moved away from the fatalism implicit in Freudian theory,

Erik H. Erikson and Joan Erikson Erikson became a leading figure in the psychosocial study of human growth and development, formulating nine stages, with a "conflict" or "crisis" to be resolved at each stage if healthy development is to occur. He and his wife Joan collaborated on writing about and refining his theory through his early nineties.

challenging Freud's notion that the personality is primarily established during the first five to six years of life. He observed that if everything goes back to early childhood, then everything becomes someone else's fault, and this undermines trust in one's own capabilities.

Erikson concluded that the personality continues to develop over the entire life span. His more optimistic view emphasizes success, greatness, and the flowering of human potential. As his work progressed, Erikson also departed from Freud in another respect. He wove the external landscapes provided by culture, society, and history into Freudian notions of the internal dimensions of the mind.

The Nature of Psychosocial Development Erikson's chief concern is with **psychosocial development,** or development of the person within a social context. Erikson basically formulated eight major stages of development (see Table 2.1), but after his death in 1994, his wife Joan published his theory about a ninth stage in very old age (which Erikson experienced himself). Each stage poses a unique developmental task and simultaneously confronts individuals with a crisis that they must resolve (Erikson preferred the term *opportunity*). As the term is employed by Erikson (1968a, p. 286), a crisis is not "a threat of catastrophe but a turning point, a crucial period of increased vulnerability and heightened potential." More important, he said, "Remember that conflict and tension are sources of growth, strength, and commitment" (Erikson & Erikson, 1997). He would see great people of history, such as German Reformationist Martin Luther, Indian philosopher and peace-keeper Mohandas Gandhi, American civil rights activist the Reverend Martin Luther King, Jr., Pope John Paul II, and Mother Teresa of Calcutta as achieving greatness by virtue of the fit between their personal crises and the crises of their times. Their solutions—as expressed in

TABLE 2.1 Erikson's Nine Stages of Psychosocial Development

Stage	Developmental Period	Characteristics of Stage	Favored Outcome
Trust vs. mistrust	Infancy (birth to 1 year)	Come to trust or mistrust themselves and others	Develop trust in self, parents, and the world
Autonomy vs. shame and doubt	2 to 3	With increased mobility, decide whether to assert their will	Develop sense of self-control without loss of self-esteem
Initiative vs. guilt	4 to 5	Are curious and manipulate objects	Learn direction and purpose in activities
Industry vs. inferiority	6 to puberty	Are curious about how things are made and how they work	Develop a sense of mastery and competence
Identity vs. identity confusion	Adolescence	Explore "Who am I?" question	Develop a coherent sense of self and ego-identity
Intimacy vs. isolation	Early adulthood	Are able to reach out and connect with others	Become intimate with someone and work toward career
Generativity vs. stagnation	Middle adulthood	Look beyond self to embrace society and future generations	Begin family, develop concern for those outside family
Integrity vs. despair	Late adulthood	Take stock of one's past	Get sense of satisfaction from looking at past
Hope and faith vs. despair	Very old age (late 80s and beyond)	Face new sense of self over failing bodies and need for care	Achieve a new sense of wisdom and transcendance

their ideas—become cultural solutions to broader social problems.

According to Erikson (1959, 1982; Erikson & Erikson, 1997), individuals develop a "healthy personality" by mastering "life's outer and inner dangers." Development follows the **epigenetic principle,** a term he borrowed from biology—"anything that grows has a ground plan, and . . . out of this ground plan the parts arise, each having its time of special ascendancy, until all parts have arisen to form a functioning whole" (Erikson, 1968b, p. 92). Hence, according to Erikson, each part of the personality has a particular time in the life span when it must develop if it is going to develop at all. If a capacity does not develop on schedule, the rest of the individual's personality development is unfavorably altered. The individual's capacity to deal effectively with reality is then hindered. However, Erikson did insist that there must be a healthy balance between both sides of each crisis that we encounter. For instance, a healthy mastery of the first stage culminates in a preponderance of *trust* but also produces a healthy dose of *mistrust:* You cannot trust every person you meet and avoid mishap—you must develop a bit of mistrust to get along in this world. But in the end you should interact with the world from a position rooted in trust, not mistrust, to further healthy psychosocial development (Rothbaum & Trommsdorff, 2007).

Erikson's Nine Stages   Erikson was the first theorist to offer a model of development that extended over the entire life span. Table 2.1 depicts Erikson's nine stages, beginning with "trust vs. mistrust" and ending with "hope and faith vs. despair."

Appraisal of Erikson's Work   Erikson's work provides a welcome balance to traditional Freudian theory. Although he does not neglect the powerful effects of childhood experience, Erikson draws our attention to the continuous process of personality development that takes place throughout the life span. Whereas Freud was primarily concerned with pathological outcomes, Erikson holds open the prospect of healthy and positive resolutions of our identity crises. Erikson's portrait of the life cycle allows "second chances" for opportunities missed and paths not taken. It has always been a general tenet of American individualism that people can improve themselves and continually refashion their fate by changing their social situation, so Erikson's perspective has captured the imagination of the U.S. public. The language Erikson provided—"identity," "identity crisis," "the life cycle"—plays a major role in thinking about adolescence and, beyond this, about the widest range of adult trials and tribulations (Terkel, 1987).

One criticism of Erikson's work is that all of the subjects of his psychobiographies and most of his case samples were males (Josselson, 1988). However, since the

Carol Gilligan   Dr. Gilligan has been a pioneer in research on the development and psychological health of U.S. girls and teens as they navigate the passage to womanhood.

1970s, identity development in women has been looked at more closely using Erikson's identity statuses as a base (Marcia, 1991). Josselson (1988) studied women's identity statuses and found that "a woman's identity at the close of adolescence forms the template for her adulthood." The issues most important to her female subjects were social-emotional and religious, not occupational or political. Josselson agrees with Jean Baker Miller's relational theory: "Women's sense of self becomes very much organized around being able to make and then to maintain affiliations and relationships" (Josselson, Lieblich, & McAdams, 2007).

Carol Gilligan's (Taylor, Gilligan, & Sullivan, 1999) theory also views female identity as rooted in connections to others and in relationships: "Women conceptualize and experience the world in a different voice, and men and women operate with different internal models" (Gilligan, 1982a, p. 7). A comprehensive concept of identity must incorporate both female and male ways of developing (Pescitelli, 1998). (See the *Further Developments* box on page 38, "Theories of Emotions or Playing Mind Games.")

Questions

How does Erikson's theory of psychosocial development differ basically from Freud's theory of personality development? What crisis/opportunity characterizes each of Erikson's psychosocial stages, and what is the healthy outcome proposed for each stage throughout the life cycle?

FURTHER DEVELOPMENTS

Theories of Emotions, or Playing Mind Games

Have you recently experienced an emotional high (or low) by winning (or losing) a college scholarship, or by winning (or losing) a large amount of money in a lottery, at a casino, or just playing Texas Hold 'Em in the dorm? Poker has gained popularity at campuses across the nation and on the Internet and TV, and every good poker player knows that opponents can "read" a player's emotional state by his or her facial expressions, especially during "bluffing." Some celebrities are passionate about playing poker, including Ashton Kutcher, Ben Affleck, Matt Damon, Tobey Maguire, and Cameron Diaz—all experts at *showing* their emotions! Many of the strategies that people use when playing Texas Hold 'Em reveal their emotions, such as *bluff*, *edge*, *streak*, *tells*, and *tilt*.

For centuries, philosophers and researchers have tried to understand how our emotions reveal so much about us and whether emotional expressions are universal across cultures. Only recently have researchers examined emotions positively and with the same interest as they've shown in cognition. Emotions have traditionally been accorded "second status" in academia because emotions are very hard to quantify and measure. Historically, emotions have also been linked to abnormal or irrational behaviors.

Texas Hold 'Em: An Emotional Rollercoaster

Aristotle endorsed the theory that a balance of bodily fluids determines the individual's temperament. Descartes believed that ideas are innate and that the body and mind are distinct entities; he attempted to locate emotions in the nervous system. Rousseau insisted an infant is born with noble

BEHAVIORAL THEORY

As its name suggests, **behavioral theory** is concerned with the observable behavior of people—what they actually do and say. This is in contrast to psychoanalytic theory, which focuses on the mental and emotional processes that shape human personality and uses data that are derived largely from the self-observations provided by *introspection*. Behavioral psychologists, by contrast, believe that if psychology is to be a science, its data must be directly observable and measurable.

Behavioral theorists have traditionally separated *behavior* into units called **responses** and separated the environment into units called **stimuli**. Behaviorists are especially interested in how people *learn* to behave in particular ways, and hence the approach is also termed *learning theory*. Historically, behaviorism has emphasized two types of learning: (1) *classical*, or respondent, conditioning and (2) *operant*, or instrumental, conditioning (see Figure 2.3).

Ivan Pavlov: Classical Conditioning

Classical conditioning is based on the work of Ivan Pavlov (1849–1936), a Russian physiologist. Pavlov gained international renown and a Nobel Prize for his early research on the role of gastric juices in digestion in dogs. Subsequently, Pavlov pursued work on an observation he made while conducting his gastric experiments with dogs. He noted that a dog would initially salivate only when food was placed in its mouth. With the passage of time, however, the dog's mouth would water *before* it tasted the food. Indeed, the mere sight of the food or even the sound of the experimenter's footsteps would cause salivation.

Pavlov was intrigued by the anticipatory flow of saliva in the dogs, a phenomenon he termed psychic secretion. He saw the study of "psychic secretions" as a powerful and objective means for investigating the mechanisms by which organisms adapt to their environment. So Pavlov devised a series of experiments in which he rang a bell immediately before feeding a dog.

emotions, which society adulterates. Kant suggested that innate dispositions are neither good nor bad. Darwin thought that strong emotions are universal, because they are important for the survival of a species—that is, a strong emotion like *fear* in response to danger enables one to run away and live to face another day. G. Stanley Hall noted that emotions such as joy, sadness, fear, and anger tend to be expressed more frequently and intensely in childhood and youth. In adolescence, he believed, social forces start to redirect the expression of emotions, leading to other manifestations, such as violence.

Freud was intrigued with the possibilities of using hypnosis to deal with emotional conflicts in patients, which he initially attributed to birth trauma. He eventually decided that emotional disturbances differed from other neuroses more in degree than in kind. William James argued that emotion consists of the feeling or perception of changes occurring in bodily organs; that is, if one sees a dangerous object, one begins to tremble and run and *then* experiences fear, so that the emotion follows the physical movement.

In the early 1900s, several Harvard researchers countered that emotions depend on neural activity in the brain's cortex. They removed part of a cat's hypothalamus and reported that they had eliminated all angry reactions from the cat's behavioral repertoire. John Dewey thought that the brain and all other bodily structures function in harmonious relation to each other, creating a variety of feelings, depending on the environment. John Watson concluded that fear, rage, and love are inherited or developed shortly after birth, and that all other emotions are learned later through classical conditioning.

Carroll Izard (2007) is a nationally recognized authority on the emotional development of children—especially aggression in children. His cross-cultural research reveals that everyone feels the basic six emotions: happiness, surprise, fear, sadness, disgust, and anger—and that 42 muscles in the face are used to express these feelings.

More recently, the study of emotions has come to include the influence of genetic and environmental factors. Paul Ekman researched facial expressions, the physiology of emotions, and universal facial expressions in the United States, Japan, Brazil, and Papua, New Guinea. He published his findings in *Unmasking the Face: A Guide to Recognizing Emotions from Facial Expressions* (Ekman & Friesen, 2003) and *Emotions Revealed: Recognizing Faces and Feelings to Improve Communication and Emotional Life* (Ekman, 2003). He proposes that the 10,000 emotional facial expressions are largely universal, which supports Darwin's theory. Presently he consults for the security field to create devices that will restrict access to high-security areas to authorized personnel by matching images of distinctive facial expressions.

In *Emotional Intelligence: Why It Can Matter More than IQ* (1995a), Daniel Goleman drew attention to theories of emotional intelligence proposed by other researchers and spurred a profusion of empirical research. Recently, a new discipline called *social neuroscience* has emerged from Goleman's studies on the brain's interpersonal circuitry, including social encounters in online environments (Goleman, 2007).

Source: Originally adapted from Samuel Smith, *Ideas of the Great Psychologists* (1983), and Kirn, W., & Ressner, J. (2004). Poker's new face: Hot game in town. *Time, 164* (4), p. 30.

After he did this a number of times, the dog's mouth would water at the sound of the bell even though food did not follow.

In his experiments, Pavlov dealt with a behavior that is biologically preprogrammed within a dog through genetic inheritance—the salivation reflex. The reflex is an involuntary and unlearned response that is automatically activated by a given stimulus: the presence of food in the animal's mouth. By pairing the sound of the bell with food, Pavlov established a new connection between a *stimulus* (S) (the sound of the bell) and a *response* (R) (salivation) that previously had not existed. This is called **classical conditioning**—a process of stimulus substitution in which a new, previously neutral stimulus is substituted for the stimulus that naturally elicits a response. An illustration might be helpful: Consider a bright student who develops intense nausea associated with fear when confronted with a test situation. As a child, this student had a teacher who denied lunch recess to youngsters who did poorly on tests and assigned them extra work.

Classical conditioning depends on the existence of a reflex that can be activated by a new stimulus; in other words, you must already have some reflex to work with. But most people lack a preexisting unconditioned stimulus with which to link a new stimulus. Accordingly, psychologists have searched for alternative mechanisms. One of these mechanisms is probably familiar to you if you have seen animals perform tricks. When dolphins perform acrobatic jumps, they are always rewarded with food immediately afterward. In this procedure, the dolphin is signaled to *enact* the behavior and then is rewarded with fish; the food *follows* the response (the trick) and reinforces that particular behavior. When teaching a dolphin to do tricks, trainers employ **operant conditioning**—a type of learning in which the consequences of a behavior change the strength of that behavior. *Operants* are behaviors that are susceptible to control by changing the effects that follow them; they are responses that "operate," or act, on the environment and generate consequences. Thus, when a dolphin engages in behavior that is immediately followed by food, the behavior is strengthened by this consequence, and therefore the

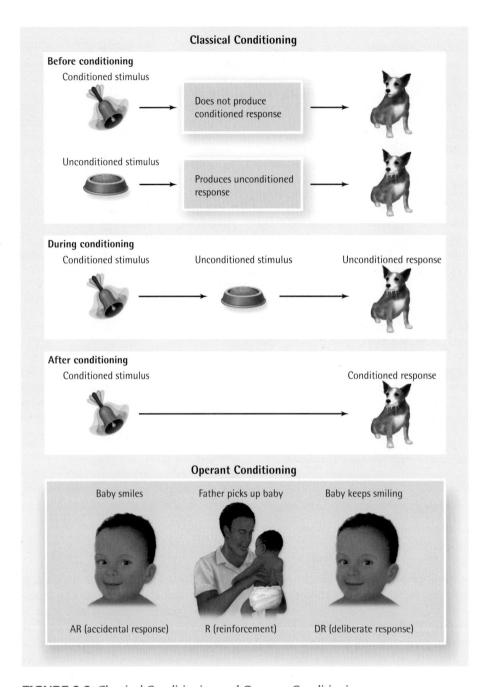

FIGURE 2.3 Classical Conditioning and Operant Conditioning

dolphin is more likely to repeat the behavior in the future. This is in contrast to classical conditioning, where the food itself directly produces the behavior (see Figure 2.3).

To summarize, classical conditioning derives from preexisting *reflexes;* a stimulus is said to elicit the response; and *antecedents* determine the response probability. Whereas operant conditioning does *not* derive from preexisting reflexes; the response is emitted; and it is determined by *consequences.*

John Watson and B. F. Skinner

We owe much to the earlier work of behaviorist John Watson (1878–1958), who said that people do not go through distinct stages but do go through a continuous process of behavior changes due to responses to environmental influences (external stimuli). During the 1950s and 1960s, no U.S. psychologist enjoyed greater prominence or had greater influence than B. F. Skinner

(1904–1990). He added to our understanding of operant conditioning, especially the role of *rewards* and *punishments*. Among the concepts popularized by Skinner is **reinforcement**—the process whereby one event strengthens the probability of another event's occurring. Skinner showed that much of life is structured by arranging reinforcing consequences, or "payoffs." For instance, businesses reward appropriate employee work behaviors with wages, commissions, bonuses, or flextime; and teachers use a variety of positive praise and rewards to motivate students who are struggling to learn a difficult concept. Also, psychotherapists lead clients to set goals to reduce ineffective behaviors or increase effective behaviors by having clients select their own rewards that are reinforcers.

Many of the principles of learning have found a use in **behavior modification.** This approach applies learning theory and experimental psychology to the problem of altering maladaptive behavior. According to behaviorists, pathological behavior is acquired just as normal behavior is acquired—through the process of learning. They claim that the simplest technique for eliminating an *unwanted* behavior is usually to stop reinforcing it. Interestingly enough, by attending to a child's inappropriate behavior (e.g., by scolding), we can reinforce exactly what we want to diminish. But behavior modification can also involve more deliberate intervention in the form of rewards or punishments. Rewards, as reinforcers, normally are selected by the individual whose behavior is to be changed. Behavior modification has helped obese people lose weight and has helped people overcome *phobias,* such as fears of high places, taking tests, sexual inadequacy, closed-in spaces, speaking before an audience, and many others. Watson and Tharp (2007) contend that people can develop their own behavior modification plan (see the *More Information You Can Use* box on page 42, "Putting Theory to Use in Your Life").

Our understanding of conditioning has undergone major transformations over the past three decades (Rosales-Ruiz & Baer, 1997). Psychologists now understand that conditioning is not simply a mechanical process that involves the association of two events that happen to occur closely in time. Organisms do not pair events in a vacuum. The environmental context is critically important. The overshadowing of some stimuli, the blocking of others, and the highlighting of still others has an impact. From a cognitive learning perspective, organisms learn only when events violate their expectations (Watson & Tharp, 2007). For example, suppose you retrieve a baseball from a bed of poison ivy, and shortly thereafter your skin becomes red and itchy with tiny blisters. You might not link the two events, but a doctor will point out that you are allergic

B. F. Skinner After World War II, B. F. Skinner (above left) became the dominant figure in American psychology. His experimental work with pigeons pioneered many facets of behavioral theory. He stressed the significant role that environmental forces play in an organism's acquisition of various behaviors. His theories are prevalent in the educational and therapeutic communities today.

to poison ivy. Then you grasp the relationship between the blisters and the offending plant. Subsequently, you take care to avoid contact with poison ivy. You have learned!

Questions

Consider the growing problem of the eating disorder anorexia nervosa. Using behavioral terminology, how would you explain the development of this condition? Using principles described in the preceding section, what would you propose as a plan to reduce this harmful behavior?

HUMANISTIC THEORY

In the past 60 years or so, a "third force" in psychology has arisen in reaction to the established psychoanalytic tenet of humans having only a few "basic drives" and the behaviorists' view that humans are motivated only by forces outside of themselves. **Humanistic psychology** maintains that humans are different from all other organisms in that they *actively* intervene in the course of events to control their destinies and shape the world around them. This takes a **holistic approach** that views the human condition in its totality and regards each person as more than a collection of physical, social, and psychological components (Schneider, Bugental, & Pierson, 2002).

MORE INFORMATION YOU CAN USE

Putting Theory to Use in Your Life

What if you could use theory to help you stop smoking, lose weight, overcome shyness, or become a more effective student? Many people have the impression that theories are grand ideas thought up by "armchair intellectuals" and that they are not relevant to everyday life concerns. How can we know whether a theory is going to work in a practical sense? The odds of success are greatly improved when the theory is backed by scientific research studies. Seeing the results of research studies tells us how good the theory is and hence how well it will work when applied to a real situation.

Two researcher/educators have compiled several research-supported theories of behavior into the book *Self-Directed Behavior* (Watson & Tharp, 2007). From these theories they designed a program for anyone to apply to change their own behaviors and ultimately to gain control over their lives. Most people have some behavior pattern that they desperately wish to change in order to improve their lives. Whether our goal is to become more assertive, to be a better friend or family member, to eliminate risky behaviors or addictions, or to increase health-promoting behaviors, each of us has room for improvement.

Watson and Tharp use self-regulation strategies, and understanding and developing the self-regulation skills leads to greater self-control. People *are* capable of regulating their own thoughts, feelings,

Believe You Can Achieve Your Goals

actions, and impulses. Depending on the situation, our self-regulation capabilities may be stronger or weaker. The good news is that we can learn to regulate our thoughts, feelings, and actions to achieve better behavioral outcomes.

Research findings show that greater self-control leads to better grades in school, a decrease in depression or anxiety, higher self-esteem, greater popularity, and greater relationship satisfaction (Baumeister, Vohs, & Tice, 2007). You might be thinking, "This sounds too good to be true. How can it possibly work for me?" Well, actually it is not the theory that will be doing the work—it is *you* who will be doing the work. The theory is the guidepost, but achieving results will require commitment, persistence, and effort.

Let's say that your goal is to lose weight. Target a specific behavior (e.g., overeating) that leads to an unwanted outcome (excess weight). One must also be clear and specific about one's goals (e.g., losing 20 pounds). Then, anticipate and manage obstacles (such as a holiday party).

The key to successful change lies with a strong self-efficacy belief (a key concept of a branch of scientific study called *positive psychology*). You must truly believe you can change and achieve your goals. Many studies show that when people *believe* they can change, they are more successful at meeting their goals (Bandura & Locke, 2003). Watson and Tharp (2007) give the example of an Olympic weightlifter who tried to break his own record. Try as he might, he could not seem to lift 500 pounds, yet he knew he could lift 499½ pounds. Unbeknownst to the weightlifter, his trainer once put 500½ pounds on the bar. The unaware weightlifter was able to lift it successfully. Here is an example of someone literally "raising the bar." We too can do this as we increase our self-efficacy beliefs.

The work involved in self-directed behavior hinges on *self-knowledge*—attained by observing ourselves in a careful and deliberate way. We must observe carefully, because studies show that we are prone to overestimating our abilities in activities that we are actually not very good at performing. We tend to underestimate how extensively we engage in health-risking behavior, while overestimating our competence level at work, as well as our educational attainments (Dunning, Heath, & Suls, 2003).

Applying scientific principles to gain self-knowledge includes observing our own thoughts, feelings, and actions. Keeping written records in order to understand and ultimately change a behavior provides evidence of when, how often, and why we engage in certain behaviors. Using the collected information as a baseline provides a means of comparing and pinpointing our behaviors over time. This then helps to mark the roadmap for change. Self-knowledge, scientific knowledge, and the guidance of theory can all be used to change your life for the better.

Source: Watson, D. L., & Tharp, R. G. (2007). *Self-directed behavior* (9th ed.). Belmont, CA: Wadsworth.

Abraham Maslow and Carl Rogers

Humanistic psychologists, such as Abraham Maslow (1908–1970) and Carl R. Rogers (1902–1987), are concerned with maximizing the human potential for self-direction and freedom of choice (Maslow, 1968; Rogers, 1970). One of the key concepts advanced by Maslow is the **hierarchy of needs,** depicted in Figure 2.4. Maslow felt that human beings have certain basic needs that they must meet before they can fulfill their other, "higher" developmental needs. At the bottom of Maslow's pyramid are fundamental requirements to satisfy physiological needs (including needs for food, water, and sex) and safety needs. Next, Maslow identified a set of psychological needs focused on belongingness (love) and self-esteem. At the top of the pyramid, he placed the need to realize one's unique potential to the fullest in a process he termed **self-actualization.** To Maslow, such people as Albert Einstein, Eleanor Roosevelt, the Reverend Martin Luther King, Jr., and Dr. Maya Angelou are good examples of self-actualizers.

Maslow constructed a composite picture of self-actualized persons (1970). According to Maslow, they are autonomous and independent. They have a firm perception of reality, accepting themselves, others, and the world for what they are, yet they are able to transcend their environment rather than merely coping with it. They are problem-centered rather than self-centered and are sympathetic to the condition of other human beings. They tend to establish deep and meaningful relationships with a few people, rather than superficial bonds with many people, but they also have a need for privacy. They have a democratic world perspective and work to promote the common good. They are spontaneous in thought and behavior but are not deliberately unconventional. Self-actualized people are creative and are susceptible to *peak experiences* (rapturous feelings of excitement, insight, and happiness) (Rathunde & Csikszentmihalyi, 2006).

Maslow and other humanistic psychologists argue that scientific inquiry should be directed toward helping people achieve freedom, hope, self-fulfillment, and strong identities. The goal of humanistic therapy is to help a person become more self-actualized—that is, to guide the client to self-directed change, building self-esteem along the way (in contrast to psychoanalysis and behavior modification, which are directed more by the therapist). Recently, some psychologists have suggested revising Maslow's pyramid to better reflect the importance of humans' evolutionary needs. They propose that self-actualization is a psychological need (mid-hierarchy) and that the pinnacle of the hierarchy consists of the evolutionary needs of mate acquisition, mate retention, and parenting (Kenrick, Griskevicius, Neuberg, & Schaller, 2010).

However, many other psychologists are skeptical about their humanistic colleagues. Indeed, important differences characterize their intellectual style (Kimble, 1984). Most clinical psychologists see increasing scientific knowledge as their primary task, adhering more to

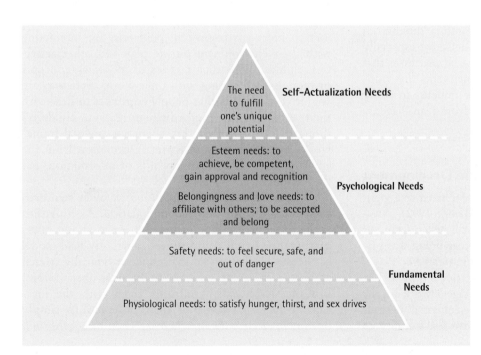

FIGURE 2.4 Maslow's Hierarchy of Human Needs According to the humanistic psychologists Abraham Maslow and Carl Rogers, fundamental needs must be satisfied before an individual is free to progress to satisfying her or his psychological needs, which in turn must be met before the person can realize self-actualization needs. *Source: Motivation and Personality,* 3rd ed. By Abraham H. Maslow. Copyright 1954, 1987 by Harper & Row Publishers, Inc. Copyright 1970 by Abraham H. Maslow. Reprinted by permission of Addison-Wesley Educational Publishers, Inc.

a "medical model" concerned with "diagnosing" and "treating" those with mental health disorders; whereas humanists focus primarily on improving the human condition and investigating behavior by relying on intuition and insight (Elkins, 2009). Also, critics charge that humanistic psychology turns people inward, encouraging an intense concern with the self. They maintain that this may breed the narcissistic view that if each of us works on becoming more fully human ourselves, then social ills such as racism, homelessness, hunger, and militarism will flourish.

Questions

What is the primary task of a humanistic psychologist? How might such a psychologist guide someone to change unwanted behavior?

COGNITIVE THEORY

Early formulations of behaviorism regarded human life as a "black box." These behaviorists viewed *input* or *stimuli* as entering the "box" at one end and coming out the other end as *responses*. What was inside the box did not concern them. But over the past 60 years, psychologists have become increasingly interested in what goes on inside the box. They call these internal factors **cognition**—acts or processes of knowing. Cognition involves how we go about representing, organizing, treating, and transforming information as we devise our behavior. It encompasses such phenomena as sensation, perception, imagery, retention, recall, problem solving, reasoning, and thinking.

Cognitive theory takes issue with a number of behaviorist tenets. Cognitive psychologists are especially interested in the cognitive structures and processes that enable a person to mentally represent events that transpire in the environment. The initial impetus to study cognition in the United States came from Jean Piaget, a Swiss developmental psychologist.

Jean Piaget: Cognitive Stages in Development

Like Freud, Piaget (1896–1980) is recognized as a giant of twentieth-century psychology (Beilin, 1992). Anyone who studies Freud and Piaget will never again see children in quite the same way. Whereas Freud was primarily concerned with *personality development*, Piaget concentrated on qualitative changes that occur in the child's *mode of thought*. Central to Piaget's work are the **cognitive stages** in development—sequential periods in the growth or maturing of an individual's ability to

think—to gain knowledge, self-awareness, and awareness of the environment (Mooney, 2006).

Adjustment as Process   When Piaget began to work with children in the early 1920s, little was known about the process by which thinking develops. Most psychologists assumed that children reason in essentially the same way as adults. Piaget challenged this view, insisting that the thought of infants and children is qualitatively distinct, not a miniature version of adult thought. For example, when they say that their shadow follows them when they go for a walk or that dreams come through the window, they are not being illogical—they are operating from a different mental framework from that of an adult. As children grow up, the form of their thought changes.

According to Piaget (1954), children engage in continuous interaction with their environment. They act on, transform, and modify the world in which they live, and in turn, they are shaped and altered by the consequences of those interactions. As children have new experiences, they interact with an existing structure or mode of thought. They then alter this structure to make it more adequate. This modified structure influences the children's new perceptions, which are then incorporated into a more complex structure. In this fashion, experience modifies structure, and structure modifies experience. Thus, Piaget viewed the individual and the environment as engaged in continuing interaction. This interaction leads to new perceptions of the world and new organizations of knowledge (Beilin, 1992; Brown, 1996).

Basically, Piaget saw development as **adaptation.** Beginning with the simple reflexes they have at birth, children gradually modify their repertoire of behaviors to meet environmental demands. By interacting with their environment during play and other activities, children construct a series of *schemas*—concepts or models—for coping with their world. **Schemas** are cognitive structures that people construct to deal with their environment. According to Piaget, children's thoughts mainly reflect the schemas or mental frameworks by which they interpret information from the environment, rather than any bits of information that they acquire.

Piaget believed that *adaptation* involves two processes: assimilation and accommodation. **Assimilation** is the process of taking in new information and interpreting it so that it conforms to a currently held model of the world. Piaget said that children typically stretch a schema as far as possible to fit new observations. But life periodically confronts them with the inescapable fact that some of their observations simply do not fit their current schemas. Then *disequilibrium* or imbalance occurs. As a result, children are required to invent increasingly better schemas or theories about the world as they grow up. **Accommodation** is the process of changing one's schema to make it better match the world of reality. Unlike assimilation, in which new 'experiences are fit into existing conceptions of the world, accommodation involves changing a conception to make better sense of the world. Imagine a child who understands that some animals, called fish, live in the ocean (this is *assimilation*). Yet as he watches whales leaping out of the ocean and listens to a tour guide's remarks during a whale watch, he discovers that whales are not fish but mammals that need to breathe air. Faced with this new information, the child makes an *accommodation* in his understanding of the animals that live in the ocean.

A balance between the processes of accommodation and assimilation is **equilibrium.** When in equilibrium, the child assimilates new experiences in terms of the models she or he arrived at through accommodation. But equilibrium eventually gives way again to the process of accommodation and the creation of new schemas or models. Thus, as viewed by Piaget, cognitive development is marked by alternating states of *equilibrium* and *disequilibrium*. Each stage consists of particular sets of schemas that are in a relative stage of equilibrium at some point in a child's development (Rathunde & Csikszentmihalyi, 2006).

Characteristics of Piaget's Cognitive Stages Piaget (1954) contended that biological growth combines with children's interaction with their environment to take them through a series of separate, age-related stages. The stage concept implies that the course of development is divided into steplike levels. Clear-cut changes in behavior occur as children advance up the developmental staircase, with no skipping of stages allowed. Although teaching and experience can speed up or slow down development, Piaget believed that neither can change the basic order of the stages (Piaget, 1970). Piaget described four stages in the development of cognition or intelligence. They are summarized in Table 2.2 and will be treated in more detail in later chapters on cognitive growth.

Appraisal of Piaget's Work Today the study of cognitive factors in development is of central interest to psychologists across the world. They credit Piaget with drawing their attention to the possibility that an unsuspected order might underlie some aspects of children's intellectual development (Levin & Druyan, 1993). Nonetheless, some followers of Piaget, such as John H. Flavell (1992), say that Piaget's notion of stages implies long periods of stability, followed by abrupt change. Flavell

Jean Piaget at Work Piaget spent more than 50 years observing children in informal settings, and he developed a stage theory of cognitive development. His work convinced him that a child's mind is not a miniature model of the adult's—a fact we often overlook when we try to teach children by using adult logic.

argues, rather, that the most important changes happen gradually, over months and years. He contends that cognitive growth is much less predictable than Piaget thought.

A mounting body of evidence also suggests that Piaget underestimated the cognitive capabilities of infants and young children. The kinds of memory Piaget found in 18-month-old babies researchers now find in babies at 6 months of age. Of course, Piaget did not have the methods, equipment, and procedures now available to scholars to measure the brain's electrical activity. The operational thinking capabilities of children from 2 to 7 years of age also are considerably greater than Piaget recognized (Novak & Gowin, 1989).

Research on other cultures has revealed both striking similarities and marked differences in children's performance on various cognitive tasks. Certain aspects of cognitive development among children in these cultures seem to differ from particular assumptions of Piagetian theory (Maynard & Greenfield, 2003). We should remember that no theory—particularly one that offers such a comprehensive explanation of development—can be expected to withstand the tests of further investigation without undergoing some criticism (Brown, 1996).

Piaget's theory has had a significant impact on our understanding of cognitive development. We would not know as much as we do about children's qualitative changes in intellectual development without Piaget's

TABLE 2.2 Piaget's Stages of Cognitive Development

Developmental Stage	Major Cognitive Capabilities	Example
Sensorimotor stage (birth to 2 years)	Infants discover the relationships between sensations and motor behavior.	They learn that their hands are part of themselves, whereas a ball is not.
	Children master the *principle of object permanence.*	Piaget observed that when a baby of 4 or 5 months is playing with a ball and the ball rolls out of sight behind another toy, the child does not look for it even though it remains within reach. Piaget contended that infants do not realize that objects have an independent existence. Around the age of 8 months, the child grasps the fact of object constancy and will search for toys that disappear from view.
Preoperational stage (2 to 7 years)	Children develop the capacity to employ *symbols,* particularly language.	Children use symbols to portray the external world internally—for instance, to talk about a ball and form a mental image of it.
	Egocentrism prevails.	Children of 4 and 5 years consider their own point of view to be the only possible one. They are not yet capable of putting themselves in another's place. A 5-year-old who is asked why it snows will answer by saying, "So children can play in it."
Stage of concrete operations (7 to 11 years)	Children show the beginning of rational activity. They are able to "conserve" mass, weight, number, length, area, and volume.	Youngsters come to master various logical operations, including arithmetic, class and set relationships, measurement, and conceptions of hierarchical structures. Before this stage children do not appreciate that a ball of clay can change to a sausage shape and still be the same amount of clay.
	Children gain the ability to "conserve" quantity.	Before this stage, children cannot understand that when water is poured out of a full glass into a wider glass that the water fills only halfway, the amount of water remains unchanged. Instead, children "concentrate" on only one aspect of reality at a time. They see that the second glass is half empty and conclude that there is less water in it. Now children come to understand that the quantity of water remains the same.
Stage of formal operations (11 years and older)	Youths acquire a greater ability to deal with abstractions.	When younger children are confronted with the problem, "If coal is white, snow is _____," they insist that coal is black. Adolescents, however, respond that snow is black.
	Youths can engage in scientific thought.	At this stage, youths can discuss Newtonian principles about the behavior of spherical objects.

monumental contributions. He noted many ways in which children seem to differ from adults, and he shed light on how adults acquire abstract concepts such as space, time, morality, and causality (Sugarman, 1987). Other researchers have attempted to integrate aspects of Piaget's theory into the cognitive learning and information-processing theories that are discussed in the next section (Brown, 1996).

Questions

Piaget is often considered to be one of the great "stage" theorists of developmental psychology. In your own words, how would you explain his stage theory of cognitive development? Why have his research findings been criticized recently?

Albert Bandura: Cognitive Learning

Piaget's work gave a major impetus to cognitive psychology and to research into the part played by inner mental activity in human behavior (Sperry, 1993). Opposing classical behavioral notions, cognitive theorists affirm that the world we live in is driven not solely by mindless physical forces but also by subjective human attitudes, values, and aims. Cognitive psychologists view the contents of conscious experience and their subjective qualities as dynamic, emergent properties of *brain activity* (inseparably interfused with and tied to the brain's cellular and biochemical properties and processes).

These psychologists are finding that mental schemes—often called "scripts" or "frames"—function as selective mechanisms that influence the information individuals attend to, how they structure it, how much importance they attach to it, and what they then do with it (Vander Zanden, 1987). As we noted earlier in this chapter, psychologists are also finding that people actively engage their environment, evaluate different stimuli, and devise their actions accordingly.

Classic behavioral theory also fails to explain many changes in our behavior that result from interactions with people in a social context. Indeed, if we learned solely by direct experience—by the reward or punishment for our actions—most of us would not survive to adulthood. If, for example, we depended on direct experience to learn how to cross the street, most of us would already be traffic fatalities. Similarly, we probably could not develop skill in playing baseball, driving a car, solving mathematical problems, cooking meals, or even brushing our teeth if we were restricted to learning through direct reinforcement.

We can avoid tedious, costly, trial-and-error experimentation by imitating the behavior of socially competent models (Eccles, 2007; Grusec & Davidov, 2007). By watching other people, we learn new responses without first having had the opportunity to make the responses ourselves. This process is termed **cognitive learning.** (It is also termed *observational learning, social learning,* and *social modeling*.) The approach is represented by the work of theorists such as Albert Bandura (1977, 1986, 2007).

The cognitive learning theory of Bandura relies heavily on notions of **information-processing theory,** which holds that through incoming sensory stimuli, individuals mentally process and then perform a series of discrete mental operations based on rules and strategies that become more sophisticated as the child develops (Bandura, 2006) (see Chapter 7). Bandura's theory emphasizes that people abstract and integrate information that they encounter in the course of their social experiences, including their exposure to models, verbal discussions, and encounters with discipline (Bandura, 2007).

Cognitive theorists reject the portrayal of children as "blank slates" who passively and unselectively imitate whatever the environment presents to them. Rather, they portray children as active, constructive thinkers and learners. Children's cognitive structures and processing strategies lead them to select meaningful information from an array of sensory input and to mentally represent and transform this information. Thus, to a considerable degree, children manufacture their own development as they interact with the environment (Flavell, 1992).

Cognitive learning theorists say that our capacity to use symbols gives us a powerful way to comprehend and deal with our environment. Language and imagery allow us to represent events, analyze our conscious

Social Modeling Often Influences Child Behavior How little we may be aware that children imitate our behaviors.

experience, communicate with others, plan, create, imagine, and engage in foresightful action. Symbols are the foundation of reflective thought and enable us to solve problems without first having to enact all the various solutions. Indeed, stimuli and reinforcements exert little impact on our behavior unless we first represent them mentally (Bandura, 1977).

By means of this abstraction and integration, individuals mentally represent their environments and themselves, particularly in terms of their expectations for the outcomes of their behavior and the perceptions they evolve of the actual effectiveness of their actions. Bandura portrayed people not as weather vanes who constantly shift their behavior in accordance with momentary influences but rather as stewards of values, social standards, and commitments. They evolve beliefs about their own specific abilities and characteristics (what Bandura called "self-efficacy") and then use these beliefs in fashioning what they say and do. Moreover, children and adults not only respond to environments, they actively seek out all sorts of environments (Grusec & Hastings, 2007).

Cognitive learning theories have been criticized for their lack of attention to significant developmental changes that can affect behavior. Bandura attempted to respond to this matter in his later theoretical writings, but he and his associates undertook little accompanying research that specifically addressed developmental issues. Consequently, approaches that emphasize more clearly age-related changes in development have moved to the forefront of interest for many developmental psychologists (Shiraev & Levy, 2007).

Lev Vygotsky: Sociocultural Theory

According to prominent Russian psychologist Lev Vygotsky (1896–1934), "All of the higher [psychological] functions originate as relations between human individuals" (Vygotsky, 1978). Interdependence is natural to human activity and offers different trajectories for development.

Vygotsky is credited with creating one of the outstanding schools of Soviet cognitive psychology and is known for his **sociocultural theory** of psychological development. Vygotsky assumes that the development of the individual is determined by the *activity of groups*. The child will interact with another person, assimilate the social aspects of the activity, and take that information and internalize it. In this way, social values become personal values (Vygotsky, 1978). According to Vygotsky, to understand the mind we must first understand how psychological processes (especially language) shape the functions of the mind. The major theses of his work are as follows:

- Development of individuals occurs during the early formative years and has a specifically historical character, content, and form; in other words, development will be different depending on when and where you grow up.
- Development takes place during changes in a person's social situation or during changes in the activities the person undertakes.
- Individuals observe an activity and then internalize the basic form of that activity.
- Systems of signs and symbols (such as language) must be available in order for individuals to internalize activities.
- Individuals assimilate the values of a particular culture by interacting with other people in that culture.

Vygotsky's theory provides a developmental perspective on how such mental functions as thinking, reasoning, and remembering are facilitated through *language* and how such functions are anchored in the child's *interpersonal relationships* (Daniels, Wertsch, & Cole, 2007). The child, according to Vygotsky, will observe something happening between others and then will be able to take that observation and mentally incorporate it. One example is the way children use language. First, a child will be told by a parent to "Say please and thank you." The child will also hear people saying "Please" and "Thank you" to each other. Then the child will begin to say these words aloud. By saying "Please" and "Thank you" aloud, the child is internalizing the words and the concepts they stand for in a social setting. Only after assimilating the words' meanings can the child individually start to act in a polite manner. It follows that development is always a social process and that child-adult interaction plays an important role (Berk & Winsler, 1995). Hence, it should come as no surprise that for Vygotsky, the way to understand development is to observe the individual in a social activity.

ECOLOGICAL THEORY

One cannot grasp human development by simply observing and measuring individuals' behavior in clinical settings that are separate from their relevant social, physical, and cultural environments. As mentioned in Chapter 1, Urie Bronfenbrenner (1917–2005) proposes an **ecological theory** that centers on the relationship between the developing individual and the changing environmental systems. Recall from Chapter 1 that Bronfenbrenner's model includes four increasingly broad, interactive, concentric levels of environmental influence: the microsystem, mesosystem, exosystem, and macrosystem (see Figure 2.5).

Urie Bronfenbrenner

Bronfenbrenner (1979, p. 27) states, "Development never takes place in a vacuum; it is always embedded and expressed through behavior in a particular environment." In proposing the ecological model as a research tool, Bronfenbrenner wants to move away from the traditional focus that sees either the environment or the person—instead of the relationship between them—as the most important aspect of development. Furthermore, he wants to focus on the process of development rather than concentrating on isolated variables at a single point in time.

Think of someone you know who considered dropping out of school. Bronfenbrenner suggests that focusing solely on factors such as the socioeconomic status of

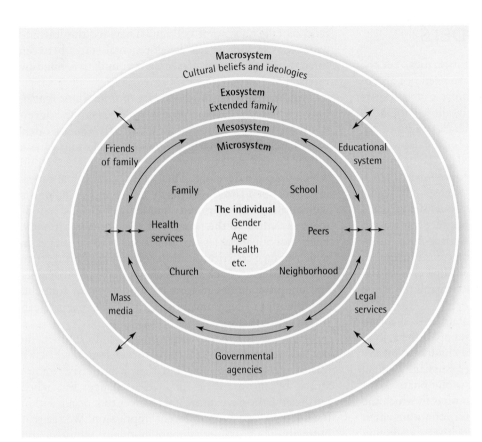

FIGURE 2.5 Bronfenbrenner's Ecological Theory of Development This diagram shows the four levels of environmental influences: the microsystem, mesosystem, exosystem, and macrosystem.

the family, intellectual ability, or ethnicity to explain the student's disengagement from school ignores most of the information relevant to this student's situation. Researchers must look at the relationships among variables in different environments. If you were to read an article in a research journal that sought to explain your friend's "dropping out" primarily in terms of distinct categories to which she or he belonged, you would probably be dissatisfied with the explanation, knowing that the reasons were much more complex than those offered by the researcher.

Finally, Bronfenbrenner's theory is important as a way of capturing how people make sense of their circumstances and how their understanding influences their behavior. You have probably been in a situation where a number of people reacted differently to the same experience. How each person perceived that situation—based on his or her personal history, expectations, feelings, and so forth—determined how he or she behaved. When studying development, it is important to remember not only that different people see things differently but also that the same person—as she or he develops cognitively, physically, and psychosocially—may see the same phenomenon differently throughout the life span. For example, a person will probably have very different reactions to a film about war if he or she sees the same film both before and having participated in a real war.

Bronfenbrenner also said change must occur over time, and he added the concept of the chronosystem to capture the dynamics of development with and across other systems. The **chronosystem** consists of changes within the individual and changes in the environment across time, as well as the relationship between the two processes. For example, a divorce that occurs in a child's family during the preschool period will have a different impact than a divorce that occurs when the child is an adolescent or young adult.

Question

Every morning when she rises, a woman from the Kiribati Islands in the Pacific pulls one hair from her head, places it in a container, and then goes out to check her fish trap. You need to come up with a reason that explains why she does this. You have two possible ways to collect data and arrive at an understanding of why she does this. You do not speak the woman's language, but you can use an interpreter for one day, or you can observe her for one week without being able to talk to her. In your opinion, which of the theories described in this chapter comes closest to explaining her behavior? Explain your decision.

CLASSIFYING THE MODELS

Each theory has its proponents and its critics. Yet the theories are not mutually exclusive; we need not accept one and reject the others. In fact, most psychologists prefer an **eclectic approach,** which allows them to select, from among all the various theories and models, whatever aspects provide the best fit for the descriptive and analytical task at hand. As stated at the beginning of this chapter, theories are simply tools—mental *constructs* that enable us to visualize (that is, to describe and analyze) something. Any theory limits the viewer's experience, presenting a tunnel perspective. But a good theory also extends the horizon of what is seen, functioning like a pair of binoculars. It provides rules of inference through which new relationships can be discovered and suggestions about how to expand the scope of a theory.

Furthermore, different tasks call for different theories. Consider language acquisition, for example. Behavioral theory helps us understand why U.S. children typically learn English and Russian children learn Russian. We shall see that ethological theory, one of the evolutionary adaptation theories, directs our attention to ways in which the human organism is neurally prewired for certain activities. In interacting with an appropriate environment, young children typically find that their acquisition of language comes rather "naturally"—a type of *easy learning.* Psychoanalytic theory alerts us to personality differences and to differing child-rearing practices that influence a child's learning to talk. Cognitive theory encourages us to consider the stages of development and the mental processes involved in the acquisition of language. Sociocultural theory reminds us of the range of influences that affect individual development—from individual attributes and family characteristics to community and cultural influences.

Continuity and Discontinuity in Development

Most psychologists agree that development follows orderly sequences of change that depend on growth and maturation as individuals interact with their environment—that is, on *continuity* of development. Those that say development produces smooth, gradual, and incremental change typically fall within the mechanistic camp. However, other psychologists emphasize discontinuity in sequences of change. They usually fall within the organismic camp.

The distinction between the two different models of development can be clarified by considering two analogies. According to the *continuity* or *mechanistic model,* human development is analogous to the growth of a leaf. After a leaf sprouts, it grows by simply becoming larger. The change is gradual and uninterrupted. Psychologists who emphasize the part that learning plays in behavior

tend to take this point of view. They see the learning process as lacking sharp developmental states between infancy and adulthood. Learning is cumulative, building on itself.

According to the *discontinuity* or *organismic model,* however, human development is analogous to the developmental changes that produce a butterfly. Once a caterpillar hatches from an egg, it feeds on vegetation. After a time it fastens itself to a twig and spins a cocoon within which the pupa develops. Then one day the pupal covering splits open and the butterfly emerges. Psychologists who adopt the discontinuity model see human development as similar to the process of insect metamorphosis. Each individual passes through a sequence of stages in which change constitutes a difference in kind rather than merely in degree. Each stage is characterized by a distinct and unique state in ego formation, identity, or thought. The theories of Sigmund Freud, Erik Erikson, and Jean Piaget are of this sort.

How we view development depends in part on our vantage point. To return to our analogies, when we observe first a caterpillar and then a butterfly, we are struck by the dramatic qualitative change. But when we observe the developmental changes that occur within the cocoon, we have a different impression. We see that butterfly-like characteristics are gradually acquired, and consequently we are more likely to describe the process as continuous (Lewis & Starr, 1979). However, if we look at a seed and then a tree, we are impressed by the magnitude of the change that has occurred.

Increasingly, psychologists recognize that much depends on one's vantage point and hence see both continuities and discontinuities across the life span (Lewis, 2001). In sum, social and behavioral scientists increasingly have come to see development as residing in a relation between organism and environment—in a transaction or collaboration: People work with and affect their environment, and it, in turn, works with and affects them.

Questions

How would you explain the distinction between the continuity models and the discontinuity models of human development over the life span? Which view do you think is more accurate? Why?

Nature Versus Nurture

Time and again it has been claimed that heredity-versus-environment questions are dead—that they have been definitively answered for all time. Yet in one fashion or another, each generation resurrects them, thrashes them out once more, and then presumes once again to set them to permanent rest. For example, a prevailing question in contemporary U.S. society is why some of our children and adolescents are so violent. Is the child's tendency to be violent due to an inherited genetic flaw, or to the type of home or school environment, or to peer influences, or to a combination of these factors? Some of the difficulties associated with the nature-nurture controversy stem from the fact that various schools of thought ask different questions and hence come up with different answers. How we phrase our questions affects the means by which the questions are answered.

Scientists began by asking *which* factor—heredity or environment—is responsible for a given trait, such as a mental disorder or a person's level of intelligence. Later, they sought to establish *how much* of the observed differences among people is due to differences in heredity and *how much* to differences in environment. Human intelligence is probably the trait about which the study of genetics has yielded the most information. Researchers are using data from the *Human Genome Project* to identify specific genes that are responsible for the heritability of intelligence (Plomin & Schalkwyk, 2007). And recently, some scientists have insisted that a more fruitful question is *how* specific hereditary and environmental factors *interact* to influence various characteristics (Buss, 2008). Each of these questions leads to its own theories, interpretations, and methods of inquiry.

The "Which" Question   Most students can recall debating the question "Which is more important, heredity or environment?" Yet most scientists today reject this formulation. They believe that phrasing the issue in terms of *heredity versus environment* has caused the scientific community, and society at large, untold difficulties. Counterposing heredity to environment is similar in some respects to debating whether sodium or chlorine is more important in ordinary table salt. The point is that we would not have salt if we did not have both sodium and chlorine (see Figure 2.6).

The "How Much" Question   As scientists recognized the inappropriateness of the "which" question, some of them reformulated the issue. Granting that both heredity and environment are essential for the emergence of any characteristic, they asked, *"How much* of each is required to produce a given trait?" They asked, "What percentage of a person's level of intelligence is attributable to heredity, and how much depends on environment?" The same question could be asked of a given mental disorder.

Scientists have traditionally sought answers to the "how much" question by measuring the resemblance among family members with respect to a particular trait

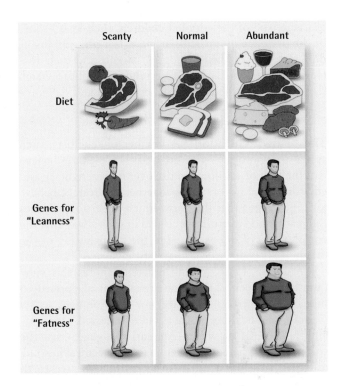

FIGURE 2.6 Gene-Environment Interaction Many traits are affected by environmental and genetic factors. A person who has a gene for "fatness" might actually weigh less than one with a gene for "leanness" if the former lives on a scanty diet and the latter on an abundant diet.
Source: Mankind Evolving: The Evolution of the Species by Theodosius Dobzhansky. Copyright © 1962 by Yale University. Reprinted by permission of Yale University Press.

(Segal, 1993). Nature occasionally provides us with the makings of a natural experiment. From time to time a fertilized egg, by some accident, gets split into two parts termed *identical* or *monozygotic twins*. Genetically, each is essentially a carbon copy of the other. The study of identical twins reared under different environmental conditions is the closest approach possible to experiments concerned with the influence of environment and heredity (see "The Minnesota Twin Project" on page 53).

In contrast to identical twins, *fraternal* or *dizygotic twins* come from two eggs fertilized by two different spermatozoa. They are simply siblings who happen to develop separately in the womb at the same time and are (usually) born at the same time. Important evidence can be obtained, and comparisons can be made between identical twins reared apart and fraternal twins reared together. Many scientists believe that such comparisons reveal valuable information about the relative contributions that heredity and environment make to a particular trait or behavior (Buss, 2008).

By studying children who were adopted at birth and reared by foster parents, one can compare some characteristic of the adopted children, such as IQ score or the presence of a particular mental or physical disorder, with that of their biological parents and their foster parents. In this fashion researchers attempt to weigh the relative influences of the genetic factor and the home environment.

The "How" Question A number of scientists, such as the psychologist Anne Anastasi (1908–2001) believe that the task of science is to discover *how* hereditary and environmental factors work together to produce behavior. They argue that the "how much" question assumes that nature and nurture are related in such a way that the contribution of one is *added* to the contribution of the other. This produces a particular behavior.

Anastasi (1986), among others, disputes this view (Smith & Thelen, 2000). She argues that as applied to human life, neither heredity nor environment exists separately. They are always interconnected, continually interacting. However, Anastasi recognizes that the role played by hereditary factors is more central in some aspects of development than in others. She thus sets forth the notion of the **continuum of indirectness.** At one end of the continuum are the most direct contributions of heredity—such as physical characteristics like eye color and chromosomal disorders like Down syndrome. At the other end of the continuum are contributions of heredity that are quite indirect—such as social stereotypes that members of a given society attach to various categories of skin color and hair texture.

Heredity and environment interact in complex ways. Genes influence the kinds of environments we seek, what we attend to, and how much we learn (Plomin & Schalkwyk, 2007). Psychologist Sandra Scarr (1997) contends that each stage in a child's psychological development is ushered in by an increment in the child's biological maturation. Only after the child is genetically receptive is the environment able to have any significant effect on her or his behavioral development. Scarr believes that children's genetic predispositions tailor their environment in three ways—passively, evocatively, and actively.

- *Passive relationship:* Parents give their children both genes and an environment that are favorable (or unfavorable) to the development of a particular capability. For example, parents gifted in social skills are likely to provide their children with an enriched social environment.
- *Evocative relationship:* A child evokes particular responses from others because of the child's genetically influenced behavior. For instance, socially engaging children typically elicit from other people more social interaction than passive, sober children do.

- *Active relationship:* Children seek out environments that they find compatible with their temperament and genetic propensities. For example, sociable children search for playmates and even create imaginary playmates if real ones are not at hand.

In short, what children experience in any given environment is a function of genetic individuality and developmental status (Buss, 2008). Scientists, then, are increasingly able to apply rigorous measurements to some aspects of the old nature-nurture controversy. In particular, valuable new insights are coming from a rapidly growing field of study (behavioral genetics) that undertakes to embrace, forge, and integrate insights from both psychology and genetics.

Questions

Historically, as scientists have studied the heredity-environment debate, what types of questions have they investigated? Where do contemporary researchers stand now?

Behavioral Genetics

Behavioral genetics focuses on individual differences and seeks answers to why individuals within a species exhibit different behaviors. There is much more acceptance in the field of psychology for the influence of genetics on individual difference (Plomin & Schalkwyk, 2007). Interest in the hereditary aspects of behavior had been subdued for nearly half a century by both behaviorism and psychoanalytic theory. The renewed interest in biological factors is due partly to exciting new discoveries in microbiology and genetics (advancing technologies enable us to examine cell structures both microscopically and chemically) and partly to the failure of social scientists to document a consistently strong relationship between measures of environmental experience and behavioral outcome. The pendulum seems to be swinging away from the environmentalists toward the side of the biologists. Indeed, some scholars worry that the pendulum is moving too rapidly toward a biological determinism that is as extreme as the earlier loyalty of some social and behavioral scientists to an environmental explanation of behavior (Plomin, Defries, & Fulker, 2006).

Jerome Kagan: Timidity Studies One area of investigation is extreme timidity ("shyness"). Jerome Kagan and his associates (Kagan & Snidman, 1991) followed 41 children in longitudinal research for eight years, studying "behavioral inhibition." The researchers found that 10 to 15 percent of those studied seem to be born with a biological predisposition that makes them unusually fearful of unfamiliar people, events, or even objects like toys. These youngsters have intense physical responses to mental stress: Their dilated pupils, faster and more stable heart rates, and higher levels of salivary cortisol (a hormone found in saliva) indicate that their nervous system is accelerated by even mildly stressful conditions.

Other researchers have found that shy biological parents tend to have shy children—even when the youngsters are adopted by socially outgoing parents (Rothbart, 2004). In addition, shy boys are more likely than their peers to delay entry into marriage, parenthood, and stable careers; to attain less occupational achievement and stability; and—when late in establishing stable careers—to experience marital instability. Shy girls are more likely than their peers to follow a conventional pattern of marriage, childbearing, and homemaking (Caspi & Shiner, 2006). A predisposition to timidity can be enhanced or reduced, but not eliminated, by nurturing child-rearing experiences. Kagan offers this additional bit of advice: "Look at whether the child is happy. Some shy kids are. And they often end up doing well in school . . . they become computer scientists, historians. We need these people, too" (quoted by Elias, 1989, p. 1D).

Identical Twins Separated at Birth Often Reveal Startling Similarities Separated as infants from Guadalajara, Mexico, identical twins Adriana Scott and Tamara Rabi were adopted into families only miles apart in the New York City area. While she was attending Hofstra, Adriana's friends mistook her for Tamara, who was attending Adelphi University. When they met, they were amazed at the similarities in their behavior and lives: Both are 5'3¾" tall, both were raised as only children, both are psychology majors with a B average, both have difficulty with math, both love music and dancing, both use similar expressions and gestures, and both lost their adoptive fathers to cancer.

Question

Briefly, how would you summarize these research findings on timidity?

The Minnesota Twin Project The results of an ongoing project at the University of Minnesota similarly suggest that genetic makeup has a marked impact on appearance, personality, health factors, and intelligence (Johnson & Bouchard, 2005). Researchers put 348 pairs of identical twins, including 44 pairs who were reared apart, through six days of extensive testing that included analysis of their blood, brain waves, intelligence, and allergies. All the twins took several personality tests, answering more than 15,000 questions on subjects ranging from personal interests and values to aggressiveness, aesthetic judgment, and television and reading habits.

Of 11 key personality traits or clusters of traits analyzed in the study, 7 revealed a stronger influence for hereditary factors than for child-rearing factors. The Minnesota researchers found that the cluster rated highest for heritability was "social potency" (a tendency toward leadership or dominance); "social closeness" (the need for intimacy, comfort, and help) was rated lowest. Although they had not expected "traditionalism" (obedience to authority and strict discipline) to be more an inherited than an acquired trait, it is one of the traits with

a strong genetic influence. The Minnesota researchers do not believe that a single gene is responsible for any one of the traits. Instead, each trait seems to be determined by a large number of genes in combination, so that the pattern of inheritance is complex—what is called **polygenic inheritance** (see Chapter 3).

Such findings do not mean that environmental factors are unimportant. It is not full-blown personality traits that are inherited, but rather tendencies or predilections. Such family factors as extreme deprivation, incest, or abuse would have a larger impact—though a negative one—than the Minnesota research reveals.

The message for parents is that it is a mistake to treat all children the same. Children can—and often do—experience the same events differently, and this uniqueness nudges their personalities down different roads. In studies of thousands of children in Colorado, Sweden, and Great Britain, researchers found that siblings often respond to the same event (a parent's absence, a burglarized home) and also interpret the same behavior (a mother's social preening) in quite different ways (Plomin, DeFries, & Fulker, 2006). Birth order, school experiences, friends, and chance events often add up to very different childhoods for siblings (Leman, 2004).

Because each child carries about her or his own customized version of the environment, it seems that growing up in the same family actually works to make siblings different. In guiding and shaping children, parents should respect their individuality, adapt to it, and cultivate those qualities that will help each child cope with life. For a timid child, good parenting would involve providing experiences in which success will encourage the child to take more risks. If another child is fearless, good parenting will involve cultivating qualities that temper risk taking with intelligent caution. Remember, though, that cultures differ in the value they place on such personality traits as risk taking and timidity, so good parenting differs from culture to culture.

Some scholars fear that the results of the Minnesota research will be used to blame the poor for their misfortunes, so they are distrustful of biological or genetic explanations of behavior. Other scholars point out that the research holds promise for preventive medicine. As researchers find a genetic predisposition for various disorders, they can work on changing the environment with diet, medication, or other interventions. For example, in 2007, research teams identified specific genes that they believe increase susceptibility to schizophrenia (Zhao et al., 2007) or bipolar disorder (also known as manic-depressive illness) (Jamra et al., 2007). Using the newest genetic-sequencing methods, researchers can better understand diseases and can then search for new ways to treat these disorders. In sum, the potential dangers of genetic research are great, but so are its potential benefits (Hartwell et al., 2008).

Questions

How would you summarize the major findings of the Minnesota Twin Project? What do we mean by polygenic inheritance?

Evolutionary Adaptation

It follows that organisms are *genetically prepared* for some responses. For instance, much learning in many insects and higher animals is guided by information inherent in the genetic makeup of the organism (Hartwell et al., 2008). The organism is preprogrammed to learn particular things and to learn them in particular ways. As we will see in Chapter 5, Noam Chomsky says that the basic structure of human language is biologically channeled by an inborn language-generating mechanism. Such a mechanism helps to explain why we learn speech so much more easily than we learn inherently simpler tasks such as addition and subtraction.

Evolutionary Psychology A newer discipline has recently arisen and is making an important contribution to our understanding of human behavior and the design of the human brain and mind. **Evolutionary psychology** is actually a reinvigorated investigation into what mental functions and behaviors are innate, or *instinctive,* which was originally proposed by Charles Darwin and William James in the late 1800s. Two of its main principles are that (1) "the brain (and therefore the mind) evolved to solve problems encountered by our hunter-gatherer ancestors," and (2) "the mind is equipped with species-specific 'instincts' that enabled our ancestors to survive and reproduce and that give rise to a universal human nature" (Workman & Reader, 2008, p. 1).

Leda Cosmides, a psychologist, and anthropologists John Tooby and Jerome Barkow co-edited *The Adapted Mind: Evolutionary Psychology and the Generation of Culture* (Barkow, Cosmides, & Tooby, 1992). Their ground-breaking work inspired research in related scientific fields that examine how the human body, organs, and mind have been shaped, or *adapted,* over time in response to biological and environmental/cultural influences. A very wide range of research includes the function of human anger, human fear, mate attraction and selection, altruism, friendship, and cooperation, among many other areas.

Ethology, the scientific study of animal behavior, holds that human babies are biologically preadapted with behavior systems such as crying, smiling, and cooing that elicit caring by adults (Buss, 2008). Similarly, babies have attributes of cuteness—large heads, small bodies, and distinctive facial features—that induce others to want to pick them up and cuddle them. Ethologists call these behaviors and features **releasing stimuli** and they function as especially potent activators of parenting. A number of psychologists, among whom John Bowlby (1969) is perhaps the most prominent, compare the development of strong bonds of attachment between human caretakers and their offspring to the imprinting encountered among some bird and animal species. **Imprinting** is a process of attachment that occurs only during a relatively short period early in life and is so resistant to change that the behavior appears to be innate.

Konrad Lorenz (1935), the Nobel Prize–winning ethologist, has shown that there is a short period of time early in the lives of goslings and ducklings when they slavishly follow the first moving object they see—their mother, a human being, even a rubber ball. Once this imprinting has occurred, it is irreversible. The object becomes "Mother" to the birds, so that thereafter they prefer it to all others and in fact will follow no other. Imprinting differs from other forms of learning. First, imprinting can take place only during a relatively short period, termed a **critical period.** (For example, the peak period for the imprinting effect among domestic chickens occurs about 17 hours after hatching and declines rapidly thereafter.) Second, as already mentioned, imprinting is irreversible; it is highly resistant to change, so that the behavior appears to be innate.

Some developmental psychologists have applied ethological notions to human development. However, many prefer the term *sensitive period* to *critical period*, for it implies greater flexibility in the time dimension and greater reversibility in the later structure. According to this concept, particular kinds of experience affect the development of an organism during certain times of life more than they do at other times (Bornstein, 1989). As we saw in our earlier discussion of Freud, the notion of sensitive periods is central to psychoanalytic thought. Freud's view was that infancy and early childhood are the crucial period in molding an individual's personality. However, most life-span developmentalists reject the idea that the first five years of a child's life are all-important.

Konrad Lorenz Here, young goslings follow the eminent Austrian ethologist rather than their mother. Because he was the first moving object that they saw during the critical imprinting period, they came to prefer him to all other objects.

Questions

Who are ethologists and what contributions have they made to our understanding of human development? How does evolutionary adaptation apply to human development?

SEGUE

In Chapter 2 we have considered several major types of theory dealing with human development. Psychoanalytic theories draw our attention to the importance of early experience in fashioning personality and to the role of unconscious motivation. Behavioral theories emphasize that one's environment plays a large part in learning. Humanistic theories attempt to maximize the human potential for self-actualization. Cognitive theories highlight the importance of various mental capabilities and problem-solving skills. Sociocultural theory focuses on the interaction between the individual and others in a social activity and on how individuals assimilate and internalize cultural meaning. Ecological theory stresses the importance of the relationship between the developing individual and the changing environment. Ethology holds that humans are biologically preadapted with behavior systems.

With Chapter 3, we begin to take you on a journey through the stages of life, from conception through birth, infancy, early childhood, middle childhood, late childhood, adolescence, early adulthood, middle adulthood, late adulthood, and dying and death. In each of these life stages, many of these developmental theories will be discussed further.

We have also written this text to help you broaden your understanding of human development from several other perspectives. In the following chapters you will encounter a prudent blend of research findings and theories from the hard sciences of biology, chemistry, and genetics, as well as from the social sciences of psychology, sociology, anthropology, history, and political science. In addition, we have included some cross-cultural research findings. You will come to realize that contemporary developmentalists live and conduct research around the world, collaborate on a global scale, and disseminate findings broadly so that the "newest" theories are more accessible than in the past. We encourage you to use your critical thinking skills to evaluate the diversity of theories you will undoubtedly encounter in our text, in your classroom, and in the online world.

SUMMARY

Theory: A Definition

1. The framework of a theory enables us to organize a large array of facts so that we can understand them. Theories about human development provide information or serve as a guide to acting on the world in a rational way, and they can inspire or stimulate further inquiry or research about behaviors.

2. Some newer theories seek to explain the development of women and nonwhites. Cross-cultural social scientists are examining the universality of older theoretical models of development in cultures across the world.

Psychoanalytic Theories

3. Sigmund Freud, the originator of psychoanalytic theory, postulated that personality development involves a series of psychosexual stages. Each stage poses a unique conflict that the individual must resolve before passing on to the next stage.

4. Freud also proposed that people operate from three states of being: the id, which seeks self-gratification; the super-ego, which seeks what is morally proper; and the ego, which is the rational mediator between the id and super-ego. Freud used a variety of therapeutic techniques to tap into the unconscious thoughts of his patients, which he believed were the source of his patients' distress.

5. Critics point out that Freudian theory is difficult to evaluate because it makes predictions about unconscious states that can neither be observed nor tested by accepted scientific procedures.

6. Freud's work is also criticized for his conclusion that early childhood is a significant stage of development, he studied mainly adult patients with disorders. Freud's daughter Anna continued her father's work, applying psychoanalytic principles to the treatment of children.

7. Contemporary feminist scholars find Freud's work problematic because he neglected to study women's development and psychological difficulties within the context of the historical time period.

8. Erik Erikson identifies nine psychosocial stages over the course of the life span, each of which confronts the individual with a major task (crisis) that the individual must successfully resolve to achieve healthy psychosocial development. Each part of the personality has a particular time period within the full life span when it must develop if it is going to develop at all.

9. More contemporary researchers, such as Carol Gilligan, propose that female identity is rooted in connections to others and in relationships.

Behavioral Theory

10. The proponents of behavioral theory, such as Watson and Skinner, believe that if psychology is to be a science, it must look to data that are directly observable and measurable and must not rely on introspection and self-observation by subjects. Behaviorists are interested in how people learn to behave in particular ways.

11. People learn to respond to the stimuli in their environment, and their responses shape their behavior. Some learning is based on classical conditioning, using a subject's reflex/innate responses; other learning derives from operant conditioning, where the consequences of the behavior alter the strength of the behavior.

12. Behaviorists deem learning to be a process called "conditioning," whereby individuals, as a result of their experience within an environmental context, establish an association or linkage between two events.

13. Behaviorists use concepts such as reinforcement (the administration of rewards or the removal of noxious stimuli) and punishment to shape desired behavior. Behavior modification is an approach that applies behavioral/learning theory to the problem of altering maladaptive behavior.

Humanistic Theory

14. Humanistic psychology maintains that human beings are different from all other organisms in that they actively intervene in the course of events to control their destinies and to shape the world around them.

Cognitive Theory

15. Cognitive theory examines internal mental representations such as sensation, reasoning, thinking, and memory. Cognition involves how children and adults go about representing, organizing, treating, and transforming information that in turn alters behavior.

16. Jean Piaget studied growing children and how they adjust to the world they live in. By playing and interacting with their world, children develop schemas, or mental frameworks.

17. Piaget proposed four progressive stages of cognitive development: the sensorimotor stage, the preoperational stage, the stage of concrete operations, and the stage of formal operations.

18. Cognitive learning theorists say that the human capacity to use symbols affords us a powerful means for comprehending and dealing with our environment. Symbols allow us to represent events; analyze our conscious experience; communicate with others; plan, create, and imagine; and engage in foresightful action.

19. Piaget underestimated the cognitive capabilities of infants and young children, and cross-cultural studies of cognitive development in children are finding aspects of his stage theory to be less applicable.

20. Cognitive learning and information-processing theorists' findings suggest that mental "schemas" function as selective mechanisms that influence what information individuals attend to, how they structure information, how important it is to them, and what they do with the information.

21. Through the process of cognitive learning (which is also called observational learning, social learning, and social modeling), people can learn new responses without first having had the opportunity to make the responses themselves.

22. Lev Vygotsky proposed sociocultural theory, which focuses on the interaction between the individual and others in a social activity and on how individuals assimilate and internalize cultural meanings. Mental functions are facilitated through language, and such functions are anchored in the child's interpersonal relationships during activities such as play.

23. Vygotsky stressed that interdependence is natural to human activity.

Ecological Theory

24. Urie Bronfenbrenner devised an ecological theory that centers on the relationship between the developing individual and four expanding levels of the changing environment, from home and family to the broader cultural context. The chronosystem captures the dynamics of development through time.

Classifying the Models

25. Each developmental theory has its proponents and critics. Yet different tasks and components of development simply call for different theories. Most psychologists prefer an eclectic approach to development.

26. Continuity theories of development suggest that human development is gradual and uninterrupted, whereas discontinuity models suggest that humans pass through a set sequence of stages, characterized by distinct states of ego formation, identity, or thought.

27. Social scientists continue the debate about the role of nature and that of nurture in human development.

28. Jerome Kagan and his associates have shown the part that genetic factors play in extreme timidity. Bouchard and colleagues at the University of Minnesota have similarly examined how the genetic makeup of twins affects personality.

29. Evolutionary psychologists investigate how the human brain, mind, and behavior have adapted through evolution. Ethologists propose that humans are biologically preadapted (via evolution) with behavior systems that elicit care by adults; these features function as especially important activators of parenting. The concept of a critical (sensitive) period for certain human development to occur is supported by some developmentalists but rejected by others.

KEY TERMS

accommodation *(45)*

adaptation *(44)*

assimilation *(44)*

behavior modification *(41)*

behavioral genetics *(52)*

behavioral theory *(38)*

chronosystem *(49)*

classical conditioning *(39)*

cognition *(44)*

cognitive learning *(47)*

cognitive stages *(44)*

cognitive theory *(44)*

continuum of indirectness *(52)*

critical period *(54)*

eclectic approach *(50)*

ecological theory *(48)*

epigenetic principle *(37)*

equilibrium *(45)*

ethology *(54)*

evolutionary psychology *(54)*

fixation *(35)*

hierarchy of needs *(43)*

holistic approach *(41)*

humanistic psychology *(41)*

imprinting *(54)*

information-processing theory *(47)*

operant conditioning *(39)*

polygenic inheritance *(53)*

psychoanalytic theory *(33)*

psychosexual stages *(34)*

psychosocial development *(36)*

reinforcement *(41)*

releasing stimuli *(54)*

responses *(38)*

schemas *(44)*

self-actualization *(43)*

sociocultural theory *(48)*

stimuli *(38)*

theory *(33)*

FOLLOWING UP ON THE INTERNET

Web sites for this chapter focus on the historical study of human development and on major theories of various aspects of development. Please access the text Web site at www.mhhe .com/crandell10 for up-to-date hot-linked Internet addresses for the following topics:

APA Society for the History of Psychology (Division 26)
http://www.apa.org/about/division/div26.aspx

Archives of the History of American Psychology
http://www3.uakron.edu/ahap/

Classics in the History of Psychology
http://psychclassics.asu.edu/

Erikson's Stages of Psychosocial Development
http://web.cortland.edu/andersmd/ERIK/welcome.HTML

A History of Women in Psychology
http://psychology.okstate.edu/museum/women/cover2
  .html

A History of Japanese Psychology
http://psychology.okstate.edu/museum/japanese/

The Jean Piaget Society
http://www.piaget.org/

Resources in the History of Psychology
http://psych.athabascau.ca/html/aupr/history.shtml

Twin Studies
http://mctfr.psych.umn.edu/

Center for Evolutionary Psychology
http://www.psych.ucsb.edu/research/cep/index.html

PART
2 BEGINNINGS

The biological foundations of heredity, reproduction, and prenatal development are discussed in Chapter 3. Today we think we know much more about the beginnings of life, yet medical research continues to astound us and makes us search for an answer to the question "When does life begin?" The Human Genome Project, a worldwide collaborative study that has mapped all human genes, continues to lead to even greater understanding of, and potential treatments for, disorders and hereditary defects. Chapter 3 explains sophisticated genetic testing and assisted reproductive technologies that have led to advances in fertility. More recent technological advances have led to the possibility of becoming pregnant after menopause. The phases of prenatal development leading up to birth have remained the same, although sophisticated imaging techniques now enable us to observe the tiniest humans readying themselves for living outside the womb.

Reproduction, Heredity, and Prenatal Development

1. What special challenges do parents face when multiple births occur through the use of fertility drugs and the implantation of multiple embryos created by in vitro fertilization? What are the costs and benefits of these reproductive technologies in light of their association with potential short- and long-term developmental complications?

2. Can you envision a time in the near future when human reproduction is accomplished primarily using technology to enhance the genetic traits of children and reduce the likelihood of illness and disease? What trait of your own would you like to see copied in your own child?

3. Why does the law allow people more freedom to destroy fetuses than to create them?

4. What should happen to women who abuse a developing fetus by exposure to some of the known biochemical agents (teratogens) that compromise the health of the developing fetus—when it is going to cost society millions, if not billions, of dollars to treat and care for children with birth defects through adulthood? Is an extensive education campaign enough, or should there be stricter penalties for repeat abusers?

5. A child dies and one parent decides to clone the child from a lock of hair or saved baby teeth—but the other parent doesn't want to do this. Who owns the DNA of the dead child?

Like all other living things, the majority of human beings are capable of producing new individuals and thus ensuring the survival of the species. With the use of assisted reproductive technologies (such as artificial fertilization, human egg and sperm donations, cryogenic preservation, and implantation techniques) and birth alternatives (such as selected surrogacy and intrauterine surgery), many humans who were previously deemed infertile can choose to reproduce. Many infertile couples and singles—both women and men—can now choose to have their own biological offspring, instead of adopting a child or remaining childless. A recent discovery has been made by Cornell researchers revealing the first fully functioning artificial human womb that could potentially revolutionize the bearing of children and childbirth in coming years. And the idea of human cloning, once merely a futuristic fantasy in science fiction novels, is a current—though ethically questionable—possibility.

It's almost as if the idea of woman + man = child is the old-fashioned way to re-create the species. What once was a private experience has become both public Internet entertainment and big business. For people with the resources, there certainly is a kaleidoscope of opportunities to procreate.

REPRODUCTION

Reproduction is the term biologists use for the process by which organisms create more organisms of their own kind. Biologists depict reproduction as the most important of all life processes. Two kinds of mature sex cells, or **gametes,** are involved in human reproduction: the male gamete, or **sperm,** and the female gamete, or **ovum** (egg or oocyte). In the process called **fertilization/fusion,** a male sperm enters and unites with a female ovum to form a **zygote** (fertilized egg). Each ovum and sperm has a unique composition of genetic material, and when they are united, the resultant structure is about the size of the period at the end of this sentence.

The Male Reproductive System

The primary male reproductive organs are a pair of **testes** normally lying outside the body in a pouchlike structure, the scrotum (see Figure 3.1). Sperm are produced and stay viable at a temperature a little lower than normal body temperature (about 96 degrees Fahrenheit). The scrotum holds and protects the testes and keeps them from being held too close to the man's warmer body. The testes produce sperm and the male sex hormones called *androgens.* The principal androgens are *testosterone* and *androsterone.* The androgens are responsible for producing masculine secondary sexual characteristics, including facial and body hair, increased muscle mass, and a deeper voice.

During sexual arousal and ejaculation, the sperm pass from the epididymis along muscular ducts into the *urethra.* On the way, they are mixed with secretions (which will nourish the sperm on their journey out of the man's body and into the woman's body) from the *seminal vesicles* and the *prostate gland.* The mixture of the sperm and secretions is termed semen, which will be ejaculated through the male's urethra—a tube that also connects with the bladder—and is surrounded by the man's external reproductive organ, the **penis.** A man's home and working environment, nutritional habits, level of exercise, health care, and sexual behaviors have a great impact on the health of his reproductive system and sperm production.

> **Questions**
>
> Can you identify the primary sex organs in males? Can you explain their functions in the process of human reproduction? What types of conditions can harm the male reproductive organs?

The Female Reproductive System

A woman's reproductive system is composed of the organs that produce ova (eggs), are involved in sexual

FIGURE 3.1 The Male Reproductive System This illustration of the male pelvic region shows the organs of reproduction.
Source: HealthWise KnowledgeBase: The Male Reproductive System, Healthwise, Incorporated, PO Box 1989, Boise ID 83702.

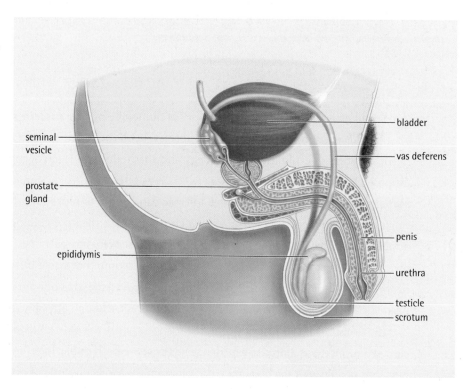

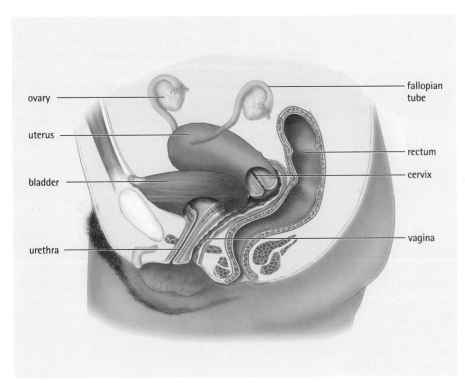

FIGURE 3.2 The Reproductive System This illustration of the female pelvic region shows the organs of reproduction.
Source: Rolin Graphics, 4080 83rd Avenue North, Suite LL, Brooklyn Park, MN 55443 1-888-500-1334.

intercourse, allow fertilization of the ovum, nourish and protect the fertilized ovum until it is developed, and are involved in giving birth. The primary female reproductive organs are a pair of **ovaries,** almond-shaped structures that lie in the pelvis (see Figure 3.2). While a female embryo is still in her mother's womb, that embryo's developing ovaries produce about 400,000 immature ova. After puberty, the ovaries produce mature ova and the female sex hormones, *estrogen* and *progesterone*. These hormones are responsible for the development of female secondary sexual characteristics, including breast (mammary gland) development, body hair, and hip development.

One or more ova are expelled typically from one of her ovaries on a monthly schedule. For most women this is about every 28 days, although for some women the cycle varies, particularly during the first few, and the last few, years of menstruation. The ovum is moved through the **fallopian tube,** or oviduct, where it may be fertilized if sperm are present. The fallopian tube is lined with tiny, hairlike projections called *cilia* that propel the ovum along its course through the fallopian tube into the womb, or uterus. This short progression takes a few days; the fallopian tube is about 6 inches long and inside has the circumference of a human hair (Nilsson & Hamberger, 2004).

The pear-shaped **uterus,** a hollow, thick-walled, muscular organ, can house and nourish what will be called the developing **embryo,** the organism from the time the **blastocyst** implants itself in the uterine wall until the organism develops into a recognizable human fetus. The muscular uterus prepares itself each month for potential conception with a blood-rich lining, which each month it sheds for four to six days (in menstruation) if conception (fertilization) does not occur. The unfertilized ovum is expelled from the body through the narrow lower end of the uterus, called the *cervix,* which projects into the vagina. The **vagina** is a muscular passageway that is capable of considerable dilation. The penis is inserted into the vagina during sexual intercourse, and the infant passes through the vagina at birth. Surrounding the external opening of the vagina are the *external genitalia,* collectively termed the *vulva.* The vulva contains the fleshy folds known as the *labia,* as well as the *clitoris* (a small, highly sensitive erectile structure comparable in some ways to the man's penis).

A woman's home and working environment, nutritional habits, level of exercise, health care, and sexual behaviors have a great impact on the health of her reproductive system.

Questions

Can you identify each of the primary female sex organs involved in the process of human reproduction? What types of conditions can harm the female reproductive organs?

How and When Fertilization Occurs

The Menstrual Cycle   **Menstruation** is the periodic discharge of blood and cells from the lining of the uterus, marking the end of one cycle and the beginning of another. The series of changes associated with a woman's **menstrual cycle** begins with menstruation and continues through the maturing of an ovum, ovulation, and the eventual expulsion of an unfertilized ovum from the body through the vagina. A healthy woman's ovaries typically produce at least one mature ovum, or egg cell, every 25 to 32 days, the average being every 28 days (U.S. Department of Health and Human Services, Office of Women's Health, 2010).

Health problems (such as illness, disease, stress, nutritional deficiencies, or excessive exercise) can affect a woman's menstrual cycle. But variations among women in the length of the ovarian cycle are normal. Irregular cycles or skipped cycles are common among young women who have just begun menstruating and among older women who are approaching or in their forties. Day 1 of a cycle is the first day of menstruation. Toward the middle of each menstrual cycle (around days 13 to 15) for a majority of women, typically one ovum reaches maturity in a follicle of an ovary and passes into one of the two passages called the fallopian tubes (also called oviducts) from the ovaries to the uterus. *Fertilization,* if it occurs, typically takes place in the fallopian tubes.

This is commonly considered the optimal time for conception to occur, because a mature ovum is viable for about 24 hours. However, researchers have found that there is hardly a day in the menstrual cycle during which some women are not potentially fertile (U.S. Department of Health and Human Services, 2010f). If there is no fusion with a sperm in the fallopian tube, the ovum begins to degenerate after 24 hours and will be expelled from the body during menstruation.

Ovulation   An ovary contains many follicles, and typically only one undergoes full maturation in each ovarian cycle. Initially a *follicle* in an ovary consists of a single layer of cells; but as it grows, the cells proliferate, producing a fluid-filled sac that surrounds the primitive ovum, which contains the mother's genetic contribution. Most women's ovaries seem to alternate, each releasing an ovum every other month, although when one ovary is diseased or has been removed, the other ovary ovulates each month.

The hypothalamus in the forebrain instructs the pituitary gland to release a surge of luteinizing hormone (LH), and the maturing follicle ruptures in the ovary. The discharge of the ovum from the follicle in the ovary is called **ovulation.** When the mature follicle ruptures, releasing its ovum, it undergoes rapid change. Still a part of the ovary, the follicle transforms itself into the *corpus luteum,* a small growth recognizable by its golden pigment. The corpus luteum secretes *progesterone* (a female hormone), which enters the bloodstream and causes the mucus lining along the inner wall of the uterus to prepare itself for the potential *implantation* of the newly fertilized egg. If conception and implantation do not occur, the corpus luteum degenerates and eventually disappears. If pregnancy occurs, the corpus luteum continues to develop and produces progesterone until the placenta takes over the same function. The corpus luteum then regresses and disappears (Stocco, Telleria, & Gibori, 2007).

> *Questions*
>
> What is the purpose of menstruation, and what happens during a typical menstrual cycle for most women? Is there an optimal time for conception during this cycle—that is, a time when conception is most likely to occur?

Fertilization   At the time of sexual intercourse, a man customarily ejaculates 100 to 500 million sperm into the woman's vagina. Sperm can ascend the *cervical canal* only during those few crucial days when the woman's *cervix* is open and produces strands of mucus that allow some of the sperm to enter the uterus and fallopian tubes. Sperm have a high mortality rate within the female tract because of its high acidity and other factors related to the health of the sperm, yet a small number of sperm are viable up to 48 hours in the female's reproductive tract. The one sperm that fuses with the ovum has prevailed against gigantic odds: several hundred million to one. The union (or fusion) of a sperm and an ovum is called *fertilization,* and when this process is successful, we say that *conception* has occurred. This normally takes place in the upper end of the fallopian tube. When there is a joining of the chromosomes from the sperm and egg, the new structure is called a *zygote,* with its unique genetic makeup (see Table 3.1). Even then, however, the new zygote is extremely vulnerable; about one-third of all zygotes die shortly after fertilization.

If fertilization fails to take place, the thickened layers of tissue lining the wall of the uterus deteriorate over a three- to seven-day period and are discharged from the vagina. Industrialized countries have seen a rise in *infertility rates* over the past three decades. It is suspected that this is due to women delaying childbirth (an older woman's ova are less likely to be fertilized than a younger woman's ova), an increase in pelvic inflammatory diseases and other sexually transmitted infections (STIs), and lower sperm counts in men (Dyer, Lombard, & Spuy, 2009).

TABLE 3.1 Conception

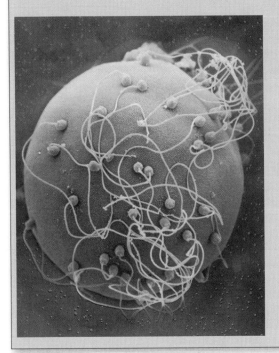

Description	Vulnerabilities
Fertilization occurs when the two gametes, ovum (egg) and sperm, have fused. Their DNA has joined, creating a new structure called a zygote. Additional sperm that did not penetrate the cell wall of the egg (normally nearly 100 or so) continue to attempt to penetrate the cell wall of the ovum. This action, plus the movement of the cilia of the tubal lining, promotes a counterclockwise motion of the zygote. The zygote will proceed down the fallopian tube, a journey of about 6 inches that will take 3 to 4 days.	The fallopian tube has about the same internal circumference as a human hair. If the fallopian tube is scarred or blocked, the zygote will be unable to proceed. Damage or obstruction to the fallopian tube can occur because of such factors as pelvic inflammatory disease (PID), sexually transmitted infections (STIs), and endometriosis, to name a few. There is potential for incomplete fusion if the sperm is defective or if the biochemistry of the cell wall of the ovum is not functioning properly.

Conception: The photo shows sperm, their tails thrashing, as they approach an ovum. One will successfully burrow into the ovum, just before depositing its genetic material.

Questions

How and where does fertilization occur? What are some factors that inhibit or prevent fertilization? What happens to the ovum if fertilization does not occur?

Multiple Conception   If more than one ovum matures and is released, the woman might conceive multiple, non-identical siblings (**dizygotic** or fraternal **twins**). Identical twins (**monozygotic twins**) result from one fertilized egg splitting into two identical parts after conception. Triplets and higher-order multiples may occur as a combination of single and/or dizygotic or monozygotic twins, but such multiples are more likely with assisted reproduction.

For couples who select assisted reproduction methods, multiple conceptions also occur in a test tube in a medical laboratory. After the resultant embryos (usually several) grow for a few days, some are transplanted into a woman's uterus in hopes that at least one will implant itself into the uterine wall and continue to develop. The incidence of multiple pregnancies has risen at an unprecedented pace over the past two decades, and in vitro fertilization (IVF) is now responsible for about one-half of all multiple births in various parts of the world. The twin birthrate in the United States was 70 percent higher in 2007 than in 1980, and the triplet and higher-order birth rates were a staggering 400 percent higher (see Figure 3.3) (Martin et al., 2010).

Reduction of Higher-Order Multiple Pregnancy
Multiple pregnancy of an order higher than twins involves far greater risks for the woman's health and also for her fetuses, which are likely to be miscarried or to be delivered prematurely with a high risk of either dying or having birth defects. In such circumstances, it may be ethically acceptable to some women to use *selective reduction* procedures to reduce the number of embryos than to do nothing. The procedure is usually performed between 9 and 11 weeks of pregnancy.

However, some women do not regard selective reduction as an acceptable method for controlling the high rate of multiple pregnancies associated with assisted reproductive technologies because of the moral, ethical, and psychological consequences of the procedure, as well as the risks it entails. Although medical professionals in the fertility business do not view this as an abortion procedure—because the intention of the mother is that the pregnancy continue—others can't bring themselves to consent to eliminating any fetus and prefer simply to leave it in the hands of a higher authority. Whatever the

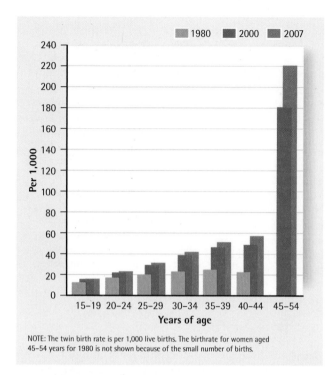

FIGURE 3.3 Twin Birthrates by Age of Mother: United States, 1980, 2000, 2007 The birthrate for twins has climbed for all age groups since 1980, and the greatest increases continue to be for older mothers, ages 45–54.

Source: Martin, J. A., et al. (2010, August). Births: Final data for 2007. *National Vital Statistics Reports, 58*(24), 1–125. Retrieved November 5, 2010, from www.cdc.gov/nchs/data/nvsr/nvsr58/nvsr58_24.pdf. Also Martin, J. A., et al. (2002, December 18). Births: Final data for 2001. *National Vital Statistics Reports, 50*(5), Table 50, 100–102. Also Martin, J. A., & Park, M. M. (1999, September 14). Trends in twins and triplet births: 1980–1997. *National Vital Statistics Reports, 47*(24), 1–17.

parents choose, it is one of life's most difficult decisions (Ferrara et al., 2008).

Questions

Where in the woman's reproductive system does conception normally occur? What is the difference between dizygotic and monozygotic twins? What are some potential risks of the continually rising rates of multiple pregnancy since 1980? What does "selective reduction" mean?

Conceiving or Avoiding Conception

Do you and your partner want to conceive a child in the near future? Or do you not want to conceive a child right now? Do you know when a woman is most likely to be "fertile"? As previously mentioned, generally at midcycle (for a majority of women, but not all) an ovum in the fallopian tube is viable for about 24 hours. Sperm are viable for fertilization for about 48 hours once they are introduced into the vagina. Women who have difficulty conceiving must become aware of their optimal time of

conception by taking their daily body temperature and/or undergoing a daily high-density ultrasound to determine their days of ovulation.

Recent investigations have discovered optimal times of the calendar year as well. In some regions of the world, people mating during the optimal fertility season have twice the chance of conceiving than they have at other times. The optimal period for conception seems to be when the sun shines for about 12 hours a day and the temperature hovers between 50 and 70 degrees Fahrenheit. It is likely that an internal biological clock, fine-tuned by the length of daylight, contributes to the seasonal differences (Sperling, 1990).

Infertility and Assisted Reproductive Technology

Since 1978 when Louise Brown, the world's first "test-tube baby" was born in England, medical researchers have created many fertility drugs and microscopic and surgical procedures that have dramatically transformed infertility treatments. In the United States, about 12 percent of women of childbearing age have sought **assisted reproductive technologies (ARTs)** to increase their chances of becoming pregnant. Worldwide, the estimate runs into millions of couples with infertility issues. In 2007 there were 483 fertility clinics in the United States, and over 1 percent of all infants born in the United States every year are conceived using ART. The goal of these fertility clinics is to offer hope to childless couples, single women, same-sex couples, and those who postpone childbearing because of illness, disease, career, or late marriage or remarriage (Centers for Disease Control and Prevention, 2009a).

There are several ART options because there are many reasons why conception might not occur naturally. A man's sperm count might be low, he might have sustained injury or disease of the testicles, or his sperm might be unhealthy or have low motility. Analysis of data on male reproductive dysfunction has revealed declining semen quality, rising infertility, and increasing rates of testicular disorders (Dyer, Lombard, & Spuy, 2009). Some researchers are suggesting that postponement of childbearing is a key factor, for sperm motility decreases markedly from one's twenties to one's forties and older (Sobotka, 2004). Moreover, a woman's fallopian tubes might be blocked, scarred, or missing as a consequence of disease, injury, or surgery. The follicles in her ovaries might not be producing healthy ova. The endometrial lining of the uterus might not be able to host a developing embryo. In some instances there is no physiological reason, and in some cases a single woman or same-sex couples may wish to have a child.

In vitro fertilization (IVF) is fertilization outside the body in a test tube in a lab environment. In an attempt to accomplish pregnancy, a woman will be given hormone injections to stimulate the ovaries to produce

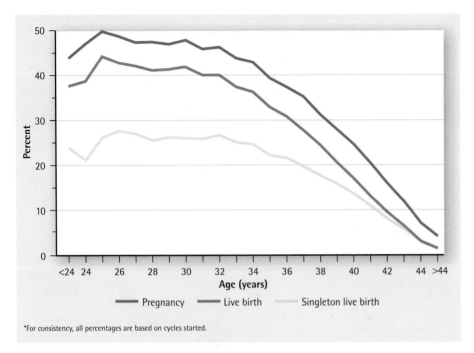

FIGURE 3.4 ART Success Rates Differ Among Women of Different Ages: 2008 A woman's age is the most important factor affecting the chances of a live birth when her own eggs are used. Among women in their 20s, pregnancy rates, live birthrates, and singleton birthrates were relatively stable, but success rates declined steadily from the mid-30s.
Source: Centers for Disease Control and Prevention, American Society for Reproductive Medicine, Society for Assisted Reproductive Technology. (2010). *2008 Assisted reproductive technology success rates: National summary and fertility clinic reports.* U.S. Department of Health and Human Services. Figure 15. Retrieved May 27, 2011.

several viable eggs using a protocol of follicle-stimulating hormones. After the injection regimen, a medical practitioner will retrieve several eggs from the ovaries. Several eggs will be fertilized with sperm of the spouse or donor. The embryos develop for three to five days in a special culture. The highest-quality embryos are placed into the uterus, and then the woman waits to see whether implantation takes in the uterus. Single-embryo transfer is proving less risky to the embryo and mother than multiple-embryo transfer. Some in vitro fertilization procedures are *GIFT (gamete intrafallopian transfer)*, *ZIFT (zygote intrafallopian transfer)*, and *ICSI (intracytoplasmic sperm injection)*.

In vitro fertilization procedures are available for a woman past menopause. These IVF procedures can use the woman's own eggs and her partner's sperm, or donor eggs and/or donor sperm. In 2006, a 59-year-old woman in the United States gave birth to twins using IVF procedures (Bone, 2006). Very-high-risk multiple births are on the rise in the United States because of these procedures (Martin et al., 2010). Contemporary practitioners are attempting to improve the chances of having a healthy, full-term fetus by using SET, or *single-embryo transfers* (rather than implanting multiple embryos), and *sperm sorting* (sperm separation) for simple medical insemination and to help prevent sex-linked diseases.

Some Cautions About ART Procedures   Worldwide, it is estimated that more than 4 million babies have been born as a result of the use of ART methods since 1978, and about one out of six couples experiences an infertility problem (Rosenwaks, Goldstein, & Fuerst, 2010). Yet more studies across several countries confirm that rates

of miscarriage, prematurity, low birth weight, infant birth defects or developmental delays, and infant mortality are higher than with normally conceived babies. Medical researchers are improving these techniques, are extending the time for embryo growth before implantation into the mother, and are implanting only a few embryos to reduce the high risks of higher-order multiples (see Figure 3.4). But present success rates per ART cycle reported among 52 countries indicate average pregnancy rates of 35 percent and only 29 percent actual births—this leaves far too many couples acutely disappointed, with unfulfilled dreams (Centers for Disease Control and Prevention, 2009a). On the other hand, those parents who give birth to twins and higher-order multiples face their own unique challenges in managing the emotional demands and expenses of such a large family.

Questions

What percent of couples in the United States are experiencing complications with fertility? What do we know about the success rate of ARTs, especially with a woman's advancing age?

Developmental Biology and Reproduction in the Twenty-First Century   **Cloning** is a form of *asexual reproduction,* which creates an embryo by a process called *somatic cell nuclear transfer (SCNT).* Researchers create a cloned embryo by taking the nucleus of a somatic cell (such as a skin cell) and inserting it into an egg cell whose own nucleus has been removed—a process called *nuclear transplantation.* This hybrid egg is then stimulated to

MORE INFORMATION YOU CAN USE

The Future of ARTs, and Some Ethical Concerns

Future Assisted Reproductive Technologies

The scientific search to help couples conceive is a worldwide research effort. The first "test-tube baby" was born in England. Australia claims the first baby born from a frozen embryo. Belgian researchers found a way to inject sperm directly into an egg cell (Lemonick, 1997). Medical researchers are conducting studies on synthetic amniotic fluid that keeps tiny premature infants alive (Christensen, Havranek, Gerstmann, & Calhoun, 2005). Also, medical researchers are developing an artificial uterus (or "womb tank")—a chamber connected to a machine that brings oxygen and nutrients to the fetus developing inside the chamber, but completely outside the woman's body. This science of **ectogenesis**, the process by which a fetus gestates in an environment external to the mother, may evoke images of Aldous Huxley's *Brave New World*, but researchers estimate that ectogenesis will be a reality within a few years (see Figure 3.5). Most recently, Cornell researchers have announced that they have cultured endometrial cells and used them to engineer a natural uterus outside of the body that sustained the implantation of embryos (Simonstein, 2009). Artificial wombs will probably be used as intensive care units for fetuses either when the mother is ill and can no longer carry the child or when the fetus is ill and needs to be removed from the mother's womb for close monitoring. We are entering a time when, for some, having a child could become a completely out-of-body experience.

Ethical Concerns with ARTs

Although critics call an artificial womb unnatural and dehumanizing and maintain that it poses moral, social, and psychological dilemmas, Farooqi (2003) from Texas A&M says, "Ectogenesis is merely an artificial means to sustain life, and, by this definition, it is no different than life support. And while ectogenesis may entail an unnatural delivery, so does a cesarean section" (see Figure 3.5). And as Farooqi and other proponents suggest, such an approach to saving very premature infants may end the abortion debate forever. An unwanted fetus could be removed from the biological mother, developed in a life-supporting artificial womb, and adopted at "birth." Yet there are other issues with developing artificial wombs. A fetus responds to its mother's heartbeat, voice, emotions, and movements. Further, the bond that exists between the two plays an important role in development (Simonstein, 2009).

The same ethical unease arose with the creation of incubators for premature babies in the late 1800s, with the first

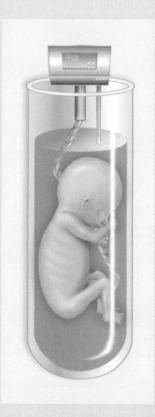

FIGURE 3.5 Ectogenesis Babies of the future may develop outside the mother's womb. Reproductive researchers predict that the controversial science of ectogenesis will be a reality within five years.
Source: Gelfand, S., & Shook, J. R. (2006). *Ectogenesis: Artificial Womb Technology and the Future of Human Reproduction.* Amsterdam-New York: Rodopi.

birth control pills in the 1960s, with the first human heart transplant in 1967 (ushering in the age of donor tissues and organ transplants), and with the first baby created by IVF in 1978. Today the public welcomes such life-saving or life-creating procedures. However, as with all new medical "miracles," there must be federal regulation and oversight because there have already been disasters. In 1957 the drug *thalidomide* was sold in Europe and Canada to ease pregnant women's "morning sickness" or insomnia. Tragically for both parents and children, over 10,000 babies were born with stunted or missing limbs. Yet more recently, thalidomide has reemerged and may be prescribed to ease the nausea of AIDS and chemotherapy) (Public Affairs Committee, 2000).

Social scientists, physicians, bioethicists, politicians, clergy, and laypeople raise legitimate questions about ARTs. How long (days or cell divisions) are embryos allowed to develop in a lab? Should embryos be "designed" to exhibit certain characteristics? What happens if an abnormality occurs? At what stage are embryos destroyed? Is this a form of eugenics? Will human fetal tissue be grown solely for transplantation (i.e., *xenotransplantation*) (Center for Biology Evaluation and Research, 2004)? Who owns the anonymous embryos developed in a lab? How will children conceived through cloning technologies feel when they find out how they were created in this manner? Will development outside a mother's body affect the natural bonding process? Researchers, fertility specialists, politicians, and venture capitalists who support ARTs, including cloning, maintain that they are not subverting any moral standard. Some say they are bringing humankind closer to God by helping infertile couples fulfill their dream to reproduce or by easing suffering (Talbot, 2001). Yet many people, especially women, still have moral reservations about redefining motherhood and humanity—and express serious concerns for the future of all humankind (Simonstein, 2009). As a result, some see artificial reproductive technology as an encroachment upon what makes us human, whereas others see the evolution of ARTs as a triumph of modern science.

begin embryonic divisions by treatment with electricity or certain ions. Thus, a new embryo may be created that is a nearly 98 percent genetic replica of the donor body cell, which some call a "clonote" (Hansen, 2004).

In *reproductive cloning,* the cloned embryo is placed into a woman's uterus, in the hope that it will implant in the uterine wall, develop into a fetus, and be born healthy. Reproductive cloning has been successfully performed in several mammalian species, such as sheep and cats. Many cloned animals exhibit puzzling developmental defects (such as obesity), which may be due to an "epigenetic phenomenon" associated with cloning procedures. No country or group of scientists has yet condoned the reproductive cloning of humans (Hartwell et al., 2008).

In *therapeutic cloning,* the resultant embryo is allowed to grow four to five days to the blastocyst stage. Then its *stem cells* are extracted and grown to become other body cells or potentially body organs (skin, blood, bone, pancreatic cells, neurons, sperm, eggs, and so on) (see Figure 3.6 on page 70). Although ardent opponents say such human embryos must not be designed solely for destruction (which ignores the sanctity of life), zealous proponents say stem cells can be used to cure illness and disease (including cancer, diabetes, Parkinson's, Alzheimer's, spinal cord injuries, and others). In a surprising advance that could sidestep the ethical debate surrounding stem cell biology, researchers have come closer in the conversion of patient's own cells into specialized tissues that might replace those lost to disease. The technique entails reprogramming a skin cell of a mouse back to the embryonic state; then the embryonic cells can be induced to develop into many of the body's tissues. If this technique could be adapted to human cells, researchers could use a patient's skin cells to generate new heart, liver, or kidney cells, without destroying human eggs (Murphey et al., 2009). (See the *Further Developments* box on page 70, "Stem Cell Research: Making Progress or Opening Pandora's Box?") Since the embryonic and differentiated cells derived from them are identical to the patient's own cells, there should be no chance of tissue rejection when the cells are transplanted into the patient's body. Other recent studies have raised concerns that even if therapeutic cloning in humans is possible, stem cells may accumulate cancer-causing mutations (Hartwell et al., 2008).

The goal of early cloning research was to create genetically identical animals; now some researchers want to help infertile or same-sex couples and individuals have their own genetic offspring. Others want to understand human or animal diseases and perhaps develop cures (Aldhous & Coghlan, 2006). Yet fertility experts at the Roslin Institute in Great Britain report that it took 277 attempts before a "normal" sheep, called Dolly, was born. The majority of the sheep embryos never implanted or died off during gestation or soon after birth. Since Dolly, other animals have been cloned: mice, cats, pigs, goats, a mule, and some endangered species. But with humans, biomedical researchers estimate that they would need millions of women's egg cells and that there would be countless failed attempts and grotesque fetal and placental distortions and maternal complications (Hansen, 2004). Great Britain, Canada, Australia, New Zealand, Japan, South Korea, and several European countries are researching therapeutic cloning, and the International Society for Stem Cell Research (ISSCR) issues daily reports online.

Questions

Can you describe the process of cloning to create a human embryo? What do you think about using human embryos for research? Where does U.S. legislation stand on these issues of life and death? If present regulations allow for cloned embryos to grow only for 14 days in a lab, do you think there will be a "slippery slope" in the future such that cloned embryos will become fetuses used solely for body parts?

FURTHER DEVELOPMENTS

Stem Cell Research: Making Progress or Opening Pandora's Box?

Stem cells are those cells that have the capacity to reproduce themselves. They divide and renew themselves for long periods, are unspecialized, and are capable of differentiating into any of the 220 types of human cells or tissues. This research is controversial because many researchers propose that the best source of stem cells for creating human tissues and organs is human fetal tissue from the blastocyst stage (a preimplantation embryo of 30 to 150 cells) (see Figure 3.6) (Murphey et al., 2009). Such embryonic stem cells (ESCs) can come from aborted fetal tissue, embryos created by IVF, and leftover or frozen embryos from IVF procedures. Yet other stem cells can be found in fetal placenta and umbilical cord tissue, and *adult* stem cells can be found in fat cells, skin, blood, bone marrow, and other body cells (Hartwell et al., 2008).

Pro-Choice

Pro-choice advocates, many biomedical scientists, some afflicted with disease or illness, and some politicians and venture capitalists predict that ESC research holds the potential for repairing tissue injury, curing degenerative diseases, or slowing normal functional declines that accompany aging (Rando, 2006). Thus, this research is known as the field of regenerative medicine.

In 2004, Harvard scientists offered other stem cell researchers free access to 17 new human embryonic stem cell lines developed without government funds, hoping to boost research (Nano, 2004). In Australia, scientists have been able to extract stem cells from cloned monkey embryos, suggesting that human therapeutic cloning is moving closer

to realization (Mitalipov, 2007). In 2007, British scientists were given the go-ahead to create hybrid animal-human embryos and then to harvest the stem cells to help study serious human illnesses (Moss, 2007).

In California, voters passed legislation that funds $3 billion worth of stem cell research through 2014. The Institute for Regenerative Medicine was created, which distributes funds and establishes research guidelines. California's constitution was amended to give biologists the right to do ESC research. The state is a global leader in this field and is drawing the most qualified biotech researchers (Hutson, 2009). It's a competitive race worth billions of dollars, and it has set up what some are calling the "biological enterprise."

Reservations

In 2003, the U.S. House of Representatives passed the Human Cloning Prohibition Act, making illegal all uses of human somatic cell nuclear transfer (SCNT), banning human cloning, and establishing criminal and civil penalties for anyone convicted of attempting or performing human cloning or of importing products derived from human cloning. In 2009, President Obama issued an executive order lifting the Bush administration's ban on federal funding of embryonic stem cell research, allowing for public funding of this research. In addition, private funding of human stem cell research has not been regulated or prohibited by law (Munro, 2007). Many bioethicists and pro-life advocates are concerned about the unregulated creation and destruction of additional embryos and the potential exploitation of women. The U.S. National Institutes of Health (2009) wants

FIGURE 3.6 Harvesting Embryonic Stem Cells for Research and Cures Worldwide, there is increasing research investigating the use of embryonic stem cells and other body cells and tissues. *Source:* Stephanie Nano. "Scientists Give Free Access to Stem Cell Lines," Associated Press, March 3, 2004. Copyright © 2004 Associated Press. Reprinted by permission.

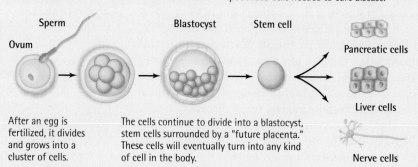

Free access to new stem cell lines

Researchers believe stem cells can be coaxed to form specialized cells needed to cure disease.

Sperm

Ovum

Blastocyst

Stem cell

Pancreatic cells

Liver cells

Nerve cells

After an egg is fertilized, it divides and grows into a cluster of cells.

The cells continue to divide into a blastocyst, stem cells surrounded by a "future placenta." These cells will eventually turn into any kind of cell in the body.

to bring all existing stem cell lines from fertility clinics available to U.S. researchers into one repository. This would allow researchers easier access, lower costs, and establish standardized conditions, uniform quality, and regulatory oversight and review of stem cell and embryonic research.

To enhance progress, a majority of infertility patients surveyed were willing to donate their frozen embryos to stem cell research. The patients' willingness to donate frozen embryos, along with governmental and private funding, could have a tremendous impact on stem cell research (Kliff, 2007). However, regulatory laws, commissions, standards, and oversight are lacking to prevent human cells from being used irresponsibly, opening the door to new high-tech eugenics. Who decides what regulatory agencies will set standards and monitor this research? Given a rising demand for human embryos, where will they come from? How long will embryonic stem cells be allowed to develop?

A Compromise

Worldwide, there is an unstoppable driving force of research, and all sides of this issue agree that using adult stem cells, placental, and umbilical cord stem cells should be explored first for cures and other life-saving advancements. Researchers continue to make progress developing adult stem cells into healthy tissues and organs. A "working compromise" that has been proposed by the National Institutes of Health (2009) would allow funding only for research using stem cell lines derived from unused embryos originally created for in vitro fertilization. It also requires that the donors of those embryos give informed consent for their use. In addition, a process known as parthenogenesis, which develops embryos by activating an unfertilized egg using chemicals, rather than fertilizing it with sperm, could result in a genuine compromise for opponents of human embryonic stem cell research.

Birth Control Methods

Contraception is the leading reason why women first seek care of a **gynecologist** (a physician who specializes in women's reproductive health), and 75 percent see such a physician by the age of 20 (Frankel, 2004). Over the past decade intensive, multipronged approaches to reducing U.S. teen pregnancy and adult unwanted pregnancy have been very successful. After peaking in the early 1990s, births for U.S. teens of all races and ethnicities are reported to be at the lowest levels ever reported. Between 1990 and 2005, there was a continuing significant *decline* in the number of births to these very young women, followed by a slight 2-year increase. By 2009, the teen birth trend continued to decline, despite the increased population of young females (see Figure 3.7). Yet U.S. teen pregnancy and birthrates, at 39 per 1,000 women aged 15 to 19, remain the highest in the industrialized world (Ventura & Hamilton, 2011).

Also, in the last decade managed-care insurance plans improved coverage such that by 2002, a majority of plans covered the five leading methods of reversible contraception: diaphragm, one- and three-month injectables, the IUD, and oral contraceptives (Sonfield et al., 2004). Since 1998 the Food and Drug Administration (FDA) has approved at least 14 new contraceptive products for women in the United States. Such essential plans provide reproductive choice for the 60 million U.S. women who are in their childbearing years. Furthermore, sexually active adolescents and adults are now better informed about other risks of sexual activity, including HIV/AIDS, sexually transmitted infections, and the socioeconomic consequences of early and repeat pregnancies. They also are more aware of the variety of birth control options to

prevent pregnancy, and they have legal access to abortion to terminate pregnancy.

Contraception   There are many contraceptive products and methods that range from reversible (condoms, injectables, and oral contraceptives) to irreversible (tubal ligation and vasectomy), but most contraceptives do not protect against HIV or other sexually transmitted

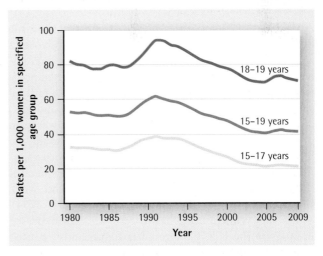

FIGURE 3.7 Birthrates for Females Aged 15–19 Years: United States, 1980–2009 By 2009, the birthrate among young U.S. adolescents aged 15 to 19 had fallen to the lowest levels ever reported.
Source: Ventura, S. J., & Hamilton B. E. (2011, February). U.S. teen birth rate resumes decline. *National Vital Statistics Reports, 58.* Hyattsville, MD: National Center for Health Statistics. Figure 1. Retrieved May 27, 2011. Menacker, F., Martin, J., MacDorman, M. F., & Ventura, S. J. (2010, September). Births to 15-19 year-old mothers 1990–2004: Trends and health outcomes. *National Vital Statistics Reports, 55*(1). Hyattsville, MD: National Center for Health Statistics.

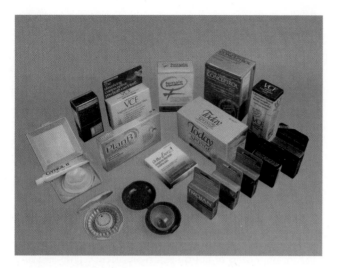

Available Contraception Products Products include reversible contraception methods, emergency contraception, and irreversible contraception methods.

infections. Various advocates of reproductive health choices are working in concert to promote a better-informed public, making options more accessible through insurance coverage, and lobbying for more effective means of birth control—including dual-action drugs (e.g., promoting hair growth *and* contraception). In some states, a range of health-care providers (PAs, FNPs, RNs, LPNs, pharmacists, and others) are distributing some contraceptives in pharmacies and community clinics. Pharmacists are also being trained to give injections for emergency contraception.

Abstinence Moral values are at the center of the issue of teen pregnancy. Hence, some public health advocates and policymakers agree that *abstinence* is a key ingredient, or the *A* in the *ABC*s of preventing unwanted pregnancy or sexually transmitted infections (*B* is "be faithful to your partner" and *C* is "if active, use a condom") (Cohen, 2004). They claim that the much lower teen pregnancy and abortion rates over the past decade are largely due to the efforts of "abstinence until marriage" or "abstinence until older" programs as a component of the publicly funded Personal Responsibility and Work Opportunity Reconciliation Act of 1996 (HR 3734). Thus, they lament that health-care legislation passed in 2010 by the U.S. Congress has significantly reduced funding for abstinence-centered programs and increased funding for comprehensive sexual education (National Abstinence Education Association, 2010).

The abstinence movement is criticized by those in the public health sector who want to teach a more comprehensive contraception program to prevent pregnancy and sexually transmitted infections (STIs). Both sides should be allies in this public health issue, however. In a national survey of 1,000 teens and 1,000 adults, most

adults (94 percent) and teens (92 percent) said it is important for society to give teens a strong message that they should not have sex until they are out of high school (Albert, 2003). And more young people are cautious about early and casual sex (Kirby, 2008). Teens realize that HIV/AIDS and STIs are big problems, and a growing number of teens, especially those in poor minority neighborhoods, are motivated to go to college and change their lives. Even though contemporary teens have greater awareness of, and access to, contraceptive choices, they also want to learn more about relationships, intimacy, love, and communicating with partners (Kirby, 2008).

Abortion Contraceptives are not foolproof, and nearly half of pregnancies among American women are unintended, but termination of the pregnancy is a legal option. **Abortion** is the spontaneous or induced expulsion of the fetus prior to the time of viability. Abortion on demand has been a legal medical procedure since the U.S. Supreme Court legalized abortion in *Roe v. Wade* in 1973. The majority who undergo abortion are young, are unmarried, and are likely to obtain an abortion within the first eight weeks of pregnancy when health risks are at their lowest. The official statistics are astonishing: From 1973 to 2008, more than 52 million abortions were reported (three states, including California, do not report abortion data) (Pazol et al., 2009). In 2008, more than 1.2 million U.S. women had abortions, yet this is a marked decline since a high in 1990 (Kost, Henshaw, & Carlin, 2010).

The striking reduction in abortions is partially attributable to increasing use of emergency contraceptive pills, which have been sold in the United States since 2000; taking a regimen of pills prevents pregnancy after unprotected intercourse (Guttmacher Institute, 2010a). Such pills work only in early pregnancy, and they are not without the potential of serious side effects. More states are training pharmacists, nurse practitioners, physician's assistants, and medical residents to distribute such emergency contraception. Various advocacy groups are lobbying for campus health centers to be able to provide a full range of reproductive, contraceptive, and emergency contraceptive services. The abortion issue has spawned a bitterly divisive conflict between two large factions of citizens, the pro-life and the pro-choice advocates—and abortion laws vary from state to state.

Pro-Life View Pro-life advocates point to the extensive loss of human life, the reported lasting psychological harm to the women who have selected this choice, and the moral decay of a society that allows this to happen. The National Right-to-Life Committee and some psychologists have identified "postabortion stress syndrome" as a cluster of symptoms some women experience after the abrupt termination of a pregnancy by elective abortion: depression, a sense of worthlessness, personal relationship disorders, sexual dysfunction, damaged self-esteem, a sense of victimization, and, for a small number of women, suicide (Rue et al., 2004).

There are over 3,000 Crisis Pregnancy Centers across the United States that are ready to help counsel women facing unplanned pregnancy and to offer medical, financial, and legal assistance ("Alternatives to Abortion," 2010). The woman who initiated the *Roe v. Wade* lawsuit to secure a safe, legal abortion in 1973 is now a pro-life advocate. An especially volatile issue is *partial-birth abortion,* performed during the last trimester when a fetus could be viable outside the womb. The procedure (called "dilation and extraction," or "D&X") involves bringing the fetus feet-first into the birth canal, puncturing its skull with a sharp instrument and sucking out its brain, and then removing it from the mother's body. President Clinton vetoed legislation to ban partial-birth abortion that the U.S. Congress passed in 1995. Then President Bush signed the Partial-Birth Abortion Ban Act of 2003, after Congress passed it. Critics of the law contend that it is vaguely worded and may restrict access to safe, affordable procedures (Greene & Ecker, 2004). In 2010, the U.S. Supreme Court upheld the federal restriction on partial-birth abortion (Sherman, 2010).

Pro-Choice View   Pro-choice advocates state that abortion provides many benefits to women and couples who choose not to have or cannot afford a baby and that every woman deserves the right to control what happens to her body. Illegal abortions performed prior to 1973 put women at a much greater health risk than those performed in medical settings today. Couples with a high risk of producing a fetus with genetic defects have a choice to continue or terminate the pregnancy. Pro-choice advocates further state that the abortion procedure, performed during early stages of pregnancy, is statistically safer for the pregnant woman than childbirth. In 2005, seven U.S. women died from complications after a legal abortion (out of a reported 820,000) (Pazol et al., 2009).

Both sides of this emotional issue are gathering greater force, affecting the outcomes of election campaigns at state and national levels, and significantly affecting the future of our society.

The Expanding Reproductive Years

Of great interest to medical professionals is the fact that about 10 percent of American and European girls are entering puberty earlier than they did 30 years ago. In the early 1900s girls did not menstruate until they were 14 years old, on average. Today some girls begin developing pubic hair and breasts as young as 5 years old and begin menstruating at 8 or 9 years of age. Judging on the basis of a recent national sample of girls, the median age is 12.2 years for Caucasian girls, 12.0 years for Mexican

American girls, and 12.0 years for African American girls (Adams Hillard, 2008). A growing body of research finds that increased rates of obesity among girls is a contributing factor (Rosenfeld, Lipton, & Drum, 2010).

Children who undergo early puberty often struggle with poor self-esteem and social pressures among peers. *Precocious puberty* is associated with earlier sexual activity, pregnancy, and alcohol consumption (Lee et al., 2007). This is a critical societal issue, because such young girls do not have the resources to support themselves and the children they are bearing. The health-care system, the social welfare system, the educational system, governing agencies, and American business and industry are collaborating to educate American youth about the risks of teen (or younger) pregnancy. In 2007, after a controversial debate, the school board governing a middle school in Maine voted to allow giving out contraceptives to girls as young as 11 through the school. Parental consent is usually necessary for health treatment at the school, but the nature of this "treatment" is protected by patient privacy laws. Although school officials feel responsible for preventing early teen pregnancy, opponents view this as a violation of parental rights (Gibbs, 2007).

Throughout history, a woman's reproductive years have typically ceased after her last menstrual cycle (averaging about age 50), a milestone called *menopause.* Yet with ART methods today, more women are attempting to have a baby during their forties, during their fifties, or after menopause. Infertile women in their thirties and forties and menopausal women undergo a careful health screening, but some are ineligible for ARTs. Those accepted are at high risk for pregnancy complications, and only a small subgroup of U.S. women can afford the cost of assisted reproduction (some have insurance coverage, and medical costs are tax deductible under current law) (Connolly, Hoorens, & Chambers, 2010). Some countries, such as Denmark, have much higher ART success rates, even for older women, because assisted conception is freely available, and funding is generous for covering the costs of ART procedures (Rice, 2007). The American Society for Reproductive Medicine launched an educational campaign targeting those who wait to conceive: *Advancing Age Decreases Your Ability to Have Children.* With advancing age, only a small percentage of women are able to get pregnant and produce a healthy child.

Questions

What are some birth control methods available to women in the United States? What are the contrasting views about abortion, and at what stage of pregnancy do most women seek abortions? How can a menopausal woman potentially have a baby, and how likely is she to be successful?

HEREDITY AND GENETICS

Perhaps at the heart of the debate about ART and the expanding range of reproductive years is our understanding that each person's genetic makeup is unique and very complex, with a range of flaws likely. With normal sexual reproduction, many things often malfunction. What will happen when scientists have free license to re-create the human species—and all its genetic combinations? How many embryos may we create and destroy before accepting the "perfect" one? Is there such a thing as the "perfect baby"? Do we really want to parent a younger physical replica of ourselves?

As mentioned earlier, a major debate in the fields of psychology, psychobiology, and sociobiology involves what contribution hereditary or environmental factors make to our unfolding physical, intellectual, social, and emotional development. This is called the nature (biology)-versus-nurture (environment) debate. Sociobiologists work to discover laws governing the evolution and biology of social behavior in many species. Psychologists tend to focus on the nature of psychological mechanisms and adaptability to one's environment. Healthy debate among professionals, including bioethicists, contributes to our knowledge about the significant role of biological inheritance.

We now take a look at our biological inheritance, referred to as **heredity**—the genes we inherit from our biological parents. Each of us has inherited a specific genetic code from our biological parents, and fertilization is the major event determining our biological inheritance. We begin life as a single fertilized cell, or *zygote,* that contains all the hereditary material passed on to us from our parents and their ancestors. Precisely blueprinted in this original cell are the 200 billion or so cells that we possess nine months later, at birth. **Genetics** is the scientific study of biological inheritance by geneticists, and in 2000 the first draft of the genetic blueprint of humans was accomplished by the Human Genome Project.

The Human Genome Project

In 1990, scientists from the U.S. Department of Energy and the National Institutes of Health began competing in an exciting scientific race with Celera Genomics, a private company that intended to patent its findings, to discover the sequencing of the **human genome,** the genetic blueprint of all the *genes* on their appropriate chromosomes within the 6 feet of DNA coiled up in every human cell (National Human Genome Research Institute [NHGRI], 2007a). The first draft of the human genome was reported jointly in 2000 by researchers from publicly funded universities and Celera. Then President Clinton announced that the human genome could not be patented, and hundreds of scientists worldwide began collaborating to convert the draft into a genome sequence with high accuracy. That sequence was completed in 2003, and there are far fewer genes than expected. The current estimate is about 20,000 to 25,000, rather than the 150,000 genes predicted by genetic researchers (see the photo on page 59) (Pennisi, 2007). Interestingly, humans have only twice as many genes as a fruit fly or a lowly nematode worm!

This sequencing of genes holds the entire set of hereditary instructions for creating, operating, and maintaining an organism and for reproducing the next generation. Each of your body's trillions of cells contains a copy of your genome. More important, a genome is information that affects every aspect of our behavior and physiology. The ultimate goal of behavioral genomics is to understand the developmental pathways between genes and behavior, not just a single gene and a single behavior, but for the system that includes all genes (the genome) and all behaviors (Than, 2010). Not only do our genes influence what we look like, but molecular errors in our genes are responsible for an estimated 3,000 to 4,000 clearly hereditary diseases. In 2005, the International *HAPMap* Project published a comprehensive map of human genetic variation that is already speeding the search for genes involved in common, complex maladies, such as heart disease, diabetes, blindness, and cancer. And in 2007, researchers found new genetic clues to the cause of Alzheimer's disease and identified new genetic risk factors for Type 2 diabetes (National Human Genome Research Institute, 2007b).

In short, the genome is divided into chromosomes, chromosomes contain genes, and genes are made of **DNA (deoxyribonucleic acid),** which in turn tells a cell how to make vital proteins. "The way genes influence your traits is by telling your cells which proteins to make, how much, when, and where" (DeWeerdt, 2001). It has been found that human beings are 99.5 percent alike in their genetic sequence—it is the 0.5 percent that gives us our differences on the outside and on the inside, at a cellular level (Cohen, 2007).

The next phase of sophisticated genetic studies continues as the *Genomes to Life* project, which has the visionary goals of (1) sequencing genomes of other animal species, (2) mapping genomes and making datasets publicly available, (3) studying variation within genomes, (4) reducing both computation time and costs for sequencing, and (5) studying specific diseases. In addition, the NHGRI-led project is designing an Encyclopedia of DNA Elements (ENCODE), which will provide an efficient way of identifying and precisely locating all of the protein-coding genes contained in the human DNA sequence (National Human Genome Research Institute, 2007c). Thanks to improving technology, within the next five years people who choose to do so should be able to have their entire genome sequenced as a routine part of their medical records for about a thousand U.S. dollars. This will allow doctors to develop individual preventive medical plans. Moreover, what research scientists learn will eventually help doctors predict, detect, and treat human diseases and conditions—and some of these "corrections" to the human genetic code might be achieved during the embryonic or fetal stages of life.

> *Questions*
>
> How do scientists study heredity and genetics? What have geneticists accomplished with the Human Genome Project to date, and what are their goals in the near future? About how many genes are there in the human genome?

Chromosomes and Genes

By the early 1900s, the use of microscopes to study cellular tissue led to the discovery of chromosomes. **Chromosomes** are long, threadlike structures made of protein and nucleic acid that contain the hereditary materials found in the nuclei of any cell. Upon fertilization, for humans, the 23 chromosomes of the ovum are combined with the 23 chromosomes of the sperm, for a total of 46 chromosomes, usually referred to as 23 pairs. Exceptions to this normal pairing will be discussed later in this section.

Each chromosome contains a linear arrangement of thousands of smaller units that divide it into regions called **genes,** which transmit inherited characteristics passed from biological parents to children. They are like beads on a string, and each gene has its own specific location on the chromosome. Each human cell contains about 20,000 to 25,000 genes and 3 billion letters of chemical code, which are composed of DNA. DNA is the active biochemical substance in genes that programs the cells to manufacture vital protein substances, including enzymes, hormones, antibodies, and other structural proteins (National Human Genome Research Institute, 2007a). This DNA code of life is carried in a large molecule shaped like a double helix or twisted rope ladder (see Figure 3.8).

Nearly all cells in the human body are formed through a kind of cell division called **mitosis,** during which every chromosome in the cell splits lengthwise to form a new pair. Through this process of nuclear division, the cell replicates itself by dividing into two "daughter" cells with the same hereditary information. Unlike other cells in the human body, the gametes—ova and sperm—have only 23 chromosomes each, not the usual 23 pairs. Gametes are formed by a more complex kind of cell division called meiosis. **Meiosis** involves two cell divisions during which the chromosomes are reduced to half their original number. Each gamete receives only one chromosome from each pair in every parental cell. This is half the usual number, enabling each parent to contribute

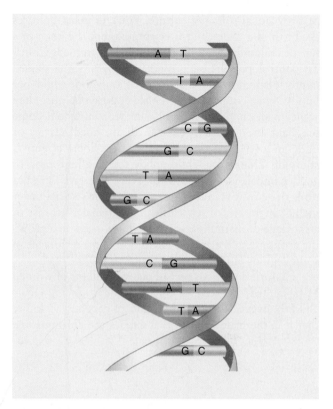

FIGURE 3.8 A Model of the DNA Molecule The double-chained structure of a DNA molecule is coiled in a helix. During cell division the two chains pull apart, or "unzip." Each half is now free to assemble a new, complementary half.
Source: Johnson & Losos. (2008). *The Living World* (5th ed.). New York: McGraw-Hill.

half the total number of chromosomes and genetic material at fertilization. Thus, upon fertilization, the newly formed zygote contains 23 pairs of chromosomes (see Figure 3.9).

Each person's genome is slightly different because of mutations—"mistakes" that occur occasionally in a DNA sequence—and some of these mutations are expressed as diseases and defects in the human organism. Geneticists predict breakthroughs over the next 10 to 15 years in the early detection and treatment of many diseases. The goal of the new science of gene therapy is to correct or replace the altered gene (Toscano et al., 2011). The gene for cystic fibrosis, the most common lethal hereditary disease among Caucasians, was discovered in 1989, and since, medical researchers have relieved the cloned cystic fibrosis disease in mice. These encouraging results suggest that in the not-so-distant future, gene therapy may help people who are suffering from this life-threatening genetic disorder. Scientists can test for these diseases directly as well as prenatally.

Determination of an Embryo's Sex

In many societies, even today, a male child is expected to inherit the family name or carry on the family business or provisional role in a culture. Thus, in many cultures the birth of a male child is celebrated, but the birth of a female child might not be. An extreme example is China. To control population growth, in 1979 China passed family-planning laws that allowed only one child per family. Some couples abort female children because they want a male child instead, and some women who become pregnant after already giving birth are fined heavily or undergo forced abortion or sterilization. Social scientists studying China's one-child policy report a high ratio of gender imbalance: six boys for every five girls. Predictions of serious resulting threats to China's social order include high rates of sex trafficking of females because of a shortage of marital partners, fewer workers in a growing economy, and a greater likelihood of male violence in some regions of the country (Fragoso, 2007).

Historical writings record many incidents of women being faulted, divorced, or killed for not producing a male child. However, through the study of genetics we know that it is the male's sperm that carries the chromosome

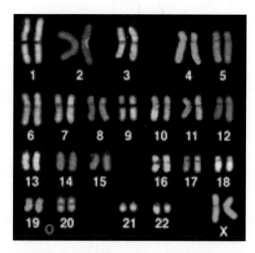

A Karyotype of a Human Male   Each cell nucleus has 23 pairs of chromosomes—two of each type. Each parent provides one member of the pair, which differ in size and shape. Scientists arrange the 23 pairs in descending order by size. The members of each chromosome pair look alike, except for the 23rd pair in males as shown in the bottom far right corner, where one can see that a male's Y chromosome is smaller than an X. A female's contribution to the 23rd pair can only be an X, and thus a male's contribution to the 23rd chromosome determines the child's sex. An XX combination of chromosomes produces a female; an XY combination produces a male.

that determines the sex of a child. Of the 46 chromosomes (23 pairs) that each human normally possesses, 22 pairs are similar in size and shape in both men and women; these chromosomes are called **autosomes.** The 23rd pair, the **sex chromosomes**—one from the mother and one from the father—determine the baby's sex. Each of the mother's ova has an X chromosome. However, a sperm can contain either an X chromosome or a Y chromosome. If an ovum with X is fertilized by a sperm with X, then the zygote will be a female (XX). If an ovum with X is fertilized by a sperm with Y, then the zygote will be a male (XY). The Y chromosome determines that a child will be male (see the photo of the karyotype of a male). About six to eight weeks into embryonic development, the male embryo starts producing the male hormone **testosterone,** which promotes the development of male characteristics.

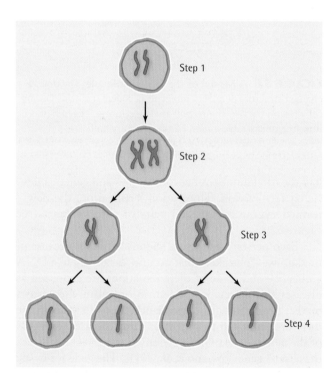

FIGURE 3.9 Meiosis   This diagram illustrates how sex cells form by meiosis. In Step 1 each chromosome teams up with its partner. In Step 2 the first meiotic division occurs; both chromosomes of each pair are duplicated. (The figure portrays only one pair, although human beings normally have 23 pairs.) Each original chromosome and its copy, termed a chromatid, are joined at the center. Step 3 involves a second meiotic division. Each of the two original chromosomes and its copy become a part of an intermediary cell. In Step 4 each chromatid—the original and its copy—segregates into a separate ovum or sperm. Thus, the intermediary cells undergo cell division without chromosome duplication. This process produces four gametes.

Questions

What are the mechanisms of heredity, and what is their function on the double helix? How many chromosomes do the mother and father contribute to the genetic makeup of a zygote? How many total chromosomes does each human normally possess? What is the genetic makeup of a female versus a male on the sex chromosome?

Principles of Genetics

Have you ever wondered how your own heredity has influenced your characteristics and development? Much of our original understanding of genes and the science of genetics came from studies conducted by an Austrian monk, Gregor Mendel (1822–1884). By crossing varieties of peas (short, tall; red flowers, white flowers) in his small monastery garden, Mendel was able to formulate the basic principles of heredity. Mendel hypothesized that independent units he called "factors" determined inherited characteristics, and today we call these units *genes.* Mendel reasoned that the genes that control a single hereditary characteristic must exist in pairs. Advances in microbiology and genetics have confirmed Mendel's hunch. Genes occur in pairs, one on a maternal chromosome and the other on the corresponding paternal chromosome. The two genes in a pair occupy a specific position on each chromosome. Each and every human gene has been mapped for both its location and its function by the Human Genome Project, as noted earlier.

Dominant and Recessive Characteristics   Each member of a pair of genes is called an allele. An **allele,** then, is one member of a pair of genes found on corresponding chromosomes that affect the same trait. There can be only two alleles per person for any characteristic, one from each parent (one on the maternal chromosome and one on the paternal chromosome). Mendel demonstrated that one allele, the **dominant character,** completely masks or hides the other allele, the **recessive character.** Mendel used a capital letter of the alphabet to signify the dominant allele (*A*) and a lowercase letter to signify the recessive allele (*a*). When both alleles from the parents are the same, this is referred to as a **homozygous** characteristic (*AA*) or (*aa*). When the two paired alleles are different, this is called a **heterozygous** characteristic (*Aa*). The characteristic of the dominant allele (*A*) will be expressed, unless the recessive alleles pair up (*aa*) (see Figure 3.10).

Not all traits are transmitted this simply. Some inherited traits, or defects, are the result of the complex interaction of many genes, which is called **polygenic inheritance.** Personality, intelligence, aptitudes, and abilities are subject to polygenic inheritance.

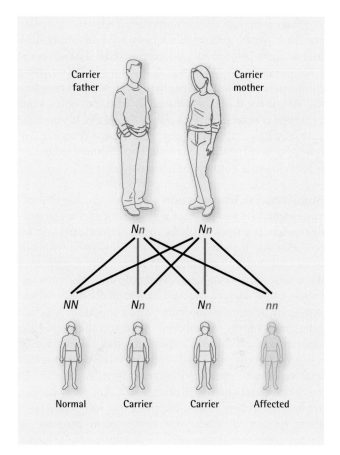

FIGURE 3.10 Transmission of Recessive, Single-Gene Defects   Both parents, who often are unaffected by the faulty gene, carry a normal gene (*N*) that dominates its faulty recessive counterpart (*n*). The odds for each child are (1) a 25 percent chance of being *NN*, normal: inheriting two *N*s and thus being free of the faulty recessive gene; (2) a 50 percent chance of being *Nn* and therefore a carrier like both parents; and (3) a 25 percent risk of being *nn*, affected: inheriting a "double dose" of *n* genes, which may cause a serious genetic disease.

Phenotypes and Genotypes   By cross-pollinating red-flowered and white-flowered pea plants, Mendel demonstrated the distinction between the **genotype,** the actual genetic makeup of an organism, and the **phenotype,** the observable (or expressed) characteristics of the organism. In human beings, the phenotype includes physical, physiological, and behavioral traits. Humans also possess dominant and recessive genes, as mentioned earlier.

As an illustration, consider your eye color. Brown is the dominant eye color in humans worldwide. Blue and green are recessive eye colors. When looking at your own eyes in a mirror (without colored contact lenses), you are observing the phenotype. Potentially, the underlying genotype could be one of three possibilities for eye color, with *B* representing brown: *BB*, *Bb*, or *bb*. If you are a brown-eyed person, you have either the *BB* or the *Bb* genotype. If you are a blue-eyed or green-eyed person, you have inherited the two recessive alleles for eye color and have the *bb* genotype. Do you have naturally dark hair or light-colored hair (blonde or red)? The observed color of your natural hair is your phenotype. Again, using *B* for brown or black, there are three possible genotypes: *BB, Bb,* or *bb.* If you have naturally dark hair color, your genotype is dominant with either *BB* or *Bb.* If you have naturally light hair color, your genotype is recessive and is *bb.* To modify what TV comic Flip Wilson used to say, what you see is not necessarily what you get.

Multifactorial Transmission   The recognition that environmental factors interact with genetic factors to produce traits is termed **multifactorial transmission.** If we consider that heredity and genetics provide us with our basic biochemical structure and an unfolding plan over the course of development, what role does our environment—or ecological systems, as Bronfenbrenner would say—play in our development? The implication was that gene-environment interactions were for the most part separate and of so little importance that they could be ignored. Recent empirical findings have demonstrated and replicated gene-environment interdependence in ways that clearly matter (Rutter, 2007). Are you who you are because of this genetic blueprint that has been passed along to you, or does your environment promote or detract from that blueprint? Do you have any influence on your own life's development?

Consider Leann Rimes, who was born with a predisposition toward musical talent. From an early age she loved singing and sang publicly. With her parents' encouragement and support (praise, lessons, time, financial sacrifice, and management), she developed her ability throughout her childhood. By her early teens, she had received recognition and praise from top professionals in the country music field. Her self-motivation and the encouragement from others promoted the development of her natural abilities. Without such encouragement and support through her early years, she might not have developed her singing talent.

Additionally, some physical characteristics are the result of multifactorial transmission. The age for the onset of puberty and the age of menopause are believed to be preprogrammed genetically, but nutrition, physical fitness, stress, illness, and disease can advance or delay these preprogrammed events (Gottlieb, 2007).

Sex-Linked Inherited Characteristics   Genes are inherited independently only if they are on different chromosomes. Genes that are linked, or appear on the same chromosome, are inherited together. Good examples of linked genes are **sex-linked traits.** The X chromosome, for instance, contains many genes that are not otherwise related to sexual traits. Hemophilia, a hereditary defect that interferes with the normal clotting of blood, is a sex-linked characteristic

carried by the X chromosome. There are about 150 other known sex-linked disorders, including a type of muscular dystrophy, certain forms of night blindness, Hunter's syndrome (a severe form of mental retardation), and juvenile glaucoma (hardening of the fluids within the eyeball).

The majority of sex-linked genetic defects occur in men, because men have only one X chromosome. In women, the harmful action of a gene on one X chromosome is usually suppressed by a dominant gene on the other chromosome. Thus, even though women themselves normally are unaffected by a given sex-linked disorder, they can be carriers. A man is affected if he receives from his mother an X chromosome bearing the genetic defect (see Figure 3.11). A man cannot receive

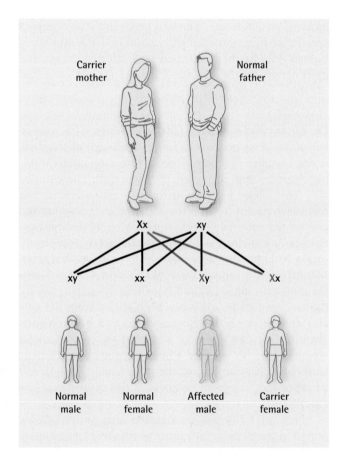

FIGURE 3.11 Transmission of Sex-Linked Genetic Defects In most sex-linked genetic disorders, the female sex chromosome of an unaffected mother (who does not show the disorder) carries one faulty chromosome (X) and one normal chromosome (X). The father carries normal X and Y chromosomes. The statistics for each male child are (1) a 50 percent risk of inheriting the faulty X chromosome and hence the disorder, and (2) a 50 percent chance of inheriting normal X and Y chromosomes. For each female child the statistics are (1) a 50 percent risk of inheriting one faulty X chromosome and hence being a carrier like her mother, and (2) a 50 percent chance of inheriting no faulty gene.

the abnormal gene from his father. Males transmit an X chromosome only to their daughters (that's what makes them females), never to their sons, who always receive a father's Y chromosome (that's what makes them males).

A common example of a sex-linked trait is male-pattern baldness, which begins with thinning hair at the crown of the man's head and can lead to extensive baldness by the late twenties and early thirties. The mother inherits this trait from her father, but she herself is not affected. However, her sons have a 50 percent chance of being affected. Another illustration of a sex-linked trait is red-green color blindness. The majority of people affected by this are males, who often do not realize they see things "differently" until they start driving and have trouble recognizing the red and green on traffic lights. To those affected, these two colors look more like a brownish color. Newer traffic lights have a shutterlike clear covering that opens up and closes quickly to emit a pulsing bright light on the red and green so that those affected with red-green color blindness can more accurately distinguish the command. Preschool and kindergarten teachers teaching color recognition are likely to be the first to spot this trait in affected children.

In rare instances a female can inherit these sex-linked disorders if the X chromosome she receives from her mother and the X chromosome she receives from her father both bear a gene for a given disease or disorder.

Genetic Counseling and Testing

Over the past 20 years or so, our increased knowledge of genetics has given rise to the field of **genetic counseling,** whereby physicians and specialists counsel couples about concerns they may have about inherited diseases in their family history. (See the *Implications for Practice* box on page 80, "Genetic Counselor.") People who are deciding whether to create a child might have concerns about inherited diseases in their family backgrounds and seek genetic counseling to learn how much risk they run of passing along this particular disorder or disease. In some genetic disorders, the disease shows up during the first year of life; in others, the symptoms do not become apparent until much later. Some disorders are much more serious than others.

A variety of diagnostic tests are now available to parents with substantiated histories of genetic disease and to couples who, for whatever reason, wish to determine whether a fetus has defects. **Prenatal diagnosis** employs various techniques to determine the health status of an unborn fetus. Congenital anomalies (existing at birth) account for 20 to 25 percent of perinatal deaths. Prenatal diagnosis is helpful for (1) managing the pregnancy, (2) determining pregnancy outcome, (3) planning for birth complications or health risks to the newborn, (4) deciding whether to continue a pregnancy,

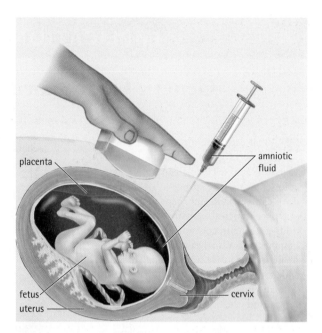

FIGURE 3.12 Amniocentesis Amniocentesis is a procedure for detecting hereditary defects in the fetus. A small amount of amniotic fluid is withdrawn. The sample is centrifuged to separate fetal cells from the fluid. The cells are then grown in a laboratory culture and analyzed for genetic abnormalities. *Source:* Yale New Haven Health System, 789 Howard Avenue, New Haven, CT 06519 Yalenewhavenhealth.Org

and (5) finding conditions that could affect future pregnancies (Chadefaux-Vekemans et al., 2006). Invasive and noninvasive techniques help to identify many genetic and chromosomal problems during prenatal development.

Amniocentesis is an invasive procedure done normally between the 14th and 18th weeks of gestation. A physician inserts a long, hollow needle through the abdomen into the uterus, drawing out a small amount of amniotic fluid surrounding the fetus. A fetal **ultrasound** is done throughout this procedure to view the positions of fetal organs and extremities (see Figure 3.12). The amniotic fluid contains fetal cells, which are grown in a culture and analyzed for various genetic abnormalities. Genetic and chromosomal defects, such as those linked to Down syndrome, spina bifida, and other inherited disorders, can be detected in this manner. With advancing age, the risk of having a baby with genetic problems is greater than the risk of miscarriage due to the procedure.

Some genetic defects are more prevalent in people of certain racial or ethnic backgrounds. Sickle-cell anemia occurs among people of African descent, and Tay-Sachs disease occurs in Ashkenazic Jews. The results of genetic testing can bring relief or inflict anguish and sorrow. Parents who decide to request genetic testing face

IMPLICATIONS FOR PRACTICE

Genetic Counselor Luba Djurdjinovic, M.S.

I am an executive director, director of genetics programs, and **genetic counselor** at the Ferre Institute. Genetic counseling is the process of helping people understand and adapt to the medical, psychological, and familial implications of genetic contribution to disease. Families pass on a health legacy in terms of lifestyle choices and genetic makeup, and some families wish to understand why and how these conditions are passed down and their options in identifying "at-risk" individuals. A person's genetic makeup provides the initial contribution to the development of common health conditions (e.g., heart disease, cancer, stroke, and others). Some families have generations with a health or physical condition.

When meeting families for genetic risk assessment and counseling, I learn the family's medical history. They collect family medical records and information, and I review their health information to provide a genetic perspective. I provide such information in an educational and psychologically sensitive manner. Families learn about inheritance, the natural history of the condition, and the chance of occurrence or recurrence in the family. Genetic testing options are explored, as well as options in treating or managing the condition. Some families are directed to research studies. Counseling is important to promote informed choices, and support is provided for adaptation to the risk information and/or genetic condition.

Genetic counselors earn a two- or three-year master of science degree with an emphasis in human genetics. Candidates for a genetic counselor training program are encouraged to have direct experience with persons challenged by disability and demonstrate an ability to appreciate the psychological challenges individuals and families might face. They learn about the professional role of genetic counselors through an internship, observation, and discussion with a genetic counselor. Genetic counselors are encouraged to take a national certification exam, and some states require licensure. Genetic counselors must complete a clinical rotation at a medical school and/or major medical center in the areas of pediatric genetics, prenatal genetics, cancer genetics, and adult disease genetics. Some clinical internships relate to neuromuscular disease, blood disorders, craniofacial disorders, and others.

Genetic counselors appear to share characteristics such as curiosity about human dilemmas and adaptations to them. They should have strong interpersonal skills and enjoy engaging the client in the genetic counseling process. Clients often feel that scientific information is "above their head," and it is the genetic counselor's role to make every effort to assist the client in learning and applying the new information. The person will be a "lifelong learner," because understanding science and medicine requires ongoing aggressive continuing education.

I especially enjoy meeting families. I am amazed at family adaptations to generations of challenges that come from some inherited conditions. I value the efforts that families undergo to learn why a condition has occurred and to understand the recurrence. Each family's experience prepares me to meet and help the next family. The society of genetics professionals in the United States is small, with a close collegial relationship.

the difficult decision of whether to have an abortion if the test results indicate a high risk of fetal defects. Parents who learn that their child is abnormal can experience psychological problems, including denial, severe guilt or shame, depression, termination of sexual relations, marital discord, and divorce. Accordingly, parents may need psychological counseling in conjunction with genetic counseling.

Questions

What is a person's genotype, and what is his or her phenotype? If a man has the genotype *Bb* for eye color, what can you say about his eye color? Can you give an example of multifactorial transmission? Why do the majority of sex-linked defects occur in males?

Even though genetic counseling can be quite beneficial in many circumstances, ethicists also debate the pros and cons of genetic counseling. How is a decision whether a fetus should live or die made? Is our society edging toward a disguised eugenics movement? Is genetic information kept private? Is genetic information a reason to excuse certain illegal behaviors in a court of law? What do we do after we test a 2-year-old for a disease and find out that the child has inherited a disorder? How much does it cost to raise a child with severe disabilities? What are the hidden emotional and social costs to the family and to society? There are many sides to this issue—and no conclusive answers.

Genetic and Chromosomal Abnormalities

Some disorders are associated with the presence of too few or too many chromosomes (rather than the normal 23 pairs, in humans). One common chromosomal disorder is Down syndrome, which occurs in 1 out of about every 800 live births (National Down Syndrome Society [NDSS], 2007). About 350,000 U.S. families have a family member with Down syndrome, and about 5,000 children with Down syndrome are born each year (National Down Syndrome Congress, 2010). As the mortality rate associated with Down syndrome declines, the number of individuals with Down syndrome in American society is increasing.

There are three causes of Down syndrome, but in about 95 percent of cases there are three copies of the 21st chromosome, a condition called trisomy 21. In these individuals the total number of chromosomes is 47 instead of the normal 46. The extra chromosome on the 21st pair alters the course of development and causes the characteristics associated with Down syndrome: flat facial profile, upward-slanted eyes, protruding lower jaw, poor Moro reflex, hyperflexibility of joints, excess skin on neck, protruding underlip, a small mouth cavity that causes the tongue to protrude, short neck, very short fifth finger on each hand, one long crease across the palm of each hand, typically mild to moderate cognitive delays, global developmental delays, and increased incidence of respiratory, cardiovascular, gastrointestinal, and other manifestations (NDSS, 2007).

Today, early intervention services help children with Down syndrome develop to their full potential. Those who receive good medical care and are included in school and community activities can be expected to adapt successfully, develop social skills, find work, participate in decisions that affect them, and make a positive contribution to society. Some adults with Down syndrome are marrying and forming their own families (children of parents with trisomy 21 have a 50 percent chance of having normal intelligence) (NDSS, 2007). There have been major advances in the public's familiarity and ease

Young Adults with Down Syndrome: Productive Members of Society Two of these young women have Down syndrome and reside in a community residence with staff that supports their need to be integrated into the community. Their goal is to become as independent as possible by developing their life skills, making many of their own decisions, developing their abilities and interests, working and contributing to their own support, and being actively engaged in community social and recreational activities.

of interaction with people who have disabilities, and support services have been expanded considerably.

Can genetic counseling predict who is likely to have a child with Down syndrome? A few relevant factors are known. Down syndrome affects people of all races and economic levels. The additional chromosome that causes Down syndrome is more likely to originate from the mother (95 percent chance) than from the father (5 percent chance). Older women have a much higher risk of having a child with Down syndrome, but the prevalence is higher among younger mothers because many more women younger than age 35 become pregnant (NDSS, 2007).

A number of other disorders are linked to sex chromosome abnormalities. For those who believe they may have a significant chance of bearing a child at risk of a genetic disorder, genetic counseling and testing can determine with a high degree of accuracy whether the fetus has this defect, can help couples prepare for the arrival of a child with a disorder, or can lead to termination of a pregnancy.

Questions

What does a genetic counselor do, and what types of diagnostic tests are available for assessment of embryonic and fetal health? What are some potential outcomes of fetal diagnostics for parents?

PRENATAL DEVELOPMENT

Centuries before people knew of sperm and eggs, Aristotle argued that the fusion creating a new person did not exist until "quickening," the first noticeable movements in a woman's womb. He reckoned that quickening occurred 40 days into pregnancy. The 40-day rule was later picked up by Jewish and Muslim religions. The Catholic Church did not adopt its current position that life begins at fertilization until 1896, when Pope Pius IX condemned abortion at any age after the moment of conception. Many Jewish theologians now argue that life begins seven days into pregnancy, with implantation of the embryo. Gene transcription starts even later, and many scientists feel human individuality cannot be said to begin until the embryo starts to use its genes. The U.S. Supreme Court takes the position that human life begins much later, when the fetus becomes capable of independent life—roughly the third trimester (Johnson & Losos, 2008). When do you think our human journey in life begins?

Whether conception occurs naturally or as a result of an assisted reproductive technique, between conception and birth the human being grows from a single cell, barely visible to the naked eye, to a mass of about 7 pounds containing some 200 billion cells. The **prenatal period** is the period between conception and birth. It normally averages about 266 days, or 280 days from the last menstrual period. Embryologists divide prenatal development into three stages: The **germinal period** extends from conception to the end of the second week; the **embryonic period** extends from the end of the second week to the end of the eighth week; and the **fetal period** extends from the end of the eighth week until birth. Developmental biology is progressing rapidly, giving us a better understanding of how the body and its specialized organs and tissues are formed (Hill, 2007).

The Germinal Period

The *germinal period* is characterized by (1) growth of the *zygote* after fertilization and (2) establishment of a linkage between the zygote and the mother's support system. After fertilization, the zygote begins a 3- to 4-day journey down the fallopian tube toward the uterus (see Figure 3.13). The zygote is moved along by the action of the cilia and the active contraction of the walls of the oviduct. Within a few hours of fertilization, growth begins with the initiation of mitosis. In mitosis the zygote divides, forming 2 cells identical in makeup to the first cell. In turn, each of these cells divides, making 4 cells. The 4 cells then divide into 8, 8 into 16, 16 into 32, and so on.

The early mitotic cell divisions in development are called *cleavage* and occur very slowly. The first cleavage takes about 30 hours; each subsequent cleavage takes 10 to 12 hours. These cell divisions soon convert the zygote into a hollow fluid-filled ball of cells termed a *blastocyst* (see Figure 3.13). The blastocyst should continue to develop and travel into the uterus. When a blastocyst remains trapped in the fallopian tube, the pregnancy is ectopic or tubal. An *ectopic* pregnancy is dangerous and will cause the mother a great deal of pain. The blastocyst will have to be surgically removed or the fallopian tube will burst, causing hemorrhaging.

Once the blastocyst enters the uterine cavity, it floats freely for 2 or 3 days. When it is about 6 to 7 days old and composed of some 100 cells, the blastocyst makes contact with the endometrium, the wall of the uterus. The endometrium in turn becomes vascular, glandular, and thick. The blastocyst "digests" its way into the endometrium through the action of enzymes and gradually becomes completely buried in it. As a result, the embryo develops within the wall of the uterus, and the organism derives its nourishment from the eroded tissue and maternal blood flow.

By the 11th day, the blastocyst has completely buried itself in the wall of the uterus, in a process called **implantation** (see Figure 3.13). The hormone progesterone from the ovary prepares the uterine lining for implantation. This increase in progesterone is also a signal to the brain that the woman is pregnant, and most pregnant women cease to menstruate (in rare instances, a woman menstruates and does not realize she is pregnant). At this stage in development, the organism is about the size of a pinhead, and the mother is seldom aware of any symptoms of pregnancy. The blastocyst, now made up of hundreds of cells, is busy surrounding itself with chemicals to prevent the uterine immune system from destroying it, and the cervix has been sealed by a plug of mucus (Brooker et al., 2008).

The blastocyst now begins to grow rapidly, initiating the formation of the membranes that will later surround, protect, and nourish it. The internal disc or cluster of cells that compose the blastocyst, called the **inner cell mass,** produces the embryo. One of these membranes, the **amnion,** will enclose the developing embryo, whereas another, the **chorion,** which forms from the **trophoblast,** will interact with the uterine tissue to form the *placenta*. The entire process is controlled by genes. Some genes turn on rapidly as the embryo develops, others turn on slowly, and still others operate throughout the prenatal period and beyond (Johnson & Losos, 2008).

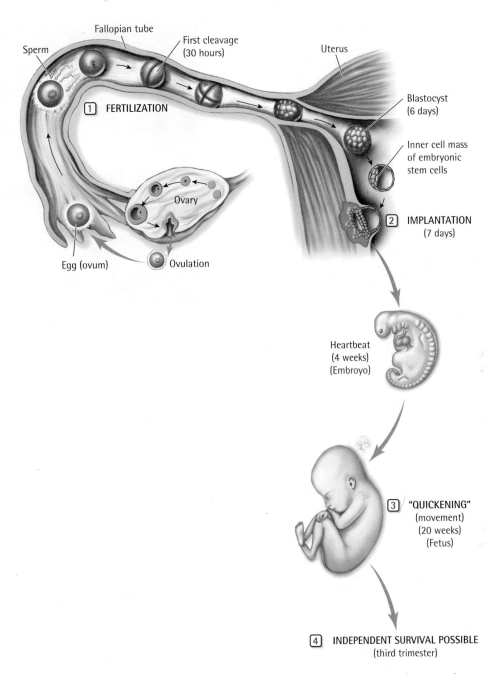

FIGURE 3.13 Early Human Development: The Course of the Ovum, Embryo, and Fetus The drawing depicts the female reproductive system, fertilization of the ovum, and the early growth of the blastocyst, which will soon become an embryo.
Source: Johnson & Losos. (2008). *The Living World* (5th ed.). p. 287.

Toward the end of the second week, mitotic cell division proceeds more rapidly. The embryonic portion of the inner cell mass begins to separate into three layers: the **ectoderm** (the outer layer), which is the source of future cells forming the nervous system, the sensory organs, the skin, and the lower part of the rectum; the **mesoderm** (the middle layer), which gives rise to the skeletal, muscular, and circulatory systems and the kidneys; and the **endoderm** (the inner layer), which develops into the digestive tract (including the liver, the pancreas, and the gallbladder), the respiratory system, the bladder, and portions of the reproductive organs (Johnson & Losos, 2008).

The Embryonic Period

The *embryonic period* lasts from the end of the second week to the eighth week. It spans that period of pregnancy from the time the blastocyst completely implants itself in the uterine wall to the time the developing organism becomes a recognizable human fetus. During this period the developing organism is called an *embryo* and normally experiences (1) rapid growth; (2) the establishment of a placental relationship with the mother; (3) the early structural appearance of all the chief organs; and (4) the development, in form at least, of a recognizably human body. All of the major organs are developing now, except the sex organs, which will begin to develop within several weeks; at that point, male embryos begin to produce the hormone testosterone, and male sex organs begin to differentiate from female organs.

The embryo becomes attached to the wall of the uterus by means of the placenta. The **placenta** is a partially permeable membrane that does not permit the passage of blood cells between the two organisms. The placenta forms from uterine tissue and the trophoblast of the blastocyst; it functions as an exchange terminal that permits entry of food materials, oxygen, and hormones into the embryo from the mother's bloodstream and the exit of carbon dioxide and metabolic wastes from the embryo into the mother's bloodstream. This feature safeguards against the mingling of the mother's blood with that of the embryo. Were the mother's and embryo's blood to intermix, the mother's body would reject the embryo as foreign material.

The transfer between the placenta and the embryo occurs across a web of fingerlike projections, the villi, which extend into blood spaces in the maternal uterus. The villi begin developing during the second week, growing outward from the chorion. When the placenta is fully developed at about the seventh month of pregnancy, it is shaped like a pancake, or disc, 1 inch thick and 7 inches in diameter. From the beginning, the **umbilical cord** links the embryo to the placenta and is a conduit carrying two arteries and one vein. This connecting structure, or lifeline, is attached to the middle of the fetal abdomen.

Development that commences with the brain and head areas and then works its way down the body is called **cephalocaudal development.** This direction of development ensures an adequate nervous system to support the proper functioning of other systems. During the early part of the third week, the developing embryo begins to take the shape of a pear, the broad, knobby end of which becomes the head. The cells in the central portion of the embryo also thicken and form a slight ridge that is referred to as the *primitive streak.* The primitive streak divides the developing embryo into right and left halves and eventually becomes the spinal cord. The tissues grow in opposite directions away from the axis of the primitive streak, a process termed **proximodistal development.** Cephalocaudal development and proximodistal development are illustrated in Chapter 4.

By the 28th day, the head region takes up roughly one-third of the embryo's length. Also about this time,

Embryo with Primitive Streak Barely 6 weeks old and measuring 15 mm (just over ½ inch), the embryo has its transparent back turned toward us. The primitive streak, visible through the thin skin, will become its spinal cord. The embryo is encircled by its amniotic sac, with the ragged chorionic villi and the umbilical cord to the right. The yolk sac hovers to the left.
Source: Lennart Nilsson. (1990). *A Child Is Born.* New York: Dell.

a brain and a primitive spinal cord become evident. As development progresses during the second month, the head elevates, the neck emerges, and rudiments of the nose, eyes, mouth, and tongue appear. Another critical system—the circulatory system—also develops early. By the end of the third week, the heart tube has already begun to beat in a halting manner.

Within four weeks of conception, the embryo is about ⅓ inch long—nearly 10,000 times larger than the fertilized egg. About this time the mother usually suspects that she is pregnant. Her menstrual period is generally two weeks overdue. She might feel heaviness, fullness, and tingling in her breasts; simultaneously, the nipples and surrounding areolas may enlarge and darken. Also at this time, about one-half to two-thirds of all pregnant women experience a morning queasiness or nauseated feeling. This "morning sickness" can persist for several weeks or months and varies in intensity from woman to woman.

The developing embryo is particularly sensitive to the invasion of drugs, diseases, and environmental toxins in the mother's body because so many of its major body systems are developing. The mother's excessive use of alcohol, nicotine, or caffeine, and her use of more potent chemical agents, such as methamphetamine, crack cocaine, heroin, and strong prescription medications, can certainly harm the development of this embryo's organs and structures. Each organ and structure has a **critical period** during which it is most vulnerable to damaging influences.

The Fetal Period

The final stage in prenatal life—the *fetal period*—begins at the end of the eighth week and ends with birth. During this time the organism is called a **fetus,** and its major organ systems continue to develop and assume their specialized functions. By the end of the eighth week, the organism definitely resembles a human being. It is complete with face, arms, legs, fingers, toes, basic trunk and head muscles, and internal organs. The fetus now builds on this basic form.

Development during the fetal period is less dramatic than that during the embryonic period. Even so, significant changes occur. By the eighth week, the fetal face acquires a truly human appearance. During the third month, the fetus develops skeletal and neurological structures that lay the foundation for spontaneous movements of the arms, legs, and fingers. By the fourth month, stimulation of the infant's body surfaces activates a variety of reflex responses. Between the fourth and fifth months, the mother generally begins to feel the spontaneous movements of the fetus (called *quickening* a sensation like a moving butterfly in the abdominal region). Also during the fifth month, a fine, downy, woolly fuzz (*lanugo hair*) begins to cover the fetal body.

At six months the eyebrows and lashes are well defined; the body is lean but strikingly human in proportions; the skin is wrinkled. At seven months the fetus (now weighing about 2½ pounds and measuring about 15 inches in length) gives the appearance of a dried-up, aged person, with red, wrinkled skin covered by a waxy coating (*vernix*). The fetus is now a viable organism and can cry weakly. At eight months, fat is being deposited around the body, the fetus gains an additional 2 pounds, and its neuromuscular activity increases.

At nine months the dull redness of the skin fades to pink, the limbs become rounded, and the fingernails and toenails are well formed. At full term (40 weeks) the body is plump; the skin has lost most of its lanugo hair, although the body is still covered with vernix; and all the organs necessary to carry on independent life are functioning. The fetus is now ready for birth—which will be discussed in Chapter 4.

The Timing of Birth Reproductive researchers have begun to understand the biochemical changes in the mother, the fetus, and the placenta that work in concert to control the timing of birth. Nobody knows exactly what initiates labor, but it is the placenta that orchestrates the timing. The placenta produces *corticotrophin-releasing*

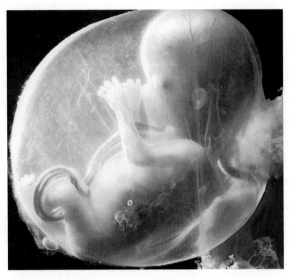

The Fetus at 3 Months At 3 months the fetus is a little more than 3 inches long and weighs nearly an ounce. Its head is disproportionately large and appears increasingly like that of a human. By now the external ears and eyelids have formed. The umbilical cord increases in size to accommodate the growing organism. The fetus is developing the skeletal and neurological structures that provide the foundation for moving in its capsule, where it floats weightlessly much in the manner of an astronaut in space.
Source: Lennart Nilsson. (1990). *A Child Is Born.* Growth. Reprinted by permission of Yale University Press.

hormone (CRH) very early in the pregnancy, but the output increases steadily until it eventually reaches a threshold. This sets in motion the release of other hormones, most notably from the adrenal glands, which boost the production of estrogen. The estrogen boost in turn stimulates the uterus to contract, ending with birth and discharge of the placenta (Tallack & Murkoff, 2006).

Like members of a highly trained orchestra appearing at the same time for a performance, precise levels of critical hormones must be released by the mother, the fetus, and the placenta, culminating in delivery. Research findings on the genes that trigger the release of CRH and other hormones associated with labor may lead to screening women at risk for premature delivery. Such women could plan to give birth at a hospital with a neonatal intensive care unit.

Questions

How long is the average prenatal period (length of pregnancy)? What are the three distinct prenatal periods, and what important developments occur in each? What is the role of the placenta and umbilical cord? How is cephalocaudal development different from proximodistal development?

Loss by Miscarriage or Stillbirth

A **miscarriage** occurs when the zygote, embryo, or fetus is naturally expelled from the uterus before it can survive outside the mother's womb. The medical term is **spontaneous abortion,** and it is often preceded by cramping or bleeding. About 15 percent of known pregnancies of U.S. women end in miscarriage during the first or early second trimester, but only 1 percent of women experience recurrent pregnancy loss (National Institute of Child Health and Human Development, 2007).

A high majority of miscarriages occur before 12 weeks of development, which may indicate a problem with the implantation of the embryo into the uterine wall, some form of genetic mutation causing abnormality of the embryo, or exposure to infectious agents. In fact, early miscarriages are sometimes referred to as chemical pregnancies, wherein the embryo didn't develop but many signs and symptoms of pregnancy existed (National Institutes of Health, 2010). Later miscarriages are usually the result of some structural problem with the uterus, problems with implantation, or a cervix that does not stay closed (Hill, 2007). Indeed, a woman's cervix may be temporarily "sewn" to prevent premature birth.

"Fetal growth restriction" is associated with stillbirth or death of a fetus after 20 weeks of gestation, and stillbirth occurs in nearly 1 in 200 pregnancies in the United States yearly (National Institute of Child Health and Human Development, 2007). The pregnant woman might also have sustained an accident, trauma, or illness that triggered a miscarriage or stillbirth. About half of all miscarriages and stillbirths remain unexplained. Women over age 35 and women in developing countries of the world have much higher rates of pregnancy complications, fetal loss, and maternal death. Many organizations are collaborating to improve services for prenatal and obstetric care (National Institutes of Health, 2010).

Substantial research documents the mother's deep emotional distress for months or years after a miscarriage, yet Western cultures have no recognized ritual to mourn the loss of a child by miscarriage. Empirical studies continue to document the psychosocial impact of this loss on all family members (Lok et al., 2010). Established support groups, visits by the clergy, and online support groups are often very helpful (Cacciatore, 2007). The Internet has sites devoted to remembering those special little ones. Some women need further support and seek it by meeting with mental-health professionals. *All* women who miscarry want to know the cause of their loss, and we are just beginning to understand the significant impact of environmental factors on prenatal development or loss.

Prenatal Environmental Influences

To most of us, the term *environment* refers to a human being's surroundings after birth. In truth, environmental influences are operating from the moment of conception if not actually before, with the mother's and father's own health. The fertilized ovum undertakes a hazardous week-long journey down the fallopian tube and around the uterus, encountering throughout a highly variable and chemically active medium. We generally think of the uterus as providing a sheltered and protected environment for prenatal development. But even after implanting itself in the uterus, the embryo is vulnerable to maternal disease, malnutrition, infections, immune disorders, use of cigarettes, prescription drugs and illegal drugs, accidental trauma or biochemical malfunctioning, and exposure to X rays.

Most pregnancies end with the birth of normal, healthy babies. Yet in the United States, about 15 percent of all conceptions result in spontaneous abortion or stillbirths. Another 3 percent of babies are born with birth defects, which are the leading cause of infant mortality (Centers for Disease Control and Prevention, 2006b). The March of Dimes (2004) defines a birth defect as "an abnormality of structure, function, or metabolism (body chemistry) present at birth that results in physical or mental disabilities" and notes that several thousand different birth defects have been identified. Genetic and environmental factors can cause birth defects. Scientists term any environmental agent that contributes to birth defects or anomalies a **teratogen,** and the field of study of birth defects is called **teratology.**

Maternal Medications   Maternal medications account for 3 percent of birth defects (Crider et al., 2009). According to medical opinion, pregnant women should not take drugs except for conditions that seriously threaten their health—and then only under medical supervision. The thalidomide tragedy in the 1960s awakened the medical profession and the public to the potential dangers of drug use in pregnant women. European, Canadian, and Australian women who had been prescribed thalidomide (a sedative) for nausea, or "morning sickness," during the embryonic stage of pregnancy gave birth to nearly 10,000 infants with serious teratogenic effects: absence of ears and arms, deafness, facial defects, and malformations in gastrointestinal systems (Rajkumar, 2004). The use of thalidomide has returned in some countries as an antinausea treatment in patients with various health problems. We learned that many drugs and chemical agents cross the placenta and affect the embryonic and fetal systems (Crider et al., 2009). Certain antibiotics used during pregnancy have been implicated in causing birth defects. Quinine (a treatment of malaria caused by a parasite) can cause congenital deafness. Barbiturates (sedating drugs) can affect the oxygen supply to the fetus and result in brain damage. Antihistamines can increase the mother's susceptibility to spontaneous abortion. Asthmatic women who require systemic steroids are more likely to have complications during pregnancy (Beckmann, 2003).

The most widely used prescription drug for women of childbearing years is Accutane and its generic versions (some sold illegally over the Internet), which are prescribed for persons with severe acne and cause known birth defects (Bérard et al., 2007). Patients sign informed consent about reproductive outcomes, must take pregnancy tests, and must use birth control while taking Accutane. In 2004 a federal registry instituted stricter guidelines because fetal deaths and congenital malformations still occur (Bérard et al., 2007). Women of childbearing years must exercise extreme caution when taking teratogenic prescription drugs.

Maternal Infectious and Noninfectious Diseases

Under some circumstances, infections that cause illness in the mother can harm the fetus. Infections can be passed along by certain raw foods (e.g., chicken, hot dogs, fish, and sandwich meats), by pets (protect hands when cleaning a cat litter box), and by exposure to people who are infected, especially children. Always wash hands after caring for children or changing baby diapers. Infections can also be passed along during vaginal, oral, and anal sex. When the mother is directly infected, viruses, bacteria, or malarial parasites can cross the placenta and infect the child (see Table 3.2 for a list of some such teratogens). In other cases the fetus can be indirectly affected by a mother's fever or by toxins in the mother's body. The exact time during the fetus's development at which an infection occurs in the mother has an important bearing.

TABLE 3.2 Teratogenic Effects of Some Maternal Infectious and Noninfectious Diseases

Name of Disease	Specific Targets of Infection/Disorder	Source of Transmission/ Acquisition	Known Teratogenic Birth Defects
Rubella (Congenital Rubella)	Skin on face, trunk, limbs	Respiratory, urine of active cases	Cardiac abnormalities, deafness, mental/physical retardation, blindness, and spontaneous abortion
Chlamydia	Vagina (PID), urethra, lymph nodes	Mucus discharges; STI	Conjunctivitis or blindness; pneumonia complications
Trichomoniasis	Vagina, vulva, urethra	Genital discharges, direct contact; STI	Born prematurely, low birth weight
Human Papillomavirus (Genital Warts)	Membranes of the vagina, penis	Direct contact with warts; STI	Born prematurely, low birth weight
Syphilis (Congenital Syphilis)	Genitalia; mucus membranes	Chancres, skin lesions; STI	Brain and spinal cord damage and/or death
Genital Herpes	Genitalia, perineum	Contact with vesicles, shed skin cells; STI	Lesions or blisters around the mouth, central nervous system damage, spontaneous abortion, infant death
Gonorrhea	Vagina (PID), urethra	Mucus secretions; STI	Conjunctivitis, blindness, pneumonia complications
Human Immunodeficiency Virus (HIV)	White blood cells, brain cells	Blood, semen, vaginal fluids; STI	Recurrent bacterial infections, cancer, swollen lymph glands, failure to thrive, neurological impairments, delayed development, early death
Diabetes Mellitus (Type 1)	Insulin-producing pancreatic cells are attacked	Heredity, metabolic complications	Congenital malformations, neurological defects, respiratory distress, spontaneous abortion, intrauterine death
Diabetes Mellitus (Type 2)	Insulin resistance/ inefficiency	Heredity, obesity, lack of exercise	Fetal obesity, labor and delivery complications, neural tube defects, respiratory distress, spontaneous abortion, stillborn

Source: Author

As described earlier, the infant's organs and structures emerge according to a fixed sequence and timetable, and each has a critical period during which it is most vulnerable to damaging influences.

HIV/AIDS   In 2010, health experts worldwide determined that the number of people infected with *human immunodeficiency virus/acquired immune deficiency syndrome* (HIV/AIDS) continues to increase markedly. There are 56,300 new HIV infections each year in the United States and 33 million people living with HIV worldwide (National Institute of Allergy and Infectious Diseases, 2010).

HIV/AIDS rates have risen to pandemic magnitude in eastern and southern Asia, Eastern Europe and Russia, central Asia, and sub-Saharan Africa (World Health Organization, 2007). In addition to increasingly higher rates of heterosexual transmission, some mothers with HIV/AIDS are drug users at risk of contracting HIV from shared needles (National Institute of Allergy and Infectious Diseases, 2010). Many people are unaware of their HIV status, and marriage and long-term monogamous relationships do not protect women from being infected. Perinatal transmission (mother to child) of HIV accounts for more than 90 percent of all pediatric AIDS cases, and experts estimate that children account for 1 in 6 AIDS-related deaths worldwide and for 1 in 7 new HIV infections (Joint United Nations Programme on HIV/AIDS, 2010).

Some mothers with HIV show no outward signs of disease, but health officials report that once these mothers are diagnosed, a three-part regimen of the drug *ZVD (zidovudine)* or *AZT (azidothymidine)* given during gestation, at birth, and to the infant at six weeks after birth reduces mother-to-child transmission of HIV from 25 percent to under 2 percent (National Institute of Allergy and Infectious Diseases, 2010).

A majority of mothers with HIV/AIDS are poor, lack medical insurance or prescription coverage, and require financial assistance and social services (unavailable in poor regions of the world). Thus, poor HIV-infected mothers breast-feed their infants, putting their infants at great risk (Joint United Nations Programme on HIV/AIDS, 2010). The World Health Organization has greatly expanded efforts for HIV/AIDS funding, education, treatment, and care (World Health Organization, 2007).

Maternal Sensitization: The Rh Factor   Pregnant women should undergo routine screening for the presence of the Rh factor in their red blood cells. There is a possible incompatibility between a protein in the mother's and child's blood cells that may produce a serious and often fatal form of anemia and jaundice in the fetus or newborn—a disorder termed *erythroblastosis fetalis.*

About 85 percent of all people have this Rh factor; they are called Rh-positive (Rh$^+$). About 15 percent do not have it; they are Rh-negative (Rh$^-$) (Talaro, 2008). The Rh factor is expressed as a superscript that follows one's blood type, such as O$^+$, O$^-$, A$^+$, B$^-$, AB$^+$, and so on.

Rh$^+$ blood and Rh$^-$ blood are *incompatible,* but adverse outcomes are preventable. Each blood factor is transmitted genetically in accordance with Mendelian rules, and Rh$^-$ is a recessive trait. Generally, the maternal and fetal blood supplies are separated by the placenta. On occasion, however, a capillary in the placenta ruptures, and a small amount of maternal and fetal blood mixes. In addition, some admixture usually occurs during the "afterbirth," when the placenta separates from the uterine wall.

An incompatibility results between the mother's and the infant's blood when an Rh$^-$ mother has a baby with Rh$^+$ blood. Under these conditions, the mother's body produces antibodies that cross the placenta and attack the baby's blood cells. Erythroblastosis fetalis can now be prevented if an Rh$^-$ mother is given anti-Rh antibodies (RhoGAM) shortly after the birth of her first child. If an Rh$^-$ mother has already been sensitized to Rh$^+$ blood by several pregnancies in the absence of RhoGAM therapy, her infant can be given an intrauterine transfusion.

Questions

What factors contribute to a spontaneous abortion, commonly called miscarriage? At what time during the prenatal period is a woman at highest risk of miscarriage? What maternal illnesses are known to compromise fetal health?

Major Drug and Chemical Teratogens

Smoking   The nicotine in tobacco is a mild stimulant drug. When a pregnant woman smokes, her bloodstream absorbs nicotine that is transmitted through the placenta to the embryo, which increases fetal activity and is linked with prematurity and low birth weight. In a longitudinal study, researchers are following the health of more than 1,000 British and Irish severely premature babies into childhood. These children have a higher range of physical and cognitive disabilities than their peers and require many more services (Marlow et al., 2005). Researchers have also found that continuing to smoke during pregnancy leads to a reduced growth of the fetal head, which could be associated with cognitive impairments (Hofman et al., 2007). Neurobehavioral decrements may also be a consequence of maternal smoking during pregnancy as well. Research studies also show that smoking during pregnancy is significantly associated with symptoms of attention-deficit hyperactivity disorder (ADHD) in offspring (Fowler et al., 2003).

Alcohol   One of the greatest tragedies of fetal alcohol syndrome (FAS) is that it occurs at all. Each year in the United States, as many as 40,000 babies are born with FAS, which is the most common cause of mental retardation that can be prevented (Astley, 2010). FAS is a pattern of anomalies occurring in children born to alcoholic women. The main features of FAS are the prenatal and/or postnatal growth retardation, low birth weight, characteristic facial abnormalities, and central nervous system dysfunction, including mental retardation. Sadly, postnatal care cannot erase the growth retardation; head and facial abnormalities; and skeletal, heart, and brain damage. The incidence of FAS in the industrialized world is roughly 1 to 3 per 1,000 children born (Astley, 2010).

Findings from international studies indicate that two-thirds of women drink at some point during their pregnancy, so it is crucial for public health care to emphasize education (Centers for Disease Control, 2009a). Other researchers suggest that alcohol consumption among pregnant women is actually higher, because figures are based on the mother's self-report of alcohol consumption and therefore sensitive to response bias (Alvik et al., 2006). Since the brain is the first organ to develop, but also the last to be complete, even small amounts of alcohol at any point in the pregnancy can lead to damaging effects (Centers for Disease Control, 2009a). It is crucial to recognize that prevention of avoidable fetal harm requires that each society take responsibility and establish programs that educate everyone about the dangers of alcohol abuse.

Marijuana   Marijuana, a psychoactive drug, is the most frequently used illicit drug in America. It has detrimental health effects on a pregnant woman, altering her mood, memory, motor control, quality of sleep, and other cognitive functions. A body of research shows that marijuana use has injurious effects on fetal development and neonatal behavior, including altered response to visual stimuli, increased activity level, a high-pitched cry, and altered neurological development, as well as impaired fetal growth (van Gelder et al., 2010). Infants exposed to marijuana in utero are sometimes identified at birth and during the neonatal period by low birth weight and size, respiratory problems, slow weight gain, and increased risk of sudden infant death syndrome (SIDS).

Oral Contraceptives   Exposure to first-generation oral contraceptives (from the 1960s through the 1970s) during the first trimester has been linked to birth defects (Nora & Nora, 1975). But today's third-generation oral contraceptives deliver reduced doses of combined estrogen and progesterone (Mosher & Jones, 2010). Surprisingly, published research is limited, and your authors found only one study linking a higher risk of congenital urinary tract anomalies with the use of oral contraceptives after conception (Li et al., 1995). There is a consistent message in current research literature that oral contraceptives are safe for most women, but each woman must exercise caution and be monitored carefully by her physician, especially if she is using continuous-use contraceptives or the birth control patch (Kuehn, 2008).

Caffeine   Increasing rates of miscarriage and birth defects among coffee drinkers prompted health care professionals to recommend that women stop or reduce their consumption of caffeinated tea, coffee, chocolate, and cola drinks during pregnancy (U.S. Food and Drug Administration, 2010). Interestingly, caffeine intake seems to have no effect on birth weight or length of gestation (Bech et al., 2007).

Cocaine and Other Hard Drugs   Fetal exposure to heroin, methadone, methamphetamine, cocaine, and its derivative "crack" produces a wide range of birth deformities (Pollard, 2007). A recent survey reported that about 4 percent of pregnant women in the 15–44 age group used illicit drugs. Newborn infants exposed in utero to heroin are identified by premature birth size and weight, excessive tremulous behavior, profuse sweating, excessive sneezing, excessive yawning, poor sleep patterns, poor swallowing ability, poor sucking or eating ability, and increased risk of SIDS (Namboodiri, 2010).

Furthermore, newborns addicted to heroin may develop neonatal abstinence syndrome (NAS), where they refuse food or fluids altogether. These newborns experience the same withdrawal symptoms as adults. "Crack babies" are small with low birth weight, and they have tremulous behavior, nasal stuffness, prolonged high-pitch crying, high temperature, poor sucking or feeding ability, respiratory problems, regurgitation problems, excessive hyperactivity, and rigidity (Hull et al., 2010). School-aged children exposed prenatally to cocaine are at risk for developing learning disabilities (LDs) or impaired intellectual functioning (Accornero et al., 2006).

Recent years have seen a significant increase in the use of methamphetamine (MA) and a growing trend of maternal use as well. Prenatal exposure to MA has devastating effects, including cardiac anomalies, fetal growth retardation, cranial abnormalities, and death (Arria et al., 2006). The movement to criminalize pregnant women who use illicit drugs is a contentious one, and state laws vary in protecting fetal rights versus maternal rights. As of this writing, no state has laws that criminalize prenatal drug use, but 36 states have expanded their child welfare policies to address prenatal drug exposure or death under civil laws as child abuse or neglect (van Gelder et al., 2010). The rates of drug addiction and poor prenatal care are highest for young, single, minority mothers, some of whom might decide not to seek prenatal care or drug treatment programs for fear of losing custody of existing children or being prosecuted (Wolfe et al., 2004).

Environmental Toxins   Pregnant women and their offspring are affected by potentially toxic agents in everyday substances these toxins include household molds, hair spray, cosmetics, pesticides, cleaning agents, air fresheners, and food preservatives. Miscarriages and birth defects also are much higher in areas where air and water are contaminated by pesticides and other agricultural products, by derivative chemicals used in industrial waste and high-tech electronics manufacturing, and by waste disposal facilities (Masters et al., 2007).

Workplace Toxins   Medical authorities are concerned about the hazards to female and male reproductive organs and processes that are found in workplaces. Studies reveal that continuous exposure to a variety of gaseous anesthetic agents used in medical facilities is associated with an increase in spontaneous abortions among female workers (Sessler & Badgwell, 1998). The University of Massachusetts School of Public Health has found that women working in clean rooms of semiconductor makers—where computer chips are etched with acids and gases—have a miscarriage rate nearly twice the national average (Meier, 1987). Prenatal exposure to the element mercury is associated with neurological and kidney disorders. Women of childbearing age are advised to follow dietary guidelines for avoiding eating certain fish, a source of the known neurotoxicant mercury. Pregnant women should also avoid exposure to cleaning solvents, lead, insecticides, and paint (Centers for Disease Control, 2010f).

A body of research in teratology and neurotoxicology reports a link between reproductive anomalies and male exposure to chemicals, radiation, and trace metals (Kalter, 2004). Mercury, solvents, various pesticides, and herbicides can affect the genes in the sperm, the structure and health of the sperm, the epididymis, seminal vesicles, and the prostate, or they can be carried in semen, causing male infertility, spontaneous abortions, and congenital malformations. In sum, working men and women with potential contact to toxins should go through training and follow exposure prevention guidelines: Wash hands regularly, wear protective clothing, avoid skin contact, keep the workplace clean, leave contaminated clothes and objects at work, and change into street clothes before leaving.

Maternal Factors

Stress   The effect of maternal emotions on the unborn infant has long been a subject of folklore. Most of us are well aware that being frightened by a snake, a mouse, a bat, or some other creature will not cause a pregnant woman to give birth to a child with a distinctive personality or birthmark. However, medical science does suggest that severe, prolonged anxiety in an expectant mother can have a harmful effect on her child (Singer et al., 2010). When the mother is anxious or under stress, various hormones such as *epinephrine* (adrenaline) and *acetylcholine* are released into her bloodstream. These hormones can pass through the placenta and enter the fetus's blood. Should a pregnant woman feel that she is experiencing prolonged or severe stress, she should consult a physician, a trained therapist, or someone in the clergy.

Maternal stress and anxiety are linked with complications of pregnancy, mainly prematurity and low birth weight for gestational age (Singer et al., 2010). Some stress and anxiety are inescapable features of expectant motherhood, but too much stress can have long-term effects on the fetus.

Age   The number of U.S. teen births has declined significantly for all ages 19 and younger since 1972. But national data indicate that teens experience high rates of abortion, miscarriage, late or no prenatal care (see Figure 3.14), premature births, very low birth weight, and perinatal deaths compared with older women of childbearing ages. African American, Hispanic, and Native American teens are more likely to delay seeking prenatal care (Child Trends Data Bank, 2008b). Such unsafe pregnancy outcomes occur despite the fact that teens are generally in better health, suffer from few chronic diseases, and engage in fewer risky behaviors than older women (Menacker, Martin, MacDorman, & Ventura, 2006).

Because young mothers are often poor and less educated, many experts assumed that their living conditions explained their pregnancy problems, but recent data show that middle-class teenagers are almost twice as likely as older women to deliver premature babies (Hamilton et al., 2010). Also, researchers find that teen mothers seem to provide lower-quality parenting. Pregnancy and motherhood are stressful to the adolescent—and even more so when her baby is preterm and has low birth weight. She is dealing with the demands of parenting concurrent with establishing her own identity and confronting the developmental tasks of adolescence, while also experiencing educational and

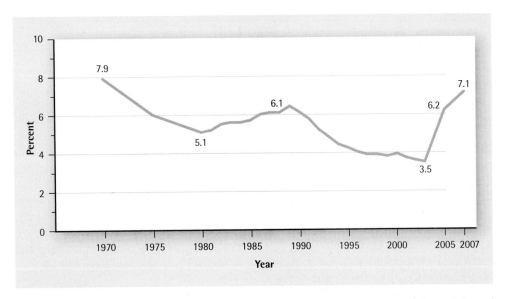

FIGURE 3.14 Percent of Births to Mothers Receiving Late or No Prenatal Care, Selected Years, 1970–2007 A high majority of U.S. women of all races are seeking early prenatal care. Prenatal care enhances pregnancy outcomes by providing health care, offering advice, and managing chronic and pregnancy-related health conditions. However, by 2007, the percent of U.S. mothers with late or no prenatal care rose to 7.1 percent (based on data from 22 states).
Source: Martin, J. A., Hamilton, B. E., Sutton, P. D., Ventura, S. J., Mathews, T. J., Kirmeyer, S., & Osterman, M. J. K. (2010, August 9). Births: Final data for 2007. *National Vital Statistics Reports, 58*(24), 1–125. Retrieved from http://www.cdc.gov/nchs/data/nvsr/nvsr58/nvsr58_24.pdf

economic limitations and complex family problems (Menacker et al., 2006).

The current consensus is that a healthy woman in her thirties or early forties enjoys a good prospect of giving birth to a healthy infant and remaining well herself, provided that she is under medical supervision. This is especially good news since more women are postponing childbirth while they complete their education or establish a career (Hamilton et al., 2010). Women over 35 are at a higher risk for fertility difficulties, diabetes, hypertension and other health issues, miscarriage, fetal chromosomal abnormalities, intrauterine death, and complications in labor and delivery. The oldest women who elect to have children after menopause (using ARTs) are more likely to experience pregnancy complications and have a significantly increased risk of fetuses with congenital malformation (National Institutes of Health, 2010).

Nutrition and Prenatal Care The unborn infant's nourishment comes from the maternal bloodstream through the placenta. Poor maternal nutrition—associated with war, famine, poverty, drug addiction, and poor dietary practice—has long-term insidious effects on brain growth and intelligence. Thus, maternal nutritional deficiencies, particularly severe ones, are reflected in changes in genes, structure, physiology, and metabolism of the

child, predisposing such individuals to other diseases in adulthood (Abu-Saad & Fraser, 2010).

Seeking early and regular prenatal care, taking prenatal vitamins and folic acid, getting moderate exercise, and not smoking or not using harmful drugs are significantly correlated with babies born with adequate birth weight and fewer birth complications. Women should make a prenatal visit as soon as they know they are pregnant and should attend scheduled visits thereafter. About 7 percent of pregnant women in the United States seek late or no prenatal care (see Figure 3.14) (Child Trends Data Bank, 2008b). Research studies over the past 30 years overwhelmingly confirm that early and regular prenatal care pays off, both in significantly improved health for newborns and their mothers and in lower costs to society (Ickovics et al., 2007).

Questions

What percentage of pregnancies ends in miscarriage? What are some prenatal environmental influences and known teratogens that are harmful to the development of the zygote, embryo, and fetus? What actions can a pregnant woman take to promote a safe pregnancy for herself and optimal health for her baby throughout the prenatal period?

SEGUE

This chapter has introduced you to the marvelous intricacies and complexities of the female and male reproductive systems. Assisted reproductive technologies (ARTs) have brought hope for those who used to be classified as infertile. The microscopic hereditary code transferred from both parents to the zygote at conception provides a blueprint for our physical makeup and a timing device for various changes in our body during our lifetime. It is truly a "miracle of life" that each of us started out with such a complex code and that it was embedded in a fertilized egg smaller than the period at the end of this sentence.

Many structures in the mother's womb must function properly to support the embryo/fetus during its course of development and birth. However, for optimal health of both mother and fetus, the mother-to-be must seek early and regular prenatal care, get proper nutrition and sleep, abstain from smoking cigarettes and from using alcohol or other drugs, avoid toxins in the home and work environments, exercise moderately to prepare for labor and delivery, and try to keep stress to a minimum.

In Chapter 4, we discuss the variety of approaches employed to prepare for the coming birth of a child, methods used to ease mothers and the fetus through labor and delivery, and the exciting and challenging first two years of infant development.

SUMMARY

Reproduction

1. Two human cells are involved in reproduction: the female's ovum and the male's sperm. Technological advances are available to help more people reproduce.

2. The male's primary reproductive organs are a pair of testes located in an external pouchlike structure called the scrotum. The testes produce the principal male sex hormones, called androgens (testosterone and androsterone), which produce male secondary sex characteristics.

3. During sexual arousal and ejaculation, mature sperm are released from the tubules, emptied into the epididymis, and mixed with nurturant fluids from the prostate gland and seminal vesicles. This is semen, which is ejaculated out of a man's body through the urethra in the man's penis.

4. A male's sperm count and health can be compromised by illness, sexually transmitted infections, and exposure to biochemical substances.

5. The primary female reproductive organs are a pair of ovaries that lie in her pelvis. Each ovary produces mature eggs (ova) and the female sex hormones estrogen and progesterone. During ovulation and menstruation, a mature egg normally is moved into the fallopian tube (oviduct), into the uterus (womb), through the cervix, into the vagina, and out of the body.

6. An ovary contains many follicles, and normally only one ovum matures in a menstrual cycle. Ovulation is the discharge of the mature ovum from its follicle.

7. The menstrual cycle is the series of regular hormonal and physical changes associated with producing a mature ovum. The cycle begins the first day the woman menstruates, and the average length of the cycle is about 28 days (with some variation). A mature ovum is usually produced toward the middle of each monthly cycle.

8. If fertilization does not take place, decreasing levels of female hormones lead to menstruation about two weeks later. For most women, this menstrual cycle continues for 30 to 40 years, unless pregnancy, disease, illness, stress, or surgical intervention occurs.

9. Fertilization occurs in the upper end of the fallopian tube, and the new organism is called a zygote. About one-third of all zygotes die after fertilization.

10. A woman might conceive dizygotic twins (nonidentical) if two ova or more are released during the same menstrual cycle. Monozygotic (identical) twins are the result of one fertilized egg splitting into two identical parts after conception. Multiple conceptions occur more frequently now, because of the use of artificial procedures to enhance fertility.

11. Many U.S. women are delaying childbirth until their thirties or older, but those over 35 have a higher infertility rate. Fertility drugs and assisted reproductive technologies (ARTs) have been created to aid in conception.

12. One infertility treatment is in vitro fertilization (IVF), where fertilization occurs outside the womb. Some postmenopausal women are also becoming pregnant and have high-risk pregnancies. But ART methods such as cloning and stem cell research to produce human embryos for reproduction or experimentation are strongly debated.

13. There are optimal times of a menstrual cycle and optimal seasons of the year for conception to occur—yet infertility rates are increasing worldwide.

14. Some biomedical researchers support research on reproductive techniques to screen embryo health and on cloning. One goal is to end infertility, but laws to protect couples and embryos do not yet exist.

15. Public education campaigns about birth control methods, including abstinence, are targeting young adolescents,

women at risk of HIV and STIs, and those with multiple sex partners.

16. Elective abortion is legal in the United States, and pro-life and pro-choice advocates dispute each other with powerful political efforts.

17. Women are conceiving at both younger and older ages. The youngest teen pregnancy rate dropped markedly since the early 1990s, yet the United States has the highest teen pregnancy rate in the developed world.

Heredity and Genetics

18. Our biological inheritance is called heredity, and genetics is the scientific study of biological inheritance.

19. The Human Genome Project has successfully mapped the human genome, the sequencing of the genetic blueprint of all the genes on their appropriate chromosomes. Our individual genome affects every aspect of our physiology and behavior. Many types of mutations result in hereditary diseases.

20. Chromosomes are long threadlike structures made of protein and nucleic acid located in the nucleus of each cell. The chromosome is shaped like a rope ladder (or double helix) and contains about 20,000 to 25,000 genes. Genes are composed of DNA (deoxyribonucleic acid), which programs cells to make substances vital to life. Upon normal fertilization, the 23 chromosomes of the ovum and the 23 chromosomes of the sperm combine to create a unique zygote with 46 chromosomes (23 pairs).

21. Mitosis is the type of cell division through which nearly all cells of the human body (except the sex cells) replicate themselves. In the cell nucleus, each single chromosome splits lengthwise to form a new pair, called "daughter" cells, which have the same hereditary code as the original.

22. Meiosis is a replication process that takes place in the gametes (the sperm and ovum). Meiosis involves two cell divisions during which the chromosomes are reduced to half their original number. Each gamete receives only 23 chromosomes, not 23 pairs as in other cells. This allows each gamete to contribute one-half of the genetic material at fertilization.

23. The male's sperm carries the chromosome that determines the sex of a child. In human chromosomes, 22 pairs are similar in size and shape in both men and women and are the autosomes. The 23rd pair, the sex chromosomes (one X from the mother and one X or Y from the father), determines the baby's sex.

24. An ovum (X) fertilized by a sperm with X will produce a female child (XX). An ovum (X) fertilized by a sperm with Y will produce a male (XY). About six to eight weeks into embryonic development, the male embryo produces the hormone testosterone, which promotes masculinization of the fetus.

25. Each member of a pair of genes at a specific place on the chromosome is called an allele. An allele can be dominant and hide traits of the other allele, creating a recessive character. A dominant character is labeled with a capital letter, such as *A*, and the recessive character is signified by a lowercase letter, in this case *a*. Some traits result from the complex interaction of many genes, which is called polygenic inheritance.

26. An organism's genotype is its actual genetic makeup, and the phenotype is its observable characteristics. In humans, the phenotype includes physical, physiological, and behavioral traits. Humans also possess dominant and recessive traits. In humans, environmental factors interact with genetic factors to produce traits, and this is called multifactorial transmission.

27. Genes can also be linked together during inheritance. The X chromosome can carry a sex-linked trait such as hemophilia, red-green color blindness, and about 150 other traits and disorders. The vast majority of sex-linked genetic defects occur in males.

28. The field of genetic counseling and testing has arisen out of genetic research to apply knowledge about genetics to reproduction, health, and well-being. Diagnostic tests are available to counsel those who are most likely to be affected.

29. Prenatal diagnosis employs various techniques to determine the health and condition of an unborn fetus. Down syndrome is a chromosomal disorder that has a higher incidence than some other genetic defects and appears in all cultures of the world.

Prenatal Development

30. The prenatal period normally lasts about 266 days, or 280 days (about 40 weeks) from the last menstrual period, and is divided into three stages: the germinal period, the embryonic period, and the fetal period.

31. The germinal period is characterized by the growth of the zygote (the fertilized egg) and the establishment of an initial linkage between the zygote and the support system of the mother through implantation in the uterus. In several days the structure called the blastocyst begins to differentiate into the chorion, trophoblast, and inner cell mass.

32. The embryonic period lasts from the end of the second week to the end of the eighth week. The embryo grows rapidly, establishes a complex physical membrane exchange with the mother through the placenta, and differentiates the chief organs in early structural form.

33. In the embryonic stage, structures develop in accordance with two principles: cephalocaudal development (brain and head first, then on down to trunk and toes) and proximodistal development (tissues grow in opposite directions away from the earliest structure of the spinal cord).

34. A woman may be unaware of her pregnancy until about four weeks after conception, when she does not menstruate. The early developing embryo is highly sensitive to the mother's ingestion of drugs, medications, and environmental teratogens.

35. The fetal period, during which the organism is a fetus, begins with the ninth week and ends with birth. Differentiation of major organ systems continues, and the organs assume specialized functions. The fetus becomes a sensory aware and active being.

36. A miscarriage occurs when the zygote, embryo, or fetus is naturally expelled from the uterus before it can survive outside the mother. Up to 15 percent of pregnancies end in miscarriage, and most miscarriages occur by the 12th

week. Families experience emotional distress after miscarriage and need social support.

37. Toxic environmental substances (called teratogens) in the home, workplace, and social-recreational settings can affect the organism from the moment of conception and throughout the prenatal period, potentially resulting in birth defects. The woman must get skilled prenatal care, proper nutrition, plenty of sleep, and moderate exercise, and must avoid excessive stress, to prepare for a healthy pregnancy, labor, and delivery.

KEY TERMS

abortion *(72)*

allele *(77)*

amniocentesis *(79)*

amnion *(82)*

assisted reproductive technologies (ARTs) *(66)*

autosomes *(76)*

blastocyst *(63)*

cephalocaudal development *(84)*

chorion *(82)*

chromosomes *(75)*

cloning *(67)*

critical period *(85)*

dizygotic twins *(65)*

DNA (deoxyribonucleic acid) *(74)*

dominant character *(77)*

ectoderm *(83)*

ectogenesis *(68)*

embryo *(63)*

embryonic period *(82)*

endoderm *(83)*

fallopian tubes *(63)*

fertilization/fusion *(62)*

fetal period *(82)*

fetus *(85)*

gametes *(62)*

genes *(75)*

genetic counseling *(79)*

genetic counselor *(80)*

genetics *(74)*

genotype *(77)*

germinal period *(82)*

gynecologist *(71)*

heredity *(74)*

heterozygous *(77)*

homozygous *(77)*

human genome *(74)*

implantation *(82)*

in vitro fertilization (IVF) *(66)*

inner cell mass *(82)*

meiosis *(75)*

menstrual cycle *(64)*

menstruation *(64)*

mesoderm *(83)*

miscarriage *(86)*

mitosis *(75)*

monozygotic twins *(65)*

multifactorial transmission *(78)*

ovaries *(63)*

ovulation *(64)*

ovum *(62)*

penis *(62)*

phenotype *(77)*

placenta *(84)*

polygenic inheritance *(77)*

prenatal diagnosis *(79)*

prenatal period *(82)*

proximodistal development *(84)*

recessive character *(77)*

reproduction *(62)*

sex chromosomes *(76)*

sex-linked traits *(78)*

sperm *(62)*

spontaneous abortion *(86)*

stem cells *(70)*

teratogen *(86)*

teratology *(86)*

testes *(62)*

testosterone *(76)*

trophoblast *(82)*

ultrasound *(79)*

umbilical cord *(84)*

uterus *(63)*

vagina *(63)*

zygote *(62)*

FOLLOWING UP ON THE INTERNET

Web sites for this chapter focus on heredity, genetics, and human reproduction. Please access the text Web site at www.mhhe.com/crandell10 for up-to-date hot-linked Internet addresses for the following organizations and topics:

American Fertility Association
http://www.theafa.org/

American Social Health Association
http://www.ashastd.org/

American Society for Reproductive Medicine
http://www.asrm.org/

The International Society for Stem Cell Research
http://www.isscr.org/

Research Ethics and Stem Cells: National Institutes of Health
http://stemcells.nih.gov/info/ethics.asp

National Geographic Society: The Human Family Tree
http://channel.nationalgeographic.com/channel/human-family-tree-3706-interactive

The Visible Embryo Project
http://www.visembryo.com/

PART 3 BIRTH AND INFANCY
THE FIRST TWO YEARS

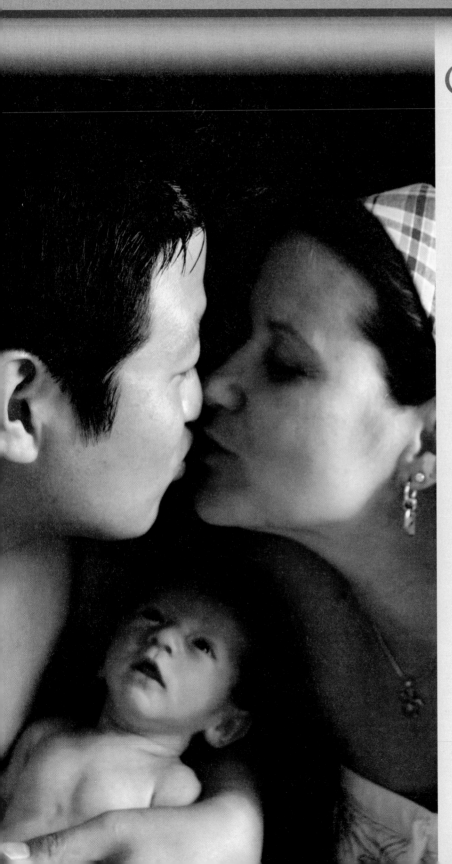

Chapter 4 describes the preparation of the mother for labor, delivery, birth, and motherhood. We discuss several birth and delivery methods, including natural, or prepared, childbirth. The significance of early caregiver-infant bonding within diverse family structures is also discussed. We next examine potential birth complications and birth defects. Then we turn to the infant's physical, motor, and sensory development during the first two years. In Chapter 5, we examine the cognitive and language development that enables infants to take greater command of their environment. Chapter 6 describes the emotional and social development of infants, including the significant influences of attachment, temperament, and parenting practices.

4 Birth and Physical Development
The First Two Years

Extensive research in prenatal development over the past 40 years has revealed that the tiny human demonstrates physical, sensory, cognitive, and emotional behaviors. Routine use of non-invasive diagnostic and imaging technologies have made it possible for us to view the developing embryo and fetus as it prepares for birth. For most expectant parents, the first time they see a fetal ultrasound or hear a fetal heartbeat is a thrilling experience.

Touch, the first sense to develop and the cornerstone of human experience and communication, begins in the womb (Arabin, 2004). The first dramatic movement, one that symbolizes life itself, is the first heartbeat at 3 weeks after conception. At 10 weeks, a fetus can use its hand to touch its head, mouth, and face, and it can open and close its mouth and swallow (Arabin, 2004). The fetus lives in a stimulating environment of sound, vibration, and motion (Kisilevsky et al., 2003). Voices reach the womb, and patterns of pitch and rhythm as well as music reach the fetus. A mother's voice is particularly powerful (Hepper, 2006). The fetus reacts to amniocentesis (usually done between weeks 14 and 18) by shrinking away from the needle, a reaction easily observed on the ultrasound. Rapid eye movement sleep, a manifestation of dreaming, is observed as early as 23 weeks of gestation, although the eyelids remain closed (Hopson, 1998).

Most full-term infants arrive at birth with all sensory systems functioning. Newborns are real, separate persons, not the "blank slates" they were thought to be only a few decades ago. Tests made at birth reveal that infants have exquisite taste and odor discrimination and definite preferences, and visual and auditory tests demonstrate how remarkably a newborn can imitate a variety of facial expressions and vowel vocalizations (Meltzoff & Prinz, 2002). When newborns are awake, their eyes constantly seek out the environment (Johnson, Slemmer, & Amso, 2004). Throughout the newborn's first two years of life, extraordinary emotional and social developments accompany the maturation of its physical, sensory, and cognitive systems.

BIRTH

A Child Is Born into a Family

Today, babies are born into a shifting composition of American families and households, and American families are composed of fewer children. Demographic trends in rates of marriage, cohabitation, divorce, single parenthood, fertility, and mortality influence family composition, and all these factors affect the quality of life of our most precious resource—our children. Although a small proportion of men and women remain childless or experience infertility, more than 80 percent of U.S. adults will be the parent of a child by the age of 35 (Child Trends DataBank, 2002). The U.S. National Center for Health Statistics reports that after annual declines in births in the 1990s, births rose to their highest level—more than 4 million babies were born each year since 2000. Rates began to decline again in 2008, and this dip appeared to be linked to the economic recession that began in late 2007 (Livingston & Cohn, 2010).

American infants are entering households that include fewer biological married parents, but more unmarried parents, parents and stepparents, single parents, same-sex parents, grandparents, adoptive parents, foster parents, and the various configurations of siblings that accompany these family structures. In 2007, the birthrate for women 20 to 24 remained relatively stable, whereas birthrates continue to climb for women in their thirties and forties (see Figure 4.1). Significantly, nearly 4 out of 10 American babies are born to single women. The fertility rate for white, African American, Asian, and Native American women rose very slightly in 2008 (Martin et al., 2010). After a sharp rise in recent years, the birthrate for Hispanic women decreased slightly in 2008 (Hamilton, Martin, & Ventura, 2010).

Motherhood itself is changing too. There are more older and more well-educated mothers today than 20 years ago. In 2008, 14 percent of mothers of newborns were aged 35 or older compared to 9 percent in 1990, and over half of all new mothers had at least some college education, whereas only 40 percent had attended college in 1990. One thing has remained the same, though, through the ages: Many mothers in 2008 said they decided to have children because of the joy of it, while others said there was no reason at all; it merely happened to them (Livingston & Cohn, 2010). Tracking fertility rates and living arrangements of families helps agencies plan for services and allocation of resources.

Preparing for Childbirth

In the 1940s, English obstetrician Grantly Dick-Read (1944) began popularizing the view that pain in childbirth could be greatly reduced if women understood the

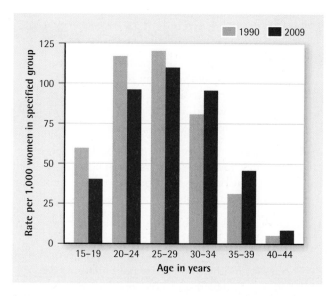

FIGURE 4.1 U.S. Birthrates by Age of Mother, per 1,000 Women: 1990 and 2009 Note the declining rate of births for nearly all ages in 2009. However, rates for women aged 40–44 and 50 and over continue to rise. Overall, this constitutes the largest decline in fertility rates since 1973.
Source: Hamilton, B. E., Martin, J. A., & Ventura, S. J. (2010, December 21). Births: Preliminary data for 2009. *National Vital Statistics Reports, 59*(3), 1–19, Figure 3 and Table 2.

birth process and learned to relax properly. Childbirth, he argued, is essentially a normal and natural process. He trained prospective mothers to relax, to breathe correctly, to understand their anatomy and the process of labor, and to develop muscular control of their labor through special exercises. He also advocated training the father as an active participant in both prenatal preparation and delivery.

During the same period, Russian doctors began to apply Pavlov's theories of the conditioned reflex to delivery practices, reasoning that society conditioned women to be tense and fearful during labor. If pain was a response conditioned by society, it could be replaced by a different, more positive response. Accordingly, the **psychoprophylactic method** evolved, which encouraged women to relax and concentrate on how they breathed when a contraction occurred.

In 1951, Fernand Lamaze (1958), a French obstetrician, visited maternity clinics in the Soviet Union. When he returned to France, he introduced the fundamentals of the psychoprophylactic method. Lamaze emphasized the mother's active participation in every phase of labor. He developed a precise and controlled breathing system in which women in labor respond to a series of verbal cues by panting, pushing, and blowing. The Lamaze method has proved popular with U.S. physicians and prospective parents, and nearly every hospital and many private medical organizations offer Lamaze childbirth preparation classes, which encourage the father or a close relative or friend to participate in the birth process.

Natural Childbirth The term **natural childbirth** refers to an awake, aware, and unmedicated mother-to-be. A woman proceeding through a Lamaze delivery might use a number of cognitive techniques that distract her from the activities of the labor room and provide support. These techniques include using a visual focus and sucking on hard candies or ice chips (Lothian & De Vries, 2010).

Natural childbirth offers a number of advantages. Childbirth education classes can do much to relieve the mother's anxiety and fear. Many couples find their joint participation in labor and delivery a joyous, rewarding occasion. The mother takes no medication or is given it only sparingly in the final phase of delivery, at her request. There is conflicting research on the effects of these analgesic and sedative drugs (Briggs & Wan, 2006). Some studies show that using certain medications can reduce the need for *cesarean sections* (surgical delivery) and reduce delivery time (Votipka, 1997). Safe obstetric practice suggests caution in the administration of these drugs, however, because what passes into the mother's system might affect the baby during labor and delivery.

Medical authorities conclude that women should not labor and deliver alone (Bruggemann et al., 2007). Evidence suggests that women who have a companion with them during childbirth have faster, simpler deliveries, have fewer complications, and are more affectionate toward their babies. This insight has led to the reemergence of *doula* services (*doula* is a Greek word meaning "one who ministers"). Doulas and *midwives,* as acknowledged members of the maternity care team, provide emotional care and physical comfort and are usually licensed and often affiliated with **obstetricians** (physicians who specialize in conception, prenatal development, birth, and the woman's postbirth care). This returns to women an element of childbearing that was the norm until the medicalization of childbirth in the United States in the 1920s. Before that time, women typically delivered babies surrounded by female relatives and often were assisted by a midwife. Research shows that the presence of a doula during childbirth can positively influence the mother's relationship to her child; mothers with doulas reported more confidence in their mothering skills than mothers who chose standard hospital care (Campbell, Scott, Klaus, & Falk, 2007).

Doulas can also provide essential cultural knowledge to help nurses care for immigrant women. A large teaching hospital in the Minneapolis–St. Paul area initiated a program using Somali doulas for Somali mothers. The

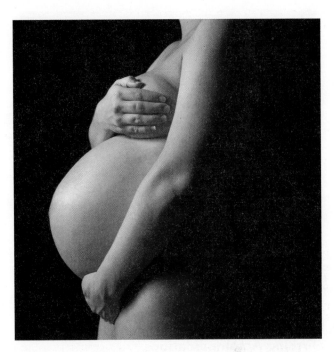

Preparing for Childbirth A woman's body changes dramatically over the nine months of pregnancy, giving her time to prepare herself for the most significant change in her life—motherhood. The majority of contemporary American women have two children.

women from this refugee population, many of whom had undergone genital cutting (infibulation) as a rite of passage, had special medical needs in childbirth. Nurses at the hospital reported that the presence of the Somali doulas aided them greatly in understanding how to provide cultural and medically sensitive care, including Somali words for key phrases and sentences used during childbirth. The rate of cesarean section for Somali women attended by doulas was significantly lower than that for Somali women who were not attended by doulas (Dundek, 2006).

Although natural childbirth offers advantages for many couples, it is more suitable for some couples and some births than others. In some cases, the pain becomes so severe that wise and humane practice calls for medication. Although the average intensity of labor pain is quite high, women differ substantially in their experience of it. Despite their pain and discomfort, most women say that childbirth is one of the greatest experiences of their lives (Picard, 1993). Both proponents and critics of natural childbirth agree that women who are psychologically or physically unprepared for it should not consider themselves inadequate or irresponsible if they resort to medication during childbirth. Indeed, many practitioners view natural childbirth training and pain-relief remedies as compatible, complementary procedures.

FIGURE 4.2 Cesarean Births
Continue to Increase in the United
States: 1990–2007
Source: Martin, J. A., Hamilton, B. E., Ventura, S. J.,
Matthews, M. S., Kirmeyer, S., & Osterman, M. J. K.
(2010). Births: Final data for 2007. *National Vital Statistics
Reports, 58*(24), 1–125.

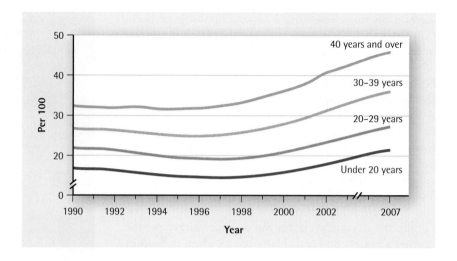

Birthing Accommodations

Most couples now seek an obstetrician and a hospital that view uncomplicated pregnancies as a normal process rather than as an illness. Parents are rebelling against regimented and impersonal hospital routines. They do not want the delivery of their babies to be a surgical procedure (cesarean section, or C-section) unless such surgery is necessary or planned. Nevertheless, 99 percent of babies born in 2007 in the United States were delivered in hospitals, and the cesarean rate continued to rise to nearly one-third of all births (Martin et al., 2010) (see Figure 4.2). Two out of three nonhospital births took place in a residence, and just over one-quarter took place in a community birthing center (Martin et al., 2010).

Although the great majority of all babies born in hospitals were delivered by physicians, other options exist. Among the maternity-care options more widely available is **midwifery.** Midwives attended almost one out of ten U.S. births in 2007 (Martin et al., 2010). Most of this increase is due to more certified midwife–attended births in hospitals (American College of Nurse-Midwives, 2007). The highest level of expertise is a *certified nurse-midwife* (CNM), and this person will have a nursing degree, will have had midwifery training and certification, and might work with doctors. Midwives who are not nurses are seeking legal status. The demand for the use of midwives is now being fueled by women who prefer a more personal birthing experience and by women who lack access to or cannot afford the high costs of traditional obstetrical and gynecological care (Lyndon-Rochelle, 2004). In most countries of the world, the majority of births are assisted by trained midwives (Wagner, 2006).

In response to the home-birth movement, many hospitals have introduced **birthing rooms** that have a

homelike atmosphere. The woman can give birth assisted by a nurse-midwife or an obstetrician and her husband, partner, or other family members. The trend of having family members present during birth is highly valued by women from many ethnic groups. A survey of mothers from various ethnic groups by student nurses at Hawaii Community College found that many cultures emphasize companionship and support for the mother while she labors, followed by extensive physical support for the mother and the baby during the first month after the birth (see Table 4.1). The mother and child might then return home about 6 to 24 hours after an uncomplicated delivery, but birthing rooms allow for close proximity to a regular delivery room and life-saving equipment in case it is needed.

Other hospitals have introduced family-centered hospital care. Usually the mother has **rooming in,** an arrangement in which the infant stays in a bassinet beside the mother's bed, allowing the mother to get acquainted with her child and integrating the father early in the child-care process. This practice runs counter to the longtime U.S. hospital practice of segregating infants in a sterile nursery. Under the supervision of the nursing staff, parents gain skill in nursing/feeding, bathing, diapering, and caring for their infant. Women who desire to breast-feed their babies can begin the process with the help and support of the trained hospital staff.

Birthing centers are open in many urban areas. These primary care facilities are used only for low-risk deliveries because they lack high-tech equipment. Should complications arise, patients are transferred to nearby hospitals (DeWitt, 1993). Another recent trend has shortened hospital stays for new mothers and their newborns. In today's cost-conscious climate of U.S. managed health care, maternity stays have declined from the

TABLE 4.1 Traditional Cultural Beliefs and Practices About Labor and Delivery Among U.S. Ethnic Groups

Culture	Practice	Belief
African American	A knife under the pillow will cut the pain of labor. Traditionally, granny-midwives delivered babies. Making loud sounds during delivery is acceptable.	The placenta has a spirit of its own and must be secretly buried so it can never harm the child. Talismans are used to protect the child and connect it to the ancestors and the spirits of nature. New mothers are to rest for four to eight weeks and are cared for by the family and the community.
Chinese	The father has no role at the first birth, although he may be present at subsequent births. The mother's mother assists at the first birth. Crying out during labor will attract evil spirits to the child.	The placenta must be kept and buried in a safe place because it is essential for rebirth. The child must have the placenta when it dies and enters heaven. The mother is encouraged to have total bed rest for one month—the "sitting month." Twelve days after the birth, the family serves soup to friends and family to celebrate the happy event.
Hispanic	Natural birth is desirable. Most Hispanic women prefer to have their families with them as they labor. Vocalization during labor is avoided. Traditionally, the door was shut as delivery approached to prevent the evil eye from entering.	The placenta should be buried in the family's yard to prevent blindness and stomach pains in the child. The family provides complete care for mother and baby for forty days.
Portuguese	Women friends support the mother during labor. Screaming during labor is a sign of weakness.	The mother and father must burn the umbilical cord and bury the ashes to bring good luck to the baby. The husband and grandfather must burn the placenta and bury the ashes to protect the baby from evil spirits. Female family members care for mother and baby for up to two months.
Japanese	Husbands are not present during labor and delivery. Stoicism during labor is highly valued.	The placenta and cord should be buried to protect the child. Mothers are encouraged to stay indoors with their child for one month to protect the baby from infection. Mothers and grandmothers help with the baby.
Samoan	Males are not present during labor and delivery. Female family members support the mother during the labor. The mother is not supposed to show evidence of pain, and pain medication is to be avoided.	The placenta is buried near a fruit tree. If the tree grows large, it will feed the baby. If the tree does not thrive, the baby will be sickly. The family has a day-long party to welcome the mother and baby. Elder women in the community advise and support the new mother.
Vietnamese	If the husband is present, the baby will not come out or the mother will have a difficult birth.	The placenta may be kept if the mother is strong and healthy. The mother may eat the placenta to promote good health. The mother has strict bed rest for one month.

Source: Division of Nursing and Allied Health. (2005, July 7). Information collected from pregnant women by nursing students at Hawaii Community College, 2003–2006. Retrieved October 26, 2007 from http://www.hawcc.hawaii.edu/nursing/transcultural.html

weeklong sojourn in the 1950s (which is still prevalent in many European nations) to a national average of about 2.5 days in 2005 (DeFrances & Hall, 2007). Three days is now typical for cesarean births. Not surprisingly, many health professionals criticize the fact that most health insurance allows only such abbreviated stays, saying that mothers need more hospital time to rest and recover and acquire basic child-care skills. Although problems with newborns might surface early, some conditions, including jaundice and heart murmurs, tend to appear within the first few days, and the mother herself might experience medical complications hours after delivery (Goulet et al., 2007).

Questions

How do giving birth in a birthing room in a hospital, giving birth in a medically supervised birthing center, and giving birth in a home delivery with a midwife or doula attending differ? What are some factors to consider in making this important decision?

Stages of the Birth Process

Birth is the transition between dependent existence in the uterus and life as a separate organism. In less than a day, a radical change occurs. The fetus is catapulted from its

MORE INFORMATION YOU CAN USE

Options You May Have for a Birth Plan

Onset of Labor
Spontaneous
Self-induced
  Walk
  Enema
  Castor oil
  Nipple stimulation
  Thumb sucking
  Accupressure
Medically Induced
  Prostaglandin gel
  IV pitocin
  Amnitomy

Clothes
Own clothing
Hospital gown

Empty Bladder
Walk to toilet
Bedpan
Catheterization

Monitoring
None
Intermittent
Continuous
Internal
Telemetry unit

Pain Relief
Epidural
  Soon as possible
  When uncomfortable
  At 5 cm
  Only if I ask
Narcotic
  Definite
  Offer please
  Only if I ask
Relaxation Techniques
  Vocalization
  Relaxation
  Breathing
  Imagery/visualization
  Close eyes
  Focal point

Hydration
Drinking fluids
Popsicles/ice chips
Suckers/lollipops
Mouthwash
Heparin lock
IV fluids
No liquids

Comfort Measures
Dim lights
Music
TENS unit
Heating pad
Hot/cold packs
Water
  Shower, bathtub,
  Jacuzzi
Massage

Comfort Items
Pillow
Tennis balls
Rolling pin
Wooden roller
Lotion/powder

Positions
Walk
Lunge
Sitting in chair
Sitting on side of bed
Rock
Stand
Pelvic rock
Dangle
Back-to-back
Hands & knees
Squat
Leaning over bed

Speed up Labor
Nipple stimulation
Position changes
Break amniotic bag
Pitocin
Prolonged pushes

Episiotomy
Forceps/vacuum extractor

Pushing
Spontaneous
Directed
Prolonged

Perineal Care
Massage
Warm compresses
Episiotomy
Prefer tear to episiotomy

Cesarean
Partner present
Doula present
Remain alert
Infant with mother in recovery
Describe events
Video/pictures

Cutting Cord
Partner
Mother
Doctor/midwife
Wait until pulsing stops

Baby's Warmth
On mother's abdomen
In warmer
Warmer if medically indicated

Apgar Scores
At birth
As needed

Eye Care
Delayed 1 hour

Mementos
Footprints
Video/pictures

Rooming In
24-hour with mother
Nursery at mother's request
Partner rooming in

Permission granted by Jennifer Vanderlaan, Colonie, New York, from www.birthingnaturally.net

warm, fluid, sheltered environment in the womb into the larger world, where the infant must depend exclusively on its own biological systems. Birth, then, is a bridge between two stages of life. The mother's body sends hormonal signals, including *oxytocin,* from the pituitary gland to the blood, prompting uterine contractions and labor, which normally begins at some point between 38 and 42 weeks of prenatal development. In this section we will explain the stages of the birth process, labor, and delivery.

A few weeks before birth, the head of the infant generally turns downward, which ensures that it will be born head first. (A small percentage of babies are born buttocks or feet first, in the *breech position.* This most often requires a surgical delivery.) The uterus undergoes **lightening** by simultaneously sinking downward and forward, which "lightens" the mother's discomfort. She now breathes more easily, because the pressure on her diaphragm and lungs is reduced. At about the same time the mother might begin experiencing mild contractions (*Braxton-Hicks contractions*) that are a prelude to the more vigorous contractions of labor.

Labor   The birth process consists of three stages: labor, delivery, and afterbirth. Either at the beginning of labor or sometime during it, the *amniotic sac* that surrounds and cushions the fetus ruptures, releasing the amniotic fluid. The duration of this first stage of labor varies considerably, depending on several factors: the age of the mother, the number of prior pregnancies, and potential complications of the pregnancy. During **labor** the strong muscle fibers of the uterus rhythmically contract, pushing the infant downward toward the birth canal (the vagina). Simultaneously, the muscular tissue that forms the neck of the uterus (the cervix) relaxes, becoming both shortened and widened.

Initially, the uterine contractions are spaced about 15 to 20 minutes apart and last for about 25 to 30 seconds. As the intervals shorten to 3 to 5 minutes, the contractions become stronger and last for about 45 seconds or longer. Sometimes epidural anesthesia is administered as a means for pain relief from the waist down during labor (see Figure 4.3). As the mother's uterine contractions increase in intensity and occur more frequently, her cervix opens wider (dilates). Eventually it will expand enough to allow the baby's head and body to pass through (see Figure 4.4).

Electronic Fetal Monitoring   Normally during the process of labor and delivery in a hospital setting, a strap connected to an electronic monitor is placed so that it encircles the mother's abdomen and back. The fetal heartbeat is monitored continuously and registered on a strip of paper. The baby's pulse slows down during strong contractions, but it regains its original rate

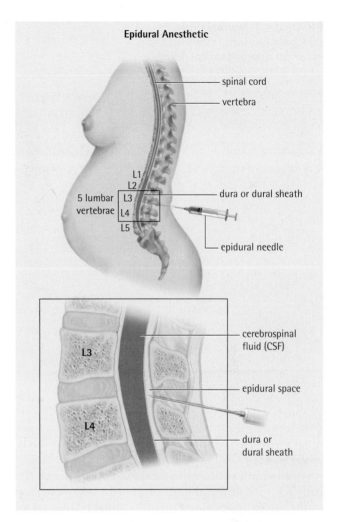

FIGURE 4.3 An Epidural Anesthetic   An epidural injection places anti-inflammatory medicine into the epidural space between vertebrae to reduce the pain in the lower body from contractions during labor and birth. It may also be used during delivery by cesarean section.
Source: MyDoctor.Com.au Epidural: What You Need to Know

in between. Its heartbeat is likely to be twice as fast as the mother's. Even though normally the baby's body is well prepared to withstand the stress of delivery, surgical intervention can be necessary if the heart-rate monitor indicates that the fetus is in distress. Using this monitor and newer computer devices can be crucial to the survival of some babies.

Delivery   **Delivery** begins once the infant's head passes through the cervix and ends when the baby has completed its passage through the birth canal. This stage generally lasts 20 to 80 minutes but can be shorter in deliveries of subsequent children. During delivery, contractions last for 60 to 65 seconds and come at 2- to 3-minute intervals. The mother aids each contraction by pushing with her abdominal muscles at recommended

FIGURE 4.4 Normal Birth The principal movements in the mechanism of normal labor and vaginal delivery. *Source:* Northwestern Memorial Hospital, http://health_info.nmh.org/hwdb/images/hwstd/medical/obgyn/n5551690.jpg

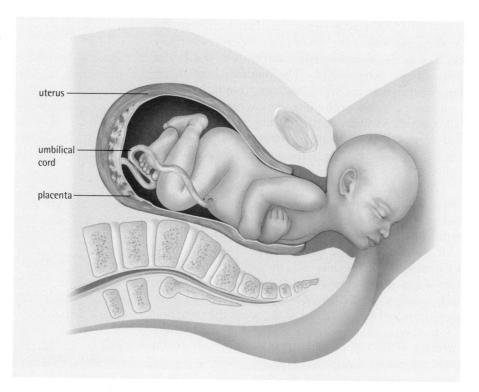

times. With each contraction, the baby's head and body emerges more.

Crowning occurs when the widest diameter of the baby's head is at the mother's vulva (the outer entrance to the vagina). Sometimes there is natural tearing, or an incision called an *episiotomy* is made between the vagina and the rectum if the opening of the vagina does not stretch enough to allow passage of the baby's head. This type of surgical intervention has come under much criticism, but it may be necessary to prevent complications of delivery in some births. Once the head has passed through the birth canal, the rest of the body quickly follows (see Figure 4.4).

The second stage of labor is now over, unless there are multiple births. The doctor or health professional will quickly suction mucus from the baby's throat. The newborn, called the **neonate,** is still connected to the mother by the *umbilical cord.* The newborn will be quickly assessed for its level of alertness and health and might be placed on the mother's warm body or quickly cleaned of the *vernix caseosa* (a white, waxy substance that covers its body) and placed into the parent's waiting arms.

Afterbirth   After the baby's birth, the uterus commonly stops its contractions for a few minutes. The contractions then resume, and the placenta and the remaining umbilical cord are expelled from the uterus through the vagina. This process, which expels the **afterbirth** (placenta), may last for about 20 minutes. During this process, the father of the baby may cut the clamped umbilical cord to separate the baby from the mother. Some midwives suggest that it is best to wait to cut the cord until it stops pulsating on its own. During these first minutes of the baby's life, the cord continues to provide oxygen to the baby while it learns to breathe (Harper, 2005). See the *Further Developments* box on page 106, "Childbirth in America."

Some hospitals offer a technique that collects and preserves the blood from the placenta and umbilical cord by means of *cryopreservation* for potential later transplantation. The "progenitor" cells (normally found in bone marrow) in the cord blood are effective in treating such life-threatening diseases as leukemia, some types of cancer, and some immune or genetic disorders ("Cord Blood Banking Industry," 2004).

Most parents cherish the birth experience. Yet circumstances can temper reactions to the birth of a baby. Was this baby planned for and wanted? Has the mother's health been compromised in some way? Is the baby's father present at the birth? Is it already known that the child has a birth defect? Is the family already overburdened with many children? Is this a young teenager's first pregnancy? Is this baby the product of rape or incest? Is this a surrogate pregnancy? Does the mother plan to give up her legal right to the child so it can be adopted? These types of situations certainly affect the mother's and father's level of acceptance and emotional reaction at the first sight of their newborn child.

Questions

What choices do parents have in selecting care providers for pregnancy, childbirth, and delivery? What are the events that occur in the progressive stages during labor and delivery, culminating in birth and expulsion of the afterbirth?

The Baby at Birth

In 1975 Frederick Leboyer, a French obstetrician, captured popular attention with his best-selling book *Birth Without Violence* (1975). Birth for the baby, says Leboyer, is an exceedingly traumatic experience. Leboyer calls for a more gentle entry into the world via lowered sound and light levels in the delivery room, the immediate soothing of the infant through massaging and stroking, and a mild, warm bath for the newborn.

Leboyer's claims are controversial in the scientific community. Researchers report that the stresses of a normal delivery are usually not harmful. The fetus produces unusually high levels of the stress hormones *adrenaline* and *noradrenaline* that equip it to withstand the stress of birth. This surge in hormones protects the infant from asphyxia during delivery and prepares it to survive outside the womb (Lagercrantz & Slotkin, 1986). The hormones also increase the blood flow to vital organs and raise the white-blood-cell count, enabling the baby to fight off infections. The baby's journey through the birth canal also squeezes amniotic fluid out of its lungs, making the first breath easier (Riley, 2006).

Although many physicians have rejected some of Leboyer's claims, one element of his philosophy has had a lasting effect on obstetrical practice. Parents can take comfort from knowing that from the baby's standpoint, the stress of labor during normal birth is more beneficial than common sense might suggest, for the neonate's blood flow must reverse itself, a specific valve in the heart must close, and the baby's lungs must begin to function on their own. By the same token, Leboyer fostered a more humane view of childbirth management. Today's babies no longer receive that rough slap on the backside to encourage them to breathe.

Newborn Appearance   At the moment of birth, infants are covered with *vernix,* a thick white waxy substance. Some newborns still have their *lanugo,* the fetus's fine, woolly facial and body hair, which disappears by age 4 months. Many babies are born with *milia,* or small white and yellow pimples, on their faces. These usually go away within the first few weeks.

On average, a full-term newborn is 19 to 22 inches long and weighs 5½ to 9½ pounds. Their heads are often misshapen and elongated as a product of *molding,* the process by which the soft skull "bones" become temporarily distorted to accommodate passage through the birth canal. Babies born by C-section do not have this same elongated look. Most infants have receded chins and underdeveloped lower jaws. Bowleggedness is the rule, and the feet might be pigeon-toed. These are all normal physical characteristics of a newborn's physical appearance, and they usually change over time.

The Apgar Test   Several aspects of a newborn's physical condition are monitored closely to see whether intervention is necessary. The average birth weight for babies is about 7 pounds 5 ounces (3.3 kilograms) (Martin et al., 2006). More babies are being born at lower birth weight because of the increasing number of multiple births. But weight is only one factor in assessing a neonate's health. The normalcy of the baby's condition at birth is usually appraised by the physician or attending nurse in terms of the **Apgar scoring system,** a method developed by anesthesiologist Virginia Apgar (1953). The infant is assessed at one minute and again at five minutes after birth on the basis of five conditions: heart rate, respiratory effort, muscle tone, reflex irritability (the infant's response to a catheter placed in its nostril), and body color. Each of the conditions is rated 0, 1, or 2 (see Figure 4.5). The ratings of the five conditions are then summed (the highest possible score is 10). For U.S. births in 2004 at five minutes after birth, less than 1 percent of all infants received scores of 0 to 3, which is poor. About 88 percent had scores of 9 to 10, excellent (Martin et al., 2006). A score of less than 5 indicates the need for prompt diagnosis and medical intervention. Infants with the lowest Apgar scores have the highest mortality rate.

Brazelton Neonatal Behavioral Assessment Scale and the Clinical Neonatal Behavioral Assessment Scale   Dr. T. Berry Brazelton, a noted pediatrician, author, and television and Internet physician, devised the *Neonatal Behavioral Assessment Scale (NBAS)* to be used several hours after birth or during the week after birth. It is used by many researchers studying infant development. An examiner uses the 27 subtests of the NBAS to assess four categories of development: physiological development, motor development, development and regulation of alertness, and levels of interaction with people (Brazelton & Nugent, 1995). A low score might indicate potential cognitive impairment in a neonate or a need for more stimulation through early intervention methods. The *Clinical Neonatal Behavioral Assessment Scale (CNBAS)*, the updated version of Brazelton's scale, consists of 18 behavioral and reflex items designed to assess the newborn's alertness and physiological, motor, and social capacities (Brazelton, 2001).

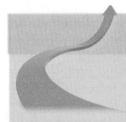

FURTHER DEVELOPMENTS

Childbirth in America

We think of the U.S. history of childbirth as a march toward continual progress. It is true that in the twenty-first century, the number of U.S. maternal and infant deaths is much lower than in 1915, when 44 babies per 1,000 live births died (U.S. Bureau of the Census, 1960). By 2007, that number had declined to just under 7 babies per 1,000 live births (Xu, Murphy, & Tejada-Vera, 2010). Antibiotics, the ability to monitor the developing fetus, greater access to prenatal care, and medical technology have made it possible for the majority of babies to arrive safely and begin a healthy childhood.

Still, many nations have higher rates of survival at childbirth than the United States, including some developing countries with fewer resources. How can we explain this? This is a complex, emotionally charged issue. The present U.S. childbirth medical model differs from practices in many other countries. And research findings are revealing elements of this model that are associated with higher risk to both newborns and mothers.

Perhaps the most distinct element of the U.S. model is that childbirth is viewed as a medical case instead of a natural process. Physicians manage most U.S. births, and most hospitals have what is known as a "24-hour rule." That is, the mother should deliver her baby within 24 hours of hospital admission (Block, 2007). If she does not, then medical staff often intervenes to hasten the birth process in such ways as rupturing the amniotic sac to hasten the onset of labor (known as "breaking the waters"), using drugs to start labor and intensify contractions, and performing cesarean sections when complications arise from medical interventions. Each procedure has potential risks for the mother's and child's health. Rupturing the sac increases infection risk that might compromise both the mother and the baby. *Cytotec,* a drug often used to induce labor, is not approved by the FDA for use in labor and delivery. In fact, it is linked with the risk of uterine rupture (Wagner, 2006).

Although surgical delivery of babies at risk is a medical breakthrough that has saved many lives, the U.S. rate of C-sections has increased rapidly in the past decade. The World Health Organization estimates that 5 percent of births require C-section (AbouZahr & Wardlaw, 2001). Notably, *one-third* of all U.S. hospital births were done by C-section in 2008—a 50 percent increase since the mid-1990s (Hamilton, Martin, & Ventura, 2010). What explains this unusually high rate? Studies examining this critical issue repeatedly cite the doctor's preference. A surgical delivery planned for certain conditions or convenience is quicker than a vaginal delivery, and the doctor and hospital are paid more. Malpractice insurance premiums for obstetricians are so high that doctors must carefully scrutinize the economics of staying in business. Also, some doctors believe that a surgical birth reduces the chance that they will be sued (Block, 2007).

More U.S. doctors seem to be willing to intervene in the natural birth process. The use of **epidural narcotics** (see Figure 4.3) to manage the pain of labor leads to maternal fever in about 20 percent of cases. Such drugs can slow the labor process, leading to a diagnosis of "failure to progress." A common side effect of epidural drugs is a sudden drop in

FIGURE 4.5 Apgar Scoring for Newborns
A score is given for each sign at 1 minute and 5 minutes after birth. If the baby has problems, another score is given at 10 minutes. A score of 7–10 is normal, a baby scoring 4–7 might require some resuscitative measures, and a baby with an Apgar of 3 or below requires immediate resuscitation. (Note that the five signs are indicated by words that not only describe the conditions being assessed but also begin with letters that spell out the originator's last name.)
Source: Adapted from V. A. Apgar, "A proposal for a new method of evaluation of the newborn infant," *Current Researches in Anesthesia and Analgesia,* Vol. 32 (1953), pp. 260–267. Reprinted by permission of Lippincott Williams & Wilkins.

	Sign	0 Points	1 Point	2 Points
A	Activity (muscle tone)	Absent	Arms and legs flexed	Active movement
P	Pulse	Absent	Below 100 bpm	Above 100 bpm
G	Grimace (reflex irritability)	No response	Grimace	Sneeze, cough, pulls away
A	Appearance (skin color)	Blue-gray, pale all over	Normal, except for extremities	Normal over entire body
R	Respiration	Absent	Slow, irregular	Good, crying

the mother's blood pressure, leading to concern about the fetus's oxygen levels. *Pitocin,* often used to intensify and increase the frequency of contractions, might cause irregularities in the fetus's heart rate. Any of these complications can lead to an emergency C-section (Block, 2007).

U.S. doctors use drugs for labor pain management that are different from those used in other industrialized nations. In countries such as Sweden, Canada, and Great Britain, *nitrous oxide* mixed with oxygen is widely used. It is not a narcotic, it does not slow down the labor process, and it is safe for the babies because they are born fully alert. Also, it is not associated with maternal fever. Yet this option is largely unavailable to American women. Anesthesiologists oppose its use because women can administer it themselves using a gas mask (Rooks, 2007).

The recent U.S. medical model of childbirth is not typical in other nations. Women in many countries rely on *midwives,* both for home and hospital births (Harper, 2005). Midwives see birth as a natural process and are committed to being with the mother through labor and delivery. The majority of births attended by midwives proceed with little or no medical intervention. Midwives help the woman find the most comfortable position for labor and delivery (maybe squatting rather than reclining) and provide emotional support and encouragement through the process.

More U.S. nurses and midwives are calling upon the medical profession to focus on preventing C-sections and are concerned about an increasing maternal mortality rate. In 2008, the World Health Organization reported that 49 nations had lower maternal mortality rates than the United States (see Table 4.2) (WHO/UNICEF/UNFPA/World Bank, 2010). Nurses and midwives are also concerned about research findings that link difficulty with breast-feeding to epidural narcotic use and C-section (Torvaldsen et al., 2006).

To decrease risk during childbirth, parents can find caregivers who will support their choices during prenatal

TABLE 4.2 Maternal Mortality Rate in Selected Countries: 2000 and 2008*

Country	2000	2008
Ireland	4	3
Italy	4	5
Denmark	5	5
Canada	7	12
Switzerland	7	10
Poland	8	6
Japan	9	6
Australia	9	8
United Kingdom	12	12
United States	**14**	**24**
Iran	59	30
Pakistan	340	260
Republic of Tanzania	920	790
Afghanistan	1800	1400

*Maternal deaths per 100,000 live births.

Source: WHO/UNICEF/UNFPA/World Bank (2010). Trends in maternal mortality: 1990–2008. Estimates developed by WHO, UNICEF, UNFPA and the World Bank. Geneva: World Health Organization. In the *International Statistical Classification of Diseases and Related Health Problems,* Tenth Revision, 1992 (ICD-10), WHO defines maternal death as: The death of a woman while pregnant or within 42 days of termination of pregnancy, irrespective of the duration and site of the pregnancy, from any cause related to or aggravated by the pregnancy or its management but not from accidental or incidental causes.

development, labor, and delivery. Understanding the range of options and risks for pain management is important. Avoiding C-sections, unless medically indicated, will decrease risk to the mother and baby and increase the likelihood that subsequent children will be delivered vaginally (Wagner, 2006). A medical provider giving comfort and emotional support to a mother during labor and delivery is crucial.

Circumcision   Each year within a few hours or days of birth, more than one-third of U.S. male newborns undergo a surgical procedure that many medical professionals now believe should be based on parental discretion (Provencio-Vasquez & Rodriguez, 2009). Circumcision is the surgical removal of the foreskin (prepuce) that covers the tip (glans) of the penis. Through the centuries this procedure has been a religious rite for Jews and Muslims. Among some African and South Pacific peoples, circumcision is performed at puberty to mark the passage of a youth to adulthood. In contrast, circumcision has never been common in Europe. Yet more medical researchers promote circumcision as a health measure and as protection against cancer of the penis, sexually transmitted infections, urinary tract infections, and, in female sexual partners, cancer of the cervix (Fergusson, Boden, & Horwood, 2006). Generally, though, physicians maintain that there are few valid

medical indications for routine infant circumcision, and there can be surgical complications. The practice has been on the decline in the United States as parents have become better informed about the pros and cons of removal of foreskin tissue and the potential for altering adult sexual function (Storms, 2010).

Patient Protection and Affordable Care Act   In 2010, the U.S. Congress passed President Barack Obama's health-care reform legislation, the *Patient Protection and Affordable Care Act* (PL 111-148). The goal of this law is to make health care affordable and accessible to *all* Americans by requiring insurance companies to cover preventive services and by eliminating deductibles, coinsurance, and copayments. The expectation is that women and children will see improved health outcomes because of expected ease of access to health care. It is projected that well-baby and well-child visits and services to ensure healthy pregnancies will be covered (U.S. Department of Health and Human Services, 2010b). The plan has not been popular among a majority of Americans because of concerns about costs and penalties, control, and choice, and it is not yet known what the practical outcomes and ultimate fate of the legislation will be. Because implementation is to be phased in over several years, it is also unclear what impact the legislation will have on health-care costs, delivery, services, and professionals.

Questions

What do we know about the baby's own birth experience? What are a typical neonate's appearance and activity level at birth? How might a newborn's health be assessed at birth?

Caregiver-Infant Bonding

During most of human history, babies have been placed immediately on their mothers' bodies after birth. According to the studies by anthropologist Meredith Small (1998), in most cultures around the world babies are still placed on their mothers this way. Research on the concept of parental bonding has undergone a drastic change in the last few decades. Although it was studied as a psychological/medical construct in the West in the 1970s, it is now more widely viewed from a cross-cultural perspective. Earlier research focused on European Americans and promoted an Anglo/Eurocentric perspective. As the findings from cross-cultural studies of caregiving emerge and as previous practices are seen in historical perspective, a different picture becomes clear. As Rogoff (2003) explains, "The cultural research draws attention to community aspects of infants' and caregivers' attachments to each other, including the health and economic conditions of the community, cultural goals of infant care, and cultural arrangements of family life." For example, one study compares cultural models of infant development between rural Africans and urban Europeans (Keller, 2001). Health-care and human services professionals must become aware of these cultural beliefs and practices because one out of every four American children today comes from an immigrant family (Migration Policy Institute, 2008).

Researchers have been interested in the concept of infant attachment since the mid-twentieth century. In the 1950s, Harry Harlow conducted and published results from his experiments on infant monkey attachment. He found that infant monkeys deprived of contact with their own mothers preferred to cling to a surrogate mother covered in cloth rather than to a wire surrogate mother with no cloth but with a bottle for feeding. Harlow concluded that the baby monkeys sought comfort with the cloth surrogate mothers (Harlow, 1971). John Bowlby's attachment theory, based on a research interest that grew from his experiences with children who had

been separated from their parents during World War II, proposes that attachment is a mechanism of evolutionary survival. Mary Ainsworth (1992), building on the work of Bowlby, constructed an experiment in which infants were placed in a strange situation by being separated briefly from their mothers. She drew conclusions about patterns of child-mother bonding from the way the children reacted when they were reunited with their mothers. Her work is now being replicated with larger samples, including a variety of ethnic groups. Research studies take into account the impact of government policy on caretaking beliefs and practices (Ahnert & Lamb, 2001).

The practice of separating babies from their mothers at birth has arisen only in the past century and only in Western cultures. In the 1890s, Martin Cooney invented one of the first incubators to aid premature infants. He advocated separation of mother and child for health reasons (this was back when microorganisms were first discovered). By the 1940s, incubators for most newborns had become standard practice in hospitals. During this period, more mothers chose to give birth in hospitals than at home. The new mother, often heavily sedated, was given only a glimpse of her baby before being moved to the maternity ward to recuperate; her baby was whisked to the nursery. By the late 1960s, birthing practices had begun to change in the Western world. In 1976, two obstetricians, Marshall Klaus and John Kennell, theorized that there is a critical early period of 16 hours for mother-infant bonding. In 1978, the American Medical Association proclaimed that promoting infant-mother bonding was its official policy (Small, 1998).

Maternal Bonding Ideas about maternal bonding have also changed, and its role in society is under debate. Evolutionary biologists argue that it is natural (adaptive) for mothers and their newborns to bond in a process that requires close proximity, constant interaction, and emotional attachment. In this view, bonding is especially crucial in our species because human infants are dependent beings who need much care, protection, and teaching. Other scholars "believe [that the notion of maternal bonding] fosters unwarranted social stereotypes that portray motherhood as the 'font of emotional support'" (Eyer, 1992). **Parent-infant bonding** is considered by most as a *process* of interaction and mutual attention that occurs over time and forges an emotional bond.

Some argue that natural childbirth facilitates emotional bonding between parents and their child. The intimate time immediately after birth, when parents and child gently touch and gaze at each other, is only the beginning of parent-infant bonding. Some mothers choose to breast-feed their newborn immediately, but mothers who have cesarean deliveries or parents who adopt children should not conclude that they have missed out on something fundamental to a healthy child-parent relationship. A growing body of research suggests that parents who do not have contact with their infant immediately after delivery typically can bond just as strongly with the youngster as parents who do have such contact (Eyer, 1992).

A father can play an important role in initiating bonding after a cesarean section by holding the newborn on his bare chest, providing skin-to-skin contact (known as *kangaroo care*) during the period the infant is separated from his or her mother. One study found that babies of fathers who provided this care cried less than other babies and were able to adjust to breast-feeding more quickly. The researchers hypothesized that skin-to-skin contact provided comfort so the babies did not have to use energy for crying and could instead use energy to initiate breast-feeding when they were reunited with their mothers. The researchers considered the father to be the primary parent while the neonate was separated from its mother after cesarean section (Erlandsson et al., 2007).

Bonding with several caretakers is required in some societies that live communally. Researchers have shown that the Efé forest-dwellers of Congo practice a very flexible form of child rearing (Ivey, 2000). Infants are cared for by a number of adults in the village. An Efé infant might spend 50 percent of its day with other caretakers and might be nursed by any of several women who are lactating. Yet the baby clearly knows who its mother and father are (Ivey, 2000).

Developmentalists recognize that some mothers and fathers have difficulty forming an attachment to their newborn. Attachment can be difficult for mothers who have had a particularly complicated labor and birth or whose infants are premature, malformed, or initially unwanted. Because some births are high risk, not every parent-child relationship begins calmly.

Paternal Bonding   In many cultures, expectant fathers often experience **Couvade syndrome**—complaints of uncomfortable physical symptoms, dietary changes, and weight gain because of their partner's pregnancy (Small, 1998). A study of 147 expectant fathers in the Milwaukee area found that about 90 percent of them experienced "pregnancy" symptoms similar to those of their wives. For instance, the men had nausea in the first trimester and backaches in the last trimester. The majority of the men reported weight gains ranging from 2 to 15 pounds, and they all lost weight in the first four weeks after the babies were born. Couvade syndrome may be one way in which fathers express sympathy with the expectant mother (Lewis, 1985). Expectant fathers commonly become concerned about their ability to provide for and protect an expanding family (Kutner, 1990). These findings are supported by the results of a 2007 study of British men who experienced these same physical and psychological symptoms during their partners' pregnancies. The study indicated that health-care professionals should be mindful of the needs and concerns of the fathers-to-be and of the effect of their physical and emotional health on the

pregnant women (Brennan, Marshall-Lucette, Ayers, & Ahmed, 2007).

Anthropologists have found that biological fathers have a very important parenting role in societies where family life is strong, women contribute to subsistence, the family is an integrated unit of parents and offspring, and men are not preoccupied with being warriors. Although the degree of fathering across cultures varies, the potential for human males to contribute to infant care is great. There is also increasing evidence of the importance of fathers' involvement in their children's development (Horn & Sylvester, 2004).

To their benefit, many contemporary American fathers are visiting the obstetrician with the mother-to-be to hear the baby's heartbeat, see the first ultrasound, or be present during amniocentesis. These fathers often help plan for the baby's arrival, attend childbirth preparation classes, participate in the birth, cut the umbilical cord, and help care for the baby after its birth by changing diapers, feeding, bathing, and so on. Research reviews indicate that the father's love and caring is just as important as the mother's for their children's cognitive, emotional, and physical health (Rohner & Veniziano, 2001). A father's close involvement with the daily life of his child is likely to increase his sense of well-being and his interactions with the larger society; this is true across racial groups and socioeconomic categories.

After the birth, new fathers and mothers report similar emotions when they first see the newborn. When given a chance, fathers explore a new baby's body in the same pattern as mothers do: fingers first, then palms of hands, arms, legs, and then trunk. New fathers, like mothers, also instinctively raise the pitch and cadence of their speech (speaking what is called "**motherese**" or "**parentese**") with

Father-Infant Bonding Studies reveal that involvement of fathers in the nurturing and development of their children confers many benefits on both. Note how a smiling father, Paulo from Dar Es Salaam, Tanzania, carefully holds his infant close, promoting father-infant bonding.

their newborn. Clearly, the more fathers interact with their babies, the more mutual attachment occurs (Small, 1998).

Father Involvement   Fathers parent differently than mothers do. Mothers tend to be more verbal with children, whereas fathers tend to be more physical. Fathers often engage in rough-and-tumble play with their sons, which we are finding serves as practice for boys to help them develop control over their aggression. Both the mother's and the father's nurturing contribute to the childhood experience. Fathers usually provide positive role models for daughters as well. Both father love and mother love have a significant impact on a child's personality and psychological development. Some evidence suggests that father love is even more strongly associated with some aspects of development (Rohner & Veniziano, 2001). A father's positive active involvement in his child's life reinforces the mother's parenting skills when they are strong and compensates for weak maternal parenting as well (Martin, Ryan, & Brooks-Gun, 2010).

Fathers provide a different style of caring, discipline, and parenting; these traits also promote the development of both physically and psychologically healthier children who feel cared about. Studies have shown that the presence and involvement of fathers in the nurturing and development of their children confer benefits that are irreplaceable by any father substitute, whether the substitute is the state, a grandparent, a male friend, or a stepparent (East, Jackson, & O'Brien, 2006).

Unfortunately, though, some American men (from all racial, ethnic, and socioeconomic statuses) do not bond with or support the children they are producing. Some lead dysfunctional lives or are abusive, some are incarcerated, and some men father many children by several women without regard to the future welfare of the mothers or babies. There are far-reaching harmful social and economic consequences for many neglected or abandoned children and for American society at large.

Co-sleeping   One way some parents bond with their children is through co-sleeping. In the United States, there is controversy about the risks and benefits of an adult caregiver co-sleeping, or sharing a bed, with an infant. American caregivers are advised by doctors and child-care experts to put the baby in its own crib, on its back, for safety during sleep. Americans worry about an increased risk of SIDS or accidental suffocation (McKenna & McDade, 2005). Yet anthropologists studying cultures around the world have discovered that for most of human history, babies and children have slept with their mothers, or with both parents and the rest of the family, because they lived in one-room dwellings and because their society believed that an infant should not be left alone (Small, 1998). The non-Western view of co-sleeping appears to promote attachment with the infant,

whereas Western cultures value independence and self-sufficiency in their children (Small, 1998).

> **Questions**
>
> What are some factors that promote caregiver-infant bonding? In what ways can fathers promote bonding with infants? How do parents from different cultures view co-sleeping with an infant?

Complications of Pregnancy and Birth

Although most pregnancies and births proceed without complications, there are exceptions. Currently in the United States, about 1 in 10 women experiences some type of complication during labor and delivery in a hospital setting that results in surgical intervention besides cesarean sections (Martin et al., 2006). The purpose of good prenatal care and diagnostics under medical supervision is to minimize complications. But if complications develop, much can be done through medical intervention to help the mother and save the child. Fetal ultrasounds and other diagnostics should be administered routinely to check for potential complications.

For example, about 1 percent of babies are born with **anoxia,** oxygen deprivation caused when the umbilical cord becomes squeezed or is wrapped around the baby's neck during delivery. With **placenta praevia,** the placenta covers the cervix, preventing natural birth. As we noted in Chapter 3, in some pregnancies the mother and baby have incompatible Rh factors in their blood, and medical procedures can prevent serious complications. Whereas efforts used to focus on saving the mother when complications arose, saving both the mother and the infant is a high priority today.

At-Risk Infants   Development of at-risk infants is a topic of increasing importance. Advances in medical technology are saving many newborns who previously would not have survived. The number of babies born early and unusually small is rising in the United States; in 2008, about 8 percent of babies born were **low birth weight,** or less than 5.5 pounds (2,500 grams). This percentage has been rising steadily since the 1980s (Hamilton et al., 2010).

In an average week in the United States:*

83,004 babies are born

10,512 babies are born preterm

6,814 babies are born low birth weight

548 babies die before reaching their first birthday

Source: March of Dimes. *Perinatal Overview: United States, 2010.* From the National Center for Health Statistics, period linked infant birth/death data. Retrieved October 3, 2010.

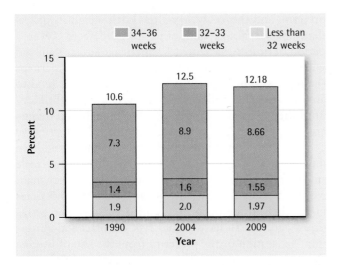

FIGURE 4.6 Percentage of Preterm Births: United States, 1990, 2004, 2009

Source: Hamilton, B. E., Martin, J. A., & Ventura, S. J. (2010, December 21). Births: Preliminary data for 2009. *National Vital Statistics Reports, 59*(3), 1–19, Table 9, p. 15.

Preterm Infants   A **preterm infant** has been traditionally defined as a baby having a gestational age of less than 37 weeks, and such births account for most infant complications or death. In 2009, the number of preterm births declined some, to about 12 percent of all U.S. births (see Figure 4.6). The highest preterm rate, about 17 percent, was for black infants. Babies classified as *very preterm* are born at less than 32 weeks of gestation, and that rate remained close to 2 percent. The number of babies who were born *very low birth weight,* defined as weighing less than 3 pounds 3 ounces (1,500 grams) declined to about 1.5 percent, the lowest level in several years (Hamilton et al., 2010). Although low birth weight is associated with prematurity, apparently it is developmental immaturity rather than low birth weight per se that is the primary source of the difficulties. More than half the low-birth-weight babies born in the United States are not preterm; **small-for-term infants,** whether singletons, twins, or multiple births, typically do well. The number of multiple births continues to increase because of ART procedures, which can lead to high rates of preterm and low-birth-weight deliveries and other complications (Centers for Disease Control and Prevention, 2010f).

For preterm infants, survival rate correlates closely with birth weight; larger and more mature infants have better survival rates. Treating premature babies is hardly routine and costs thousands of dollars a day. In 2005, the cost to the U.S. economy of care of preterm babies was over $26 billion (March of Dimes, 2007a). Significantly, the March of Dimes (2007b) reports that prematurity/low birth weight is the second leading cause of all infant

deaths and the leading cause of infant deaths among African Americans. Research suggests that progesterone may reduce the incidence of preterm birth. Since infection seems to be linked to preterm labor, antibiotics can sometimes prevent it. Dietary supplementation with fish oil has also been found to be an effective preventive, although more research needs to be done (Lamont & Jaggat, 2007).

For some infants, prematurity can lead to developmental delays, neurological problems, chronic respiratory problems, and vision and hearing impairment in addition to greater risk of infant mortality (March of Dimes, 2007a). But many preterm infants become healthy children and productive adults.

Larger urban hospitals usually have a **neonatal intensive care unit (NICU)** staffed with *perinatologists* and *neonatologists* who specialize in managing complicated high-risk pregnancies, birth, and the postbirth experience. In a NICU, a preterm baby stays in a see-through incubator called an *isolette* and may receive oxygen through plastic tubes inserted in the nose or windpipe. Banks of blipping lights, blinking numbers, and beeping alarms of electronic equipment and computerized devices monitor the baby's vital signs. Technological innovations, such as steroid therapy, ventilator techniques, surfactant therapy, and enhanced nutrition have decreased infant mortality rates. The result has been a reduction in the overall complications and mortality associated with preterm birth (Wilson-Costello, 2007).

Preterm infants are more likely to survive if they have gentle touch and "comfort care"—that is, normal skin contact, massage, and other stimulation, especially from the parents. A program called "kangaroo care" promotes the recovery of premature babies through skin-to-skin, chest-to-chest contact between the mother or father and the child while sitting in a quiet, dimly lit neonatal infant care unit. Health benefits to preterm infants include decreased levels of motor activity, less oxygen required, less behavioral distress, greater daily weight gain, more restful sleep, and fewer blood transfusions (Ferber & Makhoul, 2004). Health benefits to mothers include a better style of interaction with their babies, a feeling of efficacy in coping with the trauma of preterm birth, a decrease in emotional stress, and a stronger bond with their babies (Tallandini & Scalembra, 2006).

One longitudinal study compared 23 sets of extremely-low-birth-weight children to their full-term siblings using standardized medical, social, cognitive, motor, and language tests. The results showed that the extremely-low-birth-weight children were lighter, were shorter, and had a smaller head circumference. The study concluded that preschool-age cognitive and language functioning were affected by both preterm status and

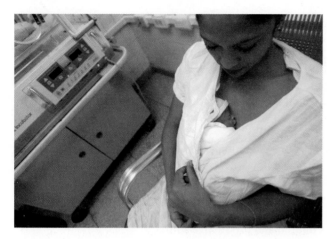

Kangaroo Care in a NICU in Havana, Cuba A NICU (pronounced "nickyou") setting provides a high level of intensive care to premature or ill newborns and infants. Services include better temperature and respiratory support, vision and hearing supports, isolation from risk of infection, specialized feeding, and access to specialized equipment and professional resources.

socioeconomic variables (Kilbride, Thorstad, & Daily, 2004).

Questions

What are some of the causes of preterm birth? What are some other complications that can arise during labor and delivery of the neonate? How does the medical community save many of these babies born at high risk?

Postmature Infants   A baby that is delivered more than 2 weeks after the usual 40 weeks of gestation in the womb is classified as a **postmature infant.** Most postmature babies are healthy, but they must be watched carefully for a few days. Some babies are heavier because their mothers are diabetic or prediabetic; in these cases, an extra amount of sugar has crossed the placenta. Such babies might have metabolic problems for the first few days after birth and require close medical scrutiny. Postmature infants are likely to be larger, posing more complications for both mother and infant during delivery. A mother's options include induced labor and cesarean delivery.

Infants Born with Drug Exposure   Because of the potential legal consequences in several states (which include being charged with a misdemeanor, child abuse, or criminal homicide), many pregnant women who are addicted to drugs, including alcohol, resist prenatal care. More states are taking an aggressive stand on pregnant women who use drugs (Coleman & Miller, 2006–2007). Drug-exposed babies are likely to be deprived of nutrition, blood, and oxygen and are likely to be born

preterm, and they may have low birth weight, smaller-than-normal heads, and other birth defects. Over a period of time these neonates experience severe pain and withdrawal symptoms, of which seizures are perhaps the most striking sign. When held, these babies tend to arch their backs, pull away, and cry in a high, shrill cry until they exhaust themselves. Cocaine-exposed infants are jittery, have high muscle tension, are hard to move because they are stiff, don't like to be touched, and have difficulty feeding (Crump, 2001). The first large-scale study of *methamphetamine* (meth) use by pregnant women reveals that meth-exposed infants are 3.5 times more likely to be born preterm, to be small for gestational age, and to have higher risk for placental abruption (separation of the **placenta** from the site of uterine implantation) and fetal distress (Smith et al., 2006).

Infant massage can help drug-exposed babies develop. Researchers have found that drug-exposed infants who are massaged gain significantly more weight, have fewer postnatal complications, and score higher on the *Brazelton Neonatal Behavior Assessment Scale* in motor behaviors. Infants who are massaged are better able to regulate their sleep and wake behaviors, or states, and their social interaction improves more rapidly than that of infants who are rocked but do not receive massage. Despite these proven benefits, massage is provided to infants in NICUs in only about half of U.S. hospitals (Field, Diego, & Hernandez-Reif, 2010).

The child's own behaviors can further influence how the parents or caretakers treat the baby and how the child is likely to grow and learn. Reevaluation of the studies on cocaine use of pregnant women has not found detrimental long-term effects for the children's development. Perhaps more detrimental is the media stigma attached to "crack kids" and the socioeconomic factors that hamper social, emotional, physical, and mental development of these children (Frank et al., 2001).

Babies Born with HIV   HIV is the insidious virus that causes AIDS. Most children with HIV acquired the infection from their mothers during pregnancy, birth, or breast-feeding. Current estimates suggest that more than 2 million children worldwide are infected, mainly in sub-Saharan Africa and Asia (UNAIDS/WHO, 2009). The U.S. Public Health Service promotes routine, voluntary prenatal HIV testing and (when HIV is present) *zidovudine* therapy to reduce the transmission from mother to child. The best recommendation for a pregnant woman with HIV is to see her health-care provider early and often during the pregnancy to maintain her own health and her fetus's health and to plan for the infant's birth and care. Getting treatment with *antiretroviral* medications during pregnancy, labor, and delivery, coupled with *protease inhibitors* for the infant, can dramatically reduce the risk of transmission of the virus (U.S. Public Health

Service Task Force, 2002). With early diagnosis and early medical treatment, a high percentage of children with HIV are living much longer, many into adolescence and adulthood (Storm et al., 2005).

Babies with Fetal Alcohol Spectrum Disorder (FASD)   Research has shown that when the mother-to-be drinks alcohol during her pregnancy, not only does the placenta easily absorb it, but the alcohol remains in the amniotic fluid longer than it does in the mother's system. Having as few as two drinks a day in early pregnancy or four drinks at once (a binge episode) can kill the baby's developing brain cells and alter developing body organs. Drinking alcohol during pregnancy can lead to a range of effects known under the umbrella term **fetal alcohol spectrum disorders (FASD),** among them fetal alcohol syndrome (FAS) (see Chapter 3).

Symptoms of FASD can include growth deficiencies both before and after birth, central nervous system dysfunction resulting in lowered IQ and learning disabilities, physical malformations of the face and cranial areas and growth retardation, and other organ dysfunctions. Babies born to mothers who drank heavily during pregnancy often suffer permanent nerve damage (Sokol, 2003). An individual afflicted with FASD can incur health-care costs of over $1.4 million over his or her lifetime (National Organization on Fetal Alcohol Syndrome, 2010). *FASD is the leading known preventable cause of developmental disability,* and it appears in every race, social class, and culture. FASD affects more than 40,000 infants annually—more than Down syndrome, cerebral palsy, and spina bifida combined (National Organization on Fetal Alcohol Syndrome, 2010). Some children are diagnosed with *fetal alcohol effects* (*FAE*), which is a manifestation of fewer of these effects.

Like other children born with birth defects, children born with FASD are eligible from birth for early intervention services. Parents, caregivers, and teachers should realize that these children may have difficulty staying focused, recognizing and understanding patterns, predicting "commonsense" outcomes, and/or mastering math and reading. They may have short attention spans, memory problems, and difficulty with problem solving. Children do not outgrow FASD (National Organization on Fetal Alcohol Syndrome, 2010).

Incarceration of pregnant women with alcoholism is controversial, and laws about treatment versus incarceration vary from state to state. Incarceration opponents point out that if pregnant alcoholics know they could be jailed, they are likely to avoid any prenatal care and that treatment for alcoholism is often not available in jails (HealthNewsDigest, 2007). Brief counseling sessions effectively supported a population of low-income Hispanic women as they abstained from alcohol (O'Connor & Whaley, 2007). Currently, North Dakota, Oklahoma, and South Dakota may commit pregnant alcoholic women to treatment facilities if a judge determines that it is in the best interest of the fetus. Minnesota and Wisconsin have similar laws (U.S. Department of Health and Human Services, 2009b).

Babies with Prenatal Exposure to Chemical Toxicants
A developing embryo or fetus is quite vulnerable to what we are exposed to and ingest. In the 1950s in Minimata Bay, Japan, babies, children, and adults were exhibiting physical deformities and severe brain damage because the poisons that corporations had pumped into the bay had contaminated the fish that local residents ate. In the early 1960s, American and European societies experienced a similar high incidence of miscarriage and limb deformities with the widespread use of the prescription drug *thalidomide* for pregnant women's "morning sickness." Veterans exposed to Agent Orange during the Vietnam War produced children with birth defects. The high incidence of miscarriages and birth deformities in the 1970s in Love Canal, near Buffalo, New York, were proved to be directly related to air and water contamination.

According to a recent five-year study, more than 100,000 Gulf War veterans have reported symptoms such as fatigue, muscle and joint pains, rashes, memory loss, attention problems, and sleep disturbances (Ozakinci, Hallman, & Kipen, 2006). These veterans were exposed to a number of different "reproductive toxicants," such as the anthrax vaccination, antibotulism medicine, and depleted uranium. A high percentage of children born to returning veterans were born with congenital birth defects or are sick. Also, female Gulf War veterans may be more vulnerable to spontaneous abortion and ectopic pregnancy (Sartin, 2006).

Affected families suffer emotional strain, financial drain, and disbelief that their health needs were not initially acknowledged by the U.S. government, military, medical, and insurance systems. The U.S. Congress approved the inclusion of medical services for these veterans in the *Veterans Benefits Act of 2001* (Gallegly, 2001). Health-care providers, educators, and mental-health professionals need to be aware of the special needs of this population of families that live with chronic illness.

Support for Babies with Disorders   Parents who give birth to an infant diagnosed with any disorder at birth might want to get connected immediately with local professionals and support groups that focus on that disorder. Knowledge can alleviate much fear and anxiety at this early stage and give parents the hope they need to parent this child as effectively as possible. There are many online support groups for families who live in more remote locations or have a child with a rare disorder. Although pediatricians continually learn more about the physiological aspects of many disorders, their

Speech-Language Therapy   Speech-language therapists diagnose, treat, and help to promote correct speech, language, cognition, communication, voice, swallowing, speech fluency, and other related disorders.

medical training often does not include learning about the social and emotional consequences of raising a child with a difficulty. Organizations such as the *National Down Syndrome Society* (*NDSS*) provide invaluable information, support, research, and a place to connect with other parents who share the same concerns.

Public Law 99-457: Early Intervention Services for Infants Born at Risk   Public Law 99-457, enacted by the U.S. Congress in 1986, was designed to provide early intervention services (free education, training, and therapeutic services) to families with children from birth to 5 years who have disabilities and special needs. The program seeks to enhance the development of infants and toddlers with disabilities and to enhance their families' ability to meet their needs. There is an infant component for those from birth to age 2 and a preschool component for those aged 3 to 5. One goal of early intervention is for fewer children to need special education classes during their formal schooling years. Another goal is for more children to achieve independent living at home and in the community, thus decreasing the need for institutionalization. The law was amended in 1991 and is now known as the **Individuals with Disabilities Education Act (IDEA).** Congress and President George W. Bush reauthorized IDEA as the *Individuals with Disabilities Education Improvement Act* (PL-108-446) in 2004.

Early intervention services are defined as "services that are designed to meet the developmental needs of each child eligible . . . and the needs of the family related to enhancing the child's development." It is significant that the act seeks to involve parents and caregivers to the greatest extent possible. Assessments must be made from a multidisciplinary approach and preferably in a child's natural settings (Addison, 2004). Along with the parents or guardian, it takes the input of various trained professionals to provide as complete a picture as possible of the child. Those who might be involved in this process include audiologists, family therapists, nurses, nutritionists, occupational therapists, pediatricians, physical therapists, psychologists, speech therapists, social workers, and teachers.

Infant Mortality   We do not expect babies to die; it feels contrary to the natural order of life. Consequently, the death of an infant is a traumatic experience—most say it is the worst experience in life. Parents, family, and friends will go through a period of grief and mourning, just as when an older loved one dies. **Infant mortality** is the death of an infant within the first year of life. The leading causes of infant death continue to be birth defects, premature birth and low birth weight, SIDS, maternal complications, and unintentional injuries (accidents) (Xu, Kochaneck, Murphy, & Tejada-Vera, 2010). In 2007, more than 29,000 infants died in the United States. Although the U.S. infant mortality rate has decreased since the 1940s, it is still higher than the rate in many industrialized nations (see Figure 4.7) (Xu et al., 2010). Black infants are far more likely than white infants or infants in other racial groups to die before age 1 (Schempf et al., 2007). Many of these deaths are attributable to preterm birth. Researchers do not fully understand why more black mothers experience preterm birth, but one study found that poverty plays a clear role (Sims, Sims, & Bruce, 2007).

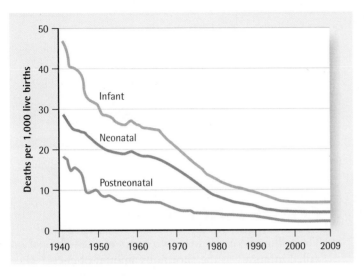

FIGURE 4.7 Infant, Neonatal, and Postneonatal Mortality Rates: United States, 1940–2009
Source: Kochanek, K. D., Xu, J., Murphy, S. L., Miniño, A. M., & Kung, H. C. (2011, March 16). Deaths: Preliminary data for 2009. *National Vital Statistics Reports, 59*(4), 1–69, Table 4. Kochanek, M. A., Murphy, S. L., Tejada-Vera, B. (2010, May 20). Deaths: Final data for 2007. *National Vital Statistics Reports, 58*(19), 1–135.

Infant mortality rates are highest for women under 20 years of age and lowest for women between the ages of 30 and 39 (March of Dimes, 2007a). Infant mortality rates were higher for women who did not receive prenatal care, women who smoked during pregnancy, and women with less education. Infant mortality rates were higher for male infants, preterm and low-birth-weight infants, and infants in multiple births (MacDorman, Munson, & Kirmeyer, 2007).

Questions

What are some serious conditions that can compromise a neonate's health during and after birth? What is an early intervention program, and which babies and families are eligible for these services? What are the leading causes of U.S. infant mortality?

Postpartum Experience for Mom and Dad

Whether a newborn is born healthy or at risk, every new mother needs time to adjust and adapt, both physically and emotionally, after delivery of her child. Society and the media perpetuate the myth that motherhood is equated with total fulfillment and joy. These myths create unrealistic expectations for women. Normally the *postpartum period* lasts several weeks, but some women need several months to adapt to the fatigue and the new responsibilities in their life. Often during this period, the high expectations the mother had before giving birth and the hard reality of being a new parent collide. Each woman experiences a range of hormone fluctuations after giving birth. Her progesterone levels were elevated during the pregnancy. Now her endocrine system is attempting to bring her body back to prepregnancy levels, and this can promote mood swings. Mothers of babies born prematurely experience a higher level of anxiety and postpartum depression than mothers who deliver full term, and mothers of twins or multiples are at higher risk for anxiety and depression during the prenatal and postpartum periods.

The postpartum period is a time of adjustment for the father, too. He is most likely trying to manage at home and work, while beginning to adapt to his role with the new baby. The mother will need his help more than ever, especially if she is recuperating from surgery or if the baby was born at risk. Although a high percentage of new moms experience the "baby blues," including anxiety, insomnia, and weepiness, approximately 10 percent of new mothers experience what is called **postpartum major depression (PMD)**. PMD has a biochemical basis and may include feelings of being unable to cope, thoughts of not wanting to take care of the baby, unrealistic fears, and/or thoughts of wanting to harm the baby (Epperson, 1999). A recent study indicates that some new fathers also experience some level of postpartum depression, especially if their partners are depressed. The depression may be expressed as anger or anxiety rather than as sadness in these men (Melrose, 2010). Those working closely with new families can help by following up with fathers and by providing information about when and where to seek help.

Health-care professionals now realize that a new mother struggling with depression needs support, both for her health and for the health of the baby. Postpartum depression may contribute to a shorter period of breast-feeding early in a baby's life when frequent breast-feeding is important for the physical and emotional development of the baby. Early intervention from groups such as La Leche League or the WIC programs in county health departments and peer support groups is very important (McCarter-Spaulding & Horowitz, 2007). The distress some new mothers feel should never be minimized by health-care workers but should be acknowledged, and the women should be supported with empathy and sensitivity, without criticism (Bilszta, Eriksen, Buist, & Milgron, 2010).

Any intervention to provide support for a new mother should be culturally aware. Some cultures highly value self-discipline and expect individuals to fulfill their social roles regardless of the circumstances. Women who share these values might feel shame and be reluctant to seek professional help. Health-care workers should be aware of the social, cultural, and personal barriers that might prevent a new mother from seeking help (Bilszta et al., 2010). Alternative strategies of support might include home-based visits, telephone support, and careful avoidance of Western-based terms such as "depression."

Newborns demand a great deal of time and attention, both night and day, and might spend quite a bit of time crying—*I am hungry. I need to be changed. I am sleepy. I am cold. I need comfort. I am sick. I want attention.* No one else will be as dependent on us as a newborn! The National Association of Neonatal Nurses recommends that clinicians conduct screening using the *Postpartum Depression Predictors Inventory (PDPI) Revised* to identify women most at risk of PMD, especially mothers of infants in the NICU ("Recognizing and Screening for Postpartum Depression," 2003).

Dr. Tiffany Field (2006) has been researching the effects of maternal depression and has found that "the newborns have elevated stress hormones, brain activity suggestive of depression, show little facial expression, and have other depressive symptoms as well" (Field, 1998). Depressed infants are slower to learn to walk, weigh less, and are less responsive. To develop normally, infants need eye contact, need to be spoken to, need gentle massages, and need to be played with.

Questions

How does a mother bond with her newborn? What are some signs of postpartum depression, and what should a mother or father do if she or he experiences these symptoms? What might you suggest as an intervention strategy for a new mother or father who is experiencing depressive symptoms?

DEVELOPMENT OF BASIC COMPETENCIES

The hallmark of the first two years of life—the period called **infancy**—is the enormous amount of energy children spend exploring, learning about, and mastering their world. Once infants begin walking, they are often referred to as "toddlers." Few characteristics of infants are more striking than their relentless and persistent pursuit of competence. They seek stimulation from the world around them. In turn, they act on their world—chiefly on caretakers—to achieve the satisfaction of their needs.

Sleep researcher James McKenna and other infant researchers have discovered that infant biology is intimately connected to the biology of the adults who are responsible for their care. This symbiotic relationship, called **entrainment,** is "a kind of biological feedback system across two organisms, in which the movement of one influences the other. . . . The physiology of the two individuals is so entwined that, in a biological sense, where one goes, the other follows, and vice versa" (Small, 1998, p. 35). Entrainment is first and foremost a physical relationship (touching, nursing, cleaning, massaging, and so on). The connection is also visual and auditory: A newborn recognizes its mother's voice (and usually its father's voice, too) and prefers it over other sounds.

The Postpartum Period Is a Time of Adjustment for the New Parents
Source: © Lynn Johnston Productions, Inc./Dist. By the United Features Syndicate, Inc.

Child development experts point out that a baby's most powerful, adaptive, and vital skill is the ability to engage an adult on a social level to meet its needs (Small, 1998). Child expert T. Berry Brazelton (1998) says that this synchronicity of movements and physical reactions between parents and infant is vital to infant development. He suggests that infants who fail to thrive lack this physical engagement with their mother (as can happen when the baby is institutionalized or the mother is severely depressed or addicted to drugs and doesn't attend to the infant's needs). **Failure to thrive (FTT)** is a term used to describe a condition where an infant does not take nourishment and therefore is severely underweight based on weight charts for its age and gender. FTT can stem from inherited physiological and biochemical anomalies, virus infections, size of parents, food allergies or intolerance to certain foods caused by conditions such as celiac disease or obstructive sleep apnea syndrome, or parental abuse and neglect (Sanderson, 2004). Once diagnosed, such a serious condition may be ameliorated by clinical-nutritional interventions and home visits to educate caregivers (Black, Dubowitz, Krishnakumar, & Starr, 2007).

Newborn States

Interest in neonate sleeping patterns has been closely linked with interest in newborn states. According to Wolff (1966), the term **states** refers to a continuum of alertness ranging from regular sleep to vigorous activity (see Table 4.3). Pediatrician T. Berry Brazelton (1978) says that states are the infant's first line of defense. By means of changing state, infants can shut out certain stimuli and thereby inhibit their responses. It is also through a change in state that infants set the stage for actively responding. Thus, the newborn's use of various states reflects a high order of nervous system control (Korner et al., 1988). The *Brazelton Neonatal Behavioral Assessment Scale* evaluates early behavior by assessing how the baby moves from sleep states to alert states of consciousness (Brazelton & Nugent, 1995).

Reflexes   The newborn comes equipped with a number of behavioral systems, or reflexes. A **reflex** is a simple, involuntary, and unlearned response to a stimulus, a response that is triggered automatically through built-in circuits. Some reflexes, such as coughing, blinking, and yawning, last throughout life. Others disappear over the first weeks and reappear as learned voluntary behaviors as the infant's brain and body develop. Reflexes are the evolutionary remains of actions seen in animals lower in the phylogenic scale (Cratty, 1970). Reflexes are excellent indicators of neurological development in infants (Goddard, 2005). Table 4.4 illustrates a few.

Sleeping   The major activity of newborns is sleeping. Newborns normally sleep 16 or more hours per day in

TABLE 4.3 Infant States
Regular Sleep: Infants are at full rest; little or no motor activity occurs; facial muscles are relaxed; spontaneous eye movement is absent; respirations are regular and even.
Irregular Sleep: Infants engage in spurts of gentle limb movements and more general stirring, squirming, and twisting; eye movement is occasional and rapid; facial grimaces (smiling, sneering, frowning, puckering, and pouting) are frequent; the rhythm of respiration is irregular and faster than in regular sleep.
Drowsiness: Infants are relatively inactive; on occasion they squirm and twist their bodies; they open and close their eyes intermittently; respiratory patterns are regular but faster than in regular sleep.
Alert Inactivity: Although infants are inactive, their eyes are open and have a bright, shining quality; respirations are regular but faster than during regular sleep.
Waking Activity: Infants may be silent or moan, grunt, or whimper, spurts of diffuse motor activity are frequent; their faces may be relaxed or pinched, as when crying; their rate of respiration is irregular.
Crying: Vocalizations are strong and intense; motor activities are vigorous; the babies' faces are contorted; their bodies are flushed bright red. In some infants, tears can be observed as early as 24 hours after birth.

seven or eight naps. Sleep and wakefulness alternate in roughly four-hour cycles—three hours in sleep and one hour awake. Unless they are ill or uncomfortable, neonates will sleep wherever they are (in a crib, in a stroller, or cradled in a sling on a parent's back). By six weeks, the naps become longer, and infants take only two to

Customs and Baby Sleep Arrangements   Culture, customs, and traditions influence whether a baby sleeps swaddled on a mother's back, in a woven basket, in a hammock, on a futon, on a mattress made of bamboo, in a crib, or co-sleeps with parents. This child is napping with her mother in Bhaktapur town near Kathmandu, Nepal.

TABLE 4.4 Some Newborn Reflexes

Reflex	Description	Reflex	Description
Sucking 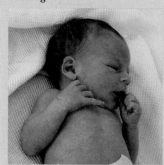	When a newborn's mouth or lips are touched, she automatically sucks on the object in her mouth.	Tonic neck 	When the baby's head is turned to one side, her arm on that side will straighten and the other arm will bend as in a fencing position.
Stepping 	When the baby is held upright with the soles of the feet touching a firm surface, he will deliberately take "steps," as if walking. This behavior disappears after the first week then reappears in several months as learned, voluntary behavior.	Palmar/Grasping 	When an object is placed on the baby's palm, he will close his hand around it and grasp it firmly.

four naps during the day. Around this age, many begin to sleep through most of the night, although others will not sleep through the night for many months yet. As the infant matures into a 1- to 2-year-old toddler, sleep time is usually reduced to one naptime during the day and an extended sleep at night.

Sudden Infant Death Syndrome (SIDS)   Although the rate of **sudden infant death syndrome (SIDS)** deaths has generally been on the decline since the start of the national Back to Sleep campaign in the 1990s, it remains one of the leading causes of postneonatal death in the United States, after birth defects and accidents. It is most likely to occur between 2 and 4 months of age, although it can happen up to a 1-year-old ("Sudden Infant Death Syndrome," 2004). The mortality rate from SIDS in 2009 was 52.5 per 100,000 live births, a significant decrease from the 1990s (see Figure 4.8) (Kochanek, Xu, Murphy, Miniño, & Kung, 2011). Parents put their seemingly healthy baby down to sleep and return to find that the infant has died. A related warning is given to caretakers of infants to place

the infant in his or her own uncluttered bed to avoid accidental suffocation and strangulation in the parental bed—such infant deaths have quadrupled since the mid-1980s (Shapiro-Mendoza, Kimball, Tomashek, Anderson, & Blanding, 2009).

Although overall SIDS rates declined markedly in the last decade for most ethnic groups, the incidence of SIDS is highest in Native American and African American families, and rates are lowest among Mexicans and Hispanics (National SIDS/Infant Death Resource Center, 2007). The measures suggested to prevent SIDS include getting regular prenatal care, providing good nutrition for the baby, refraining from smoking and using drugs, avoiding teen pregnancy (especially multiple teen births), and waiting at least a year between births. Caregivers should put the infant on its back to sleep, use a firm mattress with nothing in the bed, avoid overheating the baby's room, avoid exposing the baby to tobacco smoke and persons with respiratory ailments, avoid overdressing the baby, and consider using a baby monitor (American SIDS Institute, 2004).

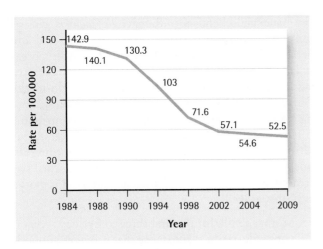

FIGURE 4.8 SIDS Infant Death Rates: United States, 1984–2009
Source: Kochanek, K. D., Xu, J., Murphy, S. L., Miniño, A. M., & Kung, H. C. (2011, March 16). Deaths: Preliminary data for 2009. *National Vital Statistics Reports, 59*(4), 1–69. Shapiro-Mendoza, C. K., Kimball, M., Tomashek, K. M., Anderson, R. N., & Blanding, S. (2009, February). U.S. infant mortality trends attributable to accidental suffocation and strangulation in bed from 1984 through 2004: Are rates increasing? *Pediatrics, 123*(2), 533–539.

Crying Crying in the newborn is an unlearned, involuntary, highly adaptive response that incites the parents to caretaking activities. Humans find few sounds more disconcerting than the infant's cry. Physiological studies reveal that the sound of a baby's cry triggers an increase in parents' blood pressure and heart rate (Donate-Bartfield & Passman, 1985). Some parents feel rejected because of the crying and reject the child in turn. But simply because caretakers have difficulty getting babies to stop crying does not mean they are doing a bad job! Crying is the chief way that babies communicate. Different cries—each distinctive in pitch, rhythm, and duration—convey different messages.

The Language of Crying Most parents typically learn the "language" of crying rather quickly (Bisping et al., 1990). Babies have one cry that means hunger, one that means they are too cold or too warm, one that signals their need for attention, one that means frustration, and others for such problems as pain or illness. An infant's cries become more complex over time. By the second month, the irregular or fussy cry appears (Fogel & Thelen, 1987). At about 9 months, the child's cry becomes less persistent and more punctuated by pauses, and the older youngster checks how the cry is affecting a caregiver (Bruner, 1983).

Babies exposed prenatally to cocaine and other drugs by their mothers present special problems. These newborns commonly experience withdrawal symptoms consisting of irritability and incessant shrill crying, inability to sleep, restlessness, hyperactive reflexes, tremors, and occasionally convulsions. But symptoms often subside after the infant has gone through withdrawal (Hawley &

Disney, 1992). In many non-Westernized cultures, babies are wrapped tightly next to the mother's front or back during the day; these babies cry less and are more subdued than American babies tend to be (Small, 1998).

Shaken Baby Syndrome If they cannot get the baby to stop crying, some parents or caretakers wind up feeling distraught and helpless and act out angrily toward the baby. **Shaken baby syndrome (SBS)** occurs when a baby's head is violently shaken back and forth or strikes something, resulting in bruising or bleeding of the brain, spinal cord injury, and eye damage. Health-care and child-care professionals look for a glassy-eyed look or lethargy if they suspect that a baby has been shaken or abused. Bruises and vomiting can also indicate SBS (Duhaime et al., 1998). Infants less than 6 months old are particularly vulnerable to SBS. Of those diagnosed each year, one-third die, one-third suffer brain damage, and one-third recover.

Researchers have found that men (fathers or boyfriends) are more likely than women to inflict this injury, followed by female baby-sitters and then mothers. Boy babies are more likely to be the victims of this abuse than girl babies (Duhaime et al., 1998). SBS usually results from an impulsive, angry response to an infant's crying. Parents should take extra precaution to select baby-sitters carefully and never to leave a child with a person they do not know well. If a parent feels frustrated and fears hurting a crying child, he or she should leave the room, shut the door, go to another room, and calm down. Calling a trusted family member or friend to come help might provide some relief.

If a child cries regularly and incessantly, the infant needs to be examined carefully by a pediatrician to check for **colic**—a condition of discomfort, of unknown cause, in which the baby cries for an hour or more, typically every day at about the same time, for up to several weeks. One study found that a Breathing Bear—a stuffed bear that makes "breathing" movements at a rate that matches that of the colicky infant—helps reduce the fussy crying associated with colic and enables mothers to get through this difficult phase of a baby's development with less stress and depression (Novosad & Thoman, 2003).

Soothing the Infant Meeting physical and emotional needs is likely to soothe a crying baby. If a baby is crying because it is hungry or sleepy, it will probably soon soothe itself by sucking its own fingers. Infants who can learn to comfort themselves are learning to meet their own needs.

When a baby is crying, check to see that the baby is warm enough, has a clean diaper, is not hungry, and feels comfortable. Many older infants like to have a comfort object, such as a specific blanket or stuffed animal, at naptimes or at particularly stressful times. Some infants like rhythmic behaviors, such as rocking in a chair or riding in a stroller. In many cultures of the world, babies spend most of their time carried in a sling on the back or side of an adult, which is warm as well as physically soothing. Most important, parents should try to remain calm and not show anger and stress around babies, for the infant's behavior often mirrors its caretakers' behavior. (Recall the concept of "synchronicity" between child and caretaker mentioned earlier in this chapter.)

Feeding   The first few weeks of feeding a newborn can be worrisome, because a baby will feed only when its internal state signals that it needs nutrition. After a few weeks, the caretaker will be more aware of the baby's pattern of feeding. When fully awake, neonates spend a good deal of time feeding. Indeed, their hunger and sleep patterns are closely linked. Newborns might feed 8 to 14 times during the day. Some infants prefer to feed at short intervals, perhaps every 90 minutes, all day. Others feed at intervals of 3 to 4 hours or longer.

Fortunately, infants come to require fewer daily feedings as they grow older. Most seem to eat three to five meals a day by the time they are 1 year old. As they grow into toddlers, all babies begin to vary in how much they will eat at one time and in what they will eat. Child health experts suggest that changing eating habits are normal and that young children experience "growth spurts"— occasional periods of time when they need considerably more energy to accommodate their bodies' growth.

On-Demand Feeding Versus Scheduled Feeding   Several decades ago, doctors recommended strict feeding schedules for infants. But today many pediatricians recognize that babies differ markedly, and they encourage parents to feed their baby when it is hungry. In on-demand feeding, caregivers let the infant pick its own times in the 24-hour cycle to feed. Typically, pediatricians recommend scheduled feedings for twins and multiples. Whatever schedule parents and caretakers follow, they must decide whether the baby will be breast-fed or bottle-fed. Before 1900, the vast majority of mothers breast-fed their babies or employed a "wet nurse" to do this (a wet nurse is a lactating woman employed to nurse others' babies). But in the ensuing years, as women began to leave homes to work in factories, bottle-feeding with infant formulas became increasingly popular, and by 1946 only about one-third of women left the hospital with a nursing baby. By 1956, this figure had dropped to 20 percent. Since then, breast-feeding has gained in popularity. By 2007, nearly 75 percent of U.S. babies were breast-fed for some time after birth (CDC, 2010).

Breast-Feeding   There is a large body of evidence that breast-feeding the infant for the first several months of life is the best source of nutrition (Wright & Lo, 2007).

The beneficial chemical messenger *oxytocin* is released into the mother's bloodstream before, during, and after birth. Oxytocin promotes release of the mother's breast milk and also causes a mother to be calmer, more relaxed, and more attuned to her baby's needs. The skin-to-skin contact of nursing is also important to the baby, making it feel secure, warm, and comforted and contributing to baby-mother bonding (World Health Organization, 2010). The release of oxytocin during breast-feeding also causes the woman's uterus to shrink back to normal size. Breast-feeding offers several other advantages for mother and baby, as well:

- Mother's milk for the first three to five days contains **colostrum,** a substance that provides antibodies that build up the newborn's immune system, protecting the infant from a variety of infectious and noninfectious diseases.
- Breast-feeding reduces the chance that the infant will develop diarrhea, allergies or asthma, and ear infections.
- Digesting breast milk is usually easier because it is more watery than formula-based milk.
- Breast-feeding improves maternal health by reducing postpartum bleeding, helps mothers return to their prepregnancy weight, and may lower the risk of premenopausal breast cancer and ovarian cancer.

The chief drawback of breast-feeding is that the mother must be available to the infant every few hours, night and day. This is difficult if she has to return to work, unless she uses a breast pump and expresses her milk and stores it in bottles so that the father and other caretakers can feed the child. A breast-feeding mother does not know how much milk the baby is getting, but a breast-feeding baby who is gaining weight and eliminating several times daily is getting adequate nutrition. While breast-feeding, the mother may need to limit her intake of caffeine, which is a mild stimulant. Her eating certain other foods (such as broccoli, cauliflower, cabbage, and spicy foods) can also affect the baby's developing gastrointestinal system and cause crying, crankiness, or irritability. Also, if the mother herself has a preexisting illness, such as HIV or AIDS, or is taking medications, she might not be able to breast-feed.

Formula (Bottle-Feeding)   Today, more than 50 formulas are available, including standard dairy-based, standard for preterm infants, lactose-free, soy-based, and other specialized formulas for infants who cannot tolerate other formulas (Wright & Lo, 2007). The advantage of formula (bottle-feeding) is that it gives mothers physical freedom and enables fathers and other caregivers to become involved in feeding the infant. It also provides a feeding alternative for mothers who are taking medications (such as antidepressants, anticonvulsants, insulin, or AZT). Commercial formulas tend to fill babies up more, so they can go longer between feedings. However, formula-fed babies tend to pass bulkier stools and are more likely than breast-fed babies to experience the discomfort of constipation.

Additional Cautions Regarding Infant Nutrition   Breast-feeding infants should be monitored regularly by a health-care professional if the mother is taking medications or drugs. Also, the Committee on Nutrition of the American Academy of Pediatrics recommends that breast-fed infants be given certain supplements, such as vitamin D, iron, and fluoride.

Mothers in developing countries, who are vigorously targeted by suppliers of infant formula, might inadvertently prepare formula with contaminated water, putting the baby's health at risk ("Spotlight on the Baby Milk Industry," 1998). Pediatricians have discovered that cow enzymes and antibodies are likely to be factors in infant colic, because babies' immature digestive and excretory systems are unable to process these enzymes and antibodies. Formulas with a soy base (vegetable base) do not contain such agents. Some infants cannot digest milk-based or soy-based formulas but can tolerate goat's milk or a special pediatric formula to meet their nutritional needs for development.

Graduating to "Regular" Foods   Pediatricians presently recommend breast-feeding for the first six months, followed by the introduction of mashed vegetables before sweet cereals or fruit. During the first two years of development, a child will begin to eat "regular" table foods and beverages. An adequate balanced diet is extremely important for continued health and brain growth. Two developmental milestones occur when a child can pick up food using the forefinger and thumb (the *pincer grasp*) and hold a cup and drink from it unaided by adults. It is highly recommended that parents use moderation in giving the child sweetened foods and beverages, since the child's baby teeth could begin to decay. All infants exhibit likes and dislikes when it comes to the flavors and textures of foods, but it is a good idea to introduce a variety of tastes and textures (such as solid foods, soft foods, and liquid foods) into the child's diet during the first few years. How much a child can eat at one time varies from child to child and from age to age in development.

Mastering Toilet Training   By about 1½ to 2 years of age, or later, most young children show an interest in toilet training. This is an especially important developmental milestone in American families, because many of our youngsters are taken into public settings, such as child care and preschool, for long periods of time each day.

When the developing muscles in the toddler's anal and urinary tract are strong enough, the child will let a caretaker know that he or she is ready to be toilet trained. When the child begins to demonstrate such understanding, providing "big boy" or "big girl" underpants and praising success will reward the child's efforts. No young child should be forced to sit on a toilet for long periods of time or be left alone on the toilet. Freud said in his psychoanalytic theory that attitudes toward one's sexuality form during toilet-training times, and shaming a child for something he or she cannot yet control does a great deal of harm. Words used to refer to body parts and elimination vary from culture to culture, within cultures, and within families.

Infant Checkups and Immunizations   Regularly scheduled medical checkups are essential so each infant can get proper medical care and immunizations. All children must get several shots before entering child care, preschool, or public and private school settings. Most local health clinics administer checkups and required vaccinations free or for a minimal fee. By helping a child's immune system function effectively, vaccinations provide immunity to a disease before it has a chance to make the child sick. Government-mandated child vaccinations have increased since the early 1990s. Some infants get their first shot (hepatitis B) after birth before leaving the hospital. Other vaccinations begin at 2 months of age. Some parents oppose vaccinating babies on the recommended schedule because of concerns about the safety of preservatives used in vaccines, religious restrictions, or distrust of pharmaceutical companies. Medical practitioners can guide parents in making such important decisions (Fraleigh, 2009).

> ### Questions
>
> What are several states that babies are learning to regulate during the first few years of life? In what ways does an infant begin to regulate its internal states? What factors might promote or detract from a child's healthy growth and development over the first two years?

Brain Growth and Development

Infants grow at a surprising rate and change in wonderful ways. Their development is especially dramatic during the first two years of life. These maturational changes take place because of growth in key systems of the body. The pituitary gland in conjunction with the hypothalamus (a structure at the base of the brain composed of a tightly packed cluster of nerve cells) secretes hormones that play a critical part in regulating children's growth (Guillemin, 1982).

Predictable changes occur at various age levels. Many investigators have analyzed the developmental sequence of various characteristics and skills (Gesell, 1928;

FIGURE 4.9 Synaptic Density in the Human Brain A single neuron can connect with as many as 15,000 other neurons. The incredibly complex network of connections that results is impacted by proper nutrition, experience, and environmental stimulation.

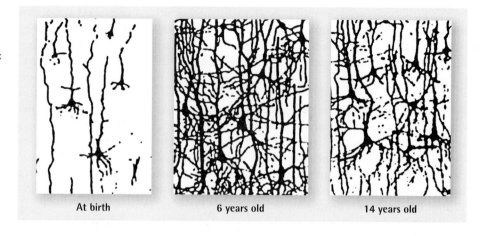

At birth   6 years old   14 years old

Meredith, 1973). From these studies psychologists have evolved standards, called **norms,** for evaluating a child's developmental progress relative to the average of the child's age group. Although children differ considerably in their individual rates of maturation, they show broad similarities in the sequence of developmental change. Among infants, length and weight are the indices most strongly correlated with behavioral development and performance (Lasky et al., 1981).

Charts in pediatricians' offices that are based on norms show relatively smooth continuous curves of growth, suggesting that youngsters grow in a steady, slow fashion. In contrast, parents often say that their growing child "shot up overnight." Intriguing findings by Michelle Lampl and her colleagues seem to show that babies grow in fits and starts, with long intervals between growth spikes (Lampl et al., 1995). Additionally, it seems that a few days prior to growing rapidly, youngsters often become hungry, out of sorts, fussy, agitated, and sleepy.

Growth of Key Systems and the Brain

Not all parts of the body grow at the same rate. The reproductive system grows very slowly until adolescence, at which point its growth accelerates. The internal organs, including the kidneys, liver, spleen, lungs, and stomach, keep pace with the growth in the skeletal system, and these systems show the same two growth spurts in infancy and adolescence.

The Newborn and Brain Development The nervous system develops more rapidly than other systems. At birth the brain already weighs about 350 grams; at 1 year it is about 1,400 grams; by 7 years of age, the brain is almost adult in weight and size (Restak, 1984). The circumference of the baby's skull is measured to verify continued cerebral cortex growth with ultrasound imaging while in the womb, at birth, and at every scheduled medical checkup during childhood. Those parts of the

hindbrain that control basic processes such as circulation, respiration, and consciousness are operative at birth.

Most neonatal reflexes, such as sucking, rooting, and grasping, are organized at the subcortical level (the part of the brain that guides basic biological functioning, including sleeping, heart rate, hunger, and digestion). The parts that control processes less critical to immediate survival, including physical mobility and language, mature after birth. The rapid growth of the brain during the first two years of life is associated with the development of neural pathways and connections among nerve cells, particularly in the cerebral cortex (the part of the brain responsible for learning, thinking, reading, and problem solving). Brains that are unusually efficient are characterized by complex neuronal interactions and rich synaptic connections (see Figure 4.9). This is why essential nutrition and extensive sensory experience and stimulation play a vital role in brain maturation and cognitive functioning (Chugani & Phelps, 1986).

Environmental Stimulation Factor Researchers now confirm that the way parents interact with children in the early years and the experiences they provide have a major impact on an infant's emotional development, learning abilities, and later functioning (Yarrow et al., 1984). A baby is born with an unfinished brain, one that lets the child develop neural pathways in direct response to its world. Researchers are finding that the quality of caregiving has an even greater effect on brain development than most people previously suspected. Of course, heredity also plays a role. Recent research suggests that the expression of parental love affects the way the brain forms its complex connections: Looking into the baby's eyes and holding and stroking the baby stimulates the brain to release hormones that promote growth; singing and talking to a baby stimulates the sense of hearing ("Brain Facts," 2009). Some researchers refer to this as promoting "emotional intelligence." If an infant's brain is not exposed to visual or auditory experiences, the child will have difficulty mastering language and will have difficulty with visual and auditory tasks (Thompson, 2001). Every caregiver, as well as every family member, is potentially a source of love, learning, comfort, and stimulation that promotes brain growth.

Principles of Development   Human development proceeds according to two major principles. Development according to the **cephalocaudal principle** proceeds from the head to the feet. Improvements in structure and function come first in the head region, then in the trunk, and finally in the leg region. At birth the head is disproportionately large. In adults the head makes up only about one-tenth to one-twelfth of the body, but in newborns it is about one-fourth of the body. In contrast, the arms and legs of newborns are disproportionately short.

From birth to adulthood the head doubles in size, the trunk trebles, the arms and hands quadruple in length, and the legs and feet grow fivefold (Bayley, 1956). Motor development likewise follows the cephalocaudal principle. Infants first learn to control the muscles of the head and neck. Then they learn to control the arms and the abdomen; last, they learn to control the legs. Thus, when they begin to crawl, they use the upper body to propel themselves, dragging the legs passively behind. Only later do they begin to use the legs as an aid in crawling. Similarly, babies learn to hold their heads up before they acquire the ability to sit, and they learn to sit before they learn to walk (Bayley, 1936).

The other major pattern of human development follows the **proximodistal principle:** development from near to far—outward from the central axis of the body toward the extremities. Early in infancy, babies must move their head and trunk to orient their hands when grasping an object. Only later can they use their arms and legs independently, and it is still longer before they can

The Cephalocaudal Principle of Development   Physical development and motor development come first in the head and neck region, then in the trunk and upper body, and finally in the legs and feet. Thus, when infants begin to crawl, they use their upper body to propel themselves, dragging their legs behind. Then they get up on all fours, using the legs to aid in crawling.

make refined movements with their wrists and fingers. On the whole, control over movement travels down the arm as children become able to perform increasingly precise and sophisticated manual and grasping operations. In general, large-muscle control precedes fine-muscle control. Thus, the child's ability to jump, climb, and run (activities involving the use of large muscles) develops ahead of the ability to draw or write (activities involving smaller muscles).

Motor Development

Reaching, grasping, crawling, and walking—behaviors that infants learn to perform with considerable proficiency—have proved to be highly complex and problematic tasks for engineers who design computers and robots that can perform these tasks. Not surprisingly, a great deal of the early psychological research devoted to motor development was primarily descriptive, much as we might describe the mechanical activities of a computer or robot (McGraw, 1935).

To crawl, walk, climb, and grasp objects with precision, babies must have reached certain levels of skeletal and muscular development. As their heads become smaller relative to their bodies, their balance improves. As children's legs become stronger and longer, they can master various locomotor activities. As their shoulders widen and their arms lengthen, their manual and mechanical capacities increase. Motor development occurs in accordance with maturational processes that are built into the human organism and are activated by a child's interaction with the environment (Thelen, 1986, 1995).

Rhythmic Behaviors   Probably the most interesting motor behavior displayed by young infants involves bursts of rapid, repeated rhythmic movements of the limbs, torso, or head (Thelen, 1986, 1995). Infants kick, rock, bounce, bang, rub, thrust, and twist. Such behaviors are closely related to motor development and provide the foundation for the more skilled behaviors that will come later. Hence, rhythmic patterns that involve the legs, such as kicking, gradually increase at about 1 month, peak immediately prior to a child's initiation of crawling at about 6 months, and then taper off. Likewise, rhythmic hand and arm movements appear before complex manual skills. Thus, bouts of rhythmic movement seem to be transitional behaviors between uncoordinated activity and complex voluntary motor control. They represent a state in motor maturation that is more complex than that found in simple reflexes yet less variable and flexible than that found in later, cortically controlled behavior.

Locomotion   The infant's ability to walk, which typically evolves among U.S. youngsters between 11 and

15 months of age, is the climax of a long series of developments (Thelen, 1995). These developments progress in a sequence that follows the cephalocaudal principle. First, children gain the ability to lift up the head; later, they can lift the chest. Next, they achieve command of the trunk region, which enables them to sit up. Finally, they achieve mastery of their legs as they learn to stand and walk. For most infants the seventh month brings a surge in motor development. Usually, children begin by *crawling*—moving with the abdomen in contact with the floor. They maneuver by twisting the body and pulling and tugging with the arms. Next, they may progress to *creeping*—moving on hands and knees while the body is parallel with the floor. Some children also employ *hitching*—sitting and sliding along the floor by "digging in" and pushing themselves backward with the heels. In this form of **locomotion** they often use the arms to aid in propulsion. Indeed, an occasional infant varies the procedure by sitting and then, using both arms to lift its body, bouncing across the floor on its buttocks.

At 8 months children pull themselves to a *standing* position but usually have difficulty getting back down again. The urge to master new motor skills is so powerful in infants at this age that bumps, spills, falls, and other obstacles discourage them only momentarily. Before age 1, many infants are *cruising* (standing and walking while holding on to furniture). A major milestone of motor development that brings both excitement and caution occurs when an infant begins walking unaided. Walking is the culmination of physical and motor development that brings with it greater independence and mobility. Caregivers are cautioned to get down to "child level" and childproof the environment against hazards.

Our knowledge of the stages and timing of motor development are based largely on studies of infants from Western cultures. But the possibility that the timing of motor development varies considerably among cultures has been raised by a number of studies of African infants (Ainsworth, 1967; Keefer et al., 1982). Geber and Dean (1957a, 1957b) tested nearly 300 infants living in an urban area of Uganda. They found that these babies were clearly accelerated in motor development relative to American white infants. The Ugandan infants' precocity is greatest during the first six months of life, after which the gap between the two groups tends to decrease. It closes by the end of the second year. The timing of motor development is not universal. North African children develop motor skills sooner than Western children do, and American Indian and East Asian children develop them later (Field, 2006). Cultural variables play a part in the differences between the timetables according to which children in different groups reach developmental milestones. As Rogoff (2003, p. 159) explains, "In some communities walking sooner is valued; in others, it is not desired. In Wogeo, New Guinea, infants were not allowed to crawl

and discouraged from walking until nearly 2 years of age so that they know how to take care of themselves and avoid dangers before moving about freely."

Manual Skills The child's development of manual skills proceeds through a series of orderly stages in accordance with the proximodistal principle—from the center of the body toward the periphery. At 2 months of age, infants merely make swiping movements toward objects with the upper body and arms; they do not attempt to grasp objects. At 3 months of age, their reaching consists of clumsy shoulder and elbow movements. Their aim is poor and their hands are fisted. After about 16 weeks, children approach an object with hands open and spend a considerable amount of time looking at their own hands. At the age of about 20 weeks, children become capable of touching an object in one quick, direct motion of the hand; occasionally, some of them succeed in grasping it in an awkward manner.

At 36 weeks they coordinate their grasp with the tips of the thumb and forefinger. Caretakers must take extra precautions once infants can pick up small objects, because infants seem to put all objects in their mouth for the next several months. By about 52 weeks, infants master a more sophisticated forefinger grasp (Ausubel & Sullivan, 1970). By the age of 24 months, most children can hold and use such items as eating utensils, a crayon or paintbrush, a ball, and a toothbrush.

> **Questions**
>
> What is the typical developmental progression of physical and motor skills from newborn to 2 years of age? If you worked on staff with a local pediatrician, how would you explain to a concerned parent why her healthy infant is not walking by 14 months of age?

Sensory Development

What is the world like to the infant? Increasingly, sophisticated research and monitoring equipment is enabling us to pinpoint what the infant sees, hears, smells, tastes, and feels. A goal of such research is to increase parental knowledge of child development and health care, while informing pediatricians about cultural beliefs and practices—because in the United States, one out of every five children is from an immigrant family that is likely to be unaware of empirical findings (Bornstein & Cote, 2007). During the first six months of life, there is a considerable discrepancy between infants' vast sensory capabilities and their relatively sluggish motor development. Their sensory apparatus yields perceptual input that far exceeds their capacity to use it. As a result of maturation, experience, and practice, they have already acquired the ability to extract information from the environment at a phenomenal rate. The child surges ahead when these perceptual abilities become linked with the big spurt in motor development that begins around the seventh month. Hence, 10 to 11 months later, at 18 months of age, the child is an accomplished social being. Let us consider the processes of sensation and perception. *Sensation* is the reception of information by our sense organs. *Perception* consists of the interpretation or meaning that we assign to sensation.

Vision   Infants born preterm are at higher risk of visual delays and difficulties. Full-term newborns are typically equipped at birth with a functional and intact visual apparatus, but their eyes are immature. The retina and the optic nerve, for instance, are not fully developed (Valenti, 2006). The muscles that control the lenses are not fully developed for visual accommodation. As a result, their eyes sometimes focus too close and sometimes too far. In contrast to earlier research findings that suggested infants see from 7 to 10 inches in front of their face best, more recent research suggests that "infants are generally farsighted at birth" outgrowing it over the first years of life (Hamer & Skoczenski, 2001). As one would expect, infants' visual scanning capabilities become progressively more sophisticated with the passage of time, which in turn affects the development of neural structures (Dobson et al., 2009). Let us take a closer look at the developing visual capabilities of infants by examining a number of specific components (Hamer & Skoczenski, 2001):

- *Visual acuity* (detail vision). By about 2 to 3 months of age, most infants can focus accurately. By 8 months, the infant's nervous system has matured so it is nearly as good as normal adult acuity (nearly 20/20).
- *Eye coordination.* A newborn infant's eyes are not perfectly coordinated, and eyes may wander, even in different directions. By 3 months, generally, an infant's eyes are well coordinated.
- *Ability to follow (tracking).* Newborns can follow objects, often with jerky motions. By 3 months, infants can normally follow objects more smoothly.
- *Color vision.* Infants as young as 2 weeks of age have color vision, distinguishing red from green. Infants can also see large colored patterns and black-and-white patterns.
- *Object and face recognition.* At birth an infant's eyes tend to be attracted to the borders of objects, although they have enough detail vision to see the larger features of a face. Newborns ranging from 12 to 36 hours of age produce significantly more sucking responses in order to see an image of their mothers' faces than they do to see an image of strangers' faces (Walton, Bower, & Bower, 1992).

- *Visual constancy.* Three- to 5-month-old infants are able to recognize object boundaries and object unity by detecting surface separations or contours (Spelke, von Hofsten, & Kestenbaum, 1989).
- *Depth perception.* It appears that at birth, infants have two-dimensional vision. Three-dimensional vision requires good muscle coordination of the eyes, sufficient brain and nerve cell maturation, and lots of visual experience. Infants' binocular vision—the ability to tell the distances of various objects and to experience the world three-dimensionally—undergoes a sudden burst between 3 and 5 months of age (Nawrot, Mayo, & Nawrot, 2009).

A family vacation to the Grand Canyon led Eleanor Gibson to undertake a *visual cliff experiment* with the assistance of one of her students, Richard D. Walk (Gibson & Walk, 1960). They devised a technique where an infant is placed on a glass surface on which she or he can crawl (see Figure 4.10). The shallow side is covered on the underside with a checkered material. At the deep side, an illusion of a cliff is created by placing the checkered material several feet below the glass. The infant's mother stands alternately at the shallow and deep sides and coaxes the infant to crawl toward her. If infants can perceive depth, they should be willing to cross the shallow side but not the cliff side, because the cliff side looks like a chasm.

Gibson and Walk tested 36 infants between 6½ and 14 months of age. Twenty-seven of the infants crawled across the shallow side toward their mothers. Only three could be enticed to cross the cliff side. A number of infants actually crawled away from their mothers when beckoned from the deep side; others cried, presumably because they could not reach their mothers without crossing the chasm. Some patted the glass on the deep side, ascertaining that it was solid, but nonetheless backed away. Apparently, they were more dependent on the visual evidence than on the evidence provided by their sense of touch. This research suggests that the vast majority of babies can perceive a dropoff and avoid it by the time they become capable of creeping. Infants have already developed rather sophisticated visual-perceptual capabilities by the time they reach 6 to 14 months of age (Younger, 1992).

Hearing   At the time of birth, normally the hearing apparatus of the neonate is remarkably well developed. Indeed, the human fetus can hear noises three months before birth (Chelli & Chanoufi, 2008). For several hours or even days after delivery, the neonate's hearing might be somewhat impaired. Vernix and amniotic fluid frequently stop up the external ear passage, while mucus clogs the middle ear. These mechanical blockages disappear rapidly after birth.

FIGURE 4.10 The Visual Cliff Experiment In the visual cliff experiment, the child is placed on a center board that has a sheet of glass extending outward on either side. A checkered material is placed on one side about 40 inches below the glass, which provides the illusion of depth. Despite its mother's coaxing and the presence of a safe glass surface, a 6-month-old infant generally will not crawl across the "chasm." The infant will, however, venture across the shallow side of the apparatus to reach its mother.

Source: Adapted from E. J. Gibson and R. D. Walk, "The Visual Cliff," *Scientific American,* Vol. 202 (1960), p. 65.

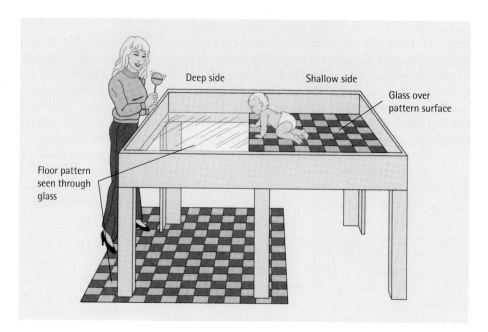

On average, each day in the United States, 33 babies (12,000 annually) are born with permanent hearing loss, and four or five per thousand have a hearing impairment (Gaffney et al., 2010). *It is imperative to identify hearing-impaired babies as early as possible,* and most states have early hearing detection and intervention laws (American Speech-Language-Hearing Association, 2007). This is a safe, simple, painless assessment, and an infant who is identified will be referred to a pediatric audiologist.

Ear infections are the second most common ailment in infancy (after colds) and are caused by a variety of factors. The most obvious sign of ear infection is persistent high-pitched crying, often after the infant has been lying down for a while. If an infant doesn't respond to a parent's voice or to loud noises by showing a startle reflex or by crying or doesn't make babbling or cooing sounds within the first few months of life, he or she should be checked immediately for a hearing problem. Without professional intervention, an infant who cannot hear will acquire neither the sounds of human language nor the cognitive or social skills that provide the foundation for success in later schooling. Hearing-impaired and deaf infants are eligible for early intervention services. Clearly, parents will also want to learn sign language to communicate with their baby. Educators have long recognized that hearing plays a crucial part in the process by which children acquire language. But research by Condon and Sander (1974a, 1974b), purporting to show that newborns are attuned to the fine elements of adult speech, surprised the scientific community. The researchers videotaped interactions between neonates and adults and analyzed them frame by frame. To ordinary viewers, the hands, feet, and head of an infant appear uncoordinated,

clumsily flexing, twitching, and moving about in all directions. But Condon and Sander say closer analysis reveals that infant movements are synchronized with the sound patterns of the adult's speech. For example, if an infant is squirming about when an adult begins to talk, the infant coordinates the movements of brows, eyes, limbs, elbows, hips, and mouth to start, stop, and change with the boundaries of the adult's speech segments (phonemes, syllables, or words). The newborns, who were from 12 hours to 2 days old, were equally capable of synchronizing their movements with Chinese or English.

Hearing Assessment Before a Newborn Leaves the Hospital Hearing screening by an audiologist is safe, simple, and painless. It is imperative to identify hearing-impaired infants as soon as possible.

Condon and Sander conclude that if infants, from birth, move in precise, shared rhythm with the speech patterns of their culture, then they participate in millions of repetitions of linguistic forms long before they employ them in communication. More recent research has yielded consistent findings about infant rhythmic behaviors and social interaction with caregivers (Jaffe, Beebe, Feldstein, Crown, & Jasnow, 2001).

Taste and Smell Both taste (gustation) and smell (olfaction) are present at birth. Infant taste preferences can be determined by measuring sucking behavior (Blass & Ciaramitaro, 1994). Young infants relax and suck contentedly when provided with sweet solutions, although they prefer sucrose over glucose (Beauchamp & Mennella, 2009; Engen, Lipsitt, & Peck, 1974). Infants react to sour and bitter solutions by grimacing and breathing irregularly (Beauchamp & Mennella, 2009). The findings for salt perception are less clear; some researchers find that newborns do not discriminate a salty solution from non-salty water, whereas other investigators find that salt is a negative experience for newborns (Bernstein, 1990). Crook and Lipsitt (1976) found that newborns decrease their sucking speed when receiving sweet fluid, which suggests that they savor the liquid for the pleasurable taste. This would indicate that the hedonistic aspects of tasting are present at birth (Acredolo & Hake, 1982). At 3 months, infants become more accepting of new tastes (Slater & Lewis, 2007).

Much of the time the olfactory system monitors the environment without the organism being aware of the process. The familiar simply fades into the background. But when novel odors come into sensory range, the system promptly brings them to conscious awareness. It is this feature—alerting the organism to potential danger and so increasing the organism's chances for survival—that accounts for the system's evolutionary value (Engen, 1991).

Infants respond to different odors, and the vigor of the response corresponds to the intensity and quality of the stimulant. Engen, Lipsitt, and Kaye (1963) tested olfaction in 2-day-old infants. At regular intervals they held a cotton swab saturated with anise oil (which has a licorice smell) or asafetida (which smells like boiling onions) under an infant's nose. A polygraph recorded the babies' bodily movements, respiration, and heart rate. When they first detected an odor, infants moved their limbs, their breathing quickened, and their heart rate increased. With repeated exposure, infants gradually came to disregard the stimulant. The olfactory thresholds decreased drastically over the first few days of life, meaning that the neonates became increasingly sensitive to nasal stimulants. Other researchers have confirmed that neonates possess well-developed olfactory abilities (Bartocci et al., 2000).

Cutaneous Senses Heat, cold, pressure, and pain—the four major cutaneous sensations—are present in neonates (Humphrey, 1978). Kai Jensen (1932) found that a bottle of hot or cold milk (above 124 degrees Fahrenheit or below 72 degrees Fahrenheit) caused an irregular sucking rhythm in neonates. On the whole, neonates are relatively insensitive to small differences in thermal stimuli. Neonates also respond to body pressure. Touching activates many of the reflexes discussed earlier in the chapter. Finally, we infer from infants' responses that they experience sensations of pain. For instance, observation of neonate and infant behavior suggests that gastrointestinal upsets are a major source of discomfort. As infants receive required vaccination injections during the first few years of life, it is quite obvious that they sense pain and discomfort (Izard, Hembree, & Huebner, 1987). And male infants increase their crying during circumcision, providing additional evidence that neonates are sensitive to pain (Taddio, Goldbach, Ipp, Stevens, & Koren, 1995).

Interconnections Among the Senses Our sensory systems commonly operate in concert with one another. We expect to see things we hear, feel things we see, and smell things we taste. We often employ information we gain from one sensory system to "inform" our other systems (Acredolo & Hake, 1982). For instance, even newborns move both their head and their eyes in efforts to locate the source of sounds, especially when the sounds are patterned and sustained.

Developmental psychologists, psychobiologists, and comparative psychologists have advanced two opposing theories about how the interconnections among systems evolve. Take the development of sensory and motor coordination in infants. One viewpoint holds that infants only gradually achieve an integration of eye-hand activities as they interact with their environment. Infants are seen as progressively forging a closer and sharper coordination between their sensory and motor systems in the process of adapting to the larger world. According to Jean Piaget, infants initially lack cognitive structures for knowing the external world. Consequently, they must actively construct mental schemas that will enable them to structure their experience.

The opposing theory holds that eye-hand coordination is biologically prewired in the infant's nervous system at birth and emerges according to a maturational schedule. T. G. R. Bower (1976) favors this interpretation. Bower finds that newborn infants engage in visually initiated reaching. Apparently, when neonates look at an object and reach out for it, both the looking and the reaching are part of the same response by which the infants orient themselves toward the object (von Hofsten, 1982).

In ensuing months an increase in visual guidance occurs during the approach phase of reaching (Ashmead et al., 1993). A cautious conclusion to be drawn from this research is that the eye-hand coordination of newborns and very young infants is biologically prewired. But visual guidance in eye-hand coordination becomes more important as older babies monitor and progressively reduce the "gap" between the seen target and the seen hand (McKenzie et al., 1993). So for this later sort of reaching, the youngster must attend to its hand. In sum, eye-hand coordination changes early in life from using the felt hand to using the seen hand (Bushnell, 1985). Development is often characterized by patterns of skill acquisition, loss, and reacquisition on new foundations and levels.

Questions

Which sensory systems are already functioning well at birth? What can you tell new parents about when their infant will see clearly, hear acutely, and distinguish qualities of smell, taste, and touch? How do infant senses interconnect?

SEGUE

As any parent knows, infants actively search out and respond to their environment. Scientific research on infants' developing motor and sensory abilities bears out the truth of this observation. Children are predisposed to begin learning how the world operates around them. As they mature, they refine their ability to take information from one sense and transfer it to another. All the senses, including seeing, hearing, smell, taste, and touch, create a system that acts as a whole. Information gained from multiple systems is often more important than that gained from one sense, precisely because it is interactive.

A growing body of contemporary research points to the multicausal, fluid, contextual, and self-organizing nature of developmental change, the unity of motor behavior and perception, and the role of exploration and selection in the emergence of new behavior (Smith & Thelen, 2003).

In Chapter 5 we will turn our attention to cognition and to maturing intellectual abilities, such as use of language, which grows from the roots in motor behavior, sensation, perception, caretaker attachment behaviors, and experiential factors that we have discussed in this chapter.

SUMMARY

Birth

1. The number of births in the United States peaked in 2007 at its highest level in two decades but began to decline again in 2008. Families vary widely in composition and are having fewer children. About 40 percent of births are to unmarried women.
2. A variety of natural childbirth approaches help a mother prepare for delivery.
3. Women might choose to deliver in hospital birthing rooms, in birthing centers, or in home delivery with an experienced midwife attending. Most American women are attended by obstetricians who specialize in prenatal care, birth, and postnatal care.
4. American hospitals and birthing centers offer family-centered hospital care in which childbirth can be a family experience. Natural childbirth and rooming in are common features of these programs.
5. The period of gestation for a human baby from conception to birth is nearly nine months.
6. A few weeks before birth, most fetuses normally position themselves head downward and lower in the uterus. Fetal diagnostics at this later stage are warranted to ensure a healthy delivery or discovery of the need for medical intervention. Most women experience mild contractions for a few weeks before birth.

7. The birth process consists of labor, delivery, and afterbirth. At the beginning of labor, the amniotic sac ruptures. The first contractions are periodic and come more quickly and intensely as delivery nears. Delivery begins when the baby's head passes through the cervix and ends with the passage of the baby through the birth canal. Birth concludes when the mother's body expels the afterbirth.
8. The Leboyer method of birth reflects the view that infants need a gentler delivery, lower sound and light levels, a warmer delivery room, newborn massage, and a warm bath.
9. In a hospital setting, electronic fetal monitoring and computers continually assess the status of the fetus to determine whether the fetus needs surgical delivery. Cesarean deliveries now account for one-third of births in U.S. hospitals.
10. A full-term neonate is usually 19 to 22 inches long, weighs 5½ to 9½ pounds, is covered with a substance called vernix, and often has fine body hair. The first several weeks of life are called the neonatal period.
11. Other health factors are assessed at one minute and five minutes after birth via the Apgar scoring system: heart rate, respiratory effort, muscle tone, reflex irritability, and skin tone. Other assessment measures may be used to evaluate physical behaviors, reflexes, and social capacities.

12. The practice of routine circumcision for infant boys is declining.
13. Parent-infant bonding is a process of interaction and mutual attention between parents and their infant. Attachment occurs over time with close proximity, constant interaction, and emotional attachment.
14. Complications might arise during pregnancy and childbirth. Much can be done to help the mother and infant through medical intervention and technology, such as neonatology units to help premature, very-low-birth-weight, or at-risk infants survive.
15. Postmature infants, those delivered more than 2 weeks after the usual 40 weeks of gestation in the womb, are usually larger and healthy.
16. Although the majority of American infants are born without complications, a small percentage are born as preterm infants or are full term but small. Some are born with genetic disorders or birth defects from prenatal exposure to chemical toxicants, and some experience birth complications.
17. Infants who are determined to be at risk from birth or during the neonatal period are eligible by law for early intervention services from birth through preschool age.
18. Infant mortality occurs because of such conditions as birth defects, prematurity or low birth weight, sudden infant death syndrome (SIDS), maternal pregnancy complications, complications caused by medical interventions, and respiratory disease syndrome.
19. After birth, some mothers and fathers experience postpartum depression (PMD). This depression has a significant impact on the infant's behavior, emotional responsiveness, and cognitive development.

Development of Basic Competencies

20. The first two years of life after birth are called infancy. Some infant researchers have discovered that infant biology is intimately connected to the biology of the adults responsible for infant care.
21. Sleeping, crying, feeding, and eliminating are the newborn's chief behaviors. An infant's responses at any given time are related to its states, which include regular sleep, irregular sleep, drowsiness, alert inactivity, waking activity, and crying.
22. Neonates are born with good indicators of neurological development called reflex behaviors, which are simple, involuntary, unlearned responses, such as sucking, coughing, blinking, yawning, and stepping.
23. The major activity of newborns is sleeping. It may be weeks or months before infants sleep through the night, and they normally take one nap a day.
24. Annually, nearly 3,000 U.S. families experience the devastating tragedy and agony of sudden infant death syndrome (SIDS), or crib death. There has been a decline in SIDS deaths over the past decade, although there was a slight uptick in 2007. The overall decline in deaths is attributed to the national education campaign urging caregivers to place infants on their back to sleep and to avoid smoking around a baby.
25. Crying is the language of the newborn. It is an unlearned, involuntary, highly adaptive response that incites the parents to caretaking activities. Different cries convey different messages to caretakers.
26. Some caregivers become so annoyed with infant cries that they harm the infant out of frustration, causing shaken baby syndrome. A child's incessant crying could be a sign of colic, a condition of lengthy crying for an unknown cause.
27. Newborns spend much of their waking time feeding, and pediatricians encourage parents to feed their baby when it is hungry. Extensive research suggests that breast-feeding is best for promoting healthy mothers and infants.
28. Toddlers' anal and urinary tract muscles begin to strengthen and develop over time, allowing children to be toilet trained on their own schedules.
29. Parents should schedule regular medical checkups and vaccinations to help a child's immune system function effectively. Proof of vaccinations is required for entry into child care, preschool, and kindergarten.
30. Infant researchers have come up with predictable changes that occur at various age levels and have established standards of growth and maturation, called norms, or averages for the child's age group.
31. Normal development follows two patterns: the cephalocaudal principle and the proximodistal principle. Infants first gain motor skills over muscles controlling the head muscles, then the trunk muscles, and finally the leg muscles. The child's development of manual skills proceeds through a series of orderly stages in accordance with the proximodistal principle—from the center of the body toward the extremities (out to the fingertips).
32. Young infants display bursts of repeated rhythmic movements of the limbs, torso, and head that are closely related to motor development and provide the foundation for later, more skilled actions.
33. The development of locomotion proceeds in a specific sequence, but children vary in their rate of development.
34. Healthy infants are born with their sensory systems functioning, but over the course of the first several months of life, these systems and the brain are constantly growing, adapting, and adjusting to clearly interpret sensations of their new world.
35. At birth a neonate's eyes are immature. It will be several months before infant eyes can focus clearly and work in coordination. A neonate can see in shades of black, white, and gray; within a few months the cells of the retina develop so that colors and contrasts will be more evident. Infants typically undergo a patterned sequence of changes in their method of focusing and organizing visual events.
36. The fetus can hear before birth, and at birth neonate hearing is normally well developed. Hearing plays a very important role in the process by which infants acquire language. Ear infections are the second most common ailment in infancy (after colds).
37. Taste and smell are present at birth, and infants show distinct preferences. Skin/cutaneous senses of heat, cold, pressure, and pain are also present at birth.
38. Infants are actively searching out and responding to their environment. Information gained from their senses is interactive with environmental experiences and the quality of caretaker involvement.

KEY TERMS

afterbirth *(104)*

anoxia *(110)*

Apgar scoring system *(105)*

birth *(101)*

birthing centers *(100)*

birthing rooms *(100)*

cephalocaudal principle *(123)*

colic *(119)*

colostrum *(120)*

Couvade syndrome *(109)*

crowning *(104)*

delivery *(103)*

entrainment *(116)*

epidural narcotics *(106)*

failure to thrive (FTT) *(117)*

fetal alcohol spectrum disorders (FASD) *(113)*

Individuals with Disabilities Education Act (IDEA) *(114)*

infancy *(116)*

infant mortality *(114)*

labor *(103)*

lightening *(103)*

locomotion *(124)*

low birth weight *(110)*

midwifery *(100)*

motherese/parentese *(109)*

natural childbirth *(99)*

neonatal intensive care unit (NICU) *(111)*

neonate *(104)*

norms *(122)*

obstetricians *(99)*

parent-infant bonding *(108)*

placenta *(112)*

placenta praevia *(110)*

postmature infant *(112)*

postpartum major depression (PMD) *(115)*

preterm infant *(111)*

proximodistal principle *(123)*

psychoprophylactic method *(98)*

reflex *(117)*

rooming in *(100)*

shaken baby syndrome (SBS) *(119)*

small-for-term infants *(111)*

states *(117)*

sudden infant death syndrome (SIDS) *(118)*

FOLLOWING UP ON THE INTERNET

Web sites for this chapter focus on preparation for birth and delivery, neonate assessment, infant development, and parent-infant attachment. Please access the text Web site at www.mhhe.com/crandell10 for up-to-date hot-linked Internet addresses for the following organizations and resources:

American College of Nurse-Midwives
http://www.acnm.org/

American Association of Birth Centers
http://www.birthcenters.org/

Association of Women's Health, Obstetric and Neonatal Nurses
http://www.awhonn.org/

CDC: National Center on Birth Defects and Developmental Disabilities
http://www.cdc.gov/ncbddd/index.html

CDC: Sudden Infant Death Syndrome (SIDS) and Sudden Unexpected Infant Death (SUID): Home
http://www.cdc.gov/sids/

Childbirth.org
http://childbirth.org

Depression After Delivery
http://Depressionafterdelivery.com

March of Dimes Perinatal Center
http://www.marchofdimes.com/peristats/

National Center for Cultural Competence
http://www11.georgetown.edu/research/gucchd/nccc/

National Center for Hearing Assessment–Pediatric Diagnostic Audiology
http://www.infanthearing.org/audiology/index.html

National Newborn Screening and Genetics Resource Center
http://genes-r-us.uthscsa.edu/

National Organization of Fetal Alcohol Syndrome
http://www.nofas.org/

Neonatology on the Web
http://www.neonatology.org/neo.links.html

U.S. Department of Health: Administration on Developmental Disabilities
http://www.acf.hhs.gov/programs/add/

Infancy
Cognitive and Language Development

Critical Thinking Questions

1. Learning is defined in terms of three criteria: There must be some change in behavior, this change must be relatively stable, and the change must result from experience. Can learning take place if only two of the three conditions are present? Why or why not?

2. What would it be like to live in a country where a language was spoken that you did not know and where no one else knew your language? How would you communicate your needs, desires, fears, concerns, and hopes? How is this similar to what a young child might feel before he learns to use language?

3. A researcher in Japan developed a handheld electronic gadget called the "Bow-lingual" that he claims can translate a dog's barking into six basic categories of "emotions." "Happy," "fun," "annoyed," and "frustrated" are just a few of the options. The invention, which uses a microphone on the dog's collar to record the bark, relays to the owner up to 200 words about the dog's "feelings," together with relevant pictures. Do you think it will be possible for researchers to invent a device that translates the variety of cries of human babies into human language? Why or why not?

4. Speech develops through a series of stages, ending in the construction of two- and three-word sentences for the beginning language learner. Do you think you could learn a second language easier and faster today if you went through a similar process?

Outline

Our cognitive and language abilities are probably our most distinctive features as human beings. Cognitive skills enable us to gain knowledge of our social and physical environment. Language enables us to communicate with one another. Without either, human social organization would be impossible. Even if we lacked these abilities, we might still have families as many other animals organize themselves in family groups. However, our cognitive and language abilities allow us to structure families in a way that is distinctly human. Without cognitive and language abilities, we would lack rules about such things as incest, marriage, divorce, inheritance, and adoption. We would have no political, religious, economic, or military organizations; no codes of morality; no science, theology, art, or literature. We would have virtually no tools. In sum, we would be without culture, and we would not be human (White, 1949). This chapter surveys the processes by which cognition and language develop during the early years of infancy, from birth through age 2.

COGNITIVE DEVELOPMENT

As discussed in Chapter 2, **cognition** is the process of knowing and encompasses such phenomena as sensation, perception, imagery, retention, memory, recall, problem solving, reasoning, and thinking. We receive raw sensory information and transform, elaborate, store, recover, and use this information in our daily activities (Neisser, 1967). Some infants exhibit superior abilities to communicate using their native language, compared to the majority of infants who are on-time with communication skills. Others are identified as having specific language impairments (SLIs)—that is, hearing impairments or deafness, severe developmental delays, neglect or caregiver deprivation and abuse, and autism, a pervasive developmental disorder that typically appears in early childhood and is characterized by marked deficits in communication and social interaction.

Making Connections

Mental activity enables us to "make something" out of our perceptions by relating some happening to other events or objects in our experience. Humans also perform complex and varied behaviors, such as driving and solving mathematical problems, because the brain is able to use the different regions independently and simultaneously. We use information from our environment and our memories to make decisions about what we say and do. Because these decisions are based on available information and on our ability to process the information intelligently, we view them as rational (Bauer, 2006). This capacity allows us to intervene in the course of events with conscious deliberation.

For instance, if we show youngsters aged 13 to 24 months the simple steps involved in "making spaghetti" with clay, a garlic press, and a plastic knife and then allow them to undertake the task for themselves, they are able to recall the sequence of events and repeat them—sometimes eight months later. Clearly, these youngsters are obtaining knowledge from their senses, imitating others' actions, and remembering the information—all evidence of higher cognitive functioning. Indeed, a body of evidence suggests that 16- and 20-month-olds are capable of organizing their recall of novel events around causal relations—they know that "what happens" occurs in such a way that one event ordinarily follows another event and that this same sequence of events will again unfold in the same manner in the future (Knopf, Kraus, & Kressley-Mba, 2006).

Today psychologists, neuroscientists, pediatricians, and other developmentalists view infants as very complex creatures who are capable of experiencing, thinking about, and processing enormous amounts of information (Cohen & Cashon, 2006). Building on the developing competencies in the early months of their lives, infants begin to form associations between their own behavior and events in the external world. They progressively gain a conception of the world as an environment that exhibits stable, recurrent, and reliable components and patterns. Such conceptions allow them to begin functioning as effective beings who cause events to happen in the world about them and who evoke social responses from others (Bedrova & Leong, 2007). They also begin to refine their conceptual thinking (Mandler, 2004). Let us begin our exploration of these matters with a consideration of infant learning.

Learning: A Definition

Learning is a fundamental human process. It permits us to adapt to our environment by building on previous experience. Psychologists have traditionally defined learning in terms of three criteria:

- There must be some change in behavior.
- This change must be relatively stable.
- The change must result from experience.

Learning, then, involves a relatively permanent change in a capability or behavior, and it results from experience. As we discussed in Chapter 2, theories of learning fall into three broad categories:

1. Behavioral theories emphasize that people can be conditioned by positive or negative reinforcers.
2. Cognitive theories focus on how to fashion the cognitive structures by which individuals think about their environment.
3. Social learning theories stress the need to provide models for people to imitate.

These three kinds of theories highlight some of the common influences on individuals that facilitate learning.

When Infants Start Learning

A growing body of worldwide research confirms that fetuses in the last trimester are learning while in the womb. Anthony DeCasper and other researchers have investigated fetal and infant auditory perception (DeCasper et al., 1994). They found evidence that fetuses can discriminate between low-pitched notes that are within the range of normal human speech, and they propose that it is possible that fetuses can sense the mother's emotions by differentiating among different types of speech patterns, such as those produced by anger or happiness (Henry, 2001). They believe that some kind of fetal learning is occurring, although its exact mechanism is not understood. The researchers devised a nipple apparatus that activates a tape recorder. By sucking in one specific pattern, newborns would hear their own mother's voice; by sucking in another pattern, they would hear another woman's voice. The babies (some just hours old) tended to suck in a way that would allow them to hear their mother's voice. The researchers concluded that the infants' preferences were affected by their auditory experiences before birth.

In earlier tests, 16 pregnant women read Dr. Seuss's *The Cat in the Hat* to their unborn children twice a day for the last six weeks of gestation—for a total of about 5 hours. After they were born, the infants were allowed to choose, by means of their sucking behavior, to hear either a recording of their mother reading *The Cat in the Hat* or a recording of their mother reading stories by other authors having a different meter. By means of their sucking responses, the infants chose to hear *The Cat in the Hat*. Since this initial research, other studies have indicated that by the 30th week of pregnancy, the fetus can hear and distinguish among sounds and can demonstrate physiological responses, such as accelerated or lowered pulse, to those familiar sounds after birth (Saffran, Werker, & Werner, 2006).

In similar cross-cultural research, Kisilevsky and colleagues studied Chinese fetuses for auditory perception of language and found that fetal heart rates increased when a recording of the mother's voice was played near the mother's abdomen. The fetuses got "excited" as they recognized their mothers' voice and distinguished her voice from the voices of strangers. This research confirms that a fetus is learning in the womb, is capable of memory, and can sustain attention (Kisilevsky et al., 2003). Fetal auditory perception for music was also studied during the last two trimesters of pregnancy. Fetal responses to 5-minute piano recordings of Brahms's *Lullaby* varied from younger

fetuses to older fetuses. Fetuses older than 33 weeks of gestation showed sustained acceleration in heart rate, and those older than 35 weeks showed changes in body movements as well as changes in attention (Kisilevsky et al., 2004).

It appears that infants are born with an innate perception of the *prosody* of music—that is, the rhythm and intonation (Saffran et al., 2006). Jónsdóttir (2001) notes that by the third trimester, fetuses are sensitive to music and clearly hear the *whoosh* and flow of the womb, the mother's heartbeat, and her digestive and breathing sounds. Some suggest that language develops from this innate musical knowledge, since linguists have classified spoken languages according to their rhythmic properties (Loewy, 2004). Parents might interpret these findings to mean that they can give their infants a developmental head start by reading to them or playing classical music before they are born. The findings of DeCasper and colleagues (1994) have prompted research about the development of premature babies and their exposure to the many loud and sometimes harsh sounds in neonatal intensive care units (NICUs), such as beeping machines, alarms, and the conversations of strangers, that might be harmful to the babies' health and progress.

Music therapists continue to study infant crying, babbling, and language development to devise early intervention methods for those children with delayed language. Some parents believe that viewing electronic educational media, such as *Baby Einstein* or *Brainy Baby* videos, can accelerate a baby's language learning and cognitive development. But the American Academy of Pediatrics (2010) issued a policy statement that parents should not allow infant viewing and listening to television for the first two years and that televisions should not be placed in children's bedrooms (see the *Further Developments* box, "Babies in Diapers, Media Viewing, and Cognitive and Language Outcomes"). Many of the responses that babies show are adaptations to specific stimuli for which newborns appear to be biologically prepared (Sirois & Mareschal, 2004), so in a moment we will take another look at Piaget's work, particularly his ideas regarding the sensorimotor period.

Newborn Learning   Developmentalists have long been interested in knowing whether newborns can learn—or whether they can adjust their behavior according to whether it succeeds or fails. Arnold J. Sameroff (1968) conducted a study on infant learning involving neonatal sucking techniques and suggests that the answer is yes. It is generally recognized that two nursing methods are available to newborns—*expression* involves pressing the nipple against the roof of the mouth with the tongue and squeezing milk out of it, and *suction* involves creating a partial vacuum by reducing the pressure inside the mouth and thus pulling the milk from the nipple.

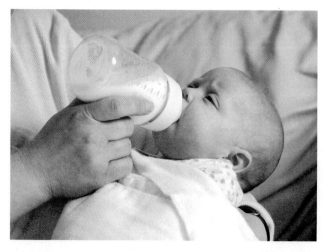

Can a Fetus Learn? Anthony DeCasper conducted research on learning in fetuses and newborns. While pregnant, a baby's mother regularly read a story aloud. After the baby's birth, the infant's sucking is much higher when his mother reads the story (via a recording) than when a stranger reads it.

FURTHER DEVELOPMENTS

Babies in Diapers, Media Viewing, and Cognitive and Language Outcomes

Do you watch television or play DVDs with babies or young children present? As you hold an infant in your arms, are you watching *Monday Night Football* or *American Idol*? Or are you watching *Blue's Clues, Dora the Explorer,* or *Sesame Street*? What about the effects of many hours of television and baby DVD viewing (and hearing) on the cognitive and language development of infants under age 2? Recent studies find that most parents believe the positive educational claims made by the marketing experts (Zimmerman, Christakis, & Meltzoff, 2007). Whereas infants from earlier generations were introduced to language through adult and sibling communication and print media, babies today are being raised in an environment inundated with electronic media. A nationwide survey of more than 1,000 parents reported by the American Academy of Pediatrics in 2007 found that nearly all homes had two or more TVs and two or more DVD or VCR players, almost half had video game equipment, 80 percent had a computer, and three-quarters had an Internet subscription (Vandewater et al., 2007). Yet we just might be placing our infants and toddlers at risk by saturating their early environments with home theaters and large HDTV screens with surround-sound (Kirkorian, Wartella, & Anderson, 2008).

This same survey revealed that infants and toddlers spent an *average* of more than 2 hours daily with television, video, or computer screens. Almost all American families with children under the age of 2 have at least one television in their homes, and close to 20 percent of these young children have a television in their bedrooms. *Two-thirds* of these infants watch TV *every day.* Fewer parents are monitoring children's TV viewing time or content; only about 20 percent of parents believe their children watch too much TV (see Figure 5.1) (Vandewater et al., 2007).

The American Academy of Pediatrics (AAP) (2010a) recommends that caregivers not expose children under age 2 to electronic media—television, videos, DVDs, CDs, computer games, or large-screen movies and that children not have a TV in their rooms. This advice is based on empirical findings showing the harmful effects of aggression and violence in media on preschool and older children (Christakis & Zimmerman, 2007). Children have less interaction with others when media are used in the home or in child-care settings, and this reduced interaction hinders vocabulary development and expressive language (Linebarger & Walker, 2005). Sedentary behaviors such as watching TV and playing video/computer games contribute to obesity in young children

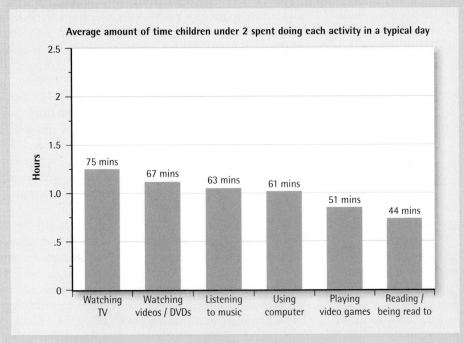

FIGURE 5.1 Daily Activities of Infants Results of a recent parent survey revealed the amount of time that children under age 2 spent, on average, viewing and listening to electronic media on screens.
Source: Vandewater, E. A., Rideout, V. J., Wartella, E. A., Xuan, H., Lee, J. H., & Shim, M. (2007). Digital childhood: Electronic media and technology use among infants, toddlers, and preschoolers. *Pediatrics, 119*(5), 1006–1015.

continued

(Burdette & Whitaker, 2005). Despite these findings, more television programs, DVDs, and computer software are being produced for infants, such as *Baby Einstein* and *Brainy Baby* products. Yet research shows that children under the age of 2 learn better from real-life experiences than from electronic media (Kirkorian et al., 2008). In fact, studies show that children who are exposed to child-directed programs as infants, toddlers, or preschoolers have no greater vocabulary skills or school readiness than those who are not exposed to such material (Barr, Lauricella, Zack, & Calvert, 2010).

Program Content Matters

Children who watched *Dora the Explorer, Blue's Clues, Arthur,* and *Clifford* used more single- and multiple-word utterances than nonviewers. These TV programs have specific strategies embedded into curricula to promote expressive language and vocabulary. *Blue's Clues* and *Dora the Explorer* have characters speaking directly to the child, actively eliciting participation, labeling objects, and providing opportunities for the child to respond. Children who watched *Sesame Street* produced fewer single- and multiple-word utterances; watching Disney videos was unrelated to single- and multiple-word utterances.

An Important Case Study

Caregivers cannot rely solely on television programming to teach language to children. In a classic study, Sachs, Bard, and Johnson (1981) reported on a 3-year-old boy with deaf parents who was exposed to the English language only by television. By age 3 he had acquired some vocabulary, but his grammar was dysfunctional.

Ethnic and Economic Factors

In 2009, researchers at the University of Pennsylvania surveyed more than 1,400 parents. The study found that African American and upper-income young children were more likely to have screen media in their homes. African American children had more traditional screen media, such as TVs and video game systems, whereas Asian American children tended to have the newer media, such as computers with high-speed Internet access. Children living in single-parent homes were more likely to have a TV in their bedrooms. Overall, Latino and African American children had access to fewer books in the home. Boys of all ethnic and economic groups were more likely than girls to play video games. Children of all ethnic backgrounds from higher-income families tended to have fewer media in their bedrooms but more in their homes (especially computers) and to have greater access to books (Lapierre, Piotrowski, & Linebarger, 2010).

This research itself is in its infancy, and longitudinal studies need to be conducted with baby participants. In the meantime, professionals who work with infants and toddlers should discuss media use and viewing habits with their families to help educate them about the possible benefits and drawbacks of the use of electronic media by young children (Conners, Tripathi, Clubb, & Bradley, 2007).

Sameroff devised an experimental nipple that permitted him to regulate the supply of milk an infant received. He provided one group of babies with milk only when they used the expressive method (squeezing the nipple); he gave the second group milk only when they used the suction method.

He found that the infants adapted their responses according to which technique was reinforced. The group that was given milk when they used the expressive method diminished their suction responses—indeed, most abandoned the suction method during the training period. In a second experiment, Sameroff (1968) was able to induce the babies, through reinforcement, to express milk at one of two different pressure levels. These results show that learning can occur among 2- to 5-day-old, full-term infants.

Newborns can also categorize varieties of speech rhythm and can discriminate between sounds made in two languages (Ramus, 2002). It appears that rhythm, phonemes (basic units of sound such as *ba*), syllable structure, and eventual word learning are linked (Houston, Jusczyk, & Jusczyk, 2003). When we first hear a foreign language, we cannot detect the boundaries between words. *Itisasifeverythingrunstogether.* (It is as if everything runs together.) Yet we perceive word boundaries when listening to a language *we have learned.* This is part of the pacing and rhythm of an infant's native language (see Table 5.1 and Figure 5.2).

Autobiographical Memory　In the early 1900s, Freud posed a theory of what he called infantile amnesia or childhood amnesia. Today a spate of books and articles explore many facets of infant memory (Bauer, 2007; Rovee-Collier, Lipsitt, & Hayne, 2000). Most theorists agree that the age of 3 marks a turning point for *autobiographical* memory—the memory of events that happened to oneself.

Consistent with his developmental stage theory, Freud believed that two stages characterize childhood amnesia. In the first stage (before 3 years), people remember little if anything. During the second stage (between the ages of 3 and 7), people remember somewhat but not as much as an adult (considering average rates of forgetting). Freud attributed this amnesia to a person blocking or repressing unacceptable impulses, but today's theorists discredit this view (Brown et al., 2006).

TABLE 5.1 How Do Infants Learn to Distinguish the Sounds of Language?

Young infants can distinguish the patterns of sounds within words and at the ends of words. The waveform in Figure 5.2 represents the sentence "Where are the silences between words?" At the Infant Learning Lab in the Psychology Department at the University of Wisconsin, Madison, the infant sits in the parent's lap and listens to such sounds playing from speakers. This research focuses on tone, rhythm, sequence, memory, and word segmentation. The blue-gray lines indicate silent points in the phrase, which often fall in the middle of a word rather than between words. Note that there is a silent point in the middle of the word *between* and no silent point at the boundary of *between* and *words*.

Source: Professor Saffran's Infant Learning Lab, Psychology Department, University of Wisconsin, Madison. Adapted by permission.

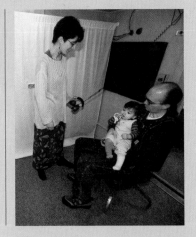

How Do Infants Learn to Distinguish the Sounds of Language? Psychology professor Jenny Saffran stands in a sound-proof room and helps situate David Niergarth and his son Harper, who have volunteered to participate in an infant auditory test study at the Waisman Center Infant Learning Laboratory at the University of Wisconsin–Madison.

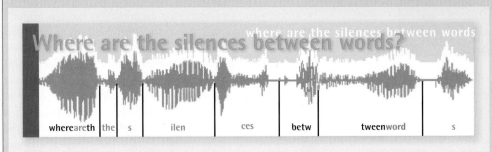

FIGURE 5.2 How Do Human Infants Learn to Use Language?

Current theorists believe that infants lack memory because they never formed memories in the first place. Neisser (2004) says that young children have fewer skills than adults, are less knowledgeable than adults, and do not structure their experience in memorable ways. The difference between child and adult memory takes into account differing cognitive perspectives, or lenses, through which they see the world. Thus, children who do not have adult language capabilities may encode their memories visually. Because the language lens dominates the way memories are encoded, the old, visually encoded memories are "pushed out."

Another lens might be based on the characteristics and values associated with a person's life stage at the time the remembered event occurred. For example, remembering the anxiety of your first day at kindergarten is probably very different from your memory of the first day of a new job. Your coping strategies and storehouse of past experiences made these two events qualitatively different; hence, your memory will also be qualitatively different. Another aspect of the cognitive lens explanation is that because children are physically smaller than adults, the people and objects around them are often remembered as being bigger than they actually were.

Another explanation for childhood amnesia is cognitive development. Piaget believed that infants up to 1½ to

2 years of age (in the sensorimotor stage, to be discussed below) are incapable of symbolically representing the world. They need to see the object in front of them to conceive of it. Similarly, they cannot hold an event in their cognitive storehouse so that it can be recalled later. Even so, this would account for amnesia only up to age 2. Piaget postulates that because children lack the ability to effectively organize their experiences in terms of time, their ability to remember is hampered. It is in the preoperational stage (from ages 3 to 6) that they develop the ability to understand time sequencing. The development of a sense of self at this stage may also play a part in the appearance of autobiographical memory (Howe & Courage, 1993). Having a sense of self provides an organizing principle around which to build a personal history.

A sociocultural approach adds the elements of social interaction and culture (Wang, 2006). According to this view, autobiographical memory is developed as the person interacts with others who share the memory. As parents recall their memories of an experience, the cognitive and linguistic advances the parents possessed at the time of the event help to fill the memory gaps of the young child. Children develop an appreciation of reminiscing through the process of sharing memories with others and thereby being socialized to remember. Thus, according to the socioculturalists, memory is socially constructed.

Infant Memory It is very unlikely that this child, under age 3, will remember his delight in playing with his new pet.

Questions

In what ways have researchers demonstrated that a fetus and a neonate can learn? What theories explain what a young child remembers and why?

Piaget: The Sensorimotor Period

As we saw in Chapter 2, the Swiss developmental psychologist Jean Piaget contributed a great deal to our understanding of how children think, reason, and solve problems. Perhaps more than any other person, Piaget was responsible for the rapid growth of research interest in cognitive development over the past 60 years. Initially, the breadth, imagination, and originality of his work overshadowed other research in the field.

Piaget charted a developmental sequence of stages during which the child constructs increasingly complex notions of the world, and he described how the child acts at each level and how this activity leads to the next level. His most detailed analysis was of the first two years of life, which he calls the sensorimotor period. In Piaget's terms, *sensorimotor* refers to the coordination of motor activities with sensory inputs (perceptions), which is the major task of the **sensorimotor period.** He noted six progressive stages within the sensorimotor period, from a newborn responding with inborn reflexes at birth, to coordinating those reflexes, to becoming more aware and responding to people and objects, to actively and purposefully exploring his or her environment. Over the first two years, the

infant comes to integrate the sensory, motor, and perceptual systems; develops the capacity to look at what she or he is listening to; and learns to grasp and walk by visual, auditory, or tactile cues. Infants learn to *habituate*—that is, they look at and attend to novel stimulation and then look away when no longer interested (Schöner & Thelen, 2006). By age 2, Piaget said, the child is like a little "scientist," continually learning by trial and error and *deferred imitation*—copying behaviors witnessed earlier.

Babies also develop the capacity to view the external world as a permanent place. Infants fashion a notion of **object permanence**—they come to view a thing as having a reality of its own that extends beyond their immediate perception of it. As adults, we take this notion for granted. But infants do not necessarily do so during the first six to nine months in the sensorimotor period. Between six and nine months, a baby becomes capable of searching for an object that an adult has hidden under a cloth. The child will search for it on the basis of information about where the object went. In so doing, infants demonstrate their understanding that the object exists even when it cannot be seen. At this time a caregiver first plays "peek-a-boo," and the child quickly learns to remove the cloth or hands from the person's face and is delighted with the caregiver's reappearance. Likewise, the child wants to cover his or her face and reappear to you! Recent research findings from a study of Swedish infants indicate that infants imitate from memory (deferred imitation) well before their first birthday. These imitation skills are related to communication abilities that develop about five months later (Heimann et al., 2006).

According to Piaget, another characteristic of the sensorimotor period is the inability of infants to represent the world to themselves internally. They are limited to the immediate here and now. Because they cannot fashion symbolic mental representations of the world, they "know" the

Peek-a-Boo Between 6 and 9 months of age, children enjoy taking turns with a caregiver playing a game of "peek-a-boo," which reflects an understanding of object permanence.

world only through their own perceptions and their own actions on it. For example, infants in the sensorimotor stage know food only as something they can eat and manipulate with their fingers. According to Piaget, infants are unable to form a static mental image of food "in their heads" in the absence of the actual visual display. "Out of sight, out of mind" is an appropriate description of how the infant perceives the external world during the sensorimotor stage.

In sum, during the sensorimotor period, infants coordinate the ways they interact with their environment, recognize the environment's permanence, and begin to "know" the environment, although their knowledge of the environment is limited to their sensory and motor interactions with it. The child then enters into the next developmental period ready to develop language and other symbolic ways of representing the world.

Sensorimotor Development and Craniosacral Therapy

The Western understanding of the craniosacral system comes from ancient traditions of healing massage in India, China, the Middle East, and North America. Underlying an infant's ability to develop sensorimotor skills is a critical physiological system in the body called the **craniosacral system**—a closed system that involves the pumping, or inflow and outflow, of cerebrospinal fluid within the membranes around the brain and spinal cord. *Cerebrospinal fluid (CSF)* circulates between cells of the brain and spinal cord and fills the spaces between the cells or *neurons*. This fluid helps the brain float, serves as a shock absorber for any sudden movement of or blow to the cranium, provides nutrients to the brain and spinal cord, and washes away metabolic waste products and toxic substances, among other functions (Upledger, 2004). The fluid within the craniosacral system flows in a constant but rhythmic cycle. Cranial bones make minute adjustments to allow for this rhythmic flow.

Injury to a newborn's skull, face, or neck prior to birth, during birth, or after birth can restrict the natural rhythmic flow of the cerebrospinal fluid—creating excessive or restricted fluid pressure on various areas of the delicate brain or spinal cord. The overlap of a neonate's cranial bone plates that allows for easier passage through the birth canal should correct itself in a few days, but in some babies it does not. Other babies that have craniosacral problems are those born with abnormal head shapes and spinal, pelvic, and hip problems. Infants who develop a flattened skull from being placed on their backs in their cribs for many hours also benefit from *craniosacral therapy (CST)*.

The goal of craniosacral therapy is to have each child reach his or her optimal functional state—allowing for full sensorimotor development. Doctors of osteopathy, physical therapists, massage therapists, and chiropractors are learning CST light-touch massage techniques to help babies and children develop normally.

Post-Piagetian Research

Piaget's work has encouraged others to investigate children's cognitive development. They are intrigued by the idea that infants do not think in the same ways that adults do, and they have particularly studied object permanence, habituation, and deferred imitation in infants (Bremner et al., 2007). This body of research is refining Piaget's insights. For example, researchers have found that infants possess a set of object search skills more sophisticated than Piaget had imagined (Rochat & Striano, 1998). By 4 months of age, they might understand that an object continues to exist when their view of it is blocked, even though they might not yet be capable of coordinating their movements to search for it (Bertenthal & Longo, 2007).

Playing Is Learning   Developmental psychologists find that children do not develop an interest in objects and object skills in a social vacuum, and play is essential to healthy development. When caregivers play with babies, they give the babies clues to what they should do, how to do it, and when they should do it (Ginsberg, 2007). By playing with infants, parents and caregivers provide experiences that youngsters cannot generate by themselves (Vygotsky, 1978). More contemporary parents are substituting organized activities or media viewing (television, video, and computer) for playtime because of hurried lifestyles and an increased focus on academic preparation. Researchers find that playing with children is one of the cornerstones of healthy family life, which includes listening, caring, guiding, and having fun together (Ginsberg, 2007).

In the course of play activities, infants acquire and refine their capacities for social interaction, so that by the end of the first year they share attention, emotional

Play Activities Are Essential for Learning Infants enjoy coordinating their sensory and motor capabilities during play as they develop social, cognitive, and emotional skills.

feelings, and intentions with others. All the while infants gain a sense of their society's culture and acquire some of the skills essential to living in that culture. Caregivers—the curators of culture—transmit the knowledge, attitudes, values, and behaviors essential for effective participation in society, and they help to gradually transform infants into genuine social beings capable of manipulating objects and acting in concert with others. In playing with their youngsters, caregivers provide sociocultural guidance for the children's later cognitive and language performance (Rogoff et al., 2007). Mothers are typically prominent in the infant's learning environment, so the mother's emotional states can influence development.

Consequences of Maternal Depression   Clinically depressed mothers might have such debilitating symptoms that they are virtually incapable of meeting their children's needs. Clinical depression is an emotional disorder characterized by a mood drop that can last for months, even years. As depression deepens, it commonly involves insomnia, lack of interest in work, low energy, loss of appetite, reduced sexual desire, persistent sadness, hopeless feelings, and profound overall emotional despair. In this condition, even routine tasks become hard to perform. Depressed people report difficulty concentrating, remembering things, and getting their thoughts together. Some suffer considerable anxiety as part of their depression. Postpartum depression occurs in at least 10 percent of U.S. women, but the rate for women with a history of postpartum depression is higher (Sohr-Preston & Scaramella, 2006).

The children of depressed mothers are susceptible to developmental deficits because of disturbances in the mother-infant interaction. Research shows that depressed mothers often appear sad, are given to frequent sighs, fail to interact playfully with their youngsters, seem insensitive to their babies' needs, and focus their gaze downward (Knitzer, Theberg, & Johnson, 2008).

Because depressed mothers have a reduced capacity for caregiving, nurturing, and stimulating their infants, their youngsters tend to lag behind in their cognitive adaptations, including emotional, language, and social development. Kaplan, Bachorowski, and Zarlengo-Strouse (1999) observed that mothers suffering from depression are unlikely to use child-directed speech—that is, the singsong melodic speech that engages and maintains infant attention. Rather, depressed mothers tend to talk to their infants in a monotone that does not engage the infant's attention.

The babies of depressed women are more withdrawn, unresponsive, and inattentive than other youngsters. They may cry and fuss a good deal, appear apathetic and listless, have problems sleeping and feeding, and fail to grow normally, which is sometimes diagnosed as **failure to thrive (FTT).** Current thinking about FTT is that there is problematic mother-infant interaction, especially

less touching between mother and child. Some researchers suggest, "It is possible that the behavioral characteristics of the infant with failure-to-thrive may be related to underlying physiologic response patterns, specifically, activity of the autonomic nervous system" (Steward, Moser, & Ryan-Wenger, 2001, p. 162).

Matters can be complicated by a mother's disciplinary ineptness. Depressed mothers tend to be inconsistent and may alternately ignore their children and lash out at them with strict prohibitions. Such behavior is confusing to youngsters, and they may respond by being negative, challenging limits, resenting punishment, and becoming unusually argumentative. A vicious cycle is likely to ensue wherein this difficult behavior reinforces the mother's depression and sense of parental inadequacy. Clinical depression is usually a treatable disorder that responds to antidepressant medication and other psychiatric interventions. Before depression can be treated effectively, however, it must be recognized and brought to the attention of appropriate medical personnel who provide close monitoring of medication effects and make recommendations for skilled psychotherapy.

Questions

Why does Piaget call infancy the sensorimotor period, and what are an infant's major cognitive accomplishments during the first two years of life? What is craniosacral therapy? How does a mother's depression affect an infant's cognitive development?

Bruner on Modes of Cognitive Representation

One of the first U.S. psychologists to appreciate the importance of Piaget's work was Jerome S. Bruner. Bruner, a distinguished psychologist, has served as president of the American Psychological Association. Many of his research papers show a strong Piagetian influence, especially in the way he treats the stages of cognitive development.

Through the years, however, Bruner and Piaget developed differences of opinion about the roots and nature of intellectual growth. The two disagreed over Bruner's (1970) view that "the foundations of any subject may be taught to anybody at any age in some form." Piaget, in contrast, held to a rigorous stage approach, in which knowledge of certain subjects can be gained only when all the components of that knowledge are present and properly developed.

One of Bruner's main contributions to our understanding of cognitive development concerns the changes that occur in children's favored modes for representing the world as they grow older (Bruner, 1990). According to Bruner, at first (during Piaget's sensorimotor period) the representative process is *enactive:* Children represent the world through their motor acts. In the preschool and kindergarten years, *ikonic representation* prevails: Children use mental images or pictures that are closely linked to perception. In the middle school years, the emphasis shifts to *symbolic representation:* Children use arbitrary and socially standardized representations of things; this enables them to internally manipulate the symbols that are characteristic of abstract and logical thought. Thus, according to Bruner, we "know" something in three ways: through doing it (enactive), through a picture or image of it (ikonic), or through some *symbolic* means such as language (symbolic).

Take, for instance, our "knowing" a knot. We can know the knot by tying it; we can have a mental image of the knot as an object on the order of either a pretzel or "bunny ears" (or a mental "motion picture" of the knot being formed); and we can represent a knot linguistically by combining four alphabetical letters, *k-n-o-t* (or by linking utterances in sentences to describe the process of tying string). Through these three such general means, humans increase their ability to achieve and use knowledge.

Continuity in Cognitive Development from Infancy

Psychologists have long been interested in knowing whether mental competence and intelligence later in life can be predicted from cognitive performance in infancy. Until recently, psychologists believed that there was little continuity between early and later capabilities. But now they are increasingly concluding that individual differences in mental performance in infancy are, to a moderate extent, developmentally continuous across childhood and perhaps beyond (Cronin & Mandich, 2005). Thus, U.S. prevention policies and early intervention agencies have been established, reflecting the conviction that efforts to assist infants with cognitive and language delays should begin during the early months of life. The concept of cognitive continuity has implications for social policy and future research (Dawson, Ashman, & Carver, 2000).

Decrement and Recovery in Attentiveness Information-processing models of intelligence have contributed to this reassessment. For people to mentally represent and process information concerning the world about them, they must first pay attention to various aspects of their environment. Two components of attention seem most indicative of intelligence in youngsters:

- *Decrement of attention*—losing interest in watching an object or event that is unchanging
- *Recovery of attention*—regaining interest when something new happens

Youngsters who tire more quickly when looking at or hearing the same thing are more efficient processors of information. So are those who prefer the novel over the familiar. These infants typically like more complex tasks, show advanced sensorimotor development, explore their environment rapidly, play in relatively sophisticated ways, and solve problems rapidly. Similarly, the rapidness with which adults learn something is associated with measures of their intelligence. Given equivalent opportunities, more intelligent people learn more than less intelligent people in the same amount of time. Not surprisingly, then, psychologists are finding that decrement and recovery of attention seem to predict childhood cognitive competence more accurately than do more traditional tests of infant development.

The patterns children reveal in attending to information reflect their cognitive capabilities and, more particularly, their ability to construct workable *schemas* (à la Piaget) of what they see and hear. As Harriet L. Rheingold (1985) points out, mental development proceeds through transformations of novelty into familiarity. Each thing in the environment begins as something new, so development progresses as infants turn something new into something known. In turn, once you know something, it provides a context for recognizing what is new, so the known provides the foundation for further mental development. Both the familiar and the novel, then, compel attraction and are reciprocal processes central to lifetime adaptation.

Questions

Do you agree with Bruner that "the foundation of any subject may be taught to anybody at any age in some form"? Should parents make efforts to boost their babies' brain power as early as possible? What research evidence supports early intervention efforts for those infants with physical, cognitive, and language delays?

LANGUAGE AND THOUGHT

Humans are set apart from other animals by their possession of a highly developed system of language communication. This system enables them to acquire and transmit the knowledge and ideas provided by the culture in which they live. To be sure, a number of scientists claim that skills characteristic of the use of language have been developed in a dozen or so chimpanzees (Savage-Rumbaugh et al., 1993). But even though chimps exhibit skills clearly related to human skills, the manual gestures they can learn for about 100 conventional signs

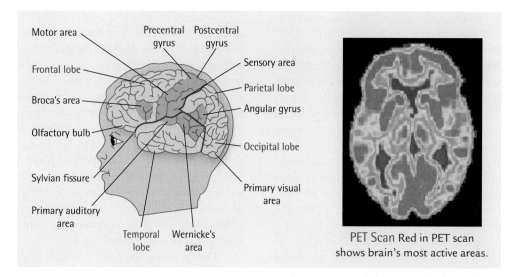

FIGURE 5.3 Where and How Babies Process Sound and Language The drawing at the left shows the left hemisphere of the cerebral cortex. The temporal lobes of each hemisphere interpret the sounds heard by each ear. Often one side is more "dominant" in hearing, though both sides hear a given sound. For most individuals, speech-language is located in Broca's and Wernicke's areas. The child is learning language by observing a speaker's mouth and facial expressions and is also using the visual/occipital cortex. It really is a whole brain effort! Note the full brain involvement in language on the PET scan to the right.

are hardly equivalent to our intricate and subtle language capacity (MacWhinney, 2005). And the methods by which chimps typically must be trained are quite different from the spontaneous ways in which children learn a language. Apes learn to deal with signs sluggishly and often only after being plied with bananas, cola, and M&Ms (Gould, 1983).

Language is a structured system of sound patterns (words and sentences) with socially standardized meanings. Language provides a set of symbols that rather thoroughly catalog the objects, events, and processes in the human environment (DeVito, 1970). Humans process and interpret language in the left cerebral cortex (see Figure 5.3).

The Functional Importance of Language

Language makes two vital contributions to human life: It enables us to communicate with one another (*inter*-individual), and it facilitates individual thinking (*intra*-individual). First, **communication** is the process by which people transmit information, ideas, attitudes, and emotions to one another. This feature of language enables human beings to coordinate complex group activities. They fit their developing lines of activity to the developing actions of others on the basis of the "messages" they provide one another. Thus, language provides the foundation for family and for economic, political, religious, and educational institutions—indeed, for society itself.

The second contribution of language is that it facilitates *thought* and other cognitive processes. Language enables us to encode our experiences by assigning names to them. It provides us with concepts by which we discern the world around us and categorize new information. Thus, language helps us partition the environment into manageable areas relevant to our concerns. Language also allows us to deal with past experiences and to anticipate future experiences. It enlarges the scope of our environment and experience. This second function, the relation of language to thought, has been the subject of intense debate. Let us examine each of these functions more closely.

Thought Shapes Language

Those who believe that thought shapes language argue that thought takes place whether or not language exists. They believe that words are necessary only for conveying thoughts to others and that we do not need language to understand our own thoughts. For instance, some types of thought are visual images and "feelings." You become aware of language only when someone asks you to describe something—the view from your room, the main street in your hometown, a person you know. You try to translate a mental picture into words. But you may find that the task of verbally describing images is complex and difficult.

Piaget (1952, 1962) took the view that structured language presupposes the prior development of other kinds of mental representation. On the basis of his studies, Piaget concluded that language has only a limited role in a young child's mental activity. According to Piaget, children form mental images of objects (water, food, a ball) and events (drinking, sucking, holding) that are based on mental reproduction or imitation, not on word labels. Thus, the child's task in acquiring words is to map language onto her preexisting concepts.

However, we will see that Piaget oversimplifies matters. In some areas, representation does precede language. For instance, William Zachry (1978) finds that solid progress in mental representation is necessary for some forms of language production. He suggests that children gain the ability to represent certain activities internally as images. Thus, the various actions associated with bottles would come to be represented by such mental pictures as holding a bottle, sucking a bottle, and pouring from a bottle. Later, the child comes to represent the "bottle activities" by the word *bottle*. The word *bottle* then becomes a semantic, or meaning, "marker" that represents the qualities associated with a bottle—holdable, suckable, pourable, and so on. In this manner, Zachry says, words come to function as semantic markers for mental pictures.

Young children have a tendency to search for hidden, nonobvious features when learning the meaning of words (Graf Estes, Evans, Alibali, & Saffran, 2007). More specifically, children seem predisposed to "whole object" meanings for nouns: They assume that a new noun refers to an entire object rather than to one of its parts. For example, consider the noun *dog*. Youngsters must learn that dog can refer both to a specific object (for instance, Fido) and to the category Dog, yet the word *dog* does not apply to individual aspects of the object (for instance, its nose or tail); to relationships between the object and other objects (for example, between a dog and its toy); or to the object's behavior (for instance, the dog's eating, barking, or sleeping). Were children to weigh these and countless other possible meanings before arriving at the correct mapping of the word *dog,* they would be overwhelmed by an unmanageable sea of dog-related inputs. Research also indicates that young children keep the generic image of an object in their long-term memory (Gelman & Raman, 2007).

Some researchers believe that young children practice "fast mapping" when they learn language. This means they are often able to remember the meaning of a word after one exposure (Schafer & Plunkett, 1998). In addition, children are cognitively biased toward an assumption that words refer to mutually exclusive categories. In other words, if a child knows the word for an object, she will reject another word for the same object (Gelman, 2003). So we see that some aspects of linguistic development are linked to a preexisting level of conceptual development.

Infants as young as 4 months of age possess the ability to partition the color spectrum into four basic hues—blue, green, yellow, and red. For example, infants respond differently to two wavelengths selected from adjacent adult hue categories, such as "blue" at 480 millimicrons and "green" at 510 millimicrons. Yet infants do not respond differently to two wavelengths selected from the same adult hue category such as "blue" at 450 and "blue" at 480 millimicrons. It seems, then, that the mental representations of infants are organized into blue, green, yellow, and red, and not into the subtle shades of these colors. They do not respond to exact wavelength codes, which, for adults, make up the color spectrum (Bornstein & Marks, 1982). Only later do the children come to name these categories.

Such findings suggest that color organization precedes, and is not a product of, the categories (the verbal labels *blue, green, yellow,* and *red*) provided by language and culture (Soja, 1994). Additional research confirms that infants spontaneously form categories during the *prelinguistic period* (Roberts, 1988). In some respects, then, children's knowledge of language depends on a prior mastery of concepts about the world to which words will refer (Coldren & Colombo, 1994).

Language Shapes Thought

The second viewpoint is that language develops with, at the same time as, or even prior to the development of thought. According to this viewpoint, language shapes thought. This theory follows in the traditions of George Herbert Mead (1934), Benjamin L. Whorf (1956), and Lev Vygotsky (1962).

This perspective emphasizes the part that concepts play in our thinking. Life becomes more manageable when stimuli are partitioned into classifiable units and into areas relevant to our concerns. Through **conceptualization**—grouping perceptions into categories on the basis of certain similarities—children and adults alike can identify and classify informational input. Without the ability to categorize, life would seem chaotic. By using categories, adults and infants "tune out" certain stimuli and "tune in" others (Needham & Baillargeon, 1998). Categorization enables us to view an object as being the same despite the fact that it varies from perspective to perspective and from moment to moment. And people are able to treat two different but similar objects as equivalent—as being the same kind of thing. For example, two flowers of different sizes, shapes, or colors are still both recognized as flowers. Categorization, and making the mental leap from the specific to the general, allows for more advanced cognitive thinking. Recent research indicates that infants are more likely to categorize when images are not accompanied by an auditory stimulus or by spoken words or labels (Robinson & Sloutsky, 2007).

Concepts also perform a second service. They enable individuals to go beyond the immediate information provided to them. People can mentally manipulate concepts and imaginatively link them to fashion new adaptations. This attribute of concepts allows humans to make additional inferences about the unobserved properties of objects and events (Birney et al., 2005). Humans have an advantage over other animals in that we can use words in the conceptualization process. Some social and behavioral scientists claim that the activity of *naming*, or verbally labeling, offers three advantages:

- It facilitates thought by producing linguistic symbols for integrating ideas.
- It expedites memory storage and retrieval via a linguistic code.
- It influences perception by sensitizing people to some stimuli and desensitizing them to others.

Critics contend, however, that it is easy to oversimplify and overstate the relationship between language and various cognitive processes. Lenneberg (1967) and Nelson (1973) note that a child's first words are often sounds strung together that parents interpret as words (*da da* becomes "daddy") and the naming of favorite objects (*bir* becomes "bird," for the family pet). First words typically occur around the child's first birthday and are considered a major cognitive milestone (Evans, 2007). As noted previously, color organization in infants precedes learned categories provided by language. The suggestion here is that language is not the sole source for the internal representation on which thought depends. Nor is language the sole source for the representation of information in memory (Perlmutter & Myers, 1976). And language has at best only a minor impact on perception.

Even though these perspectives stand in direct contrast, many linguists and psychologists believe that there are many ways to look at the relationship between language and thought. Some theorists believe that language and thought need not be mirror images of each other. Many aspects of language change over time as a consequence of cultural forces and interpretation of meaning (Malt, Sloman, & Gennari, 2003).

Question

Historically, there have been two opposing views in scientific circles regarding the relationship between language and thought. The first view is that thought shapes language, and the second is that language shapes thought by providing the concepts or categories into which individuals mentally sort their perceptual stimuli. Do you think, then, that someone who is both blind and deaf is without thoughts—or even without language?

THEORIES OF LANGUAGE ACQUISITION

How are we to explain the development of speech in children? Is the human organism genetically and biologically "preprogrammed" for language usage? Or is language acquired through learning processes? These questions expose a nerve in the long-standing nature-versus-nurture controversy: *Nativists* (hereditarians) and environmentalists vigorously disagree on their answers—and the most recent empirical research supports the interplay of both genetic and environmental influences. Recent theories take an evolutionary approach to language acquisition in humans (Fisher & Marcus, 2006). Combining the information from recent developments in the fields of linguistics, psychology, genomics, and neuroimaging, researchers have developed a view of language as a complex series of adaptations occurring on an evolutionary scale.

Nativist Theories

Youngsters are said to begin life with the underpinnings of later speech perception and comprehension, just as they begin life with the specialized anatomy of the vocal tract and the speech centers in the brain. Nativists (hereditarians) contend that human beings are "prewired" by their brain circuitry for language use—that the potential for language acquisition has been "built into" humans by genes and needs only to be elicited by an appropriate "triggering mechanism" in the same way that nutrition triggers growth. They view humans as having evolved in ways that make some kinds of behavior, such as language acquisition, easier and more natural than others. And a growing body of empirical findings supports a variety of genetic contributions.

Significantly, recent studies report that there are auditory genes and mutations of genes associated with deafness. Research is progressing rapidly to discover the molecular mechanics underlying hearing and hearing impairments. And there are other exciting genetic studies from Harvard Medical School that are illuminating the mystery of hearing and hearing impairments (Resendes, Williamson, & Morton, 2001). Notably, over the past decade British and American researchers have discovered further details about the role of genes in language production.

Research by Noam Chomsky (1957, 1965, 1980, 1995), Eric H. Lenneberg (1967, 1969), Peter D. Eimas (1985), and Steven Pinker (1994, 2001) also focuses on the biological endowments that human beings bring to the environmental context of language development.

Noam Chomsky's Nativist Theory
Noam Chomsky, a renowned linguist at the Massachusetts Institute of

TABLE 5.2 Some of the 42 Phonetic Sounds in Modern English

An infant's first "cooing" sounds are simple vowel sounds, with the mouth open and little work done by the tongue or lips.

Phoneme	Spelling(s) and Example Words	Meaningful Names
/A/	a (table), a_e (bake), ai (train), ay (say)	Long A; Fonzie's greeting
/E/	e (me), ee (feet), ea (leap), y (baby)	Long E; shriek
/I/	i (I), i_e (bite), igh (light), y (sky)	Long I
/O/	o (okay), o_e (bone), oa (soap), ow (low)	Long O; Oh, I see

Technology, has provided a nativist theory of language development that has had a major impact on education and psychology over the past 50 years (Chomsky, 1957, 1965, 1975). Supporters and critics alike acknowledge that Chomsky's theoretical formulations have provided many new directions in the study of linguistics.

Central to Chomsky's position is the observation that mature speakers of a language can understand and produce an infinite set of sentences, even sentences they have never before heard, read, or uttered and therefore could not have learned. The explanation for this, argues Chomsky, is that human beings possess an inborn language-generating mechanism, which he terms the **language acquisition device (LAD).** Chomsky sees the human brain as wired to simplify the chaos of the auditory world by sorting through incoming frequencies and shunting speech sounds into 42 intelligible **phonemes** (the smallest units of language, such as long *A*, as in the word *bake*) (see Table 5.2). In the process of language acquisition, children merely need to learn the peculiarities of their society's language, not the basic structure of language. Although Chomsky's theory has attracted a good deal of attention as well as controversy, it is difficult to test by established scientific procedures and hence remains neither verified nor disproved.

In support of his view, Chomsky points out that the world's languages differ in *surface structure*—for example, in the words they use. But they have basic similarities in their composition, which he calls *deep structure*. The most universal features of deep structure include having nouns and verbs and the ability to pose questions, give commands, and express negatives. Chomsky suggests that through preverbal, intuitive rules—*transformational grammar*—individuals turn deep structure into surface structure, and vice versa.

The Twins' Early Development Study Plomin and colleagues (Colledge et al., 2002; Plomin & Dale, 2000) have been studying 3,000 twin pairs born in the years from 1994 to 1996 in England and Wales in the *Twins' Early Development Study (TEDS)*. The goal of this longitudinal study in behavioral genetics is to chart a course to identify specific genes in multiple-gene systems that influence language abilities and disabilities (Colledge et al., 2002; Plomin & Dale, 2000). Extensive data were collected and analyzed on DNA samples and measures of early language delay in these young participants at ages 2, 3, and 4. The results at age 2 for these participants demonstrate substantial differences in the etiology, or cause, of individual differences within the normal range and the low-performance range.

Research on a group of 4-year-old twins from the TEDS investigated whether language impairment is as much affected by genetic factors as language ability is. The results of this study confirmed the findings of four previous twin studies that indicated substantial genetic influence on language impairment. The study found that language disability is more influenced by genetic factors than language ability (Spinath et al., 2004). Another study of 4-year-old twins found that although there is some difference, genetic and environmental influences on language impairment are similar for boys and girls (Viding et al., 2004).

The Cambridge Language and Speech Project British researchers estimate that between 2 and 5 percent of children who are otherwise unimpaired have significant difficulties in acquiring language, despite adequate intelligence and opportunity (Lai et al., 2001). Steven Pinker (2001) and colleagues (Lai et al., 2001) have identified a mutated form of the *FOXP2* gene in a three-generational British family that has a severe speech/language disorder.

Although Pinker does not believe language impairments can be linked to one single gene, the *FOXP2* mutation appears to be responsible for the specific language disorder in this family. This gene produces actions on a group of proteins affecting the brain at an early stage in development, leading to abnormality in the brain circuitry needed for normal speech and language. This is the first discovery of a direct link between a speech/language disorder and a specific gene. Subsequent research findings dispute the link between specific language impairments and the *FOXP2* gene (Newbury et al., 2002). However, it has been known for some time that specific language impairments (SLIs) often run in families: "First degree relatives of affected individuals are 7 times as likely to develop SLI as a member of the general population" (Williams et al., 2001, p. 1).

Since 1982, researchers at the Institute for Behavioral Genetics in Boulder have studied over 200 pairs of identical twins and 150 pairs of same-sex fraternal twins in which at least one twin in the pair met the criteria for reading disability (using many performance measures). Significantly, in two-thirds of the pairs of identical twins, both members of the pair were affected, whereas same-sex fraternal twins shared a concordance rate of about one-third (DeFries, 1999).

International Molecular Genetics Study of Autism Autism is a neurological disorder that appears in "normal" children at about age 2 who regress and show significant deficits in communication and social interaction, language impairment, preoccupation with fantasy, and unusual repetitive or excessive behaviors (Weismer, Lord, & Esler, 2010). Autism and related disorders occur in as many as 1 in 110 children (1 in 70 boys and 1 in 315 girls) (Centers for Disease Control and Prevention [CDC], 2009b), and the Autistic Society reports that the incidence of cases is escalating around the world. However, some research indicates that some of this apparent increase is due to children who were previously diagnosed with another disorder being later re-diagnosed with autism (Bishop, Whitehouse, Watt, & Line, 2008).

Autistic children require speech and language therapy, occupational therapy, and adaptive physical education and often need life-long supervision and care. The cost over a lifetime to care for a person with autism can exceed $3 million, with yearly costs for medical and nonmedical needs totaling around $70,000 (CDC, 2009b). Over the past 20 years, family and twin studies of autism in England, Germany, and the United States have revealed that genes play a significant role in most cases of autism. Furthermore, these studies also suggest that the same genes may be involved in the development of other developmental disorders, such as Asperger's syndrome and other, milder difficulties of communication and social interaction. (See the *Further Developments* box on pages 172–173 in Chapter 6, "The Rising Incidence of Autism," for more information about autism.)

Findings from recent data reveal that autism is influenced by complex, yet strong, genetic factors linked to specific locations on chromosomes 2, 7, and 16 (Palferman, Matthew, & Turner, 2001). Monozygotic (identical) twins show a relatively high concordance for autism, whereas dizygotic (fraternal) twins show a smaller concordance. The recurrence risk for siblings is far greater than for the general population (Hallmayer et al., 2002). These are just a few of the examples of current research findings that support the nativist view of language/speech development and impairments. The goal of these researchers is to discover the mutated genes, identify those infants and young children most likely to be affected with these auditory/speech/language disorders, and design medical/pharmacological intervention methods that will improve the children's language/communication skills. Other researchers are investigating possible genetic, environmental/toxic, or pharmaceutical causes of autism (Lathe, 2008).

Most Children Acquire Language with Little Difficulty Even very young children master an incredibly complex and abstract set of rules for transforming strings of sounds into meanings. By way of illustration, consider that there are 3,628,800 ways to rearrange the 10 words in the following sentence:

> Try to rearrange any ordinary sentence consisting of ten words.

However, only one arrangement of the words is grammatically meaningful and correct. Nativists say that a youngster's ability to distinguish the one correct sentence from the 3,628,799 incorrect possibilities cannot arise through experience alone (Allman, 1991). Likewise, consider how formidable a foreign language such as Japanese or Arabic seems to you.

Adult Speech Is Inconsistent, Garbled, and Sloppy Reflect for a moment on how a conversation carried on in an unfamiliar language sounds to you; it probably sounds more like one giant word than neat packages of words. Or listen to a conversation between two adults; it is full of false starts, "ums," and many "filler phrases" such as "you know." Indeed, linguists have experimentally shown that even in our own language, we often cannot make out a word correctly if it is taken out of context. From recorded conversations, linguists splice out individual words, play them back to people, and ask the people to identify the words. Listeners can generally understand only about half the words, although the same words were perfectly intelligible to them in the original conversation (Cole, 1979).

Children's Speech Is Not a Mechanical Playback of Adult Speech Children combine words in unique ways and also make up words. Expressions such as "I buyed," "foots," "gooder," "Jimmy hurt hisself," and the like reveal that children do not imitate adult speech in a strict fashion. Rather, according to nativists, children are fitting their speech in underlying language systems with which they are born, so exceptions are not initially mastered.

Concurrent to the exciting findings by geneticists, growing numbers of psychologists and other social scientists are exploring the role of input in the language acquisition process (Mueller Gathercole & Hoff, 2007) and the influence of language experience on speech perception and production in infants (Polka, Rvachew, & Mattock, 2007).

Babies Communicate with Caregivers Through their own gestures and sounds, babies are communicating before they can speak a formal language.
Source: Brian and Greg Walker: *Hi and Lois.* November 5, 2007.

Learning and Interactionist Theories

Some researchers have followed in the tradition of B. F. Skinner (1957), who argued that language is acquired in the same manner as any other behavior—through learning processes of reinforcement. Researchers using computer simulations of parental speech as input have been successful in simulating the patterns of children's language development (Gobert, Freudenthal, & Pine, 2004). Some believe that language acquisition depends on social interaction (Bohannon & Bonvillian, 2009). Other researchers, most notably Lev Vygotsky, believe that complex mental activities, such as speech, have their origins in social contexts. We will consider Vygotsky's theories further in Chapter 7, because his ideas have been applied mostly to older children. Others have studied the details of interaction between caregivers and youngsters and how that contributes to the acquisition of language (Baumwell, Tamis-LeMonda, & Bornstein, 1997). Indeed, language use might begin quite early.

As we noted earlier in the chapter, DeCasper's research suggests that babies have sensitivity to speech that starts even before birth. While they are in the uterus, they apparently hear "the melody of language." After birth this sensitivity provides them with clues about which sounds belong together. The ability of neonates to discriminate between speech samples spoken in their mother's native language and samples spoken in an unfamiliar language could derive from the unique melodic qualities found in the linguistic signals to which they were exposed prenatally (Fernald, 1990). Young infants respond more calmly to lower-pitched tones than to higher-pitched tones, and they especially seem to enjoy the melody of common lullabies. Every culture has its own renditions of melodies and rhythms that seem to calm a baby. If you haven't heard one lately, take a few seconds and listen to a common lullaby (some can be heard at www.babycenter.com under Lullaby Lyrics). Here is a common one:

Twinkle, twinkle, little star
How I wonder what you are!

Up above the world so high
Like a diamond in the sky
Twinkle, twinkle, little star
How I wonder what you are

Other researchers suggest that babies intensively tune in to the subtleties of their native language for the first six to eight months before refining their listening practices and that they eventually come to ignore sounds that do not exist in their native language (Werker & Stager, 1997).

Caregiver Speech Much recent research has focused on caregiver speech. In caregiver speech, mothers and fathers systematically modify the language they use with adults when addressing infants and young people. **Caregiver speech** differs from everyday speech in its simplified vocabulary, higher pitch, exaggerated intonation, short simple sentences, and high proportion of questions and imperatives. Parents use caregiver speech with preverbal infants in numerous European languages, Japanese, and Mandarin Chinese (Fernald & Morikawa, 1993).

For their part, young infants show a listening preference for caregiver speech with its higher overall pitch, wider pitch excursions, more distinctive pitch contours, slower tempo, longer pauses, and increased emphatic focus (Fernald, 1985). Researchers believe that levels of auditory recognition in infants are predictive of cognitive abilities in early childhood.

Speech characterized by the first two characteristics of caregiver speech—simplified vocabulary and higher pitch—is termed baby talk. Baby talk has been documented in numerous languages, from Gilyak and Comanche (languages of small, isolated, preliterate Old World and New World communities) to Arabic and Marathi (languages spoken by people with literary traditions). Furthermore, adults phonologically simplify vocabulary for children—*wa-wa* for "water," *choo-choo* for "train," *tummy* for "stomach," and so on. Researchers have found that caregiver speech varies according to caregivers' level of education, yet there is a common pattern of increase within each caregiver group across age of the child (Huttenlocher et al., 2007).

The Interactional Nature of Caregiver Speech   The interactional nature of caregiver speech actually begins with birth (Rheingold & Adams, 1980). Hospital staff, both men and women, use caregiver speech with the newborns in their care. The speech focuses primarily on the baby's behavior and characteristics and on the adult's own care-taking activities. Moreover, the caregivers speak as though the infants understand them. Their words reveal that they view the newborns as persons with feelings, wants, wishes, and preferences. Similarly, a burp, smile, yawn, cough, or sneeze typically elicits a comment to the infant from the caregiver (Snow, 1977). Often the utterances are in the form of questions, which the caregivers then answer as they imagine the children might respond. If a baby smiles, a parent might say, "You're happy, aren't you?" Or if the child burps, the caregiver might say, "Excuse me!"

Indeed, caregivers impute intention and meaning to infants' earliest behavior, making the babies appear more adept than they in fact are. These imputations facilitate children's language acquisition much in the manner of self-fulfilling prophecies. Infants with depressed mothers are handicapped in this respect, because their mothers are less likely to use the exaggerated intonation contours of "parentese" and because their mothers are slower to respond to their early attempts at vocalization (Bettes, 1988). Recent research in eight developing countries looks at the relationship between maternal depression and the impact of reduced mother-infant interaction, which is a risk to infant health and language development (Stewart, 2007).

Motherese, or Parentese   When infants are still in their babbling phase, adults often address long, complex sentences to them. But when infants begin responding to adults' speech, especially when they start uttering meaningful, identifiable words (at around 12 to 14 months), mothers, fathers, and caregivers invariably speak what is called *motherese* or (more recently) **parentese** in some research literature—a simplified, redundant, and highly grammatical sort of language.

When speaking parentese, parents tend to restrict their utterances to the present tense, to concrete nouns, and to comments on what the child is doing or experiencing. And they typically focus on what objects are named ("That's a doggie!" or "Johnnie, what's this?"), the color of objects ("Bring me the yellow ball. The yellow ball. No, the yellow ball. That's it. The yellow ball!"), and where objects are located ("Hey, Lisa! Lisa! Where's the kitty? Where's the kitty? See. On the steps. See over there on the steps!").

The pitch of the caregiver's voice is correlated with the child's age: the younger the child, the higher the pitch of speech. A study on the impact of infant-directed speech (IDS) versus adult-directed speech (ADS) found that IDS increased neural activity in infants. Younger infants exhibited increased neural activity only for familiar words

Acquiring Language   An infant learns language from someone speaking directly to him or her saying one or a few words with exaggeration, and within about 8 to 10 inches of the child's face. When the child repeats the sound, the caregiver rewards the child with a big smile and words of pleasure, such as "Good girl!" Infants demonstrate receptive language skills before being able to speak that word.

(Zangl & Mills, 2007). Parentese seems to derive less from parents' intent to provide brief language lessons than from their efforts to communicate to their youngsters. And as we will see later in this chapter, infants also use intonation effectively to express desires and intentions before they master conventional phonetic forms (Lewis, 1936/1951).

Parentese is also frequently accompanied by gestures, object motion, and touch, making it a multisensory communication device (Gogate & Bahrick, 2000). In a fascinating observation, infants, even before the one-word stage of language development, spontaneously produce gestures, just as do infants with hearing impairments. Mothers often translate these gestures into words, which facilitates language learning (Goldin-Meadow, 2007).

A Resolution of Divergent Theories

Most psychologists agree that language has a biological basis, but they continue to disagree over how much the input from parents and other caregivers matters. The most satisfactory approach seems to be one that looks to the strengths of each theory and focuses on the complex and many-sided aspects of the development of language capabilities. Indeed, language acquisition cannot be understood by examining learning or genetic factors in isolation. No aspect by itself can produce a language-using human. Instead of asking which factor is most important, we need to study the ongoing process by which the factors dynamically come together.

Infants are biologically adapted to acquire language. They possess a genetically determined plan that leads them toward language usage. Their attentional and perceptual apparatus seems biologically pretuned to make phonetic distinctions. Human beings possess a biological predisposition for the development of language, but this does not mean that environmental factors play no part in language acquisition. Indeed, language is acquired only in a social context (Tamis-LeMonda et al., 2006). Youngsters' earliest vocalizations, even their cries, are interpreted by caregivers, who in turn use these interpretations to determine how they will respond to the youngsters.

Can We Make Babies Smarter?   Regardless of which theory about learning languages is more accurate, most parents want their babies to learn quickly and speak as soon as possible. At one time it was thought that the brain was hardwired and that its wiring could not be changed. However, a mounting body of evidence suggests that enriched environments can produce physical changes in the developing brain. Imaging studies using techniques such as positron emission tomography (PET) scans reveal a positive correlation between positive environmental changes and an increase in synaptic connections among brain cells. Stimulating the brain through enrichment experiences—good nutrition, toys, playmates, learning opportunities, and parental counseling—can prevent a substantial amount of mental retardation and developmental disability and can overcome stumbling blocks for culturally deprived youngsters. Early intervention can make the future brighter for many youngsters whose development would otherwise be stunted (Lanzi, Ramey, & Ramey, 2007).

However, many children who are pressured to learn through inappropriate methods begin to dislike learning. Young children learn best from their own experience—from self-directed activity, exploring real objects, talking to people, and solving real-life problems, such as how to balance a stack of blocks. And they benefit from having stories read to them regularly. When caregivers intrude in children's self-directed learning and insist on imposing their own priorities on the child's learning, such as math, reading, or violin, they interfere with children's own impulses and initiative. Parents and caregivers, then, must consider the style of learning appropriate for the very young (Elkind, 1987).

Questions

Nativists insist that human beings possess an inborn language-generating mechanism, whereas learning/interactionist researchers argue that language is learned within an environmental context. Which position do you take regarding language/speech acquisition? Is it possible to make a child smarter in infancy?

LANGUAGE DEVELOPMENT

What is involved in learning to talk? This question has fascinated people for centuries. The ancient Greek historian Herodotus reports on the research of Psammetichus, ruler of Egypt in the seventh century B.C.—the first attempt at a controlled psychological experiment in recorded history. The king's research was based on the notion that vocabulary is transmitted genetically and that children's babbling sounds are words from the world's first language:

> Psammetichus . . . took at random, from an ordinary family, two newly born infants and gave them to a shepherd to be brought up amongst his flocks, under strict orders that no one should utter a word in their presence. They were to be kept by themselves in a lonely cottage, and the shepherd was to bring in goats from time to time, to see that the babies had enough milk to drink, and to look after them in any other way that was necessary. All these arrangements were made by Psammetichus because he wished to find out what word the children would first utter. . . . The plan succeeded; two years later the shepherd, who during that time had done everything he had been told to do, happened one day to open the door of the cottage . . . [and both children ran up to him and] pronounced the word "becos." (Herodotus, 1964, pp. 102–103)

When the king learned that the children had said, "becos," he undertook to discover the language to which the word belonged. From the information produced by his inquiries, he concluded that *becos* was the Phrygian word for "bread." As a consequence, the Egyptians reluctantly yielded their claim to being the most ancient people and admitted that the Phrygians surpassed them in antiquity.

Communication Processes

Becoming competent in a language is not simply a matter of employing a system of rules for linking sounds and meaning (Thiessen, Hill, & Saffran, 2005; Tomasello, 2006). Language also involves the ability to use such a system for communication and, furthermore, to keep such systems separate when one has access to two or more.

Nonverbal Communication, or Body Language   The essence of language is the ability to talk to one another. Yet spoken language is only one channel or form of message transmission. We also communicate by body language (also termed **kinesics**), which is the nonverbal communication of meaning through rhythmic movements of hands or head and through voice and gestures (Loehr, 2007). For instance, we wink an eye to demonstrate intimacy; we lift an eyebrow in disbelief; we tap our fingers to show impatience; we rub our noses or scratch our heads in puzzlement; we produce the "tsk" sound to express exasperation; and many in the United States slap a "high five" or exchange "fist bumps" when greeting. Every society develops its own patterns and meanings of such body movements and gestures—thus such communication can be misunderstood when one travels in or moves to another country. Likewise, when immigrant children enter the public school system, there is a lot of confusion about teachers' gestures and nonverbal cues. Some sociologists interested in communication and languages have created Web sites devoted to nonverbal communication from cultures around the world.

We also communicate by *gaze:* We look at the eyes and face of another person and make eye contact. One way we use gazing is in the sequencing and coordination of speech. Typically, speakers look away from a listener as they begin to talk, shutting out stimulation and planning what they will say. At the end of the utterance, they look at the listener to signal that they have finished and are yielding the floor; and in between they give the listener brief looks to derive feedback.

By the end of the second year, most children seem to pattern their eye contact in the way adults in their environment do: looking up when they are done speaking to signal that they are finished and looking up when the other person is through speaking to confirm that the floor is about to be theirs again. Even so, children show considerable differences in the consistency and frequency of these behaviors (Rutter & Kurkin, 1987). And some groups actually avoid eye contact, such as African Americans, who view staring as aggressive, and Native Americans, who view staring as rude.

Another nonverbal behavior is *pointing.* Pointing can be observed in infants as young as 2 months old, although intentional pointing usually begins around 12 months of age and indicates communicative intent (D'Entremont & Seamans, 2007). Pointing is a nonverbal precursor of language, and researchers believe that when 12-month-old infants point at adults, they are trying intentionally to influence their mental states. Furthermore, the researchers found that pointing depends on skills and motivations that are unique to human beings (Tomasello, Carpenter, & Liszkowski, 2007). Mothers commonly employ pointing when talking to their youngsters. Children use the gesture to mark out features of a book, to call attention to an activity, or to indicate something they want.

Another form of communication is **paralanguage**— the stress, pitch, and volume of vocalizations by which we communicate expressive meaning. Paralanguage involves *how* something is said, not *what* is said. Tone of voice, pacing of speech, and extralinguistic sounds (such as sighs) are examples of paralanguage. By the late babbling period, infants already control the intonation, or pitch modulation,

Pointing By 1 year of age, infants use pointing as a nonverbal precursor of language. Children often use this gesture to call attention to an activity or to something they want.

of their utterances (Moskowitz, 1978). By about 9 months, new social cognitive competencies emerge in joint attention, social referencing, and communicative gestures (Tomasello et al., 2007).

Most of the research on language development has focused on language production, the ability of children to string together sounds so as to communicate a message in a meaningful fashion. Until recently, little research dealt with **language reception,** the quality of receiving or taking in messages. Yet children's receptive capacities occur first, before the ability to produce language. For instance, even very young babies are able to make subtle linguistic discriminations—such as that between the sounds *p* and *b* (Eimas, 1985).

Older children similarly make finer distinctions in comprehension than they reveal in their own language productions (Bates, Bretherton, & Snyder, 1988). Consider the now somewhat classic conversation that the linguist Roger Brown had with a young child (Moskowitz, 1978): The child made reference to "fis," and Brown repeated "fis." The child was dissatisfied with Brown's pronunciation of the word. After a number of exchanges between Brown and the child, Brown tried "fish," and the child, finally satisfied, replied, "Yes, fis." Although the child was not yet able to make the distinction between *s* and *sh* in his pronunciation, he knew that such a sound difference did exist.

The Sequence of Language Development

Until a couple of decades ago, linguists assumed that children merely spoke an imperfect version of adult language, one that reflected a child's handicaps of limited attention, limited memory span, and other cognitive deficits.

TABLE 5.3 Milestones in Language Development

Age	Characteristic Sounds
Birth–1 month	Cries; makes small throaty noises.
2 months	Begins producing vowel-like cooing noises
3 months	Cries less, coos, gurgles at the back of the throat, squeals, and occasionally chuckles.
4 months	Cooing becomes pitch-modulated; vowel-like sounds begin to be interspersed with consonantal sounds; smiles and coos when talked to.
6 months	Vowel sounds are interspersed with more consonantal sounds (f, v, th, s, sh, z, sz, and n are common), which produce babbling (one-syllable utterances); displays pleasure with squeals, gurgles, and giggles, and displays displeasure with growls and grunts.
8 months	Displays adults' intonation in babbling; often uses two-syllable utterances such as "mama" or "baba"; imitates sounds.
10 months	Understands some words and associated gestures (may say "no" and shake head); may pronounce "dada" or "mama" and use holophrases (words with many different meanings).
12 months	Employs more holophrases, such as "baby," "bye-bye," and "hi"; many imitate sounds of objects, such as "bow-wow"; has greater control over intonation patterns; gives signs of understanding some words and simple commands (such as "Show me your nose").
18 months	Possesses a repertoire of 3 to 50 words; may begin using two-word utterances; still babbles, but employs several syllables with intricate intonation pattern.
24 months	Has repertoire of more than 50 words; uses two-word utterances more frequently; displays increasing interest in verbal communication.
30 months	Rapid acceleration in learning new words; speech consists of two or three words and even five words; sentences have characteristic child grammar and rarely are verbatim imitations of adult speech; intelligibility of the speech is poor, although children differ in this regard.
36 months	Has a vocabulary of some 1,000 words; about 80 percent of speech is intelligible, even to strangers; grammatical complexity is roughly comparable to colloquial adult language.
48 months	Language well established; deviations from adult speech are more in style than in grammar.

Adapted from Frank Caplan, ed., *The First Twelve Months of Life*. New York: Grosset & Dunlap, 1973; and Eric H. Lenneberg, *Biological Foundations of Language*. New York: Wiley, 1967, pp. 128–130.

However, linguists now generally accept that children speak their own language—a language with characteristic patterns that develop through a series of stages (Berko Gleason, 2005; Jaswal & Fernald, 2007).

Children reveal tremendous individual variation in the rate and form of language development (Fenson et al., 1994). Indeed, some children don't begin to talk until well into their third year, whereas others are producing long sentences at this point. Such variations do not appear to have implications for adult language skill, provided that the child is otherwise normal. Table 5.3 summarizes the typical milestones in language development of the "average" child.

From Vocalization to Babbling   Crying is the most noticeable sound uttered by the newborn. Although it serves as the infant's primary means of communication, crying cannot be considered true language (although some mothers say they can easily distinguish meaning among different cries). Young infants also produce a number of other sounds, including yawns, sighs, coughs, sneezes, and belches.

Between the sixth and eighth week, infants diversify their vocalizations and, when playing alone, employ new noises, including "Bronx cheers," gurgling, and tongue noise games. Around their third month, infants begin making cooing sounds and squealing-gurgling noises, which they sustain for 15 to 20 seconds.

Babbling   Around the sixth month, infants in all cultures produce sequences of alternating vowels and consonants that resemble one-syllable utterances, such as *"da-da-da."* Indeed, infants seem to play with sounds, enjoying the process and exploring their capabilities. Frequently babbled sounds consist of *n, m, y, w, d, t,* or *b,* followed by a vowel such as the *eh* sound in *bet.* It is probably no coincidence that in many languages, the words for mother and father begin with these sounds (for example, *mama, nana, papa, dada, baba*). Consonants such as *l, r, f,* and *v* and consonant clusters such as *st* are rare.

MacNeilage and Davis (2000), researchers at the University of Texas, analyzed audiotapes of several infants from 6 to 18 months and concluded that four patterns of consonant-vowel combinations are common to babies' babbling and first words in several languages. They state that these patterns are created by basic open (vowels) and close (consonant) movements of the mouth and jaw during speech, and they do not attribute babbling to any genetic or inborn language mechanism—in contrast to the thinking of traditional linguists. (See Figure 5.4.)

Infant *laughter* typically appears around this time, as well.

Deaf infants also go through the *cooing* and *babbling* phase, even though they may never have heard any spoken sounds. Oller (2005) reports that, contrary to much earlier research based on small samples of deaf infants, these infants babble in a different fashion from hearing infants and produce different sounds. Yet there is a suggestion that a hereditary mechanism underlies the early cooing and babbling process. During the second six months of life, typically deaf babies' babbling sounds have a more limited range than hearing children's. Whereas a deaf infant might say *ba* or *da*, a hearing infant will say *bababa* or *dadada*. Furthermore, unless congenitally deaf children are given special training, their language development is delayed (Folven & Bonvillian, 1991).

Early Communication: Cooing About 3 months of age, infants make "cooing" sounds that are simple vowel sounds such as *ooooh, eeeeeh,* and *ahhhh.* By around 6 months, she or he will enjoy making "bubbles" with the saliva from the mouth, with simple spitting. The infant is learning to move the tongue and lips in readiness for language.

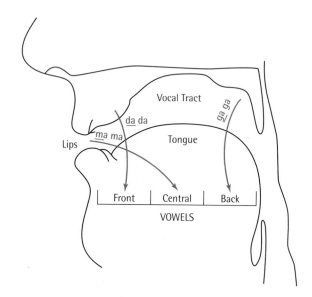

FIGURE 5.4 Sequence of Early Infant Sound Patterns
Illustrated are the sequences of early infant sound patterns called babbling. Each is a consonant-vowel combination. Try saying them and feeling where they are formed in the mouth. *Da da* is formed in the front of the mouth, behind the lips, for example. *Ma ma* is formed in the central area of the mouth with the lips coming together. Where in the mouth do you think other baby sounds, such as *goo goo, pa pa, na na,* and *ba ba,* are formed?
Source: MacNeilage, P. F., & Davis, B. L. (2000). Origin of the internal structure of words. *Science, 288,* 527–531, http://www.utexas.edu/features/archive/2005/babble.html

Research conducted by Goldin-Meadow (2000) with deaf infants from American and Chinese cultures confirmed that infants have a strong bias to communicate in language-like ways. The parents in this study differed in their native language, in their child-rearing practices, and in the way that gesturing was used in relation to speech—yet the children themselves spontaneously introduced language-like structure into their gestures. Researchers have also compared and studied the development of gestures in hearing and deaf children (Volterra, Iverson, & Castrataro, 2006).

Other researchers find that deaf babies of deaf parents babble with their hands in the same rhythmic, repetitive fashion in which hearing babies babble with their voices (Petitto et al., 2001). Sounds such as *googoo* and *da-da-da* that hearing babies make arise around the same time that the babbling signs and motions arise among deaf youngsters. Most of the hand motions of the deaf infants are actual elements of *American Sign Language*—gestures that do not in themselves mean anything but that have the potential to indicate something when pieced together with other gestures. (See the *More Information You Can Use* box, "Should Babies Learn Sign Language?")

Language Development in Children with Hearing Impairments Significantly, deaf children pass through the same stages and at the same times as are observed in the vocal babbling of hearing children: They string together signs and motions in much the same way that hearing youngsters string together sounds. Such gestures appear to have the same functional significance as the babble noises of hearing babies, for they are far more systematic and deliberate than the random finger flutters and fist clenches of hearing youngsters (Kyle, McEntee, & Ackerman, 1998). Such findings suggest that language

MORE INFORMATION YOU CAN USE

Should Babies Learn Sign Language?

Sign language has been promoted as a way for deaf or hearing-impaired people to communicate with the hearing world since 1817, when Thomas Gallaudet, founder of the American School for the Deaf, began to encourage its use. For years, deaf children and children with special needs have learned sign language to enable them to communicate with others. However, some parents today teach sign language to babies who have normal hearing.

Two researchers who have done extensive work in this area are Linda Acredolo and Susan Goodwyn. They discovered that babies between 10 and 24 months were using simple symbolic gestures to communicate ideas and wishes and needs that they could not express using words. For example, a baby might sniff when she was trying to communicate that she was thinking about a flower, or she might flap her arms when she was thinking about a bird. With National Institutes for Health funding, Acredolo and Goodwyn developed a program called *Baby Signs,* which enables infants and parents to communicate without spoken words using nonverbal symbols or signs adapted from American Sign Language. (See Figure 5.5.)

Most babies already use signs or signals like shaking their heads to indicate yes or no or waving their hands to say goodbye. Acredolo and Goodwyn (2009) believe that babies use other signs as well and can be taught many more to enhance early communication. They believe that teaching signing to a baby actually enhances and speeds up language acquisition and use. However, the advantages they found seem to have a greater effect early in a baby's life and appear to fade after 36 months. They postulate that a baby's ability to use signs to communicate shows that the baby has already done much of the cognitive work needed to understand

words and language and their symbolic functions (Acredolo & Goodwyn, 2009). Researchers who have reviewed their work believe that until more studies are done, a direct cause-and-effect relationship between learning sign language and developing early verbal skills cannot be confidently established (Barnes, 2010). However, teaching sign language to babies seems to have no negative effects on verbal development, and the increased parental attention and stimulation are benefits in and of themselves.

FIGURE 5.5 Baby Signs
Source: Reprinted with permission from www.babysigns.com

is distinct from speech and that speech is only one of the signal systems available to us for communication with one another. In addition, the research suggests that babbling, whether manual or vocal, is an inherent feature of the maturing brain as it acquires the structure of language.

These observations suggest that although vocal behavior emerges spontaneously, it flourishes only in the presence of adequate environmental stimulation. And deaf babies, of course, are incapable of "talking back"—the process of vocal contagion and model imitation noted by Piaget. Children do not seem to learn language simply by hearing it spoken. To learn a language, children must be able to interact with people in that language (Hoff-Ginsberg & Shatz, 1982).

In the United States, through universal newborn hearing-screening programs, those with hearing loss are identified by audiologists and speech-language therapists and are eligible for early intervention services. Although some learn sign language, new technology has produced cochlear implants that can sometimes "awaken" the hearing in year-old infants and preschool children who are affected with hearing impairments and can improve speech perception and speech production (Kileny, Zwolan, & Ashbaugh, 2001).

Receptive Vocabulary   Between 6 to 9 months, caregivers will notice that the child understands some words. This is a favorite time for parents, who begin to ask the

Learning Sign Language Both babies who can hear and those with hearing impairments pass through the same maturing stages at about the same months of age. Around 6 to 8 months, babies can learn gestures and signs to communicate before they can actually express words.

baby questions: "Where is Mommy's nose?" and the baby points to mommy's nose. Or Daddy might say, "Wave bye-bye to Daddy" as he leaves the house, and the child demonstrates understanding by waving bye-bye. A child who is not yet speaking can respond appropriately when asked to go get things, such as his or her toys or the pots and pans in the kitchen. All of these actions demonstrate that children have developed a **receptive vocabulary** long before they speak their first word—that is, long before they have an **expressive vocabulary,** using their own words to effectively convey meaning, feeling, or mood.

Holophrases The majority of developmental psychologists agree that most children speak their first word at about 10 to 13 months of age. However, the precise age at which a child arrives at this milestone is often difficult to determine. The child's first word is so eagerly anticipated by many parents that they read meaning into the infant's babbling—for instance, they note *mama* and *dada* but ignore *tete* and *roro*. Hence, one observer might credit a child with a "first word" when another observer would not. Behavioral theorists suggest that at this time parents reinforce, or reward, the infant with their smiles and encouragement. In turn, the child repeats the same expression over and over, such as *da*, which quickly becomes *dada* (or what we interpret to be *daddy*). The *d* sound is easier for the infant to say; the *m* sound (as in *mama*) requires the child to purse the lips together, so it might not be heard for another few months.

Children's first truly linguistic utterances are **holophrases**—single words that convey different meanings

depending on the context in which they are used. Using a holophrase, a child can imply a complete thought. G. DeLaguna (1929) first noted the characteristics of holophrases more than 80 years ago:

> It is precisely because the words of the child are so indefinite in meaning, that they can serve such a variety of uses. . . . A child's word does not . . . designate an object or a property or an act; rather it signifies loosely and vaguely the object together with its interesting properties and the acts with which it is commonly associated in the life of the child. . . . Just because the terms of the child's language are themselves so indefinite, it is left to the particular setting and context to determine the specific meaning for each occasion. In order to understand what the baby is saying, you must see what the baby is doing.

The utterance *mama*, not uncommon in the early repertoire of English-language youngsters, is a good illustration of a holophrase. In one situation, it may communicate "I want a cookie"; in another, "Let me out of my crib"; and in another, "Don't take my toy away from me." A holophrase is most often a noun, an adjective, or a self-invented word. Only gradually do the factual and emotional components of the infant's early words become clearer and more precise.

Nelson and colleagues (1978) found that children typically pass through three phases in their early learning of language. About 10 to 13 months of age, they become capable of matching a number of words used by adults to already existing concepts, or mental images, such as the concept "bottle" discussed earlier in the chapter. The average child of 13 months understands about 50 words. Yet the average child does not speak 50 words until six months later, with a smaller percent speaking much earlier and some speaking much later (Tomasello & Bates, 2001). It is also interesting to note that caregivers have successfully taught preverbal children signs for words such as *more, cat,* and *hungry,* which they use in place of spoken language.

In the second phase, which usually occurs between 11 and 15 months of age, most children themselves begin to speak a small number of words. These words are closely bonded to a particular context or action.

Overextension By the age of 16 months, the child knows about 150 words (Fenson et al., 1994). In the third phase—from 16 to 20 months—children produce many words, but they tend to *extend* or *overgeneralize* a word beyond its core sense or grammatical form. For instance, a child might first apply the word *tick-tock* to a watch but then broaden the meaning of the word, first to include all clocks, then all watches, then a gas meter, or any item with a round dial. In general, children overextend meanings on the basis of similarities of movement, texture, size, and shape. Overgeneralization is also exemplified by a child saying "I goed there" instead of "I went there." Researchers have been interested in finding out when a child first uses these forms and how the child eventually eliminates the incorrect forms. One explanation is that the frequency of occurrence plays a role. Tomasello (2006) argues that the more frequently a child hears the correct form of a particular utterance, the less likely the child is to overgeneralize and use an incorrect form.

Children tend to first acquire words that are related to their own actions or to events in which they are participants (Shore, 1986). Nelson (1973) noted that children begin by *naming* objects whose most salient property is change—the objects *do* things like roll (ball), run (dog, cat, horse), growl (tiger), continually move (clock), go on and off (light), and drive away (car, truck). The most obvious omissions in children's early vocabulary are immobile objects (sofas, tables, chests, sidewalks, trees, grass).

Children also typically produce a holophrase when they are engaged in activities to which the holophrase is related. Marilyn H. Edmonds (1976, p. 188) observed that her subjects named the objects they were acting on, saying "ball" as they struggled to remove a ball from a shoe; they named where they placed objects, saying "bed" as they put their dolls to bed; they named their own actions, saying "fall" when they fell, they asserted possession, saying "mine" as they recovered objects appropriated by siblings; they denied the actions of their toys, yelling "no" when a toy cow fell over; and so forth.

Very often, a child's single-word utterances are so closely linked with action that the action and speech appear fused: In a Piagetian sense, a word becomes "assimilated" to an existing sensorimotor *scheme*—the word is fitted or incorporated into the child's existing behavioral or conceptual organization (see Chapter 2). Edmonds (1976, p. 188) cites the case of a child 21 months old who said "car" 41 times in 30 minutes as he played with a toy car.

Two-Word Sentences   When they are about 18 to 22 months old, most children begin to use two-word sentences. Examples include "Allgone sticky," said after washing hands; "More page," a request to an adult to continue reading aloud; and "Allgone outside," said after a door is closed behind the child ("allgone" is treated as one word because "all" and "gone" do not appear separately in these children's speech). Most of the two-word sentences are not acceptable adult English sentences, and most are not imitations of parental speech. Typical constructions are "More wet," "No down," "Not fix," "Me drink," "Allgone lettuce," and "Other fix" (Clark, Gelman, & Lane, 1985). Two-word sentences represent

attempts by children to express themselves in their own way through their own unique linguistic system. Young children do not simply imitate adult speech; rather, they use words in unique combinations (Lieven et al., 2003).

As with holophrases, one often must interpret children's two-word sentences in terms of the context. Lois Bloom (1970), for instance, observed that one of her young subjects, Kathryn, employed the utterance "Mommy sock" in two different contexts with two different meanings. "Mommy sock" could mean that Mommy was in the act of putting a sock on Kathryn, or it could mean that Kathryn had just found a sock that belonged to Mommy.

Children's actual utterances are simpler than the linguistic structures that underlie them. Slobin (1972, p. 73) observes that even with a two-word horizon, children can convey a host of meanings:

> Identification: "See doggie."
> Location: "Book there."
> Repetition: "More milk."
> Nonexistence: "Allgone thing."
> Negation: "Not wolf."
> Possession: "My candy."
> Attribution: "Big car."
> Agent-action: "Mama walk."
> Agent-object: "Mama book" (meaning, "Mama read book").
> Action-location: "Sit chair."
> Action-direct object: "Hit you."
> Action-indirect object: "Give papa."
> Action-instrument: "Cut knife."
> Question: "Where ball?"

Children also use intonation to distinguish meanings, as when a child says "*Baby* chair" to indicate possession and "Baby *chair*" to indicate location.

Telegraphic Speech   Children who begin to use short, precise words in two- or three-word combinations are demonstrating **telegraphic speech** and the first understanding of grammar. The third word frequently fills in the part that was implied in the two-word statement (Slobin, 1972). "Want that" becomes "Jerry wants that" or "Mommy milk" becomes "Mommy drink milk."

Psycholinguist Roger Brown (1973) characterizes the language of 2-year-old children as telegraphic speech. Brown observes that words in a telegram cost money, so that we have good reason to be brief. Take the message "My car has broken down and I have lost my wallet; send money to me at the American Express in Paris." We would word the telegram, "Car broken down; wallet lost; send money American Express Paris." In this manner, we omit eleven words: *my, has, and, I, have, my, to, me, at, the, in.* The omitted words are pronouns, prepositions, articles, conjunctions, and auxiliary verbs. We retain the nouns and verbs. This type of abbreviated speech is similar to that used in texting today.

Between 12 and 26 months of age, a child is most likely to be using nouns and verbs, with some adjectives and adverbs, such as "Daddy go bye-bye," "Me go out," "Me want drink" (Brown, 1973). Children especially love having parents and caregivers read to them in an exaggerated way.

By 27 to 30 months, a child is starting to form plurals: "Annie want cookies," "Mommy get shoes." The articles *a, an,* and *the* are now evident in speech: "The cat goes meow," or "I want a cookie." Some prepositions (indicating placement) are also used: "Jimmy in bed now." Whereas first-language acquisition has predictable milestones, the time course and ultimate attainment of skills in a second language are highly variable ("Reaction Time Studies," 2005).

Bilingualism

Although children are less proficient than adults in overall cognitive capabilities, newborns are language universalists. It seems that normal, healthy infants can learn any sound in any language and distinguish among the vocal sounds that human beings utter (Bjorklund & Green, 1992). In contrast, adults are language specialists. They have considerable difficulty perceiving speech sounds that are not in their native tongue. For instance, Japanese infants can distinguish between the English sounds *la* and *ra,* but Japanese adults cannot because their language does not contrast these sounds (Kuhl et al., 2006).

Some linguists contend that there is a critical period of language acquisition and that language learning occurs primarily in childhood. Some aspects of the nervous system seem to lose their plasticity with age, so that by the onset of puberty the organization of the brain is basically fixed, making the learning of a new language difficult (Lenneberg, 1967). However, this assumption has recently been challenged by findings that suggest that it is the level of language proficiency—not when the language is learned—that leads to bilingual acquisition (Perani et al., 2003).

Given this state of affairs, it is hardly surprising that proficiency in a second language is related to the age at which exposure to the language begins (Baker, Trofimovich, Flege, Mack, & Halter, 2008). To put it another way, adults who learned a second language early in childhood are more proficient with the language than adults who learn a second language later in life. Similar results are found for older children or adults with hearing deficiencies who learn American Sign Language as their first language (Baker et al., 2008).

Evidence suggests that, regarding the ability to acquire a second language, there is a gradual decline across childhood rather than a sudden discontinuity at puberty. Indeed, the decline begins very early in life. Patricia K. Kuhl and her colleagues (1992) report that experience alters sound perception by 6 months of age. For instance, experiments with 6-month-old babies in the United States and Sweden reveal that American youngsters routinely ignore the different pronunciations of the *i* sound because in the United States they hear the same sound. But American infants can distinguish slight variation in *y* sounds. The reverse is true of Swedish babies—they ignore variations in *y* sounds but notice variations in the *i* sound.

These findings have substantial implications for educators. The best time to learn a new language is early in life. The cognitive structures of young children seem especially suited for learning both a first and a second language. This ability is gradually lost across the childhood years. Although adults are able to acquire a second language, they rarely attain the same proficiency as individuals who acquire the language in childhood (Bjorklund & Green, 1992). It appears that bilingual infants learn to distinguish between similar-sounding words later than monolingual infants. The researchers postulate that this may be due to the greater cognitive load involved with learning two languages (Fennell, Byers-Heinlein, & Werker, 2007).

As we shall see in later chapters on childhood, the large influx of immigrant children into the United States over the past decade has stimulated a flurry of research on bilingualism. The results of a recent study on acquisition of a second language suggest that Spanish-speaking children who were identified as "rapid learners" need about three to five years to become proficient in academic settings using English as a second language. However, other children may be much slower in learning English as a second language ("Reaction Time Studies," 2005).

The Significance of Language Development

Parents anxiously await normal language development in their young children, for in many cultures, language expression and understanding are considered indicators of intellectual ability or intellectual delay. Children vary in their timing of their expressive language. Parents and grandparents generally speak constantly to a firstborn child, and firstborns are the most likely to speak early or within the expected range of development. Later-born children with siblings sometimes do not have to speak to get what they want; if older siblings take care of a child and anticipate the child's needs, it is likely that this child will simply delay expressing language. Some children speak very little, and then suddenly they surprise everyone by speaking in short sentences!

However, if caregivers notice that a child does not follow simple instructions or does not speak simple sounds or words according to a normal timetable, they are advised to schedule a checkup with the child's pediatrician. Some children with delayed speech have hearing impairments; others may be eligible for speech therapy to promote normal speech development. We do know that children who have language delays or cannot be understood when they speak are at a risk for later social isolation upon entering group activities, such as child care, preschool, or kindergarten.

Some American parents are enrolling their toddlers in nursery or preschool programs where instruction in a second language is the norm, whereas parents who recently immigrated into this country are struggling to immerse their children in the English-speaking culture. Some children have bilingual parents and seem to learn both languages with ease at home.

Questions

What are the several milestones in infant language development from vocalizations, such as crying, to speaking an actual sentence? Who or what motivates the child to communicate? How easy is it for a young child, compared to an adult, to acquire a second language? Explain your answer.

SEGUE

The issue of the increasing numbers of non-English-speaking young children in the United States has prompted much debate on when language learning should begin, what teaching methods are most effective in the earliest years, what language or languages should be spoken in the child's home, and how all of these programs will be funded. People who work in such areas as health care, social services, teaching, early child care, and criminal justice are particularly aware of how difficult it is to communicate without a common language.

In Chapter 6, we discuss the influential role that the home environment and caregivers play in the young child's emotional development and the expanding social contexts within which the child's developing sense of self evolves.

SUMMARY

Cognitive Development

1. Chapter 5 surveys the processes of cognitive and language development through infancy—that is, from birth through age 2. Although some infants exhibit superior abilities in cognitive and language development, others are born with, or develop, cognitive delays and specific language impairments.

2. Cognition is the process of knowing and remembering. As infants receive raw sensory information (stimuli), they transform these data into meaningful information. Infants can experience and process enormous amounts of sensory information.

3. Learning enables us to adapt to our environment by building on previous experience and is defined as a change in behavior that is stable and results from experience. To facilitate learning, we can condition people, provide a model for them to imitate, or shape and fashion the cognitive structures by which individuals think about their environment.

4. DeCasper and other researchers studying fetal and infant auditory perception have found that infants' preferences and physiological responses are affected by their auditory experiences before and after birth.

5. Sameroff and others found that newborns can learn to control which of two sucking methods they use and to express milk at one of two pressure levels when feeding. These different neonatal sucking techniques and reinforcement principles show that infants can learn to adjust their behavior according to whether it succeeds or fails.

6. Researchers believe young children cannot remember events in their lives (autobiographical memory) until the age of 3 years. They differ about why children have few memories before that age.

7. Jean Piaget characterized children's cognitive development during the first two years of life as the sensorimotor stage. The child's major task during infancy is to integrate the perceptual and motor systems to arrive at more adaptive behavior. Some infants may improve sensorimotor functioning through craniosacral evaluation and therapy methods.

8. Another hallmark of the sensorimotor period is the child's progressive refinement of the notion of object permanence. Six- to 9-month-old infants come to know that objects exist, even when the objects cannot be seen.

9. Neo-Piagetians find that infants possess skills more sophisticated than Piaget had imagined. Infants must be

provided with experiences that they cannot generate by themselves, such as playing with others.

10. Caregivers transmit to infants the knowledge, attitudes, values, and behaviors essential for later effective participation in society. Depressed mothers have a reduced capacity for caregiving and for nurturing, stimulating and talking with their infants. In turn, their infants are more withdrawn, unresponsive, and inattentive. They also have problems sleeping and eating and may be diagnosed with failure to thrive.

11. According to psychologist Jerome Bruner, children first represent the world through their physical/motor actions. Young children use mental images called ikonic representations (images or pictures), whereas school-age children begin to use symbolic representations (letters, numbers, and words).

12. Individual differences in mental performance in infancy are probably developmentally continuous across childhood and beyond. Children's patterns of attending to information reflect their cognitive capabilities, particularly their ability to construct workable schemas of their visual and auditory worlds.

13. Early intervention enrichment experiences for infants with delayed cognitive development—including good nutrition, toys, playmates, learning opportunities, and effective parenting—can produce physical changes in the developing brain and boost intellectual development. Caregivers need to provide positive feedback about their infant's accomplishments, encourage exploratory behaviors in a safe setting, and make efforts to bond with their infants.

Language and Thought

14. Human beings are set apart from other animals by their highly developed system of language communication. Language allows for communication with one another (interindividual communication) and facilitates thought (intraindividual communication).

15. Historically, there have been two opposing scientific views on the relationship between language and thought. One view is that thought takes place independent of the existence of language, and the other is that language shapes thought by conceptualization. Categories are the basis for more advanced cognitive thinking. Naming, or verbally labeling, offers many advantages.

Theories of Language Acquisition

16. Nativists (hereditarians) and learning/interactionists (environmentalists) take opposing views about the determinants of language. Research is progressing rapidly to discover the genetic, chemical, and molecular mechanics underlying the sense of hearing, hearing impairments, and the production of language.

17. The findings from a longitudinal study in behavioral genetics suggest that verbal delay appears to be highly heritable. Girls scored significantly higher on verbal measures than most boys, and boys and girls scored about the same in nonverbal measures.

18. British researchers estimate that between 2 and 5 percent of children who are otherwise unimpaired have significant difficulties acquiring language, despite adequate intelligence and opportunity. Specific language impairments (SLIs) often run in families.

19. Over the past 20 years, family and twin studies in three countries have confirmed that genes on specific chromosomes play a significant role in autism and other developmental disorders. Identical twins show a high concordance for autism.

20. Learning researchers (environmentalists) argue that language is learned through the processes of reinforcement. Babies "tune in" to the sounds of their native language for the first six to eight months. When infants begin responding, caregivers begin to use a new pattern of speaking called parentese. Babies communicate using sounds, nonverbal cues, and gestures. Researchers agree that an enriched environment can help a young child learn, but they caution caregivers to avoid pressuring a child to learn rapidly or through inappropriate methods.

21. The acquisition of language requires complex interactions among genetic influences, biochemical processes, maturational factors, learning strategies, and the social environment.

Language Development

22. The essence of language is the ability to understand and transmit messages. Some linguists suggest that there is a critical period of language acquisition. The best time to learn a second language is early in life.

23. People, including infants, also communicate through nonverbal body language, which includes gazing, pointing and gesturing, and a variety of vocal stress, pitch, and volume, called paralanguage. Infants understand much of what is said to them before they produce language themselves.

24. Linguists now recognize that early communication and speech develop through a series of stages: early vocalizations (primarily crying), cooing and babbling, holophrases, two-word sentences, and three-word sentences. Deaf children and those with hearing loss pass through the same stages by stringing together a variety of gestures that are self-produced.

25. Through universal newborn hearing screening programs, those with hearing loss are identified and eligible for early intervention services. Cochlear implants can "awaken" the hearing in year-old infants and preschool children who are affected with hearing impairments. Deaf infants pass through the same language stages using their own self-generated gestural sign language.

26. Infants' first true words are holophrases; a holophrase is a single word that conveys different meanings. Two- and three-word combinations demonstrate telegraphic speech and the first use of the structure we call grammar. By 27 to 30 months, a child is normally beginning to use plurals, articles, and prepositions.

27. Children vary greatly in when they begin to use language. Although some speak early, others show signs of delay and may need to be tested by an audiologist or speech-language therapist to be eligible for early intervention services.

KEY TERMS

autism *(146)*

caregiver speech *(147)*

cognition *(133)*

communication *(142)*

conceptualization *(143)*

craniosacral system *(139)*

expressive vocabulary *(154)*

failure to thrive (FTT) *(140)*

holophrases *(154)*

kinesics *(149)*

language *(142)*

language acquisition device (LAD) *(145)*

language reception *(150)*

learning *(133)*

object permanence *(138)*

paralanguage *(150)*

parentese *(148)*

phonemes *(145)*

receptive vocabulary *(154)*

sensorimotor period *(138)*

telegraphic speech *(155)*

FOLLOWING UP ON THE INTERNET

Web sites for this chapter focus on cognitive and language development in infancy. Please access the text Web site at www.mhhe.com/crandell10 for up-to-date hot-linked Internet addresses for the following organizations, topics, and resources:

Autism Society of America
http://www.autism-society.org/site/PageServer

National Institute of Deafness and Communication Disorders
http://www.nidcd.nih.gov/

Society for Research in Child Development
http://www.srcd.org/

Infant Learning Lab at University of Wisconsin, Madison
http://www.waisman.wisc.edu/infantlearning/Welcome.html

Communication Science & Disorders Research, University of Texas at Austin
https://webcms.utexas.edu/CSD/research/index
.htm?ssSourceNodeId=972

Baby Signs
https://www.babysigns.com/

Jean Piaget Society
http://www.piaget.org/index.html

American Speech-Language Hearing Association (ASHA)
http://www.asha.org/

Normal Speech Development
http://www.nidcd.nih.gov/health/voice/speechandlanguage
.html#mychild

International Society of Infant Studies
http://www.isisweb.org/

6 Infancy
The Development of Emotional and Social Bonds

Critical Thinking Questions

1. How would you feel if your baby consistently preferred to be held by other people instead of you? Would you try to change your baby's preferences?

2. Why do we sometimes experience two emotional states simultaneously? For example, a child will laugh and cry at the same time. Have you ever loved and hated someone at the same time? Is it really possible?

3. Babies are said to have different temperaments: Some are difficult, some are slow to warm up, and some are easygoing. If you and your baby ended up at opposite ends of the temperament continuum, how would you handle this? What practical steps would you take to understand, nurture, encourage, and live with someone who approaches life so differently than you?

4. You suspect, but are not sure, that a relative or a neighbor is abusing or neglecting her child. How would you feel? What would you be concerned about? How would you react?

Outline

I n Chapters 4 and 5, we focused on the infant as a growing and cognitively developing being. With those areas of development as a foundation, we now examine multiple ways in which young children are socialized into the larger human group. In America, many families have moved away from the three-generational model of child care in the home that is evident in many other countries.

The demographics of family life are changing in the United States. The trend is toward fewer two-parent families and more families headed by single parents (U.S. Bureau of the Census, 2009a). The number of women in the workforce has steadily increased over the last generation. Almost two-thirds of mothers with children under the age of 5 are in the workforce (U.S. Department of Labor, 2010d). One of every five American children has a foreign-born parent and is likely to live below poverty levels. Thus, the number of families who tap into assistance from the larger community to provide high-quality care and supervision for children continues to grow.

Young children in the United States are supervised (and therefore socialized) by a larger array of people than ever before. A number of programs have evolved over the past three decades to assist in the important task of child care. Television has also come to be a powerful socialization influence. This is of great concern to social scientists who study attachment, because the emotional ties that children form in their early years are extremely significant and serve as models for their later relationships. Perhaps most important, the child's own personality and temperament are underlying factors in the successful development of emotional and social bonds.

EMOTIONAL DEVELOPMENT

Emotions play a critical part in our daily existence and in making us human. Emotions set the tone for much of our lives, and at times they override our most basic needs: Fear can preempt appetite, anxiety can wreak havoc on a student's performance on an exam, and extreme happiness can lead a person to hugging a total stranger!

Most of us have a gut-level feeling of what we mean by the term *emotions,* yet we have difficulty putting the feeling into words. Even psychologists and other developmental scientists have characterized emotions in different ways. Some have viewed them as a reflection of physiological changes that occur in our bodies, which include rapid heartbeat and breathing, muscle tension, perspiration, and a "sinking feeling" in the stomach. Others have portrayed emotions as a subjective experience—the labels we assign to a set of particular states of arousal. Still others have depicted emotions as the visible expressive behaviors we display, including crying, moaning, laughing, smiling, and frowning.

Yet emotions are best characterized as a combination of all these components. We can say that **emotions** are the physiological changes, subjective experiences, and expressive behaviors involved in feelings such as love, joy, grief, and anger.

The Role of Emotions

Emotions, then, are not simply "feelings" but rather are processes by which individuals establish, maintain, and terminate relations between themselves and their environment (Campos et al., 1993). Researchers have learned that human emotions perform a number of functions:

- *Emotions help humans survive and adapt to their environment.* For instance, fear of the dark, fear of being alone, and fear of strangers are adaptive because there is an association between feared things and potential danger. On a positive note, as a 3-month-old infant gives her first big smile to a parent and gets instant feedback of pleasure from the parent, the whole process of socialization is set in motion.
- *Emotions guide and motivate human behavior.* Our emotions influence whether we categorize events as dangerous or beneficial, and they provide the motivation for patterning our subsequent behavior. A young boy is happy after he learns to dress himself for the first time and is rewarded with praise and smiles from caregivers. Thus, he is likely to continue dressing himself each day.
- *Emotions support communication with others.* By reading facial, gestural, postural, and vocal cues of others, we gain indirect access to their emotional states. Knowing that a friend is happy or sad allows us to more accurately predict the friend's behavior and to respond to it appropriately (Mayer, Ciarrochi, & Forgas, 2001).

Being able to "read" another person's emotional reactions permits **social referencing,** the practice whereby an inexperienced person relies on a more experienced person's interpretation of an event to regulate his or her subsequent behavior. Before they are 1 year old, most infants engage in social referencing by looking at their parents when confronted with new or unusual events (Seifert, 2007). They then base their behavior on the emotional and informational messages their parents communicate. Their ability to control their emotions develops over time as a result of neurophysiological growth (Cole & Tan, 2007a).

Meltzoff and Moore (1983, 1997) have demonstrated that social referencing begins during the first days of infancy, or even hours after birth, with infants' innate ability to imitate their parents' facial expressions of mouth opening and tongue protrusion (see photo on page 164). Youngsters 10 months of age use others' emotional expressions to appraise events such as those encountered in the visual cliff experiments conducted by Gibson and Walk (1960) and others (see Chapter 4). When they approach the illusory "drop-off," they look to their mothers' expressions and modify their own behavior accordingly. When their mother presents an angry or fearful face, most youngsters will not cross the "precipice." But when their mothers present a joyful face, they will cross it. Infants show similar responses to their mothers' vocalizations that convey fear or joy (Jaswal & Fernald, 2007).

Around 12 months, an infant begins to respond positively to strangers when his or her mother welcomes them. At this age, the infant also takes cues from the mother about how to react to pretend situations, such as when the mother pretends to eat from an empty bowl (Nishida & Lillard, 2007). Infants use social referencing to understand how to interpret new situations and to learn about potentially dangerous situations (Laible & Thompson, 2007).

Emotional Development in Infancy

From birth, infants have emotions. Newborns cry when they are unhappy and when they hear other newborns cry. They demonstrate a relaxed body posture when they are contented. Over the next 36 months, the tiny human acquires the capacity to express and recognize a much fuller range of emotions (Field, 2006; Lewis, 2007). Researchers offer a variety of theories about how and why emotional development occurs. In the second half of the twentieth century, *ethological theory* began to play an important role in psychological theory (see Chapter 2). Ethologists are influenced by Charles Darwin's theory and explain human adaptation by looking at the evolutionary function of changes. Researchers in neurobiology have been influenced by ethologist Paul Ekman's work (1980, 1994; Buss, 2008). Ekman believes that "affective processing [is] an evolutionary antecedent to more complex forms of information processing" and that "higher cognition requires the guidance provided by affective processing" (Adolphs & Damasio, 2001, p. 45).

Ekman and other researchers have shown participants from different cultures photographs of faces that people from Western societies would judge to display six basic emotions: happiness, sadness, anger, surprise, disgust, and fear. They found that individuals from around the world label the same faces with the same emotions. Ekman argued from these findings that the human central nervous system is genetically prewired for the facial expression of emotion: The face provides a window by which other people can gain access to our inner emotional life and by which we gain similar access to their inner life. Cross-cultural research supports the theory that humans associate specific emotions with specific facial expressions, and such research focuses on identifying body movements and vocalizations in different types of emotional situations (Camras & Fatani, 2008).

Psychologist Carroll E. Izard has been a central figure in the study of children's emotional development and has introduced the "differential emotions theory" (Izard & King, 2009). Like Paul Ekman, Izard contends that each emotion has a distinctive facial pattern. But Izard says that a person's facial expression colors what the thinking brain "feels." For example, he argues that muscular responses associated with smiling make you aware that you are joyful. And when you experience rage, Izard says, a specific pattern of muscle firings physiologically linked with anger "informs" your brain that you feel rage (rather than, say, anguish or humiliation). Thus, according to Izard, the feedback from sensations generated by your facial and related neuromuscular responses yield the distinctive subjective experiences that you recognize as different types of feeling (see Table 6.1).

Izard finds that babies have intense feelings from the moment of birth. But at first their inner feelings are limited to *distress, disgust,* and *interest.* In the course of their maturation, new emotions—one or two feelings at a time—develop in an orderly fashion. Izard says that emotions are preprogrammed on a biological clock: The infant's **social smile** (joy) emerges around 6 to 10 weeks in response to adult smiles and interactions; anger, surprise, and sadness at about 3 to 4 months; fear at 5 to 7 months; shame, shyness, and self-awareness at about 6 to 8 months; and contempt and guilt during the second year. Izard and others continue to develop intervention strategies to foster social competence (Izard et al., 2002).

Psychologist Joseph Campos argues that instead of merely registering a response to an event, emotions serve a function—that is, they emerge and are expressed as an individual seeks to accomplish something in interaction with his or her environment (Campos et al., 1993).

TABLE 6.1 Ten Fundamental Emotions

In his book *The Psychology of Emotions,* Izard (2004) explains the characteristics of what cross-cultural research reveals as 10 fundamental emotions. Because of high interest on the part of students, Izard also addresses the emotion of *love,* a feeling or state of relatedness with many others (parents, siblings, grandparents, spouse, partner, children, and friends).

Interest	Disgust
Enjoyment	Fear
Surprise	Shyness
Sadness	Shame
Anger	Guilt

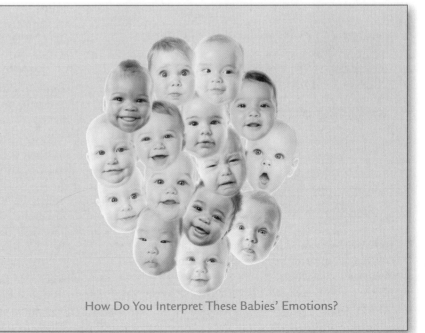

How Do You Interpret These Babies' Emotions?

Although Izard identifies the emotions that infants demonstrate with their facial expressions as the "basic emotions" (such as *interest, joy, fear, anger, disgust* and *sadness*), Campos says that other emotions (such as *shame, guilt, pride,* and *love*) are just as basic because of the function they play as an infant interacts with and adapts to his or her social world. He argues that all the basic emotions are in place at birth in a prewired process and that many of an infant's emotions do not become apparent to observers until after the infant first experiences them.

Whether emotions are present at birth or emerge only in the course of maturation, we know that infants show an increasing ability to discriminate among vocal cues and facial expressions—particularly happy, sad, and angry ones—in the first five months of life. In addition, their faces express their own emotions of joy, sadness, disgust, fear, and even anger within the first eight months. However, emotional expressions become more graded, subtle, and complex beyond the first year of life (Lewis, 2007).

Self-Regulation   One of the main tasks during the first two years is learning to regulate one's emotions, which is among the key building blocks of mental health. Infants are also learning to regulate sleep patterns, crying patterns, and feeding patterns. In the realm of emotions, **self-regulation** consists of an infant's growing ability to control negative emotions and integrate his

or her emotions adaptively into daily social interactions (Shonkoff & Phillips, 2000). Put another way, self-regulation is the child's ability to follow the everyday customs and norms valued by his or her culture (Keller, 2007).

The ability to self-regulate appears in the second half of the first year in healthy babies, although infants who have been abused or neglected and those who have physiological challenges may be on a different timetable (Calkins & Howse, 2004). Most infants learn this task in the context of their relationship with their mother, and research has found that in Western cultures, mothers who provide warm and sensitive caregiving are more likely to help them learn this important task (Keller, 2007). Parents should be aware that temperament may shape how infants manage stress, soothe themselves, or cope with frustration (Grolnick, McMenamy, & Kurowski, 2006).

> **Questions**
>
> How do various theorists view the development and role of emotions? What are the differences among Ekman's, Izard's, and Campos's theories of why emotions develop? When might we expect an infant to demonstrate emotional self-regulation, and why is that important?

Stages in Children's Emotional Development   Child psychiatrist Stanley Greenspan and Nancy Greenspan, a former health economist with the federal government, were among the first researchers to propose a model of emotional development of the typical healthy child from birth to age 4 (Greenspan & Greenspan, 1985). According to the Greenspans' model, even in infancy children are actively constructing and regulating their environments. The Greenspans' stages and timetable are shown in Table 6.2.

Early attachment relationships lead to purposeful communication and then to the toddler's creation of a coherent, positive sense of self. These early accomplishments lay the foundation for the young child's use of language, pretend play, and engagement in "emotional" thinking (Hyson, 1994). The Greenspans stress that the more negative factors interfere with a child's achieving emotional milestones, the more likely it is that the child's intellectual and emotional development will be compromised later. For example, teachers can see that a young child will have difficulty mastering the ABCs if Mom and Dad have just separated.

The *Greenspan Social-Emotional Growth Chart* is a basic scale for early identification of a child's social and emotional functioning (ages birth to 42 months) and can be completed by a parent or caregiver. Dr. Greenspan and colleagues developed the *Functional Emotional Assessment*

Social Referencing and Infant Imitation   Dr. Andrew Meltzoff began studying imitative facial and hand gestures of newborn human infants in 1977, and his discoveries have transformed our understanding of infant cognition, personality, and brain development.
Source: A. N. Meltzoff & M. K. Moore, "Imitations of facial and manual gestures by human neonates." *Science,* 1977, *198,* 75–78.

TABLE 6.2 The Greenspans' Model of Infant and Young Child Emotional Progress

The typical healthy child from birth through age 4 should be observed displaying these emotional behaviors.

Age	Milestones of Emotional Development	Observed Behaviors
0 to 3 months	Self-regulation and interest in the world	Infants learn to calm themselves, and they develop a multisensory interest in the world.
2 to 7 months	"Falling in love"	Infants develop a joyful interest in the human world and engage in cooing, smiling, and hugging.
3 to 10 months	Developing intentional communications	Infants develop a human dialogue with the important people of their lives (for instance, they lift their arms to a caretaker, give and take a toy offered to them, gurgle in response to a caretaker's speech, and enjoy peek-a-boo games).
9 to 18 months	Emergence of an organized sense of self	Toddlers learn how to integrate their behavior with their emotions, and they begin to acquire an organized sense of self (for example, they will run to greet a parent returning home or lead a caretaker to the refrigerator in order to show hunger, instead of simply crying for dinner).
18 to 36 months	Creating emotional ideas	Toddlers begin to acquire an ability to create their own mental images of the world and to use ideas to express emotions and regulate their moods.
30 to 48 months	Emotional thinking—the basis for fantasy, reality, and self-esteem	Young children expand these capacities and develop "representational differentiation," or emotional thinking; they distinguish among feelings and understand how they are related; and they learn to tell fantasy from reality.

Source: Greenspan, S., & Greenspan, N. T. (1985). *First feelings.* New York: Viking Press.

Scale that can be administered by clinicians (Greenspan, DeGangi, & Wieder, 2001). Dr. Greenspan's further explanation of typical emotional development from birth through age 5 can be found at the Web site of the Interdisciplinary Council on Development and Learning Disorders (www.icdl.com).

Stability of Emotional Expression   Izard and others have also turned up evidence of continuity, or stability, of emotional expression in children (Abe & Izard, 1999). The amount of sadness a child shows during a brief separation from his mother seems to predict the amount of sadness the same child shows six months later (Izard & Malatesta, 1987). Izard does not deny that, in some measure, learning conditions and experience modify a child's personality. A mother's mood affects how her infant feels and acts (Carver & Vaccaro, 2007). When mothers of 9-month-old youngsters display a sad face, their children often display the same facial expression. Izard believes that "the interactional model of emotional development is probably correct. Biology provides some thresholds, some limits, but within these limits, the infant is certainly affected by the mother's moods and emotions" (quoted by Trotter, 1987, p. 44). Much parental socialization is directed toward teaching children how to modulate their feelings and expressive behavior to conform to cultural norms.

Attachment

Attachment is an affectional bond that one individual forms for another and that endures across time and space (Ainsworth, 1992, 1993, 1995). An attachment is expressed in behaviors that promote proximity and contact. Among infants these behaviors include approaching, following, clinging, and signaling (smiling, crying, and calling). Through these activities a child demonstrates that specific people are important, satisfying, and rewarding. Some writers call this constellation of socially oriented reactions "dependency," whereas laypeople refer to it simply as "love."

What Is the Course of Attachment?   Schaffer and Emerson (1964) studied the development of attachment in 60 Scottish infants over their first 18 months of life. They identified three stages in the development of infant social responsiveness:

- During the first two months of life, *infants are aroused by all parts of their environment.* They seek arousal equally from human and nonhuman aspects.
- Around the third month, *infants display indiscriminate attachment.* During this stage, infants become responsive to human beings as a general class of stimuli. They protest the withdrawal of any person's attention, whether the person is familiar or strange.

- When they are about 7 months old, *babies show signs of specific attachment.* They begin displaying a preference for a particular person and, over the next three to four months, make progressively more effort to be near this attachment object.

Children differ greatly in the age at which specific attachment occurs. Among the 60 babies in the Schaffer and Emerson study, 1 showed specific attachment at 22 weeks, whereas 2 did not display it until after their first birthdays (Van IJzendoorn & Sagi, 1999).

Cross-cultural differences also play a part in this development. Mary Ainsworth found that infants in Uganda show specific attachment at about 6 months of age—a month or so earlier than the Scottish infants studied by Schaffer and Emerson (1964). Similarly, it was found that separation protest occurred earlier among infants in Guatemala than among those in the United States (Lester et al., 1974). Researchers attribute the precocity of the Ugandan and Guatemalan infants to cultural factors. Ugandan infants spend most of their time in close physical contact with their mothers (they are carried about on their mother's back), and they are rarely separated from her. Generally, American infants are placed in their own rooms shortly after birth. Such separation is virtually unknown in Guatemala, where most rural families live in a one-room rancho. Other research findings with a small sample of Colombian mothers and infants support Ainsworth's concepts of attachment theory (Posada et al., 2004).

Schaffer (1971, 1996) suggests that the onset of separation protest, or separation anxiety, is directly related to a child's level of *object permanence.* Social attachment depends on the ability of infants to differentiate between their mother and strangers and on their ability to recognize that their mother continues to exist even when she is not visible. In terms of Piaget's cognitive theory (outlined in Chapter 5), these abilities do not appear until late in the sensorimotor stage. Indeed, Sylvia M. Bell (1970) finds that in some instances the concept of **person permanence**—the notion that an individual exists independently of immediate visibility—might appear in a child before the concept of object permanence. Studies by other researchers also confirm that protests over parental departures are related to a child's level of cognitive development (Kagan, 1997; Klaus & Klaus, 1998).

How Do Attachments Form?   Psychologists have advanced two explanations of the origins or determinants of attachment, one based on an *ethological* perspective and the other on a *learning* perspective. Psychoanalytically oriented ethologist John Bowlby (1969, 1988) said that attachment behaviors have biological underpinnings that can best be understood from a Darwinian evolutionary perspective. The human species survived, despite an

Fostering Secure Infant-Parent Attachment   Close proximity and contact promote affectional bonds that individuals form for one another. Hteik Soe, an 18-year-old from Taung Pet village in Myanmar (formerly Burma) in Southeast Asia, cuddles her 8-days-old newborn baby.

extended period of infant immaturity and vulnerability, because mothers and infants are endowed with innate tendencies to be close to each other. This reciprocal bonding functioned to protect the infant from predators when humans lived in small nomadic groups (Bowlby, 1969, 1988).

According to Bowlby, human infants are biologically preadapted with a number of behavioral systems ready to be activated by appropriate "elicitors" or "releasers" within the environment. Close physical contact—especially holding, caressing, and rocking—often soothes and quiets a distressed, fussing infant. Indeed, an infant's crying literally compels attention from a caregiver, and smiles accomplish much the same end (Grossman, Grossman, & Kindler, 2005). Rheingold observes:

As aversive as the cry is to hear, just so rewarding is the smile to behold. It has a gentling and relaxing effect on the beholder that causes him to smile in turn. Its effect upon the caregiver cannot be exaggerated. Parents universally report that with the smile the baby now becomes "human." With the smile, too, he begins to count as a person, to take his place as an individual in the family group, and to acquire a personality in their eyes. Further-more, mothers spontaneously confide that the smile of the baby makes his care worthwhile. In short, the infant learns to use the coin of the social realm. As he grows older and becomes more competent and more discriminating, the smile of recognition appears; reserved for the caregiver, it is a gleeful response, accompanied by vocalizations and embraces. (Rheingold, 1969a, p. 784)

Clinging, calling, approaching, and following are other kinds of behavior that promote both contact and proximity. Viewed from the evolutionary perspective, a child is genetically programmed to a social world and "in this sense is social from the beginning" (Ainsworth, Bell, & Stayton, 1974). Parents, in turn, are said to be genetically predisposed to respond with behaviors that complement the infant's behaviors (Ainsworth, 1993). The baby's small size and distinctive body proportions apparently elicit parental caregiving (Alley, 1983). Although attachment occurs universally across cultures, recent studies of twin infants have found that environmental influences are more significant than genetic factors in explaining whether an infant was securely attached or not (Bokhorst et al., 2003).

Bowlby's research focused on the infant's relationship with the mother; he theorized that the emotional nurturance the mother provided was the primary source of secure attachment for her child. Learning theorists look at the mother's contribution to attachment from a different angle; they attribute attachment to socialization processes. According to psychologists such as Robert R. Sears (1972) and Jacob L. Gerwitz (1972), the mother is initially a neutral stimulus for her child. She comes to take on rewarding properties, however, as she feeds, warms, dries, and snuggles her baby and otherwise reduces the infant's pain and discomfort. Because the mother is associated with satisfaction of the infant's needs, she acquires secondary reinforcing properties—her mere physical presence (her talking, smiling, and gestures of affection) becomes valued in its own right. In brief, attachment develops.

Learning theorists stress that the attachment process is a two-way street. The mother also finds gratification in her ability to terminate the child's piercing cries and to allay her own discomfort associated with the nerve-wracking sound. Also, infants reward their caregivers with smiles and coos. Thus, as viewed by learning theorists, the socialization process is reciprocal and derives from a mutually satisfying and reinforcing relationship (Adamson, 1996).

Ethologically oriented psychologists point out that attachment has adaptive value in keeping infants alive. It promotes proximity between helpless, dependent infants and protective caregivers. But attachment also fosters social and cognitive skills.

Programmed to Elicit Parenting? Ethologists believe that human beings are genetically programmed for parenting behavior and that caretaking tendencies are aroused by "cuteness." Apparently, short faces, prominent foreheads, round eyes, and plump cheeks all stir up parental feelings.

Who Are the Objects of Attachment? In their study of Scottish infants, Schaffer and Emerson (1964) found that the mother was most commonly the first object of specific attachment. However, in 5 percent of cases the first attachment was to the father or to a grandparent. And in 30 percent of cases, initial attachments to the mother and to another person occurred simultaneously. Also, the number of a child's attachments increased rapidly. By 18 months, only a small percent displayed attachment to only one person, but almost one-third of the babies had five or more attachment persons. Indeed, the concept of attachment as originally formulated was too narrow (Bronfenbrenner, 1979). Because infants have ongoing relationships with their fathers, grandparents, siblings, and a network of extended family or caregivers, some psychologists suggest that theory and research should focus on the infant's social network—a web of ties to significant others (Lamb, 2010b; Lewis, 2007).

Maternal Responsiveness and the Strange Situation Mary Ainsworth and her colleagues devised a procedure called the "Strange Situation" to capture the quality of attachment in the infant-parent relationship (Ainsworth, 1983). In the **Strange Situation** study, a mother and her infant enter an unfamiliar playroom where they find interesting toys as well as a stranger. After a few minutes, the mother leaves the room and the child is given an opportunity to explore the toys and interact with the unfamiliar adult. When the mother returns, the infant's behavior is observed, and then the procedure is repeated a total of eight times with slightly different variations. Ainsworth became intrigued by differences in the children's behavior, especially the way they reacted upon reunion with their mothers (Ainsworth & Wittig, 1969):

When their mother returned to the room, **securely attached infants** (pattern B attachments) would greet her warmly, show little anger, or indicate they wanted to be picked up and comforted by their mother. About 60 percent of the infants used the mother as a secure base from which to explore the unfamiliar environment and as a source of comfort following separation. Securely attached infants seemed to have received consistent, sensitive, and responsive mothering (Ainsworth, Bell, & Stayton, 1974).

Insecure/avoidant infants (pattern A attachments), about 20 percent, ignored or avoided the mother on her return. Subsequent studies have repeated and extended the Strange Situation research, suggesting that these infants show little distress at being released from the parent's hold and tend to treat a stranger with a response similar to that given to the parent. Typically, these infants are easily consoled by a stranger (Wilson, 2001).

Insecure/resistant infants (pattern C attachments), about 10 to 15 percent, were reluctant to explore the new setting when they entered the playroom and would cling to the mother and hide from the stranger. However, when the mother returned after her brief absence, the infant would initially seek contact with the mother only to reject her by squirming and pushing her away, with continued crying. Ainsworth (1993) finds that these children display more maladaptive behaviors and tend to be angrier than the infants in the other groups. Using the Strange Situation method, Main and Solomon (1986) identified another attachment category:

> **Disorganized/disoriented infants** (pattern D attachments). D-pattern youngsters seem to lack coherent coping strategies during separation episodes, and upon parental return, they indicate confusion and apprehension toward their mothers (Jacobsen, Edelstein, & Hofmann, 1994). Moreover, D-pattern youngsters apparently are at greater risk for social maladaptation in childhood (Vondra et al., 2001). D patterns are likely to be linked to parents who suffered from abuse or deep emotional loss and have not yet resolved these issues.

Ainsworth contended that the A, B, and C patterns of attachment behavior in the Strange Situation reflect the quality of maternal caregiving that children receive during their first 12 months of life. She traced the origins of the A and C patterns to a disturbed parent-child relationship, one in which the mother was rejecting, interfering, or inconsistent in caring for the child. The mothers would often over- or understimulate their baby; fail to match their behavior to that of the child; be cold, irritable, and insensitive; and provide only perfunctory care. Not all children classified as either anxiously or insecurely attached suffer from attachment disorders, but researchers have found that a subgroup of insecurely attached young children have *reactive attachment disorder,* which is described later in this chapter (Wilson, 2001).

A secure attachment relationship, in which the caregiver provides warm and consistent care while feeding, holding, comforting, and playing with an infant, leads the young child to expect that interactions with others will be positive. As the child moves from infancy to the second year, this secure base enables the child to expand his or her world. Even as a toddler moves toward greater independence, the presence of a sensitive parent enables him or her to learn to cope with stressful situations, often through social referencing. Toddlers facing frightening or confusing new situations often turn to an adult they trust for cues about their physical and verbal responses. Researchers have found that children who have secure attachment relationships tend to exhibit more emotional understanding, to be more cooperative, and to demonstrate less aggression in close relationships (Thompson & Lagattuta, 2006).

For about 40 years, social scientists have been studying the significance of infant attachments to fathers as well as mothers (Lamb, 2010a). Researchers continue to find that secure attachments to both mothers and fathers strongly predicted the emotional behavior of young adults. When parents play together with infants in ways that promote exploration, cooperation, and autonomous problem solving, their children are highly likely to grow into adults who ask for help, value close relationships, and appropriately regulate their emotions in stressful situations (Lamb, 2010a). With the changing arrangement of many modern families, researchers have expanded their study of attachment and of the role of stepfathers, divorced fathers and custodial and noncustodial parenting, and gay fathers (Lamb, 2010b). Yet research on the role of fathers in Asian and African countries is in its infancy (Nsamenang, 2010; Schwalb, Nakazawa, Yamamoto, & Hyun, 2010).

Stranger Anxiety and Separation Anxiety   A maturing infant reacts very strongly in two stressful situations: when encountering strangers and when a significant caregiver leaves. Wariness of strangers, an expression of the fear-wariness behavior system, usually emerges about a month or so after specific attachment begins. **Stranger anxiety,** a wariness of unknown people, seems to be rather common among 7- to 8-month-old infants, seems to peak at 13 to 15 months, and decreases thereafter. When encountering a strange person, particularly when a trusted caregiver is absent, many youngsters frown, whimper, fuss, look away, and even cry (Waters, Matas, & Sroufe, 1975). Even at 3 and 4 months of age, some babies stare fixedly at a strange person, and occasionally this prolonged inspection leads to crying (Bronson, 1972).

Stranger Anxiety Between 8 and 15 months or longer, infants show wariness of strangers, such as a new caregiver, those dressed in costumes, or a photographer who gets too close.

Another behavior that 8-month-old infants commonly display is **separation anxiety,** crying and exhibiting other signs of distress when a familiar caregiver leaves. This stage may last for 8 months or so, and it may return in later stages of development during times of stress. Separation anxiety emerges at about the same age for Guatemalan Indian, Israeli, and African bush infants (Buss, 2008). There is a biological basis for separation distress; infants experience a decrease in endorphins, the hormones that control feelings of well-being, when separated from their mothers (Cozolino, 2006). (Mothers also experience this decrease in endorphins, and they often report anxiety when they are separated from their babies.) The distress behaviors of the infant experiencing separation anxiety serve the evolutionary function of keeping caregivers nearby (Abe & Izard, 1999).

Reactive Attachment Disorder Young children who experience frequent changes in caregivers, whose caregivers do not respond to their attempts to elicit caretaking, or who are severely deprived of care or maltreated during the period of infancy do not form bonds with others and are diagnosed with **reactive attachment disorder (RAD)** (DSM-IV and ICD 10). Zeanah and Gleason (2010) suggest there are two subtypes. The *emotionally withdrawn/inhibited RAD subtype* of children are emotionally withdrawn or inhibited, rarely look to others for comfort, and rarely react when comfort is given. The *indiscriminate RAD subtype* consists of children who

look for affection from anyone, even from strangers, and who fail to show expected reserve with unfamiliar adults.

RAD sometimes develops in children who are adopted out of abusive or neglectful circumstances. Since the 1990s, researchers have been studying the physical, emotional, cognitive, and social development of more than 100,000 Romanian infants and children who were raised in orphanages in the late 1980s and later adopted by American, Canadian, and European families. After the collapse of the dictatorship and the Romanian economy in 1989, it was discovered that thousands of Romanian infants and young children had been abandoned to orphanages. The infants, raised in crowded, stark institutions where they were deprived of normal stimulation and nurturance by caregivers, received only food and shelter. They were severely deprived of cognitive, emotional, and social attention because of overcrowding and understaffing (Zeanah, Smyke, Koga, & Carlson, 2005). These institutionalized children showed many more serious attachment issues and signs of RAD than children raised in other settings.

The English and Romanian Adoptees Study Team continues to research the negative impact of severe early deprivation on adopted survivors. Two groups of children were randomly selected from a pool of Romanian adoptees: those adopted before 24 months of age and those adopted between 24 months and 42 months of age. The researchers' findings from extensive assessment at age 4 and age 6 indicate that children exposed to longer periods of deprivation exhibited greater deficits in cognitive, social, physical, and medical well-being (i.e., malnourishment, smaller head circumference, and delays in growth). The younger the infant was at adoption, the greater the resiliency following adversity, and the researchers found that psychosocial interventions played a significant role in enabling the children to catch up their cognitive skills (Kreppner et al., 2007).

Ongoing research has found that the length of time the Romanian children experienced deprivation has proved to be the strongest predictor of future cognitive abilities. Indeed, even though researchers had theorized that education might foster improvements in cognitive development, they found that five years of schooling had not produced an increase in IQ for the children from Romanian institutions (Beckett et al., 2006). In 2010, the English and Romanian Adoptee Project team reports: "The follow-ups at 15 years of age, and into young adulthood, have revealed unusual patterns of persisting, specific patterns of deficits and problems that appear to be deprivation-specific, out of which arise a number of emotional, conduct and peer-relationship problems" (Holmes, 2010). Children who experience abuse from caregivers are more likely to show aggression toward themselves and controlling behaviors toward caregivers (Hardy, 2007). Children who experience multiple primary caregivers (such as those who live in successive foster homes) are at risk of being diagnosed with RAD (Hardy, 2007).

IMPLICATIONS FOR PRACTICE

Carole A. Rosen, Licensed Certified Social Worker

I am a licensed certified social worker at the High Risk Birth Clinic in Binghamton, New York, and I presently work with families who have children with disabilities or who have had babies born at risk. My main tasks are to complete child and family assessments, to provide short-term and crisis intervention counseling, and to act as a liaison with community agencies. I am fluent in American Sign Language and am called in to help parents who are deaf or who have infants or young children with disabilities to access necessary services.

I earned a bachelor's degree in sociology and humanities and a master's in social work (MSW). I am certified to practice in New York State (LCSW) and am an American Certified Social Worker (ACSW). When I was a social worker at a developmental center, I planned, evaluated, and implemented clinical goals for mentally retarded, developmentally disabled, and head-injured clients, and I conducted orientation, training, and supervision of new social workers within the treatment team in counseling and behavior management techniques. I have also worked in a community college in New York,

providing individual, vocational, and academic counseling; administered a foster-care program for court adjudicated youths in a four-county region of upstate New York; and provided psychotherapy for individuals, couples, and families, including play therapy for children in an agency and in private practice.

The characteristics a person should have to enjoy working as a social worker are compassion, patience, and tolerance. Anyone seeking an internship, supervised clinical experience, or work experience needs to enjoy working with diverse families; to have knowledge of health-related and social issues and developmental disabilities; and to have knowledge of community services and the ability to assess individuals and families for treatment. Also, you need to be flexible regarding work settings and family circumstances.

I believe that social work is an absolutely wonderful profession because you can work in many different settings with such a wide variety of people. It is an exciting field where you are always learning from the people with whom you serve, as well as from the constant research being done in the field.

Infants who are disabled, unwanted, "difficult," lethargic, or chronically ill, or who experience extended separation from parents, run a higher risk of experiencing attachment difficulty (Biringen, Fidler, Barrett, & Kubicek, 2005). Family social problems (i.e., separation, neglect and abuse, or foreign adoptions) may augment the frequency of this disturbance (Wimmer, Vonk, & Bordnick, 2009). There is support available for adoptive parents to help them deal with the effects of their children's earlier physical, emotional, and social neglect. Research shows that children diagnosed with RAD may be helped through treatment by therapists trained in attachment therapy (Wimmer et al., 2009).

Facilitating Secure Attachment   Classifications derived from the Strange Situation predict social functioning in preschool with teachers and peers. Youngsters judged to have secure attachments to their mothers are socially more competent in preschool, sharing more and showing a greater capacity to initiate and sustain interaction. Such children

are also more accepting of their mothers' showing attention to their older brothers and sisters, and secure older siblings are more likely to assist and care for their younger brothers and sisters than are insecure older siblings (Teti & Ablard, 1989). And the B-pattern children seem more resilient and robust when placed in stressful or challenging circumstances (Stevenson-Hinde & Shouldice, 1995).

These findings are consistent with the speculation of attachment theorists that young children who enjoy a secure attachment to their parents develop internal "representational models" of their parents as loving and responsive and of themselves as worthy of nurturance, love, and support. By contrast, youngsters with insecure attachments develop "representational models" of the caregiver as unresponsive and unloving and of themselves as unworthy of nurturance, love, and support (Bowlby, 1969, 1988). Some evidence suggests that the various patterns of attachment might be transmitted across generations via parents' states of mind—their internal working models of attachment relationships that they subtly communicate to their children (Bowlby, 1969; Steele, 2002).

Goodness of Fit   Thomas and Chess (1987) have introduced the notion of **goodness of fit** to refer to the match between the characteristics of infants and their families. In a good match, the opportunities, expectations, and demands of the environment are in accord with the child's temperament. A good match fosters optimal development. Conversely, a poor fit makes for a stormy household and contributes to distorted development and maladaptive functioning. Thomas emphasizes that parents need to take their baby's unique temperament into account in their child-rearing practices. Children do not react in the same ways to the same developmental influences. Domineering, controlling parental behavior can make one child anxious and submissive and lead another to be defiant and antagonistic. As a consequence, Thomas and his colleagues (1963, p. 85) conclude, "There can be no universally valid set of rules that will work equally well for all children everywhere."

Parents with difficult babies often feel considerable anxiety and guilt, wondering what they might be doing wrong. The knowledge that certain characteristics of their child's development are not primarily due to parental malfunctioning has proved helpful to many parents. A given environment does not have identical functional consequences for all children. Babies are individuals from the moment they draw breath. Pregnant women sometimes notice temperamental differences between successive children while the babies are still in the womb! Researchers highlight the importance of adjusting child-rearing practices to the needs of individual children.

Sometimes caregivers encounter children who overreact to sensory stimulation, are highly excitable, or have behavioral "meltdowns." A. Jean Ayres, an occupational therapist who worked with children with developmental disabilities, developed *sensory integration theory* about brain-behavior relationships. **Sensory integration** is "a normal developmental process that allows one to take in, process and organize sensations one receives from one's body and the environment" (Ayres, 1972, p. 11). Although people are familiar with the senses of sight, touch, sound, taste, and smell, most do not know that specialized parts of the nervous system also sense the force of gravity and sense body movement and position (these are referred to as the *vestibular* and *proprioceptive systems*). It is important to a child's well-being not only that the sensory systems function effectively, but also that all of the senses work well together.

A child who is overly sensitive or avoids stimulation can be referred to as *sensory defensive*. Such a child exhibits the fight-or-flight reaction to an otherwise non-threatening sensation. Thus, a child may perceive touch, sound, taste, or movement as threatening or even painful. For example, it is well known that children with autism

have unusual sensory-perceptual issues (Bogdashina, 2003; Grandin, 2008). A child who underreacts will seek out stimulation in greater intensity and duration than the typical child, sometimes hurting himself (i.e., banging his head or running into walls). These issues may adversely affect a child's ability to adapt to behavioral demands of daily life within a family, and a referral to an occupational therapist with training and expertise in sensory integration may be appropriate (Bundy, Lane, & Murray, 2002).

Cross-Cultural Views of Attachment   Although the behaviors that indicate an infant's attachment to a caregiver are universal, how we interpret the meaning of those behaviors must be understood in its proper cultural context (Cole & Tan, 2007b). For example, researchers found that Japanese infants were much more highly stressed when they were separated from their mothers than were German infants during the Strange Situation experiment. Was this because the Japanese infants were more insecure, as we would assume if a Western baby exhibited this behavior? In fact, it is just the opposite. Because Japanese mothers are physically close to their children all day and rarely allow them to feel distress, their infants felt higher levels of stress when separated from their mothers than did Western infants, who are accustomed to brief separations (van den Boom, 2001).

Measurements of social attachment are not easily and seamlessly transferable from culture to culture (Antonucci, Akiyama, & Takahashi, 2004). When Japanese infants were assessed using this method, their responses did not correspond with Ainsworth's A, B, and C patterns of attachment. This anomalous finding may reflect the differences between Japanese and U.S. social values and practices of raising children (Rothbaum, Weisz, Pott, Mayake, & Morelli, 2000).

Carlson and Harwood (2003) found that Puerto Rican mothers, who value proper demeanor in their children very highly, used much more physical control with their very young infants than did Anglo American mothers while they were feeding them or teaching them to be calm and well-behaved. This mothering style is considered intrusive in an Anglo American mother; the social goal of Anglo American mothers is to teach their children to be independent and explore their worlds for themselves. But the overall social goal of the Puerto Rican mothers is to teach their children proper demeanor. The researchers reported that, contrary to their expectations, the Puerto Rican children exhibited secure attachments to their mothers at 12 months. They concluded that their results "call into question the use of a single, universal definition of maternal sensitivity" (Carlson & Harwood, 2003, p. 53). Recent cross-cultural research in Japan, China, Korea, and Africa reveals that mothers and fathers cultivate attachment in culturally sensitive ways (Nsamenang, 2010; Shwalb, Nakazawa, Yamamoto, & Hyun, 2010).

FURTHER DEVELOPMENTS

The Rising Incidence of Autism

Autism is a lifelong developmental disability characterized by impaired attachment and social interaction, sensory-perceptual differences, speech difficulties, and unusual, repetitive patterns of behavior. These impairments begin to appear before the age of 3 (Centers for Disease Control and Prevention, 2009b). One heart-wrenching factor is that the child appears to develop normally but begins to regress. The number of U.S. children diagnosed with autism has risen by 600 percent since 1990 (Lord & Bishop, 2010). The CDC's Autism and Developmental Disabilities Monitoring Network (2009) states that this is "a national health emergency." By 2009, based on studies with 8-year-olds in ten states, 1 in 110 U.S. children (1 in 70 among boys) has been diagnosed with an **autism spectrum disorder (ASD)** (CDC, 2009). ASD is a classification of neurological disorders characterized by impairment in social and cognitive functioning that ranges from mild to disabling. Some children also have medical issues such as seizures, sleep problems, and gastrointestinal, metabolic, and immunological challenges (U.S. Department of Health and Human Services, 2010g).

Kanner (1943) reported the first case histories of U.S. children diagnosed with autism. A small percent of children were diagnosed each year until the 1990s, and Figure 6.1 shows the dramatic rise in ASD cases that has occurred since then. Environmental changes and exposures may have contributed to the rising incidence of ASDs, and some children in special education were rediagnosed as having an ASD (Bishop, Whitehouse, Watt, & Line, 2008). The diagnostic criteria published in the American Psychiatric Association's *Diagnostic and Statistical Manual* (DSM-IV) were broadened in 1994. How autism is defined and measured plays a role in this rapid rise.

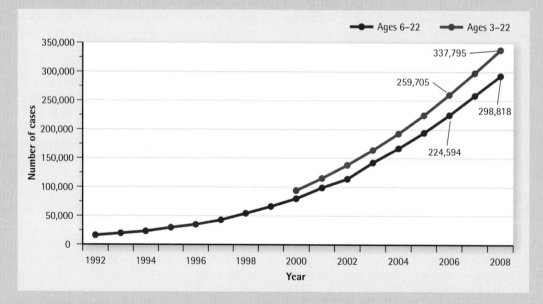

FIGURE 6.1 U.S. Child Population with Autism Spectrum Disorders, 1992–2008 The number of children diagnosed with autism spectrum disorders continues to increase rapidly and is considered a "national health emergency."
Source: http://www.idea.org, Centers for Disease Control.

Temperament

Issues of continuity and discontinuity in children's emotional expressions invariably lead investigators to the matter of infant temperament and, more particularly, to differences in temperament among youngsters.

Generally, children's personality and temperament are underlying factors in their ability to successfully develop emotional and social bonds. These connections are difficult for children with autism or other pervasive developmental disorders (PDDs) because of their inability to

The Autism Society of America (ASA) reminds us that each person with autism is a unique individual with his or her own personality, but there are some common characteristics. People with autism may exhibit the following traits (listed from mild to severe):

- Resistance to change; tantrums
- Difficulty expressing needs; use of gestures or pointing instead of words
- Repeating words or phrases in place of normal, responsive language
- Laughing, crying, showing distress for reasons not apparent to others
- Abnormal or repetitive movements
- Prefer to be alone; difficulty mixing with others
- Sustained odd play; inappropriate attachments to objects
- May not want to cuddle or be cuddled
- Little or no eye contact
- Unresponsive to normal teaching methods
- Oversensitivity or undersensitivity to pain
- No real fear of danger
- Physical overactivity or extreme underactivity
- Uneven gross/fine motor skills
- Not responsive to verbal cues despite normal hearing
- Overactive or underactive senses

What Causes Autism?

The cause of autism spectrum disorder is unknown, but genetic and environmental factors appear to be involved (Autism Society of America [ASA], 2008). Autism is not caused by bad parenting. There are differences in brain-neuronal structure and biochemistry in autistic children (Johnson & Myers, 2007). Several studies with conflicting findings have been published about the association between vaccines containing *thimerosal* (a preservative that contains ethyl mercury, a neurotoxicant) and autism (Mutter, Naumann, Schneider, Walach, & Haley, 2005). Since 1990, infants were given more vaccines than in previous cohorts. In 1999 the CDC asked pharmaceutical companies to remove thimerosal from childhood vaccines (some still have thimerosal). Even though a CDC study found that use of thimerosal-containing vaccines is not associated with ASD (Price et al., 2010), other researchers, parents, and investigators dispute these findings (Olmstead, 2007). As of 2011, a CDC "Vaccine Safety" site still said, "Immunization providers should use the vaccines [containing thimerosal] available in their stock" (CDC, 2011).

Some scientists are looking into the link among heredity, genetics, and medical problems such as viral infections, metabolic imbalances, and environmental chemicals. Higher rates of autism occur among children with other genetic anomalies (ASA, 2008). The Autism Genome Project found specific evidence that genetic mutations were implicated in at least some cases of ASD (Buttenschøn et al., 2009; Pinto et al., 2010). The best supposition about cause is that a genetic propensity combines with environmental factors (such as parental age or exposure to toxins or infections) to produce ASD (U.S. Department of Health and Human Services, 2010g). A recent study at the University of California, San Diego, used functional MRI scanning to observe the brains of children as young as 14 months old who had been diagnosed with autism. Even at the earliest ages, the brains of autistic children seem to work differently than those of normal children. This work could make possible the earlier diagnosis and treatment of children with autism (Wang, 2010).

How Is Autism Diagnosed?

There is no one medical or biological test to diagnose autism. Any child suspected of having autism should be evaluated by a *multidisciplinary team*, including a child psychologist or psychiatrist, a speech pathologist, an occupational therapist trained in sensory integration, and a developmental pediatrician or pediatric neurologist.

Effective Approaches for Autism

Diagnosing younger children is vital because the sooner the therapy begins, the more effective it can be. Children from birth to age 3 with the diagnosis of autism are eligible for early intervention services, and after age 3 they get services through their school districts. Children with autism require many types of therapies. Parents must engage a pediatrician who is knowledgeable about the health-care needs of children with ASDs (Myers, Johnson, and the Council on Children with Disabilities, 2007).

The average lifetime cost to care for a child with an ASD is estimated to be $3 to 5 million, which significantly affects the entire family and society (Lord & Bishop, 2010). Parents must provide constant supervision; they experience higher levels of stress, conflict, and marital discord; and such parents undergo stages of grief and are often in social isolation (Seligman & Darling, 2007). The child affected by this disorder needs lifelong care. But progress is being made, and lives of people with autism are improving thanks to daily developments in the field.

understand social cues (Bogdashina, 2003; Izard, 2001). (See the *Further Developments* box, "The Rising Incidence of Autism.")

The term **temperament** refers to the relatively consistent, basic dispositions that underlie and modulate much of a person's behavior. The temperamental qualities that developmental psychologists most often study are those that are obvious to parents. The qualities that parents and researchers value vary across cultures. In Western industrialized cultures, the "Big Five" are extraversion, conscientiousness, agreeableness, absence of neuroticism, and openness to experience. Other cultures might have a different list of priorities, which might include devotion to parents, emotional self-sufficiency, or proper demeanor (Cole & Tan, 2007b).

Western cultures tend to value extraversion highly. In American culture, uninhibited people are typically more popular than inhibited ones, and timid youngsters are often pressured by parents and others to be more outgoing. As we noted in Chapter 2, Jerome Kagan (1997) finds that some children are born with a tendency, or "vulnerability," toward extreme *timidity* when faced with an unfamiliar person or situation, whereas other children are not. This difference persists as they grow up and has profound social consequences. Timid youngsters remain quietly watchful at the outskirts of activities, whereas uninhibited youngsters are eager to approach new experiences. Kagan believes we should provide our children with an environment that is, within reason, respectful of individual differences. He notes that although we push our inhibited children toward the uninhibited end of the scale, other cultures, such as China and Japan, tend to view uninhibited behavior as disrespectful and unseemly.

Individuality in Temperament   Alexander Thomas and his associates have come to conclusions quite similar to those of Kagan from their studies of more than 200 children (Thomas & Chess, 1987). They found that babies show a distinct individuality in temperament during the first weeks of life that is independent of their parents' handling or personality styles. Thomas views temperament as the stylistic component of behavior—the *how* of behavior, as opposed to the *why* of behavior (motivation) or the *what* of behavior (content). Thomas names the three most common types of babies:

> *Difficult babies.* These babies wail and cry a great deal, have violent tantrums, spit out new foods, scream and twist when their faces are washed, eat and sleep in irregular patterns, and are not easy to pacify (10 percent of infants are difficult babies).
>
> *Slow-to-warm-up babies.* These infants have low activity levels, adapt very slowly, tend to be withdrawn, seem somewhat negative in mood, and show wariness in new situations (15 percent of infants are slow to warm up).
>
> *Easy babies.* These infants generally have sunny, cheerful dispositions and adapt quickly to new routines, foods, and people (40 percent of all infants are easy babies).

The remaining 35 percent of infants show mixtures of traits that do not readily fit into these categories. Thomas and Chess (1987) also found that all infants possess nine

---

TABLE 6.3 Nine Components of Temperament

Activity level: The proportion of active versus inactive periods

Rhythmicity: The regularity of hunger, sleep, bowel movements

Distractibility: The degree to which extraneous stimuli alter behavior

Approach/withdrawal: The response to a new person or object

Adaptability: The ease with which a child adapts to changes

Attention span and persistence: The amount of time a child pursues an activity, and whether he or she is easily distracted

Intensity of reaction: The energy of response

Threshold of responsiveness: The degree of stimulation needed to evoke a response

Quality of mood: The amount of pleasant, friendly behavior versus unpleasant and unfriendly behavior

---

components of temperament that emerge quickly after birth and continue relatively unchanged into adulthood (see Table 6.3).

Researchers have long thought of temperament in terms of genetic heritage, but recently ethologists have begun to explore the connections between biology and temperament. An intriguing study found that children who were rated as shy were most likely to have been conceived during the months of longest sunlight—late July to late September in the Northern Hemisphere and January and February in the Southern Hemisphere. The first four months of gestation for these children were months when daylight was decreasing. Researchers theorize that biochemical changes in the mother, such as increases in melatonin and decreases in serotonin, may have increased the likelihood that a fetus that was genetically predisposed toward shyness would develop into a shy child (Kagan & Fox, 2006).

There is evidence that some aspects of temperament are present with more regularity in one gender than in the other. Girls tend to show more ability to control impulses and to focus attention better, whereas boys tend to externalize problems through aggressive behavior. Boys, to a slight degree, are more active, enjoy intense external stimuli, and are less shy than are girls (Else-Quest, Hyde, Goldsmith, & Van Hulle, 2006).

Environment can also shape perceptions of an infant's temperament. Parents who are stressed or depressed may rate their infants as more fearful, less easy to soothe, and less happy than independent observers would. In addition, parents who are depressed are likely to respond by interacting less with their infants, speaking to them less frequently, and showing less affection. This can have important developmental consequences for the child (Räikkönen et al., 2006).

Can Temperament Be Moderated?   Until the 1990s, most researchers focused on the degree to which an infant's temperament predicted adult behavior. Since then, researchers have come to look more often at ways in which environment moderates infant temperaments. Several studies have found that fearful infants are less likely to be aggressive at school age when their parents use a gentle style rather than a harsh style of parenting. Fearful infants with harsh parents are more likely to be rated aggressive by teachers when they reach school age. One trait that research has linked with changes in a child's environment is inhibition; inhibited children are more likely to become more outgoing when they are cared for, during a good part of the day, out of the home during the first few years (Rothbart & Bates, 2006). A number of studies have found that girls are more likely than boys to become less inhibited (Martin & Fox, 2006). Enough studies have found a link between environment and moderation of temperament to lead some researchers to use the term *vulnerability* or *tendency* rather than *temperament* to suggest that a child's environment may foster change.

Questions

What are the various views about how infant attachment occurs, the functions of attachment, and what the expected stages of attachment are for an infant over the first few years of life? What role does the caregiver play in this important process? In what way does the infant's temperament play a role?

THEORETICAL APPROACHES TO SOCIAL-EMOTIONAL DEVELOPMENT

Over the past three decades, changes in family structure and stability for many families have led to an increasing sense of urgency among parents and society at large to discover the "best" parenting practices that promote the healthiest emotional-social development for all infants and children. When parents are sole caregivers or are overworked or unemployed, chronically stressed, overtired, depressed, or unwell, they have little time or energy to properly nurture, stimulate, or protect infants and young children. It is important for those working in health, education, psychology, and human services to understand the major personality theories that have been formulated and researched over the past century.

In the early 1900s, psychoanalytic and psychosocial scientists began to focus on the long-term impact of healthy emotional development in infancy and early childhood. Later, behavioral and cognitive theories emerged. In the mid-to-late twentieth century, ecological and biological/ethological theories were proposed (Thomas, Chess, & Birch, 1970).

The Psychoanalytic View

In the early 1900s, Sigmund Freud revolutionized the Western view of infancy by stressing the part that early infant and childhood experience plays in fashioning the adult personality (see Chapter 2). Central to Freud's thinking was the idea that adult *neurosis* has its roots in childhood conflicts associated with the meeting of instinctual needs, such as sucking, expelling urine and feces, assertion of self, and pleasure (Freud, 1930/1961). Freud's views have had an important influence on child-rearing practices in the United States. According to Freudians, the systems of infant care that produce emotionally healthy personalities include breast-feeding, a prolonged period of nursing, gradual weaning, an on-demand nursing schedule, delayed and patient bowel and bladder training, and freedom from excessive punishment.

Many pediatricians, clinical psychologists, and family counselors have accepted major tenets of Freudian theory, especially as popularized by the late Dr. Benjamin Spock in his best-selling book *Baby and Child Care.* Published through many revisions between 1946 and 1998, it is said to have sold more copies worldwide (in 39 languages) than any other book except the Bible. Freud stated that infants become "fixated" in the oral stage if they are not allowed to continue to nurse at the breast or suck from a bottle until they are physically ready and motivated to drink from a cup. Similarly, Dr. Spock promoted an on-demand feeding schedule during infancy, in contrast to a rigid feeding schedule as advocated by pediatricians of the early twentieth century. He urged parents to cuddle babies and give them affection to make them happier and more secure. Pediatricians and other experts continue Dr. Spock's legacy at the www.drspock.com Web site.

Many psychologists, especially those influenced by the Freudian tradition, hold that children's relationships, especially with their mothers, in their early years are extremely significant and serve as prototypes for their later relationships. Viewed from this perspective, the health, maturity, and stability of a person's relationships derive from her or his early emotional-social ties. The goal of psychoanalytic therapy is to use therapeutic techniques to discover and discuss any traumatic events from early childhood that are concealed in the patient's subconscious and may be causing adult personality disturbances.

Psychoanalytic research, however, has produced few empirical findings, relying more on case studies and observational recordings. In an extensive study of child-rearing practices, Sewell and Mussen (1952) found no tie between the types of feeding children had received as infants and their oral symptoms, such as nail-biting, thumb-sucking, and stuttering. Many psychologists believe that children are considerably more resilient and less easily damaged by traumatic events and emotional stress than Freud thought (Werner, 1990).

The Psychosocial View

As we noted in Chapter 2, Erikson maintained that the essential task of infancy, the **oral-sensory stage,** is the development of a basic trust in others, which occurs as a caregiver is responsive and consistent in feeding the infant. He argued that during infancy, children learn whether the world is a good and satisfying place where one's needs are met by others—or a source of discomfort, frustration, and misery. If the child's basic needs are met with genuine and sensitive care, the child develops a "basic trust" in people and a foundation of self-trust (a sense of being "all right" and a complete self).

In Erikson's view, a baby's first social achievement is the willingness to let its mother move out of sight without undue anxiety or rage, because "she has become an inner certainty as well as an outer predictability" (Erikson, 1963, p. 247). The psychosocial psychologists highlight the importance of resolving progressive conflicts for healthy emotional and social development throughout life.

Erikson's theories about stages of development were developed in the context of a Judeo-Christian industrial society, and his psychosocial theory does not transfer to all societies. For example, Japanese mothers seek to cultivate *amae,* or the merging of the child's self with her own self (Shiraev & Levy, 2007). In Erikson's theory of development, this would be considered an unhealthy dependence because the child would be perceived as failing to move toward the desired goal of autonomy.

The Behavioral (Learning) View

The strict behaviorism (also called learning theory) of John Watson in the early 1900s, and later B. F. Skinner, had nearly banished the study of emotions from the curriculum of behavioral science by the 1950s. Watson claimed he could take a dozen healthy infants and form them into anything he wanted them to be. Behaviorists recognize that infants are endowed with innate emotions (including fear, rage, and love), but they are unconcerned about the child's subconscious or inner feelings. They are concerned with noting the outward display of emotions through observable behaviors and then with rewarding "appropriate" behaviors or extinguishing "inappropriate" behaviors.

Through keen observation and a system of rewards or punishments, children's behaviors can be shaped or controlled. Reinforcement schedules, time-outs, and other behavioral techniques are used to create desired patterns of behavior and expression of emotions. Most early childhood education programs that follow principles of traditional behavioral theory do not give priority to emotional development (Hyson, 1994). By mastering specific academic and self-regulatory skills, children are supposed to gain positive feelings and self-confidence.

The Cognitive View and Information Processing

Since the 1960s, a growing number of developmentalists and cognitive psychologists have focused their research on components and stages of cognitive growth, building on the legacy of Jean Piaget's body of work on cognitive development in children. Legions of child psychologists and neuroscientists devote their attention to how children reason and solve problems, starting with the infant's experience of sensory stimulation. In the past, they have viewed emotion as peripheral, of interest mostly when it interfered with rational thought or found deviant expression in the form of disruptive behavior or mental illness.

However, a renewed interest in the study of emotions is correcting the predominantly behavioral or cognitive view of human development. In the process, information-processing researchers and psychologists are rejecting the image of humankind as simply a "stimulus-response black box" or a "thinking machine" (Kagan, 1993). Contemporary theories attempt to examine cognitive information-processing mechanisms that link affect (emotions) to thinking and behavior (Forgas, Baumeister, & Tice, 2009).

Within the context of an increasing prevalence of behavioral and emotional problems in the United States and other countries, and mounting cross-cultural research on children's emotional well-being, pediatricians are more concerned than ever about identifying and treating children with emotional and/or psychosocial impairments. About 20 to 30 percent of U.S. preschoolers, school-age children, and adolescents display psychosocial problems (mental, emotional, or behavioral)—yet only about half receive treatment (Merikangas, 2009; National Center for Health Statistics, 2010b). Thus, pediatricians agree that the *Pediatric Symptom Checklist* (*PSC*) should become a mandated part of all well-child checkups (Hacker, Williams, Myagmarjav, Cabral, & Murphy, 2009). The PSC (Figure 6.2) has been devised to reflect parents' perceptions of their children's psychosocial functioning.

Pediatric Symptom Checklist (PSC)

Emotional and physical health go together in children. Because parents are often the first to notice a problem with their child's behavior, emotions, or learning, you may help your child get the best care possible by answering these questions. Please indicate which statement best describes your child.

Please mark under the heading that best describes your child:

			NEVER	SOMETIMES	OFTEN
1.	Complains of aches and pains	1	_____	_____	_____
2.	Spends more time alone	2	_____	_____	_____
3.	Tires easily, has little energy	3	_____	_____	_____
4.	Fidgety, unable to sit still	4	_____	_____	_____
5.	Has trouble with teacher (6- to 16-year-old children only)	5	_____	_____	_____
6.	Less interested in school (6- to 16-year-old children only)	6	_____	_____	_____
7.	Acts as if driven by a motor	7	_____	_____	_____
8.	Daydreams too much	8	_____	_____	_____
9.	Distracted easily	9	_____	_____	_____
10.	Is afraid of new situations	10	_____	_____	_____
11.	Feels sad, unhappy	11	_____	_____	_____
12.	Is irritable, angry	12	_____	_____	_____
13.	Feels hopeless	13	_____	_____	_____
14.	Has trouble concentrating	14	_____	_____	_____
15.	Less interested in friends	15	_____	_____	_____
16.	Fights with other children	16	_____	_____	_____
17.	Absent from school (6- to 16-year-old children only)	17	_____	_____	_____
18.	School grades dropping (6- to 16-year-old children only)	18	_____	_____	_____
19.	Is down on him or herself	19	_____	_____	_____
20.	Visits the doctor with doctor finding nothing wrong	20	_____	_____	_____
21.	Has trouble sleeping	21	_____	_____	_____
22.	Worries a lot	22	_____	_____	_____
23.	Wants to be with you more than before	23	_____	_____	_____
24.	Feels he or she is bad	24	_____	_____	_____
25.	Takes unnecessary risks	25	_____	_____	_____
26.	Gets hurt frequently	26	_____	_____	_____
27.	Seems to be having less fun	27	_____	_____	_____
28.	Acts younger than children his or her age	28	_____	_____	_____
29.	Does not listen to rules	29	_____	_____	_____
30.	Does not show feelings	30	_____	_____	_____
31.	Does not understand other people's feelings	31	_____	_____	_____
32.	Teases others	32	_____	_____	_____
33.	Blames others for his or her troubles	33	_____	_____	_____
34.	Takes things that do not belong to him or her	34	_____	_____	_____
35.	Refuses to share	35	_____	_____	_____
	Total score		_____	_____	_____

Does your child have any emotional or behavioral problems for which she/he needs help?   ( ) N   ( ) Y

Are there any services that you would like your child to receive for these problems?   ( ) N   ( ) Y

If yes, what services? _____

FIGURE 6.2 Pediatric Symptom Checklist (Available in English and Spanish)   A parent completes this questionnaire as part of a routine health-care visit, which facilitates recognition of children's behavioral/emotional problems. The following scale is used: 0 - not true (as far as you know); 1 - somewhat or sometimes true; 2 - very true or often true. For children aged 2 to 5, the scores on items 6, 7, 14, and 15 are ignored, and the total score is based on the 31 remaining items. The cutoff score for young children aged 2 to 5 is 24 or greater. For older children, a total score of 28 or higher is indicative of significant psychosocial problems.

Source: From *Psychosocial Problems, Screening, and the Pediatric Symptom Checklist,* Michael Jellnik, M.D., and J. Michael Murphy, Ed.D., Boston, Massachusetts, 1999, http://www.dbpeds.org

The Ecological View

Urie Bronfenbrenner's ecological theory (1997) posits that a variety of environmental influences—ranging from a child's family, school, and community resources through government policies and global economic forces—contribute to the emotional and social development of children (see Chapter 2). The nuclear family (siblings, single parent, grandparent, stepparent, cohabiting partner, or main caregiver) will have the greatest influence. Many young children are also in child-care or preschool environments, which means teachers and caregivers exert their influence several hours per day. The availability of high-quality child care, low-cost nutrition programs, and low-cost health care in a community directly affects each child's development. Opportunities for employment in a community can make or break a family—and economic decline and joblessness are more prevalent now.

The policies established by state legislators also affect the services offered at a local level to families, especially for education and after-school programs, housing, and health care. Federal decisions to allocate funds to preserve economic stability by helping commercial banks and large corporations mean there will be less funding for health-care or child-care programs. Federal welfare laws can either keep families together or, through judicial decrees, keep the father out of the home or ensure that he is only minimally involved, leading to even greater poverty.

On a cultural level, a society may have fluctuating views on the value of women and children, traditional nuclear families, single-parent families, stepfamilies, cohabiting families, same-sex families, foster families, and immigrant families.

The Biological View

Recently, researchers have begun to search for ways to integrate knowledge about biology and knowledge about environmental effects to create new models of understanding how human emotions develop. Some of this work has focused on how genetics determines a child's response to stress. For example, researchers have found that children with high levels of a certain enzyme are more likely than other children to respond to maltreatment with antisocial behavior (Bugental & Grusec, 2006). Some researchers are going even further in their quest to understand how genetics and environment interact. They have found that when an infant who has a genetic predisposition toward aggression is placed in a situation of chronic stress, such as abuse, his or her body may produce the hormones that "turn on" the aggression gene, resulting in higher levels of aggressive behavior in childhood and adulthood. Researchers are also examining the role of genetic predisposition for autism spectrum disorders, as well as many other child disorders.

This research is in its early stages. To date, it has focused on stressful early experiences such as deprivation and abuse, and researchers are eager to learn more about how sensitive nurturing interacts with genetics to produce positive, appropriate behaviors (Repetti, Taylor, & Saxbe, 2007).

Questions

What is the central focus of healthy personality development during the early years of life for each of the psychoanalytic, psychosocial, behavioral, cognitive, ecological, and biological views? Is there any one theory that you believe covers all aspects of infant social-emotional development? Explain your perspective.

SOCIAL DEVELOPMENT

Above all else, infants are social beings who need to become socialized into their own human group. As developmental psychologist Harriet L. Rheingold puts it, "The human infant is born into a social environment; he can remain alive only in a social environment; and from birth he takes his place in that environment" (1969, p. 781). Humanness, then, is a social product (O'Connor & Rutter, 2000). And children's "humanness" is learned within a family environment.

The number of single-parent families continues to increase, but about two-thirds of U.S. children live with married-parent families. Adding to this mix of societal concerns is the changing demographic nature of young children in the United States (see Figure 6.3). As of 2010, nearly 74.5 million children up to age 17 constituted about 25 percent of the U.S. population. The U.S. Census Bureau projects increasing numbers of children under age 19 by 2050, but they will represent a smaller proportion of the full population (U.S. Bureau of the Census, 2009b).

What might this mean for those pursuing careers working with children and their families? A steady increase of infants and preschool children has significant implications for long-term employment opportunities in professions such as child care, preschool or Head Start, pediatric medicine, nursing, dental hygiene, speech therapy, physical therapy, occupational therapy, audiology, optometry, child psychology, social work, psychiatry, and many health and social science professorial or consulting occupations—in addition to opportunities for those who wish to write books or design software, playgrounds, toys, clothing, or furniture for infants and young children.

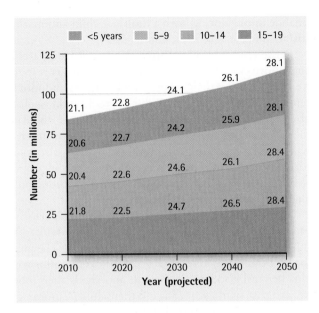

FIGURE 6.3 Projected Numbers of U.S. Children, 19 and Under, by Age Groups: 2010–2050. The U.S. Census Bureau projects a steady increase in the number of young children in the United States over the next 40 years (note the upward trend for all age groups). Children now make up about 25 percent of the population, but they are becoming a smaller *proportion* of the total U.S. population because there are over 230 million adults—and that number too is increasing.
Source: U.S. Bureau of the Census. (2008). 2008 National population projections 2010–2050. Retrieved November 30, 2010 from http://www.census.gov/population/www/projections/2008projections.html

Early Relationships and Child Rearing

During the first few years of life, children begin to learn emotional skills that will become more sophisticated as they age. They learn to trust caregivers who consistently provide for their needs. They learn to soothe themselves when they face upsetting or unexpected stimuli. They learn to seek help. They learn to shift their attention away from negative or distressing situations toward a more positive stimulus. Some of these skills begin to emerge even before a child reaches 6 months of age, and they continue to develop and expand as the child moves into toddlerhood (Calkins & Howse, 2004).

Clearly, it is very important that the child receive adequate and warm caregiving during the first several years. But who is the best provider of care for infants? In U.S. society, more than 60 percent of mothers of young children are in the labor force, often by necessity (Livingston & Cohn, 2010b). Yet many mothers of infants who work feel conflicted; they want to be at home with their babies, but the household needs their income.

A 2007 poll of working mothers found that less than one-third of working women felt that full-time employment was ideal for them. Most favored part-time employment over staying at home or working full-time. But the majority of fathers felt that full-time work was

the best situation for them. In this poll, both women and men seemed to agree that having the mother spend significant amounts of time with young children is desirable (Pew Research Center, 2007).

Household Labor and Infant Care   Caring for infants involves more than playing with them and meeting their physical needs. Infant care also involves a lot of physical work: doing housework and laundry, shopping for groceries and household needs, washing dishes, vacuuming, cooking, picking up toys, and so forth. A study that looked at how married couples allocate housework found that in the 1980s and 1990s, husbands of women who worked full-time began doing more housework than husbands of women who did not work full-time. A shift in behavior and social norms has taken place, and couples have begun to view housework in a more egalitarian way. When a woman works full-time, most partners assume that men will do some of the housework (Cunningham, 2007).

However, women still carry a disproportionate share of the responsibility for child care and housework, whether they are employed or not. One study of 20 industrialized countries found that fathers do only about one-third of the housework, regardless of whether their wives are employed (Hook, 2006). Disagreements and stress about housework have a direct impact on marital satisfaction, especially when a baby arrives. Mothers who feel supported by fathers in the area of housework and child care are more likely to feel that their partnership with the father is successful (Meier, McNaughton-Cassill, & Lynch, 2006). The following section looks at recent research about the contributions and effects of various caregivers of children in the first few years of life.

The Mother as Caregiver

Freud (1940, p. 188) saw the child's relationship to the mother as having lifelong consequences, calling it "unique, without parallel, established unalterably for a whole lifetime as the first and strongest love-object and as the prototype of all later love relations—for both sexes." The psychoanalytic tradition has strongly influenced U.S. life; researchers, clinical psychologists, psychiatrists, sociologists, and the court system have for many decades focused almost exclusively on the mother-child tie.

In the mid-twentieth century, some social scientists suggested that biological predeterminers contribute to a more nurturant, "maternal" disposition in women and to a more instrumental, "paternal" disposition in men (Erikson, 1964; Harlow, 1971). Others suggested that the differences between men and women are products of the socially defined roles assumed by mothers and fathers (Parsons, 1955). Today, researchers look at a combination of biological and social factors as they study the role mothers play in the emotional development of infants. A consensus has developed that mothers' interactions with their infants fulfill four important functions. First, her verbal and physical interactions lay the groundwork for the infant's understanding of himself or herself and others as beings with intentions that they act to fulfill. Second, a mother's care helps the infant develop a secure attachment. Third, mothers' verbalizations with their babies foster more complex forms of communication and the development of language and simple socialization.

Finally, mothers play an important role in the emotional development of their infants. For example, when a mother plays a game in which she runs her fingers up a baby's tummy, pauses to wait for the baby's smile or gurgle of pleasure, and then reinforces that behavior with cooing or tickling, she is helping her baby experience joy. Mothers and children from different cultures tend to play and pretend in similar ways, although Argentine and Japanese mothers and children indulge in play that is more symbolic while American children and mothers play in more exploratory ways. This interaction helps babies learn to regulate their emotions—for example, by introducing visual distractions to soothe an overly excited or fussy child (Cote & Bornstein, 2005).

The Father as Caregiver

In the 1950s, the television version of parenthood was that mothers stayed at home full-time and fathers were in the workplace as "breadwinners." This was the societal norm that most media accepted as reality, even though some mothers were working outside the home. Attitudes and research about the role of fathers in the American family began to change by the 1970s. Lamb defined the construct of paternal involvement to mean "the father's direct contact with his child, through caretaking and shared activities" and accessibility for interaction with the child (Pleck & Masciadrelli, 2004, p. 223). Since the 1990s, there has been a revolution in the thinking of U.S., European, and Asian social scientists about the importance of fathers in young children's emotional, cognitive, and social development (Lamb, 2010a). Contemporary U.S. social scientists are just beginning to study the role in child well-being that is played by Latino fathers (men from many Mexican, Central American, and South American subgroups) (Cabrera & Garcia Coll, 2004).

Increasingly, researchers conclude that fathers are just as good as mothers at taking care of, nurturing, and bonding with children, even in early infancy, leading to better cognitive outcomes for the children (Lamb, 2010b). Also, fathers are more likely to continue caring for their children when they become involved in caring for them as infants. A father's caring for his infant is a dynamic in promoting both a healthier child and marital satisfaction (Pleck & Masciadrelli, 2004).

Parke (1979) observed the behavior of U.S. parents of newborns and found that fathers were just as responsive as mothers to their infants' vocalizations and movements. Fathers touch, look at, talk to, rock, and kiss their babies in much the same fashion as mothers do. And when alone with their infants, fathers are as protective, giving, and stimulating as mothers. Fathers also play more physical games with their children, such as tossing the baby in the air and later, with growing children, more rough-and-tumble games (Parke, 1996).

Studies consistently show that a mother performs better in the parenting role when the father provides her with emotional support and encouragement. The man who gives warmth, love, and ego gratification to his wife helps her feel good about herself, and she is then more likely to pass on these feelings to their child (Cummings, Goeke-Morey, & Raymond, 2004).

Moreover, being a father contributes to a man's self-concept, personality functioning, and overall satisfaction with life (Pleck, 2010). By the 1990s, more men were "stay-at-home dads," doing much of the child care, while the mother earned income. Also, some fathers take on the role of custodial parent when a marriage ends (Amato & Dorius, 2010). Today, about 3 percent of U.S. children are living with single-parent fathers (U.S. Bureau of the Census, 2009c).

In 2009, more than 41 percent of U.S. births were to unmarried women (Hamilton, Martin, & Ventura, 2010b). In the first national survey of unmarried fathers,

Fathers Figure Significantly in the Lives of Their Children The presence of a positive father-child relationship improves a child's overall academic achievement and IQ test performance, self-esteem, social competence, and ability to develop self-control and avoid unhealthy behaviors.

TABLE 6.4 Prevalence of Fathers' Involvement After Nonmarital Birth: Mothers' Reports

In this study, the majority of non-wed, nonresident fathers maintained some type of contact with their child over five years. However, by their fifth birthday, nearly two-fifths of children born to unmarried parents have had no contact with their fathers in the previous two years.

	Year 1 % of M (n = 3,234)	Year 3 % of M (n = 3,113)	Year 5 % of M (n = 3,037)
Nonresident fathers (%)	47.6	55.9	62.9
All nonresident fathers			
Saw child since previous survey	87	70.9	63.2
Saw child more than once in past month	62.7	47	43.1
Mean number of days father saw child (range 1–30)	8.36	6.28	5.26
Fathers who saw child more than once in past month			
Mean number of days father saw child (range 1–30)	13.33	13.35	12.21
Mean engagement in activities (range 0–7 days)	2.08	2.1	1.51

Source: Carlson, M. J., & McLanahan, S. S. (2010). Fathers in fragile families. In M. E. Lamb (Ed.). *The role of the father in child development* (pp. 241–269). Hoboken, NJ: Wiley.

social scientists used the term *fragile families* to describe families that include dads who are younger than most married men, are of minority status, have a high school education or less, are unemployed or work few hours per week, have health and social-emotional issues (including drug use), and/or have engaged in criminal behavior or been incarcerated (Carlson & McLanahan, 2010). Those children who continue to have contact with—and economic support from—their fathers are less likely to have behavior problems and more likely to do well in school. The more contact with their fathers, the better the outcomes for the child. In this national study, some nonresident fathers remain involved with their child, but mothers report that for many, such involvement declines considerably over years 3 and 5 (see Table 6.4).

Studies of fathering across cultures reveal that men engage with their infants in emotionally warm ways. In the Aka ethnic group in the forest region of the Central African Republic, fathers cuddled their children during leisure time and played with their babies with tickling and bouncing. Indian fathers in New Delhi displayed affection for their babies while holding them. Major social changes related to paternal involvement with children continue to occur in Japan, Korea, and China—where cultural norms have traditionally viewed mother-child relations as more important for child well-being (Schwalb et al., 2004).

Good, Better, Best? One should not conclude that either mothering or fathering is superior. Each parent affords the child somewhat different kinds of experiences. The ability to nurture is not a property of one sex or the other, and societies differ considerably in their definitions of the parenting roles. For instance, in a survey of 141 societies, fathers in 45 societies (nearly one-third)

maintained a "regular, close" or "frequent, close" proximity to the infant. At the other extreme, in 33 societies (23 percent), fathers rarely or never were in close proximity to the infant (Crano, 1998).

All of this is not to say that mothers and fathers are interchangeable; both make their own contributions to children's care and development. Research suggests that the mother-child and father-child relationships may be qualitatively different and may have different influences on a child's development (Tamis-LeMonda, Shannon, Cabrera, & Lamb, 2004). Lamb and Lewis (2004) find that mothers most often hold babies to perform caretaking functions, whereas fathers spend four to five times as much time playing with their infants as they do in providing physical care for them. Fathers' positive interactions with their children directly benefited their children's language and cognitive development. Good, consistent paternal involvement from men across the economic spectrum produced high-quality impacts on the child's development (Tamis-LeMonda et al., 2004). Infants learn a good many lessons from the daily continuities in these early relationships. It seems that small moments—not dramatic episodes or traumas—give rise to most of the expectations that children evolve and bring to their later relationships.

Grandparent or Kinship Care

The term **kinship care** has evolved to mean an arrangement in which a relative or someone else emotionally close to a child takes primary responsibility for rearing the child (Lutman, Hunt, & Waterhouse, 2009). Researchers, policymakers, human services professionals, school officials, clergy, and medical professionals noticed a substantial increase in children living with other relatives since the 1990s, with the greatest growth occurring among grandchildren living with grandparents—and no parent present. Divorce, child abuse, and parental drug abuse are the most common reasons why children live with grandparents, other kin, or foster parents—although teen pregnancy, mental illness, economic problems, the incarceration of a parent, and the disability or death of a parent are also reasons (Poehlmann et al., 2008).

In 2009, about 3 million American children were living with their grandparent(s), with other relatives, in foster care, or with a nonrelative. White and black children are much more likely to live with grandparents than are Hispanic and Asian children (Federal Interagency Forum on Child and Family Statistics, 2011). One in five grandparent caregivers lives below the poverty line, and many of the grandchildren lack health insurance. Caring for grandchildren often stretches household resources, and grandparents typically experience a period of grieving over the family circumstances that brought a grandchild into their home. But most grandparents feel satisfaction with their new familial role and would make the same choice if they had it to do over again (Poehlmann et al., 2008).

Knowing a family's structure—and the presence or absence of parents—helps providers understand the needs of these families and their eligibility for services for the grandchildren (Gleeson et al., 2009). For example, grandchildren living with a grandmother only and no parent present have the highest poverty rate. The Urban Institute report *Identifying and Addressing the Needs of Children in Grandparent Care* helps those who work with families understand the full impact of this relationship on both grandparents and young grandchildren. The AARP Web site now provides links to many grandparenting and kinship care resources in your state and community: www.aarp.org/families/grandparents. Many caregiver grandparents are unaware of community resources and may not want to seek public aid, but all across the country, grandparents are establishing support groups through senior citizen centers and churches and are sharing ideas, resources, and comfort.

Gay and Lesbian Parenting

When social scientists first studied the well-being of children living in homes headed by people in same-sex relationships, most child subjects had been born or raised for a time in a traditional family and then later became the subjects of research when one of the parents decided to move into a same-sex relationship (Bos, van Balen, & van den Boom, 2007). Critics of same-sex couples' raising children argued that children of lesbian or gay parents would experience psychosocial maladjustment because of the absence of one biological parent and because of stigmatization from peers. There were confounding effects on child well-being research because the children

were often coping with parental divorce, a mother's coming out as lesbian or a father's coming out as gay, and establishing a new family life with a parent's new partner. There is a very large body of empirically sound research on the effects of marital discord and divorce on children's psychological well-being, behavior, and cognitive outcomes (Woolsley, Dennis, Robertson, & Goldstein, 2009). It is natural for any child to feel divided between two homes with different values (Telingator & Patterson, 2008). For such children in same-sex families, there are also social-emotional issues that arise, just as in a stepfamily situation (Barrett, 2010).

Critics of these initial studies cite small numbers of subjects and samples that are not representative, but lesbian mothers were often facing legal reprisals or court-ordered loss of custody of children. Moreover, interviews with young children often result in children saying what the interviewer wants to hear. And of course, longitudinal investigations of child outcomes into adulthood are ongoing. Certainly such children face adjustments in addition to those faced by a child conceived and raised by a biological parent and a "social parent."

By the 2000s, family life became an increasingly important component of many same-sex relationships, but lesbian and gay parents represent a diverse group (Riskind & Patterson, 2010). A growing number of gay and lesbian couples began families through adopting and bearing children, as a few states began to legalize civil unions, domestic partnerships, and same-sex marriage. Thus, recent research focuses on the development of children adopted or born by in vitro fertilization within the relationship of same-sex parents (Riskind & Patterson, 2010). Generally this research concludes that most children of lesbian and gay parents show no difference in development from children raised by heterosexual parents (Patterson & Hastings, 2007). Results suggest that regardless of family type, children feel secure and have high self-esteem when they have close, loving relationships with caring adults and that a parent's sexuality does not affect that person's ability to parent effectively (Fairtlough, 2008). However, children with same-sex parents may experience varying levels of homophobia in social and school situations. This tends to be enhanced in countries with lower acceptance of homosexuality (Bos, van Balen, Gartrell, Peyser, & Sandfort, 2008).

Lesbian biological and "social mothers" rate their satisfaction with their relationships highly, and overall they state a strong commitment to the children they raise together. The children of these mothers benefit from this high level of commitment to parenting (Bos et al., 2007). Children of lesbian and gay parents are often raised in the context of, and benefit from, an extensive social network of caring adults, called "families of choice" (Patterson & Hastings, 2007). They often develop a strong sense of empathy for others as the result of being raised in a context where their parents and members of their extended network experience prejudice and discrimination (Riggle, Whitman, Olson, Rostosky, & Strong, 2008).

Sibling Relationships

The birth of a new baby has a significant impact on older siblings. They will have to adjust and accept less attention from their parents, while still getting their needs met within the family situation. Some siblings become "initiators" with parents to get their needs met; others withdraw and appear to resent the baby (Thompson & Halberstadt, 2008). Wise parents prepare older children in age-appropriate ways for the arrival of a new baby in the family. Some families have older children attend the new sibling's birth; others decide to introduce the new baby to siblings when they bring the baby home from the hospital.

Most siblings display a strong degree of caring, attachment, and protectiveness toward a new child in the family. From the wealth of research on infant cognitive, social, and emotional development over the past 40 years, we know that babies need and appreciate sensory and emotional stimulation, and an older sibling is the perfect person to assist. Infants learn from their siblings how to play teasing games, how to enter into a shared world of imagination, and how to predict emotional responses in others (Dunn, 2007).

There appear to be cultural differences in the relationship of older siblings to younger ones in terms of voluntary responsibility, sharing of a wanted object, and allowing the younger child freedom of choice (Mosier & Rogoff, 2003). Older siblings typically serve as the models for younger siblings, and younger siblings often want to "tag along" with older children. This can create conflict at times, but siblings normally learn to get along with each other and to share with each other. In many non-Western cultures, older siblings play a crucial role as caregivers of infants and toddlers (Dunn, 2007). As we shall see in Chapter 18, we normally have our longest-lasting relationships with siblings (Bank & Kahn, 1997).

Cultural Differences in Child Rearing

Child-rearing practices differ from one society to another, with greater contrast between industrialized and nonindustrialized countries. In Chapter 4, we learned that in many cultures of the world the mother cradles her baby next to her body during the day—even if she is working in the fields—and, at night, continues to share sleeping quarters for at least a few years. Attachment patterns differ also (Harwood, 1992). A-pattern infants are relatively more prevalent in Western European nations and C-pattern infants in Israel and Japan (Van IJzendoorn & Kroonenberg, 1988). Whereas U.S. women and men

Sibling Interactions and Culture While both her parents work, this 8-year-old girl watches and cares for her baby sister. Americans are shocked to see young children caring for babies in other cultures, but people from other cultures are shocked to find out that American babies spend a lot of time alone in infant carriers, cribs, and strollers.

have the benefit of a maximum of 12 weeks of unpaid maternity or paternity leave, Western European nations such as Sweden have well-developed and competent national child-care systems, and parents are paid for one year for staying at home to raise children (see Table 6.5) (Heymann et al., 2007).

Multiple Mothering Traditionally in the United States, the preferred arrangement for raising children has been the **nuclear family,** which consists of two parents and their children. The view that mothering should be provided by one figure has been extolled by many professionals as the key to good mental health. Yet this view is a culture-bound perspective, for children throughout the world are successfully reared in situations of **multiple mothering**—an arrangement in which responsibility for a child's care is dispersed among several people.

In some cases, one major mother figure shares mothering with a variety of mother surrogates, including aunts, grandmothers, older cousins, non-kin neighbors, or co-wives. For instance, Jacquelyne Faye Jackson (1993) shows that within the United States, a multiple caregiver arrangement—based on shared caregiving by a number of parent figures irrespective of maternal marital status—is normative

TABLE 6.5 Maternity Leave in a Few Selected Countries, 2010

Country	Mandated Length of Leave	Percentage of Wages Paid	Provider of Benefit
Sweden	480 days	80	Social insurance
Denmark	52 weeks	100	Municipality and employer
United Kingdom	52 weeks	90	Employer and government
Italy	5 months (20 weeks)	80	Social insurance
Canada	17 weeks	55	Government
France	16 weeks	100	Social security
Austria	16 weeks	100	Government or employer
Germany	14 weeks	100	Government and employer
Mexico	12 weeks	100	Social security
United States	12 weeks	0	—

Source: United Nations, Statistics Division. (2010). *Statistics and indicators on women and men: Maternity leave benefits.* New York: United Nations. Retrieved November 15, 2010 from http://unstats.un.org/unsd/demographic/products/indwm/tab5g.htm

for African American infants. Another example of diffused nurturance is that found among the Ifaluk of Micronesia:

> For the Westerner, the amount of handling the infant receives is almost fantastic. The infant, particularly after it can crawl, is never allowed to remain in the arms of one person. In the course of a half-hour conversation, the baby might change hands ten times, being passed from one person to another.... The adults, as well as the older children, love to fondle the babies and to play with them, with the result that the infant does not stay with one person very long.... Should an infant cry, it is immediately picked up in an adult's arms, cuddled, consoled or fed.... There is little distinction between one's own relatives and "strangers." If he needs something, anyone will try to satisfy his need. Every house is open to him and he never has to learn that some houses are different from others. (Spiro, 1947, pp. 89–97)

Another approach to child care is found in the collective form of social and economic life in Israeli agricultural settlements (*kibbutzim*). From early infancy, children were reared in a nursery by two or three professional caregivers, with communal sleeping at night. Originally, their own mothers visited them regularly, but the concept of communal infant sleeping at night away from parents has been abandoned in favor of sleeping at the parental home (Tikotzky, Sharabany, Hirsch, & Sadeh, 2010).

Despite this arrangement of "concomitant mothering," systematic observation, testing, and clinical assessment have demonstrated that kibbutz children are within the normal range in intelligence, motor development, mental health, and social adjustment (Aviezer et al., 1994). The kibbutzim model continues to evolve with the economic success and incorporation of younger workers into this worker cooperative–social engineering experiment (Rosner, 2000).

Questions

Who is most likely to perform child-care duties in a two-parent family and why? In what ways does a mother's or father's involvement with the infant benefit the family? To date, what do researchers find about the well-being of children being raised in same-sex families? If you have siblings, how important were they in your "growing-up" years?

CHILD CARE FOR YOUNG CHILDREN

Presently, the U.S. Department of Health and Human Services is conducting the largest and most comprehensive longitudinal study ever undertaken, *The National Children's Study,* in which researchers from a consortium of 40 agencies will examine the effects of many environmental influences (including social and emotional) on the health and development of more than 100,000 children from before birth through age 21. The study is using the evolutionary psychological approach to human development to examine the effects of a child's environment on his or her health and development. This is the largest-scale study of its kind, and its goal is to improve child health and well-being and develop strategies and guidelines to prevent disease and encourage healthy growth ("Growing Up Healthy," 2010). Child-care arrangements are among the main variables under scrutiny, because early experiences with people shape a child's personality, mind, and behaviors (Phillips & Adams, 2001).

Caregiver-Child Interaction

Child-care quality is of great concern to social scientists, because they stress that children's emotional ties in their early years are extremely significant for their physical, cognitive, and emotional development and serve as models for later relationships. Since the 1970s, many American families have moved away from the three-generation model of child care in the home that prevails in many other countries. For example, in Japan, China, India, and Mexico, it is the norm for grandparents to live with their children and help care for their grandchildren. In the United States, grandparents and others in the extended family often live nearby, but many live hundreds or thousands of miles away.

Compounding the effects of this unraveling of the traditional family model is the rapid growth in maternal employment to provide economic security for families, high rates of divorce and single parenting, and nonmarital childbearing (Phillips & Adams, 2001). The U.S. Department of Labor (2010d) reports that almost two-thirds of married mothers with children ages 3 and under were employed either full-time or part-time. More than half of unmarried mothers (never married, divorced, separated, and widowed) with children under age 3 were employed either full-time or part-time. This is a steep increase in the number of mothers who have infants and are in the workforce (it is a 33 percent increase since 1975). Thus, young children in the United States are supervised and socialized by fewer parents and are cared for by a larger array of nonfamilial persons than ever before. Child care for infants and toddlers is the most scarce and expensive source of help, and children in working-poor families are at highest risk for poor-quality care. Child care is expected to be among the occupations that will see the largest growth over the next decade (U.S. Department of Labor, 2010a). Figure 6.4 sheds light on U.S. child-care arrangements (Federal Interagency Forum on Child and Family Statistics, 2010a).

A wide variety of programs, federal policies, and funding subsidies have evolved—and continue to evolve—to assist families in securing daily child care for a growing number of babies and toddlers. The 1993, *Family and Medical Leave Act* (FMLA) authorized 12 weeks of unpaid job-protected leave for employees of companies with more than 50 employees to deal with family or medical issues, which could include the birth or adoption of a child (U.S. Department of Labor, 2011). In 2002, California passed the *Paid Family Leave Act,* allowing both female and male employees up to 6 weeks of *paid* leave to spend time with newborn or newly adopted children. Washington (2007) and New Jersey (2008) have enacted similar paid-leave policies (Fass, 2009). In most states, whether a new parent receives paid parental leave depends solely on the company policy where the parent works. A survey of some top employers (e.g., IBM, General Mills, Ernst and Young, Discovery Communications, and Bank of America) shows that almost one-third of these companies provide at least 9 weeks of paid maternity leave, whereas no company provides more than 6 weeks of paid paternity leave (Institute for Women's Policy Research, 2007). However, the United States lags acutely behind many other countries in paid maternal or paternal leave for infant or child care (Heymann et al., 2007). (See Table 6.5.) The *Healthy Families Act* (2009) was introduced in Congress but has not become law. It would require employers with more than 15 employees to allow their workers up to 7 paid sick days a year, which would include time to care for a sick child.

Child-Care Centers

Many U.S. families need the income that working women bring to the household. In 2006, women's income contributed over one-third of household income. More than 60 percent of U.S. mothers with children under 6 are now in the workforce; this includes all racial and ethnic groups. Yet over one-quarter of the mothers of children under age 3 earn less than the federal minimum wage and must use a much higher percentage of their income to pay for child care (U.S. Department of Labor, 2010d). The convergence of these factors inflicts great financial and emotional pressure on low-income mothers who seek quality child care for their children. Researchers have identified access to affordable quality child care as a particularly important component of mothers' ability to participate in the labor force and achieve enough economic security to raise their children out of poverty (Lippman, Vandiver, Keith, & Atienza, 2008).

About one of every four families in the United States needs some form of help to provide child care for their children, including assistance from relatives, local food bank programs, and federal programs (U.S. Department of Labor, 2010d). Higher-income families are more likely to have access to free child care from relatives. But lower-income single parents of children under 5 are far more likely to need assistance from federal programs (Giannarelli, Sonenstein, & Stagner, 2006).

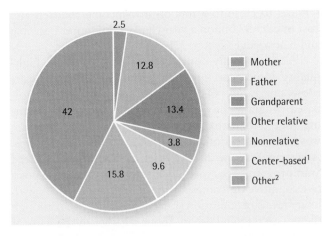

FIGURE 6.4 Child-Care Arrangements for Children, Birth to 4, When Mother Is Working, 2006 (by Percentage)

[1]Center-based care includes day-care centers, nursery schools, preschools, and Head Start programs. Home-based care or other nonrelative care includes family day-care providers, babysitters, nannies, friends, neighbors, and other nonrelatives providing care in either the child's or the provider's home. Other relatives include siblings and other relatives. Mother care includes care by the mother while she worked.
[2]Other includes children in kindergarten or grade school, in self-care, and with no regular arrangement, but it does not include school-based activities, which were deleted as categorical choices for preschoolers.

Source: Federal Interagency Forum on Child and Family Statistics. (2010). *America's children: Key national indicators of well-being, 2010.* Federal Interagency Forum on Child and Family Statistics, Washington, DC: U.S. Government Printing Office.

In 1996, the *Personal Responsibility and Work Opportunity Reconciliation Act (PRWORA)* mandated that women, including mothers of young children, move into the workforce and off the Aid to Families with Dependent Children program. The federal law exempted mothers of children under 1 year old, but some state laws require, in effect, that mothers of infants as young as 3 months enter the workforce (Farrell, Rich, Turner, Seith, & Bloom, 2008). Policymakers did not balance the need for mothers to work with increased funding for child-care centers, and the supply of child care is not able to keep up with demand as a new pool of children enter child-care centers (Farrell et al., 2008). In some states, the result of this pressure was that fewer child-care providers in subsidized child-care centers had a high school education or the required credentials (Witte & Queralt, 2006).

Infants are more likely to be cared for by their mothers or in another home at age 6 months, but by the time they are 3 years old, they are more likely to be cared for in a child-care center (National Institute of Child Health and Human Development [NICHD], 2006). Scholars and parents have proposed new federal policies to enable mothers to balance employment and child care. These include mandating proportional pay for part-time work (as the European Union has done), making family and medical leave paid leave, expanding the scope of the FMLA by decreasing the 50-employee limit, and giving employers incentives to adopt flexible workplace policies (Williams & Cooper, 2004).

Since the early 1990s, researchers commissioned by the NICHD have been studying more than 1,300 young children at 10 child-care study sites. The *NICHD Study of Early Child Care and Youth Development* is the most comprehensive study of its kind. Its goal is to determine how variations in child care for children from birth to age 3 are related to child development. Just how do child characteristics and child-care characteristics influence developmental outcomes? The study found that children who experienced higher-quality child care showed somewhat better cognitive functioning and language development during the first three years of life than those who did not. The most important factor in this was the type and quantity of language that caregivers used to interact with children. When caregivers asked questions, responded to children's talking, and engaged in other forms of conversation, children did better cognitively and linguistically than children whose caregivers did not focus on these types of language interactions (NICHD, 2006). (See the *More Information You Can Use* box, "What Is Quality Child Care?")

However, the NICHD researchers found that the strongest predictor of a child's development is family life and the child's relationship with his or her parents. These have a greater influence on a young child's development than child care. In other words, families who have well-organized routines and provide family activities have children who are more likely to be advanced socially and cognitively. The quality of mother-child interactions is the most consistent and important predictor of a well-adjusted child. The more attentive mothers are to their children, the more they engage in cognitively stimulating ways with their children, the more likely it is that their children will do well socially and cognitively. This is true regardless of whether the child is in child care or is cared for exclusively by the mother for the first three years. The study found that cognition, language, and social development were the same for children who were in child care and children who were cared for by mothers (NICHD, 2006).

Many social scientists and policymakers have lobbied for higher federal funding, legislation, and guidelines to regulate child-care centers and quality of staffing, though more stringent regulation and monitoring might raise the costs of child care and move higher-quality childcare out of the financial reach of lower-income families (Sosinsky, Lord, & Zigler, 2007).

Early Head Start Program   The Early Head Start program is a federally subsidized program established in 1994 for infants and toddlers up to age 3 in low-income families. Caregivers in Early Head Start programs must have a child development associate credential or the equivalent within 1 year of being hired. The program seeks to improve early child development with an array of coordinate services that also include child development services provided in the home, parenting education, health care, and family support (McLoyd, Aikens, & Burton, 2006). In 2009, about 1,600 programs provided Early Head Start services to close to a million low-income children at a cost of over $7 billion a year (Early Childhood Learning and Knowledge Center, 2010).

A recent study compared the outcomes of a high-quality Head Start program with a school-based state pre-K program in Oklahoma and found that the school-based program showed better results in literacy learning (but not math), whereas the Head Start program was more successful in health effects (Gormley, Phillips, Adelstein, & Shaw, 2010). Other studies show that Head Start programs are especially effective in producing positive cognitive outcomes for the children of mothers with lower levels of education (Jung & Stone, 2008). Although there is an ongoing debate about whether the benefits of Head Start justify the costs, many researchers believe that the program produces long-term positive effects and is worthwhile (Ludwig & Phillips, 2008).

The program provides support for parents as well, and participating mothers and fathers tend to be more emotionally supportive of their children and to read to them daily (McLoyd, Aikens, & Burton, 2006). Despite the developmental advantages that the Early Head Start program provides, only 10 percent of eligible children were enrolled in Early Head Start in 2007 (Hough, 2007).

MORE INFORMATION YOU CAN USE

What Is Quality Child Care?

The NICHD *Study of Early Child Care and Youth Development* has identified key features of quality child care. See the Positive Caregiving Checklist below. Mark in "How Often?" each time the caregiver does each action and then decide the rating. The higher the total rating score, the higher the quality of caregiving.

The Positive Caregiving Checklist

Date: _____   Set Amount of Time: (For example, 30 minutes) _____

How Often Does the Caregiver . . .	How Often?	Rating: 1 = Hardly any of the time; 2 = Some of the time; 3 = A fair amount of the time; 4 = A lot of the time	Total
Show a positive attitude: Is the caregiver generally happy and encouraging in manner? Is he or she helpful and upbeat? Does the caregiver smile often at the child?	_____	_____	_____
Have positive physical contact: Does the caregiver hug the child, pat the child on the back, or hold the child's hand? Does the caregiver comfort the child?	_____	_____	_____
Respond to vocalizations: Does the caregiver repeat the child's words, comment on what the child says or tries to say, or answer the child's questions?	_____	_____	_____
Ask questions: Does the caregiver encourage the child to talk by asking questions that the child can answer easily, such as "yes" or "no" questions, or asking about a family member or toy?	_____	_____	_____
Talk in other ways			
• **Praising or encouraging:** Does the caregiver respond to the child's positive actions with positive words, such as "You did it!" or "Well done!"?	_____	_____	_____
• **Teaching:** Does the caregiver encourage the child to learn or have the child repeat learning phrases, such as saying the alphabet out loud, counting to 10, naming shapes or objects? For older children, does the caregiver explain what words or names mean?	_____	_____	_____
• **Telling and singing:** Does the caregiver tell stories, describe objects, or sing songs?	_____	_____	_____
Encourage development: Does the caregiver help the child to stand up and walk? Does the caregiver encourage tummy time activities with the child? For older children, does the caregiver help finish puzzles, stack blocks, or zip zippers?	_____	_____	_____
Advance behavior: Does the caregiver encourage the child to smile, laugh, and play with other children? Does the caregiver support sharing between the child and other children? Does the caregiver give examples of good behaviors?	_____	_____	_____
Read: Does the caregiver read books and stories to the child? Does the caregiver let the child touch the book and turn the page? For older children, does the caregiver point to pictures and words on the page?	_____	_____	_____
Eliminate negative interactions: Does the caregiver make sure to be positive, not negative, in the interactions with the child?	_____	_____	_____
Overall Total	_____		_____

Ultimately, the goal is high-quality training and care for infants and toddlers in *all* care settings.

Early Education Across Cultures

The United States represents one extreme of a spectrum of attitudes about government-sponsored child care. It is seen as "welfare," with all the negative associations that word carries in U.S. culture. Individual parents are responsible to find the best child-care option, and child-care centers compete for their business. The government provides assistance in paying for child care to only a small percentage of the poorest families.

However, many countries in the European Union see child care as the responsibility of the entire society. Child care is regarded as an educational service rather than as a welfare program. These countries often provide paid leave or cash subsidies so that a mother or father can care for children under age 2 at home (Heymann et al., 2007). When the children reach age 3, they are typically enrolled in government-sponsored child care (Lamb & Ahnert, 2006). These services are not "free," however, as reflected by the relatively high individual and corporate tax rates paid by individuals and corporations in these countries (European Commission, 2010). The European Union countries are also experiencing economic crises, and availability of affordable high-quality care is of great concern (only three of their member states guarantee access to child care) (Commission of the European Communities, 2008).

> **Question**
>
> In what ways are young children cared for in the United States and in European countries?

YOUNG CHILDREN AT RISK

Children are the most vulnerable members of our society. They depend on their families and caregivers for support and protection from harm. Yet, tragically, each year hundreds of thousands of children suffer from the effects of poverty, neglect, and abuse. Poverty is closely connected with abuse and neglect, although children from all economic groups experience abuse.

Researchers have found several factors that seem to "buffer" children from being abused. The following factors make it less likely that a mother will abuse her child: having strong social support systems that offer help with life and financial crises, being involved in community activities, having less rigid expectations about what children should be able to do, receiving treatment for any mental-health issues, encountering fewer stressful life events, having a supportive partner/spouse, making a conscious decision not to repeat the history of abuse,

having had positive school experiences as a child, and having a strong, supportive religious affiliation (New York Society for the Prevention of Cruelty to Children, 2010).

Poverty

Almost 15 million U.S. children (20 percent) are living in poverty, and as a consequence of the economic downturn, that number continues to increase (U.S. Bureau of the Census, 2010h). The vast majority of poor children live with their single mothers. African American and Hispanic children are among the most vulnerable; although Caucasian children have a lower risk, they make up the largest numbers of children in poverty because of their large population. Children living in poverty live in environments with an increased risk of child abuse, health risks, limited learning opportunities, and severe emotional distress due to family disintegration caused by economic strains. Their families cannot afford adequate housing, adequate nutritious food, or quality child care. This means that more than one out of five children in the United States suffers in the following ways:

- *Health:* An increased risk of stunted growth, anemia, and less chance that the child will survive to her or his first birthday.
- *Education:* More repeated school years, lower test scores, and less education due to dropping out or expulsion.
- *Work:* Lower wages and lower overall lifetime earnings.

In economic terms, the cost of keeping poverty-stricken children in schools longer, as well as having to supply them with free breakfasts and lunches, special education services and tutoring, coupled with large medical expenses due to initial poor health, means that every year that we decide *not* to address issues of child poverty translates into a monetary loss of as much as $500 billion a year (Holzer, Schanzenbach, Duncan, & Ludwig, 2008). Children raised in poverty are more likely to die from accidents, fire, infectious disease, and other diseases. Seen from a developmental perspective, children's health, emotional and cognitive growth, and social interactions are all adversely affected by the harsh environments caused by poverty. In short, poverty steals the promise from a child's future and, in the end, negatively impacts the child, the family, and society (Engle & Black, 2008). These effects are all worsened during times of economic recession as more families fall into poverty due to unemployment.

Child Neglect and Abuse

The majority of American children are adequately or well cared for by their parents. However, according to the U.S. Department of Health and Human Services (2010e), almost 3.3 million reports of abuse or neglect were filed

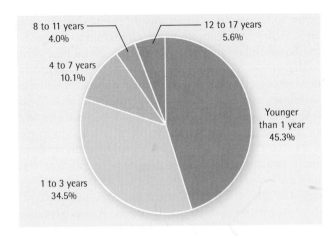

FIGURE 6.5 Child Abuse and Neglect Fatality Victims by Age, 2008 The number of U.S. child fatalities has been increasing the past few years, and there were at least 1,740 child fatalities in 2008. Very young children, especially those under age 4, are the most frequent victims of child fatalities. Fathers and mothers' boyfriends are most often the perpetrators in abuse deaths, but mothers are more often at fault in neglect fatalities.
Source: Child Welfare Information Gateway. (2010, April). Child abuse and neglect fatalities: Statistics and interventions. U.S. Department of Health and Human Services, Administration on Children, Youth, and Families. Retrieved December 5, 2010 from http://www.childwelfare.gov/pubs/factsheets/fatality.pdf

with child protective services agencies in 2008. After investigations, it was determined that 772,000 children were victims of abuse or neglect, and infants have the highest verified rates. Obviously, there are unreported cases. Tragically, 1,740 U.S. children died of neglect and abuse in 2008, and that number has risen over the past few years. Parents make up the majority of the perpetrators of this serious crime. The rate of abuse is significantly higher for children under age 3 than for older children (see Figure 6.5) (U.S. Department of Health and Human Services, 2010e).

Neglect is defined as the absence of adequate social, emotional, and physical care, and neglect can occur regardless of socioeconomic status. Neglect cases make up the majority of cases in the child protection system, and they result in the majority of young child deaths (U.S. Department of Health and Human Services, 2010e). **Child abuse** is defined as nonaccidental physical attack on, or injury to, children by individuals caring for them (sexual abuse is discussed in Chapter 8).

Increasingly, researchers are looking at child maltreatment from an ecological perspective and examining the complex social context in which the behavior is embedded. Child abuse is not confined to lower-socioeconomic-status households; it is found across the socioeconomic range. Child abuse is also related to economic and social stress in families. For instance, high levels of marital conflict, interspousal physical violence, housing stress, the burden of balancing work and child care, drug and alcohol abuse, parental mental illness, parental history of

being abused in childhood, child conduct problems, and unemployment are associated with a higher incidence of child maltreatment (Barth, 2009). Families that are socially isolated and outside support networks are more likely to abuse children than are families with strong social ties. Families in which there is evidence of these kinds of issues should receive priority help from service providers (Thomas, 2007).

Question

What have we learned about the effects of poverty or abuse and neglect on child outcomes?

Signs of Abuse and Maltreatment Maltreated children show a variety of symptoms. Because child-care staff and preschool teachers are the only adults outside the family whom many infants or toddlers see with any consistency, they are often in a position to detect signs of child abuse or neglect and to begin to remedy the situation by reporting it to a local child protective services agency or police department (U.S. Department of Health and Human Services, 2010e). In fact, most states require teachers, health-care workers, and human services professionals to report cases of child abuse, and the law provides them with legal immunity for erroneous reports made in good faith. Professionals account for the highest percentage of those reporting abuse and neglect. The U.S. Department of Health and Human Services Child Welfare Information Gateway describes the signs that teachers, health-care workers, and other concerned individuals should look for as possible tip-offs of child abuse or neglect:

- Does the child have unexplained bruises, welts, burns, or contusions?
- Does the child complain of beatings or maltreatment?
- Does the child frequently arrive early at school or stay late?
- Is the child frequently absent or late?
- Is the child aggressive, disruptive, destructive, shy, withdrawn, passive, or overly compliant and friendly?
- Is the child inadequately dressed for the weather, unkempt, dirty, undernourished, tired, in need of medical attention, or frequently injured?

Toddlers who are neglected or abused do not learn to recognize, express, or understand emotions as nonabused children do. They might, for example, react to the distress of a playmate with fear or anger rather than empathy. This, among other reasons, is why it is hard for them to make friends in child-care centers or play-groups. Also, they find it more difficult to pay attention. Yet some children can recover from early abuse to live healthy, productive lives. Researchers are studying resilience factors in young maltreated children to learn what the predictors of recovery are (DuMont, Widom, & Czaja, 2007). A good many other events in children's lives—for instance, their natural abilities, their temperaments, their networks of social support, and their participation in therapy—may mediate the adverse consequences of child abuse and neglect (Thomas & Hall, 2008).

The Intergenerational Cycle of Violence   Evidence suggests that the pattern of violence within families is transmitted from parent to child generation after generation, in what researchers and professionals have called a "cycle of violence." Mothers in violent relationships are typically unable to respond warmly toward their infants and may become angry with them, thus disrupting the crucial process of attachment (Levendosky et al., 2006). Proponents of social learning theory say that violent, aggressive children have learned that behavior from their parents, who are powerful models for children (Tomison, 1996). Some researchers contend that there is a biological or genetic component to aggressive behavior and that aggressiveness is an individual characteristic based on the child's own temperament (Fauble, 2009)—that is, the child's inherited disposition perpetuates the cycle of maltreatment.

The third explanation for intergenerational transmission of violence is the interaction of environmental (social learning) and biological/genetic factors. Kaufman and Zigler (1993, quoted in Tomison, 1996) suggest that a genetic component for the expression of antisocial behavior puts the individual at risk for expressing violent behavior, and the interaction of both genetic and environmental factors produces the greatest risk for acting violently. It is generally acknowledged that no single factor can explain how maltreatment is transmitted generationally.

Having been abused does not always lead to being abusive. However, the greater the frequency of violence experienced in childhood, the greater the chance that the victim will grow up to be an abusive parent (Milner et al., 2010). Abusing parents often select one child to be the victim. Some children are more at risk for abuse than other children; those more likely to be victimized include premature infants, children with congenital anomalies or other disabilities, children with medical problems, those born to single mothers or cohabiting families, and those who are unsupervised (Fauble, 2009). Parents who are at risk of abusing their children can be helped by individual and family counseling, parenting programs, family interventions and home visits, and strengthened social support systems (Centers for Disease Control and Prevention, 2009d). Most parents want to be good parents. Parent education programs often help prevent fathers or mothers who have abused their children from doing so again (Barth, 2009).

Breaking the Cycle of Violence   Researchers find that there are a number of factors that seem to "buffer" children against being abused. Fry (1993) suggests these approaches to breaking the cycle of violence:

- Promote a cultural attitude that physical force is unnecessary and unacceptable (outlawing corporal punishment).
- Train all children in nonviolent conflict resolution and problem solving.
- Train parents in healthy child-rearing techniques.
- Intervene in abusive situations as soon as possible.

Questions

What are the factors associated with child neglect and abuse? Is there an association between these harmful behaviors and socioeconomic status or parenting style? What social/cultural limits and/or educational policies can be employed to reduce or eliminate child abuse and neglect?

SEGUE

This chapter has documented social and behavioral scientists' long-standing interest in how children's personality development is related to their early emotional and social experiences. Initially, social scientists focused on maternal deprivation, believing that it was enough simply to ask about the mother's influence on the child. As time passed, research began to focus on fathers, and then on siblings, grandparents, aunts, uncles, extended family members, and same-sex parents. The circle has widened further in recent years to include child-care providers and preschool teachers.

In the United States, sharply divergent views exist regarding the desirability of child-care facilities. The impulse to decide whether child care is "good" or "bad" has at times seemed more a matter of ideology than an issue for science. In any event, modern societies and social scientists are increasingly confronting this question: How are we to manage the successful care and rearing of future generations of children when parents spend a substantial portion of their time at work away from home?

As we shall see in the next chapter, children during the preschool and early elementary school years continue to grow, exhibit remarkable cognitive development, and experience a diversity of social influences.

SUMMARY

Emotional Development

1. Emotions seem to have evolved as adaptive processes through which humans establish, maintain, and terminate relationships in their environment to enhance survival. We "read" others' emotions from a combination of their facial, gestural, postural, and vocal cues.
2. Contemporary researchers suggest that emotions (a) help humans survive and adapt to their environment, (b) serve to guide and motivate human behavior, and (c) support communication with others.
3. Ethologists maintain that the human nervous system is genetically prewired for emotional action and responsiveness and that humans associate specific emotions with specific human facial expressions.
4. Izard formulated the "differential emotions theory," which suggests that emotions result from feedback consisting of sensations generated by facial and neuromuscular responses. Thus, each emotion has its own distinctive facial pattern.
5. Stranger anxiety and separation anxiety emerge at about 8 months in most infants. This is true across cultures.
6. Self-regulation is one of the major emotional tasks of the first two years of infancy. Sensitive mothering helps the infant to integrate emotions to fit cultural norms.
7. From birth to age 5, infants and children progress through several stages in emotional development. The Greenspans' Functional Emotional Assessment Scale identifies children with atypical emotional development.
8. Attachment to a significant person profoundly influences an infant's mind, body, social development, and values.
9. Early attachment (bonding) patterns predict a child's later functioning and success (peers, academics, marriage, parenting).
10. Most commonly the mother is the object of infant attachment, but it can be the father, a grandparent, another family member, or an unrelated caregiver. As the child matures, the number of people he or she is attached to increases.
11. Young children who have been traumatized or severely deprived do not form attachments with their caregivers and often exhibit a range of maladaptive behaviors.
12. An infant's temperament is her or his basic disposition. Cultures place different values on temperamental qualities, such as shyness, assertiveness, and dependence.
13. Researchers find continuity and stability of emotional expressiveness in young children. A caregiver's responsiveness can modify a child's emotions.
14. Thomas and Chess propose that parents take into account their infant's unique temperament in their child-rearing practices.

Theoretical Approaches to Social-Emotional Development

15. Freudians stress the psychoanalytic view that the development of an emotionally healthy personality is associated with a prolonged period of breast-feeding, gradual weaning, a self-demand feeding schedule, delayed and patient bowel and bladder training, and freedom from excessive punishment.
16. Erikson's psychosocial view stresses an infant's need to develop a basic sense of trust in the mother and/or father. The maturing child needs to resolve a series of conflicts during progressive stages of emotional and social development.
17. Behaviorists (learning theorists) focus on the outward display of emotions, not on the thoughts that caused the emotions. A system of rewards and punishments shapes infant behaviors.
18. Contemporary cognitive psychologists study the information-processing mechanisms that link emotions to thinking and behaviors.
19. Bronfenbrenner's ecological theory states that a young child's social-emotional development is affected by a variety of environmental influences.
20. Biological researchers study how genetics and the environment interact to "turn on" genes that shape emotions and behaviors.

Social Development

21. Mothers play a key role in helping infants adjust to their social world. A mother's verbalizations with her infant encourage language development. A mother's playful interactions encourage him or her to experience emotions.
22. Mothers and fathers make equally important contributions to a child's development.
23. Fathers who care for and play with their infants are more likely to be involved parents when the child reaches age 5.
24. Fathers who provide warm and loving support to their partners help create an environment in which a mother can be warm and loving with her children.
25. Women whose male partners assist with housework in significant ways during child-rearing years are more likely to feel that they have made a successful match.
26. Children whose fathers maintain frequent contact with them are less likely to be disruptive in school and are more likely to do well academically. In this way, unmarried fathers can provide some degree of protection to at-risk children born to unmarried mothers.
27. In the United States, more grandparents than ever are the caregivers of grandchildren. As caregivers, older adults require financial resources, social support, and child-care assistance.
28. Family life has become an increasingly visible component of gay and lesbian life. Gay and lesbian parents tend to be deeply committed to parenthood, and their children show no differences in development from children raised by heterosexual parents.
29. The birth of a baby has a significant impact on older siblings. Infants learn important social and emotional behaviors from their siblings.
30. Worldwide, infants are raised under a variety of conditions, including multiple mothering, home care, child day care, and kibbutzim.

Child Care for Young Children

31. Two-thirds of working mothers of young infants and toddlers are in the paid workforce. This creates a large demand for child-care services.
32. The NICHD Study of Early Child Care and Youth Development found that family relationships, especially with the mother, are stronger predictors of a child's academic and emotional success than whether or not the child was cared for in a child-care center.
33. The Early Head Start program is a federally funded program for at-risk children from birth to age 3. It provides a range of services to children and their parents with the goal of improving child development and parenting skills.

Young Children at Risk

34. Millions of young children in the United States experience the adverse effects of poverty, including a higher incidence of health and safety risks, lower educational attainment, and lower earning capacity over their whole lifetime.
35. The incidence of child abuse and neglect is on the rise, and the impact is far-reaching. Adult abusers are likely to have been abused as children. New programs are being created to break this cycle of violence. Many professionals who come in contact with children are mandated to report neglect and abuse.

KEY TERMS

attachment *(165)*

autism *(172)*

autism spectrum disorders (ASD) *(172)*

child abuse *(189)*

disorganized/disoriented infants *(168)*

emotions *(162)*

goodness of fit *(171)*

insecure/avoidant infants *(168)*

insecure/resistant infants *(168)*

kinship care *(181)*

multiple mothering *(183)*

neglect *(189)*

nuclear family *(183)*

oral-sensory stage *(176)*

person permanence *(166)*

reactive attachment disorder (RAD) *(169)*

securely attached infants *(168)*

self-regulation *(164)*

sensory integration *(171)*

separation anxiety *(169)*

social referencing *(162)*

social smile *(163)*

Strange Situation *(167)*

stranger anxiety *(168)*

temperament *(173)*

FOLLOWING UP ON THE INTERNET

Web sites for this chapter focus on emotional and social development in infancy. Please access the text Web site at www.mhhe.com/crandell10 for up-to-date hot-linked Internet addresses for the following organizations, topics, and resources:

Society for Research on Child Development
http://www.srcd.org/

National Association for the Education of Young Children
http://www.naeyc.org/

National Children's Study
http://www.nationalchildrensstudy.gov/Pages/default.aspx

Early Childhood News
http://www.earlychildhoodnews.com/

National Child Care Information Center
http://nccic.acf.hhs.gov/

Grandparents Raising Grandchildren
http://www.childwelfare.gov/preventing/supporting/resources/grandparents.cfm

Institute for Research on Poverty
http://www.irp.wisc.edu/

Administration on Developmental Disabilities
http://www.acf.hhs.gov/programs/add/

Child Abuse Prevention Network
http://child-abuse.com/

PART 4
EARLY CHILDHOOD
2 TO 6

Chapter 7 is the first of two chapters focusing on early childhood, the developmental stage between 2 and 6 years of age. During this period children acquire greater autonomy, evolve new ways of relating to other people, and gain a sense of themselves and their effectiveness in the world. Healthy children experience physical growth, coordination of motor skills, and an energetic zest for play. Proper nutrition, good health, and stimulating sensory experiences provide a foundation for continued cognitive growth and language development. Children also begin to learn a sense of right or wrong based on preoperational thought processes. In Chapter 8, we will examine the young child's growing self-awareness in the domains of emotions and gender. Within the social context of family and friends, child-care settings, and kindergarten, young children acquire a set of guidelines about expressing their emotional needs.

Early Childhood
Physical and Cognitive Development

1. Mealtimes have become extremely frustrating for the parents of a finicky eater. What is causing this problem? Do you think this behavior is dangerous to the child's health?

2. A certain 5-year-old girl can hear a piece of music once and then sit at the piano and play it perfectly, but she does not know her name and will never learn to read words or music. Is she intelligent? What does it mean to be intelligent, and how do we measure intelligence?

3. Ask a 6-year-old and a 25-year-old to describe what occurred in their lives the day before. What details will each remember? In what order will they be remembered? Will the child remember the past the same way an adult will? Why are there differences in their recollections and perspectives?

4. Imagine that you are shipwrecked on an island where everyone wears masks so that you cannot see each other's faces. How would you be able to figure out what other people were really thinking? And how do you think your communication would be different?

Between the ages of 2 and 6, children enlarge their repertoire of behaviors. As young children develop physically and cognitively, they become capable beings in their own right. Most are healthy, energetic, and curious about mastering their world. Their growing bodies and increasing strength permit them to climb higher, jump longer, yell louder, and hug harder. For young children, every day is truly a new day. They are expanding their vocabulary, asking questions, and entertaining with their own wit and humor.

As Erikson suggests, young children begin to struggle with their own conflicting needs and rebel against parental controls, while acquiring a sense of autonomy or independence. These occasional upheavals are popularly called "the terrible twos," when toddlers begin to assert their own will and have temper tantrums. At the same time, children come to see themselves as individuals who are separate from their parents, though still dependent on them (Erikson, 1963). How does the young child's mind operate to remember what is significant and what is trivial? We will examine several theories of early cognitive development and memory, as well as physical and moral development.

PHYSICAL DEVELOPMENT AND HEALTH CONCERNS

Early childhood lays the cognitive and social foundations for the more complex life of the school years. Underpinning these intellectual skills are continued brain growth, physical development, refinement of gross and fine motor skills, and maturation of the sensory systems. Among the most encompassing factors that impede both physical and cognitive development in early childhood is living in poverty. A special section of this chapter is devoted to health risk factors for many children in the United States, particularly minority children.

Physical Growth and Motor-Skill Development

As we have noted in earlier chapters, growth is unevenly distributed over the first 20 years of life. From birth to age 5, the rate, or velocity, of growth in height declines sharply. You may have heard it said that "young children sprout like weeds," because about twice as much of this growth occurs between the ages of 1 and 3 as between the ages of 3 and 5. Young children maintain the top-heavy look—the head being large relative to the body—until the end of the preschool years, but they become thinner and lose the baby fat that characterizes the infant and toddler.

Children under 2 tend to be chubby, whereas children 2 to 6 years old are, for the most part, slim, although variations in height and weight stem from both genetic and environmental factors. After age 5, the rate of increase in height levels off and is practically constant until puberty. Parents should keep in mind, however, that their child's growth, although normal, can be markedly different from another child's development; these variations are not typically a cause for concern (American Academy of Pediatrics, 2010b).

During the preschool and early elementary years, children also become better coordinated physically. Walking, climbing, reaching, grasping, and releasing are no longer simply activities in their own right but have become the means for new endeavors. Their developing skills give children new ways to explore the world and to accomplish new tasks (see Table 7.1). Pediatricians use a variety of screening tools to test the development of physical skills in young children (Schonwald, Horan, & Huntington, 2009).

Gross Motor Skills   Healthy young children aged 2 to 6 are constantly active. At this age, children run, jump, or hop every chance they get. They can make such large body movements because their arm and leg muscles are developing. Children in this age group need and benefit from plenty of exercise, and they should get about an hour

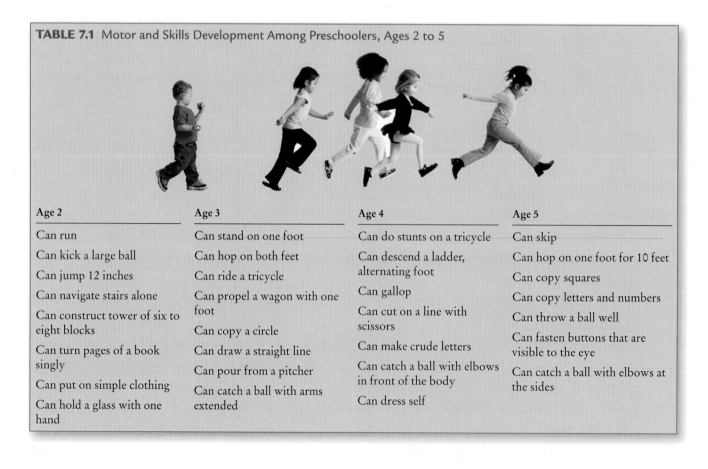

TABLE 7.1 Motor and Skills Development Among Preschoolers, Ages 2 to 5

Age 2	Age 3	Age 4	Age 5
Can run	Can stand on one foot	Can do stunts on a tricycle	Can skip
Can kick a large ball	Can hop on both feet	Can descend a ladder, alternating foot	Can hop on one foot for 10 feet
Can jump 12 inches	Can ride a tricycle	Can gallop	Can copy squares
Can navigate stairs alone	Can propel a wagon with one foot	Can cut on a line with scissors	Can copy letters and numbers
Can construct tower of six to eight blocks	Can copy a circle	Can make crude letters	Can throw a ball well
Can turn pages of a book singly	Can draw a straight line	Can catch a ball with elbows in front of the body	Can fasten buttons that are visible to the eye
Can put on simple clothing	Can pour from a pitcher	Can dress self	Can catch a ball with elbows at the sides
Can hold a glass with one hand	Can catch a ball with arms extended		

of play activity each day (Ginsburg, 2007). It is important to give children opportunities to learn new physical skills such as throwing, kicking, and catching in a caring and supportive environment (Gallahue & Ozmun, 2006). The American Academy of Pediatrics (2009) recommends that caregivers limit hours of passive activity, such as watching TV and videos and playing computer games, to no more than 2 hours per day. Young children should not have unsupervised access to media sources. Parents should not place TVs and computers in children's bedrooms, and they should watch and discuss the content of video material with their children. Caregivers should use discernment in choosing media for their children (Graf, Pratt, Hester, & Short, 2009).

4-Year-Olds   Four-year-olds are more comfortable with their bodies and push their physical limits by exploring jungle gyms and other play structures. Coordination between upper and lower body develops; young children go through three distinct stages while learning to walk and reach a mature pattern of walking by approximately 4 years of age (Snapp-Childs & Corbetta, 2009). Tasks like running are accomplished much more efficiently. Four-year-olds are beginning to master skills such as kicking and catching a ball (Gallahue & Ozmun, 2006).

5-Year-Olds   Five-year-olds can be daredevils; they swing, jump, and try acrobatics that cause their parents to hold their breath. It is hard to believe that the 5-year-old who proficiently skates and skips found it difficult to walk very far without falling down just a few years previously. Children with any type of physical disability should still be encouraged to be active so they can develop strength and coordination skills and enjoy the physical act of movement. **Recreational therapists** (see photo) and **occupational therapists** can suggest activities that individual children can accomplish. Occupational therapists help children not only to improve basic motor functions and reasoning abilities but also to compensate for permanent loss of function.

6-Year-Olds   Caregivers need to set boundaries and limits and should constantly offer reminders about safety rules and use of safety equipment, because 6-year-olds actively seek more independence in expanding community environments. Six-year-olds show increased interest in daring adventures and games. They enjoy testing the limits of their bodies by running fast, throwing hard, leaping farther and climbing higher. They enjoy riding bikes, climbing trees and fire escapes, and jumping from higher walls and steps. They may gain (or lose) confidence in their physical abilities as they begin to participate in sports activities in individual or team sports. Parents need to be cautious about overscheduling a 6-year-old's activities.

Recreational Therapist   Someone who works with children providing services that help restore function, improve mobility, relieve pain, and prevent or limit permanent physical disabilities of patients suffering from injuries or disease.

Fine Motor Skills   Whereas gross motor skills are the capabilities that involve larger body parts, fine motor skills involve small body parts such as hands and fingers. Fine motor skills develop more slowly than gross motor skills, so 3-year-olds who no longer need to concentrate intently on the task of running still require mental energy to stack blocks, construct with Legos, use a paintbrush, sculpt with clay, maneuver a crayon, or tap keys on a computer keyboard. They still tend to force a puzzle piece into the hole or slide and wiggle it until it pops into place. Five-year-olds normally have their hands, arms, legs, and feet under tight command and are bored with the simple acts of coordination, preferring instead to walk on a balance beam, build high block structures, and begin the task of tying shoelaces. Fine motor skills are required for success in such activities as getting dressed, printing the alphabet and numerals, cutting, pasting, coloring within the lines, and putting puzzles together.

Children with Coordination Problems   Some 5 percent of youngsters have noticeable difficulties with coordination and may be diagnosed with developmental coordination disorder (Wann, 2007). About half of the children who have these problems at age 5 still have them at age 9. Increasingly, psychologists and teachers are paying attention to these children with poor physical coordination. Helping less adroit children become more successful at physical activities can be important. Motor skills form a large part of youngsters' self-concepts and how they perceive others. Researchers find that children with coordination problems are at greater risk for significant social problems later in elementary school, because clumsiness often interferes with youngsters'

Fine Motor Skills Involve More Complex Hand-Eye Coordination Putting together blocks, beads, and puzzle pieces requires extensive use of fine motor skills and are favorite activities of young children.

social relationships (Sugden & Chambers, 2005). Virtual reality games that have become widely available for home use in recent years, such as *Dance Dance Revolution* and Nintendo's *Wii Sports* games, encourage children to be physically active (Graf et al., 2009).

Questions

Why would a pediatrician be concerned if a child's growth or motor skills seemed delayed for the age of the young child? What types of services are available for young children diagnosed with physical and motor delays?

Sensory Development

Most young children delight in the novel sensory experiences of using various colors and textures of objects, but a small percentage have difficulty integrating sensory information. Toddlers enjoy the sensation of putting objects in the mouth, but preschool children typically do not, although occasionally a child will suck a thumb or fingers as a self-comforting behavior. Along with new sensory experiences, the children are expanding descriptive language to categorize experiences such as slippery sand, crunchy colorful leaves, warm water, fluffy snowflakes, prickly cactus, cuddly kittens, and so forth.

Visual, Tactile, and Kinesthetic Senses To develop their visual and tactile senses, young children not only explore objects visually but also enjoy touching them, especially interesting materials such as sand, water, food, grass, finger paints, Play-Doh, soap, washcloths, feathers, and insects. They use their eyes, hands, and feet to help them discover all the fascinating differences among

the objects in their environment. Some children, however, might say that sound, touch, and light may "hurt." Such children would benefit from a professional assessment for sensory integration difficulties and from services with an occupational therapist.

Caregivers responsible for a child's eye health and safety should look carefully at a young child's eyes for crossing eyes, a "lazy" or wandering eye and unusual appearance, and excessive rubbing, watering, or redness of the eyes. Optometrists and pediatric ophthalmologists recommend scheduling vision exams by 3 to 4 years old, because serious eye problems occur in 2 to 5 percent of preschool children (Hartmann et al., 2006). Even so, a recent national survey of pediatricians found that by age 5 only about two-thirds of children had had a vision screening before entering school (Kemper, 2006). Untreated eye problems can lead to serious health, learning, and self-esteem problems. New screening devices are being developed for preliterate children, using common symbols rather than the alphabet. Young children with visual impairments are eligible for early intervention services (see Figure 7.1).

Sensory experiences also help young children use language skills to classify things (e.g., big or small, hot or cold, wet or dry, smooth or bumpy, loud or soft, pleasant or scary, safe or dangerous). Eventually, most children are able to utilize the maturing visual, tactile, and kinesthetic senses of the muscles for deliberate movements.

Hearing and Language Development A child's language capabilities depend on a healthy auditory system as well as on the growth and development of muscles in the mouth, tongue, and larynx. Babies less than a year old make sounds that are considered "universal" across cultures, and a child can listen to and learn the sounds of more than one language during this time (Chomsky, 1975). The auditory sense can be temporarily or seriously impaired by colds, ear infections, sinus congestion, sore throats, and allergies (often phlegm blocks the tubes from the back of the throat to the ears if the child is allergic to dairy products). A common illness of early childhood is **otitis media,** a painful infection in young children that causes fluid buildup in the middle ear. Typically, the child will be tugging at the ear and crying or screaming in the middle of the night; lying down for a period of time causes the fluid to settle in the ear, which causes pain. Often medication is needed to reduce the fluid. It is important to get medical attention for such children; a child who has a series of ear infections or for whom medical attention is delayed might experience hearing loss.

Chronic hearing problems interfere with learning and using language and can therefore cause serious delays in cognitive development if left undetected. If a young child does not seem to respond to parental

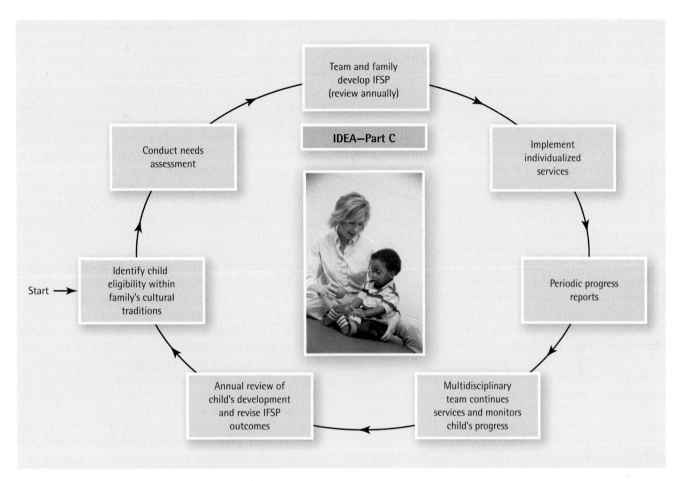

FIGURE 7.1 Implementation of the Early Intervention Services Annual Process An Individualized Family Service Plan (IFSP) provides ongoing services and supports to facilitate development of a young child (birth to 2, or 3 to 5) with delay, disability, or poverty risks. A service coordinator works with the family, agencies, and the local school to plan for school transition.

requests or to turn in the direction of sounds, a checkup is in order. An *otolaryngologist* (a specialist who treats ear, nose, and throat problems) may make a small incision in the eardrum to drain fluid or may temporarily insert a ventilation tube in the eardrum if ear infections persist. When a young child is diagnosed with severe to profound deafness, a cochlear implant or a hearing aid may help (Nicholas & Geers, 2007). Also, there are many accommodations in private and public school environments and a wealth of resources on the Internet to help the child develop his or her communication potential. Children with hearing impairments are also eligible for early intervention services.

Olfactory and Gustatory Sensations Children in any culture exhibit a wide range of responses to smells and tastes of foods and beverages. Also, children must be taught about what is safe or not safe to put in their mouths. Identifying for children what a smell is (a rose) or what a taste is (strawberry) helps them learn to recognize and cognitively categorize smells and tastes. Because

both smell and taste are involved in eating foods, mealtime is when parents notice a "finicky" eater; a small percentage of children are overly sensitive to olfactory or gustatory stimuli or are allergic to specific foods. The intensity of sensations as new foods are introduced into the child's diet can make for challenging mealtimes. Do not try to force a child to eat. Do not bribe a child with sweets, thus reinforcing poor eating habits. The child won't starve, and he or she will get adequate nutrition over the course of several days if a balanced diet is provided (Davis et al., 2007).

The Brain and the Nervous System

The brain and nervous system continue rapid development during early childhood. If the child has stimulation of his or her senses and social interaction, a rich connectivity among the axons and dendrites of neurons will develop. Increased *myelination* provides insulation around axons that helps to enhance the speed of neurochemical signaling in the brain and body. The messaging system between the two hemispheres of the brain also becomes more efficient because of growth and myelination of the band of nerve fibers called the *corpus callosum* that connects the two hemispheres. At age 5 the child's brain will weigh about 90 percent of its adult weight, but the child's body will be only about one-third of its adult weight (Sampaio & Truwit, 2001).

Recall, too, from general psychology that each hemisphere of the brain is dominant in performing certain functions—and that the left hemisphere controls the right side of the body and the right hemisphere controls the left. By preschool age, most children prefer to use their right hand to perform tasks, and a smaller percentage prefer using their left hand. Cherbuin & Brinkman (2006) found that a large sample of left-handed individuals have a thicker corpus callosum and tend to have more efficient interaction between the hemispheres. Although for centuries it was the custom in most cultures to force a child to use the right hand, today impeding a child's own genetic potential is considered unwise. Also in these years, the *frontal cortex* of the brain is developing, which helps young children improve in simple problem-solving and self-regulatory behaviors. Yet most behaviors require a whole-brain effort. Thus, it is no surprise that preschool children can perform increasingly complex cognitive tasks and physical actions. They can think and speak more quickly; their vocabulary is increasing, and their sentences are longer and more descriptive; their memory is improving; and most can move faster and with more precision.

Children at Risk of Cognitive Delays

As children's physical worlds expand, they are confronted with new developmental requirements. They actively seek new opportunities for manipulating and regulating their environment, and in doing so, they achieve a sense of their own effectiveness. These processes underlie and stimulate healthy cognitive development. But some young children experience cognitive delays because of birth defects, premature birth, forms of severe developmental delays, and other health problems that show up in early childhood, such as attention-deficit hyperactivity disorder or depression, pervasive developmental disorders such as autism or a milder form called **Asperger's syndrome**, seizure disorders, and HIV/AIDS. Well-designed early intervention programs can help children who live in high-risk settings and those with neurodevelopmental disabilities (Shonkoff & Phillips, 2000).

Congenital Birth Defects   Children who are born at risk (as a consequence of premature birth, birth defects, or being born into poverty, for example) are likely to experience delayed physical development and slower maturation of their senses and therefore may not get the opportunity to develop to their full potential. These children are eligible for intensive early intervention services, such as Early Head Start. For such children from ages 3 to 5, county health department case workers will develop an Individualized Family Service Plan (IFSP), while working with the family and public school district to help a child transition to a school setting (see Figure 7.1). Poor families may face obstacles to accessing services for their children such as lack of transportation, not being able to get time off from work to take children to doctors or other service providers, and lack of money to pay for medication, even when the cost is partially covered by federal and state programs. A growing number of poor immigrant families also face language barriers (Farel, 2005).

Young Children with Behavior Problems   In the United States, about 14 percent of children aged 5 to 11 suffer from mental, emotional, or behavioral problems that limit their activities (National Center for Health Statistics, 2010b). Around 2 to 3 percent of these children are disabled by their condition (Farel, 2005). When a preschool child appears inactive, depressed, or troubled, is overly active, or constantly runs, fights, or bites, he or she could have a serious emotional/behavioral problem. A significantly increasing number of young children, especially boys, either privately insured or on Medicaid, are diagnosed with attention-deficit disorder, pervasive developmental disorder, severe depression, mood disorders, or disruptive behavior disorder. Only about half of these children receive formal mental-health services (Olfson, Crystal, Huang, & Gerhard, 2010).

Joseph Coyle (2000) of Harvard Medical School says no empirical evidence exists to support psychotropic drug treatment in very young children. However, these young children are likely to be prescribed stimulants, antidepressants, and neuroleptics (used as antipsychotics). **Methylphenidate** (brand name *Ritalin*) is a mild stimulant of the central nervous system used to treat hyperactive behavior disorders in children, commonly labeled as ADD (attention-deficit disorder) or ADHD (attention-deficit hyperactivity disorder). Newer medications prescribed for hyperactivity include *Adderall*, *Concerta* (a re-formation of Ritalin), *Atomoxetine*, *Clonidine*, and *Guanfacine* (Dopheide & Pliszka, 2009). When children take psychotropic drugs, the side effects may include emotional outbursts, sleep disturbances, decreased appetite and lower growth rates, and repetitive behaviors (Kuehn, 2007).

Demographically, white children are most likely to receive these medications, followed by African American children (Zito et al., 2007). American children are prescribed psychotropic medications at a rate more than double that in the Netherlands and three and a half times more frequently than children in Germany (Zito et al., 2008). Worldwide, the use of stimulant medications for hyperactive children has increased substantially, and doctors are calling for more cautious monitoring (Scheffler et al., 2007). They believe the pharmaceutical industry has had a profound influence in funding ADHD studies, has published drug promotions extensively to doctors, and has advertised directly to consumers on television (Diller, 2002).

Pediatricians also recommend treatments in addition to drug therapy. These include cognitive-behavioral therapy, psychosocial treatment, emotional counseling, and early intervention services (see Figure 7.1). Polyunsaturated fatty acids from fish oil, acetyl-L-carnitine, and iron supplements have proved effective as dietary treatments (Dopheide & Pliszka, 2009). Increased structure at home, with support and training for parents (Vaughan, Wetzel, & Kratochvil, 2008), as well as examination of the child's classroom environment, may be helpful (LaForett, Murray, & Kollins, 2008). In 2005, the U.S. surgeon general paid special attention to early childhood development and mental-health problems and issued a special report that placed greater emphasis on "improving the body, mind, and spirit of the growing child" ("U.S. Surgeon General," 2005).

Chemical Exposure in Young Children   Caregivers of young children must take precautions to limit exposure to known and questionable toxic substances. Some young children experience compromised physical, motor, and brain functioning associated with their exposure to chemical toxicants emitted from industrial factories and old storage facilities, pesticides sprayed on farm crops and golf courses, toxic chemicals buried in landfills, and polluted water supplies.

Unfortunately, many common household objects are made of or treated with toxins. Flame-retardant chemicals (PBDEs) are found in home furniture, rugs, and children's clothing. Though effectual in fire protection, they are under close research scrutiny as neurotoxin risks to children (Hays et al., 2003). Bisphenol A (BPA) from plastic water and baby bottles and radiation emitted by cell phones are proving to be harmful to children's health (O'Callaghan, 2010). Certain pesticides sold for home use have been found to increase the rate of childhood brain tumors (Nielsen et al., 2010), PCBs from common household items are suspected in the rise of childhood leukemia (Ward et al., 2009), and both pesticides and PCBs are suspected as contributing to ADHD (Kuehn, 2010).

Further Resources for Young Children with Mental-Health Issues and Other Developmental Delays
Preparing an Individualized Family Service Plan (IFSP) for any eligible young child includes investigating a variety of resources in these areas:

- early identification and assessment of disabling conditions in children

- related services, including transportation
- developmental, corrective, and other supportive services (including speech-language pathology and audiology services)
- psychological services
- physical and occupational therapy; recreation, including therapeutic recreation
- social work services; counseling services, including rehabilitation counseling, orientation, and mobility services
- medical services, except that such medical services shall be for diagnostic and evaluation purposes only, as may be required to help a child with a disability to benefit from special education

Questions

Why should a young child have many types of sensory experiences? What changes are taking place in children's sensory systems, and what types of sensory disorders and health issues impede normal cognitive development? What types of services are available to help those with delays?

Nutrition and Health Issues

Pediatricians normally recommend that young children eat a "mixed diet" that includes a variety of foods and beverages so that over time the child will get the proper nourishment for normal growth (Kleinman, 2004). By age 2, toddlers are able to eat most family foods. Preschoolers need the same variety of fruits, vegetables, grains, and proteins that adults do, but in smaller portions. However, most children aged 2 to 6 do not eat enough grains and fruits and ingest too much cholesterol, sodium, and sugar (Federal Interagency Forum on Child and Family Statistics, 2007). The majority of U.S. children are healthy, but the rate of obese children aged 2 to 5 has nearly doubled in a decade—and child obesity is correlated with many health risks and a shorter life span (National Center for Health Statistics, 2007b).

Commercially prepared foods might provide some nutrition, but restaurant and take-out foods tend to be high in sodium, fats, and/or sugars. Young children who consume sugar-sweetened beverages are at a higher risk for obesity. Poor eating habits include skipping breakfast, eating at fast food restaurants, eating large portion sizes, snacking on high-calorie foods, and not eating with the family (Davis et al., 2007). Other factors contributing to the rise in overweight preschoolers are declining physical activity at home and school and increasing engagement in sedentary behaviors. Even though having a television and other media in a child's room has been associated with excess weight (Davis et al., 2007), new active video games, such as *Wii Sports* and *Dance Dance Revolution*,

MORE INFORMATION YOU CAN USE

Video Games with Health Benefits

The media have long been reviled for their negative effects on children's physical and mental health. Various studies have raised concerns about the association of childhood exposure to media, including video games, with aggression, sexual behavior, substance abuse, and eating disorders and academic struggles (Strasburger, Jordan, & Donnerstein, 2010). Video games have been blamed for both sedentary behavior and passivity. A large proportion of children over 2 years of age are obese or overweight, including as many as 4 out of 10 children enrolled in federally funded health programs (Graf et al., 2009; Wojcicki & Heyman, 2010). Obesity has been linked to physical inactivity, to which video gaming, as well as television viewing and computer work, has contributed (Graf et al., 2009). One feature of First Lady Michelle Obama's "Let's Move" campaign, launched in 2009, is the charge to increase the opportunities that children have to be physically active (Wojcicki & Heyman, 2010).

A new category of video gaming has emerged, however, called "exergaming" (Graf et al., 2009). The most popular of these new games are the *Wii Sports* suite of software and *Dance Dance Revolution* (DDR). Because these games require players to stand and move during play, children expend energy at a rate 172 percent higher during exergaming than when watching television or playing traditional sedentary video games; this output is similar to a child's walking at a low to moderate rate, such as skipping, jogging, or stair climbing (Graf et al., 2009; Mhurchu et al., 2008). Even video games such as *Guitar Hero* and *Rock Band*, which require players only to stand, burn more calories than sedentary video games (Kasland, 2008).

As these active video games gain in popularity, they are being put to use by a variety of groups. Nintendo and *USA Today* teamed up to sponsor a Family Fitness Challenge by donating *Wii* systems to families to help them shape up (Hellmich, 2010). DDR and other exergames have been included in school physical education programs (Kasland, 2008). For children with physical or brain injury, "Wiihab" has become part of their rehabilitation program. Exergames

Exergaming Promotes Exercise

require both mental processing and physical movement, which can be a great benefit to those recovering from injury (Kasland, 2008).

Video gaming may not be a substitute for traditional exercise for children, such as bicycling, running, or swimming, but there are measurable benefits to the exergaming phenomenon (Kasland, 2008). Researchers hope that the increase in popularity of video and computer games will counter the effects of sedentary behavior (Graf et al., 2009). Children in studies who were provided with active rather than passive video games engage in more physical activity, play fewer video games overall, and improve their waist measurements (Mhurchu et al., 2008).

---

can be beneficial to children (Graf et al., 2009) (see the *More Information You Can Use* box, "Video Games with Health Benefits). Also, many children's television programs advertise food products with poor nutritional content, such as sugary cereals (Powell et al., 2007).

It is recommended that by age 3 and thereafter, children should get most of their calories from grain products, fruits, vegetables, low-fat dairy, beans, lean meat,

poultry, fish, and nuts (Dietary Guidelines Advisory Committee, 2005). Most young children do not readily accept spicy, strong-tasting, bitter, or pungent foods. Consequently, pharmaceutical companies add sweeteners to children's vitamins and medications.

Variability in Eating Behaviors Among Children

Like everyone else, young children will feel hungry; their

bodies tell them when to eat, but their hunger might not coincide with the family mealtime. Young children also go through "growth spurts," and during such times they experience periods of greater hunger. Children can become difficult or disruptive at mealtimes if caregivers impose strict eating behaviors, such as requiring them to finish all of something and to try everything (Satter, 1998). Again, some children react severely to the taste and texture of certain foods, and sensory integration methods may help. Other children have allergies to specific foods, and caregivers must pay special attention to removing that food from the child's diet. Also, a small percentage of children have a swallowing disorder and may need a special diet.

When a Child Refuses Certain Foods
Some foods, such as broccoli, cabbage, Brussels sprouts, spinach, cauliflower, olives, and onions, taste very bitter to the sensitive taste buds of young children—and other foods may be rejected because of texture (children often dislike liver, for example). It might be better to reintroduce these foods in tiny portions at several time intervals during development, but it may be the case that the child will never come to like certain foods that will always taste bitter to him or her. Also, certain foods may not taste good to a child because he or she is genetically more sensitive to bitter tastes than most people. For all these reasons, a parent and a child may live in different sensory worlds when it comes to how food tastes (Menella, Pepino, & Reed, 2005).

When given a variety of healthy foods to choose from, children tend to eat what their body needs, although not from every food group every day. Leach (1998) cites a study conducted at a nursery in London revealing that when children were offered trays of a wide range of suitably cooked and cut-up foods three times each day, they selected for themselves diets that were balanced over the long term. Some would prefer protein one day, fruits other days. Some days they ate more, some days less. A routine checkup with a pediatrician will determine whether the young child is growing adequately for gender, age, and body type. Also, a parent or caregiver can easily track a child's growth with growth charts by gender provided by the CDC at www.cdc.gov/growthcharts.

Mealtimes should be enjoyable; food should never be used as a reward, punishment, bribe, or threat. The important thing to remember is that early childhood is a time of exploration. It's important not to overreact when a child refuses to eat. There's no nutritional advantage to eating three meals a day; this is just a social custom. Having a variety of healthy snacks that children can eat throughout the day will help ensure adequate nutrition (Wardlaw & Smith, 2007).

Eating Frequency
Young children need something to eat when they wake up, as well as a midmorning snack, lunch, a mid-afternoon snack, an evening meal, and maybe a snack before bedtime. When hungry children must wait too long to eat, their blood sugar levels dip, causing energy drain, lack of patience, and a "cranky" attitude. Child-care providers must be prepared to offer children proper nutrition at various times of the day.

Most preschool children and 5- and 6-year-olds in kindergarten classes need the energy boost of the midmorning or mid-afternoon snack to think clearly and participate in activities (Leach, 1998). Some children are larger or more energetic than others and might need to snack more between mealtimes. Other children are smaller and less energetic and might simply require fewer calories. Gender, ethnicity, and geographic climate have all been examined as influential factors in determining how much energy young children need to expend (Goran et al., 1998).

Cultural background affects what and how much children eat. Children whose families practice fasting to honor religious requirements are expected to fast for days or even weeks, eating only one or two meals per day.

Dental Health Affects Nutritional Intake
The most common chronic health issue of early childhood is dental *caries* (tooth decay, or cavities), and today's children aged 2 to 5 have more cavities in baby teeth (Young, Lyon, & Acevdeo, 2010). Between the early 1990s and 2007, the rate of decay in baby teeth increased from 25 percent to almost 30 percent (Dye et al., 2007). Dentists recommend that primary care physicians examine children's teeth for defects and cavities when they emerge and at every well-child visit (Casamassimo, 2004). However, a recent national study found that less than half of the children aged 2 to 5 had visited a dentist in a one-year period (Dye et al., 2007). Free dental screenings for U.S. children are offered in some states, but the full impact of the 2010 health-care reform legislation (*Patient Protection and Affordable Care Act*) on coverage for child dental care is unclear at this time.

To prevent decay of both baby teeth and permanent teeth, children should not be given sweet foods before they go to sleep. The American Academy of Pediatrics recommends that children 1 to 6 years old drink no more than 6 ounces of fruit juice each day and avoid sweetened soft drinks (Wardlaw & Smith, 2007). Other factors that promote healthy tooth development include training toddlers and children to clean their teeth regularly, having regular dental checkups, and providing fluoride in local water supplies. Around the age of 5 to 6, baby teeth begin to come out and permanent ones come in. Parents and caregivers should teach and model proper

TABLE 7.2 Food Allergies May Be Life Threatening

The most common symptoms of food allergies and anaphylaxis are

- Hives
- Vomiting
- Diarrhea
- Abdominal cramping
- Swelling of the throat, lips, or tongue
- Difficulty breathing or swallowing
- Metallic taste or itching in the mouth
- Generalized flushing, itching, or redness of the skin (hives)
- Nausea
- Increased heart rate
- Plunging blood pressure (and accompanying paleness)
- Sudden feeling of weakness
- Anxiety or an overwhelming sense of doom
- Collapse
- Loss of consciousness

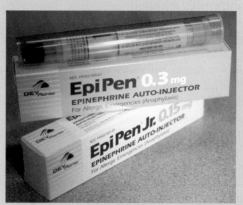

EpiPen All child caregivers should familiarize themselves with signs of anaphylaxis and with the EpiPen, a tool for quickly administering epinephrine, a form of adrenaline that reverses the effects of an allergic reaction.

dental hygiene and provide supplies. Programs such as Head Start and WIC provide dental supplies for low-income families, and contemporary policymakers are urging that dental checkups be included as part of universal health care.

Improper tooth development can impair a child's ability to eat and speak—not to mention affect a child's appearance, level of comfort, or health in later years (some children never smile because of decayed, irregular, or missing teeth).

Allergies The Food Allergy and Anaphylaxis Network (FAAN) estimates that over 3 million U.S. children have an allergic reaction to certain foods, which can happen immediately or within hours. For children with food allergies, the organs most affected are the mouth, skin, gastrointestinal tract, and respiratory system. The foods that most commonly cause allergic reactions are milk, eggs, peanuts, tree nuts, wheat, soy, fish, and shellfish (FAAN, 2007). Severe allergic reactions, called **anaphylaxis** (anna-phi-lax'-iss), can result in death if not treated medically. Parents, child-care workers, school nurses, and teachers must know which children are at risk of anaphylaxis due to allergies to food and other allergens. Insect stings—including those from bees, hornets, wasps, and fire ants—can also be life-threatening to some children. Some children have serious allergies to animal dander, specific medications, or latex ("Information about

Anaphylaxis," 2005). The common symptoms of food allergy are noted in Table 7.2, and all caregivers of children should equip themselves with this life-saving information. The only way to prevent an allergic reaction is strict avoidance of the allergy-causing food, animal, insect, or substance (FAAN, 2007).

In 2006, Congress passed the Food Allergy and Anaphylaxis Management Act, which called for national guidelines for managing food allergies and anaphylaxis in schools (FAAN, 2006). School nurses, teachers, and other caregivers should be aware that one-quarter of the allergic reactions to food that take place at school happen to children who were not aware they had a food allergy.

For generations, medical practitioners and the dairy industry convinced parents that children's bones would not grow without daily intake of cow's milk, but today it is known that some children's digestive systems do not handle cow's milk well. Some children are lactose intolerant; they experience abdominal pain and cramping or episodes of passing foul-smelling gas or stools shortly after eating dairy foods. These children can get the necessary nutrients from soy products, tomatoes, and green and leafy vegetables (Sicherer, 2006).

A Vegetarian Diet Children in vegetarian families commonly get their carbohydrates and protein from a range of bean, legume, and nut dishes and possibly from egg, cheese, or dairy dishes. Feeding a strict vegetarian diet to a growing child is questionable, and parents should seek dietary advice from a nutritionist or medical professional. The diet of a vegetarian child should include enough protein, vitamin B-12, iron, and zinc (Wardlaw & Smith, 2007). The other trace minerals and vitamins that children need for healthy bones, teeth, blood, and neural growth are usually found in a diet with plenty of fresh fruits and vegetables.

Good Health Also Means Sufficient Calories Children need an adequate number of calories daily to keep their bodily functions running smoothly and to provide the fuel needed for growth of their brain and body systems. Staple carbohydrates, eaten in different forms all over the world, include rice, wheat, potatoes, corn, beans, yams, and sweet potatoes. Children can get an ample supply of protein from meat, fish, poultry, eggs, or foods that contain eggs, cheese, yogurt, peanut butter, and similar foods (Leach, 1998).

In areas of the world with limited food supply, many children develop forms of life-threatening malnutrition called *marasmus* or *kwashiorkor* from diets chronically deficient in carbohydrates, protein, and fat. Malnourished children have little energy, are lethargic, are likely to have a large protuberant abdomen from protein deficiency, and are at high risk of early death (Douglass et al., 2007).

Effects of Poverty on Nutrition and Health The term **food security** is used to mean having access at all times to enough food to support a healthy, active life. This means having enough food that is nutritious and safe without needing to rely on sources such as food pantries. Because food security is directly related to income and monetary resources, children who live in poverty are much more likely to experience food insecurity. The percentage of children living in food-insecure situations is slowly declining; in 2007, 16 percent of households that included children in the United States were classified as food insecure, and in 8 percent of those households, the children themselves were food insecure (Nord, 2009). The diet quality of these children is poor; that is, they do not get enough nutritious food to meet the needs of their growing bodies (Federal Interagency Forum on Child and Family Statistics, 2007). This insufficiency has implications for their entire lives. Poor nutrition early in life creates cognitive deficits in adulthood, even when an individual catches up in physical growth (Fisher, Nager, & Monaghan, 2006). Countrywide, there is a movement to provide schools and consumers with more local foods, which are fresher, less processed, more nutritious, and lower in cost (Martinez et al., 2010).

Safety Practices in a Young Child's Environment Accidental injuries are the leading cause of children's visits to emergency rooms and include falls, being struck by an object or person, animal and insect bites, poisoning, traffic accidents, and cuts. Thus, all dangerous items, such as sharp knives, matches and lighters, loaded guns, fireworks, and household cleansers, should be kept out of a child's reach, as should plants with poisonous leaves. Windows, doors, wall sockets, and pool gates should have child safety locks to prevent injuries. Keys should be in a safe place so a curious child cannot imitate starting the car, lawnmower, or all-terrain vehicle. When disposing of old appliances, such as refrigerators or dishwashers, make sure the doors are removed.

When exploring new tastes, young children will try new and different items, some of which are poisonous, such as pills, mothballs, and many household cleansers, and some of which pose a choking hazard, such as marbles, coins, and hard candies. The effects of neurotoxins from lead dust and paint chips include seizure, coma, and death (Centers for Disease Control and Prevention, 2004). (See the *Further Developments* box on page 206, "Household Lead Poisoning: Still a Problem.") Preschool children should be supervised at every moment.

> *Questions*
>
> What types of nutrition and eating behaviors are critical for a child's healthy growth and brain development, and what are some of the chronic health conditions that affect young children today? How can one keep busy, growing children safe from accidents?

Self-Care Behaviors

An important aspect of a young child's development is training in self-care behaviors, such as daily bathing and shampooing, cleaning teeth, brushing hair, wiping the nose, wiping the bottom and washing the hands after toileting, washing hands before and after eating, and dressing appropriately for weather conditions (putting on boots, coat, and mittens when it is cold and snowy, for example). Cultures differ in how much independence they promote in children regarding self-care behaviors. Many school-readiness tasks expected of a child aged 4 or 5 are related to self-care behaviors.

Toilet Training Elimination training is a big developmental milestone during early childhood, and there is considerable variance in age of mastery. On average, in Westernized cultures children demonstrate self-control of these bodily functions by the third year. In nonindustrial societies, mothers respond to their child's elimination rhythms by using natural infant hygiene (Bauer, 2001). Parents and caregivers should realize that patience and a sense of humor help both them and the child get through this time of maturation and development. Children who

FURTHER DEVELOPMENTS

Household Lead Poisoning: Still a Problem

Although overall blood lead level (BLL) rates have been steadily declining over the years, lead poisoning continues to be a serious public health issue, especially for young children. One major source of lead exposure is deteriorating house paint in the form of dust, paint chips, and lead pipes (especially in buildings built before 1978). Nearly half of all U.S. homes in which children under the age of 6 live still have lead paint, and lead dust is easily spread during rental or home renovations. Children are exposed to lead by breathing or swallowing lead dust, by swallowing water from old lead pipes, or by eating soil or paint chips containing lead (U.S. Department of Housing and Urban Development, 2003).

In 2007 the U.S. Consumer Product Safety Commission (CPSC) began issuing recalls of more than 21 million toys manufactured in China because they contained lead paint or parts. Almost 90 percent of toys in the United States are manufactured abroad, including toys sold by leading manufacturers, and over 70 percent come from China. However, China is not the only culprit; lead also has been found in toys manufactured in Canada, Mexico, Thailand, and the United States itself. The CPSC attempts to monitor toys entering the country, but its staff has been cut by over half since 1973, even though it is still responsible for monitoring 300 U.S. ports (Schmidt, 2008).

Lead can also be found in other children's products over which the CPSC has no control, including children's jewelry and games made from vinyl. Although vinyl may not release much lead during mouthing, chewing or swallowing could expose children to extremely high levels of lead (Schmidt, 2008). Other, more unexpected sources of lead poisoning include folk remedies for illness, imported condiments and candies, lead pellets and bullets, and dust from imported mini-blinds (Gorospe & Gerstenberger, 2008). Children whose parents work in a lead-contaminated environment may be exposed to lead dust from a parent's clothing or a buildup of dust in the home (Khan, Qayyum, Saleem, Ansari, & Khan, 2010).

Researchers continue to study the health effects associated with lead exposure, which include damage to the brain and nervous system, behavioral and learning problems, and hormonal effects that delay puberty (Canfield et al., 2003). Lead poisoning causes decreased appetite, stomachache, sleeplessness, learning problems, constipation, vomiting, diarrhea, tiredness, lowered IQ, and anemia ("Lead Poisoning," 2005). A pediatrician can order a blood test to determine a child's blood lead levels.

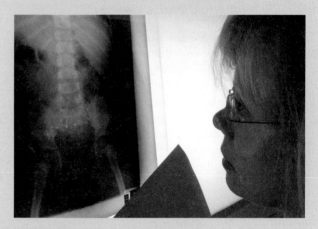

Lead Paint Is Still Injuring Children Lead paint chips sparkle in the intestines of a 2-year-old girl who swallowed them.

These health effects appear to be long-term and irreversible. *Chelation therapy* (cleansing the bloodstream) does not seem to provide sustained improvements to cognitive, behavioral, or neuropsychological function (Rischitelli et al., 2006). The CDC continues to find harmful effects at lower levels in the blood. The U.S. Department of Health and Human Services set a new goal to eliminate BLLs greater than 10 milligrams per deciliter in children 6 years of age and under by the year 2010. However, studies show that impairments occur at concentrations well below that goal (Jusko et al., 2008).

Prevention is the only way to protect children from lead exposure. Homes should be tested for lead paint and repainted frequently to prevent peeling of old layers of lead paint. Old lead pipes should be replaced, but water filters can remove some of the lead. Caregivers who live in older homes or work with children in old buildings should have the facility and outside soil checked for lead contamination, wash children's toys and hands regularly, dust and wash floors and window sills regularly, make sure there are no loose paint chips, ensure that the children's toys do not contain lead, and avoid exposure to lead dust when remodeling or renovating. Parents must read labels on all toys, check the list of recalled toys, and remember that there is no way to regulate used toys that are resold or donated (Marder, 2007). A list of recalled toys can be found at http://www.cpsc.gov.

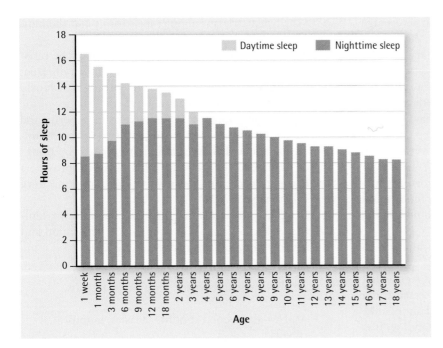

FIGURE 7.2 Hours of Daytime and Nighttime Sleep Change with Increasing Age Daytime sleep gradually decreases over the first three years, with an increase in night-time sleep. By age 4 or 5, many children do not take a daytime nap.
Adapted with permission of Simon & Schuster Adult Publishing Group, from *Solve Your Child's Sleep Problems* by Richard Ferber. Copyright © 1985.

master self-care skills and can self-regulate their own behaviors are likely to develop greater self-esteem and self-confidence, and this can lead to many other positive outcomes as the child matures.

Sleep Studies show that children's sleep patterns and sleep problems are influenced by cultural and social factors (Liu et al., 2005). Parents are often concerned about their young children's sleep behaviors (Thiedke, 2001). Daytime sleep gradually decreases over the first three years, and by age 4 most children no longer require a daytime nap (see Figure 7.2). Night awakenings are common throughout early childhood; about a third of children under age 4 wake up in the night and need soothing from parents to fall back asleep (Thiedke, 2001). There are two schools of thought about young children's sleep habits: (1) the child needs a daily routine of one early afternoon nap and a reasonable evening bedtime so that he or she will get 10 to 12 hours of sleep per night, or (2) the child's sleep schedule can vary at times to meet the parents' needs.

In actuality, sleep schedules are based on parental and caregiver tolerance about sleep habits, the number of caregivers, whether the child goes to child care, and timing of the parents' workday. Today, with over 60 percent of mothers working, many young children awaken early, are transported to a child-care center for the day, and return home for only a few hours before bedtime. An overtired child can be whiny and cranky and will probably be difficult or lethargic. It is unfair to punish a child for unruly or uncooperative behavior when the parents are not providing enough rest, relaxation, or sleep time for an energetic, growing child.

Parents who establish a consistent bedtime routine will find it easier than those who reinforce a lot of rocking, getting up many times, walking around, or overplaying. It relaxes children at bedtime to have a warm bath, to have a story read to them, or to share a quiet talk with a caregiver. Young children who are allowed to stay up late and run around the house at all hours are likely to be in control of the family over this sleep issue.

Sleep Disturbances in Young Children Children aged 3 to 8 often have sleep problems, although we do not know what causes *nightmares* or *night terrors* ("Sleep Problems: Nightmares," 2001). "Night terrors occur approximately 90 minutes into sleep. . . . The child suddenly sits bolt upright and screams and is inconsolable for up to 30 minutes before relaxing and falling back to sleep" (Thiedke, 2001, p. 279).

Preschoolers can have problems with initiating, maintaining, and resisting sleep. Parents need to set firm limits when the child pleads for one more drink of water or one more story (Thiedke, 2001). A preschool or kindergarten-age child experiences many daytime stresses or fears—such as attending a new school, the birth of a new sibling, moving to a new home, separation of parents, or death of a significant person or pet—that can trigger bad dreams. Also, young children today are exposed, in various media, to graphic displays of violence that are very disturbing and likely to cause sleep disturbances (Thompson & Christakis, 2005).

An estimated 5 to 7 million American children (and a higher percentage of boys) experience nocturnal *enuresis* (bed wetting). By 5 years of age, about 1 out of 4 children still wets the bed, and that is when physicians consider a diagnosis of enuresis. By age 12 a small percentage of boys and girls are still enuretic (Thiedke, 2003). The causes of enuresis are multifactorial: Primary nocturnal enuresis is caused by small bladder capacity and the child's failure to awaken to the sensation of a full bladder; secondary enuresis may be a sign of medical issues, genetic factors, psychological concerns, behavior problems, bladder problems or infections, and sleep disorders (Ramakrishnan, 2008). Children who still wet the bed after age 5 should be examined by a physician. Treatment plans include bed-wetting alarms, medication, encouragement, and support (Thiedke, 2003). Parents should avoid instilling guilt, shame, or fear of punishment in the child (Ramakrishnan, 2008).

A young child does not have the vocabulary to understand or express the anxiety she or he is experiencing, and chronic sleep disturbances can be a signal that the child is not coping well. Parents can reassure the child by giving him or her extra love and attention, talking about the child's fears, and being understanding. It is unlikely that a young child has mastered the distinction between fantasy and reality.

Illness and Immunizations   With more children in early childhood education programs or receiving out-of-home care in a nursery, child-care center, preschool, pre-K, Early Head Start or Head Start, children are with other children daily and at greater risk for contracting childhood diseases. For children aged 1 to 4, the most common causes of child hospitalization are diseases of the respiratory system; endocrine, metabolic, and immunity diseases; infectious and parasitic diseases; injuries; and diseases of the digestive system (U.S. Maternal and Child Health Bureau, 2010).

Most states require proof of immunizations before a young child can be enrolled in child care or in public preschool or kindergarten classes. Even though a small percentage of children have extreme reactions to certain vaccinations, the vast majority will experience better health if their parents maintain the recommended inoculation schedule. Between 2004 and 2009, the number of reported U.S. cases of pertussis (known as whooping cough) rose from 6,000 to 17,000, with 14 deaths nationally (Centers for Disease Control and Prevention, 2010g; U.S. Department of Health and Human Services, 2006). In 2010, there were increasing outbreaks of pertussis in several states, and infants are at high risk for serious illness. Pertussis is a vaccine-preventable disease, but some parents are refusing this immunization on the basis of personal religious or health concerns. The MMR (measles-mumps-rubella) immunization is also under close scrutiny by U.S. research teams and other countries for its potential association with pervasive developmental disorders. Parents with questions about the use of certain preservatives in immunizations are advised to confer

with their pediatricians about vaccinations and the individual child.

Immigrant parents of young children may be resistant to the idea of immunization because of their different cultural understanding of illness. According to Chinese medical practice, illness is caused by an imbalance of the body's energies; some cultures believe in supernatural sources of illness, such as curses and fixes; other immigrant groups may believe that illness is caused by thinking or doing evil (Lecca et al., 1998). Medical providers are being trained to be sensitive to these immunization fears (Betancourt, 2003).

Here are the recommended vaccinations for children aged 4 to 6 years ("Recommended Childhood and Adolescent Immunization Schedule," 2005):

- *IPV*—the fourth booster: poliovirus
- *DtaP*—the fifth booster: diphtheria, tetanus, pertussis
- *MMR*—the second shot for measles, mumps, rubella

Childhood Asthma   Asthma is the leading chronic pediatric disease. The rate of childhood asthma has increased dramatically since the 1980s, and today almost 10 percent of children suffer from asthma in some parts of the country. The rate of asthma is highest among Puerto Rican and black children, and black children are much more likely to die from the disease than white children (Akinbami, 2006). **Asthma** is a chronic lung disease characterized by inflammation and narrowing of small airways in the lungs in response to *allergens,* which trigger the asthma attack. Such "triggers" include pet dander (from home or classroom pets), pollen, dust, and dust mites, as well as exposure to tobacco smoke, household cleansers, changes in the weather, and environmental pollutants (Akinbami, 2006).

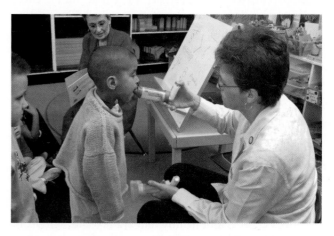

Asthma Is a Main Cause of Child Hospitalizations   In 2007, 13 percent of American children were diagnosed with asthma, and diseases of the respiratory system were the major causes of hospitalization for children aged 1 to 4.

It is the most common reason why children are admitted to the hospital and a major cause of school absences (U.S. Department of Health and Human Services, 2006).

Symptoms include coughing, wheezing, shortness of breath, and tightness in the chest, making it very difficult to breathe (Akinbami, 2006). Caregivers must decrease or eliminate a child's exposure to allergens, thereby decreasing asthma symptoms. After being diagnosed, some children take inhaled medications to improve their breathing (quick-relief drugs), whereas others get regular allergy shots and other medications (long-term control). Families whose children have serious allergies and asthma need to have an emergency *epinephrine* (see Table 7.2) kit available and should ensure that their child's school has a protocol in place for administering a "rescue medicine" (McIntyre et al., 2005).

Public School Health Care   Children in the U.S. public school system are checked annually by a health-care professional for physical and health problems, such as malnutrition, obesity, and curvature of the spine; respiratory illnesses such as asthma; sensory capabilities, through vision and hearing screenings; and overall health and self-care skills, with attention to bathing, head or body lice, and such. The combination of proper nutrition for growth and development, required sleep for physical maturation and increased alertness, and childhood immunizations protecting against specific diseases helps to lay a healthy foundation for central nervous system development and cognitive functioning.

Demographic Trends and Implications for Child Health

The total number of children under 18 has increased by over 50 percent since 1950, which has implications for health care, education, child care, and other services. There were 74.5 million children in the United States in 2009, representing 24 percent of the total population. The number of children is expected to rise to over 82 million by 2021 (Federal Interagency Forum on Child and Family Statistics, 2011). The percentage of U.S. children who are of Hispanic background has more than doubled since 1980 to 22 percent; the percentage of U.S. children of Caucasian background was about 55 percent in 2009 (Federal Interagency Forum on Child and Family Statistics, 2011).

Figure 7.3 shows estimated statistics for 2009 for child population by race-ethnicity. Population experts project that while the number of Hispanic children under 18 will continue to increase, the black, Asian, and white populations of children will remain relatively stable. The changing demographics in the United States have important implications for the overall population. With increasing numbers of persons representing

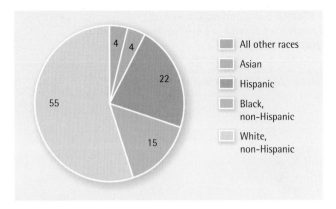

FIGURE 7.3 Estimated Percentages of U.S. Children Ages 0 to 17, by Racial-Ethnic Group: 2009 In 2009, there were 74.5 million children, and racial and ethnic diversity continues to increase.
Source: Federal Interagency Forum on Child and Family Statistics. (2010). *America's Children: Key National Indicators of Well-Being, 2010.* Retrieved November 12, 2010, from http://www.childstats.gov/americaschildren/glance.asp

diverse ethnic groups, there are large numbers of individuals unable to speak English—a great deterrent to getting proper health care and other services. Translation services are needed to ensure that members of minority racial-ethnic groups will be able to converse with professionals about their health needs. It is common for adult immigrants to bring a 4- or 5-year-old child who is learning English to be their interpreter at a visit to a doctor! But it is also likely that they won't seek health care until their health condition is serious, and this delay leads to increased costs for health services and to more negative health outcomes.

Child Mortality Rates and Causes

A reduction in both early and late childhood mortality rates in the United States indicates an improvement in the health status of the child population. But even with decreasing mortality rates, since 1960 male children have died at a greater rate than female children (Federal Interagency Forum on Child and Family Statistics, 2011).

Causes of Death for Young Children   In 2007, the leading cause of death for children aged 1 to 4 was unintentional injuries (see Figure 7.4). Motor vehicle accidents are the leading cause of death for children ages 1 to 4, followed by drownings (Xu, Kochanek, Murphy, & Tejada-Vera, 2010).

Since motor vehicle crashes are the most common cause of death from accidental injury, any child from birth to age 7 should always be secured in a safety seat appropriate for the child's weight and height (U.S. Maternal and Child Health Bureau, 2006). For children under 40 pounds, this means a front-facing safety seat. Children over 40 pounds should use a booster seat in the back seat

FIGURE 7.4 Leading Causes of
Death for Children Ages 1 to 4:
2007
Source: Xu, J., Kochanek, K., Murphy, S. L., &
Tejada-Vera, T. (2010). Deaths: Final data for
2007. *National Vital Statistics Reports, 58*(19),
27–31.

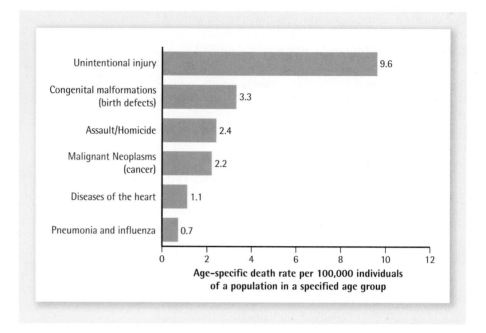

of the vehicle until the vehicle's seat belts fit them properly (Glassbrenner & Ye, 2007). Burns from flammable
liquids or burning clothing are another risk for children
under 4 (Bessey et al., 2006). Adults must always supervise children near any type of water, including a bathroom tub, kiddie pool, or jacuzzi. Keep the child in sight
and within reach 100 percent of the time. Turn off the cell
phone and *do not* multitask.

Child Mortality in Minority Communities   Despite
overall reductions in childhood mortality, there are substantial differences across racial-ethnic groups. Black
children have the highest death rate of all racial-ethnic
groups, followed by Hispanic children, white children,
and Asian and Pacific Islander children (Federal Interagency Forum on Child and Family Statistics, 2007).
This may be linked to the fact that so many American
black children live in poverty. One leading cause of death
for black children is house fires; many children in this
group live in older urban housing that is not required to
meet updated building codes (Pressley et al., 2007).

Future Directions   Many private and public sector
partners are collaborating in a national initiative called
Healthy People 2020. Families, child health professionals,
federal, state and community representatives, and private
organizations have come together to identify health priorities, increase public awareness, provide measurable
goals, strengthen policies, and identify research needs in
42 areas of health. The plan presents strategies for delivering services to help all people improve the quality of
their lives that can be achieved by 2020 ("Healthy People
2020," 2010). Most components of the federal *Affordable
Care Act* do not take effect until 2014.

Questions

What variables will a health-care practitioner examine
to determine whether a young child is healthy and
developing normally? What are some of the more
common childhood disorders and disabilities that
compromise healthy development, and what services
are available for those affected? What are the main
causes of accidents to and the death of young children?

COGNITIVE DEVELOPMENT

Preschool children who receive adequate nutrition,
sleep, and varied stimulation normally experience a rapid
expansion of cognitive abilities. They become more adept
at obtaining, ordering, and using information. Gradually,
these abilities evolve into the attribute called intelligence.
Whereas sensorimotor processes largely dominate development during infancy, a significant transition occurs
after 18 months toward the more complex processes of
reasoning, inference, and problem solving. Preschool
children continue to use their senses to absorb the world
around them, and preschool educators use many sensory
experiences to teach about the world. By the time children are 7 years old, they have developed a diversified
set of cognitive skills that are functionally related to the
elements of adult intelligence (Sternberg, 1990).

Intelligence and Its Assessment

For laypeople and psychologists alike, the concept of
intelligence is a rather fuzzy notion (Sternberg, 1990).

In some ways intelligence resembles electricity. Like electricity, intelligence "is measurable, and its effect, but not its properties, can be only imprecisely described" (Bischof, 1976, p. 137). Even so, David Wechsler (1896–1981), a psychologist who devised a number of widely used intelligence tests, proposed a definition that has won considerable acceptance (Wechsler, 1975). He viewed **intelligence** as a global capacity to understand the world, think rationally, and cope resourcefully with the challenges of life. In Wechsler's view, intelligence is a capacity for acquiring knowledge and functioning rationally and effectively, rather than the possession of a fund of knowledge. Intelligence has captivated the interest of psychologists for a variety of reasons, including a desire to devise ways of teaching people to better understand and increase their intellectual abilities (Sternberg, 1986).

Intelligence: Single or Multiple Factors? One recurrent divisive issue among psychologists is whether intelligence is a single general intellectual capacity or a composite of many special independent abilities. Alfred Binet (1857–1911), the French psychologist who in 1905 devised the first widely used intelligence test, viewed intelligence as a general capacity for comprehension and reasoning. His test used many different types of items, and Binet assumed that he was measuring a general ability that was expressed in the performance of many kinds of tasks.

In England, Charles Spearman (1863–1945) quickly rose to eminence in psychological circles by advancing a somewhat different view. Spearman (1904, 1927) concluded that there is a general intellectual ability—the g (for "general") factor—that is used for abstract reasoning and problem solving. He viewed the g factor as a basic intellectual power that pervades all of a person's mental activity. However, because an individual's performance across various tasks is not perfectly consistent, Spearman identified two elements of intelligence: general intelligence (the g factor), which is universal, and specific intelligence (the s factor), which is particular to certain tasks, such as arithmetic or spatial relations. This approach is known as the **two-factor theory of intelligence** (see N. Brody, 1992). J. P. Guilford (1967) carried the tradition further by identifying 120 factors of intelligence. Not all psychologists are happy, however, with such minute distinctions. Many prefer to speak of "general ability"—a mixture of abilities that can be more or less arbitrarily measured by a general-purpose intelligence test.

Multiple Intelligences Psychologist Howard Gardner (1983, 1993a, 1993b, 2000a, 2000b, 2006a, 2006b, 2008) has been conducting research with gifted children for decades. On the basis of his research, he proposes that instead of just one factor called intelligence, there are **multiple intelligences (MIs).** That is, humans have at least nine distinctive intelligences that interact (see Figure 7.5): verbal-linguistic, logical-mathematical, visual-spatial, musical, bodily-kinesthetic, interpersonal (knowing how to deal with others), intrapersonal

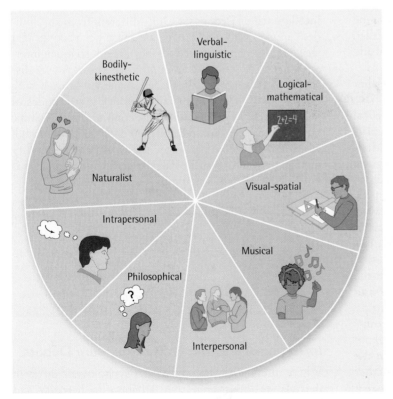

FIGURE 7.5 Multiple Intelligences Howard Gardner proposes that there is not just one factor called intelligence but, rather, that there are multiple intelligences (MIs). That is, humans have at least nine distinctive intelligences that interact. Thus, children have different learning strengths and weaknesses. Gardner suggests that educators vary instructional and evaluation methods to accommodate a variety of learners (Gardner, 2006).

(knowledge of oneself), naturalist (knowledge of the natural world), and existentialist (philosophical knowledge about existence). Gardner argues that children have different learning strengths and weaknesses and that educators should vary their instructional and evaluation methods to accommodate more than visual-linguistic and logical-mathematical learners (Gardner, 2000a).

Gardner contends that these separate intelligences are located in different areas of the brain (Gardner, 2000a). Youngsters who are advanced in one area are often unremarkable in others. In fact, people with retardation whose mental ability is lower in most areas occasionally exhibit extraordinary ability in a specific area, such as mathematical calculation or music (Treffert, 2001). These observations led Gardner to say that the intelligence quotient (IQ) ought to be replaced with an "intellectual profile." Gardner's proposed theory has been embraced by teachers who work daily with children and readily see their different capabilities (Gardner, 2000a). But critics such as John White (2006) dispute Gardner's theory, saying that some of the intelligences Gardner has identified are really expressions of emotion, not types of reasoning. His critics have difficulty using the word *intelligence* for what people typically label human abilities, aptitudes, or virtues.

Spatial Ability, Music, and Intelligence   Gardner defines **spatial ability** as skills pertaining to the ability to form mental images, visualize graphic representations, and recognize interrelationships among objects (Gardner, 1983, 2000a). Spatial skills are used to move objects around (including oneself) in any environment (as in playing sports, strategizing in a game of chess, or becoming skilled at a computer video game) and to solve mathematical and engineering problems later in life.

Along similar lines, psychologist Fran Rauscher (1996) and neuroscientist Dee Joy Coulter (1995) have argued that singing, rhythmic movement, musical games, listening, and early training in musical instruments are neurological exercises that introduce children to speech patterns, sensorimotor skills, and vital rhythm and movement strategies. All of these nonverbal activities are independent of language, they suggest, and promote brain development in the same neural pathways used for spatial skills (Baney, 1998). Rauscher (1996) conducted a study in 1993 in which ten 3-year-old children took either singing or piano lessons. When tested later, the children's scores improved 46 percent on the Object Assembly Task of the *Wechsler Preschool and Primary Scale of Intelligence–Revised*. In a later study that took place over eight months with three groups of preschool children, the preschoolers taking piano lessons scored a significant 34 percent higher than the groups not taking piano lessons. Heyge (1996) further states that music is essential to children's lives because it

Cultural Bias in Intelligence Testing A culture influences what an individual is likely to learn. It would be invalid to give these youngsters the Stanford-Binet intelligence test, which was designed by and for English-speaking residents of the United States.

optimizes brain development, enhances multiple intelligences, facilitates genuine bonding between adult and child, builds social/emotional skills, promotes attention to task and inner speech, develops impulse control, enhances motor development, and communicates creativity and joy.

In sum, these psychologists and neuroscientists recommend both incorporating music into children's lives as early as possible to build neural connections and revitalizing music programs in the public schools.

Intelligence as Process   Quite different from an "abilities" approach to intelligence are those perspectives that view intelligence as a *process*—they are not so much interested in *what* we know as in *how* we know. As we discussed in Chapter 2, Jean Piaget concerned himself with the stages of development during which given modes of thought appear. He focused on the continual and dynamic interplay between children and their environment through which children come to know the world and to modify their understanding of it. Piaget's preoperational stage is discussed later in this chapter.

Questions

How have various theorists defined the concept of "intelligence" over time? What theory do you think applies to the differences in individual abilities and capacities, such as being classified as "gifted"?

Intelligence and the Nature-Nurture Debate

Where intelligence is concerned, psychologists differ in the relative importance they attribute to heredity and to environment. As we discussed in Chapter 2, some investigators of the nature-nurture issue have asked the "which" question, others the "how much" question, and still others the "how" question. And because they ask different questions, they come up with different answers.

The Hereditarian Position Hereditarians tend to phrase the nature-nurture question primarily in terms of the "how much" question and to seek answers in family resemblance studies (see Chapter 2) based on intelligence tests (Jensen, 1984). Psychologists have devised tests of intelligence, employing a single number called the **intelligence quotient, or IQ,** to measure intelligence. An IQ, let's say 120, is derived from the ratio of tested mental age to chronological age, usually expressed as a quotient multiplied by 100. Today's intelligence tests provide an IQ score based on the test-taker's performance relative to the average performance of other individuals of the same age.

Many psychologists say that the assessment of intellectual abilities is one of their discipline's most significant contributions to society. But other psychologists say that it is a systematic attempt by elitists to "measure" people so that "desirable" ones can be put in the "proper" slots and others rejected. Research reveals that the median IQ correlation coefficient of separated identical (*monozygotic*) twins in three studies is +.72. The median IQ correlation coefficient of fraternal (*dizygotic*) twins is +.62. In sum, identical twins reared in different homes are much more alike in IQ than fraternal twins raised together (Jensen, 1972). Hereditarians typically conclude that 60 to 80 percent of the variation in IQ scores in the general population is attributable to genetic differences, and the remainder to environmental differences (Herrnstein & Murray, 1994).

The Environmentalist Rebuttal A number of scientists dispute the claim that differences in intelligence are primarily a function of heredity. Some disagree with the formulation of the nature-nurture question in terms of "how much" and insist that the question should be *how* heredity and environment interact to produce intelligence. Leon J. Kamin (1974, p. 1) goes so far as to assert, "There exist no data which should lead a prudent man to accept the hypothesis that IQ test scores are in any degree heritable." Psychologists in agreement with Kamin's view, commonly called *environmentalists,* argue that mental abilities are *learned.* They believe that intellect is increased or decreased according to the degree of enrichment or impoverishment provided by a person's social and cultural environment (Bradley, 1993; Molfese, Modglin, & Molfese, 2003).

Kamin (1974, 1981, 1994) has vigorously challenged the adoption and identical-twin research that the advocates of heredity use to support their conclusions. He

insists that it is improper to speak of individuals as being reared in differing environments simply because they were brought up in different homes. In some cases identical twins were raised by relatives or they lived next door to one another or went to the same school even though they lived in different homes. Similarly, environmentalists charge that studies of adopted children are biased by the fact that adoption agencies attempt to place children in a social environment that is similar—in race-ethnicity and religion—to the one into which they were born.

Contemporary Scientific Consensus Most social and behavioral scientists believe that any extreme view in the nature-nurture controversy is unjustified. Estimates based on twin and adoption studies suggest that hereditary differences account for 40 to 80 percent of the variation found in the intelligence test performance of a population. Bouchard and colleagues (1990) found that 70 percent of the IQ differences among people are attributable to genetic factors, but other experts think that a 70 percent heritability estimate is too high.

Jencks (1972), employing path analysis, which is a statistical technique used to partition the amount of variance within a group, estimated that 45 percent of IQ differences is due to heredity, 35 percent to environment, and 20 percent to gene-environment interaction. Jencks introduced the third element of gene-environment interaction because he felt that dividing IQ into only hereditary and environmental components oversimplifies the matter. Similarly, Loehlin and colleagues (1975) contend that we need to consider these three components:

- *Genetic endowment* when intellectual stimulation is held constant
- *Environmental stimulation* when genetic potential is held constant
- *Covariance of heredity and environment*—how these two components vary relative to each other

If genes and environment reinforce each other, then the added component of variance cannot logically be assigned to either nature or nurture. Rather, it is a result of the association of their separate effects.

Questions

What is intelligence? How have the explanations of intelligence changed over time? Why is intelligence difficult to measure? What are the differences between the hereditarian view of intelligence and the environmental view?

Piaget's Theory of Preoperational Thought

Jean Piaget (1896–1980), the Swiss developmental psychologist who pioneered the study of the development of intelligence in infants and children, called the years between 2 and 7 the **preoperational period** (1952, 1963). The principal achievement of that period is children's developing capacity to represent the external world *internally* through the use of symbols. *Symbols* are things that stand for something else. For example, letters of the alphabet can be symbols; in English, c-a-t represents a four-legged animal. And numbers, such as 3, are symbols for specific quantities of something.

The ability to use symbols frees children from the rigid boundaries of the here and now. They can use symbols to represent not only present events but past and future ones as well. Acquiring language and numeration facilitates children's ability to employ and manipulate symbols.

Difficulties in Solving Conservation Problems   Piaget observed that although children make major strides in cognitive development during the preoperational period, their reasoning and thinking processes have a number of limitations. These limitations can be seen in the difficulties preschool children have when they try to solve conservation problems. The term **conservation** refers to the concept that the quantity or amount of something stays the same regardless of changes in its shape or position.

For example, if a ball of clay is shown to a child and then rolled into a long, thin, snakelike shape, the child will say that the amount of clay has changed simply because the shape has changed. Similarly, if we show a child under age 6 two parallel rows of eight evenly spaced pennies and ask which row has more pennies, the child always correctly answers that both rows have the same amount. But if, in full view of the child, we move the pennies in one of the rows farther apart and again ask which row has more pennies, the child will reply that the longer row has more (see Figure 7.6). The child fails to recognize that the number of pennies does not change simply because we made a change in another dimension, the length of the row. Piaget said that the difficulties preschoolers have in solving conservation problems derive from the characteristics of preoperational thought. These characteristics inhibit logical thought by posing obstacles that are associated with centering, transformations, reversibility, and egocentrism.

Centration   Preoperational children concentrate on one feature of a situation and neglect other aspects, a process called **centration.** A preoperational child cannot understand that when the water that fills a tall thin glass is poured into a short wide glass, the amount of water remains the same. Instead, the child sees that the new glass is half empty and concludes that there is less water than before; the child cannot attend simultaneously to both the amount of water and the shape of the container.

(A)

(B)

FIGURE 7.6 Conservation Experiment with Pennies
Children are first shown two rows of pennies arranged as in A. The experimenter asks if both rows contain the same amount of pennies. Then with the children watching, the experimenter spreads out the pennies in the bottom row, as in B. Children are asked again if both rows contain the same number of pennies. Preoperational children respond that they do not.

To solve the conservation problem correctly, the child must "decenter"—that is, attend simultaneously to both height and width. Likewise, in the case of the pennies, children need to recognize that a change in length is compensated for by a change in the other dimension, density, and that there is no change in quantity. Piaget said that the ability to decenter—to explore more than one aspect of the stimulus—was beyond the capabilities of preoperational children.

States and Transformations   Another characteristic of preoperational thinking is that children pay attention to *states* rather than *transformations*. In observing water being poured from one glass into another, preschool children focus on the original state and the final state. The intervening process (the pouring) is lost to them. They do not pay attention to the gradual shift in the height or width of the water in the glasses as the experimenter pours the liquid.

Preoperational thought fixes on static states. It fails to link successive states into a coherent sequence of events. Here's a more common example: If you offer a preoperational child a cookie and the child complains that it is too small, simply break the cookie into three pieces and place it next to a whole cookie. The odds are that the young child will think there is less in the cookie split into three pieces.

Their inability to follow transformations interferes with preschool children's logical thinking. Only by appreciating the continuous and sequential nature of various operations can we be certain that the quantities remain the same. Because preoperational children fail to see the relationship between events, their comparisons between original and final events are incomplete. Thus, according to Piaget, they cannot solve conservation problems.

Nonreversibility   According to Piaget, the most distinguishing characteristic of preoperational thought is the child's failure to recognize the **reversibility of operations**—that a series of operations can be gone through in reverse order to get back to the starting point. After we pour water from a narrow container into a wider container, we can demonstrate that the amount of water remains the same by pouring it back into the narrow container. But preoperational children do not understand that the operation can be reversed. Once they have carried out an entire operation, they cannot mentally regain the original state. Awareness of reversibility is a requirement of logical thought.

Egocentrism   Still another element that interferes with the preschool child's logical understanding of reality is **egocentrism**—lack of awareness that there are viewpoints other than one's own. According to Piaget, preoperational children are so absorbed in their own impressions that they fail to recognize that their thoughts and feelings might be different from those of other people. Children simply assume that everyone thinks the same thoughts they do and sees the world from the same perspective that they do.

Both Piaget (1963) and sociologist George Herbert Mead (1934) pointed out that children must overcome an egocentric perspective if they are to participate in mature social interaction. For children to play their role properly, they must know something about other roles. Most 3-year-olds can make a doll carry out several role-related activities, revealing that the child has knowledge of a social role—for example, the child can pretend to be a doctor and examine a doll. Four-year-olds can typically act out a role, relating one social role to a reciprocal role. For instance, they can pretend that a patient doll is sick and that a doctor doll examines it, in the course of which both dolls make appropriate responses. During the late preschool years, children become capable of combining roles in more complicated ways—for example, being a doctor and a mother at the same time. Most 6-year-olds can pretend to carry out several roles simultaneously.

Critiques of Piaget's Egocentric Child   More recent research by neo-Piagetians suggests that although egocentricity is characteristic of preoperational thinking, preschool children are nonetheless capable of recognizing other people's viewpoints on their own terms. Even though toddlers can be quite self-centered emotionally, they are not necessarily egocentric in the sense of not understanding other perspectives (Newcombe & Huttenlocher, 1992). Researchers are uncovering many *sociocentric* (people-oriented) responses in young children. Indeed, some researchers have questioned the characterization of children as egocentric.

Prosocial Behavior   Researchers have found evidence of prosocial behavior—behavior that is kind and helpful when there is no expectation of benefit to oneself—even in very young children. When children spontaneously share toys, take turns, or try to comfort a friend or parent who is sad or upset, they are demonstrating prosocial behavior (Bierman & Erath, 2006). For some children, this behavior emerges in the second year of life when their mothers are distressed. Prosocial behavior increases with age and spreads to include other family members and peers (Eisenberg, Fabes, & Spinrad, 2006).

If egocentricity is seen as the inability to psychologically "connect" with someone else, then prosocial behavior points to the child's ability to reach out and relate to another individual. If, however, egocentricity is seen as a "distortive interpretation of other people's experiences, and actions or

Prosocial Behavior   Developmental psychologists are discovering that young children are considerably less egocentric and more prosocial than earlier studies indicated.

persons or objects, in terms of one's own schemas" (Beard, 1969), then even prosocial acts could be labeled "egocentric."

The Montessori Mind   One of the better-known early childhood programs with a set of altruistic priorities different from those of a traditional preschool is the Montessori "Children's Community" founded in 1907 by Dr. Maria Montessori. Her first school was made up of 60 inner-city children. She developed a child-centered philosophy of "education for life" directed toward the development of each child's interests, abilities, and human potential. But her vision also expanded beyond an academic curriculum to promote *prosocial behavior* in young children.

Montessori schools today give children the sense of belonging to a family and help them learn how to live with other human beings. By creating bonds among parents, teachers, and children, Montessori sought to create a community where children could learn to be a part of families and where they could learn to care for younger children, learn from each other and older people, trust one another, and find ways to be properly assertive rather than aggressive. Dr. Montessori envisioned her movement as essentially leading to a reconstruction of society. Montessori schools today are found all over the world, including Europe, Central and South America, Australia, New Zealand, India, Sri Lanka, Korea, and Japan (Rathunde & Csikszentmihalyi, 2005).

In sum, newly developing lines of research reveal that, in our efforts to understand children, we have been hampered by adult-centered concepts and by our preoccupation with the adult-child relationship—in other words, by *adult* egocentrism. Psychologists have moved increasingly away from Piaget's notion of broad, overarching stages to a more complex view of development (Case, 1991). Rather than searching for major overall transformations, they are scrutinizing separate domains such as causality, memory, creativity, problem solving, and social interaction. Each domain has a somewhat unique and flexible schedule affected not only by age but also by the quality of the environment (Demetriou, Efklides, & Platsidou, 1993). Chapter 9 will consider prosocial behavior at greater length.

> **Questions**
>
> In what ways is Piaget's stage of preoperational thought different from the sensorimotor stage during infancy and the toddler years? What are some criticisms of Piaget's cognitive theory by neo-Piagetians?

The Child's Theory of Mind

Research in the **theory of mind** probes children's developing conceptions of major components of mental activity. When a child begins to comprehend that the mind exists,

this paves the way to rudimentary distinctions such as that of being part of the environment while also being separate from it. Furthermore, the child can begin to understand that people can think about objects differently.

For example, a researcher might show a 5-year-old a candy box and ask the youngster what is in it. "Candy," responds the child. But when the youngster opens the box, she is surprised to discover that it contains crayons rather than candy. The researcher then might inquire of the child, "What will the next child who has not opened the box think is in it?" "Candy!" the child will answer, grinning at the trick. When the researcher repeats the same procedure with a 3-year-old, the child typically responds to the first question as expected: "Candy!" But she responds to the second with the answer "Crayons!" The 3-year-old also says "Crayons" when asked to recall what she herself had initially thought would be found in the box.

The 3-year-old, unlike the 5-year-old, fails to understand that people can hold beliefs different from what he or she knows to be true. The 3-year-old believes that because she knows there is no candy in the box, everyone else automatically knows the same thing to be true (Wellman, 1990). It seems that 3-year-olds struggle with, and typically fail to understand, what 4-year-olds and older children do understand: People have internal mental states, such as beliefs, that represent or misrepresent the world, and people's actions stem from their mental representation of the world rather than from direct objective reality. Piaget's sweeping account of children's reasoning was an early attempt to broach the topic of "mind"—the notion of an instrument that can calculate, dream, fantasize, deceive, and evaluate others' thoughts.

More recently, research has been done on children's developing understanding of their mental world (Hughes et al., 2005; Hughes, Fujisawa, Ensor, Lecce, & Marfleet, 2006). Even 3-year-olds can distinguish between the physical and the mental and they possess some understanding of what it means to imagine, think of, and dream of something (Flavell, 1992). For example, if a 3-year-old is told that one child has ice cream and another child is only thinking of ice cream, then the 3-year-old will be able to say which child's ice cream can be seen by others, as well as which child's ice cream can be touched or eaten. This understanding is facilitated where youngsters enjoy a rich "database" derived from interactions with siblings, caregivers, and peers (Hughes et al., 2005; Hughes et al., 2006a).

Implicit Understanding and Knowledge   Piaget's theories have also tended to underestimate many of the cognitive capabilities of preschool children. Toddlers seem to possess a significant implicit understanding or knowledge of certain principles (Reber, 1993; Seger, 1994). Here we will consider two spheres of conceptual knowledge: causality and number concepts.

Causality The principle of **causality** involves our attribution of a cause-and-effect relationship to two paired events that recur in succession. Causality is based on the expectation that when one event occurs, another event—one that ordinarily follows the first event—will follow it again. Piaget concluded that children younger than 7 or 8 fail to grasp cause-and-effect relationships. When he asked younger children why the sun and the moon move, they would respond that heavenly bodies "follow us about because they are curious" or "in order to look at us." These types of explanations for events led Piaget to emphasize the limitations associated with young children's intellectual operations.

But contemporary developmental psychologists who investigate the thinking of young children find that they already understand a good deal about causality. Apparently, the rudiments for the causal processing of information are already evident among 3-month-old infants ("If I cry, Mom will come"). And by the time youngsters are 3 to 4 years old, they seem to possess rather sophisticated abilities for discerning cause-and-effect relationships (Gelman & Kremer, 1991). The versatility with which young children grasp causality has led some psychologists to conclude that humans are biologically prewired to understand that cause-and-effect relationships exist (Pines, 1983).

Number Concepts Piaget also de-emphasized children's counting capabilities, calling counting "merely verbal knowledge" and asserting that "there is no connection between the acquired ability to count and the actual operations of which the child is capable" (Piaget, 1965, p. 61). Yet young children seem to have an implicit understanding of some number concepts. Preschool youngsters can successfully perform tasks that require modified versions of counting procedures and can judge whether a puppet's performance in counting to demonstrate the concepts of *more* and *less* is correct (Gelman & Meck, 1986). Counting is the first formal computational system that children acquire. It enables youngsters to make accurate quantitative assessments of amount, rather than having to rely solely on their perceptual or qualitative judgments. If you ask 2- or 3-year-olds how old they are, they invariably hold up fingers and say the number.

> **Questions**
>
> According to Piaget, how do we know that a young child is developing preoperational thought processes? What are some of the other theories about how young children's thought processes develop?

Language Acquisition

Young children often show a lag between comprehending language (which involves *receptive language*) and producing language (which involves *expressive language*).

Children younger than 1 year old demonstrate time and again that they understand what we say. Say "Where's Mommy?" and the child looks for Mommy. Between the ages of 2 and 3, most children can begin to express their own needs in more than one- or two-word expressions. A 3-year-old might utter the following sentence after knocking on the door, "Is everybody not home?" meaning "Is anybody home?" It is important to remember that while children are acquiring language, they understand and use it in ways that represent how and what they know about the world at that particular point in their development.

At this stage of language development, children move beyond two-word sentences such as "Doggy go" and begin to display a real understanding of the rules that govern language and to master the different sounds within the language, which is known as **phonology.** Past tenses are used (first using "goed" and then "went" as past tense for *go*), as well as plurals ("girls" and "boys") and possessives ("Jim's" and "mine," although at first many children say "mines"), which are all examples of how a word can change form, or what is known as **morphology.**

Around the age of 3, children will begin to properly ask the *wh-* questions (Why? What? Which? When? Who?), which shows an understanding of **syntax,** the ways in which words must be ordered in a sentence. The study of the way words are meaningfully combined is called **semantics,** the rudiments of which youngsters begin to grasp. Young children also enjoy hearing nonsensical words, such as in Lewis Carroll's poem "Jabberwocky." And between the ages of 3 and 5, children learn what types of language they can use in different social environments, or the **pragmatics** of language.

Developmental Phonological Disorders Some language disorders involve difficulty in learning to use easily understood speech by age 4, and these disorders tend to run in families. The child may be experiencing difficulty storing the sound(s), saying the sound(s), or using the rules of language (Bowen, 1998). Various methods are available to evaluate and treat the many varieties of phonological disorders for most children.

Stuttering Most young children go through periods of *disfluency* as they are learning to speak. However, frequent disruption in the fluency of speech is called *stuttering* or *stammering.* Disfluency in the child's speech is typically classified as prolongations ("Mmmmme too"), periods of silence called blocks ("St—op that"), and repetitions ("N-n-n-n-n-o"). Geneticists have found that stuttering may be inherited and that boys are more susceptible to stuttering (Bowen, 2001). The general guideline today is that parents should seek the help of a pediatrician or a speech-language pathologist if they begin to notice consistent stuttering in a young child (Fraser, 2001). A child who stutters is eligible for early intervention services, and a variety of scientific approaches are used to help improve the child's fluency. See the *Implications for Practice* box, "Speech-Language Pathologist."

Language Development in Bilingual Children   By 2007, the National Center for Education Statistics reported that at least 20 percent of American children are speaking a language other than English at home and are classified as learning English as a second language (called English language learners, or ELLs) (Aud, Fox, & KewalRamani, 2010). A majority of ELLs are of Hispanic ethnicity and speak Spanish. Young ELLs must do very intense learning in each school year. Children who are ELLs typically undergo a silent period when they first encounter the English language setting. During this time the child is focusing on listening and understanding the new language. Speech experts suggest that the ideal learning situation for young bilingual children would be learning in their first language most of the time, and in English a small percentage of the time, through first grade. Children who learn in this way understand what they are hearing and are able to build a good cognitive and linguistic foundation for future learning (American Speech-Language-Hearing Association, 2007).

California voters reversed bilingual instruction in 1998 after schools experienced poor results, and now ELL children spend a year in structured English classes before being placed in an English-only class. Other states, such as Texas, use the bilingual approach (Wiese & Garcia, 2006). Cheung and Slavin (2010) from Johns Hopkins have conducted a thorough review of the most effective reading programs for ELLs and report that, judging on the basis of empirical studies, bilingual instruction appears to be the more effective approach.

Language Development in Adopted Chinese Children
More than 44,000 young Chinese children, mainly girls, have been adopted into American families. Tan and Yang (2005) investigated the expressive language development of young Chinese girls adopted into American families. It took about 16 months for the adoptees to catch up with native-speaking children. The researchers speculate that the adoptive families' socioeconomic background and the adoptive mother's educational status were responsible for such remarkable acquisition of expressive language.

Chomsky's Linguistic Theory   Noam Chomsky (1965, 1980) proposes that a linguistic theory ought to be able to adequately explain language structure, while taking into account the messy input children receive and from which they construct meaningful sentences. He says that humans are born possessing a **language acquisition device (LAD)** that takes all of the sounds, words, and sentences an infant hears and produces

More Children Than Ever Before in the United States Are Bilingual Learners   Some speech experts suggest that young bilingual children do best when instruction is in their first language most of the time and in English a small percentage of the time until first grade.

grammar consistent with these data (Lillo-Martin, 1997). Chomsky argues that this must be the case because it would be impossible for an infant to learn language simply by induction—that is, by simply reusing the sentences it had already heard. If that were the case, then a youngster would not be able to utter a novel sentence, but we all know that youngsters come up with some extremely novel sentences.

Late Talkers   Provided that the child's hearing is good and that the child is healthy and in an environment to hear speech, there are some reasons why a young child might not use expressive language (words) until 2, 3, or even 4 years of age: The baby may be a quiet baby. Other reasons for speech delay include premature birth and resulting health problems, being a twin (twins often develop their own private language), and being male (boys often talk later). The baby may live in a bilingual home, or older siblings may speak for the child. A study conducted with several hundred same-sex twin pairs with early language delay at ages 2, 3, and 4 revealed that heritability was a factor for a small percentage of the children, but environmental factors shared by both twins were associated with early language delay. Bishop and colleagues (2003) conclude that there is less concern with low expressive language skills in a 2-year-old unless there is a family history of speech or language impairment. Parents whose child has a speech delay should consult their pediatrician, who may refer the child for audiology testing or speech therapy.

Cross-Cultural Practices in Teaching Children to Speak   Children learn to speak in a variety of ways across cultures. In Papua, New Guinea, Kaluli mothers

IMPLICATIONS FOR PRACTICE

Speech-Language Pathologist Aleshia Brewer, SLP

I am a speech-language pathologist at The Resource Center, which provides services to persons with disabilities in Chautauqua County, New York. My clients are cognitively impaired or have suffered a traumatic brain injury or are children who are behind on speech/language milestones through the early intervention program. I provide language and articulation therapy for people unable to communicate verbally, build communication systems for nonverbal people, and provide swallow evaluations and guidelines for staff to follow to allow a person to eat in the safest manner possible.

I earned an associate's degree in liberal arts from Jamestown Community College in New York, a bachelor's degree in the education of the speech and hearing handicapped from SUNY Fredonia, and a master's degree in speech pathology from SUNY Fredonia. To obtain a provisional teaching license, I had to pass the Liberal Arts and Sciences Test (LAST) and the Elementary and Secondary Assessment of Teaching Skills–Written (ATS–W). To obtain licensure, I passed the *Praxis* examination for speech-language pathology.

To enjoy working as a speech-language therapist, a person should be creative, able to think quickly, and organized but open to change, as clients will sometimes change the direction

of therapy. The populations I work with need hundreds of repetitions to learn something new. *Patience* is an extremely important characteristic. I had supervised clinical experience working at a school, a nursing home, a speech-language clinic, and then at my current position before being hired.

My advice to students considering being an SLP is to keep an open mind about what type of population they want to work with until they have completed all clinical experience. I did not work with the developmentally disabled until my last semester in graduate school, and now I cannot imagine doing anything else. Working with this population is the most rewarding, fun, and fulfilling of all the populations that I have worked with. I really enjoy that each day I get to do new things and really make a difference in people's lives. Through the use of alternative and augmentative communication, I have been part of setting up communication systems with voice output for people in their fifties and sixties who have never been verbal because of physical disabilities. It is extremely fulfilling to help people express their opinions and make choices for the first time and watch their world expand with their new experiences.

carry their infants so that they face outward and can be part of the social flow. The mothers believe their children cannot understand conversation or converse, so they speak for them using language that would be appropriate for an older child. Some Mayan infants in Mexico rely heavily on nonverbal communication and learn to speak by listening to the conversations around them. In the Solomon Islands, parents use an emotionally powerful process called "shaping the mind" to teach their children traditional knowledge as they learn to speak (Shweder et al., 2006). All of these children learn to speak fluently, of course, in ways that meet the expectations and needs of their cultures.

Learning to use speech is empowering for children because it enables them to communicate their needs, relate to others, learn about and take command of their environment, and become normal social beings rather than isolates (Sachs, 1987). Thus, an evaluation by an

audiologist or speech pathologist may be warranted for children with early language delay. Some children with speech and/or language disabilities make some progress without intervention, but early intervention can dramatically increase the rate of progress (Camarata, 1996). Children who have speech/language impairment may co-present with motor difficulties, which must also be addressed (Gaines & Missiuna, 2006).

Vygotsky's Perspective   Learning language and furthering cognitive development are not tasks that children can accomplish in the privacy of their cribs—they need to be in a social setting. Lev Vygotsky (1896–1934) first conceived of how language and thought are intertwined with culture and society and therefore proposed that cognitive growth occurs in a sociocultural context dependent on a child's social interactions (Vygotsky, 1962). This led to the well-known concept of the **zone of proximal development (ZPD):** Tasks that are a little too hard for children to accomplish alone can be mastered by children when a more skilled partner helps them (Bodrova & Leong, 2007). The zone of proximal development will be different for each child at any given time. Think back to when you began reading. Your parents, grandparents, or teacher provided encouragement, suggestions, corrections, and praise as you worked through the process of learning to read. Little by little you began to read by yourself, but it was only through the interaction between you and an older, more accomplished person that you were able to master this new skill.

Notice that there is a striking difference here between Vygotsky and Piaget: Piaget thought that children learn as independent explorers, whereas Vygotsky asserted that children learn through social interactions. Thus, Vygotsky put forth a sociocultural view that stresses the social aspects of cognitive development that Piaget did not emphasize. Vygotsky believes that children's minds develop when they are engaging in activities with more skilled people on tasks that are within the child's ZPD. Furthermore, Vygotsky maintains that when a child and adult are engaged in activities, the child incorporates the language of the adult that pertains to the activity and then reuses that language to transform her or his own thinking.

Implications of Vygotsky for Early Education

Vygotsky's theories have helped educators understand the developmental tasks that preschoolers are able to accomplish when they are in peer groups, such as in a day-care center or an Early Head Start classroom. Four- and 5-year-olds are further developing the skill of self-regulation. They are beginning to understand generalized rules that provide the basis for social interaction and thus call for self-control. When Kadin steals Melissa's purple crayon in pre-kindergarten and is told not to steal her crayon, he probably understands that this means he shouldn't steal the crayons of his other classmates, either. The next time he wants a purple crayon, he remembers what happened and asks his neighbor if he can borrow the purple crayon. He is building his knowledge and regulating his behavior to meet social expectations.

Similarly, in play activities with other children, preschoolers are learning skills they will need very soon. Anisa may not be able to sit still during storytime, even with guided support from her teacher. But when she is playing school with her friends, she is completely absorbed and can concentrate on being a "student" for longer periods of time (Bodrova & Leong, 2007). According to Vygotsky, "In play the child is always behaving beyond his age, above his usual everyday behavior; in play he is, as it were, a head above himself. . . . Play is a source of development and creates the zone of proximal development" (quoted in Bodrova & Leong, 2007, p. 132).

Vygotsky's Zone of Proximal Development (ZPD) Young children often learn from others. Tasks that are a little too hard for a child to accomplish alone can be mastered with help from a more skilled partner.

Language and Emotion

Young children's vocabularies generally are limited, consisting mainly of words that refer to things and action words, with a smaller percentage of words that express *affective* (emotional) states (James, 1990). Research has shown that when children are operating from an emotional state, such as fear, hurt, pain, or stress, they are not able to concentrate on learning tasks. Their energy is concentrated in the processing going on in the limbic (emotional) system of their brains. After reading the next few sentences, stop and try this yourself. Recall a recent hurtful experience. Try to remember the details, picture the faces of the people involved, and feel the emotions you felt when this event occurred. Close your eyes now, and give yourself several minutes.

Now answer this question: *What are the main principles of Chomsky's linguistic theory?* You read about this just a short while ago, but do you now feel a little confused or somewhat overwhelmed, after reliving that hurtful experience? Teachers who have done the exercise you just finished have often commented, "I just can't think" (Rodriguez, 1998).

Some of the healthy ways in which young children can communicate their feelings are through drawing and physical movement; such activities release the energy built up by the limbic system. This is one of the reasons why child-care centers and preschools usually make available a variety of papers, paints, crayons, and colored pencils; small slides and climbing toys; and/or music time and dance time. All of these resources allow children to "express" themselves. Multisensory experiences also allow children to learn to process information from a variety of sources, which helps them develop important skills for advanced learning.

Talking and Communicating Garvey and Hogan (1973) found that during the greater part of the time that children 3 to 5 years of age spend in nursery school, they interact with others, largely by talking. Although some of their speech is **private speech** (directed toward themselves or nobody in particular), most of their speech is mutually responsive and adapted to the speech or nonverbal behavior of a partner (Spilton & Lee, 1977). Rheingold, Hay, and West (1976) have shown that children in their second year of life share with others what they see and find interesting. Preschool, pre-K, and kindergarten teachers know how to foster this type of social behavior by periodically scheduling a "show-and-tell time" when children bring special objects from home to talk about. Rheingold and her colleagues (1976, p. 1157) concluded:

> In showing an object to another person, the children demonstrate not only that they know that other people can see what they see but also that others will look at what they point to or hold up. We can surmise that they also know that what they see may be remarkable in some way and therefore worthy of another's attention. That children so young share contradicts the egocentricity so often ascribed to them and reveals them instead as already able contributors to social life.

Disabilities in Cognitive Development Some children experience moderate to severe difficulties and/or delays in cognitive development and language skills during early childhood. Children with central nervous system or genetic disorders (i.e., intellectual disability, cerebral palsy, autism), sensory impairments (such as blindness or deafness), motor-skill delays (such as muscular dystrophy, paralysis, missing limbs), social damage (such as abuse, neglect, institutionalization, homelessness, isolation), or serious illness and injuries will progress at a pace slower than is normally expected for their age.

Those who receive early intervention services are likely to make more progress than at-risk children not enrolled in such programs. Additionally, as we mentioned in Chapter 6, children who have experienced social neglect because of moving from foster home to foster home or from community to community, or because they are deliberately isolated from society, will also be cognitively delayed and will need extensive stimulation and interaction to develop their potential. Table 7.3 lists some early warning signs of developmental delays.

TABLE 7.3 Early Signs of Developmental Delay in Preschool Children

Language

Pronunciation problems

Slow vocabulary growth

Lack of interest in storytelling

Memory

Trouble recognizing letters or numbers

Difficulty remembering things in sequences (e.g., days of the week)

Attention

Difficulty sitting still or sticking to a task

Motor skills

Problems with self-care skills (fastening buttons, combing hair)

Clumsiness

Reluctance to draw

Other functions

Trouble learning left from right

Difficulty categorizing things

Difficulty "reading" body language and facial expressions

Source: Lisa Feder-Feitel, "Does She Have a Learning Problem?" *Child,* February 1997. Copyright © 1997 by Lisa Feder-Feitel. Originally published by Gruner & Jahr USA Publishing in the February 1997 issue of *Child* Magazine. Used with permission.

Questions

How do we know that children from ages 2 to 6 are acquiring language skills in the normal sequence of language development? What language disorders should caregivers be concerned about, and what services are available to help children diagnosed with specific language impairments? Explain Chomsky's and Vygotsky's theories of language development.

INFORMATION PROCESSING AND MEMORY

Memory is a critical cognitive ability. In its broadest sense, the term **memory** refers to the retention of what has been experienced. Without memory we would react to every event as though we had never before experienced it. What's more, we would be incapable of thinking and reasoning—of any sort of intelligent behavior—if we could not use remembered facts. Hence, memory is critical to information processing.

Information Processing

Memory includes recall, recognition, and the facilitation of relearning. In **recall** we remember something that we learned earlier, such as the definition of a scientific concept or the lines of a play, without memory aids. In **recognition** we perceive something that we have previously encountered, with the assistance of cues. In the *facilitation of relearning,* we find that we can learn material that is already familiar to us more readily than totally unfamiliar material.

On the whole, children's recognition memory is superior to their recall memory. In recognition, the information is already available. One of the first things young children can recognize is the McDonald's sign or a jingle in a television ad. Recall, in contrast, requires children to retrieve information from their own memory. Four-year-olds usually can recall only a small proportion of items from a list of words (Flavell, Freidrichs, & Hoyt, 1970). But children in that age group do better if they are asked to retrieve memory about something they have already done. For example, when 3- and 4-year-olds were asked to recall "What happened when you went to McDonald's?" the children remembered on average 11 separate acts that took place when they went to the fast food restaurant (Bauer, 2007).

Parents can help children develop memory by talking with them about past events. Such discussions are important because the child is often a central figure in these memories, or the events involve people, places, or things that are familiar to the child. This kind of talk also helps the child understand what types of things are worth remembering (Gauvain & Perez, 2007).

We store different types of information in memory for different periods of time. Some psychologists distinguish sensory information storage, short-term memory, and long-term memory (see Figure 7.7). In **sensory information storage,** information from the senses is preserved in the sensory register just long enough to permit the stimuli to be scanned for processing (generally less than 2 seconds). This provides a relatively complete, literal copy of the physical stimulation. For instance, if you tap your finger against your cheek, you note an immediate sensation that quickly fades away.

Early Memory

During infancy and childhood, we learn a great deal about the world, yet by adulthood our memories of early experiences have faded (Rovee-Collier, 1987). This phenomenon is called *childhood amnesia.* As adults,

generally we remember only fleeting scenes and isolated moments prior to the time we reached 7 or 8 years of age. Although some individuals have no recollections prior to 8 or 9 years of age, many of us can recall something that took place between ages 3 and 4. Commonly, first memories involve visual imagery, and most of the imagery is in color. In many cases we visualize ourselves in these memories from afar, as we would look at an actor on a stage (Nelson, 1982).

Just why early memories should wane remains an enigma (Newcombe & Fox, 1994). Freud theorized that we repress or alter childhood memories because of their disturbing sexual and aggressive content. Piagetians and cognitive psychologists claim that adults have trouble recalling early childhood events because they no longer think as children do—that is, adults typically employ mental habits as aids to memory that young children cannot employ.

Still others say that the brain and nervous system are not entirely formed in the young and do not allow for the development of adequate memory stores and effective retrieval strategies. Others contend that much learning during the first two years of life occurs in emotion-centered areas of the brain and that this learning is subject to limited recall in later years. Most types of earliest memories that we recall are associated with the emotion of fear. What early experiences do you remember? Do you feel the emotions associated with these memories?

Mark Howe and Mary Courage (1993) argue that the problem derives not from memory per se but from the absence of a personal frame of reference for making one's memories uniquely autobiographical (in other words, there is no developed "self" present as a cognitive entity). For whatever reasons, our childhood memories often remain relatively elusive.

Short-Term Memory In **short-term memory,** information is retained for a very brief period, usually not more than 30 seconds. For example, you might look up an e-mail address and remember it just long enough to type it in the address box of an online form, whereupon you promptly forget it. Another common short-term memory experience is your introduction to a stranger. How easily do you recall the person's name 10 minutes later? Typically, information is fleeting unless there is some reason or motivation to remember it longer. For example, nursing students are motivated to do well in a course on human development because they know they must eventually pass a state certification exam for registered nurses that includes questions on human development.

Long-Term Memory Information is retained in **long-term memory** over an extended period of time. A memory might be retained because it arose from a very intense single experience or because it is repeatedly rehearsed. Through yearly repetition and constant

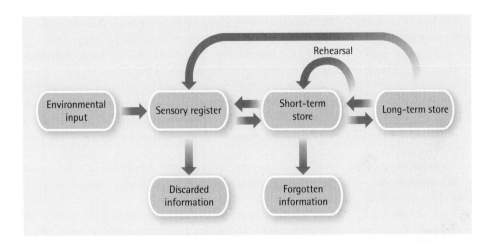

FIGURE 7.7 Simplified Flow Chart of the Three-Store Model of Memory Information flow is represented by three memory stores: the sensory register, the short-term store, and the long-term store. Inputs from the environment enter the sensory register, where they are selectively passed on to short-term storage. Information in the short-term store may be forgotten or copied by the long-term store. Individuals can rehearse information in order to keep it in active awareness in short-term storage. Complicated feedback operations take place among the three storage components.

media reminders, you come to remember that Memorial Day is in late May and that Labor Day is in early September. Researchers have studied memory from many perspectives (Tulving & Craik, 2000). Schacter and Tulving (1994) postulate that we use five major systems of human memory to operate in daily life:

- *procedural memory*—learning various kinds of motor, behavioral, and cognitive skills
- *working memory*—elaborating on short-term memory, allowing one to retain information over short periods of time
- *perceptual representation*—identifying words and objects
- *semantic memory*—acquiring and retaining factual information about the world
- *episodic memory*—remembering events seen or experienced throughout life

Metacognition and Metamemory

As children mature cognitively, they become active agents in their remembering process. The development of memory occurs in two ways: through changes in the biological structuring of the brain (its "hardware") and through changes in types of information processing (the "software" of acquisition and retrieving). Researchers have observed striking changes as a function of age, both in children's performance on memory tasks and in their use of memory strategies. As they grow older, children acquire complex skills that enable them to control just what they will learn and retain. They come to "know how to know" so that they can engage in *deliberate* remembering (Moore, Bryant, & Furrow, 1989).

Individuals' awareness and understanding of their own mental processes is termed **metacognition.** Young children attempt to learn in ways that suit themselves. Young children sometimes say, "I can't do that" or "Let me do that." These are signs of awareness of their own mental abilities. Overall, memory ability catapults upward from birth through age 5 and then advances less rapidly through middle childhood and adolescence (Chance & Fischman, 1987).

Humans require more than the factual and strategic information that constitutes a knowledge base. They must also have access to this knowledge base and apply strategies appropriate to the demands of a task (*How am I going to remember to spell this word? to walk home from kindergarten? to throw this ball to home base?*). This flexibility in calibrating solutions to specific problems is the hallmark of intelligence. Flexibility reaches its zenith in the conscious control that adults bring to bear in their mental functioning. This conscious control of strategies and awareness of these strategies continue to expand throughout adolescence and adulthood in both cognitive and socio-moral domains (Schrader, 1988). Children's awareness and understanding of their memory processes is called **metamemory.** A common example of metamemory is the intentional approach children use to memorize their address and phone number. Because many young children are away from home during the day, they must learn this vital information as early as possible. Does the child repeat this over and over out loud, or does the child ask to look at the phone number and address on a sheet of paper? Research reveals that even 3-year-olds engage in *intentional* memory behavior. They appear to understand that when they are told to remember something, they are expected to store and later retrieve it. Even 2-year-olds can hide, misplace, search for, and find objects on their own (Flavell, Green, & Flavell, 2000; Wellman, 1990).

By the time children enter kindergarten, they have developed considerable knowledge of the memory process. They are aware that forgetting occurs (that items get lost in memory), that spending more time in study helps them retain information, that it is more difficult to remember many items than a few, that distraction and interference make tasks harder, and that they can use records, cues, and other people to help them recall things (Fabricius & Wellman, 1983). They also understand such words as *remember, forget,* and *learn* (Lyon & Flavell, 1994).

Memory Strategies

Children (and adults) might use a variety of strategies to help themselves remember and recall information they are learning or want to remember. If you had to remember the names of five people in the study group you were just introduced to this morning, how would you approach this task? Would you make a list and verbally repeat the list? Would you put names on flashcards and shuffle through the flashcards? Would you make a word out of the first letter of each of their names, such as taking Harriet, Angela, Paul, Peter, and Yvonne and making the word HAPPY? Then you could think, "We are a *happy* group" to remember their names. Or would you use some other approach?

Rehearsal as a Memory Strategy   One strategy that facilitates memory is **rehearsal,** a process in which we repeat information to ourselves. Many individuals adept at remembering people's names cultivate the talent by mentally rehearsing a new name several times to themselves when they are introduced to a person. Researchers have demonstrated that children as young as 3 are capable of various rehearsal strategies. For instance, if 3-year-olds are instructed to remember where an object is hidden, they often prepare for future memory retrieval by extended looking at, touching, or pointing to the hiding place (Flavell, Green, & Flavell, 2000; Wellman, Ritter, & Flavell, 1975). Hide-and-seek activities also help young children develop various memory strategies.

As children grow, their rehearsal mechanisms become more active and effective (Halford et al., 1994). Some researchers believe that the process is facilitated through language, as children become increasingly skillful at verbally labeling stimuli. According to these investigators, the organizing and rehearsing process inherent in naming is a powerful aid to memory (Rosinski, Pellegrino, & Siegel, 1977). As children begin to process information in more sophisticated ways and learn how and when to remember, they become capable of making more decisions for themselves. Parents and teachers can cultivate children's decision-making skills.

Categorization as a Memory Strategy   Another strategy that facilitates remembering is to sort information into meaningful categories. Rossi and Wittrock (1971) found that a developmental progression occurs in the categories children use to organize words for recall.

In this experiment children ranging from 2 to 5 years old were read a list of 12 words (*sun, hand, men, fun, leg, work, hat, apple, dogs, fat, peach, bark*). Each child was asked to recall as many words as possible.

The responses were scored in pairs in terms of the order in which a child recalled them: rhyming (*sun-fun, hat-fat*), syntactical (*men-work, dogs-bark*), clustering (*apple-peach, hand-leg*), or serial ordering (recalling two words serially from the list). Rossi and Wittrock found that rhyming responses peak at 2 years of age, followed by syntactical responses at 3, clustering responses at 4, and serial-ordering responses at 5.

In many respects the progression is consistent with Piaget's theory, which depicts development as proceeding from *concrete* (seeing and touching something) to *abstract* functioning. Other research confirms that changes occur in children's spontaneous use of categories during the developmental span from age 2 to adolescence (Farrar, Raney, & Boyer, 1992). Recall increases with age (Farrar & Goodman, 1992). In comparison with older children, children aged 4 to 6 show less grouping of items into categories in recall tasks, fewer subordinate categories in tasks that ask them to group similar items together, and lower rates of consistency in assigning items to selected categories (Best, 1993). Adolescents adopt more sophisticated strategies, grouping items into logical categories, such as people, places, and things or animals, plants, and minerals (Chance & Fischman, 1987).

Questions

What do cognitive scientists tell us about early memory, short-term memory, long-term memory, and children's understanding of their own thought and memory processes? What types of strategies can young children employ to remember, recognize, and recall information or events, and what strategies do *you* use to remember information?

MORAL DEVELOPMENT

Social feelings first appear during the preoperational stage. For the first time, feelings can be represented, recalled, and named. The ability to recall feelings makes moral feelings possible. When a child can remember what someone did in the past and the emotional response linked to the action, the beginnings of moral decision making are in place.

Piaget's Theory

According to Piaget, during the sensorimotor stage, children cannot reconstruct past events and experiences because they lack representation skills. Once the child has the capacity to reconstruct both the cognitive and the affective past, he or she can begin to exhibit consistent emotional behavior.

Evolution of Moral Reasoning

When Piaget first studied moral development, he looked at the evolution of moral reasoning in children. He believed that moral feelings in young people pointed to what it was necessary to do, not just to what was preferable. He also proposed that moral norms have three characteristics:

- They are generalizable to all situations.
- They last beyond the situations and conditions that engender them.
- They are linked to feelings of autonomy.

But, according to Piaget (1932/1999),

From two to seven years, none of these conditions is met. To begin with, norms are not generalized but are valid only under particular conditions. For example, the child considers it wrong to lie to his parents and other adults but not to his comrades. Second, instructions remain linked to certain represented situations analogous to perceptual configurations. An instruction, for example, will remain linked to the person who gave it, and finally, there is no autonomy. . . . Good and bad are defined as that which conforms or fails to conform to the instructions one has received.

Reciprocity of Attitudes and Values

Piaget (1932/1999) asserts that reciprocity of attitudes and values is the foundation for social interchange in children. **Reciprocity** leads a child to value another person in a way that allows him or her to remember the values that the interactions bring forth. The following scenario is an example of how this plays out in children:

Two young children meet at the park and play. One of the children, Neiko, gives the other child, Kiri, some candy because she obviously wants some. They end up sharing their toys and having a nice time. By labeling Neiko's behavior as "good," Kiri can recall that scene the next time they encounter each other at the park. She might give Neiko something of hers or at least be nice to her owing to the recollection of warm feelings that seeing Neiko conjures up for Kiri.

Playing by the Rules

Piaget based his views on children's moral development by observing local boys playing marbles, which he considered to be a social game with a set of rules. By interviewing these boys, Piaget found two developmental stages in young children's knowledge of rules: the *motor stage* and the *egocentric stage*. In the motor stage, children are not aware of any rules. For example, a young child in this stage might build a nest out of the marbles and pretend to be a mother bird. He

or she does not understand the game of marbles. Between the ages of 2 and 5, the egocentric stage, children become aware of the existence of rules and begin to want to play the game with other children. But the child's egocentrism prevents the child from playing the game socially. The child continues to play alone without trying to compete. For example, a child will throw a marble at the pile and yell, "I won!" At this stage children believe that everyone can win. They see rules as fixed and as coming from a higher authority.

Intentionality Versus Accident

Piaget (1932/1999) also interviewed children to find out how they viewed *intentionality* versus *accident.* The children found it very difficult to separate the act from the reason for the act. For example, children were told the following two stories:

Once there was a little girl named Heidi who was playing in her room when her mother called her to come to dinner. Since they were having guests, Heidi decided to help her mother and got a tray and then put 15 cups on the tray so she could carry them into the dining room. As she was walking with the tray, she tripped and fell and broke all of the cups.

Once there was a little girl named Gretchen who was playing in the kitchen. She wanted some jam and her mother was not there. She climbed up on a chair and tried to reach the jam but it was too high. She tried for 10 minutes and became angry. Then she saw a cup on the table so she picked it up and threw it. The cup broke.

Children younger than 7 usually see the first girl, Heidi, as having committed the worse act because she broke more cups than Gretchen. The children judge the act on the basis of the quantitative results of the action, with no appreciation of the intention behind the action. For preoperational children, morality is still based mainly on perception. Although young children have the rudiments of moral feelings, they are limited in their ability to comprehend justice as long as they do not understand the intentionality of an action.

Kohlberg's Theory

Lawrence Kohlberg's theory of moral development was influenced by John Dewey's philosophy of development and by Jean Piaget's idea that people develop moral reasoning in progressive stages through their social experiences (Gibbs, 2003). Kohlberg was a developmental psychologist who researched the development of moral reasoning by studying differences in children's reasoning about moral dilemmas. According to Kohlberg, preschool children tend to be superficial in their moral judgment because they have difficulty, on a cognitive level, in keeping several pieces of information simultaneously in mind. They begin to be obedient to authority from threat or from punishment, which he categorized as Level 1, the *preconventional stage.*

Kohlberg said that children at this first level of moral reasoning are egocentric and unable to consider the perspectives of others. He rejected a focus on values and virtues (such as compassion), for he believed such concepts to be too complex for children at this stage. In his view, the child will advance in moral reasoning as he or she goes through progressive stages of moral development within social experiences (Nucci, 1998). Although Kohlberg's stage theory of moral development has been criticized for not addressing differences between male and female conceptions of morality, his theory on moral development opened a new path of research in pyschology. Later research refutes some of Kohlberg's findings by demonstrating that young children are able to make moral judgments based on their values about justice and empathy rather than on extrinsic factors such as obedience and fear of punishment (Turiel, 2006a, 2006b).

Questions

How are memories of emotion linked to moral reasoning, and what evidence do we have that children are maturing in moral development in early childhood? According to researchers, what healthy attitudes and values should be taught to young children? Although Piaget and Kohlberg both propose that moral reasoning occurs in progressive stages, how do their views differ?

SEGUE

The physical, sensory, and cognitive maturation and skills acquired during the early childhood years have profound implications for children's ability to function fully as members of society (Stipek, Recchia, & McClintic, 1992). We do not develop in isolation. To enter into sustained social interaction with others, we must impute meaning to the people around us. All of us, children and adults alike, confront the social world in terms of categories of people—we classify them as parents, family, cousins, adults, doctors, teachers, teenagers, business people, and so on. Society does not consist merely of isolated individuals. It is composed of individuals who are classed as similar because they play similar roles.

And just as we impute meaning to others, we must also attribute meaning to ourselves. We have to develop a sense of ourselves as distinct, bounded, identifiable units. In Chapter 8, we will examine the young child's growing self-awareness in the domains of emotions and gender. Within the social context of family and friends, child-care settings, and kindergarten, young children acquire a set of guidelines about expressing their emotional needs.

SUMMARY

Physical Development and Health Concerns

1. The early childhood years, ages 2 to 6, encompass physical development, brain growth, the refinement of gross and fine motor skills, and sensory system maturation.

2. Preschool children are more coordinated now and spend most of their time exploring their environments. Recreational and occupational therapists provide services that improve strength, coordination, sensory capacities, and range of motion for those children with delays and disabilities.

3. Fine motor skills develop more slowly. By age 5, most children have mastered the fine motor skills needed to dress themselves and control writing instruments.

4. Sensory development for preschoolers, especially visual, tactile, and kinesthetic senses, occurs rapidly. Caregivers need to watch for sensory impairments and to seek professional help, if indicated, for diagnoses and early intervention services.

5. The brain and nervous system continue to develop rapidly with rich connectivity of neurons and myelination of axons and the corpus callosum. Sensory stimulation is a key factor in promoting neural growth.

6. Some young children experience cognitive delays because of congenital birth defects, sensory difficulties, autism, mental retardation, attention-deficit hyperactivity disorder (ADHD), seizures, premature birth, and other health concerns. Children can improve functioning with the assistance of intervention services.

7. Psychotropic medications are increasingly prescribed for young children diagnosed with emotional, behavioral, or mood disorders.

8. Caregivers try to prevent young children's exposure to neurotoxins, which can impair cognitive development and physical functioning or cause serious health effects or death.

9. Children should consume a variety of foods and beverages to get proper nourishment for brain and body growth. There is variability in their eating behaviors, preferences, and frequency.

10. Some children are severely allergic to specific foods and substances that can be life-threatening if consumed or inhaled. Such children should have a rescue medication available.

11. Poverty has a distinct impact on the health of young children. Inadequate nutrition in early childhood affects cognitive development into adulthood.

12. Accidental injury is the leading cause of death of young children, and caregivers must supervise children and provide a safe environment for playing, eating, and sleeping.

13. Young children should be taught self-care behaviors that promote cleanliness, healthfulness, self-regulatory skills, and social acceptance.

14. Ten to 12 hours of sleep and a consistent bedtime routine are recommended for young children. Sleep-deprived children can be difficult, lethargic, inattentive, or accident-prone. From age 3 to age 8, children are prone to sleep disturbances.

15. Children should get immunizations during routine check-ups with health-care practitioners.

16. At least 6 million American children have asthma, the most common pediatric disease and the main reason for child hospital admissions. Caregivers should eliminate the child's exposure to known allergens.

17. Children need proper nutrition, exercise, plenty of sleep, and health care, including childhood immunizations, to support the developing body systems and cognitive functioning. Children in public schools get annual checkups by health-care professionals.

18. Racial-ethnic minority and immigrant children may come from families that have alternative views on health, illness, and wellness. However, all children must have vaccinations to enter a nursery school, child-care center, preschool, and kindergarten.

19. The leading causes of death among young children are unintentional injuries. Children from some minority groups experience higher risk of death.

Cognitive Development

20. If preschool children receive adequate nutrition and sensory stimulation, they experience a rapid expansion of cognitive abilities, which gradually evolve into intelligence.

21. Psychologists differ in the relative importance that they attribute to the roles of heredity and environment in fashioning an individual's intelligence, and different tests have been devised to measure a child's intelligence quotient (IQ).

22. Howard Gardner's theory of multiple intelligences suggests that children have different strengths and weaknesses in their intelligence systems and that educators should instruct in such a way as to accommodate different kinds of intelligence.

23. Jean Piaget pioneered the study of children's cognitive development. He called the years between 2 and 7 the preoperational period, when there is an increase in the child's capacity to represent the external world internally through the use of symbols, such as words and numbers.

24. Piaget held that preoperational children operate from egocentrism, are absorbed in their own feelings and thoughts, and are often not able to recognize others' thoughts and feelings. Neo-Piagetians say that young children have more reasoning capability and show evidence of prosocial behavior.

25. Research in the theory of mind has focused on children's understanding of their own thought processes. From ages 2 to 6 children gain a clearer understanding of their world, people's actions, their own thought processes, number concepts, and causality of events.

26. Children acquire language in a sequence. Children from ages 2 to 6 begin to internalize the rules of language: phonology, morphology, syntax, semantics, and pragmatics.

27. Learning to use speech enables children to communicate their needs and relate to others socially. Yet some young children experience language disorders. Typically children can improve linguistic skills with early speech therapy.

28. Young children who are English language learners undergo a silent period when they first encounter spoken English while they focus intensely on learning English. There is controversy about whether bilingual education or all-English instruction is better.

29. Lev Vygotsky said learning takes place in a sociocultural context. The zone of proximal development means that with help from a more skilled partner, children master tasks that are too hard to accomplish alone.

30. A small percentage of children experience difficulties in cognitive reasoning and language. Caregivers must watch for signs of atypical development so a child can be diagnosed and receive appropriate services.

Information Processing and Memory

31. Memory is an integral component of cognition that allows for thinking or reasoning. Information-processing skills include recall, recognition, and the facilitation of relearning. Young children's recognition memory is superior to their recall memory.

Moral Development

32. Piaget argued that children's moral reasoning evolves and that it begins with reciprocity of attitudes and values. The ability to recall thoughts and feelings from memory makes moral thought possible. As young children mature, they come to know more about attitudes, values, and the "rules" of accepted behavior.

33. Kohlberg said young children are obedient to authority from fear of threat or punishment and called this first stage of moral development the preconventional stage. Kohlberg also thought that young children are egocentric (centered on self) and unable to see the perspective of others.

KEY TERMS

anaphylaxis *(204)*

Asperger's syndrome *(200)*

asthma *(208)*

causality *(217)*

centration *(214)*

conservation *(214)*

egocentrism *(215)*

food security *(205)*

intelligence *(211)*

intelligence quotient (IQ) *(213)*

language acquisition device (LAD) *(218)*

long-term memory *(222)*

memory *(221)*

metacognition *(223)*

metamemory *(223)*

methylphenidate *(200)*

morphology *(217)*

multiple intelligences (MIs) *(211)*

occupational therapist *(197)*

otitis media *(198)*

phonology *(217)*

pragmatics *(217)*

preoperational period *(214)*

private speech *(221)*

recall *(222)*

reciprocity *(225)*

recognition *(222)*

recreational therapist *(197)*

rehearsal *(224)*

reversibility of operations *(215)*

semantics *(217)*

sensory information storage *(222)*

short-term memory *(222)*

spatial ability *(212)*

syntax *(217)*

theory of mind *(216)*

two-factor theory of intelligence *(211)*

zone of proximal development (ZPD) *(219)*

FOLLOWING UP ON THE INTERNET

Web sites for this chapter focus on young children's physical, cognitive, language, and moral development. Please access the text Web site at www.mhhe.com/crandell10 for up-to-date hot-linked Internet addresses for the following organizations and resources:

American Academy of Pediatrics
http://www.aap.org/

National Institute for Early Education Research
http://nieer.org/

National Association for the Education of Young Children
http://www.naeyc.org/

Journal of Early Intervention
http://jei.sagepub.com/

Early Childhood Research and Practice
http://ecrp.uiuc.edu/

Contemporary Issues in Early Childhood
http://www.wwwords.co.uk/ciec/content/maincontents.asp

The Food Allergy and Anaphylaxis Network
http://www.foodallergy.org/

U.S. Consumer Product Safety Commission—Recalled Toys
http://www.cpsc.gov/cpscpub/prerel/category/toy.html

Early Childhood
Emotional and Social Development

1. An American couple adopts a 1-year-old female child from an orphanage in China. Would this young child develop a sense of emotional self-development and emotional regulation from the Chinese or the American culture?

2. How would you explain the parenting style your parents used in raising you? Were they highly restrictive, permissive, or more democratic? In what ways has their approach affected your self-esteem? If you are a parent, do you parent in the same way or differently?

3. When there is a divorce in a family, or the death of a parent or sibling, or a major move to a new home, people often say of a young child, "Oh, she's young, she'll adjust" or "He's young, he's flexible." Do you think this is an accurate appraisal of young children's emotional capabilities?

4. You are the parent of a 3-year-old whose grandmother baby-sat him for the past year while you worked full-time. Now the U.S. Congress has passed legislation mandating compulsory all-day pre-kindergarten for *all* 4-year-olds in the United States beginning the next school year. What are your concerns for the transition of your young child?

Cognitive factors play an important part in setting the tone for the emotional life of youngsters, and social factors have an impact on maximizing or minimizing intellectual ability. Through social interactions, children acquire guidelines that mentally or cognitively mediate their inner experience and their outer expression of emotion (Demo & Cox, 2000). Many researchers are now using the Emotions as Social Information (EASI) model to explore how emotions affect others' behavior (Van Kleef, 2009). Until the 1980s most children in the United States spent their early years at home with family members until they entered school. Many of the classic research studies on the child's emotional regulation and sense of gender identity and on the effectiveness of parenting styles were conducted mainly with intact middle-class families in the 1950s to 1970s. Today, young children's development occurs within a variety of household and social environments.

EMOTIONAL DEVELOPMENT AND ADJUSTMENT

Since the 1980s the United States has seen fewer two-parent families, many more single parents and nonresident fathers, and a major exodus of mothers leaving the home to enter the ranks of the employed. More recently, employment data reveal that more mothers of young children are choosing to remain home rather than pursuing employment during those early years (Macunovich, 2010). However, a record number of young children are being cared for in child-care, preschool, pre-kindergarten, and full-day kindergarten programs and in the homes of nonrelatives. Research summarizing the results of three studies found strong evidence of long-term positive outcomes when children attend quality preschool programs to prepare for kindergarten (Bracey & Stellar, 2001). The young child's ability to understand emotions is a crucial component of **social competence**—the ability to understand causes of emotions, predict the emotional reactions of others, know when emotional display is appropriate, and successfully participate in social groups (Fabes, Gaertner, & Popp, 2006). A substantial body of research indicates that unless children achieve a minimal social competence by age 6, there is a high probability that they will develop emotional and/or behavioral disorders by adulthood (McClelland & Katz, 2001).

Recent cross-cultural studies of immigrant Hispanic, Asian, and Middle Eastern families are shedding light on how and when young children demonstrate sociocultural standards of emotional self-regulation and conformity to gender roles. It is within this broader context of social influences that we examine the more recent research findings on the emotional and social development of young children from age 2 to age 6.

Thinking Tasks Are Critical to Emotional Development

The process of emotional development and emotional self-regulation might seem slow to parents and caregivers, and young children vary considerably in their display of emotions and self-regulation. Many changes occur in emotional expression and emotional regulation during early childhood, and researchers are attempting to identify factors that promote or inhibit children's social competence and healthy adjustment (Calkins, 2007).

Emotions Are Central to Children's Lives Child psychologists and early childhood experts believe that children's emotions are central to their lives and should be central to the nursery school, preschool, and early elementary school curriculum. Hyson notes (1994, p. 4)

that emotional development and social development are intertwined and that "current theory and research support the belief that all behavior, thought, and interaction are in some way motivated by and colored by emotions. Thinking is an emotional activity, and emotions provide an essential scaffold for learning. In fact, children's feelings can support or hinder their involvement in and mastery of intellectual content."

Teaching Effective Problem-Solving Skills Youngstrom and colleagues (2000) studied thinking tasks that are integral to social competence and healthy adjustment in a large sample of children in Head Start at age 5 and again at age 7 in first grade. Caregivers, parents, and independent evaluators rated children who, at age 5 and age 7, generated more effective prosocial solutions to problems as more socially competent. They noted that these children had fewer attention problems and exhibited fewer disruptive behaviors than their peers. In contrast, children at age 5 and again at age 7 who proposed forceful (e.g., hitting, shouting, grabbing) and ineffective solutions were rated as less socially competent, less attentive, and more disruptive. By age 7, most of the children in the sample used fewer forceful solutions and generated more prosocial responses. These researchers conclude that young children must be taught effective problem-solving skills if they are to achieve social competence.

Learning Parents' Expression of Emotions Eisenberg and colleagues (2001) examined the relationship between parental emotional expressivity (toward the child or in general in the home) and children's adjustment and social competence. Their findings suggest that children who display social competence, emotional understanding, prosocial behaviors, higher self-esteem, and security of attachment have parents high in warmth or positive emotion and low in negativity in interactions with their children and in non-child-directed interactions within the home. They found that positive and supportive parents helped their children cope successfully with stressful situations. Children from such families are learning to imitate self-regulation and develop appropriate emotional strategies and behaviors. These children are likely to be motivated to comply with parental requests out of a sense of trust and reciprocity (Eisenberg et al., 2001).

Some exposure to negative emotions—expressed appropriately and on a limited basis—is important for learning about emotions and how to regulate them. For example, the expression of such nonhostile emotions as sadness, embarrassment, and distress has been positively associated with showing sympathy (Eisenberg et al., 2001). Demo and Cox's (2000) research supports the finding that young children who grow up in a secure family environment are likely to display healthier emotions and earlier self-regulation of emotions, whereas children who were born prematurely, have developmental disabilities, and experience maltreatment or whose parents divorce are more likely to be delayed in self-regulation of emotions and to demonstrate poor social competence.

Timing and Sequence of Emotional Development

Two-year-olds have few skills for regulating their emotions. When they do not get what they want, they are apt to respond by crying or demonstrating anger. With increased physical development, preschool children have better control of their facial muscles, can facially display more complex emotions, and begin to learn how to control their behavior (Hyson, 2004). This key accomplishment has implications for their success in school and with their peers (Rothbart, Posner, & Kieras, 2006).

Facial Expressions, Gestures, Body Language, and Voice Quality   Much developmental research has focused on the young child's face as the conduit for expressing emotions, yet parents and other caregivers would be wise to learn to read the language of children's entire bodies. Young children can use increased large- and fine-muscle control to express feelings in a more complex, deliberate way than they did during toddlerhood. They can jump, wave their arms, clap their hands together, or verbally express their delight (Hyson, 1994). Observe American children exhibit approval with a "thumbs up" or a "high five." At this age, children are only beginning to understand the concept of hiding emotion (Pons & Harris, 2005).

Yet in some cultures, the gestures that Americans use convey different meanings, even insulting or sexual messages. Often the use of a simple gesture is confusing for immigrant children to learn—such gestures probably conflict with their traditional patterns of socialization (Hojat et al., 1999). Child-care professionals should familiarize themselves with the meanings of such culturally related gestures when attempting to help young immigrant children acculturate into American society.

Psychologists have also discovered that particular voice qualities, such as loudness, pitch, and tempo, can convey specific social-emotional messages, such as fear, anger, happiness, and sadness (Scherer, 1979). As children get older, sound and vocal quality continue to be important tools for conveying feelings. Words accompany the emotion as well. "Don't touch my toys!" expresses meaning both loudly and emotionally. Words also enable children to convey feelings about themselves and others. A 2-year-old might say, "I sad. Daddy make better." Children's understanding of emotion at an early age is a good predictor of their skill at later stages (Pons & Harris, 2005).

Pretend Play Young children really enjoy pretend play, also called "make believe" play, which allows children to try on different roles. Common household items, such as cardboard boxes, costume jewelry, old hats, adult shoes and clothing, and pots and pans, can serve the child's imagination.

Pretend Play   Young children really enjoy pretend play, also called "make believe" play, which allows them to try on different roles (Frost, 2010). A child's toys, as well as common household items, such as cardboard boxes, costume jewelry, old hats, and adult shoes and clothing, can serve the child's imagination. Note that researchers are finding that pretend play with elements of violence and televised or virtual violence (as in video games) also affect brain development (Frost, 2010).

Play Behaviors and Emotional-Social Development

Play may be defined as voluntary activity undertaken for enjoyment or recreation and for no other purpose. As healthy children mature from age 2 to age 6, they display an increasingly complex array of emotions, cognitive skills, physical feats, and communication strategies through predictable developmental stages of play (Paludi, 2002):

- *Functional play* is repetitive (rolling a ball or model car around).
- *Constructive play* involves manipulating objects or toys to create something else (using blocks to build a tower).
- *Parallel play* involves solitary play near others (putting a puzzle together alone).
- *Onlooker play* is observational (watching others play a game).
- *Associative play* involves two or more children sharing toys and materials (sharing a box of crayons while they color something separately).

- Ultimately, *cooperative (collaborative) play* involves interacting, communicating, and taking turns (playing board games, jumping rope, or playing a game of kickball).

During the first two years, children's play shifts from the simple manipulation of objects to make-believe, involving ever more complex and cognitively demanding behaviors (Frost, 2010). There are many forms of play, including *pretend play, exploration play, games, social play*, and *rough-and-tumble play*. Some of the benefits of supervised play, such as during recess, include getting physical activity, nourishing the brain and body; contributing to academic success and relieving stress; appreciating nature and the outdoors; learning to be creative; and learning socialization skills such as following rules, acting cooperatively, trying out roles of leading and following; making friends; and coping with depression, mental-health issues, and trauma (Frost, 2010). Children often say that unstructured play time (or recess) is their favorite time of the day. Yet more and more U.S. schools are reducing recess time to concentrate on academic pursuits (Ramstetter, Murray, & Garner, 2010).

The social function of play activities has interested researchers for decades (Frost, 2010; Piaget, 1962). Recently, pretend play has captivated the interest of many psychologists who view make-believe or fantasy behavior as an avenue for exploring the "inner person" of the child and as an indicator of underlying cognitive changes. A young child will pretend to play "school" with another friend, or a pet, stuffed animal, or doll may be a substitute companion. During such play, the conversation will mimic what parents and caregivers say and do. Pretend play with other youngsters increases with age, especially for those children who have stories read to them or who get to explore a variety of environments. It appears that pretend play may be one of the building blocks of the skills of reading and writing that young children will be developing in a few years (Kavanaugh, 2006).

Imaginative Play Is Inexpensive but Priceless

Far too often parents buy very expensive toys that sit in a corner and are never used. Children learn to be creative by finding things around their home to play with, and they enjoy discovering how to create things out of common objects, such as pots and pans, cardboard, plastic cups, water, string, tape, or pebbles. For example, putting a blanket over the back of two chairs spread apart can create a "cave" or secret hiding place that can easily be removed and re-created. A simple large cardboard box can become a boat, a plane, a cave, a tree house, a car, a dollhouse, or any structure or place the child might imagine!

Imaginary Friends

Between the ages of 3 and 7, many youngsters engage in a form of make-believe play in which they create an **imaginary friend** who becomes a regular

Differences in Play for Boys and Girls In general, boys tend to play in larger groups, to engage in more rough-and-tumble play, and to enjoy motor activities such as running, jumping, climbing, throwing objects, and wrestling—play with overtones of competition and dominance. Girls tend to play in small groups, to be verbal during play, and to hold hands or stay close to each other.

part of their daily lives—an invisible character whom they name, refer to in conversations, and play with, assuming an air of reality that lacks an objective basis (Taylor et al., 2004). Firstborns and very intelligent children often have imaginary friends. Caregivers are advised not to scold children for using their imaginations. Children experience the same benefits of help and nurturance from imaginary friends as their real friends provide (Gleason & Hohmann, 2006). Eventually children outgrow their imaginary companion as they interact with real playmates.

Gender Differences in Play

One difference in play behavior is that boys tend to select games that require a larger number of participants than those selected by girls—but these differences in the play activities of boys and girls are often fostered by the socialization practices of parents and other caregivers. The two genders have somewhat different play styles (Hines, 2004). Boys' play has many rough-and-tumble physical qualities to it and strong overtones of competition and dominance. Girls engage in more intimate play than boys do, and their play is more apt to be cooperative and enabling of others (Ruble, Martin, & Berenbaum, 2006). Girls in U.S. culture are more likely than boys to disclose personal information to a friend and to hold hands and display other signs of affection.

Play Benefits Emotional Well-Being

Many early childhood professionals regard play as a primary way for children to communicate their deepest feelings (Erikson, 1977). Typically, from age 3 to age 5, young children are egocentric; that is, their thoughts, words, and feelings are limited in outlook to their own needs. Thus, they believe they may have caused something bad to happen (e.g., an argument between parents, the illness of a sibling, or the death of a pet or loved one). Also, preschool and elementary-age children simply do not know the vocabulary they would need to speak about such feelings as anxiety, depression, jealousy or resentment, rejection or shame, or the despair caused by loss, abandonment, or abuse. However, in therapeutic play children demonstrate behaviors, reveal innermost feelings, and express thoughts and fears. Research studies confirm that such play decreases anxiety and aggression and increases expression of emotions, social adjustment, and a sense of control (Frost, 2010).

Cultural Differences in Play Theories about play were typically based on studies of middle-class white children from Western industrialized societies. Only recently have historical, cultural, and ethnic differences in play been studied (Chen, French, & Schneider, 2006; Smidt, 2011). American parents typically tend to encourage exploration, imagination, and independence in play and are likely to play with their children; and they view play as essential for development and tend to control their children's play activities (Scarlett et al., 2004).

However, studies reveal that parents across cultures have different attitudes about play. Although some view play as unnecessary, undesirable, or unsafe, in other settings play might be difficult to achieve because time, space, materials, or playmates are lacking. Children in developing countries have a very different experience of childhood. They fill their days with home chores, sibling care, or work and school obligations and are encouraged by parents to work hard, take responsibility, and show initiative. "Play is at best tolerantly accepted by adults, and often it is discouraged or prohibited" (Harkness & Super, 1996, p. 359). Variations in play and social interaction are shaped by what adults believe children need so that they become productive members of their society.

Regardless of a child's cultural or ethnic background, the significance of play is recognized as a universal value in Article 31 of *The United Nations Convention on the Rights of the Child:* "Every child has the right to rest and leisure, to engage in play and recreational activities appropriate to the age of the child and to participate freely in cultural life and the arts" ("The Convention on the Rights of the Child," 2001).

Emotional Response and Self-Regulation

The rules for displaying expressions of culture and emotion differ among ethnic and national groups (Safdar et al., 2009). Deliberate holding back of feelings is difficult for children until after age 3 (Thompson & Goodvin,

2007). Also, individual cultural expectations dictate the norms for the expression or inhibition of emotions by boys or girls. Some believe children should be able to "let their feelings out," whereas others believe children need to learn to hide their feelings.

Emotional self-regulation is a complex task that must be mastered in a healthy way for children to develop a positive relationship with others. Self-regulation develops at each child's pace and proceeds gradually and unevenly. Vygotsky encourages preschool-age children to "let their feelings out" in sociodramatic (make-believe) play that he says promotes expressive language, shows that the child is developing culturally valued competencies, and serves to help the child develop self-regulation. To play a role, a child has to inhibit impulsive behaviors (Elias & Berk, 2002). Children who cry, whine, hit, bite, or scream to get their way certainly will not be well liked, and neither will the sad or timid child who sits quietly in a corner away from others.

Culture Transmits Expectations Contemporary social scientists are studying cross-cultural expectations or unwritten "rules" for expressing emotions. Young children learn by imitation and modeling to convey culturally prescribed emotions through gestures and body language. In Western industrialized cultures, parents tend to support **individualism,** the view that individual autonomy is paramount. Western parents promote values such as freedom of expression, independence, individuality, creativity, and competition, and they encourage their children to exhibit feelings more openly (Safdar et al., 2009). For example, it is common to witness a young American child crying loudly or having a "temper tantrum" in public. In contrast, Native Americans often convey emotions through nonverbal communication and tone of voice (Paniagua, 2005).

Asian American Expectations Asian parents traditionally stress **collectivism,** a view that fosters in children a strong emotional bonding and feeling of oneness with parents, denial of individual desires in order to do what is best for the group, obedience to authority, and show of respect to elders (Friedlmeier & Trommsdorff, 1999). Children from Asian cultures are typically encouraged not to show their emotions and to comply with their parents' wishes (Cole & Tan, 2007a). The Chinese concept of *chiao shun,* which means "training in appropriate behaviors," also shows the valuing of collectivism. Chinese parents tend to be very directive with their children and focus their interactions on obtaining obedience. Chinese mothers value respect and obedience as the highest goals of parenting. They attribute their children's success in school not to individual capabilities but to the respect the children have for their families—their children's success is an asset and honor to the entire family. Chinese children are socialized to be sensitive to the social environment and to transcend their personal concerns (Lynch & Hanson, 2004).

This growing community in the United States includes three general ethnicities: (1) *East Asians,* including Chinese, Japanese, and Koreans; (2) *Southeast Asians,* largely composed of Indochinese from Vietnam, Thailand (e.g., Hmong immigrants), Cambodia, Laos, Myanmar, and the Philippines; and (3) *Pacific Islanders,* mostly Hawaiians, Samoans, and Guamanians (Coloma, 2006). These groups and their subgroups differ in sociocultural traits, beliefs, and values.

Latino American Expectations The Latino American cultural stereotype for a male child is summed up in the word *macho,* derived from *machismo,* which connotes both positive and negative aspects about the role of a male: to be strong and dominant, to take responsibility for the well-being of his family, to work hard to provide for his family, to treat women with respect, and to be a good son, husband, and father. In contrast, *marianismo* is the Latino American cultural stereotype for a female. She is expected to be feminine, to learn self-sacrifice, to provide joy in and take responsibility for her family, and to subjugate her needs to prepare herself to live in a patriarchal subculture.

Typically there is a strong family cohesion called *familismo* (Paniagua, 2005). Hispanic children also live within a collectivist culture, and family beliefs, values, and traditions are a significant influence on behavior and emotional expression. Their parents are more relaxed about child development than some other ethnic groups. Cooperation, warmth in personal relations, and loyalty to the extended family group are important values that parents instill in their children (Lynch & Hanson, 2004).

African American Expectations Often, black American adults use eye contact and facial expression to discipline their children. A teacher with a class of African American children may use a certain look that quiets most of the class. However, this is not effective with all African American children (King, Sims, & Osher, 2001). Some are taught by caregivers to refrain from direct eye contact, which people from other cultural backgrounds might misinterpret as shyness or evasiveness (Hyson, 2004).

In her book *I'm Chocolate, You're Vanilla,* Marguerite A. Wright (1998), a developmental psychologist, states that preschool children do not attach any social or emotional meaning to skin color or race, unless their families stress this. Before children can understand the role race plays in their lives, they must first realize that skin color is permanent. Preschool children cannot categorize people into different racial-ethnic groups (e.g., African, Arab,

Chinese, and Mexican). They delight in trying on different roles, and they demonstrate a pure appreciation for people as individuals. "White preschoolers share with their black peers an innocence about racial differences" (Wright, 1998, p. 32). Around age 7, children begin to develop the cognitive skills to categorize people into different racial-ethnic groups, using physical characteristics and social cues.

American black children come from families with a history of oral tradition in their songs, tales, proverbs, stories, and jokes. These were preserved over the generations and eventually formed the basis of African American music—the Negro spiritual, jazz, the blues, and contemporary rap music. African American language, passed along to young children, uses creativity, poetic beauty, emotional intensity, and rich, colorful imagery ("Parenting Empowerment Project," 2001).

Muslim American Expectations Most adult American Muslims emigrated from various countries, but many of their children were born in the United States and negotiate Islamic religious values at home and a Western secular culture in public schools. Ahmad and Szpara (2003, p. 299) state that "Muslim children belong to Muslim communities with distinct religious and cultural identities." Syed (2007) says, "As Muslims, our educational aim is to develop the personalities of our children to the end that they will be conscious of their responsibility to God (the Creator) and to fellow humans." Muslim children are taught the importance of good manners and character.

Caregivers and teachers need to be sensitive to Muslim practices regarding observing prayers and religious festivals, wearing appropriate clothing (especially for girls in co-ed gym classes), providing permissible foods (no pork or foods that contain lard, for example), and separating the sexes where possible (Ahmad & Szpara, 2003). While young girls may choose whether or not to wear a *hijab* (head scarf), once they reach puberty, their religion requires them to remain covered in public. Also, families expect young Muslim children to pray several times each day, and some fast during the day during Ramadan, a religious observance that takes place during the ninth month of the Islamic calendar. Understanding Muslim cultural practices enables a Muslim child to develop integrity and self-esteem.

Cultural Competence and Effective Teaching, Health Care, and Social Services Understanding a child's home and values and the practices of her or his community culture is vital to a child's self-esteem, identity development, and sense of belonging—characteristics correlated with overall academic achievement (Gilliard, Moore, & Lemieux, 2007). Training in cultural competence has become an important aspect of social work, teaching, and the provision of health care. Many professional associations provide training in cultural competence and publish resources so that teachers, service providers, and healthcare workers can learn more about appropriate styles of interaction. Teachers and early intervention specialists need to familiarize themselves with the customs and practices of the young children they work with, learn some words of that child's language, and create developmentally appropriate, culturally sensitive, and adaptable curriculums and instruction (see Table 8.1) (Feng, 1994).

Acquiring Emotional Understanding

During the preschool years, children begin to use significantly more words to talk about emotions. They begin to understand the causes of emotional reactions, both within themselves and within other people. They can predict that if a friend loses her favorite toy, she will feel sad, for example. They can understand that when there is a discrepancy between what a person wants and what actually happens, a person will probably feel unhappy. The emotion they identify most easily and most often is happiness (Thompson & Lagattuta, 2006).

The Link Between Feeling and Thinking   Emotions are central to children's lives and help them organize their experiences in order to learn from them and develop other behaviors. Although cultures differ in their norms for the expression of feelings by girls and boys, Table 8.2 shows the general progression of emotional development in American children from age 2 through age 6. Past research suggested that it is not until 8 or 9 years of age

TABLE 8.1 The Influence of Cultural Identity: Contrasting Beliefs, Values, and Practices

Culture	Beliefs and Values	Practices
Dominant Anglo-European Culture 	Individualism/privacy/self-help Nuclear and immediate family bonds Independence Human equality Competition Directness/openness/honesty Time-sensitive/efficiency Rational/empirical orientation Tendency toward more democratic family structure	Marital bond stressed Strong expectations regarding child development Less value/respect toward the elderly Frequently, independent living arrangements for older parents Future orientation Action/goal/work orientation Materialism Death less ritualized Human equality
African American Ethnicity 	Collective orientation Kinship and extended family bonds High-context communication style Religious, spiritual orientation	More authoritarian child-rearing practices Greater respect for elderly and their role in the family More oriented to the situation than time-oriented
Latino Roots 	Collective orientation Interdependence Foster group identity Saving face Relaxed about time Emphasis on personal relations Spiritual belief orientation	Tendency toward more patriarchal family structure More relaxed toward child development More overt respect for the elderly Extended family system more pronounced Death more ritualized

TABLE 8.1 Continued

Culture	Beliefs and Values	Practices
Traditional Asian Roots 	Collectivist social orientation Mutual interdependence Hierarchy, role rigidity, status assigned Conformity Cooperation, nonconfrontation Family-centered Continued dependence on family Parent-child bond stressed Parental expectations of unquestioning obedience, submission to structure	Children seen as extension of parents Older children responsible for siblings' actions Communication indirect—in nonverbal ways Goal-oriented Emotionally controlled Modest, self-effacing Polytheistic, spiritualistic Traditions and past-orientation Self-denial, self-discipline Decision making not democratic
Middle Eastern and Muslim Roots 	Informal support system Children brought up to live interdependently More flexible time schedule for eating, sleeping, and toilet training Less freedom for independent learning and exploration	Respect for elderly, spiritual maturity, and wisdom For children, decision making not independent Dependent living arrangements: older parents with adult children Identity defined by family achievement

Source: Lynch, E. W., & Hanson, M. J. (2004). *Developing cross-cultural competence: A guide for working with children and their families* (3rd ed.). Baltimore: Brooks Publishing.

that children can begin to understand mental (rather than situational) causes of feelings, but more recent research by Lagattuta (2005) shows that 3- and 4-year-olds can explain emotions in terms of current external situations and that 4- and 5-year-olds have substantial knowledge about mind and emotion.

Responding to Emotions of Others Toddlers and preschoolers deliberately seek out information about others' emotional reactions. Preschoolers learn a great deal about emotions in their friendships with peers. For example, children's emotional response to the distress of others seems to motivate them to comfort and help their caregivers and peers. As young children develop emotionally, they need help in understanding these emotions in a secure environment, and adults who model appropriate emotional responses are especially helpful. Children also require support for regulating their emotions (Hyson, 2004). They might appear to be fascinated by "getting a rise out of" their parents and caregivers (what at first

might seem to be a game of repeatedly asking "Why?" can become irritating). Children who have supportive friendships are more likely to exhibit prosocial behaviors. Conversely, children who experience conflict in their early friendships are more likely to exhibit aggression and rejection of peers (Sebanc, 2003). Helping young children form warm and caring friendships is an important aspect of teaching them to be effective citizens.

Forming Emotional Ties Forming positive relationships with parents, siblings, extended family, and caregivers is a key task in the development of a child's sense of self-awareness. Emotional attachment is demonstrated by such behaviors as clinging, smiling, and crying. Children in child-care settings can develop close, affectionate bonds with caregivers, for example, without necessarily having physical contact (Hyson, 2004). The sibling relationship helps children acquire **social understanding**—the capacity to predict the intention of another person, manage conflict, talk about feelings and why people

TABLE 8.2 Progression of Emotional Development, Ages 2 to 6

Age Group	Emotional Expression
2-year-olds	These children begin to show facial expressions of shyness, pride, shame, embarrassment, contempt, fear, and guilt.
	Parallel play—that is, playing independently near others without interaction—is common in 2-year-olds.
	Play is more likely to be simple manipulation of objects.
	Deliberate holding back of feelings, called emotional self-regulation, is unlikely at this early age.
	Sometimes toddlers deliberately try to elicit emotional responses from caregivers.
	Children definitely begin to use the word *no.*
	Toddlers can also develop close, affectionate bonds with caregivers, demonstrated by smiling, clinging, and crying.
	Two-year-olds demonstrate emergence of the interpersonal self (e.g., reacting happily when mother comes to pick up the child at the end of the day).
	"Watch me do this!"
	Young children conceive of the self strictly in physical terms, pointing to the head, for example.
	Plants and animals also have selves and minds.
	Gifted children master their environment quickly and thoroughly and appear to be self-directed.
3-year-olds	Increased large-muscle and fine-muscle control allows expression of feelings in a more complex, deliberate way.
	Children can now jump, wave arms, clap hands together, and verbally express delight.
	Voice qualities, such as loudness, pitch, and tempo, vary, conveying specific feelings (e.g., "Don't touch my toys!").
	They begin to demonstrate a complexity of emotions through play materials in their environment.
	Associative play is more common, with children beginning to interact with one another and sharing play materials.
	Playing cooperatively begins toward the end of this year.
	There is some evidence of emotional self-regulation.
	This age group learns about expectations of emotional self-regulation from observing others, from imitating the behaviors of others, and from receiving direct instruction.
	Gifted children often display leadership qualities and often say, "I can do it myself!"
3- to 4-year-olds	This age group has a tendency to explain feelings in terms of external events ("I sad. He hit me.")
	They are more likely to deliberately elicit emotional responses from caregivers.
	They are likely to want to help with tasks and to help others.
4-year-olds	This age group has better control of facial muscles and can display more complex emotions at one time.
	They begin to verbally express more complex feelings.
	They can accurately identify a commonly expressed emotion and can describe an eliciting situation.
	Boys seem to prefer to engage in more rough-and-tumble competitive play in larger groups, whereas girls seem to engage in two-person groups with more intimate behaviors, such as talking and holding hands.
	Some children this age have an imaginary friend.
	Four- and 5-year-olds show substantial knowledge about mind and emotion.
	A gender identity is usually established.
5- to 6-year-olds	Members of this age group have greater mastery of thinking and remembering.
	They show evidence of an emerging distinction between the mental self and the physical self.
	They show evidence of a greater variety of temperaments and behaviors.

behave as they do, and engage in teasing and imaginative play. All of these activities are important milestones in the task of understanding the thinking and feelings of others (Dunn, 2007).

> *Questions*
>
> In early childhood, how do children acquire emotional understanding and, in turn, increase their ability to develop healthy emotional self-regulation? What are some examples from cross-cultural studies about various influences on children's emotional development?

THE DEVELOPMENT OF SELF-AWARENESS

As we have seen, emotional development is an essential component of a child's sense of self-awareness. In Western cultures, we are concerned about a child's own sense of self-worth or self-image, which is part of the overall dimension called **self-esteem.** Some children develop what is referred to as positive self-esteem; others develop a more negative view of themselves, referred to as low self-esteem. Enhancing children's self-esteem is an important goal for many parents and most preschool and kindergarten programs, and there is considerable evidence that children's self-esteem can have lifelong effects on their attitudes and behavior, performance in school, relationships with family, and functioning in society (Hong & Perkins, 1997). In this section, we examine the factors that influence a child's developing self-esteem.

The Sense of Self

Among the cognitive and social achievements of a child's early years is a growing self-awareness—the human sense of "I." At any one time, we are confronted with a greater variety of stimulation than we can attend to and process, and we must select what we will notice, learn, infer, or recall. Selection does not occur randomly but depends on our use of internal cognitive structures—mental "scripts" or "frames"—for processing information. Of particular importance to us is the cognitive structure that we employ for selecting and processing information about ourselves. This structure is the **self**—the system of concepts we use in defining ourselves.

The development of a sense of self as separate and distinct from others is a central issue of children's early years (Brownell, Zerwas, & Ramani, 2007). The self provides us with the capacity to observe, respond to, and direct our own behavior and distinguishes each of us as a unique individual, different from others. This fundamental cognitive change facilitates numerous other changes in social development. Youngsters come to view themselves as active agents who produce outcomes. They insist on performing activities independently, resulting in behavior sometimes pejoratively labeled "the terrible twos." Common directives from young children include "I do it myself!" and "Watch me!"

During the preschool years, young children conceive of the self strictly in physical terms—body parts (the head), material attributes ("I have blue eyes"), and bodily activities ("I walk to the park") (Johnson, 1990). Children view the self and the mind as simply parts of the body (Damon & Hart, 1982). Young children locate the self in the head, although they might also cite other body parts, such as the chest, or the whole body. And they often say that toys, animals, plants, and dead people also have selves and minds, which is called *animism.* Piaget's writings suggest that children "are naturally animistic until they develop more advanced, rational, and correct understandings of the world around them" (Harvey, 2006, p. 14). The Disney organization has capitalized on the beliefs of young children since 1928, from *Mickey Mouse* to today's *Toy Story* series (and beyond!).

Between 6 and 8 years of age, children begin to distinguish between the mind and the body (Inagaki & Hatano, 1993). They begin to recognize that people are unique not only because each of us looks different from other people but also because each of us has different feelings, traits, and thoughts. Hence, children come to define the self in *internal* rather than *external* terms and to grasp the difference between psychological and physical attributes.

Parents' and caregivers' overall support and unconditional love provide the foundation for a child's developing self-concept. The **self-concept,** or *self-image,* is the image one has of oneself. One theory is that a child's self-image develops as a reflection of what others think about the child. Parents' facial expressions, tone of voice, and patient or impatient interactions reflect how the parents value their child. The child's own personality contributes to his or her growing self-awareness and to the parents' conceptions about the child. That is, a parent might recognize that her child is "shy" or "happy-go-lucky" or "strong-willed"—traits that appear to be inherent in this particular child's nature.

Children from some cultures understand "self" differently than do children in the dominant culture. They develop a stronger self-concept and can negotiate their relationship to the dominant culture better when their sense of ethnic identity is strong. Studies have examined children from a wide variety of ethnic groups in the United States, including Mexican, Central American, Vietnamese, Chinese, Indian, and Pakistani. Children of the Pikuni ethnic group, part of the Blackfoot Confederacy, are taught not to point at another person, because this distinguishes him or her as a separate being, apart from the collective group. In a classroom exercise to teach young children identity, they are told to close their hands into fists and move their hands in a circle to encompass everyone they see while saying "Me, you, all of us. . . . We're Pikuni." A Hawaiian educator of young children stresses that parts of the body are locations that connect the child to the collective whole, past and present. The fontanel in the skull of an infant connects the child to the spiritual beliefs of his or her people, the navel connects the child to the ancestors, and the reproductive organs connect the child to future generations. Children raised in these cultures will have a very different understanding of "self" than will children raised in the dominant culture. They are taught that their actions affect the entire collective into which they were born (Nee-Benham & Cooper, 2000).

Children with a secure ethnic identity are more able to cope with stressful situations and master new skills, and are less likely to be depressed or feel lonely, than children whose ethnic identity is not as strong (Phinney & Ong, 2007). Again, it is important for caregivers to educate themselves about the cultural values of the ethnic groups of the children with whom they interact so they can positively reinforce these values.

Measuring a Child's Self-Esteem

Sometimes adults recognize a young child's lack of self-esteem by the child's withdrawn, sad, or acting-out or antisocial behaviors and realize that the child might need intervention to boost self-esteem for better mental health and social functioning. Psychologists have devised a variety of psychometric instruments used to assess the accuracy of such observations. Harter and Pike (1984) developed the *Pictorial Scale of Perceived Competence and Social Acceptance in Young Children.* This has become a commonly used self-report measure, where children are asked to report on their own behavior and receive separate scores for cognitive and physical competence, maternal acceptance, and peer acceptance. An alternative approach to self-esteem measurement is the *Behavioral Rating Scale of Presented Self-Esteem in Young Children,* used by parents and teachers to assess inferred self-esteem (Haltiwanger & Harter, 1988). Ratings include such behaviors as initiative, preference for challenge, social approach/social avoidance, social-emotional expression, and coping skills.

The Gifted Child's Sense of Self   The gifted child has extraordinary capabilities and potential—often in particular areas, such as in an academic field, in the arts, or in an area such as leadership. The skills and potential of gifted children reach beyond the domain of talent and into the realm of the extraordinary. Giftedness is associated with high IQ, but some children who are gifted in

one domain may be classified as learning disabled in another area. Interestingly, gifted children may not perform above average in school (think of the genius inventor Thomas Edison, who was described as "addled" by one of his schoolteachers). Gifted children come from every racial and ethnic group and every socioeconomic group (Carpenter, 2001). Children with extraordinary abilities tend to share the personality characteristics of independence, unconventionality, openness, flexibility, and risk taking (Moran & Gardner, 2006).

What makes some children gifted? Elizabeth Maxwell of the Gifted Development Center in Denver finds that "it is difficult not to notice the assertive drive of gifted and highly gifted young children to master their environment as quickly and as thoroughly as possible, far beyond the age expectations of developmental timetables. They appear to be self-directed, their sense of self-awareness arriving early and thrust in the face of parents and the environment in general" (Maxwell 1998, p. 245). Lovecky (1994) calls this **entelechy,** a particular type of motivation, need for self-determination, inner strength, and vital force directing life and growth to become all one is capable of being.

Gifted children are active learners with their own agendas, and they learn remarkably quickly, yet they may be difficult to teach or to manage. They do not automatically show respect for adults, are likely to see themselves as equal to adults, might demonstrate a strong will, and can present unique challenges to parents and teachers. A common, highly charged directive from highly intelligent children is "I can do it myself!" Even so, they are likely to share easily with others, to have a strong sense of justice, and to display leadership qualities (Maxwell, 1998).

Questions

What are some cognitive and social factors that promote a young child's growing self-awareness? What factors or behaviors might a psychologist assess to determine a child's self-esteem?

GENDER IDENTIFICATION

One of the attributes of self acquired early in life is **gender,** the state of being male or female. A major developmental task for the child during the first six years of life is to acquire gender identification. All societies appear to have seized on the anatomical differences between women and men to assign **gender roles**—sets of cultural expectations that define the ways in which the members of each sex should behave.

Societies throughout the world display considerable differences in the types of activities assigned to women and men (Aboim, 2010; Murdock, 1935). In many societies, girls are socialized to identify with the mother's nurturant, caregiving role, and boys are prepared to identify with the father's provisional-protector role. In some societies, though, women do most of the manual labor. In others, as in the Marquesas Islands, cooking, housekeeping, and baby-tending are male occupations.

Gender Identity

Children develop gender identities that are reasonably consistent with the gender-role standards of their society. **Gender identity** is the conception that a person has of himself or herself as being male or female. Since the 1960s in the Western world, a good deal of research has explored the process by which children come to conceive of themselves in *masculine* or *feminine* terms and to adopt the behaviors considered culturally appropriate for them as males or females. It has also activated debate about the psychology of gender differences and gender stereotypes. Feminist researchers point out that from the moment children are born, parents assign particular roles and expectations. Thus, some children do not have an opportunity to develop a gender identity that suits their personalities, because the dominant culture imposes rigid expectations about what it means to be a boy or a girl (Harrison & Hood-Williams, 2002). It would be fair to say that in U.S. society, gender roles have become more versatile over the past 30 years.

How children are treated in any culture because of their gender significantly affects how children feel about themselves. You can see how most parents quickly plan to assimilate their child into the appropriate gender role beginning with the fetal ultrasound: What color paint and curtains are planned for the baby's room? What color and style of clothing is chosen prior to the birth? What types of toys are purchased to put in the child's crib? What potential names are selected for the child-to-be?

Children's understanding about gender identity changes from age 3 to age 7. During this period, they search for cues about gender in every experience; researchers Carol Martin and Diane Ruble (2004) call them "gender detectives." They illustrate:

> In an Italian restaurant, a four-year-old noticed his father and another man order pizza and his mother order lasagna. On his way home in the car, he announced that he had figured it out: "Men eat pizza and women don't." (Bjorkland, quoted by Martin & Ruble, 2004, p. 67)

This little boy was in the beginning phase of learning about gender-related characteristics. This phase begins around ages 3 and 4 through socialization experiences with parents and extended family, preschool experiences, and media influence (Maccoby, 2002; Sinno & Killen,

2009). Between ages 5 and 7, children consolidate their gender identity—one is either all-male or all-female to them. After age 7, they are able to be more flexible about their understanding of gender (Martin & Ruble, 2004).

Influence of Biology, Brain, and Hormones

The study of gender and sex differences related to cognitive abilities and behavior continues to provoke a great deal of heated controversy (Halpern, 2000). In the past, cultural stereotypes about male or female abilities or behaviors have done great harm, and they still do in some areas of the world where females are devalued. But neuroscientists and psychobiologists persist in attempting to determine both similarities and differences in the size, structure, or functioning of particular regions of the brain and the relationship to gender identity, behavior, sexual orientation, cognitive processes, and neurodevelopmental disorders. In general, studies on brain specialization find that boys tend to be more logical, analytical, spatial, and mathematical, whereas females tend to be more verbal at an earlier age, more emotionally expressive, and more interested in people-oriented activities (Halpern, 1997). Witness the number of little boys who enjoy playing "superhero" or video games and sports that are based on spatial relations, and the number of little girls who enjoy activities such as having a "tea party" or playing "school" that are based on language and social skills.

Other researchers continue to investigate the influence of hormones (chemical messengers of the endocrine system) on gender behaviors throughout the life span (Ruble, Martin, & Berenbaum, 2006). Both sexes have some male and female hormones, although the proportions vary in males and females. The hormones our brains are exposed to in the womb do much to shape how we express being male and female. Males are typically exposed to higher levels of androgens, and females to higher levels of progesterone and estrogen. But there is a spectrum within each gender. The prevalence of androgens tends to make boys more physically active, more aggressive, and less likely to be able to sit still than girls (Hyde, 2005; Maccoby & Jacklin, 1974). And girls who are exposed to higher levels of androgens may prefer sports and have little interest in playing with dolls (Leaper & Friedman, 2007). Eleanor Maccoby (1980), after repeated reviews of research studies on sex behaviors, concluded, "The tendency of males to be more aggressive than females is perhaps the most firmly established sex difference and is a characteristic that transcends culture."

Gender Identity Problems Although most young children are collecting information about their gender identity and are certain that they are a boy or a girl, a small percentage of children begin to exhibit signs that gender identity is more problematic. Some children are *intersexed;* that is, they are born with genitalia that are not clearly male or clearly female. An intersexed child might be born with a vagina and an incompletely formed penis or with some other combination of male and female genitalia. For decades, researchers and physicians felt that it was best to assign a clear gender identity to such children as early as possible through surgery, if necessary, and through intensive gender socialization. This position is now being called into question by researchers (Ruble, Martin, & Berenbaum, 2006). Research has shown that gender is not determined by biology alone or by culture alone, and a consensus is growing that it is best to let intersexed individuals choose their own gender identity when they are ready. Families of intersexed children face many difficult decisions and need medical, psychological, and community support. A good source of information is the Intersex Society of North America's Web site at www.isna.org.

Social Influences on Gender Behaviors

Environmental influences play a significant role in gender behaviors. Certainly each individual child's family experience and cultural socialization patterns influence gender behaviors. Culture typically seeks to bring our behavior into conformity with narrower expectations. Clearly, anatomy in itself does not provide us with our gender identity. Boys receive more toy action vehicles, sports equipment, machines, toy animals, and military toys; girls receive more dolls, dollhouses, and domestic toys. Although the sexual revolution has reshaped many aspects of U.S. life, it has failed to reach very deeply into the toy box. Behind many parents' concerns about the types of toys their children play with are unexpressed fears about homosexuality, yet there is little evidence that children's toy preferences are related to their sexual orientation (Williams & Pleil, 2008).

By the age of 3, most children show a clear preference for gender-differentiated play. One meta-study concluded that in the preschool years, boys and girls engage in such different play behaviors that they are "almost like two separate cultures" (Ruble, Martin, & Berenbaum, 2006, p. 869). Girls most often play dress-up and choose dolls and kitchen sets, and their fantasy play involves home life and glamour. Boys most often play with cars, trucks, and construction toys, and their fantasy play involves aggression, danger, and action hero figures. Girls seem to be more willing to play with toys considered "male"; but boys seem less flexible about playing with toys typed "female," although there are always some children who cross the norms.

Even though women give birth and men do not, little evidence exists to support the popular notion that somehow biology makes women kinder and gentler beings (Whiting & Edwards, 1988). Psychologist Jerome Kagan,

Gender Awareness Mothers and fathers typically react to male and female children in distinct and consistent ways. In American society, boys are likely to be described as "big," "strong," and "well coordinated," whereas girls are likely to be described as "beautiful," "delicate," or "cute."

who has spent more than 35 years studying children, speculates that any propensity women might have for caretaking can be traced to an early *awareness* of their role in procreation:

> Every girl knows, somewhere between the ages of 5 and 10, that she is different from boys and that she will have a child—something that everyone, including children, understands as quintessentially natural. If, in our society, nature stands for the giving of life, nurturance, help, affection, then the girl will conclude unconsciously that those are the qualities she should strive to attain. And the boy won't. And that's exactly what happens. (Kagan, quoted by Shapiro, 1990, p. 59)

Theories Regarding the Acquisition of Gender Identity

Social and behavioral scientists have proposed a number of theories regarding the process by which children psychologically become masculine or feminine. Among these theories are the psychoanalytic, psychosocial, cognitive learning, and cognitive developmental approaches.

Psychoanalytic Theory According to Sigmund Freud, children are psychologically bisexual at birth. They develop their gender roles as they resolve their conflicting feelings of love and jealousy in relation to their parents. A young boy develops a strong love attraction for his mother but fears that his father will punish him by cutting off his penis. The usual outcome of this Oedipal complex is for a boy to repress his erotic desire for his mother and learn to identify with his father. As a consequence of coming to identify with their fathers, boys later erotically seek out females. Meanwhile, Freud said, young girls fall in love with their fathers. A girl blames her mother for her lack of a penis. But she soon comes to realize that she cannot replace her mother in her father's affections, so most girls resolve their Electra complex by identifying with their mothers and later by finding suitable men to love. These complexes are normally resolved by age 5 or 6. Although Freud's theory about gender identity remains controversial, it is common to hear a 4- or 5-year-old child proclaim, "When I'm older, I'm going to marry Daddy (or Mommy)."

Psychosocial Theory Erikson, who accepted Freud's psychoanalytic theory of gender identity, showed how certain gender traits are assimilated by social interaction. Erikson said that between the ages of 3 and 6, children strive exuberantly to do things and to test their developing abilities. Erikson called this the psychosocial period, during which the child attempts to resolve the conflict of **initiative versus guilt** by gaining more independence. Children at this age usually try to model their behavior after the same-sex adults and siblings in their environment. At the time of Erikson's writing, boys were expected to become self-sufficient, while girls were expected to establish close relationships. Traditionally, *if Daddy is washing the car, then little Jimmy will want to help. If Mommy is baking cookies, then little Jill will want to help.* Erikson would say that if the parents approve and let them help, with supervision, then they are experiencing initiative. If, on the other hand, Jimmy and Jill decide they want to turn on the stove, they might be scolded that they are too little, and they are likely to experience a sense of guilt, disappointment, or inhibition. Erikson would say that there is a balance in this process of always wanting to learn and do and being told "No, you are too little" or "You can't; only grown-ups do this." The authors have a friend who was told by his traditional mother (in the 1950s) that "boys don't do things in the kitchen; that was her place."

Young American children today are likely to learn skills from mothers who are airplane mechanics or police officers and from fathers who are nurses or preschool teachers. Children who learn how to suitably regulate their drive for initiative are developing what Erikson called the "virtue of purpose" (Erikson, 1982). At this

age, children might begin to say of themselves, "I am good" or "I am bad," depending on the level of encouragement, discouragement, or punishment they get from their parents and caregivers.

Cognitive Learning Theory Cognitive learning theorists take the view that children are essentially neutral at birth and that the biological differences between girls and boys are insufficient to account for later differences in gender identities. They stress the parts that *selective reinforcement* and *imitation* play in the process of acquiring a gender identity. Viewed from this perspective, children reared in a nuclear family setting are rewarded for imitating the behavior of the same-sex parent. Cognitive theorists hold that boys and girls are actively rewarded and praised, both by adults and by their peers, for what society perceives to be sex-appropriate behavior, and they are ridiculed and punished for behavior inappropriate to their sex (Smetana, 1986).

Albert Bandura (1973; Bussey & Bandura, 1984) points out that in addition to imitating the behavior of adults, children engage in *observational learning.* According to Bandura, children mentally encode a model's behavior as they watch it, but they will not imitate behavior they have observed unless they believe that it will have a positive outcome for them. He says that children discern which behaviors are appropriate for each sex by watching the behavior of many male and female models. In turn, they employ these abstractions of sex-appropriate behavior as "models" for their own imitative actions.

Cognitive Developmental Theory Still another approach, which is identified with Lawrence Kohlberg (1966; Kohlberg & Ullian, 1974), focuses on the part that cognitive development plays in children's acquisition of gender identities. This theory claims that children first learn to label themselves as "male" or "female" and then attempt to acquire and master the behaviors that fit their gender category. This process is called *self-socialization.* According to Kohlberg, children form stereotyped conceptions of maleness and femaleness—fixed, exaggerated, cartoonlike images—that they use to organize their environment. They select and cultivate behaviors that are consistent with their ability to understand gender concepts (see Table 8.3) ("Gender Identity," 1998).

Kohlberg distinguishes between his approach and cognitive learning theory in these terms. According to the cognitive learning model, the following sequence occurs: "I want rewards; I am rewarded for doing boy things; therefore I want to be a boy." In contrast, Kohlberg (1966, p. 89) believes that the sequence goes like this: "I am a boy; therefore I want to do boy things; therefore the opportunity to do boy things (and to gain approval for doing them) is rewarding."

TABLE 8.3 Kohlberg's Stages of Gender Development

Stage 1: Gender Labeling	Children can identify themselves and other people as girls or boys (mommies or daddies). However, gender is not seen as stable over time or across changes in superficial physical characteristics (e.g., length of hair and type of clothes).
Stage 2: Gender Stability	Children recognize that gender is stable over time: Boys will grow up to be daddies, and girls will grow up to be mommies. However, the unchanging nature of gender—that it remains the same regardless of changes in superficial appearance or activity choice—is not yet appreciated.
Stage 3: Gender Consistency	Children have a full appreciation of the permanence of gender over time and across situations.

Source: Kohlberg, L. (1966). A cognitive-developmental analysis of children's sex-role concepts and attitudes. In E. Maccoby (Ed.), *The development of sex differences.* Stanford, CA: Stanford University Press.

Genital anatomy plays a minor part in young children's thinking about sex differences. Instead, children notice and stereotype a relatively limited set of highly visible traits—hairstyle, clothes, stature, and occupation. Children use *gender schemes* or *models* to actively structure their experiences and to draw inferences and interpretations regarding gender behaviors (Bem, 1993). Children develop a rudimentary understanding of gender and invoke gender schemes to process information. These schemes begin developing during the second year of life (Serbin, Poulin-Dubois, Colburne, Sen, & Eichstedt, 2001).

Evaluation of Theories   The theories considered here stress an awareness of children's knowledge about **gender stereotypes** (exaggerated generalizations about male or female behaviors) as powerful determinants of sex-typed behavior. Each emphasizes that behavioral differences between the sexes are at least in part perpetuated by the fact that most children are more inclined to imitate the behavior of same-sex models than they are to imitate the behavior of opposite-sex models. Each of the theories has some merit (Jacklin & Reynolds, 1993). Instead of counterpoising these theories in an either/or fashion, many psychologists prefer to see them as supplementing and complementing one another.

Mothers, Fathers, and Gender Typing

Social and behavioral scientists suggest that gender stereotypes arise in response to a society's division of labor by

sex and serve to rationalize this division by attributing to males and females basic personality differences (Johansson, 1998). The family household configurations (married parents, single parent, cohabiting, or same-sex parents), whether a mother works outside the home, and the family's culture intervene to shape gender.

Evidence suggests that in U.S. society, parents socialize girls and boys differently about gender. In the dominant U.S. culture, fathers are more likely to engage in active play with their young children. Mothers are more likely to provide direct care and to use toys and books when they spend time with their children. Another example is found in sports. Girls and boys participate in sports in almost equal numbers, but many parents view their sons as more competent in sports than their daughters (Leaper & Friedman, 2007). The way parents speak to their young children also conveys gender messages. Fathers use much more directive speech ("Do this"; "Go over there"), whereas mothers use much more supportive speech ("Keep trying!"; "You did that just right!") than fathers. Mothers also emphasize interpersonal closeness with their daughters and autonomy with their sons (Leaper & Friedman, 2007). Fathers are more apt to give their sons nicknames that speak of strength ("Tiger" or "Buster"); with their daughters they use words that describe emotions ("happy" or "angry") (Gleason & Ely, 2002). Both fathers and mothers are more eager to push their sons toward masculinity than to push their daughters toward femininity. Parents generally express more negative reactions when boys make choices culturally defined as feminine than when girls make choices culturally defined as masculine (Lewis & Lamb, 2003). Fathers' fears of homosexuality, in themselves or in their sons, lead many men to inhibit displays of love and tenderness toward their sons (Parke, 1995). The acceptance of men in child-care settings has varied drastically through the years, with parents seeing them as an unexpected but necessary male influence or as suspect because of their male sexuality (Willett, 2008).

Children whose mothers work outside the home tend to have less stereotyped views of gender roles for women. Girls whose parents model egalitarian roles have fewer symptoms of depression when they reach adolescence and do better in math and science in middle school than children whose parents model more traditional roles. Also, children who live with only one parent rely less on gender stereotyping. Early research on the parenting styles of same-sex parents suggests that they provide more flexible and egalitarian gender-role models for their children. Parents in each of these configurations convey many messages each day about gender and shape their children's understanding of what it means to be male or female (Bornstein, 2006).

How do these differences in socialization affect how male and female children express gender identity? Repeated studies have shown that male infants are more emotionally expressive than female infants for the first six months. They express more joy and anger, they are fussier when they are unhappy, and they gesture toward their mothers more often than girl babies. But by the age of 2, boys are less verbally expressive about emotion than girls, and one study found that by the age of 6, even their mothers couldn't tell what they were feeling by looking at their faces (they *could* tell what their daughters were feeling) (Levant, 2001). Sometime between infancy and age 6, little boys are taught to conceal their emotions. Conversely, parents encourage girls to express their emotions (Bornstein, 2006). Researchers have found that children who are emotionally expressive and who express *positive* emotions are more socially successful, are more positively evaluated by teachers as teachable students, and achieve more in school (Denham, 2006). Emotional expressiveness is also linked to mental and physical health (Bornstein, 2006).

Questions

Which biological and sociocultural factors play a role in a child's gender identity? What are the major theoretical views of children's acquisition of gender identity?

FAMILY INFLUENCES

Children are newcomers to the human group, strangers in an alien land. Genes do not convey *culture*, the socially standardized lifeways of a people. Clyde Kluckhohn (1960, pp. 21–22), a distinguished anthropologist, provides an illustration of this point:

Some years ago I met in New York City a young man who did not speak a word of English and was obviously bewildered by American ways. By "blood" he was as American as you or I, for his parents had gone from Indiana to China as missionaries. Orphaned in infancy, he was reared by a Chinese family in a remote village. All who met him found him more Chinese than American. The facts of his blue eyes and light hair were less impressive than a Chinese style of gait, Chinese arm and hand movements, Chinese facial expression, and Chinese modes of thought. The biological heritage was American, but the cultural training had been Chinese. He returned to China.

Families Convey Cultural Standards

The process of transmitting culture, of transforming children into functioning members of society, is called **socialization,** through which children acquire the knowledge, skills, and dispositions that enable them to participate effectively in group life. Infants enter a society that is already formed, and they need to be fitted to their

people's unique social environment. They must come to guide their behavior by the established standards, the accepted dos and don'ts, of their society. The child is first introduced to the requirements of group life within the family. By the time a child reaches the age of 2, the socialization process is already well under way. Developmental psychologists David P. Ausubel and Edmund V. Sullivan (1970, p. 260) observe:

At this time parents become less deferential and attentive. They comfort the child less and demand more conformity to their own desires and to cultural norms. During this period [in most societies] the child is frequently weaned, is expected to acquire sphincter control, approved habits of eating and cleanliness, and do more things for himself. Parents are less disposed to gratify his demands for immediate gratification, expect more frustration, tolerance, and responsible behavior, and may even require performance of some household chores. They also become less tolerant toward displays of childish aggression.

By their fourth birthday most children have mastered the complicated and abstract structure of their native language, and they can carry on complex social interactions in accordance with their own cultural patterns. Jay Belsky (1990; Belsky & Barends, 2002) proposes that the family is a network of interacting individuals functioning as a system, such that a minimum of three dyadic units are interacting: mother-father, mother-child, and father-child. Other influences affect the family system, including cultural norms, quality of marital relations, parental employment (dual-earner vs. single-earner), division of labor among family members, parenting practices, and infant-child behavior development.

Demographic Trends Affect Families Many researchers are studying how children are affected by the shifting cultural trends in marriage, divorce, nonmarital childbearing, migration of families, immigration patterns, education, work, income, poverty, cohabitation, and same-sex unions (Hetherington & Stanley-Hagan, 2002). These trends are related to major demographic and economic transformations over the past 100 years (Walsh, 2006): (1) the shift from farm to industrial to service work, (2) a significant reduction in family size, (3) greater educational attainment for men and women, (4) women's increasing participation in the labor force, (5) an increase in single-parent families and nonresidential or absentee fathers, (6) an increase in childhood poverty, (7) elders living longer, and (8) the movement for same-sex unions.

In addition to these trends, the ethnic diversity of American families and children will continue to increase, with the proportion of Hispanic American children increasing rapidly. It is projected that by 2023, more than half of U.S. children will be nonwhite. These major trends will certainly shape U.S. culture in interesting ways. Researchers are just beginning to study how various ethnic groups parent and socialize their children in the context of U.S. society.

Determinants of Parenting

Until relatively recently, most socialization research focused on how parents' child-rearing strategies and behaviors shape and influence children's development. Parenting styles vary by social class, by religious-ethnic group, and by the way parents themselves were raised. For the most part, psychologists and psychiatrists neglected the part children play as active agents in their own socialization and in influencing their caregivers' behavior.

This focus has changed over the past two decades, resulting in a more balanced perspective (Bornstein, 2006). Jay Belsky (1997) has provided a framework that differentiates among three major determinants of parental functioning: (1) the parents' personality and psychological well-being, (2) the child's characteristics, and (3) the contextual sources of stress and support operating within and upon the family (see Figure 8.1).

The Parents' Characteristics   Parenting, like other aspects of human functioning, is influenced by the personality of a man or woman (Belsky, 1990). So, as one

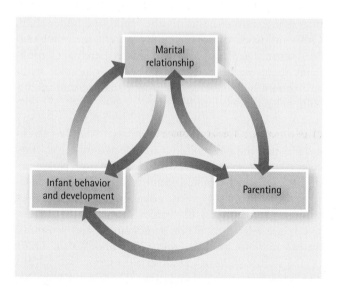

FIGURE 8.1 A Scheme for Integrating the Disciplines of Family Sociology and Developmental Psychology During the Infancy Years   The family is a network of interacting individuals functioning as a system—with interrelated influences that marital relations, parenting, and infant/child behavior/development may have on each member of the system. Positive affect (smiling, affection) between the wife and husband influences positive affect toward the child. And negative affect between wife and husband (hostility, verbal criticism) results in negative affect toward the child.

Source: Belsky, J. (1981). Early human experience: A family perspective. *Developmental Psychology, 17,* 6.

might expect, troubled parents are more likely to have troubled children (Emig, Moore, & Scarupa, 2001). A six-year study of 693 families found that more than half of the children with emotionally troubled mothers had psychological problems; nearly half of the children had problems in families where only the father had symptoms; and a majority had problems when both parents were disturbed (this was double the rate for children with two healthy parents) (Parker, 1987). Other researchers find that parental discord or stress can have an adverse effect on children (Lamb & Lewis, 2010). Many studies find that children of depressed mothers suffer adverse effects in childhood and call for effective prevention and intervention strategies to lessen adverse developmental effects in children (Guajardo, Snyder, & Petersen, 2009).

In contrast, children whose parents are happily married have more secure emotional ties to their parents and, as a result, seem to enjoy intellectual and other advantages over children of unhappily married people (Lamb & Lewis, 2010). Findings from a study that investigated family structure and child well-being indicated that mothers in two-parent biological families reported that their children had fewer behavioral problems, and fathers in two-parent biological families reported that they spent more time with their children and had higher family cohesion than parents in all other types of family structures (Lansford et al., 2001). Overall, though, researchers suggest that it is the processes within families that are important determinants of well-being, regardless of family structure (Lamb & Lewis, 2010).

The Child's Characteristics   Children's characteristics influence the parenting they receive (see Figure 8.2) (Sanson & Rothbart, 1995). These characteristics include such variables as age (Fagot & Kavanagh, 1993), gender (Kerig, Cowan, & Cowan, 1993), and temperament (Sanson & Rothbart, 1995). And some children are simply more difficult to rear than others (Shaw et al., 2006). Evidence suggests that parents and other caregivers typically react to disobedient, negative, and highly active youngsters with negative, controlling behavior of their own (Belsky, 1990).

Sources of Stress and Support   Parents do not undertake their parenting in a social vacuum. They are immersed in networks of relationships with relatives, friends, neighbors, and coworkers. These arenas of social interaction can be sources of stress or support or both. For instance, difficulties or arguments at work are likely to be followed by disagreements between a husband and wife (Bodenmann, Ledermann, & Bradbury, 2007). Yet social support networks, throughout life, have beneficial effects on us whether or not we are under stress (Ellis, Nixon, & Williamson, 2009). When we are integrated in social networks and groups, we have access to positive experiences and a set of stable, socially rewarding roles in the community (Cochran & Niego, 1995). Studies show that when teenage parents, particularly fathers, have support from their own parents, they are more likely to parent their own child in positive ways (Fagan, Bernd, & Whiteman, 2007).

Not surprisingly, then, research undertaken among Japanese and U.S. mothers shows that the adequacy of a woman's mothering is influenced by the perception she has of her marital relationship (see Figure 8.1). When a woman feels she has her husband's support, she is more likely to involve herself with her infant (Lamb & Lewis, 2010). Likewise, researchers find that parents with little social support do a poorer job of parenting than parents who are integrated in well-functioning support systems.

Key Child-Rearing Practices

Most authorities agree that parenting is one of the most rewarding yet difficult tasks any adult faces. Moreover, most parents are well intentioned and desire to succeed at parenting. Because this complex task encompasses many years and consumes much energy, parents have often looked to pediatricians or experts in child psychology to provide them with guidelines for rearing mentally and physically healthy youngsters (Morrow & Malin, 2004). But parents who turn to "authorities" can become immensely frustrated, for they will be confronted with an endless array of child-rearing books, conflicting information, and gimmickry. In the United Kingdom, social programs have been developed to help parents better use the information available to them (Morrow & Malin, 2004).

As we have already noted, until relatively recently psychologists assumed that socialization effects flow essentially in one direction—from parent to child. For some 50 years, roughly from 1925 to 1975, they dedicated themselves to understanding how different parenting practices shape a child's personality and behavior. This research found three dimensions to be significant:

- the *warmth or hostility* of the parent-child relationship
- the *control or autonomy* of the disciplinary approach
- the *consistency or inconsistency* that parents show in using discipline

The Warmth-Hostility Dimension   Many psychologists have insisted that one of the most significant aspects of the home environment is the warmth of the relationship between parent and child (Grolnick, 2003). Parents show warmth toward their children through affectionate, accepting, approving, understanding, and child-centered behaviors. When disciplining their children, parents who are warm employ frequent explanations, use words of encouragement and praise, and only infrequently resort to physical punishment. Hostility, in contrast, is shown through cold, rejecting, disapproving, self-centered, and highly punitive

behaviors (Grolnick, 2003). Wesley C. Becker (1964), in a review of the research on parenting, found that love-oriented techniques tend to promote children's acceptance of responsibility and to foster self-control through inner mechanisms of guilt. In contrast, parental hostility interferes with development of conscience and breeds aggressiveness and resistance to authority.

Parents who are substance abusers have a history of aggression, marital conflict, and negative interactions that correlate with behavioral maladjustment in children, especially for boys (Blackson et al., 1999), but whether treatment of the parents' substance abuse helps any but the youngest of children is unclear (Phillips, Gleeson, & Waites-Garrett, 2009). Children surviving in such dysfunctional home environments suffer through incidents of physical abuse, neglect, and repeated removal from the home by child protective services (McFarlane et al., 2003).

The Control-Autonomy Dimension   The second critical dimension is the range of restrictions that parents place on a child's behavior in such areas as sex play, modesty, table manners, toilet training, neatness, orderliness, care of household furniture, noise, obedience, and aggression toward others (Becker, 1964; Sears, Maccoby, & Levin, 1957). On the whole, psychologists have suggested that highly *restrictive* parenting fosters dependency and interferes with independence training (Grolnick, 2003; Maccoby & Masters, 1970). However, as Becker (1964, p. 197) observes, psychologists have had difficulty coming up with a "perfect" all-purpose set of parental guidelines.

Combinations of Parenting Approaches   Rather than examining the warmth-hostility and control-autonomy dimensions in isolation from one another, a number of psychologists have explored their four combinations: warmth-control, warmth-autonomy, hostility-control, and hostility-autonomy (Becker, 1964).

Warm but Restrictive Parenting   Warm but restrictive parenting is believed to lead to politeness, neatness, obedience, and conformity. It also is thought to be associated with immaturity, dependency, low creativity, blind acceptance of authority, and social withdrawal and ineptness (Becker, 1964). Eleanor E. Maccoby (1961) found that 12-year-old boys who had been reared in warm but restrictive homes were strict rule enforcers with their peers. Compared with other children, these boys also displayed less overt aggression, less misbehavior, and greater motivation toward schoolwork.

Warm with Democratic Procedures   Children whose homes combine warmth with democratic procedures (autonomy) tend to develop into socially competent, resourceful, friendly, active, and appropriately aggressive individuals (Grolnick, 2003). Where parents also encourage

Parenting Is One of the Most Rewarding but Difficult Tasks Any Adult Faces
Source: Lynn Johnston Productions Inc./Dist. By United Features Syndicate, Inc.

self-confidence, independence, and mastery in social and academic situations, the children are likely to show self-reliant, creative, goal-oriented, and responsible behavior. Where parents fail to foster independence, permissiveness often produces self-indulgent children with little impulse control and low academic standards.

Hostile (Rejecting) and Restrictive Parenting Hostile (rejecting) and restrictive parenting interferes with the child's developing sense of identity and self-esteem. Children come to see the world as dominated by powerful, malignant forces over which they have no control. The combination of hostility and restrictiveness is said to foster resentment and inner rage. These children turn some of the anger against themselves or experience it as internalized turmoil and conflict. This can result in "neurotic problems," self-punishing and suicidal tendencies, depressed affect, and inadequacy in adult role playing (Whitbeck et al., 1992).

Hostile and Permissive Parenting Parenting that combines hostility with permissiveness is thought to be associated with delinquent and aggressive behavior in children. Rejection breeds resentment and hostility, which, when combined with inadequate parental control, can be translated into aggressive and antisocial actions. When such parents do employ discipline, it is usually physical, capricious, and severe. It often reflects parental rage and rejection and hence fails as a constructive instrument for developing appropriate standards of conduct (Becker, 1964).

Discipline   Effective discipline is consistent and unambiguous and builds a high degree of predictability into the child's environment. Although it is often difficult to be consistent in how one disciplines a child, Parke and Deur (1972) reveal that erratic punishment generally fails to inhibit the punished behavior. Researchers have found that the most aggressive children have parents who are permissive toward aggression on some occasions but severely

punish it on others (Sears, Maccoby, & Levin, 1957). Inconsistency can occur when the same parent responds differently at different times to the same behavior. It can also occur when one parent ignores or encourages a behavior that the other parent punishes (Belsky, Crnic, & Gable, 1995).

Any discussion of discipline raises the controversial issue of corporal punishment. Although antispanking advocates feel very strongly about this issue, a 2004 survey found that over half of U.S. parents felt that spanking was appropriate as a regular form of punishment (Crary, 2004). Yet research shows that spanking has harmful effects that may affect a child for years. Young children who are punished with physical violence are likely to have behavior problems later, such as aggression, delinquency, mental-health problems, and criminality (Lansford et al., 2005).

Spanking also has harmful effects on a child's self-esteem. One study examined three groups of children over a period of two weeks: those who had experienced no physical punishment, those who had experienced low levels of physical punishment (one or two times), and those who had experienced high levels of physical punishment (three or more times). Researchers found that both groups of children who experienced physical punishment had lower self-esteem than the children who were not punished physically. These findings were the same for children from both rural and urban areas and regardless of the emotional climate of the family or race-ethnicity (Aucoin, Frick, & Bodin, 2006). Physical punishment is correlated with other forms of violence within the family, including sibling abuse and spouse assault (Zolotor et al., 2007).

Child Maltreatment

Many people have difficulty determining exactly where the line falls between legitimate effective discipline and child abuse. Most Americans define child abuse and neglect as leaving young children home alone, living in a filthy home and lacking food, and hitting a child hard enough to cause bruises. The federal Child Abuse Prevention and Treatment Act defines **child maltreatment** as

> Any recent act or failure to act on the part of a parent or caretaker, which results in death, serious physical or emotional harm, sexual abuse, or exploitation, or an act or failure to act which presents an imminent risk of serious harm. (Child Welfare Information Gateway, 2007)

Child Abuse and Neglect   In 2008 about 3.6 million American children were reported as victims of child abuse or neglect to Child Protective Services (CPS), with more than 770,000 confirmed victims. A high majority of victims experienced neglect, followed by physical abuse, sexual abuse, emotional abuse, and medical neglect. Slightly more girls than boys were victimized. The highest victimization rates were for the youngest age group (birth to age 3) followed by those aged 4 to 7 (see Figure 8.2). Nearly 1,800 American children died from abuse and neglect in 2009—and a high majority were age 4 and under (U.S. Department of Health and Human Services, 2010e). Most of these children were killed by their parents, acting alone or together. Female parents were the perpetrators of neglect and physical abuse for the highest percentage of child victims. Male relatives, parents, and strangers were identified as the perpetrators of sexual

abuse for the highest percentage of victims. Researchers believe that many cases of child abuse and neglect go unreported (Child Welfare Information Gateway, 2007). A small sample of children who experienced abuse before age 4 were followed from age 4 to age 10, and "anxiety/depression and attention problems emerged and grew more pronounced over time" (Thompson & Tabone, 2010).

Sexual Abuse of Children   **Sexual abuse** of children is "a type of maltreatment that refers to the involvement of the child in sexual activity to provide sexual gratification or financial benefit to the perpetrator, including contacts for sexual purposes, molestation, statutory rape, prostitution, pornography, exposure, incest, or other sexually exploitative activities" (Child Welfare Information Gateway, 2007). In 1974, the federal government passed the *Child Abuse Prevention and Treatment Act* (PL 93-247), which set identification standards, reporting policies, and management policies for these maltreatment cases, while empowering individual states to investigate abuse and provide child protective services (CPS). Public Law 108-36 reauthorized this law (*New Child Abuse Prevention and Treatment Act*). Many complex problems, issues, and costs to society arise regarding sexually abused children and the legal system (Bull, 2004).

Males are reported to be the abusers in a majority of cases (Kellogg, 2005). A national survey found that girls reported being sexually abused three times more often than boys, and most research has dealt with the sexual abuse of females (Kellogg, 2005). Researchers at the national level cautiously report a 40 percent decline in substantiated child sexual abuse cases over the past decade, partially due to a change in reporting practices, a more cautious approach to identification of abuse, more prevention/awareness programs, and more criminal convictions (Finkelhor & Jones, 2004).

Sexual contact typically consists at first of fondling and masturbation. The behavior continues over time and might proceed to intercourse or sodomy. Child molesters often disguise themselves as trusted, caring family members, neighbors, and responsible citizens. They spend a lot of time manipulating (grooming) a family so they will not be suspected of abusing children. Thus, child sexual abuse is often unreported. Male children are particularly reluctant to report abuse (Miller-Perrin & Perrin, 2007).

Children who have been sexually abused are more fearful, have post-traumatic stress disorder more often, exhibit more behavior problems and sexualized behaviors, and have lower self-esteem than other children (Finkelhor et al., 2005). Even though children might be too young to know that the sexual activity inflicted on them is "wrong," they will develop behavioral or physical problems resulting from their inability to cope with the

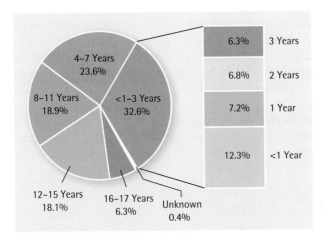

FIGURE 8.2 U.S. Child Victims of Maltreatment by Age, 2008 Children younger than 4 years of age account for a high percentage of child maltreatment that is reported and substantiated. In 2008, one or both parents were involved in the majority of child maltreatment cases, and in the majority of child fatalities as well.

Source: U.S. Department of Health and Human Services, Administration on Children and Families. (2010). *Child maltreatment 2008*. Washington, DC: U.S. Government Printing Office.

overstimulation. Children who have been abused become experts at reading subtle signals that a perpetrator is angry (Dubow, Huesmann, & Greenwood, 2007). Often there are no obvious physical signs of child abuse, only signs that a physician can detect, such as changes in the genital or anal area. Behavioral signs are likely to include any of the following:

- unusual interest in, or avoidance of, all things of a sexual nature
- sleep problems, nightmares, bedwetting
- depression or withdrawal from friends or family
- sexually inappropriate behaviors with others or knowledge beyond the child's years
- statements that their bodies are dirty or fear that there is something wrong in the genital area
- refusal to go to school or delinquent behaviors
- aspects of sexual molestation in drawings, games, fantasies
- unusual aggressiveness, secretiveness, suicidal behaviors (even in a younger child), or other severe behavior changes

Sexually abused children are usually afraid to tell others about their experiences because the abuser will control/manipulate the child by saying such things as "Mommy won't love you anymore" or "No one will believe you since you are a child." When a father sexually abuses his daughters, he places them at greater risk of sexual abuse by other male relatives and family friends. Female victims tend to show lifetime patterns of shame and stigmatization, and they tend to see themselves as less powerful in their relationships with others (Bugental & Grusec, 2006).

Because boys are socialized to gain control of themselves and their environments, boys may feel their masculinity has been destroyed when they are sexually abused. Complicating matters, male victims often face the additional problem of stigmatization as homosexual, because the large majority of abusers are male (Finkelhor et al., 2005).

Reporting and Prevention   Sexual abuse (and any type of suspected abuse) should always be reported to authorities; and law enforcement officers, child-care workers, teachers, social workers, and medical and dental professionals are mandated by law to do so. Adults should never dismiss a child's complaint of maltreatment. Many prevention programs have been designed that use multiple modes of multimedia technology (film, video, audiotape, and filmstrip) and format (storybooks, coloring books, songs, anatomical dolls, and board games). Numerous criminal justice, government, and human services agencies have responded to the problem of child abuse and offer a wide range of perspectives from which to combat it (Finkelhor et al., 2005).

Questions

What are some effective, healthy child-rearing practices? What are the various forms of child abuse, and which children are most at risk for severe abuse? What are some behaviors exhibited by children who are victims of sexual abuse, and what can be done to protect them from harm?

Parenting Styles

Developmental psychologist Diana Baumrind (1971, 1980, 1996) examines the relationship between parental child-rearing styles and social competence in children of preschool and school age. From 1968 through 1980, she conducted research for *The Family Socialization Project,* examining family socialization practices, parental attitudes, and factors of development at three crucial stages in a child's life: preschool, early childhood, and early adolescence. She included both parents and children from white middle-class families in her sample. In her studies of white middle-class nursery-school children, Baumrind (1971) found that different types of parenting tend to be related to quite different behaviors in children. Among other findings in this longitudinal study, she distinguishes among authoritarian, authoritative, permissive, and harmonious parenting.

Authoritarian Parenting   The **authoritarian parenting** style attempts to shape, control, and evaluate a child's behavior in accordance with traditional and absolute values and standards of conduct. Obedience is stressed, verbal give-and-take is discouraged, and punitive, forceful discipline is preferred. More commonly, parents who use this style of parenting are said to be operating from the *rejecting-demanding dimension.* The offspring of such authoritarian parents tended to be discontented, withdrawn, and distrustful (see Figure 8.3).

Authoritative Parenting   The **authoritative parenting** style provides firm direction for a child's overall activities but gives the child considerable freedom within reasonable limits. The parent provides reasons for given policies and engages in verbal give-and-take with the child, meanwhile responding to the child's wishes and needs. (It may help you to distinguish authorita*tive* from authoritarian by using the mnemonic device of *give*-and-take with authorita*tive*.) Authoritative parenting was often associated with self-reliant, self-controlled, explorative, and contented children. In later research, Baumrind (1996) found that an authoritative parenting style is especially helpful when parenting adolescents.

Baumrind believes that authoritative parenting gives children a comfortable, supported feeling while they

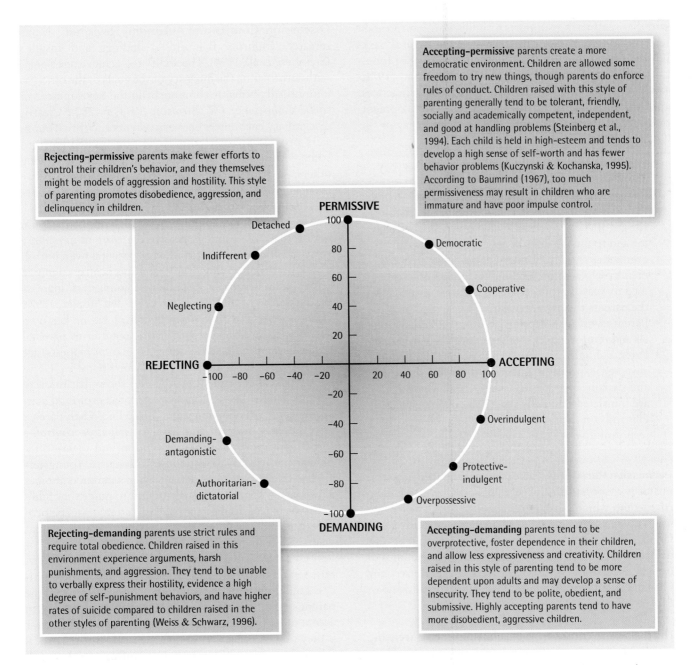

Rejecting-permissive parents make fewer efforts to control their children's behavior, and they themselves might be models of aggression and hostility. This style of parenting promotes disobedience, aggression, and delinquency in children.

Accepting-permissive parents create a more democratic environment. Children are allowed some freedom to try new things, though parents do enforce rules of conduct. Children raised with this style of parenting generally tend to be tolerant, friendly, socially and academically competent, independent, and good at handling problems (Steinberg et al., 1994). Each child is held in high-esteem and tends to develop a high sense of self-worth and has fewer behavior problems (Kuczynski & Kochanska, 1995). According to Baumrind (1967), too much permissiveness may result in children who are immature and have poor impulse control.

Rejecting-demanding parents use strict rules and require total obedience. Children raised in this environment experience arguments, harsh punishments, and aggression. They tend to be unable to verbally express their hostility, evidence a high degree of self-punishment behaviors, and have higher rates of suicide compared to children raised in the other styles of parenting (Weiss & Schwarz, 1996).

Accepting-demanding parents tend to be overprotective, foster dependence in their children, and allow less expressiveness and creativity. Children raised in this style of parenting tend to be more dependent upon adults and may develop a sense of insecurity. They tend to be polite, obedient, and submissive. Highly accepting parents tend to have more disobedient, aggressive children.

FIGURE 8.3 **Baumrind's Research Expands on the Interaction of Parenting Dimensions** Two parenting dimensions have been observed in all societies: the permissive-demanding dimension and the accepting-rejecting dimension (Rohner & Rohner, 1981). Some research findings indicate that parental choice of these dimensions—especially for the demanding style—may be influenced by the parent's genetic makeup; other findings suggest that the parent's own upbringing has a significant bearing on parental practices (Plomin, DeFries, & Fulker, 2006).

Adapted from Schaefer, E. S. (1959). A circumplex model for maternal behavior. *Journal of Abnormal and Social Psychology, 59,* 232; and M. L. Hoffman and L. W. Hoffman. (1964). *Review of Child Development Research*. Reprinted by permission.

explore the environment and gain interpersonal competence. Such children do not experience the anxiety and fear associated with strict, repressive parenting or the indecision and uncertainty associated with unstructured, permissive parenting. Laurence Steinberg and colleagues (1989) also found that authoritative parenting facilitates school success, encouraging a healthy sense of autonomy

and positive attitudes toward work. Adolescents whose parents treat them this way are more likely than their peers to develop positive beliefs about their achievement and so are likely to do better in school.

In addition, authoritative fathers and mothers seem more adept than other parents at scaffolding (helping a child learn at his or her own level). Vygotsky (1962, 1978) said that **scaffolding** supports a child's learning through interventions and tutoring that provide helpful task information attuned to the child's current level of functioning. On the basis of her research, Baumrind (1971, 1980, 1996) found a number of parental practices and attitudes that seem to facilitate the development of socially responsible and independent behavior in children:

- Parents who are socially responsible and assertive and who serve as daily models of these behaviors foster these characteristics in their children.
- Parents should use firm enforcement policies to reward socially responsible and independent behavior and to punish deviant behavior. Parents can be even more effective if their demands are accompanied by explanations and if punishment is accompanied by reasons that are consistent with principles the parents themselves live by.
- Parents who are accepting are more attractive models and reinforcing agents than rejecting parents.
- Parents should emphasize and encourage individuality, self-expression, initiative, divergent thinking, and socially appropriate assertiveness. These values are translated into daily realities as parents make demands on their children and assign them responsibility.

Permissive Parenting   The **permissive parenting** style provides a nonpunitive, accepting, and affirmative environment in which the children regulate their own behavior as much as possible. The children are consulted about family policies and decisions. The parents make few demands on the children for household responsibility or orderly behavior. The least self-reliant, explorative, and self-controlled children were those with permissive parents (see Figure 8.3).

Harmonious Parenting   The **harmonious parenting** style seldom exercises direct control over a child. These parents attempt to cultivate an egalitarian relationship—one in which the child is not placed at a power disadvantage. Parents typically emphasize humane values, rather than the predominantly materialistic and competitive values operating within mainstream society. The harmonious parents identified by Baumrind were only a small group. Of the eight children studied from such families, six were girls and two were boys. The girls were extraordinarily competent, independent, friendly, achievement-oriented, and intelligent. The boys, in contrast, were cooperative but notably submissive, aimless, dependent, and not achievement-oriented. Although the sample was too small to be the basis for definitive conclusions, Baumrind tentatively suggests that these outcomes of harmonious parenting might be sex-related.

Discussion: Control and Autonomy Revisited   Much research confirms Baumrind's findings and insights (Steinberg et al., 1994). The ability to "achieve one's goals without violating the integrity of the goals of the other" is undoubtedly a major component in the development of social competence (W. Bronson, 1974, p. 280). Clearly, disciplinary encounters between parents and their youngsters provide a crucial context in which children learn strategies for controlling themselves and for controlling others, so parents who model competent strategies are more likely to have children who also are socially competent (Regalado, Sareen, Inkelas, Wissow, & Halfon, 2004).

By way of illustration, consider Erik Erikson's (1963) notion that how toddlers resolve the issue of *autonomy* versus *shame and doubt* is linked to parental overcontrol. The 2-year-old's saying "No!" is a spectacular cognitive achievement because it accompanies youngsters' increasing awareness of the "other" and the "self" (Spitz, 1957). *Self-assertion* (the child's expression of his or her own desire), *defiance* (deliberately acting counter to parental requests), and *compliance* (doing as a parent requests) are distinct dimensions of toddler behavior.

Crockenberg and Litman (1990) show that the way parents handle these autonomy issues has profound consequences for their youngsters' behavior. When parents assert their power in the form of *negative control*—threats, criticism, physical intervention, and anger—children are more likely to respond with defiance. Youngsters are less likely to become defiant when a parent combines a directive with an additional attempt to guide the child's behavior in a desired direction. This latter approach provides the child with information about what the parent wants, while inviting power sharing.

This approach is consistent with Baumrind's *authoritative* style of parenting and keeps the negotiation process going, allowing the toddler to "decide" to adopt the parent's goal. It seems that children are more willing to accept other people's attempts to influence their behavior if they perceive that they are participating in a reciprocal relationship where their attempts to influence others will also be honored (Kochanska & Aksan, 1995).

Guidance alone seems less effective than guidance combined with control. An invitation to comply ("Could you pick up the toys now?") seems to offer the toddler a choice, and the child might feel free to turn it down in the absence of a clear and firm expression of parental wishes. This approach of guidance without control is consistent with Baumrind's *permissive* style of parenting and seems to be linked to less competent child behavior. When toddlers assert themselves and their parents follow with a power directive ("You better do what I say or I'll spank you!"), the children might interpret the behavior as an assertion of parental power and a diminution of their own autonomy—an approach in keeping with Baumrind's *authoritarian* style of parenting (Silk, Morris, Kanaya, & Steinberg, 2003).

Overall, it seems that parents who are most effective in eliciting compliance from their youngsters and deflecting defiance are quite clear about what they want their children to do but are prepared to listen to their children's objections and to make appropriate accommodations in ways that convey respect for their youngsters' individuality and autonomy (Gralinski & Kopp, 1993). These parental behaviors encourage and elicit competent behavior from the child (Belsky et al., 2008).

Questions

According to Diana Baumrind, what are the four main styles of parenting and which is considered most effective? How does each style affect the child's behavior?

Gaining Perspective on Parenting The parenting dimensions and styles that we have considered thus far have focused on broader patterns and practices. But they are much too abstract to capture the subtleties of parent-child interaction. In everyday life parents exhibit a great variety of parenting behaviors, depending on many factors: the situation; the child's gender and age; the parents' inferences regarding the child's mood, motives, and intentions; the child's understanding of the situation; the social supports available to the parent; the pressures parents feel from other adults; and so forth (Dix, Ruble, & Zambarano, 1989).

The child's response to being disciplined also modifies the parent's behavior and the parent's choice of future disciplinary measures. And the way the child perceives the actions of the parent can be more decisive than the parent's actions in themselves. Children are not interchangeable; they do not all respond in identical fashion to the same type of caregiver behavior (Kochanska, 1995).

The Harvard Child-Rearing Study A classic study helps us clarify some of these matters. In the 1950s three Harvard psychologists carried out one of the most enterprising U.S. studies of child rearing ever undertaken. Robert Sears, Eleanor Maccoby, and Harry Levin (1957) attempted to identify parenting techniques that make a difference in personality development. They interviewed 379 mothers of kindergartners and rated each mother on about 150 different child-rearing practices. Some 25 years later, other Harvard psychologists led by David C. McClelland (McClelland et al., 1978) contacted many of these children, who were then 31 years old. Most were married and had children of their own.

McClelland and his associates interviewed them and administered psychological tests. They concluded that not much of what people think and do as adults is determined by the specific techniques of child rearing their

parents used during their first five years. It is how parents *feel* about their children that they found made a difference. The Harvard researchers express their conclusion as follows:

> How can parents do right by their children? If they are interested in promoting moral and social maturity in later life, the answer is simple: They should love them, enjoy them, and want them around. They should not use their power to maintain a home that is designed only for the self-expression and pleasure of adults. They should not regard their children as disturbances to be controlled at all costs. (McClelland et al., 1978, p. 53)

American Family Structures According to the Federal Interagency Forum report *America's Children in Brief: Key National Indicators of Well-Being, 2009,*

- 67 percent of children under 18 currently live with two married parents (including biological, adoptive, and stepparents)
- 26 percent of children live with a single parent (80 percent with a single mother)
- 6 percent live with a parent or parents who are cohabiting
- 5 percent of children live with fathers only
- 4 percent live with neither parent (with grandparents, with other relatives, or in foster care)

Family structure has an impact on the poverty rate of children. In 2008, female-headed households with no father present had a poverty rate five times that of two-parent households (Federal Interagency Forum on Child and Family Statistics, 2011). Figure 8.4 provides data on poverty rates by family type. Children in low-income families experience economic insecurity, poor health, nutrition, and/or medical problems, developmental delays, and problems learning in school. They also tend to drop out of school, become single parents, and experience unemployment as adults (Federal Interagency Forum on Child and Family Statistics, 2011). In 2008, nearly one of out five children was living in poverty—the highest rate since 1998; the poverty rate is even higher for many minority families. The National Center for Children in Poverty estimates that over one-third of the nation's children live in families that do not earn enough income to support them (Fass & Cauthen, 2007). For more about the impact of poverty on preschool children, see the *More Information You Can Use* box on page 255, "Preparing the Nation's Most Vulnerable Children for Kindergarten."

Divorce The divorce rate in the United States peaked in 1981 and has been declining ever since. Today, the divorce rate of 3.6 per 1,000 married couples is the lowest it has

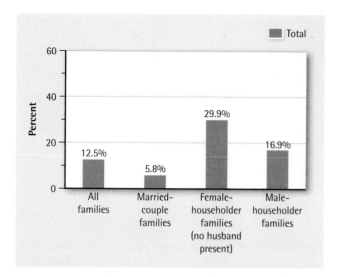

FIGURE 8.4 Poverty Rates by Family Type: 2009 In 2009, the poverty rate was the highest in 11 years, with more than 14 percent of all U.S. residents considered to be living in poverty. In 2009, the poverty line for a family of four was $21,954; for a family of three it was $17,098. People in female-householder families had a poverty rate five times greater than their counterparts in married-couple families.

Source: DeNavas-Walt, C., Proctor, B. D., & Smith, J. (2010). *Income, Poverty, and Health Insurance Coverage in the United States: 2009*. U.S. Census Bureau, *Current Population Reports* (P60-238,Table 4). Washington, DC: U.S. Government Printing Office. Retrieved January 3, 2011, from http://www.census.gov/prod/2010pubs/p60-238.pdf

been since 1970. The divorce of parents has a major impact on children's lives. Divorce is a process that begins well before parents separate and continues long afterward (Barber & Demo, 2006). The most common family arrangement in the period immediately following a divorce is for the children to live with their single mothers and to have only intermittent contact with their fathers.

Many of the stressors that parents experience following divorce and the accompanying changes in their lifestyles are reflected in their relationships with their children (Sandler, Miles, Cookston, & Braver, 2008). Hetherington and colleagues (1976, p. 424) found that the interaction patterns between the divorced parents and their children differed significantly from those encountered in the intact families:

Divorced parents make fewer maturity demands of their children, communicate less well with their children, tend to be less affectionate with their children and show marked inconsistency in discipline and lack of control over their children in comparison to parents in intact families. Poor parenting seems most marked, particularly for divorced mothers, one year after divorce, which seems to be a peak of stress in parent-child relations. . . . Two years following the divorce, mothers are demanding more . . . [independent and] mature behavior of their children, communicate better and use more explanation and reasoning, are more nurturant and consistent and are

better able to control their children than they were the year before. A similar pattern is occurring for divorced fathers in maturity demands, communication and consistency, but they are becoming less nurturant and more detached from their children. . . . Divorced fathers were ignoring their children more and showing less affection [while their extremely permissive and "every day is Christmas" behavior declined].

Hence, many single-parent families had a difficult period of readjustment following the divorce, but the situation generally improved during the second year. Hetherington has found that much depends on the ability of the custodial mother to control her children. Children whose mothers maintain good control show no drop in school performance (Hetherington & Kelly, 2003).

Joint-Custody Arrangements   Researchers find that the quality of the child's relationships with *both* parents is the best predictor of her or his postdivorce adjustment (Amato, 2000). Children who maintain stable, loving relationships with both parents appear to have fewer emotional scars— they exhibit less stress and less aggressive behavior, and their school performance and peer relations are better— than children lacking such relationships (Bauserman, 2002). Children in joint-custody arrangements were found to be better adjusted than those in sole-custody arrangements but no different from those in intact families (Bauserman, 2002). With **joint custody,** both parents share equally in making significant child-rearing decisions, and both parents share in regular child-care responsibilities. The child lives with each parent a substantial amount of time—for example, the child might spend part of the week or month in one parent's house and part in the other's. Joint custody eliminates the "winner/loser" character of custodial disposition and much of the sadness, sense of loss, and loneliness that the noncustodial parent frequently feels (Hetherington & Kelly, 2003).

But joint custody is not an answer for all children. Critics point out that parents who cannot agree during marriage cannot reach agreement on rules, discipline, and styles of parenting after divorce. Alternating between homes interferes with a child's need for continuity in his or her life. Furthermore, the mobile nature of contemporary society and the likelihood that parents will remarry render a good many joint-custody arrangements vulnerable to collapse (Hetherington & Kelly, 2003). Initial evidence suggests that joint-custody arrangements do not differ from sole-custody arrangements in children's adjustment to divorce (Donnelly & Finkelhor, 1992).

With respect to school achievement, social adjustment, and delinquent behavior, the differences are small or nonexistent between children from one- and two-parent homes of comparable social status (Amato, 2000, 2005). Some research suggests that children and adolescents from

MORE INFORMATION YOU CAN USE

Preparing the Nation's Most Vulnerable Children for Kindergarten

Each fall millions of 4- and 5-year-olds begin a new phase of cognitive and social development when they enter kindergarten (see Figure 8.5). School staff, government officials, and researchers realize that a child's transition to kindergarten is an important event for the entire family. "Research has made it increasingly clear that children's school and later life success depends not only on children's cognitive skills, but also on their physical and mental health, emotional well-being, and ability to relate to others" (Hair, Halle, Terry-Humen, Lavelle, & Calkins, 2006, p. 440). Thus, a consensus has developed that a child's attendance in a high-quality preschool program is a strong predictor for success in school (Magnuson & Waldfogel, 2005).

Preschool programs are particularly important for children whose families live in poverty, for children of immigrant parents, and for black and Hispanic children. Each of these social groups faces multiple challenges as they raise their children. Many parents in these families work two jobs to support the family. Some are single-parent families. Immigrant families are also working hard to blend the values of their own culture with the values their children encounter through the media and at school. But they all share one common goal—they want their children to do well in school.

Researchers measure school readiness using five categories: physical well-being and motor development, emotional and social development, learning style, language skills, and general knowledge (Hair et al., 2006). Poverty affects all five areas. Children who live in poverty are more likely to be low-birth-weight babies, which has an effect on cognitive development in the preschool years. They are more likely to live in areas where they are exposed to lead and toxic chemicals, affecting cognitive development and health. Their parents' employment is more likely to be insecure, causing stress at home and even food insecurity. Poor children are less likely to be read to by a parent, which affects the development of language skills. Poor children are more likely to live in households where there are high levels of stress from abuse, neglect, and maltreatment. Poverty takes a heavy toll on the development of young children, and this puts them at a disadvantage as they enter the school system (see Figure 8.5).

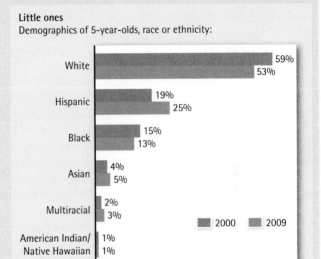

Little ones
Demographics of 5-year-olds, race or ethnicity:

White 59% / 53%
Hispanic 19% / 25%
Black 15% / 13%
Asian 4% / 5%
Multiracial 2% / 3%
American Indian/Native Hawaiian 1% / 1%

■ 2000 ■ 2009

FIGURE 8.5 Actual U.S. Kindergarten Enrollment: Class of 2010–2011 (in percent) Increasing numbers of American children will be enrolling in kindergarten programs in the next decade. These kindergartners will come from more racially diverse families.
El Nasser, H., & Overberg, P. (2010, August 27). Kindergartens see more Hispanic, Asian students. *USA Today Weekend*. p. 1A. Retrieved from http://www.usatoday.com/news/nation/census/2010-08-27-1Akindergarten27_ST_N.htm

What types of interventions work in helping children overcome obstacles to school success? High-quality preschool for all children, not just those whose parents can afford it, would do much to close the gap in readiness associated with race-ethnicity (Magnuson & Waldfogel, 2005). Multiple studies have shown that preschool programs that include the parents of young children are far more likely to improve a child's success in school than programs that interact with the child only. Programs that include parents increase the likelihood that immigrant children will attend preschool and stay in preschool. An important issue for immigrant families is how well a preschool program fits their beliefs and values regarding education.

single-parent homes show less delinquent behavior, less psychosomatic illness, better adjustment to their parents, and better self-concepts than those from unhappy intact homes (Demo & Cox, 2000). Even so, either an unhappy marriage or a divorce entails adverse outcomes for

children. Each alternative brings its own sets of stressors (Amato, 2000, 2005). In many cases, divorce reduces the amount of friction and unhappiness a child experiences, leading to better behavioral adjustments (Maldonado, 2009). Overall, research strongly suggests that the quality of children's relationships with their parents matters much more than the fact of divorce (Hetherington & Stanley-Hagan, 2002).

Society has increasingly come to recognize that the single-parent home is a different, but viable, family form. The nation's public and private schools, communities, and churches are assisting the increasing number of single-parent families with before-school and after-school child-care programs and with summer school enrichment or remedial classes for children of all ages. Some school districts have restructured the school day or extended the school year to 12 months with periodic breaks, to meet the particular needs of single-parent families.

Summing Up Clearly, parenting is not a matter of employing a guaranteed set of formulas. Cultures differ, parents differ, and children differ. Parents who employ identical "good" child-rearing techniques have children who grow up to be exceedingly different (Plomin et al., 2001). Furthermore, situations differ, and what works in one setting can boomerang in another. The essence of parenting resides in the parent-child relationship. In their interactions, parents and children evolve ongoing accommodations that reflect each other's needs and desires. Parent-child relationships differ so much, both within the same family and among families, that in many respects each parent-child relationship is unique (Elkind, 1974; Plomin et al., 2001). There is no mysterious secret method that parents must master. It is the child that matters, not the technique, although child-rearing experts believe that parents should not use severe punishment. On the whole, most parents do very well.

> ### Questions
>
> What types of parenting styles seem to promote emotionally healthy children? In addition to the traditional biological, two-parent family, what are some other types of family household structures evident in the United States today? What factors are associated with a young child's healthy emotional adjustment to parental divorce?

Sibling Relationships

A child's relationships with sisters and brothers within the family are very important (Dunn, Slomkowski, & Beardsall, 1994). For children who are experiencing stress, siblings represent an important support system (Gass, Jenkins, & Dunn, 2007). A child's position in the family and the number and sex of his or her siblings are thought to have major consequences for the child's development and socialization (Volling & Belsky, 1992). These factors structure the child's social environment, providing a network of

Sibling Interactions Are Important in All Societies The fact that each child occupies a different position in the birth order of her or his family establishes a somewhat different social web or environment for every sibling. Siblings typically maintain strong bonds throughout life.

key relationships and roles (E. Brody et al., 1994). An only child, an oldest child, a middle child, and a youngest child all seem to experience a somewhat different world because of the different social webs that permeate their lives, even though they usually receive the same style of parenting.

Some psychologists contend that these and other environmental influences operate to make two children in the same family as different from each other as are children in different families (Daniels, 1986). These psychologists say that there is a unique *micro environment* in the family for each child. In this view there is not a single family but, rather, as many "different" families as there are children to experience them. These psychologists conclude that the small degree of similarity in personality found among siblings results almost totally from shared genes, rather than from shared experience.

The "pioneering function" of older brothers and sisters can persist throughout life, providing role models for how to cope with such life events as getting a job, going to college, bereavement, retirement, or widowhood (Rosenthal, 1992). Indeed, as a consequence of today's frequent divorces and remarriages, the sibling bond has received closer research attention (Sheehan et al., 2004). Sibling relationships typically become more egalitarian, but also less intense, as youngsters move into later childhood and adolescence (Buhrmester & Furman, 1990).

Children and Birth Order Worldwide, across many cultures, firstborns are more likely than later-borns to have elaborate birth ceremonies, to become a namesake (receive the paternal name), to inherit privileges and rank, and to have authority over and respect from siblings. Firstborn sons generally have more control of property, more power in the society, and higher social positions (Leman, 2009; Sulloway, 1997). Moreover, older siblings act as caregivers for their younger siblings in a good many cultures (Dunn, 2007).

Firstborn children continue to be the focus of much research, for they appear to be fortune's favorites (Sulloway, 1997). They tend to be high achievers in many professional fields, and they make up a majority of U.S. presidents and Supreme Court appointees. Findings from many studies suggest that (1) firstborns are viewed as intelligent, obedient, secure, and responsible; (2) middle children are viewed as ambitious, caring, friendly, and thoughtful; (3) lastborns are believed to be the most creative, emotional, friendly, disobedient, and talkative—and the least responsible; and (4) only children are viewed as independent and self-centered (Leman, 2009). Leman (2009) finds that later-borns seem to possess better social skills than firstborns.

Research reveals that parents attach greater importance to their first child (Sulloway, 1997). More social, affectionate, and caretaking interactions occur between parents and their firstborn (Leman, 2009). Firstborns have more exposure to adult models and to adult expectations and pressures (Sulloway, 1997). Parents and others tend to react differently toward firstborn and later-born children, which in turn reinforces personality stereotypes.

A second explanation of the differences between first- and later-born children derives from **confluence theory,** a model devised by Zajonc and Mullally (1997). Confluence theory gets its name from the view that the intellectual development of a family is like a river, with the inputs of each family member flowing into it. According to Zajonc, the oldest sibling experiences a richer intellectual environment than younger siblings do. A third theory, the **resource dilution hypothesis,** says that in large families, resources (parental time, material goods, and cultural opportunities) get spread thin, to the detriment of all the offspring. Additional siblings reduce the share of parental resources available to each. These resources have an important effect on children's educational achievement and socioemotional development (Zajonc & Mullally, 1997).

Another explanation, which was first advanced by Alfred Adler, stresses the part that sibling power and status rivalry play in a child's personality formation (Adler, 1964). Adler viewed the "dethroning" of the firstborn as a crucial event in the development of the first child. With the birth of a sister or brother, the firstborn suddenly loses his or her monopoly on parental attention (Dunn, 1986). This loss, Adler said, arouses a strong lifelong need for recognition, attention, and approval that the child, and later the adult, seeks to acquire through high achievement. Another critical factor in the development of the later-born child is the competitive race for achievement with older and more accomplished siblings. In many cases the rancor disappears when individuals get older and learn to manage their own careers and married lives (Dunn, 1986).

> **Questions**
>
> In what ways do older siblings influence younger ones in terms of motivation, self-esteem, and social support? In general, how does a child's position in the birth order of a family affect her or his personality?

NONFAMILIAL SOCIAL INFLUENCES

We have seen that children enter a world of people, an encompassing social network. With time, specific relationships change in form, intensity, and function, but the social network itself stretches across the life span. Yet social and behavioral scientists mostly ignored the rich tapestry of children's social networks until the past two decades. They regarded social intimacy as centering on one relationship, that between the infant and mother, and treated young children's ties with other family members and with agemates as if they did not exist or had no importance.

However, a growing body of research points to the significance of other relationships in the development of interpersonal competencies. In this section we explore children's peer relationships and friendships. **Peers** are individuals who are approximately the same age. Early friendship is a major source of a youngster's emotional strength, and a child who does not have friends can face lifelong risks (Newcomb & Bagwell, 1995).

Peer Relationships and Friendships

From birth to death we find ourselves immersed in countless relationships. Few are as important to us as those we have with our peers and friends (Newcomb & Bagwell, 1995). Children as young as 3 years of age form friendships with other children that are surprisingly similar to those of adults (Verba, 1994). Some child relationships are reminiscent of strong adult attachments; others, of relationships between adult mentors and protégés; and still others, of the camaraderie of adult coworkers. Although young children lack the reflective understanding that many adults bring to their relationships, they often invest in their friendships with an intense emotional quality (Selman, 1980). Some young children bring a considerable measure of social competence to their relationships, and most eventually develop a high level of give-and-take (Doyle & Smith, 2002).

As we saw in Chapter 6, attachment theory predicts that the quality of the mother-child tie has implications for the child's close personal relationships. Researchers

All Young Children Enjoy and Benefit from Peer Relationships and Friendships

confirm that preschoolers with secure maternal attachments enjoy more harmonious, less controlling, more responsive, and happier relationships with their peers than do preschoolers with insecure maternal attachments (Lucas-Thompson & Clarke-Stewart, 2007).

A variety of studies reveal that with increasing age, peer relationships are more likely to be formed and more likely to be successful (Doyle & Smith, 2002). Children of preschool age sort themselves into same-sex play groups (Maccoby, 1990). In a longitudinal study, Eleanor E. Maccoby and Carol N. Jacklin (1987) found that preschoolers at 4½ years of age spent three times as much time playing with same-sex playmates as they did with opposite-sex playmates. Moreover, preschool girls tend to interact in small groups, especially two-person groups, whereas boys more often play in larger groups (Eder & Hallinan, 1978). Four-year-olds spend about two-thirds of the time when they are in contact with other people associating with adults and one-third of the time with peers. By 6½ years of age, the youngsters were spending a majority of time with same-sex peers.

Eleven-year-olds spend about an equal amount of time with adults and with peers (Wright, 1967). Several factors contribute to this shift in interactive patterns: (1) As children grow older, their communication skills improve, facilitating effective interaction (Eckerman & Didow, 1988). (2) Children's increasing cognitive competencies enable them to attune themselves more effectively to the roles of others (Verba, 1994). (3) Nursery, preschool, pre-K, and elementary school attendance offers increasing opportunities for peer interaction. (4) Increasing motor competencies expand the child's ability to participate in many joint activities. Children play an important

part as reinforcing agents and behavioral models for one another, a fact that adults at times overlook. Much learning takes place as a result of children's interaction with other children (Ladd, Buhs, & Seid, 2000).

Aggression in Children

Aggression is behavior that is socially defined as injurious or destructive to people, animals, and objects. Children—both boys and girls—begin to exhibit aggressive behavior as early as 12 months of age (Alink et al., 2006). The proportion of aggressive acts of the undirected temper-tantrum type decreases gradually during the first three years of life and then shows a sharp decline after the age of 4. In contrast, the relative frequency of retaliatory responses increases with age, especially after children reach their third birthday. Although physical aggression typically decreases between the ages of 3 and 4, verbal aggression increases from the age of 3 (Alink et al., 2006). Some researchers posit that the decline in physical aggression is attributable to increasing language skills and a growing capacity for empathy.

In the preschool years, most children learn to regulate this behavior and use other techniques besides violence. However, some children do not, and these children are at a high risk of serious antisocial behavior in their teenage and adult years (Tremblay et al., 2004). Certain aspects of family life are predictors that a child will not learn to regulate aggression. Those children whose mothers started childbearing very early, whose mothers have a history of antisocial behavior during their school years, and whose mothers smoke during pregnancy are less likely to learn to control aggression. Children in households where income is inadequate and children whose parents have serious difficulties living together are also at high risk of being unable to learn to regulate aggression (Tremblay et al., 2004). Youngsters who see and hear angry exchanges among adults become emotionally distressed and respond by aggressing against their peers (Vuchinich, Bank, & Patterson, 1992). Toddlers and preschool children who have been maltreated, especially those who have been physically abused, are more likely to engage in levels of aggressive behavior that are beyond the norm for their age groups (Zoccolillo, Paquette, & Tremblay, 2005). Boys in single-parent households, particularly when the mother has limited education, appear to benefit from intervention, however (Benzies, Keown, & Magill-Evans, 2009).

Girls and boys differ in how they express their aggression toward peers. Boys tend to harm others through physical and verbal aggression; their concerns typically center on getting their way and dominating other youngsters. Girls, in contrast, tend to focus on relational aggression; they attempt to harm others by damaging their friendships or their sense of peer-group inclusion by such acts as spreading negative rumors, excluding the child from a play group, and purposefully withdrawing friendship or acceptance (Alink et al., 2006).

More aggressive children, particularly boys, report that aggression produces tangible rewards and reduces negative treatment by other children (Trachtenberg & Viken, 1994). Aggression, hostility, bullying, defiance, and destructiveness are signs of **antisocial behavior,** which involves *persistent* violations of socially prescribed patterns of behavior (Tremblay et al., 2004). Between 4 and 6 million children in schools have been identified with conduct disorder, and the numbers are rising (Kazdin, Marciano, & Whitley, 2005). Research (Tremblay et al., 2004) suggests that aggressive, antisocial behavior among children is not "just a phase" to be outgrown; antisocial behavior in early childhood is the most accurate predictor of delinquency in adolescence. If an antisocial behavior pattern is not altered by the end of third grade, it can become chronic, and prevention and early intervention are the best hopes we have of diverting children from this path.

Some intervention programs for aggressive preschool children have proved effective. Removing stressors in a child's family life helps break the link between child maltreatment and aggression. Toddlers who benefited from nurse visit interventions grew up to be adolescents who were less likely to abuse substances, to be arrested, or to be sexually promiscuous. Early intervention is key; intervention programs that target school-age children are much less successful than those that target preschoolers (Cavell et al., 2007). Children must be screened over time to monitor their likelihood of aggression (Benzies, Keown, & Magill-Evans, 2009).

Questions

What role do early friendships play in a child's emotional development? What are the research findings on aggressive behaviors in early childhood?

Preschools and Early Childhood Programs

A consensus has developed that a child's attendance in a high-quality preschool program is a strong predictor for success in school (Magnuson & Waldfogel, 2005). With a majority of mothers working and with more children being born at risk since the 1990s, increasing numbers of children in the Western world are in early intervention programs, child care, and preschools long before they enter the public school arena.

That early childhood programs have a powerful impact on the development of young children is an understatement, and a flurry of research in emotional development of children is being undertaken with renewed vigor. As Edward Zigler says,

> Today's children are spending less and less time with their parents, who are forced by economic necessity to work longer hours and to place even their very young children in [nursery and] preschool settings. The nature of the early childhood curriculum, its developmental appropriateness, and the emotional tone its practice creates are becoming increasingly important. (1994, Foreword)

The children in early childhood settings are just beginning to construct their personal social universes. They are experiencing for the first time many of their own emotional responses and those of others. A key should be to help young children at this stage of life learn desirable ways of expressing feelings and develop healthy patterns of understanding and regulating their emotions (Hyson, 2004).

Public kindergarten programs were originally established in the 1950s to support and nurture the young child's emotional and social development—to provide a healthy transition time from the emotional support at home to the cognitive tasks ahead. In the 1960s, Zigler (1970) directed the earliest days of the *Head Start* program, which had been designed to provide children from low-income families with early intervention education in nursery school settings. Educators believed that appropriate services from outside the family could compensate for the disadvantages these youngsters experienced from the effects of poverty during their early years.

In the 1980s, lawsuits and charges of sexual abuse of young children in preschool and child-care programs forced such programs to focus on the children's intellectual development, rather than on their emotional growth, in order not to allow any pretext for inappropriate physical contact. Many professionals and parents concerned about child development believe that undue emphasis has been placed on formal academics (understanding the alphabet, time, number, volume, and space), although they agree that a certain amount of intellectual preparation should be a component of these programs. Like child-care programs, the preschool experience has been seen by a number of educators, child psychologists, and political leaders as a possible solution to many of the massive social problems of illiteracy, underachievement, poverty, and racism that confront Western nations.

In recent years, long-term data have become available that reveal that SES-disadvantaged children in a variety of such programs do indeed get a head start (Gormley, Phillips, Adelstein, & Shaw, 2010) and that they benefit from long-term effects as well (see the *Further Developments* box on page 261, "Head Start: Affecting the Heart,

Hands, Health, and Home"). The payoff of Head Start programs has been not only in education but also in dollars, for in the long run its participants are less likely to need remedial programs as children and economic support systems like welfare as adults (Schweinhart et al., 2005). But as some disadvantaged and disabled youngsters grow older, they continue to need the same comprehensive services. For years the federal government provided some monies for pre-kindergarten, after-school, and summer enrichment programs for this group of youngsters in elementary schools. However, because of the economic recession, by 2010 school districts in nearly every state had been forced to eliminate some of these programs in order to reduce budget deficits (Center for Public Education, 2010).

Family literacy programs also have proved promising for low-income and immigrant families. In these programs, immigrant parents learn English-language skills, get information about child development, and are informed about available social services. At the same time, their children attend bilingual early childhood development programs (Takanishi, 2004). Examples of family literacy programs include the Inter-generational Literacy Program in Massachusetts, the Jane Addams School for Democracy in Illinois, and the AVANCE Program in Texas (Caspe, 2005; Takanishi, 2004). The federal *Even Start* program for teen mothers and their young children also provides family literacy programs. After a year of participation in a family literacy program, 90 percent of children who were considered to be at risk were assessed as prepared for kindergarten, and the benefits of the family literacy program followed them into later school years (National Institute for Literacy, 2007; U.S. Department of Education, 2007).

Preschool Programs Include Children with Disabilities

Early perceptions about people with disabilities or differences lay the groundwork for attitude formation. In fact, by the age of 5, children have already formed perceptions, positive or negative, about youngsters with disabilities (Gifford-Smith & Brownell, 2003). Without thoughtful planning and strategies to promote acceptance, these early attitudes are often negative (Favazza & Odom, 1996). Teachers can address the three key influences in attitude formation by setting up a classroom to promote a positive, accepting attitude on the part of the class and positive self-esteem in children with a disability: Through *indirect experiences,* teachers allow children to see children with disabilities in photographs, books, and other instructional materials that depict children with various special needs. Through *direct experiences,* children share in assisting classmates with disabilities. And through *primary social group experiences,* parents, teachers, and perhaps adults with disabilities model appropriate interactions (Favazza, 1998).

Media Influences

Television, other electronic media, and computer software are powerful socializing agents and educators of children. U.S. preschool children watch television, commercial videos, and small computer screens more than 32 hours each week, according to Nielsen (Chozick, 2010). Preschoolers also average about 1 hour a day using the computer (Hinchliff, 2008). Some studies show that media use has certain benefits for young children, such as increased collaborative play, school readiness, language use, and adaptation for children with special needs. Some higher-quality educational programs for young children, such as *Sesame Street, Barney, Blue's Clues,* and *Dora the Explorer,* contribute to children's school readiness, letter and number skills, and vocabulary, regardless of parent education, income, native language, or quality of the home environment (Huston & Wright, 1998). Watching prosocial programs that offer parent-guided activities increases children's prosocial behaviors (Wright & Huston, 1995).

Increasingly, educational programming (DVDs, computer software, video games, and hand-held video games) is marketed to parents to help infants and young children develop language and cognitive skills—a multi-billion-dollar industry (Garrison & Christakis, 2005). Of course, the media used must be appropriate to children and framed by adult supervision and interaction (Hinchliff, 2008). Media providers seem to be divided into two major camps: those favoring traditional storytelling, led by Disney, and those favoring more curriculum-based programming, including Nickelodeon (Chozick, 2010). It is true that age-appropriate, educational programs can enhance cognitive development, but poor choices when it comes to general TV programming may interfere, over the long term, with a child's learning (Kirkorian, Wartell, & Anderson, 2008).

Harmful Effects of TV and Viewing Computer Screens   After more than 50 years of research on media viewing, leading authorities conclude that young children's school readiness and achievement are affected in these areas: attention and comprehension, language, creativity and imagination, social interactions, identity and gender role, health habits and eating behaviors, level of aggression, family life, vulnerability to advertising, sexuality, and moral values (Vandewater et al., 2007). Studies have repeatedly found that children's viewing of violence in the media contributes to childhood and adult aggression, especially for those prone to aggressive behavior (Strasburger, 2007). Children view more cartoons and comedies with age, and such programs are saturated with aggression, mayhem, and violence (Huston et al., 1990). The American Academy of Pediatrics (2009) points out that children who watch 3 to 4 hours of television a day see 8,000 TV murders by the time they finish grade school. In 2010, Nintendo issued a warning to parents *not* to

FURTHER DEVELOPMENTS

Head Start: Affecting the Heart, Hands, Health, and Home

Since 1965, more than 27 million preschool-age children have been provided with high-quality preparation for kindergarten in nursery and preschool settings through the *Head Start* program, which is the largest U.S. school readiness program (Early Childhood Learning and Knowledge Center, 2010). Begun in 1965 and reauthorized in 2007, Head Start provides children from low-income families with early intervention education via literacy, numeracy, and vocabulary skills training. It also provides "medical, dental, nutritional and family support services." Educators believed that providing these services to the child and to the family could compensate for the educational disadvantages the children experienced as a consequence of poverty. Congress created the *Early Head Start* program in 1995 to address the needs of children younger than 3 and low-income pregnant women (Children's Defense Fund, 2003).

The project also annually provides about 1 million young children (about 1 out of 10 have disabilities) with essential health-care services and teaches parents better parenting skills. This program's effectiveness is increased by involving the parents and bringing them into partnership with the educational enterprise. In 2010, about 850,000 parents volunteered. Any bad experiences that parents had in their own schooling need to be addressed so that they will be less likely to pass on negative attitudes to their youngsters (Waanders, Mendez, & Downer, 2007).

Head Start continues to be one of the most thoroughly researched government-funded programs; and at a cost of about $9 billion annually, accountability is an essential component. But in 2007 Congress suspended a controversial assessment component that involved administering tests of vocabulary, letter recognition, and math skills to every kindergarten-bound child (Friel, Smallen, & Dick, 2007). The National Black Child Development Institute and the National Council of La Raza argued that relying only on cognitive tests of very young children fails to take into account such hallmarks of their school readiness as developmental progress in social, emotional, and motor skills. Indeed, many variables (such as the mother's education, the family's ethnicity, and any childhood speech-language impairment) can affect children's vocabulary skills and other literacy abilities in Head Start (Hammer, Farkas, & Maczuga, 2010).

Yet long-term data are available that reveal that children in quality preschool programs do indeed get a head start and benefit from long-term effects as well (Garces, Thomas, & Currie, 2000). In 2004 the report *Lifetime Effects: The High/*

Quality Preschool and Head Start Programs Make a Difference Researchers find that quality Head Start and preschool programs can make a long-term difference for poor youngsters that extends well beyond the child's school years. Parents' involvement in Head Start also contributes to their own positive growth (Schweinhart et al., 2005).

Scope Perry Preschool Study Through Age 40 was released (Schweinhart et al., 2005). This longitudinal study examined the long-term effects of a high-quality program, Perry Preschool. David Weikert, a preschool founder, and his colleagues began the study in 1962 with 123 children at 3 years of age. Subjects were randomly assigned to groups that either received treatment (preschool) or did not. Data was collected until the participants reached age 40 in 2002.

Study findings revealed that the children who received preschool had significantly higher high school graduation rates than those who did not. The group that received treatment (preschool) had significantly higher employment rates, earned over $5,000 more yearly, were more likely to be homeowners, were more likely to be parents raising their own children, and were more likely to have a bank/savings account (Kirp, 2004). These long-term effects are important

continued

for the participants but also for the legacy of benefits from early education and family services for the generations to follow. Head Start is not the only source of quality preschool programming, but it has been shown to increase health-related aspects of children's lives more than other preschool programs (Gormley, Phillips, Adelstein, & Shaw, 2010).

In the United States, the education of children through the age of 4 is largely a private, family matter; from the age of 5, all children have access to public kindergarten. However, children from low-income families are less likely to be enrolled in quality preschool programming. This, combined with there being less chance of these children receiving preschool skills

at home, means they are doubly disadvantaged (Bainbridge, Meyers, Tanaka, & Waldfogel, 2005). The importance of Head Start as a public school-readiness program endures.

Questions

What is the purpose of Early Head Start and Head Start, and what population of children and families are served? How do children and parents benefit from quality preschool programs?

allow their children under age 6 to play its newly released three-dimensional games because children's eyes are still developing (Wingfield, Hobson, & Wakabayashi, 2010). In sum, an accumulating body of literature suggests that television provides a wide variety of entertainment for children—but that it can act as a powerful negative socializer as well (Christakis & Zimmerman, 2007).

Recommendations   During the preschool years when viewing habits are established, parents and caregivers have the most control to influence children's viewing habits (Garrison & Christakis, 2005). The American

Academy of Pediatrics (2009) recommends that parents forbid media use for children under the age of 2 and that preschoolers be limited to 2 hours of television or computer use per day (Table 8.4 will give you some idea of how much today's reality differs from these recommendations.) Even having the TV on in the background is disruptive to a child's focus when playing with toys (Schmidt, Pempek, Kirkorian, Lund, & Anderson, 2008). Hinchliff (2008) recommends that parents establish guidelines for their children's general media exposure. It is unrealistic to completely rule out children's use of digital media, but limiting it to such products as educational

TABLE 8.4 Media and Technology Use in Children Aged 3 Through 6
Note how much time very young children view television and other digital screens.

Parameter	3- to 4-year olds	5- to 6-year-olds
Watched television	82%	78%
Average minutes of television	89.67	73.99
Watched video/DVD[a]	42%	29%
Average minutes of video/DVD	86.82	78.88
Played video game (console/hand-held)[a]	13%	16%
Average minutes of video game (console/hand-held)	60.5	51.59
Used computer[a]	20%	27%
Average minutes of computer use	45.8	50.5
Read electronic book[a]	20%	10%
Average minutes of reading electronic book	36.5	47.2
Listened to music[a]	85%	77%
Average minutes of music	57.4	51.4

[a]The children were asked if they did the activity either yesterday or on the last typical day. The percentages of those who said they did are shown.

Source: Vandewater, E. A., Rideout, V. J., Wartella, E. A., Huang, X., Lee, J. H., & Shim, M. S. (2007). Digital childhood: Electronic media and technology use among infants, toddlers, and preschoolers. *Pediatrics, 119*(5), 1006–1015, doi:10.1542/peds.2006-1804

software, *Wii* games, Nintendo DS, and LeapFrog handhelds may be a practical solution.

Research shows that parents should avoid putting a TV in a child's bedroom, check movie ratings, preview videos and shows, restrict children's screen time or use V-chip devices, and spend more time doing other activities with their children. Media and technology have not replaced children's traditional favorite activities: being read to, listening to music, and playing outdoors (Hinchliff, 2008). Very young children actually learn better from real-life experiences than from technology-based information (Kirkorian, Wartell, & Anderson, 2008). However, television and media programming are ubiquitous, and parents and caregivers would be wise to diligently limit and monitor their children's use of technology.

Questions

What are some ways in which children can be encouraged to accept children with disabilities into the group? Do you agree that television and other screen media are "silent" socializers? In what ways does research reveal that young children's lives are enhanced or impaired by media viewing? Who is responsible?

SEGUE

In this chapter we discussed variables that can promote or detract from a young child's emotional and social development. Each child's whole development—physical, intellectual, emotional, social, and moral—is unique. Even when adults attempt to rush the child from one stage of development to another, these natural developmental processes move along at the appropriate pace for each young child. A child's emotional self-regulation and self-image are influenced and reflected back by a variety of factors: the child's own developing sense of self within a cultural context; encouragement or discouragement from family members and caregivers; association with, acceptance by, or dissociation from peers; and, in industrialized cultures, the extent of media influence. Children need to feel accepted and loved by the significant people in their lives if they are to maximize their own potential and to have a positive image of themselves. A healthy emotional-social foundation prepares young children for the demands of the middle childhood stage of development, from ages 7 to 12, which we will turn to next in Part 5, Middle Childhood.

SUMMARY

Emotional Development and Adjustment

1. Research on emotions documents that all behavior, thought, and interactions are motivated by emotions. The path of emotional development varies within a diversity of home and social environments.

2. Children need to achieve minimal social competence by age 6. Children who do not reach this milestone by this age risk emotional and behavior disorders by adulthood.

3. Thinking is an emotional activity, and children's feelings can either support or hinder intellectual/academic mastery.

4. Parents and caregivers can promote social competence for young children by teaching them effective problem-solving skills.

5. Parents directly influence social-emotional competence in their children. Children whose parents are negative or hostile are least likely to comply with parental directives, and they display more negative emotions and behaviors that reveal emotional insecurity.

6. Facial expressions, body language, and gestures appear with greater frequency during the preschool years, reflecting greater cognitive ability and awareness of cultural values and standards.

7. Play enables children to improve cognitive capacities and to communicate their deepest feelings. There are many benefits of play activities.

8. Boys tend to play in larger groups and seem to prefer rough-and-tumble, competitive play, whereas girls tend to prefer two-person groups conducive to verbal interaction and displays of affection.

9. Young children use pretend play to explore their feelings. They use their imaginations and play creatively with objects in their environment.

10. Young children are egocentric: Their thoughts, feelings, and words revolve around themselves. Therapeutic play benefits young children with emotional and behavior disorders by offering an outlet for their feelings, thoughts, and aggression.

11. Self-regulation of emotions proceeds gradually at each child's own pace and is unlikely to appear until after age 3. Cultural norms related to the control of boys' and girls' emotions vary.

12. Parents in Western societies encourage individualism in their children, allowing for exploration, imagination, and independence in play, whereas parents from Asian and Latino collectivist cultures emphasize a child's relatedness to the entire culture and a sense of responsibility for the group.

13. Teachers, child-care professionals, early intervention specialists, social workers, and health-care personnel need to familiarize themselves with cross-cultural standards and views as more immigrant families are entering American society.

14. Young children demonstrate extensive understanding of emotional information and reactions. They can develop close, affectionate bonds with family members and other caregivers.

The Development of Self-Awareness

15. Emotional development is essential to self-awareness. A child's understanding of self as separate from others continues to develop during the preschool years.

16. Gifted children demonstrate high motivation and self-direction. Typically, they tend to be active learners and demonstrate a strong will.

Gender Identification

17. Recognition of one's gender is a major developmental task during the first six years of life. Cultural socialization experiences help a child between the ages of 3 and 4 to develop a gender identity.

18. Biology, the brain, and hormones influence the display of gender behaviors.

19. Each child's cultural socialization patterns and family experience influence gender behaviors.

20. Some children are born intersexed; they have genitalia of both genders. A consensus is growing that it is best to let intersexed children choose a gender when they are ready to do so.

21. Psychoanalytic theory suggests that early experience plays a significant role in gender identity.

22. Erikson's psychosocial theory proposes that children attempt to resolve the conflict of initiative versus guilt by acting with purpose on their world.

23. Cognitive learning theory proposes that modeling/imitation plays a major role in gender identity.

24. Cognitive developmental theory states that children acquire a mental model of a female or male, or traditional gender stereotypes, and then adopt that model's gender-related characteristics.

25. In U.S. society, parents socialize girls and boys differently. Girls are taught to be emotionally expressive, and boys are taught to conceal their emotions.

Family Influences

26. Young children must come to understand and adopt the established standards that make up their society's cultural ways, in a process called socialization. Within a cultural context, the family is a network of interacting individuals functioning as a dynamic system.

27. Love-oriented parenting techniques tend to promote the formation of a child's conscience and sense of responsibility. In contrast, hostile and rejecting parents interfere with the child's development of conscience and breed aggressiveness and resistance to authority. Children's own personality and temperament also exert a reciprocal influence on the parenting they receive.

28. Restrictive parenting tends to be associated with well-controlled, fearful, dependent, and submissive behaviors. Permissiveness, although it fosters outgoing, sociable, assertive behaviors and intellectual striving, also tends to decrease persistence and increase aggressiveness.

29. Effective discipline is consistent and unambiguous. The most aggressive children have parents who are inconsistent with discipline.

30. In American society there is strong debate about using spanking as a disciplinary method. No parent should use severe punishment, which causes serious physical, emotional, and behavioral problems in victims.

31. Sexual abuse of children alters a child's cognitive and emotional orientation to the world, causing a loss of control and a sense of powerlessness, stigmatization, and a sense of betrayal by a trusted person.

32. All professionals who work with young children are mandated by law to report any suspected child maltreatment. The highest rate of abuse is in the age group up to 4 years old; child abuse rates decline as children get older.

33. Baumrind distinguishes among authoritarian, authoritative, permissive, and harmonious parenting.

34. Family structure affects the well-being of families and children. There are many known detrimental effects for children living in poverty. Female-headed households have a poverty rate five times that of married two-parent households.

35. Divorce is a stressful experience for both children and their parents for a period of time. Parents typically change interaction patterns with their children. Much of the children's well-being depends on the custodial parent's interaction style, time spent with the children, and discipline.

36. With joint custody, parents share in regular child-care responsibilities and decision making. Overall, the quality of a child's relationship with both parents is most important.

37. There seem to be differences between firstborns and laterborns. One theory posits that resources in large families are spread thin with each successive child and that younger children do not get as many resources as firstborn children. Sibling rivalry plays a role in the formation of each child's personality, as each child competes for attention and recognition in a family.

Nonfamilial Social Influences

38. Young children enjoy and benefit from peer relationships and friendships, which occur more often with increasing age. Children serve one another as reinforcing agents and behavioral models.

39. Friendship functions as cognitive stimulation, allows children to self-regulate, provides for socialization, fosters a sense of identity, and enables children to deal with fears.
40. Young children tend to spend more time with same-sex playmates. Girls interact in two-person or small groups, and boys often play in larger groups.
41. As children grow older, their aggression becomes less diffuse, more directed, more retaliatory, and more verbal. Boys display aggression both physically and verbally, whereas girls display aggression by using harmful words, practicing exclusion, and withdrawing friendship.
42. Children who participate in quality preschool, Early Head Start, and Head Start programs do achieve a higher academic level than children who did not go to preschool. Parents of children in Head Start also benefit from a guidance and support network.
43. For 50 years, research findings have indicated that viewing televised violence is highly associated with aggressive behaviors in children. Pediatricians recommend that young children's television viewing be limited to 2 hours daily and that TVs not be placed in children's bedrooms.

KEY TERMS

aggression *(258)*

antisocial behavior *(259)*

authoritarian parenting *(250)*

authoritative parenting *(250)*

child maltreatment *(249)*

collectivism *(234)*

confluence theory *(257)*

egocentric *(234)*

entelechy *(240)*

gender *(240)*

gender identity *(241)*

gender roles *(240)*

gender stereotypes *(244)*

harmonious parenting *(252)*

imaginary friend *(233)*

individualism *(234)*

initiative versus guilt *(243)*

joint custody *(254)*

peers *(257)*

permissive parenting *(252)*

play *(232)*

resource dilution hypothesis *(257)*

scaffolding *(252)*

self *(239)*

self-concept *(239)*

self-esteem *(239)*

sexual abuse *(249)*

social competence *(231)*

social understanding *(237)*

socialization *(245)*

FOLLOWING UP ON THE INTERNET

Web sites for this chapter focus on early childhood emotional, self-esteem, gender, and identity issues. Please access the text Web site at www.mhhe.com/crandell10 for up-to-date hot-linked Internet addresses for the following organizations, topics, and resources:

Center on the Emotional and Social Foundations for Early Learning
http://csefel.vanderbilt.edu/

Cultural Competency
http://minorityhealth.hhs.gov/templates/browse
    .aspx?lvl=2&lvlID=11

Child Care and Early Education Research Connections
http://www.researchconnections.org/childcare/welcome

Advances in Child Development and Behaviour
http://www.sciencedirect.com/science/bookseries/00652407

Association for the Gifted
http://www.cectag.org/

The Division for Early Childhood
http://www.dec-sped.org/

National Association for the Education of Young Children
http://www.naeyc.org/

Exceptional Parent
http://www.eparent.com/

U.S. Administration for Children & Families: Office of Head Start
http://www.acf.hhs.gov/programs/ohs/index.html
http://www.acf.hhs.gov/programs/ohs/about/index
    .html#factsheet

Middle childhood, the time during the elementary school years, is a period of slower physical growth but faster intellectual development than occurs during the preschool years. In Chapter 9 we will see that children experience greater cognitive sophistication, acquire more socialization skills, and do a better job understanding and coping with their emotions. Cognitive maturation enables the child to deal with fearful and stressful events and to imitate prosocial behaviors. In Chapter 10 we will see that children at this stage are industrious, inquisitive, and more socially aware than before. Peer groups begin to exert a stronger influence on preadolescent children than in earlier years. Youth become more aware of social standings such as popularity, acceptance, and rejection. Most children learn to control their emotions in school, in other group settings, and around peers and friends. Some children, however, need help with academic performance, controlling their behavior, or making friends.

Middle Childhood
Physical and Cognitive Development

Critical Thinking Questions

1. What does it mean to say someone is gifted or a genius? For example, if Mozart had been taken at the age of 20 to a Pacific island where the inhabitants did not know or understand Western music, if he had no musical instruments and no means of expressing his musical talents except by humming or singing, would the islanders have considered him a genius? Or would they have thought he was disabled?

2. How do you perceive others? Think back to when you were a child and compare the perception you had of your parents then to the perception you have now. In what ways has your perception of them changed?

3. If you were going to try to teach a "hardened criminal" how to be moral, which of the following approaches would you use, and how would you implement your plan? (a) Place the criminal in a very moral environment and assume that morality would rub off. (b) Teach the criminal the basic principles of morality and then send the person to live in mainstream society. (c) Use examples of crime and deviancy to teach the criminal about morality and ethics.

4. Why don't we hold children to adult standards of morality? Why don't we treat adults like children and give them the same treatment for offenses?

In the middle childhood years, children get to rest up a bit after the dramatic physical development of early childhood and prepare for the onset of puberty and adolescence. From a developmental perspective, the changes during this time appear so smooth and uneventful that we might think nothing is happening. The greatest changes will be in cognitive growth, and we will discuss concrete operational thought, intelligence and its measurement, individual differences, and children with special learning needs.

These children capably use complex classifications and enjoy making collections of everything from sports cards to butterflies. They start paying attention to counts and amounts, what is bigger, and who has more; and their knowledge of the physical world grows by leaps and bounds. A significant part of children's work during these years involves learning appropriate cultural and social skills. The patterns and habits of social interaction that are established now will not only affect the child's adolescence but also persist into adulthood. We conclude this chapter with an examination of learning language skills and moral development, two significant issues in contemporary U.S. society.

PHYSICAL DEVELOPMENT

Writer Robert Paul Smith (1957) recalls his elementary years with best friends as a constant whirlwind of play and activity in his book *"Where Did You Go?" "Out." "What Did You Do?" "Nothing."* Their "doing nothing" included swinging on swings, sliding on slides, going for walks, sitting in boxes, riding bikes, reading on back porches, climbing on roofs, sitting on tree limbs, playing hide-and-seek, standing in the rain and in the snow, skipping, hopping, jumping, galloping, whistling, humming, and screaming. Such carefree experiences with childhood friends are the things we recall with nostalgia as we age. In some ways, childhood today is the same, yet we shall see some differences in how children now spend their middle childhood years.

One of those differences is in the increasing numbers of children who will be passing through elementary and middle schools over the next decade (see Table 9.1). Note that an increase of nearly 8 percent each decade is projected for children aged 5 to 14, who will be attending schools, requiring out-of-school supervision, needing medical and dental care, participating in sports or other unsupervised play activities, and growing up in a technically sophisticated world.

As these millions of children grow, there will be individual variations in development, as well as variation due to gender, race-ethnicity, and socioeconomic status. For example, African American children tend to mature more quickly (as measured by bone growth, percentage of fat, and number of baby teeth) than Americans of European descent. Asian Americans appear to have the slowest rate of physical change and are less likely to show signs of puberty during middle childhood. Studies are currently being conducted to determine whether body image is linked to ethnicity (Baugh, Mullis, Mullis, Hicks, & Peterson, 2010). Although variations in size and maturity are normal, children who fall at one extreme or the other on the continuum can feel deficient because of their physical differences. The feelings associated with body dissatisfaction are often reinforced by peers and can become a source of psychological and social maladjustment for both boys and girls (Nishina et al., 2006).

Growth and Body Changes

Children grow more slowly during the years of middle childhood than in early childhood or adolescence. With adequate nutrition, the typical child gains about 5 or 6 pounds and grows about 2 inches per year. Girls and boys have similar growth patterns, except that girls tend to have more body fat, and they mature a bit faster than boys.

Most children gain fine motor skills and hand-eye coordination for writing, getting dressed, tying shoes, and performing other tasks. Gradually, their baby teeth begin to come out, and larger permanent ones come in. Children must be taught to perform daily dental care, and periodic dental cleanings should be scheduled. But dental *caries* (cavities) is the most chronic health problem during childhood years, more common even than asthma and hay fever (National Center for Health Statistics, 2011). Dental sealants and fluoridated water help to prevent dental caries. Children who have dental caries or lose permanent teeth will resist talking, reading aloud, and smiling and will become less confident of using language. Disparities exist in children's oral health partly because of the cost of dental care and limited access to dental or health insurance, as well as because of inadequate caregiver education (Edelstein & Chinn, 2009). The American Academy of Pediatric Dentistry (2005) recommends that children participating in contact sports wear mouth guards, helmets, and facial shields to protect permanent teeth and facial bones.

If we look at children during this time period, generally they appear thinner or slimmer because as they grow taller, their body proportions change. However, a growing percentage of U.S. children are considerably overweight, a topic discussed later in this chapter. Muscles become bigger and stronger, and children can kick and throw a ball farther than in the earlier years. An increase in lung capacity bestows greater endurance and speed, of which children make full use. Some variations in height, strength, and speed are due partly to nutrition, particularly in developing countries, but most of the differences among children are the result of heredity. There are differences not only in size but also in rate of maturation. This is particularly noticeable at the end of middle childhood, when some children begin to undergo the changes of puberty and find themselves quite different from their peers in height, shape, strength, and endurance.

TABLE 9.1 Projected Population of U.S. Children, Ages 5 to 14: 2010–2050

Year	Projected Population (in millions)
2010	41.3
2020	45.3
2030	48.8
2040	52.0
2050	56.4

Source: Statistical Abstract of the U.S.: 2008. Population Projections. No. 10 Resident Population Projections by Sex and Age: 2010 to 2050.

Question

What are the expected growth and body changes for a child during the middle childhood years?

Motor Development

During their middle years, children become more skilled in controlling their bodies. Their rate of physical growth has slowed down temporarily, giving them time to feel comfortable with their bodies (unlike in earlier years) and an opportunity to practice their motor skills and increase their coordination. Seven- or 8-year-olds might still have difficulty judging speed and distance, but they have improved their skills sufficiently to be successful in games like soccer and baseball. Jumping rope, skate-boarding, rollerblading, snow-boarding, and riding bicycles are also activities they can enjoy. Which specific skills are developed depends somewhat on the children's environment (for example, on whether they learn games played in snow or in the tropics and on whether the culture favors soccer or football). Whatever activities children choose, they lead to greater coordination, speed, and endurance. Gender differences are minimal during this time period, although girls tend to have greater flexibility and boys have greater forearm strength. Age and experience are much more important determinants than gender, and we can see this in team sports where girls and boys are equally likely to score goals or hit home runs. Both also enjoy doing cartwheels, somersaults, and other gymnastic maneuvers.

Brain Development

As stated in earlier chapters, with regular proper nutrition, health care, and adequate sleep, a child's brain and nervous system continue to develop by both progressive myelination and regressive pruning processes. As a result, assertions that "the die has been cast" by the time the child enters grade school are not supported by neuroscience and can create unwarranted pessimism about the potential efficiency of intervention programs initiated after the preschool years (Thomas & Johnson, 2008). During this time period, the capacity, speed, and efficiency of the child's mental processes typically increase as well (Kuhn & Siegler, 2006). The use of functional MRI has shown a shift in patterns of brain activation—a shift that is consistent with activity becoming less diffuse and more focal and is related to enhanced cognitive performance in middle childhood (Durston et al., 2006). Proper nutrition is essential for brain development (Rosales, Reznick, & Zeisel, 2009), and abuse, neglect, malnourishment, sensory deprivation, and growing up in a dangerous or toxic environment are all manifest risks for healthy brain development and long-term potential (Bornstein & Lamb, 2005).

Memory span increases fairly steadily during the childhood years. One type of improved efficiency is simply faster response time (Durston & Casey, 2005). Speed of response is important even at birth and may be a predictor of later facility in speech acquisition (Sheridan et al., 2010).

Faster response is due in part to the physical development that occurs in the brain, but also to the fact that children at this age are becoming adept at using more cognitive strategies to help them solve more complex tasks.

Studies utilizing imaging of the brains of young children have revealed that children's brains appear to be organized differently than adult brains. The incredible adaptability, or plasticity, of the child's brain often makes possible the restoration of cognitive function after brain injury, so much so that some researchers suggest that evaluations about the effects of brain injury to children should not be finalized before adulthood (Horneman & Emanuelson, 2009). As a result, recovery from brain injury is greater in children than in adults. For example, a stroke in a young child of 6 or 7 might have no subsequent effect on the child's language development, whereas the same kind of stroke in an adult would normally cause permanent loss of language abilities. As mentioned earlier, brain researchers are finding that trauma, neglect, and abuse often have severe effects on a child's developing brain. Yet plasticity of the brain allows for amelioration of those effects if children are placed in a loving and supportive environment (Baltes, Lindenberger, & Staudinger, 2006).

Sex differences are consistently found in developmental studies, with relatively less loss of gray brain matter in girls and relatively greater white brain matter development in boys (Wilke, Krägeloh-Mann, & Holland, 2007). A number of studies suggest that the greater loss of gray brain matter in boys could be associated with psychiatric disorders (e.g., schizophrenia) that have adolescent onsets with differential sex ratios. Early-onset psychotic disorders show variance by gender, with girls more vulnerable at earlier ages, while boys are more likely to relapse somewhat later (Gearing & Mian, 2009). Sex differences in cognitive skills, such as generally higher verbal skills in girls and spatial skills in boys, have also been linked to differential brain development. A growing body of research finds that, generally, the female brain is "hard-wired" for empathy and socialization, and the male brain shows advantages in understanding and building systems (spatial and mathematical abilities). Yet there are individuals who are not typical of their gender (Baron-Cohen, 2005).

Question

What are the typical changes in body growth and brain maturation during these childhood years?

Dyslexia   The learning disorder **dyslexia** is diagnosed when an otherwise normally intelligent, healthy child or adult has extreme difficulty recognizing written words, affecting reading comprehension and writing. Some theories suggest that dyslexia stems from visual difficulties, but others find that dyslexia originates with speech and hearing problems. There are more boys with dyslexia than girls (Hawke, Olson, Willcut, Wadsworth, & DeFries, 2009). Those affected often have an average or above-average IQ and tend to learn math skills more easily (Dowker, 2006). Neuroscientists are studying this brain disorder and so far have discovered, from imaging, diagnostics, and limited autopsies of dyslexics, that in the language area of the cerebral cortex in the left hemisphere, the layers are disorganized, whirled with primitive, larger cells. Turn this book upside down and try to read the words fluently. This is what reading tasks are like for children with dyslexia, who are at a greater risk of lower achievement in school, poor self-esteem, dropping out of school, and having limited occupational opportunities. Some children with dyslexia learn to compensate for their underlying condition and develop adequate reading skills, but others do not (Hoeft et al., 2011). Interestingly enough, some of these children are also identified as gifted or talented (Montgomery, 2009), and teachers and researchers are beginning to examine children with disabilities for various types of giftedness (Manning & Bestnoy, 2008).

In an ongoing study at Stanford University, medical researchers are investigating whether functional or structural brain measures could predict reading improvement over time: "dyslexic readers who showed gains in reading did so by depending on a right-hemisphere pathway [prefrontal cortex], in contrast to the left-hemisphere pathway that characterizes typical reading" (Hoeft et al., 2011, p. 362). Other recent neuroimaging studies find white matter differences in temporal, right inferior parietal, right middle occipital, and many frontal regions (Rollins et al., 2009). Thus it makes sense that teachers who work with children with dyslexia find these children are more successful when teaching is multisensory, using sight, sound, touch, and movement.

Genius and Giftedness   Neuroscientists and psychobiologists have found that more efficient brains have rich neuronal interactions and a multiplicity of synaptic connections. It has been hypothesized that child geniuses may have more complex synaptic connections in the association areas of the cerebral cortex or that their neurochemical transmissions may be more efficient. The controversy over the relative contributions of heredity and environment to intelligence is likely to continue for some time due to the complexity of issues involved. However, important progress has been made in distinguishing differences in genetic and environmental contributions to high intelligence. For example, developmental genetic research indicates that the heritability of intelligence increases with age and that genetic factors contribute to age-to-age change, especially during the transition to middle childhood (Hardman, Drew, & Egan, 2008). As

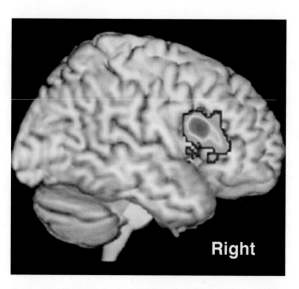

Right Prefrontal Brain Mechanisms May Be Critical for Reading Improvement in Dyslexia
Source: Bruce McCandliss, Vanderbilt University.

gifted children age, they actively select, modify, and even create environments that complement their genetic dispositions. The areas in which some children have displayed genius range from piano playing to mathematical problem solving. In fact, the term *gifted* is now accompanied by the terms *creative* and *talented* to account for multiple abilities beyond simple intelligence (Sternberg, 2006). A standard IQ score of 130 or above, or scoring in the 90th to the 99th percentile in reading or math on standardized achievement tests, usually qualifies a child for a pullout program, in-class enrichment, or advancing a grade.

About 6 percent of children are identified as gifted and talented during the middle childhood years and need additional intellectual challenges to avoid boredom and to develop their abilities (Snyder & Dillow, 2010). Many schools, but not all, provide special assignments or programs for these students. In large cities, students compete to enter specialized schools. Some colleges and universities offer special weekend and summer programs to stimulate the sharp minds of these students. Some universities, including Johns Hopkins, Duke, Northwestern, University of Denver, and University of California, Irvine, sponsor annual talent searches. The University of Connecticut hosts the National Research Center on the Gifted and Talented, and most colleges have centers or summer programs that serve local youth. Also, with online courses, children with special talents can pursue their interests despite schools' cutting budgets for enrichment programs. Some competitive contests for highly intelligent, creative youth are Odyssey of the Mind, American Mathematics Contest, Science Olympiad, Scripps Spelling Bee, Invention Convention, National Geographic Bee, and MENSA programs. The National Society for the Gifted and Talented is an excellent resource. Those of you who are preparing to become educational or school psychologists, teachers, or school administrators may want to find out more about the special needs of gifted and talented youth by contacting one of these special programs that is near you.

Health and Fitness Issues

Typically, children are much healthier in the middle childhood years than at any time since birth. The rate of illness is lower, with most children in elementary schools reporting four to six acute illnesses in a year. The most common childhood illness is upper respiratory infection, although rates of childhood asthma have been rising, as much higher numbers of black and Hispanic youth with asthma are seeking care at emergency rooms (Boudreaux et al., 2003). In 2004, limitation of activity due to chronic health conditions was reported for 7 percent of children under the age of 18 years. Among school-age children 5 to 11, learning disabilities and attention-deficit hyperactivity disorder were frequently reported as a cause of activity limitation.

Unintentional injuries, rather than illness, are the major cause of death for youth of all racial-ethnic groups during this time period, and the most common cause is being killed in a car accident—hence our recent, stricter seat-belt and booster seat laws. However, mortality rates for children aged 5 to 14 have been decreasing over the years. Since 1980, overall child mortality rates have declined nearly one-third in this age group for both male and female children and for all races/ethnicities. Nevertheless, children in middle childhood still need adult supervision and care. The greatest number of sports injuries for children in this age group occurs when they are playing basketball, football, or baseball; bicycling; or using playground equipment.

Establishing healthy habits in youth can help prevent many chronic health problems later in life that are attributable to unhealthy eating, sedentary lifestyle, drug abuse, and being overweight. Schools can play a crucial role in improving the health of children by developing programs that focus on supporting positive environmental influences that increase physical activity and improve healthy eating (Franks et al., 2007). Further, researchers have found that the daughters of sedentary parents are more likely to become sedentary themselves and that higher levels of TV viewing among parents affect both boys and girls (Jago, Fox, Page, Brockman, & Thompson, 2010). Thus, to promote physical activity in children, parents need to design environments that support active living, and they should limit access to television viewing at home.

Obesity The CDC uses the term *overweight* when referring to children and the term *obesity* with adults. Being **overweight** is defined as having a body mass index

TABLE 9.2 Children Who Are Overweight by Gender, 1976–2006 (by percent)

Here is the breakdown, by percentage, for children in the United States classified as overweight (at or above the 95th percentile in body mass index). Eating high-fat snacks accompanies sedentary activities such as watching TV and playing video games or computer games. These behaviors are correlated with being overweight and at risk for serious health problems.

	Total	Male	Female
1976–1980	5.7%	5.5%	5.8%
1988–1994	11.2	11.8	10.6
1999–2000	15.0	15.7	14.3
2001–2002	16.5	18.0	15.1
2003–2004	18.0	19.1	16.8
2005–2006	16.5	17.2	15.9

Source: Centers for Disease Control and Prevention. (2010). Overweight children ages 6–17: Percentage has increased from 6 percent in 1976 to 17 percent in 2006. Retrieved from http://www.cdc.gov/Features/dsOverweightchildren/

(BMI) at or above 25 (see CDC growth charts online or Table 9.2). The proportion of overweight children quadrupled, since the 1970s, to nearly one-third of children aged 6 to 11 in 1980. By 2006 overall rates had declined, with Hispanic and black youth the most at risk. A recent study of poor black children shows that most obese children do not outgrow obesity, as many researchers had assumed (Lee et al., 2010). Thus, doctors refer to the increasing rate of overweight children as an epidemic for many communities (Jolliffe & Janssen, 2006). Major health risks include high cholesterol and blood pressure, leading to early cardiovascular disease, higher risk of diabetes mellitus, orthopedic problems, sleep apnea, and skin disorders (National Center for Health Statistics, 2010b). The psychosocial well-being of overweight children is also affected, causing depression (a result of negative self-image), low self-esteem, teasing and rejection, and withdrawal from peer interactions (Fulkerson & Strauss, 2007). Teachers and parents have been shown to misunderstand obesity and often have unhelpful attitudes toward children who are obese (Jiménez-Cruz, Castellón-Zaragoza, García-Gallardo, Bacardí-Gascón, & Hovell, 2008). Some researchers suggest the need for mental-health treatment as one component of obesity treatment (Walker & Hill, 2009).

Obesity is caused by high caloric intake, low activity, and (in rare cases) genetic or thyroid hormone factors. However, the body's regulation of energy use may be programmed during the preschool years, infancy, and even while children are in utero (Olstad & McCargar, 2009).

Factors such as the following are related to increasing rates of overweight children: (1) lifestyle changes such as moving to the suburbs and car-pooling; (2) fears about child kidnappings and drive-by shootings; (3) increasing work hours for both parents; (4) exercise time limited to organized sports and little or no unstructured playtime; (5) fewer physical education classes due to school budget cuts; (6) soft drink and snack food vending machines in schools; and (7) more sedentary time spent with TV, video games, and computers (Thompson et al., 2007). Ultimately, however, parental obesity may be the primary factor in predicting childhood obesity (Olstad & McCargar, 2009).

We know that obese adults and children take in more calories and exercise less than others of the same age, socioeconomic status, and gender who are not overweight. Studies of twins separated at birth by adoption and reunited in adulthood indicate that children have a genetic tendency toward fatness or thinness; however, behavior has a larger effect on weight (Crothers, Kehle, Bray, & Theodore, 2009). Adults should act as good role models, provide healthy foods and encourage children to make healthy food choices when at school, promote regular exercise (one hour per day for children), and reduce sedentary activities, such as playing computer games and television viewing (Vandewater et al., 2005). Lifestyle interventions as a treatment for childhood obesity have been shown to significantly reduce a child's weight both in the short term and into adulthood (Wilfley et al., 2007). Developing life-long habits of engaging in physical activity during leisure time is one of the best ways to avoid obesity (Waller, Kaprio, & Kujala, 2008).

Too many schools have allowed the installation of vending machines that sell soft drinks and high-caloric snacks. In 2010, a federal law was passed that establishes "nutrition standards for foods sold in schools during the school day. The standards would require schools to serve more fruits and vegetables, whole grains and low-fat dairy products, to offer healthier lunch options, restrict student access to junk foods, or remove such vending machines" (Pear, 2010). Ironically, free and reduced-price school lunches may be contributing to the obesity problem (Schanzenbach, 2009). Children who bring their own lunch to school are less likely to be obese than children who eat school lunches, even though they enter kindergarten with similar rates of obesity (Kirkendoll, 2010).

Eating Disorders   In many countries, a growing number of elementary and middle school children (as young as 4), mainly girls, are diagnosed with the eating disorders of anorexia and bulimia (Bryant-Waugh, 2006). Family environment and interactions, media portrayal of girls and women, and friends are powerful influences on children's eating behaviors (O'Brien et al., 2007). Anorexia is so prevalent a part of society that controversial pro-anorexia, or *pro-ana* Web sites are found on the Internet (Custers & Van den Bulck, 2009).

A child's refusal of regular nourishment causes poor health, fatigue, or even death. It is imperative that parents, teachers, school nurses, and pediatricians learn about the typical physical and behavioral signs and causes of these disorders. Researchers have found that psychotherapy is the best treatment for eating disorders (Lock & Fitzpatrick, 2009), although mental-health practitioners must be careful in passing younger patients on to adult mental-health services (Arcelus, Bouman, & Morgan, 2008). Eating disorders are discussed further in Chapter 11.

Role of Play and Exercise   Public school children are required to participate in physical education classes unless they have an illness or disability. However, daily gym class in schools is becoming obsolete as a consequence of budgetary constraints and emphasis on raising children's test scores. Schools, communities, and policymakers need to provide regular, quality physical education for all youth, ideally in the form of activities that can become lifelong habits (Ginsburg, Committee on Communications, & the Committee on Psychosocial Aspects of Child and Family Health, 2007). Also, middle schools offer extracurricular sports for both boys and girls, such as indoor and outdoor soccer, basketball, track, football, baseball or softball, field hockey, lacrosse, volleyball, and tennis. Increased physical activity promotes overall fitness, improves cognitive functioning, improves overall mental health, reduces the effects of stress, and builds self-esteem (Wilfley et al., 2007).

All children should develop a regular routine of physical activity and maintain it throughout high school, and throughout life, to keep their immune and cardiovascular

Exercise Promotes Healthy Children Recreation and health experts recommend turning off the TV and computer and encouraging play activities that children enjoy. Research indicates that girls enjoy more singular types of energetic endeavors (walking, jogging, or social dancing), whereas boys typically enjoy competitive sports.

systems healthy. Yet research reveals age-related declines in physical activity and participation, particularly for girls. Dowda and colleagues (2004) recommend that PE classes be made more enjoyable and relevant for girls. Girls report that they enjoy walking, rollerblading, aerobics, jogging or running, bicycling, swimming, jumping rope (double-dutch), and social dancing, whereas boys report that they enjoy participating in traditional competitive activities. A growing body of research shows that reducing television viewing allows children time for play activities, improving their overall health (Gable, Chang, & Krull, 2007). Healthy girls and boys of this age have a difficult time sitting in a classroom all day without being able to expend their tremendous energy. For some—but not all—gym class is their favorite activity of the week because that is where they experience their greatest success!

Questions

What are the common causes of childhood chronic illness and death? What factors promote healthy growth and physical and cognitive development?

COGNITIVE DEVELOPMENT

An important feature of the elementary school years is an advance in children's ability to learn about themselves and their environment (Kuhn & Siegler, 2006). During this period they become more adept at processing information as their reasoning abilities become progressively more rational and logical (Bialystok & Craik, 2006). A study examining children's mental strategies in solving math problems found that metacognition accounts for much of the variance of successful math performance in 8- to 9-year-olds (Despete, 2001).

Piaget's Period of Concrete Operations

From Piaget's perspective, there is a qualitative change in children's thinking during middle childhood as children begin to develop a set of rules or strategies for examining the world. Piaget calls middle childhood the **period of concrete operations.** By an "operation" Piaget means an integration of such powerful, abstract, internal schemas as identity, reversibility, classification, and serial ordering. The child begins to understand that adding something results in more, that objects can belong to more than one category, and that these categories have logical relationships. Such operations are "concrete" because children during these years are bound by immediate physical reality and cannot transcend the here and now. Consequently, during this period, children still have

Concrete Operational Thought and Conservation Skills According to Piaget, children in the concrete operational stage of thought can decenter, thus attending simultaneously to both width and height. They assimilate transformations, such as the gradual shift in the height or width of the fluid in a container as it is poured by the experimenter. Also, they attain reversibility of operations, recognizing that the initial state can be regained by pouring the water back into the original container.

difficulty dealing with remote, future, or hypothetical (or abstract) matters.

Despite the limitations of concrete operational thought, during these years children make major advances in their cognitive capabilities. For example, in the preoperational period before 6 or 7 years of age, children arrange sticks by size in their proper sequence by physically comparing each pair in succession. But in the period of concrete operations, children "mentally" survey the sticks and then quickly place them in order, usually without any actual measurement. Because the activities of preoperational children are dominated by actual perceptions, the task takes them several minutes to complete. Children in the period of concrete operations finish the same project in a matter of seconds, because their actions are directed by internal cognitive processes: They can make the comparisons in their minds and do not have to physically juxtapose the sticks and view them side by side.

Conservation Tasks   The difficulty younger children had solving conservation problems is due to the rigidity of their preoperational thought processes. Let's look at how children use concrete operations to solve these kinds of problems when they are a bit older. **Conservation** requires recognition that the quantity of something stays the same despite changes in appearance. It implies that children are mentally capable of compensating in their minds for various external changes in objects. Elementary school children come to recognize that pouring liquid from a short, wide container into a tall, narrow one does not change the quantity of the liquid; they understand that the amount of liquid is *conserved*. Whereas preoperational children fix ("center") their attention on either the width or the height of the container and ignore the other dimension, concrete operational children decenter, attending simultaneously to both width and height. Furthermore, concrete operational children assimilate transformations, such as the gradual shift in the height or width of the fluid in the container as it is poured by the experimenter. And most important, according to Piaget, they attain reversibility of operations. They recognize that the initial state can be regained by pouring the water back into the original container. (Decentering, transformations, and reversibility were discussed in Chapter 7.)

> **Question**
>
> How does the acquisition of concrete operations enable a child to perform Piaget's conservation tasks?

Classification, or the concept of class inclusion, is usually understood by the age of 7 or 8. This development in children can be seen when they play a game similar to "20 Questions." Children aged 6 to 11 were shown a group of pictures and were told to ask questions to figure out which one the researcher "had in mind." ("Is it alive?" "Is it something you would play with?" etc.) The questions asked were divided into two basic types: strategy (categories) and no strategy (guessing). Six-year-olds typically resorted to guessing particular objects ("Is it a banana?"); older children asked categorical questions ("Is it something that you eat?") (Denney, 1985). Multiple classifications also develop when children start collections of favored objects, such as *Pok-e-mon* or sports cards, comic books, action toys, American dolls, stamps, coins, rocks, and so forth. With such collections, children come to classify by actual name or by size, value, color, first-to-last, etc. (Lightfoot, Cole, & Cole, 2009).

According to Piaget, children in the period of concrete operations develop the ability to use *inductive logic:* Given enough examples or provided with multiple experiences, children can come up with a general principle of how something operates. For example, if they are given enough problems of the form of 3 + 4 = ? and 4 + 3 = ?, they can induce that the order of the numbers in addition is not significant. They know that they will always get the same answer, 7. On the other hand, they are not very good at moving from the general to the specific, which is *deductive logic.* Starting with a concept or rule and then generating its application is difficult for them, because

Favorite Collections Teach Multiple Classification Skills
During this stage, children start collections of favorite objects, and they begin to classify these things by name, size, color, order, cost, and so on.

it involves imagining something they may never have experienced. Despite the cognitive advances made in concrete operations, most children in this period are still "concrete" and in some degree dependent on their own observations and experiences. Thus, teachers and many parents often plan field trips to sites where children can see, hear, touch, and experience real events.

As is true of other cognitive abilities, children acquire some conservation skills earlier and some later (see Figure 9.1). Conservation of discrete quantities (number) occurs somewhat before conservation of substance. Conservation of weight (the heaviness of an object) follows conservation of quantity (length and area) and is in turn followed by conservation of volume (the space that an object occupies). Piaget gave the name *horizontal décalage* to this sequential development, wherein acquiring each new skill is dependent on the acquisition of earlier skills. **Horizontal décalage** implies that repetition takes place within a single period of development, such as the period of concrete operations. For example, a child acquires the various conservation skills in sequential steps. The principle of conservation is first applied to one task, such as the quantity of matter—the notion that the amount of an object remains unchanged despite changes in its position or shape. But the child does not apply the principle to another task, such as the conservation of weight—the notion that the heaviness of an object remains unchanged

Conservation Skill	Basic Principle	Test for Conservation Skills	
		Step 1	Step 2
Number (Ages 5–7)	The number of units in a collection remains unchanged even though they are rearranged in space.	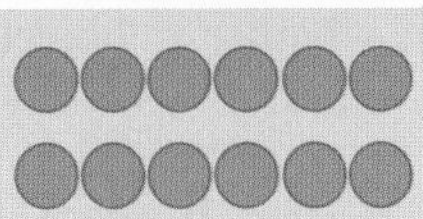 Two rows of pennies arranged in one-to-one correspondence	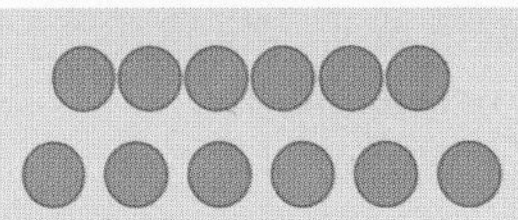 One of the rows elongated or contracted
Substance (Ages 7–8)	The amount of a malleable, plastic-like material remains unchanged regardless of the shape it assumes.	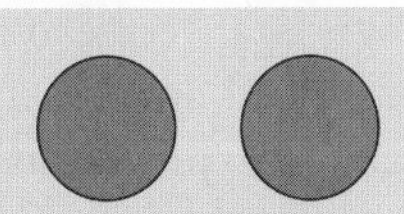 Modeling clay in two balls of the same size	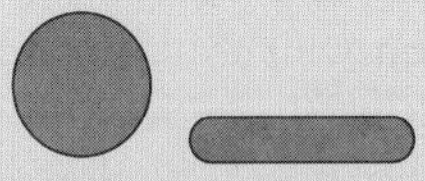 One of the balls rolled into a long, narrow shape
Length (Ages 7–8)	The length of a line or object from one end to the other end remains unchanged regardless of how it is rearranged in space or changed in space.	Strips of cloth placed in a straight line	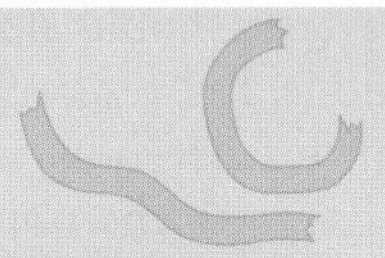 Strips of cloth placed in altered shapes
Area (Ages 8–9)	The total amount of surface covered by a set of plane figures remains unchanged regardless of the position of the figures.	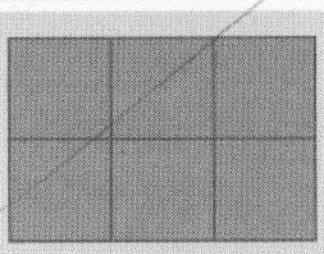 Square units arranged in a rectangle	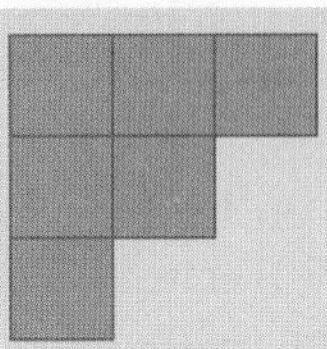 Square units rearranged
Weight (Ages 9–10)	The heaviness of an object remains unchanged regardless of the shape that it assumes.	 Units placed on top of each other	 Units placed side by side
Volume (Ages 12–14)	The space occupied by an object remains unchanged regardless of a change in its shape.	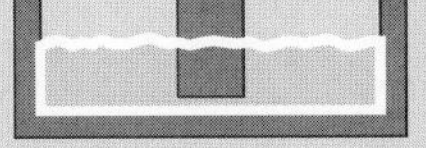 Displacement of water by object placed vertically in the water	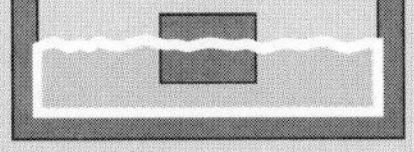 Displacement of water by object placed horizontally in the water

FIGURE 9.1 Sequential Acquisition of Conservation Skills Piaget says that during the period of concrete operations, children develop conservation skills in a fixed sequence. That is, they acquire the concept of conservation of number first, then that of substance, and so on.

regardless of the shape that it assumes. It is not until a year or so later that the child extends the same type of conservation operation to weight.

The general principle is the same with respect to both quantity and weight. In each case, children must perform internal mental operations and no longer rely on actual measurement or weighing to determine whether an object is larger or weighs more. However, children typically achieve the notion of the invariance of quantity a year or so before that of the invariance of weight (Flavell, 1992).

Post-Piagetian Criticism   The difference in acquisition times does not necessarily fit with Piaget's notion of stages. If, as Piaget says, each stage is a "cohesive whole," then we should find that children of any given age apply similar logic to a wide range of problems. A child who has concrete operations should be able to use operational logic on all tasks presented. Similarly, for children who are capable of operational logic, the amount of particular knowledge they have about the content of a task should not affect their use of these basic operations. But research has shown that it appears to make a difference how much *experience* or expertise a child has with the objects involved, for children can perform more complex operations on tasks they are familiar with than on tasks that are novel to them (Bornstein & Lamb, 2005).

Other research has focused on whether the development of concrete operations can be accelerated, not just by general experience with objects, but through specific training on how to do conservation tasks. Jerome S. Bruner (1970) states, "The foundations of any subject may be taught to anybody at any age in some form." Learning theorists reject Piaget's stage formulations and disagree with Piaget's view that children below the age of 6 cannot benefit from experience in learning conservation because of their cognitive immaturity.

In the early 1960s any number of psychologists attempted to teach young children conservation skills. For the most part, they were unsuccessful. Subsequently, a number of researchers successfully used cognitive learning methods to train children in conservation. Furthermore, psychologists are finding that the content of a task decisively influences how a person thinks (Spinillo & Bryant, 1991). By altering the cognitive properties of a task, one often can elicit preoperational, concrete operational, or formal operational thinking from a child (Smith, 1992). Issues of this sort have stimulated research in creativity. (For more on this subject, see the *More Information You Can Use*, "Fostering Creativity.")

Cross-Cultural Evidence   Piaget realized that "culture played a role in cognitive development, and he was aware of cross-cultural variations in the timing of the

appearance of cognitive stages" (Maynard, 2008, p. 56). Since the 1950s, children throughout the world have been subjects for a variety of Piagetian experiments "using culturally relevant tools, in familiar domains and situations" (Maynard, 2008). Research has been conducted in over 100 cultures and subcultures, from Switzerland to Senegal and from Alaska to the Amazon (Feldhusen, Proctor, & Black, 1986). The Six Cultures Study of Socialization began in the 1950s, with researchers studying child development in Mexico, New England, Okinawa, the Philippines, and India. The results show that regardless of culture, children do appear to move through Piaget's four hierarchical stages of cognitive development when allowed to use culturally relevant tools and situations. But some research suggests that there is a developmental lag in the acquisition of conservation among children in non-Western, nonindustrialized cultures. Not entirely clear is whether this lag is due to cultural differences or to flaws in research procedures that use materials and tasks alien to some cultures. Another study of Chinese children performing the Piagetian water-level task found an association between cognitive development and the instruction effect (Li, 2000).

The research also raises a question about whether the acquisition of conservation skills in the period of concrete operations occurs in the invariant sequence (horizontal décalage) postulated by Piaget. Children in Western nations, Iran, and Papua New Guinea exhibit the expected Piagetian pattern. Thai children, however, appear to develop conservation of quantity and weight simultaneously (Boonsong, 1968). Some Arab, Indian, Somali, and Australian aborigine subjects conserve weight before quantity (deLemos, 1969; Hyde, 1959). Children of pottery-making families in Mexico performed better on conservation-of-substance tasks than did their peers from other families (Ashton, 1975). Greenfield (1966) found, in her studies of Wolof children in Senegal, West Africa, that it made a difference whether the experimenter or the children poured the water in the test involving wide and narrow containers. Two-thirds of children under 8 years old who themselves transferred the water achieved the concept of conservation. Yet a smaller number who watched the experimenter pour the water realized that the amount of water was the same. The children attributed the experimenter's feat to a "magical action."

Today's cross-cultural psychologists continue to find that cultures vary in the use of tools, the goals parents set for their children, availability of resources to children, and values and motivations. Some cultural groups do not attain the state of formal operations, though. Whereas Asian parents want their children to reach the stage of formal operations, Mayan parents want their children to become good storytellers and weavers (Maynard, 2008).

MORE INFORMATION YOU CAN USE

Fostering Creativity

We commonly value creativity as the highest form of mental endeavor and achievement. Whereas intelligence implies quick-wittedness in learning the predictable, **creativity** implies original and useful responses and creations. Often we assume that high intelligence and creativity go hand in hand. In fact, psychologists find that although high intelligence does not ensure creativity, low intelligence seems to work against it. Above-average intelligence—though not necessarily exceptional intelligence—seems essential for creative achievement (Sternberg, 2006).

In some cases too much brainpower can even get in the way of creativity. Psychologist Simonton (1991) studied renowned creators and leaders of the 1900s and found that the optimal IQ for creativity is about 19 points above the average of people in a given field. Nor is formal education essential. Many famous scientists, philosophers, writers, artists, composers, and entrepreneurs never complete college (examples include Bill Gates of Microsoft and Steven Jobs of Apple). Formal education often instills rote methods for doing things and discourages offbeat but creative solutions. Albert Einstein felt stifled by formal education: "The hitch in this was the fact that one had to cram all this stuff into one's mind for the examinations, whether one liked it or not. This coercion had such a deterring effect on me that, after I had passed the final examination, I found the consideration of any scientific problem distasteful for an entire year" (Einstein, 1949, p. 17).

Sternberg (2009) describes the matrix of attributes that contribute to creativity as *WICS*—wisdom, intelligence, creativity, and synthesis—and posits that all must work together and be cultivated. If children do not fully utilize their imagination, explore possibilities, try new things, consider new actions, invent and experiment, they will not be able to discover who they are, what they are capable of, and what is acceptable in their family, school, peer group, and culture (Spodek & Saracho, 2006). Adults should both support children's imaginative play and experimentation and provide feedback, structure, and appropriate values through differentiated education (Tomlinson & Hockett, 2007). If such experiences are available to children, they can develop mature forms of creative talent and may contribute in a meaningful fashion to society. Psycholinguist Vera John-Steiner (1986) finds that scientists and artists mention that their talent and interest were revealed early in life and that they were often encouraged and nurtured by their parents or teachers.

Although creative people may have innate talent, they must nurture their creativity with discipline and hard work. Purnell (2009), when teaching origami to children, talks about the necessity of *quiet focusing* to develop creativity.

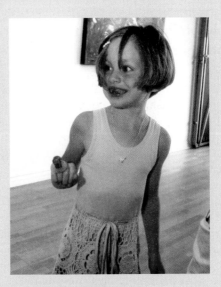

The Gift of Creativity Psychologists agree that a natural gift is not sufficient to produce creative effort. What is required is the convergence of innate talent and a receptive environment, and such talents and interests are revealed early in life. Artist Marla Olmstead began painting at age 2 and has attracted the attention of international art collectors (and skeptical media). You might enjoy watching her express her creativity at http://www.marlaolmstead.com or view the DVD *My Kid Could Paint That.*

Here are some other tips to encourage creative thinking and originality in children:

- Respect children's questions and ideas, and their right to initiate their own learning.
- Respect children's right to reject the ideas of caretakers in favor of their own.
- Encourage children's awareness and sensitivity regarding environmental stimuli.
- Confront youngsters with problems, contradictions, ambiguities, and uncertainties.
- Give children opportunities to make something and then do something with it.
- Use provocative and thought-producing questions, and give children opportunities to describe what they learned and accomplished.
- Encourage children's sense of self-esteem, self-worth, and self-respect.

In addition, parents and teachers should be aware of creativity in historically neglected groups, including girls, children with disabilities, and children from different ethnic/cultural and socioeconomic groups.

In short, situational, cognitive, motivational, and personality characteristics all play a part in creativity.

Questions

What is the developmental sequence of Piaget's conservation skills? What are some post-Piagetian and cross-cultural findings? How do we identify a child's accomplishment as creative?

Information Processing and Cognitive Development

In Chapter 7, we indicated that some theorists ask children to report what they are doing intellectually while they perform a task. How does the child process the information she or he is given to solve a problem? How do these intellectual processes change with age?

This is quite different from Piagetian theorists, who ask what overall structure of logic the child uses and how these structures change over time. According to the information-processing view, we need to understand whether there is a change in the basic processing capacity of the system (hardware) and/or whether there is a change in the types of programs (software) used to solve a problem. For instance, there are certain limitations to the number of operations a computer can perform at one time and to the speed at which it can perform them. Just like an executive, children at this age might be better at dividing tasks into more manageable segments. For example, with regard to memory, children at this age might become more efficient at using the mnemonic strategies of rehearsal and categorization, as discussed in Chapter 7.

Individual Differences   Much of our thinking so far has centered on how the typical child develops cognitively through this middle childhood period. We have described the changes in the use of concrete operations with advancing age and have shown that the developmental process is predictable to a certain extent. We have also noticed variations in the rate at which children change and in the overall amount of change that takes place in this period. Piaget believed that only 30 to 70 percent of adolescents and adults perform at the next level, formal operations (Piaget, 1963). Likewise, some children take quite a while to develop operational logic for any task, whereas other children learn some academic skills quite easily and yet struggle with other skills that appear quite similar operationally. School and home environments alone do not seem to account for the individual variability in conceptual ability.

Children's Perception of Others   The elementary school years are a time of rapid growth in children's cognitive understanding of the social world and of the requirements for social interaction (Kuhn & Siegler, 2006). Consider what is involved when we enter the wider world. We need to assess certain key statuses of the people

we encounter, such as their age and sex. We must also consider their behaviors (walking, eating, reading), their emotional states (happy, sad, angry), their roles (teacher, sales clerk, parent), and social contexts (home, school, church, restaurant) (Vander Zanden & Pace, 1984).

Accordingly, when we enter a social setting, we mentally attempt to "locate" people within the broad network of possible social relationships. By scrutinizing them for a variety of clues, we place them in social categories. For instance, if they wear wedding rings, we infer that they are married. Only in this manner can we decide what to expect of others and what they expect of us. In sum, we activate **stereotypes**—certain inaccurate, rigid, exaggerated cultural images—that guide us in identifying the mutual set of expectations that will govern the social exchange. Livesley and Bromley (1973) traced developmental trends in children's perceptions of people. The study reveals that the number of dimensions along which children conceptualize other people grows throughout childhood. The greatest increase in children's ability to distinguish people's characteristics occurs between 7 and 8 years of age. This observation led Livesley and Bromley (1973, p. 147) to conclude that "the eighth year is a critical period in the developmental psychology of person perception."

Children under 8 years of age describe people largely in terms of external, readily observable attributes. Their conception of people tends to be inclusive, embracing an individual's personality, family, possessions, and physical characteristics. At this age children categorize people in a simple, absolute, moralistic manner and employ vague, global descriptive terms such as *good, bad, horrible,* and *nice.* Consider this account by a 7-year-old girl of a woman she likes:

> She is very nice because she gives my friends and me toffee. She lives by the main road. She has fair hair and she wears glasses. She is forty-seven years old. She has an anniversary today. She has been married since she was twenty-one years old. She sometimes gives us flowers. She has a very nice garden and house. (Livesley & Bromley, 1973, p. 214)

When they are about 8 years old, children show rapid growth in their vocabularies for appraising people. Their phrases become more specific and precise. After this age children increasingly come to recognize certain regularities or unchanging qualities in the inner dispositions and overt behaviors of individuals. Here is a description of a boy by a 9-year-old girl:

> David Calder is a boy I know. He goes to this school but he is not in our class. His behavior is very bad, and he is always saying cheeky [impudent] things to people. He fights people of any age and he likes getting into trouble for it. (Livesley & Bromley, 1973, p. 214)

This suggests the rapid development that occurs during middle childhood in children's abilities to make inferences about the thoughts, feelings, personality attributes, and general behavioral dispositions of other people (Erdley & Dweck, 1993). As children's cognitive ability of "person perception" matures, their vocabulary increases, and so does their ability to express their needs and to communicate with others (Livesley & Bromley, 1973).

Questions

How does Piaget describe children's cognitive development from age 7 to age 12, and why are some of his theories less applicable in some other cultures? Why is it important to encourage creativity in children? Why do younger children employ stereotypes?

Language Development in Middle Childhood

The development of communication skills, language, and literacy denotes significant accomplishments. Almost all children succeed at learning language. As a result, people often tend to take the process of language learning for granted. But learning a language is the most complex skill that a human being will ever master (Shonkoff & Phillips, 2000). This may be a more complicated task for multilingual children, since the rate of learning may not be consistent from language to language (Goswami, 2008). By age 6, children have mastered most of the basic vocabulary and grammar of their language. The cognitive abilities described in this chapter help school-age children to combine words in a meaningful manner. Children with persistent language difficulties are at risk for social and academic problems, which could be expressed as a learning disability or social isolation, as discussed later in this chapter.

Learning any language is a lifelong process. Children from age 6 to age 12 continue to acquire subtle phonological distinctions, vocabulary, semantics, syntax, formal discourse patterns, and complex aspects of pragmatics in their first or second language (Gleason, 1993). During this time, children are usually in school and add to speech the cognitively complex systems of reading and writing. Some schools use Conversation Stations to promote purposeful, one-on-one language interaction between adults and children (Bond & Wasik, 2009). As children grow older, they grow wiser, and the complexity and cognitive level of their language increases as a reflection of their academic studies and life experiences. Let's take a closer look at the changes in language that take place during middle childhood—in particular, changes in vocabulary, syntax, and pragmatics.

Vocabulary   Kagan and Herschkowitz (2005) report that a fifth-grader learns as many as 20 new words a day and achieves a vocabulary of nearly 40,000 words by age 11. Some of this increase is basic academic vocabulary, because children in school are exposed to a wide range of subjects requiring them to understand and use specific new terms. The concrete operational child is also able to learn and understand words that might not be tied to his or her personal experience, such as *ecology, discrimination,* and *social justice.* They are able to describe objects, people, and events in terms of categories and functions rather than just physical features. They are more likely to describe their family dog in terms of its breed, its personality traits, and the kinds of things it can do. They can compare their dog to other dogs and contrast their dog as a pet with the kinds of pets others have. Children begin to understand that words have multiple meanings, and they can use this new skill to tell jokes and ask riddles. By third grade, children typically love to tell and make up their own "knock-knock" jokes. [Knock-Knock. *Who's there?* Abby. *Abby who?* Abby birthday to you!]

Syntax and Pragmatics   Children now begin studying grammar, for they understand that rules apply to language. They might still speak incorrectly, improperly using pronouns and agreement of subject and verb, but they can learn the correct form and can recognize errors in syntax. The structure of their sentences becomes more complex—they use other conjunctions besides *and,* and they use adverbs, adjectives, and prepositional phrases. Their cognitive abilities are sufficiently developed to allow the correct use of auxiliary verbs such as *can, must, will, may, might,* and *should* (Nelson, Aksu-Ko, & Johnson, 2001).

A second type of growth occurs in the child's pragmatic language. As we noted in Chapter 7, pragmatic language is use of language in a particular context or situation. In middle childhood, children recognize that they can (and should) modify their voice, volume, and even their vocabulary, depending on the context of the interaction. For example, they will adopt a more formal style of vocabulary and syntax when talking with a teacher than when talking to their parents or close friends. This ability of *code switching,* or changing from one form of speech to another, indicates that the child has developed an awareness of the social requirements in a given context. It also allows children a certain freedom in speech when talking with peers, enabling them to express themselves using casual—often emotional—words, including slang and swear words. Caregivers are sometimes alarmed by the use of slang and swear words among children, but they often represent experimentation in the use of language. However, children must learn appropriate boundaries in using informal language (Aitchison, 2006).

Question

What changes do we see in the way children use and understand language from age 7 to age 12?

Educating Children Whose Communication Skills Are Below Standard　Since the 1980s, dramatically increasing numbers of immigrant children with **limited English proficiency (LEP)** have had an impact on U.S. schools. These are students who were not born in the United States or whose native language is not English and who cannot participate effectively in school because they have difficulty speaking, understanding, reading, and writing English. Educators refer to these children as **English language learners (ELLs)**. In the 2007–2008 school year, more than 10 million English language learners received services in public schools, and most speak Spanish (see Table 9.3) (National Center for Education Statistics, 2010). Another group has also emerged: **Long-term English learners (LTELs)** are those students who arrive in secondary schools seven or more years later and still lack proficiency in English and (as a consequence) lag behind in academic skills (Olsen, 2010).

In 2002 when the *No Child Left Behind* (NCLB) legislation was signed into law, the National Association for Bilingual Education (NABE) endorsed its passage. However, the law has so far done little to address the needs of all ELL children (funds for training teachers, providing instructional materials, and creating adequate facilities are limited) (A. Lewis, 2007). The Hispanic population represents the fastest-growing U.S. minority population (Federal Interagency Forum on Child and Family Statistics, 2010). As a result, the use of the English language in our schools is a hurdle to some of our newest schoolchildren. Children who are recent immigrants are more likely to have difficulty speaking English because many speak another language at home (U.S. Department of Education, 2010). It is estimated that, more than one-third of American schoolchildren in the western states speak a second language with family (National Center for Education Statistics, 2010).

Few Hispanic children start kindergarten with pre-school experience, so their lack of preparedness and their inability to communicate in English put them at a great disadvantage (Coltrane, 2003). Earlier studies revealed significant shortages in teachers of bilingual education. Today, however, school districts are hiring more teachers and classroom paraprofessionals who are bilingual to teach students who do not speak English (Tenore, Dunn, Laughter, & Milner, 2010).

American educators and administrators are pressured to get increasing numbers of LEP students to pass standardized tests, and even the billions of dollars distributed through the federal and state budgets for education are not sufficient to meet this goal (Office of Management and Budget, 2011). Many approaches are proposed to "rectify the deficiency" and provide mainstream education for children, family literacy, parent outreach, and teacher training programs. The four main approaches are described here (U.S. Department of Education, 2005, p. 25).

English as a Second Language (ESL)　The **English as a second language (ESL) approach** is focused on teaching children English as quickly and efficiently as possible. Thus, children might learn English in a separate class all day until they reach some standard of proficiency. Then they enter the regular classroom and receive full-time instruction in all academic areas in English. That is, the child is taught specific vocabulary and the rules of grammar and has practice in speaking and interpreting English. The obvious question then is, When is a child ready to join the mainstream and exit the ESL class?

One important variable is the level of competency and/or formal instruction the child has had in the primary language. A child whose first language is well developed might reach age- and grade-level norms in English in 3 to 5 years. If the child has received no formal education in the first language, it can take 7 to 10 years (Hoff & Shatz, 2007). In general, late-exit programs have resulted in higher academic achievement than early-exit programs. Another concern is that these children may come to devalue their first language, refusing to speak it at home and in the community. This limits the quality and quantity of their interactions with their families and hinders their development of cultural identity (Crawford, 2007).

TABLE 9.3　Immigration's Contribution to the School-Age Population of English Language Learners

State	School-Age Population (Ages 5–17)	
	Percent with Immigrant Mothers	Number with Immigrant Mothers in Thousands
California	46.8%	3,250
Nevada	29.6	134
New York	28.9	989
Hawaii	27.1	56
Arizona	28.7	294
Florida	26.7	807
Texas	26.4	1,180
New Jersey	26.3	429
Colorado	19.4	161
Maryland	18.5	182
Massachusetts	18.0	205
Illinois	17.7	405
Entire Country	19.2	10,272

Source: Center for Immigration Studies Analysis of March 2005 Current Population Survey.

Bilingual Education   A second approach, **bilingualism,** provides instruction in both languages by teachers who are proficient in both. This approach seems ideal to some, who argue that because children receive instruction in their first language, they can continue to acquire both academic skills and language skills. Using their first language, they are able to express more complex ideas, read higher-level texts, and increase their basic vocabulary, which in turn enables them to learn a second language (English) more easily. It has been documented that cognitive and academic development in the first language has an extremely important and positive effect on second-language schooling (Hoff & Shatz, 2007).

Bilingual programs have consistently shown the greatest gains for children in academic skills and in social and emotional skills. The child is able to interact with family and community with increasing complexity and greater meaning and can feel that her or his first language is on an equal basis with English. When children are tested in their second language, they typically reach and surpass native speakers' performance across all subject areas after 4 to 7 years in a quality bilingual program (Hoff & Shatz, 2007).

Bilingual education programs are controversial, however, and have become a complex issue in nearly all states (Escamilla et al., 2003). In spite of the benefits of bilingual education, California and Arizona voters approved a referendum in the late 1990s requiring that teachers teach only in English, and by 2006 about half of all states had some form of English-only law for classroom instruction (de Jong, 2008). Apparently the majority of voters in these states believed the bilingual approach was not successful and was too great a tax burden since districts had to hire more staff that spoke every child's language. Significantly, many parents did not want their children segregated in schools by pullout bilingual programs. Voters in many states prefer, instead, an instructional approach called total immersion.

Total Immersion   In **total immersion programs,** children are placed in regular classrooms (with or without support in their first language), and English is used for all instruction. This eliminates "separate" education or classes and gives every child an opportunity to observe and learn social communication in English with peers. The theoretical basis of total immersion is that language is best learned not when it is an academic subject but when it is useful, and that children are motivated to learn the language to understand what is going on around them. However, the process is quite lengthy, and learning is directed purposefully to the child's linguistic and cognitive level. That is, we don't teach our 2-year-olds the language of the scientific method. Immersion programs seem to work best when the children are young and the family has positive feelings about this approach.

Two-Way Bilingual Instruction   Some U.S. schools provide instruction in both English and Spanish, and the intended outcome is that all children will become bilingual.

During the middle school years, children begin to understand sentence structure and grammar, extend their vocabularies, write coherently, use school and public libraries or the Internet to find information, and give oral presentations in class. They also utilize their language skills in the community through membership in clubs and activities or by helping neighbors, working as newspaper carriers, volunteering, and so forth. Children this age learn that they have a right to voice their concern about various environmental and societal issues. A command of the English language is a symbol of empowerment for both these children and their parents.

Two-Way Bilingual Programs   In **two-way bilingual programs,** also called *dual-language* programs, both native-speaking students and nonnative speakers receive instruction in English and in another language—such as Spanish or Chinese. Instruction is equally divided between the two languages. All students would eventually become proficient in both languages and achieve *biliteracy,* or literacy in two or more languages. There are nearly 400 such programs in the United States (Center for Applied Linguistics, 2010). Many view biliteracy as a great advantage in seeking college admission, employment, and civic engagement. For such programs to be successful, instruction should begin in preschool and pre-K, and they require teachers who are bilingual, trained, inventive, and strong leaders (de Jong, 2008).

Will They Work?   The success of any of these methods will depend on curriculum planning and implementation; assessment and accountability; teacher quality and professional development; community support and resources; as well as on parental efforts to encourage children, the language spoken in the home, and the skills and motivation of the student (Howard, Sugarman, Christian,

Lindholm-Leary, & Rogers, 2007). Further, acquiring English as a second language remains a very controversial topic in the United States. Providing enough taxpayer funding, resources, and bilingual teachers and mentors for these programs is one of the greatest challenges facing the U.S. educational system. The future success of children learning English as a second language will depend on both family support and the support of U.S. society at large.

Questions

Do you think children should be "allowed" to speak a language besides English in school? What are some of the various instructional approaches for children learning English as a second language? Should colleges require all graduates to become bilingual to be able to communicate with an increasingly diverse ethnic population?

Global Assessment in Math, Science, and Literacy

International comparisons of academic achievement on tests in mathematics and science are becoming more important as global economic competition becomes more intense. A country's ranking is often viewed as a barometer of its economic strength. Comparisons are often made between the United States and other industrialized nations. Although U.S. students in fourth and eighth grade improved their scores above the international average in math and science in 2003 and 2007, the *Trends in International Mathematics and Science Study* (*TIMSS*) found that since 1995, they have been consistently outperformed by students in several Asian countries: Singapore, Hong Kong SAR, Chinese Taipei, Japan, and the Republic of Korea (see Table 9.4) (Gonzales et al., 2009). Still, the average mathematics scores for U.S. students in both grades were higher in 2007 than in 1995, so improvements in math can be seen. U.S. fourth- and eighth-grade students' average science scores in 2007 were not measurably different from those in 1995. In general, U.S. boys scored slightly higher in math than U.S. girls in both grades (Mullis et al., 2008).

Results from another global assessment of fourth-grade students in 2006, *Progress in International Reading Literacy Study* (*PIRLS*), indicate that the top-performing countries in reading literacy were the Russian Federation, Hong Kong SAR, and Singapore. In all countries, girls had higher reading achievement scores than boys. "Only about half the students across the PIRLS 2006 countries agreed that they enjoyed reading and appreciated books, reflecting a troubling downward trend since 2001" (TIMSS & PIRLS International Study Center, 2007). Students worldwide took the next TIMSS and PIRLS tests in 2011, and the results were to be published

TABLE 9.4 *TIMSS* Rankings of Average Math Achievement Scores of Eighth-Graders, Selected Countries: 1995–2007

Country	1995 N = 41	1999 N = 38	2003 N = 48	2007 N = 48
Chinese Taipei	N/A	3	4	1
Korea	2	2	1	2
Singapore	1	1	2	3
Hong Kong	4	4	3	4
Japan	3	5	5	5
Hungary	13	9	8	6
England	22	19	20	7
Russian Federation	14	12	10	8
United States	25	18	14	9
Australia	16	13	18	14

Source: Mullis, I. V. S., et al. (2008). *TIMSS 2007 International Mathematics Report: Findings from IEA's Trends in International Mathematics and Science Study at the Fourth and Eighth Grades.* Chestnut Hill, MA: TIMSS & PIRLS International Study Center, Boston College. Mullis, I. V. S., Martin, M. O., & Foy, P. (2005). *TIMSS 2003 International Report on Achievement in the Mathematics Cognitive Domain: Findings from a Developmental Project.* Chestnut Hill, MA: TIMSS & PIRLS International Study Center, Boston College. Mullis, I. V. S., et al. (2000). *TIMSS 1999 International Mathematics Report: Findings from IEA's Repeat of the Third International Mathematics and Science Study at the Eighth Grade.* Chestnut Hill, MA: TIMSS & PIRLS International Study Center, Boston College. Harmon, M., et al. (1997). *Performance Assessment in IEA's Third International Mathematics and Science Study (TIMSS).* Chestnut Hill, MA: TIMSS International Study Center, Boston College.

in 2012. However, a recent national report card from the National Assessment of Educational Progress (NAEP) presented results indicating that U.S. fourth- and eighth-graders' scores in mathematics and reading were much higher in 2007 (Lee, Grigg, & Donahue, 2007).

Assessment of Intelligence

When we think about intelligence, we think about the ways in which individuals differ from one another in their ability to understand and express complex ideas, adapt effectively to their environment, learn from experience, and solve problems. (The concept of intelligence was defined in Chapter 7.) Although the children's differences in their ability to do those things may be tremendous, their abilities can also appear to vary as a consequence of the time at which we assess them, the methods used, and the specific tasks we ask them to perform (Daniel, 1997). Historically, what we know about differences in school-age children is based on academic performance in school and intelligence testing using standardized psychometric tests. This makes sense because in school these differences play a major role in determining how children learn and what educational programs best meet their cognitive needs. Given that, two questions come to mind. First, what tests should we use to measure children's cognitive abilities? Second, how should the information we get from the assessment be used to determine specific educational plans? For a cross-cultural perspective on academic performance, see the *Further Developments* box on page 286, "Why Asian Children Strive for Excellence."

Types of Intelligence Tests Intelligence tests come in many formats. Some use only a single type of item or question; examples include the *Peabody Picture Vocabulary Test* (a measure of children's verbal intelligence) and *Raven's Progressive Matrices* (a nonverbal, untimed test that requires inductive reasoning about perceptual patterns). Other tests use several different types of items, including verbal and nonverbal (performance), to measure a wide range of abilities instead of one specific construct such as spatial ability or verbal intelligence. The Wechsler scales and the *Stanford-Binet* test ask the test-taker to give meanings of words, complete a series of pictures, copy a block design, and complete analogies. Performance on these tests can be measured in several domains (subscores), as well as by an overall score relating to general intelligence. The scores are standardized, with a *mean* of 100 and a *standard deviation* of 15. This permits us to make statements such as "95 percent of the population scored within 2 standard deviations of the mean" (between 70 and 130) and compare the person's score to the norming population (the population the test-taker is being compared with).

In contrast to these psychometric tests, other tests give us insight about a person's ability in a specific type of task. If we want to measure spatial ability, we might measure the length of time it takes a person to find a certain place in a new town or unfamiliar setting, or we might measure linguistic ability by asking a person to give an extemporaneous talk. Schools primarily use the more conventional measurements such as the *Stanford-Binet* or *WISC-IV* (*Wechsler Intelligence Scale for Children-IV*), because the reliability and validity of such tests are documented, the scores are stable at least for school-age children, and they correlate well with, and are predictive of, academic performance.

The EQ Factor: Emotional Intelligence Learning emotional self-regulation, a component of **emotional intelligence,** is not an easy task. Consider this short interaction and how emotional intelligence is displayed:

> Three twelve-year-olds are heading to a soccer field for gym class. The two athletic looking boys are walking behind and snickering at the third, a somewhat chubby classmate. "So, you're going to try to play soccer," one of the two says sarcastically to the third. The chubby boy closes his eyes for a moment and takes a deep breath, and in a calm, matter-of-fact voice replies, "Yeah, I'm going to try, but I'm not very good at it." After a pause, he adds, "But I'm great at art, show me anything, and I can draw it real good . . ." Then, pointing to his antagonist, he says, "Now you, you're great at soccer, really fantastic!"

> At that, the first boy, his disdain now utterly disarmed, says in a friendly tone, "Well, you're not really that bad. Maybe I can show you a few things about how to play." (Goleman, 2007)

Here, a volatile situation that could easily have led to a fight, may lead to a new friendship instead. The use of emotional intelligence may also help the growing number of children who are turning to violence when social conflict arises. Some children in middle schools and high schools are bringing weapons to school and concealing them in lockers and book bags. Large urban and suburban schools have resorted to using metal detectors, 24-hour video security systems, and police officers to patrol hallways. When confrontations arise, as they always will, some youngsters have not been able to control their anger, rage, or fear. A few have taken tragic courses of action, killing innocent peers and school personnel. Drive-by shootings, in which youth in cars randomly shoot innocent children and adults for the thrill of it, have become all too common. We will return to the topic of emotional maturation in Chapter 13, where we discuss early adulthood.

Limitations of IQ Tests Many times children are included in or excluded from specific educational programs on the basis of their intellectual functioning, but the intellectual functioning of children with limited English proficiency often cannot be determined. For example, special education services for mental retardation (now called intellectual disability) or cognitive impairment are available only to children who are tested using a standard measure of intelligence (an IQ test) and obtain an IQ score (full scale) of less than 75. A child with a score below 75 is assumed to be achieving lower than 97 percent of the population tested. Yet we know that a child's academic performance cannot be totally explained by this one score. In fact, other factors play a role in the child's success in school, such as the child's motivation, social and language skills, self-concept, family and ethnic values, and familiarity/comfort with the person administering the test. Socioeconomic causes may also blur the significance of IQ tests. Children with mild intellectual disability from poor households are often subject to poor nutrition and medical care, unstable living situations, and limited access to learning opportunities at home (Children's Defense Fund, 2008). The question of the relative effects of genetics and sociocultural background in determining intelligence is sometimes referred to as the *nature-versus-nurture controversy.* The combination of ill effects from both genetic and sociocultural factors as a determinant in intelligence is known as *cultural-familial* intellectual disability.

More recently, some schools have turned to a *multidisciplinary team assessment.* This comprehensive look at the child might include teacher input on achievement

FURTHER DEVELOPMENTS

Why Asian Children Strive for Excellence

Asian Students Excel Since 1995, Asian schoolchildren have performed at the highest levels of math and science on the TIMSS and of literacy on the PIRLS—international assessments administered to schoolchildren from nearly 50 countries. Asian parents demand excellence and work with their children for long hours, and schools provide a longer school year and an orderly and focused education.

Achievement consists of hard work and never giving up, states Chinese philosopher Hsun Tzu (pronounced *Sun Zi*) (Zhang, 2005). Asian students consistently have much higher scores than students from other countries in the TIMSS and PIRLS studies. Shen (2005) suggests that Asian schools take a more central position in the lives of their children. Also, in 2011 Amy Chua, distinguished professor of Law at Yale Law School, wrote in the *Wall Street Journal* about her life growing up as a first-generation Chinese child in the United States and about her own parental approach as a Chinese-American mother raising her two daughters. She has authored three books, and one of them, *Battle Hymn of the Tiger Mother,* has caused a heated debate. She spoke out about "how Chinese parents raise such stereotypically successful kids" (Chua, 2011). She says that whereas Western parents *think* they are strict, most Chinese parents actually *are.* Western parents are also very concerned about their child's self-esteem and happiness. Not so most Chinese mothers (she calls them "tiger mothers"). Chinese mothers spend many hours daily working with their child(ren), believing that "academic achievement reflects successful parenting," that "to get good at anything you have to work," and that "tenacious practice, practice,

practice is crucial for excellence." Her children spend at least two hours a day practicing music, completing homework (plus earning extra credit), and taking lessons from a Chinese tutor. Chinese mothers believe their children can be the best and assume that they will get nothing less than an A grade. Chinese parents put in long hours "tutoring, training, interrogating, and spying on their kids."

Chua says that Chinese parents would give up anything for their child(ren) and believe they know what is best—which is to prepare them with skills, work habits, and inner confidence for their future. This practice contrasts with the Western view of respecting a child's individuality and encouraging a child to follow her or his passion. Her two daughters could not attend a sleepover, have a playdate, be in a school play, watch TV or play computer games, choose their own extracurricular activities, get any grade less than an A, be less than the number one student in each subject except gym or drama, or play an instrument other than piano or violin. When Chua mentioned some of her cultural parenting practices in front of other women, the American mothers expressed great alarm. She says it's just a different style of parenting, designed to raise successful children. Indeed, her older teenage daughter has performed at Carnegie Hall. But her younger daughter rebelled against the strict regimen of study and practice. Subsequently, Chua has become more flexible with her younger daughter's violin practice time and has allowed her 14-year-old daughter to attend her first sleepover.

Japanese parents also have high regard for education and teach children to count to 100 and tell time on clocks before they enroll in elementary school (Sugiyama, 2001). Learning the Japanese numeral system is relatively easy: A child learns to count from 1 to 10 and then learns one simple rule that enables him or her to count to 100 (there is less to memorize than in the decimal system). By second grade, all Japanese students learn their multiplication facts (*ku ku*), using various songs and mnemonics (Sugiyama, 2001). The Japanese school system has a *no failure policy;* thus teachers must pay special attention to low-achieving students.

Source: Chua, A. (2011, January 8). Why Chinese mothers are superior. Can a regimen of no playdates, no TV, no computer games and hours of music practice create happy kids? And what happens when they fight back? *Wall Street Journal, 257*(6), C1–C2. Retrieved from http://online.wsj.com/article/SB10001424052748704111504576 059713528698754.html

and effort, parent and community reports of how the child functions, observations by a school psychologist of the child in the classroom, review of the child's portfolio or work samples, and recommendations from various professionals and others who have knowledge about the child (e.g., speech therapist, resource room teacher). These additional pieces of information provide a more global understanding of the child's abilities. Nevertheless, it is useful to obtain standard measures as well, to prevent bias or prejudice in the child's placement in a special education program.

It is well documented that certain groups of children are identified more frequently than others as being in need of special education services, even with the use of standard scores. For example, more African American children than white children are being placed in special education classes, even though there is no evidence of underlying differences in their abilities (LeBeauf, 2008). To ensure proper placement for all children, school psychologists, educational psychologists, and teachers must continue to pursue theoretical as well as practical knowledge about how children learn, the role of intellectual ability, and curriculum and instructional methods that best match children's learning needs.

Individual Cognitive Styles   Have you ever wondered why some subjects come easier to you than others? Have you ever felt stupid or out of place in a classroom? Did you feel that you couldn't understand the information being presented, no matter how hard you concentrated? Although intelligence plays a role in all learning, not everyone learns in the same way. Some people learn best using visual information; others prefer to hear the spoken word. Yet others learn faster and retain the information longer when they involve all of their senses in hands-on learning (such as laboratory experiences). Still others, such as some students with autism, "think" in pictures instead of in words, storing images "as if they were on a CDROM" (Grandin, 2008). These differences in how individuals organize and process information have come to be called cognitive styles.

Cognitive styles are powerful heuristics that cut across traditional boundaries between intelligence and personality and influence a person's preferred way of perceiving, remembering, and using information (Crandell, 1979, 1982; Sternberg & Grigorenko, 1997). Psychologists have been researching cognitive styles for over 50 years and have identified a number of different cognitive-style models, including Witkin's field-dependence versus field-independence, Kagan's impulsive versus reflective, Hill's educational cognitive style, the Myers-Briggs Type Indicator, the Dunn & Dunn Learning Style, the Kirtin Adaption-Innovation, and others (Messick, 1984). Research shows that when students are matched to instruction based on their preferred style of learning, they process information faster, retain it longer, and are motivated to continue to learn (Dunn, Beaudry, & Klavas, 1989). Several features of this book were developed with students' various learning strengths in mind.

Putting theory into practice is difficult because teachers utilize many methods of teaching (such as speaking, writing on the board or on transparencies, acting or modeling, using manipulatives, showing videos, presenting PowerPoint slides, and arranging active learning in a lab). Teacher education programs are becoming more innovative, developing new delivery and testing strategies, requiring proficiency in a second language, and offering training in multimedia and multisensory approaches to accommodate the students' different learning styles. The concept of *portfolio assessment* has been an outgrowth of learning styles: Any student is a whole being, not simply one who writes and speaks and calculates. Some are artistic, some are mechanical, some are musical, and some are quite adept socially. Proponents of portfolio assessment believe that a whole year of a child's academic life should not be reduced to a grade point average. These teachers keep a portfolio of the best of a child's performances for the year. The portfolio might include examples of a child's best work (such as photographs of a class play or sports events, a science fair or a talent show, an original poem, or notes on a car the child helped build for *Odyssey of the Mind* competition), in addition to the child's best essays and math exams of the year.

Questions

Why do Asian children consistently outperform U.S. children on international assessments in math and science? How do we measure individual differences in cognitive abilities? In what ways is the process of cognitive development universal? Are there individual and group differences in the way people process information?

Students with Disabilities

The *Education for All Handicapped Children Act,* PL 94-142, enacted in 1975, gave every American school-age child the right to a free, equal, and appropriate education in the least restrictive environment possible. Since then, American children with disabilities have been able to attend public schools and prepare for a meaningful future. This law was reauthorized by the *Individuals with Disabilities Education Act (IDEA)* in 1990. And the *Individuals with Disabilities Education Improvement Act of 2004* updated regulations (Learning Disabilities Roundtable, 2005). Classifications are more specific now, and Figure 9.2 shows the disability distribution for students aged 3 through 21 receiving special education and related

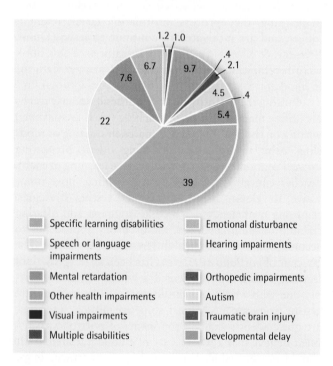

Specific learning disabilities   Emotional disturbance

Speech or language impairments   Hearing impairments

Mental retardation   Orthopedic impairments

Other health impairments   Autism

Visual impairments   Traumatic brain injury

Multiple disabilities   Developmental delay

FIGURE 9.2 Distribution of Disabilities for U.S. Students Aged 3 to 21 Receiving Special Education and Related Services Under IDEA: 2007–2008 (by percentage)

Source: Snyder, T. D., & Dillow, S. A. (2010, April). *Digest of Education Statistics 2009* (NCES2010-013). 1–732. Washington, DC: U.S. Department of Education, National Center for Education Statistics.

services under IDEA (Bender, 2008). In 1975 scholars estimated that 2 percent of the school-age population had learning disabilities; in the 1990s this figure had reached 5 percent; and by 2007–2008, nearly 14 percent of all students were receiving a wide range of special education services (Snyder & Dillow, 2010). In 2008, the largest disability category (39 percent of those receiving special education services) was specific learning disabilities (Snyder & Dillow, 2010). Most students diagnosed with a disability are identified by third and fourth grade, and a majority of those students continue receiving special services throughout their school years (Snyder & Dillow, 2010).

Mental Retardation/Intellectual Disabilities   In 2010, federal law (called *Rosa's Law*) changed the classification of mental retardation to **intellectual disabilities.** This change affects the classification for 7 to 8 million Americans and for any federal agency, reporting agencies, and federal education, health, and labor laws; school programs; and Social Security (Roach, 2010). Children and adults with intellectual disabilities have below-average mental functioning and limitations in adaptive skills, and a diagnosis must occur before the child reaches age 18. Since 1976, far fewer children have been classified with mental retardation (MR); in 2008, only 1 percent of the total school-age population was classified with such intellectual disabilities—probably because of more refined prenatal diagnostics and more children being classified with learning disabilities (Hardman, Drew, & Egan, 2011). "Intellectual disabilities" can result from genetic or chromosomal disorders (such as Down syndrome or fragile X), prenatal teratogen effects (such as fetal alcohol syndrome), birth complications (such as oxygen deprivation), nutritional and/or environmental deprivation after birth, childhood head injuries or exposure to teratogens, and unknown causes.

IQ scores of approximately 75 to 70 and lower are used to classify the severity of cognitive limitation into four categories: *mild, moderate, severe,* and *profound.* When both ability and measured intelligence are low, clearly intellectual disability exists. However, discrepancies between ability and measured intelligence usually indicate a learning disability. Youth with MR/intellectual disability experience limitations in academics, communication, daily life skills, social skills, leisure, and work—although there are more opportunities for development to full potential when therapeutic services begin with early intervention at birth.

Learning Disabilities (LDs)   In 2007–2008, 2.5 million children aged 3 to 21 years (5 percent of total school enrollment) were classified with a learning disability; more boys than girls have a learning disability (Snyder & Dillow, 2010). The 2004 law defines a *learning disability* as "a disorder in one or more of the basic psychological processes involved in understanding or in using language,

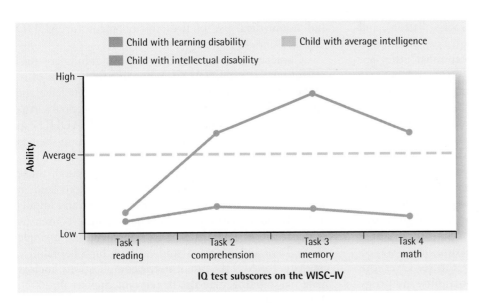

FIGURE 9.3 Hypothetical Profile of a Child with a Learning Disability, a Child with an Intellectual Disability, and a Child of Average Intelligence on the *WISC–IV* IQ Test

spoken or written, which may manifest itself in an imperfect ability to listen, think, speak, read, write, spell or do mathematical calculations" (Bender, 2008).

Educators employ the term **learning disabilities (LDs)** as an umbrella concept to refer to difficulties that children, adolescents, college students, and adults encounter with school-related or work-related material despite the fact that they appear to have normal intelligence and lack any demonstrable physical, emotional, or social impairment (some prefer the term *differently abled*). In practice, the notion implies that a discrepancy exists between a student's estimated ability and his or her academic performance. Youngsters are usually diagnosed as having a learning disability when their achievement falls two or more grade levels below their ability, as predicted by a standardized IQ test score (see the hypothetical example in Figure 9.3).

Specific learning disabilities continues to be the most prevalent category of disability among students in elementary school through high school, accounting for more than 40 percent of the total of all children receiving special education services (see Figure 9.2). Nearly four times as many boys as girls are formally classified with reading disabilities, yet just as many girls have reading disabilities as boys (Bender, 2008).

A variety of youngsters are designated as "learning disabled." There are some whose eyes see correctly but whose brains improperly receive or process the informational input. Or instead of zeroing in on what is directly in front of their noses, they take a global view (Cramer & Rosenfield, 2008). They might get letters mixed up, reading *was* as "saw" or *god* as "dog." Others have difficulty selecting, from a mass of sensory information, the specific stimulus that is relevant to the task at hand. Still

others might hear but fail to remember what they have heard because of an auditory-memory problem. They might turn to the wrong page in the book or attempt the wrong assignment when they rely on oral instructions. The sources of such disabilities are varied and include combinations of genetic, social, cognitive, and neuropsychological factors (Bursuck & Damer, 2007).

High-tech brain-imaging techniques, including PET scans, suggest that signal-processing regions such as the thalamus might be implicated. The thalamus is a structure that takes incoming signals from the eyes, ears, and other sensory organs and routes them to different areas of the brain. Those with a learning disability have problems in reading (*dyslexia*), writing (*dysgraphia*), mathematics (*dyscalcula*), or auditory and visual processing. Students identified as dyslexic make up a large percentage of the LD population, and a significant longitudinal study of youth from first grade to twelfth grade reveals continuing difficulty with phonological awareness (distinguishing the sounds of the phonemes of words), which impacts reading fluency (Dowker, 2006). Recent research using (fMRI) reveals that the brain structures for reading are malleable, and their disruption in children with learning disorders may be remediated by proper reading interventions that work on these designated areas (Shaywitz, Lyon, & Shaywitz, 2006).

Such disabilities are often called "the invisible handicap," but learning disabilities do not necessarily lead to low achievement. Many accomplished scientists (Thomas Edison and Albert Einstein), political leaders (Woodrow Wilson and Winston Churchill), authors (Hans Christian Andersen), artists (Leonardo da Vinci and Tommy Hilfiger), sculptors (Auguste Rodin), actors (Tom Cruise and Henry Winkler), famous athletes (Magic Johnson and Nolan Ryan), military figures (George Patton), and entertainers (Jay Leno) have had learning disabilities. Such individuals are called "twice exceptional"; they are exceptional both because they are gifted and because they have learning disabilities (Nicpon, Allmon, Sieck, & Stinson, 2011).

The placement of children in a category such as "learning disabled" is a serious matter. From a positive perspective, classification provides services that can facilitate learning, improve a child's sense of self-worth, and foster social integration. It is important for teachers and the public to be aware that the labels are not used for obscure, covert, or hurtful purposes (Shaywitz, 2003). Up until 1975, children with disabilities were not offered a public education; most stayed at home with no prospects for the future. Over the past three decades, the doors of opportunity and progress have opened. Each child and her or his family can determine to what extent they will take advantage of this opportunity.

Attention-Deficit Hyperactivity Disorder   A condition that has implications for learning and cognitive development is **attention-deficit hyperactivity disorder (ADHD)**. ADHD involves a collection of vague and global symptoms. Typically, youngsters who are impulsive and cannot stay in their seats, wait their turn, follow instructions, or stick with a task are viewed as having ADHD. (One well-known person diagnosed with ADHD is carpenter-designer Ty Pennington, who appears on ABC's *Extreme Makeover Home Edition*.) Three subtypes of ADHD are recognized: hyperactive-impulsive, inattentive, and combined hyperactive and inattentive (Zentall, 2006). In 2007, Bloom and Cohen reported that 4.5 million children aged 3 to 17 were diagnosed with ADHD. Boys were more than twice as likely as girls to have ADHD (11 percent versus 4 percent), although a new finding suggests that research on children with ADHD has focused on Caucasian males from middle-class and upper-middle-class families. Less attention was directed at females, children from low socioeconomic backgrounds, and children from diverse racial-ethnic backgrounds. This narrow focus may have affected prevalence rates and gender differences in ADHD treatments (Daly et al., 2007).

Some of these children also have learning disabilities and some do not. Many children with ADHD and many with both ADHD and a learning disability are often prescribed medication (Bloom & Cohen, 2007). Recent research suggests that combining medical and behavioral therapies is an especially effective approach to treating ADHD. However, research on long-term effects of medications for ADHD is ongoing. Psychostimulants are the most effective agents available at present. One serious concern is the sharp rise the past few years in teen abuse

and nonmedical use of prescription meds for ADHD (Setlik, Bond, & Ho, 2009).

Clinicians report that some afflicted adults are successful not in spite of ADHD, but in part because of it. These people, though easily distracted, often have the uncanny ability to "hyperfocus" and can become virtually immune to distractions. Ironically, while ADHD can put those with high IQs and good social skills at the top of their field (e.g., emergency room physicians, sales personnel, stock-market traders, and entrepreneurs), those with ADHD and who lack such attributes can land in prison, led astray by their zeal for risk taking and impulsive behaviors (Barkley, 2001). There is little consensus on what causes ADHD or even whether it has a single cause. Twin and adoption studies show high heritability estimates for ADHD, but obstetric complications, such as maternal smoking, may also be relevant (Stein et al., 2007). Associations have been found with specific gene variants, particularly in the dopaminergic and noradrenergic systems. Genes related to dopamine signaling (a chemical messenger in the brain) have been seen as modulators in attention. Those diagnosed with ADHD have been described as having low levels of dopamine, which correlate with diminished attention spans (Waldman & Gizer, 2006). Further, the dopamine transporter has been linked to cerebral blood flow to the basal ganglia, a major factor in effective ADHD treatment (see Figure 9.4) (Pliszka, 2007). As a result, an interactive model combining genetic and environmental influences might best explain the development of ADHD in childhood (Stein et al., 2007).

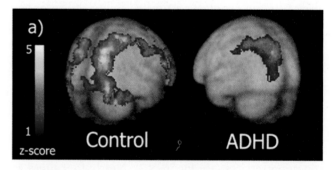

FIGURE 9.4 Brain Scans Give New Hope for Diagnosing Individuals with Attention-Deficit Hyperactivity Disorder (ADHD)   Research from the University of Queensland, Australia, using functional magnetic resonance imaging (fMRI) shows that 8- to 12-year-old boys with ADHD have less activity in the left-temporo-parietal brain areas while performing attention-demanding, problem-solving tasks than boys in the control group. This strengthens the evidence for a biological cause of ADHD, and intervention techniques are under study to provide remediation for changes in brain function.
Source: Dr. Ross Cunnington. The University of Queensland, Australia. (2007, September 24). Young children have biological reason for attention deficit hyperactivity disorder. *University of Queensland News.* Retrieved January 5, 2008, from http://www.uq.edu.au/news/index.html?article[H11005]13050

Most nations, such as France and England, still treat unruly youngsters as behavior problems rather than as patients. Many professionals and members of the public fear that overreliance on prescribing amphetamines to "hyperactive" children has led to abuses and acceptance of drug therapy for children who might not benefit or who might actually be harmed by it. Recently, some doctors have turned to advocating exercise as an ADHD treatment for children, rather than prescribing drugs. Studies reveal that after physical activity, children diagnosed with ADHD displayed an increase in attentiveness and calmness (Azrin, Ehle, & Beaumont, 2006).

Individualized Education Plans (IEPs)   All students classified as having any disability, including a learning disability, are to be provided with an **individualized education plan (IEP).** This plan, which is developed in a collaborative effort by the school psychologist, the child's teachers, an independent child advocate, and the parent(s) or guardian, is a legal document that ensures that the child with special learning needs will receive the needed educational support services in the least restrictive environment possible. The children themselves may also sit in on the process and contribute to their own plans. Goals and objectives for a child, based on current levels of functioning, are outlined by everyone involved in planning and providing services.

For the school year 2007–2008, 13 percent of public school students, or 6.6 million children, had a special education individualized education plan (IEP) (Snyder & Dillow, 2010). In 2007, 13 percent of boys in grades K–3 had an IEP, but only 3 percent of girls of the same age had IEPs (Child Trends Databank, 2010f).

The development of an IEP gives caregivers the opportunity to work with educators as equal participants to identify a child's needs. The IEP is a commitment in writing to the educational program and resources the school agrees to provide. Periodic IEP review serves as an evaluation of the child's progress toward meeting the educational goals decided upon by the caregivers and school professionals. The IEP is an important legal document.

Inclusion   In the past, many children with disabilities were schooled at home or in segregated or expensive private settings. Since 1975, shifts in laws and educational policy formed the basis for inclusive education, often called *mainstreaming* or *inclusion* (Bricker, 2000). **Inclusion** gives these children the opportunity to attend the school they would have attended if they were not disabled (National Association of School Psychologists, 2009). They receive additional support, while participating in classes with peers their age. Annual placement occurs as a result of appraisal of child characteristics, family expectations and ability to access information,

teacher training, availability of services, and supports in the school system. (See the *Implications for Practice* box on page 292, "Special Education Teacher.")

Placement in pre-kindergarten or kindergarten is often fully inclusive yet becomes more restrictive as academics are more challenging in each grade (Hanson et al., 2001). Therefore, the presence of children with special needs in regular classrooms does not guarantee academic or social success. It works well when leaders are committed to making it work through designing, implementing, and supporting appropriate restructuring of the educational enterprise (Hanson et al., 2001). A significant relationship exists between teachers' prior experience, knowledge of disabilities, and attitudes about inclusion (Burke & Sutherland, 2004). Special education teachers are particularly prone to burnout, which is often occasioned by large caseloads, the broad range of disabilities among students, and the burden of paperwork and other regulatory issues (Emery & Vandenberg, 2010).

Through the *Individuals with Disabilities Education Improvement Act of 2004*, transition planning and services from preschool through graduation are supposed to be incorporated into an IEP for students with learning disabilities or other disabilities. To prepare for post-school life, more are experiencing vocational training and work experience and then are (1) eventually transitioning out to sheltered workshop employment, regular employment, or military endeavors; (2) graduating from high schools; or (3) entering and graduating from college programs where special services are provided to accommodate the student's individual learning needs. More of these youth are integrating into the mainstream of society, becoming productive, fully integrated members of society; others sustain themselves minimally on social services and welfare (Bakken & Obiakor, 2008).

Questions

What process is used to identify a child as "learning disabled"? Why do some children need an individualized education plan? What do we mean when we speak of an inclusive education for children?

What Is Known About Effective Schools

Public education performance is starting to improve from over two decades ago, yet society demands highly trained and skilled citizens for today's jobs. Some researchers have concluded that successful schools foster expectations that order will prevail and that learning is a serious matter (Johnson, 1994). Much of the success of private and Catholic schools has derived from their ability to provide students with an orderly environment and strong academic demands, but their enrollment is

IMPLICATIONS FOR PRACTICE

Special Education Teacher, James Crandell

I have been a consultant-teacher of special education in the sixth grade at Chenango Forks Central School District (New York) for 19 years. Primarily, I am responsible for providing services to 15 students classified with learning disabilities. I also spend time instructing another 35 regular education students.

I wear a lot of hats! My primary role is to develop and deliver classroom lessons that I modify to reflect the various learning preferences and challenges of my students. The remainder of my time is spent on the following: collaborating and planning with my two co-teachers, offering instructional ideas and deciding how our individual lessons will actually be presented; using a variety of behavior modification strategies to provide immediate, predictable, and consistent consequences to those children who have limited self-control; grading various classroom assignments; and planning how to assess the content taught so that each child has an equal opportunity for success.

I have a bachelor's of science in psychology from SUNY Cortland and a master's degree in special education from Alfred University. Special education teachers are required to complete student-teaching experience under the guidance of a certified teacher. I was required to pass a state certification exam to qualify for my degree. My previous job experience includes working at a day treatment center with individuals with developmental disabilities.

Foremost, a special education teacher needs to possess a high degree of flexibility. Due to new state regulations regarding the inclusion of students with disabilities in the mainstream classroom, I provide services to my students in other teachers'

classrooms. Sometimes it is difficult to work closely with educators who have philosophical differences, but I focus on being helpful because the children are ultimately those who are impacted. Another essential personality trait is patience. These children often make slow progress due to the cycle of failure they experience in their schooling. I am determined to help these students realize that, despite their limitations (i.e., reading-decoding disability), they all have strengths. One of my students is well below grade level in his reading skills, yet he is a phenomenal artist and knows every part of an auto engine. Finally, you must be creative and investigate nontraditional methods for teaching students with special needs. For example, rather than use a vocabulary matching quiz, I ask the child to recognize a picture of the vocabulary term as a way to reflect the child's understanding.

You have to love children to think about being a teacher. Unlike computers, children cannot be programmed—especially middle-schoolers with special needs who are going through major emotional-social developmental changes. Teachers must accept that these feelings may disrupt a well-planned lesson. Skilled teachers know how to provide the students with appropriate ways to express feelings and are able to help children transfer their passion into class work.

The most enjoyable aspects of my job include seeing children be successful, especially those who encounter mostly failure, and relating with my co-teachers who share my love for teaching. I truly enjoy developing a unique strategy for teaching a concept that completely engages the children in the material. I am never bored in my job.

---

declining due to the rise in tuition costs (Meyer, 2007). Some researchers question whether private schools are really doing a better job, or whether *selection bias* (private schools may select their student population, whereas public schools must be open to all) is the underlying reason for their apparent success (Goyal, 2009).

The principal of a Blue Ribbon School in Frankford, Delaware—also a National Distinguished Title

I School—was honored as a National Distinguished Principal. She believes these five qualities are associated with student achievement and school success: (1) systematic, specific interventions in place for low achievers, including many opportunities for one-on-one support; (2) collaborating teams of teachers that also provide leadership—her teachers have procured $750,000 in grant monies to integrate technology instruction into the curriculum; (3) use of data to evaluate programs and drive continuous improvement; (4) extensive support from family and community members as mentors; and (5) support for staff development and leadership capacity at all levels (Brittingham, 2005).

No Child Left Behind   After federal officials reviewed the slightly above average U.S. student results from international exams, such as TIMSS and PIRLs, in 2001, the *No Child Left Behind* (NCLB) education reform plan became law (U.S. Department of Education, 2001). Although school reform, higher achievement expectations for *all* students, teacher training, regular program evaluation, and accountability are clearly necessary, the education community has many criticisms of the mandates, such as inadequate funding and the constant emphasis on students' passing standardized tests.

In 2010, the U.S. Department of Education called for congressional reauthorization and revision of NCLB, officially known as the *Elementary and Secondary Education Act* (ESEA) (U.S. Department of Education, 2010). The revision plan emphasizes producing career- and college-ready students, with better tools for assessing students; placing the best teachers and administrators and providing them with support and rewards; supporting all students, including those with LEP and learning disabilities; raising the bar for assessment of schools and rewarding those with the best plans; and promoting innovation and continued improvement. Some fear that the new goals of NCLB may counteract effective teaching for students with special needs (Fuchs, Fuchs, & Stecker, 2010).

Family Influences on Academic Achievement   Researchers studying Western-style parental influences have focused on the impact of the general patterns and philosophy of child rearing on children's overall orientation toward achievement. The family variables shown to enhance a child's motivation to succeed in the classroom are general emotional warmth and supportiveness in the home, valuing of achievement, support for academic goals, and appropriate discipline tactics (Grusec & Hastings, 2007). Parents need to structure their children's learning activities to support the child's sense of autonomy and to foster high levels of achievement, motivation, and engagement. For example, reading to one's preschool children and then providing books and magazines in the home for children to read on their own boosts the children's later reading achievement and motivation (Grusec & Hastings, 2007). However, some parents who are active in their child's education at home believe that public school education could be better. "Fed up" with public schools, some parents are turning to evangelical schools, private-tuition schools, and charter or magnet schools, as well as other government-sponsored alternative schools, or to homeschooling.

Since 1993, when it became legal to homeschool children in the United States, the number of children in homeschools has risen considerably—in Canada and Great Britain as well. Recent data show that over 2 million U.S. children aged 6 to 17 are homeschooled, and the numbers are rising every year (National Center for Education Statistics, 2010). A majority of homeschooled children live in two-parent families, and most mothers do not work outside the home. Christian families make up a majority of those who do homeschooling, but American Muslims are the most rapidly growing subgroup. On average, homeschoolers perform at least one grade level above age level (Basham, Merrifield, & Hepburn, 2007). Homeschooled students consistently perform above the national average on standardized tests and on SAT and ACT college admissions tests and are earning more National Merit Scholarships ("Academic Statistics on Homeschooling," 2004). The main reasons why parents choose to homeschool their children are child safety, character development, and maintaining family values versus peer-secular values. Accordingly, we now turn to that central issue of character development, or moral development, during the middle childhood years.

Questions

What types of programs are mandated for children with learning or other disabilities? Why are more children being classified as having a learning disability? Why are more parents placing their children in alternative school settings?

MORAL DEVELOPMENT

As humans, we live our lives in groups. Because we are interdependent, one person's activities can affect others' welfare. Consequently, if we are to live with one another—if society is to be possible—we must share certain conceptions of what is right and what is wrong. Each of us must fulfill our needs and pursue our interests, be they work, food, shelter, clothing, pleasure, power, fame, education, or recreation and leisure, within the context of a moral order governed by rules. Morality shapes how we go about distributing the benefits and burdens of a cooperative group existence (Wilson, 1993). People in societies have different views on morality: "Western cultures are based on a morality of personal rights and individual autonomy, whereas in non-Western cultures the concept of rights is not central because of a moral orientation to the group and interdependence" (Turiel, 2006b, p. 25). But universally, "humans express moral disapproval and apply sanctions against those who violate the social rules" (Fry, 2006, p. 405). Such consequences might include gossip, sarcasm, ridicule, nasty looks, infliction of injury, ostracism, retaliation or revenge, or even execution (Fry, 2006).

Thus, all societies require that their standards of morality be passed on to children, so that moral development will take place in its young. **Moral development** is the process by which children adopt principles and values that lead them to evaluate given behaviors as right and others as wrong and to govern their own actions in terms of these principles. If media interest is any indication, many Americans are quite concerned with the moral status of contemporary youngsters, and although some rely on their own formal practices of faith, others expect schools and educators to teach values and fill what they deem to be a moral vacuum.

A century ago, Freud believed that children develop a conscience through feeling a sense of guilt for their actions. Certainly, development of conscience is an ongoing process throughout the middle childhood years. Children of this age are not self-interested opportunists with a punishment-and-obedience orientation to moral compliance. Rather, development of conscience is rooted in their efforts to understand the desires and interests of other people. The incentive for moral development arises not only through the discipline of parents and authorities, but also from the mutual goodwill that arises from close relationships of trust—or the *reciprocity principle*: Do unto others as you would have them do unto you (Fry, 2006). Children learn about moral values from the way parents talk about rules and from the consequences of violating them, but they learn even more when parents talk about people's feelings and how those feelings are affected by the child's conduct (Killen & Smetana, 2006). The developing conscience is closely tied to cognitive and emotional growth and to the self-regulating emotions of guilt and shame and other-oriented emotions, such as empathy, that are powerful catalysts for moral understanding as well as self-understanding. Thus, conscience development is closely tied to children's experiences in close relationships, their developing psychological understanding, and their emerging self-awareness as morally responsible individuals (Killen & Smetana, 2006).

Perhaps most valuable is the view that young children are intuitive moralists who begin to understand values in the context of relationships that are significant to them. Young children develop an intuitive morality from the socialization efforts of caregivers in helping to shape their own sensitivity to the feelings and thoughts of others and their developing grasp of normative standards of behavior (Damon & Lerner, 2006). They are moral apprentices, striving hard to understand, creating their own intuitive morality, but also aided by the sensitive guidance of adult mentors in the home and others in the community. More recent theories about moral development come from the field of cognitive research.

Cognitive Learning Theory

The discussion of cognitive learning theory in Chapter 2 emphasized the important part that imitation plays in the socialization process. According to psychologists such as Albert Bandura (1977, 1986, 1999) and Walter Mischel (1977), children acquire moral standards in much the same way that they learn any other behavior, and social behavior is variable and dependent on situational contexts. Most actions lead to positive consequences in some situations and not in others. Consequently, individuals develop highly discriminating and specific response patterns that do not generalize across all life circumstances (Bussey, 1992).

Studies carried out by cognitive learning theorists have generally been concerned with the effect that models have on other people's resistance to temptation (Bandura, Ross, & Ross, 1963). In such research, children typically observe a model that either yields or does not yield to temptation. Walters, Leat, and Mezei (1963) conducted such an experiment. One group of boys individually watched a movie in which a child was punished by his mother for playing with some forbidden toys. A second group saw another version of the movie, in which the child was rewarded for the same behavior. And a third group, a control group, did not see any movie. The experimenter took each boy to another room and told him not to play with the toys in the room. The experimenter then left the room.

The study revealed that boys who had observed the model being rewarded for disobeying his mother disobeyed the experimenter more quickly and more often than did the boys in the other two groups. The boys who had observed the model being punished showed the greatest reluctance of any of the groups to disobey the experimenter. In short, observing the behavior of another person does seem to have a modeling effect on children's obedience or disobedience to social regulations (Speicher, 1994). Other research reveals that dishonest or deviant models often have a considerably greater impact on children than honest or nondeviating models (Grusec & Hastings, 2007).

These findings provide a context for evaluating the prevalent notion that violent/aggressive children's social cognitions, attitudes, and thinking patterns contribute to their violent behavior. Clinical psychologists have often viewed violence as symptomatic of "internal conflicts" or "antisocial personality traits" within individual children. In other words, they assume that the children have deficient or distorted cognitions that contribute to their violent behavior.

Cognitive Developmental Theory

Cognitive learning theorists view moral development as a cumulative process that builds on itself gradually and continuously, without any abrupt changes. In sharp contrast to this idea, cognitive developmental theorists like Jean Piaget and Lawrence Kohlberg conceive of moral

DENNIS THE MENACE

"HOW DO YOU KNOW WHEN THE YELLOW LIGHT MEANS SLOW DOWN AND WHEN IT MEANS TO SPEED UP?"

Children's Models Cognitive learning theorists have generally been concerned with the effect that models have on other people's resistance to temptations. Children are observant of "models" in their environment who either yield or do not yield to temptation.
DENNIS THE MENACE used by permission of Hank Ketchum and by North America Syndicate.

development as taking place in stages, with clear-cut changes between them, such that a child's morality in a particular stage differs substantially from that child's morality in earlier and later stages. Although the learning and developmental perspectives are frequently counterpoised to one another, they nonetheless provide complementary and interdependent analyses of human social interaction (Gibbs et al., 1992).

Jean Piaget The scientific study of moral development was launched about 80 years ago by Jean Piaget. In his classic study *The Moral Judgment of the Child* (1932), Piaget said that there is an orderly and logical pattern in the development of children's moral judgments. This development is based on the sequential changes associated with children's intellectual growth, especially the stages that are characterized by the emergence of logical thought. In keeping with a constructivist perspective, Piaget argued that moral development occurs as children act on, transform, and modify the world they live in. As they do, they in turn are transformed and modified by the consequences of their actions. Hence, Piaget portrayed children as active participants in their own moral development. In this respect Piaget differed from the cognitive learning theorists, according to whom the environment acts on and modifies children, and children

are passive recipients of environmental forces. Cognitive learning theorists picture children as learning from their environment rather than, as Piaget would have insisted, in dynamic interaction with their environment, including through social activities (Carpendale, 2009).

Piaget formulated a two-stage theory of moral development. The first stage, that of **heteronomous morality,** arises from the unequal interaction between children and adults. During the preschool and early elementary school years, children are immersed in an authoritarian environment in which they occupy a position decidedly inferior to that of adults. Piaget said that in this context, children develop a conception of moral rules as absolute, unchanging, and rigid.

As children approach and enter adolescence, a new stage emerges in moral development—the stage of **autonomous morality.** Whereas heteronomous morality evolves from the unequal relationships between children and adults, autonomous morality arises from the interaction among status equals—relationships among peers. Such relationships, when coupled with general intellectual growth and a weakening in the constraints of adult authority, create a morality characterized by rationality, flexibility, and social consciousness. Through their peer associations, young people acquire a sense of justice—a concern for the rights of others, for equality, and for reciprocity in human relations. Piaget described autonomous morality as egalitarian and democratic, a morality based on mutual respect and cooperation.

Lawrence Kohlberg Lawrence Kohlberg refined, extended, and revised Piaget's basic theory of the development of moral values. Like Piaget, Kohlberg focused on the development of moral judgments in children rather than on their actions. He saw the child as a "moral philosopher." Like Piaget, Kohlberg gathered his data by posing questions about hypothetical moral dilemmas. One of these stories has become famous as a classic ethical dilemma:

In Europe, a woman was near death from a special kind of cancer. There was one drug that the doctors thought might save her. It was a form of radium that a druggist in the same town had recently discovered. The drug was expensive to make, but the druggist was charging ten times what the drug cost him to make. He paid $200 for the radium and charged $2,000 for a small dose of the drug. The sick woman's husband, Heinz, went to everyone he knew to borrow the money, but he could only get together about $1,000, which is half of what it cost. He told the druggist that his wife was dying and asked him to sell it cheaper or let him pay later. But the druggist said, "No, I discovered the drug and I'm going to make money from it." Heinz got desperate and broke into the man's store to steal the drug for his wife. Should the husband have done that? (Kohlberg & Colby, 1990, p. 241)

TABLE 9.5 Kohlberg's Stages of Moral Development

Level	Stage	Child's Sample Response to Theft of Drug
I Preconventional	1	• Heinz shouldn't steal the drug because he might be caught and go to jail. • Heinz should steal the drug because he wants it.
	2	• It is justified because his wife needs the drug and Heinz needs his wife's companionship and help in life. • Theft is condemned because his wife will probably die before Heinz gets out of jail, so it will not do him much good.
II Conventional	3	• Heinz is unselfish in looking after the needs of his wife. • Heinz will feel bad thinking of how he brought dishonor on his family; his family will be ashamed of his act.
	4	• Theft is justified because Heinz would otherwise have been responsible for his wife's death. • Theft is condemned because Heinz is a lawbreaker.
III Postconventional	5	• Theft is justified because the law was not fashioned for situations in which an individual would forfeit life by obeying the rules. • Theft is condemned because others may also have great need.
	6	• Theft is justified because Heinz would not have lived up to the standards of his conscience if he had allowed his wife to die. • Theft is condemned because Heinz did not live up to the standards of his conscience when he engaged in stealing.

Source: Lawrence Kohlberg, "The Development of Children's Orientations Toward a Moral Order," *Vita Humana,* Vol. 6 (1963), pp. 11–33; "Stage and Sequence: The Cognitive-Development Approach to Socialization," in D. A. Goslin (ed.), *Handbook of Socialization Theory and Research* (Chicago: Rand McNally, 1969), pp. 347–480; "Moral Stages and Moralization," in T. Lickona (ed.), *Moral Development and Behavior: Theory, Research, and Social Issues* (New York: Holt, Rinehart & Winston, 1976), pp. 31–53.

On the basis of responses to this type of dilemma, Kohlberg identified six stages in the development of moral judgment. He grouped these stages into three major levels:

1. *The preconventional level* (Stages 1 and 2)
2. *The conventional level* (Stages 3 and 4)
3. *The postconventional level* (Stages 5 and 6)

Kohlberg's stages of moral development are summarized in Table 9.5, with typical responses to the story of Heinz. Note that the stages are based not on whether the moral decision about Heinz is pro or con but on what reasoning is used to reach the decision. According to Kohlberg, people in all cultures employ the same basic moral concepts, including justice, equality, love, respect, and authority; furthermore, all individuals, regardless of culture, go through the same stages of reasoning with respect to these concepts and in the same order (Walker, de Vries, & Bichard, 1984), and individuals differ only in how quickly they move through the stage sequence and how far they progress along it. It is Kohlberg's view that what is moral is not a matter of taste or opinion—there is a *universal morality.* Researchers have begun to question the universality of Kohlberg's claims, however. Krebs and Denton (2005) believe that Kohlberg does not really acknowledge the pragmatic basis of everyday moral decisions. Lotfabadi (2008) finds that Kohlberg did little

empirical study of the fundamental values of other cultures. In actuality, early moral theorists studied people in their own culture, whereas cross-cultural research is more recent.

Carol Gilligan   Research by Carol Gilligan (1982a) suggests that Freud's, Piaget's, and Kohlberg's moral theories were limited to men's understanding, but not women's moral development. Gilligan's work reveals that women and men have differing conceptions of morality: Men have a *morality of justice,* the one described by Kohlberg, and women have a *morality of care* (Brown & Gilligan, 1992; Gilligan, 1982a). There is considerable merit to Kohlberg's position that the course of moral development tends to follow a regular sequence, particularly in Kohlberg's first four stages. Even so, differences exist among individuals and between genders, both in the order and in the rate of attainment of given levels.

Question

What are the major differences among cognitive learning theory, cognitive developmental theory, Piaget's theory, Kohlberg's theory, and Gilligan's theory of moral development?

Correlates of Moral Conduct

As discussed in the previous section, moral conduct tends to vary among individuals and within the same individuals in different contexts. Research on morality has focused on developmental transitions and universal processes more than on cultural or individual differences. Questions regarding individual differences are somewhat discomforting, for they imply that some people are more moral than others. And most of us are loath to label youngsters as uncaring and unprincipled (Hastings et al., 2000). Even so, a number of researchers have attempted to specify which personal and situational factors are most closely associated with moral/ethical behaviors (Davidson & Lickona, 2007).

Biology   There is some evidence that childhood moral development has a biological explanation. That is to say, we are by nature moral creatures. Even Charles Darwin concluded, in *The Descent of Man* in 1871, that the "golden rule" was the foundational principle of morality (Fry, 2006). Many sociobiologists today agree that altruism and empathy witnessed in young children are a result of evolution. In this view, the capacity for empathy and altruistic characteristics evolved from natural selection pressure, especially among mammals (Killen & Smetana, 2006).

The biological processes that support empathy could help explain some individual differences in moral conduct, when varying life experiences produce changes in the physiological systems that are necessary for empathy (Volbrecht et al., 2007). Humans carry with them their genetically encoded and experientially shaped individual propensities to experience empathy more or less easily and with greater or lesser intensity (Stoff & Sussman, 2005). In general, females tend to exhibit higher degrees of empathic concern than males (recall from this chapter that neuroscientists are making this finding as well). But children's heritable temperaments influence empathic responses (Volbrecht et al., 2007). Primarily as a consequence of ethical constraints, the vast majority of studies conducted on the aspects of human physiological functioning and moral conduct have been correlational. That is to say, "These are the biological events that occur when one feels empathy," instead of "When these biological events occur, one feels empathy" (Eisenberg, 2006). Future research will involve establishing gene-based explanations for these evolutionary theories on natural moral development.

Intelligence   Maturity in several of the aspects of moral reasoning described by Piaget and Kohlberg tends to be positively correlated with IQ. The relationship between IQ and honesty declines when the context is nonacademic or when the risk of getting caught is low. Overall, being smart and being moral are not the same. The character education proponents in U.S. public schools say that *performance* character and *moral* character should be integrated. They say it is not enough for schools to spend so much time and effort helping children succeed academically (e.g., pass tests or get high grades)—schools also need to attend to the moral/ethical domain. And most teachers agree that they should be guiding children to develop moral character outcomes of integrity, justice, caring, respect, responsibility, and cooperation (Davidson & Lickona, 2007).

Age   Research provides little evidence that children become more honest as they grow older. There may be a small correlation between age and honesty, but it seems to be due to other variables that also correlate with increasing age, such as an awareness of risk and an ability to perform the task without the need to cheat (Burton, 1976). Whether a child of a particular age is able to "tell the truth" factually comes up in some legal proceedings.

Gender   In the United States, girls are commonly stereotyped as being more honest than boys, but research fails to confirm this notion. Studies undertaken during the last half century show both genders capable of deception and aggression (Turiel, 2006a). However, Gilligan (1982a) suggests that boys and girls experience attachment differently. Girls identify and are attached to their mothers, but boys' attachment changes from the mother to the father, where they identify with the father as a person of authority and power. Boys also become more independent and generally develop a moral orientation toward justice and rights, whereas girls generally develop a morality of care for others.

Group Norms   Research by Hartshorne and May (1928) revealed that one of the major determinants of honest or dishonest behavior was the group code. When classroom groups were studied over time, the cheating scores of the individual members tended to become increasingly similar. Thus, group social norms were becoming more firmly established. Today, a body of research confirms that groups (siblings, friends, peer groups, and gangs) play a very influential part in providing guideposts for the behavior of their members and in channeling their members' behavior (Smetana, 2006). Bullying behaviors are usually endorsed by a peer group and inflicted on someone peripheral to the group (Duffy & Nesdale, 2008).

Motivational Factors   Motivational factors are a key influence in determining honest or dishonest behavior. Some children have a high need for achievement and a considerable fear of failure, and they are likely to be deceptive or to cheat if they believe they are not doing as well on a test as their peers. (Adults can view this behavior on a golf course!)

How Do Children Learn Prosocial Behaviors? Initially, expectations regarding proper and improper behavior are external to children, and some children are very aggressive about getting what they want. Moral development involves replacing aggressive or self-serving behaviors with prosocial behaviors—ways of getting along with other children through cooperative, helpful, sympathetic, comforting, rescuing, and giving acts.

Prosocial Behaviors

Moral development, or what some call character education, is not simply a matter of learning prohibitions against misbehavior (Killen & Smetana, 2006). It also involves acquiring **prosocial behaviors**—ways of responding to other people through sympathetic, cooperative, helpful, rescuing, comforting, sharing, and giving acts. Some psychologists distinguish between helping and altruism. *Helping* involves behavior that benefits or assists another person, regardless of the motivation that underlies the behavior (Eisenberg, 2007). *Altruism,* in contrast, involves behavior carried out to benefit the other person, without the expectation of an external reward. Thus, we label a behavior altruistic only if we are fairly confident that it was not undertaken in anticipation of return benefits. Younger children report more self-oriented motives and older ones more genuine concern for others (Grusec & Hastings, 2007). According to Piaget, a child younger than 6 or 7 is too egocentric to understand another person's point of view. Yet, one needs only to spend a short while in a preschool classroom to observe young children's sharing and caring in action.

There is a growing misperception about violence perpetrated against or by older youth who are approach-

ing their teen years. Children under the age of 13 who commit delinquent acts have an increased likelihood of committing future delinquent acts and are also apt to be delinquent for a longer time (Loeber & Farrington, 2000). Research on violence indicates that violent or aggressive behavior is often learned early in life, and steps need to be taken in families and communities to help children deal with their emotions without using violence (Barr & Higgins-D'Allesandro, 2009). Consequently, many teacher education programs are training future teachers in conflict resolution methods. One of the strongest findings was that children "do what they see," and it is important that we take care not to model violence (Tisak, Tisak, & Goldstein, 2006). Television and realistic video or computer games produce violent images and reward children for being more aggressive. Some E-rated computer games (suitable for everyone) depict violence, sex, and use of tobacco and alcohol (Anderson, Gentile, & Buckley, 2007). The perceived status of cliques within schools also has a strong influence on prosocial behavior and aggression: Aggression was found to be highest in both the most-popular and the least-popular cliques, and prosocial behavior was lowest in unpopular cliques. Aggression was also found among those jockeying for position within the same clique (Closson, 2009).

Parents have been shown to have the greatest influence on children's prosocial development. Research suggests that warm, affectionate parenting is essential for the development of helping and altruistic behaviors in children (Grusec & Hastings, 2007). Yet nurturing parenting is not enough; parents must be able to convey a certain sensitivity regarding their own concern for other living things. If a cat is hit by a car, what matters in the development of a child's prosocial behavior is whether the parent appears to care about the cat—speaks about the cat's suffering and attempts to do something to alleviate it—or seems callous and unconcerned. Yet there is a fine line between encouraging altruism and fostering guilt; parents should not inject too much intensity into such situations lest their youngsters become overanxious. Moreover, parental warmth and nurturing alone can encourage selfishness. Interestingly, there may also be a genetic contribution to prosocial behavior (Gregory, Light-Häusermann, Rijsdijk, & Eley, 2009). Parents need to provide guidelines and set limits on what youngsters can get away with (see our discussion in Chapter 8 of what Diana Baumrind calls the authoritative style of parenting).

Altruism and helping are often associated with **empathy**—feelings of emotional arousal that lead an individual to take another perspective and to experience an event as the other person experiences it. Swiss researchers have found prosocial behavior to increase with increased sympathy (Malti, Gummerum, Keller, & Buchmann, 2009). Indeed, some psychologists deem empathy to be the foundation of human morality, particularly in inducing cooperation among strangers and provoking guilt in wrongdoers. Researchers found that a mother's parenting style predicted children's reports of making reparative actions after causing harm to one of their peers (Killen & Smetana, 2006). Interestingly, the single most powerful predictor of empathy in adulthood was how much time the children's fathers had spent with them. Youngsters who saw their fathers as sensitive, caring beings were themselves more likely to develop these traits. Also, mothers' tolerance of their children's dependency—reflecting their nurturance, responsiveness, and acceptance of feelings—was related to higher levels of empathic concern among adults (Grusec & Hastings, 2007).

Culture and gender also influence the degree to which children exhibit prosocial behaviors. Several researchers have found that children in a more collectivist culture are more empathic, altruistic, helpful, or cooperative than children in individualist cultures (Eisenberg, 2006). This may be due to collectivist cultures' de-emphasis of individual needs or goals and emphasis on the needs of the broader community. Further, to some extent, boys and girls differ in biological predispositions, experience different socialization from parents and peers, and receive sex-type expectations from media and other conveyers of cultural norms. Thus, simply identifying gender may serve to capture an array of socializing forces that favor more or stronger prosocial (female) outcomes or fewer or weaker prosocial (male) outcomes (Eisenberg, 2006).

We need to emphasize that human behavior occurs in physical and social settings (see our discussion of the ecological approach in Chapter 2). Historically, when searching for what it takes to get people to live together harmoniously and without violence, sociologists have looked to larger social forces. Beginning with Émile Durkheim (1893/1964), sociologists have stressed that people, including children, need to feel that they are part of something. They must bond with some social entity, such as a family, church, neighborhood, or community. Moreover, children require a clear set of standards that tells them what is permissible and what impermissible. In sum, children need to feel bonded to a larger social whole. Once they are part of this entity, then standards make a difference to them. Counseling, education, or therapeutic intervention may bring about improvement in prosocial behaviors (Cooper et al., 2010; Oberst, 2009).

> **Questions**
>
> How does a child develop a conscience and establish moral and prosocial values during middle childhood? Do all children develop these? Why or why not?

SEGUE

Children experience substantial growth in all areas during middle childhood, and in this chapter we have looked at the physical and cognitive aspects of this growth: Children become comfortable with using their bodies and minds in new and exciting ways, and their abilities and skills become more pronounced, as some children are advanced—or delayed—either physically or intellectually in comparison to their peers. Concepts such as intelligence and morality start to become important because children are entering, often without parental or caretaker supervision, into their first social groups (e.g., sports teams, Girl Scouts, Boy Scouts, YMCA or YWCA, Boys and Girls Club, 4-H, summer camp). In addition to family, schools, religious institutions, sports teams and other social groups, and communities become important sources of interaction for children. Cognitive maturation and the increasing opportunities to interact socially with others provide children a myriad of possibilities for emotional and social development, and we look at those significant issues in Chapter 10.

SUMMARY

Physical Development

1. Children grow more slowly during middle childhood and become more skilled in controlling their bodies.
2. With regular proper nutrition, health care, and adequate sleep, a child's brain and nervous system will continue to develop by both progressive myelination and regressive pruning processes. Still, a small percentage of children during these years are identified as having learning disabilities and/or as being gifted.
3. This is the period when most children are healthiest. Yet rates of dental caries, asthma, attention-deficit hyperactivity disorder, and obesity in this age group are rising. Risks include accidents, contagious illness, eating disorders, and sedentary lifestyles.

Cognitive Development

4. An important feature of the elementary school years is a marked growth in children's cognitive sophistication. Piaget

calls this the period of concrete operations, and most children achieve mastery of conservation problems over time.

5. Considerable controversy exists about whether the acquisition of conservation skills in the period of concrete operations occurs in the invariant stage sequence that Piaget reported—and about whether understanding conservation tasks can be accelerated.

6. Using the computer as a model for the brain, information-processing theorists ask whether during childhood there are changes in the basic processing capacity of the system (hardware) or in the type of the programs (software) used to solve problems.

7. Although the developmental process is somewhat predictable, children vary in their rate and overall amount of change. Individual differences in abilities become more evident.

8. The number of dimensions along which children conceptualize other people grows throughout childhood, and they exhibit an increasing ability to distinguish people's characteristics by 7 to 8 years of age.

9. Children between the ages of 6 and 12 continue to acquire subtle phonological distinctions, vocabulary, semantics, syntax, formal discourse patterns, and complex aspects of pragmatics in their first language.

10. A growing segment of the U.S. child population is bilingual and identified as English language learners, or ELLs. The four main approaches used in the United States to open the doors to mainstream education are English as a second language, bilingualism, total immersion, and two-way bilingualism.

11. Schools primarily use conventional intelligence measurements, such as the *Stanford-Binet* test or *WISC-IV* (*Wechsler Intelligence Scale for Children-IV*). The reliability and validity of such tests are documented, the scores are stable for school-age children, and they correlate well with and are predictive of academic performance or the need for special education services.

12. There is greater understanding today that children do not all learn in the same way; thus, there is a growing body of research and instructional materials to meet different cognitive-style needs.

13. More U.S. children are being provided with special education services and individual education plans. The largest percentage of these youth is classified as having learning disabilities. Such children might have problems in reading (dyslexia), writing (dysgraphia), mathematics (dyscalcula), auditory/visual perception, or other sensory areas. A child can be classified as having a learning disability in one area but may also be classified as gifted in another area.

Moral Development

14. Morality involves how we go about distributing the benefits and burdens of a cooperative group existence and includes an understanding of behavior and actions that are considered right or wrong. Cultures vary in what moral/ethical values children are taught; thus there seems to be no one set of universal moral standards.

15. Cognitive learning theory views moral development as a gradual and continuous process whereby children acquire moral standards and values primarily through imitating the observable behavior of others.

16. Cognitive developmental theorists conceive of moral development as taking place in sequential stages, with clear-cut changes distinguishing one stage from the next. Given the differing views of moral values across cultures, their theories may not apply everywhere.

17. A number of researchers have attempted to specify which personal and situational factors are most closely associated with moral behavior. Biological, intelligence, age, and sex differences play only a small part in moral conduct. Group codes and motivational factors have a much larger role.

18. Moral development involves much more than simply learning prohibitions against misbehavior. It also involves acquiring prosocial behaviors. Schools, churches, and community organizations promote healthy moral development through various character education programs.

KEY TERMS

attention-deficit hyperactivity disorder (ADHD) *(290)*

autonomous morality *(295)*

bilingualism *(283)*

cognitive styles *(287)*

conservation *(275)*

creativity *(279)*

dyslexia *(271)*

emotional intelligence *(285)*

empathy *(298)*

English as a second language (ESL) approach *(282)*

English language learners (ELLs) *(282)*

heteronomous morality *(295)*

horizontal décalage *(276)*

inclusion *(291)*

individualized education plan (IEP) *(291)*

intellectual disabilities *(288)*

learning disabilities (LDs) *(289)*

limited English proficiency (LEP) *(282)*

long-term English learners (LTELs) *(282)*

moral development *(294)*

overweight *(273)*

period of concrete operations *(275)*

prosocial behavior *(298)*

stereotypes *(280)*

total immersion program *(283)*

two-way bilingual program *(283)*

FOLLOWING UP ON THE INTERNET

Web sites for this chapter focus on physical, cognitive, and moral development of youth in middle childhood. Please access the text Web site at www.mhhe.com/crandell10 for up-to-date hot-linked Internet addresses for the following organizations, topics, and resources:

Centers for Disease Control Growth & BMI Charts
http://www.cdc.gov/growthcharts/clinical_charts.htm#Set1

National Center for Learning Disabilities
http://www.ncld.org/

Council for Exceptional Children
http://www.cec.sped.org//AM/Template.cfm
    ?Section=Home

Learning Ally
http://www.learningally.org

National Association for Gifted Children (NAGC)
http://www.nagc.org/

National Society for Gifted and Talented
http://www.nsgt.org/

National Board for Professional Teaching Standards
http://www.nbpts.org/

National Clearinghouse for English Language Acquisition
http://www.ncela.gwu.edu/accountability/

Homeschool Organizations
http://www.hslda.org/orgs/

U.S. Office of English Language Acquisition
http://www2.ed.gov/about/offices/list/oela/index.html

TIMSS and PIRLS International Study Center
http://timss.bc.edu/

Center for the 4th and 5th Rs (Respect and Responsibility)
http://www2.cortland.edu/centers/character/

10 Middle Childhood
Emotional and Social Development

As children progress into middle school, ability differences among peers become more apparent. A few excel, and others experience difficulty. Immigrant children need services to improve their English communication skills. Children with physical, cognitive, or behavioral problems are assigned to special education services. Schools must meet the needs of all students in ways that attend to inclusion, diversity, national academic standards, and discipline.

Children in middle childhood are ready to learn to build things, play on teams, enjoy a family outing to a science museum, cook, or play a musical instrument. These activities do more than teach them new skills; they are crucial for development. While they are learning and doing these things, children are also learning to inhibit impulsivity, delay gratification, and respond to the demands of the task. In other words, they are learning self-control. Parents who provide a warm and supportive environment for these activities are helping their children develop emotionally, cognitively, and socially.

From the ages of 7 to 12, children form friendships through a variety of pursuits. When both parents are employed, some children are left on their own for a period on weekdays. After-school programs might be an option for these children, but some find such programs too restrictive compared with the freedom they are used to. In this chapter we will examine the research on these and other emotional-social issues in middle childhood.

THE QUEST FOR SELF-UNDERSTANDING

In interacting with significant adults and peers, children get clues about how others appraise their desirability, worth, and status. Through the accepting and rejecting behaviors of others, children continually receive answers to these questions: "Who am I?" "What kind of person am I?" and "Does anyone care about me?" Even young children seem to have a concept of self-understanding, and caregivers have an important influence in this development (Goodvin, Meyer, Thompson, & Hayes, 2008).

Erikson's Stage of Industry Versus Inferiority

According to Erikson's psychosocial model of development, children in middle childhood experience the fourth stage of the life cycle—**industry versus inferiority.** Think back to your own childhood, and you will probably remember this period as the time when you became interested in how things were made or how they worked. Erikson's notion of industry captures children's ability and desire to try their hands at building and working, through activities such as building models, cooking, putting things together and/or taking them apart, and solving problems of all sorts. A child who has difficulty in these areas can develop a sense of inferiority if compared with children who easily accomplish such tasks.

Erikson argued that good teachers are capable of instilling in students a sense of industry rather than a sense of inferiority. Likewise, if children are not given the opportunity to try their hand at constructing, acting, cooking, painting, fixing, and so forth but are restricted to watching adults perform these tasks, they will develop a sense of remaining inferior to the adult who is able to accomplish these tasks while they are relegated to observer status. Imagine children who want to help make a pizza and are told they may only watch because they might make a mess if they were allowed to actively participate. Extracurricular offerings that encourage children to "jump right in" and try out a variety of skills include sports, clubs, and activities such as Odyssey of the Mind, Science Olympiad, Invention Convention, talent shows, science fairs, the school newspaper, cooking or computer instruction, scouting programs, and 4-H, to name just a few. Much of children's most exciting learning happens outside of the school classroom!

Self-Image

Self-image is the overall view that we have of ourselves. When children are constantly praised or belittled, it is not uncommon for them to internalize this input and start to perceive themselves as "good" or "unworthy."

Self-Appraisals as Reflected Appraisals How we perceive ourselves is powerfully influenced by how others respond to us. Children who are respected and approved of for what they are have more self-esteem and self-acceptance than children who don't have this advantage. This self-confidence is reflected in their achievements.

Self-concept is a domain-specific assessment that children make about themselves. You might hear a child say, "I am a good athlete" or "I am horrible at math," which is very different from equating poor math performance with being a horrible person. For instance, Theresa is happy, confident, outgoing, and independent. She eagerly accepts new challenges and is not afraid to tackle problems. She thinks she is a nice, intelligent, friendly, caring child. In contrast, Lorri considers herself dumb, clumsy, and lacking in confidence. She cannot handle being singled out for praise or criticism. She does not actively engage in new projects and tends to watch from the sidelines. Theresa is typical of the child with a high self-image, whereas Lorri is a child with a low self-image.

Self-Esteem

Since the early 1900s, social psychologists and neo-Freudian psychiatrists have theorized that self-conceptions emerge from social interaction with others and that self-conceptions in turn influence and guide our behavior (Cooley, 1909; Mead, 1934; Sullivan, 1953). Thus, conventional social-psychological theory states that if children are accepted, approved, and respected for who they are, they are likely to acquire positive, healthy **self-esteem,** or a favorable evaluation of themselves. But if the significant people in their lives belittle, neglect, or abuse them, they are likely to evolve low or unhealthy self-esteem. Psychologists further divide self-esteem into the categories of earned and global. Children attain *earned self-esteem* as a result of their hard work and actual achievement, and this type is encouraged because it is based on work habits and effort in home and school. *Global self-esteem* is a sense of pride in oneself that is likely to be based on an inflated opinion of oneself or on empty praise (Rees, 1998).

Since the 1960s, numerous studies have suggested that low self-esteem is the root cause of many U.S. social and economic ills, such as drug abuse, teen pregnancy, spousal abuse, child abuse, poor school or work performance, and higher poverty and crime rates. Nurturing parental style—and caring mothers in particular—have a positive effect on their children's self-esteem (DeHart, Pelham, & Tennen, 2006). However, an evaluation of 9,000 students in grades 1 to 3 who graduated from federal Head Start programs and entered schools promoting self-esteem, schools with traditional instruction, or combination schools found that the schools that provided the tools for academic success were far more effective because the students improved in both academic achievement and earned self-esteem (Rees, 1998). The type of school that children attend may also have an effect on their development of self-esteem and achievement; for example, a growing body of research finds that students have higher educational achievement in same-sex schools than in co-ed schools (Gibb, Ferguson, & Horwood, 2008; McTaggart, 2009; Yaratan & Yucesoylu, 2010). Researchers are finding that self-esteem does not build success; rather, success builds self-esteem. A healthy sense of self-esteem provides a resource that children can draw on during stressful and disruptive times in their lives (Cast & Burke, 2002).

Although conventional wisdom suggests that high self-esteem is desirable, adaptive, and an indicator of emotional well-being, a word of caution is advised: School and athletic programs that superficially bolster a child's ego, with little effort from the child, promote artificially high self-esteem that is often viewed by others as conceit, pride, or arrogance. But low self-esteem can also cause problems. Children with a low self-concept can be more likely to engage in school violence. That is, children who believe that they do not do well in certain areas or activities associated with school, such as math or science or music or sports, are more likely to be disciplined at school for aggressive behaviors (Taylor, Davis-Kean, & Malanchuk, 2007).

Stanley Coopersmith (1967) devised the *Coopersmith Self-Esteem Inventory* and studied the kinds of parental attitudes and practices associated with the development of healthy levels of self-esteem, using a sample consisting of 85 preadolescent boys. He found that three conditions were correlated with high self-esteem in these children:

- *The parents had high levels of self-esteem and were very accepting toward their children.* The mothers of children with high self-esteem are more loving and have closer relationships with their children than do mothers of children with less self-esteem. . . . The child also appears to interpret her interest and concern as an indication of her significance; basking in these signs of her personal importance, she comes to regard herself favorably. This is success in its most personal expression—the concern, attention, and time of significant others.

- *The parents enforced clearly defined limits.* Enforcement of limits gives the child a sense that norms are real and significant, contributes to self-definition, and increases the likelihood that the child will believe that a sense of reality is attainable. Such children are more likely to be independent and creative than those reared under open and permissive conditions.

- *The parents showed respect for the children's rights and opinions, although parents of children with high self-esteem did set and enforce limits for their children's behavior.* The parents supported their children's right to have their own points of view and to participate in family decision making.

These findings from Coopersmith's study are reinforced by Diana Baumrind's studies on parenting styles (1967, 1980, 1996), which found that competent, firm, accepting, and warm parenting is associated with the development of high self-esteem. By providing well-defined limits, parents structure their children's world so that the children have effective standards by which to gauge the appropriateness of their behavior. And by accepting their children, parents convey a warm, approving reflection that allows children to fashion positive self-conceptions. In contrast, factors such as obesity and too much TV watching can damage self-esteem (McClure, Tanski, Kingsbury, Gerrard, & Sargent, 2010).

Adding to the research on self-esteem is the work of Susan Harter (1983), whose *Self-Perception Profile for Children* measures five domains of children's conceptions of self: (1) scholastic competency, (2) athletic competency, (3) physical appearance, (4) social acceptance, and (5) behavioral conduct. Harter asked 8- to 12-year-olds to rate themselves in these domains and to specify how their competence in each domain affected their self-perceptions. Most children listed physical appearance as most important, followed by social acceptance.

The construct of self-esteem appears on a continuum from very low to healthy levels to very high levels that are considered egotistical or narcissistic. Although it is possible to raise a child's self-esteem, it is more difficult to teach humility to one with an unfounded sense of superiority over others. In essence, all children's self-esteem will be affected by their own competencies, attributes, and behaviors and by the support they receive from immediate and extended family, friends, their community, and society.

Gender and Age Trends in Self-Esteem   Frost and McKelvie (2004) conducted a cross-sectional study using the *Culture-Free Self-Esteem Inventory* with elementary, high school, and university students. Results from their study support emerging trends: Girls under age 13 had higher self-esteem than boys, but adolescent boys have higher self-esteem than adolescent girls. This trend suggests that between childhood and adolescence, girls generally experience a drop in self-esteem, whereas boys experience an increase in self-esteem. Elementary school girls had a better body image than elementary school boys—across all three age groups, boys wished to gain weight. Girls' lowered self-esteem and body image with age appear to be related to satisfaction with their weight. BMI is directly linked to self-esteem, although the effect is less marked in African American than Caucasian girls (Biro, Striegel-Moore, Franko, Padgett, & Bean, 2006).

Studies show that as more girls get involved in sports, they are more likely to be fit and stay healthy, have positive body images, have higher self-esteem and self-confidence, and earn higher test scores, as well as be more likely to graduate, more likely to attend college, less likely to get pregnant at an early age, and less likely to use drugs or stay in an abusive relationship (Colletti, 2007). Presently, one out of three girls participates in a sport. But at the same time that more youth are involved in sports, the number of other children who are significantly overweight has increased substantially. Even though the Girl Scouts' program *GirlSports* has developed programs linking successful female athletes with girls' sports clinics, girls' participation in athletic activity declines substantially between middle school and high school, depriving them of a significant source of self-esteem just as they enter puberty. By the time they are 12, almost half of America's young people are not engaging in vigorous physical activity, and a substantial minority of girls aren't getting any physical exercise at all (President's Council on Physical Fitness and Sports, 2007). Parents play an important role in encouraging daughters to participate in team sports and to continue their participation through their adolescent years (Jacobs, Vernon, & Eccles, 2005).

Race/ethnicity can also be linked to self-esteem. African-American girls are less likely to report low esteem than other teens, but Hispanic boys are at a higher risk than their peers for developing problems with self-esteem (McClure et al., 2010).

More Girls Are Participating in Sports   Research indicates that sports participation bolsters girls' self-esteem, resulting in improved school attendance, higher grades, and more positive body images.

Questions

What factors in an elementary-age child's environment are likely to influence the child's sense of self-worth? Which of these factors, if any, are found to be more significant for boys or for girls?

Self-Regulated Behaviors

By the time children reach the elementary school years, they are expected to regulate their emotions and behaviors to a much greater degree than during the preschool years. This ability, whereby a child learns to regulate his or her impulse to respond or act on a given emotion, which is also related to the child's developing conscience, is called **effortful control** (Rothbart, Sheese, & Posner, 2007). As children are developing emotional competence, they can pay attention for a longer time without prompting from an adult. They can stop an activity, even one they enjoy, when it's time to do so. They can talk quietly when it's necessary and understand when those times are (Simonds et al., 2007). Children often exhibit prosocial behaviors toward peers during these years, and sympathy is strongly linked with prosocial behavior (Malti, Gummerum, Keller, & Buchmann, 2009). Positive marital conflict and genetics are also factors in the development of prosocial behavior (Gregory, Light-Häusermann, Rijskijk, & Eley, 2009; McCoy, Cummings, & Davies, 2009).

However, some children exhibit negative, antisocial behaviors during middle childhood. Lying, stealing, fighting, bullying, and other antisocial behaviors are manifestations of emotional and behavioral problems. In educational and expanded societal settings, adults apply higher standards of behavior to fourth- through sixth-grade children than to younger age groups. Children who regularly cannot get along with their peers and cannot (or will not) control their overimpulsive, defiant, or highly aggressive behaviors are likely to be classified by schools as *socially maladapted,* as *behaviorally challenged,* or as a child with *oppositional defiance* or *emotional disability* (*ED*).

Public school personnel are supposed to identify these youngsters (whom peers and teachers alike are afraid of), conduct an assessment of the child's needs, develop an individualized education plan (IEP), and place the child in an appropriate educational setting where he (and a majority are boys, though some are girls) will no longer hurt or intimidate the teacher and classmates. Central to this situation is the child's ability—or inability—to use self-regulatory behaviors.

In some children, such as those with *attention-deficit hyperactivity disorder* (*ADHD*) (see Chapter 9), their biochemistry makes it difficult for them to control behaviors such as excessive impulsivity, short attention span and inability to focus, yelling out in class, jumping around, grabbing or hitting others, and spilling things. Other children have never been taught acceptable social or self-regulatory skills by their caregivers. And some parents encourage an aggressive child, thinking that the aggressiveness shows that the child can handle himself or herself in unpredictable situations—an ability that is often a necessity for survival in inner-city neighborhoods. In any case, these children are at high risk of being rejected by most peers except those like themselves.

Understanding Emotions

Cognitive factors also play an important part in setting the tone for the emotional life of youngsters. Recall from Chapter 6 that *emotion* involves the physiological changes, subjective experiences, and expressive behaviors associated with feelings such as love, joy, grief, and rage. As children interact with others, they acquire guidelines that mentally or cognitively mediate their inner experience of emotion and their outer expression of it. This is particularly the case in a child's interactions with his or her peer group. Children strive to present themselves in a way that will win approval of their peers and are able to control their emotions as part of this agenda (Rutland, 2005).

By the middle childhood years, boys and girls have already deeply ingrained familial and societal expectations about expressing emotions. They perceive that females are regarded as more emotional than boys and that, in general, mainstream society does not value emotionality highly. Young boys already know that expressing anger is more acceptable for them than it is for girls. But they also know that they are expected to conceal other emotions. Thus, by the elementary school years, boys have begun to hide emotions such as sadness, and girls have learned to suppress expressions of anger. Girls

are more likely to express feelings of empathy by this age (Ruble, Martin, & Berenbaum, 2006).

Children's knowledge of their own emotional experiences changes markedly from ages 7 through 12, as they mature cognitively and learn display rules, determined by their culture, for the appropriate expression of behavior (Buntaine & Costenbader, 1997). They learn to "read" facial expressions with greater precision, although girls are more skilled than boys at decoding the emotions of others (Ruble, Martin, & Berenbaum, 2006). They better understand that emotional states can be mentally redirected (such as by thinking happy thoughts when in a sad state), and they are able to identify their inner states and attach labels (such as anger, fear, or happiness) to them, although boys have begun to suppress their awareness of emotions regarded as negative (Ruble, Martin, & Berenbaum, 2006). Children also come to realize that the emotions they experience internally need not be automatically turned into overt action, especially if they know there is someone who will listen.

> *Questions*
>
> What do we mean by emotional self-regulation? Why do you think U.S. parents treat girls and boys differently when they display the same emotions?

Anger   *Anger* is frequently associated with acts of aggression. Boys and girls are equally likely to experience the emotion of anger, but they are socialized to express anger differently (see Figure 10.1). Research on gender and aggression reveals that boys are more likely than girls to react with direct/physical aggression when they become angry (Card, Stucky, Sawalani, & Little, 2008). This finding occurs across age levels, ethnicity, and socioeconomic status (Cole, Bruschi, & Tamang, 2002). Also, when fourth- and fifth-grade boys and girls were posed hypothetical situations, the girls were better at attending to the behavior's intent (accidental versus deliberate) and attending to the social cues in such situations and thus did not respond as aggressively. One of Buntaine and Costenbader's (1997) major findings was that urban children reported a significantly higher level of anger than children from suburban or rural schools. The researchers suggest that differential patterns of socialization occur in response to real-life events occurring in the child's inner-city environment. For some children the emotion of anger may lead to displays of repeated aggression, which are associated with delinquency, rejection by peers, lower levels of academic achievement, and more mental-health interventions.

Fear and Anxiety   Fear plays a protective role in the lives of children of all ages. Psychologists define **fear** as an unpleasant emotion aroused by impending danger,

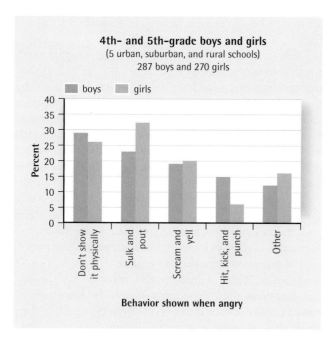

FIGURE 10.1 How Children Express Anger Boys and girls are socialized to handle their emotions differently. Boys are more likely to show aggression when they are angry, whereas girls are more likely to sulk or pout.
Source: Derived from data in Buntaine, R. L., & Costenbader, V. K. (1997). Self-reported differences in the experience and expression of anger between girls and boys. *Sex Roles: A Journal of Research, 36*(9), 625–638.

pain, or misfortune, whereas **anxiety** is a state of uneasiness, apprehension, or worry about future uncertainties (Gullone, 2000). Distinguishing between fear and anxiety can be difficult, and the terms are often used interchangeably. Both emotions are normal and involve feelings of apprehension and physiological stress reactions, but normal anxiety is differentiated from *clinical anxiety* by the degree to which it interferes with normal life. Fears, and the intensity of fears, change as children mature. Younger children report more fears at higher levels of intensity than older children and adolescents, and females report more fears with greater intensity than males, but the intensity of fears decreases over time (King et al., 2005). This finding is consistent with other studies that suggest that as normal children mature, they become better able to verbalize their fears and anxieties and to learn effective ways of coping. However, children who are nonverbal and those with severe developmental delays may not be able to verbalize their concerns and are likely to act out their feelings.

Psychologists also distinguish between fear and phobia. Whereas fear is viewed as a normal reaction to threatening stimuli, a **phobia** is an excessive, persistent, and maladaptive fear response—usually to benign or ill-defined stimuli, such as riding in an elevator or seeing snakes. Some children at this age develop what is called *school phobia.* Children who experience school phobia need professional

counseling to help them cope with their excessive fear and anxiety and return to school. (One author knew of a girl in fifth grade who refused to attend school for weeks; finally the family revealed that her mother was undergoing cancer treatments, and the child refused to attend school when she thought her mother might die. She did *not* have school phobia.)

As children move through elementary school, their fears change as their cognitive and emotional understanding matures. Gullone (2000) examined a century of cross-national and cross-cultural studies on normal developmental fears. Her review revealed a predictable pattern of developmental fears. Preschool children have fears of being left alone and imaginary fears—of darkness, large animals, and monsters. Elementary-aged children have fears of failure and criticism, bodily injury and illness, loss of family or pets, and supernatural phenomena, such as ghosts. Adolescents have more global, abstract, and anticipatory fears, such as fear of failure and criticism, social evaluation, economic and political concerns, and violence. Throughout all life stages, fears of danger, death, and injury are common.

Cross-cultural findings of normative fear are consistent with the most common fears by developmental age and gender, although cultural norms and practices significantly influence the levels and types of fears reported (i.e., danger-related fears or social-evaluative fears, which concern negative evaluations by others) (Gullone, 2000). Children are now more likely to suffer from post-traumatic stress disorder (PTSD), obsessive-compulsive disorder, and other social phobias and anxiety disorders (Muris & Broeren, 2009). Unfortunately, their anxiety and fears have intensified because of the September 11, 2001, terrorist attacks on the United States. Widespread media coverage of natural disasters such as the Hurricane Katrina floods along the southeastern U.S. border and New Orleans have raised children's anxiety levels. Finally, the direct effects of the death of military family members serving in the war in Iraq and Afghanistan and the possibility that a family member will die there cause fear (Cozza, Chun, & Polo, 2005). The effect of a parent's deployment is cumulative—the longer the parent is gone, the more a child's anxieties build—and these effects persist even after the return of the parent (Lester et al., 2010). See the *More Information You Can Use* box, "Services for Children of Veterans."

Patricia Owen (1998) examined the fears of nearly 300 children in San Antonio, Texas: Nearly half of the children were of either middle or low socioeconomic status (SES). The findings indicate that children from low-SES families report a greater number of intense fears than the middle-SES children; there were no significant ethnic differences, however. In this same study, girls and boys both reported significant fears of social violence. Hispanic and Anglo children differed minimally, and both

MORE INFORMATION YOU CAN USE

Services for Children of Veterans

The wars in Iraq and Afghanistan have taken a significant toll on members of the military. One population sometimes overlooked in the discussion of the cost of war is the children of military service members. However, many professional and government groups are now turning their attention to the wars' youngest sufferers in order to serve them better as they cope with the sacrifices their parents have made.

While homelessness among vets overall is dropping, homelessness among returning women is increasing. Only seven of the almost 500 homeless shelters run by the U.S. Department of Veterans Affairs (V.A.) accommodate families (Fitzpatrick, 2010). However, a new program, Supportive Services for Veteran Families, has been designed to provide services for children of veterans who are at risk of becoming homeless (C.D. Publications, 2010).

Returning female vets, including mothers and prospective mothers, often have difficulty negotiating a medical system still focused on male soldiers (Fitzpatrick, 2010). The V.A. has only one Center of Excellence for Women's Health, and it was not until 2010 that the Veterans Administration became authorized to care for newborns (Fitzpatrick, 2010).

Because military families no longer live together on bases, and because of the complicated deployment schedules some military members must contend with, social workers across the country are facing the difficulties of serving military veterans and their families (Savitsky, Illingworth, & DuLaney, 2009). A parent's service in the military can complicate many child-care issues, including custody or guardianship (Sullivan, 2010). Many social work professionals are calling for colleagues in their profession to educate the public on the unique needs of serving military veterans

Children Welcome Home Operation Desert Storm Veterans

and their families (Savitsky, Illingworth, & DuLaney, 2009). This impetus to understand the needs of military families has been paralleled in the legal profession (Sullivan, 2010).

Anyone trying to serve the needs of the children of veterans can turn to the Internet. Web sites such as United Children of Veterans and Veterans' Children include everything from scholarly articles addressing intergenerational post-traumatic stress disorder (PTSD) to personal accounts of children dealing with veteran parents. Even the Veterans Administration itself has launched a Web site, V.A. Kids, to educate children and adults about the lives of military service personnel and veterans, and to increase awareness of their needs and concerns.

reported significant fears of social violence. Children from low- and middle-SES families differed little in their fears, which centered on social violence. Fears pertaining to death and social dangers were prominent in this study, just as in past research. The pervasiveness of real-life fears (drive-by shootings, gangs, street drugs) is affecting many American children at younger ages.

Parents of fearful children can take comfort in the research finding that parenting is responsible for childhood anxiety in only a small percent of instances. Genetics and environmental factors account for the greatest share of children's anxiety (McLeod, Wood, & Weisz, 2007). Although fear can sometimes get out of hand and take on incapacitating and destructive qualities, it does serve an essential "self-preservation" function. If we did

not have a healthy fear of fierce animals, fire, getting lost, and speeding automobiles, few of us would be alive today. Appropriate screening can help parents discover problematic anxiety in their children, and school counselors are well-informed resources (Simon & Bögels, 2009).

Question

American children used to worry about doing well in school, being liked by classmates, and meeting their parents' expectations, though only a small percentage of children developed phobias. In comparison, what types of fears do American children aged 7 to 12 report today?

Stress   The image of children in pain and anguish stirs our adult sense of concern and indignation. We are moved to intercede and attempt to heal, and some of us go into social work, psychology, or medical professions to do just that. Yet all children must confront distressing situations. And without some stress, we would find life drab, boring, and purposeless. Stress can be beneficial if it contributes to personal growth and increases our confidence and skills for dealing with future events. Stress is an inevitable component of human life, so coping with stress is a central feature of human development.

Psychologists view **stress** as a process involving the recognition of and response to a threat or danger. Stress can also accompany positive experiences such as graduating to junior high, going to a first dance, competing in a sport, performing in a school concert, or taking home a good report card. We usually talk about stress in children in terms of physiological effects—butterflies in the stomach or having a stomachache, a headache, a backache, a rash or hives; being short-tempered; going on crying jags; having dizzy spells, sleepless nights, or asthma attacks: and, in a some children, bed-wetting. Children as well as adults experience and react to stress. The American Psychological Association's (2010) recent nationally representative survey of more than 2,000 children found that (1) overweight children reported significantly more stressful events in their lives than children of normal weight and (2) more than half of American children aged 8 through 12 were sad, worried, or frustrated when they felt their parents were stressed (see Figure 10.2). In some of these children, these feelings are carried over to a behavior problem at school.

As all of us confront difficult situations, we seek ways of dealing with them. **Coping** involves the responses we make in order to master, tolerate, or reduce stress (Diehl & Hay, 2010). There are two basic types of coping: problem-focused coping and emotion-focused coping (Folkman & Lazarus, 1985). *Problem-focused coping* changes the troubling situation, whereas *emotion-focused coping* changes one's appraisal of the situation.

As psychologists have come to recognize that children are not miniature adults, they have turned to the study of stress, coping, and resilience among children (Kochenderfer-Ladd & Skinner, 2002). In conducting this research, psychologists are finding inaccuracies in popular notions. Children's individual *perceptions* of such events greatly influence their stress reactions. Many stressors long cited by clinical psychologists as very stressful, such as the birth of a sibling, are actually experienced by children as less stressful than worrying about grades in school and relationships with peers (LaRue & Herrman, 2008).

Yet adults and children are alike in that people who feel in *control* of a situation experience a sense of empowerment (Whisman & Kwon, 1993). Individuals with a high sense of mastery believe that they can control most aspects of their lives. But those who are unable to gain mastery—to exert influence over their circumstances—feel helpless. Both children and adults with a low sense of mastery believe that their attempts at control are futile. A sense of mastery moderates the negative effects of stress and encourages problem-focused, as opposed to emotion-focused, coping.

Researchers find that an important moderator of our experience of stress is **locus of control**—our perception of *who* or *what* is responsible for the outcome of events and behaviors in our lives. When people perceive the outcome of an action as the result of luck, chance, fate, or powerful others, they believe in *external control.* When they interpret an outcome as the consequence of their own abilities or efforts, they believe in *internal control* (Kliewer & Sandler, 1992). Internal control typically increases with the age of a child. Scores on psychological measures of internal/external control tend to be relatively external during the third grade, with internality increasing by the eighth and tenth grades.

In evaluating matters of stress, coping, and locus of control, three factors stand out in the emerging body of research as being of particular importance: (1) the child's characteristics, (2) developmental factors, and (3) situation-specific factors:

- *Dispositional and temperamental differences among children play a central role in influencing their coping responses* (Kagan, 1983). Some show signs of greater arousal and distress in response to events than others, so they must cope with a greater number of stressful situations than more stress-resistant youngsters. Moreover, children differ in the ways in which they react once they are aroused or threatened (see Figure 10.1).

- *Developmental factors also play a part.* In middle childhood, children's emerging sense of self makes them more vulnerable to events that threaten their self-esteem than when they were younger. Children who change schools two or more times a year experience more stress, behavior problems, and problems in school (Crnic & Low, 2002). As they move into middle school, students with learning problems or developmental delays experience more stressors associated with the increased academic and social challenges for preadolescents (Martínez & Semrud-Clikeman, 2004).

- *Situational factors influence how children experience and deal with stress.* Healthy parents often mediate many of the effects of stressful crises (Sorensen, 1993). A caregiver's irritability, anxiety, self-doubt, and feelings of incompetence are likely to intensify a child's fear of hospitalization or of moving to a new school. Emotional support and acceptance

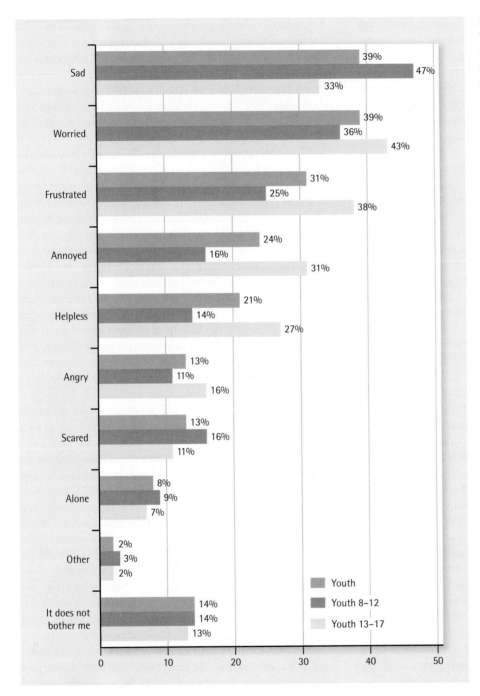

FIGURE 10.2 How Children Feel When Their Parents Are Stressed: 2009 In a sample of more than 2,000 children, nearly one-third of children aged 8 to 17 believed that a parent was often worried or stressed about things during the past month. Children are also vulnerable to a variety of health problems when parents are stressed.
Source: American Psychological Association. (2010, November 9). *Stress in America: Mind/body health: For a healthy mind and body, talk to a psychologist.* 1–68. Retrieved from http://www.apa.org/news/press/releases/stress/national-report.pdf

from the family and economic security can have a steeling effect, buffering the influence of stressors (White & Rogers, 2000).

Questions

A child who is experiencing stressful life events is likely to complain about what types of physical symptoms? What is the difference between external control and internal control? What are the three major factors in a child's coping responses to stress?

Trauma Research has shown that *traumatic events* are pervasive in children's lives. In 2008, over 3.7 million U.S. cases of child abuse and neglect were reported, with more than 770,000 confirmed cases; 4 percent of children who died were aged 8 to 11 (Gaudiosi, 2010). A child's emotional and psychological well-being can be harmed by any exceptionally stressful naturally occurring event, such as hurricanes and earthquakes, or by human-made events, such as the Space Shuttle *Challenger* explosion. Other events are more personal, such as being abused or neglected; witnessing the death of a parent, sibling, friend, or pet; being homeless; witnessing domestic violence; seeing a parent arrested and jailed; witnessing a home burning down; moving repeatedly from foster homes; witnessing a fatal accident; or experiencing war; and the effects are worse when parents have ineffective coping skills (Goldfinch, 2009). Some children live with chronic health conditions, and others experience one sudden episode of severe trauma (Cook-Cottone, 2004).

Children clinically classified with **post-traumatic stress disorder (PTSD)** (also called *post-traumatic stress reaction,* or *PTSR*) exhibit a range of physiological stress symptoms and behavioral symptoms, including learning and concentration problems; numbness and detachment from others; a feeling of helplessness; increased irritability and aggressiveness; extreme anxiety, panic, and fears; an exaggerated startle response; sleep disturbances; and regressive behaviors such as bed-wetting, clinginess, or refusing to go to school. Preadolescent youth and teens may also present with self-injurious behaviors, suicidal intentions or attempts, conduct problems, or substance abuse (Cook-Cottone, 2004).

To help such children reduce their stress, social workers, school psychologists, teachers, and families need to plan intervention strategies to restore a sense of security, stability, and safety for the child and reintegrate the child into school. Today there are more assessment tools available to clinical and school psychologists for identifying PTSD. Child-trauma experts believe that *art therapy* and *play therapy* illuminate a younger child's inner distress much more effectively than conventional adult talk therapies. Some children need long-term therapy to reduce distress symptoms. Research indicates that cognitive behavioral therapy methods are very effective (Eisen, 2007). School psychologists or social workers play a key role in the child's recovery, individualized education plan, and reintegration at school. Attentive caregivers and professionals need to understand that they are dealing with each individual child's personality and developmental issues, as well as with the aftermath of a recent trauma (Eisen, 2007).

War has the potential to disrupt every aspect of a child's life. A child may lose family members, may be separated from caregivers, and may lose members of his or her peer network. Children living in a war environment often assume caretaking roles for younger siblings or for incapacitated adults. Their schools may be destroyed or their schooling may be disrupted in other ways. War also affects the cognitive development of children. The mental maps a child has constructed to organize daily life are suddenly inaccurate. He or she may be forced to see, hear, and smell things that are incomprehensible, such as recently killed bodies or bombed homes or schools that were safe places. Beliefs about who belongs to his or her social network may be challenged in ways the child cannot assimilate, as may occur if neighbors or family friends take actions the child perceives as

disloyal. Children in these circumstances cannot predict the future, much less what will happen on a daily basis. Their past beliefs and values are no longer applicable to wartime events.

Klingman (2006), an Israeli psychologist with extensive experience helping children cope with war, finds that one of the most important messages caregivers and professionals can give to young children during a war is a positive message about the future. Klingman emphasizes the resilience of children and focuses on providing the types of support they need to cope with the high levels of anxiety and stress that are normal reactions to the horrifying events of war. Children whose parents, older siblings, or other family members are serving in the war also experience unusual levels of stress, even when the war is raging in a faraway place. These children worry that their loved one will be hurt or killed. Their fears are vivid and detailed because of the gruesome combat scenes they see on television and in the print and electronic news media. And when the family member returns from the war, the dynamics of the family system must change, and the family may experience new stress as the parents and children settle into their postwar roles.

Impulsivity and Risk Taking Youngsters differ in their willingness to take risks. Some children are drawn to the excitement of risk more than others, but accidents (unintentional injuries) are the leading cause of the death of children, adolescents, and young adults (Xu, Kochanek, Murphy, & Tejada-Vera, 2010). Young children and those with cognitive delays especially lack the cognitive awareness of harmful consequences. Also, children with attention-deficit hyperactivity disorder are more prone than others to impulsivity and injury. More boys than girls seek out stimulation in ways that concern their parents, caregivers, and teachers—and they are more likely to act on dares taunted by peers to save face. Risk taking finds different avenues of expression, and much depends on the child's environment and parenting style (Boles et al., 2005). Children who excel in athletics, music, art, acting, or leadership routinely take risks that their peers avoid—behaviors we deem "creative" or "courageous." But the pursuit of novelty and excitement can also lead children to take unsafe risks such as running away from home, stealing, experimenting with drugs, or setting fires. Parents (such as those who allow a 5-year-old boy to roam a neighborhood all day without supervision) may also affect their child's willingness to participate in risky behaviors (Morsünbül, 2009). Interestingly, although participation in school sports programs makes white male students less prone to risk-taking with regard to their health and well-being, males from other ethnic/racial groups are more likely to risk their health in spite of team sports activity (Taliaferro, Rienzo, & Donovan, 2010).

Our consideration of emotional development, fear, anxiety, stress, trauma, and risk taking leads us to inquire next how children encounter and manage social situations that involve morality (such as deciding whether to participate in online bullying of other students) through family influences, a broadening social environment, and the world of school.

> **Questions**
>
> What behaviors will a child exhibit who has experienced a major stressor or trauma? What actions can adults take to help such a child? What behaviors should concern us in a child who is impulsive and takes risks?

CONTINUING FAMILY INFLUENCES

It is important to see how children are faring on academic performance measures, but as we saw in Chapter 9, children's experiences within family and neighborhood environments are also vital to their emotional well-being and social development. Social scientists at the University of Michigan Institute of Social Research (ISR) have been conducting a longitudinal study on the daily lives of a nationally representative sample of more than 2,000 children and their families since 1968 (and their extant 7,000 families; in all, 65,000 individuals are still participating in this study) (Hofferth, 1998; 2010; Juster, Ono, & Stafford, 2004). How children spend their time provides insight into a variety of issues that directly affect their physical, intellectual, social, emotional, and moral development.

Analysis of time diaries reveals that children spend their time very differently than they did just 10 years ago, when children were more active and many families did not have computers. Overall, today's children aged 6 to 17 spend more time in school and more time studying, but they spend almost 2 hours a week less on sports and outdoor activities than children did 40 years ago. Children aged 6 to 11 spend an average of 6 to 7 hours daily in school settings (before-school programs, regular school day, and after-school programs), but less time in recess, an "activity" that is crucial for their cognitive, social, and emotional development (Ramstetter, Murray, & Garner, 2010). Children's free time, or unstructured play, has declined, and middle-class children today are in many scheduled activities (see Figure 10.3) (McIntosh et al., 2008; Veitch, Salmon, & Ball, 2010).

Children spend an average of several hours daily after school watching TV, playing video games, and using the computer (Hofferth, 2010). Many children have televisions in their bedrooms, and nearly two-thirds

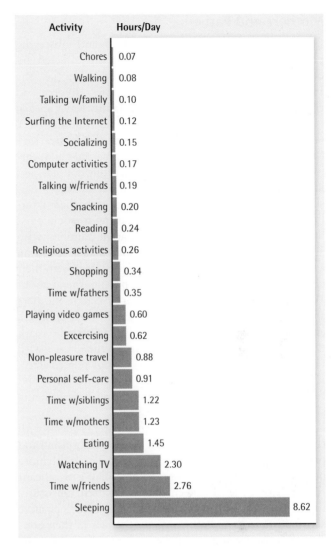

FIGURE 10.3 How U.S. Children Aged 8 to 10 Spend Their Time Each Day: 2008 Family life shapes how children spend their time, which affects their physical, intellectual, social, emotional, and moral development. Children today spend more time in school and in before- and after-school programs, in structured activities, and using the computer and video games, which did not exist 25 years ago. In general, they spend far less time on play and outdoor activities.
Source: McIntosh, W. A., Dean, W., Jan, J., Torres, C., Nayga, R., Kubena, K., & Anding, J. (2008, July 28). Parental work and time children spend in eating and non-sedentary activities. Paper presented at the annual meeting of the Rural Sociological Society. Manchester, New Hampshire. Lareau, A. (2003). *Unequal childhoods: Class, race, and family life.* Los Angeles, CA: University of California Press.

say the TV is on during mealtimes (Rideout, Foehr, & Roberts, 2010). A 2009 Kaiser Foundation study found that 70 percent of U.S. children have TVs in their rooms (Rideout, Foehr, & Roberts, 2010), and a Nielsen (2009) study showed that 98 percent of U.S. households own televisions, and the number is rising. Thus, media have a significant influence on today's children. Children devote little time each week to reading or just "playing."

Mothers and Fathers

Children learn from interacting with and observing parents, but they are increasingly being affected by demands on their parents' time. *Public policy* (i.e., the Healthy Marriage Initiative, welfare laws, divorce and child-support laws, taxation policies, family leave, special education laws, criminal laws, Medicaid funding, etc.), *family resources* (SES), and *changes in family structure* (decline in married couples, rise in nonmarital childbearing and single parenthood, rise in cohabiting couples, and kinship or foster care arrangements) affect the emotional-social relationship that children have with their families (Seefeldt & Smock, 2004). According to sociologist Sandra L. Hofferth (1998), two-parent families with a male wage earner and a female homemaker spend an average of 22 hours per week in direct contact with their children. When both parents work, parents spend about 19 hours per week with their children. Single mothers spend an average of 9 hours a week with their children, and much of this time is on weekends. Parents who work nonstandard hours may spend more daytime hours with their children but may miss evening school-related activities, such as teacher conferences or science fairs, and may "pay" for the time spent with children by sacrificing sleep (Wight, Raley, & Bianchi, 2008).

However, the quality of the time parents spend with their children is what matters, and a warm relationship and parents' expectations of closeness are associated with more positive behaviors in children. Fathers play a significant role in shaping the self-esteem of their children. One study found that fathers who talk about their children's positive accomplishments and affirm positive values in their conversations can do much to foster self-esteem. Conversely, fathers who put their children down and make them feel stupid, call them names, or use body language to express disapproval are likely to be cultivating low self-esteem in their children (Bulanda & Majumdar, 2009).

Supportive Mothers   Since 1970, maternal employment rates have risen markedly for both married and single mothers with children aged 6 to 17 in school. In 2009, almost 10 million married women with school-age children—nearly three-fourths of married mothers—were employed. Over 3.5 million single mothers with school-age children were employed—nearly three-fourths of single mothers (divorced, separated, or widowed) (U.S. Department of Labor, 2010). Thus, it is common for children to be in other-relative (kin) care, nonrelative care, after-school programming, or self-care (home alone). Some employed mothers and fathers adjust their work schedule to make sure a child is at home with a parent or older sibling when not in school.

Research shows that even though they often feel tired or rushed, mothers who work outside the home have greater self-esteem because they feel more economically secure, more competent, and generally more valued (Cunningham, 2008). And when a mother feels better about herself and her situation, she is more likely to be better able to nurture her children and will be a more effective parent. Also, Hofferth's (1998) findings indicate that the mother's verbal ability is associated with her children's higher verbal and math achievement scores. Mothers who are warm and close to their children, who do activities with their children, who are involved in their children's schooling, and who expect their children to complete college are most apt to rate their children's behavior more positively (Hofferth, 1998).

However, a common feeling among some working mothers is a sense of guilt for not always "being there" for their infants and young children. On the other hand, if their mothers are working, children are encouraged to be more independent. This sense of independence benefits girls especially, as they become more competent, have more self-esteem, and perform better in academics (Bronfenbrenner & Crouter, 1983). Mothers play an important role in the lives of their children during the preschool and elementary school years, and they play a crucial role in providing the stability and security a child needs to do well when he or she ventures outside the house to go to school or participate in after-school activities.

Mothers who encourage children to join in productive activities such as team sports, learning a musical instrument, attending church youth events, or joining organizations such as Scouts or 4-H are giving their children opportunities to develop coping skills for confronting challenges. In these activities, their children are also learning how to make decisions that lead to achieving a goal. Family life also provides such opportunities when children of both genders participate in preparing family meals or visiting a local museum or science center together. Mothers who create many opportunities for their children to learn new skills are creating a **stimulus-rich environment**—that is, an environment in which a child has many opportunities to learn about and try new things. Researchers link stimulus-rich environments to higher levels of self-regulation and fewer behavior problems at school (Bradley & Corwyn, 2005).

The great value of a stimulus-rich environment at home raises the issue of economic status. Does family income matter? Do children from households with lower income have a disadvantage at school? A growing body of empirical research suggests that the answer is "It depends." Researchers are finding that a warm, stimulating, responsive home environment provides a buffer against the effects associated with growing up in a low-income home. Although they generally experience a stimulus-rich environment, children from affluent families are prone to substance abuse, eating disorders, anxiety, and depression caused by pressure to excel, isolation from parents, and having less discipline and a sense of entitlement (Luthar & Latendresse, 2005).

Questions

In general, how do supportive mothers and fathers contribute to child well-being? How might a mother's employment benefit her children?

Caregiving Fathers   Today there is substantial research and public interest in the involvement of (or absence of) fathers, stepfathers, or father figures in the lives of children (Hymowitz, 2007a). Most children still live with a biological father or a stepfather for at least part of their childhood, and the presence or absence of a father is considered to be a significant variable affecting a child's well-being and school achievement (Mo & Singh, 2008). Recent studies reveal that many men see their family role as being just as important as their working role, and some children are more used to having fathers as at-home caregivers (Sinno & Killen, 2009).

A father's time, availability, engagement in shared activities, and warmth are known to be critical to a child's development. Yet many factors have affected the presence and role of fathers for U.S. children since the 1970s: the rising divorce rate, which has stabilized since the mid-1990s; the high rates of remarriage (about 75 percent will remarry); the rising rate of childbearing by single women (40 percent of babies are born to a single mother); the rising rates of unmarried couples (cohabiting) with children (with biological fathers or an unrelated father figure); the rising rate of nonresident biological fathers; and increasing rates of children conceived by artificial insemination by same-sex couples or single adults (Goldscheider, Hofferth, Spearin, & Curtin, 2009; Hymowitz, 2007b). Current estimates suggest that one of every three children will live with a stepparent (usually a stepfather) or a mother's cohabiting partner before age 18. Sociologists Hofferth and Anderson (2003) examined the engagement, availability, participation, and warmth of *residential fathers* with a representative sample of more than 2,500 children. The children's "father" sample comprised married and unmarried biological fathers, married stepfathers, and unrelated father figures in cohabiting families, reflecting the complexity of contemporary fatherhood.

Biological Fathers   Hofferth and Anderson's findings (2003) are consistent with research showing that married biological fathers generally invest more time, resources, and warmth in their own and in adoptive children. Married biological fathers report higher levels of educational attainment and higher incomes than other fathers—which generally results in a higher standard of living for children, more effective co-parenting, and fewer stressful

Children Benefit from Their Father's Involvement Children and mothers benefit significantly when fathers spend quality time with their children, and fathers serve as role models for future behaviors.

events (Amato, 2005). Two exceptions are that biological fathers in father-stepmother families report the highest amount of time spent with children, and biological single-parent fathers spend significantly more time with their residential children (about 5 percent of children live with a single father). Biological fathers with sons tend to increase their involvement; but biological fathers with daughters only or young children only, or who work long hours, tend to engage in fewer activities with their children (Wood & Repetti, 2004). In an extensive study that is the first of its kind, young men who reached adulthood in two cohorts (1985 and 2004) were surveyed for the presence of fathers in their own lives and for their own fatherhood status today. The young men aged 20 to 26 from the 2004 cohort who grew up with a stepfather or nonresident father were much more likely to become young, nonresident fathers themselves. Young men from both cohorts who grew up in socioeconomic disadvantage have higher rates of becoming young, nonresident fathers (Goldscheider, Hofferth, Spearin, & Curtin, 2009).

Mothers still engage in a greater proportion of child-rearing activities than fathers. A recent study found that children perceive mothers as more competent as caretaker than fathers, but both girls and boys accepted both parents' working (Sinno & Killen, 2009). Fathers tend to spend more time with sons, especially in sports activities. But fathers spend more time with children of both genders when mothers are employed outside the home. They help their children get ready for school and for bed, they help them with homework and read to them, they play with them, and they attend school meetings about them. Fathers who decrease their weekly work hours often increase the amount of time they spend with their children (Wood & Repetti, 2004). It is very beneficial for children to see both parents engaging in multiple roles and to have access to their father's time and emotional resources. But the story is different for nonresidential biological fathers and their children (Juby et al., 2007). A significant change in American family life has been the decline in the number of children growing up with two biological parents (Amato, 2005).

Divorced Fathers   When a marital or cohabiting relationship breaks down, some biological fathers disavow or abandon children, which is a heartbreaking emotional and economic loss for children. The break with children is often related to unresolved hostility with the ex-wife or partner, disengagement due to emotional distress, and anguish about developing a new role and identity (often as a noncustodial father with support payments to make) (Trinder, Kellet, & Swift, 2008). In Baum's study (2004), two-thirds of stepchildren reported minimal or no contact with a nonresident, biological father—but one-third reported frequent contact with a nonresident, biological father. Whereas married biological fathers have legitimate legal protections and obligations to support children, such protections and obligations are ambiguous for cohabiting fathers, nonresidential fathers, same-sex fathers, and those who are "father figures."

Fathers who are divorced face several emotional challenges, and their ability to meet these challenges is a key factor in whether they will be able to be warmly engaged with their children after the divorce. First, they must mourn the loss of their home, marriage, and family life. Fathers who do not go through the mourning process are more likely to be distant and disengaged from their children. Second, they must emotionally disengage from their previous identity as the partner of their children's mother. Some divorced fathers have difficulty disengaging from their ex-spouses and remain engaged in conflict with their former wives as a way to preserve their former identities as spouses. These men have not reached the stage where they can see themselves as fathers but not husbands. Researcher Nehami Baum says that they turn the process of divorce into "a lasting present" rather than

moving on into a new future with a new identity (Baum, 2004, p. 322). These behaviors are obstacles to a warm and nurturing relationship with their children. Children whose parents have high levels of conflict exhibit higher levels of anxiety, depression, and antisocial behaviors (Trinder, Kellet, & Swift, 2008).

Factors that predict a nonresident father's involvement with his children after divorce include the father's close relationship with his children from the time of birth, his ability to have a cooperative and low-conflict relationship with the mother, and his consistent contact with his own biological father. Thus, a father who is closely involved with the lives of his family members and is willing to cooperate is more likely to be an engaged father after divorce. This is true regardless of SES, although for a low-income father, stability of employment is an important factor in his ability to have a good relationship with his children after divorce. Fathers who do not feel that they are good providers are more likely to withdraw from their children (Holmes & Huston, 2010).

Stepfathers   In Hofferth and Anderson's (2003) study, stepfathers were significantly younger than biological fathers and generally had lower earnings. The younger the children are in a stepfamily, the more likely the stepfather is to engage in activities and invest in a warm relationship with them. Stepfathers in this study scored lower than married biological fathers on measures of desirable parenting practices and fathering attitudes with stepchildren, perhaps for two reasons: (1) stepfathers were often committed to providing resources, time, and emotional support to their own biological children from a former marriage or relationship; and (2) if a divorced biological father maintains a close, supportive relationship with his children, a stepfather is less likely to develop a close relationship with these stepchildren. Stepfathers were least engaged with adolescent stepchildren.

Stepfathers who had no biological children of their own in the household rated themselves as having low amounts of activity or warmth with children. Generally, stepchildren received significantly more time and attention in a *blended family* (mother's children and father's children residing together) than in a nonblended family. Results from one 20-year study with adult children from stepfamilies suggest that given time, more than half of the adult children perceived a close relationship with a stepparent (more said so about stepfathers than about stepmothers) (Ahrons, 2007).

Cohabiting Father Figures   Cohabitation is defined as a man and a woman living together in a marriage-like relationship (National Marriage Project, 2010). Today, children are more likely to be living in a cohabiting household (see Table 10.1). In 2002, nearly 60 percent of women in a large sample aged 19 to 44 reported

TABLE 10.1 Births Outside Marriage in Selected European Union and Other Countries: 2007, 2008*
Marriage rates are down in most European countries and in the United States, and more children are living with single parents or in cohabitation households.

Country	Percent of Total Births
Iceland	66
Sweden*	54.7
Norway	54
Slovenia*	52.8
France*	52.6
Bulgaria*	52.1
Denmark	46.1
United Kingdom*	46
Finland	40.6
United States (2008)	40.6
Netherlands	39.5
Austria	38.3
Ireland (2006)	33.2
Germany	30
Spain (2006)	28.4
Italy	21
Cyprus	8.9
Greece	5.9
Japan	2

Sources: Eurostat European Commission. (2010). Europe in figures. *Eurostat Yearbook 2010.* © European Union, 2010. DOI: 10.2785/40830. Martin, J. A., Hamilton, B. E., Sutton, P. D., Ventura, S. J., Mathews, T. J., & Osterman, M. J. K. (2010, December 8). Births: Final data for 2008. *National Vital Statistics Reports,* 59(1), 1–72. Retrieved from http://www.cdc.gov/nchs/data/nvsr/nvsr59/nvsr59_01.pdf. Hamilton, B. E., Martin, J. A., & Ventura, S. J. (2010, December). *National Vital Statistics Reports,* 59(3), 1–29. Retrieved from http://www.cdc.gov/nchs/data/nvsr/nvsr59/nvsr59_03.pdf

cohabiting (Popenoe, 2009). Today, more than half of nonmarital births are to cohabiting couples (Mincieli et al., 2007). Early studies on cohabitation focused on cohabiting stepfamily households and suggested that children in cohabiting families fare worse behaviorally, economically, and academically than children in married families and stepfamilies (Wu, Costigan, Hou, Kampen, & Schimmele, 2010). But if a cohabiting partner shares his resources with family members, then the children are likely to benefit (Manning & Brown, 2006). Based on the early studies, a mother's cohabiting partner reported the lowest income of all "father" types. These men also reported the least amount of time engaged in activities with residential children. Thus, children in cohabiting families reported less warmth and attention from cohabiting father figures than in other "father" types of families, leaving these children vulnerable to other negative influences (Wu et al., 2010).

A recent study of cohabiting two-biological-parent households (never-married) with young children revealed economic insecurities, levels of maternal depressive symptoms, and poorer child well-being similar to

those found in cohabiting stepfamilies (Artis, 2007). Children who live in a cohabiting household are much more likely to experience dissolution of the household (Popenoe, 2009). This research suggests that those who marry have different personality characteristics from those who choose to cohabit (Artis, 2007). To date, no studies in the United States have shown that cohabitation before marriage ensures the strength of a subsequent legal union (National Marriage Project, 2010). In order to strengthen marriage and ensure strong families for children, Popenoe (2009) recommends education programs for prospective couples and parents and suggests that divorce laws be revised so that they better address the needs of children.

Absentee or Nonresident Fathers   As of 2009, about one out of every four American children was living in a home where no biological father was present; thus for nearly 20 million children, their time with their father ranges from negligible to custody-related visitation time (U.S. Bureau of the Census, 2011a). The national study *Father Facts,* by the National Fatherhood Initiative (Horn & Sylvester, 2004) reports that about 40 percent of children in father-absent homes have not seen their father at all during the past year, and half of these children have never visited their father's home (some absent fathers live out of state or are incarcerated). Researchers have described children in households without fathers as living in a fragile state (National Marriage Project, 2010).

The absence of fathers from U.S. children's lives is considered a crisis by those concerned with the welfare of children (Kelly, 2007). The factors associated with father absence in children's lives include a legal system that often grants custody to a mother or creates an adversarial situation between parents seeking custody; limited and strict visitation times; maternal hostility toward paternal involvement that puts children in the middle; a father who chooses to be marginally involved in his children's lives; either parent moving away; single women who bear children and who cannot or refuse to identify the father; parental remarriage and starting a new family; and paternal mental illness, substance abuse, incarceration, homelessness, and paternal child abuse (Kelly, 2007). After reviewing the extensive data on fathers' time, availability, engagement in shared activities, and warmth with children, social scientists suggest that a healthy, supportive relationship with a father matters to the overall well-being of children (Kelly, 2007). A father serves as a significant role model for his children's future behavior.

Child advocates encourage the use of alternatives to court-ordered decisions regarding separation and divorce disputes, such as mediation or integrative family therapy. With either approach, each parent's concerns are heard and recognized, with the ultimate goal of conflict resolution. Various professionals in the field of mediation assist couples in making more balanced legal decisions about restructuring their family lives and promoting involvement of both parents (Katz, 2007). A large body of research finds that when caring, supportive fathers are involved in children's lives, mothers and children experience many economic and social-emotional benefits (Ahrons, 2007).

> **Questions**
>
> How does a father's involvement, or lack of it, affect children's lives? In general, how are stepparents and unrelated cohabiting "father figures" involved with the children that reside with them?

Sibling Relationships

Even though U.S. families are smaller than they were a few generations ago, more than 80 percent of children in America are growing up in a home with at least one sibling (see Table 10.2) (U.S. Bureau of the Census, 2011a). If you grew up with siblings, you probably remember having a much more intense relationship with them than with your friends. Siblings do not have the luxury of choosing each other, as friends have, so it is necessary to work on cooperation as they live daily life. Likewise, siblings know that an angry confrontation does not end the relationship. Even when they temporarily harbor bad feelings for each other, siblings know that they must continue to live together. Good sibling relationships are often marked by positive processes for resolving conflict (Recchia & Howe, 2009). Older siblings normally play a role in helping younger siblings "learn the ropes"— whether doing homework, coping with issues such as puberty changes, sex or drugs, or learning the values and mores of society (Cicirelli, 1994).

Siblings who learn to resolve their own conflicts without assistance from adults are learning important life skills. Conflict is more likely to be resolved when both children are thinking of the future rather than dwelling on accusations about past behavior and injustice. Siblings are also better able to resolve conflict when both children can be flexible about their plans and are willing to compromise. When siblings take account of the position of their brother or sister in their negotiations, both siblings learn that they are interdependent and can rely on each other to find solutions to their problems (Recchia & Howe, 2009). Siblings who play together are learning skills such as sharing, cooperation, and empathy. These are prosocial behaviors that will serve them well throughout life (Pike, Coldwell, & Dunn, 2005). In contrast, children who have distant or conflictual relationships with their siblings are at increased risk for maladaptive behavior in peer relationships. They also are less able to adjust to stressful changes such as the transition from elementary to junior high school and changes in family life (Kim et al., 2007). Some children report feelings of jealousy toward siblings, which girls are more likely to report than boys (Thompson & Halberstadt, 2008). Siblings who learn to resolve their own conflicts without adult intervention learn important life skills of compromise and negotiation. For more comprehensive research, Dr. Kevin Leman has authored *The Birth Order Book*, which sheds light on personality variables in firstborns, middle children, and the "baby" of the family.

The chronic illness or disability of a sibling creates significant levels of stress for everyone in a family, and it is more common for such children to be raised at home today. In fact, both asthma and autism rates are rising rapidly, so more and more families are affected (Ross & Cuskelly, 2006). Able-bodied children may not be getting enough attention from their parents, and they may be asked to contribute to family life above and beyond what is expected of their peers. Whether the family member is ill or disabled, healthy siblings are often thrust into caretaking roles, both physical and emotional, at younger ages—and this can cause psychosocial problems. Such families need support and access to resources that will help them strategize about how to meet the needs of all of the children in the household. With information and support from medical and human services professionals, many families can function and provide effective support for all members when a disability or chronic illness touches their lives (O'Brien, Duffy, & Nicholl, 2009).

Researchers are beginning to explore the ways in which ethnicity shapes the experiences of siblings. Siblings in African American, Hispanic, Asian American, American Indian, and other ethnic groups share family traditions that are important to their ethnic group. One study found that African American siblings with positive sibling relationships were more likely to have a strong ethnic identity. They also support each other in coping with the experience of discrimination in the larger society.

TABLE 10.2 Presence of Siblings in American Families: 2009

	Number	Percent
Under 18 Years of Age	74,230,000	100
1 sibling	28,795,000	39
2 siblings	18,270,000	25
0 siblings (only child)	15,751,000	21
3 siblings	7,521,000	10
4 siblings	2,293,000	3
5 or more siblings	1,600,000	2

Source: U.S. Bureau of the Census. (2011). *America's families and living arrangements: 2009.* Table C5. Retrieved from http://www.census.gov/population/www/socdemo/hh-fam/cps2009.html

African American siblings with a weaker ethnic identity are more likely to have distant relationships (McHale et al., 2007). We have much more to learn about the interrelationship between ethnicity and an individual's experience of family life.

> #### Questions
>
> What are the general findings about the role of siblings in a child's life? How is a child's life different if a sibling has a chronic illness or disability? How does a child's ethnicity affect the sibling relationship?

Children of Divorce

Each child reacts differently to the breakup of a family, depending on the child's age and temperament and the parents' competence in handling the situation (Lansford, 2009). Programs have been established in many states for children of divorced parents, but there is a need for more such programs nationwide (Pollet, 2009). Children aged 6 to 12 need to know what the separation is about (younger children are likely to think it is their fault). Their concerns are very different from the concerns of parents, and parents can be too preoccupied to notice. Children of separated or divorced parents have loyalty stresses (Schlesinger, 1998). High levels of parental conflict have a significant impact on children regardless of family structure and affect both biological and adopted children equally (Amato & Cheadle, 2008). To adjust to the divorce, children need a sense of safety and closeness to their parents and need to have their basic needs met. Children feel lower levels of conflict when their parents cooperate in matters related to child care.

Wallerstein and Kelly (1980; Wallerstein, Lewis, & Blakeslee, 2000) found that children have six psychological tasks to complete after a divorce, and the ease of completing these tasks is related to how well the parents handle the divorce. These "tasks" are (1) accepting that the divorce is real; (2) getting back into previous routines, such as school and other activities; (3) resolving the loss of the family, which means having a distant or absent parent, restructured family traditions, and loss of security; (4) resolving anger and self-blame, followed by forgiveness; (5) accepting that the divorce will be permanent; and (6) believing in relationships. Many schools offer children the opportunity to join support programs such as *Banana Splits*. Children get together in peer groups with a school social worker or school psychologist to share their feelings and experiences. These programs teach children how to cope with their feelings of loss, fear, helplessness, anxiety, or anger.

Divorce affects children's development in complex ways, with many confounding factors involved. Although most children adjust in time, some are troubled for many years (Kelly, 2007). In one study, children were interviewed a few years after their parents had divorced (the children were aged 6 to 8 at that time), and a majority of the girls and boys were well adjusted. Most children lived with their mothers, about 5 percent lived with their fathers, and the rest lived with other kin (often grandparents) or in foster homes. Overall, children who have a stable, loving relationship with both parents have fewer emotional scars (Ahrons, 2007).

Several factors affect the development of children whose parents divorce:

1. *Age of the child.* Young children respond differently than older children because they are in a different stage of development. Also, young children tend to visit their fathers more frequently than adolescents (Kelly, 2007).
2. *Level of parental conflict.* High conflict before, during, and after divorce is very harmful to children's development.
3. *Gender of the child and custodial parent.* Children living with a same-sex parent (girls with mothers and boys with fathers) were happier, more mature, and more independent, and they had more self-esteem.
4. *Nature of custody.* Researchers find that child satisfaction in custody arrangements is variable, and much depends on the availability, emotional well-being, degree of supportiveness, and economic resources of the custodial parent. More liberal visitation policies and joint legal custody (also called shared physical custody) have become more prevalent over the past 20 years as "best interest" statutes have been passed, and there are more father-custody families (Kelly, 2007).
5. *Income and resources.* Often the significant drop in income for mother-custody families creates considerable stress because the family must move to lower-standard housing. The children lose the comfort and security of familiar neighborhoods, friends, and schools, along with experiencing the disruption of family routines.

Single-Parent Families

The family structure is associated with child well-being and with many future outcomes, such as rate of high school completion or dropout, substance abuse, criminal behavior, age at becoming a parent, economic security and lifetime earnings, and repeating the parents' marriage or nonmarriage pattern. An extensive amount of research comparing findings from the 1960s through the present suggests that children born to single mothers, regardless of the age of the mother, are more likely to grow up in poverty, to spend their childhood without two parents, and to become single parents themselves (Bramlett & Mosher, 2002). However, child outcomes are generally more positive when single mothers are employed. Children growing up in homes with single-parent fathers are likely to fare better because males are more likely to be employed and generally earn higher wages, and single-parent fathers report spending more time in activities with their children (Hofferth & Anderson, 2003).

As of 2009, the proportion of children in married, biological-parent families continued to decrease, comprising only 52 percent (Pew Research Center, 2010c). Nearly 25 percent of U.S. children live with their mother only, and about 5 percent live with their father only (Federal Interagency Forum on Child and Family Statistics, 2010a). With cohabitation rates rising, more children are living with their unmarried biological parents (Mincieli et al., 2007). The highest rate of single parenting is in black families, with more than half of black children residing with mothers or in kin/grandparent-headed families. In 2008, 72 percent of black women who gave birth were single (Pew Research Center, 2010c).

Mothers-by-Choice   There are increasing numbers of single-by-choice mothers (also called "choice mothers"), and these are typically women in their late thirties to forties, college educated and established in a career, who choose to have a child by adoption or artificial insemination (AI), with a same-sex partner or without a marriage partner (Nelson, 2006). Originally, assisted reproductive technologies served married women who had difficulty conceiving, but in 2006 the American Society for Reproductive Medicine Ethics Committee called for equal access to fertility treatment for gays, lesbians, and singles. The CDC reports that in 2009 the number of U.S. births for single women aged 30 and older increased slightly from the number of such births in 2008 (Hamilton, Martin, & Ventura, 2010a).

Legally, children conceived in such ways have no knowledge of their biological fathers—and men are protected from any legal recourse that might otherwise be sought by the many children they might be creating, unless they are "open identity" donors (allowing their identity to be given to adult children) (Egan, 2006). This is creating a profound cultural transformation, with increasing numbers of "fatherless children" (Hymowitz, 2007b). Initial studies with teenage children of "choice mothers" reveal that they are very curious about their fathers and feel that they could learn a lot more about themselves (Scheib, Riordan, & Rubin, 2005). However, children of lesbian mothers who were conceived by donor insemination have been found to develop no differently than children of two heterosexual parents, and lesbian co-mothers are often more involved in their children's lives than fathers (Brewaeys, 2010).

Stepfamilies

Between 75 and 80 percent of divorced parents remarry, and most of these marriages involve children (Bramlett & Mosher, 2002). These families are labeled *reconstituted,* or *blended,* families, and successfully integrating family members is a complicated, emotional process. It is common for children to feel insecure and vulnerable, thus "younger children want their parents to reunite, while older children want to oust the stepparent" (Pacey, 2005, p. 368). Children often find it difficult to adjust to new stepparents who have their own children, and the stress from trying to acclimate to the new family dynamics can lead to emotional and behavioral problems. Stepfathers are usually accepted by boys but can come between girls and their mothers. Thus, girls are more likely to reject the stepfather (Bray & Hetherington, 1993). Stepparents usually adopt a laissez-faire attitude with stepchildren in regard to discipline, and eventually they find that there are fewer conflicts if the biological parent does the disciplining.

Men and women bond with stepchildren in different ways. Stepmothers are more likely to slip into the day-to-day activities with their stepchildren, whereas stepfathers are generally less involved with their stepchildren's activities (Hofferth & Anderson, 2003). Stepfathers are less likely to invest their financial resources in the children of their partners. One study found that a man was over five times less likely to give money for college to his stepchildren than he was to his biological children (Buss, 2008).

As children enter later childhood, no matter what the family type or the degree of harmony within the family, they seek close peer relationships outside the family to provide a support system associated with resilience and life satisfaction (Nickerson & Nagle, 2004).

> *Questions*
>
> How do children learn to cope with parental separation and divorce? What do we know in general about a child's well-being in a single-parent family? In a stepfamily?

LATER CHILDHOOD: THE BROADENING SOCIAL ENVIRONMENT

Later childhood is a time when children significantly enlarge and refine their cognitive and social skills. Social scientists often refer to this time as *preadolescence.* Preadolescents become increasingly self-directed and begin to choose their own social contacts with peers, and with some they form close friendships. From age 6 to age 14, children's conceptions of friendship show an increasing emphasis on mutual caring, trust, and loyalty, and a child's ability or inability to develop peer relationships can affect his or her overall psychological well-being (Klima & Repetti, 2008). Supportive friends are positively correlated with achievement in school, healthy self-esteem, and psychosocial adjustment (Nickerson & Nagle, 2004).

The World of Peer Relationships

During preadolescence, there is a developmental change in what children consider important to know about a friend. Children begin focusing on a friend's preferences, such as her or his favorite games, activities, and people. As they transition to adolescence, young people become increasingly concerned about a friend's internal feelings and personality traits. Hence, there is a progressive shift from concern with the observable and external qualities of a friend (he's my friend because he has a new computer) to concern with a friend's internal psychological world (she's my friend because she and I like the same things, she's fun to be with, and I trust her). Clearly, peer relationships assume a vital role in children's development (Nickerson & Nagle, 2004).

Developmental Functions of Peer Groups

Most boys and girls desperately want to fit in with peers during the middle childhood years. Getting along with peers requires considerable social skill, including prosocial behaviors, negotiating skills, empathy, and emotion regulation (Underwood, Mayeux, & Galperin, 2006). There are many different kinds of peer relationships and groups: a friendship, a school or neighborhood clique, a scout troop, a basketball or soccer team, a youth group at a place of worship, a gang, and so on. Children may be simultaneously involved in a number of peer relationships, which provide them with a world of children, in contrast to a world of adults. Peer groups serve a variety of functions:

- *Peer groups provide an arena in which children can exercise independence from adult controls.* Because of peer-group support, children gain the courage and confidence they need to weaken their emotional bonds to their parents. The peer culture also operates as a pressure group, by creating peer standards for behavior. The peer group becomes an important agency for extracting concessions for its members on matters such as bedtime hours, dress codes, choices of social activities, and amounts of spending money.
- *Peer groups give children experience with relationships in which they are on an equal footing with others.* In the adult world, children often are subordinates, with adults directing, guiding, and controlling

Children Comfort Friends Loyalty to friends and comforting a friend in distress are examples of prosocial behaviors that children begin to exhibit in the middle childhood years.

their activities. Peer-group membership is characterized by sociability, self-assertion, competition, cooperation, and mutual understanding among equals (Newman, Lohman, & Newman, 2007). By interacting with peers, children learn the functional and reciprocal basis for social rules and regulations.
- *The peer group is the only social institution in which the position of children is not marginal.* Children can acquire status and realize an identity in which their own activities and concerns are supreme. Furthermore, the "we" feeling—the solidarity associated with group membership—furnishes security, companionship, acceptance, and a general sense of well-being.
- *Peer groups are agencies for the transmission of informal knowledge, superstitions, folklore, fads, jokes, riddles, games, and secret modes of gratification.* Upstairs, behind the garage, on the street, and in other out-of-the-way places, children acquire and develop many skills essential for the management of adult life.

By middle childhood, most children have an expectation that friendships will produce positive experiences. Their peers provide a sense that they belong and are included, as well as a context in which to strive for achievement. When they have an upsetting experience, most children feel better after they talk with friends. Friendships also provide a context in which children can work through conflicts and disagreements, and most children will work to sustain a close friendship when problems arise (Underwood, Mayeux, & Galperin, 2006).

Questions

Why is it so important that children get along with peers and develop friendships? What are some of the major functions of children's peer groups?

Gender Cleavage

A striking feature of peer relationships during the elementary school years is *gender segregation,* or **gender cleavage**—the tendency for children to separate themselves into same-sex peer groups. For many children, same-gender friendships are closer and more intense in late childhood and early adolescence than in any other phase of the life span. Although social distance between the genders is present at preschool age, it increases during the elementary school years and remains strong through middle childhood (Baines & Blatchford, 2009).

In the early school years, peers intensify the pressure for gender segregation. A few children might try to play with opposite-sex peers, but they are often rejected. Although first-grade children nearly always name members of their own gender as best friends, girls and boys are observed playing together on playgrounds during recess. By the third grade, though, children divide themselves into two gender camps, and gender separation peaks around fifth grade. Much of the interaction between boys and girls at the fifth-grade level consists of bantering, teasing, chasing, name calling, and displays of open hostility. This "them-against-us" view serves to emphasize the differences between the genders and may function as a protective phase in life during which children can fashion a coherent gender-based identity (perhaps you recall putting a sign on your bedroom door or clubhouse that said "No Girls Allowed!" or vice versa).

Whatever characteristics may differentiate the genders, the way boys and girls are socialized in Western countries magnifies the differences greatly. Children feel great pressure to conform to expectations for their gender and are severely sanctioned by their peers for cross-gender behavior. This pressure is greater for boys than for girls; it is worse for a boy to be regarded as a "sissy" than for a girl to be seen as a "tomboy" (Sani & Bennett, 2004). Boys are told in many ways that asking for help, showing emotion, seeking greater connectedness with friends, and exhibiting vulnerability are unacceptable behavior. Those who demonstrate these behaviors (which are encouraged in girls) are called "wimps," "mamma's boys," and "fags." These epithets tell boys that they are not being masculine in a way mainstream society will accept. Dr. William Pollack, director of the Centers for Men and Young Men at Harvard University, calls the intense pressure boys experience to meet society's expectations about masculinity a war on boys (Pollack, 2006).

Pollack finds that despite a mask of bravado and invulnerability, many boys feel profoundly sad and isolated by these social demands. The needs of such boys are often not recognized by parents, teachers, or even psychologists. Caregivers and clinicians are sometimes fooled by the masks that boys feel pressured to wear. This social pressure not only affects boys emotionally but also

Gender Cleavage Gender cleavage, or gender segregation, increases during the elementary school years and remains strong through middle childhood, peaking around the fifth grade.

can undermine their performance in school. Research has shown that boys are doing less well academically, particularly in reading and writing, than they did in the past and that they have more difficulty adjusting to school. Pollack has found in his extensive counseling work with boys and young men that they are not "lone rangers" but instead long for connection.

In contrast, many studies have shown that girls benefit from this period of gender segregation. It gives them a time when they can focus on developing close friendships in which they experience trust, affection, acceptance, validation, loyalty, and nurturance. They hone the skills of connectedness that many of them will use for the rest of their lives. These supportive friendships provide an arena where girls can learn to solve problems by facing them and talking about them.

The prevalence of this childhood gender cleavage provided Sigmund Freud with his concept of the *latency period.* In Freud's view, once children no longer look on the parent of the opposite sex as a love object (thereby resolving their Oedipus or Electra conflict), they reject members of the opposite sex until they reach adolescence. Hence, according to Freud, the elementary school years are a kind of developmental plateau during which sexual impulses are repressed.

> *Questions*
>
> Did you experience gender cleavage in elementary school? Who were your friends? Why do you think same-gender friends are so prevalent during this stage of life?

Popularity, Social Acceptance, and Rejection

Peer relationships often take on enduring and stable characteristics, in particular the properties of a **group,** which is defined as two or more people who share a feeling of unity and are bound together in relatively stable patterns of social interaction. Group members have a psychological sense of oneness; they assume that their own inner experiences and emotional reactions are shared by the other members. This sense of oneness gives individuals the feeling that they are not merely *in* the group but also *of* the group. A group's awareness of unity is expressed in many ways. One of the most important is through shared **values,** which are the criteria that people use in deciding the relative merit and desirability of things (themselves, other people, objects, events, ideas, acts, and feelings). Values play a critical part in influencing people's social interaction. They function as the standards—the social "yardsticks"—that people use to appraise one another. In short, people size up one another according to various group standards of excellence, which can range from prosocial to antisocial.

Peer groups are no exception. Elementary school children arrange themselves in ranked hierarchies with respect to various qualities. Even first-graders have notions of one another's relative popularity or status. Consequently, children differ in the extent to which their peers desire to be associated with them. Recent research has also indicated that when children perceive their peer group to be "different" in some way, the bonds between members are much stronger (Nesdale et al., 2009).

Body Image and Popularity   Physical attractiveness is culturally defined, and different cultures define it differently. Children begin to acquire these cultural definitions by about 6 years of age. By the age of 8, as their thought processes shift to the period of concrete operations, they come to judge physical attractiveness in much the same manner as adults (Tremblay & Limbos, 2009). Stereotypes and appraisals of body configurations are also learned relatively early in life. "Lean and muscular," "tall and skinny," and "short and fat" are all bodily evaluations that influence the impressions people form of one another. As we noted in Chapter 9, negative attitudes toward "fatness" are already well developed among today's young children. Among boys, a favorable stereotype of the *mesomorph* (the person with an athletic, muscular, and broad-shouldered build) is evident at age 6, although boys' desire to look like a mesomorph does not appear until age 7 and is not clearly established until age 8.

Although researchers have found many qualities that make children appealing in the eyes of preadolescent and teen peers, physical development, attractiveness, and body build are their main concerns. Many studies with teens have consistently reported a significant relationship between physical attractiveness and popularity (Akos & Levitt, 2002). Phares, Steinberg, and Thompson's (2004) cross-sectional study with elementary and middle school students revealed significant concerns about weight and

Young Girls Feel the Pressure to Have a Perfect Body

body image—with girls reporting greater body dissatisfaction than boys. Girls as young as 6 in this study had tried to lose weight by dieting, and most children were knowledgeable about weight-control methods. Boys typically grow bigger and stronger, which is consistent with cultural ideals for males, so they struggle less with body image dissatisfaction (Maine, 2000). Friedman (1998) reports that at ages 10 and 11, a great majority of girls are convinced that they should be thinner. In one study with 11- to 14-year-old girls, more than one-third reported dieting activity (Byely et al., 2000). Obese youth are more at risk for developing mental-health problems related to their bodies than adolescents who are overweight or of normal weight (Goldfield et al., 2010).

Mainstream U.S. society's somewhat unrealistic standard of an ideal weight for women affects girls as young as preschool. One study found that half of the girls surveyed selected an ideal size that was smaller than their current size, even though only a small proportion of the girls were overweight. Girls watch television, read magazines, and consume other media and then internalize ideal body images (Tremblay & Limbos, 2009), not realizing that many photographs of women in magazines are altered or that actresses and models starve themselves to reach a certain weight for a particular job. Girls who reject unrealistic, idealized images of females in the media have higher self-esteem about their bodies.

Parents also influence children by transmitting weight-related attitudes and opinions. Mothers place more emphasis on body image, weight, and dieting than fathers do (Phares, Steinberg, & Thompson, 2004). Teasing by peers and family members about facial features, body weight, or body shape has a strong influence on the development of eating disorders and weight concerns for boys as well as girls. Researchers find that gender differences related to body image, physical attractiveness, and weight develop years before any puberty changes and argue that it is imperative to address concerns about weight and body image well before adolescence (Phares, Steinberg, & Thompson, 2004). Because body dissatisfaction is the single strongest predictor of developing an eating disorder, school counselors and mental-health experts suggest intervention strategies that increase self-esteem (Akos & Levitt, 2002). Such interventions in peer-group settings help girls disrupt the internalization of media images of women and may increase the self-esteem of girls and young women at a crucial point in their development (Clark & Tiggemann, 2006).

Behavioral Characteristics A range of behavioral characteristics are related to children's peer acceptance. Both children and teachers tend to describe model popular children as active, outgoing, alert, self-assured, helpful, and friendly. They show interest in others, act in prosocial ways, and are confident but not boastful (Newcomb, Bukowski, & Pattee, 1993). Recent studies of popular boys in grades 4 to 8 find that some preadolescent children consider boys who are "tough" or oppositional to be the most popular (Rodkin, Farmer, Pearl, & Van Acker, 2006). Boys of ethnic minority groups typically nominate as "most popular" those boys who are low achievers, disobey the rules, put little effort into school, and are good at sports. Thus, both popular prosocial and popular antisocial boys are central members of cliques in which they enjoy high levels of prominence. Tough boys have the highest self-perception of their popularity (Rodkin, Farmer, Pearl, & Van Acker, 2006).

In contrast, unpopular children have distinctive traits. *Social isolates* are physically listless, lethargic, and apathetic (or they might be experiencing a periodic chronic illness). Some children are simply introverted, timid, and withdrawn. Other children who are unpopular are overbearing or aggressively hostile and are described by their peers and teachers as noisy, attention-seeking, demanding, rebellious, and arrogant (Taylor, Davis-Kean, & Malanchuk, 2007). Significantly, early peer rejection in the first two months of kindergarten forecasts less favorable school perceptions among youngsters, higher levels of school avoidance, and lower performance levels. Children who encounter early rejection are likely to experience serious adjustment problems in later life.

Bullying Behaviors Whereas appearance is a central determinant of social status among girls, competitive, tough, and aggressive behaviors are often status markers for boys (Rodkin, Farmer, Pearl, & Van Acker, 2006). **Bullying** is deliberate, repeated aggressive behavior toward another person that involves *an imbalance of power or strength* (Nansel et al., 2003). The aggressor might be an individual or a group, and the victim might be an individual or a group. Such harmful actions include making faces, using "dirty" gestures, name calling, teasing, pinching, hitting, kicking, restraining actions, threatening

Popularity, Bullying, and Exclusion Elementary and middle school–aged children are reliant on peers for social support. Yet children who are perceived as different in some way—because of their physical appearance, ability, intellect, or race-ethnicity, or even because they are shy—are likely to be excluded from or bullied by the "in" group at school. Various intervention programs can be used to promote acceptance and a safe school climate for all children.

harm, stealing money and possessions, harassing sexually, sending mean notes or e-mail, spreading rumors or lies on a social network, or excluding others from a group. Boys are more likely to be bullied physically, but girls are likely to be the targets of rumors, sexual comments, and social exclusion (Nansel et al., 2001). Victims are likely to be "different" physically, intellectually, racially, socioeconomically, culturally, or in sexual orientation. They are often weaker and younger, are timid and lack confidence, or are not good at sports. Bullying behavior can be seen as a way to create and enforce cultural norms (Hamarus & Kaikkonen, 2008). Cyberbullying on the Internet is a form of bullying that inflicts serious psychological harm (Mason, 2008). An American Association of University Women (AAUW) study, *Hostile Hallways* (2001b), reports that four out of five girls experience sexual harassment in school.

The victims, or targets, of bullying experience injurious psychological and physical effects, such as depression, loneliness, anxiety, low self-esteem, stress-related illness, sleep disturbances, headaches, thoughts of suicide, or even, in a small number of cases, a final episode of violent revenge or suicide (Limber, 2002). Studies also reveal negative outcomes for the aggressor, such as being involved in a fight, theft, drugs, truancy, dropping out of school, later criminal convictions (e.g., gun or drug possession in school), or imprisonment (Nansel et al., 2003).

Schools have a legal responsibility, under the provisions of Title IX of the Education Amendments of 1992, to ensure that a safe environment is available to all students, although researchers have found that bullying communication is often hidden from teachers (Hamarus & Kaikkonen, 2008). Researchers say the effects of bullying have become a public health problem, and the negative effects on victims are long-lasting (Dracic, 2009). School intervention programs that focus on increasing empathy, teaching students to solve social problems fairly, and developing prosocial behavior have been shown to promote positive leadership and reduce social aggression among girls (Capella, 2006).

Questions

What personality characteristics distinguish a model popular child from a "tough popular" child? What traits are likely to make a child unpopular? What are some behavioral traits of a bully and victim?

Racial-Ethnic Awareness and Prejudice

A key aspect of many children's peer experiences involves relations with members of different racial-ethnic groups. A growing body of research indicates that children as young as 3 can correctly identify some differences between blacks and whites, and by the age of 7 a majority of children can make such racial-ethnic identifications accurately (Katz, 2003). By age 5 youngsters demonstrate a capacity for strong in-group bias and high levels of same-group cohesion (Aboud, 2003). Children's perceptions and understanding about racial-ethnic differences follow a developmental sequence similar to that for other stimuli (Wright, 1998). Their own social identities as members of particular racial-ethnic groups evolve slowly with age, as they subjectively identify with a group and assimilate notions of race-ethnicity and belonging within their self-concepts (Berry et al., 2006). Labeling oneself as a member of a racial-ethnic group is one of the earliest expressions of a child's social identity and is acquired by 7 to 8 years of age. Parents must be especially sensitive to their own beliefs about race in order to help their children avoid racial insensitivity (Vietze & Hildebrandt, 2009).

However, there is some doubt that all children, especially younger schoolchildren, show coherent, consistent **prejudice**—a system of negative conceptions, feelings, and actions regarding the members of a particular religious or racial-ethnic group. In-group bias can develop in young children, but prejudice is not a general characteristic of young children. *Discrimination* occurs when people act on the basis of their prejudicial beliefs (Levy & Hughes-Milligan, 2009). Young children in the preoperational stage classify things and people by the most salient features: big-small, tall-short, or black-white. (Thus when a young child notices a person on the street with purple hair, she or he may blurt out, "That girl has purple hair!" Recognizing and acknowledging the

obvious feature does not mean the child is prejudiced toward or against those with purple hair.) Children may also express bias in situations where it is expected of them (Monteiro, de França, & Rodrigues, 2009). Children surely observe adults behaving badly and shouting obscenities toward opposing teams at sporting events—and then mimic that behavior.

There are several theories about how children develop prejudice, ranging from psychodynamic theory (projecting subconscious anger onto others); social learning theory (learning by observing and imitating others); lack of exposure (fear of strangers); cognitive learning theory (children focus on people like themselves and then acquire social cognitive skills); and evolutionary theory (favoring members of one's own tribe over others) (Levy & Hughes-Milligan, 2009). Much research shows that how people act in a diverse racial-ethnic group situation bears little or no relation to how they feel or what they think (Vander Zanden, 1987). The social setting in which individuals find themselves does much to determine their specific responses. Thus, a public show of blatantly racist and discriminatory behavior is commonly defined as counter to American democratic ideals and is wrong, or even illegal.

There are various approaches to reducing prejudice and improving intergroup behaviors (Levy & Hughes-Milligan, 2009). Friendship among diverse groups is promoted by policies that foster positive intergroup contact at early ages in child-care settings, preschool, elementary schools, and neighborhoods—and integration should begin at the earliest possible time. Adjusting to new environments and avoiding negative stereotypes is more difficult for older students than for younger ones. Indeed, the junior high school and middle school years can be the worst period in which to start integration (Berry et al., 2006). One successful method for reducing racism is for community and authority figures to condemn prejudice and discrimination and to group students into mixed cooperative learning teams, which (like sport teams) knit members together in a shared endeavor that often leads to friendships among racial-ethnic groups (Levy & Hughes-Milligan, 2009).

Questions

How do children develop racial-ethnic prejudices? What types of behavioral interventions can be employed, and at what ages, to promote positive views among children who differ in race-ethnicity?

THE WORLD OF SCHOOL

The nature and mission of schools have been disputed through the ages, and Americans are no more in agreement about their schools than were the citizens of

Rome 2,000 years ago. Controversies persist over the content of school curricula, separation of church and state, teaching approaches, busing students to realize better racial-ethnic and socioeconomic mixes, school financing and taxation, special programs for youth with exceptionalities and for immigrant youth, academic freedom versus the need to prepare students to demonstrate achievement that meets standards set by *No Child Left Behind* or *Race to the Top,* preparing youth with technological skills, and school safety. School is a child's first big step into the larger society. When they attend school, children are away from family or their neighborhoods for several hours a day, especially if they are enrolled in before- and after-school programs while parents work. In school, children encounter a diverse population of teachers and children. These children move with them through a series of grades, so the school environment has a major impact on the development of a child's personality, self-esteem, intellectual capabilities, interpersonal skills, values, civic values, and social behavior.

Parents have choices about how to educate their children, and more parents are taking advantage of school-choice options (Grady, Bielick, & Aud, 2010). Alternative schools include public, private (religious and nonsectarian), charter or magnet schools (more freedom in curriculum design), and homeschools. Homeschooling continues to gain in popularity in the United States; more than 2 million K–12 students were homeschooled in 2010, and the numbers are rising yearly (Ray, 2010). The reasons cited for homeschooling include customization of education for a certain child's needs, more expansive pedagogical methods, opportunities to engage in community service and civic life, provision of religious or moral instruction, and dissatisfaction with available public instruction (National Center for Education Statistics, 2009). As a group, homeschooled students consistently achieve higher academic scores on standardized tests than traditionally educated students (Cogan, 2010; Ray, 2011). Homeschooled students are predominantly white. A recent survey of more than 11,000 homeschool students indicated that 98 percent of their parents are married, and about two-thirds of their parents had earned a bachelor's degree or higher (Ray, 2010).

For the school year 2008–2009, there were a record 49.3 million children in U.S. public schools and more than 7 million enrolled in parochial (Catholic) schools (Sable & Plotts, 2010; Snyder & Dillow, 2010). The U.S. Department of Education projects a need for more teachers because "total public school enrollment is expected to increase 8 percent between 2009 and 2018" (Snyder & Dillow, 2010). Since the 2011 federal and state budgets crises, many districts have been releasing teachers. But the employment outlook is good for teachers "in high-demand fields, such as mathematics, science, and bilingual education, and in

less desirable urban or rural school districts" (U.S. Bureau of Labor Statistics, 2011a).

Developmental Functions of Schools

Elementary schools serve many functions. First, the cognitive skills they teach—primarily the "core" subjects of language, math, social studies, and science—are similar across the world. However, the extent to which students gain skills, particularly social skills, in school is a function of the interaction of school, family, environment, and the characteristics of the individual child (Samanci, 2010). In general, U.S. students are continuing to fall far short of the Pacific Rim countries in the TIMSS and PIRLS tests of international comparison in the core subjects of math, science, and English, even though their scores have risen in the past decade (see Chapter 9) (Gonzales et al., 2009; Mullis, Martin, & Foy, 2008). The annual National Assessment of Education Progress (NAEP) assesses student performance in the fourth, eighth, and twelfth grades in reading, math, and other subjects. Children's average scores have gone up only a few points since 1992 (Federal Interagency Forum on Child and Family Statistics, 2010).

Second, schools share with the family the responsibility for transmitting any society's dominant cultural goals and values. Like schools in the United States, schools in Japan, China, and Russia stress patriotism, national history, obedience, diligence, personal cleanliness, physical fitness, and the correct use of language. Schools also attempt to instill general skills, such as being on time, paying attention, sitting quietly, collaborating in classroom activities, and completing assignments and meeting deadlines, preparing youth for future work conditions (Apple, 2004). Even the school evaluation system of A to F has its parallel in the merit system of wage and salary scales as a device for motivating individuals.

Third, to one degree or another, schools function as a "sorting and sifting agency" that selects young people for upward social mobility. Some families influence the careers of their children by socializing them to higher educational and occupational aspirations and providing them with the support necessary for achieving their goals (Southerland, 2006). Successful elementary and middle school experiences are very important in launching children into this process. Although early academic success does not ensure later success, early academic failure strongly predicts later academic failure (Hamre & Pianta, 2005).

Fourth, schools attempt to help children overcome deficits or difficulties that interfere with adequate social functioning and participation. Schools work in collaboration with parents and guardians, school psychologists, social workers, guidance personnel, school nurses and local doctors, physical therapists, speech therapists, occupational therapists, social services, parole officers, and the juvenile justice system. Schools also serve a custodial function, providing a day-care service that keeps children from potential harm on the streets (see the *Further Developments* box on page 328, "After-School Care and Supervision"). In higher grades, they function as a dating and marriage market. And compulsory education, coupled with child labor laws, typically serves to keep younger children out of the labor market, thus prolonging childhood until the late teenage years.

Motivating Students

Most of us assume that people do certain things because the outcomes somehow meet their needs. This premise underlies the concept of motivation. **Motivation** involves the inner states and processes that prompt, direct, and sustain activity. Motivation influences the rate of student learning, the retention of information, and performance (Eccles & Wigfield, 2002). Significantly, a gradual, overall decline occurs in various indicators of academic motivation—attention in class, school attendance, and self-perception of academic competence—as youth move from elementary to middle school or junior high (Eccles & Wigfield, 2002). Here we will examine a few aspects of motivation that are most relevant to our consideration of the schooling process.

Intrinsic and Extrinsic Motivation   Mark Twain once observed that work consists of whatever we are obligated to do, whereas play consists of whatever we are not obligated to do. Work is a means to an end; play is an end in itself. Many psychologists make a similar distinction between extrinsic motivation and intrinsic motivation. **Extrinsic motivation** involves activity undertaken for some purpose other than its own sake. Rewards such as school grades, honor rolls, scholarships, wages, and promotions are extrinsic because they are independent of the activity itself and are controlled by someone else. **Intrinsic motivation** involves activity undertaken for its own sake. Intrinsic rewards are those inherent to the activity itself and over which we have a high degree of personal control (Brophy, 2004).

As we noted earlier in this chapter, children want to feel effective and self-determining in dealing with their environment. Regrettably, formal education often undermines children's spontaneous curiosity and desire to learn. Children become more extrinsically motivated and less intrinsically motivated to do their schoolwork as they transition into middle and junior high schools. At this same age, many—especially boys and minority youth—"turn off" to school and education (Brophy, 2004). Most psychologists agree that punishment, anxiety or distress, and being ignored impede classroom learning. But they have also become more aware that even rewards can be the enemies of curiosity and exploration (Brophy, 2004). Teachers must learn to be more supportive and less controlling of students' motivation (Katz, Kaplan, & Gueta, 2010; Reeve, 2009).

Research by Lepper and Greene (1975) revealed that parents and teachers can unwittingly undermine intrinsic interest in many activities by providing youngsters with extrinsic rewards such as lavish praise, gold stars, money, toys, or treats to undermine children's intrinsic interest in many activities. They suggest that parents and educators should use extrinsic rewards only when necessary to draw children into activities that do not at first attract their interest. And even in these cases, extrinsic rewards should be phased out as quickly as possible.

Attributions of Causality   Closely linked to the issue of rewards is another matter—people's perceptions of the factors that produce given outcomes (Buehner & May, 2009). Consider the following experience. You have been watching a game involving your favorite football team. With 5 seconds left in the game and the score tied, a player on your team intercepts a pass and races for the goal line. As the player stumbles into the end zone, the gun sounds, ending the game. Your team has won. Your friend, who favored the other team, says, "Your guys were just lucky!" You respond, "Luck my eye! That was true ability." "Naw," exclaims another friend. "Your guys were more psyched up. They put out more effort." Then a fourth observer interjects, "It was an easy interception. No one was between him and the goal line!" Four people had four different explanations of causality for the same event: luck, ability, effort, and the difficulty of the task (Weiner, 1993).

Youngsters also attribute their academic successes to these differing explanations. And it makes a considerable difference which explanation they employ. Educational psychologists find that when students attribute their successes to high ability, they are more likely to view future success as highly probable than when they attribute their success to other factors. The perception that one has failed because one has low ability is considerably more devastating than the perception that one has failed because of bad luck, lack of effort, or task difficulty (O'Laughlin & Malle, 2002).

It seems that both success and failure feed on themselves. Students with histories of performing better than their peers commonly attribute their superior performances to high ability, so they anticipate future success. Should they encounter periodic episodes of failure, they attribute them to bad luck or lack of effort. But youngsters with histories of low attainment typically attribute their successes to good luck or high effort and their failures to poor ability. Consequently, high attainment leads to attributions that maintain a high self-concept of high ability, high academic motivation, and continued high attainment. It is otherwise for those youngsters with low attainment (Elliot & Dweck, 2005).

FURTHER DEVELOPMENTS

After-School Care and Supervision

The number of children in the United States who routinely spend part of the day unsupervised is of great concern. According to the National Institute on Out-of-School Time (NIOST) in 2009, about 14 million school-age children spend time without adult supervision on a regular basis when out of school. The possible consequences of lack of supervision torment many parents and concern the scientific community, child welfare advocates, and the juvenile justice system. Almost half of school-age children are cared for by relatives after school (see Figure 10.4). But children who do not have adult supervision after school are at risk of harm.

The National Safe Kids Campaign says that 4.5 million children 14 and under are injured at home annually and that most injury-related deaths occur when children are unsupervised after school (Karasik, 2000). Serious juvenile crime rates triple on school days between 3 and 6 P.M., and young children are often victimized. Children who must care for themselves after school are most likely to be from lower-SES groups and are already at risk. Self-care is linked with lower academic performance and higher levels of anxiety and depression among children who live in high-crime neighborhoods (Lord & Mahoney, 2007).

Of the 49,700 U.S. public elementary schools, more than half now offer various after-school programs located within their schools to about 50,000 students. Such programs include fee-based programs, day care, academic instruction and tutoring, and other broad-based programs (Parsad & Lewis, 2009). Children who attend after-school programs glean many benefits, such as better work habits and more homework completed, improved social skills, improved school attendance, higher grades and test scores, fewer hours watching television, more hours in sports and activities, and better conduct in school compared with peers (National Institute of Child Health and Human Development Early Child Care Research Network, 2004). Some children also participate in organized after-school activities such as sports, religious activities, and fine arts programs (Federal Interagency Forum on Child and Family Statistics, 2010).

Successful programs depend on well-trained staff, structured programming, and appropriate levels of supervision (Munton, Blackburn, & Barreau, 2002). Consequently, over the past decade many U.S. schools—with federal funding and in partnership with YMCAs, YWCAs, Boys & Girls Clubs, and scouting programs—have established after-school and summer programs at both the elementary and middle school levels. These programs provide safety and supervision, nutrition, activities, and adult care for children who would otherwise be unsupervised while parents work. Although many agencies and schools provide after-school child supervision, some parents cannot afford after-school programs.

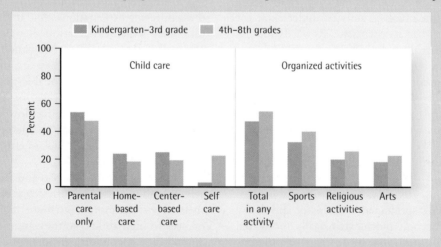

FIGURE 10.4 Percentage of Children in Kindergarten Through Eighth Grade by Weekday Care and Activities: 2005 More employed parents choose relative care, including care provided by grandparents, siblings, and other relatives, although a growing number of single parents and two working parents are selecting after-school programs.
Source: Federal Interagency Forum on Child and Family Statistics. (2010). Indicator Fam3.C. *America's Children in Brief: Key National Indicators of Well-Being, 2010.* Washington, DC: U.S. Government Printing Office. Retrieved from http://www.childstats.gov/pdf/ac2010/ac_10.pdf

Locus of Control   The research on attributions of causality has been influenced by the concept of locus of control. Earlier in this chapter we noted in our discussion of stress that *locus of control* refers to people's perception of who or what is responsible for the outcome of events and behaviors in their lives. Many studies have shown a relationship between locus of control and academic achievement (Elliot & Dweck, 2005). It seems that locus of control plays a crucial role in determining whether students become involved in the pursuit of achievement. Externally controlled youngsters tend to assume that no matter how hard they work, the outcome will be determined by luck or chance; they have little incentive to invest personal effort in their studies, to persist in problem-solving efforts, or to change their behavior to ensure success.

In contrast, internally controlled youngsters believe that their behavior accounts for their academic successes or failures and that they can direct their efforts to succeed in academic tasks. Not surprisingly, pupils with an internal sense of control generally show superior academic performance (Elliot & Dweck, 2005). Children's belief that they are competent and can achieve success with hard work declines from a very strong belief in self-ability (in the preschool years) to a much more guarded belief (by the college years) that hard work will pay off. Researchers theorize that this is because the U.S. education system places an increasing emphasis on academic competition as students get older (Eccles et al., 2006). Low educational attainment is often associated with socioeconomic disadvantage and the effects of poverty, a topic that is being subjected to extensive empirical scrutiny by behavioral scientists (Thernstrom & Thernstrom, 2003).

School Performance, Social Class, Ethnicity, and the Gender Gap

Many studies have shown a close relationship among school performance, socioeconomic status, race-ethnicity, and gender (Alexander, Entwisle, & Olson, 2001).

Social Class   Rather than looking at whether schools improve socioeconomic status, Heyneman (2005) feels that schools should be judged on how well they socialize students. However, this relationship is evident regardless of the measure employed (occupation of main wage earner, family income, or parents' education). Studies have shown that the higher the SES of children's families: (1) the greater the number of formal grades the children will complete, the more academic honors and awards they will receive, and the more elective offices they will hold; (2) the greater their participation in extracurricular activities; (3) the higher their scores on academic achievement tests; and (4) the lower their rates of failure,

"HOW DO YOU KNOW I'M AN UNDERACHIEVER? —MAYBE YOU'RE JUST AN OVERDEMANDER!"

Achievement Is Relative
Source: Drawing by Baloo, from the *Wall Street Journal*—Permission, Cartoon Features Syndicate.

truancy, suspension, and premature dropping out of school. Among the hypotheses that have been advanced to explain these facts are the middle-class bias of schools, differences attributable to race-ethnicity, a gender gap for boys, and educational self-fulfilling prophecies.

Middle-Class Bias   Boyd McCandless (1970, p. 295) has observed that "schools succeed relatively well with upper- and middle-class youngsters. After all, schools are built for them, staffed by middle-class people, and modeled after middle-class people." Even when teachers are originally from a different social class, they encourage the development of middle-class values such as thrift, punctuality, respect for property and established authority, sexual morality, ambition, and neatness. In the past decade, school districts nationwide have begun to hire administrators, teachers, and teachers' aides from diverse racial, ethnic, and SES backgrounds—especially those who are bilingual—to serve the increasing mix of first-generation immigrant students who are likely to live in poorer neighborhoods.

Some middle-class teachers, perhaps unaware of their prejudice, find youth from lower-SES families as difficult or disobedient (Auwarter & Aruguete, 2008). These students sense the lack of acceptance and respect and respond by taking the attitude "If you don't like me, I won't cooperate with you!" The result is that some of these children fail to acquire basic reading, writing, and math skills and become disillusioned with the educational system, which typically is the only avenue available to them to improve their well-being in the long run (Vaught & Castagno, 2008).

Race-Ethnicity   Children of different racial-ethnic groups and social classes, especially black and Hispanic students, bring somewhat different experiences and attitudes into the school situation, and some of these differences are related to the education achievement gap (Mo & Singh, 2008). Most racial-ethnic groups in the United States have a painful history with the U.S. government regarding education. Blacks were denied education under slavery and given unequal education resources for generations after that. American Indian children were forcibly removed from their parents and taught English and were given an education that their parents did not want for them. Many immigrant groups experienced great pressure to leave their language and cultural values behind and become "Americanized," and this pressure persists even today. These experiences still shape the cultural attitudes of ethnic groups in the United States toward education. Many parents are wary of trusting teachers and school systems, even as they want their children to do well in school to prepare for a good career in adulthood (Spring, 2007). Most parents teach their children about their ethnicity, stressing cultural values, the history of discrimination against their racial-ethnic group, and the importance of questioning the values of the dominant U.S. culture (Hughes et al., 2006c). These complex histories can create competing arenas for children, as they experience conflict between loyalty to their racial-ethnic group and their desire to do well in schools that often do not address their cultural needs or accommodate their learning styles (Spring, 2007).

Middle-class parents generally make it clear to their children that they are expected to apply themselves to school tasks. But not all groups subscribe to this value, and some directly oppose it (Thernstrom & Thernstrom, 2003). Therefore, children vary in their level of preparedness for school—for example, in their attitudes regarding punctuality; the use of books, pencils, and paper; numerals and the alphabet; and completing homework assignments.

Perhaps even more important, middle-class children are much more likely than disadvantaged youngsters to have embraced the conviction that they can affect their environments and their futures. When fourth-grade Latino and black students were asked which students at school they admired, boys and girls both chose students who were high academic achievers of their same gender. When seventh-grade Latino and black students were asked the same question, the focus of the male students had shifted toward same-gender students who were low achievers academically. They had opted out of academic achievement as an arena where success was possible— and perhaps they did not even regard it as desirable. These findings reflect the racial-ethnic inequality in U.S. society. Black and Latino boys often perceive their interactions with teachers as unsupportive and feel that the school climate is hostile and unfair to them. Indeed, harsh discipline is used disproportionately with these boys, leading them to question their ability to succeed (Taylor & Graham, 2007).

A recent meta-analysis of teachers' attitudes toward students from ethnic and racial groups found that teachers have more negative expectations about the performance of Hispanic students than they do for black and Asian students, and that their expectations for all three groups are lower than those they have for European American students. These expectations are conveyed in subtle ways; teachers speak more positively to European American students and give non–European American students less positive feedback and fewer opportunities to respond in class (Tenenbaum & Ruck, 2007).

The Gender Gap   It appears that a gender reversal of achievement and engagement in schools has been occurring over the past 30 years. This is attributable to federal legislation such as Title IX and to the efforts of organizations such as the American Association of University Women to help girls excel in school. From 1992 to 2009, girls in the fourth, eighth, and twelfth grades achieved higher scaled scores on a standardized reading and writing exam (NAEP and PIRLS) (see Table 10.3). However, boys achieve higher scaled scores on standardized math and science exams (NAEP and TIMSS) (Gonzales et al., 2009; U.S. Department of Education, 2011). Girls from age 5 to age 12 are less likely to repeat a grade. Boys are more likely to get into a fight on school property, but these rates have declined since 1995. In all but a few years since 1972, more males dropped out of high school than girls—until 2008, when slightly more girls than boys dropped out (Chapman, Laird, & Kewalramani, 2010).

TABLE 10.3 Gender Differences on Results of the National Assessment of Education Progress (NAEP) Exams in Reading and Science: 1992–2009

Average Scaled Scores in Reading for Fourth- and Eighth-Graders, by Sex. The scale ranges from 0 to 500.

	Fourth-Graders		Eighth-Graders	
	Boys	Girls	Boys	Girls
1992	213	221	254	267
2003	215	222	258	269
2009	218	224	259	269

Average Scaled Scores in Science for Fourth- and Eighth-Graders, by Sex

	Fourth-Graders		Eighth-Graders	
	Boys	Girls	Boys	Girls
1996	151	149	151	149
2005	153	149	150	147
2009	151	149	152	148

Note: Accommodations for students with any special needs were not permitted for the 1992 assessment.

Source: U.S. Department of Education. (2011). National Assessment of Education Progress (NAEP), 1990–2009. National Center for Education Statistics. Retrieved from http://nces.ed.gov/nationsreportcard/

The gender gap begins early: Girls' fine motor skills develop earlier (the nerves on boys' fingers develop later than girls', so it is more difficult for boys to hold a pencil and write clearly). Girls are better at sitting still, paying attention, abiding by rules, being verbally competent, and dealing with interpersonal relations (Garbarino, 1999). Boys' hormones surge several times a day, causing the urge to move, but they may be lucky to get even one recess to expend that energy (boys are more likely to be kept in at recess to get extra help or be disciplined for rough behaviors, not paying attention, or causing interruptions in class). Boys' female teachers may not know how to help boys harness their energy constructively. Boys outnumber girls in special education classes by 2 to 1 (Haggerty, 2009), and more boys are diagnosed with attention-deficit hyperactivity disorder (Bauermeister et al., 2007).

Overall, males achieve higher scores on standardized tests such as the SAT and ACT; but females take more Advanced Placement courses, attend college in greater numbers, and earn more than half of all bachelor's and master's degrees and as many doctoral degrees as males do (Snyder & Dillow, 2010). Parents, schools, and communities must begin to focus on developmentally appropriate learning for both girls and boys, for this trend affects employment rates, lifetime income, marriage and child outcomes, and other lifelong socioeconomic factors.

Educational Self-Fulfilling Prophecies   Children of lower socioeconomic status and minority children are frequently the victims of **educational self-fulfilling prophecies,** or the effects of teacher expectations (Eccles et al., 2006). Some children fail to learn because those who are charged with teaching them do not believe that they will learn, do not expect that they can learn, and do not act toward them in ways that motivate them to learn (Auwarter & Aruguete, 2008). The goal is to get more college graduates from ethnically diverse backgrounds to enter the teaching profession, for they will have a better

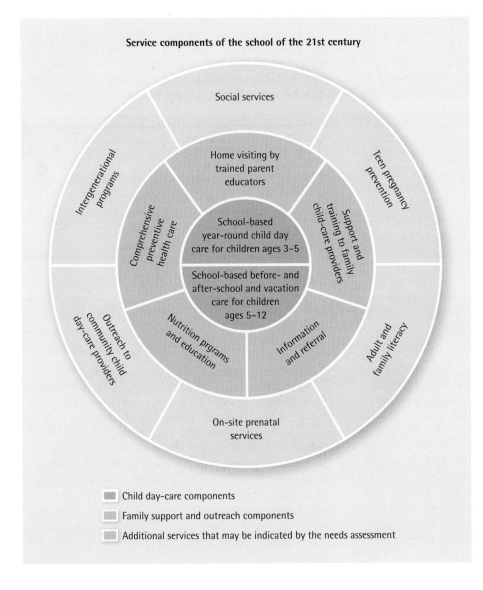

FIGURE 10.5 A Model of the School of the Twenty-First Century The school is now a central location for providing comprehensive services that benefit children and their families: education, child care, health care, and social services.
Source: Zigler, E. F., Finn-Stevenson, M., and Marsland, K. W. Child day care in the schools: The school of the 21st century, *Child Welfare, 74*(6), 1303. Copyright © 1995 by Child Welfare League of America, Inc. Reproduced with permission of the Child Welfare League of America, Inc. via Copyright Clearance Center.

understanding of children's diverse backgrounds and serve as models to the younger generation.

James Vasquez (1998) writes that children brought up in Hispanic homes come to school with a sense of loyalty to the family and that the family is their basic support group throughout life. This is in direct contrast to the sense of individualism instilled in many other American youth. Consider the difference in these two forms of hypothetical teacher praise: "This is good work, Maria. You should be proud of yourself." Or "Maria, this is good work. I'm going to send it home for your family to see." Vasquez also states that Hispanic youth thrive in an environment of cooperation with the group, which differs significantly from the mainstream value of individual competition and striving to be at the top at someone else's expense. Vasquez suggests a student-centered, three-step sequence for teachers to develop instructional strategies for adapting instruction to student cultural traits: (1) Identify cultural traits of individual students, (2) consider the content to be taught, the context in which it will be taught, and the mode or delivery method, and (3) write down and practice new instructional strategies. All teachers would do well to educate themselves about the cultural values of ethnic groups in the United States, attend presentations on multicultural education, and read research on multicultural education to enhance their knowledge of the distinctive learning traits of students (Frye & Vogt, 2010; Hwang & Vrongistinos, 2010).

Moreover, communities need to become involved, because schools and school districts do not provide equal learning opportunities, particularly facilities, equipment, and teacher quality. American inner-city school districts often cannot afford to upgrade the infrastructure of their schools. Black and Hispanic students are often disadvantaged by schools in very much the same ways that their communities are disadvantaged in their interactions with major societal institutions (Gore & Aseltine, 2003).

Schools of the Twenty-First Century   Many school reform initiatives have been implemented and are under close scrutiny, in association with researchers and federal education leaders. Such efforts are put into practice in charter schools, magnet schools, and ventures such as *Atlas Communities, The Modern Red Schoolhouse, Success for All,* Stanford's *Accelerated Schools,* and Yale's *School of the 21st Century (21C)* to create the best possible educational environment for all students. 21C is a comprehensive community model of shared work dedicated to the healthy growth and development of all children from birth to age 12. More than 1,300 traditional U.S schools have been converted into year-round multiservice centers that are accessible to children and parents all day, providing guidance and support for parents, including classes in English, preschool programs, before- and after-school and vacation care for children, health education and services for children, networks and training for community child-care providers, and information and referral for families (see Figure 10.5). A central goal is meeting the needs of the continuing influx of immigrant students and their families (see Figure 10.5). Initial evaluations of two 21C schools are very positive in terms of the schools' effects on variables such as absenteeism, reading at higher grade levels, grade retention, special education students, and school suspensions (Zigler & Finn-Stevenson, 2010).

Questions

In what ways do you think contemporary schools in the United States contribute to or detract from a child's overall achievement and well-being? How are U.S. schools changing to meet the needs of children and families from diverse cultural backgrounds in the twenty-first century?

SEGUE

Many interrelated factors are involved in children's healthy physical, cognitive, emotional, and social development throughout the elementary and middle school years. Most middle-class children have the benefit of protective forces—an intact family structure, economic support, school curriculum and teacher support, friendships, community activities and recreational programs, and supervised after-school programs. Other children, particularly some who are at a socioeconomic disadvantage, do not develop in a healthy, resilient way because of inconsistent family supervision and the unsupportive nature of the social environments in their lives. The following factors are associated with healthy child development and competency: (1) good self-esteem, (2) optimism and a sense of hope, (3) resilience, (4) the ability to cope with fears and stress, (5) the ability to experience a range of emotions and to self-regulate emotions, (6) sociability, (7) cognitive abilities to problem-solve, (8) responsibility for regular chores at home, and (9) participation in school, church, or extracurricular activities ("Determinants of Health in Children," 1996). These traits provide a solid foundation for thriving in junior high and high school environments during the adolescent stage of development, which is discussed in Chapter 11.

SUMMARY

The Quest for Self-Understanding

1. Erikson's psychosocial stage during middle childhood is industry versus inferiority. Children desire to try many new things and to develop their abilities. Those who are prevented from trying new activities, don't get the opportunity to try, or don't experience success in comparison to the group are likely to develop low self-esteem.

2. Children's self-concepts develop as they get feedback about their worth or status from the significant people in their lives. Children acquire positive, healthy self-esteem if they are accepted, approved, and respected.

3. In expanded social settings, children must also learn to regulate their own emotions to get along with the group (classmates, friends in the neighborhood, teammates, relatives). The peer group typically rejects children who cannot self-regulate their behaviors.

4. Anger, fear, anxiety, and stress play an important part in the lives of young children. Generally, girls experience more fears, anxiety, and stress than boys—especially as they enter middle school years.

5. All children experience stressful situations in response to perceived threats or dangers, yet they can learn coping strategies to deal with stress. Two important aspects of coping with stress are a child's own sense of mastery and locus of control. Children of veterans are likely to experience long-term, repeated stress.

Continuing Family Influences

6. The lives of children in the United States have become more structured as parents' lives have changed. Children's unstructured play time has declined sharply.

7. Research findings indicate that more positive behaviors in children are associated with a warm parental relationship, parents' expectations for closeness, and parents' expectation that the child will complete college.

8. Mothers play an important role during the middle years of their children's development by supporting them in their efforts to engage in productive activities.

9. Most children still live in a family that includes a biological father or stepfather during at least part of their childhood. But fathers differ in the amount of time they spend with children, in the activities they share with them, and in the degree to which they take on the responsibilities of parenting. When fathers are involved in children's lives, both children and mothers benefit.

10. Divorced fathers must go through a process of grieving and accepting the end of their relationship with the mother of their children to prepare for their new relationship with their children. Fathers who do not do this emotional work often find it difficult to stay emotionally close to their children after divorce.

11. Siblings normally feel loyalty and support for each other, but they may also experience conflict. Sibling relationships are good places for children to learn important conflict-resolution and negotiating skills.

12. Children vary in their reactions to divorce, depending on the child's age and temperament and on parental

competence in managing the divorce. Children's concerns about this loss are normally quite different from their parents' concerns. Studies find that children experience less stress when parents cooperate in matters concerning the children.

13. The number of children living in single-parent families increased throughout the 1990s and 2000s. The majority of single-parent families are headed by women, but the number of single-parent families headed by fathers is slowly rising.

14. Between 75 and 80 percent of divorced parents remarry, creating stepfamilies. Children can find it difficult to adjust to the authority of a new parent, who may or may not bring new children into the reconstituted family.

Later Childhood: The Broadening Social Environment

15. Peer groups provide children with situations in which they are independent of adult controls, give them experience in egalitarian relationships, furnish them with status in a realm where their own interests reign supreme, and transmit informal knowledge.

16. During the years of gender segregation, girls benefit by learning relationship skills. In contrast, boys are more likely to be taught to conceal their emotions.

17. Elementary school children arrange themselves in hierarchies with regard to various standards, including physical attractiveness, body build, and behavioral characteristics. This affects which children are accepted and which are not accepted by a peer group.

18. Children's self-conceptions tend to emerge from others' feedback regarding their desirability, worth, and status. Through their interactions with others and through the effects they produce on their material environment, they derive a sense of their energy, skill, and industry.

19. Bullying behaviors emerge during middle childhood. Both boys and girls participate in bullying. Intervention programs to increase prosocial behavior and develop positive leadership and cooperative behavior among peers have been successful in reducing bullying.

20. Most children can make accurate racial-ethnic identifications by 7 years of age. However, it is doubtful whether children, especially younger school children, show coherent and consistent prejudice.

The World of School

21. Schools teach specific cognitive skills (primarily the "core" subjects of language, math, history, and science), general skills associated with effective participation in classroom settings, and the society's dominant cultural goals and values.

22. Motivation influences the rate at which students learn, their retention of information, and their performance. Ideally, motivation comes from within (intrinsic motivation).

23. As some children from racial-ethnic groups move from early childhood to preadolescence, they come to believe

that they cannot succeed in school because racial-ethnic discrimination presents insurmountable obstacles. This is especially the case for Latino and African American males.

24. Cross-cultural research shows that children of different racial-ethnic groups or immigration histories differ in behaviors, beliefs, and norms about children working, playing, reading, or learning new skills.

KEY TERMS

anxiety *(308)*

bullying *(324)*

cohabitation *(316)*

coping *(310)*

educational self-fulfilling prophecies *(331)*

effortful control *(306)*

extrinsic motivation *(327)*

fear *(307)*

gender cleavage *(322)*

group *(322)*

industry versus inferiority *(304)*

intrinsic motivation *(327)*

locus of control *(310)*

motivation *(327)*

phobia *(308)*

post-traumatic stress disorder (PTSD) *(312)*

prejudice *(325)*

self-esteem *(305)*

self-image *(304)*

stimulus-rich environment *(314)*

stress *(310)*

values *(323)*

FOLLOWING UP ON THE INTERNET

Web sites for this chapter focus on social-emotional issues, family and school influences, and continued identity development of children in middle childhood. Please access the text Web site at www.mhhe.com/crandell10 for up-to-date hot-linked Internet addresses for the following organizations, topics, and resources:

Erikson's Latency Stage
http://web.cortland.edu/andersmd/ERIK/stage4.HTML

National Association for Single-Sex Public Education
http://www.singlesexschools.org/home-introduction.htm

National Center on Fathers and Families
http://www.ncoff.gse.upenn.edu/

National Home Education Research Institute
http://www.nheri.org/

U.S. Department of Education and Teacher Loan Forgiveness
http://studentaid.ed.gov/PORTALSWebApp/students/english/cancelstaff.jsp

National Education Association Character Education Resources
http://www.nea.org/tools/40672.htm

National Stepfamily Resource Center
http://www.stepfamilies.info/

Yale's School of the 21st Century
http://www.yale.edu/21c/index2.html

PART 6 ADOLESCENCE

Adolescent youth generally experience rapid physical, intellectual, social, and emotional changes during the time of puberty. Chapter 11 discusses issues of maturity that accompany the adolescent growth spurt and fertility for males and females. Variations in timing of sexual maturation occur and influence both adolescent personality and behavior. Cognitive growth includes the ability to use logical and abstract thought and to plan for the future. Adolescents become more egocentric and are influenced by peers more than at any other time of development. Social pressures to belong to a group or conform to group norms cause some teens to experience anxiety, eating disorders, or depression or to engage in risky behavior. In Chapter 12 we will discuss how teens continue to develop a sense of identity, to establish autonomy, and to explore vocational choices. Some teens begin to question authority, experiment with alcohol or other drugs, or become sexually active or pregnant; they are also more likely to drop out of school. A small number exhibit antisocial behaviors and end up in the juvenile justice system. Most adolescents navigate through adolescence into early adulthood in a healthy fashion.

11 Adolescence
Physical and Cognitive Development

Critical Thinking Questions

1. During adolescence some children develop much faster than others. Should we separate students at this age into different schools or tracks based on how much they have developed physically or cognitively?

2. Two lifelong friends accidentally wear exactly the same outfit to parties at ages 6, 16, and 60. At which age do you think this will have the most impact on them and why?

3. Think back to when you first became concerned with such things as the environment, your own nudity, politics, and whether you wanted to be seen publicly with your parents. Chances are, your awareness of these issues occurred during adolescence. Why would this be so?

4. Imagine that you are a high school student, and one afternoon you and several friends are milling about near the varsity football field. It's there you happen to witness an incident involving bullying between two people who go to your school. There's no violence yet, just some low-level taunting that centers on humiliating the victim. Complicating matters, the bully is someone you used to like, and the victim is a boy who just moved into the school district—someone who's been having trouble fitting in. In fact, you've heard your friends say they don't like him, but they're vague about the reasons. Would you get involved in confronting the bully? Would you be affected by what your friends thought of the reputation of each person? What would you say to the bully? What would you say to your friends?

For the first time since the 1970s, the number of 13- to 19-year-olds is surging, and this increase is expected to continue until the year 2050 (U.S. Bureau of the Census, 2010k). In the United States, adolescence is depicted mainly as a carefree time of physical attentiveness and attraction, vitality, robust fun, love, enthusiasm, and risk-taking activities. Although the majority of American teens manage to get through their adolescent years with relatively minor problems, some find it to be a much more difficult period. In contrast, in much of the world, adolescence is not a socially distinct period in the human life span. Although young people everywhere undergo puberty, many assume adult status and responsibility by age 13 or younger.

This chapter focuses on the dramatic physical changes, cognitive growth, and moral challenges that adolescents experience as they make the transition from childhood to emerging adulthood. During this transition they begin to experiment with what they see as "adult" behaviors, such as driving, working, smoking, drinking, and having sex. It is truly an exciting and sometimes frightening time, for it is probably the last time they will experience so many novel experiences, emotions, and sensations in such a short period of time.

PHYSICAL DEVELOPMENT

During adolescence young people undergo truly radical changes in growth and development. After a lifetime of inferior size, they suddenly catch up to or surpass many adults in physical size and strength. Females typically mature earlier than males, and this becomes more evident in sixth and seventh grades, when many girls are taller than most boys. Accompanying these changes is the less evident development of the reproductive organs that signals sexual maturity. Remarkable chemical and biological changes are taking place that will, over time, fashion girls into women and boys into men.

Signs of Maturation and Puberty

Puberty is the period in the life cycle when sexual and reproductive maturation becomes evident. Puberty is not a single event or set of events but a crucial phase in a long and complex process of maturation that begins prenatally. However, unlike infants and young children, older children experience the dramatic changes of puberty through a developed sense of consciousness and self-awareness. Their emerging capacity for abstract thought, coupled with the biological and psychological changes associated with puberty, can have a significant bearing on adolescent development (Euling et al., 2008).

Hormonal Changes During Puberty

The dramatic changes that occur in children at puberty are regulated, integrated, and orchestrated by the central nervous system and the glands of the endocrine system. Recall from general psychology that the *hypothalamus* is part of the midbrain that sits above the *pituitary gland,* a pea-sized structure found at the base of the brain. At puberty some type of genetic timing triggers a cluster of neurons within the *hypothalamus* to stimulate secretion of gonadotropin-releasing hormone (GnRH) (see Figure 11.1) (DiVall & Radovick, 2008). The hypothalamus then releases GnRH in intermittent bursts to the pituitary. The pituitary gland, called the "master gland," secretes hormones into the bloodstream that in turn stimulate other glands to produce their specific kinds of hormones. The pituitary steps up its production of the growth hormones, follicle-stimulating hormone (FSH), and luteinizing hormone (LH) that stimulate the manufacture of *estrogen* and *progesterone* in females and stimulate cells of the testes in males to

FIGURE 11.1 The Brain and the Endocrine System During Puberty
Genetic timing triggers the hypothalamus to release gonadotropin-releasing hormone (GnRH), thus activating the "developmental clock" of pubertal development by age 10 or 11, or earlier. GnRH in turn stimulates the pituitary gland to secrete FSH and LH sex hormones (which biologists call *gonadal steroid hormone secretions*) into the young person's bloodstream. The arrows indicate that there is a continuous neuroendocrine feedback loop between the reproductive glands (the ovaries and testes) and the brain that excites the GnRH neurons. In about four years, the physiological capacity and desire for human sexual reproduction are set in motion.
Source: Sisk, Cheryl L., & Foster, Douglas L. (2004, October). The neural basis of puberty and adolescence. *Nature Neuroscience, 7*(10), 1040–1047.

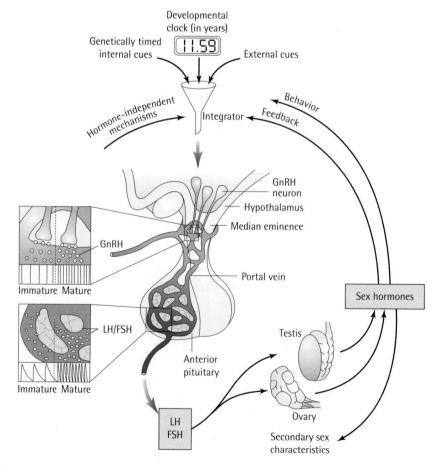

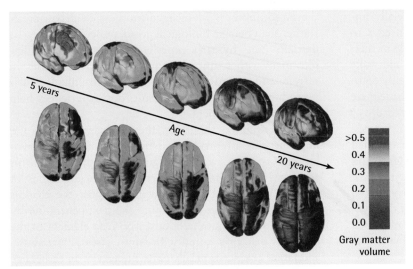

FIGURE 11.2 The Dynamic Sequence of Gray Matter Maturation over the Cortical Surface The sidebar shows a color representation in units of gray matter volume.
Source: Lenroot, R. K., & Giedd, J. N. (2006). Brain development in children and adolescents: Insights from anatomical magnetic resonance imaging. *Neuroscience and Biobehavioral Reviews, 30,* 718–729.

manufacture and secrete the masculinizing sex hormone, *testosterone* (Ge, Natsuaki, Neiderhiser, & Reiss, 2007; Sisk & Foster, 2004).

Banerjee and Clayton (2007) explain that pubertal timing "is triggered in every healthy individual at any time over a 4-year period (males during 10–14 years and females during 9–13 years)." The initial visible physical changes that occur in both males and females, called **secondary sex characteristics,** include growth in height and weight, breast development in girls, appearance of body hair, voice changes in boys, and so forth. We shall discuss these shortly. A second signaling pathway from the hypothalamus to the pituitary produces hormones in the bloodstream that activate the *adrenal glands* (on top of the kidneys) to secrete *androgens* (male hormones) in both males and females (see Figure 11.1). Androgens cause underarm, facial, and pubic hair to grow; activate sweat glands in the armpits; and sometimes cause acne (Steingraber, 2007). Male production of testosterone also causes increased muscle size and mass, changes in vocal cords and a deeper voice, and changes in skeletal and bone structure and facial shape.

A woman's eggs were created in an immature state while she was a fetus in her mother's womb. Hence, puberty is the time when a hormonal system that was established prenatally becomes reactivated (Steingraber, 2007). By late puberty, the brain and glandular changes will trigger the ovaries to release one mature egg (*ovum*) on a "monthly" cycle for about 35 years of her life, typically. Unlike females, males first begin to produce mature sex cells, called *sperm,* during puberty, and they continue to do so throughout life, unless their testes are affected by illness or injury or are removed. The attainment of *fertility,* the ability to reproduce, is the culmination of this 4.5-year process. The anatomical parts of the body specific to human reproduction are known as the primary sex characteristics of males and females (see Chapter 3 on reproduction).

Biological and Brain Changes During Puberty The brain's circuitry is also resculpted during puberty (see Figure 11.2). Researchers using neuroimaging find that brain wave patterns change in adolescence, a process that generally improves cognitive functions related to abstract thinking, consideration of values in making judgments, capacity to consider alternative viewpoints, autonomy, and social behaviors (Coch, Fischer, & Dawson, 2007). Although overall brain size remains about the same, pruning of gray matter results in regional changes (the principle "use it or lose it" applies): White matter increases (fibers that establish long-distance connections between brain regions) and new synapses form; axon diameters and myelination increase, resulting in faster conductivity; the prefrontal cortex, corpus callosum, and temporal lobe structures increase in size, with slight gender variance (Posthuma et al., 2002). These changes improve the speed of neural transmission, allowing for improved reasoning, planning, and impulse control (Coch, Fischer, & Dawson, 2007).

On the other hand, as part of the pruning process, the brain loses plasticity, some of its capacity to recover from injury, and some of its ability to assimilate new complex skills, such as learning to play a new musical instrument or achieving athletic prowess at a new sport (Steingraber, 2007). The changes in the brain's circuitry that are required for new attachments during adolescence can also lead to confusion, disorientation, and depression. Research reveals that adolescents actually experience emotions more acutely, as is discussed in Chapter 12. Unfortunately, these shifts are fraught with dangers related to an increased vulnerability to risky behaviors and substance abuse (Cozolino, 2006).

Studies have also shown that sleep is especially important during brain maturation. Adolescents need 8 to 9 hours of sleep daily, but the sleep-awake cycle in their brain shifts, and teens naturally fall asleep later and wake up later (Wolfson & Carskadon, 2008). Yet roughly 65 to 70 percent of U.S. high school students get an inadequate amount of sleep on an average school night, especially as they go through high school from ninth to twelfth grade (Eaton et al., 2010). Recent research has also outlined the relationship between inadequate sleep patterns and the rising hostility being reported among contemporary adolescents (Ireland & Culpin, 2006). With early school hours and active lives, many teens suffer sleep deprivation effects, which have been associated with increased health problems, injuries, and accidents (Coch, Fischer, & Dawson, 2007).

One brain disorder that affects about 1 percent of people during later adolescence is *schizophrenia*. Symptoms include disordered thinking, hallucinations, delusions, unusual speech or paranoid behavior, and social withdrawal—any and all of which limit the individual's ability to interact with others and manage life. In fact, several genes have been discovered that are associated with the onset of schizophrenia (Crespi, Summers, & Dorus, 2007). Medical intervention is imperative for this disorder, and the earlier treatment begins, the better the outcome (Cannon et al., 2008).

Questions

What physical changes in the nervous system, endocrine system, and reproductive system are expected in girls and in boys during puberty? What triggers the onset of this maturational process?

Ethological Theory *Life history theory* presents a framework in which to view pubertal timing from an evolutionary developmental perspective. It is focused on the study of survival, growth, development, and reproduction in an ecological context (Buss, 2008). Some developmental psychologists contend that the timing of the onset of puberty, which takes one from the prereproductive to the reproductive phase in the life cycle, has significant ramifications both socially and biologically (Banerjee & Clayton, 2007; Ellis, Figueredo, Brumbach, & Schlomer, 2009). Thus, biological factors have consequences for teenagers' social relationships.

Jay Belsky (1997, 1999, 2001) has advanced an *ethological theory,* proposing that some young mothers are responding to a pattern in human evolution that induces individuals who grow up with insecure attachment to bear children early and often. In so doing, he addresses a matter that has troubled a good many U.S. policymakers, social scientists, and health-care practitioners—namely,

the large numbers of teenage mothers in urban areas. Rather than being a biological given, puberty is said to be partially "set" by early experience. Thus human beings, like many other animals, adjust their life histories in response to environmental conditions to enhance their reproductive success. As a result, our experiences help shape our development.

According to this view, these teenage mothers are implementing a reproductive strategy that, from an evolutionary perspective, makes good sense. Belsky and his associates argue that girls growing up in conditions of insecure attachment are "primed" to boost the chances of having their genes survive into the next generation by initiating sex and motherhood early. One element of the theory is that girls reared with family stress, child abuse, and father absence typically enter puberty at an earlier age than girls reared in households where care, nurturance, and father presence are more abundant and predictable (Matchcock & Susman, 2006). Further, the effect of father absence was found to be associated with early menarche, early first sexual intercourse and first pregnancy, and duration of first marriage (Buss, 2008; Steingraber, 2007).

Extensive research in Western societies demonstrates that early pubertal maturation in girls is correlated with a number of negative health and psychosocial outcomes for some girls (Ellis et al., 2009; Ge et al., 2007). Girls who mature early—a condition called *precocious puberty*—are at higher risk later in life for unhealthy weight gain, breast cancer, and a variety of other cancers affecting the reproductive system (Raneri & Constance, 2007). Precocious puberty is now defined as less than 7 years for U.S. white girls and less than 5 years among U.S. black girls (Steingraber, 2007). Girls with early pubertal timing have earlier sexual activity and higher teen pregnancy rates, more low-birth-weight babies, and more emotional concerns such as anxiety and depression (Walvoord, 2010). A growing body of research finds that precocious girls demonstrate more conduct disorders and higher rates of victimization, delinquency, and aggression, as well as early smoking, alcohol use, and drug abuse (Oldenhinkel, Verhulst, & Ormel, 2010; Reardon, Leen-Feldner, & Hayward, 2009).

Some developmental psychologists have expressed skepticism regarding ethological formulations. For instance, Eleanor E. Maccoby (1991, 1999) favors a simpler explanation for the earlier pregnancies of girls from troubled homes: They receive less parental supervision. Other dissenters point out that girls tend to enter puberty at the same age as their mothers did, by virtue of genetic factors (Bornstein & Lamb, 2005). Girls who develop sexually at earlier ages are more likely to date and marry early, but they are also more likely to make the "worst" marital choices and to terminate their marriages with divorce. So the girls whose parents are divorced might simply have had mothers who also tended to have undergone puberty at an earlier age. Sociologists also distance themselves from these ethological

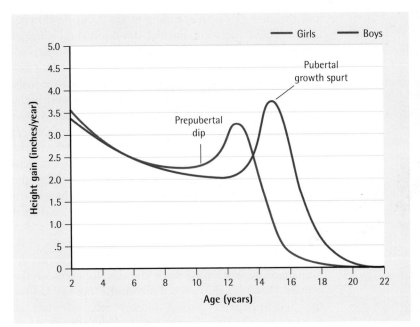

FIGURE 11.3 Adolescent Growth Spurt
The rapid increase in height and weight that accompanies pubertal growth tends to occur two years earlier in girls than in boys.
Source: Stützle, W., Gasser, T., Molinari, L., Largo, R. H., Prader, A., & T., & Huber, P. J. (1980). Shape-invariant modeling of human growth. *Annals of Human Biology, 7*(6), 507–528.

formulations, contending that the more immediate cause of teenage sexuality and pregnancy is the lack of jobs and the presence of severe poverty in inner-city neighborhoods (Lynne et al., 2007).

The Adolescent Growth Spurt

During the early adolescent years, most children experience the **adolescent growth spurt,** evidenced by a rapid increase in height and weight (see Figure 11.3). Usually, this spurt occurs in girls two years earlier than in boys (Euling et al., 2008; Grumbach & Styne, 2003). This means that many girls are taller than most boys in late middle school and junior high. The average age at which the peak is reached varies somewhat, depending on the people being studied. Among British and North American children, it comes at about age 12 in girls and age 14 in boys. For a year or more, the child's rate of growth approximately doubles. Consequently, children often grow at a rate they last experienced when they were 2 years old. The spurt usually lasts about two years, and during this time, girls gain about 6 to 7 inches and boys about 8 to 9 inches in height. By age 17 in girls and age 18 in boys, the majority of young people have reached 98 percent of their final height. James M. Tanner (1972, p. 5), an authority on adolescent growth, writes that practically all skeletal and muscular dimensions of the body take part in the growth spurt, although not to an equal degree:

> Most of the spurt in height is due to acceleration of trunk length rather than length of legs. There is a fairly regular order in which the dimensions accelerate; leg length as a rule reaches its peak first, followed by the body breadths, with shoulder width last. Thus a boy stops growing out

of his trousers (at least in length) a year before he stops growing out of his jackets. The earliest structures to reach their adult status are the head, hands, and feet. At adolescence, children, particularly girls, sometimes complain of having large hands and feet. They can be reassured that by the time they are fully grown, their hands and feet will be a little smaller in proportion to their arms and legs, and considerably smaller in proportion to their trunks.

Physical Growth   The term **asynchrony** refers to the dissimilarity in the growth rates of different parts of the body. As a result of asynchrony, many teenagers have a long-legged, or coltish, appearance. Asynchrony often results in clumsiness and misjudgments of distances, which can lead to various minor accidents, such as tripping on or knocking over furniture, and to exaggerated self-consciousness and awkwardness in adolescents.

The marked growth of muscle tissue during adolescence contributes to differences between and within the sexes in strength and motor performance (Kaplowitz, 2008). A muscle's strength—its force when it is contracted—is proportional to its cross-sectional area. Males typically have larger muscles than females, which accounts for the greater strength of most males. Girls' performance on motor tasks involving speed, agility, and balance has generally been found to peak at about 14 years of age, although this statistic is based on past performance and does not reflect the increasing rate of female participation in junior high, high school, college, and professional sport competition. The performance of boys on similar tasks improves throughout adolescence.

At puberty the head shows a small acceleration in growth after remaining almost the same size for six to

Gender Differences A 10-year-old fourth-grade girl and a 9-year-old fourth-grade boy compare their heights. (Is it our imagination, or does he look a little unhappy about the differential?)

seven years. The chin and jaw are the last bony elements to reach adult proportion (Golub, 2000). The heart grows more rapidly, almost doubling in weight. Most children steadily put on subcutaneous fat between 8 years of age and puberty, but the rate drops off when the adolescent growth spurt begins. Indeed, boys actually tend to lose fat at this time, but girls simply experience a slowdown in fat accumulation. Overall, the sequence of events in the pubertal process is similar across cultures and ethnicities, but the timing varies (Shiraev & Levy, 2007).

Maturation in Girls

In addition to incorporating the *adolescent growth spurt,* puberty is characterized by the development of the reproductive system (see Figure 11.4). The complete transition to reproductive maturity takes place over a few years and is accompanied by extensive physical changes. As in the case of the adolescent growth spurt, girls typically begin their sexual development earlier than boys.

When puberty begins in girls, the breasts begin to increase in size—growth that generally takes three to four years (DiVall & Radovick, 2008). On average, this change starts at about age 9 or 10 and is called the *bud stage* of breast development. The appearance of pubic down (soft hair in the pubic region) may precede the bud stage of breast development or appear after the bud stage. Also during puberty, the pelvis widens, an increase in fatty and supportive tissue appears in the buttocks and hip region,

and the skin gets oilier (Euling et al., 2008; Kaplowitz, 2008). These perfectly normal developmental changes prompt some girls in their early teen years to begin dieting or exercising to excess, which can lead to eating disorders. Many contemporary adolescent girls erroneously think their bodies should be as slender as they were in the childhood years. Another visible change in puberty is the growth of axillary (underarm) hair. Internal anatomical changes are occurring as well: The vagina lengthens, the ovaries grow in size, and the uterus expands, more than doubling in length (Grumbach & Styne, 2003). Near the end of puberty, rising levels of estrogen cause the growth plates in long bones to *ossify,* or turn to bone, and final adult height is reached (Golub, 2000).

Menarche   The ovaries, uterus, and vagina mature simultaneously over time with the development of the breasts. However, the onset of **menarche** (me när′ key)— the first menstrual period—occurs relatively late in puberty, usually following the peak of the growth spurt. Menstruation is the most visible phase of the monthly *menstrual cycle* in which the blood-rich uterine lining is shed, causing some females to experience cramping or discomfort. The timing of menarche differs markedly among girls from different racial and ethnic groups (Euling et al., 2008). Early menstrual periods tend to be irregular, perhaps for a year or more. Furthermore, *ovulation* (the release of a mature ovum/egg from an ovary) usually does not take place for about 10 months after the first menstruation (Papathanasiou & Hadjiathanasiou, 2006). Thus, it is difficult to determine exactly when a girl is fertile and capable of reproduction.

A Trend Toward Earlier Onset of Menarche   Since 1900, mainly in industrialized countries, the average age of menarche has been reported to be declining steadily; this earlier onset appears to be associated with increased caloric consumption and longer life expectancy (Matlin, 2008). Tanner's (1972) earlier findings indicated that among well-nourished Western populations, including the United States, the average onset of menarche occurs between 12 and 13 years of age (Balter & Tamis-LeMonda, 2006). While minority youth were not included in the earliest U.S. studies, they were included in studies since the 1970s (Walvoord, 2010). More recent findings indicate that African American and Hispanic girls start puberty and menarche earlier than white girls. The National Health Examination Survey conducted from 1966 to 1970 showed menarche occurring on average at 12.1 years in black girls, 12.2 in Hispanic American girls, and at 12.6 in white girls (McDowell, Brody, & Hughes, 2007). The latest menarcheal ages are found among peoples with scarce food resources. Thomas and colleagues' (2001) review of international variability reveals that in countries such as Nepal, Senegal, New Guinea,

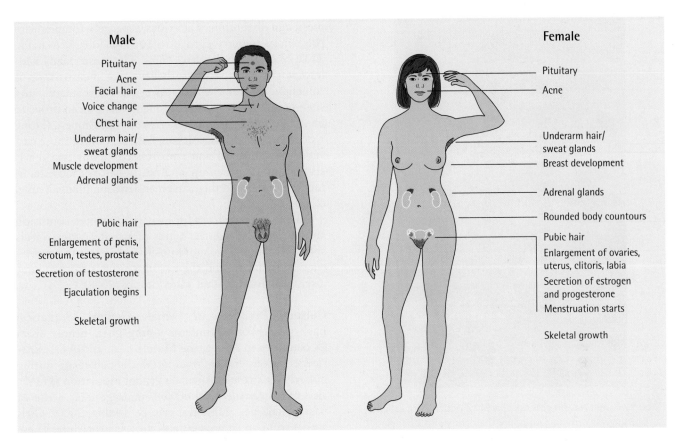

FIGURE 11.4 Effects of Sex Hormones on Development at Puberty At puberty, the pituitary gland secretes gonadotropins (follicle-stimulating hormone and luteinizing hormone) that stimulate the adrenal glands and the ovaries and testes to secrete their sex hormones. This prompts the growth spurt and the development of secondary sex characteristics. By late puberty, the sex hormones create changes in body tissues and functions that lead to reproductive maturity in males (ejaculation of sperm) and females (menstruation and ovulation).

and Bangladesh, the average age of menarche is about 15. In contrast, the earliest average ages of menarche are in Congo-Brazza, Greece, Italy, Spain, Thailand, and Mexico, around the age of 12.

Note that a statistical average does not mean that all girls will begin menstruating at that age. More girls today begin puberty as early as 7 or 8 years old (or earlier), according to a study involving 17,000 American girls aged 3 through 12. In this PROS (Pediatric Research Office Settings) study, conducted in the early 1990s, nearly 10 percent of subjects were black and 90 percent were white. By 8 years of age, nearly half of black girls and 15 percent of white girls had begun developing breasts, pubic hair, or both (Cesario & Hughes, 2007; Herman-Giddens, 2007). A higher proportion of Asian American girls reach menarche at 14 or later (Matlin, 2008). Menarche can also be delayed by strenuous physical exercise, and it occurs about 15 years of age or later among dancers and athletes (especially in ballet, running, swimming, and bicycling) (Halpert & Warren, 2004). This condition is diagnosed as exercise-induced *amenorrhea*.

Researchers conducting studies with large, nationally representative samples of girls find that earlier onset of puberty is associated with increased nutrient intake and *phytoestrogens* (chemicals that mimic estrogens and are found in plant foods such as beans, soybeans and soy products, seeds, and grains), obesity and low physical activity, and exposure to cigarette smoke (Steingraber, 2007). Rose E. Frisch (1978) advances the hypothesis that menarche requires a critical level of fat stored in the body. She reasons that pregnancy and lactation impose a great caloric drain. Consequently, if fat reserves are inadequate to meet this demand, a woman's brain and body respond by limiting her reproductive ability. Frisch suggests that the improvement in children's nutrition contributes to an earlier onset of menarche because youngsters reach the critical fat/lean ratio, or "metabolic level," sooner.

Consistent results show strong positive associations of early onset of puberty with obesity (measured as body mass index), and there is a significantly higher incidence in Hispanic and black girls (Himes, Park, & Styne, 2009). Higher proportions of Hispanic and black girls also

Puberty Rites Navajo girls take part in a puberty rite called the Blessingway ceremony to honor their entry into Changing Woman status. The ceremony features songs that include blessings of beauty, harmony, success, order, and well-being. Navajo believe that the Changing Woman, who is also associated with mothers about to give birth, is closest to the personification of the earth and the natural order of the universe (Wyman, 1970).

experience early menarche, and a recent study reconfirms that early-maturing girls showed patterns of depression along with pubertal changes (Herman-Giddens, 2007).

The Significance of Menarche   Menarche is a pivotal event in an adolescent girl's experience. Most girls are both happy and anxious about their first menstruation (Matlin, 2008). It is a symbol of a girl's developing sexual maturity and portends her full-fledged status as a woman. As such, menarche plays an important part in shaping a girl's image of her body and her sense of identity as a woman. Post-menarcheal girls report that they experience themselves as more womanly and that they give greater thought to their reproductive role. However, some researchers report an accentuation of conflict between the mother and the daughter shortly after menarche. This development is not necessarily negative, because it often facilitates the family's adaptation to pubertal change (Pulkkinen & Caspi, 2002). Some cultures, in fact, celebrate pubertal maturation with communal rituals for both girls and boys, declaring that the child now has adult status.

Yet menstruation is often associated with a variety of negative events, including physical discomfort, mood-

iness, and disruption of activities, especially for girls with precocious puberty aged 6 to 10 (Hawkins & Matzuk, 2008; Short & Rosenthal, 2008). The westernized adolescent girl is often led to believe that menstruation is somehow unclean, embarrassing, even shameful, and such negative expectations of menstruation can prove to be self-fulfilling prophecies. A study of Chinese (Hong Kong) girls found that although 85 percent of those surveyed felt annoyed and embarrassed, about two-thirds also felt more grown up, and nearly half felt more feminine in response to their first menstruation (Tang, Yeung, & Lee, 2003).

Thus, preparedness for menarche reduces confusion and anxiety. Indeed, the better prepared a woman feels she was as a girl, the more positive she rates the experience of menarche and the less likely she is to encounter menstrual distress as an adult (Stubbs, 2008).

Cultural Practices of Female Genital Mutilation
Each year about 2 million young girls, mainly from 28 countries in Africa, the Middle East, and Asia, experience serious health risks or death before or during puberty as a result of female genital mutilation (FGM), also called *female circumcision*, undergone as a rite of passage (Barber, 2010; Rahman & Toubia, 2000). Girls aged 4 to 12 are at greatest risk for this procedure. These centuries-old cultural practices in such patriarchal societies are related to controlling a girl's sexuality, ensuring chastity, and increasing a future bride's monetary worth in exchange for her "purity" (Hosken, 1998). With increasing numbers of women emigrating to Western countries, this puberty rite for girls has been exposed—as families try to continue this practice with their daughters. Health services professionals in the United States, the United Kingdom, Europe, and Australia continue to see evidence of this practice being inflicted on daughters of immigrants from Somalia, the Sudan, Ethiopia, Kenya, Nigeria, and some other Muslim countries (although FGM is not sanctioned in the Koran).

Female genital mutilation can take several forms, including *clitoridectomy,* where all or part of the clitoris is removed; excision, where all or parts of the labia minora are removed; and the most extensive—infibulation. This means that the entire clitoris and the labia minora are cut away and the two sides of the labia majora are partially sliced off or scraped raw and then sewn together, often with catgut. The girl is immobilized for several weeks until the wound of the vulva has closed, except for a small opening that is created by inserting a splinter of wood or bamboo (Hosken, 1998). Bloodborne pathogens, such as HIV and hepatitis B virus, are easily transmitted during these procedures. Many girls die from infection, and those who survive often have health problems, such as urinary tract infections, pelvic inflammatory disease, complications of pregnancy and delivery, or infertility.

Young Girls Wait for Female Circumcision These young girls are awaiting female circumcision in Cooperstown, Liberia.

(In these cultures, an infertile woman can be divorced at will and shamed for life.)

The World Health Organization (2010) continues to sponsor educational campaigns in African and Middle Eastern communities in an effort to eradicate this damaging and life-threatening practice. Young women have sought asylum in other countries to avoid FGM, but that decision carries the consequence of isolation from family, friends, and culture (Nandutu, 2008). FGM has been outlawed in Western countries, but the practice still continues as a consequence of long-held beliefs (Barber, 2010).

Maturation in Boys

Herman-Giddens, Wang, and Koch (2001) reported an important study on boys' pubertal development, with over 2,000 racially-ethnically diverse participants aged 8 to 19. They found much earlier ages for the onset of pubic hair and genital growth than the 11 to 11.5 years of age in Marshall and Tanner's (1970) study. They also found significant differences by racial-ethnic groups by age 8. Some African American boys began the onset of puberty by age 8, followed by some white and Hispanic American boys 1 to 1.5 years later. Axillary and facial hair generally make their first appearance about two years after the beginning of pubic hair growth, though in some males axillary hair appears before pubic hair. Boys also acquire additional weight and size in the form of increased muscle mass. Furthermore, the most striking expansion in males takes place in the shoulders and rib cage (American Academy of Pediatrics, 1996).

By age 15, all boys in this study attained pubertal development, which includes full testes and scrotum growth, penis lengthening and thickening, voice changes as the larynx enlarges and the vocal folds double in length (resulting in a boy's voice cracking), and prostate gland fluid that can be ejaculated during orgasm. Mature sperm appear in the ejaculatory fluid about a year later, with wide variation among individuals. By full maturation, boys have "wet dreams," involuntary emissions of *seminal fluid* during sleep. For most males, their first ejaculation elicits both very positive and slightly negative responses. Given the open, extensive public education about sexuality and reproduction the exists today, most boys are somewhat prepared for the event.

Some boys experience dramatic changes in body shape from junior high through high school, which creates a time of adjustment. American society seems to equate greater male height with popularity, sex appeal, and success. Most boys want to be tall and talk about this a great deal during this growth time. Tall girls, however, may feel more self-conscious about their height during adolescence.

The Impact of Early or Late Maturation

Children show enormous variation in the timing and rates of growth and sexual maturation. Some children do not begin their growth spurt and the development of secondary sexual characteristics until other children have virtually completed these stages (Tanner, 1973; Walvoord, 2010). The average age of menarche for girls across the world ranges from 10.5 to 15.5 years (Kotch, 2005). Thus, one cannot appreciate the facts of physical growth and development without taking account of individual differences.

The majority of youth in the United States move in chronological lockstep through elementary, middle, and secondary school. Consequently, fairly standardized criteria are applied to children of the same age with respect to their physical, social, and intellectual development. But because children mature at varying rates, they differ in their ability to meet these standards. Individual differences become most apparent at adolescence. Several studies over the past two decades confirm that adolescents' early or late maturation has important consequences for them in their relationships with both adults and their peers (Walvoord, 2010).

Because of different rates of maturation, some adolescents have an advantage in the "ideals" associated with height, strength, physical attractiveness, and athletic prowess (Balter & Tamis-LeMonda, 2006). Hence, some young people receive more favorable feedback regarding their overall worth and desirability, which in turn influences their self-image and behavior. For example, the value placed on manly appearance and athletic excellence means that early-maturing boys often enjoy the admiration of their peers. In contrast, late-maturing boys often receive negative feedback from their peers, are likely to experience bullying and teasing, and are more susceptible to having a less positive self- and body image (Balter & Tamis-LeMonda, 2006). Researchers at the University of California at Berkeley studied the physical and psychological characteristics of a large group of individuals over an extended period of time. On the basis of this work, Mary Cover Jones and Nancy Bayley (1950, p. 146) reached the following conclusion regarding adolescent boys:

> Those [boys] who were physically accelerated are usually accepted and treated by adults and other children as more mature. They appear to have relatively little need to strive for status. From their ranks came the outstanding student-body leaders in senior high school. In contrast, the physically [delayed] boys exhibit many forms of relatively immature behaviors: this may be in part because others tend to treat them as the little boys they appear to be. Furthermore, a fair proportion of these boys give evidence of needing to counteract their physical disadvantage in some way—usually by greater activity in striving for attention, although in some cases by withdrawing.

A follow-up study of the early- and late-maturing males in the Berkeley sample was conducted when the men were 33 years old. Their behavior patterns were surprisingly similar to the descriptions of them recorded in adolescence (Jones, 1957). The *early maturers* were more poised, relaxed, cooperative, sociable, and conforming. *Late maturers* tended to be more eager, talkative, self-assertive, rebellious, and touchy. Boys who perceived themselves to be late maturing also tended to exhibit feelings of inadequacy, negative self-concept, and feelings of rejection. These feelings were coupled with a rebellious quest for autonomy and freedom from restraint (Mussen & Jones, 1957). Interestingly, recent research shows a positive correlation between obesity and late maturation in boys (the opposite is true for girls, where obesity is correlated with early maturation) (McCabe, Ricciardelli, & Holt, 2010).

Hayward and colleagues (1997) reported the findings of a longitudinal study of growth and development with over 1,400 ethnically diverse girls from San Jose, California. Participants were in sixth to eighth grade when the study began. Using self-report instruments, diagnostic interviews, and psychiatric assessment, the girls were evaluated over several years to determine the relationship between age of puberty and onset of any mental health issues or disorders. The girls who had gone through early puberty (the earliest 25 percent) were twice as likely as those who matured later to develop symptoms such as depression, substance abuse, eating disorders, and disruptive behavior disorders. Recent findings further suggest that those girls who go through puberty early remain at increased risk for developing these specific disorders even after they enter high school (Arnett & Tanner, 2006).

So what are we to conclude? The answer may lie largely in the *ecological context:* A dynamic interplay between differing individual temperaments and the social environment produces substantially differing outcomes

among young women (Buss, 2008). Additionally, the situation for girls is more complicated than that for boys. Psychologists point out that early-maturing girls are more likely to be a little heavier and to develop a stocky physique. In contrast, late-maturing girls are more likely to be thin and to acquire a slim, slight body build. Thus, over the long run, later maturation in girls may be associated with factors other than maturation itself that function as assets in social adjustment. A general guideline for anyone seriously concerned about a child's experiencing early or late puberty is to consult an *endocrinologist*, a physician who specializes in hormonal and glandular disorders.

Questions

What are the differences between girls and boys in physical growth and maturation during puberty? What are some of the factors that account for pubertal variability in males and females?

Self-Image and Appearance

The image that adolescents have of themselves is particularly susceptible to peer influences. Adolescents are quick to reject or ridicule age-mates who deviate in some way from the physical norm. Indeed, few words have the capacity to cause as much pleasure—and as much pain—to adolescents as the word *popularity*. Among boys, athletic prowess and a muscular body with a large chest but slim waist bring social recognition and popularity, but a slim overall body is associated with U.S. girls' popularity (McCabe, Ricciardelli, & Holt, 2010). To say that teenagers are preoccupied with their physical acceptability and adequacy is an understatement. These concerns arise during adolescence, when the nature and significance of friendships are undergoing substantial developmental change and when affect (feeling good about oneself and feeling happy) and self-worth are undergoing change as well (Thompson & Cafri, 2007). The ability to establish close, intimate friendships becomes more integral to social and emotional adjustment and well-being during adolescence than it was during preadolescence. Adolescent friendships have been studied in the context of developmental stage, network of interpersonal relationships, and gender (Richard & Schneider, 2005).

Puberty brings with it an intensification of gender-related expectations, especially in the context of physical appearance. Adolescents, both boys and girls, express considerable concern about their facial features, including their skin and hair. The American Society of Plastic Surgeons (ASPS) (2010) reported that in 2009, more than 210,000 plastic surgery procedures were performed on U.S. teens aged 13–19. More than 4,000 adolescents aged 13–19 had breast reduction surgery in 2009; that number includes males. Adolescent girls often feel troubled about the development, size, and shape of their breasts. Most cosmetic surgeries performed on teens are for non-medical reasons that include "misshapen nose, protruding ears, overly large breasts, asymmetrical breasts, or severe acne and scarring" (American Society of Plastic Surgeons, 2010). Significantly, the idealized media models (teen magazine cover girls, television actresses, and music idols) tend to be taller and weigh less (many are actually underweight) than young women in general, and the gap between the two is growing (Hargreaves & Tiggemann, 2009). Television shows sponsored by advertisers that market cosmetic and plastic surgery to teens do a great disservice to adolescent females and males, who are already highly self-critical of their own appearance. As consumers, they do not get the full story.

Questions

What concerns about appearance or self-image did you have as an adolescent? Have you resolved your concerns, or do you still worry about some of these things? If so, which ones and why?

HEALTH ISSUES IN ADOLESCENCE

What does it mean to be healthy? You might think of yourself as being fairly healthy or as having been a healthy adolescent. Indeed, the majority of adolescents are free of disabilities, weight problems, and chronic illnesses, but a recent national health report indicated that between 7 and 30 percent of adolescents aged 12 to 17 suffer from at least one chronic health problem that limits activity, and many youth are in need of counseling or other health services (National Center for Health Statistics, 2010). Among adolescents aged 12 to 17, learning disabilities and attention-deficit hyperactivity disorder (ADHD) were the most common chronic conditions, followed by other mental health problems (such as eating disorders, major depression, mood disorders, obsessive-compulsive disorder, anxiety disorders, and drug dependence), mental retardation (now known as intellectual disability), speech problems, and asthma (National Center for Health Statistics, 2010).

Additionally, what sorts of risky behaviors do adolescents engage in that lead to concerns about their health? It is during the adolescent years that many of us drink our first beer, experiment with other psychoactive substances, try smoking, and have our first sexual experiences with members of the opposite sex, the same sex, or both sexes. Many adolescents are also stressed by attempting to earn money by working in part-time jobs to help their families, especially with more teens in single-parent families, in minority families, or living with an unemployed parent. Teens living in poverty are at much higher risk of having chronic health problems, such as asthma and other respiratory illness and developmental disabilities. And it is expected that the general health of adolescents will become worse over the next few decades, simply because the increasing size of the adolescent population means that more young people will be poor (Kotch, 2005). Some of the negative health factors associated with poverty are premature birth; poor nutrition; lack of or poor-quality medical, dental, and eye care; lack of required immunizations; higher risk of exposure to health hazards; and greater incidence of high-risk behaviors.

Many parents become indifferent about annual check-ups for teenage children because they seem so healthy. Parents and caregivers may be unaware of the recommended immunizations for adolescents. The Advisory Committee for Immunization Practices (ACIP) in 2010 recommends that adolescents aged 11 through 18 receive the following vaccines: Tdap (tetanus, diphtheria, and pertussis; HPV (human papillomavirus); meningococcal; and influenza (yearly). Other vaccines, such as those for *meningitis* and *hepatitis B,* are required for students traveling abroad or for college admission. Recently, the CDC recommended that parents get daughters vaccinated at age 11 or 12 against the *human papillomavirus* (HPV) to prevent genital warts and cervical cancer. This vaccine is also recommended for females 13 to 26 years of age who were not vaccinated previously (Kuehn, 2006). HPV is the most common sexually transmitted viral infection in U.S. women, with more than 6 million women infected annually—but not all women infected with HPV will develop cervical cancer. As of 2010, 19 states have enacted legislation to either require, fund, or educate the public about the HPV vaccine (National Conference of State Legislatures, 2010b). A few states have enacted laws requiring vaccination for girls entering sixth grade, which has raised parental concerns and prompted public outcry about compelling girls alone to submit to a new vaccine to continue their education, when boys are just as likely to get this virus (Gostin & DeAngelis, 2007).

Public school health officials conduct annual hearing and vision exams, and students who participate on school sports teams are required to have an annual physical. Of course, some adolescents themselves refuse to go to the doctor because they associate this with "childhood" behavior. Thus, a large proportion of adolescents are likely to neglect regular health exams and immunizations. Many at this age believe that they can take care of themselves, even though they might be participating in risky behaviors (sleep deprivation, poor nutrition, alcohol or substance abuse, sexual activity, driving under the influence of alcohol or while texting, and the like). We now discuss some of the most common health risks for the U.S. adolescent cohort.

Questions

What are some chronic health issues that affect adolescents? How does their self-image become distorted and their body shape misperceived? What types of treatments are suggested to help victims become healthier?

Nutrition and Eating Disorders

What did you eat for lunch yesterday? A hamburger, a candy bar, pizza, French fries, chips, or soda? Junk food is very tempting for most of us. Owing to our busy schedules, we do not want to sit down, relax, and eat if we can grab a snack or pick up a quick bite to eat. However, most "fast food" has very little nutritional value—yet it has high caloric content from sugars and fats. Currently, eating disorders are estimated to affect 8 million individuals in the United States (7 million women and 1 million men), and a high majority of them developed the eating disorder during their childhood or adolescent years (Ayala et al., 2007).

Some researchers suggest that culture exerts great influence on family eating habits. That is why they believe that eating disorders are more prevalent in white women in Western cultures—which value "thinness." More recent evidence suggests this is not the case. It was the underrepresentation of ethnic minorities in research populations that led investigators to believe that eating-related problems were less common in these populations than among whites. Yet when compared with whites, African American and Hispanic females are found to be suffering from bulimia nervosa at a much higher percentage than white females (Ayala et al., 2007). Some suggest that family life and eating behaviors play a far greater role in producing eating disorders, especially when a family is preoccupied with perfection, control, appearance, and weight (Benninghoven et al., 2007). The interactionist view suggests that both culture and family environment are influential (Haworth-Hoeppner, 2000).

Adolescents are usually deficient in calcium, iron, zinc, and vitamin D (important for calcium absorption and bone growth), which can lead to problems such as thinning of the bones (half of peak bone mass is accumulated during the adolescent years) (Barclay & Morata, 2008; Gordon, DePeter, Feldman, Grace, & Emans, 2004). Certain types of cancers, stroke, and even diabetes mellitus have been associated with long-term deficiencies in diet. Consequently, good nutritional diets in adolescence will result in fewer health problems in adulthood (Kotch, 2005). Typically, four disorders prevalent among contemporary U.S. teens stem from poor nutritional habits: anorexia nervosa, bulimia, binge-eating disorder, and obesity.

Anorexia Nervosa   The eating disorder **anorexia nervosa** is a serious, complex mental health condition that primarily affects females—at least 10 percent or more of adolescent and adult women report symptoms of eating disorders, although a small percentage of anorexics are males—and the number of affected teens is increasing (Chao et al., 2008). A person with this eating disorder becomes obsessed with looking thin and is terrified of becoming fat. Anorexics perceive food as being a threat to their bodies rather than a source of nutrition and pursue a regimen of self-starvation, often accompanied by excessive exercise. Anorexia nervosa is most common in countries where food is plentiful and attractiveness is equated with thinness.

About half of the people who are anorexic also develop binge-and-purge eating behaviors called **bulimia.** Unlike anorexics, people with bulimia often are of normal weight for their age and height. About 4 percent of college-age women have bulimia. (See the *Further Developments* box on page 350, "Understanding Anorexia and Bulimia.") Some teens are also affected by **binge-eating disorder (BED)**, consuming unusually large amounts of food at least a few times a week and not purging or exercising. Those with BED are usually very overweight (Hudson et al., 2007).

Obesity   Since the 1960s, there has been a significant increase in the number of overweight and obese children and adolescents (see Figure 11.5). Obesity is defined several ways, and diverse factors such as body frame, status of adolescent growth spurt, genetics, and activity level make it impossible to generalize across the entire population. We define **obesity** as the excess accumulation of body fat, or *adipose tissue,* and it is the most common eating disorder in the United States. Overweight adolescents often face social prejudice, peer rejection, and bullying, and they are likely to experience depression, low self-esteem, health concerns, problematic dietary behaviors, or, in some cases, suicide (McCabe, Ricciardelli, & Holt, 2010).

Results from the National Health and Nutrition Exam Survey (NHANES) indicate that nearly 20 percent of adolescents aged 12 to 19 are significantly overweight (Ogden et al., 2006). For all ethnic groups except blacks, obesity occurs more among males than among females. Asian American and Hispanic adolescents born in the United States are more than twice as likely to be obese as are their parents who were first-generation residents of the 50 states (Popkin & Udry, 1998).

The recent findings for adolescents are of great concern, for overweight adolescents are at increased risk of becoming overweight adults with serious obesity-related health conditions (McCracken, Jiles, & Blanck, 2007). A large proportion of adolescents want to change their weight—they perceive themselves as "too heavy." The overweight adolescent is at a serious health and social disadvantage (LaFontaine, 2008). In fact, a stigma

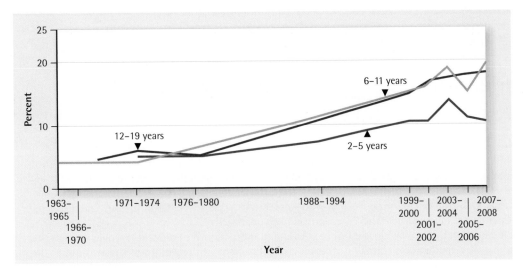

FIGURE 11.5 Trends in Obesity Among Children and Adolescents in the United States: 1963–2008
Note: Obesity is defined as body mass index (BMI) greater than or equal to sex- and age-specific 95th percentile from the 2000 CDC Growth Charts.
Sources: CDC/NCHS. National Health Examination Surveys II (ages 6–11) and III (ages 12–17); National Health and Nutrition Health Examination Surveys (NHANES) 1–III; and HANES 1999–2000, 2001–2001, 2003–2004, 2005–2006, and 2007–2008.

is associated with obesity in the United States. Given this state of affairs, particularly for females, it is hardly surprising that adolescent girls are extremely sensitive regarding their body configurations and that even a moderate amount of fat generates intensely negative feelings and distorted self-perceptions. What makes such distortions so cruel is that our body image and our self-esteem are linked, so when we dislike our bodies, we find it difficult to like ourselves.

Health Consequences   Obesity in adolescents portends poorly for their health in adulthood:

> At 5 feet 6 inches and 216 pounds, Tyshon represents an alarming new health trend: the sharp increase in the number of children with Type 2 diabetes, also known as adult-onset diabetes, an incurable and progressively damaging disease that can cause kidney failure, blindness and poor circulation. . . . Doctors long believed that the disease occurred mostly during middle age or later. "Ten years ago we were teaching medical students that you didn't see this disease in people under 40, and now we're seeing it in people under 10," said Dr. Robin S. Goland, co-director of the Naomi Berrie Diabetes Center. (Thompson, 1998)

Indeed, researchers find that adolescent obesity is even more strongly linked to serious health risks and mortality earlier in adult life (Baker et al., 2007). Compared with other women, those who are overweight during their teens and early twenties are less likely to get married, are more socially isolated, are more apt to live in poverty, and get an average of four months' less schooling (Pickett et al., 2005). Thus, the fact that obesity in childhood and adolescence has increased significantly is of great concern. Federal and state public policy health experts are promoting changes regarding nutritious school lunches, removal of vending machines in schools,

and promotion of increased physical and recreational activities that motivate teens to get more exercise (Gillis et al., 2009; Kubik et al., 2010).

Factors Associated with the Increase in Adolescent Obesity
Both genetic and environmental factors are implicated. Studies of families and twins have clearly demonstrated a strong genetic component in resting metabolic rate, feeding behavior, and changes in energy level due to overfeeding. Environmental factors associated with obesity include socioeconomic status, race, region of residence, season, urban living, and being part of a smaller family (Sanchez et al., 2007). Sanchez and colleagues (2007) suggest that parental health behaviors are associated with adolescents' health behaviors. Thus, both parental diet and sedentary behaviors have been linked to children's potential for obesity. Not surprisingly, effective interventions have concentrated on increasing physical activity and nutritional awareness for the whole family (Velde et al., 2007).

How Can We Prevent or Reduce Obesity?   Complicating matters, obesity has proved quite difficult to treat (Neumark-Sztainer et al., 2006). In fact, a mounting body of evidence suggests that dieting can make matters worse, leading to counterproductive binge eating and a perpetual cycle of fruitless dieting (Keener et al., 2009). Some psychiatrists argue that obesity is a response to psychological disorders (e.g., women who are fearful of men subconsciously gain weight to create a protective shell and keep men at a distance). Another explanation is that fat babies and fat children develop a permanent excess of fat cells. This excess provides them with a lifelong storehouse of fat cells. When such individuals become adults, the existing fat cells enlarge but are not thought to increase in number. Still another popular theory postulates the existence of a metabolic regulator or "set point"

FURTHER DEVELOPMENTS

Understanding Anorexia and Bulimia

Anorexia nervosa is a self-imposed disorder in which the person consciously suppresses appetite, resulting in self-starvation. About 1 percent of females and 0.3 percent of males are affected, but the prevalence of eating disorders among children and adolescents is on the rise (Gonzalez, Kohn, & Clarke, 2007). The victims are obsessed with their plan of self-starvation, have a morbid terror of having any fat on their bodies, and deny that they are thin or ill, insisting that they feel good even when they are so weak they can barely walk. One scenario follows:

> Jeannette was always a bit chubby until she entered junior high, when she decided one day to lose a little weight. She lost 12 pounds in three weeks and received quite a few compliments from her friends, family, and teachers . . . [and] it was soon apparent to her family that something else was going on with their daughter . . . . Her mother describes a meal on a family trip. . . . "There was the way she would eat her food . . . how she would separate each bit of food, cut it into tiny, precise shapes, and repeatedly calculate calories on a small counter that she clicked." (Sacker & Zimmer, 1987)

Patients diagnosed with anorexia are usually diagnosed with other psychosocial disorders such as mood, anxiety, impulse-control, or substance use disorders (Hudson et al., 2007). Anorexia has the highest mortality rate of all mental health disorders. Western societies emphasize being thin, and this powerful message is promoted by the mass media that target teens and young adults with "ideal," rather than realistic, body images (Kirsh et al., 2007). Some experts suspect a disturbance of the hypothalamus; others suggest that the cause of anorexia might be traced to inadequate coping skills, whereby the person feels that the only thing under her (or, in fewer cases, his) control is body weight. Some believe it is an attempt to avoid adult responsibilities. The female with anorexia diets away her secondary sex characteristics: Her breasts diminish, her periods cease entirely, and she resembles a prepubescent child. In this view, such women are seeking a return to the comfort and safety of childhood (Fassino, Daga, Piero, & Delsedime, 2007). By studying chromosomes and family histories, some researchers are examining the disorder in a new way (Bulik, Slof-Op't Landt, van Furth, & Sullivan, 2007).

As girls mature during puberty, they experience a "fat spurt"—that is, their bodies naturally accumulate more fat in subcutaneous tissues. Early maturers are at greater risk for eating disorders, because they are likely to be heavier than their peers (Dorn et al., 2006). The refusal to eat is likely to be preceded by "normal" dieting, often prompted by casual comments by family or friends that the youth is "putting on weight" or "getting plump." The victim's misperception of body size increases with the severity of the illness. Ironically, the disorder entails self-induced starvation by women who desperately want to be beautiful but end up being grotesquely unattractive.

Although most victims of anorexia recover or improve, some die of the disorder. Left untreated, anorexia can contribute to osteoporosis, heart problems, infertility, depression, other health and dental issues, or death. Adolescents with the disorder are especially prone to depression, anxiety, substance abuse, and suicidal behavior (Brunner & Resch, 2006). Treatment requires a combination of various long-term antidepressants and individualized psychotherapy—often in inpatient settings. One effective intervention has been the dissonance-based program, in which those with body image concerns voluntarily engage in verbal, written,

Disturbed Eating Behaviors Among the Victims of Bulimia
Victims of bulimia repeatedly eat excessively (binge) in response to stress, depression, and low self-esteem. To offset weight gain, victims purge in several ways: self-induced vomiting, fasting, excessive use of laxatives and diuretics, and compulsive exercising.

and behavioral exercises in which they critique this ideal (Stice et al., 2007). A short-term, outpatient strategy involving a form of family therapy might be successful as well (Le Grange, Crosby, Rathouz, & Leventhal, 2007).

Bulimia is now a more common eating disorder characterized by repeated episodes of compulsive bingeing, often on high caloric foods—followed by purging through self-induced vomiting, laxatives, enemas, diuretics (water pills), or fasting. About 1.5 percent of adolescent girls and 0.5 percent of males suffer from bulimia (Hudson et al., 2007). Sacker and Zimmer (1987) describe how a bulimic person feels: "The whole purge process was cleansing. It was a combination of every type of spiritual, sexual, and emotional relief I had ever felt in my life. Purging became the release for me. First, I felt a tremendous rush that you could really call orgasmic. Then, I relaxed completely and fell asleep. After a while, I was hooked."

Bulimics often appear to be within normal weight range and may look healthy, but they are ashamed and depressed about their eating habits and conceal their eating behaviors. Some experts consider *binge eating disorder (BED)* to be a subset of bulimia—bingeing but not purging—and those affected are likely to be overweight or obese (Hudson et al., 2007). Bulimics experience ulcers, hernias, hair loss, dental problems (stomach acid destroys the teeth), electrolyte imbalance (resulting in heart attacks), or death (Jenkins, 2007). Some researchers believe that a hereditary form of depression underlies some forms of both disorders, and some patients who seek treatment do indeed respond to antidepressant medication and behavior therapy (Costin, 2007).

Researchers, health practitioners, and social psychologists are calling on insurance companies to provide comprehensive coverage to help adolescents who suffer from these serious and life-threatening disorders, especially those from poor and minority populations—since eating disorders often require repeated hospitalizations or long-term care (Miller & Golden, 2010).

(Ogden, 2010; Ogden & Flegal, 2010). According to this view, each of us has a built-in control system, a kind of fat thermostat that dictates how much fat we should carry. Some of us have a high setting and tend to be obese; others of us have a low setting and tend to be lean. Long-term studies of weight reduction in children have shown that even if some lose weight, 95 percent return to their original weight within five years (National Eating Disorders Screening Program, 2001).

Today, many obese people challenge the prevailing social stereotypes and prejudices. Unlike the physically handicapped, obese people tend to be held responsible for their condition. They are the object of much concern and a frequent target of criticism, derision, and overt discrimination (Wang, Brownell, & Wadden, 2004). Negative attitudes seem to intensify during adolescence, particularly among females. But increasingly, obese people are "fighting back" against discrimination by defining obesity as a disability, in an attempt to make it illegal to discriminate against persons who are obese.

Still, medical practitioners are familiar with the long-term effects of obesity and promote getting up, getting regular aerobic activity, and changing one's diet and lifestyle for a higher-quality, longer life. The Centers for Disease Control and Prevention offers 24 useful strategies for communities to help prevent obesity (Keener, Goodman, Lowry, Zaro, & Kettle Khan, 2009). Yet findings from the most recent national School Health Policies and Programs Study (conducted in 2006) reveal that only a small percentage of high schools across the country require daily physical education, about one-third offer classes three times per week, about one-third have a cardiovascular fitness center, and nearly half offered intramural activities or physical activity clubs (Lee, Burgeson, Fulton, & Spain, 2007).

> **Questions**
>
> Why has there been an increase in the number of adolescents who have eating disorders, and what are the consequences of being seriously underweight or overweight when entering adulthood?

Smoking and Tobacco Products

The majority of adolescents who use tobacco do so by smoking cigarettes. Other ways to ingest tobacco include cigars, pipes, and *bidis* (leaf-wrapped Indian cigarettes) or *kreteks* (clove cigarettes). Additionally, "smokeless" or "spit" tobacco is used by a surprisingly large number of young people, considering the unattractive nature of its use (Johnston, O'Malley, Bachman, & Schulenberg, 2010). The 2010 Monitoring the Future Survey (MTF) reports that "despite the demonstrated health risks associated with smoking, young people have continued to establish regular cigarette habits during late adolescence in sizeable proportions" (Johnston et al., 2010). The MTF explains that for adolescents, smoking usually begins in grades 6 through 9, with initiation generally trailing off by grade 12, although some light smokers in twelfth grade make the transition to heavy smoking in the first two years after high school (Johnston et al., 2010).

Judging on the basis of survey results, rates appear to be declining more among high school students since the late-1990s, despite heavy exposure to tobacco marketing campaigns in the media, state cuts in funding for antismoking campaigns, and teens not always having to show proof of age to purchase cigarettes (Federal Interagency Forum on Child and Family Statistics, 2010). Data from across all states in the 2009 High School Youth Risk Behavior Survey reveal that between 9 and 26 percent of teens were smoking cigarettes (Eaton et al., 2010). Effective antismoking strategies continue to be implemented in markets where more teens smoke, and new strategies are being devised to continue to decrease tobacco use among teens (Hershey et al., 2005). Some public service ad campaigns have been very effective because teens used to be pressured into smoking by peers, but now teens are being pressured *not* to smoke because "It's not the cool thing to do."

Interestingly, there has been an increase in negative attitudes toward the use of cigarettes among middle school students, which may account for the recent decline in tobacco use (Bachman et al., 2007). In addition, teens cite being turned off to smoking by the antihygienic aspects of smoking, such as bad breath, darker teeth, and lingering smoke odors (King, 2005). Most young people today understand that there is considerable risk associated with smoking because smoking has serious long-term health-related consequences.

Alcohol and Other Substance Abuse

In 2009, social scientists who conducted the annual national survey Monitoring the Future reported a continuing decline in the percentage of teens aged 12 to 17 using alcohol and drugs (see Figure 11.6) (Johnston et al., 2010). One reason for the decline in alcohol use among

teenagers is their increased awareness that alcohol can cause them serious harm (Substance Abuse and Mental Health Services Administration, 2010). Current programs designed to educate teenagers on the risks associated with alcohol abuse have had some effect. Those teens who reported alcohol use were less likely to perceive great risk in using alcohol than were those who did not report use (Office of Applied Studies, 2007). Part of this problem of perception may be how alcohol is presented in the media. Recent longitudinal studies suggest a correlation between exposure to advertising and other media that centers on alcohol consumption and the likelihood that adolescents will begin to drink, or the likelihood that baseline drinkers will increase their drinking (Anderson et al., 2009).

It's not only that young people are drinking but also the *way* they drink that puts them at such high risk for alcohol-related problems. Alcohol use and binge drinking are highest among those between 18 and 21. Many more males than females reported alcohol use and binge drinking. Adolescent white males and Hispanic males report the highest rates of alcohol consumption, whereas Asians and blacks report low rates of alcohol use (Johnston et al., 2010). "Among the most powerful predictors [of heavy episodic alcohol use] were proportion of friends who get drunk, disapproval of heavy drinking, and cigarette and marijuana use" (Johnston et al., 2010). Such risky drinking often leads to tragic consequences, most notably alcohol-related traffic fatalities (National Institute on Alcohol Abuse and Alcoholism, 2006). Too often today's headlines bring news of yet another alcohol-related tragedy involving a young person, especially during prom and graduation periods.

Researchers continue to report that regular alcohol or drug abuse interferes with adolescent educational performance, disengagement from dependence on parents, development of relationships with peers, and important life choices (such as completing high school, avoiding unprotected sex, securing and keeping employment, and maintaining family relations). Furthermore, sustained alcohol use in adolescence is a strong predictor of alcohol abuse later in life (Patrick, Wray-Lake, Finlay, & Maggs, 2010).

Substance abuse is the harmful use of various drugs (including prescription drugs) or alcohol, lasting over a prolonged period that puts oneself or others in hazardous situations. Although state laws set age 21 as the minimum legal drinking age, underage drinking remains America's number one youth drug problem (Davies, 2009). Besides alcohol, such drugs include cigarettes, marijuana, pain relievers, ecstasy, amphetamines, methamphetamines, inhalants, cocaine/crack, heroin, LSD and other hallucinogens, narcotics, sedatives (barbiturates), tranquilizers, and steroids (see Figure 11.7). Results of the annual Monitoring the Future national study, with more than 50,000 participants, show continuing reductions in use of illicit

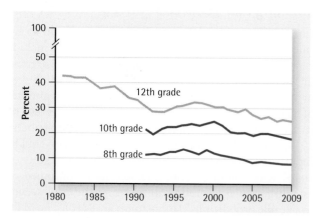

FIGURE 11.6 Percentage of Eighth-, Tenth-, and Twelfth-Grade Students Who Reported Having Five or More Alcoholic Beverages in a Row in the Past Two Weeks (by Grade), 1980–2009 Note: Data for 10th grade in 2008 are not included because estimates are considered to be unreliable as a consequence of sampling error.
Source: Johnston, L. D., O'Malley, P. M., Bachman, J. G., & Schulenberg, J. E. (2009). *Monitoring the Future national survey results on drug use, 1975–2008: Volume I, Secondary school students* (NIH Publication No. 09-7402). Bethesda, MD: National Institute on Drug Abuse.

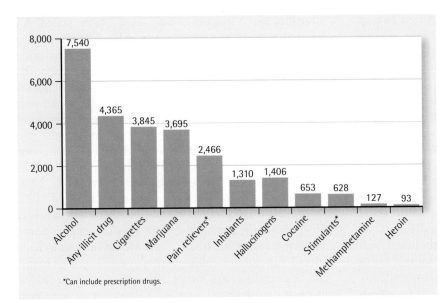

FIGURE 11.7 Use of Psychoactive Substances: Number of U.S. Adolescents Aged 12 to 17 Who Used Cigarettes, Alcohol, or Illicit Drugs for the First Time on an Average Day, 2008
Source: Office of Applied Studies. (2010, April 29). *The OAS Report: A day in the life of American adolescents: Substance use facts update.* Rockville, MD: Substance Abuse and Mental Health Services Administration.

drugs occurring in all grades; only a few categories have remained stable by twelfth grade—alcohol, marijuana, and cigarettes (Johnston et al., 2010). Also, using or mixing over-the-counter and prescription medicines to "get high" (teens call this "pharming") is more prevalent among those aged 12 to 25 (Substance Abuse and Mental Health Services, 2008). Inhalant use is more common among middle school students because these substances are easy for them to obtain and cost little. Such abuse includes breathing fumes from glues, white-out fluids, aerosol cans, paint thinners, butane lighters, and nail polish remover—and the outcome can be deadly.

Most adolescents do not abuse drugs (note that school dropouts are not included in these national surveys). Although half of twelfth-grade respondents in the 2009 MTF national survey report they have *never used illicit drugs*, only about 25 percent report never using alcohol, so there is a discrepancy in their understanding of "illicit" drug. Also, MTF researchers examined data retrospectively since 1970 and found that twelfth-graders who use illicit drugs began using some substance by or before ninth grade (Johnston et al., 2010). Most parents surely believe their homes are safe, but teens cite other people's homes as the most common setting for drinking ("Underage Drinking," 2005). Those who do use illicit drugs regularly run the risk of substance dependency, have a much higher chance of becoming adult drug addicts, and are more likely to become criminals to support their addictions. About 8 percent of all persons admitted to publicly funded treatment facilities for substance abuse in 2005 were aged 12 to 17 (Substance Abuse and Mental Health Services Administration, 2007). Moreover, more adolescent boys than girls drive while intoxicated, and alcohol is a factor in most deaths for 15- to 24-year-olds: traffic accidents, homicides, suicides,

and accidental overdoses. One-third of drivers aged 16 to 20 who died in traffic crashes in 2006 had measurable alcohol in their blood (National Institute on Alcohol Abuse and Alcoholism, 2006). Sadly, auto accidents are the major killer of children aged 2 to 14.

More high school chapters of SADD (Students Against Destructive Decisions) have been established to promote better decisions and safe teen driving. Classroom programs in elementary and middle schools, such as DARE, help students recognize, resist, and strategize about the cultural and peer pressures that influence them to experiment with alcohol, tobacco, marijuana, inhalants, or other drugs. The serious issue of peer influence on substance use and abuse is discussed in Chapter 12.

Sexually Transmitted Infections

Results from the nationally representative 2009 Youth Risk Behavior Surveillance (YRBS) study indicate that by the eleventh grade, about one-half of adolescents engage in sexual intercourse (see Table 11.1) (Centers for

TABLE 11.1 Adolescents Who Reported Having Had Sexual Intercourse at Least Once During Their Life, by Grade Level: 2009

Grade	Females (percent)	Males (percent)
12	65	59.6
11	52.5	53.4
10	39.6	41.9
9	29.3	33.6

Source: Centers for Disease Control and Prevention. (2010, June 4). Youth risk behavior surveillance—United States, 2009. *MMWR, 59*(SS-5), 1–142.

Disease Control and Prevention, 2010h). About 14 percent of sexually active adolescents have had four or more partners and tend to have riskier attitudes toward contraceptive use (Ball, 2007; Centers for Disease Control and Prevention, 2010). "More than two dozen bacterial, viral or parasitic infections are known to be transmitted largely or exclusively through sexual contact" (Guttmacher Institute, 2009). Government statistics show that of the 19 million cases of sexually transmitted infections that are diagnosed annually, people in the 15- to 24-year-old age bracket account for half of them (Wildsmith, Schelar, Peterson, & Manlove, 2010). Further, early adolescent sexual initiation has become a more serious problem behavior (Madkour et al., 2010).

In the 2009 YRBS study, with several thousand high school students, about one-half of sexually active females did not use a condom at last sexual episode, and only one-third of sexually active males did not use a condom during last sexual intercourse. Thus, they are more vulnerable to unplanned pregnancy or **sexually transmitted infections (STIs)** (Centers for Disease Control and Prevention, 2008). STIs are infections that are transmitted during sexual activity; they cause symptoms that, if left untreated, can lead to disease and infertility. Some, such as syphilis and HIV/AIDS, are very serious and, if left untreated, can become life-threatening. Teenagers give the following reasons and others for not using condoms: I was drunk; we decided on the spur of the moment; I was embarrassed to buy them; it spoils the romance. In 2009, *chlamydia* was the most frequently reported STI—and the number of cases, 1.2 million, was the highest ever reported for any condition (Division of STD Prevention, 2009). Women aged 15 to 24 years old have the highest rates of chlamydia, but rates are also increasing for males of this age group (see Figure 11.8) (Wildsmith et al., 2010). Chlamydia is caused by atypical *bacteria* and can lead to

infertility and blindness in women, if left untreated. An infected woman can pass on the chlamydia parasite to her infant as the baby passes through the birth canal. Five percent of female college students have been diagnosed with chlamydia. Fortunately, it is curable with antibiotics.

Human papillomavirus (HPV) is the most common sexually transmitted *viral* infection among Americans—more than half of sexually active men and women are infected with HPV at some time in their lives, and about half of those infected are between the ages of 15 and 24 (Centers for Disease Control and Prevention, 2008; Dunne et al., 2007). With more than 100 types of HPV, some are low risk and resolve without treatment, whereas others produce genital warts or cervical cancer. Sexually active female adolescent teens would be wise to have annual *Pap test* screenings with a gynecologist or health practitioner. In 2006, a new HPV vaccine was licensed for use with females aged 9 to 26. A controversy has arisen because a few states mandated that administration of this HPV vaccine be compulsory for 12-year-old girls (Colgrove, 2006). Even though the FDA has approved *Gardasil* as safe, there are still concerns about its safety and long-term effects and reports of some girls having had serious adverse reactions (Fitton, Farrell, & Millspaw, 2008).

Syphilis is a bacterial infection that can be passed on to a fetus through the placenta. Syphilis develops in four phases, beginning with incubation and ending in the final phase some five years later. Death is possible if the infected person is left untreated. *Gonorrhea* is caused by bacteria that pass from one infected mucous membrane to another. Young women and men between the ages of 15 and 24 have the highest rates of gonorrhea (Centers for Disease Control and Prevention, 2008).

Of more concern to health professionals is the number of teens who are having oral sex, their misperception

FIGURE 11.8 Chlamydia: Teens and Young Adults Have the Highest Rates in the United States, 2009 Chlamydia, a bacterial infection that can be treated with antibiotics, is the most prevalent STI among teens, especially for females. Many poor and ethnic minority teens do not have health insurance to pay for treatment.
Source: Division of STD Prevention. (2010, November). *2009 Sexually Transmitted Diseases Surveillance.* Atlanta, GA: Centers for Disease Control and Prevention.

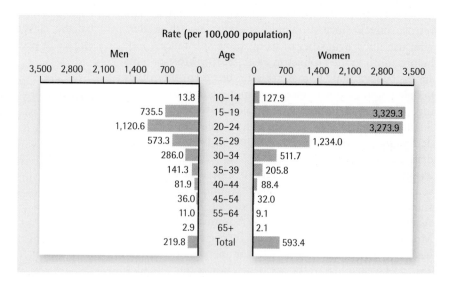

that oral sex is more acceptable and less risky than vaginal sex, and their lack of understanding about the health, social, and emotional consequences of this form of sexual relations. Song and Halpern-Felsher (2011) report findings of a longitudinal study on teen oral sex with more than 600 ninth-grade males and females. Participants report oral sex as more prevalent than vaginal sex and say they consider it more acceptable and less a threat to their values and beliefs. Teens have coined the term "friends with benefits" for their casual sex partners, who are not in close, committed relationships. In one study, girls report "feeling bad about themselves and feeling used" after oral sex (Brady & Halpern-Felsher, 2007). The truth is that STIs, including HIV, are caused by bacteria and viruses that like moist places such as the mouth and genital area—and STIs can and do spread from the mouth to the genital area and from the genital area to the mouth. It is just as important to talk to a partner about his or her sexual history before having oral sex as it is if considering vaginal sex. And the use of some type of barrier method is definitely advised, as well as regular health screenings for both males and females.

Many adolescents are not aware of how they can avoid STIs, cannot identify common symptoms, and do not know what action to take once they show signs of being infected. High school and college health practitioners are a ready source of information. De Rosa and colleagues (2010) surveyed nearly 5,000 middle-school students about their sexual behaviors and recommended that "interventions addressing oral sex, intercourse and multiple partners should begin before sixth grade and continue throughout the middle school years."

Adolescent Risk for HIV/AIDS

Many adolescents frequently engage in sexual intercourse and/or oral or anal sex, and some have had multiple partners and tend to have riskier attitudes toward contraceptive use (Ball, 2007). Since the 1980s, HIV/AIDS has become the most feared sexually transmitted infection because at that time it was a premature death sentence. Tragically, it still is a death sentence (called the "wasting disease") for millions in poor countries of the world that cannot provide the expensive antiretroviral treatment regimen. Of Americans aged 15 to 24, 160 died of HIV in 2007 (Xu, Kochanek, Murphy, & Tejada-Vera, 2010).

The *human immunodeficiency virus (HIV)* eventually causes AIDS, which damages the immune system and prevents the body from fighting infections. This insidious virus is spread primarily by sexual contact with multiple partners (including oral sex) and by sharing needles for injection drug use. Although most early AIDS victims were either gay males or intravenous drug users, HIV also spread rapidly among heterosexuals. In 2006, more than 1 million people in the United States were living with HIV, and it is estimated that 25 percent

were unaware of their infection (Glynn & Rhodes, 2005). African Americans and younger gay males (13 to 24) are at the highest risk (Centers for Disease Control, 2007c). It appears that more gay males have become complacent about HIV transmission because today there are antiretroviral treatments that are prolonging life (Cole, 2006). The progression of HIV to AIDS infection now depends on crucial factors: testing, awareness of diagnosis, access to health care, being prescribed the appropriate medications, taking the medications as prescribed, and following up to see whether the medications are working. Rapid HIV tests play an important part in detection (Greenwald et al., 2006).

Public health experts worry about young people, who are currently the high-risk HIV/AIDS group (especially homosexual males). Based on Hall and colleagues' (2008) first direct estimate of Americans in 50 states, about 16,000 to 22,000 adolescents and young adults (ages 13 to 29) have HIV infection. A discharge of mucus from chlamydia or gonorrhea increases the risk of HIV transmission 3 to 5 times; ulcers from syphilis or genital herpes increase the risk to 9 times the rate for noninfected individuals (National Institute of Allergy and Infectious Diseases, 2006).

For years, millions of teens were part of abstinence-only programs in schools to discourage premarital sex, the spread of various STIs, and unwanted pregnancy. Kim and Rector's (2010) research review of abstinence programs found that 17 of 22 studies report statistically positive findings: "better psychological well-being and higher educational attainment than those who are sexually active." One landmark study compared the effectiveness of abstinence courses to that of safe-sex courses with sixth- and seventh-graders. Within two years only one-third of abstinence-only students had become sexually active, compared with about half of those who completed the safe-sex program (Jemmott, Jemmott, & Fong, 2010). In 2009 the Obama administration eliminated all federal funding for abstinence education programs, while increasing funding for comprehensive sex education programs (Stein, 2010). Such educational programs mainly emphasize contraceptive use.

Most high schools and colleges have a staff nurse who can be a well-informed, safe resource person to counsel students who suspect they have contracted a disease, but many youth don't have access to health care. Rates of abstinence, adolescent sexual experience, types of sexual activity, and effective contraceptive practice are important determinants of adolescent health and well-being, changes in pregnancy rates, and opportunities for an adolescent's future.

A new form of sexual vulnerability called "sexting" also affects the teen culture today (see the *More Information You Can Use* box on page 356, "Sext" Messaging: Harmless Activity or Criminal Act?).

MORE INFORMATION YOU CAN USE

"Sext" Messaging: Harmless Activity or Criminal Act?

Sexting—"the sharing of sexually explicit photos, videos, email, text, and chat by cell phone or online"—is a new phenomenon that has surfaced among teenagers and some adults (O'Donovan, 2010). An Associated Press-MTV poll in 2009 found that more than 25 percent of teens have "sexted" in some form (Associated Press, 2009). And because this practice has attracted notoriety in the wake of several teen suicides, U.S. lawmakers are deliberating whether harsh penalties need to be meted out to offenders convicted of "cyberbullying," prosecuting them no differently from those tried under existing child-pornography or child-exploitation laws. The U.S. Senate has proposed the Safe Internet Act in 2009, but it has not become law. Yet others question whether this trend is simply a harmless part of adolescence and, as such, should be dealt with by parents or education programs. Teenage sexters often trade nude pictures of themselves or others via cell phone. A recent *Wall Street Journal* article reports that the percentage of teens who have engaged in sexting is "roughly 4 percent to 25 percent" (Koppel & Jones, 2010). Is such behavior just an example of freedom of expression, an innocuous part of growing up? Or is it dangerous, no different from other crimes involving sexual exploitation? Well, that depends on which side of the wall you stand on. Those who believe sexting is harmless maintain that if it is self-created, and if individuals share it consensually, it should not be judged in the same way as other types of pornography.

Still, there are those who argue that such pictures, once broadcast, have a way of becoming permanently available on the Internet, leading to humiliation of the victims of sexting, who are often unaware of the unintended consequences of such public exhibitionism. They argue that it may encourage or attract sexual predators, subjecting kids to danger. Those who sext may be naïvely unaware of how the images get used. Mary Leary, a law professor at the Catholic University

A Parent Whose Daughter Took Her Own Life After a Sexting Incident Speaks to Congress About Internet and Wireless Safety Issues

of America in Washington, DC, who specializes in issues involving the exploitation of children, says, "The notion that this is simply innocuous behavior among juveniles ignores the fact that this involves the circulation of images for eternity, beyond the control of the kids who are the subject of the images" (Koppel & Jones, 2010). In one Pennsylvania school, "officials discovered photographs of nude and partially clothed teenage girls on several students' cellphones. Male students, the officials learned, had been trading the images over their phones" (Koppel & Jones, 2010).

Making the debate even more complicated is "the range of forms that sexting can take. It may be the exchange of a revealing photo between two romantic partners or a rapid-fire humiliation campaign, with a photo spreading throughout a school. A single photo may start out as the former and end up as the latter" (Koppel & Jones, 2010).

Questions

What are the current trends in the incidence of sexually transmitted infections in teenagers? Which teens are at high risk for contracting STIs and HIV? What are some of the reasons you would give teenagers for using condoms?

Teenage Pregnancy

Despite the reported decrease in sexual activity and the increase in safer sexual practices, some teens do become parents. In 2008 the nonmarital birth statistic for all U.S.

women rose to its highest level yet, 40.6 percent, and six out of seven pregnant teens are unmarried when they become parents (Hamilton, Martin, & Ventura, 2010). National campaigns to curb teen pregnancy reported significant success from 1990 to 2005, when birthrates fell 34 percent for U.S. teens in all age groups, to the lowest levels ever reported in the nation (Hamilton et al., 2010). But U.S. teen birthrates are still higher than rates in other developed countries (Wingo, Smith, Tevendale, & Ferré, 2010). Public policy analysts are examining the 5 percent increase in teen births for 2006 and 2007, but many complex factors are involved: an increase in the number

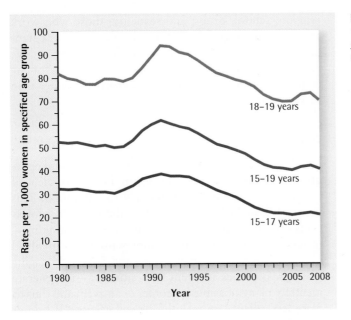

FIGURE 11.9 Birthrates for Teens by Age: United States, 1980–2006 and Preliminary Data for 2007 and 2008
Source: Hamilton, B. E., Martin, J. A., & Ventura, S. J. (2010, April 6). Births: Preliminary data for 2008. *National Vital Statistics Reports, 58*(16), 1–13.

of teens, lower abortion rates not seen since 1974, an increasing, ethnically diverse population of single teens having babies (higher rates for Hispanic and black teens), less fear and concern about HIV/AIDS, and the desire of some teenage girls to become mothers rather than continuing their education (Guttmacher Institute, 2008). Yet U.S. teen births declined 2 percent overall again in 2008 (see Figure 11.9) (Hamilton et al., 2010). The life-changing emotional, social, and socioeconomic consequences of teen pregnancy are discussed in Chapter 12.

Body Art and Tattooing

Today, more teens and college students are getting tattoos and body piercings than in any previous American generation. Yet body art has been practiced in every culture for centuries, and the show *Body Art: Marks of Identity* at the American Museum of Natural History confirms its legitimacy (Tanne, 2000). Tattooing, body piercing, and body art are found on people of all ages, occupations, and social classes. An estimated one-third of the North American population between the ages of 18 and 30 now have tattoos (Zinn, 2009). A growing body of research finds a relationship between getting tattoos, piercings, and body art and lower perceived mental health and high-risk behavior among adolescents (Preti et al., 2006). For example, an Italian study of a sample of 829 adolescents found a significant association between the presence of tattoos or piercings and engaging in smoking and the use of alcohol (Bosello et al., 2010). Studies show that adolescents indulge in body art for the following reasons (Armstrong et al., 2004): to demonstrate social identity, membership, or class; to commemorate a special event; to express intimacy (tattooing a lover's name); or to be entertained.

Potential health risks from body piercing include hepatitis B, tetanus, and skin infections. In the United States and many other countries, this remains an unregulated industry for the most part. A lawsuit was filed in 2005 against nine tattoo ink companies for metal toxicity in the colorants of ink, which could cause cancer, birth defects, or other reproductive harm (McGovern, 2005). A poorly placed piercing can cause nerve damage, and a tongue stud can lead to speech problems and chipped teeth. Having a dermatologist remove a single tattoo can cost $2,000 to $2,500 or more. Recently, scarification (cutting), branding, and stretched earlobe holes have made their way into the body art scene.

As adolescents look for novel ways to express themselves, it is obvious that many of these adornments have been accepted in American work environments. As we recall our own teen years, we recognize that every adolescent cohort finds interesting ways to distinguish itself from the adult generation—including "slang," characteristic types of music, hairstyles, length and fit of clothing, and use of body and facial adornments.

Stress, Anxiety, Depression, and Suicide

The rates of adolescents describing themselves as "seriously considering suicide" have dropped significantly since 1980 and now range from 12 to 18 percent for more than 16,000 teens reporting across states in grades 9 to 12. In 2009, the overall rate of suicide attempts was 2 percent (attempts resulting in treatment by a doctor or nurse for self-injury, poisoning, or overdose) (Centers for Disease Control and Prevention, 2010h). Teenage females were much more likely than males to report considering suicide throughout this past decade. Moreover, females report attempting suicide at double the rates of males for grades 9 to 12—yet males are more likely to actually end their lives (often by firearms). In 2007, suicide was the third leading cause of death, taking the lives of more than 4,000 young persons aged 15 to 24 (Xu et al., 2010).

Because stress, anxiety, and depression often occur within the context of adolescent-parent relationships, peer-adolescent relationships, and boyfriend-girlfriend and same-sex relationships, we will discuss the range of reactions and coping strategies adopted to deal with anxiety, stress, fear, loss, social isolation, and attacks on self-esteem and self-worth in Chapter 12.

Brain Development and Decision Making   As stated earlier, the majority of adolescents are healthy and full of energy, and they typically "squeeze" many physical/recreational, academic, social, and family activities into their daily lives, while their sleep-wake cycle shifts to later hours. As we have just seen, they are also at a stage of life when they seek more freedom from parental and adult authority and supervision and are tempted to take risks or engage in unhealthy behaviors—behaviors they mistakenly believe are more adultlike but for which they cannot foresee the outcomes.

When participating in the risky behaviors mentioned earlier, tragically some teens make decisions that will harm them for life or even end their lives. Since a majority of teens begin to drive at around the age of 15 or 16, with little skill and experience, driving accidents are the major cause of death for adolescents (typically, excessive speed, alcohol, and texting while driving are factors). Many high schools and parent-teacher organizations now offer extravagant alcohol-free prom nights and graduation events in an attempt to keep every student alive during periods of intensely emotional celebration. The other main causes of teen loss of life, in descending order, are other accidents and injuries, assault (homicide), suicide, cancer, and heart disease (Kung et al., 2008).

Questions

Why do many young people begin experimenting with smoking, drinking, drugs, sex, body art, and other risky behaviors during adolescence? What are the main causes of adolescent death?

COGNITIVE DEVELOPMENT

During adolescence, young people gradually acquire several substantial new intellectual capacities. They begin to reflect about themselves; their parents, teachers, and peers; and the world they live in. They develop an increasing ability to use *abstract thought*—to think about hypothetical and future situations and events. In our society they also must evolve a set of standards regarding family,

religion, school, drugs, and sexuality; those who work at jobs during high school must also develop work standards. Often teens learn things the "hard" way—and we call this "the school of hard knocks," an idiom for the education one gets from real-life experience rather than formal education.

Piaget: The Period of Formal Operations

Jean Piaget called adolescence the **period of formal operations,** the final and highest stage in the development of cognitive functioning from infancy to adulthood. This mode of thought has two major attributes. First, adolescents gain the ability to think about their own thinking—to deal efficiently with the complex problems involved in reasoning. Second, they acquire the ability to imagine many possibilities inherent in a situation—to generate mentally many possible outcomes of an event and thus to place less reliance on real objects and events: "If I don't come home at my curfew time with Dad's car, then . . . or . . . will happen." In sum, adolescents gain the capacity to think in logical and abstract terms.

Formal operational thought so closely parallels scientific thinking that some call it "scientific reasoning." It enables people to mentally restructure information and ideas so that they can make sense of a new set of data. Through logical operations, individuals can transfer the strategic skills they employ in a familiar problem area to an unfamiliar area and thus derive new answers and solutions. In so doing, they generate higher-level analytical abilities to discern relationships among various classes of events.

Formal operational thought is quite different from the concrete operational thought of the previous period. Piaget said that children in the period of concrete operations cannot transcend the immediate. They are limited to solving tangible problems of the present and have difficulty dealing with remote, future, or hypothetical matters. For instance, a 12-year-old will accept and think about the following problem: "All three-legged snakes are purple; I am hiding a three-legged snake; guess its color" (Kagan, 1972, p. 92). In contrast, 7-year-old children are confused by the initial premise because it violates their notion of what is real. Consequently, they can be confused and refuse to cooperate.

Likewise, if adolescents are presented with the problem "There are three schools, Roosevelt, Kennedy, and Lincoln schools, and three girls, Mary, Sue, and Jane, who go to different schools. Mary goes to the Roosevelt school, Jane to the Kennedy school. Where does Sue go?" they quickly respond "Lincoln." The 7-year-old might excitedly answer, "Sue goes to Roosevelt school, because my sister has a friend called Sue and that's the school she goes to" (Kagan, 1972, p. 93). Similarly, Barbel Inhelder and her mentor, Jean Piaget, found that before 12 years

Adolescents Seek Freedom from Parental Authority and Take Risks Without Realizing the Consequences As adults, we fail to remember that we probably did something similar—or worse!
Source: Jerry Scott & Jim Borgman, ZITS, January 22, 2008.

of age most children cannot solve this verbal problem (Inhelder & Piaget, 1964, p. 252):

Edith is lighter than Suzanne.

Edith is darker than Lily.

Which is the darkest of the three?

Children under 12 often conclude that both Edith and Suzanne are light-complexioned and that Edith and Lily are dark-complexioned. Accordingly, they say that Lily is the darkest, Suzanne is the lightest, and Edith falls in between. In contrast, adolescents in the stage of formal operations can correctly reason that Suzanne is darker than Edith, that Edith is darker than Lily, and that therefore Suzanne is the darkest girl.

Piaget suggested that the transition from concrete operational to formal operational thought takes place as children become increasingly proficient in organizing and structuring input from their environment with concrete operational methods. In so doing, they come to recognize the inadequacies of concrete operational methods for solving problems in the real world—the gaps, uncertainties, and contradictions inherent in concrete operational processes (Labouvie-Vief, 1986).

Not all adolescents, and for that matter not all adults, attain full formal operational thought, especially those with intellectual or developmental disabilities. Therefore, some fail to acquire its associated abilities in logical and abstract thinking and will require social services and additional supports as they transition into adult living. People who score below average on standard intelligence tests show this lack of ability, for instance. Indeed, as judged by Piaget's strict testing standards, less than 50 percent of U.S. adults reach the stage of formal operations. Some evidence suggests that secondary schools can provide students with experiences in mathematics and science that expedite the development of formal

operational thought. And some psychologists speculate that various environmental experiences might be necessary to its development (Kitchener et al., 1993).

However, Piaget's stages have been criticized on many grounds. One flaw in his theory is that some children and adolescents are intellectually gifted and often grasp ideas and are able to perform operations earlier than Piaget found (Porath, 2006). Another problem is that cognitive development across domains typically is uneven; rarely does a child think in stage-typical ways across all topics (e.g., mathematics, science, or history) (Schunk, 2008). Furthermore, cross-cultural studies fail to demonstrate the full development of formal operations in all societies. For example, rural villagers in Turkey never seem to reach the formal operational stage, yet urbanized educated Turks do reach it (Kohlberg & Gilligan, 1971). Overall, a growing body of research suggests that full formal operational thinking may not be the rule in adolescence. Even so, considerable research confirms Piaget's view that the thought of adolescents differs from that of young children (Marini & Case, 1994).

Adolescent Egocentricity

Piaget (1967) said that adolescents produce their own characteristic form of **egocentrism,** and this view was expanded by the psychologist David Elkind (1970) in terms of two dimensions of egocentric thinking: (1) the *personal fable* and (2) the *imaginary audience.* As adolescents gain the ability to conceptualize their own thought, they also achieve the capacity to conceptualize the thought of others. But adolescents do not always make a clear distinction between the two. In turning their new powers of thought introspectively, adolescents simultaneously assume that their thoughts and actions are equally interesting to others. They conclude that other people are as admiring or critical of them as they are themselves. They tend to view the world as a stage on which they are the principal actors and all the world is the audience. According to Elkind, this characteristic accounts for the fact that teenagers tend to be extremely self-conscious and self-preoccupied: The preoperational child is egocentric in the sense that he is unable to take another person's point of view. The adolescent, on the other hand, takes the other person's point of view to an extreme degree.

As a result, adolescents tend to view themselves as somehow unique and even heroic—as destined for unusual fame and fortune. Elkind dubs this romantic imagery the **personal fable.** The adolescent feels that others cannot possibly understand what she or he is experiencing, and often this leads to the creation of a story, or personal fable, that the adolescent tells everyone, even though it is a story that is not true. If you have ever thought something like, "They will never understand the pain of unrequited love; only I have been through this torture," then you have created your own personal fable.

The **imaginary audience,** another adolescent creation, consists of the adolescent's belief that everyone in the local environment is primarily concerned with the appearance and behavior of the adolescent. The imaginary audience causes the adolescent to be very self-critical and/or extremely self-admiring. The adolescent really believes that everyone she or he encounters thinks solely about her or him night and day. Remember how devastating a pimple was in high school because you thought every eye would be glued to your affliction? You probably never suspected that your peers were too concerned and preoccupied with their own pimples to notice yours. Elkind believes that adolescents can eventually distinguish between real and imaginary audiences, and he also acknowledges that the adolescent's imaginary audience and personal fable are progressively modified and eventually diminished.

Other psychologists, such as Robert Selman (1980), also find that young adolescents become aware of their own self-awareness, recognizing that they can consciously monitor their own mental experience and control and manipulate their thought processes. However, only later in adolescence do they become capable of distinguishing between conscious and nonconscious levels of experience. Hence, although they retain a conception of themselves as self-aware beings, they realize that their ability to control their own thoughts and emotions has limits. This gives them a more sophisticated notion of their mental self and what constitutes self-awareness.

The growing self-awareness of teenagers also finds expression in the increasing differentiation of the *self-concept* during adolescence. Notably, William James proposed in the 1890s a framework for the multidimensional self that still applies: The *material self* includes one's body and material possessions; the *social self* comprises

characteristics of one's self that are recognized by others (such as "s/he's musically talented"); and the *spiritual self* is the inner core of one's being and includes thoughts, values, and moral judgments. James visualized these dimensions of self in a hierarchy, ranging from the material, to the social, to the spiritual, which occupies the most precious part of the self (Harter, 1999). For James Baldwin, *imitation* of others is particularly powerful in children's developing a sense of self, and sometimes we come to "own" some of those behaviors as part of ourselves (Harter, 1999). Recently, using brain-imaging techniques, Goleman (2007) provides evidence that emotional intelligence (EQ) is a stronger indicator of human success than intelligence (IQ); and he defines emotional intelligence in terms of an emotional sense of self and others, motivation, and the ability to be in healthy relationships (Van Bockern, 2006).

In the past, the home and a family's place of worship provided training for a teen's developing a healthy sense of self and "soul-filled" education. But now U.S. public schools must present their version of "character" education while maintaining separation of church and state (Van Bockern, 2006, p. 218). Their task is difficult: Contemporary teens are bombarded hourly with sensational marketing and media images of popular teenage celebrities exhibiting public intoxication, drug abuse and rehab, eating disorders, indecent public acts and random sexual encounters, early pregnancy, and rebellion toward authority. Sadly, millions of young teens who are still developing a sense of "self" imitate those teens who have a disturbed or "soul-less" sense of "self" (Hymowitz, 2003).

For several decades, studying the "self" waned as behaviorists were concerned with external, observable behaviors. As humanistic and cognitive psychology emerged in the last four decades, with a wealth of research in self-concept, self-esteem, self-worth, self-help, and individual differences, study of the construct of "self" has reemerged (Harter, 1999). Thus, more contemporary social scientists have contributed to our understanding of how we become who we are—and how we can improve our "selves" if we are motivated.

What are you *really* like with different people? Adolescents provide different self-descriptions in different social contexts (see Figure 11.10). Teenagers assign differing self-attributes depending on whether they are describing their *role* in relation to their mother, father, close friends, romantic partners, or classmates, or their role as child, student, employee, athlete, artist, musician, dancer, and so forth. The self they depict with their parents might be open, depressed, or sarcastic; with friends they might be caring, cheerful, or rowdy; and with a romantic partner they might be fun-loving, self-conscious, flirtatious, or controlling. With cognitive maturation, teenagers make greater differentiations among role-related attributes. At the same time, the differing expectations

What I am like with different people

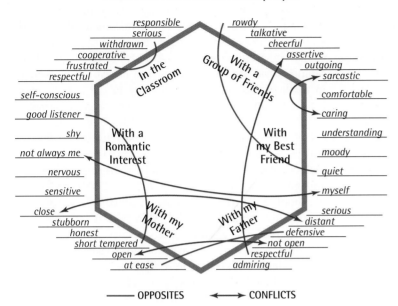

— OPPOSITES   ←→ CONFLICTS

FIGURE 11.10 What Are Teens Like with Different People? With increasing cognitive maturation, and in response to expectations from a variety of significant others in their lives, teens are able to differentiate the self with respect to varying social roles. Note the great variety of descriptors that this 15-year-old girl assigns to her "selves."

Source: Susan Harter. (1999). *The construction of the self: A developmental perspective.* Guilford Press, p. 70. Reprinted by permission.

of significant others in different social contexts compel adolescents to differentiate the self with respect to varying social roles (Harter, 1999). We will discuss adolescent egocentrism in its social context in Chapter 12.

> **Questions**
>
> How does a typical adolescent develop cognitively during the junior high to high school years? What are various personal and social factors that influence a teen's developing sense of self?

Educational Issues

Most teenagers look forward to moving from the more structured middle school or junior high to high school. Students get an opportunity to select a few courses and a daily schedule, along with enrolling in state-mandated courses (mathematics, English, social studies, science, and foreign language). Students with an aptitude in vocational careers select from courses such as computer science, carpentry, mechanical drawing, auto mechanics, technology, child care, veterinary care, food service, cosmetology, horticulture, and prenursing. Many large high schools offer "schools within a school," such as a core of special courses for students who are highly gifted or talented in the fine arts, along with a mentoring experience in—typically—music, drama, or computer art and design.

Of significant interest is the educational performance of those youth in junior high who were in the Head Start programs as preschoolers. Results from the Chicago Longitudinal Study indicate that at-risk children who participated in follow-up programs for three or more years after early intervention services had significantly higher

reading achievement in the seventh grade, had a lower rate of being held back a grade, and were less likely to receive special education services (Reynolds et al., 2007). Further investigation with this long-standing study of childhood intervention indicates other long-term positive outcomes, such as higher rates of educational attainment, economic and health well-being, and lower rates of juvenile or adult arrest (Reynolds et al., 2007).

Students who are high achievers can select Advanced Placement (AP) or International Baccalaureate (IB) courses that challenge their problem-solving and critical thinking skills and enable them to earn college credits while in high school. More high schools today have graduation requirements of community service and are also offering *Service Learning* and mentoring opportunities in nonprofit, government, and human service agencies where students volunteer time and effort in real-world settings (Barrios Marcelo, 2007). Typically, high schools offer a variety of extracurricular activities that give adolescents real-world opportunities to try out potential career skills. Such activities might include working on the school newspaper or yearbook, competing on sports teams, singing in concert choirs and performing in orchestras, acting in dramas, debating on mock-trial teams, assisting with the operation of an on-campus store for supplies, being an officer of a club, participating in a community service club, or being a class officer.

Adolescents with low or limited intellectual capacity take part in some regular high school classes, but they are also eligible to receive life-skills training in specific vocational programs that include work experience. Their preparation during high school is called the "aging out" process, and these students are eligible to remain in academic and skills-training programs until they are 21 years old, should they choose to do so.

Students with high intellectual abilities who have had positive experiences during their school years typically enjoy the challenge of high school and anticipate furthering their education. But those who have not experienced academic success or social acceptance begin to transition out, both physically and psychologically—displaying erratic school attendance, an unmotivated attitude toward schoolwork, disagreements with or aggression toward adults, increased substance abuse, and sometimes trouble with the law. The *status dropout rate* includes persons aged 16 to 24, since many high school dropouts return to get their GED (graduate equivalency diploma). More males than females drop out of high school. Each year, more than 1.2 million students do not complete the requirements for a high school degree. In 2007–2008, the average of 8 percent across the 50 states did not reflect the much higher dropout rates in large U.S. cities (Aud et al., 2010). The rates vary by race-ethnicity: black and Hispanic youth drop out at much higher rates than white or Asian youth. Although few in numbers, students of American Indian/Alaska Native heritage have a high dropout rate. By district size and locale, minority students in large city schools have the highest dropout rate (Alliance for Excellent Education. 2009; Aud et al., 2010).

These youth are highly aware of when they can "quit" school, and some are at risk of dropping out well before the legal age by disappearing into the community or becoming a PINS youth (person in need of supervision). Many communities now have group homes for some of these teenagers, where they receive more structure, education, supervision, and support than they may have experienced before.

Pregnant teenage girls are a growing group at risk of never earning a high school diploma. The *Even Start* program is federally sponsored and administered through many large urban high schools. Surprisingly, federal funding for Even Start has declined recently, but the goals of this program remain and are threefold: (1) to help young mothers earn a high school diploma while learning effective parenting skills; (2) to physically nurture and intellectually stimulate the infants and preschool children of these teenagers in a nearby setting where mothers can interact with their children during the school day; and (3) to nurture the self-esteem of mother and child and provide healthy role models who encourage the teenage mothers to develop their abilities and talents.

Academic Standing and Global Comparisons

Today's classrooms are changing—and secondary education will continue to change dramatically to meet the needs of the ever-increasing population of twenty-first-century adolescents aged 15 to 19, which is expected to increase to more than 26 million by 2050 (U.S. Bureau of the Census,

2004). As part of *No Child Left Behind,* teacher certification requirements are more rigorous to provide a new generation of highly trained educators, especially in math and science (Corcoran, 2007). Even with increased professional and technological support, American high school seniors performed well below the international average in mathematics and science literacy in the largest international study of student achievement ever undertaken every four years—*The International Mathematics and Science Study* (*TIMSS*), which was first released in 1998 by Boston College (Forgione, 1998). This large-scale study includes more than 500,000 students from 49 countries, and it assessed students in 1995, 2003, and 2007 in all types of schools and programs (Martin, Mullis, & Foy, 2009).

Results from the 2007 TIMSS tests reveal that U.S. fourth-grade and eighth-grade students achieved above-average scores compared to other industrialized countries (the students with the highest achievement were those in Chinese Taipei, Korea, Singapore, Hong Kong SAR, and Japan). However, students in the states of Massachusetts and Minnesota had much higher achievement in both math and science, nearing the scaled scores recorded in Pacific Rim countries. U.S. student average scaled scores for the fourth and eighth grade have improved slightly since 1995 in mathematics and have remained about the same in science (Martin et al., 2009).

In 2000, a national commission released a report titled *Before It's Too Late,* with guidelines to improve the quantity, quality, and working environment for math and science teachers and to raise curriculum and evaluation standards for teaching U.S. children (Glenn, 2000). Since the *No Child Left Behind* (*NCLB*) legislation in 2001, standards have been raised, and students are required to take more rigorous math and science courses. NCLB has come in for its share of criticism, but standard reading, math, and science scores for fourth- and eighth-graders across the nation had reached their highest levels after six years of NCLB, although twelfth-grade scores had remained about the same (National Center for Education Statistics, 2005a; 2007c). In 2010 most high school student scores on the SAT college-entrance exam revealed little progress, except for Asian Americans, "who continue to outperform all other test takers" (see Table 11.2) (Banchero, 2010). Without major improvements, American youth will be at a disadvantage for employment in this age of scientific and technological advances. But all is not bleak. According to Banchero (2010), college entrance exam results indicate that "students who took a core curriculum in high school—defined as four years of English and three of math, science and history—scored, on average, 151 points higher than those who didn't take the curriculum."

Effective Classroom Instruction

Merely reading textbooks does not spark every student's imagination, but computer and digital access opens up a world of active

TABLE 11.2 U.S. High School Students' SAT Scores in 2010 Reveal Little Progress

U.S. students' SAT scores by population group

White	Average Score	1-Year Change	10-Year Change
Reading	528	0	0
Math	536	0	+6
Writing	516	−1	N.A.
Black			
Reading	429	0	−5
Math	428	+2	+2
Writing	420	−1	N.A.
Asian American			
Reading	519	+3	+20
Math	591	+4	+26
Writing	526	+6	N.A.
Mexican American			
Reading	454	+1	+1
Math	467	+4	+7
Writing	448	+2	N.A.

Source: Banchero, S. (2010, September 14). Students' SAT scores stay in rut. *Wall Street Journal*, p. A4.

learning. For example, teachers report that students are more engaged in assignments and collaborative projects when using wireless laptops (Joyner, 2003). Curriculum-specific expertise and technological preparedness are essential for teachers using iPods or iPads and other MP3 players, DVDs, CDROMs, multimedia presentations, Internet-based lessons and homework assignments, and distance-learning courses. Technical and computer expertise is needed to plan, develop, and access Web sites to gather and disseminate course information and homework assignments. Teachers also need to learn classroom management and conflict-resolution skills to diffuse potential aggressive or violent behaviors.

Today's U.S. students are a much more culturally diverse population; some are more intellectually gifted or more challenged than others; some have disabilities; and a growing percentage have limited English proficiency. More research reveals the great variance among the physical, cognitive, and emotional needs of contemporary teens. Competent and highly qualified teachers must come to the classroom well prepared to stimulate, motivate, educate, and evaluate. And students demand practical relevance in the course content they are learning. Rideout, Foehr, and Roberts (2010) conducted a longitudinal survey of more than 2,000 youth nationwide, aged 8 to 18, who also kept weekly diaries of media use. They report that Millennial-generation students use a record number and variety of electronic devices and media in their homes and bedrooms on an average of 7.5 hours daily (a 2-hour daily increase since 1999) (see Table 11.3).

More students are *media multitasking*, or using several devices at one time, while trying to complete homework (for example, they might be downloading music and texting on a cell phone, while a DVD is playing on the TV) (Rideout, Foehr, & Roberts, 2010). One expert on children, identity, and digital culture says it is common for teens to have four media screens on at one time, which of course affects their ability to pay attention and focus on the task at hand (Turkle, 2003).

High school classes are not an end in themselves, at least not for most students. High school instruction should be like a springboard, providing a firm foundation while launching the young adult on to new heights. Supporting the classroom teacher's efforts to provide the best education for every student are classroom aides, special education teachers, guidance counselors, school psychologists, school nurses, librarians, school administrators, and clerical staff.

Use of Media and Computer Technology The exciting diversity and richness of the world is opening up to our youth—and to all of us—through high-speed computer networks and digital technology. There is a high rate of job growth and opportunity for today's adolescent in the technology and computer industries. The network wiring of schools and colleges with "wireless" networks is now the Internet connection of choice. However, some parents and faculty are concerned that computer games, Internet access, social networking sites, and cell phone texting take time away from the three Rs or may lead to ethically questionable—or even dangerous—activities (see Table 11.3).

Modes of instruction using the computer, hand-held notepads, and PDAs, such as distance-learning options and e-books, are expanding. Today nearly all research journals, magazines, newspaper articles, and textbooks are available via the Internet. Schools, colleges, and local libraries are now considered "Information Resource Centers." Many parents have purchased computers for home use and consider this an investment in their child's future. However, there are some concerns with the displays of violence that adolescents witness daily via TV, movies, games, and the Internet. The results of a recent study strongly suggest that habitual exposure of high school students to violent video games is positively correlated with high levels of aggression and violence (Anderson, Gentile, & Buckley, 2007). Also, the age of *cyberbullying*, another form of "relational aggression," has arrived—and some teens are victims while others are perpetrators (Adams, 2010). Today, it is well known that computers are used in nearly all occupations and that they are indispensable in managing and recording nearly every aspect of life. We must prepare today's adolescent cohort to thrive in the technologically oriented future and to avoid the pitfalls that may attend it.

TABLE 11.3 Average Daily Media Use Among 8- to 18-Year-Olds: 1999–2009

In 2009, adolescents spent an average of about 7.5 hours each day on media activities. Do you think that figure has changed since 2009? (Except for the row of entries marked %, all entries are in hours and minutes.)

Among all 8- to 18-year-olds, average amount of time spent with each medium in a typical day

	2009	2004	1999
TV content	4:29	3:51	3:47
Music/audio	2:31	1:44	1:48
Computer	1:29	1:02	:27
Video games	1:13	:49	:26
Print	:38	:43	:43
Movies	:25	:25	:18
Total media exposure	10:45	8:33	7:29
Multitasking proportion	29%	26%	16%
Total media use	7:38	6:21	6:19

Notes: **Total media exposure** is the sum of the times spent with all media. **Multitasking proportion** is the proportion of time that is spent using more than one medium concurrently. **Total media use** is the actual number of hours out of the day that are spent using media, taking multitasking into account.

Source: From Rideout, V. J., Foehr, U. G., & Roberts, D. F. (2010). *Generation M2: Media in the lives of 8- to 18-year-olds.* Menlo Park, CA: Kaiser Family Foundation. Retrieved November 23, 2010, from http://www.kff.org/entmedia/upload/8010.pdf. This information was reprinted with permission of The Henry J. Kaiser Family Foundation. The Kaiser Family Foundation, based in Menlo Park, California, is a nonprofit, independent national health-care philanthropy and is not associated with Kaiser Permanente or Kaiser Industries.

Questions

Why do you think American students' academic performance in math and science ranked above average in international comparison but were well below the highest scores of Asian students in Pacific Rim countries in the international TIMSS study? What would you recommend to improve instruction and the academic achievement of U.S. teens? Does technology help?

MORAL DEVELOPMENT

At no other period in life are people as likely to be as concerned with moral values and principles as they are during adolescence. A recurrent theme of American literature, from *Huckleberry Finn* to *Catcher in the Rye,* has been the innocent child who is brought at adolescence to a new awareness of adult reality and who concludes that the adult world is hypocritical, corrupt, and decadent. *Adolescent idealism,* coupled with *adolescent egocentricity,* frequently breeds "egocentric reformers"—adolescents who assume that it is their solemn duty to reform their parents and the world following their own personal standards. Some two and a half millennia ago, the Greek philosopher Aristotle came to somewhat similar conclusions about the young people of his time:

> [Youths] have exalted notions, because they have not yet been humbled by life or learned its necessary limitations; moreover, their hopeful disposition makes them think themselves equal to great things—and that means exalted notions. All their mistakes are in the direction of doing things excessively and vehemently. They love too much, hate too much, and the same with everything else.

The Adolescent as a Moral Philosopher

Significantly, young people have played a major role in many of the social movements that have reshaped the contours of history. In Czarist Russia, the schools were "hot-beds of radicalism." In China, students contributed to the downfall of the Manchu dynasty and again to the political turmoil of 1919, the 1930s, and 1988 to 1989. And German students were largely supportive of different forms of right-wing nationalism from the mid–nineteenth century on and, in student council elections, showed support for the Nazis in the 1930s (Lipset, 1989).

As we saw in Chapter 9, Kohlberg and his colleagues found that in the course of moral development, people tend to pass through an orderly sequence of six stages. These six stages of moral thought are divided into three major levels: the *preconventional,* the *conventional,* and the *postconventional.* Preconventional children are responsive to cultural labels of good and bad out of consideration for the kinds of consequences of their behavior—punishment, reward, or the exchange of favors. Persons at the conventional level view the rules and expectations of their family, group, or nation as valuable in their own right. Individuals who pass to the postconventional level (and Kohlberg says that few people do consistently) come to define morality in terms of self-chosen principles that they view as having universal ethical validity and application for the good of all.

Neo-Kohlbergians focus on the shift from a conventional view of cooperation to a postconventional perspective and describe it as a central feature of adolescence and adult development. However, they view cognitive growth as the plausible entry point into the study of moral functioning. That is, new forms of moral thinking develop over time, and these new developments are improvements over the older conceptions. These newer conceptions are better, in the philosophical sense, by leading to more justifiable applications (Killen & Smetana, 2006). As a result, the impetus for moral development results from increasing cognitive sophistication of the sort described by Piaget. Consequently, postconventional morality becomes possible only with the onset of adolescence and the development of formal operational thought. Thus, postconventional morality depends primarily on changes in the structure of thought, rather than on an increase in the individual's knowledge of cultural values (de Vries & Walker, 1981). In other words, Kohlberg's stages tell us *how* an individual thinks, not *what* she or he thinks about given matters.

James Fowler has devised a stage theory based on a broad definition of faith called *faith development theory* (*FDT*). Older teenagers often begin to struggle with identity issues of "Who am I?" and "What is the meaning of life?" and "What am I going to do with my life?" Various forms of religiosity often appeal to young people at this stage, whereas for others a quest for spiritual understanding outside of formal religious groups becomes more important. Drawing on the disciplines of philosophy and psychology, Fowler explores the stages of faith and identity development (Fowler & Dell, 2004). Fowler describes several different types of "faithful" people who exhibit similar patterns in their expression of faith.

Fowler's theory of faith development includes a hierarchy of six stages that are sequential and do not vary. These stages range from an early imaginary, fantasy stage around ages 3 to 6 to various steps in accepting or struggling with conventional religious doctrines (with symbols and rituals) as the individual matures. Few humans ultimately become what Fowler describes as *universalists,* who are "feeling at one with God" and are willing to make great sacrifices for their beliefs (Fowler, 2001).

Questions

In what ways is adolescent egocentrism different from the egocentrism of a 4-year-old? How does a typical adolescent's moral development change from sixth grade to twelfth grade?

The Development of Political Thinking

The development of political thinking, like the development of moral values and judgments, depends to a considerable extent on an individual's level of cognitive development. The psychologist Joseph Adelson and his colleagues have interviewed large numbers of adolescents between 11 and 18 years of age. Their aim has been to discover how adolescents of different ages and circumstances think about political matters and organize their political philosophies. Adelson (1972, p. 107) presents adolescents with the following premise:

Imagine that a thousand people venture to an island in the Pacific to form a new society; once there they must compose a political order, devise a legal system, and in general confront the myriad problems of government.

Each subject is then asked a large number of hypothetical questions dealing with justice, crime, the citizen's rights

and obligations, the functions of government, and so on. Adelson (1975, pp. 64–65) summarizes his findings as follows:

The earliest lesson we learned in our work . . . is that neither sex, nor race, nor level of intelligence, nor social class, nor national origin is as potent a factor in determining the course of political thought in adolescence as is the youngster's sheer maturation. From the end of grade school to the end of high school, we witness some truly extraordinary changes in how the child organizes his thinking about society and government.

Adelson finds that the most important change in political thought that occurs during adolescence is the achievement of increasing abstractness. This finding echoes Piaget, who described the hallmarks of formal operational thought in terms of the ability to engage in logical and abstract reasoning. Consider the answers given by 12- and 13-year-olds when they are asked, "What is the purpose of laws?"

They do it, like in schools, so that people don't get hurt. If we had no laws, people could go around killing people. So people don't steal or kill. (Adelson, 1972, p. 108)

Now consider the responses of subjects two or three years older:

To ensure safety and enforce the government. To limit what people can do. They are basically guidelines for people. I mean, like this is wrong and this is right and to help them understand. (p. 108)

An essential difference between the two sets of responses is that the younger adolescents limit their answers to concrete examples such as stealing and killing. Eleven-year-olds have trouble with abstract notions of justice, equality, and liberty. In contrast, older adolescents can usually move back and forth between the concrete and the abstract:

The young adolescent can imagine a church but not the church; the teacher and the school but not education; the policeman and the judge and the jail but not the law; the public official but not the government. (Adelson, 1975, p. 68)

Another difference between the political thinking of younger and older adolescents is that the former tend to view the political universe in rigid and unchangeable terms. Younger adolescents have difficulty dealing with historical causes. They fail to understand that actions taken at one time have implications for future decisions and events.

There is also a sharp decline in authoritarian responses as the child moves through adolescence. Preadolescents are more one-sided in their views toward lawbreakers. They see issues in terms of good guys and bad guys, the strong against the weak, and rampant corruption versus repressive cures. They are attracted to one-person rule and favor coercive and even totalitarian modes of government. By late adolescence, children generally have become more liberal, humane, and democratic in their political perspectives (Helwig, 1995). Thus, they see many sides to the issues evolving from the September 11, 2001, attacks. Some support war; others want peace.

Adelson finds some national variations among young people of different political cultures. Germans tend to dislike confusion and to admire a strong leader. British adolescents stress the rights of the individual citizen and the government's responsibility to provide an array of goods and services for its citizens. Americans emphasize social harmony, democratic practices, the protection of individual rights, and equality among citizens.

Questions

Why and in what ways do adolescents generally become more morally and politically aware as they progress through high school, graduate from high school, and enter college, the military, or the world of work?

SEGUE

We have seen how adolescents enter the life-changing stage of puberty and have discussed the physical and cognitive changes linked to this period in life. Maturation brings with it certain responsibilities and temptations that many adolescents find difficult to come to terms with. It is no surprise, then, that some adolescents begin to engage in behaviors that adults see as "risky" or "destructive," although most adolescents come through these years unscathed. A review of the research on physical development and health issues in adolescence reveals that today's teens are dealing with many serious concerns on a daily basis. As we shall see in Chapter 12, at a time when teens are presented with many challenges and choices, they become more reluctant to discuss these significant issues with parents or caretakers and turn to friends for information, advice, support, and comfort. In Chapter 12 we will turn our attention to the individual adolescent's developing self-concept and self-esteem, family and peer influences, and continuing preparation for a healthy adult life.

SUMMARY

Physical Development

1. During adolescence, young people experience the adolescent growth spurt, a very rapid increase in height and weight. The spurt typically occurs two years earlier in girls than in boys.
2. Adolescence is also characterized by the development of the organs and glands of the reproductive system, which are called primary sex characteristics. The complete transition to reproductive maturity takes about 4.5 years on average and is accompanied by extensive external and internal physical changes.
3. Children of the same chronological age show enormous variations in growth and sexual maturation. Because of different rates of maturation, some adolescents have an advantage in height, strength, physical attractiveness, and athletic prowess.
4. Any difference from the peer group in growth and development tends to be a difficult experience for the adolescent, especially if the difference places the individual at a physical disadvantage or in a position of unfavorable contrast to peers, such as early maturation for girls and late maturation for boys.
5. Many teenagers are preoccupied with their physical acceptability and adequacy. These concerns arise during a time of substantial developmental change in the nature and significance of friendships.

Health Issues in Adolescence

6. Three disorders stem from abnormal nutritional habits: anorexia nervosa, bulimia, and obesity.
7. Substance abuse is the harmful use of drugs or alcohol, lasting over a prolonged period, that endangers self or others.
8. Unprotected sex often leads to the spread of STIs, and sexually active teens are at high risk for several serious bacterial and viral infections.

Cognitive Development

9. Jean Piaget called adolescence the period of formal operations. Its hallmarks are logical and abstract reasoning.

Not all adolescents—nor all adults—however, attain this stage or acquire the capacity for logical and abstract thought that is associated with it.

10. Adolescence produces its own form of egocentrism and centering of attention on one's self. In turning their new powers of thought on themselves, adolescents assume that their thoughts and actions are as interesting to others as they are to themselves.

11. Students are divided into different ability groups in school during this period. Special programs help make the transition from school to work less problematic for many adolescents. Teens are using digital, Internet, and cell phone technology daily at record high rates.

Moral Development

12. At no other period of life are individuals as likely to be concerned with moral values and principles as they are during adolescence. Some, but not all, adolescents attain Kohlberg's postconventional level of morality. In the process, a number of young people go through a transitional phase of moral relativism. Fowler describes stages of development in his faith development theory.

13. During adolescence young people undergo major changes in the way they organize their thinking about society and government. Maturation appears to be the most potent source of these changes. As children move through adolescence, their political thinking becomes more abstract, less static, and less authoritarian.

KEY TERMS

adolescent growth spurt *(341)*

anorexia nervosa *(348)*

asynchrony *(341)*

binge-eating disorder (BED) *(348)*

bulimia *(348)*

egocentrism *(359)*

imaginary audience *(360)*

menarche *(342)*

obesity *(348)*

period of formal operations *(358)*

personal fable *(360)*

primary sex characteristics *(339)*

puberty *(338)*

secondary sex characteristics *(339)*

sexually transmitted infections (STIs) *(354)*

substance abuse *(352)*

FOLLOWING UP ON THE INTERNET

Web sites for this chapter focus on physical, cognitive, and moral maturation in adolescence. Please access the text Web site at www.mhhe.com/crandell10 for up-to-date hot-linked Internet addresses for the following organizations, topics, and resources:

Adolescent Health from the American Medical Association
http://www.ama-assn.org/ama/pub/physician-resources/
   public-health/promoting-healthy-lifestyles/
   adolescent-health.shtml

The Journal of Adolescent Health
http://jahonline.org/current

Society for Adolescent Health and Medicine
http://www.adolescenthealth.org

Academy for Eating Disorders
http://www.aedweb.org

National Eating Disorders Association
http://www.nationaleatingdisorders.org/

Monitoring the Future Surveys
http://monitoringthefuture.org/

AIDS Prevention Education
http://www.aidshealth.org/

TIMSS & PIRLS International Study Center at Boston College
http://timss.bc.edu/

National Center for Education Statistics
http://nces.ed.gov/

12 Adolescence
Emotional and Social Development

The concept of adolescence is a Western phenomenon. Non-Western cultures do not recognize an adolescent stage of development between youth and adulthood. The Western model of segregating youth from the adult world has given rise to youth culture. Its obvious features revolve around the notion of a generation gap and various peer-group trademarks (such as style of music or the latest electronic gadgets). Teens must make difficult adjustments regarding their lifestyle choices and their sexual identity and expression. As they enter the adult environment, teens experience many exciting activities for the first time, such as learning to drive, selecting high school courses directed toward a career path, joining clubs and activities, volunteering in their community, taking a first job, or taking a trip to a foreign country.

Most American adolescents make a successful transition into young adulthood. Still, some teens are likely to engage in high-risk behaviors, such as substance abuse, eating disorders, indiscriminate sexual activity, pregnancy, abortion, suicide attempts, delinquency, tattooing or cutting, and school failure, with little or no transition into employment. On the other hand, teens who continue to experience a healthy self-concept are likely to finish high school and college, pursue advanced degrees, and continue building a foundation for their adult life.

In this chapter, we examine the influential factors that enhance or detract from an adolescent's self-worth and how—and with whom—an adolescent successfully navigates this challenging stage of life.

DEVELOPMENT OF IDENTITY

Older teenagers spend a good deal of time focusing on the question "Who am I?" Through social interactions with family members, friends, classmates, teammates, teachers, coaches, advisors, and mentors, most adolescents come to a firmer understanding of their abilities and talents. Some want to make their mark in the world using their unique talents. Others decide to follow in a parent's footsteps or enter into a family-owned business. Many decide to enter college or the military, which allows them time to postpone declaring a vocation or career. A smaller number drop out of high school and mainstream society because they are dissatisfied with or unsuccessful in the school system, or because they need to go to work to help support a family (as is the case with many immigrant youth). Unfortunately, those who do not earn a high school degree put themselves at risk for unemployment, teen pregnancy, teen parenting, health problems, criminal activity, and the far-reaching effects of poverty. In 2009, about 9 percent of youth between the ages of 16 and 19 were neither working nor enrolled in school, with males more likely than females to be in this situation (Child Trends Databank, 2010c). However, some dropouts are able to enter the entry-level world of work, which we address later in this chapter. As we shall see, several theories attempt to explain why adolescence seems a pivotal point in an individual's life.

Hall's Portrayal of "Storm and Stress"

The notion that adolescence is a distinct and turbulent developmental period gained momentum in 1904 with the publication of G. Stanley Hall's monumental work *Adolescence.* Hall, one of the major American figures in the development of the field of psychology, depicted adolescence as a stage of **storm and stress,** characterized by inevitable turmoil, maladjustment, tension, rebellion, dependency conflicts, and exaggerated peer-group conformity. This view was subsequently taken up and popularized by Anna Freud (1936) and other psychoanalysts (Blos, 1962). Indeed, Anna Freud (1958) went so far as to assert that "the upholding of a steady equilibrium during the adolescent process is itself abnormal." Viewed from this Western perspective, the adolescent undergoes so many rapid life changes that a restructuring of identity or self-concept is required if these changes are to be properly integrated into the individual's personality.

Further complicating matters, biological and hormonal changes influence the adolescent's sense of emotional and psychological well-being and generate—in some youth—substantial mood swings, irritability, and restlessness (Sisk & Zehr, 2005). Adolescence was originally conceived of as the "troubled waters" one had to pass over when voyaging from the more peaceful world of childhood to the demanding "real world" called adulthood. Aspects of Hall's theory of adolescence have stood the test of time, particularly his focus on adolescent depression, sensation-seeking, and peer relations, as well as how biological development during puberty influences adolescent behavior (Arnett, 2006b). Yet some social scientists reject Hall's notion that adolescence is inevitably stormy (Arnett, 2001).

Sullivan's Interpersonal Theory of Development

One of the first theorists to propose that adolescents go through stages of development was Harry Stack Sullivan (1892–1949). He emphasized the importance of relationships and communication for teenagers in *The Interpersonal Theory of Psychiatry* (Sullivan, 1953). Sullivan's theory—in contrast to Freud's psychosexual stage theory—explains the principal forces in human development as being social instead of biological. His social theory is enlightening when used to examine adolescent development and the impact on individuals of peer groups, friendships, peer pressure, and intimacy. Sullivan states that positive peer relationships during adolescence are essential for healthy development and that negative peer relationships will lead to unhealthy development, such as depression, eating disorders, drug abuse, delinquency, or criminal behavior. We will focus on three periods of Sullivan's theory: preadolescence, early adolescence, and late adolescence.

Preadolescence   Preadolescence (ages 10 through 14 and called the "tween" years by marketing executives) begins with a powerful need for an intimate relationship with a same-sex playmate (Hymowitz, 2003). During this time, personal intimacy involves interpersonal closeness but typically does not involve genital contact. It ends when the adolescent begins to experience a desire for genital sexuality. Sullivan says best friends are likely to have many of the same characteristics (same sex, social status, and age) and share love, loyalty, emotional intimacy, and the opportunity for self-disclosure, but they do not have a sexual relationship and do not experience what Sullivan calls "lust dynamism." By having a best friend, the preadolescent gains insight into how others see the world, which helps reduce most forms of egocentric thought.

Early Adolescence   With the onset of puberty, most adolescents experience genital maturation over about four years. Sullivan (1953) says that the intimate personal relationship that preadolescents had with their same-sex friends is challenged at puberty because of the emerging drive for sexual intimacy. The advent of early adolescence brings three separate needs: a need for sexual satisfaction,

Identity Formation in Adolescent Girls Some recent studies suggest that teenage females develop a poorer self-image and less confidence in themselves and their abilities than they had in late childhood.

Source: For Better or for Worse © 2005 Lynn Johnston Productions. Distributed by University Press Syndicate. Reprinted with permission. All rights reserved.

a continued need for personal intimacy, and a need for personal security (i.e., a need to be seen as socially acceptable by potential sexual partners).

Security issues include positive self-esteem, value as an individual, and an absence of anxiety. For adolescents, the new importance of their genitals as an indicator of their worth is enough to throw them into a state of disequilibrium. Remember what it was like when you became aware that other people perceived you as a sexual being? Or how you felt when you first wanted to kiss someone? If you were to observe young adolescents today in malls or schools, the first thing you would probably notice would be their various attempts to catch someone's eye by teasing, flirting, or performing some act of bravado.

Late Adolescence In Sullivan's theory, the period of late adolescence begins once the individual has established a method of satisfying sexual needs and ends with the establishment of a relationship that is both sexually and personally intimate. Love is the result of fusing intimacy and lust, and love with another person often leads to a stable long-term relationship in adulthood. In late adolescence, the ability to sexually reproduce merges with the capacity for close interpersonal relationships.

Sullivan's theory attempts to explain the details of why adolescents go through stages of development, in contrast to Hall's theory, which painted a much more general picture of adolescence as a tumultuous period. Hall and Sullivan both wanted to explain certain aspects of adolescence in terms of how the young person makes the transition to adulthood. Hall looks at generalities; Sullivan looks at relationships. Neither emphasizes adolescent introspection or young people's psychological task of trying to make sense of the internal and external changes characteristic of adolescence.

Sullivan's Theory and Contemporary Adolescence
Although Sullivan's theory held true for several teen generations, a small percentage of today's teens engage in sexual behaviors at very young ages as a consequence of the highly sexualized nature of teen music, MTV, magazines, movies, pornographic cable television and Web sites, and ad campaigns targeting tweens (and very young children) for "sexy" underwear and clothing (Brown, Halpern, & L'Engle, 2005). For two decades, abstinence and abstinence-plus programs have been delivered to this cohort of vulnerable youth, and some researchers find that making private virginity pledges is associated with delaying the onset of sexual activity by a few years (Bersamin et al., 2005). Critics of abstinence programs say that when these adolescents do become sexually active, many are not protected against STIs (Sullivan, 2005). In 1999, the PBS series *Frontline* broadcast a startling exposé on "The Lost Children of Rockdale County" that described a syphilis outbreak in a white, affluent neighborhood where more than 200 teens (most under 16, some as young as 12) were involved in after-school orgies of group sex, oral sex, and multiple sex partners (Loftus, 2001). More recently, researchers are finding that "oral sex with an opposite-gender partner is an established component of youths' initial sexual experiences, regardless of virginity status" (Brewster & Tillman, 2008). These teens point to their parents' working long hours, being too busy, and being unaware of their damaging behaviors.

Critics of safe-sex education in public schools say that some teens interpret it as adult permission to engage in sexual activity, but proponents point to the necessity for sexually active teens to protect themselves from serious infections, disease, and pregnancy. Let us now turn to Erik Erikson, the psychosocial stage theorist who looks a little more closely at the additional personal challenges that teens struggle with during adolescence.

Erikson: The Crisis of Adolescence

Erik Erikson's (1902–1994) work has focused attention on the struggle of adolescents to develop and clarify their identity. His view of adolescence is consistent with a long tradition that portrays it as a difficult period. As described in Chapter 2, Erikson divides the developmental life span into nine psychosocial stages. Each stage poses a significant challenge during development that requires the individual to move in either a positive or a negative direction. Erikson's fifth stage covers the period of adolescence and consists of the search for **identity.** He suggests that an optimal feeling of identity is experienced as a sense of well-being: "Its most obvious concomitants are a feeling of being at home in one's body, a sense of 'knowing where one is going,' and an inner assuredness of anticipated recognition from those who count" (Erikson, 1968a).

Erikson observes that adolescents, like trapeze artists, must release their safe hold on childhood and reach in midair for a firm grasp on adulthood. Some have a "safety net" if they falter, but others do not. The search for identity becomes particularly acute because the adolescent is undergoing rapid physical change while confronting many imminent adult tasks and decisions (Makros & McCabe, 2001).

The older adolescent must often make an occupational choice: continue formal schooling, apply for an apprenticeship for various jobs, seek employment, enter the military, or simply drop out. Other environmental aspects of adolescence provide testing grounds for a concept of self: broadening peer relationships, sexual contacts and roles, moral and ideological commitments, moving out of a parental home and into one's own, and emancipation from adult authority. Recent research has begun to use Erikson's concept of identity crisis to understand how gay, lesbian, and bisexual teens develop a self-identity and how ethnic identity develops in adolescence (Potoczniak, Aldea, & DeBlaere, 2007).

Role Identification   Adolescents must synthesize a variety of new roles to come to terms with themselves and their environment. Erikson believed that because adolescent identities are tentative, adolescents often feel lost. This ambiguity and lack of stable anchorage can lead many adolescents to overcommit themselves to cliques or gangs, allegiances, loves, and social causes. To keep themselves together, they temporarily overidentify with the heroes of cliques and crowds, and some apparently lose their sense of individuality completely. Teens Dylan Klebold and Eric Harris are notorious for killing 13 people and wounding 20, before killing themselves, at Columbine High School in 1999. They wore swastikas, admired the Nazis, and were self-proclaimed "rebels" who identified with the hitmen in *Pulp Fiction* and the computer hacker in *The Matrix.* Seung-Hui Cho, a loner who also wrote stories of violence and killing, admired the Columbine killers; in 2007 he massacred 32 people at Virginia Tech.

Adolescent love can be an attempt to find one's identity by projecting a diffused self-image on another and seeing it reflected back and gradually clarified. This is why young love is so often marked by conversation. Today such "conversation" can be by cell phone, text messaging, or hours in online chat rooms. Clarification can also be sought by destructive means. Young people can become clannish, intolerant, and cruel in their exclusion of others who are different in skin color, cultural background, looks or abilities, tastes and talents, and often entirely petty aspects of dress and gesture arbitrarily selected as the signs of being "in" or "out." (As teens, the Columbine and Virginia Tech mass murderers were considered "outcasts" and "misfits" by some of their peers.)

According to Erikson, this clannishness explains the appeal that various extremist and totalitarian movements have for some adolescents; in other words, you do not see many 75-year-old "skinheads." In Erikson's view, every adolescent confronts a major danger: that he or she will fail to arrive at a consistent, coherent, and integrated identity. Consequently, adolescents may experience *identity diffusion*—a lack of ability to commit oneself, even in late adolescence, to an occupational or ideological position and to assume a recognizable station in life. Another danger is that adolescents may fashion a **negative identity**—a debased self-image and social role. Still another course taken by some adolescents is formation of a **deviant identity**—a lifestyle at odds with, or at least not supported by, the values and expectations of society.

Other researchers have followed Erikson's lead. James E. Marcia (1991, 2007) examines the development and validation of ego identity status in terms of achievement, moratorium, foreclosure, and diffusion. Marcia interviewed college students to learn their feelings about future occupations, their religious ideology, and their worldview. From these interviews Marcia found that students could be classified according to four types of identity formation:

1. **Identity diffusion.** A state in which the individual has few, if any, commitments to anyone or to any set of beliefs. There is no core to the person that one can point to and state, "This person stands for X, Y, or Z." Those who are identity diffused do not seem to know what they want to do in life or who they want to be. *Example: Henri joins one cause this week and another next week. He is a strict vegetarian this month and an avid carnivore next month. He cannot tell you why he believes what he does except in very vague terms, such as "Because that's the way I am."*
2. **Identity foreclosure.** The avoidance of autonomous choice. Foreclosure is premature identity formation.

The adolescent accepts someone else's (such as parents') values and goals without exploring alternative roles. *Example: Carmen wants to be a doctor and has wanted to be a doctor since her parents suggested it at age 7. Now, at 18, she does not think twice about the idea because she has internalized her parents' expectations.*

3. **Identity moratorium.** A period of delay, during which adolescents can experiment with or try on various roles, ideologies, and commitments. It is a stage between childhood and adulthood when the individual can explore various dimensions of life without having to choose any yet. Adolescents might start or stop, abandon or postpone, implement or transform given courses of action. *Example: André joined the Peace Corps because he didn't quite know what he wanted to do after college and he thought this would give him a chance to "find himself."*

4. **Identity achievement.** A period when the individual achieves inner stability that corresponds to what others perceive that person to be. *Example: Everyone agrees that when Jamella walks into the room she will handle the situation in a professional manner and refuse to divulge confidential information afterward. In fact, this is exactly what happens. Everyone knows that Jamella is trustworthy, and she sees herself in the same light.*

David Elkind (1998, 2001), in *All Dressed Up and No Place to Go* and *The Hurried Child*, warns that American culture has accelerated the pressures on adolescents to have higher school achievement, to take more rigorous courses, to become healthy and fit, to be the best in sports and other activities, to be attractive and to fit in, to better prepare for the jobs of the twenty-first century, and so on. Elkind argues that because of these pressures to become more adultlike, identity formation can no longer be put off until late adolescence.

Questions

In what respects do Hall, Sullivan, Erikson, and Elkind view the developmental tasks of adolescence similarly? In what ways do these theorists differ in their views of adolescent identity formation?

Cultural Aspects of Identity Formation

Social scientists suggest that the transition to adulthood is more difficult in Western nations, although globalization, increasing industrialization, and worldwide emigration/immigration shifts are complicating the transition to adulthood in many cultures (Larson & Wilson, 2004). Adolescents often receive contradictory messages. They are expected to stop being children, yet they are not expected to be men and women; they are told to "grow up," yet they are still treated as dependents; they are financially supported by their parents, yet they are frequently viewed by society as untrustworthy and irresponsible. In critical social essays in *Liberation's Children*, Hymowitz (2003) observes that many of today's U.S. adolescent cohort have been raised by adults who expect to have successful children, lavish them with name-brand clothing, put the latest electronic gadgets and TVs in every room, and reward every endeavor. But such teens flounder in loneliness when parents working long hours find it easier to be nonjudgmental "friends." In our sexualized and materialistic culture, many teens are floundering in a "sea" of moral confusion and impoverished identity (Brown, Halpern, & L'Engle, 2005). In their efforts to make meaningful life decisions, their response to nearly any question will be "Whatever." Yet so many adults ask, "What's wrong with today's kids? They just don't seem to have any values." Is it any wonder, then, that these conflicting cultural messages and adult expectations generate an identity crisis among U.S. and European youth?

In contrast, many non-Western societies provide rites of passage, or **puberty rites**—initiation ceremonies that symbolize a clearer transition from childhood to adulthood (Arnett, 2001; Spencer, 2006). Rites of passage occur across cultures, have existed throughout history, are often collective (involving several young people of the same age), and include specific rituals: seclusion from society, instruction from elders, tests of strength or endurance, a transition ceremony, and a return to society with recognition of adult status (Kottak, 2008). Ceremonies include physical and spiritual cleansing, prayers and blessings, traditional clothing, traditional foods or fasting, and traditional music. Puberty rituals bestow feelings of solidarity and togetherness and mark a psychological break with childhood. In some cultures, young boys no longer live with their mothers once they have undergone their rite of passage (Ferraro, 2006). It is not simply the rite but the extensive time spent with elders that helps many adolescents make a healthier transition to adult status (Kottak, 2008).

Western societies provide less obvious rites of passage. Examples include going through the Jewish *bar* or *bat mitzvah* or the Christian confirmation, securing a driver's license at age 16 or 17, voting at age 18, graduating from high school or college, entering a seminary or doing a year of missionary service, joining the military and undergoing boot camp training, and undergoing fraternity or sorority hazing (Kottak, 2008). In Latin American countries and now in many Hispanic American families, a 15-year-old girl celebrates the *quinceañera* to mark her transition from girl to woman (the rite starts with Mass, which is followed by an elaborate ritualized celebration and a lavish meal with parents, godparents, guests, and 14 special couples). Although some American girls have

Sweet 16 parties, for most American youth the demarcation between childhood and adulthood is less clearly defined, and self-initiation is more common. It may include cigarette smoking, alcohol consumption, or sexual activity—changes that generally occur among peers without an adult presence. Thompson and Barker (2008) say that American boys are looking for some type of masculinity "test," with guides and companions, that requires commitment and courage. They also note that boys without fathers or strong male role models are often drawn to gang membership, and gang members typically mark rites of passage with deviant behaviors and criminal activities.

Teens with a strong ethnic heritage must decide how they will present themselves to their peers and the larger society in terms of their ethnicity (Spencer, 2006). A multicultural identity is especially difficult for teens, because these are the years when membership in a peer group is so important to identity formation. Parents often intensify their efforts to impart racial-ethnic identity and cultural heritage to their adolescents (Phinney & Ong, 2007). They may relate their racial-ethnic group's history of discrimination and alert their children to barriers they may face in mainstream society. This process, known as *ethnic-racial socialization,* usually combines a sense of racial-ethnic pride and a high valuation of the achievements and strengths of the family's heritage group. Multicultural teens find socialization easier when they attend diverse high schools that offer a variety of racial-ethnic identities and that offer them opportunities to be part of a peer group that shares many experiences and challenges. This enables them to negotiate an identity, including an ethnic identity, in the context of a peer group that is familiar with their cultural issues without worrying that they will be rejected because they are different from their peer group (French et al., 2006).

When multicultural persons feel others are evaluating their heritage culture positively, they are more likely to feel accepted. One study found that **collective self-esteem,** or how individuals evaluate their social group and how they feel their social group is evaluated by the public, is a key factor in shaping how an individual balances racial-ethnic identity with an identity in the mainstream culture. People who experience high collective self-esteem are more likely to feel accepted in a variety of contexts and are more likely to share intimate details of their lives with friends and coworkers who are not members of their heritage culture.

Conversely, individuals who experience low collective self-esteem, who feel that their heritage group is not accepted in mainstream society, sometimes adopt a chameleonlike strategy. With their heritage group, they present themselves as members of that racial-ethnic group; with members of mainstream society, they compartmentalize their racial-ethnic identity, present themselves as members of the mainstream group, and avoid talking about their heritage. Researchers have found that

Quinceañera: A Rite of Passage to Womanhood for 15-year-old Latino Girls Teens whose families have strong ethnic identities face a complex set of decisions about the role ethnicity will play in their identity. An emotional part of the *quinceañera* ritual is for the father to change his daughter's shoes from flats to high heels.

multicultural individuals who adopt the chameleon strategy have less intimate relationships with others when they feel their heritage culture is being devalued, which in turn undermines their ability to function in daily interactions (Downie et al., 2006).

Research further shows that a positive ethnic identity fosters academic achievement. Students whose parents have socialized them about their racial-ethnic heritage have higher grades than multicultural students who know nothing about their heritage. However, racial-ethnic socialization is a delicate task. It is important that knowledge of a history of discrimination be coupled with strategies for coping with bias and a clear emphasis on cultural pride and heritage. Finding the right balance for each of their children is the challenge facing parents (Hughes et al., 2006b).

Adolescence: Not Necessarily Stormy or Stressful?

Psychologist Albert Bandura (1986, 1997) stresses that the stereotyped storm-and-stress portrait of adolescence most closely fits the behavior of "the deviant 10 percent of the adolescent population that appears repeatedly in psychiatric clinics, juvenile probation departments, and . . . the newspaper headlines." Bandura argues that the "stormy-decade myth" is due more to cultural expectations and the representations of teenagers in movies, literature, and other media than to actual fact. Bandura's theory holds if certain elements are in place in relations between parents and children. One study followed a group of ethnically diverse young people from working-class and middle-class families from childhood to preadolescence to determine the relationship between parenting style and social adjustment, which the researchers defined as the ability of the young person to regulate his or her emotions. They found that parents who used a warm and positive parenting style were more likely to raise children who were less likely to be angry and aggressive. This finding was strong regardless of the economic status of the family. The researchers looked at the style of parenting of children at age 7 and were able to accurately predict which children would be well adjusted as they entered adolescence (Eisenberg et al., 2005).

Young people who enter high school with high aspirations and positive self-concepts are likely to retain these advantages at least five years beyond high school (Turbin et al., 2006). Hence, students in graduate and professional schools typically have high self-esteem that mirrors the positive self-images they possessed five years earlier. Similarly, the poor self-images of dropouts are already established before these adolescents withdraw from school. Such individual differences are quite stable across time (Turbin et al., 2006).

However, the adolescent years can be a bumpy time. In the period 1999 to 2005, about one-quarter of the teens in grades 9 through 12 reported that they had felt sad or hopeless for at least two weeks in the previous year. Changes in social environment and family structure, including parental military deployment or forced transfers, parental separation or divorce or loss, school changes, a new home environment, and demands to achieve in school and other activities—all can cause depression and lowered self-esteem (Van Voorhees et al., 2008). **Depression** is an emotional state usually characterized by prolonged feelings of gloom, despair, and futility, profound pessimism, and a tendency toward excessive guilt and self-reproach. Other symptoms of depression include fatigue, insomnia, poor concentration, irritability, anxiety, reduced sexual interest, boredom, and overall loss of interest. At times, depression appears in the guise of other disorders, such as vague pains, headaches, or recurrent nausea (Van Voorhees et al., 2008). Girls are more likely than boys to experience depression, socioeconomic status also plays a role, and the rate of depression is higher for nonwhite youth of both genders (Van Voorhees et al., 2008).

Adolescents and Self-Esteem   Self-esteem can change in a variety of ways during adolescence. Over half of students in grades 6 through 8 maintain high levels of

Girls and Self-Esteem Carol Gilligan and others feel that girls develop their identities within a collectivist model. That is, they develop positive self-esteem and strong interpersonal skills from their relationships and interactions with their peer group.

self-esteem or show an increase. But the remaining students experience a steep decline or chronically low self-esteem (Arnett, 2001). Researcher Susan Harter (1999) finds that the self-image of adolescents hinges on degree of success in eight domains: academic competence, acceptance by peers, skill in athletics, physical appearance, success in holding a part-time job, romantic appeal, behavioral conduct, and the presence of at least one close friend.

Identity Formation in Adolescent Girls   The American Association of University Women (AAUW), which examined self-esteem and academic achievement and outcomes in adolescent girls for many years, published its original findings in its 1992 report *How Schools Shortchange Girls*. Carol Gilligan, who assisted with this study, states that girls in elementary school generally are confident and assertive and feel positive about themselves. But by junior high school and high school, most have a poorer self-image, lower expectations, and less confidence about their abilities (Brown & Gilligan, 1992). When Gilligan wrote in the early 1990s, few girls were enrolling in rigorous high school math, science, or computer science courses, which are factors related to college acceptance, scholarship, and employment opportunities in a technologically driven society.

Since the publication of the AAUW report that was a catalyst for change (Taylor, Gilligan, & Sullivan, 1999), females have made tremendous gains and are closing the gender gap. By 2004 more female high school graduates than males completed advanced science and math courses. By 2005 more females than males were graduating from high school and going to college. By 2007–2008, more women than men were earning associate's, bachelor's, master's, doctoral, and some professional degrees. However, far fewer female degree recipients are majoring in computer science, engineering, math/statistics, and physical sciences (Snyder & Dillow, 2010).

Critics of Gilligan's studies contend that from grade school through college, girls earn higher grades, higher class ranking, and more honors than boys (except in science and sports) and that boys experience more behavioral and academic difficulties (Thompson & Barker, 2008). Yet if girls are performing better academically than boys, why do we see a decrease in self-esteem and an increase in depression when they are doing well in school? The answer hinges on societal attitudes toward women, less access to strong female role models, the life choices that a young woman perceives as available to her, and her family's economic resources to help her transition into adulthood.

One clue lies at home. High self-esteem in adolescence has been positively linked with opportunities for teens to make their own decisions (Gutman & Eccles, 2007). Many parents, however, treat their teen sons and daughters differently: Sons are given more autonomy than daughters, perhaps because of fear that a daughter might get pregnant (Denmark, Rabinowitz, & Sechzer, 2005). Low self-esteem may also come from a teenage girl's beliefs about her physical attractiveness, a concern that emerges by middle school as one of the key factors in how children choose members of their peer group (Pedersen et al., 2007). Girls who feel their bodies don't measure up to mainstream society's standard of female beauty are likely to experience depression in their teen years (Arnett, 2001).

Gilligan contends that girls are more likely than boys to develop a *collectivist* or *connected* model for the self and are likely to feel good about themselves from being sensitive to, connected to, and interdependent on others. Adolescent girls who attend large junior high or high schools can lose the connectedness that promotes meaningful relationships. In contrast, boys are likely to feel more positive about themselves by being independent, separate, and competitive (Thompson & Barker, 2008).

In brief, Gilligan finds that adolescent girls begin to doubt the authority of their own inner voices and feelings and their commitment to meaningful relationships. As 11-year-olds they assert themselves and still speak their minds, yet in adolescence they come to fear rejection and anger, so they mute their voices and repress their autonomy. Western culture, Gilligan says, calls on young women to accept the image of the "perfect" or "nice" girl—one who avoids being mean and bossy and instead projects an air of calmness, quietude, and cooperation. Schools contribute to the problem by educating primarily for individuality, competition, and autonomy, while neglecting the pursuit of rewarding relationships.

More recently, Gilligan has turned her attention to developing programs that encourage young women to write authentic and meaningful scripts for their own lives. A symposium of experts that discussed the 2001 AAUW report *Beyond the Gender Wars* urged that educators address the needs of all youth by making schools safe and improving instruction using character education, multiple learning styles, active learning, and collaborative approaches (Taylor, 2001).

Clinical psychologist Mary Pipher (1994), author of the exposé *Reviving Ophelia: Saving the Selves of Adolescent Girls,* based her research on 20 years of counseling adolescent girls. Her work not only supports Gilligan's theories but also warns that American culture (schools, media, the advertising industry) is destroying the identity and self-esteem of many adolescent girls. She provides recommendations for healthier identity formation, since too many young adolescent girls model their appearance and behavior after famous, wealthy, child-behaving female celebrities, many of whom appear to be vacuous sex symbols, have substance abuse issues, and violate the law.

Identity Formation in Adolescent Boys Michael Gurian, a therapist and educational consultant, has devoted a great deal of study to the identity development of boys. Gurian and Stevens's 2005 book *The Minds of Boys: Saving Our Sons from Falling Behind in School and Life* describes what boys need to become strong, responsible, sensitive men. His theory about male identity development is centered on the fact that brain and hormone differences basically regulate the way in which males and females operate. Two decades of research on the brains of females and males confirm the structural and behavioral differences that Gurian discusses (Coch, Fischer, & Dawson, 2007).

Gurian states that when a boy reaches puberty, the influence of testosterone on both brain and body increases. A male's body will experience five to seven surges of testosterone a day (Gurian & Stevens, 2005). A male has more dopamine in his brain that can increase impulsive behaviors. A boy will frequently bump into things, be moody and aggressive, require a great deal of sleep, lose his temper, have a massive sexual fantasy life, and masturbate often (Halpern et al., 2000). Between tasks, the male brain needs to renew, recharge, and reorient itself. Thus, boys have difficulty attending to lecture-style teaching; they learn by imitation and practice. Boys frequently get more low grades, are more likely to have learning disabilities, are more likely to be diagnosed with attention and behavioral disorders, and are less likely to earn a high school or college degree (Gurian & Stevens, 2005).

In Gurian's view, boys need a primary and extended family, relationships with fathers or mentors (relatives, tutors, coaches, neighbors, friends, members of faith communities and service agencies), and intense support from school and community. Without healthy adult models

Boys and Mentors Teen boys can benefit from a healthy mentoring relationship that provides an opportunity to develop communication-relational skills, to learn about careers and hobbies, and to discuss issues they do not feel they can discuss with parents.

and support, adolescent boys are prey to gang and criminal activities or sexual misconduct. This is confirmed by the high rate at which young males commit crimes (teen and young adult males commit most violent crime) and also by how many are incarcerated or killed. Gurian states that "boys are acting out against society and parents because neither is providing them with enough modeling, opportunity, and wisdom to act comfortably within society" (Gurian, 1996, p. 54).

Gurian's theory is supported by a study of teen boys and adult male mentors in a community-based organization. The boys and their mentors reported a great deal of emotional closeness in their relationship. But these relationships were focused on doing activities together. Sometimes it took six months for boys to trust their mentors enough to discuss important emotional issues. In the course of joint activities, the boys opened up and discussed issues they couldn't discuss with women. When they did open up, the boys learned valuable skills, such as managing anger and learning how and when to ask for help. In short, a good father or male mentor can help an adolescent boy learn valuable life

skills in the realms of managing emotions and relationships (Spencer, 2007).

Using Social Resources to Weather Adolescence
Research on adolescence reveals that despite the challenges of these years, teens remain resilient. Many available social resources encourage and support positive development. These include participating in sports and other after-school activities, belonging to community organizations, belonging to a supportive church or faith community, having positive adult role models, having friends who model responsible behavior, having parents and teachers who encourage a young person to aim high and do well, living in a safe neighborhood and feeling safe at school, and living in a community that values and supports young people (Benson et al., 2006). For example, the Boy Scouts developed a *Venturing* program for boys and girls aged 14 and older, based on responsible mentoring in settings of adventure, that meets Gurian's criteria. Given these resources, researchers conclude that "all youth have the inherent capacity for positive growth and development" (Gurian, 1996, p. 896).

Unfortunately, not all young people have access to such resources. What of the adolescents living in the inner city in unsafe neighborhoods, where housing is inadequate and unhealthy, where jobs are scarce or nonexistent, and where the adult generation lives in such dire poverty as to have more in common with residents of nonindustrialized nations than with the rest of American society? These teens, marginalized from mainstream society, strive to complete the emotional and developmental tasks of adolescence in dangerous and unhealthy environments. Indeed, research shows that these teens are at much higher risk for depression, anxiety, post-traumatic stress disorder, and thoughts of suicide (Fitzpatrick et al., 2005). One study concluded that the best approach is to take the view that "all soil can be enriched . . . to nourish all flowers." In other words, fix the environment so young people can grow up healthy rather than trying to fix the young people themselves (Lorion & Sokoloff, 2003).

Yet some young people in this situation show great strength and resilience. If *any* of the social resources listed above are available to them, they use them for the maximum benefit. Researchers have found that a key resource for African American youth is the extended family. When parents, grandparents, aunts, and uncles are available and supportive, and the family shares meals together, teens are less likely to experience symptoms of depression. A close family life where the young person can discuss daily problems helps to insulate him or her against the harsh and unhealthy environment of the inner city. Having strong and positive connections to school also helps African American teens develop resiliency. However, these findings were stronger for girls than they were for boys (Fitzpatrick et al., 2005).

Questions

How does culture affect a teen's developing identity? What are some factors that enhance or detract from adolescent female and adolescent male identity development?

PEERS AND FAMILY

Historically, we have had an image of adolescence as a time when the world of peers and the world of parents are in continual conflict with each other. However, we derive a quite different picture from psychological and sociological research. Western industrial societies not only have prolonged the period between childhood and adulthood but also have tended to segregate young people. The notion of a **generation gap** has been widely popularized since the 1970s, implying misunderstanding, antagonism, and separation between youth and adults. The organization of schools into grades on the basis of age means that students of the same age spend a considerable amount of time together—and influence each other greatly. In both academic and extracurricular activities, schools form little worlds of their own. Middle-aged and older adults also tend to create a kind of psychological segregation through the stereotypes they hold of adolescents. They frequently define adolescence as a unique period in life, one that is somehow set apart from—even at odds with—the integrated web of human activity. Let's examine these matters more carefully.

Certainly there are exceptions to the generations experiencing constant conflict with one another. In 2011, about 2 million U.S. students were being homeschooled (Slatter, 2011). Many parents who homeschool their children want to maintain a close and influential relationship with their children, and they often provide moral as well as academic instruction. National reports reveal that many homeschooled students are earning higher grades on standardized tests than students from private or public schools. Such youth are winning the National Spelling Bee and the National Geography Bee and are earning more Presidential and National Merit Scholarship awards to attend college (HSLDA, 2009). Contrary to concerns that these children are social isolates, homeschoolers and their families are more involved in society (see Figure 12.1). They network and share information via the Internet, often graduate from high school two years early, earn higher SAT scores, and start college early. Parents who homeschool say their children are well-adjusted, well-rounded, and less affected by negative peer influences (Gathercole, 2007).

The Adolescent Peer Group

To the extent that young people are physically and psychologically segregated, they are encouraged to develop

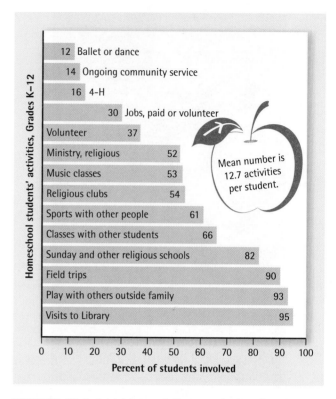

FIGURE 12.1 Activities and Community Involvement of Homeschoolers Students might be involved in more than one activity so the total for the list of activities is greater than 100 percent.

Source: Ray, Brian D. (2001). *Home Education in Ohio: Family characteristics, academic achievement, social and civic activities, and college admissions officers' thoughts.* Table 13. Social activities of those children and youth ever home educated and age 6 and older. Salem, OR: National Home Education Research Institute, www.nheri.org.

their own unique lifestyles (Brown & Huang, 1995). Some sociologists say that Western societies prolong the transition to adulthood by segregating their youth, giving rise to a **youth culture**—a large body of young people with standardized ways of thinking, feeling, and behaving. The first youth culture, the Baby Boomers, arrived after World War II (they were born between 1946 and 1964). Many teens had free time, extra money, and unstructured energy. Football teams, cheerleaders, Elvis, rock 'n' roll and jukeboxes, and television appeared (Zoba, 1999). Generation X (born between 1965 and 1980) is more ethnically diverse and better educated than the boomer generation and has dominated the college culture and work environment for the past 25 years. It is often called the "me" generation—one that is independent and self-sufficient, is technically adept, and attempts to balance work with daily living.

The Millennials make up the group born between the early 1980s and 2010. This is the largest cohort in American history: It numbers 78 to 80 million and is expected to grow even larger with child immigration. Strauss and Howe, authors of *Millennials Rising,* and others (Lovern, 2001; Taylor & Keeter, 2010) describe the following characteristics of the Millennial generation:

- They show signs of altruistic values, such as optimism, fairness, morality, renewed spiritual awareness, and appreciating diversity (many are from recent immigrant families).
- They exhibit a greater sense of social responsibility about community, politics, and service to others (as students, they have learned the value of teamwork and volunteerism).
- They advocate strongly for improving the environment, poverty issues, and global concerns.
- They demonstrate ambition, drive, and a strong work ethic (in school and at work).
- They back away from unprotected sex and teen pregnancies and embrace more conservative marriage and family values.
- They take more time for themselves and want less structured lives than during their earlier heavily scheduled childhoods.

Additionally, Taylor and Keeter (2010) report that Millennials are more ethnically and racially diverse than older adults (see Chapter 11) and are likely to become the best-educated generation in American history. Even so, some studies point out that Millennials may be less prepared for academic work than previous generations and less able to integrate their skill with technology into the work world (Charsky et al., 2009; Stewart, 2009).

The most obvious features of youth culture revolve around various peer-group trademarks: preferred music and dance styles; celebrity and sports idols; body art (tattooing and piercing); fashionable clothes and hairstyles; and distinctive jargon and slang. These features separate teenagers from adults and identify adolescents who share related feelings. Such trademarks facilitate a **consciousness of oneness**—a sympathetic identification in which group members come to feel that their inner experiences and emotional reactions are similar. Adolescents also feel they lack control over many of the changes occurring in their lives. One way they take back control is by assuming the distinctive trademarks of the peer group. They cannot control whether they get acne, but they do have control over what music they listen to, what clothes they wear and how they adorn their bodies, and how they wear their hair.

Among the central ingredients in a youth culture are various ideas about the qualities and achievements that reveal an individual's masculinity or femininity. Traditionally, for boys the critical signs of manhood are physical mastery, athletic skill, sexual prowess, risk taking, courage in the face of aggression, and willingness to defend one's honor at all costs. For girls, the most admired qualities are physical attractiveness (including popular clothing), proper behavior and obedience to rules, the ability to delicately manipulate various interpersonal rela-

tionships, and skill in exercising control over sexual encounters (Pipher, 1994). Some scholars believe that the concept of youth culture overshadows individuality in adolescence, since most are motivated to join a peer group over time in order not to feel isolated (Ryan, 2001).

The Developmental Role and Course of Peer Groups

Conformity to peer groups plays a prominent role in the lives of many teenagers, and *peer pressure* is an important mechanism for transmitting group norms and maintaining loyalties among group members. Although peers serve as major socialization agents in adolescence, peer pressure varies in strength and direction across grades. Clique membership seems to take on a growing significance for many sixth-, seventh-, and eighth-graders, but then group membership drops off during high school as the individual aspects of social relationships take on greater importance (de Bruyn & Cillessen, 2008).

Furthermore, studies of peer pressure have tended to focus on pressure to engage in deviant behavior, and perhaps their findings are not valid for teens in other situations. A study of over 3,600 ethnically diverse males and females from age 14 to age 18 found that, contrary to previous findings, peer pressure steadily increased over this age group and then declined after age 18. The researchers concluded that although teens begin to develop autonomy from parents at around age 14, they need the next four years to consolidate their own beliefs and learn to stand up to the influence of their peers. During that time they depend on their peers for a social life and are not ready to challenge their friends.

This study challenges typical understandings of the direction of resistance to peer pressure among adolescents. Interestingly, the researchers found that girls are more likely than boys to stand up to peers and that teenage girls are more autonomous than boys. The researchers wrote, "perhaps it is time the field abandoned the stereotype of the soft-spined female popularized in depictions of young women written in the 1960s" (Steinberg & Monahan, 2007, p. 1540). In addition, African American teens reported greater resistance to the influence of their peers than did teens from other ethnic groups.

However, our search for similarities among young people should not lead us to overlook the individual differences that also exist among them (Closson, 2009). Many of these differences arise from differences in socioeconomic and racial-ethnic backgrounds (McLoyd et al., 2009). Every high school typically has several "crowds"—cliques that are often mutually exclusive. Moreover, a "cycle of popularity" seems to bring some teenagers together within relatively stable cliques (for instance, cheerleaders and athletes). In due course, many "outsiders" come to resent and dislike their "popular" counterparts, whom they define as "stuck up." Even so, leading-crowd members tend to exhibit higher self-esteem and self-confidence than "outsiders" do. Level of self-esteem has been found to have an effect on susceptibility to peer pressure, on grades, and on use of alcohol (Crocker & Park, 2004).

The Expanding Role of Teen Social Networking Sites   Today's teens are constantly immersed in a ubiquitous techno-social world. The explosive popularity of online social networking sites, such as *Facebook*, *MySpace*, and *Twitter*, provides opportunities to strengthen existing friendships, make new friends, or flirt with total strangers, who may be questionable at best. Such social networking sites include a blog, pictures, songs, videos, and messages. Think of these sites as "virtual" town malls where teens gather 24 hours a day with little or no adult presence. *MySpace* is open to anyone, and users can create whatever type of profile they want. *Facebook* originally reflected real-world communities, such as colleges; it has become more open but still requires users to register using their real names (Lenhart et al., 2007). A 2006 national study finds that more than half of all teens (thus millions of them) use social networks and have created online profiles, revealing private information and photos in a public setting. Through creating such sites, teens are developing their personal identities (and often alternative identities), literacy skills, and computer literacy skills—considered to be job tools of the twenty-first century (Willard, 2007). Using mobile devices, about 20 percent of teens are staying connected constantly to social networking sites nearly all the time. Medical researchers call this "hyper-socializing" and "hyper-texting," and an initial study finds that teens who engage in these activities without parental supervision have higher rates of various health risk behaviors (Frank, Dahler, Santurri, & Knight, 2010).

Most teens say they limit access to their personal profiles; but because they post very personal information, parents, school officials, and government leaders are concerned about their potential vulnerability to victimization by online predators. (Advertisers also have access to users' personal information.) Some teens post sexual photos; harmful or nasty rumors and lies; or violent or intimidating threatening content (a possible criminal violation). Offensive or threatening content about others is referred to as "cyberbullying" or "cyberthreats"—and about one-third of teens have experienced this, ranging from benign to criminal. Cyberbullying involves repeated and willful attacks on victims through the use of text messages, e-mail, cell phones, chat rooms, and Internet sites (Dilmaç & Aydoğan, 2010; Mishna, Cook, Gadalla, Daciuk, & Solomon, 2010). Traditional bullying differs from cyberbullying (Dilmaç, 2009). Traditional bullies are known by others in school, whereas cyberbullies are usually anonymous. Victims of traditional bullying are often children who are "considered overweight,

Being Social Made Easy Technology has significantly changed how teens shape their identity. Cell phones with video, other mobile devices such as iPads, and Internet networking features such as *Twitter*, *MySpace*, *Facebook,* and *Skype* are resources teens now use to explore and express their evolving identities and to connect with friends and others. Excessive use is called "hyper-networking" or "hyper-socializing."

physically weak, disabled, or unpopular," but all students are potential victims of cyberbullying, which can happen at any time. The intention of cyberbullying is to harass, to inflict pain, or to humiliate unsuspecting victims.

Cyber-bullying messages or images can be spread instantly to a wider audience by downloading to mobile devices for text messaging and may remain permanent, thus making the damage even more devastating to victims (Dilmaç, 2009). (See the *Further Developments* box, "Text Messaging and Teens: whr R U now?") In 2006 a 13-year-old girl committed suicide because of a cruel cybercrime committed by the parents of a peer. In 2008 *MySpace* agreed to take steps to protect youth from online sexual predators and bullies, including searching for ways to verify users' ages. While networking sites attempt to improve privacy regulations of cyberspace, adolescents must learn to engage in responsible online behavior—or suffer the consequences. "The 'MySpace Generation' is both concerned about privacy and yet readily discloses personal information" (Livingstone, 2008). In a striking paradox, they are setting up an identity in such sites to be visible to hundreds of friends *and* strangers, while at the same time they do not want

FURTHER DEVELOPMENTS

Text Messaging and Teens: whr R U now?

A recent article in the *Wall Street Journal* reports that 13- to 17-year-olds send and receive about 3,000 texts a month—roughly 100 per day (see Figure 12.2). Yet this convenient though cryptic form of staying in touch comes with opportunities for misunderstanding (Rosman, 2010). The tendency among teens is not necessarily to write elaborate or even in-depth communiqués, as a survey of college students reveals. Asked to comment on their attitudes toward phone calls and text-messaging, they confided that their main goal was "to pass along information in as little time, with as little small talk, as possible" (Rosman, 2010). Instead of planning things in advance, those who text resort to what Rich Ling, "a professor at IT University in Copenhagen who studies teens and technology, has named 'micro-coordination'—'I'll txt u in 10 mins when I know wh/ restrnt'" (Rosman, 2010). Although "texting saves us time, it steals from quiet reflection" (Rosman, 2010).

Today's youth are history's first "always connected" generation, with more than 8 out of 10 acknowledging that they sleep with their cell phone near the bed, "poised to disgorge texts, phone calls, emails, songs, news, videos and wake-up jingles" (Taylor & Keeter, 2010). Quiet reflection is an antidote as well as a necessary foundation to build upon for deeper understanding, which works to counteract the "always on" frenetic impulses of those whose days may be filled with technological multitasking.

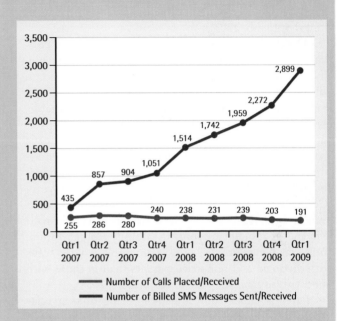

FIGURE 12.2 Teens Text at Incredible Rates This graph shows the average number of texts and phone calls each quarter between 2007 and 2009 for U.S. teens aged 13–17. Note the changes between 2007 and 2009.
Note: SMS stands for Short Message Service.
Source: The Nielson Company. (2009, June). How teens use media: A Nielsen report on the myths and realities of teen media trends. Retrieved from http://blog.nielsen.com/nielsenwire/reports/nielsen_howteensusemedia_june09.pdf

parents to view content. In one study (Livingstone, 2008), Jason says,

> You don't mind [other] people reading it, but it's your parents, you don't really want your parents seeing it, because I don't really like my parents sort of looking through my room and stuff, because that's like my private space. (p. 11)

Maintaining a social network site can be very time-consuming as well as socially isolating, and it can significantly reduce time spent studying or participating in other activities (Livingstone, 2008). Also, some college admissions counselors and employers now search an applicant's digital scrapbook for youthful indiscretions. School districts, parents, and the criminal justice system must develop comprehensive, effective policies for acceptable Internet use (Smith, White, & Moracco, 2009). Parental

subscriptions to *SafetyWeb* and *SocialShield* send alerts about their children's online "discussions that relate to drugs, sex, violence, alcohol or suicide" (Kessler, 2010).

Questions

In what ways are various peer groups important for identity development in adolescence? What cliques do you recall from your school years? How do you think social networking sites help teens to develop an identity and "fit in" (or not)?

Adolescents and Their Families

The parent-child relationship changes at puberty. The amount of time spent with parents, the sense of emotional closeness, and the degree to which teens yield to parents in decision making all decline from early adolescence to late adolescence. In intact families, the parent who is the same gender as the teen typically has a greater influence on teen socialization (Wang, Pomerantz, & Chen, 2007). Other studies have found that mothers continue to engage in more frequent interactions with teens and play a greater role in their adolescents' peer relationships. Fathers typically continue to be involved with teens' scholastic achievement and extracurricular performances (Lewis & Lamb, 2003).

The quality of the parents' marital relationship continues to be associated with the parent-child relationship. Those who are warm and accepting tend to have children who are more socially competent (Updegraff et al., 2004). But hostile sibling relationships and coercive, irritable, inconsistent, or absent parenting (stepparenting or foster parenting) during childhood and early adolescence have a strong influence on transforming what is merely noncompliance in earlier childhood into antisocial behaviors and associating with deviant peers in the teen years (Collins et al., 2000). Although the vast majority of children in stepfamilies do not show serious behavior problems and are resilient in coping with family reorganization, antisocial behaviors are more common in older teens with divorced and remarried parents than in those with nondivorced families (Amato & Cheadle, 2008).

Parental supervision and monitoring of peer relations are increasingly important through the teen years. A higher level of parental monitoring was associated with lower rates of delinquency, substance use, and aggression in a sample of African American adolescents. Whereas boys report less monitoring by parents, they also experience higher levels of delinquency, physical aggression, drug and alcohol use, and criminal offenses than girls (Goncy & van Dulmen, 2010). This finding holds for boys in other ethnic groups as well, including boys living in small towns (Dodge, Coie, & Lynam, 2006). Parents should maintain close ties to their teens, offering them encouragement in making their own decisions to help them develop psychological autonomy and their unique personalities. Teens who feel close to their parents are much more likely to talk with them about problems and concerns, even about behavior that breaks family rules or puts them at risk (Soenens et al., 2006).

Influence in Different Realms of Behavior   Both the family and the peer group are influential in the lives of most teens. Both provide adolescents with different kinds of experience, and the influence of the two groups varies with the issue at hand. When the issues pertain to finances, education, and career plans, adolescents overwhelmingly seek advice and counsel from adults, particularly their parents. Parental time centers on household activities such as eating, shopping, performing chores, and viewing television. And family interaction more closely parallels the socialization goals dictated by the

African American Teens Gain Strength and Resilience from Strong Family Ties   Over time, the cohesion or emotional closeness between parent(s) and children evolves from dependency to a more balanced connectedness that permits the adolescent to mature as a distinct individual capable of assuming adult status and roles.

larger community. Contrary to some psychoanalytic formulations, adolescents do not seem to develop autonomy and identity by severing their ties with their parents. Rather, teens benefit in their development by remaining connected with their parents and by using them as important resources in their lives. This effect is most notable when the parenting style is authoritative, the more democratic style (Collins et al., 2000).

For many youth, the *right* to choose friends is more important than the choice itself. It signals that their parents recognize their maturity and growing autonomy. Some evidence suggests that adolescents who believe that their parents are not providing them with sufficient space—that their parents are not relaxing their power and restrictiveness—are apt to acquire more extreme peer orientations and seek out more peer advice (Beveridge & Berg, 2007). Both psychological overcontrol and undercontrol of behavior places youngsters at greater risk for problem behaviors (Collins et al., 2000). Disagreements between parents and their teenagers occur primarily over differing interpretations of issues and over the extent and legitimacy of the youngsters' personal jurisdiction (such as what clothing to wear or the setting of a curfew) (Player, 2006).

Shift in the Family Power Equation   From early to late adolescence, the emotional closeness between parent and child ideally becomes transformed from one of considerable dependency to a more balanced connectedness that permits the youngster to develop as a distinct individual capable of assuming adult status and roles. Across adolescence, parents typically make increasingly less use of unilateral power strategies and more use of strategies

Being Able to Communicate with a Concerned Parent Is Crucial to an Adolescent's Development
Source: © 2008 ZITS Partnership. Distributed by King Features Syndicate.

that share power with their youngsters. But nearly all young teens report varying degrees of conflict along the path to independence (Allison & Schultz, 2004). Parents report the most intense conflicts with high school teens over such issues as irritating/disruptive behaviors at home, negative personal/moral characteristics, home and school performance, punctuality/curfews, and personal autonomy. Less intense conflicts occur over room care, household chores, inconsiderate behavior, television viewing and computer time, personal appearance, and personal hygiene (Allison & Schultz, 2004).

Maternal Role and Involvement   Mothers typically are better informed and more concerned about their adolescents' social relations because they spend more time in caretaking and monitoring their teens' where-abouts and activities (Lamb & Lewis, 2010). Thus, they experience more conflicts with their teens than fathers do (Updegraff et al., 2001). Indeed, many adolescents can describe their mothers much more fully than they can describe their fathers, a clear indication that their relationship with their mother is the closer one (Besser & Blatt, 2007). A child's relationship with his or her mother becomes tricky during the teen years. Boys are seeking autonomy, but when boys perceive that their mother is being psychologically controlling, their self-esteem decreases (Ojanen & Perry, 2007). However, girls are still learning about connected relationships, and if their father is the available parent rather than the mother, they are more likely to exhibit depression, anxiety, and physical complaints (Besser & Blatt, 2007).

Although a mother must walk a fine line to satisfy the emotional needs of her children, she is a crucially important figure in building their self-esteem. The emotional style she chooses during disciplinary events can produce strikingly different results in this area. When girls perceive that their mothers are warm and affectionate, even during discipline, their self-esteem increases.

Despite the bravado and impatience teenagers exhibit in interacting with their mothers, they still care very much what mothers think about them. Notably, McNeely and colleagues (2002) analyzed data from thousands of teens in the National Longitudinal Study of Adolescent Health. Their findings revealed that mothers' values and beliefs, and relationship satisfaction, strongly influence the timing of daughters' first sexual experience.

Paternal Role and Involvement   More men today are involved in their children's lives than in previous generations, so the research on paternal influence is evolving across cultures (Lamb & Lewis, 2010). Paternal involvement varies depending on whether the parents are residing together, cohabiting, or apart. Men's involvement with their children is greater when they have a good relationship with their child's mother. One researcher found that father-child interaction (play, companionship, and care) peaked during the preschool years and slowly declined during childhood. Baumrind's style of parenting (authoritarian, permissive, authoritative, or indifferent) is associated with a father's level of involvement with his children as well—fathers tend to be stricter and less patient with younger children. Fathers who are involved in their child's education help to promote greater achievement (Lamb & Lewis, 2010). Fathers who are "physically playful, affectionate, and socially engaged" teach their children about effective social relations. And "the teen-agers' sense of self-worth is predicted by the quality of their play with their fathers some 13 years earlier" (Lewis & Lamb, 2010, p. 125). Generally, fathers tend to spend less time and have few conversations with adolescent children—but they tend to be more involved with their sons than with their daughters (Lewis & Lamb, 2010). Overall, "there is a long-term association between reported paternal involvement and psychosocial adjustment of adolescents" (Lamb & Lewis, 2010, p. 128). With more female single-parent families, however, many more

U.S. children are growing up without the regular influence and economic support of a concerned and caring father. Child (and teen) poverty rates rise dramatically in the absence of a resident father—which portends difficulties for those teens (Lamb & Lewis, 2010).

Question

In what areas do teens typically seek out friends for advice and support, and under what circumstances do they seek out family members for advice and support?

SEXUALITY, COURTSHIP, AND LOVE

One of the most difficult adjustments for adolescents, and perhaps the most critical, revolves around their developing sexuality. Biological maturity and social pressures require that adolescents come to terms with awakening sexual impulses. At the same time, they are being bombarded by the highly sexualized messages of the culture in movies, on the Internet, on television, and in advertising—all encouraging them to express their sexuality at ever-younger ages (Brown, L'Engle et al., 2006). As a result, sexual attraction and sexual considerations become dominant forces in their lives (Brown, L'Engle et al., 2006). Indeed, first sexual intercourse is a developmental milestone of major personal and social significance and is often viewed as a declaration of independence from parents, an affirmation of sexual identity, and a statement of capacity for interpersonal intimacy. The age of sexual initiation is often a matter of contention among teens, parents, public policymakers, health officials, and school personnel. Adolescent sexuality is a matter that commands considerable societal concern. Since the 1980s rising rates of nonmarital adolescent births and STIs have become symbols of such social ills as poverty, welfare dependence, child neglect and abuse, and AIDS.

Differing Romantic Behavioral Patterns

Youth vary a good deal in the age at which they first experience intercourse. A large proportion of sexual exposure of females before the age of 14 is involuntary. Sociologist J. Richard Udry (1988) and his colleagues report strong evidence for a hormonal basis of sexual motivation and behavior, particularly in adolescent males. When parents reinforce school-based prevention curricula, adolescent sexual behavior is affected (Blake et al., 2001). Young people who remain virgins longer than their peers are more likely to value academic achievement, enjoy close ties with their parents, report stricter moral standards, begin dating later, and exhibit more

conventional behavior with respect to alcohol and drug use. However, virgins are decidedly not "maladjusted," socially marginal, or otherwise unsuccessful. They report no less satisfaction and no more stress than nonvirgins, and they typically achieve greater educational success. In many cases teenagers, especially girls, select as their friends individuals whose sexual behavior is similar to their own (Adamczyk, 2009; McLoyd et al., 2009).

Aspects of family life also affect adolescent sexual behavior. Generally, the earlier the mother's first sexual experience and first birth, the earlier the daughter's sexual experience. And teenagers with older sexually active siblings are more likely to begin sexual intercourse at an earlier age (Kornreich et al., 2003). Living in poverty also tends to be associated with early sexual activity and early pregnancy. Unwed adolescent pregnancies are several times more likely to occur among youth with poor academic skills and those from economically disadvantaged families. Moreover, adolescents, especially daughters, from single-parent households typically begin sexual activity at younger ages than their peers from two-parent families. A number of factors contribute to the higher rates of sexual activity among teens in single-parent families (Kinsman et al., 1998): (1) There is often less parental supervision in single-parent households; (2) single parents are themselves often dating, and their sexual behavior provides a role model for their youngsters; and (3) adolescents and parents who have experienced divorce tend to have more permissive attitudes about sexual activity outside of marriage.

In sum, behavior is shaped by the characteristics of the communities in which teens live with their cohort (Gardner & Steinberg, 2005). A concentration of poverty, crowded housing conditions, high levels of crime, higher rates of unemployment, marital dissolution, and scarce public services engender a social climate of apathy and fatalism (McLoyd et al., 2009). These communities have fewer adult role models of economic and social success. Where few adult women are able to find stable, sufficient employment, the potential costs of sexual activity in terms of future occupational attainment appear minimal to some female adolescents. Indeed, a variety of social factors encourage teenage girls to become pregnant. In some ethnic groups, having a baby symbolizes maturity and entrance into adulthood (getting one's own apartment, a welfare check, Medicaid for health coverage, and food stamps), and peers often ridicule teens who remain virgins.

Courtship

In the United States, high school dating traditionally was the framework for fostering and developing sexual relations through prescribed "courtship." Dating began with a young man inviting a young woman for an evening's entertainment, at his expense. The first invitation was often given during a nervous conversation on the phone days or weeks in advance. The man would call for the woman at the appointed hour in a car and return her by car. Over time, holding hands, putting an arm around shoulders, and light kissing were early steps of courtship. Girls were more likely than boys to report being in a "steady" dating relationship, and the boy gave his class ring to his girlfriend (Hays, Forman, & Sikes, 2009). Societal norms forbade a single woman from having sex outside of marriage. New patterns of courtship swept in with the youth movement of the early 1970s. Dating itself was largely replaced by "hanging out" and "getting together" among groups of youth. A more relaxed style governed the interaction between the sexes, including informal get-togethers and roving in groups through malls. Since the late 1990s, courtship does not seem to exist; rather, the terms *friends with benefits* and *hooking up* are used to describe the casual sex patterns that teens report. Such behaviors (which are likely to entail neither prior friendship nor commitment) have "trickled down from campuses into high schools and junior highs" (Denizet-Lewis, 2004). Social networking and cell phones have made such liaisons easier. Teen boys say that with so many girls willing to "hook up," there's no need to get into a relationship—and it's easy to find *str8-up sex* with Web sites such as BuddyPic.com and FacetheJury.com (Denizet-Lewis, 2004).

Many teenage males report that they do not date—or refuse to admit to it. Growing numbers of young men "do not want to look soft" to their friends. This fear, along with a desire to demonstrate their manhood, leads many teenage males to use, abuse, or show disrespect to girls (behaviors carried into young adulthood). Teenage males (and some females) report that they gain popularity by yelling explicit propositions at or fondling females/ males who pass by, all the while competing with one another to demonstrate the most flair and audacity in "talking trash" and "making moves." An American Association of University Women (AAUW) report, *Hostile Hallways: Bullying, Teasing, and Sexual Harassment in School* (2001b), revealed that a majority of adolescent boys and girls say they experience harassment, and a smaller percentage report being the perpetrators. All these behaviors are physically and emotionally unhealthy, and random sex leads to unintended pregnancy and higher rates of STIs, including HIV.

Love

In the United States nearly everyone hopes to fall in love eventually. TV shows, soap operas, magazines for brides, movies, the Internet, and popular music reverberate with themes of romantic ecstasy. In many non-Western countries, however, marriage is often preplanned by the parents of the prospective bride and groom, and there is some financial exchange for assurance of the virginity of

The Concept of Romantic Love Social scientists find it difficult to define romantic love. Some say it can be measured by physiological arousal, some say it is a unique chemical reaction that activates the brain's pleasure centers, and others say it is associated with a special transcendent feeling. From a cross-cultural view, the concept of romantic love is not universal.

the bride. Clearly, different societies view romantic love quite differently (Kottak, 2008). At one extreme are societies that prefer arranged marriages and consider a strong love attraction to be a laughable or tragic aberration (think of *Romeo and Juliet*). At the other extreme are societies that define marriage without love as shameful. It seems that the capacity for romantic love is universal, but its forms and the extent to which the capacity gets translated into everyday life are highly dependent on social and cultural norms (Kottak, 2008).

All of us are familiar with the concept of romantic love, yet social scientists find it exceedingly difficult to define, so it is no wonder that American teenagers are uncertain about what mature love is supposed to feel like and how they can recognize the experience. Some social psychologists conclude that *romantic love* is simply an agitated state of physiological arousal that individuals come to define as love. The stimuli producing the agitated state might be sexual arousal, gratitude, anxiety, guilt, loneliness, anger, confusion, or fear. What makes these diffuse physiological reactions love, they say, is that individuals label them as such.

Some researchers are finding that love has a unique chemical basis and that love and romance are among the most powerful activators of the brain's pleasure centers. Intense romantic attraction triggers neurochemical reactions that produce effects much like those produced by a manic state: persistent elevated alertness, thoughts of the beloved person, feelings of overwhelming joy, efforts to sustain proximity to the person, and altered sleep patterns (Brand et al., 2007). Fisher (2004) scanned the brains of people who identified themselves as having fallen "madly" in love. She found that attraction is related to elevated levels of dopamine and other neurotransmitters that produce intense focus and concentration, as well as exhilaration, increased energy, a pounding heart, sleeplessness, and loss of appetite. Her research reveals that when you fall in love, specific "reward" regions of the brain show increased blood flow, creating the strong emotion of romantic passion. Also, elevated levels of testosterone in both men and women stimulate the sex drive (Fisher, 2004). As a romantic relationship becomes more serious, couples become more passionate (lustful), intimate (sexual), and committed (attached) (Gao, 2001).

Questions

How are today's U.S. teens meeting needs for sexual intimacy? Is the idea of romantic love a universal concept? How does the feeling called love manifest itself in physical, psychological, or emotional ways?

Sexual Expression and Behavior

Although we commonly equate adolescent sexuality with heterosexual intercourse, sexual expression takes a good many different forms. Furthermore, sexuality begins early in life and merely takes on more adult forms during adolescence.

Development of Sexual Behavior Both male and female infants show interest in exploring their own bodies, initially in a random and indiscriminate fashion. Even at 4 months of age, babies respond to genital stimulation in a manner that suggests that they are experiencing pleasure. Between 2 and 3 years of age, they will curiously investigate their siblings or playmates' genitals. With strong social prohibitions, children are socialized to restrain these behaviors.

Masturbation, or erotic self-stimulation, is common among children. In many cases, children experience their first orgasm through self-stimulation (Komisaruk, BeyerFlores, & Whipple, 2006). It might occur through the fondling of the penis or the manual stimulation of the clitoris or by rubbing against a bedcover, mattress, toy, or other object. Boys often learn about masturbation from other boys, whereas girls learn to masturbate primarily through accidental discovery (Halpern et al., 2000; Kinsey et al., 1953).

Many children also engage in some form of sex play with other children prior to adolescence. The activity is usually sporadic and typically does not culminate in orgasm. On the basis of his research, Alfred C. Kinsey and his associates (1953) found that the peak age for sex play among girls was 9, when about 7 percent engaged in heterosexual play and 9 percent in homosexual play. The peak age for boys was 12, with about equal participation in heterosexual and homosexual play. But Kinsey believed that more girls and the vast majority of boys engage in sex play with other children before reaching puberty.

Adolescent Sexual Expression Adolescent sexuality finds expression in masturbation, nocturnal orgasm, heterosexual petting, heterosexual intercourse, oral sex, and homosexual activities. Teenage masturbatory behavior is often accompanied by erotic fantasy. Various myths have attributed harmful effects to masturbation, but the physiological harmlessness of the practice has now been thoroughly documented by medical authorities. Even so, some individuals might feel guilty about the practice for social, religious, or moral reasons. Researchers in this area of human sexuality report that teenagers are very reluctant to discuss masturbation, so there is serious underreporting in studies (Bancroft, 2003). Adolescent boys commonly begin experiencing nocturnal orgasms, or "wet dreams," between the ages of 13 and 15. Erotic dreams that are accompanied by orgasm and ejaculation occur most commonly among men in their teens and twenties and less frequently later in life. Women also have erotic dreams that culminate in orgasm, but they seem to be less frequent among women than among men.

Adolescent Sexual Activity Rates Since the early 1990s, the rates of teenage sexual experience per 1,000 teens have declined for most ethnic groups, according to national self-report surveys (see Chapter 11) (Eaton et al., 2010). The Centers for Disease Control and Prevention (CDC) reported that slightly less than half of the high school students surveyed nationwide in 2009 had engaged in sexual activity. Of those adolescents, about three out of five reported that they or their partner had used a condom, and condom use decreased from grade 9 to grade 12 for females. Survey results also indicated that the highest average prevalence of sexual activity was among black youth (65 percent), followed by Hispanic youth (49 percent), and white youth (42 percent). One out of four black males also reported that they first had sexual intercourse prior to age 13 (Eaton et al., 2010). A limitation of this study is that only teens who remain in high school are surveyed.

Multiple Sex Partners Social scientists also see a downward but stable trend in the number of teens in high school who are engaging in sex with multiple partners (four or more), and rates rise by twelfth grade. The CDC reports that an average of 14 percent of respondents have had multiple partners (Eaton et al., 2010). Prevalence of multiple sex partners is lower among female students (11 percent). The higher rate of multiple sexual partners among American teens compared with teens in other developed countries explains why American teenagers have higher rates of sexually transmitted infections (STIs) (Centers for Disease Control, 2007c; 2009c).

Teenage Pregnancy

The U.S. teen pregnancy rate declined significantly for nearly 20 years since its peak in 1990 (Hamilton, Martin, & Ventura, 2010). In 2005–2007 there was a slight increase in teen births, mainly attributable to a higher rate for adolescent Hispanic American females giving birth. But from 2008 to 2009 the teen birthrate fell by a record 6 percent, to the lowest rate in seven decades of reporting (see Chapter 11). Teen Hispanic American childbearing also decreased by 10 percent from 2008 (Hamilton, Martin, & Ventura, 2010). But the rate in the United States is still significantly higher than that in other industrialized nations (see Figure 12.3) (United Nations, 2007).

By 2009, the precentage of teens who had had sex before age 14 had declined to the lowest on record. The younger a girl is at the onset of sexual activity, the more likely it is that the sexual activity is unwanted or involuntary (Menacker, Martin, MacDorman, & Ventura, 2004). In addition, many teens use some method of contraception the first time they have intercourse. Although many use condoms, a significant proportion of older teen girls use birth control pills, demonstrating planning and a sense

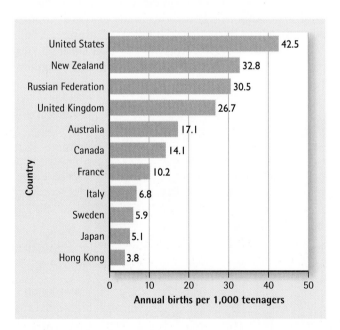

FIGURE 12.3 Early Motherhood in the Industrialized World, 2008 Although the U.S. adolescent birthrate has fallen since 1991, it is still much higher than the rate in other industrialized countries.
Source: United Nations. Department of Economic and Social Affairs. (2009). *Demographic Yearbook 2008.* New York: United Nations. Retrieved January 13, 2011, from http://unstats.un.org/unsd/demographic/products/dyb/dyb2008.htm

of responsibility about their sexual behavior. Yet one in five sexually active females uses no method of contraception, and it is this group that accounts for most teen pregnancy in the United States. Teen girls with older male partners are more likely to have unprotected sex and unplanned pregnancies (Kaiser Family Foundation, 2005). One confounding factor in pregnancy data is the increasing use of nearly two dozen brands of emergency contraception pills that can be purchased by prescription, online, or over the counter (Office of Population Research, 2010).

The Teenage Mother A teenage mother is particularly vulnerable to emotional stress. She must cope with many issues that her peers do not need to think about, such as whether the father will be emotionally and financially supportive to her and the baby, how her family will react to the news of her pregnancy, how she can learn to be a parent when her own journey to independent adulthood is not yet complete, and whether and how she can continue her education so she can support her child. A recent study found that teen mothers are particularly stressed during the third trimester of pregnancy and when their children are toddlers. Yet a comparison between childbearing teens and those who have not had a child revealed that financial stress, rather than the experience of childbearing itself, was most closely linked to stress and depression among the young women in the study. However, the study found that teen mothers are vulnerable in a unique way; if they have experienced violence at the hands of a family member, their response to parenthood is more likely to be negative (Milan et al., 2004).

A teen mother must negotiate complex new relationships with her own parents and with the father of her child. Close relationships with her parents can help a teen develop a sense that she is a competent mother. This is often facilitated when the young mother lives with her parents in a three-generation household. The confidence she develops as a mother in this structure helps her be more welcoming to the father of her child, thus paving the way for a crucial relationship between her child and its father. Fathers who have conflict-filled relationships with their child's grandmother are less likely to be involved with their child over time. It is important for the maternal grandparents of the child to be sensitive to the fact that many of the father's parental roles are co-opted when the mother lives with her parents. Grandmothers play an important role in including fathers in the life of the child (Krishnakumar & Black, 2003).

African American teen mothers in one study reported that their contact with the child's father declined significantly over the first three years after birth (Gee & Rhodes, 2003). Both fathers and mothers reported more positive relationships with their partners over time and less parenthood stress when their relationships to their own parents were close (Florsheim et al., 2003).

The Teenage Father About 25 percent of first-time unmarried fathers are under the age of 20, and unmarried fathers are more likely to come from minority ethnicities (Carlson & McLanahan, 2010). Teen fathers have a crucial role to play in the development of their children. Fathers who see their children at least once a week have a positive effect on the children's adjustment to school, achievement in reading skills, and cooperation with teachers (Howard, Lefever, Borkowski, & Whitman, 2006). But before a young male can be a father, he needs to understand his legal rights and responsibilities, especially if he is unmarried. The first step is establishing paternity, which is usually done through a blood test. If the couple is sure of paternity, then the father should sign a form at the hospital when the baby is born, acknowledging that he is the father of the child. This legal document is the basis for all subsequent rights and responsibilities, so it is wise for the teen father to have a trusted adult review the document before he signs it. Establishing paternity gives the child rights to the father's Social Security, military benefits, and health-care coverage through the father's workplace (Sickels, 2007).

If needed, the father can then negotiate with the mother about visitation or custody rights. If both parents agree, establishing these rights starts with filing a signed agreement with the local family court. Teen fathers are responsible for providing child support to their children, and courts will work to make sure that they pay the monthly amount that has been established. If the father does not pay, the courts can take money directly from his wages and can even seize his personal property, such as his car. In this situation no one wins, because the court retains part of the money to cover its costs, the mother

and child do not get the full amount, and the father's credit is ruined (Hardcastle, 2008).

Fathers are equally legally responsible with mothers to ensure that their child is safe and well cared for. Many teen fathers are eager to be involved with their child. If both the father and the mother can negotiate the new territory of parenthood, which often involves new and complex roles with both sets of grandparents, the child will benefit from the care and support of both parents. However, Carlson and McLanahan (2010, p. 250) studied unmarried couples' relations after the birth of a child and found that nearly half of couples report that they have "no relationship." These researchers found that father absence is "associated with a greater risk of adverse outcomes for children and youth."

Contraception and Abstinence Education Since the 1970s, many more adolescents became sexually active, creating a spike in teen births. However, since 1991 teen sexual behavior has changed considerably, with major declines in teen birthrates. The decline was attributable to three types of intervention programs: increasing use of contraceptives and emergency contraceptives, effective programs combining abstinence and safe-sex education that encourage teens to delay having sex, and youth development programs that keep teens constructively involved in service and community activities (see Figure 12.4) (National Campaign to Prevent Teen and Unplanned Pregnancy, 2007). While some teens report delaying sexual intercourse until high school or later, other teens use birth control when they have intercourse (Guttmacher Institute, 2006).

Since the mid-1990s, programs that offer either safe-sex education or abstinence education and blended programs

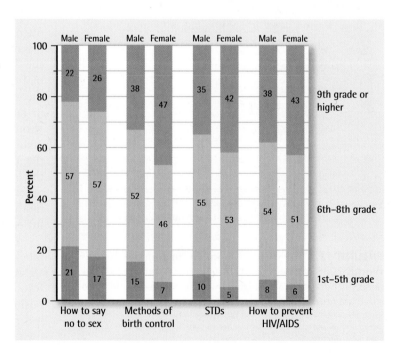

FIGURE 12.4 Grade in Which U.S. Teenagers 15–19 First Received Formal Sex Education, by Topic and Gender: 2006–2008
Source: Centers for Disease Control and Prevention, National Center for Health Statistics (2010, September). *NCHS Data Brief*, No. 44.

that combine these approaches have been funded with billions of federal dollars (Hoffman, 2006). Abstinence-only education requires that educators teach about the social, physiological, and health gains achievable by abstaining from sex (Dailard, 2003). Some researchers find that abstinence programs do help some teens to delay the onset of sexual activity up to a year or much longer (Bersamin et al., 2005). Critics want contraception and STI prevention included. A national ongoing study with students from 10 middle schools examined the success of a comprehensive safe-sex program. Results from grade 7 to grade 9 indicate that a multifaceted program promotes a later age of initiating sexual behaviors (Tortolero et al., 2010). Then, in 2010, the Obama administration awarded millions to comprehensive safe-sex teen pregnancy prevention programs and cut most grants to abstinence programs (Stein, 2010). To further confound the matter, in 2010, the results from a randomized controlled study of the use of five different intervention strategies with students in grades 6 to 7 found that after two years, "abstinence-only interventions may have an important role in preventing adolescent sexual involvement" (Jemmott, Jemmott, & Fong, 2010).

In results of national surveys, teens say that their parents are the most important influence on their decisions about sexual activity. But parents underestimate their influence, and one-third of teens report that they have never had a conversation about sex or contraception with a parent. Further, two-thirds of sexually active teens say they wish they had waited longer (Albert, 2007). Parents who communicated their views about sex and maintained strong relationships with their daughters had a significant influence on the girls' decisions to abstain from sex. It is worth noting that this study defined "abstinence" as refraining from vaginal intercourse; it does not reveal whether the girls were delaying sexual behavior altogether (Maguen & Armistead, 2006).

Abortion Since 1990, the number of legally induced abortions for teenagers aged 15 to 19 years has declined to levels not reported since 1973 (see Table 12.1) (Guttmacher Institute, 2008). This decline is attributed to many factors: More teens are carrying babies to term and raising their children; attitudes about abortion have changed; contraceptive use has increased, including the use of the "patch" and injectables that last three months; there is easier access to various morning-after pills; and unintended pregnancies have decreased.

During this period, laws regarding teen abortions changed in some states to require teens to notify parents that they plan to have an abortion; in other states they must obtain parental consent. Although the rate of abortion among teens dropped in states with the new laws, the rate also dropped in states without the new restrictions. An analysis concluded that teen abortion rates are declining for the reasons stated above and that the restrictive laws have

TABLE 12.1 Percentage of High School Students Who Are Sexually Active, by Grade Level, Gender, and Race/Ethnicity: 1995 and 2009

	1995	2005
Grade		
9th	23.6	21.4
10th	33.7	29.1
11th	42.4	40.3
12th	49.7	49.1
Gender		
Male	35.5	32.6
Female	40.4	35.6
Race-Ethnicity		
White, Non-Hispanic	34.8	32
Black, Non-Hispanic	54.2	47.7
Hispanic	39.3	34.6
All Students	37.9	34.2

Sexually active youth are more likely to engage in sexual behaviors that increase their risk of acquiring an STI, such as having unprotected sex and having multiple sex partners. (*Sexually active* is defined as having had sexual intercourse within the past three months.)

Source: Child Trends Databank. (2011). Sexually active teens. Retrieved from http://www.childtrendsdatabank.org/sites/default/files/23_Sexually _Active_Teens.pdf

little effect on the decision a young woman makes about whether to terminate a pregnancy (Lehren & Leland, 2006).

Questions

As adolescents begin to express themselves sexually, what do U.S. national trends reveal regarding sexual activity rates and teen pregnancy? How do teen mothers and fathers cope with having a child? What might a comprehensive safe-sex education program include, and what factors are believed to be associated with a declining incidence of U.S. teen abortions?

Sexual Orientation

Because contemporary American society is more open about sexuality issues, sexual orientation among adolescents is receiving more research attention than in the past. Studies show that some children begin to question their sexual orientation as early as age 9 (Carver, Egan, & Perry, 2004). By age 18, most youth deem themselves to be heterosexual or homosexual, though some 5 percent are still "unsure" of their orientation (Russell & Joyner, 2001). This is by no means the last word on an individual's sexual orientation; many gay adults gradually realize their sexual orientation after an unsuccessful period of trying to conform to heterosexual norms.

Gay, Lesbian, Bisexual, Transgendered, and Intersexed Teens   A body of evidence makes it clear that growing up lesbian or gay is a difficult journey toward self-acceptance (Russell & Joyner, 2001). The social pressures are intense during adolescence, when conformity is celebrated and minor differences can bring humiliation and ostracism. In middle and high schools, name-calling is a fact of life, but few labels are more hurtful than the words *fag, dyke,* and *sissy* when they are used to insult gay or lesbian teens and exclude them from a peer group. The National Mental Health Association (2008) reports that sexual-minority teens hear these and other words over 20 times a day at school and that many times these verbal assaults escalate to threats and actual violence. These pressures put enormous stress on such youth at a time when peer groups are crucial to development and teens are exploring romantic relationships. Especially troubling is the adolescent's fear of disclosing his or her sexual orientation to family and friends. One study found that although a small number of sexual-minority youth are at a greater risk for attempted suicide, it is not accurate to characterize all sexual-minority youth as at risk (Savin-Williams & Ream, 2003).

A few adolescent homosexual experiences do not necessarily predict a lifetime of homosexuality. Genital exhibition, demonstration of masturbation, group masturbation, and related activities are not uncommon among group-oriented preteen boys (Katchadourian, 1985). This prepubescent homosexual play generally stops at puberty. Most teenage boys do not regard their playful sexual contact with other boys as "homosexual" and transition to predominantly heterosexual relationships.

A small percentage of people are born with inconclusive gender identities. They may have female genitalia but a brain that is hormonally male, or vice versa. Known as transgendered individuals, these are people whose biological or psychological makeup does not conform to mainstream beliefs about what it means to be male or female. Transgendered individuals are not necessarily gay. These youth report that they were aware of their condition from early childhood. As they become teenagers, their feeling that they were born with the wrong body intensifies. Thus, the task of forming a stable identity is complex as the pressure to begin dating increases. Until recently, psychologists and physicians were reluctant to consider sex reassignment for adolescents because they feared that a young person might not make a good decision or would be unhappy after surgery. But research has not supported these fears (Cohen-Kettenis, 2002). The present thinking is that earlier sex reassignment surgery will contribute to the mental health and well-being of the transgendered person and help him or her complete the developmental tasks of adolescence. Studies corroborate that transgendered teens who have undergone sexual reassignment go on to live stable and well-adjusted lives (Smith, Van Goozen, Kuiper, & Cohen-Kettenis, 2005).

Intersexed individuals display a variety of biological sexual characteristics of both females and males. An intersexed person is "born with a reproductive or sexual anatomy that doesn't seem to fit the typical definitions of female or male. For example, a person might be born appearing to be female on the outside, but having mostly male-typical anatomy on the inside" (Intersex Society of North America, 2010). Sometimes this isn't discovered until the child goes through puberty.

One reason why fewer nonheterosexual teens are at risk than even a decade ago is the growth of school- and community-based support groups for gay, lesbian, bisexual, transgender, queer, and intersex (GLBTQI) teens. These groups take two forms: (1) support groups for teens only, which provide places where they can form peer groups and discuss issues relevant to their social and psychological needs and (2) support groups that include both gay and non-gay teens, called gay-straight alliances, whose members work together to find common ground. These forms of social support help these teens form healthy self-images. Their existence makes it possible for young people to disclose their sexual identity to family and friends much earlier than was the case 20 years ago, thus diminishing a significant social anxiety and developmental obstacle (Potoczniak, Aldea, & DeBlaere, 2007).

National organizations such as PFLAG (Parents, Families, and Friends of Lesbians and Gays) help parents provide support for their GLBTQI children and provide advocacy for legislative changes to fight discrimination and gender-related harassment (Meyer, 2008). The national organization GLSEN (Gay, Lesbian, and Straight Education Network) helps GLBTQI students and their supporters, teachers, school administrators, and parents form school-based groups that foster safe schools and inclusive education for all students. These groups urge school districts to include sexual orientation in their antibullying policies. GLSEN's research has shown that bullying and violence against gay teens decreases when such policies are in place (GLSEN, 2005).

> *Questions*
>
> Why are nonheterosexual teens often fearful about disclosing their sexual identity? How might high schools and communities foster greater understanding and tolerance for adolescents exploring their sexual identity?

CAREER DEVELOPMENT AND VOCATIONAL CHOICE

In addition to questioning themselves about "Who am I?" most teens in late adolescence are also wrestling with "What am I going to do with the rest of my life?" A critical developmental task confronting adolescents involves making a variety of vocational decisions. In the United States, as in other Western societies, the jobs people hold have significant implications for their adult development life course. The positions they assume in the labor force influence their general lifestyle, the quality of the neighborhoods in which they reside, important aspects of their self-concept, their children's life chances, and most of their relationships with others in the community (Moody-Ayers et al., 2007). Further, employment ties individuals into the wider social system and gives them a sense of purpose and meaning in life.

Preparing for the World of Work

One focus of the transition from childhood to adulthood is preparation for finding and keeping a job in the adult years. Given the importance of the job-entry process, many adolescents are ill prepared to make vocational decisions and to be successful in college in order to prepare for jobs of the twenty-first century (Zimmer-Gembeck & Mortimer, 2006). Most teens have only vague ideas about what they are able to do successfully, what they would enjoy doing, what requirements are attached to given jobs, what the current job market is like, and what it will probably be like in the future. Complicating matters, schools tend to emphasize a college-preparatory curriculum; many youth do not see a relationship between their current academic endeavors and their future employment opportunities; there is a gap between the skills that employers need and the abilities of the workforce; and often they must rely on personal connections and resources when leaving high school (Cochran & Lekies, 2008). The twenty-first century is a "knowledge economy" rather than an industrial one, but today's youth can be prepared with the necessary skills and workforce preparation through various school, after-school, and work-based programs (apprenticeships and field experience) to help them transition to the workforce (see Table 12.2) (Cochran & Ferrari, 2009).

Youth with serious health risks and antisocial behaviors are also at risk for low academic achievement and school failure; this compromises their later job marketability. Of course, many teenagers work (some estimates are as high as 80 to 90 percent), but their ability to balance work and school is very important. Most teens work a moderate number of hours (averaging about 14 hours a week or less) along with attending school and learn effective time-use strategies, which facilitates educational attainment for high school and later years (Staff & Mortimer, 2007). However, teens who work so many hours that their school attendance and grades suffer are more likely than others to turn to alcohol and substance abuse (Marsh & Kleitman, 2005).

Some teens encounter special difficulties in entering and staying in the job market, especially single female

---

TABLE 12.2 Skills for Success in the Knowledge Economy

Thinking Skills

Critical thinking, problem solving, creativity, and innovation

Communication

The ability to communicate effectively using the variety of methods and tools available in today's environment

Teamwork and Leadership

The interpersonal skills to work effectively in a team and to provide leadership through collaboration, motivation, and leveraging the strengths of others

Lifelong Learning and Self-Direction

Continually improving one's capabilities by taking responsibility to set goals, improve skills, and show initiative

Technology Adoption and Application

A firm foundation of technology skills, including concepts and operations, selecting appropriate tools, and solving problems with appropriate technology

Professionalism and Ethics

Personal accountability and effective work habits: punctuality, working productively with others, and time and workload management

Source: Cochran, G., & Lekies, K. (2008). Skills for success in the knowledge economy. *Preparing Youth for the 21st Century Knowledge Economy.* Retrieved from http://www.ohio4h.org/workforceprep/documents/SkillsforSuccess-ActionBriefMay2008.pdf

---

teens with a child, teens with disabilities, teens from racial-ethnic minorities, and teens who have not completed high school (Hooker & Brand, 2009). Gender differences surface early, mirroring those of the adult work world (Mau & Kopischke, 2001). Young men are more likely than young women to be employed as manual laborers, newspaper deliverers, and recreation aides, whereas young women are more likely to work as clerical workers, retail sales clerks, babysitters or child-care workers, health aides, and education aides. Gender segregation also occurs within industries. Among food service workers, for example, young men more often work with things (they cook food, bus tables, and wash dishes), whereas young women more often work with people (they fill orders and serve as waitresses and hostesses).

Changing Employment Trends in the United States

More recently, high rates of unemployment have been the lot of many young people—even for summer employment. For young people aged 16 to 24, the Bureau of Labor Statistics (2010) reports, "July 2010 marked the first time on record that less than half of all youth 16 to

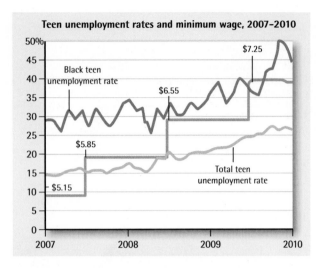

FIGURE 12.5 The Young and the Jobless This graph traces the unemployment rate for black teens and for all teens, along with the minimum wage, from 2007 to 2010.
Source: U.S. Bureau of Labor Statistics (2010).

24 years old were employed in that month. The sharp decline in recent years reflects continued weak labor market conditions experienced during the recession that began in December 2007." Since 1989, the summer labor force participation rate for this age group has trended down significantly. Those employed typically work in the leisure, hospitality (includes food service), and retail trades. In July 2010, the unemployment rate for youth aged 16 to 24 was 19 percent, the highest on record since 1948, reflecting the weak job market. Black and Hispanic teens, and those with disabilities, have the highest rates of unemployment (Bureau of Labor Statistics, 2009). The *Wall Street Journal* ("The young and jobless," 2010) reports a trend of joblessness for teens related to the rising minimum wage (see Figure 12.5).

In late 2010, national unemployment statistics hovered between 9 and 10 percent, but teens who were searching for jobs had the highest unemployment rate—around 25 percent; blacks had the second highest unemployment rate—near 16 percent (Bureau of Labor Statistics, 2010–11). Young people in the United States used to find a job in manufacturing, construction, or sales and expect to make a career of it. But contemporary young Americans without skills, and often those *with* skills, cannot count on good wages and steady work. The contributing factors include the economic effects of globalization, U.S. corporate downsizing and relocations, and the technological paradigm shift, whereby computer work can be done 24 hours a day, at a lower cost, in other countries. At present, college graduates are most likely to secure employment, especially in the fields of accounting, network systems and data communication, health care, education, and biomedical engineering, and as physician assistants (Bureau of Labor Statistics,

2011). The National Association for Colleges and Employers (NACE) reports that employers expect to increase their hiring of graduates in 2011 (Bureau of Labor Statistics, 2010–11).

Jobs for adolescents that support rather than displace academic pursuits and provide learning opportunities lead to lower rates of school deviance, alcohol use, and arrests among twelfth-graders (Mortimer, 2010). However, when adolescents work more hours, it results in lower grades, lower educational goals, dropping out of school, and emotional alienation from parents, as well as increased delinquency and use of tobacco, alcohol, and marijuana (Paternoster et al., 2003). Many school-to-work programs are available to teens, including After School Matters, Upward Bound, Gear Up, Job Corps, AmeriCorps, Jobs for America's Graduates (JAG), National Guard Youth Challenge, Junior ROTC, Knowledge Is Power (KIPP), Opportunities Industrialization Centers (OIC), Youth Build U.S.A., and Youth Services and Conservation Corps, among many others (Hooker & Brand, 2009).

Balancing Work and School

More than one-third of today's teens are already working while attending high school (National Youth Employment Coalition, 2008). How many hours a teenager works is important. A study of 12,000 students in grades 7 to 12 reveals that teens who work 20 hours or more a week during the school year are more likely to be emotionally distressed, drink, smoke, use drugs, and have early sex. About one-third of teens surveyed said that work limits their participation and achievement in school, sports, and social activities (Gehring, 2000). The bottom line, say counselors, parents, and therapists, is that these youth struggle with balancing daily responsibilities. Good working conditions can boost a teen's morale and motivation to continue an education, but bad working conditions can hurt morale, lower self-esteem, and be a factor in dropping out of high school (Teixeira et al., 2004).

Graduation Rates and Dropout Rates

A U.S. national study revealed that the overall average public high school graduation rate in 2007–2008 was nearly 75 percent for more than 2.9 million teens who were in ninth grade four years earlier (Stillwell, 2010). The findings show a big disparity in graduation rates between various states: The highest graduation rates are in upper mid-western states and a few New England states; the lowest rates are in Nevada, the District of Columbia, and southern states. Graduation rates continue to improve in 36 states (Stillwell, 2010). However, there remains a considerable disparity in high school completion rates on the basis of race/ethnicity (see Table 12.3).

TABLE 12.3 Academic Achievements of U.S. Youth Aged 18 and Older, by Race/Ethnicity: 2008 (by percent)

Overall, 87 percent of adults 25 and older had a high school diploma or more in 2009, and 30 percent had earned at least a bachelor's degree.

Race/Ethnicity	Without High School Diploma	High School Graduate	Bachelor's Degree or Advanced Degree	Bachelor's Degree	Ph.D. or Professional Degree
Hispanic	38	62	33	13	1
Black	15	85	44	15	1.3
Asian	11	89	69	53	6
White, Non-Hispanic	9	87	60	33	3

Source: U.S. Bureau of the Census. (2009). 2008 Annual Social and Economic Supplement. *Current Population Survey.*

Dropout Rates   Although the *number* of white students dropping out of high school is much higher, minority students have higher *rates* of dropping out (see Table 12.3). More males than females drop out of school. In 2008, the national dropout rate was reported to be 8 percent for 16- to 24-year-olds who dropped out of school and had not yet earned a high school diploma or an equivalency diploma (GED) (National Center for Education Statistics, 2010).

The actual U.S. high school dropout rate is a multifaceted figure and is difficult to determine because school districts, states, and federal agencies use different definitions, calculations, and jargon. The age until which students must attend school varies among the states from 16 to 18. Student mobility may not be tracked, and districts are not required to report middle school dropout statistics (Kronholz, 2001). It is difficult to track home-schooled students, students who attend private and charter schools, and those who earn a GED later. Thus, other studies report that the high school dropout rate is much higher (Greene & Winters, 2005).

Moreover, dropout rates vary greatly by student socioeconomic status: more students from poor families, racial-ethnic minorities, pregnant teens and teen parents, and those with academic difficulty (Hood, 2004). Adding to this complex task are many more students who are English language learners, and classes are increasing in size as many thousands of U.S. teachers are laid off because of budget cuts (Greene & Winters, 2005; Lewin & Dillon, 2010). Many high schools have consolidated from small neighborhood schools into large, sprawling facilities that have become impersonal (Green & Winters, 2005).

High school students who drop out of school place themselves at risk in an economy where entry-level jobs are scarce. In 2009, 9 percent of young people aged 16 to 19 were not enrolled in school and were not working (Population Reference Bureau, 2010). The most vulnerable groups were black and Hispanic American. Males in this situation often get involved in illegal activities to find money, and females often turn to the welfare system. Young people who are in the juvenile justice and foster care systems are particularly vulnerable when they drop out. They are often ineligible for government services intended to help them transition to adulthood (Child Trends Databank, 2010b). Fortunately, over half of them eventually earn a high school diploma or general equivalency diploma (GED), which opens up employment opportunities and increases their lifetime earnings (Bureau of Labor Statistics, 2010). Because of the technological advances, teens who do not complete high school or who fail to acquire basic reading, writing, and math skills cannot find work or must settle for entry-level jobs at minimum wage (or below) with limited opportunities for advancement.

U.S. governors and business leaders (such as Microsoft's Bill Gates) have held National Education Summits to discuss how to improve the performance of the nation's high schools. As a result of such strategic planning, many states have raised high school graduation requirements, requiring more core courses (math, science, and English) as well as improvements in career guidance and college preparation. Also, employers and college faculty have developed course work that prepares graduates to think analytically, write more, develop good work and study habits, learn to use problem-solving skills, and develop work-related computer skills (Balz, 2005).

Questions

How are adolescents preparing for careers and vocations? Who is most likely to drop out of high school? Why? What are some recommendations for improving the preparation of high school graduates for employment in the twenty-first century?

RISKY BEHAVIORS

Even teenagers who do not perceive themselves as having "problems" may be seen by adult society as engaging in risky or deviant behaviors. Because adults control the seats of power, including legislative agencies, the courts, the police, and the mass media, they are in a better position than adolescents to make their definitions and values "stick" in the realm of everyday life. And indeed, some risky behaviors are common for this age group, including drinking, illicit drug use, suicide and self-harm (such as cutting), delinquency, and exposure to Internet victimization. These behaviors are risky because they interfere with the person's long-term health, safety, and well-being.

Social Drinking and Drug Abuse

Nowadays, everyone talks about drugs, but the word itself is imprecise. If we consider a drug to be a chemical, then everything that we ingest is technically a drug. To avoid this difficulty, *drug* is usually arbitrarily defined as a chemical that produces some extraordinary effect beyond the life-sustaining functions associated with food and drink. A drug might heal, put to sleep, relax, elate, inebriate, produce a mystical experience or a frightening one, and so on. Our society assigns different statuses to different types of drugs. Through the federal Food and Drug Administration (FDA), the Bureau of Narcotics, and other agencies, the government takes formal positions on whether a given drug is "good" or "bad" and approves or bans its use. Sociologists note that some drugs have official approval. Caffeine is a mild stimulant that is societally approved through coffee breaks and soda machines. The consumption of alcohol, a central nervous system depressant, has become so prevalent in recreational, entertainment, private, and business settings that nonusers of the drug are relatively rare. Until about two decades ago, the same was true of the use of nicotine (from tobacco), a drug usually categorized as a stimulant.

Any drug can be abused. **Drug abuse** is the excessive or compulsive use of chemical agents to the extent that it interferes with one's health, one's social or vocational functioning, or the functioning of the rest of society. Among adolescents, as among their elders, alcohol is the most frequently abused drug in the United States. According to a 2009 national Youth Risk Behavior Survey conducted by the National Institute on Drug Abuse, nearly 10 percent of the respondents had driven a car under the influence of alcohol within the previous 30 days, and one-third reported riding in a vehicle with a driver who had been drinking. Tragically, a high majority of serious injuries, disability, and deaths among teens and young adults are alcohol- and motor-vehicle related (Eaton et al., 2010).

Adolescent Binge Drinking   Binge drinking is often the result of peer pressure. Binge drinking in adolescence increases the risk of alcohol dependency in adulthood. It may also cut a life short; one in three traffic deaths among teens is related to alcohol use. High school students who plan to go to college are less likely to engage in binge

drinking. (See the *More Information You Can Use* box, "Determining Whether Someone You Know Has an Alcohol or Drug Problem.")

Nationwide, nearly three out of four teens report having had at least one alcoholic drink in their lives (with high rates by later high school years) (Eaton et al., 2010). Also, **binge drinking,** defined as downing five or more drinks in a row (for males) and four or more (for females) over the previous 2 hours, begins in the high school years. In 2009, nearly one out of four students reported having participated in binge drinking, with higher rates (up to one out of three) among high school juniors and seniors (Eaton et al., 2010). Males are much more likely than females to binge drink. White and Hispanic high school students are more likely to engage in heavy drinking at all ages. Risk factors associated with teens drinking heavily include having alcoholic parents, having little parental support or supervision, and having friends who drink. Other consequences of heavy drinking include poor academic performance, unprotected sex, increased vulnerability to rape, pregnancy, STIs, other illicit drug use, auto accidents, criminal behaviors, or even death from alcohol poisoning (Child Trends Databank, 2010a).

Other Drug Use   A growing problem in drug abuse is the illegal use of anabolic steroids. In 2009 both male (4 percent) and female (2 percent) students reported taking steroids to build their muscles and enhance their athletic performance (Eaton et al., 2010). Adolescents, whose bodies are still developing, are at risk for adverse effects from steroids such as stunted growth, mood changes, long-term dependence, acne, fluid retention, breast development in males, masculinization of females, high blood pressure, and reversible sterility in males. Teens might find steroid use appealing because of their concerns about their appearance, peer approval, and "being large and strong enough to make the team" in competitive sports (Eaton et al., 2006). Given the easy accessibility of marijuana in the peer culture, it is not surprising that more than one-third report using marijuana by twelfth grade (Eaton et al., 2010). Of very serious concern is the increasing teen use of prescription drugs (such as *Vicodin, OxyContin, Robitussin* cough syrups, and *Dramamine*) for nonmedical purposes (Office of Applied Studies, 2010). In such "pharming," teens collect pills from their parents' and friends' medicine cabinets (or purchase pills on the Internet) and mix the pills for consumption by partygoers. The federal government is reporting an "epidemic" of teen abuse of prescription drugs, because emergency room visits for drug abuse have tripled in just a few years (Office of Applied Studies, 2010). But these findings show that adolescents who frequently use drugs are often maladjusted, showing a distinct personality syndrome marked by increased loneliness, social isolation, poor impulse

MORE INFORMATION YOU CAN USE

Determining Whether Someone You Know Has an Alcohol or Drug Problem

How Can I Tell If My Friend Has a Drinking or Drug Problem?

It might be difficult to tell because most people will try to hide their problems, but here are questions that you can ask yourself about their behavior (or your own):

1. Do they get drunk or high on a regular basis?
2. Do they lie about how much they drink or do drugs, or do they lie in general?
3. Do they avoid people in order to get drunk or high?
4. Do they give up activities they used to do, such as playing sports or hanging out with friends who do not get drunk or use drugs?
5. Do they plan the day or activity around the act of drinking or getting high?
6. Do they have to increase the amount of alcohol or drug to maintain the same high?
7. Do they believe that drinking or drugs are necessary to have fun?
8. Are they frequently incapacitated because they are recovering from a "fun night"?
9. Do they pressure others to take drugs or condemn those who do not consume alcohol?
10. Do they take risks, such as careless driving or sexual risks, or otherwise act invincible?
11. Do they have blackouts where they have no recollection of what happened while high?
12. Do they talk of being depressed or about committing suicide?

If you see these signs, chances are that your friend (or you) need help. Being under the influence of substances can cause people to engage in unsafe behaviors, such as driving while intoxicated, having unsafe sex, and trying dangerous "stunts." The person may develop serious psychological problems (such as depression, suicidal thoughts, and thoughts of harming others) and physical problems (such as liver damage, brain damage, fetal damage if pregnant, and—of course—overdose).

What Would Cause My Friend to Have This Problem?

Sometimes these problems run in families, much like heart disease. If a family has a history of substance abuse, it is more likely that your friend could develop a dependency. Some people take drugs or drink to avoid things that bother them—stress, work pressures, feelings that they are different

Adolescent Binge Drinking   Binge drinking is often the result of peer pressure. It can start as early as junior high. Binge drinking in adolescence increases the risk of alcohol dependency in adulthood. It may also cut a life short: One in every three traffic deaths among teens is related to alcohol use.

from others, or they are not worthy, or they are unhappy with their situation. However, they will become anxious or depressed when the high wears off and they have to face the same problem repeatedly (Schulenberg et al., 1997). It is very difficult for most people to admit they have a serious problem. If they are young, they believe that nothing bad can happen to them. It can seem easier to isolate oneself than to constantly hide evidence of the problem. It is difficult to see a problem once someone withdraws.

How Can I Help My Friend?

You have several options:

- Talk to someone you trust—a counselor, teacher, doctor, or member of the clergy can give you another perspective on what to do.
- Wait until your friend is sober to talk with him or her. Approach him or her in a spirit of support. Encourage your friend to get professional help.
- Try not to accuse or blame your friend. Give examples of what you have noticed that worry you.
- Offer to accompany your friend to seek help.

continued

What Does My Friend Have to Do to Get Help?

First, your friend must admit that there is a problem. This is difficult because it will mean admitting to having shown poor judgment. Your friend cannot solve this problem alone and will need professional help. Many people benefit from groups such as Alcoholics Anonymous (Al-Anon), Alateen (for younger members), or Narcotics Anonymous (NA). These groups often meet on campus at your own campus counseling center. In the end, it is your friend who must make the decision to get help.

control, and significant emotional distress, including suicidal thoughts, all of which interfere with social-emotional adjustment (Dube et al., 2003). For these young people, experimentation with drugs is highly destructive—or even deadly. Nearly 400 U.S. teens, aged 12 to 17, are admitted daily to publicly funded substance abuse treatment facilities (Office of Applied Studies, 2010).

Why Do Teens Use Drugs?   Factors that may predispose teenagers to use drugs include a family history of substance abuse, a pattern of antisocial behavior, a temperament of low impulse control, low levels of support and discipline from parents, failure in school with resulting low aspirations, and peer influence. This is a heady brew of ideas, and researchers have much work to do before we understand why teens use drugs (Johnston et al., 2006).

The recreational use of illegal drugs has become central to many adolescent peer groups in the past 30 years. Most adolescents who use drugs move in peer groups that use drugs in daily life. Another contributing factor is the influence of prescription drugs being sold on television as "helpful" or "harmless" and the fact that their parents use drugs—such as alcohol, tranquilizers, barbiturates, and stimulants. Perhaps seeing famous athletes using steroids and celebrities using other illicit drugs has led to greater curiosity about and increased teen use of drugs. Nearly all U.S. adolescents report that their family has a rule against illicit drugs, yet many mimic their parents' drug use. In this context, adolescent drug use is a juvenile manifestation of adult behavior, so it is perhaps more accurate to view drug abuse as a society-wide problem.

Teenage Suicide

In the United States, suicide ranks as the third leading cause of death (after accidents and homicides) among young persons aged 15 to 24 (Eaton et al., 2010). More than 4,100 suicides were reported in 2007 for those aged 15 to 24, with four times more males than females taking their own lives (Xu, Kochanek, Murphy, & Tejada-Vera, 2010). Although a small percent of the population, Native American males have the highest rates of suicide (Child Trends Databank, 2010). The overall suicide rate among young people has slowly declined over the past decade.

The self-destructive behavior in these adolescents is alarming and devastating to family and friends left behind. Because stigma is often attached to suicide in Western countries, medical personnel frequently report a suicidal death as resulting from an accidental injury or as a death from natural causes.

The national Youth Risk Behavior Surveillance Study found that during the previous 12 months, 14 percent of high school students surveyed had seriously thought about attempting suicide and nearly one out of ten had made a plan to attempt suicide. More than 6 percent had already attempted suicide, and nearly 2 percent had made a suicide attempt that resulted in injury, poisoning, or overdose requiring emergency medical attention (see Figure 12.6). Girls are almost twice as likely as boys to consider suicide (Eaton et al., 2010). At especially high risk are gay, lesbian, and bisexual youths, who attempt suicide three times as often as other adolescents. They report more family tension over their gender-atypical behavior, inner turmoil over their sexuality, and victimization by peers over their sexual orientation (D'Augelli, Grossman, Salter, Vasey, Starks, & Sinclair, 2005).

Risk Factors Associated with Suicide   A constellation of familial, biological, psychological, and environmental factors are implicated. These factors include a sense of hopelessness, a family history of suicide, impulsiveness, aggressive behavior, social isolation, a previous suicide attempt, easier access to alcohol, use of illicit drugs, lack of emotional support from a family, negative life events, and access to lethal suicide methods. In many cases, depression underlies suicide and suicidal attempts (Walsh & Eggert, 2007).

Suicide Prevention   The ability to screen for suicide risk is the most important part of suicide prevention. Second is linking at-risk individuals with community mental-health services. The strongest risk factor for completed suicide is the presence of a firearm in the home (King & Apter, 2003). A broader societal focus on reducing substance abuse and poor family functioning includes both community and family interventions, which means

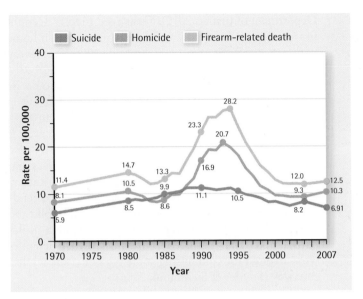

FIGURE 12.6 Rates (per 100,000) for Homicide, Suicide, and Firearm-Related Deaths of Youth Aged 15 to 19, 1970–2007
Source: Child Trends Databank. (2010g). Teen homicide, suicide, and firearm deaths. Retrieved from http://www.childtrendsdatabank.org/?q=node/124

educating parents and educators (King & Apter, 2003). The following protective psychosocial factors enhance adolescent health: regular physical exercise, healthy eating habits, dental care, safety behaviors, adequate sleep, religiosity, a commitment to school, having friends who take part in conventional youth activities and community volunteer work, an orientation toward parents, positive relationships with adults, church attendance, and involvement in prosocial activities (Jessor, Turbin, & Costa, 1998).

Treatment of adolescents with suicidal tendencies usually involves a combination of psychotherapy and medication for depression (Eskin, Ertekin, & Demir, 2008). The therapist seeks to help the teen describe his or her problems and learn more effective techniques for coping with life and stressful circumstances. Dramatic progress has been made in recent years in the treatment of depression with antidepressant medications and cognitive-behavioral therapy intervention (Walsh & Eggert, 2007).

Antisocial Behaviors and Juvenile Delinquency

The problem of youthful "deviance" has been reported by societies throughout human history. Young males are responsible for an overwhelming proportion of the nation's crime, and men of this age group are also involved disproportionately with the criminal justice system. Although the rate of adolescents in juvenile detention has been declining since 1997, black males continue to be the most likely to be detained in custody. Youth who are placed in juvenile detention facilities have a mortality rate that is four times higher than that of youth in the population at large, and a majority of youth who are detained will be incarcerated later in life. Research shows that a high percentage of males and females in juvenile

detention have underlying mental-health problems that are not adequately treated while they are in detention (Child Trends Databank, 2007d).

The media have sensationalized school shootings, leading the public to believe youth crime is on the rise, but youth crime rates have declined significantly, except for arrests for substance abuse and property crimes. The availability of firearms gives a few emotionally disturbed males a lethal weapon that kills more victims. And there is mounting controversy about imprisoning juveniles convicted of substance abuse and possession alongside criminals who have committed serious felony crimes. Psychologists, sociologists, and criminologists increasingly conclude that more responsible parenting, closer home and school supervision, and rehabilitation programs—not the police and jails—could reduce most youth crime.

Youth Violence   Male youth remain the largest subgroup to be both victims and perpetrators of violent acts—and alcohol and other drugs are implicated (Sedlak & Bruce, 2010). In fact, about 85 percent of 101,000 juveniles (most are aged 16 to 17) incarcerated for serious crimes were male (Sedlak & Bruce, 2010). Since 1999, there have been several cases where young males opened fire on students, teachers, and authorities—killing or wounding people before killing themselves or being subdued. There were multiple fatalities at Columbine High School, Red Lake High School, an Omaha shopping mall, and Virginia Tech, and in 2011, Jared Loughner, age 22, shot Arizona Representative Gabrielle Giffords in the head and randomly killed 6 and wounded 14. Such senseless, violent crimes inflicted by young males on innocent victims were highly sensationalized by the media. Such lurid images leave the nation with the mistaken impression that youth crime is high. In fact, most serious offenses are property-related, and fatalities at school are rare (Robers, Zhang, & Truman, 2010; Sedlak & Bruce, 2010).

The increasing use of social networks, such as *Twitter* and *Facebook*, has unleashed a new type of teen violence that often includes destructive behaviors, crimes, serious injuries, and even deaths—violent behavior that teens record for *YouTube* and instant notoriety. The crowds that gather to perpetrate these crimes are called *flash mobs* or *flashgangs*. What began only a few years ago with many performing artists converging in one place to entertain and then disperse quickly has turned into ugly mob behavior, as some teens in large cities create such spontaneous-seeming events to commit theft, create chaos, and harm innocent victims and bystanders. Civic leaders and those in school systems, criminal justice, and health care are making efforts to curb this unprecedented "electronic aggression" (Solecki & Goldschmidt, 2011).

This and other youth crime and victimization can decline further with continued interventions by government, criminal and juvenile justice, social, and school security programs. By 2004, overall adolescent crime, including assaults by firearm, had decreased significantly for those aged 15 to 24, although rates rose slightly by 2007 (see Figure 12.6) (Child Trends Databank, 2010; Miniño et al., 2007). In 2008 the majority of homicides for juvenile victims aged 13 and older continued to be committed by firearm (Puzzanchera, 2009).

Abductions and Runaway Youth   About 800,000 children under age 18 are abducted each year, and 200,000 of these children are abducted by a family member (Sedlak, Finkelhor, Hammer, & Schultz, 2002; U.S.

Department of Justice, 2010). Teens aged 15 to 17 account for most runaway children, although many return home within a week (Snyder & Sickmund, 2006). Yet every child abduction/runaway case must be taken seriously. All children, even teens, and especially girls, should be taught the rules: *Do not go out alone*; *tell an adult where you are going*; and *yell "NO" when threatened* (Howard, Broughton et al., 2004). The classification of runaway is considered a subset of homeless and missing youth—also called "thrownaway" children. Many are homeless and are forced to commit crimes, such as theft or prostitution, to survive. If these youth become violent juvenile offenders, they pose a challenge to both the general public and the juvenile justice or adult criminal justice system (Miles & Okamoto, 2008). In 2003, more than 123,000 juveniles were arrested for committing some type of crime while a runaway (Snyder & Sickmund, 2006).

The majority of adolescents are law-abiding citizens, but adolescent antisocial behaviors, such as delinquency, conduct disorders, driving while intoxicated, substance abuse, and assaults, are linked to a wide variety of troublesome adult behaviors, including criminality, drug addiction, economic dependency, educational failure, employment instability, marital discord, and child abuse. Even so, some juvenile delinquents later become law-abiding citizens.

Question

Why are so many risky behaviors prevalent among adolescents, and what are some potential negative outcomes for those who start these behaviors in early adolescence?

SEGUE

In the United States the social boundaries surrounding adolescence are rather ill defined. By tradition, the shift from elementary school to junior high school signaled entry into adolescence. But with the advent of the middle school, this distinction became blurred. It is also not clear when a person leaves adolescence and enters young adulthood. Roughly speaking, adolescence is regarded as having ended when the individual assumes one or more adult roles, such as marriage, parenthood, full-time employment, military enlistment, or financial independence. The extension of adolescence and youth has posed two related problems for society and for young people. Society has the problem of providing the young with a bridge to adult roles through appropriate socialization, educational and vocational preparation, and role allocation.

As we shall discuss in Chapter 13, emerging adults have the problem of establishing a stable identity, achieving independence, and deciding among future alternatives. Many Western industrialized nations have put off the entrance of adolescents into adulthood for economic, educational, and other reasons. Today, college postpones full adult status for many socially and economically advantaged young people. Unemployment and underemployment produce a somewhat similar effect among less advantaged groups. At the same time, children are reaching puberty earlier than they did a century ago. Thus, physically mature people are told that they must wait 10 or more years before they can assume the full rights and obligations of adulthood.

SUMMARY

Development of Identity

1. Hall views adolescence as characterized by inevitable turmoil, maladjustment, tension, rebellion, dependency conflicts, and exaggerated peer-group conformity. Some social scientists believe this storm-and-stress view has been exaggerated and is not accurate today.

2. Sullivan's theory, in contrast to Freud's, explains the principal forces in human development as being social instead of biological; the three periods he defines are preadolescence, early adolescence, and late adolescence.

3. The crisis in Erikson's fifth stage of psychosocial development is the search for identity—an optimal feeling of identity experienced as a sense of well-being.

4. Marcia proposes that identity formation can be further classified in terms of four different statuses: achievement, moratorium, foreclosure, and diffusion.

5. The United States and other Western countries promote an extended adolescence. Conflicting generational expectations create an identity crisis among U.S. and European youth.

6. Depression is an emotional state characterized by prolonged feelings of gloom and futility. Adolescent girls are twice as likely as boys to experience depression.

7. Some studies indicate that females emerge from adolescence with a poorer self-image, relatively lower expectations for life, and considerably less confidence in themselves and their abilities. But today, girls' high school and college graduation rates and test scores are higher than boys' in many academic areas.

8. Gurian has studied identity development in boys and proposes accepting their biological differences and providing adolescent males with role models and opportunities to learn to act responsibly.

9. Societies that prolong the transition to adulthood and segregate their youth create a youth culture with standardized ways of thinking, feeling, and acting that are often at odds with the rest of society.

10. Social resources such as parental support, after-school activities, participation in extracurricular activities, and having positive adult role models can help teens develop the resilience to overcome the challenges of adolescent development.

Peers and Family

11. Both the family and the peer group are anchors in the lives of most teenagers. However, their relative influence varies. Adolescents segregated by age in high schools are influenced by their peers but are normally not at war with their parents. Teens benefit from ties with their parents and seek advice from them on issues of finance, education, and careers.

12. Teens seek advice from peers on topics such as clothes, hairstyles, dating, and music.

13. Conformity to a peer group and to peer pressure play a prominent role in the lives of most teenagers, but there are many types of teen groups. A small percentage of adolescents are isolated or associate with delinquent/deviant groups.

14. For teens, the demand to make their own choices is a signal of maturation and growth. Parental supervision of teenagers is important, yet interactions with teens that encourage them to make their own decisions support the growth of self-esteem.

15. Mothers play a significant role in helping daughters increase their self-esteem and learn about connected relationships and in helping sons gain emotional maturity and autonomy.

Sexuality, Courtship, and Love

16. Some of the most difficult adjustments for adolescents as they make the transition to adulthood revolve around their sexuality, sexual orientation, and sexual expression. Sexual attraction and sexual concerns become dominant forces in their lives.

17. Adolescent sexual behavior can be shaped by the degree of parental supervision and by peer-group pressures.

18. Social scientists find it difficult to define romantic love, and cross-cultural studies suggest that it is not a universal concept.

19. Adolescent sexuality finds expression in a number of ways, including masturbation, nocturnal orgasm, heterosexual petting, oral sex, heterosexual intercourse, homosexual activity, and bisexual activity.

20. The rates of teenage sexual activity increased throughout the 1980s, plateaued by the early 1990s, and declined until 2005–2006 and then declined again. Teens have become more consistent contraceptive users. More teens are abstaining from sex until they are older.

21. Although teen birthrates have been declining, U.S. childbearing by unwed teens is still high.

22. Teen mothers can be quite resilient if they receive support from family, particularly from their mothers.

23. Teen fathers play a crucial role in the development and support of their children. They have legal rights and responsibilities to their children.

24. Sex education, safe-sex education, and abstinence-only sex education for teens have been criticized on a number of fronts. The most effective approach includes both abstinence and safe-sex practices.

25. The number of teen abortions is declining to near-record lows.

26. By age 18, most youth deem themselves to be heterosexual or homosexual, although about 5 percent are still "unsure" of their orientation.

27. The growth of support organizations for gay, lesbian, bisexual, transgender, queer, and intersex youth has enabled many to have a less difficult time in adolescence. School-based organizations include both GLBTQI and non-gay members.

28. Transgender teens face difficult challenges as puberty approaches. With the correct standard of physical and psychological care, and with proper levels of family and social support, transgender teens can develop into healthy and well-adjusted individuals if they undergo sex reassignment surgery.

Career Development and Vocational Choice

29. Adolescents need to make decisions about career development and vocational choice. Employment is associated with many positive outcomes as adults, but employment in high school can complicate the picture for teens.

30. The high school dropout rate is higher among the poor, minorities, and pregnant teens; yet there are fewer employment opportunities for these teens and an association with low socioeconomic status as adults.

Risky Behaviors

31. Some risky behaviors common for this age group are drinking, illicit drug use, suicide, and delinquency, all of which typically interfere with a person's immediate or long-term health, safety, and well-being.

32. Certain familial, biological, socioeconomic, mental-health, and environmental factors are associated with substance abuse and suicide among youth.

33. Childhood antisocial behavior, such as juvenile delinquency, conduct disorder, assaults, and violent outbursts, is linked to a wide variety of dysfunctional adult behaviors, including criminality, drug addiction, economic dependency, educational failure, employment instability, marital discord, and child abuse.

34. Most adolescents are law-abiding citizens.

KEY TERMS

binge drinking *(394)*

collective self-esteem *(374)*

consciousness of oneness *(379)*

depression *(375)*

deviant identity *(372)*

drug abuse *(394)*

generation gap *(378)*

identity *(372)*

identity achievement *(373)*

identity diffusion *(372)*

identity foreclosure *(372)*

identity moratorium *(373)*

negative identity *(372)*

puberty rites *(373)*

storm and stress *(370)*

youth culture *(378)*

FOLLOWING UP ON THE INTERNET

Web sites for this chapter focus on emotional and social issues, career development, and risky behaviors. Please access the text Web site at www.mhhe.com/crandell10 for up-to-date hot-linked Internet addresses for the following organizations, topics, and resources:

Child Trends Data Bank: Teens
http://www.childtrendsdatabank.org/

Healthy Youth
http://www.cdc.gov/healthyyouth/

Youth Risk Behavior Surveillance
http://www.cdc.gov/features/riskbehavior/

Teen Pregnancy
http://www.childtrendsdatabank.org/

Education Week—Graduation Mapping Tool
http://www.edweek.org/apps/maps/

Understanding Adolescent Depression and Suicide
http://www.teensuicide.us/

Monitoring the Future Survey (American Secondary Students)
http://monitoringthefuture.org/

Office of Applied Studies: Substance Abuse and Mental Health Services Administration
http://oas.samhsa.gov/newpubs.htm

U.S. Bureau of Labor Statistics
http://www.bls.gov/

Chapters 13 and 14 focus on the dynamic life stage of young adulthood, which extends from the late teens until the mid-forties, and discuss various theories of adult development. Contemporary young adults in the United States are known as either Gen X or the Millennials and are more ethnically diverse, better educated, and less religious than previous generations, as well as more likely to delay marriage by cohabiting. Most young adults are more active and health conscious than ever before. Recent findings suggest that most are more open-minded about sexual behavior and are protecting themselves from HIV/ AIDS and STIs. A smaller number engage in unhealthy behaviors, such as alcohol use, drug abuse, or unprotected sexual activity with multiple partners, which leads to a higher risk of mental-health issues, HIV/AIDS, or unplanned pregnancy. Most are training for careers, attending college, joining the military, or going to work. Friendships and social relationships are of prime importance to young adults, who are searching for a compatible intimate partner during this stage of life, often via social networking. Cohabitation prior to marriage is more common today than in the past; the average age at marriage is now in the mid-twenties. Most young adults are delaying childbearing while working and establishing careers. At present, though, some find themselves among the ranks of the unemployed or underemployed and are living at home longer while establishing careers.

13 Early Adulthood
Physical and Cognitive Development

Today in American society, the line of demarcation between adolescence and adulthood is much less clear than it was a few decades ago. Some social scientists have suggested that adolescence extends well into the twenties, with more young adults living at home with parents during their expensive college years and when launching a career, and others returning home after a short-lived marriage, or perhaps as a single parent. Many middle-class young adults expect to maintain a lifestyle equivalent to or better than that of their parents while they struggle through these early adult years.

Following the lead of psychologists such as Carl Jung, Erik Erikson, Robert Kegan, Bernice and Dale Neugarten, Paul and Margret Baltes, Jeffrey Arnett, and others, the social science community has come to recognize that adulthood is not a single monolithic stage sandwiched between adolescence and old age. Developmentalists now understand that individuals undergo change across the entire life span. The contemporary view is of a *process of becoming*. Thus, adulthood is now seen as an adventure that involves negotiating ups and downs and changing direction to surmount obstacles. In this chapter, we examine several views of the stage called early adulthood, including typical physical and cognitive changes, the differing moral domains of men and women, and the impact of the diversity of values that adults impose on society.

DEVELOPMENTAL PERSPECTIVES

The category *adulthood* lacks the concrete boundaries of *infancy, childhood*, and *adolescence*. Even in the scientific literature, it has functioned as a kind of catchall category for everything that happens to individuals after they "grow up." Sigmund Freud, for instance, viewed adult life as merely a ripple on the surface of an already set personality structure. Jean Piaget assumed that no additional cognitive changes occur after adolescence, and Lawrence Kohlberg saw moral development as reaching a lifetime plateau after early adulthood. Many middle-aged American parents are asking themselves, *When is my son or daughter going to be an adult, capable of working and living independently of our resources?* Developmentalists have no firm answer to their question today, and it seems to be quite an individual matter (Kins, Beyers, Soenens, & Vansteenkiste, 2009).

In the United States, adulthood generally begins when a person leaves high school, attends college, takes a full-time job, enters the military, gets married, or becomes a parent. Yet becoming an adult is a rather different matter for various segments of each society. In Western societies, men have traditionally emphasized such issues in development as autonomy, independence, and identity. In contrast, women, some ethnic minorities, and non-Western societies have typically assigned greater importance to issues of relatedness, such as closeness within a family or friendship network (Neff & Harter, 2003). Arnett (2000) proposed a distinct developmental stage unfolding between ages 18 and 25 called **emerging adulthood**, a time that for many allows greater exploration of life's possibilities in work, love, and worldviews and lays a foundation for the remainder of adult life. We provide more information about this newly recognized stage in Chapter 14.

Demographics of Early Adulthood

People's feelings, attitudes, and beliefs about adulthood are influenced by the individuals who are adults and their life perspectives. In the United States, major population and demographic changes are under way that will have important social and economic consequences. The group of all adults in the United States presently comprises five generations—but *early adulthood,* the focus of this chapter, comprises the youngest two generations. (See Table 1.1 on page 12 for specific traits of the generations.) The oldest U.S. generation of adults still living, which is made up of those born between 1900 and 1925, is called the GI Generation. In their youth, members of this generation experienced World War I, Prohibition, and (in 1920) passage of the Nineteenth Amendment to the Constitution, which gave women the right to vote. Many were immigrants who came to America because

of economic hardships in Europe and elsewhere. In 2009, this generation was represented by about 6 million people, out of a total U.S. population of over 310 million (U.S. Bureau of the Census, 2010a). The next oldest segment of the U.S. adult population, whose members were born between 1925 and 1945, is known as the Silent Generation—a cohort that now numbers about 32 million and lived through the Great Depression of the 1930s and World War II. We address the needs of these two generations more specifically in the chapters of this text on late adulthood.

The baby-boom generation (born between 1946 and 1964 and now often called the boomers) represents more than 78 million graying adults—a demographic tidal wave. In the 1950s and early 1960s, the birth of the baby boomers transformed the United States into a child-oriented society full of new schools, suburbs, shopping malls, and station wagons. As children and teenagers, they lived through the turmoil of the civil rights struggle and protests over the Vietnam conflict, the assassinations of a president and of civil rights leaders, the excitement of space exploration and the Beatles, and social changes such as more women entering colleges and professional careers, the sexual revolution, and the iconic event known as Woodstock.

About two-thirds of the baby boomers are still in middle adulthood and number about 58 million adults. The oldest baby boomers are now in their mid-sixties and are reaching retirement age and the threshold of late adulthood. Those at the "tail end" of the boomers are now approaching 50 years old and presently number about 23 million. We will focus more fully on the baby boomers in the chapters on middle adulthood. As the last of the baby-boom generation is passing into middle adulthood, the next two generations of young adults, Generation X and the Millennials, are coming of age. They are more racially and ethnically diverse than older generations (see Figure 13.1).

> ### Question
> Think of your favorite television shows. What do the main characters and the issues that are explored say about the values and characteristics of these various "adult" generations?

Generation X

The cohort of people born from 1965 to the early 1980s constitutes about 60 to 62 million Americans. Generation X is more ethnically diverse than older generations, and this cohort shares an appreciation for individuality and an acceptance of diversity in race-ethnicity, family structure, sexual orientation, and lifestyle (Stoneman, 1998). Members of this generation were raised in a variety of family

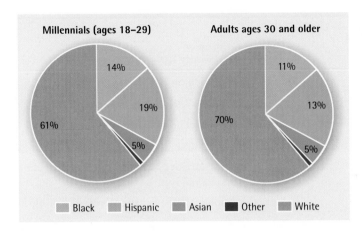

FIGURE 13.1 The New Face of America: 2009
Source: Pew Research Center. (2010, February 17). *Millennials, A portrait of Generation Next: Confident. Connected. Open to change.* Retrieved December 28, 2010, from http://pewsocialtrends.org/files/2010/10/millennials-confident-connected-open-to-change.pdf

structures; often both parents worked outside the home. More than 40 percent of Gen Xers spent time in a single-parent home by the age of 16 because of the increase in the divorce rate (U.S. Bureau of the Census, 2007b). The National Survey of Children, a longitudinal study of people born in the late 1960s, found that one-fourth of this generation had received psychological treatment for emotional, learning, or behavioral problems by the time they reached adulthood (Peterson & Zill, 1986). Yet Gen Xers are generally self-reliant and independent, having grown up with less parental supervision. Whereas boomers at this age had goals that were family- and work-related, Gen Xers' goals focus on their education and leisure pursuits. This calls into question the traditional understanding of the developmental tasks of young adulthood—that starting a career and a family are the signs of becoming an adult (Bangerter, Grob, & Krings, 2001).

Gen Xers share some attributes with the Millennials because they too grew up in a computer-oriented society. They are technologically literate and expect the immediate gratification of quick and easy access to people and information via the Internet and cell phones. Translating their independence and technological savvy into careers, many Gen Xers were involved in creating and working in computer and Web industries. Many seek greater monetary success and new experiences by hopping from job to job. Having tasted quick success, some Gen Xers in the fields of finance and technology lived lavish lifestyles only to have them curtailed when the dot-com industry collapsed in the early 2000s and in the recession that began in 2008 (U.S. Bureau of Labor Statistics, 2010b). Gen Xers are also facing a future in which they must support an aging baby-boom population, while maintaining their own lifestyle and paying for their children's rising educational costs (Reynolds, 2004). Add to this the uncertainty of the future of the American economy and of Social Security, and society can only hope that Gen Xers continue to draw on their

problem-solving and creative abilities in the future (see Table 13.1).

The Millennial Generation

The largest cohort in recent history is defined as the group of people born between the early 1980s and the early 2000s—and they are the most ethnically diverse of any U.S. cohort (see Figure 13.1). The main reason for the large size of this generation is the fact that many baby boomers decided to delay childbirth. The Millennial generation includes several subsets of children, but the oldest is now emerging-adult age or even a bit beyond. In 2009, this sector of the U.S. adult population, aged 18 to 29, numbered about 78 to 80 million (U.S. Bureau of the Census, 2010a).

Millennials are characterized as being wanted, sheltered, and made to feel valued (recall the advent of "Baby on Board" signs and of legislation mandating that infants be placed in car seats). They share the technical expertise and ambition of the Gen Xers, but they differ from them in their sense of being team players. As they come of age, the Millennials are interacting with boomers and Gen Xers who may be their college professors, employers, and workmates (see Table 13.1).

Despite efforts to categorize young adults such as the Gen Xers and Millennials with labels and generational characteristics, a new way to think about adulthood was put forth by Dr. Jeffrey Arnett in 2000. Arnett believes that the transition from adolescence to adulthood has changed significantly over the past half-century in industrialized societies and that researchers should regard the period from age 18 to age 29 as a distinct developmental phase called *emerging adulthood.* During this time, many young people in industrialized societies delay marriage and parenthood and focus on self-development as they try out various options in love and work. We will discuss this important idea in Chapter 14.

TABLE 13.1 Highlights of Two U.S. Generations in Early Adulthood

	Generation X Born 1965–1981	Millennial Generation Born early 1980s–early 2000s
Size	About 60 to 62 million	About 78 to 80 million (depending on end year)
Family Life	Adult-oriented from an early age	"Special" children—eagerly anticipated
	Less parental supervision than in any previous generation	Lowest parent-to-child ratio ever
	Little peer interaction in childhood	Protected and sheltered
Work	First generation to seek work-life balance	Many are underemployed
	Not constrained by time or place	More discretionary income than any previous group
School Life	First generation to be less educated than their parents by both choice and circumstance	Most educated generation
	Large segment of online learners	Expect active learning in classrooms but study less than any previous generation
		Volunteerism part of requirement to graduate
Significant Cultural/ Political Events	Berlin Wall comes down	Columbine High School shootings
	Challenger explosion	September 11, 2001
	AIDS epidemic	War in Iraq and Afghanistan
	Gulf War	Political strife between liberals and conservatives
	Personal computer	Social networking
Other Traits	Self-reliant	Optimistic and more liberal
	Adaptable	Racially diverse
	Resourceful	Pressured to achieve and succeed
	Distrust authority	Value healthy family and social relationships

Sources: Baker College: Effective Teaching and Learning Department, pp. 20–33. Flint, MI: Baker College. Alsop, R. (2008). *The trophy kids grow up* (p. 5). San Francisco, CA: Jossey-Bass.

Question

How would you concisely compare the general traits and values of Generation X and the Millennial generation to those of the previous generation of adults from the baby-boom generation, most of whom are now in middle adulthood and entering late adulthood?

Conceptions of Age Periods

Historical evidence suggests that age distinctions were more blurred and that chronological age played a less important role in the organization of U.S. society before 1850 than it does today. In the early nineteenth century, a person was either a child or an adult. Most young men became adults when they completed an apprenticeship for a trade or when they got married; a small number of young men from more wealthy families went to college. For young women, the transition occurred at marriage. Consciousness of discrete stages has grown over the past 160 years in response to developments in education, medicine, and psychology (including the psychology of

advertising). Public school systems used to impose strict age criteria for each grade. In the early twentieth century, sociological evidence regarding the relationship between work and health afforded a rationale for age legislation regarding child labor, school attendance, and pension benefits. And in medicine, *pediatrics* emerged as a specialty in the 1930s, and the study of old age became known as *gerontology* in the mid-1940s. Popular culture, as expressed in the media, song lyrics, birthday celebrations, and advice columns of popular magazines, picked up and helped disseminate the notion that there are appropriate ages for experiencing various life events.

For the most part, Americans perceive adults of all ages favorably. Nevertheless, older adults are viewed less favorably and as less desirable to be around than younger adults (unless you are an older adult, in which case you may prefer to be around people your own age). Such attitudes are influenced by a variety of factors. Adults who have had more formal education and more experience with a range of older adults have more positive attitudes toward older people than is true of the population generally. Adults who encounter burdens or conflicts associated with the elderly have more negative attitudes toward them.

College students tend to see young people as more adaptable, more capable of pursuing goals, and more active than older people. But overall, people's age, in and of itself, seems to be less important in determining their attitudes toward the elderly than other types of information, such as their personality traits. People also evaluate the stages of the life cycle differently depending on their current age. Americans have some difficulty specifying the age at which an average man or woman becomes old. Much depends on the person's health, activity level, and related circumstances.

According to surveys of adult Americans, two-thirds perceive themselves as being younger than they actually are, although those under 30 years of age often perceive themselves as being older than they actually are (Kotter-Gruhn, Kleinspehn-Ammerlahn, Gerstorf, & Smith, 2009). It seems that younger people desire to be grown up and to dissociate themselves from potential social stigmas and disadvantages attached to being "too young." Once individuals reach middle age, however, they think of themselves as being 5 to 15 years younger than they are. Indeed, people frequently say that they feel about 30 or 35 years old, regardless of their actual age. The thirties seem to have eternal appeal. In addition,

as is consistent with the notion that "you're only as old as you feel," aging people's own conceptions of their age seem to be better predictors of their mental and physical functioning than their chronological age is. However, as adults near the end of life, they report being less satisfied with aging and feeling older than they are (Kotter-Gruhn et al., 2009).

Question

In what ways do social scientists distinguish various life stages during adulthood, and what are those stages?

Age Norms and the Social Clock

We commonly associate adulthood with **aging**: biological and social change across the life span. **Biological aging** consists of changes in the structure and functioning of the human organism over time. The term **social aging** refers to changes in an individual's assumption and relinquishment of roles over time. Therefore, the life course of individuals is punctuated by **transition points**—the relinquishment of familiar roles and the assumption of new ones. Some of these transition points help to define adulthood (see Table 13.2).

TABLE 13.2 Differing Conceptions of Adulthood

Ethnic-racial groups in the United States have differing standards for defining adulthood. All agree that self-sufficiency is the key marker of adulthood, but the chart below illustrates interesting differences among four U.S. cultural groups.

	African American %	Latino %	Asian American %	White %
Accept responsibility for the consequences of your actions	89	85	93	91
Decide on personal beliefs and values independently of parents or other influences	80	72	82	82
Financially independent from parents	72	79	75	71
Less self-oriented, greater consideration for others	75	75	80	73
Avoid drunk driving	62	64	72	60
Use contraception	63	65	65	56
Make lifelong commitments to others	42	46	52	37
Employed full time	43	50	35	19
Married	14	32	13	5
Reach age 18	41	52	35	34
Reach age 21	43	47	40	30
Finish education	23	24	32	14
Have at least one child	16	32	10	5

Note: The questionnaire used in this survey asked participants to "indicate whether you think each of the following must be achieved before a person can be considered an adult." N = 109 whites, 122 African Americans, 96 Latinos, and 247 Asian Americans.

Source: Arnett, J. J. (2006). What does it mean to be an adult? Young people's conceptions of adulthood. In L. Balter & C. S. Tamis-LeMonda (Eds.). (2006). *Child psychology: A handbook of contemporary issues* (p. 485). New York: Psychology Press.

Each society or community reckons age as a set of behavioral expectations associated with given points in the life span. Many behaviors are prescribed for us in terms of society's "dos and don'ts." Conformity to these expectations generally has favorable results; violation of them has unpleasant ones. Such dos and don'ts are termed **social norms**—standards of behavior that members of a group share and to which they are expected to conform, such as the unacceptability of pushing and shoving when entering or exiting a subway car. Social norms are enforced by positive and negative sanctions. For example, drivers who obey traffic laws enjoy freedom of movement. But drivers who exhibit road rage or drive under the influence of alcohol are likely to lose their licenses for a time.

Social norms that define what is appropriate for people to be and to do at various ages are termed **age norms.** Age norms tend to define the "best age" for a man or woman to get a driver's license, to marry, to have babies, to finish school, to settle on a career, to hold a top job, or to become a grandparent. Other examples include compulsory school attendance laws, laws about the minimum voting age, the age at which youth may purchase alcoholic beverages, the age at which it is possible to enter military service, and the age at which individuals retire and become eligible for Social Security benefits. According to the World Bank, the average U.S. life span is increasing (it is near age 80 now), and the United States (like most other countries around the world) is experiencing a longevity revolution that is already creating a shift in age norms (World Bank, 2010). In general, young adults are leaving home later, couples are marrying much later if at all, women are having babies much later, and people are retiring later.

Age norms can also represent informal expectations about the kinds of roles appropriate for people of various ages. At times, such expectations are only vague notions about who is "too old," "too young," or "the right age" for certain activities. The appeal "Act your age!" pervades a great many aspects of life. Variations on this theme are often heard in such remarks as, "She's too young to wear that style of clothing" and "That's a strange thing for a man his age to say" and "Couldn't he have found someone more age-appropriate?"

Age grading at the social level—the arranging of people in social layers that are based on periods in the life cycle—creates a **social clock,** a set of internalized concepts that regulate our progression through the age-related milestones of the adult years. The social clock sets the standards that individuals use in assessing their conformity to societal expectations. For example, most think it appropriate to be impulsive in adolescence but not in middle age.

Although the members of a society tend to share similar expectations about their life cycle, some variations do occur. *Social class* is one important factor. The lower the socioeconomic status, the more rapid the pacing of the social clock tends to be. The higher the social class, the later individuals generally leave school, acquire their first job, get married, begin parenthood, secure their top job, and begin grandparenthood. New generations believe they can reset the social clock. For instance, compared to women of earlier generations, young women currently prefer earlier ages for educational and occupational events and later ages for family events. It is not uncommon today for professional women to wait until their late thirties or even their forties to have a first child. Assisted reproductive technology has made it possible (albeit expensive) for significant numbers of women to conceive and carry a child to term at later ages than was ever possible before.

Neugarten and Neugarten (1987) believe that distinctions between life periods are blurring in the United States. They note the appearance of the category "young-old"—retirees who are healthy and vigorous, relatively well off financially, and actively engaged in community life. A young-old person could be 55 or 90. The line between middle age and old age is no longer clear. What was once considered "old" now characterizes a minority of elderly people—the "old-old," a particularly vulnerable group who often are in need of special support and care. The Neugartens observe that increasingly we have conflicting images rather than firm stereotypes of age: It is common to see an 18-year-old who is married and supporting a family, but it is also common for an 18-year-old college student still to live at home. At the other end of the age spectrum, some 70-year-olds move about like elderly people, but some run marathons.

A more fluid life cycle affords many people new freedoms. But each person has an internal timetable for life accomplishments. Young adults might feel they are failures if they have not "made it" in their profession by the time they are 35. And a young woman might delay marriage or childbearing to focus on a career but then hurry to bear children in her late thirties and early forties—or later.

Questions

What evidence do we see that traditional age-grade norms are "blurring," as Neugarten states? How have you been affected personally by age norms or age grading?

Age-Grade Systems

Age norms are embodied in an age-grade system in a number of African societies (Foner & Kertzer, 1978). Members of each grade are alike in chronological age or life stage and have certain roles that are age-specific. For instance, the Latuka people of Sudan distinguish among five age grades: children, youth, rulers of the village, retired elders, and the very old. In such societies the individuals of each age grade are viewed as a corporate body and move as a unit from one age grade to another. For example, among the African Tiriki, uninitiated boys may not engage in sexual intercourse, must eat with other children and with women, and are permitted to play in the women's section of the hut. After initiation by puberty ritual, they may engage in sexual intercourse, are expected to eat with other men, and are forbidden to enter the women's section of the hut. In India, young women who marry become the caretakers of everyone in the household, and the older mother or mother-in-law in the home finally enjoys higher social status and a more leisurely life.

Furthermore, age grades differ in the access they afford their members to highly rewarded economic and political roles. In Western societies, people's chronological age is but a partial clue to their social locations. Socioeconomic class and ethnic factors cut across lines of age stratification and provide additional sources of identity.

All societies are faced with the fact that aging is inevitable and continuous. Hence, they all must make provision for the perpetual flow of one cohort after another by fitting each age group into an appropriate array of social roles. In the United States, no collective rituals mark the passage from one age grade to another. High school and college graduation ceremonies are an exception, but even here, not all individuals in a cohort graduate from either high school or college, and some intellectually gifted children skip grades in elementary school and enter college early. With corporate downsizing, takeovers, and outsourcing, it is now common to see middle-aged college students retraining for a second career in the workforce. At the older age levels, too, flexibility often operates: Within some companies and some occupations, older workers may either retire early or work well beyond the age at which retirement typically begins.

The *Age Discrimination in Employment Act* of 1967, or ADEA, is intended to protect U.S. workers over age 40 from age discrimination—mainly workers in labor organizations, government agencies, and (in the private sector) companies with 20 or more employees. Older workers are vulnerable to layoff or termination today because they typically earn higher wages and "cost more" in benefits than younger workers. ADEA applies to job applicants and employees and prohibits discrimination because of age regarding "any term, condition, privilege of employment, including hiring, firing, promotion, layoff, compensation, benefits, job assignments, and training" (Milodragovich, 2011).

In 1990, Congress passed the *Older Workers Benefit Protection Act* (OWBPA) to strengthen ADEA with more protections in the areas of early retirement provisions and termination (Mitchell, 1992).

Life Events

People locate themselves across the life span in terms of social timetables. They also do so in terms of **life events.** But some events are considered nonnormative—that is, largely independent of age or stage. Examples include being in a serious automobile accident, winning a lottery, undergoing a "born again" conversion, being alive when Pearl Harbor or the World Trade Center was attacked, or experiencing the feeling of awe when Neil Armstrong became the first person to walk on the moon. We often employ major events as reference points or time markers in our lives, speaking of "the day we got married," "the day I had my first baby," and "after the World Trade Center attack." Such life events define transitions. Events that produce traumatic or reflective consequences include the death or disappearance of a loved one, divorce, being fired from a job, and being the victim of a serious crime. These life events cause one to ask questions about oneself or society. Some of the effects of child sexual abuse are discussed in the *Further Developments* box on page 410, "The Long-Term Effects of Childhood Sexual Abuse." Also see Figure 13.2.

Life events may be examined in a great many ways by different people (Villalonga-Olives et al., 2010). For instance, some life events are associated with internal growth or aging factors such as puberty or old age. Others, including wars, national and international economic crises such as the recession that began in 2007, revolutions, and events such as the terrorist attacks and anthrax scare of 2001 and the 2009 acts of the Ft. Hood shooter and the Christmas Day airplane bomber are the consequences of living in society. Others derive from events in the physical world, such as fires, floods, hurricanes such as Katrina in 2005, tidal waves, and earthquakes. And then there are those events with a strong inner or

Changing Notions of the "Right Time" for Life Events
Age norms reflect what each society determines appropriate for people to be and to do at various ages. To some extent, age norms are variable regarding the "best age" for a woman to have babies. This woman was 57 when she conceived her twin daughters via assisted reproductive technologies.

FURTHER DEVELOPMENTS

The Long-Term Effects of Childhood Sexual Abuse

Men and women who survive childhood sexual abuse face a number of obstacles on the path to adulthood. Many experience emotional reactions to stimuli that do not affect individuals who did not experience childhood sexual abuse. Often their behavior and reactions seem strange or inappropriate to their friends or partners. The smallest or most innocuous event may trigger a response in their body and emotions that seems hard to understand, even for the survivor who is experiencing the reaction. Yet at one time, the period when they were being abused, the reaction they exhibit *was* appropriate. It is not until adulthood that some survivors can begin to sort out what is an appropriate reaction to stressors and what behaviors are no longer necessary and can be changed. Often this process requires the help of a supportive therapist or counselor.

Healing from childhood sexual abuse on an emotional level is a challenging process that yields rich rewards. The survivor may realize how strong he or she was to survive the trauma, which may have lasted for years. Survivors may also notice what adaptive strategies they used to survive and may learn how to apply those personality strengths in healthy ways in their work life and social life.

But the experience of being sexually abused leaves hidden scars in the body as well. One study found that adult survivors of childhood trauma responded to a startling sound much more intensely than adults who did not experience trauma. They blinked rapidly and more often, they sweated more, and they reported more intense feelings of anxiety, danger, anger, and helplessness. The researchers theorized that life-threatening experiences in childhood affect the developing nervous system and alter the child's sensitivity to threats. In effect, the nervous system is "tuned" to a higher sensitivity that stays with the person into adulthood. The researchers in this study were interested to learn how childhood trauma might affect the responses of police officers, firefighters, and other emergency services providers to threatening situations, particularly with regard to predicting job-related post-traumatic stress (Pole et al., 2007).

Another way in which abuse resets the body's functioning has to do with women's menstrual cycles. Even though a woman's experience of abuse might have happened before the onset of menstruation, the exposure to severe stress apparently alters her neurobiology during a crucial period of physical development. As a result, her entire physiology is more sensitive to stressors, even mild ones, in adulthood. Women who were abused in childhood are more likely than other women to experience severe daily emotional and physical symptoms associated with the menstrual cycle. Their moods are produced by the responses of their neuroendocrine systems to the physical stress of ovulation in what the researchers call "an adaptation gone awry" that "continues to prepare

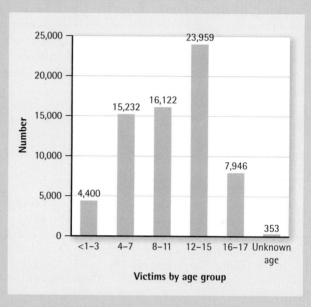

FIGURE 13.2 Confirmed Child Victims of Sexual Abuse by Age, United States: 2008
Source: U.S. Department of Health and Human Services, Administration on Children, Youth and Families. (2009). *Child Maltreatment 2008.* Washington, DC: U.S. Government Printing Office. Retrieved November 20, 2010, from http://www.acf.hhs.gov/programs/cb/pubs/cm08/cm08.pdf

the survivor for a severe stressor that no longer exists but somehow remains encoded in the brain" (Girdler et al., 2007).

Both men and women who were sexually abused in childhood are at some risk of self-harming behaviors such as cutting or burning one's own body, yet recent research indicates that the association is not strong (Klonsky & Moyer, 2008). However, studies show that the adverse physical effects of childhood sexual abuse can add the equivalent of eight years of aging to a victim's life (Talbot et al., 2009). In general, men and women respond to their childhood trauma in different ways. Both genders are highly likely to experience post-traumatic stress long after the trauma has ended. The effects can last a lifetime (Draper et al., 2008). Men are more likely to react to this state by becoming irritable, angry, or violent. Women are more likely to be anxious and depressed. Men are more likely to describe their childhood sexual abuse in somewhat neutral ways, but women are more likely to describe it in negative ways. Women are also more likely to believe that they are damaged and that they should have been able to prevent the abuse from occurring. Researchers are just beginning to learn about gender differences in the expression of post-traumatic stress. This research should be very useful in aiding adult survivors as they continue the lifelong journey of growth and healing (Tolin & Foa, 2006).

psychological component, such as a profound religious experience, the decision to adopt a child, the realization that one has reached the zenith of one's career, or the decision to leave one's spouse. Any of these events we might view as good or bad, a gain or a loss, controllable or uncontrollable, and stressful or unstressful. The type of life event largely determines whether people organize social support systems to assist others in buffering the change. In the United States, for example, we have extensive, organized social support systems for helping infants in need of early intervention; for ushering children through formal schooling, including special education; for getting and staying employed; for getting married; and for making the transition to retirement.

The Search for Periods in Adult Development

Many psychologists have undertaken the search for regular, sequential periods and transitions in the life cycle. They depict adulthood as being, like childhood, a sort of stairway—a series of discrete, steplike levels. The metaphor of the life course as being divided into stages, or "seasons," has captured the imagination of philosophers and poets, as well as other writers. One of the most popular versions of the stage approach is contained in Gail Sheehy's best-selling books *Passages* (1976) and *New Passages* (1995). Sheehy views each stage as posing problems that must be resolved before the individual can successfully advance to the next stage. In these passages from one stage to the next, each person acquires new strengths and evolves an authentic identity. Such an identity has many of the qualities that humanistic psychologist Abraham Maslow associates with the self-actualized person.

Other psychologists have taken exception to the stage approach. Some believe that an individual's identity is fairly well established during the formative years and does not fundamentally change much in adulthood. According to this view, people might change jobs, move to new addresses, even cosmetically alter their faces and bodies to appear younger, but their personalities persist, much as adult height and weight do, with only minor changes. As we noted in our treatment of developmental continuity and discontinuity in Chapter 2, this approach views aging as a continuous yet dynamic process. The discontinuity approach stresses the differences between stages and the uniqueness of the issues for each stage.

Questions

How does the stage perspective of adult development differ from the view that adult development is a continuous process of change over the life course? What significant life events do you recall?

PHYSICAL CHANGES AND HEALTH

Our physical organism changes across the life span. But in and of themselves, such changes may be less important than what people make of them. As we pointed out earlier, cultural stereotypes and social attitudes have a profound effect on our perceptions of biological change and our experience of it. Whereas the physical changes associated with puberty are comparatively easy to identify, later changes (with the possible exceptions of prostate problems and menopause) are less easy to pinpoint as marking stages in adulthood.

Physical Performance

Most individuals believe that getting older means losing a measure of physical attractiveness, vigor, and strength. Yet although physical changes take place throughout adulthood, in early adulthood they generally have only minimal implications for an individual's daily life. The years from 18 to about 30 are peak years for speed and agility. Most Olympic athletes fall between these ages, although exceptions include Lance Armstrong, two-time Olympian and seven-time winner of the Tour de France; Cal Ripkin, who retired from professional baseball at age 41; and Dara Torres 2008 Olympic medalist in swimming, at age 41. TV's first physical fitness expert Jack LaLanne, who was also a proponent of good nutrition, a motivational speaker, and the inventor of fitness machines, exercised every day and died from pneumonia complications at age 96.

Both men and women complete their physical growth in early adulthood, although women reach full height before their twenties and men continue to grow until age 30. Both genders achieve peak bone mass by age 35, and both genders reach their capacity to work at their maximum rate without fatigue by this age. Both muscle strength and coordination peak when a person is in his or her 20s and 30s. The heart's maximum output is reached in early adulthood, too, between the ages of 20 and 30. Men and women reach peak respiratory function in their 20s, women around age 20 and men around age 25 (Polan & Taylor, 2003). In short, the human machine functions at its highest level in early adulthood.

Physical Health

Adult health is a function of a wide variety of factors, including heredity, nutrition, exercise, recreational pursuits, prior illness, ability to pay for health care and access to health insurance, and the demands and constraints of the social environment. For the most part, we

IMPLICATIONS FOR PRACTICE

Family Nurse Practitioner, Ronald Dingwell

I am a family nurse practitioner (FNP), and I work in a hospital setting as well as in private practice. I work with both children and adults. My main job tasks are to provide primary and emergency care to an inner-city population of uninsured minorities.

I earned my bachelor's degree in nursing (BSN) from Queen's College in New York City, my master's degree in nursing (MSN) from SUNY Downstate, and my family nurse practitioner (FNP) degree from SUNY Stonybrook on Long Island. Prior to becoming an FNP, I worked as an emergency room nurse for seven years. For students interested in entering this profession, you need to get clinical experience in both primary

care (office practice setting) and acute care (hospital setting). Prior experience as a nurse in such settings as an ICU (intensive care unit), ER (emergency room), or pediatrics is also valuable. Such experience will help you determine where your competency or comfort level is as an FNP.

I believe that to enjoy working as a family nurse practitioner, you need to be self-motivated, to have a desire to serve society, and to have the ability to practice independently. What I enjoy most about my profession is helping patients who otherwise would not be able to afford or access health care.

assess people's health by how well they are able to function in their daily lives and adapt to a changing environment. Health, then, has a somewhat different meaning for a young pregnant woman, a nursing-home resident, a college professor, a presidential candidate, a high school basketball player, an astronaut, a construction worker, and a surgeon (Van Mechelen et al., 1996).

The provision of medical care is a multifaceted, costly issue that is hotly debated from the federal level to the kitchen table. Many people living in the United States (about 50 million, or 16 percent of the population in 2009) cannot afford their own health insurance (U.S. Bureau of the Census, 2010j). Federal funding for Medicaid and Medicare is meant to provide a safety net for a majority that cannot afford health coverage. In 2007, as a first in the nation, the Massachusetts legislature passed a law requiring all citizens of the state to have health insurance (Belluck, 2007). Residents are required to prove medical coverage on tax returns, and penalties are imposed on those who have the financial ability to pay toward health coverage but do not. Those who legitimately cannot afford to pay for health insurance are subsidized on a sliding scale. As of July 2009, Vermont and Maine had similar plans, and fourteen other states were considering similar health-care proposals (Kaiser Family Foundation, 2009).

Health-Care Reform   On March 23, 2010, President Obama's *Patient Protection and Affordable Care Act*

(PPACA) became law, mandating major changes in health insurance and health-care delivery by 2014. The law outlines comprehensive health insurance reforms. Its goal is to lower health-care costs, guarantee more choice, and improve the quality and accessibility of health care for Americans (U.S. Department of Health & Human Services, 2010b). One provision affecting young adults is that parents' health plans will offer coverage for adult children through the age of 26.

However, the law is controversial and lacks widespread support because many people fear it will lead to rationed and reduced care with less individual choice among providers of medical services at a higher cost. Some individuals and businesses have found their health insurance rates increasing dramatically in response to the law's requirements. Lawmakers disagree about how to enact or fund the law's provisions. At present, 20 states have sued the federal government to block the law's implementation, because much of the mandated costs (billions) will fall on the states (Adamy, 2010). As a constitutional matter, unprecedented penalties will be imposed on adults who do not purchase health-care insurance. A major concern is the impending lack of enough health-care providers to serve millions more people—and the restructuring of systems for delivering health care (Iglehart, 2010). The impact this legislation will have on immigrants, minorities, the poor, employed and unemployed people without health-care insurance, uninsured women, and young adults is not yet known.

Increasing Access to Affordable Health Care   Having access to affordable health care remains an important issue in the United States. The populations most likely to lack health insurance are blacks and Hispanics, persons aged 18 to 24, and persons living in households of less than $25,000 annual income (U.S. Bureau of the Census, 2010b). Millions of undocumented persons get health care in hospital emergency rooms that are required by law (EMTALA) to treat the uninsured, with no compensation to the physician or the hospital. Thus, many uninsured get medical treatment in high-tech and costly emergency rooms. Also, between 300,000 and 350,000 "anchor" babies are born annually in the United States. That is, women who are in the United States illegally are delivering babies in U.S. hospitals so that their babies will be American citizens. This makes the infant and his or her family eligible for welfare and medical aid. Hospitals provide at least $34 billion worth of uncompensated care for the uninsured every year (National Coalition on Health Care, 2008). By 2007, more than 75 hospitals in southern California had been forced to close, and some physicians and surgeons are leaving areas of the country that are the most affected by the influx of undocumented persons (Cosman, 2005).

However, many uninsured people come from working families whose employers do not provide health insurance. Also, employee contributions to health insurance premiums have risen, and benefits for new or retired employees have been reduced. Some employees cannot afford to pay their share of the premium for health insurance (National Coalition on Health Care, 2008). Even though the federal Medicaid program insures millions of persons who are poor or have disabilities, others live near or below the poverty line. In 2010 a family of four earning $22,050 or above was ineligible for coverage (U.S. Department of Health and Human Services, 2010a). The United States spends nearly $100 billion a year in health care for uninsured individuals; as a result, most states have large budget deficits due to the cost of providing medical care for the uninsured. For common illnesses, more affordable care can be found in the nearly 800 walk-in clinics that pharmacies and retailers such as CVS, Walgreen's, and WalMart have opened in over 26 states. These clinics are operated in partnership with local health-care providers, and costs are 30 to 40 percent less (Shapiro, 2009). (See the *Implications for Practice* box on page 412, "Family Nurse Practitioner.")

Women are more likely to lose health insurance, because they are more likely to be covered as dependents under a spouse's policy. When divorced or widowed, they may lose their coverage. One in every five women aged 18 to 64 in the United States cannot afford her own health insurance coverage. Among this group are single parents, those without high school diplomas, Latina or Native American or Aleut/Eskimo women, undocumented immigrants, and those under the age of 24. Many uninsured women need care but don't get it or have no regular doctor. Even when they see a doctor, many do not fill prescriptions because they cannot afford the cost of the medicine (Kaiser Family Foundation, 2007). In some communities, retired physicians and other health-care professionals are providing free health care on a limited basis through county health departments.

Government policy has affected the number of women who have health insurance, particularly poor women who depend solely on Medicaid coverage. The *Personal Responsibility and Work Opportunity Reconciliation Act of 1996* set a five-year time limit, after which recipients had to leave public assistance. The result was that many families became ineligible for Medicaid. Policymakers thought that full-time employment would provide workers with health-care coverage, but full-time employment no longer guarantees essential health-care coverage.

Most young adults enjoy good to excellent health, but college graduates are much more likely to be in excellent health than peers who did not attend college (Barnes, Adams, & Schiller, 2003). In fact, 25 percent of young adults actually choose not to carry health insurance because of the high cost and their perception that they are and will remain healthy (U.S. Bureau of the Census, 2010b). To help students stay healthy, many colleges and universities have upgraded gymnasiums into recreation, fitness, and wellness centers for students, staff, alumni, and community members. Comprehensive offerings include expanded intramural programs, fitness assessment, personal training, and individualized exercise programs and goals (Blumenthal, 2004).

Chronic Conditions and Common Illness   Certain diseases emerge in 6 percent of adults aged 18 to 44 that can limit daily activity or incapacitate. Most common are arthritis and musculoskeletal conditions, followed by mental-health issues, and cardiovascular conditions (National Center for Health Statistics, 2010b). Three-quarters of lifetime cases of mental illness emerge by age 24 (Park et al., 2006). The most common illnesses in this age group are infectious diseases—particularly colds, upper respiratory infections, and sexually transmitted infections. Employers can expect to lose more workdays to sickness among young adults than to sickness among older adults. Common diseases among college students include mononucleosis, asthma (especially among ethnic-minority groups), migraine headaches, and urinary tract infections (Rimsza & Kirk, 2005).

Causes of Mortality   In 2008, car accidents and other unintentional injuries were the leading causes of death for young adults aged 15 to 24, and the rate for men was

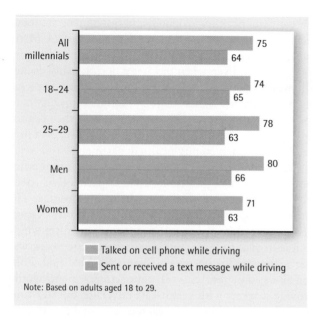

FIGURE 13.3 The Majority of Millennials Have Talked or Texted While Driving

Source: Pew Research Center. (2010, February 17). *Millennials, A portrait of Generation Next: Confident. Connected. Open to change.* Retrieved December 28, 2010, from http://pewsocialtrends.org/files/2010/10/millennials-confident-connected-open-to-change.pdf

components of staying fit, yet by the time they reach their 20s, only half the population is getting the recommended level of exercise, which is at least 20 minutes of vigorous exercise on three or more days a week. Gender, race, and level of education are all associated with whether a person gets enough exercise in adulthood. In general, men exercise more hours each week than women. White people are more likely than people of other races to exercise for fitness. And people who attended or graduated from college are far more likely to exercise regularly than those who did not (Baum, Ma, & Payea, 2010). Research findings suggest that college students and graduates develop a sustainable sense of responsibility toward achieving a successful life, but another factor is also involved: the ability to earn enough money in a reasonable number of hours so that there is enough time left to take proper care of one's body (Mirowsky & Ross, 2003).

After completing high school, most young adults enter into new routines that affect how active they are—some enter environments that include time for exercise, whereas others take on responsibilities that prevent them from being as active as they were during adolescence. One survey of physical activities among Americans over 18 found that fear of injury was a significant barrier to exercise for individuals whose annual income was less than $25,000. Perhaps being able to report to work is a more salient factor for workers who earn hourly wages and who are also less likely to have medical benefits (Keenan, 2006).

Men and women seem to exercise in different ways and for different reasons. Women report that they exercise to improve their health or to control their weight. Men are more likely to report that they exercise as a way of socializing with other people. Men prefer group sports, running, and weight training. Women prefer walking (Keenan, 2006). There are physiological differences in how men and women's bodies experience exercise as well. Women's bodies are more subject to heat stress because they have fewer sweat glands and produce less sweat than men. Women start sweating at higher temperatures than men do, and the fat in women's bodies acts like insulation and inhibits heat dissipation. For these reasons, in warmer temperatures, women have to work harder than men to achieve similar workloads (Robbins, Powers, & Burgess, 2008).

Exercise has benefits that are particular to the health needs of young adults. Research by the American Heart Association (2007a) has found that fitness levels in young adulthood predict whether a person will develop cardiovascular disease in middle age. People whose fitness level is low or moderate have an increased risk for diabetes, high blood pressure, and heart disease. The good news is that improving one's fitness level can cut that risk in half (McCoy, 2003). A similar study

significantly higher than the rate for women (National Highway Traffic Safety Administration, 2010; National Safety Council, 2010). Failure to use seatbelts, distracted driving using cell phones and texting, driving under the influence of alcohol or drugs, and accidental overdose or alcohol poisoning contribute significantly to accidental death among young people (see Figure 13.3). The other leading causes of mortality for those 15 to 24 are homicide, suicide, cancer, and heart disease. For young adults aged 25 to 44, other leading causes of death are cancer, heart disease, homicide, and suicide (Miniño, Xu, & Kochanek, 2010).

Questions

What types of common conditions and behaviors are detrimental to health or contribute to the higher death rates at this age? What are some health-promoting practices recommended for young adults?

Dieting, Exercise, and Obesity Being healthy is not something that just happens to you, especially as you get older. At age 25, most U.S. adults can expect to live at least 50 to 55 more years. How well their bodies function during that half-century is largely up to them. Having and maintaining good health consists of choosing certain patterns of behavior and avoiding others. A healthy diet and regular exercise are two important

found that young adults who exercised an average of five times a week and expended 300 calories in each session reduced their risk of hypertension significantly (ScienceDaily, 2007).

Exercise can even improve cognitive functioning among young adults. One study found that young people who jogged for 30 minutes two or three times a week improved their performance on computer-based memory tests. However, the test scores fell if the study participants stopped running. The researchers concluded that the test scores went up because of increased oxygen to the brain (Cocke, 2002).

Of great concern for many young adults today is the ever-increasing waistline. The average weight for U.S. adults has increased by about 25 pounds for both women and men since 1960. That in itself is a concern; even a slight weight gain brings an increased risk of cardiovascular disease. But of greater concern is how that weight gain is distributed in the population. Since 1980, the U.S. population has become much heavier, and now more than one-third of adults are classified as *obese* (see Figure 13.4). For women, **obesity** is defined as 30 percent of body weight being fat; for men it is 25 percent. The National Institutes of Health has adopted the **body mass index (BMI)** as a way to classify overweight and obesity. This index compares weight to height and calculates what percentage of a person's weight is fat. It offers ranges for normal weight, moderate overweight, obesity, and extreme (or morbid) obesity. In the 20–39 age group, about one-fourth of men and one-third of women can be categorized as obese (with a BMI of 30 or greater), but about two-thirds of men and women in this age group are overweight (with a BMI of 25 or greater). These numbers are even higher for older adults (Flegal, Carrol, Ogden, & Curtain, 2010).

The Causes of Obesity   Weight is gained when more calories are consumed than are expended in physical activity. Some researchers point to the prevalence of eating out rather than eating home-cooked meals, and indeed, over one-third of adults in the 18–24 age group eat out four or more times a week. Most restaurant meals are higher in calories and saturated fat than home-cooked meals (National Center for Health Statistics, 2007b). In addition, today's restaurant portions are significantly larger than in the past, much larger than the serving sizes recommended by the government (Condrasky, Ledikwe, Flood, & Rolls, 2007).

But obesity is much more complex than simply a matter of calories consumed and calories expended. Scientists still don't fully understand the physiology of obesity. Some advocate the fat-cell theory, which holds that overweight and obesity may be caused by too many fat cells or larger-than-normal fat cells. (Whether a person is born with too many fat cells or adds them through overeating is unknown.) Those who are more than 40 percent overweight probably have too many fat cells and larger fat cells (Insel, Turner, & Ross, 2010). Other scientists adhere to the set-point theory, which says that the body regulates itself to maintain a certain weight. The body's set-point mechanism responds to signals that the fat cells send out about how much fat needs to be stored. Individuals who have a normal number of fat cells can lose weight by reducing the size of fat cells, while still sustaining an adequate volume of fat. Individuals who have excess fat cells have a harder time losing weight because the body will work to maintain the size of the fat cells; it will go into starvation mode if a person diets too strenuously (Farias, Cuevas, & Rodriguez, 2010). Science does lend some credence to the argument that genetics plays a role in obesity, although researchers are careful to say that one can inherit a *tendency* toward obesity and that this tendency can usually be controlled (Robbins et al., 2008).

Obesity Increasing Across Cultures   In 2002, the Worldwatch Institute announced that for the first time in history, the number of overweight people in the world rivaled the number of malnourished people. The World Health Organization (WHO) coined the new term "globesity" and listed obesity as one of the top 10 risks to human health around the globe (Eberwine, 2002). A decade later, Delpeuch, Maire, Monnier, & Holdsworth

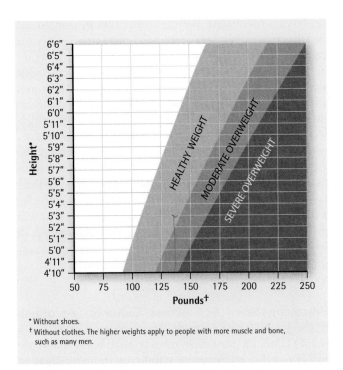

FIGURE 13.4 Recommended Weight for Adults by Height
Source: NIDKK. (1998). Understanding adult obesity. Retrieved January 17, 2008, from http://www.medhelp.org/NIHlib/GF-382.html

(2009) described globesity as "out of control" and stated that there are now more people overweight than malnourished.

You might assume that the problem of obesity existed mostly in industrialized nations, but the rate of obesity is increasing faster in most developing countries than it is in developed nations (WHO, 2010). Countries such as Samoa, China, India, Egypt, Albania, and South Africa have rapidly increasing rates of overweight and obesity, especially in urban areas and among women (Misra & Khurana, 2008). WHO attributes this alarming trend to what it calls the "worldwide nutrition transition" brought about by globalization and increased access to Western-style diets and fast food restaurants (WHO, 2010). In addition, poor people in developing countries often cannot afford to eat healthy foods and turn, by default, to foods full of sugar and carbohydrates (Kim, Stein, & Martorell, 2007). WHO predicts that by 2015, about 400 million adults will be obese (WHO, 2010).

In the case of diet and nutrition, development has been a mixed blessing. The peasant populations that used to live off the land and produce healthy food can no longer afford to buy it. WHO notes the links between obesity and respiratory difficulties, heart disease, type 2 diabetes, certain cancers, and gallbladder disease and points out that developing nations will find it difficult to meet the health-care needs of a rapidly increasing obese population (WHO, 2010).

In contrast to many other societies of the world, Western societies put a premium on being thin. Being overweight, or even viewing oneself as overweight, can place a Westerner in a precarious emotional state. Only after adolescents emerge into adulthood and the concomitant changes in lifestyle do the effects of poor diet and little exercise begin to show. It is therefore no coincidence that dieting is so common among adults in the United States. A recent study showed that a majority of men and women were either dieting to reduce weight or watching their food intake to prevent weight gain (Millstein et al., 2008). One major concern regarding diets is the constant on-again, off-again pattern of weight loss and gain that dieting produces. And as we noted in Chapter 11, dieting can lead to eating disorders such as bulimia and anorexia. Clearly, a combination of a healthy diet and regular exercise promotes better health.

Questions

Which adults are most likely to become overweight or obese, and what are the causes? How can young adults reduce their weight and improve their health and well-being?

Use of Contraceptives to Prevent Pregnancy and STIs   The Guttmacher Institute (2010) reports that most U.S. women want to have only a few children and want to be responsible and provide for the ones they have. To achieve that goal, they need to practice contraception for about three decades. A majority of sexually active women have used at least one method of contraception, but the methods women choose vary by age, race, and marital status. Since the early 1980s, the most common methods have been hormonal means (pills, patches, and devices), IUDs, condoms, and sterilization. White women and younger women tend to use the pill and condoms, and older women and Hispanic and black women are more likely to choose sterilization—but neither the pill nor sterilization offers any protection from STIs (Guttmacher Institute, 2010a).

Which method of contraception a woman uses has much to do with how much influence she has in her relationship with her sexual partner. Women who do not have influence in their relationships, or women in violent relationships, often cannot convince their partners to use a condom (Senn et al., 2007). This category includes several large groups of women. Many studies have shown that women who are survivors of childhood sexual abuse are less likely to be able to negotiate with sexual partners about using condoms and are more likely to engage in risky sexual behaviors, such as not using condoms and having multiple partners (Perrino et al., 2006).

Another such group is low-income African American women, some of whom are also survivors of childhood sexual abuse or are in violent relationships. One recent study of low-income African American women found that how their partners responded to their requests for condom use revealed interesting dynamics of the women's strengths and vulnerabilities. If the partner responded angrily or argued with the woman, she was sometimes able to convince him to use a condom. But if the partner believed that the woman suspected him of infidelity, the couple was less likely to use condoms. When a request to use a condom jeopardized the relationship, the women backed down (Perrino et al., 2006). Many low-income women depend on the financial resources of their sexual partners to help support their children and so face a terrible dilemma. Asking for sexual behaviors that will protect them from STIs might put the relationship in jeopardy. Thus they don't use condoms, thereby increasing the likelihood of bearing more children who will have access to fewer resources.

Practicing Safer Sex Across Cultures   According to the Joint United Nations Programme on HIV/AIDS (2010) *Global Report*, the rate of growth in the incidence of HIV/AIDS seems to be stabilizing in many areas of the world—except it is increasing significantly in Eastern Europe and in Asia. AIDS mortality is decreasing thanks to growing access to antiretroviral (ARV) therapy, and

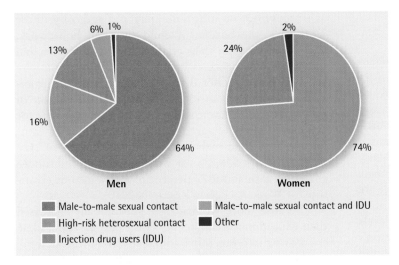

FIGURE 13.5 HIV/AIDS Transmission By 2008, the CDC reported that more than a million Americans were living with HIV/AIDS and that three out of four were males. The charts show how adolescents and adults living with HIV/AIDS are likely to have become infected with it. Note that males are more likely to get HIV/AIDS from having relations with men, whereas a majority of females are infected through heterosexual contact.
Sources: United States Statistics by Transmission Route and Gender: HIV. Retrieved December 30, 2010, from http://www.avert.org/usa-transmission-gender.htm. Centers for Disease Control and Prevention (2010, June). Diagnoses of HIV infection and AIDS in the United States and Dependent Areas, 2008. *HIV Surveillance Report*, Volume 20. 1–143. Retrieved December 30, 2010, from http://www.cdc.gov/hiv/topics/surveillance/resources/reports

the number of transmissions from mother to child is decreasing. Yet more than 33 million people are infected with HIV, and the majority of HIV infections occur during injection drug use, men having sex with men, in transgender persons, and among immigrants. For women, heterosexual sex is the main mode of HIV transmission (UNAIDS/WHO, 2010). In many regions of the world, more than half of those infected with HIV are women and girls (UNAIDS/WHO, 2010). In one U.S. study, 20 percent of men having sex with men also report having female sex partners (Harawa et al., 2004).

Many individuals falsely believe that certain forms of birth control protect them against STIs and HIV/AIDS transmission. Some young adults believe that requesting condom use is awkward because it indicates a belief that the partner may carry an STI. Research findings also suggest that once a relationship is established and partners trust one another, condom use is replaced by oral contraceptives, which seem more convenient but are not effective in providing a barrier to infections (Manlove & Terry-Humen, 2007). Many adults consider monogamy an effective way to prevent transmission of STIs and do not use condoms. Yet it is impossible to be sure that a partner is practicing monogamy.

The Kinsey Institute reports that 20 to 25 percent of men and 10 to 15 percent of women have affairs during marriage; the rate is likely to be higher among cohabiting partners (Kinsey Institute, 2010). Individuals who had multiple sexual partners before making a commitment to one partner are also more likely to have an affair (Kinsey Institute, 2007). For example, rates of infidelity are much higher in college student dating relationships; thus many relationships between young adults do not last (Allen & Baucom, 2006). Short-term serial monogamy is not an effective way to prevent transmission of STIs. To avoid the risk of getting STIs, adolescents and young adults are increasingly practicing oral sex—unaware that the main viral and bacterial sexually transmitted infections can be

transmitted via oral sex. Even though it is rare, HIV can be transmitted via oral sex (Chambers, 2007).

U.S. African American and Hispanic women are at a higher risk of contracting HIV and other sexually transmitted infections (STIs)—especially those living in large urban areas (Hall, Espinoza, Benbow, Hu, & the Urban Areas HIV Surveillance Workgroup, 2010). In 2007, more than 11,000 adult Americans, mainly aged 25 to 64, died from HIV complications (Xu, Kochanek, Murphy, & Tejada-Vera, 2010). African Americans accounted for slightly more than half of new cases in 2008. One-third of these new cases were contracted through high-risk heterosexual contact (see Figure 13.5) (Johnson et al., 2010). One study concluded that poverty, dependence on partners for income, low self-esteem, and alcohol and drug use explained the sexually risky behaviors of the HIV-positive women in the study (Centers for Disease Control and Prevention, 2005a).

The solution to reducing AIDs transmission seems so simple. A very low-cost intervention—using female or male condoms—will prevent the spread of HIV (CDC, 2010b). And yet there is nothing simple about it. Cultural factors, relationship dynamics, the degree of women's power in their relationships, and an individual's tendency for risky sexual behavior all intervene to decrease the likelihood that people will use condoms. Health-care providers and community educators need to be aware of these dynamics as they plan education programs that will be most effective. Rapid HIV testing is available in hospitals, in health department clinics, and in non-health-care settings, and individuals can be given their results on the same day. This substantially increases the chance that individuals will know their HIV status and will be able to start a regimen of medical care, as needed. An analysis of U.S. HIV testing and diagnosis from 2001 to 2009 reveals that the number of persons who have ever been tested continues to increase—yet 56,000 persons are newly diagnosed with HIV each year (Johnson et al., 2010).

Socioeconomic Status, Race-Ethnicity, and Gender

In the United States, people who are poor and lack higher education have a higher death rate than people who are wealthy and better educated (National Center for Health Statistics, 2010a). This is not surprising—poverty increases the likelihood that one will have inadequate or poor nutrition, poor housing, inadequate or no prenatal care, limited access to health-care facilities, and less education. Many studies confirm that racial-ethnic minorities and single parents are more likely to live in poverty. Poor people are eligible for Medicaid, but many do not have health insurance and cannot afford good medical care. Lower levels of education, linked to lower income, increase a person's risk of cardiovascular disease, hypertension, diabetes, and other serious health ailments (Lindelow, 2008).

a

We all know that women have a longer life expectancy than men. This is likely for three reasons. Women have two X chromosomes; scientists believe that the second X chromosome serves as a backup if something goes wrong with a gene on the first one (Austad, 2006). Women also produce larger amounts of the hormone *estrogen,* which is thought to delay the aging process. And men tend to gain weight in the stomach, which puts them at higher risk of hypertension, diabetes, heart disease, and stroke. In contrast, women tend to gain weight in the hips; this distribution is not associated as strongly with these diseases (Heid, 2010). But even though these diseases are likely to be decades away for young adults, this age group tends to engage in risky behaviors that have the potential to reduce longevity.

The National Longitudinal Study of Adolescent Health followed 10,000 young people from middle school into young adulthood during the period 1994 to 2002. Participants in the study were in grades 7 through 12 when it began, and at the time the results were published, they were aged 18 to 26. The study found that as this group of young people entered adulthood, the rate of obesity increased significantly for both genders and all racial-ethnic groups. As this U.S. cohort aged, they increasingly engaged in the risky behaviors related to the top three causes of death: tobacco use, poor diet and lack of exercise, and alcohol consumption (Harris et al., 2006). Excessive drinking among males in particular increased as they entered adulthood. Researchers pointed out that the risky behavior of this generation is jeopardizing their health in later decades. The racial-ethnic disparity in access to health care widened over the period of the study, a trend that intensified as young people left their parents' homes and aged out of Medicaid coverage or their parents' health insurance coverage.

Educational Attainment, Income, and Health Care

Gender inequities exist in several areas of adult life, such as employment opportunities, pay and authority in the workplace, the burden of child care and housework, and the conflicts in their relationships that women and men often experience as young adults. One reason why the gender gap is not disappearing is that men generally get more pay outside the home, and the balance of power within the home still rests with men (Institute for Women's Policy Research, 2010). The real median earnings for full-time male workers in 2009 were $47,127 compared with $36,278 for women working full time—who thus earn about 77 percent of men's income (Institute for Women's Policy Research, 2010).

Because more women have substantially increased their educational attainment over the past 40 years, some are moving into executive, administrative, medical, legal, engineering, and professional positions with higher incomes (see Table 13.3). But more women are in service industries that pay minimum wage with few, if any, medical benefits. On average, women contributed about 36 percent of the family income in 2008, compared with only 26 percent in 1970. Still, one in four wives earned more than her husband in 2008 (Solis & Hall, 2010). These women and their spouses sometimes contend with complex emotional issues involving power and responsibility for household matters. Interestingly, from 2000 to 2010, participation in the labor force has declined for

Education, Earnings, and Gender More women than men are earning associate's, bachelor's, and master's degrees—and women earned slightly more than half of all doctoral degrees as of 2008. Also, record numbers of women are entering the professions of psychology, engineering, dentistry, medicine, and law (National Center for Education Statistics, 2010). Colleen and Curt spent many years preparing to be board-certified physicians in their respective fields.

TABLE 13.3 Change in Numbers and Percent Change, Between 1997–1998 and 2007–2008, for U.S. Females Earning Master's, Doctoral, and First Professional Degrees

Field of Study	Number	Number of Females	Change in Number of Degrees	Percent Change for Females
Total Master's Degrees	**430,164**	**378,532**	194,859	54
Total Doctoral Degrees	**46,010**	**32,497**	17,702	68
Total First Professional Degrees	**78,598**	**45,393**	12,711	**34.7**
Law	39,331	20,572	4,438	17.9
Medicine	15,424	7,711	222	20.1
Pharmacy	3,660	7,216	7,272	193
Theology	5,873	1,974	−122	29
Dentistry	4,032	2,134	763	38.4
Osteopathic	2,110	1,651	1,122	113.6
Chiropractic	3,735	956	−1,096	−6.5
Veterinary medicine	2,193	1,924	311	33.7
Optometry	1,274	859	30	26.3
Podiatry	594	250	−39	42

Source: National Center for Education Statistics. (2010). *The Condition of Education 2010: Contexts of Postsecondary Education.* Table A-42-1: Graduate and First-Professional Fields of Study. Academic years 1997–98 and 2007–08. Retrieved December 28, 2010, from http://nces.ed.gov/programs/coe/2010/section5/table-gfs-1.asp

single women, those with no children, and those with a college education (Macunovich, 2010).

Education is the single most important predictor of future earnings. Significantly, more than half of the unemployed U.S. population in 2010 had only a high school education or less (U.S. Bureau of Labor Statistics, 2010b). Without at least some college education or apprentice training, adults will confront serious deficits in earning potential across their lifetime. They also may be forced to delay marriage; as one study pointed out, "For young men who cannot find work that pays enough to support themselves, much less a family, and for the women they might otherwise marry, postponing full adulthood may reflect painful constraints rather than welcome choices" (Hamilton & Hamilton, 2006, p. 267).

Drug and Alcohol Use

The end of high school is a major transition period for most adolescents as they enter the world of young adulthood. The usual roles that young adults take on include college student, apprentice, civilian employee, and member of the armed forces—though approximately 10 percent of young adults simply "drop out" of mainstream society (some are imprisoned, disabled or chronically ill, institutionalized, or addicted to drugs). Traditionally, common experiences for young adults have included completing college, securing full-time employment, being promoted in the workplace or military, cohabiting

or marrying, working toward advanced degrees, and parenting. Each of these experiences affects substance or alcohol use during the post–high school years, so it is useful to consider the timing of these experiences during young adulthood and how they are interrelated.

Alcohol abuse is widespread among adolescents and young adults. This is because their perception of risk is not accurate and because they engage in sensation-seeking behaviors. Drinking too much can have life-altering or life-threatening consequences: A woman whose judgment is impaired by alcohol may not accurately gauge the aggressive intentions of her date and may not take action to remove herself from a rape situation quickly enough. A soldier on leave for the holidays may get behind the wheel of a car with his buddies and end more than one life. The number of young people who wind up in emergency rooms for treatment related to alcohol consumption and unintentional injuries grows throughout adolescence, peaking in the mid-twenties for both men and women (National Center for Health Statistics, 2011). Over 1,800 college students aged 18 to 24 die each year from alcohol-related injuries (Hingson, Zha, & Weitzman, 2009). Men are three times more likely than women to get behind the wheel after drinking, and single people are twice as likely as people with mates to do so (Centers for Disease Control, 2007e).

Binge drinking is defined as having five or more consecutive drinks (for men) and four or more (for women), on one or more occasions in a few weeks. This multifaceted problem on college campuses has received national attention, and the institutions are under pressure to set policies to protect students from the serious outcomes of excessive episodic drinking on campus. A Harvard School of Public Health 14-year College Alcohol Study (CAS) with more than 50,000 participants reveals that more than 80 percent of students drink, and about half of them admitted that they had engaged in binge drinking (Wechsler & Nelson, 2008). "The CAS findings have shown that alcohol consumption at binge levels and beyond has a significant impact on college students' academic performance, social relationships, risk taking behaviors, and health" (Wechsler & Nelson, 2008, p. 3). Nearly 600,000 are injured annually from alcohol-related accidents (National Institute on Alcohol Abuse and Alcoholism, 2010). Their behaviors also negatively affect others around them (study or sleep disruption, property damage, and potential assaults that may be verbal, physical, or sexual).

Serial drinking rates on campus are highest in fraternities and sororities, followed by consumption at off-campus bars and parties—especially among first-year students—and mainly on Thursday through Saturday (Wechsler & Nelson, 2008). College students also spend more on alcohol than they spend on textbooks, soft drinks, tea, milk, juice and coffee combined—about $5.5 billion a year (Nelson et al., 2005). Although a culture of drinking has always been part of the college scene, the increase in bingeing is probably due to the greater social acceptance of drinking than of drugs. It is speculated that raising the legal drinking age has served only as a new type of prohibition—one that college-age people wanted to breach. "Young or 'emergent' adulthood is a time of great opportunity, risk and social developmental transition for young people," said Weitzman (2004).

Questions

Is there any particular segment of the young adult cohort that is most at risk for negative health outcomes? What are some recommendations to maintain or improve physical health during this period of the life span?

Mental Health

The period of young adulthood, ages 18 to 24, coincides with the peak years for onset of the most common mental-health and addiction problems among young adults—those associated with alcohol, tobacco, and other drug use; depression and anxiety disorders; and suicide. The mental-health aspect of well-being is a matter of concern at any age. Overall, two elements stand out in any consideration of mental health. First, from a social perspective, **mental health** involves people's ability to function effectively in their social roles and to carry out the requirements of group

living. Second, from a psychological perspective, mental health involves a subjective sense of well-being: happiness, contentment, and satisfaction. Mental health requires that people continually change and adapt to life experiences. People who cannot find a comfortable fit between themselves and the world can experience anxiety, stress, or depression. Further, a person's religious or cultural beliefs about what causes mental illness and the social stigma attached to various types of mental illness can contribute to prolonged denial of the condition and to ineffective coping strategies (Conrad & Pacquiao, 2005). For example, one of your authors attended a cross-cultural training workshop on mental-health issues given by respected members of local ethnic groups. An elderly, dignified Vietnamese gentleman said that if a man were to experience any mental-health issues, from his culture's view it was the wife's responsibility to make him happy. People from Laos's Hmong culture attribute any form of mental illness to a malevolent spirit called a *dab* that can overtake a person; the rituals of daily life are designed to avoid the *dab* (Fadiman, 1998). In contrast, from an American perspective, we know that poor health, stress, alcohol and drug use, depression, poverty and joblessness, and family dysfunction are interrelated.

Depression Young adulthood is often the time when one of the leading disorders emerges—depression (Mental Health America, 2008). Depression is treatable in most cases, and physicians and psychiatrists speak of it as a mood disorder rather than a mental illness. In the general population, treatment for depression with antidepressant drugs has increased significantly for both genders since 1995 (National Center for Health Statistics, 2007a). Women are twice as likely as men to experience and be diagnosed with depression, a statistic that holds across all cultures. The World Health Organization attributes this disparity to a number of environmental risk factors that include violence against women, poverty, low social status, and "unremitting responsibility for the care of others" (WHO, 2008). In fact, depression is the number one disease among women worldwide; it is even more prevalent than HIV/AIDS and heart disease. A large proportion of women worldwide do not receive treatment for their depression because policies on mental-health care do not exist in their countries (WHO, 2003).

In the United States, environmental risk factors for depression include racial-ethnic discrimination, lower educational and income levels, segregation into low-status jobs, the double burden of working for wages and managing a household, and the responsibility of caring for children, either in large families or when a marriage ends and a woman becomes a single parent. Also, immigrant women contending with acculturation have higher levels of depression. Married women have higher rates of depression than single women, especially when they are caring for young children. A mother's vulnerability to depression increases with the number of children she bears. Childhood sexual abuse and violence against women also contribute strongly to depression among women (American Psychological Association, 2008a).

There are several risk factors for depression. A person is more likely to have an episode of depression if family members have experienced it. Having a close relative with bipolar disorder also increases a person's risk of developing a major depression. A person who has already had an episode of depression has increased risk of having another episode (All About Depression, 2004). For some women, hormonal and biochemistry changes associated with menstruation and pregnancy have been linked to depression. Researchers are studying the links between genetics, hormones, and experience in depression (American Psychological Association, 2008b).

Women and men cope with depression differently. Women are more likely to have a social network of support or to seek help. They tend to acknowledge and accept their emotions and to identify problems that need attention. However, men seem less willing to acknowledge emotional symptoms and are more likely to turn to alcohol or other substances to suppress their feelings of despair. The standard of masculinity in U.S. culture (and in other cultures) socializes men to be strong and to ignore pain, disease, sadness, grief, and illness. Men are more likely to go to work when they are sick, ignore symptoms of illness, and repress emotional distress instead of dealing with the cause of their pain and discomfort (Mahalik, Burns, & Syzdek, 2007).

One study compared how men seek help in the United States and in Costa Rica. The American men who had difficulty disclosing their emotions to others were more likely to seek help through an anonymous source, such as an Internet chat room. They were less likely to talk directly with male friends about problems related to depression—that is perceived as feminine behavior. Interestingly, the substance-abusing men in the study sought help from peers who had shared similar experiences. The American men with high authority and status were less likely to seek help from professionals, but Costa Rican men of similar status were more likely to seek help from doctors and other professionals (Lane & Addis, 2007).

In the United States, treatment for depression focuses on antidepressant medication and psychotherapy. These interventions can be very useful and can even save lives, but the World Health Organization identifies three main factors that protect people from depression:

- having enough autonomy to exercise some control in response to stressful events
- having access to material resources that make it possible to make choices about how to respond to stress
- having access to a supportive network of family, friends, and health-care providers

The remedies for depression in the United States seem to focus on fixing the person, whereas the World Health Organization believes it is important to focus on the larger issues of the underlying social and environmental problems that produced the depression. Both strategies are useful and necessary (WHO, 2008). Nobel Prize winner Wangari Maathai illustrates the latter response to social stress. In the 1970s, Kenyan women spent hours every day searching for firewood because of deforestation, and this activity led to high stress levels. Maathai's solution was creation of the Green Belt movement: Kenyan women started planting trees in their communities. Today Kenya has made significant progress against deforestation, firewood is not scarce, and food crops are growing again. Equally important, the women in the movement found leadership roles in their communities (Womenaid International, 2003).

Psychological disorders and disturbances result from both individual vulnerability (internal causes) and environmental stresses (external causes) (Jang et al., 2005). Some people are genetically so susceptible that it is exceedingly difficult for them to find an environment lower in stress to prevent them from having a disorder. Yet some people are so resistant to stress that few, if any, environments trigger severe disturbance in them. For example, some political or military prisoners, despite years of torture and solitary confinement, manage to retain their sanity. Recent findings suggest there is a genetic component for resiliency encoded in some brain receptors (Bradley et al., 2008). Most of us are resilient when coping with one adversity. However, multiple adversities can overwhelm our natural resistance. In sum, people differ greatly in their vulnerability to mental disorders (Bonanno & Mancini, 2008).

Stress In the course of our daily lives, most of us experience one or more demands that place physical and emotional pressure on us. We commonly call these experiences "stress." The circumstances that lead to stress are many and varied, but most are commonly perceived as being negative. In actuality, stress can also come from positive events (such as winning the lottery, driving a car for the first time, or giving birth to a baby), in which case it is called *eustress*. Negative events are associated with *distress* (such as failing an exam, losing a job, or discovering marital infidelity). Common daily stressors are called *hassles;* examples include having to look for lost car keys, getting a flat tire on your car, or going to class only to discover that it has been canceled. A significant factor is how we *perceive* an event. Some people are relieved to lose a job that makes them feel miserable!

According to a 2010 survey report, the Millennial and Gen X generations report higher levels of stress than

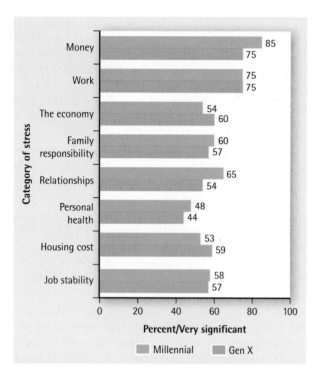

FIGURE 13.6 Causes of Stress, by Generation: 2010
Source: American Psychological Association (APA). (2010). *Stress in America Findings.* (p. 27). Retrieved November 27, 2010 from http://www.apa.org/news/press/releases/stress/national-report.pdf

older generations (see Figure 13.6) (American Psychological Association, 2010). Adults who say that they feel stress often report that they get six hours or less of sleep each night. This compares to adults who sleep seven hours and say they feel stress rarely or never. One study found that one-third of Americans reported sleeping less than six hours per night, which could lead to negative effects on physical and mental health, mood, performance, and social relationships (Bonnet & Arand, 2010). According to the National Sleep Foundation, most adults need 7 to 9 hours of sleep each night (National Sleep Foundation, 2010). Of course, some young adults are parents of newborns and infants or are juggling jobs, families, and school, and sleep deprivation for weeks or months is the norm, as difficult as it may be.

Gender Differences and Managing Stress Until the mid-1990s, women were not typically included in scientific studies of stress and hormones in humans because scientists assumed that women's monthly menstrual cycles created so much hormonal fluctuation that the results would be confounded and not be valid. This assumption was incorrect, and since that time a number of studies have yielded very interesting results about gender differences in responding to stress. Psychologist Shelley Taylor's (2002, 2008) research revealed that women's hormones account for "tending-relationship" behaviors

that challenge the scientific model of stress responses that has been accepted for the past five decades.

Both men and women produce *oxytocin,* a hormone largely associated with bonding and attachment during childbirth, and with child rearing, although it also works to reduce stress. Men, however, also produce hormones that seem to *decrease* the effects of oxytocin. In contrast, women produce *estrogen,* which amplifies the effects of oxytocin. This may be why men are more likely to develop stress-related disorders such as hypertension, aggressive behavior, and substance abuse. How does this hormonal difference shape gendered behavior in response to stress? Taylor (2002) theorizes that because of their higher levels of oxytocin, women have a drive to cultivate and maintain social relationships that is as strong as other basic drives of hunger and thirst. If women's social interactions with friends and family members fall below an adequate level, their brain signals increased levels of oxytocin, creating a "tend and befriend" response. Contacting supportive friends and family members serves a protective function that reduces stress, both emotionally and biologically. For example, a harmful hormone called *cortisol* is reduced when one receives support from other people.

Taylor also finds that oxytocin is produced by physical contact, such as when massaging a baby, giving hugs, or holding hands. She suggests that when women hug their male partners, it prompts an increase in the levels of oxytocin in the men, thus passing on the protective benefit of that hormone's stress reduction (Taylor, 2002). Several studies consistently confirm that women tend to be more distressed over family events, and men tend to be more distressed by financial or work-related problems (Matud, 2004). This is certainly the case for immigrant couples (Hiott et al., 2006).

It is possible that we can train ourselves to reduce stressful input in other ways. One study found that learning to focus attention on positive cues and events can reduce sensitivity to and fear of stressful situations. Study participants looked at a group of 16 faces in which only one had a positive and welcoming expression. They were asked to identify the individual with the positive expression as quickly as possible. Individuals in the study improved their ability to filter out the negative faces more quickly and to identify the positive facial cue more quickly. Learning to search for a smiling face in a crowd rather than focusing on negative facial cues from others may help reduce levels of stress; the process trains the brain to screen out negative input (Dandeneau et al., 2007).

Stress Reported by College Students Traditional college students are typically 18 to 24 years old, come to college directly from high school, and make up 50 percent of college students. Nontraditional students have

Early Parenthood Years Are Most Stressful Because of Sleep Deprivation The circumstances that lead to stress are many and varied. But today's new parents, both of whom are likely to be employed as well, are often the most sleep-deprived and might seek social support to ease that stress.

Source: For Better or Worse © 2004 Lynn Johnston Productions. Distributed by Universal Press Syndicate. Reprinted with permission. All rights reserved.

entered college in record numbers since the early 1990s. A *nontraditional student* is a student with multiple major roles (e.g., spouse, parent, employee, student) and at least a one-year hiatus between high school and college. The U.S. Department of Education reported that in 2009 more than 40 percent of all college students were age 24 or older; thus, many are of nontraditional status. Undergraduates who attend two-year colleges are likely to be age 30 and older.

Nontraditional students typically report more role strains because of lack of time and the pressure of more role demands. Dill and Henley (1998) suggest while all college students experience stress, higher levels of stress were more common among nontraditional students with all the demands on their time from academics, family, finances, employment, relationships and daily life. Pierceall and Keim (2007) found that nontraditional female students were more likely to be stressed than their male counterparts yet they had slightly higher grade point averages. Not surprisingly, students who felt less confident about achieving their academic goals also felt more stress. While most colleges have established activities for nontraditional students, many cannot find the time to participate. Many colleges have Web sites and offer distance learning courses specifically to meet the needs of nontraditional students. One problem for many college students of all ages who experience stress is that they cope with stress in unhealthy ways, including drinking, eating, smoking, and using illegal drugs (Pierceall & Keim, 2007).

Stages of Stress Reaction   According to a classic study undertaken by Hans Selye (1956), our bodies respond to stress in several stages. The first stage is the *alarm reaction.* The nervous system is activated; digestion slows; heartbeat, blood pressure, and breathing rate increase; and the level of blood sugar rises. In brief, the body pulsates with energy. Then the *stage of resistance* sets in. The body mobilizes its resources to overcome the stress. During this phase the heart and breathing rates often return to normal. But the appearance of normality is superficial, because adrenocorticotropic hormone (ACTH), produced by the pituitary, remains at high levels. Finally, if some measure of equilibrium is not restored, a *stage of exhaustion* is reached. The body's capacity to handle stress becomes progressively undermined, physiological functioning is impaired, and eventually the organism becomes ill or dies.

By virtue of having been linked to various physical and emotional disorders, such as heart disease, high blood pressure, ulcers, asthma, migraine headaches, and depression, stress has acquired a bad name. Yet stress is a factor in everyone's life. Indeed, without some stress we would find life quite drab and boring. Therefore, psychologists are increasingly concluding that stress, in and of itself, is not necessarily bad. Much depends on the knowledge or experience we have to problem-solve effectively or cope with the various stresses in our lives.

Stress resides neither in the individual nor in the situation alone but in how the person perceives a particular event (Harris, 2004). Psychologists find that *hardiness* is associated with an openness to change, a feeling of involvement in what one is doing, and a sense of control over events (Harris, 2004). Take the matter of a person's attitude toward change. Should a person lose a job, for example, it can be viewed as a catastrophe or as an opportunity to begin a new career. Likewise, stress-resistant individuals get involved in life: They immerse themselves in meaningful activity. Psychologically hardy people believe that they can actively influence many of

Nontraditional College Students Juggle Many Responsibilities on the Path to Graduation This young adult Hispanic mother and wife just graduated from Long Beach City College. Her extended family was no doubt a source of support to buffer some of the stress.

the events in their lives and that they have an impact on their surroundings. Other researchers find that good self-esteem and a sense of control are important buffers against the harmful effects of stress (Brougham, Zail, Mendoza, & Miller, 2009).

Because we are social beings, the quality of our lives depends in large measure on our interpersonal relationships. A particular strength of the human condition is our propensity for giving and receiving support under stressful circumstances. Social support consists of the exchange of resources among people, based on their personal interactions. Those of us with strong support systems appear better able to cope with major life changes and daily hassles. As we will see in Chapters 18 and 19, people with strong social ties live longer and enjoy better health than those without such ties. Studies covering a range of illnesses reveal that the presence of social support helps people fend off illness (Pernice-Duca & Onaga, 2009). Social support cushions us from harmful effects of stress in a number of ways: Our self-esteem is strengthened when we feel accepted by others despite our faults and difficulties. Other people help us to understand our problems and find solutions to them. Engaging in leisure-time and recreational activities with others helps us to meet our social needs and simultaneously distracts us from our worries. Other people may give us instrumental support—financial aid, material resources, and needed services—that reduce stress by helping us resolve and cope with our problems. People without a social support system who experience multiple stressors are at serious risk for despair and hopelessness. (See the accompanying *More Information You Can Use* box, "Coping with Stress.")

Suicide in Young Adulthood As at-risk populations enter young adulthood, suicide becomes an increasingly serious risk, especially for those experiencing significant stress or multiple adversities. It is the second leading cause of death for U.S. adults aged 25 to 34. Men are more likely to use a firearm and women are more likely to poison themselves. The National Center for Injury Prevention and Control (2010) reports that nearly 15,000 young adults aged 20 to 44 committed suicide in 2007. However, these numbers may not reflect the actual number of suicides, because some are reported as homicides or accidents.

Rates of *attempted* suicide are higher among adolescents and young adults than at other life stages. And men have higher rates of *completed* suicide than women: Men take their own lives at a rate four times greater than women do. Other risk factors for completed suicides include being a male with lower education and/or lower income, living alone, being divorced, and being unemployed. Other significant risk factors for young adults include having at least one psychiatric admission, having previously attempted suicide, having been sexually abused, being homosexual and having same-sex attraction, having a family member or close friend who commits suicide, or having a history of drug use (Eaton et al., 2004). The National Center for Injury Prevention and Control (2010) reports that the highest rates are among Native American males in the 15- to 24-year-old age group.

Protective factors against suicide include religious beliefs, a close connection to caring friends, close family connectedness (including having one's own children), limiting access to a gun, and gainful employment, which provides economic security and feelings of positive self-worth. Gibbs (1997) suggests young adults should make every effort to graduate from high school; go to college or enroll in job training or internship programs; and increase their opportunities for employment to mitigate the effects of the stress and depression in their lives.

Spirituality and Health A factor that helps many young adults deal with stress, anxiety, and health issues is a strong and vibrant spirituality. One study showed that young adults who nurtured their personal faith and spirituality saw themselves as healthier than those who did not. These students felt more life satisfaction and thus felt better able to deal with life stresses (Nelms, Hutchins, Hutchins, & Pursley, 2007). More religiously active people have more social relationships with people of all ages and more support overall. This gave them a stronger sense of moral guidance and greater ability to avoid harmful behaviors (King & Furrow, 2008). Yet the Pew Research Center Forum on Religion & Public Life (2010) national survey finds that about one-fourth of

MORE INFORMATION YOU CAN USE

Coping with Stress

In a national survey, the American Psychological Association (2010) found that America was an overstressed nation. Finances, the economy, family, health issues, work responsibilities or unemployment, national and international crises, and social and personal issues all contributed to what many Americans said were high stress levels that affected their physical and emotional health. Stress led to overeating, inadequate sleep, irritability, fatigue, anxiety, and lack of energy and motivation. Married women were more likely than men or single women to report high stress levels.

Both men and women often dealt with stress by reading, listening to music, or watching TV instead of engaging in healthier behaviors such as exercising or seeking professional help. Although Gen Xers reported the highest levels of stress of any group of adults, they believed they were good at managing the stress. However, they also reported the most physical symptoms of stress. Both Millennials and Gen Xers were significantly more likely to use alcohol or eating to try to manage their stress (American Psychological Association, 2010).

How do you assess the amount of stress you are dealing with? Since the late 1960s, psychiatrists Thomas Holmes and Richard Rahe have investigated the connection between stress and illness, and they developed the Social Readjustment Rating Scale (SRRS), to measure how much stress a person is experiencing from positive and negative life events. The higher the score, the more likely a person is to experience impaired physical and mental health. However, the scale cannot be used indiscriminately with people from all cultures (Woon, Masuda, Wagner, & Holmes, 1971). You can measure *your* stress level by marking on the Holmes and Rahe Social Readjustment Rating Scale the sources of stress you have experienced in the past 12 months and totaling your points. (See Table 13.4.) Once you get an idea of your score, you might then take appropriate actions to try to reduce some stress in your life for your own health and well-being.

TABLE 13.4 Social Readjustment Rating Scale (SRRS)
The following instrument is based on the premise that good *and* bad events in one's life can increase stress levels and make one more susceptible to illness and mental-health problems. Check off the events that occurred in your life during the last 12 months. Add the values in the right column that apply to you, and compare your total against these criteria: Low (<149), Mild (150–200), Moderate (200–299), and Major (>300). Copyright: Publisher, Pergamon Press. For test reliability, see Horowitz et al., 1977.

Life Event	Value	Life Event	Value
Death of spouse	100	Son or daughter leaving home	29
Divorce	73	Trouble with in-laws	29
Marital separation	65	Outstanding personal achievement	28
Jail term	63	Spouse begins or stops work	26
Death of close family member	63	Begin or end school	26
Personal injury or illness	53	Change in living conditions	25
Marriage	50	Revision of personal habits	24
Fired at work	47	Trouble with boss	23
Marital reconciliation	45	Change in work hours or conditions	20
Retirement	45	Change in residence	20
Change in health of family member	44	Change in schools	20
Pregnancy	40	Change in recreation	19
Sex difficulties	39	Change in church activities	19
Gain of new family member	39	Change in social activities	18
Business readjustment	39	Mortgage or loan of less than $100,000	17
Change in financial state	38	Change in sleeping habits	16
Death of close friend	37	Change in number of family get-togethers	15
Change to a different line of work	36	Change in eating habits	15
Change in number of arguments with spouse	35	Vacation	13
Home Mortgage over $100,000	31	Christmas	12
Foreclosure of mortgage or loan	30	Minor violations of the law	11
Change in responsibilities at work	29	Total Life Change Points:	

Source: Holmes, T. H., & Rahe, R. H. (1967, August). The Social Readjustment Rating Scale. *Journal of Psychosomatic Research, 11,* 213–218. Copyright 1967. Published by Elsevier Science, Inc. All rights reserved. Permission to reproduce granted by the publisher.

Millennial adults aged 18 to 29 are unaffiliated with any specific religion or faith, that they are less likely to attend religious services than older generations, and that fewer say religion is important in their lives.

Questions

All of us experience stress or depression about some issues in our lives, but which young adults are most likely to experience more serious bouts of stress, depression, and mental illness? What types of activities are known to mitigate the effects of significant stress, depression, other mental illness, or the potential for suicide?

Sexuality

As we all make the transition to young adulthood, sexuality takes on added importance because we need to position ourselves as competent, independent, caring individuals. "How do I meet my sexual needs?" and "How does sexuality fit in with my idea of who I am?" are questions we ask when we are deciding whether sexual relations for us will be casual, monogamous, or simply another form of "fun." At this time, gender roles are likely to become more complex and challenging. Also, the impact of HIV/AIDS and other STIs has given rise to more serious caution and changes in sexual behaviors for a majority of young adults.

Heterosexuality At the beginning of young adulthood, age 18, approximately half of all young men and women have become sexually active, and most are intimate with persons of the opposite sex. By age 25, almost all have become sexually active. By young adulthood, gender differences have all but disappeared with regard to premarital sex, and females have had nearly as many premarital sexual experiences as males. Today, for many adults there are ambiguous boundaries and commitments regarding "friends with benefits" or "hooking up" in sexual encounters, compared to the former stages of holding hands, going steady, dating, getting engaged, and eventual sexual intimacy (Owen, Rhoades, Stanley, & Fincham, 2010).

Casual sexual behaviors are more likely when one is under the influence of alcohol, and males are more likely than females to have had sex with someone they just met or did not love or to have had intercourse with more than one partner on the same day. More men than women admit that they do not tell the truth to their current sexual partners about their STI status, and both men and women admit to having affairs (Lefkowitz & Gillen, 2006). All of these risky sexual behaviors increase a young adult's serious risk of contracting an STI and/or having an unplanned pregnancy. Additionally, such casual sexual encounters often leave women with feelings of regret, low self-esteem, depression, and other mental-health issues (Owen, Rhoades, Stanley, & Fincham, 2010). If a couple decides to continue sexual intimacy within a committed relationship, it is much more likely to lead to cohabitation, which is discussed in Chapter 14.

Gay, Lesbian, and Bisexual Issues and Health Behaviors Although a majority of America's young people feel they understand their sexual orientation before or by high school, a smaller percentage become aware of their sexual preference in young adulthood (Kinnish, Strassberg, & Turner, 2005). Sexual orientation is no longer thought of in terms of either/or—individuals need not be locked into the categories of heterosexual or homosexual. Some people occupy various places on the spectrum of sexual orientation over the life course. About one-quarter of women who identify as lesbian during emerging adulthood will relinquish this identity during this period. It is important to note that only half of this group will then label themselves as heterosexual; the other half simply refuse to assign themselves a sexual orientation. They are not willing to rule out same-sex attraction but are open to other experiences (Lefkowitz & Gillen, 2006).

It is critical for health-care providers to recognize the specific issues important to lesbians and bisexual women and to know how to talk with them about their health in sensitive, knowledgeable, and understanding ways. This will enable the women to speak freely about their sexual behavior and other related issues. When women are asked to fill out a form and to check "married" or "not married," the third option "civil union/domestic partnership/other" will be more appropriate for some.

Health-care providers should also talk with all women about using condoms. Even a woman who insists that she has sex only with women needs to know about the availability and use of female condoms. Transmission of a number of STIs that are common among women requires only skin-to-skin contact; these include bacterial vaginosis, chlamydia, human papillomavirus, and herpes. Some lesbians may be falsely assuming that if they do not have sex with men, they are protected from STIs. Given how often partners do not divulge their past sexual history, and given the fact that some women, including lesbians, have affairs, one should never assume that unprotected sex with a monogamous partner is safe sex. Health-care providers need to understand the complexity of sexual identity and human sexual behavior in order to provide the information and care their patients require.

Gay men have particular health-care needs as well. In the 1990s, new and virulent strains of bacteria began emerging in the human population at large, and one strain started to hit gay men particularly hard in 2007. This bacterium is highly resistant to the antibiotic methicillin, thus its abbreviation MRSA (pronounced "mersa"), which is short for methicillin-resistant *Staphylococcus aureus*). This strain of bacteria usually starts as pimples on the skin, but it quickly invades the body to become an abscess and can go deeper, creating life-threatening infections in major body organs. It is transmitted by skin-to-skin contact and by touching contaminated surfaces. Emerging strains are resistant to some antibiotics, so early diagnosis and treatment with the right antibiotic is important to keep the bacteria from spreading (Altman, 2008; David & Daum, 2010; Maree et al., 2007). Educating gay men about the importance of washing with soap and water and about the way the bacteria are spread is essential.

Bisexual men and women also present unique health-related issues. Just as with gay men and lesbians, these issues may be difficult for them to discuss. A bisexual individual who is open about his or her identity is likely to be comfortable discussing sexual partners and behavior with a health-care provider. But a married man who is having an affair with another man may find it almost impossible to discuss the health issues his situation presents with a relative stranger in a medical practitioner's office. Men whose primary partners are women but who also have sex with men have appropriated a slang expression that originated in the African American community in the 1990s: "down low men," or "doing the DL" (DeNoon, 2004).

The practice of men having sex with men but not informing their female partners creates serious health risks. A Centers for Disease Control study of men in this category found that around one-third of men in three racial-ethnic groups had unprotected anal sex with their male partners; many also had unprotected vaginal intercourse with their female partners. Thus, these men are an HIV bridge to women. Fear of the consequences of telling their female partners (loss of relationship, loss of marriage, loss of custody of children) and of the social stigma at work and among friends and extended family keeps these men from disclosing their behavior (Centers for Disease Control, 2003c).

Same-Sex Marriage Discussion about the legalization of marriage between same-sex adults has come to the forefront of American culture, as it has in other countries. As of 2011, same-sex marriages are legal in many countries, including the Netherlands, Norway, Sweden, Belgium, Canada, Spain, Portugal, Iceland, South Africa, Mexico, and Argentina—with legislation pending in several other countries. Proponents of same-sex marriage cite the need for health insurance for their partners, full or joint custody of their children, inheritance of property for surviving spouses and children, making crucial medical decisions when a partner is incapacitated, and other legal rights that marriage confers. As of 2011 Massachusetts, Connecticut, Iowa, Vermont, New Hampshire, the District of Columbia, New York, and California (a decision by a federal district judge is being appealed) had legalized same-sex marriage, and several other states recognized civil unions or domestic partnerships (National Conference of State Legislatures, 2011). Although the rights to benefits of couples in *civil unions* and *domestic partnerships* are increasingly being recognized by businesses, industries, and colleges, the fact that only some institutions offer these benefits often limits the options of employees regarding employment.

However, many states do not recognize the legality of the same-sex marriages or unions that took place in states where these partnerships are legal. As of 2011, "voters have approved constitutional bans on same-sex marriage in 26 states since the Massachusetts court ruling, a landmark, took effect [2004]; the constitutions of four other states also limit marriage to heterosexuals" ("Same-Sex Marriage, Civil Unions, and Domestic Partnerships," 2011). It seems that the majority of adult Americans are concerned about the *deinstitutionalization* of marriage and believe that marriage between a man and a woman is the best model for raising children (Blankenhorn, 2007). But younger voters, aged 30 and under, express less opposition than older voters, according to one national poll (Kohut & Doherty, 2004).

The realization that gender is a social "construction" has led many people to question the rigid gender roles that males and females have traditionally held. Some transgendered and other individuals accept a much more fluid conception of gender that incorporates aspects of what have traditionally been called male and female characteristics (Greenberg, 2006). The Millennial generation generally has more open and accepting attitudes toward homosexuality, interracial relationships, and civil liberties (Pew Research Center, 2010b).

Lesbians and Health Care Lesbians, like gay men and bisexuals, have particular health-care needs that require practitioners to blend up-to-date knowledge with sensitivity and respect.

COGNITIVE DEVELOPMENT

The varied experiences of adult life pose new challenges and require that we continually refine our reasoning capabilities and problem-solving techniques. Whether in the realm of interpersonal relationships, college course work, military maneuvers, employment, parenting, managing homes, or participating in church or community volunteerism—or even when vacationing—we confront new circumstances, uncertainties, and difficulties that call for decision making and resourceful thought. Consequently, we must learn to identify problems, analyze them by breaking them down into their relevant components, and devise effective coping strategies.

Young adults do not have a store of life experience to help them solve many problems they encounter. Often, they cannot draw on previous experience to help them predict the outcome of a decision they make. The first time a young mother has an interview with a staff person from social services, early intervention, or a school district, she does not know what to expect or how to respond most effectively. But an older person facing this situation for the first time would probably know how to interact with the person in an effective way and would be able to draw on life experience to predict the outcome of the meeting. The advantage that younger adults have, however, is a greater belief that they will be able to find good solutions, even when they lack previous experience. This is particularly the case when the problem occurs in a familiar context, such as coping with a computer crash, not being able to understand part of a college exam, or dealing with relationship stress with one's partner. In these situations, young adults tend to believe that they have the ability to find solutions to the problems (Artistico, Cervone, & Pezzutti, 2003).

This point was underlined by a study that compared students' satisfaction with traditional classroom instruction and Web-based instruction. The intellectual content of both courses was the same, yet the students overwhelmingly reported that they were less satisfied with the Web-based course, even when researchers reduced the workload of the Internet course and even though test scores showed that the students were learning more in the Web-based course. The results helped the researchers realize that when learning is not grounded in a context of hands-on experience, young adult learners do not become actively involved in the learning process. And active involvement was what the students wanted; the advantage of higher test scores did not outweigh their need to learn in a context that helped them apply their knowledge to their lives (Maki, 2004). Young adults seem to do best with learning and problem solving when they can draw on experience from everyday life to help them acquire new knowledge and solve new problems.

Post–Formal Operations

For Jean Piaget, the stage of formal operations constituted the last and most advanced stage in cognitive development. Piaget described adolescence as opening a new horizon in thought. During this period adolescents gain the ability to think about their own mental processes, to imagine multiple possibilities in a situation, to mentally generate numerous hypothetical outcomes, and to speculate about and plan for their future. In brief, most adolescents (though not all) begin to think in logical, abstract, and creative ways.

Many psychologists have speculated about whether a fifth and qualitatively higher level of thought follows formal operations in adults (especially in science, where there are many unknowns) (Demetriou, 1988; Yang, Wan, & Chiou, 2010). Common to the various formulations of this idea is the notion that **post–formal operational thought** is characterized by these three features:

- First, adults come to realize that knowledge is not absolute but relative. They recognize that there are no such things as facts, pure and simple, but deem facts to be constructed realities—attributes we impute to experience and construe by the activities of the mind. (There are many times in the world of work when people have different visions about a project and need to learn to collaborate.)
- Second, adults come to accept the contradictions contained in life and the existence of mutually incompatible systems of knowledge. This understanding is fostered by the adult's expanding social world. In the larger community the adult is confronted by differing viewpoints, unfound solutions, contrary people, and incompatible roles. And she or he is constantly required to select a course of action from among a multitude of possibilities. (There are times when we must respect and do what our supervisor asks us to do—even if we believe it is not the best course of action.)
- Third, because they recognize that contradiction is inherent in life, adults must find some encompassing whole by which to organize their experience. In other words, adults must integrate or synthesize information, interpreting it as part of a larger totality. (Sometimes we have to look at the larger picture and realize we need to work to support ourselves and our families—even if we are not satisfied with the compensation or environment at work.)

Here, then, is a working model of post–formal operational thought. Future research will be needed to determine the validity of models that posit a fifth stage in cognitive development (Yang, Wan, & Chiou, 2010). Critics of Piaget continue to challenge his assumption that formal operations encompass adult thought. For instance, evidence suggests that younger adults seem to place greater reliance on rational and formal modes of thinking. Older adults seem to develop a greater measure of subjectivity in their reasoning, and they place greater reliance on intuition and the social context in which they find themselves (Labouvie-Vief, DeVoe, & Bulka, 1989). Further, more complex cognitive tasks place greater demands on working-memory resources that decline with increased age (Tucker-Drob & Salthouse, 2008). In any event, most psychologists now acknowledge that cognitive development is a lifelong process, a viewpoint that has gained widespread acceptance only in the past 50 years.

Thought and Information Processing

Adult thinking is a complex process. We would be little more than glorified cameras and projectors if information handling were limited to storage and retrieval. Psychologist Robert J. Sternberg (1997) has studied how we think by examining what is involved in information processing. He views **information processing** as the step-by-step mental operations that we use in tackling intellectual tasks. He examines what happens to information from the time we perceive it until the time we act on it. The various stages, or components, of this process are highlighted by an analogy problem: *Washington is to one as Lincoln is to (a) five, (b) ten, (c) fifteen, (d) fifty.*

In approaching this problem, we first encode the items, identifying each one and retrieving from our long-term memory store any information that might be relevant to its solution. For instance, we might encode for "Washington" such attributes as "president," "depicted on paper currency," and "Revolutionary War leader." Encodings for "Lincoln" might include "president," "depicted on paper currency," and "Civil War leader." *Encoding* is a critical operation. In this example, our failure to encode either individual as having his portrait on paper currency will preclude our solving the problem.

Next, we must infer the relationship between the first two terms of the analogy: Washington" and "one." We might infer that "one" makes reference to Washington's having been the first president or to his being portrayed on the one-dollar bill. Should we make the first linkage and fail to make the second, we will again be stymied in solving the problem.

Then, we must examine the second half of the analogy, which concerns "Lincoln." We must map the higher-order relationship that links "Washington" to "Lincoln." On all three dimensions the men share similarities: Both were presidents, both are depicted on currency, and both were war leaders. Should we fail to make the connection that both Washington and Lincoln are portrayed on currency, we will not find the correct answer.

In the next step we must apply the relation that we infer between the first two items ("Washington" and "one") and the third item ("Lincoln") to each of the four alternative answers. Of course, Washington appears on the one-dollar bill and Lincoln on the five-dollar bill. Here we might fail to recognize the relationship because we make a faulty application (we might mistakenly recall Lincoln as appearing on the fifty-dollar bill).

We then attempt to justify our answer. We check our answer for errors of omission or commission. We might recall that Lincoln was the sixteenth president, but if we are uncertain, we might select "fifteen," figuring that we are somewhat amiss in our recollection. Finally, we respond with the answer that we conclude is most appropriate.

Sternberg (1998) finds that the best problem solvers are not necessarily those who are quickest at executing each of the above steps. In fact, the best problem solvers spend more time on "encoding" than poor problem solvers do. Good problem solvers take care to put in place the relevant information that they might need later for solving the problem. Consequently, they have the information that they require in later stages. Thus, expert physicists spend more time encoding a physics problem than beginners do, and they are repaid by their increased likelihood of finding the correct solution. Here is a common encoding example you have probably heard—that Thomas Edison experimented with thousands of different filaments before creating and improving his first successful light bulb.

Cognitive Development in College Students   It is important that college professors—and college students—understand that students reason differently depending on their level of experience and intellectual development. Several social scientists have spent decades examining how college students mature intellectually over time. They observed that social interactions with faculty, peers, parents, and other adults especially influenced students' cognitive development from the first year in college to the senior year. William Perry (1968, 1981) studied male students at Harvard at two time intervals in 1971 and 1979. Although his theory is criticized because his subjects were all males, others who have conducted similar studies with both genders find there is some validity in his theory, in which he attempted to extend Piaget's theories of cognitive development. Perry theorized that first-year college students generally use more dualistic thinking, as in labeling things "right or wrong" or "good or bad." When asked for an opinion, they were likely to say to the professor: "You tell us. You're the teacher."

Over time and with a variety of experiences in college, they begin to use "multiplicity" in their thought. That is, they begin to recognize that there are diverse perspectives on the same subject, and they become willing to listen to them. As they continue to develop cognitively, they transition to "relativistic" thought. Applying this type of thinking, they realize that they—and others—must support and defend their position in some rational way. This happens when students move into their junior and senior years and make more commitments and as they integrate knowledge, personal experience, and self-reflection. Students demonstrate commitment when declaring a major, planning a career, choosing a religion, firming up relationships, taking a stand in politics, securing jobs, and so forth.

The Developmental Instruction Model proposed by Knefelkamp (1984) aided in operationalizing Perry's model. This model of college student cognitive development involves four components of challenge and support: structure, diversity, experiential learning, and personalism. Each exists within a continuum, such as more structure to less structure, less diversity to more diversity, low involvement in learning to experiential learning, and moderate levels of personalism to high levels of personalism in instruction. First-year college students typically appreciate more structure and social support during their first year, and they are more likely to call home for advice, rely on others, and learn through traditional classroom instruction (McAuliffe, 2006). This model has implications for instructional methods, because it suggests that first-year students might not be ready to "discuss their views" in a class—they might feel they are supposed to be told what to think, unlike a senior, who is definitely ready for a higher level of cognitive challenge. As students progress through college, they cognitively transition into making and defending their own decisions, appreciating diverse views, experiencing internships in their field, and interacting with professors and mentors for more personalized instruction. This model suggests that colleges and universities must provide students with resources and materials to support and extend their cognitive growth over time.

Research has found that many entry-level college classes place great emphasis on rote learning and on the memorization of a large body of concepts, ideas, and facts without learning to think critically about the subject matter. A better approach would be to help young adults analyze how what they are learning relates to and conflicts with their own assumptions, goals, beliefs, and decisions (Nosich, 2005). Some undergraduate students see no need for instruction that does not lead directly to a career or a marketable skill. Yet learning to identify and scrutinize—or to think critically about—one's own assumptions and those of a text or professor or presentation can lay the foundation for lifelong learning (Brookfield, 2005).

Two Generations at Work   Generation X brought distinctive values and technical skills into the workplace. Many members of this generation experienced the divorce of their parents or were latchkey kids. As a result, they are very independent, and they don't want someone always looking over their shoulder while they work. They have watched their parents withstand the vagaries of a changing employment market and are determined to remain employable. They want lots of feedback about how they are doing at work. They appreciate a more casual work environment and some flexibility and freedom in how they get their work done. They value a diverse and multicultural workforce (Thielfoldt & Scheef, 2004).

In addition, members of Generation X are highly committed to their families and are motivated to find ways to balance work life and family life in a healthy way. They want flexibility at work—for example, schedules where mothers of young children can come to work earlier in the morning so they can be at home to meet their children after school. Fathers want the ability to take parental leave when a child is born or is seriously ill. Some Gen Xers may want to telecommute—to remain employed by a company but do their work at home, either some of the time or all of the time. Others may want to adjust their work schedule so they can get more education and enhance their desirability as employees. Gen Xers are very tech savvy in the work environment, but they are easily bored and work best when listening, seeing, *and* doing (Lower & Schwarz, 2008).

The Millennial generation, about 78 to 80 million people, is already changing workplaces in significant ways (Hershatter & Epstein, 2010). Adults gave this generation more intense attention and praise in childhood (some call these adults "helicopter parents") and were rewarded with stickers and trophies. Most were made to feel that they were special and wanted. As a result, they have a great deal of self-confidence. As children, they integrated school demands, sports, a social life, and technological innovation, so they tend to be good multitaskers. They are very team-oriented and prefer collaborative work to individual work (Laughlin et al., 2006). They desire authenticity at work and in relationships but also struggle with the desire to create their own identities in multiple roles, including service to their community, because they have done so much in their personal lives (Hershatter & Epstein, 2010; Yerbury, 2010).

Members of the Millennial generation also bring a new communication style to the workplace. They grew up surrounded by technology, and they use new technology to stay connected with friends and colleagues throughout the day with cell phones, text messaging, social networking, and palm data assistants (PDAs). Some researchers have raised questions about whether their reliance on technology to communicate has caused a deficit in their interpersonal communication skills, but

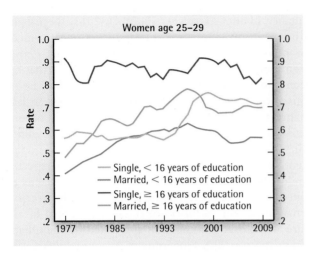

FIGURE 13.7 Labor Force Participation of U.S. Women Aged 25–29 with at Least One Child Under Age 6, by Marital Status and Level of Education, Annual Data: 1977–2009 Note the decline in labor force participation by women with young children since the late 1990s.
Source: Macunovich, D. J. (2010, November). Reversals in the patterns of women's labor supply in the United States, 1977–2009. *Monthly Labor Review, 133*(11), 16–36 (Chart 2, p. 21).

others suggest that older colleagues could benefit from Millennial mentoring in newer technological innovations such as social networking, which can benefit a company (Hershatter & Epstein, 2010).

Because they were the focus of so much attention from adults in childhood, members of the Millennial generation expect their environment to adapt to their needs. They also desire a good balance among work, family life, and volunteering. In addition, they have noticed that corporate culture is not always loyal to its employees, and loyalty—to friends, to family, to colleagues—is an important value to this generation. The result is that more members of this generation are starting their own companies—often hiring their friends as employees—or choosing self-employment (Jayson, 2006). Two-thirds of this generation is employed, either full-time or part-time, but with the economic recession, they are often the first to be let go (see Figure 13.7) (Pew Research Center, 2010b). The tension between the values and norms of this generation and the work situations available to them will produce interesting changes in the U.S. workplace culture over the next few decades.

Questions

What features characterize maturing adult cognition, and how do first-year college students think differently than college seniors and graduate students? What are some attitudinal differences between Gen X adults and the Millennials in terms of their commitment to work and families?

MORAL REASONING

As we saw in Chapter 9, Lawrence Kohlberg identified six stages in the development of moral reasoning and grouped them into three levels:

1. *Preconventional* (Stages 1 and 2)
2. *Conventional* (Stages 3 and 4)
3. *Postconventional* (Stages 5 and 6)

Of particular significance, Kohlberg's cognitive-developmental theory stresses the notion that all people go through the stages in the same order, as with the stages described by Piaget. Yet not everyone is capable of thinking at Kohlberg's highest levels of moral reasoning.

Kohlberg and Postconventional Reasoning

Even Kohlberg thought that his sixth stage, *Universal Principles,* characterized by noble ideals of brotherhood and the community good, is a lofty ideal that people often do not reach consistently (Kincheloe & Steinberg, 1993). Kohlberg said that in the postconventional Stage 5, *Social Contract and Individual Rights,* most people begin to think about society in a very theoretical way, considering the rights and values that a society ought to uphold for the good of all. He said, "A good society is best conceived as a social contract into which people freely enter to work toward the benefit of all." Even though different groups within a society have different values, he believed that all rational people would want certain basic *rights,* such as liberty and life, to be protected. Also, they would want some *democratic* procedures for improving society and changing unfair laws (Crain, 1985). In his classic moral dilemma, as you'll recall, Kohlberg poses a hypothetical situation about a husband, Heinz, stealing a drug he could not afford to save the life of his wife with cancer. Kohlberg believed a person at Stage 5 of moral reasoning would say, "From a moral standpoint, Heinz should save the life of even a stranger, since to be consistent, the value of a life means any life" (Crain, 1985).

At the highest level of moral reasoning, Stage 6, *Universal Principles,* Kohlberg said that there are universal principles of *justice* based on an equal respect for all. Has anyone ever said to you, "Walk a mile in my shoes" to explain that you should gain understanding from the other person's perspective? Kohlberg argued that participants in a moral dilemma needed to do just that to come to an understanding about such universal principles. Taking Heinz's point of view, Kohlberg himself reasoned that parties capable of Stage 6 reasoning would all agree that Heinz's wife must be saved—this would be the fair solution (Crain, 1985). Kohlberg also posited that some great moral leaders and philosophers have at times advocated civil disobedience to advance the cause of universal ethical principles—including Mohandas Gandhi, the Indian lawyer who gave up all he had to become the embodiment of human rights and change by peaceful protest, and the Reverend Martin Luther King, Jr., who changed the face of civil rights in the United States by leading and practicing nonviolent resistance. Ironically, both men's lives were abruptly ended by assassins.

In 2005, Americans struggled with a moral dilemma that will undoubtedly affect society in the future: the sanctioning of *euthanasia*. What was at issue was the court-ordered starvation of a 41-year-old (young adult) healthy but disabled woman with brain damage. Her name was Terri Schindler Schiavo. The court accepted the husband's hearsay testimony that she "wished to die rather than live like that" and ordered a simple feeding tube removed. Of note is that Schiavo required no other "life support mechanisms" but simply food, just what you and I require to live. Had she made her own wishes known in writing in a living will or advance directive, it would have been clear whether she preferred to live in a brain-damaged state or to die—and the matter would not have become such a public, contentious issue.

Various parties viewed this from many moral perspectives: the right of the law and judiciary to supersede the wishes of loving parents who wanted to care for their daughter for the rest of her natural days; the legal right of a spouse to overrule the biological parents' wishes; the rights of a legal spouse over a partner who could not speak for herself; the right of an individual to be able to move on with his life after 15 years of struggle with legal battles; the right of a spouse to deny rehabilitation efforts; the medical community's own disagreement about the level of brain damage and value of a person with brain damage; rights of all Americans (as expressed by Thomas Jefferson in the Declaration of Independence) to "life, liberty, and the pursuit of happiness"; and the personal definition of "quality of life" that causes some people to decide to die by assisted suicide.

After reading Kohlberg's reasoning at Stages 5 and 6, how do you think he would have reasoned out a "just" solution? With the "slippery slope" effect, will the court decision in Florida spread into nursing homes with their burgeoning numbers of seniors with Alzheimer's disease; into developmental centers that house those with traumatic brain injuries; and into neonatal units where babies born with severe disabilities are served? In the Netherlands, active euthanasia has been sanctioned since 1984, and more recently five regional committees, made up of a doctor, a lawyer, and an ethicist, have been appointed to oversee a network of doctors' decisions about babies born prematurely or with birth defects, citizens who are in comas, and elderly patients with no

"quality of life" (Utrecht, 2002). In 2010, the Obama administration reinserted language regarding payments for physician "end of life" planning into the *Patient Protection and Affordable Care Act*—language that had been removed to get a majority of Congress to pass the legislation earlier in the year. As you will read in later chapters, if we live long enough, each of us will become disabled in some way—living with hearing loss, immobility, intellectual and memory decline, vision impairment, and the like—and then our personal perspective on "quality of life" may change. Some U.S. citizens are concerned about the range and scope of health-care policymaking of the members of the new National Health Care Workforce Commission appointed by the Obama administration (U.S. Government Accountability Office [GAO], 2010).

For more than two decades, Carol Gilligan (1982a; Gilligan, Sullivan, & Taylor, 1995) has conducted thoughtful and systematic research involving Kohlberg's framework. She finds that as they move through their young adult years, men and women take somewhat different approaches to the moral dilemmas employed by Kohlberg in his research. Indeed, women tend to score lower than men on Kohlberg's scale of moral development. Gilligan contends that the lower scores result from bias in Kohlberg's approach, since Kohlberg used only male participants in formulating his theory.

According to Gilligan, men and women have different moral domains. Men define moral problems in terms of right and rules—the "ethic of justice." In contrast, women perceive morality as an obligation to exercise care and to avoid hurt—the "ethic of care." Men deem autonomy and competition to be central to life, so they depict morality as a system of rules for taming aggression and adjudicating rights. Women consider relationships central to life, so they portray morality as protecting the integrity of relationships and maintaining human bonding. In sum, whereas men view development as a means of separating from others and achieving independence and autonomy, women view it as a means of integrating oneself within the larger human enterprise.

These two ethical views provide somewhat different bases for finding one's identity and integrating the self. Gilligan calls on developmental psychologists to recognize that the feminine moral construction is as credible and mature as its masculine counterpart. The full response to Gilligan's proposal is not in yet. Not all researchers support her contention that women and men differ in their orientation toward moral reasoning. Some researchers have found only limited support for Gilligan's assertion that women are more attuned to issues of care in moral conflicts and men more attuned to issues of justice (Pratt et al., 1991). Still others stress that the realm of care is not an exclusively female realm, nor are justice and autonomy exclusively in the male realm. Indeed, orientations toward justice and care are frequently complementary (Gilgun, 1995).

Moral Relativism and the Millennials

Some cognitive researchers are examining the *patterns* of cognitive and moral development that continue across several levels. Stein and Dawson-Tunik (2004) are studying the impact of higher intelligence and moral reasoning in participants from the Millennial generation who grew up in the 1990s, compared to cognitive and moral development in adults who grew up as adolescents in the 1950s. Their hypothesis is that the Millennials grew up with multiculturalism, racial equality, and diversity and have adapted to the intellectual demands of the "information rich and highly complex technological and cultural innovations" of the twenty-first century. In conjunction with cognitive complexity, these investigators are studying **moral relativism,** or ethical relativism, which they describe as the belief that there are "no moral principles or guidelines by which everyone is obligated to live"; in other words, "what is ultimately 'good' or 'just' cannot be determined; and there are different ways of interpreting what it means to be moral." This is in contrast to the philosophical view of *dualism,* which holds that there are some behaviors that are simply right or wrong and some behaviors that are better for the common good.

Stein and Dawson-Tunik (2004) find that moral relativism is common in this generation and that it is embodied in such expressions as "whatever," "any opinion is as good as any other," "one can speak only for oneself," or "it's all good." This kind of relativistic

thinking has a significant impact on adult decision making, and employers are interested in understanding how degrees of relativistic thought are associated with employee decision making. Yet in real life there are situations where decisions must be made for the public good, and such decisions must be made regularly in any employment situation.

Through Internet access, adolescents and emerging adults are not as constrained by role requirements as previous generations were, and they are compelled to construct multiple frames of reference for given situations. Taking their higher cognitive capacity and moral development further, some Millennials are developing an *online alter ego* called an *avatar*—an alternate personality who can live anywhere, be anything, and be everywhere at the same time ("life beyond reality") (Montgomery, 2008). Some find it very appealing to be able to create an idealized or desired self. In Hindu philosophy, an *Avatar* is "the embodiment of a higher being in earthly form, usually as a human or animal," but on the Internet, "the meaning gets reversed as humans assume otherworldly forms" (Montgomery, 2008). Yet Stein and Dawson-Tunik (2004) find that even though emerging adults of this generation have had more college education and are "smarter" (and can create avatars), they do not have a realistic view of life after college and lack knowledge about different kinds of professional opportunities available to them.

> ### Questions
>
> What are some major differences between Kohlberg's and Gilligan's views of moral reasoning? Where do you place yourself on the continuum of dualistic to relativistic moral reasoning?

Moral Relativism Is Common in the Millennial Generation
Source: Bill Watterson, Calvin & Hobbes, 1995

SEGUE

In this chapter we have examined the physical and cognitive changes that young adults go through upon graduating from high school (or not) and embarking on the road to adulthood. It is a time when young adults are beginning to understand that there are age norms and to explore the dos and don'ts of this stage. Young adulthood is considered to be a time of increased stressors, including having to make "adult" choices such as whether to drink, smoke, or have sex. The young adult also needs to worry about other aspects of healthy development, including regular exercise, proper nutrition, and safe sex. We will consider how these changes and choices affect the individual in Chapter 14, where we look at the emotional and social dimensions of becoming an adult, especially Erikson's idea that becoming intimate with another is the "crisis" of young adulthood.

SUMMARY

Developmental Perspectives

1. Notions about what constitutes adulthood are changing as a new generation, called the Millennials, leaves high school. The new category "emerging adulthood" captures the changing social mores and expectations for the 18- to 30-year-old age group.
2. The current population of young adults consists of two generations: Generation X (born between 1965 and about 1980) and the Millennial generation (born between 1980 and the early 2000s). The members of Generation X are entering a life stage where they are raising children and supporting aging parents and other relatives. The Millennial generation is the largest generation since the baby-boom generation (born 1946 to 1964) and has in fact surpassed the boomers in size.
3. Age norms are informal expectations about the kinds of roles appropriate for people of various ages.
4. The life cycle in the United States is becoming more fluid, as adults return to college in middle and even late adulthood, young people postpone marriage, young women postpone childbearing so they can solidify careers, and older adults stay fit and active indefinitely with the proper diet and exercise.

Physical Changes and Health

5. Although young adulthood is a time of peak physical performance and good health, many young adults do not exercise regularly or do not have access to health insurance, which may compromise their health.
6. Many young adults engage in behaviors that put their health at risk, such as abusing alcohol or drugs, smoking cigarettes, not exercising, not using condoms during sex, and not eating a healthy diet.
7. Factors such as socioeconomic status, ethnicity, and gender interrelate to affect health. People who live in poverty generally experience more negative health outcomes. Men are more likely than women to choose exercise as a leisure activity.

8. Depression is a mental disorder that often emerges in adulthood. Women around the world are much more likely than men to suffer from depression.
9. Treatment for depression in the United States focuses on drug therapy and counseling. The World Health Organization recommends solutions that focus on changing the environmental factors that produce depression.
10. Men and women respond differently to stress. One explanation focuses on hormones and on how male and female bodies process oxytocin.
11. Suicide, particularly among young men, is at crisis proportions among African American and Native American populations. Men are more likely than women to successfully complete a suicide attempt.
12. A strong spirituality helps many young adults deal better with stress and can lead to a healthier lifestyle.
13. Many people feel that they know their sexual orientation before they reach the college years. However, this may be a time of exploration for some, and their conception of their sexual orientation may change during the early years of young adulthood.
14. Gays, lesbians, and bisexual individuals have particular health-care needs. Health-care providers must become aware of the health-care and social issues of special importance to these groups to be able to inform them about and prevent the spread of STIs.

Cognitive Development

15. Because young adults do not have a store of experience to help them solve problems, it is important that they learn in a context where the knowledge presented is applied to their everyday lives.
16. Some psychologists have speculated about whether a fifth, and qualitatively higher, level of thought follows formal operations. Generally, post–formal operational thought is characterized as (a) accepting that knowledge is not absolute but relative; (b) accepting the

contradictions contained in life and the existence of mutually incompatible systems of knowledge; and (c) finding an encompassing whole by which to organize experience.

17. As college students typically progress in their cognitive development through the college years and into graduate school, they learn to make important decisions, support and defend their positions, experience internships and fieldwork, and accept that a variety of perspectives exist on most issues. Students at all levels generally benefit from personalized instruction.

Moral Reasoning

18. Kohlberg's theory of moral reasoning is based on a justice orientation, defining moral problems in terms of right, rules, and a sense of justice for all of society. Gilligan argues that Kohlberg's theory reflects male moral reasoning and that women, in contrast, perceive morality as an obligation to exercise care and to avoid hurting others— the "ethic of care."

19. The Millennial generation is more likely to embrace moral relativism—a belief that there are different views about morality.

KEY TERMS

age grading *(408)*

age norms *(408)*

aging *(407)*

binge drinking *(419)*

biological aging *(407)*

body mass index (BMI) *(415)*

emerging adulthood *(404)*

information processing *(429)*

life events *(409)*

mental health *(420)*

moral relativism *(433)*

obesity *(415)*

post–formal operational thought *(428)*

social aging *(407)*

social clock *(408)*

social norms *(408)*

transition points *(407)*

FOLLOWING UP ON THE INTERNET

Web sites for this chapter focus on generational characteristics, physical changes, and health and moral issues of early adulthood. Please access the text Web site at www.mhhe.com/crandell10 for up-to-date hot-linked Internet addresses for the following organizations, topics, and resources:

Millennials: A Portrait of Generation Next
http://pewsocialtrends.org/files/2010/10/millennials-confident-connected-open-to-change.pdf

Millennials Study/PBS
http://www.pbs.org/newshour/bb/social_issues/jan-june10/millennials_02-24.html

American Obesity Association
http://www.obesity.org/AOA/

Nutrition Resources for College Students
http://nutrition.jbpub.com/resources/BMI_calculator.cfm

Harvard's School of Public Health (College Alcohol Study)
http://www.hsph.harvard.edu/cas/

Office of Victim Assistance
http://www.ojp.usdoj.gov/ovc/about/index.html

American Social Health Association
http://www.ashastd.org/

National Institute of Mental Health
http://www.nimh.nih.gov/index.shtml

U.S. Department of Labor Occupational Outlook Handbook (searchable by occupation)
http://www.bls.gov/oco/ooh_index.htm

Early Adulthood
Emotional and Social Development

Critical Thinking Questions

1. According to the National Marriage Project, the traditional sequence for major life events for most young adults in the past has followed this order: education, then work or career, next marriage, and finally children. Do you plan to do these things in this order? Why or why not? What would be the benefits and the drawbacks to following this timeline?

2. Do you believe people can fall in love with someone over the Internet without meeting face to face?

3. Would you be willing to marry someone your parents chose for you as a life partner?

4. Which of your personal characteristics would you most want to hide from your partner? From your boss? From your parents?

For young adults, the process of leaving the parental or guardian home has become increasingly complex and variable, and many young people are experiencing numerous living and work arrangements in the course of assuming adult status. Contemporary young men and women are also more accepting than previous cohorts of various sexual orientations, ethnic diversity and immigration, political liberalism, same-sex marriage, and job hopping. Since 1960, the percentage of children living with two married parents has dropped from nearly 90 percent to just over 65 percent (National Marriage Project, 2009), reflecting the trend in American society of granting greater latitude to those individuals whose lifestyle is less constrained by the "traditional" standards of a nuclear family with one man, one woman, and two children. For most contemporary young adults, the period from the late teens until the mid-forties is a time of finding oneself through self-exploration, establishing intimate relationships with family and friends, preparing for and building up an "ideal" position in the work world, committing time to community service, and looking forward with hopes and dreams for the future.

THEORIES OF EMOTIONAL-SOCIAL DEVELOPMENT

Central to any lifestyle and to our very identity are the bonds we forge with other people. Our relationships with other people involve relatively stable sets of expectations that sociologists term **social relationships.** For example, if someone asks you who you are, you might answer, "I am the daughter (or son) of _____" or "I am the husband (or wife) of _____" or "I am an employee of _____." Two common types of bonds are expressive ties and instrumental ties. An **expressive tie** is a social link formed when we invest ourselves in, and commit ourselves to, another person. Many of our needs can be satisfied only in this fashion. Through association with people who are meaningful to us, we gain a sense of security, love, acceptance, companionship, and personal worth. Social interactions that rest on expressive ties are termed **primary relationships.** We view these relationships—with friends, family, and lovers—as ends in themselves, valuable in their own right. Such relationships tend to be personal, intimate, and cohesive. One of the longest-lasting primary relationships that people normally have is with siblings.

In contrast, an **instrumental tie** is a social link formed when we cooperate with another person to achieve a specific goal. At times, this relationship can mean working with people we disagree with, as in the old political saying "Politics makes strange bedfellows." More commonly, it merely means that we find ourselves integrated in complex networks of diverse people, such as the division of labor extending from farmers who grow grain, to grocers who sell bread, to those who serve us sandwiches. Social interactions that rest on instrumental ties are called **secondary relationships.** We view such relationships as means to ends rather than as ends in their own right. Examples include our casual contacts with the cashier at the supermarket, the clerk in the registrar's office, a gas station attendant, or an acquaintance on Facebook. Secondary relationships are everyday touch-and-go contacts in which individuals need have little or no knowledge of one another. As we progress through our adulthood, our days are filled with social contacts with people to whom we have primary and instrumental ties.

Questions

Are the ties you have with family members expressive or instrumental? How do you categorize most of your "friends" in a social networking site?

Psychosocial Stages

As we saw in Chapters 2 and 13, some social scientists have taken up the search for regular, sequential stages and transitions in the life cycle. Erik Erikson, who pioneered a theory of the psychosocial stages of development, iden-

tified nine life-span stages. Four of these unfold in adulthood: early adulthood, which involves intimacy versus isolation; middle adulthood, which involves generativity versus stagnation; late adulthood, which involves integrity versus despair; and very old age, which involves despair versus hope and faith.

The principal developmental task confronting young adults in the stage of **intimacy versus isolation** is to reach out and make connections with other people. Erikson (1968b) refers to this stage as the first stage "beyond identity," which was the stage associated with adolescence. Individuals must cultivate the ability to enter into and establish close and intimate relationships with others. Should they fail to accomplish this task, they confront the hazards of leading more isolated lives devoid of society-sanctioned, meaningful bonds (for example, they might join the ranks of young-adult gang members, prisoners, the institutionalized, the unemployed, prostitutes, cults, the homeless, or the drug-addicted).

Should an individual have failed to come to terms with the critical developmental task of the previous identity stage, in young adulthood that person might temporarily drop out of college, go from job to job, or settle for an unfulfilling interpersonal relationship. Erikson expanded on Freud's succinct dictum "to love and to work," explaining that by love, Freud meant the generosity of intimacy as well as genital pleasure. A general work productiveness should not preoccupy the individual to the extent that he or she loses the capacity to be a sexual and a loving being. Isolation is the inability to take chances with one's identity by sharing true intimacy, and such inhibition is often reinforced by fears of the outcomes of intimacy, such as having children.

More young adults—especially those with social and/or dating anxiety—are connecting and communicating with others mainly through the Internet to alleviate loneliness or social isolation (Stevens & Morris, 2007). The Internet is the fourth most popular way to find a date, following work or school; family or friends; and clubs, bars, or social events (Valkenburg & Peter, 2007). The growing popularity of online dating and social networks may be due to several factors: Physical proximity doesn't matter, one can access the dating sites at any time without the help of friends or any need to "go out," and there is increased self-disclosure and communication because there is the anticipation of future interaction (Valkenburg & Peter, 2007).

There is a cultural component as well as a gender component to the experience of loneliness. Such factors include lack of social contacts or social anxiety, unfulfilling or abusive intimate relationships, relocation or significant separation or partner loss, mental-health issues, personal disabilities, having a chronic or life-threatening illness, and homelessness and other forms of social marginality (Rokach, 2007). Sadler (1978) presents a model of loneliness that many immigrants experience—that of

cultural dislocation, which is a feeling of homelessness and alienation from a previous way of life. Immigrants from South American and Asian cultures typically value family and extended family for personal support. In contrast, North Americans emphasize self-reliance, competitiveness, independence, and autonomy (Wong & Wong, 2006). Additionally, immigrants who settle in large metropolitan areas often experience unemployment, fear of crime, prejudice, and large-apartment-complex living—all of which promote reluctance to interact or get involved with others (Rokach, 2007). Rokach (2007) found that women across cultures tend to derive most of their self-worth from family and offspring. If they do not have these kinds of relationships, they can become very lonely. However, men often invest heavily in their work.

Psychiatrist George E. Vaillant and his associates found support for Erikson's formulations when they followed up a group of 392 lower-class white youth and 94 highly educated men who were first studied in the 1940s in the *Grant Study* (Vaillant & Milofsky, 1980). Like Erikson, they concluded that the post-childhood stages of an individual's life cycle must be passed through sequentially. Failure to successfully negotiate one of Erikson's stages typically precluded mastery of later stages. However, the men varied widely in the age at which they completed a given stage. In fact, one man in six was still struggling in his forties with issues characteristic of adolescence, such as "What do I want to be when I grow up?" When the researchers examined subsequent employment patterns, the men who had been least emotionally mature as boys were much more likely to have experienced significant unemployment by the time they had reached their mid-forties.

Clearly, people do not march in lockstep across the life span in developing their identities. Optimal psycho-

Separation, Isolation, Loneliness—and Excitement Establishing and maintaining close personal relationships is difficult for many young adults who relocate at a distance from family because of college attendance, job opportunities, and occupational or volunteer commitments to remote locations worldwide. This young couple is leaving to pursue graduate degrees.

logical functioning is a lifelong challenge. Fadjukoff, Pulkkinen, & Kokko (2005), researchers from Finland, have been conducting longitudinal studies with young adults up to age 42. On the basis of their findings, they expand on Erikson's theory of identity and find five domains related to optimal psychological functioning: lifestyle, intimate relationships, occupational/career, religious beliefs, and political ideology.

> **Questions**
>
> What constitutes a meaningful life for young adults, according to Erikson? What are some factors associated with social isolation or loneliness that interfere with the development of identity and intimacy?

Emerging Adulthood

We noted in Chapter 13 that in 2000, in a landmark article in *American Psychologist*, Jeffrey Arnett suggested the term *emerging adulthood* to describe young adults from 18 to 29 who began breaking many of the stereotypes of what it means to become an adult. He believes that the transition from adolescence to adulthood has changed significantly over the past half-century in industrialized societies and that researchers should regard the period from age 18 to age 29 as a distinct developmental stage (much as G. Stanley Hall documented the stage of *adolescence* a century before). Contemporary young people in industrialized societies delay marriage and parenthood and focus on self-development as they try out various options in love, work, and/or community service. Most individuals leave home during this period but delay marriage, parenthood, and commitment to any one job or career. In 2005, *Time* magazine described these young adults as *Twixters* because they are "betwixt and between" adolescence and adulthood. Ron Alsop (2008), in *The Trophy Kids Grow Up*, reports that college admissions, human resource officers, and management leaders label this cohort as *Generation Next*, *Echoboomers*, the *MyPod* generation, the *stay-at-home generation*, *Gen Rx*, and the *Boomerang Generation*, and the British call them the "kippers" (kids in parents' pockets eroding retirement savings).

According to Arnett, during this time, emerging adults are likely to move many times or even to move back with their parents for a while. They may enter a cohabiting relationship that ends after several years. Emerging adulthood typically begins with more same-sex interactions with close friends and mixed-group interactions, carrying over from adolescent years. But by the late twenties to early thirties, there is more opposite-sex or same-sex romantic socializing. However, emerging adults still depend on parents, who serve a "safe-haven" function when there is an unforeseen change in plans (Collins & van Dulmen, 2006). Often they do not have family or household obligations and are free to make independent decisions about their lives while they try out various jobs on the way to becoming self-sufficient.

In the past, graduation from high school or college, entrance into the military, marriage and parenthood, and full-time employment were the markers of the transition to adulthood. For emerging adults, the transition is not complete until they can accept responsibility for themselves, make independent decisions, and become financially independent. Yet the downturn of the economy of the 2000s in industrialized countries leaves more young adults—more likely to be college graduates—vulnerable to unemployment and entry-level jobs that they leave in record numbers (Alsop, 2008). Thus, economic uncertainty makes growing up very problematic, even for the young adult armed with advanced degrees (Skolnick & Skolnick, 2011).

Generally, emerging adults are idealistic and believe that they will eventually find their ideal romantic partner, a rewarding job, and happy family lives. They often want to try out various possibilities, including travel to foreign lands, before making commitments. For those who have had a troubling family life, it is a time to move toward a healthier place (Arnett, 2006a). The experience of this period of emerging adulthood is different for men and women and can be quite stressful. Women benefit from having more social support during these years, while men often deal with the stress of this transition through coping behaviors such as exercising and playing sports (Asberg, Bowers, Renk, & McKinney, 2008).

Stages in a Young Man's Life

A number of Yale researchers, led by psychologist Daniel Levinson, pioneered a study of adulthood from a stage perspective. Levinson and his colleagues (1978, 1986) constructed a framework for defining phases in the life-span development of adult males. Although their intent was to study men at midlife, their participants revealed much about the importance of their emerging adult years: This was a time of exploration, possibilities, and significant life events (becoming self-sufficient, renegotiating an adult relationship with parents, establishing a career, getting married, and having children). During this phase young adults are *recentering* their lives—guiding their own lives and formulating plans based on their own values and beliefs (Arnett & Tanner, 2006).

Levinson studied men in their mid-thirties to mid-forties who were blue-collar and white-collar workers in industry, business executives, academic biologists, and novelists and concluded that men go through six periods from their late teens or early twenties to their late forties. Levinson says that the overriding task throughout a man's adulthood is the creation of a *life structure*. A man must periodically restructure his life by creating a new structure or reappraising an old one. He must formulate goals; work out means to achieve them; modify long-held

assumptions, memories, and perceptions regarding himself and the world; and then initiate the appropriate goal-seeking behaviors. Transition periods tend to loom in the years on either side of the symbolically significant birthdays—20, 30, 40, 50, and 60. The German poet Goethe noted that "each ten years of a man's life has its own fortunes, its own hopes, its own desires" (Goethe, 1809). The man and his environment interact to move him developmentally through a series of new levels of life organization. This approach focuses on the underlying set of developmental tasks confronting men, rather than on the timing of major life events. Following are brief summaries of the levels.

Leaving the Family In Levinson's model, the process of entering adulthood begins for a young man in his early twenties when he leaves his family. Young men might choose a transitional institution, such as the military or college, to start them on their way, or they might work while continuing to live at home. Crossing the family boundary is the major developmental task. Levinson said this period lasts about three to five years. Leaving is actually more variable today, and many young adults are delaying leaving the family home or leave and then return because education and training take more time, and they often need significant financial support (Farner & Brown, 2008).

Entering the Adult World During this period men explore and tentatively begin committing themselves to adult roles, responsibilities, and relationships that reflect their evolving set of priorities. Through adult friendships; sexual relationships; working toward college and professional degrees; getting internships, apprenticeships, or long-term work experiences; or extended military service, the young man arrives at an initial definition of himself as an adult. A man might lay the groundwork for a career; he might develop one career and then discard it; or he might drift aimlessly, precipitating a crisis at about age 30, when the pressures become strong to achieve more order and stability within his life.

Expanding on Levinson's theory, Nurmi suggests a model of how emerging adults begin to formulate a life plan that leads to adult sufficiency: Both men and women construct a set of goals, activate those goals, evaluate their goals and achievements, and reflect on their progress (Tanner, 2006). As Arnett and Tanner (2006) report, for many, a college environment allows for a delay, or postponement, in adult role commitments. But such a delay often supports personal growth: developing competence and purpose, establishing identity, moving toward self-sufficiency, developing integrity, and maturing in managing emotions and handling personal relationships (Arnett & Tanner, 2006). Social scientists are studying young adults in the noncollege population and how they manage the developmental tasks of emerging adulthood.

Transitioning to Adulthood—We're Coming Back! Two categories of young adults are likely to return to the parental home: those who encounter such a poor job market that they cannot support themselves and those who are single parents or experience a divorce. Males are more likely than females to return home.
Source: ZITS © ZITS PARTNERSHIP, KING FEATURES SYNDICATE.

But we do know that there is an association between less formal education and lower lifetime income, more role strains, early pregnancy and marital disruption, and the risks of poverty effects.

> Mainly after age 21 people see you're adult. But you're not really an adult, you know. You're still like the mind isn't [there yet]. Like I would say around 23 . . . Reality hit me. [laughs] I need to finish school! I can't just go around doing whatever kind of job, you know. I need a career! And a sense of direction in my life. Male, between ages 24 [and] 26, from San Diego. (Settersten, 2006)

Settling Down Results from the annual *National Marriage Project* indicate that contemporary young men are much more likely to finish college or training, obtain full-time employment, and become financially independent before they contemplate marriage (Wilcox, 2010). Today the median age at which men marry is 28; in 1970, it was only 23 (U.S. Bureau of the Census, 2010d). In Levinson's model, in his early thirties a man establishes his niche in society, digs in, builds a nest, and makes and pursues longer-range plans and goals. By this time he has often evolved a dream, a vision of his own future. In succeeding years there can be a major shift in life direction when he revives the dream and experiences a sense of betrayal, disillusionment, or compromise with respect to it.

Levinson's work provides a broad outline of how individuals progress through the life course, but more recent research has shown that a young person's life experience is shaped by race-ethnicity in significant ways. Macmillan and Eliason (2003) have used the *National Longitudinal Survey of Youth* to follow a large cohort of men and women who were 14 to 22 years old in 1979 that was transitioning to adulthood in the 1980s. While white

men in this group were likely to follow the path that Levinson identified—finishing high school, beginning to work, marrying, and becoming a parent—men of other race-ethnicity were more likely to finish school, begin working, and become a parent before they married—if they married at all. In the widening experiences of work or higher education, issues of bicultural and multicultural identity become more salient, as men formulate a comfort level with their families' traditions and their ethno-American identity and way of life (Phinney, 2006).

Researchers across disciplines report that a young person's path to adulthood has become much more varied over the past few decades. In the 1990s, sociologists Heath and Cleaver interviewed young adults in their twenties in Southhampton, England, for the *Young Adults and Shared Household Living Project*. Most of them had already lived in several places—as many as five—since leaving their parental home. Some had lived with, or were living with, partners. Only a few had ever lived alone, and some had returned to live with their parents for a while. Most were working full-time in managerial or technical careers. All of them were living in shared households with a group of people their own age. Heath and Cleaver (2003, p. 184) argue that a young person's pathway to adulthood has become destandardized, largely for economic reasons. Young people without significant financial support from parents find it difficult to find work that pays enough for them to become financially independent in their twenties. As a result, there is a new transition-to-work phase in the life course of many young adults in westernized societies—one of longer dependency on relatives and delayed commitment to a career, marriage, and parenthood (Arnett & Tanner, 2006). In contrast, Phinney (2006) states that ethnic-minority and immigrant young adults are more likely to take on adult roles at earlier ages because they often provide economic support to their families of origin. Thus for some young adults, Levinson's next developmental stage of "becoming one's own man" is much later, and for others it is earlier, out of financial necessity.

> I started backwards. . . . I had the kids first. Then I skipped a couple of [those typical transitions]. . . . I tell some people: you know why white people are so successful? 'Cause when they're young, this is what their parents teach them. You go to school; then when you're done [with college, you . . .]—and other races, they don't! Not all of them do [things in the right order], you know. At least us Mexicans, not all of us, not a lot of us do. Male, between ages 24 [and] 26, from San Diego. (Settersten, 2006)

Becoming One's Own Person   Levinson found that for most men, this period tends to occur in the mid- to late thirties. A man frequently feels that no matter what he has accomplished so far, he is not sufficiently independent. He commonly believes that his superiors control too much and delegate too little. He impatiently awaits the time when he will be able to make his own decisions and get the enterprise "really going." If a man has a **mentor**—a wise older counselor, coworker, boss, or the like—he will often give up his mentor now. At this time, men want to be affirmed by society in the roles that they most value. They will try for a crucial promotion or some other form of recognition. Levinson found that in an earlier generation, many men invested much of their lives in their work role. Today—because of the recessions in the first decades of the 2000s and the massive layoffs due to corporate globalization and outsourcing jobs to foreign countries—some men have come to a more balanced understanding of their life priorities. This is not surprising, given that many have arrived at work to find a termination slip and a cleaned-out desk, even after 25 or more years of dedicated service, and must seek alternative employment (Virick, Lilly, & Casper, 2007). Some men have weathered this major change by creating new businesses, while others are existing on unemployment and community support systems or returning to college to retrain for a new job. However, recessionary periods and the financial strains they place on men can lead to serious mental-health issues, including depression and anxiety (Jenkins, Fitch, Hurlston, & Walker, 2009).

For his part, Levinson acknowledged that a life-cycle theory does not mean that adults, any more than children, march in lockstep through a series of stages. He recognized that the pace and degree of change in a person's life are influenced by personality and environmental factors (war, a death in the family, poor health, a sudden windfall). Hence, Levinson did not deny that very wide variations occur among people in any one life period. He used the analogy of fingerprints. If we have a theory of fingerprints, we have a basis for order, in that we can identify individuals because we know the basic principles around which fingerprints vary. We shall continue to discuss Levinson's theory of male transitions in Chapter 16.

Stages in a Young Woman's Life

Erik Erikson (1968a) said that the formation of *identity* in adolescence is followed by the capacity for *intimacy* in early adulthood, but he could not foresee the delay of identity formation into emerging adulthood for contemporary women and men. Now there seems to be the dual challenge of meeting these significant psychosocial needs during the emerging adult years. Nor did Levinson, who embarked on a major study of women's lives that yielded the book *Seasons of a Woman's Life* (1996), foresee a postponement period. However, his studies are still relevant and confirm that entry into adulthood is similar for men and women. Both face the four developmental tasks and the *age-30 transition.* Levinson found that although men see themselves tied to a future in terms of their career, women are much more interested in finding ways to combine work and family (and today, more years of education) (Zucker, Ostrove, & Stewart, 2002). None of the professional women in Levinson's study found that they could balance the demands of work, family, and their own well-being satisfactorily; all felt that they had slighted either career or family in the struggle to maintain both. The women also stated that they had more trouble than men finding a mate who would stay with them during their personal and career growth.

From a twenty-first-century perspective, Macmillan and Eliason (2003) found that women are more likely to follow a variety of paths to adulthood. For example, white women are apt to juggle entry into the workforce, marriage, and parenthood simultaneously, withdrawing from the workforce to care for newborn children and then reentering the world of work. But for many nonwhite women, the entry into adulthood is dominated by parenthood first and foremost. They are more likely to begin bearing and raising children before entering the labor force and, for many, before marriage, if they marry at all. However, Levinson's research about women from just 20 years ago may be outdated by women's greater participation in the workforce and their higher educational achievements. Today, many more U.S. women than men are attending and graduating from college in their twenties, thirties, forties, and beyond, earning advanced degrees, and entering professional careers (Snyder & Dillow, 2010). Thus, they are probably constructing life roles at different times, along with a new sense of identity.

These changes in how women enter adulthood have occurred rapidly. For most of the twentieth century, many young women left their parental homes to marry, although a growing number attended college and entered careers in the last 40 years. Beginning in the 1960s, women's lives changed. The birth control pill gave them more control over childbearing, and the women's movement increased their educational, career, and opportunities for self-sufficiency without marriage. By the 2000s, there was a rapid increase in the financial resources needed to establish and maintain one's own residence at the same time that the job market tightened, even for college graduates. Significantly, there was a rapid growth in cohabitation and childbearing before marriage, with an increasingly older age at first marriage (Wilcox, 2010). Some young people feel dislocated when their life takes an unexpected turn, and new paths are not clear yet. One young woman wrote,

> I am nowhere. I don't know what I'm doing, where I'm going. I don't have a fiancé anymore; we broke up. I left my job and apartment to come home, and now I'm living with my parents. I really don't know what my future is. I had a plan, and I thought I would get married, have children, get a house. Now I am nowhere. (Wolf, 2005)

In reality, broad, sustained economic and social changes have created new challenges that young women and men must meet. Many young adults struggle to make enough money to create a comfortable level of self-support, and they certainly lack the means to provide housing, food, clothing, transportation, education, and medical care for a family with children. This explains why women's labor force participation has increased significantly since the 1970s and why more young adults in close relationships share living quarters and resources to improve their standard of living. Let's now turn to the ways in which young adults develop close relationships and how they resolve the "crisis" of intimacy versus isolation.

Questions
According to social scientists, how do the stages of a young woman's life differ from those of a young man's life? What are some typical domains of identity development for the contemporary Millennial cohort in the emerging adulthood stage?

ESTABLISHING INTIMACY IN RELATIONSHIPS

As Tolstoy suggested in 1856, "One can live magnificently in this world, if one knows how to work and how to love." Love and work are the central themes of adult life. Both place us in a complex web of relationships with others. Indeed, we can experience our humanness only within our relationships with other people. Like other periods of human life, young adulthood, from the late teens until the early forties, can be understood only within the social context in which it occurs. In addition to relationships in our immediate family, our earliest social relationships are those we have with friends.

Friendship

What is a friend? One old saying goes, "A friend: One soul, two bodies." Think of your friends and see whether the following descriptors are true for you:

- You like to spend time with your friends.
- You accept your friends for who they are, and you are not interested in changing them.
- You trust your friends.
- You respect your friends.
- You would help your friends and would expect your friends to help you.
- You can confide in your friends.
- You can let down your guard with friends because you do not feel vulnerable with them.

Our friends become our major source of socializing and support during our adult years. We tend to want to spend our free time with those who are experiencing many of the same life events as we are. Women who have babies and young children tend to develop friendships with other women who have babies and young children. Single friends might begin to feel left out and gravitate toward new friends who are single, with whom they share common interests. Men tend to develop friendships within the spheres of work and recreation, and often their conversations revolve around such events.

Emerging Adulthood and Friendship In early adulthood, close friendships are a major source of support. Today, cell phones, social networking sites, and video conferencing sites such as *Skype* allow for frequent contact among friends.

Friends can become more important than siblings in adolescence and early adulthood. One study of an adult population in the Netherlands found that in the previous three months, people were much more likely to have seen their friends face-to-face at least once a week than to have seen a sibling. They were also more likely to report that they had received or given emotional support to a friend than to a sibling and were more likely to rate their relationship with a friend than their relationship with a sibling as "good" or "very good" (Voorpostel & van der Lippe, 2007). That is not to say that siblings are not still significant people in an adult's life; this research merely points out that friendships become very important.

Many of the young adults that Heath and Cleaver (2003) studied were living in mixed-gender shared housing because they could not afford adequate housing on their own incomes. Friendship was an important element in how they evaluated the quality of their lives. They noted that the experience of living with a group of friends provided the supportive environment they needed after a breakup with a romantic partner or a bad day at work (recall the popularity of the sitcom *Friends*). One participant said, "If things are bad . . . I don't have to drive to somewhere, I don't have to pick up the phone, I can just chat to the people around. And it's the same for them" (Heath & Cleaver, 2003, p. 135). For Generation X and the Millennial generation, friendship networks often provide necessary emotional support in the transition period between leaving home and entering a settled life with a romantic partner (Collins & van Dulmen, 2006). However, from the beginning to the end of early adulthood, everyday social interactions with friends change as most adults engage in more opposite-sex or same-sex romantic socializing.

With the use of the Internet, more studies are focusing on the isolation of our young-adult "technocrat" generation, who develop "friendships" in forums, chat rooms, or *Facebook* rather than across the aisle in a college classroom or across the hall in an apartment building. With Internet video-voice conferencing sites such as *Skype*, face-to-face interaction with distant friends is now possible. Despite this advantage, it is still the face-to-face interaction with best friends that provides us with much-needed social support when life gets us down. Yet, the growing trend among Millennials to develop and maintain relationships via the Internet may challenge long-held assumptions about what relationships are and how they flourish. The traditional habits and rules of social engagement and friendship may no longer apply to these young adults (Barnes, 2009). In 2009, almost three-quarters of adults aged 18 to 29 used social networking sites; most of these had a profile on *Facebook*. Using the Internet to communicate and maintain relationships was their primary goal, but young adults also used the Internet to manage their lives, to get information, to shop, to engage in civic sites, and to learn about news and health issues (Pew Research Center, 2010a).

Love

As mentioned earlier, the concept of romantic love is not universal, as is evident in the practice of arranging marriages between people who have never even met or know each other only superficially. Yet many Westerners describe themselves as being "in love" when they marry, so what do they mean? Why are certain marriages and relationships happier and longer-lasting than others? Is being in love significant for happiness and satisfaction in marriage? Traditionally, love has been divided into what are known as romantic and companionate types of love. **Romantic love** is what we think typically of when we say we are "in love" with someone. **Companionate love** is usually understood as the kind of love you have for a very close friend. Even though most people can differentiate between the two types of love, psychologists have tried to measure companionate love using a variety of measurements.

Sternberg's Triangular Theory of Love Robert J. Sternberg has proposed that companionate love consists of two other types of love: intimacy and commitment (Sternberg, 1988, 2006a) According to his **triangular theory of love** (see Figure 14.1), love is made up of these three elements:

- *passion* (sexual as well as physical attraction to someone)
- *intimacy* (having a close, warm, and caring relationship)
- *commitment* (intent and ability to maintain the relationship over an extended period of time and under adverse conditions)

When all three aspects of his triangular model exist in a relationship, Sternberg calls the emotional bond **consummate love** (Sternberg & Hojjat, 1997). A relationship that does not include all three components of a complete, consummate love—passion, intimacy, and commitment—is, says Sternberg, an emotional attachment of one of these seven kinds:

- *infatuation*—passion only
- *fatuous love*—passion and commitment but not intimacy
- *companionate love*—intimacy and commitment without passion
- *romantic love*—intimacy and passion without commitment
- *nonlove*—neither intimacy nor commitment nor passion
- *liking someone*—intimacy only
- *empty love*—commitment only

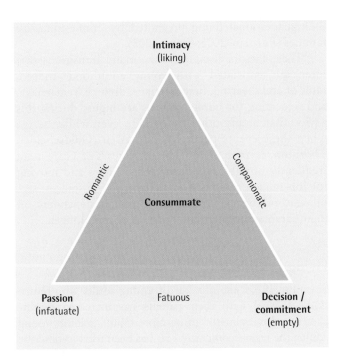

FIGURE 14.1 Sternberg's Triangular Theory of Love
According to Sternberg's theory, the ideal type of love is consummate love, comprised of passion (physical and sexual attraction), intimacy (closeness, warmth, and caring), and commitment (ability to maintain the relationship over time, even in adverse circumstances). Some close relationships have only one or two of these factors.
Source: Adapted from Janet Shibley Hyde and John D. DeLamater, *Understanding Human Sexuality,* 6th edition. Copyright © 1997 by The McGraw-Hill Companies, Inc., and used with permission of The McGraw-Hill Companies.

Significance of Romantic Love   In a study on the significance of romantic love for relationship quality and duration, Willi (1997) surveyed more than 600 adults in Switzerland and Austria ranging in age from 18 to 82. Most were married, some were single, some were divorced, and a few were widowed. Willi defined romantic love as follows:

Being in love does not simply mean a fleeting or simplistic feeling, but something that for a longer period of time leads to an intensive, erotic attraction and inner fulfillment through the idealization of the relationship with the partner. (Willi, 1997, p. 172)

On the basis of this definition, most of the participants in Willi's study said that they had fallen in love 2 to 5 times; some said 6 to 15 times; 2 percent said they had never been in love; and 1 percent said they had been in love 16 times or more. In this study, men did not fall in love more frequently than women, and being in love did not lead more frequently to a relationship for men (contrary to popular opinion). An interesting finding was that for one-third of the sample, a relationship developed with

one's great love but did not lead to living together. The majority of married individuals in this study indicated most frequently that they had lived with or continued living with their great love. For about 1 out of 10, the greatest love of their life did not lead to a relationship, mainly because their love was not reciprocated. Those who were married to their great love described themselves as significantly happier than other married respondents did, and their divorce rate was the lowest (Willi, 1997). The greatest satisfaction was reported for all groups in the areas of sexual fidelity, as well as in the security of the partnership.

Being in love seems to be a special relationship that clearly distinguishes itself from other kinds of relationships, but it does not necessarily lead to the relationship that one might expect. Being in love on the first day or "at first sight" tends to happen to those under the age of 20 and often to those who are on the rebound from another relationship or who feel a void in their lives that they want to fill as quickly as possible (Knox & Zusman, 2009). Also, one does not necessarily need to have married one's great love in order to be happy or satisfied in a relationship, although marrying one's great love is associated with marital duration. We now turn to various lifestyles in which adults express their love and desire for intimacy with another.

Questions

What are the characteristics of the triangular theory of love? How would you assess a current "love" relationship of your own?

DIVERSITY IN LIFESTYLE

People in modern complex societies typically enjoy some options in selecting and changing their lifestyles. A **lifestyle**—the overall pattern of living whereby we attempt to meet our biological, social, and emotional needs—provides the context in which we come to terms with many of the issues discussed in this chapter and the preceding one. More particularly, lifestyle affords the framework within which we work through the issues of intimacy versus isolation that Erik Erikson described. **Intimacy** encompasses our ability to experience a trusting, supportive, and tender relationship with another person. It implies a capacity for mutual trust and empathy and for both giving and receiving pleasure within an intimate context. Comfort and companionship are among the ultimate rewards to be found in a close relationship.

Overall, it appears that some elements of society and the media give citizens greater latitude in tailoring for themselves lifestyles less constrained by more traditional standards. Of course, many religious institutions and their followers maintain traditional standards for acceptable and unacceptable behaviors for men and women.

Leaving Home

Leaving home is a major step in the transition to adulthood. Prior to this transition, two generations typically live together in a single family. Until the past decade, most young Americans left the parental home between the ages of 15 and 23. Even today, the number of those living in college dormitories and military barracks spikes sharply around age 18, followed by a sharp upturn in housemate living around the ages of 19 and 20. However, in the United States and in many European countries, young people are living with their parents longer and leaving home much later. Significantly, the parental home remains the primary residence for 18 million young people aged 18 to 34 (Furman, 2005). The pathways out of the parental home are quite varied, and young adults fan out in a good many directions, with no one pattern of nonfamily living being dominant. Common arrangements include dormitory living, housemate arrangements, cohabitation, marriage, civil unions or domestic partnerships, and living alone.

Sociologists say that the transition to adulthood is particularly problematic for today's young people. They argue that the amount and duration of parental support have increased because of such factors as the longer time it takes to establish a career, recurrent economic recessions, lower salaries for entry-level jobs, higher costs of individual health care (as coverage under a parental policy ends), rising housing costs, high divorce rates, high levels of nonmarital childbearing, the havoc that drug and alcohol abuse inflict, overindulgent parenting practices, and

multigenerational living promoted by ethnic-minority families (Furman, 2005; Stern, 2007).

These factors complicate the many transitions that often are associated with young adulthood. Indeed, rates of childbearing, first marriage, divorce, remarriage, and relocating for family reasons are higher during this period than at any other time in life, even while the age when these events occur has also risen (Goldscheider, Thornton, & Yang, 2001). The early years of a career are frequently unstable, requiring job changes and moving for job-related reasons. Given these circumstances, significant numbers of young adults remain dependent on their parents into their late twenties or even longer.

Living at Home

Since the 1970s, the number of young adults who return home to live with their parents has increased significantly and is estimated to be more than 1 million young adults; the term *boomerang kids* has been used to describe them (Network on Transitions to Adulthood, 2006). Nowadays, more young people in the United States and most European Union countries remain in the parental home or return home when circumstances become difficult (see Figure 14.2). In 2009, the average U.S. college graduate had $24,000 in student loan debt at a time when there was an 8.7 percent unemployment rate for these same graduates (Project on Student Debt, 2010). They also had about $4,000 in credit card debt (Sallie Mae, 2009). Many young

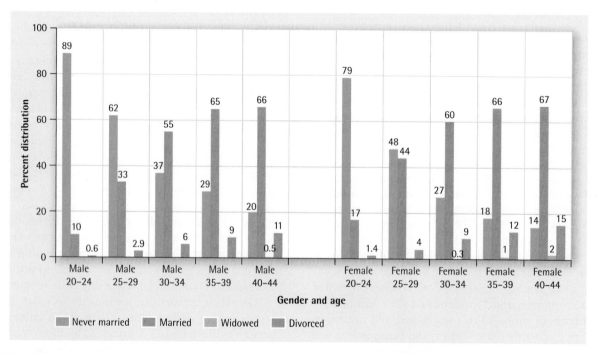

FIGURE 14.2 Marital Status of U.S. Young-Adult Men and Women, by Age and Percent: 2010

Source: U.S. Census Bureau. (2010). *America's Families and Living Arrangements: 2010.* Marital status of people 15 years and older by age, sex, personal earnings, race, and Hispanic origin, 2010. *Current Population Survey, 2010.* Washington, DC: U.S. Government Printing Office. Retrieved from http://www.census.gov/population/www/socdemo/hh-fam/cps2010.html

adults are working at entry-level jobs where starting salaries do not provide enough income for self-support. Some who were self-sufficient have lost jobs and returned home to regroup and prepare for a new career. Men are more likely than women to live with their parents in their twenties and thirties. In 2008, among the 27 members of the European Union (EU27), one-third of men but only one-fifth of women aged 25 to 34 lived with parents (Eurostat Press Office, 2010). Some married couples live with their parents while they save money for a first apartment or home. But economic pressures are not necessarily severe: Some youth merely wish to save the rent money and spend it on a car or save it to purchase a house. Among the middle classes, comfort is another reason for living in the parental nest.

Having adult children living with parents can be highly successful—or disastrous. Biological parents typically provide a sense of warmth, closeness, and emotional support during this time of transition. But stepparents and remarried (biological) parents are more likely to be unhappy with the situation. Single parents were least likely to remain positive about providing economic support (Aquilino, 2005). But the most common complaint voiced by both generations concerns the loss of privacy. Couples report that they feel uncomfortable disagreeing in front of family members. Young single adults complain that parents cramp their sex lives or their music playing, treat them like children, and reduce their independence. Parents often grumble that their peace and quiet are disturbed, the phone rings at odd hours, they lie awake at night worrying and listening for the adult child to return home, meals are rarely eaten together because of conflicting schedules, or too much of the burden of babysitting falls on them. Higher expenses might compel parents to give up long-awaited vacations, and a need for space means they must postpone a move to a smaller, less expensive townhouse, apartment, or retirement home (Furman, 2005).

Usually, the happiest refilled nests are those with ample space and open, trusting communication—and those where agreements or contracts are made for adult children to share in expenses. The boomerang situations that are most difficult involve grown children who are immature and do not contribute toward their own expenses, who have drug or mental-health problems, or who become disabled. Parents who treat a 28-year-old like a 15-year-old may find that the 28-year-old behaves like 15. Family therapists express concern that those who stay at home do not have opportunities to fully develop their sense of self-sufficiency. Staying at home tends to aggravate tendencies toward excessive protectiveness in parents and a lack of self-confidence in young people.

Staying Single

Single status among young adults under 35 years of age has sharply increased in the past decade. By 2009, about two-thirds of U.S. males and just over half of females aged 18 to 34 were single and had never been married (U.S. Bureau of the Census, 2010e). The same increasing trends of cohabitation before marriage, delaying marriage, or remaining single are common among young adults in European countries and Japan as well (Kotowska et al., 2010; Raymo & Ono, 2007). More college-educated adult women are spending time pursuing a career before settling down to marry. Japanese women are living with parents longer and marrying later and less often—a reflection of longer school enrollment and with full awareness of a cultural norm that married Japanese women are to stay home and raise the children (Raymo & Ono, 2007). Rodgers and Rodgers (2006), in *The Singlehood Phenomenon,* reveal several reasons why so many young adults are single. Young adults, they say,

- want to establish a career
- do not know how to date since they grew up socializing with groups of friends
- are concerned about divorce and separation
- are searching for the perfect mate
- view being single as the best way to live
- do not want to deal with hurt and heartbreak
- have unresolved issues from past relationships
- are afraid to admit they are looking for a partner with whom to share their life

Until a few decades ago, social stigma was attached to the terms *spinster* and *bachelor.* Even highly accomplished single people who are happy and well adjusted might be regarded as somehow incomplete, because in Western culture the nuclear family—a husband, a wife, and their offspring—continues to be the standard against which a society judges other family forms and lifestyles (Sharp & Ganong, 2007). Yet today the notion that individuals must marry if they are to achieve maximum happiness and well-being is increasingly being questioned (Coontz, 2005).

DePaulo (2006) criticizes social scientists for assuming that marriage provides the best chance for happiness for all people. She points out that single people are treated unfairly in U.S. society, from earnings (in general, married men earn more than single men) to work-related benefits packages, income-tax policies, and automobile insurance. She also states that we do not know much about the psychological development or personality traits of single people (DePaulo, 2006). People who do not marry have many valuable resources to offer society, and understanding their perspectives on happiness, attachment, work, friendship, self-esteem, and prosocial behavior would benefit a broad range of social groups.

Cohabiting

The number of unmarried couples living together has increased dramatically in the past 40 years. In 2010, it was estimated that about 25 percent of unmarried women from 25 to 39 years of age were living together

FIGURE 14.3 Number of U.S. Cohabiting, Unmarried, Opposite-Sex Couples, by Year: 1960–2009 In 2009, over 6.6 million households were classified as unmarried-partner households in the United States—a dramatic increase since 1970.

Sources: Wilcox, W. B. (Ed.) (2010). *The state of our unions, 2010.* Charlottesville, VA: National Marriage Project, University of Virginia. Retrieved from http://www.stateofourunions.org. U.S. Census Bureau. (2008). Table 62. Unmarried-Partner Households by Sex of Partners. *Statistical Abstract of the United States: 2008.* Washington, DC: U.S. Government Printing Office.

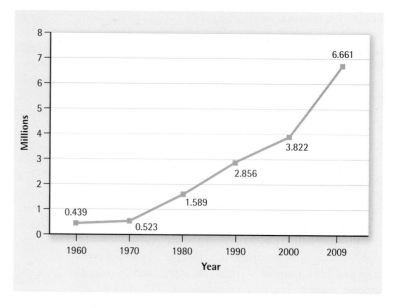

with a partner to whom they were not married, a lifestyle choice called **cohabitation.** An additional 25 percent of young women had lived with a partner in the past. Half of all first marriages are now preceded by a period of cohabitation, which was nearly unheard of 50 years ago (National Marriage Project, 2010) (see Figure 14.3). Cohabitation is higher among young adults with less education and lower income levels. Those who are more likely to cohabit include young adults who are less religious and have more permissive views about sex, those who have been divorced, those whose parents were divorced, those who grew up fatherless, and those who grew up with parents who argued a lot (National Marriage Project, 2010).

Compare this to the United Kingdom and France, where a substantial portion of people surveyed reported agreeing with the statement that marriage is an outdated institution. Northwestern European countries have the lowest age at first marriage, the highest rates of cohabitation, and the largest number of births outside marriage. Researchers from the *National Marriage Project* find that highly industrialized nations of Europe are moving in the direction of what can be called a "non-marriage culture." In contrast, in southern Europe, where family traditionalism is still strong, many young people live at home with their parents until they marry, and the rate of cohabitation is quite low (see Figure 14.4). Young people in these countries, which include Spain, Italy, and Greece, do not typically live alone before marriage (Popenoe, 2007).

Many young people believe that cohabitation improves their chance of finding out whether they and their partner are compatible before making a legal commitment to marriage. They hope to avoid entering a bad marriage that will end in unhappiness and divorce. But a growing body of research suggests that living together does not predict happier marriages. In fact, research reveals that couples who consider cohabitation to be a prelude before marrying are more likely to break up after marriage (National Marriage Project, 2010). However, it is hard to know whether this tendency toward marital instability is due to the effects of cohabitation itself or to the type of people who choose to cohabit. What *is* certain is that there is no evidence that those who choose to cohabit before marriage have stronger marriages than those who do not.

Further examination of marital versus cohabiting relationship stability in couples with children reveals that "children born to cohabiting versus married parents have over five times the risk of experiencing their parents' separation" (Osborne, Manning, & Smock, 2007). These investigators also found greater instability in cohabiting relationships when one or both of the adults had been in a prior marriage with children. An analysis of U.S. child abuse and child deaths reveals that children who are born to unmarried parents are at higher risk of poor parenting, poor developmental outcomes, child abuse, and behavioral disorders (DeKlyen, Brooks-Gunn, MacLanahan, & Knab, 2006). Another study analyzed child abuse and household composition and found that children under age 5 living in a home with a parent and an unrelated adult were *50 times* more likely to die from inflicted injuries than children living with a single biological parent or two biological parents (Kellogg & Committee on Child Abuse and Neglect, 2007). The perpetrator of such a horrific crime was often the boyfriend of the child's mother and, in fewer cases, the child's mother herself (Schnitzer & Ewigman, 2005).

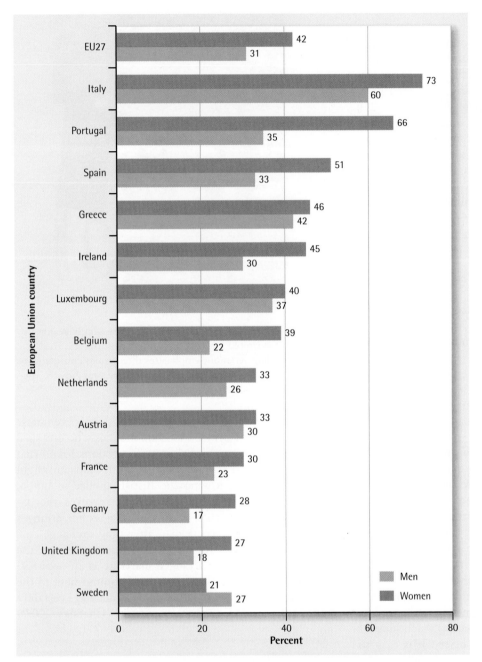

FIGURE 14.4 Percentage of European Young Adults, Aged 18–34, Living with Their Parents, by Gender and Country In Europe, one in three men and one in five women aged 25 to 34 live with their parents.
Source: Kotowska, I. E, Matysiak, A., Styrc, M., Pailhé, A., Solaz, A., & Vignoli, D. (2010, March). *Second European Quality of Life Survey: Family life and work*. Dublin, Ireland: European Foundation for the Improvement of Living and Working Conditions. Retrieved from http://www.eurofound.europa.eu/publications/htmlfiles/ef1002.htm

Some cohabiting heterosexual relationships are similar to long-term marriage. One small but growing trend is midlife couples, formerly divorced or widowed, who have decided to cohabit rather than marry because of legal, financial, health, and/or family complications (Brown, Lee, & Bulanda, 2006). But for unmarried couples who decide to separate, the emotional trauma can be every bit as severe as that experienced by married couples undergoing divorce—and just as bad for their children. There are legal complications associated with apartment leases, jointly owned property, child custody and

visitations, and inheritances. Overall, the dissolution of cohabitation resembles divorce in that the partners experience similar processes of disengagement, emotional distress, and adjustment, especially when there are children involved and no legal mechanism to adjudicate support of such children (Kenney & McLanahan, 2006). Both the U.S. federal government and state governments are presently promoting the *Healthy Marriage Initiative* to improve the economic well-being, mental and physical health, and living environments for young couples and their children (Wood, Goesling, & Avellar, 2007).

Arranged Marriages

Before the concept of romantic love came to be, arranged marriages served to sustain community cohesiveness, merge family wealth, and ensure individuals' social status through family connections. Parents wielded great power in choosing mates for their children through arranged marriages. Even today, in some cultures, girls as young as 11 or 12 are married off by their parents for social, religious, and economic considerations. The justification given for arranging marriages is that children are too young to grasp the real purpose of marriage—securing an alliance between families. But even in arranged marriages, love can sometimes be taken into consideration. For example, all of the following customs appear in various cultures:

- Parents choose the partner, no discussion or objection allowed.
- Parents choose the partner, discussion or objection is allowed.
- Parents, child, relatives, and friends come to a group decision.
- Child chooses prospective partner and parents give their approval.
- Arranged marriages and love marriages are both options.

Those who favor marriage based on love argue that it is cruel to force young people to enter into relationships with people they do not know and may not even like. Advocates for arranged marriage maintain that love is a kind of irrational distraction that interferes with the ability to make a good choice for the future. They point out that most people fall in love with someone they meet in the tiny circle of individuals with whom they are acquainted, and what's the point of *that*?

One study of young adults in India highlighted the positive and negative aspects of arranged marriages. The advantages are that these marriages receive much support from families and the approval of society. It is easy to meet a partner, and there can be the excitement of the unknown. The parents' choice can lead to a high-quality and stable marriage with someone from a compatible or desirable background, and there is time to learn to adjust to marriage. The disadvantages are that the couple does not know each other. There can be problems with the dowry. There can be incompatibility and unhappiness. The choice of mates can be limited. There can be family and in-law problems (Sprecher & Chandak, 1992). Of course, some of these pros and cons are present in marriages of choice as well!

Young women emigrants who are living in Western countries may experience uncertainty, confusion, threats of violence, or family ostracism if they object to arranged marriages; they may feel torn between traditional family values and Western social values (Zaidi & Shuraydi,

A Hindu Wedding Hindus, including those who have immigrated to the United States, favor arranged marriages. The Hindu wedding ceremony emphasizes three values considered to be essential to marriage: happiness, harmony, and growth. The color red symbolizes happiness.

2002). Transnational arranged marriages carry even more risks. A study of British Pakistani families who arranged marriages from among Pakistani kin groups found that families worry that a new spouse from Pakistan might be denied a visa, leaving the British spouse in limbo. Another form of arranged marriage involves the so-called *mail-order bride;* in this plan, a broker arranges for a woman to marry a man after they exchange correspondence. Thus, for any transnational marriage, the spouse might use the arranged marriage as an opportunity to migrate and then show little commitment to the marriage. In a global society, arranged marriage certainly does not guarantee to serve its purpose (Charsley, 2007).

Questions

Why are more young adults remaining single and residing at home with their parents? Why do young adults choose to cohabit and, in general, what do social scientists know about the well-being of couples who choose to live together? What are the benefits and drawbacks of arranged marriages?

Same-Sex Partners

As we noted in Chapter 13, the term *sexual orientation* refers to whether an individual is strongly aroused sexually by members of his or her own sex (homosexual), the opposite sex (heterosexual), or both sexes (bisexual). Most people assume that there are two kinds of people, whom they label "heterosexual" and "homosexual." A more accurate

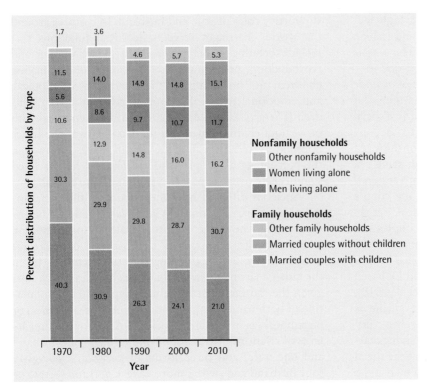

FIGURE 14.5 U.S. Household Composition: 1970–2010 The U.S. Census Bureau expects the number of nonfamily households, singles, and cohabiting couples to increase, mainly among young adults. Although the divorce rate is declining, the decision of many singles and couples to delay marriage is cited as a factor. A growing number of elderly widows contribute to the number of households made up of a single person. The number of married couples with children is declining.
Source: U.S. Bureau of the Census. (2010). America's Families and Living Arrangements: *Population Profile of the United States.* Retrieved from http://www.census.gov/population/www/socdemo/hh-fam/cps2010.html

view is that heterosexual and homosexual orientations exist at opposite ends of a continuum (in other words, one can be "more heterosexual" or "more homosexual"). At the center of this continuum, some individuals have a bisexual orientation (Crooks & Bauer, 2008). Human sexuality is quite versatile because about 1 percent of individuals identify with being *asexual* (having little or no sexual attraction to males *or* females) (Bogaert, 2004). There is great difficulty in estimating the percentage of U.S. households that are composed of gay, lesbian, or bisexual adults, because these adults and their children are likely to experience some social stigma, discrimination, harassment, or even violence (see Figure 14.5) (Kurdek, 2005).

A growing body of empirical research reveals that on standardized measures of personal adjustment and psychological well-being, gay and lesbian individuals, couples, and parents are comparable to their heterosexual counterparts; indeed, a recent study found that lesbian couples report higher levels of satisfaction with their relationships over 10 years than heterosexual couples. Heterosexual couples with children showed the most declines in relationship quality over the same 10-year period (Kurdek, 2008). Some differences that Kurdek (2005) reports are that partners from gay and lesbian couples tend to divide household labor more fairly than heterosexual couples and that they perceive more social support from friends than from family members. There are few longitudinal studies on the stability and dissolution of relationships for same-sex couples. A recent study examining the dissolution rates of several hundred

same-sex partners in Norway and Sweden revealed that "divorce" rates were considerably higher for same-sex couples (and twice as high for lesbian couples) than for heterosexual married couples (Andersson, Noack, Seierstad, & Weedon-Fekjaer, 2006).

Yet many gay and lesbian couples have stable, warm, and close relationships like those individuals in a good traditional marriage enjoy, and they also report levels of satisfaction similar to those of married couples (Kurdek, 2005). Also, same-sex partners experience conflicts from the same sources as heterosexual couples: "finances, affection, sex, being overly critical, driving style, and household tasks" (Kurdek, 2005, p. 252). Like women who marry men, lesbians report the highest levels of satisfaction when their relationship with their partner is egalitarian and when decisions are made jointly. Similarly, when both partners believe they have equal power in the relationship, they report higher levels of satisfaction (Peplau & Fingerhut, 2007). This is true for gay men in couples as well.

About one-third of people who have revealed to their families that they are homosexual find that a family member rejects them. Many gays and lesbians experience subtle or blatant discrimination from somebody several times a week. This can range from jokes about effeminate men or "butch" women to poor service in stores to hostile or threatening comments. Some experience higher levels of discrimination, such as hate crimes. One national survey found that one in three lesbian and gay respondents had been the target of physical violence, against either their property or themselves (Peplau & Fingerhut, 2007).

Needless to say, these experiences cause high levels of stress, anxiety, and depression for gay and lesbian couples (Sandfort, Melendez, & Diaz, 2007). The couple might disagree about—or not know how to respond to—prejudice, for example. Or the partners might not provide emotional support for each other at the same time that they are coping with their own stress. This is why a social network of supportive friends is so crucial to the survival and well-being of gay and lesbian relationships. At present, in many countries around the world, same-sex couples are advocating for the legality of same-sex *civil unions* or marriages. Legal marriage affords the couple more economic resources in terms of medical, retirement, and inheritance benefits. Yet same-sex couples and their children still face many legal challenges and a lack of acceptance by societies or religious groups that believe that a marital relationship and a family should be based on the traditional heterosexual model (Power et al., 2010).

Whether same-sex marriage should be available is a fiercely debated topic—for both sides believe very strongly in their position. Proponents of maintaining marriage as the traditional model are convinced that the social and religious institution of marriage between a man and a woman is the best structure for providing economic and emotional stability for children. Thus research investigating the long-term well-being of children brought into or born into same-sex households, as well as the stability and well-being of the adults in the relationship, is of great interest. One area of concern is the lack of research into, and services available for, lesbians and gay men in abusive relationships with their partners. In 2009, there were only five shelter spaces and one part-time hotline in the entire state of Massachusetts for gay and lesbian victims of domestic abuse (Preventing Domestic Violence, 2009). Some social scientists and government policymakers believe that the "slippery slope" of approving same-sex marriage will lead to demands for legally recognized multiperson group marriages, a practice called *polyamory*. An Internet search finds U.S. proponents of group sex or group marriage who believe that monogamous relationships do not work for some people, often those who are bisexual (Rust, 2003).

Questions

How is sexual orientation defined? In general, what have social scientists learned about adults in same-sex relationships, and what societal issues confront same-sex couples?

Getting Married

A lifestyle practice that appears to exist in all contemporary societies is **marriage**—a socially, legally, and/or religiously sanctioned union between a woman and a man with the expectation that they will play the mutually supportive roles of wife and husband. In cultures around the world, marriages serve basic social functions that include creating stable unions to regulate mating and reproduction, providing for a division of labor, having children, and providing for the material, psychological, and emotional needs of a couple and their young children (Ferraro, 2006). As of 2010, married couples, with or without children, made up about 53 percent of all U.S. households (U.S. Bureau of the Census, 2010o). However, the percentage of people who are married has declined significantly over the past 40 years (see Figure 14.5).

Societies differ in how they structure the social institution of marriage through laws, values, and traditions that convey how the spouses relate to one another, what marriage means, and the benefits of marriage (Blankenhorn, 2007). In some societies a child is given the father's last name, while in other societies the child is given the mother's last name or a hyphenated combination of both names. Thus, genealogy may be patrilineal or matrilineal (as in Sumatran society). Also, four main *patterns* of relationships are found: *monogamy* (one husband and one wife) and three forms of *polygamy*: *polygyny* (one husband and two or more wives), *polyandry* (two or more husbands and one wife), and *group marriage* (two or more husbands and two or more wives) (Georgas et al., 2006; Murdock, 1949). Although in the United States we use the term *polygamy* to refer to polygyny, it also includes polyandry. Monogamous marriage is prevalent in the United States, but most cultures have differing standards and practices with regard to marriage. Some countries have legalized same-sex marriage as a committed relationship between two consenting adults. At present, these include the Netherlands/Holland, Belgium, Canada, Spain, Sweden, Norway, Argentina, and South Africa (Masci, Lozano-Bielat, Ralston, & Podrebarac, 2009).

Polygyny has been widely practiced throughout the world. It is still a preferred form of marriage in many cultures in Africa, Asia, and the Middle East. The status of women in polygynous societies depends on whether a society sees women as an asset or a liability (Ferraro, 2006). Usually only the rich men in a society can afford to support more than one family (Sanderson, 2001). In contrast with polygyny, polyandry is rare among the world's societies. And in practice, women in polyandrous societies are not free to choose their mates; often polyandry simply means that younger brothers have sexual access to the wife of an older brother. Tibetan serfs practice polyandry as a way to cope with a land shortage. If brothers can marry the same women, the family can keep the family land intact rather than splitting it up among all of the brothers in monogamous unions (Ferraro, 2006).

Anthropologists disagree about whether group marriage (polyamory) genuinely exists in any society as a normatively encouraged lifestyle. There is some evidence that it might take place among the Marquesans of the

Polygyny Is Common South African President Jacob Zuma poses with his three brides. Polygyny, the practice of multiple wives, is still prevalent among many world cultures.

South Pacific, the Chukchee of Asia (men make wife-lending contracts with each other), the Kaingang of Brazil, and the Todas and Dahari of India.

Marital Satisfaction Philosophers, poets, and musicians have idealized romantic love for centuries. "And they lived happily ever after" used to be the last line in most fairy tales. Some couples in love, but not all, want to make a legal, public commitment to each other and decide to marry. Yet young-adult Americans are most likely to say that they are looking for their "soul mate" when they marry, along with sexual and emotional satisfaction and happiness, as opposed to looking for economic security or social position, as was often true in the past (National Marriage Project, 2010). In 2008 and 2009, more than 4.2 million marriages were performed in the United States (National Center for Health Statistics, 2010b). Marriage is distinguished from other types of intimate relationships by its state-sanctioned, and often church-sanctioned, status (U.S. Department of Commerce, 1998).

Living together happily in a committed marriage requires much more than the wonderful romantic feelings many couples enjoy early in their relationship. Maintaining a loving marriage is challenging at times—especially during the first year, when couples need to come to agreement about earning and spending income; meeting sexual intimacy needs; communicating fairly and resolving conflicts; deciding where to live and where to spend holidays (in-law conflicts arise); sharing household chores and errands; learning to respect each other's differences; and observing religious traditions, or not. Sometimes there already are children from a former relationship or a baby arrives within the first year, so sharing child-care responsibilities is essential.

According to marriage researchers David Popenoe and Barbara DeFoe Whitehead, several factors can influence whether a marriage will be successful and happy or not. The most likely way to find a future marriage

partner is through an introduction by family, friends, or acquaintances. Known social networks are important in bringing together individuals of similar interests and backgrounds. The more similar people are in their values, backgrounds, and life goals, the more likely they are to have a successful marriage. People who share common backgrounds and similar social networks are better suited as marriage partners than people whose backgrounds are very different. Women have a much better chance of marrying if they do not become single parents before marrying. Both women and men who are college-educated are more likely to marry, and less likely to divorce, than people with lower levels of education. College-educated women's chances of marrying are better than the chances of less-well-educated women. But the growing gender gap in college education may make it more difficult for college women to find well-educated men in the future.

Compared to those who cohabit, people who marry become economically better off (tax policy favors married couples). Marital social norms that encourage healthy, productive behavior and savings growth play a role in this. Some of the wealth of married couples results from their more efficient pooling of labor and resources and their higher rate of savings. Married couples are more likely to have emotionally and physically satisfying sex lives than single people or those who cohabit. Contrary to the popular belief, married people report higher levels of sexual satisfaction than both sexually active singles and cohabiting couples, according to surveys of sexuality. The higher level of commitment in marriage contributes to a greater sense of trust and security, less drug- and alcohol-infused sex, and more mutual communication between the couple (Popenoe & Whitehead, 2004).

On the other hand, marrying as a teenager is the highest known risk factor for divorce. People who marry in their teens are two to three times more likely to divorce than people who marry in their twenties or older. People who grow up in a family broken by divorce are slightly less likely to marry and much more likely to divorce when they do marry. According to one study, the divorce risk nearly triples if such an individual marries someone whose parents also divorced. The risk is much lower, however, if the marital partner is someone who grew up in a happy, intact family. For large segments of the population, the risk of divorce is far below 50 percent. Although the overall divorce rate in America remains close to 50 percent of all marriages, it has been dropping gradually since the mid-1980s. The risk of divorce is far less for educated people going into their first marriage, and it is even lower for those who wait to marry until their mid-twenties or older, those who haven't lived with many different partners prior to marriage, and those who are strongly religious and marry someone of the same faith (Popenoe & Whitehead, 2004). The bottom line is that if a person is somewhat well-educated and makes a decent

454   **Part Seven** Early Adulthood

salary, comes from a family not marked by divorce, has meaningful religious beliefs, does not have a baby before marriage, and marries after the age of 25, the chances for a successful marriage are actually pretty good (National Marriage Project, 2010).

Sociologists have begun to examine the points of conflict and predictors of marital satisfaction over time. One study found that married couples spent less time doing activities together in 2000 than they did 20 years earlier; fewer couples ate a main meal together, went out for leisure activities together, visited friends together, or worked together around the home than in the 1980s. Another study found that regardless of whether they worked for wages or not, wives wanted to spend more time with their husbands (Bianchi, Robinson, & Milkie, 2006). Couples often disagree about how to allocate housework and child care. Significantly, wives spend more hours on and do more of these tasks than husbands. Thus, many wives say they do a "second shift" of household labor after they finish their work for wages. We may think that helping each other do the dishes or take out the trash is minor, but the researchers reported that "perceptions of unfairness in family labor appear to seriously erode marital quality" (Amato et al., 2007, p. 170).

What are the ingredients of a happy marriage? Multiple studies have found that an egalitarian marriage is a happy marriage. Researchers have found that "people who reported equal decision making . . . reported more marital happiness, more interaction, less conflict, fewer problems, and less divorce proneness" (Amato et al., 2007, p. 170). This applies to both husbands and wives.

About Half of U.S. Households Are Married Couples
The U.S. Bureau of the Census (2010e) reports that slightly over half of households in 2010 were made up of married couples either with or without children. Thus marriage is still the dominant form of living arrangement in the United States. However, social scientists and policymakers agree that the institution of marriage is on the decline in westernized countries. (See the *Further Developments* box on page 456, "The Decline of Marriage.") Looking at Figure 14.5 (households by type from 1970 to 2010), one can see that the marital institution has declined in the past four decades. Note that "other family households," cohabiting adults with and without children, have increased by 60 percent since 1970. Thus, younger adults are remaining single longer and are postponing marriage or are living in a cohabiting relationship. For men, the median age of first marriage is now age 28; for women, the median age for first marriage is now about age 26 (U.S. Bureau of the Census, 2010d).

The U.S. divorce rate today has almost doubled since the 1960s but shows modest declines from its peak in the 1980s (National Marriage Report, 2010). National statistics collected in 2010 reveal that only 24 percent of

U.S. adults 18 and over are divorced (U.S. Census Bureau News, 2010). This is attributed to the higher number of younger couples who choose to cohabit instead of marrying (or remarrying): Statistics are not gathered for cohabitation breakups. Also, people are staying single longer and marrying later. A greater percentage of marriages are between well-educated couples who are likely to make better marital decisions that sustain marital stability. During the recession that began in 2007, the divorce rate actually fell, even though one would think that the stresses of the economic crisis might have been too much for many fragile marriages to bear. However, the drop in divorces may have been due not to strengthened marriages but simply to the fact that divorce itself is an expensive proposition. Many couples may have stayed together simply because they could not afford to legally part (National Marriage Project, 2009). In 2009, there were only 16 divorces per 1,000 people (National Marriage Project, 2010).

Historian Stephanie Coontz (2007) sees this major change in marriage patterns as being as significant as the wrenching upheavals that the Industrial Revolution caused in work patterns. She states that the basis for marriage changed in the 1700s from a means for controlling family property to a focus on romantic love. From that time until the 1960s, a number of factors kept married couples together even if the marriage was unhappy: women's and children's economic and legal dependence on men; an absence of birth control; religious teachings; and the influence of relatives, neighbors, and the larger community in pressuring a couple to stay married.

Significant change has taken place in each of these factors. Civil rights, affirmative action, employment and labor laws, and business contracts have changed to make women and men more nearly equal. Women can now earn their own income, make investments, and get their own credit at banks. (One of your authors was denied an auto loan as a young adult after college in 1972, unless her father would co-sign, even though she was employed full-time as a college faculty member and had little debt.) The birth control pill became available in the 1960s, and women were able to have fewer, if any, children. Today, various forms of birth control are widely available, except to women in countries with high poverty or religious sanctions. Finally, our mobile society has nearly eradicated the close knit multigenerational neighborhoods that provided significant social support for couples when children were young or times were hard. For people without strong religious beliefs, the main glue that holds contemporary marriages together is the ideal of romantic love (Coontz, 2005).

As a society we are skilled at planning elaborate weddings, but many of us are not prepared to cultivate and maintain satisfying relationships with our partners. With *no-fault divorce*, it is easy to get out of relationships that don't satisfy us, but we need to learn more about how to tend relationships that can be strengthened in difficult times. Researchers and clinical practitioners have learned that a core set of behaviors within a marriage or partnership will strengthen commitment and maintain bonds. The behaviors include (Harvey & Weber, 2002)

- being positive and cheerful
- being open and talking about how you feel, especially about the relationship
- giving positive messages to your partner
- demonstrating love and faithfulness
- spending time together with friends and family
- sharing tasks
- doing activities together
- expressing affection and being sexually intimate
- being spontaneous

Even in the happiest of marriages, the first years are a time of intense adjustment and learning as a couple finds what issues create conflict and how each partner reacts to stress. Couples who work through their hot-button issues in the first decade of marriage often go on to have long and deeply satisfying marriages. Conflict in marriage over everyday issues is not the end of the world (Kasen et al., 2006). Women and men tend to see conflict in marriage differently. Women tend to react to immediate events, while men's behavior tends to be shaped by their understanding of the entire relationship. Women's brains seem to be wired to pay attention to the fine details of everyday life; men's brains seem to be wired to see and assess events through a big-picture schema (Sanford, 2007). Thus, learning to communicate fairly so that both adults' views are heard is critical to a happy relationship. Showing affection and a good sense of humor and being able to laugh about daily hassles can prevent little things from being blown out of proportion (Driver & Gottman, 2004).

Being understood by one's spouse is an aspect of marriage that both men and women rate highly. Women especially like to *discuss* things that bother them and want to have their *feelings* recognized; men usually want to *solve* the problem ("What do you want me to *do*?"). Differences not uncovered before the marriage will show up. These differences can seem devastating ("How could I be married to someone who thinks *that*?"), but they can also be a source of growth. Working to understand how and why a partner has certain opinions will add to the growing store of knowledge that couples can draw on throughout the marriage. Husbands and wives who demonstrate trust and respect for each other are likely to deal with conflict in constructive and positive ways (Sanford, 2006).

Forgiveness is another important element, no matter what the length of a relationship. When a hurtful event happens in a marriage, willingness to forgive is predictive of the level of marital satisfaction one year after the

harmful event took place. When goodwill exists between partners, benevolence toward a spouse who has done something hurtful paves the way for a stronger relationship. But unresolved conflict or an unwillingness to say "I'm sorry" appears to decrease the store of forgiveness within a marriage (Fincham, Beach, & Davila, 2007).

Some researchers claim that the women's movement is responsible for the decline of the social institution of marriage, having brought about increased rates of female sexual experimentation, changes in divorce laws, increased participation in the labor force and emphasis on financial independence, and the emphasis on wives' emotional and intellectual needs. But Coontz (2007) points out that men report higher levels of happiness than men did in the 1970s. Because the economic well-being of a family is shared, they benefit emotionally from their caretaking roles with children, and they have experienced more flexible roles in the workplace (Coontz, 2007).

Women's expectations within marriage have increased since the 1970s. One 20-year analysis of marriage patterns found that married couples experienced greater conflict in the early years of the marriage, a time when women demanded change to make the relationship more equitable (Kasen et al., 2006). Most women expect their husbands to be emotionally close and supportive—of them and their children. The top item on their checklist of support is the sharing of household and child-care chores after they have worked all day (Coontz, 2007). If their husbands were not willing to help with household and child-care responsibilities, they could choose to end their marriage, for many of them had graduated from college and/or were employed. They could support themselves and their children, although probably at a greatly reduced standard of living.

Questions

What factors presently undermine the status of marriage in industrialized countries? In what ways has the American institution of marriage changed over the past 50 years? How have men's and women's marital expectations changed, and why?

FAMILY TRANSITIONS

For more than half of all American households, the traditional family remains a central and vital institution. Over the course of their lives, most Americans find themselves members of two family groups. First, a person belongs to a **nuclear family** that often consists of oneself and one's father, mother, and siblings. This group is called the individual's *family of origin* or *family of orientation*. Second, because over 90 percent of Americans marry at least once, the vast majority of American adults are members

FURTHER DEVELOPMENTS

The Decline of Marriage

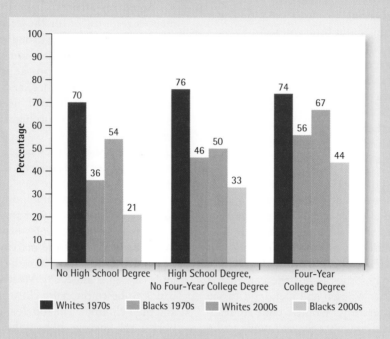

FIGURE 14.6 Percentage of 25- to 60-Year-Olds in Intact First Marriage, by Race, Education, and Decade
Source: Wilcox, W. B. (Ed.) (2010). *The state of our unions, 2010.* Charlottesville, VA: National Marriage Project, University of Virginia. Retrieved from http://www.stateofourunions.org

In the 1960s, a dramatic retreat from marriage began in the United States. Why? Federal welfare laws and the federal welfare program *Aid to Families with Dependent Children* (AFDC) that went into effect in the 1960s discouraged the father's being in the home. (If he lived there, a welfare check would not be issued unless he was unemployed.) Thus, poor women with children were most likely to seek welfare—and the amount of the check increased with the birth of each child. "In 1960 only 4 percent of the children getting welfare had a mother who had never been married; the rest had mothers who were widows or had been separated from their husbands" (Wilson, 2002). Contrast that with the fact that *more than 70 percent* of black children *and more than 40 percent* of white children born today are born to single mothers. Thus, the single-parent trend has moved into middle-class groups of both blacks and whites. Since the 1960s, federal laws and judicial decrees added Food Stamp and Medicaid eligibility to welfare recipients' support. Welfare-to-work programs replaced AFDC in 1996 (Batlan & Gordon, 2011). Today, to their great detriment, millions of U.S. children are growing up without the influence and support of fathers.

The National Marriage Project (2010) analyzed this trend by looking at people in three socioeconomic groups:

those without a high school education (the least educated), those with a high school but not a four-year college degree (the moderately educated), and those with a degree from a four-year college (the highly educated). The U.S. trend is for the moderately educated core, like the least educated, to be *less* likely to form good, stable marriages, while the highly educated group (about one-third of the population) is increasingly embracing marriage (see Figure 14.6). Like the families of the least educated, moderately educated families are at greater risk of widespread divorce and cohabitation, serious financial concerns, and high levels of family conflict, stress, and tension. In this group, there is increasing nonmarital childbearing with absent fathers and troubled children.

For both blacks and whites, children are far more likely to live with both of their parents when their mothers are highly educated than when they are not (National Marriage Project, 2010). This growing trend away from stable marriages is a great societal concern because, according to the National Marriage Project (2010), "Marriage is not merely a private arrangement between two persons. It is a core social institution, one that helps ensure the economic, social, and emotional welfare of countless children, women, and men in this nation" (p. xi). The conclusion of the National Marriage Project's research is that this retreat from marriage "makes the lives of mothers harder and drives fathers further away from families. It increases the odds that children . . . will drop out of high school, end up in trouble with the law, become pregnant as teenagers, or otherwise lose their way. . . . A social and culture divide is growing" (p. xii). This trend away from marriage is connected, in part, with the diminishing influence of churches, unions, and civic organizations. In the past, people turned to these groups to support the lifestyles and habits that sustained strong marriages and families. Another cause is the drastic cultural and economic changes that have occurred in America since the 1960s.

The bottom line is that no matter what one's race, the more highly educated one is, the more likely one is to be in an intact marriage and to have the resources to support one's own family. The dividing line between those who marry and those who do not is no longer racially based, as it was 50 years ago; now it is based on class and educational level. If this trend is not reversed, then strong, stable marriages may become a luxury that only the wealthy or highly educated can attain, and only they will have access to the stability and socioeconomic benefits that marriage offers a family.

of a nuclear family in which they are one of the parents. This group is called the individual's *family of procreation.*

Psychologists and sociologists have sought to find a framework for describing the typical transitions that occur across a person's life span that are related to these shifts in family patterns (Cowan & Cowan, 2003). They devised the concept of the **family life cycle**—the sequential changes and realignments that occur in the structure and relationships of family life between the time of marriage and the death of one or both spouses. The family-life-cycle model views families, like individuals, as undergoing development that is characterized by identifiable phases, or stages. Traditionally, as viewed by Hill (1964) and other sociologists, the nuclear family begins with the husband-wife pair and becomes increasingly complex as children are added, creating new roles and multiplying the number of interpersonal relations. The family then stabilizes for a brief period, after which it begins shrinking as each of the adult children is launched. Finally, the family returns once again to the husband-wife pair and then terminates with the death of a spouse. However, in contemporary societies, the traditional family life cycle does not apply for divorced families, stepfamilies, single-parent families, same-sex families, grandparents-raising-grandchildren families, foster families, some immigrant families, and the institutionalized population; thus multifaceted research is ongoing. Family transitions are also greatly influenced by culture and the historical period, which includes economic trends (McGoldrick & Carter, 2003).

Pregnancy

Within the life cycle of a couple, and particularly of a woman, the first pregnancy is an event of unparalleled importance (Harwood, McLean, & Durkin, 2007). The first pregnancy signals that a couple is entering into the traditional family cycle, bringing about new role requirements. Thus, the first pregnancy functions as a major marker or transition and confronts a couple with new developmental tasks. Recall from Chapter 3 that more women from westernized countries are postponing childbearing, and an increasing number of women are experiencing infertility and seeking assisted reproductive technologies to become pregnant. Such factors increase a woman's anxiety and stress, because there is no guarantee of successful fertility or birth and because the fees are high; also, the chance of having a multiple birth is greater with fertility treatments.

Pregnancy requires a woman to marshal her resources and adjust to a good many changes. Unfortunately, in many cases a woman's earliest experiences of pregnancy are somewhat negative. She might be an unmarried adolescent; she might have morning sickness, vomiting, and fatigue. Pregnancy can also compel a woman to reflect on her long-term life plans, particularly as they relate to marriage and a career. And pregnancy can cause her to reconsider her sense of identity. Many women seek out information on birth and motherhood to help them prepare for the new role. The woman's partner faces many of these same concerns. The partner might have to reappraise his or her conception of age, responsibility, and autonomy. Similarly, pregnancy contributes to changes in the couple's sexual behavior. Few events equal pregnancy in suddenness or significance, and many couples experience the initial phase of pregnancy as being somewhat disruptive, requiring marital adjustments.

On the broader social level, relatives, friends, and acquaintances commonly offer judgments on numerous matters, including whether the woman has a marital relationship with the father-to-be or will remain a single parent. An employed woman may have to adjust to changing hours at work, changing jobs, working from home, or leaving employment temporarily. As an extreme example, women carrying more than one child are often bedridden for the last few months of pregnancy. If the mother-to-be should leave the paid workforce in preparation for childbirth, she could find that her domestic situation also changes. When a new baby enters the household, the more egalitarian values and role patterns of dual-career couples may give way to the stereotyped gender-role responsibilities typical of traditional nuclear families, although fathers increasingly express their frustration about their lack of time to be with the new baby.

Researchers have identified four major developmental tasks confronting a pregnant woman. First, she must come to accept her pregnancy. She must define herself as a parent-to-be and prepare for impending parenthood. This process requires developing an emotional attachment to her unborn child, something that is now easier to do earlier in the pregnancy, thanks to images and sound from fetal ultrasound technology. Women typically are preoccupied with the developing fetus, and around the time that they begin to detect clear movements of the child in the uterus, they ascribe personal characteristics to the fetus and often talk or sing to it. It is not uncommon for women across cultures to say they experience an intuitive or spiritual communication with their unborn child (Hall, 2006).

Second, as a woman's pregnancy progresses, she must come to differentiate herself from the fetus and establish a distinct sense of self. She might accomplish this task by reflecting on a name for the infant and imagining what the baby will look like and how it will behave. This process is expedited when her increasing size brings about alterations in her clothing and she assumes a "pregnancy identity." Third, a pregnant woman typically reflects on and reevaluates her relationship with her own mother. This process often entails the woman's reconciliation with her mother and the working through of numerous feelings, memories, and identifications. Fourth, a woman must come to terms with the issue of dependency. Her pregnancy and impending motherhood often arouse anxiety concerning her loss of certain freedoms and her reliance on others for some measure of support, maintenance, and help. Such concerns are frequently centered on her relationship with her husband or partner.

The accomplishment of these developmental tasks is improved by attending childbirth-training classes or by developing a relationship with a midwife, or doula, who prepares women for what to expect during pregnancy and labor (Kennedy, Erickson-Owens, & Davis, 2006). The pregnant woman gains knowledge and emotional support from the classes that give her a measure of "active control." Finally, when husbands or partners participate in the training classes, mothers-to-be find additional social support and assistance. Both preparation in pregnancy and a partner's presence are positively associated with the quality of a woman's birth experience. Indeed, much that happens before birth influences what transpires between parent and child after birth. What a woman experiences during prenatal development is discussed in Chapter 3.

Transition to Parenthood

Psychologists and sociologists who view the family as an integrated system of roles and statuses have often depicted the onset of parenthood as a "crisis" because it involves a shift from a two-person to a three-person system (Lawrence et al., 2008). The three-person system is thought to be inherently more stressful than the two-person system. Sociologists also find other reasons why the transition to parenthood could pose a crisis:

> The birth of a child is not followed by any gradual taking on of responsibility, as in the case of a professional work role. It is as if the woman shifted from a graduate student to a full professor with little intervening apprenticeship experience of slowly increasing responsibility. The new mother starts out immediately on 24-hour duty, with responsibility for a fragile and mysterious infant totally dependent on her care. (Rossi, 1968, p. 35)

We should note that not all marriages or relationships change in exactly the same way, and important individual differences occur in the ways in which spouses respond to parenthood (Brock & Lawrence, 2008). A three-year longitudinal study by Brock and Lawrence (2008) reveals fresh insights about the transition to adulthood and parenthood in the examination of three variables: spousal support, chronic role strain, and marital satisfaction. Overall, after the birth of a baby, couples typically experience a modest decline in the overall quality and intimacy of their marital life. Husbands and wives often have less time to show each other affection, and they share fewer leisure activities (especially if the couple has multiples). But on the positive side, there is an increase in a couple's sense of partnership and mutual caretaking. Spousal support is a key factor in marital satisfaction.

Couples who are most likely to report marital problems in early parenthood are those who held the most unrealistic expectations of parenthood. One of the biggest postbirth problems is the division of labor; this problem is also called role strain. The wife frequently assumes a disproportionate share of the household chores, and this can lead her to have negative feelings toward her husband. A shared division of responsibilities between husband and wife is especially important for the maintenance of ongoing intimate relationships and marital satisfaction (Helms, Walls, Crouter, & McHale, 2010). A large body of research suggests that family routines and rituals are embedded in the cultural context of family life. Such family rituals may include religious observances, a certain type of greeting when the spouse returns

Transition to Parenthood and Role Strains Most parents are unprepared for the total dependency of a new baby, their own physical adjustments and sleep deprivation, and trial-and-error parenting. A shared division of responsibilities and adequate sleep are especially important for marital satisfaction. A network of supportive people is crucial.
Source: For Better or For Worse © 2004 Lynn Johnston Productions. Dist. By Universal Uclick. Reprinted with permission. All rights reserved.

home, routine meal times, a special weekend activity, or an annual vacation (Ahmadi & Hossein-abadi, 2009).

Postpartum Depression A majority of new mothers get the *baby blues* from about the fourth day to the tenth day after delivery, and the symptoms may include weeping, sadness, anxiety, or confusion (Bina, 2008). But about one of every eight new mothers experiences what is called **postpartum major depression (PPD)**. Symptoms include irritability, waves of sadness, frequent crying spells, difficulty sleeping, diminished appetite, and feelings of helplessness and hopelessness. The episode may be mild and last only a short time (up to a few weeks), or it may be much longer. Similar symptoms often appear in women who adopt a child, and some new fathers also report that they feel "down in the dumps." One study reported that nearly all new mothers experience some symptoms that have been traditionally associated with postpartum depression. Further, if a woman has had a postpartum depression, she is at higher risk for PPD with the next baby (Oppo et al., 2009).

The dramatic hormonal changes associated with childbirth and metabolic readjustment to a nonpregnant state influence a woman's emotional and psychological state. Following childbirth, rapid changes occur in the levels of various hormones, and fluctuations occur in thyroid, adrenal, and ovarian hormones. Such changes contribute to depressive reactions (Paris, Bolton, & Weinberg, 2009). Other explanations emphasize the psychological adjustments required of a woman in her new role as a mother (Mauther, 1999). Some women experience a sense of loss of independence, of being tied down and trapped by the new infant. Other women feel guilty about the anger and helplessness they feel when their infants cry and cannot be comforted. And others feel overwhelmed by the responsibility of caring for, rear-

ing, and shaping the behavior of another human being. Women with multiples, temperamentally difficult babies, premature babies, or babies born with a disability find that child care severely taxes their emotional and psychological resources, contributing to depression. Although mothers cannot alter their infant's basic temperament, they can cope with stress by developing a network of supportive people. In fact, a lack of a support system and the absence of extended family members to support the new mother may significantly contribute to postpartum depression in Western societies. In cultures where there is strong social support for women, the rates of postpartum depression appear to be low (Bina, 2008).

In a small percent of cases, a child's birth can catalyze severe mental illness in women who are predisposed to *schizophrenia* or *bipolar* (manic-depressive) *disorder*. This *postpartum psychosis* is characterized by bizarre behavior, disorganized thoughts, hallucinations, and delusions. It requires immediate intervention to prevent suicide or infanticide (as in the case of Andrea Yates, who drowned her five young children in 2001 after years of postpartum depression with psychosis) (Paris, Bolton, & Weinberg, 2009). Women should not be afraid or ashamed of seeking help. Treatment options include psychotherapy, antidepressant medication, participation in a support group, family counseling, and, if circumstances warrant, hospitalization (Leis, Mendelson, Tandon, & Perry, 2009).

Parenthood and Depression Evenson and Simon (2005) examined data from the *National Survey of Families and Households* to test their hypothesis that parents generally have more depression than people who are not raising children. They found that men and women raising children both reported higher levels of depression than people who are not parents. People raising children, especially young children, experience so many demands on their resources that they are likely to feel that the emotional demands of having children outweigh the emotional rewards. All types of parents reported higher levels of depression: biological parents with resident children, stepparents, single parents, and parents who do not have custody of their children (Evenson & Simon, 2005). Also, chronic *fatigue* is highly associated with stress and depression, and most new parents go months without getting sufficient sleep (Loutzenhiser & Sevigny, 2008).

With adequate sleep, and with spousal or partner or parental support, most parents have a more positive outlook about child-care responsibilities. Generally parents find great joy in their interactions with their children. But modern parents have less social support from extended families than was available in previous generations. Today's couples typically raise their children with only occasional visits from family and friends. Some grandparents live far away, and some are still working. Single parents with new babies are more likely than others to return to their parental home for support. The burden of raising children, holding down jobs, paying mortgages or rent, and putting food on the table often rests on just the two parents (and increasingly on only one parent).

Parental Stress and Child Abuse As we saw in Chapter 10, the adult who abuses a child is most likely to be a parent, a stepparent, or the unmarried live-in partner of a biological parent. One of the strongest predictors is a person's belief that aggression toward a child (hitting, slapping, yelling, shaking, belittling) is acceptable discipline. Another predictor is a caretaker's belief that a child is responsible for misbehavior that a child his age cannot yet control (beliefs such as "my son thinks he is the boss" when the son is only 3 years old). Parents who were themselves physically abused in childhood or who have a history of verbal or physical aggression are more likely to abuse their children. Parents who are depressed or overwhelmed by the responsibilities of caring for energetic children are also at risk of committing child abuse. Parents who hold a grudge against their child, are excessively demanding of the child, hover over their child to make sure they comply with every demand, and get into long arguments with their young child are more likely to overreact and become physically abusive.

It is important to note that these traits and behaviors can occur in any household regardless of race, socioeconomic status, or education. Although stress about finances and work can increase parental stress, researchers found that the behaviors listed above were far more likely to predict aggression toward a child than other variables (Slep & O'Leary, 2007). Social workers, health-care providers, teachers, dentists and dental hygienists, child-care workers, and other pediatric professionals should be aware of these warning signs in their interactions with parents and young children and should be ready to inform them of resources to mitigate their stress; they must also be prepared to comply with laws that compel them to report suspected abuse.

Questions

How do a pregnant woman and her partner best prepare for the transition to parenthood? What are some warning signs of postpartum depression? Why does parenthood change the nature of a marriage? What factors are associated with child abuse?

Same-Sex Parenthood

Lesbians may choose various pathways to parenthood, including parenting children from a former heterosexual relationship, donor insemination, adoption, and stepparenting. Some lesbian mothers are hesitant to be open about their sexual orientation for fear of losing their children in custody disputes or losing their jobs. It is still possible for a lesbian mother in a custody dispute to lose custody of her children. In some courts of law, lesbian mothers have been deemed "unfit" as parents on a number of grounds, and these decisions can vary widely, depending on the state and the judge hearing the case (Chamberlain, Miller, & Bornstein, 2008). In fact, however, there is no evidence that lesbian mothers are emotionally unstable or that they might sexually abuse their children. A growing body of research comparing psychosocial adjustment and school outcomes for children from different types of families (same-sex parents or opposite-sex parents) reveals that the children of same-sex parents adjust and function well. Also, adolescent romantic relationships and sexual behavior were not associated with family type. The quality of the parent-child relationship is a better predictor of child outcomes than family type (Fairtlough, 2008). Also, in one study, the children of lesbians were shown to function well in peer relationships and reported high-quality friendships especially if their relationships with their mothers were close (Wainright & Patterson, 2008).

Research shows that there are few differences between heterosexual and lesbian mothers, because it is motherhood—not sexuality—that emerges as the dominant identity marker for these women. Lesbian women choose to become parents for the same reasons as heterosexual parents. But they face issues that heterosexual mothers do not face, such as homophobia and societal disapproval (Ryan & Berkowitz, 2009). These factors place additional stress on the lesbian mother that can lead her to develop feelings of self-doubt, ambivalence, or having to overachieve. Lesbian couples with children reported greater sexual and interpersonal satisfaction than those lesbian couples who remained childless. Furthermore, lesbian couples tend to divide housework and child care more equitably than other couples (Shechory & Ziv, 2007).

Gay men who choose to raise children face more challenges than do lesbians. Their path to parenthood is very different from that of heterosexual men, and their decision to become parents is the first in a long and often difficult journey (Berkowitz & Marsiglio, 2007). They most often adopt children, and often the children they adopt are multiracial. They sometimes encounter homophobia in the adoption agencies they choose. Another path is through surrogacy, with a woman who is willing to carry a child created with the sperm of one of the men. One advantage that gay men have in their attempts to have children is that their combined financial resources are likely to be higher than those of either heterosexual or lesbian couples. Another advantage is that gay fathers are not bound by rigid gender roles and can experiment to find which parent is best suited to child rearing and household tasks. One study found that gay men who became parents often found growing acceptance from their families who may not have accepted their sexual orientation before the men became parents (Appell, 2008).

To date, little research has been conducted about the dynamics within gay-headed families. It is clear that gay men who adopt want to be parents and are overwhelmed with emotion when a child is placed in their arms. Thirty years ago, it was a wild dream for a gay man to consider fatherhood. Now, through reproductive technology and a more accepting society, "father" and "gay man" do not have to be mutually exclusive identities (Ryan & Berkowitz, 2009).

Question

What are the findings of studies on the psychological effects of parenting for same-sex parents and for children growing up in a same-parent home?

Separation and Divorce

U.S. divorce rates have been declining since the early 1980s, but they are still fairly high. About one-third of married couples will divorce within 10 years, and overall about half of longer-term marriages eventually end in divorce (Fine & Harvey, 2006). When divorce occurs, it seriously affects everyone involved in the family, but the experience does not affect all couples in the same ways. For instance, some spouses continue to have sex even after they are separated or divorced and get along fairly well. But for most, the negative effects are long-lasting. People who have gone through separation or divorce have increased risk of mental-health issues, depression, alcoholism or substance abuse, weight loss or weight gain, and sleep disorders (Fine & Harvey, 2006).

The effects on young children can continue into young adulthood, with children of divorce having a decreased capacity for intimacy (Piemont, 2009). And parental divorce is associated with an increased risk of offspring divorce, especially when wives or both spouses have gone through the experience of their parents' divorce (Fine & Harvey, 2006). Traditionally, women are granted either sole custody or joint custody of children and may be awarded a regular child-support stipend by the courts, which might or might not be paid. (See Figure 14.7.)

One study compared couples who divorced and couples who stayed married to look for variables that predicted a greater likelihood of divorce within the first decade of marriage. Couples who divorced after seven years of marriage were likely to have been the couples who make most of us either jealous or annoyed; they were so in love that they couldn't keep their hands off each other in public. They tended to have whirlwind courtships and seemed giddy with love in the first period of their relationship. However, once the intensity of romantic feelings diminished over the first year, the couples in the study felt disillusioned and increasingly

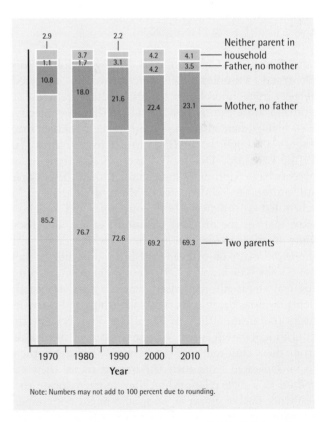

FIGURE 14.7 Living Arrangements of U.S. Children for Selected Years: 1970 to 2010   Note that about two-thirds of children reside in homes with two parents, but nearly one-fourth of children live with a single-parent mother, and close to 4 percent live with a single-parent father.
Source: U.S. Census Bureau. Current Population Survey, Annual Social and Economic Supplement, 1970, 1980, 1990, 2000, 2005, and 2010.

ambivalent about their partners. The researchers concluded that "whereas 35 years ago such couples may have remained married, contemporary couples . . . may believe that a marriage is not worth sustaining if it is no longer as meaningful, fulfilling, and intense as it once was" (Huston et al., 2001).

Researchers and therapists inform new couples about the risk of relying solely on their partners for emotional support. Young adults who delay marriage until their late twenties or older often have networks of friends who provide social support during their single years. Individuals who marry with this rich social resource and maintain these friendships are more likely to weather the storm of marriage once the honeymoon period ends. The idea that one can find a soul mate and retreat into a cozy enclave of domestic bliss is rather unrealistic, even though this is increasingly what young adults seem to look for as they seek a mate (National Marriage Project, 2010). While it is necessary for the health of their relationship to spend time together, the partners in a marriage need to visit friends, stay in touch with family members, and socialize with people nearby or from work as well (Coontz, 2006). Increasing the number of trusted and reliable people who can help you understand and cope with life's problems is a wise idea (Fine & Harvey, 2006).

Well-Being of Children and Young Adults from Divorced Families Offspring raised in divorced, single-parent households report greater life satisfaction and more positive emotional life (higher subjective well-being) than offspring raised in high-conflict marriages—although this finding varies across cultures (Yu, Pettit, Lansford, Dodge, & Bates, 2010). If divorced parents have continuing high conflict, then the children still suffer the consequences. Most often they make scheduled visits between both households and somehow must manage the differing traditions, values, and discipline practices in each parent's home, while coping with the emotional pain of losing the life and traditions they once knew (Piemont, 2009). Young children are often resilient about enforced visits, whereas teens eventually demand more flexible visits as friendships and activities begin to consume their lives. Fathers often become the nonresident parent and may begin to distance themselves from their children. It is often very painful for them to be separated from their children or to see their ex-spouse in a new relationship; they might relocate to a residence farther away; an ex-spouse might not cooperate with visitation guidelines; or a remarriage may occur with new children (Kelly, 2007). For both boys and girls, continuing conflict between parents has long-term, negative consequences including poorer school achievement, conduct disorders, psychological adjustment, lower self-concept, and difficulties with social relations (Harold, Aitken, & Shelton, 2007).

Gohm, Oishi, and Darlington (1998) conducted a cross-cultural study investigating the effects of parental divorce on the subjective well-being of adult children. They collected international data from 1995 to 1996 as part of a larger study of issues related to cultural differences in subjective well-being. Participants were several thousand college students from 39 countries (14 Asian countries, 13 European countries, 5 African countries, 4 South American countries, plus Australia, the United States, and Puerto Rico). In some cases, parental divorce increased the well-being of offspring, but for some, being raised in a second marriage was much more difficult (Chase-Lansdale, Cherlin, & Kiernan, 1995). Analysis of 37 studies of young-adult offspring found that both boys and girls experience the difficult impact of divorce (Amato, 2001).

In terms of remarriage and the newly formed family, "the subjective well-being of offspring in remarried households is not much greater than that of offspring in a high-conflict marriage, and sometimes it is lower" (Gohm, Oishi, & Darlington, 1998). In fact, Wilson and Daly (1997) report a considerably higher incidence of child abuse and homicide in remarriage families than in intact families, particularly for children under age 3. Cherlin (2004) proposes that Americans lack norms of behavior about the way members of stepfamilies should act toward each other. Offspring raised in a remarried household where parental conflict is low report life satisfaction similar to that of offspring from average marriages and of offspring from single-parent, divorced homes.

Cherlin (2004) finds that the relatively high rate of divorce and remarriage has contributed to the erosion of marriage lasting a lifetime. Changes in norms include the changing division of labor in the home, childbearing outside of marriage, repeated cohabitation, and domestic partnerships. The extended social network found in *collectivist* cultures (those with extended kinship patterns) appears to provide greater psychological and emotional support for children experiencing the trauma of marital conflict and divorce (Gohm, Oishi, & Darlington, 1998). Children often become the forgotten casualties of divorce as parents attempt to restructure their own lives and economic resources.

Single-Parent Mothers

In 2009, more than 4 out of 10 U.S. births were to single women, although a decline in births to single teens and single young-adult women was found. For births in 2009 to unmarried women, one-quarter of such births were to white single women, and about half were to Hispanic single women. Close to three-quarters of black women who gave birth were single (Hamilton, Martin, & Ventura, 2010b). Increasing numbers of women in Western nations are bearing children outside of marriage, but the highest rate is in the United States. Single parenthood is evident at all socioeconomic levels. Although the numbers are highest for women who live in poverty and black women, the most rapid rate of increase is seen among women who have attended college for at least a year and among women with professional or managerial jobs. As women become more financially independent and are able to rely on other relatives for child care, it becomes more feasible to be a single mother or adoptive parent. As noted earlier in this chapter, the traditional *nuclear family* is not a reality for a growing number of Americans.

In single-parent families the responsibilities fall on one adult rather than two, so single parents must allocate their time to cover both their own and their children's economic, physical, social, and psychological needs. The matter is complicated by the fact that many schools and workplaces have inflexible hours, and these hours do not coincide—although more businesses now have flex-time scheduling or on-site child care. More U.S. schools are providing both before-school and after-school care, as well as all-day summer programs for youth. Single mothers frequently suffer from a lack of free time, spiraling child-care costs, loneliness, and the unrelenting pressures of role overload. For some, juggling college classes adds to their stress. Being a single parent calls for a different kind of parenting. Frequently, single parents find themselves making "the speech," as one mother termed it:

> I sat down with my three children and said, "Look. Things are going to have to be different. We're all in this together and we're going to have to be partners. I'm earning a living for us now. I'm doing it all. I need your help, if this household is going to work." (McCoy, 1982, p. 21)

Women heading single-parent families often have lower levels of education, income, and social support than women in two-parent families, leading to greater stress. One study found that financial strain resulted in higher levels of depressive symptoms, which in turn had a negative effect on parenting (Jackson et al., 2000). Disruptions due to substantial income changes, residential relocation, unpredictable financial support from an ex-spouse, and changes in household composition are more likely. Not surprisingly, female heads generally report much lower self-esteem, a lower sense of effectiveness, and less optimism about the future than women in two-parent settings. However, recently divorced, separated, and widowed women experience more major life-event disruptions than women who have been single for three or more years. And even though many women do not choose single parenting, most are proud of their ability to survive under adverse circumstances (DeAngelis, 2001).

For many single mothers, kin networks are important sources of financial, emotional, and child-care support (Webber & Boromeo, 2005). Many single mothers are dependent on government programs, local charitable organizations, and churches for survival. In 1996, the federal *Welfare to Work* legislation began providing job training to enable healthy single mothers to become employed within a recommended time period. However, preliminary research findings by social scientists reveal that while about two-thirds of women have left welfare and are earning more money than before, these women and their families face significant psychological and economic challenges. In many respects a single father is in a better position than a single mother, because he is frequently viewed as a person who is doing something extraordinary.

According to the U.S. Bureau of the Census (Grall, 2009), more than eight out of ten custodial parents are women. One-third of never-married custodial parents raising children have been awarded and receive child support, while only about half of custodial divorced parents received child support that was due. U.S. divorce courts often demand the father's monetary obligation but not his presence, although more courts are awarding men joint custody. And as men start seeing their children less, they often start paying less. Among never-married mothers, only a small number get any financial help from their children's father. One-quarter of custodial parents had incomes below the poverty level. Young (under the age of 30), black, or never-married custodial parents had higher poverty rates (Grall, 2009). Thus, many never-married custodial parents depend on a variety of church, nonprofit, community, and public-assistance programs such as WIC, Medicaid, Head Start, food stamps, and the like. However, custodial parents employed full time in 2007 had about an 18 percent poverty rate (Grall, 2009).

Some families headed by women survive these hardships with few ill effects. But a disturbing number of children and parents are saddled with problems. However, one study showed that among black families headed by single women, the mother's optimism led to better outcomes for the family, especially when it was dealing with stress and other hardships (Taylor, Conger, Widaman, Larsen-Rife, & Cutrona, 2010). Children living in single-parent families are much more likely than children living with both parents to be enrolled below the grade that is customary for their age and to be experiencing difficulties in school. Juvenile delinquency rates are twice as high for children from single-parent households as for children from two-parent households. Lack of parental supervision and chronic social, health, and psychological strains are often associated with poverty (Murdock, Zey, Cline, & Klineberg, 2010).

Social isolation can create a sense of vulnerability for single mothers. Yet most women report having a partner, boyfriend, friends, or relatives who provide them with assistance on a fairly regular basis. In nearly half of all single-parent families, the parent marries within five years. This new marriage results in a "blended" or "reconstituted" family, which can produce complicated kinship networks (see Chapter 16). Where both partners have been previously married, each has to deal with the former spouse of the current partner as well as with his or her own former spouse and several sets of grandparents (some of them being ex-in-laws). Adding to the complexity are stepparent-stepchildren relationships, one's own children's reactions to the current spouse, one's own reactions to the current spouse's children, and the children's reactions to one another!

Single-Parent Fathers

In the 1970s, a father was awarded custody only if he could demonstrate in court that the mother was totally "unfit" for parenthood, and it was out of the question for single men to adopt a child. This has changed over the past 40 years. In 2009, there were more than 2.1 million father-child families in the United States (U.S. Bureau of the Census, 2011b). The number of men who become single parents as a result of their wife's death has declined. But the number of single fathers has grown as more men are awarded custody of children in divorce proceedings and as gay men adopt children.

Although the expectations attached to the father role in a two-parent family are fairly explicit, they are not so explicit for a father in the single-parent family. (See the *More Information You Can Use* box, "The Diversity of Fathers Today.") A number of studies have shown that even though single fathers are confronted with adjustment requirements, most of them raise their children successfully (Goldscheider & Kaufman, 2006). But juggling work and child care commonly poses difficulties for single fathers, as it does for single mothers, especially for those with preschool youngsters. Compared with single mothers, however, fathers often make more money and have greater economic security and job flexibility (Leininger & Ziol-Guest, 2008). Overall, the single father is neither the extraordinary human being nor the bumbling "Mr. Mom" depicted in popular stereotypes. To provide care for their children, fathers tend to gravitate toward nurseries and child-care centers where they feel that the staff have a professional commitment to children.

Generally, single fathers seem better prepared for the physical aspects of parenting—shopping, cooking, cleaning, taking the child to the doctor, and the like—than for dealing with their children's emotional needs. Men who adeptly juggle work schedules to stay home and nurse a sick child report that they fall apart in the face of a vigorous temper tantrum. Single fathers also tend to express more anxiety over the sexual behavior of their daughters than of their sons. And many are concerned about the absence of adult female role models within the home. Many single fathers admit that they

have had to learn to deal with their children's emotional needs and to develop their own nurturing skills (Gibson-Davis, 2008).

Questions

What are the stages that make up a traditional family life cycle? What do we know about the different challenges faced by two-parent and single-parent mothers and fathers raising children?

WORK

Because the cost of living is continually rising, Americans are working longer to achieve the same standard of living they had years ago. Thus, an increasing portion of the adult life span today is spent at work, and American men and women are working years longer. Since the 1990s there has been a reversal of a century-long trend toward a shorter workday (Bureau of Labor Statistics, 2007). Americans are juggling work and family life in a process marked by conflicting career goals and personal needs. Moen and Roehling (2005) find that a majority of men and women would prefer to work fewer hours than they do. The net result for Americans is a decline in their happiness and an erosion of their collective ability to care for children, do housework, sleep, and enjoy life (Ilies et al., 2007). Some resolve this conflict by adapting to the job requirements, thus delaying having children. Others opt to meet their families' needs by varying their work schedules, working from home, working part-time, or exiting the workforce, which of course has ramifications for future employment.

For a growing number of young Americans (nearly half of all 18–24-year-olds in 2008), the transition to adult occupational roles is postponed by attending college (see Figure 14.8), but a college degree is usually well worth the investment over a lifetime of work (Snyder & Dillow, 2010). Most youth view a college education primarily as a means to a better job rather than as a vehicle for broadening their intellectual horizons. One of the most significant developments in higher education in recent years is that U.S. colleges are enrolling more adult "nontraditional" students. These are students who have been out of high school for a year or more, are over 23, and have put off getting a degree, or students (both women and men) who already have a degree and have worked in business or industry for many years, are now unemployed, and want to retrain for a new career. Over the past 25 years, the number of nontraditional students enrolled in colleges and universities grew by over 70 percent. The adult nontraditional students are more likely to come from working-class backgrounds, have family and work responsibilities, do not want to waste any time in

MORE INFORMATION YOU CAN USE

The Diversity of Fathers Today

Remember how television shows shaped your ideas about what a "good" father is supposed to be? The 1950s–1960s shows (which are still re-run today), such as *The Adventures of Ozzie and Harriet, Father Knows Best, Leave It to Beaver, The Andy Griffith Show,* and *My Three Sons,* and later *The Waltons* and *Happy Days,* portrayed white middle-class American families with fathers dosing out wit and wisdom to their happy families. In these shows, the fathers were idealized dads, the kind most of us might think we would like to have: good providers, wise disciplinarians, loving role models, calm under pressure, and concerned about and responsive to their children. In the late 1960s to mid-1970s, *The Brady Bunch* broke ground with stories of a blended family led by the caring father/stepfather Mike Brady, portrayed as a professional with a strong sense of ethics.

This caring image began to change when the obnoxious Archie Bunker, of *All in the Family,* became the first of many TV fathers who undermined the idealized father figure. In the mid-1980s, Bill Cosby portrayed a successful African American father, Cliff Huxtable. He and Steve Keaton, from *Family Ties,* both seemed more realistic as they tried to find their place in a new world of working women, divorce, widowhood, remarriage, and crumbling respect for the father. More recent TV dads are likely to be portrayed as weak yet domineering, ignorant, flawed, and foolish; consider Homer Simpson of *The Simpsons.* The 2009 TV show *Modern Family* portrays different kinds of fathering arrangements: an older father, a gay couple that adopts, and a stepfather—all are portrayed more realistically.

The original TV father image and today's image are both shallow and incomplete. In reality, there are many kinds of fathers parenting in different ways, including low-income to rich fathers, heterosexual and gay fathers, fathers of healthy or developmentally disabled children, immigrant fathers, military fathers, and absent fathers—all real fathers who are confronted with many challenges and opportunities.

Socioeconomic status is a main factor. Many poor fathers *want* to be involved in child support, but they may lack the skills and resources. They live in poor neighborhoods, or rural areas, or they may be incarcerated with few job or educational prospects. Often, these fathers are not married to their children's mothers and do not live with their children. Yet research shows that fathers' involvement in children's lives leads, at the very least, to improved language and cognitive development. They are often labeled as *deadbeat dads,* yet studies show that most low-income dads want to be accessible to their children. But in addition to economic constraints, their involvement depends on the father's relationship with the mother (Tamis-LaMonda & McFadden, 2010).

Gay Parenting Is Challenging Because of Social Stigma Most gay men fathered children from former heterosexual relationships, but some are becoming fathers via adoption or surrogacy.

Gay men may become fathers from a prior heterosexual relationship, from adoption, or through a surrogacy arrangement. It has become acceptable for fathers to be primary caregivers for children, so this somewhat lessens the stigma of gay parenting. The challenge for many gay fathers is how to prepare their children for the prejudice they often face in the community toward their family (Golombok & Tasker, 2010). The legalization of same-sex marriage may produce a growing acceptance of gay men as fathers.

Fathers of children with disabilities, such as deafness, blindness, autism, genetic syndromes, or intellectual disabilities, have been portrayed as disengaged. Current research findings dispute this, and more study is being done to assess how these fathers are faring psychologically and how involved they are with their children. Many fathers are more involved with their children because extended family members may not be close by. Since the 1980s, more individuals with disabilities have been raised in their family's home (not institutionalized), necessitating more paternal involvement. The father's emotions of grief and worry after the birth of a disabled child are often overlooked because the focus is on the child and the mother's well-being. While a mother might seek outside support, a father tends to look to his wife or to professionals for support. Her efforts are usually focused on the child, and many clinicians have limited experience in this area (MacDonald & Hastings, 2010).

Research on the role of Asian fathers is growing. Confucianism led to a great respect for fathers, the ideal parenting model being "strict father, kind mother." Yet this

continued

model is fading as Asian cultures have modernized, reducing the effects of Confucianism. In Asian countries, there is an increasing understanding of the importance of fathers in their children's lives. Yet in China, Japan, and Korea, most fathers tend to believe they should sacrifice and work long hours to provide for their children's education, often neglecting to spend time with their children (Shwalb, Nakazawa, Yamamoto, & Hyun, 2010).

More recently, immigrant fathers are being studied. Immigration is viewed as a big risk factor for families. Immigration can radically change a father's role, identity, employment, and social status, as well as his children's outcomes. But emerging research reveals that the immigration of a man and his family can be a sign of resilience and determination to seek opportunities to improve their lives. Family adjustment to migration depends on many factors: country of origin, educational level and skills, language fluency, the host country's attitudes toward immigrants, and parenting styles. Host countries and agencies can help

immigrant fathers by offering good work opportunities and training, providing training in language skills, and pointers on how to cope with the host culture's differences (Strier & Roer-Strier, 2010).

In Europe, favorable public policies toward participative fatherhood allow more balance between work and family demands. Fathers can be more active in their children's social, emotional, economic, and educational lives (O'Brien & Moss, 2010). There are generous paid-parental-leave policies after birth in many European countries. The mother and father divide the allotted time as suits each couple. One issue is the high cost of arrangements like this for the employers and the governments—and families pay very high taxes.

The goals of cross-cultural research on fatherhood include identifying the challenges and responsibilities fathers face, bringing about improvements in integrating work and family, distributing study results to professionals working with families, and ultimately helping men to be the best fathers they can be.

---

getting a degree, and strive to do their best. These adults aspire to prepare themselves for a better job or a career.

The Significance of Work for Women and Men

People work for a great many reasons. "Self-interest" in its broadest sense, which includes the interests of one's family and friends, is an underlying motivation of work in all societies. However, self-interest is not simply the accumulation of wealth. For instance, among the Maori,

a Polynesian people of the Pacific, a desire for approval, a sense of duty, a wish to conform to custom, a feeling of emulation, and the pleasure of being skilled in crafts also contribute to economic activity (Hsu, 1943).

Even in the United States, few activities seriously compete with work in providing basic life satisfaction (Moen & Roehling, 2005). In a study conducted in the 1980s and the 1990s, two large samples of Israeli adults were asked whether they would continue working if they inherited enough money to live comfortably. The findings agree with early lottery studies: About 90 percent would

FIGURE 14.8 U.S. Civilian Labor Force Participation Rates, Percent Distribution by Gender and Age: 2009 Young adults from late teens through mid-forties make up most of the U.S. labor force—but more adults in midlife and older are working longer.
Source: U.S. Bureau of Labor Statistics. (2010). Household data: Annual averages: Employment status of the civilian noninstitutional population by age, sex, and race. *Labor force statistics from the Current Population Survey.* Retrieved from http://www.bls.gov/cps/cpsaat3.pdf

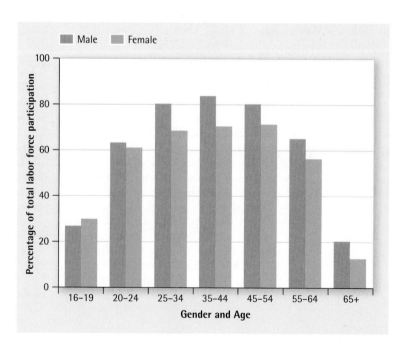

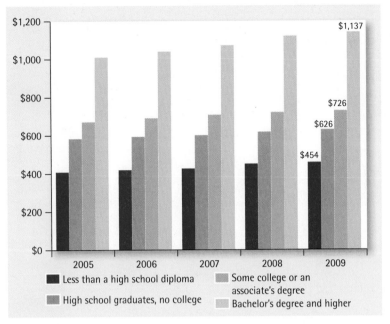

FIGURE 14.9 U.S. Labor Force: Median Usual Weekly Earnings of Full-Time Wage and Salary Workers Aged 25 Years and Older, by Educational Attainment: 2005–2009 Annual Averages More education is associated with higher rates of employment, and college graduates make more than 2.5 times the earnings of high school dropouts. *Source:* Bureau of Labor Statistics. (2010, September). Back to college: BLS Spotlight on statistics. Retrieved from http://www.bls.gov/spotlight/2010/college/home.htm

continue working, for economic factors are only one variable in overall happiness and well-being (Arvey, Harpaz, & Liao, 2004). Although it provides greater comforts, money does not buy happiness. People who have more money usually just spend more money (or they are hounded by others to give it away). Work, in addition to its economic functions, structures time, provides a context for relating to other people, offers an escape from boredom, and sustains a sense of identity and self-worth. Perhaps not surprisingly, then, only one in four winners of million-dollar lotteries quits working after hitting the jackpot. Sociologist Harry Levinson (1964, p. 20) puts it this way:

> Work has quite a few social meanings: When a man works he has a contributing place in society. He earns the right to be the partner of other men. . . . A man's work . . . is a major social device for his identification as an adult. Much of who he is, to himself and others, is interwoven with how he earns his livelihood.

And that's true of women, too!

The Millennial generation, this young-adult, more educated cohort of technologically sophisticated adults, is looking for more meaning from their jobs. They assume they are going to get employed quickly and rise rapidly into positions of leadership. They believe their ideas should be heard and incorporated by management—and if not, they quickly move on.

The *Americans with Disabilities Act (ADA)* legislation (PL 101-336), which was originally passed by Congress in 1990, recognizes the significance of work for all adults and opens the doors for more meaningful participation in higher education, work, and society for adults with disabilities.

Corporations, municipalities, industries, human service organizations, and colleges have made buildings more accessible; transit companies provide buses with wheelchair lifts and reschedule routes to get people to school or job; and communities across America are redesigning buildings and homes, doorways, restrooms, and sidewalks to facilitate their use by adults with disabilities. American corporations that receive federal contracts must demonstrate that they have hired persons with disabilities, and everyone benefits from ensuring that this segment of our adult population enjoys meaningful participation in society.

Also, work is an important socializing experience that influences who and what we are. Watson (2003) found that college-educated people are more likely than others to obtain jobs that require independent judgment, are likely to earn higher lifetime income, and are far less likely to be unemployed (see Figure 14.9). By virtue of the intellectual demands of their work, the college-educated evolve an intellectual prowess that carries over to their private lives. They often seek out intellectually stimulating activities in their community leisure pursuits (such as theater or orchestra, coaching, mentoring, or serving on boards of agencies). Typically, people who engage in self-directed work come to value self-direction more highly, to be more open to new ideas, and to be less authoritarian in their relationships with others. As parents, they pass these characteristics on to their children (Zimmerman, Aberle, Krafchick, & Harvey, 2008).

In the United States, a strong work ethic permeates the culture. Idleness seems to perpetuate a sense of hopelessness. We have seen this affect the thousands of unemployed but skilled, college-educated adults in their thirties, forties, and fifties who lost their jobs in the

FIGURE 14.10 Marital Status of Women in the U.S. Civilian Labor Force: 1975–2008 Many more American women are now in the civilian labor force, both full-time and part-time.
Source: U.S. Bureau of Labor Statistics. (2010). Employment status by marital status and sex, 2009 annual averages. *Current Population Survey.* Washington, DC: U.S. Government Printing Office. Retrieved December 21, 2010, from http://www.bls.gov/cps/wlftable4.htm

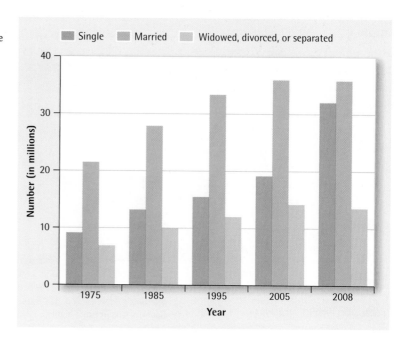

recessions of the mid-1990s and again since 2007 because of corporate layoffs, downsizing, and the "exporting" of jobs to other countries. The longer a person is unemployed, cannot find a job, and cannot support a family, the more worthless (or depressed) that person feels, whether man or woman. To be unemployed—especially for a man, whom society still views as the main wage earner—is to be a social outcast. Anthropologist Elliot Liebow (1967), in a study of "street-corner men" living in a Washington, DC, ghetto, found that the inability to gain a steady, remunerative, and meaningful job undermines an individual's self-respect and self-worth. Liebow concludes that the street-corner man tries to conceal this failure, escaping through alcoholism or substance abuse. In essence, for most people work is a truly defining activity that is vital to their health and well-being.

Family and Work   Until the 1960s in the United States and other westernized countries, a woman's life was defined primarily in terms of her reproductive role. The major events of the woman's adult years were marrying, bearing and rearing children, going through "the change of life," experiencing "the empty nest," and being the caretaker of elderly relatives. In many countries of the world, this traditional view of women has not changed. Indeed, people commonly equate the female life cycle with the family life cycle. Not surprisingly, the major psychosocial transitions in the lives of contemporary U.S. women now aged 60 and older were more likely to be associated with phases of the family cycle than with chronological age (Moen, 2003).

But today, with 90 percent of all women working for pay at some point in their lives, employment outside

the home is playing an increasingly important role in women's self-esteem and identity. Figure 14.10 provides data on the increasing employment of American women. An accumulating body of evidence suggests that women differ from men in the ways they approach tasks and in the outcomes they achieve. These differences derive from the greater complexity of women's goals for their future and from the difficulties they encounter in carrying them out. Unlike most men, many women do not report dreams in which careers stand out as the primary component. Instead, most women visualize themselves immersed in a world centered on meaningful relationships with others, particularly husbands or partners, children, friends, and colleagues. Today there are varied pathways that young women can take to fulfill a role as a marriage partner, since more young men are delaying marriage until they are older. More young women and men are cohabiting, which may or may not lead to marriage. Some young men and women decide not to marry: Some simply choose to remain single, while others decide to become single parents by assisted reproduction, adoption, or foster care. However, since the 1990s more young women have become single parents with children, without the economic or emotionally supportive benefits of marriage. Thus most of these women must work to support their children. Women struggle to balance the demands of their career and the needs of their family, and many experience guilt about work-family conflicts (Livingston & Judge, 2008). Women's increasing participation in the labor force has created a need for couples to renegotiate their roles at home. College-educated couples tend to have more egalitarian marriages than those with less education. That is, both partners tend to agree that gender roles within a marriage should be equal (National Marriage Project, 2010). But how couples interpret "equal" varies. In their lifetime women are much more likely than men to change jobs, cut hours of work, re-arrange work schedules, turn down a promotion, or refuse overtime in order to tend to the needs of their children (Maume, 2006). Some couples choose a split-shift schedule—one may work the second or third shift, for example—to ensure that one parent is with the children all the time. Unless the husbands use their time off to do their share of housework, this strategy can increase the burden on the wife. Working women tend to spend their "free" time supervising their children, and they are more likely than working fathers to report that they always feel rushed (Webber & Williams, 2008).

Most women work because of financial necessity. In the 1980s, women said that the main reason why they worked was that they liked the contact with people. Today, women rank making ends meet almost equally with contact with others as the most important reasons why they are working. Although women may need to work for financial reasons, the emotional and personal benefits of working are equally important to them (Amato et al., 2007). However, some women view parenting as the most important job of all and are willing to make sacrifices to become full-time homemakers or work part-time at home. But the popular media portray homemakers differently, because a paid job is viewed as the path to independence in the greater society and as a symbol of self-worth (Zimmerman, Aberle, Krafchick, & Harvey, 2008).

Some women have difficulty fulfilling all their work and family obligations. The *General Social Survey,* a large, annual survey of Americans, found that about one-third of women in their early thirties felt that they were not balancing work and family successfully (Donze, 2006). **Role conflict** ensues when a person experiences pressures within one role that are incompatible with the pressures that arise within another role, such as the conflicting demands made on them as a parent, spouse, and paid worker. **Role overload** occurs when there are too many role demands and too little time to fulfill them. Women who encounter these role strains—and not all women do—are more likely to experience a diminished sense of well-being, a decrease in work and marital satisfaction, and possible mental-health issues (Pearson, 2008).

Yet some scholars point out that a woman's multiple family, work, and social roles provide resources for her well-being in a number of ways: (1) Adding income to the family helps reduce financial stress; (2) variety and new perspectives broaden her understanding of the world; and (3) experiences of meeting different people expand her support network and provide a buffer against negative or difficult experiences (McNall, Masuda, & Nicklin, 2010).

Working Mothers Juggle Many Roles A job in the work-place permits participation in the larger society and compensation for one's skills. However, a shared division of responsibilities between husband and wife improves marital satisfaction and creates positive role models for children.

We should emphasize, however, that most women manage their multiple responsibilities quite well, especially if they receive social support on the job and at home. Yet it is important to note that most models that analyze how beneficial or stressful the multiple roles of work and motherhood are for women look at women in the context of two-income households. Women who are single parents face intense socioeconomic and psychological challenges that women who are partnered do not (Zimmerman, Aberle, Krafchick, & Harvey, 2008).

Reentering the Paid Labor Force Levinson finds that around age 40, men reconsider some of their commitments and often attempt to free themselves from a previously central male mentor. Levinson labeled this "becoming one's own person." In contrast, in their late thirties and early forties, some women are reentering the world of full-time work after doing part-time work; others are leaving the workforce entirely to raise children, since they are bearing children later. This is more likely to be true of white women, because economic necessity forces many ethnic-minority women to work throughout their adult years. White women and women of higher socioeconomic status are more apt to withdraw from the labor force and then reenter it after their teenagers have left home (Buddeberg-Fischer et al., 2010). Just as men can benefit, women can benefit from alternative mentorships, including peer, multiple, and collective mentoring (Tharenou, 2005). Despite current legal and social trends, there is still evidence of job discrimination against women, particularly middle-aged women, who might have stayed at home to raise children or support their husband's career. In academia and the civil service, a new trend of rehiring older, retired employees to fill part-time jobs is emerging.

Differing Work Experiences for Women and Men

The adult experience is different for women than for men (Gilligan, 1982a, 1982b; Pugliesi, 1995). As we noted in Chapter 11, Gilligan questions the traditional psychological assumption that boys and girls both struggle to define a distinct identity for themselves during adolescence. Instead, she contends that girls must struggle to resist the loss of psychological strengths and positive conceptions of themselves that they had in childhood. Therefore, a woman's development is not necessarily a steady progression. Women tend to recover in adulthood the confidence, assertiveness, and positive sense of self that Western society pressured them to compromise during their adolescence (Gilligan, 1982a, 1982b). Part of the difficulty, Gilligan says, is that women often find it hard to commit themselves to competitive success because they are socialized toward the achievement of cooperation; women focus on preserving relationships rather than on using them. But life in contemporary bureaucracies and corporations frequently rewards those who relate to others not as persons but as objects to be manipulated to get ahead.

According to Deborah Tannen (2007), Western nations socialize the two genders differently. Males often gather in hierarchical groups and teach boys how to dominate and jockey for the spotlight, often by versing them in displays of ridicule and put-downs. In contrast, female groups are structured chiefly around pairs of good friends who share secrets and forge intimacy. In large institutional settings such as companies, universities, hospitals, and government agencies, women tend to be consensus builders. When working in supervisory positions, they are inclined to ask others for their opinions. Tannen says that men often misinterpret this behavior as a show of indecisiveness. Moreover, women are less likely to call attention to their accomplishments or seek recognition. She notes a parallel in Japanese collectivist culture, where it is deemed boorish for a higher-status person to be direct or to be singled out for praise and recognition over others. Yet it is easy to overstate the differences between women and men. There is neither the "normative woman" nor the "normative man." Gender is intertwined with race, class, sexual orientation, and countless other variables of human identity. Indeed, women and men are more similar than different, and most of their apparent differences are culturally and socially produced.

> ### Questions
>
> What are some of the differing career and relationship experiences for contemporary women and men? What kinds of meaning do people derive from their work?

SEGUE

We have looked at love and the possible institutional expression of love—marriage—as they affect contemporary young adults. As individuals go through changes, or stages, they reevaluate themselves, the interactions they have with others, and the meanings that love and work have for them at the moment. For some people this evaluation can lead to transitions such as marriage, parenting, divorce, quitting a job, sexual reorientation, cohabitation, and (more likely than not) remarriage. Early adulthood is seen as the time when individuals start out on their first truly independent journey—it is a time when they are able to leave parents to explore what they "really want to do." But we have also seen that sometimes, as society changes or the economy takes a downturn, individuals themselves make changes—perhaps postponing or at least modifying their dreams. In addition, these changes lead to physical, cognitive, and social transformations, as adults in their middle years experience midlife change and reassess their life satisfaction. We will explore these significant issues in Chapter 15.

SUMMARY

Theories of Emotional-Social Development

1. Love and work are the central themes of adult life. Both place us in a complex web of relationships with others.

2. Erikson's first stage of adult development is called the crisis of intimacy versus isolation; if the challenges of this stage are not met, the person is at risk for loneliness and isolation.

3. Levinson and his associates say that the overriding task throughout adulthood is the creation of a life structure. Periodically, adults must restructure their lives by creating a new structure or reappraising an old one.

4. Levinson's model for establishing adult status is no longer salient for many adult categories, including women, racial-ethnic minorities, and people from families with lower socioeconomic status. However, its overall stage structure still applies for many white males from the middle and upper classes.

Establishing Intimacy in Relationships

5. Friends become our major source of socializing and support during our adult years. Research on love attempts to explain the real complexities involved in initiating and maintaining a meaningful, intimate relationship with another person.

6. Friendships are a source of economic and emotional support for many young people while they work to establish careers.

7. Sternberg's triangular theory of love states that three elements define a mature romantic relationship: passion, intimacy, and commitment.

8. Many studies have shown that an egalitarian marriage is more likely to be a happier marriage than marriages that use a traditional model in which the man has more power than the woman.

Diversity in Lifestyle

9. Leaving home is a major step in the transition to adulthood. Many young people experience numerous living arrangements in the course of assuming adult status.

10. An increasing number of young adults are returning to the parental home for a period of time. Most return because the job market does not offer them employment that will enable them to support themselves. Men are more likely than women to return to the parental home.

11. There has been a big increase in the number of adults 35 years of age and younger who are single. Today, emerging adults tend to postpone marriage. A majority of adult singles share housing with someone else, such as a friend, a relative, or a romantic partner.

12. The number of couples who cohabit has increased substantially, and those who follow this lifestyle do so more openly than they used to. Cohabitation is not restricted to the younger generation. More middle-aged and elderly people who are divorced or widowed also cohabit.

13. Many gay and lesbian couples have stable and warm relationships, and some choose civil unions or legal marriage. Since the 1990s, more such couples have been bearing or adopting children in order to establish families. Gays and lesbians often experience various forms of discrimination and intolerance in daily life.

14. Marriage is a lifestyle found in all societies. Marriage as an institution is declining in Western industrialized countries. Women's expectations within marriage have risen since the 1970s, and they are more likely than men to initiate divorce when they are not satisfied.

Family Transitions

15. Within the life cycle of a couple, the arrival of the first child is an event of unparalleled importance. A couple is transitioning into the family life cycle, with its attendant new role requirements. Thus, the first child functions as a major marker, and a couple is confronted with new developmental tasks that can challenge their relationship.

16. Couples who report marital difficulties following the birth of a child may have had unrealistic expectations about parenthood and child rearing. Couples who focus on positive elements of the new family situation and share in the daily tasks are likely to do well.

17. Many new mothers report postpartum depression, and new parents are more likely than nonparents to report depression. Increased stress is associated with parental child abuse; it is important to be aware of the warning signs.

18. There are few differences between heterosexual and lesbian mothers, because motherhood, not sexuality, is the dominant identity marker for these women. Lesbian mothers do, however, face additional stressful issues.

19. Although divorce rates have been declining since the early 1980s, divorce is still widespread and affects everyone involved. For those involved, most effects are negative. Remarried couples and the stepchildren face additional stressors.

20. Single-parent mothers frequently suffer from role overload from home and work, high child-care costs, loneliness, and little or no leisure time.

21. More men are becoming single-parent fathers. Even though single fathers must make adjustments, most are successful in raising their children. Like single-parent mothers, single-parent fathers have great difficulty balancing the demands of work and parenthood.

Work

22. Work plays an important part in the lives of all adults, not only because of the economic resources and benefits it brings in but also because people's identity, self-esteem, and sense of self-worth are often tied to their work accomplishments and satisfaction.

23. Men and women go through different stages as they move through adulthood. Women's participation in the labor force is often interrupted by childbearing, and women sometimes need time to finish their education and establish and develop their careers.

24. Men and women have different communication styles in the workplace. In general, unlike male managers, women in supervisory positions often solicit the opinions of others and seek consensus.

25. Americans are working longer hours, and more women are employed than ever before.

KEY TERMS

cohabitation *(448)*

companionate love *(444)*

consummate love *(444)*

cultural dislocation *(439)*

expressive tie *(438)*

family life cycle *(457)*

instrumental tie *(438)*

intimacy *(445)*

intimacy versus isolation *(438)*

lifestyle *(445)*

marriage *(452)*

mentor *(442)*

nuclear family *(455)*

postpartum major depression (PPD) *(459)*

primary relationship *(438)*

role conflict *(469)*

role overload *(469)*

romantic love *(444)*

secondary relationship *(438)*

social relationship *(438)*

triangular theory of love *(444)*

FOLLOWING UP ON THE INTERNET

Web sites for this chapter focus on the diverse social and work roles of contemporary young adults. Please access the text Web site at www.mhhe.com/crandell10 for up-to-date hot-linked Internet addresses for the following organizations, topics, and resources:

Erikson and Young Adulthood
http://web.cortland.edu/andersmd/ERIK/stage6.HTML

Network on Transitions to Adulthood
http://www.transad.pop.upenn.edu/

Alternatives to Marriage Project
http://www.unmarried.org/

Kiplinger's Setting Up a Budget
http://www.kiplinger.com/tools/budget/index.html?si=1

Unmarried Couples and the Law (Cohabitation)
http://family-law.lawyers.com/Unmarried-Couples/

Parenting and the Law for Unmarried Couples
http://www.nolo.com/legal-encyclopedia/
   faqEditorial-29095.html

Fathering Magazine
http://www.fathermag.com/

Parents Without Partners, Inc.
http://www.parentswithoutpartners.org/

American Association on Intellectual and Developmental Disabilities
http://www.aaidd.org/

National Center for Workforce and Disability & Americans with Disabilities Act
http://www.onestops.info/i.php?i=501

Bureau of Labor Statistics Occupational Outlook Handbook
 http://www.bls.gov/oco/

PART
8 MIDDLE ADULTHOOD

If we think of middle age as roughly the years between 45 and 65, middle-aged Americans now compose about one-fourth of the U.S. population—about 79 million. In 2011, the first *Baby Boomers* began turning 65—at the rate of 10,000 per day! Although the first were born right after World War II, the majority were born during the 1950s and lived out their youth during the Korean War, the Elvis–Bob Dylan–Beatles era of rock 'n' roll, the space race, the Cold War, school integration, the Vietnam conflict, the women's liberation movement, the sexual revolution and the birth control pill, the original Woodstock, and unprecedented opportunities for a college education. They entered the job market during the economic golden years of the late 1960s and early 1970s. Each one is experiencing midlife changes, and many are feeling the psychological pressures associated with the shift from the industrial age to the age of the information superhighway. As the large baby-boom cohort now occupies middle age, middle adulthood is being redefined as many try to maintain their youth and ready themselves for late adulthood.

15 Middle Adulthood
Physical and Cognitive Development

Until recently, the middle years—from about age 45 through age 65—were a time of peak earnings and well-being for many adults. Middle-aged Americans were often portrayed as being the settled "establishment" of our society, the power brokers and decision makers. However, this scenario does not reflect the plight of middle-aged Americans living in poverty, those who are unemployed long-term, or those from ethnic-minority communities who have experienced significant economic hardships and other obstacles. Additionally, while the recently crippled U.S. and European economies try to recover, corporate mergers, downsizing, international relocations, and job outsourcing continue. Newly unemployed women and men are returning to college in ever greater numbers to retrain in other careers or to become entrepreneurs. Some middle-aged Americans have lost their retirement pensions, while others are being forced into early retirement or into underemployment with no possibility of retirement. Most are already grandparents, but some in midlife are becoming first-time parents. Having learned to cope with the many contingencies of earlier life stages, middle-aged women and men have a substantial repertoire of strategies for dealing with the varied physical, intellectual, emotional, and social changes of middle adulthood.

REDEFINING MIDDLE AGE

As of 2009, the average life expectancy at birth for U.S. women has risen to 80.6 years; at birth for men, it is 75.7 years (Miniño, Xu, & Kochanek, 2010). If a man is already age 65, his life expectancy is 82, and for a women who is already age 65, it is 85 (U.S. Bureau of the Census, 2011d). In 1900 white Americans could expect to live, on average, only to age 47; on average, nonwhites lived to age 33 (Miniño, Xu, & Kochanek, 2010). By middle age, women begin to outlive men, a trend that continues through the rest of the life course (see Figure 15.1). And by midlife, various health factors shorten the life expectancy for black men and women (Miniño, Xu, & Kochanek, 2010). Although the middle of life falls statistically around age 39, we typically consider middle age as extending much later. Indeed, most of us are unsure about which years of life are the middle years. Does middle age begin at 40, 45, or 50? And does middle age end at 60, 65, or 70? The boundaries of midlife have become fluid for the 79 million Americans now at "midlife." *Chronological* or *legal age* was used in previous generations to determine where one was in the life course, but *subjective* or *personal age* reflects how young or old one perceives oneself to be (Cleveland & Lim, 2007).

A human body that has been functioning for a number of decades tends to work less efficiently than it did when it was new. At age 50 or 60, the kidneys, lungs, heart, and other vital systems, as well as the sensory organs, are less efficient than they were at 20. Yet across

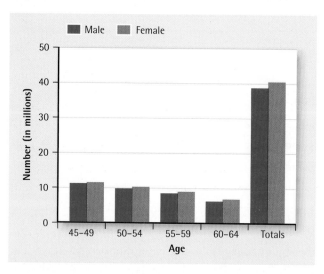

FIGURE 15.1 Middle-Aged Adults in the United States, by Age and Gender: 2009   The 79 million American baby boomers are now in middle adulthood. The boundaries of midlife have become more fluid. Note that by middle age, women outlive men.

Source: U.S. Bureau of the Census. (2011d). *The 2011 Statistical Abstract of the United States. 2008.* Table No. 7. Resident Population by Age and Sex: 1980–2009. Retrieved from http://www.census.gov/compendia/statab/2011edition.html

middle adulthood, the physical and cognitive changes that typically occur are, for the most part, not precipitous.

SENSORY AND PHYSICAL CHANGES

In most cases, sensory and physical changes in midlife are so gradual that people are often not aware of any changes until they take stock on a fiftieth or sixtieth birthday, at the wedding of a child, at the birth of a first grandchild, at a retirement celebration, upon the death of a parent or spouse, or at some other significant life event. After adolescence, most integrated bodily functions decline at the rate of about 1 percent a year. Overall, middle-aged individuals report that they are not appreciably different than they were in their early thirties. They mention that their hair has grayed (and often thinned), they have more wrinkles, they are paunchier, they may have "lost a step," they tire more easily, and they rebound less quickly. Nonetheless, by middle age some individuals have overextended themselves physically at work, at home, or during recreational pursuits and require professional assistance for rehabilitation (see the *Implications for Practice* box, "Occupational/Physical Therapist").

One caveat is that because this cohort of middle-aged adults is the largest ever, physicians are projecting a major increase in the numbers of individuals who will be affected by such age-related changes—and both their function and quality of life will decrease. Even so, except for those in poor health, middle-aged adults will, on the whole, try to carry on in much the same way they did in their younger years. The best defense against loss of strength and vitality and sensory changes consists of an active lifestyle, proper nutrition, regular exercise, and routine checkups, along with a healthy dose of humor about how life marches along.

Vision

Nearly all Americans over age 45 experience **presbyopia**, a normal condition of aging in which the lens of the eye starts to harden, losing its ability to accommodate as quickly as it did in youth. Symptoms include getting headaches or tired eyes while doing close work. Most of the baby boomers now occupying middle age need contact lenses, bifocals, or half glasses to read the newspaper, computer and I-pad screens, restaurant menus, small printed numbers on price tags, wristwatches, and prescription dosages. If this problem is not corrected, people discover that they can read printed material only by holding it farther and farther away from their eyes, until eventually, they cannot see to read even at arm's length. Eye doctors offer new laser techniques and can do corneal implants to

IMPLICATIONS FOR PRACTICE

Occupational/Physical Therapist, Merida R. Padro

I am the chief occupational/physical therapist at Broome Developmental Center (a division of the New York State Office of People with Developmental Disabilities (OPWDD). My main job tasks include being department chief for the physical and occupational departments and consultant for the pediatric-geriatric community-based population in our region. I provide staff with in-service training in areas such as back safety, cerebral palsy, handling-positioning, therapeutic dining, blind-sensory awareness, and sensory integration/modulation issues.

I hold a bachelor of science degree, PT/OT bachelor's, premedical degree of Puerto Rico, and master's degree in occupational therapy in developmental disabilities from New York University. For the past 24 years, I have worked with the cerebral palsy population in Spain, the severe cord injury unit at a Veterans Health Administration hospital, the burn/hand amputee unit in Puerto Rico, the pediatric cerebral palsy population in Laredo, Texas, and the Broome Developmental Center.

To become an occupational or physical therapist, you need to earn a degree from an accredited college in either an occupational therapy or a physical therapy program. Students must complete field work for six to nine months. In most states you also must pass a state licensure exam in either OT or PT. After earning state licensure, you apply for jobs based on your preference for clinical settings. Occupational and physical therapists might specialize in helping adults adjust to sensory and physical injuries by providing services that restore function, improve mobility, relieve pain, and prevent or limit permanent physical disabilities. To work with individuals who are mentally retarded or developmentally disabled, you need to have a great respect for people, value each one, and have compassion and understanding for every person. You need to be comfortable making eye contact, enjoy smiling at each individual, and focus on small efforts rather than big changes. In a supervisory role, you need to have knowledge, experience, and personal skills to hire, supervise, train, or terminate staff. Also, you need to motivate and train staff as professionals to enhance the quality of services for the special population you serve.

treat vision problems after diagnosis of presbyopia and aging eyes (Olson et al., 2005). Adaptation to darkness and recovery from glare also take longer, which makes night driving somewhat more taxing. Distance acuity, contrast sensitivity, visual search, and pattern recognition are also diminished (Madden, Whiting, & Huettel, 2005).

A number of other vision disorders become more common with the normal aging process. **Glaucoma,** increased pressure caused by internal fluid buildup in the eye, can damage the optic nerve and lead to blindness, if left untreated. The disorder can be detected only by a professional eye examination. **Cataracts,** or clouding of the lens, typically occur in 30 to 50 percent of people over age 65, but they can appear among individuals in their late fifties and early sixties. The condition usually requires surgery and then can be corrected by eyeglasses, a contact lens, or an implanted lens. Recently, researchers at Harvard Medical School devised new optical tests able to detect *amyloid beta proteins* in the lens of the eye—the same proteins that, found in the brain, can cause Alzheimer's disease. Early detection can slow the progression of Alzheimer's disease (Stark & Bardi, 2008).

Floaters, which can appear abruptly as annoying, blurry floating spots in the visual field, are particles suspended in the gel-like fluid of the eyeball; generally, they do not impair vision and dissipate with time. However, a severe "floating" problem, with flashes of light, could indicate the more serious problem of retinal detachment, which can be treated with laser surgery if detected early enough. The discomfort caused by **dry eye,** which stems from diminished tear production, can be eased with eye drops. Those who look at computer screens or read documents for hours are likely to experience this discomfort.

The leading cause of visual impairment and legal blindness in older adults is age-related **macular degeneration (AMD),** and about 6 percent of adults over age 40 are affected by AMD (Klein et al., 2011). AMD is caused by thinning of the layers of the retina (the photosensitive cells at the back of the eye that are responsible for vision and color perception) and/or by rupturing of tiny blood vessels. The first signs of this vision disorder are faded, distorted, or blurred central vision (Cong et al., 2008). Smoking doubles the risk of developing macular degeneration in later years (Evans, Fletcher, &

Macular Degeneration One of the eye disorders that midlife and older adults might experience is macular degeneration, the first sign of which is faded, distorted, or blurred central vision. Eating plenty of fruits and vegetables and reducing fats in the diet can promote clarity of vision and overall health of the eyes.

Wormald, 2005). Recent research has found that the two carotenoids help prevent the tissue damage in the eye that leads to AMD. Thus, a diet rich in fresh fruits and green and yellow leafy vegetables helps preserve one's vision (D'Amato & Snyder, 2000).

Hearing

The most common sensory disorder in the U.S. population, affecting at least 36 million, is hearing loss. Of those aged 40 to 49, about one-third already suffer from hearing loss (Curhan, Eavey, Shargorodsky, & Curhan, 2010). Noise levels, advancing age, certain diseases, and genetic inheritance are factors related to hearing loss and communication disorders. Recent findings from a large-scale study with white males also reveal that regular analgesic use (aspirin/acetaminophen) over a long duration is linked with higher risk of hearing loss (Curhan, Eavey, Shargorodsky, & Curhan, 2010). Mild to severe hearing loss is clearly associated with a reduced quality of life in many ways. Changes in hearing used to begin at about age 30—but one of every five of today's adolescents has some hearing loss (Shargorodsky, Curhan, Curhan, & Eavey, 2010).

In **presbycusis,** the ability to hear high-pitched sounds, such as speech, declines, but the magnitude of the change varies appreciably among individuals. The baby boomers were the first generation to listen to highly amplified music over a period of years, and they are now experiencing premature hearing loss requiring hearing aids (Kim & Barrs, 2006). By age 50 about one in every three men and one in every four women have difficulty

understanding a whisper. Almost half over the age of 75 are hard of hearing. Even a mild hearing loss can affect cognitive functioning, since areas of the brain that normally are reserved for intellectual processing must be reallocated to straining to hear (Xu, Kotak, & Sanes, 2007).

Some of the more common causes of conductive hearing loss are cochlear (nerve) damage due to prolonged exposure to loud noise from jobs or recreational pursuits, such as that experienced by miners, truck drivers, heavy equipment operators, air-hammer operators, some industrial workers, rock concert performers and stage workers, bikers, snowmobilers, race car drivers, airplane mechanics, and those who listen to their iPods and MP3 players at high volume. **Audiology testing** done by audiologists determines the extent and type of hearing loss (which can range from conduction problems to sensorineural deafness). To conduct a simple test, rub two fingers together next to each ear. If you cannot hear this slight sound, you might want to follow up with a hearing exam. Individuals often deny hearing loss because it occurs gradually, they fear the change in lifestyle and the cost, and they are often vain and embarrassed to wear one or two hearing aids (Rutherford, 2001). But hearing loss reduces quality of life, limits the ability to communicate or to drive or operate equipment safely, and can lead to social isolation and depression. Medical scientists are continually improving the quality of sound from hearing aids and cochlear implants.

Taste and Smell

Taste buds, which detect salty, sweet, sour, and bitter tastes, normally are replaced nearly every 10 days. However, in people who are in their forties, taste buds are replaced at a slower rate and smell receptors begin to deteriorate, affecting the sense of taste. Women have a better sense of taste than men do because they generally have more taste buds, and scientists believe that estrogen increases a woman's taste sensitivity. Salty and sweet are the first tastes to change, and one's appetite may become especially partial to sweet and salty foods. Yet higher salt intake, such as found in processed and restaurant foods, is associated with cardiovascular risks (Hayes, Sullivan, & Duffy, 2010).

In addition, probably half of all 65-year-olds experience a noticeable loss of their sense of smell. Tastes and flavors are almost entirely detected in the nose, so foods no longer taste as delicious. Hayes and Duffy (2008), taste-and-smell researchers, observe that women with a weakened sense of smell are more likely to gain weight as they attempt to satisfy their yearning for flavors or compensate for the loss of flavors with the gratifying texture of fat. One can compensate for the loss of flavors by holding food in the mouth longer or cooking with more flavorful seasonings or by trying new foods. Dr. Duffy also suggests that as a preventive measure, middle-aged people get the flu shot each year, because each time one catches the flu, the virus can diminish one's sense of smell!

Appearance

Losing teeth or loosening teeth might sound trivial, yet it takes time to become comfortable with a new facial appearance created by extensive dental work—and these procedures are quite costly. During midlife, the gums of the teeth begin to recede, which for some leads to a condition called **periodontal disease.** This in turn leads to loss of teeth, and dental devices might become necessary. Those who cannot afford dental work are likely to have difficulty eating nutritious foods, and their health may decline (Craddock, Yorke, & Chan, 2007). Some dental experts suggest that regular flossing and brushing and scheduled dental visits can help people keep their own teeth into their nineties.

As the skin loses tone and elasticity, it sags and wrinkles in areas where there is frequent movement, such as the face, neck, and joints. Some people also develop "droopy" eyelids as a result. Darker patches of skin ("age spots") caused by many years of exposure to the sun begin to appear by the age of 60 (Landau, 2007). Age spots are considered harmless, but they can be unattractive and give skin an older appearance. There are now therapies to remove age spots, such as laser surgery, cryosurgery (freezing), and chemical peels. Smokers have more wrinkles than nonsmokers. The facial appearance of aging men and women in American society is part of the so-called double standard of aging. As men age, they are often considered "mature" or "sophisticated" or more attractive than when they were younger. However, there are very few kind expressions for the way many older women look. American men and women spend billions of dollars each year on "wrinkle creams," bleaching products, skin lotions, facials, and electrolysis for unwanted hair removal and other dermatology and plastic surgery procedures.

Hair color changes to gray or white and is usually the most obvious physical change that marks chronological aging. During midlife or sooner, the color, thickness, and texture of hair undergo changes, such as graying, thinning, and balding. Hair coloring and hair restoration techniques can help maintain a more youthful appearance. Thinning hair is often associated with aging males, many of whom develop hair loss and balding. Women are also likely to find their hair thinning as they experience perimenopausal symptoms and hormonal changes. For those concerned with hair loss, consultation with a

dermatologist is recommended (American Academy of Dermatology, 2010).

As one ages, the skin loses collagen, fat, and oil glands; it also becomes dryer, thinner, and less elastic after years of exposure to ultraviolet rays. Skin cells grow more slowly with age, and the outer layer of skin is not shed and replaced at the same rate as in younger years. With aging, cells lose some of their ability to retain water, causing dryness. Soaps, antiperspirants, perfumes, and hot baths can aggravate this condition or cause itching.

Scaly patches of skin and any changes in skin color should be checked by a dermatologist, because they could be signs of **basal-cell carcinoma,** which can be treated. This malady could be a marker for **melanoma,** a more serious cancer. A melanoma is a tumor of the skin (which may bleed, darken in color, or itch) that can spread quickly to other body parts. If left untreated, it will be deadly. If caught early, it may be removed surgically, with radiotherapy and chemotherapy. Melanomas are caused by chronic sunlight exposure, blistering sunburns, a family history of skin cancer, and frequent exposure in a tanning booth (Lazovich, Vogel, Berwick, Weinstock, Anderson, & Warshaw, 2010). U.S. men 65 and older have twice the rate of skin cancers as women (National Cancer Institute, 2010). Regular head-to-toe examinations of the skin should be conducted by a medical professional as a necessary part of any checkup.

Women vary greatly in how they respond to looking older. When self-esteem is high, body image is often positive. A woman who was considered unusually attractive when younger may find it more difficult as she begins to look older, compared with a woman who never set great store on her looks. Women who take pride in their looks and who are concerned about looking older seem to experience this concern up to their middle and late sixties

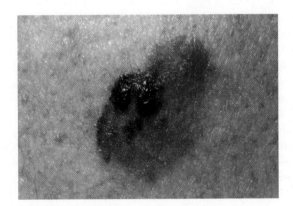

Melanoma A melanoma is a serious skin cancer caused by tumors made up of pigment-producing cells in the epidermis. It often starts in a mole and is induced by ultraviolet radiation in sunlight, blistering sunburns, and a family history of skin cancer. Early treatment is crucial. An overall skin exam should be conducted by a medical doctor or a dermatologist, who specializes in treating skin conditions.

Midlife Brings Many Physical Changes. A Good Sense of Humor Helps Keep Things in Perspective.
Source: ZITS © ZITS PARTNERSHIP, KING FEATURES SYNDICATE.

(Kite, Stockdale, Whitley, & Johnson, 2005). In contrast, middle-age lesbians and women of color tend not to conflate their sense of self-worth with their bodies (Winterich, 2007). In general, compared with women, men have better-looking skin as they age. As men take whiskers from their face each day, they also slough off dead skin cells, leaving a more youthful facial appearance.

Many women and men in middle adulthood who are at the prime of their professions want to look their best and consider it essential to retain a more youthful appearance. On the other hand, a growing number of adults in midlife are very accepting of their changing looks and find emotional comfort and satisfaction in this transitional stage of life. Many are so satisfied with their busy new social roles as grandmother or grandfather, mentor at work, and community or church volunteer that they barely focus on "looks."

Body Composition

One of the major concerns in midlife is the change in one's body composition, or proportion of muscle to fat—and the shift in location of that weight to abdominal and waist areas. Increased waist circumference is related to increased health risks (more than 40 inches for men; more than 35 inches for women) (Katzmarzyk et al., 2011). This change in appearance affects a person's body image and can lead to emotional distress and lower self-esteem. Around age 30, muscles begin to atrophy, which can diminish strength, agility, and endurance. Muscle loss also leads to an increase in body fat. Men are less likely to notice this because their muscles tend to be larger. By the time a person reaches the fifties, muscle loss is likely to be more evident and weight gain more pronounced.

It was once assumed that muscle loss was a normal function of aging and that increased fragility was inevitable. Yet research shows that muscle loss and strength loss are preventable with a regular exercise program of resistance training, toning, or weight lifting (Melov et al., 2007).

Strength training has been shown to increase leg strength in men and women in their sixties (Rosick, 2003). Exercise in middle age can also do much to prevent loss of strength in the hip muscles, which makes a person less vulnerable to falls in old age. Exercises to increase balance, such as yoga or tai chi, during midlife also produce gains that persist into old age. Researchers are shifting their focus to preventive programs to help men and women increase strength, balance, and muscle mass during middle adulthood. Healthy aging is rapidly becoming the goal for the baby-boomer generation (Choy, Brauer, & Nitz, 2007).

For women, menopause is associated with some weight gain due to hormonal changes. But regular exercise can help fight this tendency. A study of white and Chinese American women found that higher levels of exercise, particularly vigorous exercise for at least 10 minutes a day, produced lower levels of body fat and smaller waist circumference in both groups of women (Sternfield et al., 2005).

Obesity and Weight Loss   In this text, we have seen that obesity has become an epidemic in the United States. A national study finds that about 30 percent of men and women in their forties and fifties are diagnosed as obese (Centers for Disease Control, 2010d). Researchers attribute the increasing rate of obesity to a decrease in physical activity, an increase in portion sizes, and an increase in eating away from home where portion sizes are larger and the food is more likely to be unhealthy. The problem is more prevalent among middle-aged women than among middle-aged men (Ogden, Lamb, Carroll, & Flegal, 2010).

Aside from the immediate health problems that being overweight is linked with, such as a decreased rate of physical activity, being overweight in middle age is associated with serious health problems. One longitudinal study followed 17,000 people for three decades. It compared two groups of adults who had a low risk for cardiovascular disease at the beginning of the study. After controlling for other factors, the results showed that people who were obese had a much greater risk of developing and dying from heart disease and/or diabetes. Even those who were overweight, not obese, had a higher risk of death from, and hospitalization for, diabetes and heart disease (Boyles, 2008). Obesity in midlife has been linked to an increased risk of cancer of the esophagus in both men and women and to endometrial and gallbladder cancers in women (Boyles, 2008). It also increases one's risk of dementia and Alzheimer's disease (Kivipelto et al., 2005). The number of people who are classified as severely obese is increasing (100 pounds or more overweight or a BMI of 40 or higher); surgical intervention may be an option, but such surgery entails serious risks (Insel & Roth, 2008).

Research consistently shows that decreasing one's body mass index to a normal level will improve health now and in later life. As a result, more and more dietary supplements, books, products, equipment, and programs are marketed to help Americans lose weight. Many products make unrealistic claims such as "lose 21 pounds in 21 days." Herbal weight-loss products are largely untested and unregulated and may be dangerous. The only way to lose weight safely is to consume fewer calories per day than one expends in physical activity. Diet and exercise must be paired to produce the metabolic changes that will enable one to keep weight off once it is lost. See Table 15.1 for a list of popular diet plans and information about their effectiveness.

Cosmetic Procedures   Americans are bombarded with messages about the ideal body in the print and television media, in programs such as *Extreme Makeover, Nip/ Tuck, BridalPlasty,* and *Addicted to Beauty,* have fueled an obsession with physical perfection. As two feminist scholars point out, "Makeover shows continue to reinforce a certain dominant beauty ideal when they literally cut away physical features that deviate from this ideal" (Banet-Weiser & Portwood-Stacer, 2006, p. 264). Only those who have significant financial resources can afford these surgeries and procedures, which are not covered by health insurance and must be paid for out of pocket. In 2005, a single Botox injection cost on average over $350; rhinoplasty over $4,000, and liposuction almost $3,000 (Smart Plastic Surgery.com, 2008).

From 2000 to 2009, total cosmetic procedures rose markedly. Despite the high cost, about 10 million cosmetic procedures were done in the United States in 2009. Almost half of these surgeries were performed on adults aged 35 to 50. The top surgeries for women, who accounted for 9 million procedures, were liposuction, breast augmentation, eyelid surgery, nose reshaping, and tummy tucks. Men chose liposuction, nose reshaping, and eyelid surgery (American Society for Aesthetic Plastic Surgery, 2009). For U.S. adults aged 40 to 55 and over, the most common nonsurgical procedures

were Botox, soft tissue fillers, facial chemical peels, and facial microdermabrasion (American Society of Plastic Surgeons, 2010).

Anyone considering a cosmetic procedure should check the credentials of those offering services and be aware of the risks. After Botox injections, the botulism toxin that is employed can spread from the facial or neck injection site to other parts of the body, paralyzing muscles used for breathing and swallowing; this has led to several deaths (U.S. Food & Drug Administration, 2008). Silicone breast implants were reapproved by the FDA in 2006 after having been withdrawn for 14 years because of safety concerns; they have been linked with inflammatory diseases such as fibromyalgia and chronic fatigue syndrome. Implants can mask tumors during mammography, and mammography can cause the implants to burst (Santoro, 2008). Implants last several years, and if silicone has leaked, the surgery to remove the silicone is risky and may lead to chest deformities due to loss of muscle mass. The FDA recommends MRIs every two years to check for leakage, but this cost is not covered by health insurance (Ginty, 2007). Liposuction also carries risks, and organs and blood vessels can be punctured. This can cause embolisms due to clots of fat traveling into the bloodstream. The rate of death from liposuction complications is 19 in 100,000 (Free Press Release, 2010). Each cosmetic surgical procedure carries all the risks of surgery—with the added risk that the physician does not have to have specialized training.

The cosmetic surgery industry is mainly unregulated. Anyone with a medical degree (including dentists) can perform cosmetic procedures. Serious or even fatal complications involve blood clots, difficulties with anesthesia, and breathing problems. Doctors must do adequate preoperative studies of the patient's overall health. Medical ethicists have begun to call for stricter regulation of the industry, and some states now have regulations in place. The American Medical Association and the American Society of Anesthesiologists have issued guidelines, but compliance is voluntary. The American Society of Plastic Surgeons warns consumers that cosmetic surgery is a "buyer beware situation" ("Cosmetic Surgery," 2005). Consumers should choose a surgeon certified by the American Board of Medical Specialists, ask about the number of surgeries the practitioner has performed, and learn the practitioner's rate of complications. They should become informed about the specific risks, both from their surgeon and through online research (American Academy of Dermatology, 2007).

Question

What are some of the aspects of natural aging that the baby-boomer generation has challenged?

TABLE 15.1 Benefits, Effectiveness, and Risks of Popular Diet Programs

Many diet plans make extravagant claims and promise quick fixes. When it comes to weight loss, there's no such thing as a quick fix. New eating habits must be learned, particularly with regard to portion size and a balanced diet, and a good weight-loss program combines better eating habits with exercise.

Category	Examples	Claims/Method	Risks/Benefits	Effectiveness
Commercial weight-loss programs	Jenny Craig, Weight Watchers	A healthy relationship with food combined with portion control and an active lifestyle will produce weight loss.	Promotes balanced and low-fat eating. Provides information on food choices, portion size, calorie intake.	Can be safe and effective if healthy eating habits and portion control are learned. Support system is helpful.
Meal-replacement bars and drinks	Slim-Fast	Replace meals with drinks or protein bars.	Contains sugar, protein, vitamins; is low in calories.	May still be hungry; calorie intake too low. Weight often regained when diet is stopped because proper food selection hasn't been learned.
"Fat-burning" diets	Cabbage diet, grapefruit diet	Certain foods can accelerate the body's ability to burn fat. Eating them exclusively for a short period of time will cause rapid weight loss.	Promotes the idea of unrealistically rapid weight loss in a short period of time (e.g., lose 10 pounds in 7 days). Diet not nutritionally balanced; most of the weight lost is water.	No food burns fat exclusively. Weight loss caused by low calorie intake. Weight is regained easily.
Low-carb/high-protein diets	Atkins, South Beach	Claims that carbs increase insulin, which produces fat accumulation. Focuses on intake of protein and fat.	Loss of water and muscle weight causes weight loss. Early phase hard to stick with.	High fat and low calcium can contribute to future diseases. Weight is regained if eating returns to normal.
Low-fat diets	Ornish, Pritikin	Focuses on fat-free and low-fat foods, lots of fruit, vegetables, whole grains, beans.	Weight loss occurs despite eating ample amounts of low-calorie foods. Emphasizes exercise. Healthy for heart and cancer prevention.	Effective for weight loss but hard to stick with because of the lack of fats. May be low in calcium and iron if dieter isn't careful.
Diet pills	Alli, Meridia, herbal supplements with bitter orange, gurana, or hoodia	Claim to burn fat, absorb extra fat, increase metabolism, and/or suppress appetite	Bitter orange and gurana contain amphetamine-like substances that may cause jitters and heart irregularities. Alli turns stool oily and may cause loss of bowel control.	Some herbs may help some people with appetite, but lifelong eating habits aren't learned.
Glycemic index	Glucose Revolution, Good Carbs/Bad Carbs	Based on the Glycemic Index, a categorization of foods based on how quickly or slowly they break down in the body. Focuses on carbs that break down slowly (i.e., that are low on the Glycemic Index), causing a slower release of glucose, fewer fluctuations in blood sugar levels, and higher rates of fat burning.	Requires education about the Glycemic Index.	A balanced approach of consuming adequate protein, carbohydrates, and low-fat foods. Reduction in consumption of refined breads, cereals, rice, potatoes, and snacks. A sensible and healthy diet.
Insulin-resistant diets	"The Zone"	Proper ratio of carbs, proteins, and fats to combat the insulin production that may prompt fat storage. Low in carbs, high in proteins.		No scientific evidence that a diet of precise ratios puts the body in a "zone" of accelerated fat loss.

Source: Adapted from Robbins, G., Powers, D., & Burgess, S. (2008). *A Fit Way of Life*. New York: McGraw-Hill.

Changes in the Skeletal System

With the normal aging process after age 35, bones become less supple and more brittle and begin to lose their density. It is generally held that women are at greater risk of **osteoporosis** (a disorder of thinning bone mass and microarchitectural deterioration of bone tissue) than men. This is because men have 30 percent more bone mass at age 35 than women, and they lose bone more slowly as they age. Age-related decreases in bone density accelerate with menopause in women, so the earlier a woman experiences menopause, the higher the risk.

Osteoporosis is a complex condition. Usually it takes years for it to advance to the stage where it can be detected, because the skeletal structure is not visible and one does not feel the slowing in the replacement of older bone cells with newer cells. Women account for most bone fractures associated with the disease. In fact, a woman's risk of hip fracture is equal to her *combined* risk of breast, uterine, and ovarian cancer (International Society for Clinical Densitometry, 2007). Women are likely to experience bone fractures up to a decade earlier than men. A main contributing factor to bone loss in women is the major decline in the production of estrogen as a woman experiences perimenopause, menopause, and postmenopause.

Most physicians recommend that, as a preventive measure, women perform weight-bearing exercises, such as weight lifting, hiking, stair climbing, swimming, walking, and golfing. Exercise can preserve bone density; when muscle pulls on bone during exercise, it builds stronger, denser bones. Women should also avoid cigarettes and excessive alcohol consumption and begin taking calcium supplements by age 35. Noninvasive bone density testing is now suggested for adults in middle age or older. One should add calcium and vitamin D to one's diet by eating more milk products, egg yolks, leafy green vegetables, and certain shellfish or by adding calcium supplements. **Diuretics** found in caffeinated sodas and beverages and alcohol can cause loss of calcium and zinc through urine. For people who are lactose intolerant and cannot digest milk products, other foods can supply the additional calcium required. Groups that are especially vulnerable to lactose maldigestion include Native Americans, African Americans, and Asian Americans. Research shows that most lactose maldigesters can drink a cup or less of milk with each meal without ill effects, thus reducing their risk of osteoporosis (Jackson & Savaiano, 2001). We shall discuss the serious health consequences of bone loss for elderly adults in Chapter 17.

There are many types of arthritis, but **osteoarthritis,** a joint inflammation that results from cartilage degeneration and causes friction between the bones, is related to aging and is the most common. This disease causes chronic pain and functional limitations. It can be caused by aging, heredity, repetitive use of joints, or injury from trauma or disease. Various treatments may reduce joint pain and inflammation, while improving and maintaining joint function. The Japanese population has a higher incidence of osteoarthritis, although persons from all racial-ethnic groups may be affected (Shiel, 2008).

Another disorder that surfaces in some middle-aged adults is **rheumatoid arthritis,** an inflammatory disease that causes pain, swelling, stiffness, and loss of function of the joints (shoulder, knee, hip, hands, etc.). Scientists classify rheumatoid arthritis as an *autoimmune disease*—the person's own immune system attacks her or his own body tissue. People with rheumatoid arthritis may experience fatigue and occasional fever in addition to the typical symptoms. Arthritis symptoms vary from person to person and can last a few months and then disappear for years. Some people have mild forms of this disease; others live with serious disability. African Americans and Hispanics are almost twice as likely as whites to become disabled from arthritis, mainly because of lack of access to health care (contributing factors include sporadic employment, lack of transportation, and difficulty scheduling checkups), lack of health insurance, and language barriers (Song et al., 2007).

Although there is no single test for this disease, especially in its early stages, lab tests and X-rays can determine the extent of bone damage and monitor disease progression. Weight control, medication, and non–weight-bearing physical activity such as swimming or

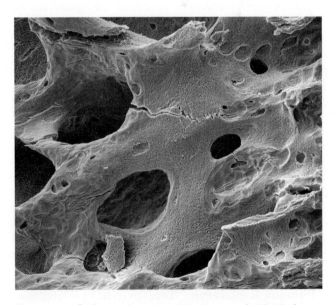

Osteoporotic Bone Osteoporosis causes a reduction in bone density and an increase in porosity, leading to increased brittleness and a greater risk of fracture. Bone densitometry is a painless test that measures bone density. It is recommended for anyone who is prone to bone loss, has a disease associated with osteoporosis, or is using medications that affect bone cells.

water aerobics can reduce the intensity of the symptoms (Insel & Roth, 2008).

Female Midlife Change

A majority of women in the baby-boom cohort have experienced *perimenopause* (also called premenopause) or **menopause**—the cessation of ovarian function and menstruation. The process leading to menopause typically takes two to four years, with intermittent periods and intervals between periods, and is referred to as **perimenopause.** Probably the most significant change is the profound drop in the production of the female hormones (primarily *estrogen*) by the ovaries. Menopause is the culminating sign of the **climacteric,** which is characterized by changes in the ovaries and in the various hormonal processes. A woman is said to have gone through menopause, or to be in **postmenopause,** when she has stopped menstruating for one year (Segal & Mastroianni, 2003).

A study of nearly 15,000 multiethnic women found that the average age range for natural cessation of menses is between 45 and 55, and the median age is 51. A small percentage of women experience premature ovarian failure, called **premature menopause,** before age 40—but it can occur as late as the sixties (Gold et al., 2001). African American and Hispanic women are 40 percent more likely to undergo early menopause than white women, and Japanese women are more likely to experience later menopause (Avis et al., 2003). A longitudinal study in the Netherlands found that heritable components from mother to daughter largely determine the natural age of menopause (van Asselt et al., 2004).

Other "clusters of symptoms" accompany the hormonal changes of menopause and vary among women, such as problems concentrating, incontinence (involuntary leaking of urine), mood disorders, sleep difficulties, and, for some women, hot flashes and vaginal atrophy (Cray, Woods, & Mitchell, 2010). These changes are considered normal reactions to the body's reduced production of sex hormones. Each woman's experience with menopause is different. Most have minimal symptoms and function quite well, but some women have more serious symptoms and need a full checkup with an **endocrinologist** (a physician who specializes in the hormone system). Menopausal women, especially those who experience early menopause, are at higher risk of hypertension, cardiovascular disease, and osteoporosis (Santen et al., 2010).

Hormone Replacement Therapy (HRT)   Troubling news emerged in the early 2000s about increased risk of serious illnesses linked with the use of **hormone replacement therapy (HRT),** a regimen of estrogen and progestin designed to slow bone loss, maintain cardiovascular fitness, slow memory loss, and maintain sexual desire (Santen et al., 2010). In 1993 the National Institutes of

Health began the largest clinical study it had ever conducted, called the *Women's Health Initiative,* of more than 161,000 multiethnic women aged 50 to 79. The goals of this research were to determine the most effective methods to prevent serious health problems in postmenopausal women: heart disease, breast and colorectal cancer, and skeletal fractures from osteoporosis (Liu, 2006). More than 16,000 women with an intact uterus volunteered in one part of this study (half got HRT and half got a placebo). Was oral estrogen, alone or with progestin, beneficial in preventing these diseases?

After five years, this study was stopped because those subjects who were taking HRT had increased risk of heart attack, stroke, blood clots, breast cancer, and dementia—although they did have lower rates of hip fractures and colorectal cancers (Liu, 2006). Yet there was no significant difference between the experimental group and the control group in the number of deaths. In another randomized trial that lasted seven years, 10,000 women without a uterus were given either estrogen alone or a placebo. Among women taking estrogen alone, there was an increased risk of blood clots and stroke and no evidence of protection from heart disease (Liu, 2006). Recent studies have linked HRT to brain atrophy, mainly in the frontal and hippocampus regions—areas that are involved in cognition and memory (Resnick et al., 2009). Consequently, women who undergo postmenopausal HRT are at greater risk for dementia and Parkinson's disease.

Recommendations   The National Institutes of Health noted that a 7 percent decline in the incidence of breast cancer in 2003 was probably linked to a reduction in the use of HRT (NIH News, 2007). The Women's Health Initiative recommends not smoking, a diet low in saturated fat, and increased exercise to reduce the risk of heart disease and osteoporosis after menopause. Many women use herbal products to mitigate postmenopausal symptoms, but clinical trials have not yet proved the effectiveness of such products. Most women can reduce the symptoms of menopause by avoiding spicy foods, alcohol, and caffeine; increasing their intake of fruits, vegetables, and grains; taking a calcium supplement with vitamin D; reducing stress; dressing in cooler clothing; getting enough sleep; and being physically active (Liu, 2006).

Contrary to the media stereotype of postmenopausal women, a poll of 1,000 women over the age of 50 by the National Center on Women and Aging found that more than half of the respondents felt that getting older was much better than they had expected (Winik, 2004). Most are relieved that they no longer have to worry about pregnancy, although a small percentage want to give birth to a child at this age (reproduction after menopause is covered in Chapter 16), and some report an improvement in their sex lives. Although conventional wisdom has linked menopause with depression, scientific studies have failed to establish a causal relationship. Indeed, research surveys consistently reveal that women are considerably more likely to suffer from depression in early adulthood than at midlife. From cross-cultural studies, we know that physical and emotional symptoms of menopause are rarer in societies such as Japan and India, where postmenopausal women gain greater power and heightened social status than they enjoyed during their reproductive years (Melby, Lock, & Kaufert, 2005). As Judith Reichman (1996) notes, "Menopause is the completion of a life cycle that started before we were born. It does not constitute a stop but actually is the start of the next phase of our lives."

Questions

What is menopause, what are its signs, and how does it affect a woman's life? What are some common health concerns for perimenopausal, menopausal, and postmenopausal women? What do we know about HRT effects, and what other recommendations are given for well-being?

Male Midlife Change

Although women's levels of the female hormone estrogen plunge during the climacteric, midlife men begin to experience about a 2 percent decline in testosterone annually over many years (see Figure 15.2). Such changes in a man's body can lead to some physical as well as psychological difficulties. Researchers find it difficult to sort out how testosterone and the adrenal hormone **DHEA (dehydroepiandrosterone)** combine to affect men's vigor. Through

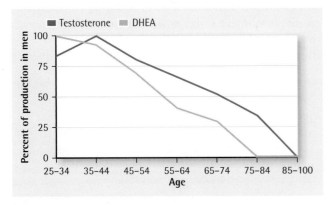

FIGURE 15.2 Testosterone Production Declines in Men
Over many years, men experience a gradual drop in testosterone production. This graph also shows the decline in DHEA hormone in men. By midlife, such declines are associated with physical, sexual, and psychological symptoms.
Source: From Geoffrey Cowley, "Attention: Aging Men," *Newsweek,* September 16, 1996, p. 68. Copyright © 1996 Newsweek, Inc. All rights reserved. Reprinted by permission.

midlife, men may experience more fatigue, increased abdominal body fat, decreased muscle mass, osteoporosis, metabolic problems, cognitive decline, loss of libido, and erectile dysfunction—a combination of factors that is referred to as *andropause* (Simon, 2008). Older men also typically lose the circadian rhythms that affect testosterone fluxes in their younger counterparts, in whom hormone levels usually peak prior to rising in the morning (this is why young men often awake with erections). These physiological changes should not be confused with masculinity or other aspects of male identity. But cultural stereotypes often depict some men in their forties and fifties as suddenly undergoing psychological disturbances, leaving steady jobs for entirely different ventures, leaving wives for much younger women, or beginning to drink to excess. Social scientists look for psychological explanations for changes in a man's life that can produce a crisis in his self-concept (Stamler, 2004). The midlife years call for physical and emotional readjustments and reassessments, some of which can be unpleasant to accept.

The prevalence of andropause varies extensively depending on the age group. It is estimated that about half of men over the age of 60 have a decline in testosterone levels (Harvey & Barry, 2009). A possible treatment for these declining levels is *testosterone replacement therapy,* but this therapy is highly controversial because of the possible risk of inducing prostate cancer (Simon, 2008). Further, prolonged testosterone replacement can damage the liver and may be linked to an increased risk of heart disease and osteoporosis. Many social scientists believe that the medical model has gained unwarranted predominance over the male body, taking too simplistic a view of male sexuality (Potts et al., 2004).

Midlife men are likely to experience an enlargement of the **prostate gland,** a walnut-sized gland at the base of the urethra (the tube that emerges from the bladder and carries urine outside the body via the penis). About 10 percent of men aged 40 already have recognizable enlargement of the prostate. The exact reasons for the enlargement of this gland are unclear. As the prostate enlarges, it puts pressure on the urethra, which contributes to decreased force in the urinary stream, difficulty in beginning urination, and an increased urge to urinate. Although the condition is not itself dangerous, it can contribute to bladder and kidney disorders, infections, and frequent urges to urinate that interrupt sleep. Should serious obstruction to the outflow of urine occur, the tissue causing the enlargement of the prostate can be removed. Some studies find about one-third of patients experience sexual dysfunction after the operation, although complete recovery of function may take up to a year. However, surgery will not restore function that was lost before the operation (National Kidney and Urologic Diseases Information Clearinghouse, 2006).

Some men experience a condition called **prostatitis,** an inflammation of the prostate gland that may be accompanied by discomfort, pain, frequent urination, infrequent urination, and sometimes fever. In addition to an annual physical examination that includes blood, urine, and possibly other laboratory tests, the National Cancer Institute and the American Cancer Society suggest talking with a physician (most likely a urologist). The physician conducts a digital rectal exam (DRE), feeling for any unusual lumps. Also, a **PSA test** will be administered; this test measures the blood level of a protein called *prostate-specific antigen (PSA)* that is made by the prostate. It is normal to find small quantities of PSA in the blood. PSA levels differ according to age and tend to rise gradually in men over age 60. PSA may become elevated as a consequence of infection (*prostatitis*), enlargement of the prostate, or cancer. In those questionable cases, other imaging techniques, such as MRI or biopsy, may be used for diagnostic purposes.

Prostate Cancer A more serious problem is prostate cancer, which is the leading cause of cancer in men throughout the Western world, but if it is caught early, it is not a death sentence (National Cancer Institute, 2011). This cancer is rarely seen in men under 50, but incidence increases with each decade of life. Japanese men have a low incidence of prostate cancer, however, perhaps thanks to dietary, genetic, or screening factors. Other lifestyle factors associated with this disease include alcohol consumption, vitamin or mineral interactions, dietary habits, promiscuity, and genital warts (National Cancer Institute, 2008). If not discovered and treated early, prostate cancer metastasizes and spreads to the bones. Males age 50 and older should have annual prostate exams. Men with higher incomes and education levels appear more likely than poor men to be screened annually for prostate cancer. Most cancers of the prostate, particularly in older men, grow at a slow pace, and there are treatments that delay ill effects.

Black men are more likely than white men to be diagnosed with prostate cancer, and they have a higher risk of dying from the disease. Various factors account for this disparity. Human genome research suggests that black men are more likely to have a genetic component to their disease (PSA Rising, 2007). Research from the University of California–Davis School of Medicine links what is called the "excess cancer burden" of black men to smoking and recommends eliminating smoking (Leistikow & Tsodikov, 2005). Black men are more likely than white men to be diagnosed in advanced stages of the disease since they are less likely to get routine PSA tests; this is because of limited access to optimal medical care and lack of health insurance (Bach et al., 2002). Black men are often unaware of their higher risk of prostate cancer, are concerned about any threats to their sexuality, and do not believe medical practitioners provide optimal care. The American medical community needs to do a much better job of informing, screening, and treating poor ethnic-minority men (Allen et al., 2007).

Male Potency Sexual activity reaffirms self-esteem, attractiveness, and gender identity and has profound psychological meaning (Wincze & Carey, 2001). One report from the large-scale Massachusetts Male Aging Study found that about one-third of men between ages 53 and 90 had some degree of **erectile dysfunction** (ED, also called impotence) and that ED increases with natural aging (Bacon et al., 2003). Erectile dysfunction can also result from drugs, medical conditions such as diabetes, cardiovascular disorders, and cancer, as well as from social habits, including smoking, alcohol consumption, and lack of exercise. Stress, depression, grief, illness, and accidents can give rise to temporary impotence (Lewis, Legato, & Fisch, 2006). Erectile dysfunction can be treated by making lifestyle changes, such as quitting smoking, getting more exercise, reducing alcohol intake, and losing weight. Counseling may help if emotional issues are involved. Oral medication is widely used to help men attain erections, although it should be used only by men in good health and should never be a substitute for treating underlying health issues that may be causing erectile dysfunction, such as hypertension, diabetes, antidepressant use, and cardiovascular disease (Bacon et al., 2003).

Men's responses to middle age are varied. Many seem to move calmly through it; others have a stormy passage. For some it can be a time of developmental defeat, leading to such problems such as depression, alcoholism, obesity, and a chronic sense of futility and failure (Sheehy, 1998). But with a positive attitude, middle age can be a time of new personality growth, a period when a man moves toward a new kind of intimacy in his marriage, greater fulfillment in his work and community service, and more realistic and satisfying relationships with his children and grandchildren.

Questions

What do we know about midlife andropause? What are some common physiological changes, health concerns, and psychological adjustments for men in middle age?

HEALTH AND LIFESTYLE

Social habits and lifestyles affect our physical and psychological health in many ways. C. Everett Koop, former U.S. Surgeon General, estimated that half of U.S. deaths in 1990 were caused by smoking, drinking, sexually transmitted infections, drug abuse, poor nutrition, guns, and motor vehicles. He observed that many of the old epidemics of the eighteenth century have been replaced by "self-induced diseases." Moreover, a mounting body of evidence suggests that strong personal social ties and connections to community networks (a collective resource called *social capital*) are conducive to physical and mental health (Poortinga, 2006). Groups provide the structure by which we involve ourselves in the daily affairs of life. Not surprisingly, therefore, living alone or feeling isolated can be hazardous to one's health. For example, men and women who lack social and emotional support are more likely to die following a heart attack than are people with a caring family and friends (Davidson et al., 2008).

Social support from family, friends, neighbors, co-workers, community groups—and even social networks on the Internet—can be of tremendous help when we are ill, are feeling down, or are looking to speak with someone who understands our issues (Moren-Cross & Nin, 2006). For instance, patients are far more likely to live at least six months after heart surgery if they draw strength from religion and participation in social groups (Davidson et al., 2008). Religious beliefs typically take on much more significance for middle-aged adults and the elderly. Research studies reveal that patients who have faith that they *will heal* often heal more quickly than those who despair over their illness. Further, prayer has been associated with both the psychological and the biological changes that are found to improve health, such as lower blood pressure, boosted immune response, positive mood states, and reduction in anxiety (Andrade & Radhakrishnan, 2009). Fortunately, more adults are smoking less, eating more sensibly, and exercising more. Yet too many continue their unhealthy ways. The *More Information You Can Use* box on pages 488–489, "A Schedule of Checkups for Midlife Adults," highlights potential physiological changes and gives a time schedule for diagnostic exams to help maintain a healthy, functional, active life.

Sleep

Individuals who get adequate healthy, restorative sleep (enough is considered to be 7 to 8 hours regularly) are better able to cope with physical pain and stress during waking hours (Hamilton, Catley, & Karlson, 2007). However, sleep changes often occur during midlife, when work and family caretaking demands are high. Such changes include shorter duration, frequent awakenings, less rejuvenating deep sleep, earlier bedtime and arising times, and, for some, the need for napping (Campbell & Murphy, 2007). The average working person gets 90 minutes less sleep per night than she or he needs, according to Dr. William Dement, founder of a sleep disorder center at Stanford University and author of *The Promise of Sleep* (2000). As one proceeds through middle adulthood, added health factors can also affect the length and quality of sleep.

Use of mild stimulant drugs, such as caffeine and nicotine, can interfere with sleep, as can prescription and over-the-counter drugs such as pain relievers, cold remedies, antihistamines, appetite suppressants, decongestants, and drugs for asthma, high blood pressure, and heart and thyroid problems. Even common foods containing sugar or caffeine (especially if eaten late at night); common beverages such as alcohol, soft drinks, cocoa, and tea; and not getting enough protein in one's diet can keep one awake or prevent sleep for an extended period of time. Adults who work irregular shift schedules are likely to experience sleep difficulties. Insomnia can also result from worry or depression. Changes in one's circadian rhythms during midlife can affect sleep patterns as well. It is quite common to be able to go to sleep when desired but to wake up only a few hours later and not be able to get back to sleep. Women experiencing perimenopause often experience this pattern, accompanied by "night sweats," or hot flashes, because of ongoing changes in their biochemistry. Sleep disturbances related to menopausal hot flashes can have an important impact on mood, and menopausal women often attribute daytime irritability to nighttime awakenings (Thurston, Blumenthal, Babyak, & Sherwood, 2006). Another factor that interferes with sleep for many midlife adults is the "waiting-up-for-teenagers-to-get-home-safely" syndrome!

Medications formulated to help induce sleep, including sleeping pills, tranquilizers, and antianxiety drugs, can actually cause more sleeplessness after discontinuation of their use. Also, these types of medications can become addictive. Because they are central nervous system depressants, their use is likely to affect alertness, aggravate memory loss, and make a person unsteady on arising, which increases the likelihood of falls or more severe injury. Use of sleeping pills for a short time or situationally (such as on vacation many time zones from home) is not likely to lead to addiction. Anyone with serious sleep disturbances should consult a sleep clinic at a local hospital or clinic for assistance—as Dement (2000) says, healthy sleep is a significant factor in longevity.

Cardiovascular Fitness

Several risk factors are associated with **cardiovascular** (heart and circulatory system) health, including high blood pressure (*hypertension*), high cholesterol, smoking, a family history of heart disease or stroke, being diabetic, and being overweight or obese (Lloyd-Jones et al., 2007). Two cardiovascular diseases that are common among U.S. adults aged 45 to 64 are heart disease, the number one cause of death in the United States, and stroke, the third most common cause of death (by midlife, cancer is the leading cause of death) (Miniño, Xu, & Kochanek, 2010). Blood pressure readings, cholesterol

MORE INFORMATION YOU CAN USE

A Schedule of Checkups for Midlife Adults

Health Checkups	Diagnosis or Potential Health Concerns	Recommendations
Vision	Presbyopia, glaucoma, cataracts, macular degeneration, dry eyes, watery eyes, "droopy" eyes, other eye conditions.	*If 40 or over,* do you have to hold this book farther and farther away to be able to read this print? *Over 60,* have an eye exam *at least once every 2 years.* This should include dilating the pupils to get a good view of the retina and optic nerve, essential in detecting diseases of the eye.
Hearing	Presbycusis, nerve deafness, or other hearing disorders. About 35% of adults age 65 and older have a hearing loss. It is estimated that 50% of those 75 and older have a hearing loss.	*Check yourself:* Can you hear a bird chirping nearby? Can you hear the telephone ringing? Are you asking others to repeat themselves? Do you have difficulty hearing in a crowded room? Can you hear the sound of rubbing your fingers together near each ear? What is the typical sound level of your work environment? Do you have a familial background of hearing loss? An audiology exam may be in order.
Skin Appearance	Look for patches of dry, scaly skin, darkening of a mole, or other skin protrusion; any bleeding or discharge from skin, sunburn.	The American Academy of Dermatology suggests that people, especially those who live in warm climates, *have a yearly skin exam* as part of a regular checkup. In between checkups, be alert for any changes in your skin.
Dental Health	Cleaning and examination; X rays for periodontal disease.	*Minimum once per year* for teeth cleaning and *every few years for dental X rays.*
Weight	Sources vary on recommendations. Some say 20% over, others say 30% over recommended weight for body size puts a person at a higher risk of heart disease, cancer, and other illnesses.	Look at muscle-to-fat ratio; consider body frame and lifestyle. Start physician-monitored exercise regimen if overweight. Make an appointment with a nutritionist.
Bone Density	Osteoporosis and other bone disorders can be diagnosed with a painless bone densitometry scan. *Osteoporosis is preventable.* Follow a diet rich in calcium and vitamin D and a lifestyle of regular weight-bearing exercise. *Those at higher risk:* small body frame, low body weight, sedentary lifestyle, anorexics and dieters.	Men and women aged 25 to 65 should have 1,000 mg calcium daily. Women near menopause or postmenopause should have 1,500 mg calcium daily. Calcium-rich foods include low-fat dairy products (cheese, yogurt, milk); canned fish with edible bones, such as salmon and sardines; dark leafy-green vegetables such as kale, broccoli, collard greens; breads made with calcium-fortified flour; juices fortified with calcium; calcium supplements with vitamin D as needed.
Cervical Cancer (women)	A Pap *smear,* or cervical biopsy if at higher risk.	A Pap smear every 1 to 3 years to detect cervical cancer. Request lab where a person examines smear; some are examined electronically. Should be done more often if at higher risk: multiple sex partners, sequential sex partners, IV drug user, have unprotected sex, previous history of STI(s), familial history of cancer, heavy smoker, postmenopausal and on HRT.
Menopause (women)	Blood test for level of FSH (follicle-stimulating hormone); begins in only 4% of women under 40. Typical age range is 45 to 55; average age is 51.	Typically if female age 40 or over and if menses are irregular or atypical, or if any other signs of menopause are indicated (hot flashes or hot flushes, sleep irregularities, etc.).
Type 2 Diabetes	In Type 2 diabetes, either the body does not produce enough insulin or the cells ignore the insulin. Insulin is necessary for the body to be able to use sugar and takes the sugar from the blood into the cells. When glucose builds up in the blood instead of going into cells, cells may be starved for energy and high blood sugar levels hurt eyes, kidneys, nerves, or heart.	The goal of treatment is to lower your blood sugar and improve your body's use of insulin with meal planning, exercise, and weight loss. There are many factors involved in controlling blood sugar levels, including diet, exercise and monitoring your blood sugar regularly. Controlling your diabetes is important to reduce the risk of long-term complications.

Health Checkups	Diagnosis or Potential Health Concerns	Recommendations
Breast Cancer (can affect both females and males)	Self-exam. Mammogram: an X-ray picture of the breast, which takes only a few seconds per breast. With aging after 40, the chances of getting breast cancer get higher. After skin cancer, breast cancer is the most frequently diagnosed cancer in U.S. women.	If you are in your forties or older, *having a mammogram every 1 to 2 years could save your life.* Look for any unusual lump or swelling lasting for a period of time; some lumps (cysts) normally occur at a certain time each month; check breasts monthly while in the shower by running hands over breasts lightly to detect any changes or lumps; also check nearby lymph glands for changes. A doctor should do an annual breast exam. Mammograms are recommended once every 2 years after 40 years old or more frequently if there is a familial or personal history of breast cancer. There is a genetic test for those with a higher familial risk of breast cancer.
Cardiovascular Fitness (age 18 and older)	Hypertension or high blood pressure. Systolic Diastolic Normal <120 <80 Prehypertension 120–139 80–89 High Stage 1 140–159 90–99 Stage 2 ≥160 ≥100	Have blood pressure taken regularly if overweight or have familial or personal history of hypertension. *To lower blood pressure:* • Maintain healthy weight (lose weight if overweight) • Be more physically active. • Choose foods low in salt (sodium). • Drink alcoholic beverages only in moderation.
Blood Cholesterol	High 240+ Borderline high 200–239 Desirable below 200.	A blood test to check for LDL and HDL for everyone aged 20 and older, every 5 years; men with no risk factors can wait until age 35; women with no risk factors can wait until age 45 (see Table 15.2).
HIV/AIDS	Blood tests to confirm absence or presence of HIV virus; gynecological cervical tests in women.	*Higher-risk factors* include unprotected sexual behaviors, homosexual male sexual behaviors, history of sexual abuse (rape), history of multiple partners, history of sequential partners, IV drug user sharing needles, history of STI(s), extreme fatigue, recurrent female pelvic diseases, female over 50 having unprotected sexual relations.
Prostate Gland (men)	Prostatitis can be caused by several types of bacteria. Symptoms include burning sensation, discharge, difficulty beginning a stream of urine. Treatment regimen is antibiotics. Prostate enlargement is more typical beginning in late 40s and symptoms are similar to prostatitis. Prostate cancer is detected by biopsy.	See a physician (a urologist perhaps, depending upon the severity of the symptoms). The physician inserts a gloved finger into the rectum to feel the prostate through the wall of the bowel. This exam is part of a *routine physical for men over 40* to detect signs of prostatic cancer—a slow-growing cancer that almost never affects young men but is seen in most elderly men.
Testicular Cancer (men)	Testicular cancer usually affects men between the ages of 15 and 35. If testicular cancer is detected early, it is very curable.	A monthly testicular self-exam (TSE) is performed to identify a number of conditions, but primarily cancer. Regularly examine the testes during a warm shower when the heat of the shower can relax the scrotum. Rotate each testicle between the thumb and forefinger, feeling for a round, firm surface. If you discover a small, painless lump on the surface of the testicle that does not appear to be epididymis, consult a physician immediately. Testicular cancer is almost always painless, so do not wait for the lump to grow or pain to develop.
Colon Cancer (also called colorectal cancer)	Among the most common cancers in the U.S. and most often occurs in men and women over 50. Associated with diets high in fat and calories and low in fiber. First-degree relatives of a person who has had colorectal cancer are somewhat more likely to develop this type of cancer themselves. Ulcerative colitis increases risk. Some types of polyps increase the risk.	Prevention requires early detection and removal of polyps. Also studies suggest a diet low in fat and calories and high in fiber for prevention. Several detection tests are used: a digital rectal exam (DRE) and a fecal occult blood test (FOBT) are used to check for hidden blood in the stool. A double contrast barium enema (DCBE) is a series of X rays of the colon and rectum. A sigmoidoscopy is an examination of the rectum and lower colon (sigmoid colon) using a lighted instrument. A colonoscopy is an examination of the rectum and entire colon using a colonoscope.

screenings, and triglyceride levels are predictors of cardiovascular fitness.

Blood Pressure   About one in every three U.S. adults has high blood pressure, called **hypertension,** which is a risk factor for other diseases affecting the heart, kidneys, and brain. Hypertension has no warning signs or symptoms. Blood pressure is the force of the blood pushing against the walls of arteries. Each time the heart beats (about 60 to 70 times a minute at rest), it pumps out blood to the arteries. Blood pressure is at its greatest when the heart contracts and is pumping the blood, which is called **systolic pressure.** When the heart is at rest, in between beats, blood pressure falls, which is **diastolic pressure.** Blood pressure is always noted as these two numbers, and both are important. They are usually written one above or before the other. The top (or first) number is the systolic pressure, and the bottom (or second) number is the diastolic pressure. A reading of 140/90 is considered high; 120/80 is normal for the heart and blood vessels (National Institutes of Health [NIH], 2006). Blood pressures can fluctuate during a regular day, depending on stress and activity level. During sleep, for instance, blood pressure goes down.

Who Is at Risk?   Anyone can develop high blood pressure, but it is more common in blacks than in whites. In the early and middle adult years, men have high blood pressure more often than women. Yet as men and women age, more women have high blood pressure than men. After menopause, women have high blood pressure as often as men of the same age. The percentage of men and women with hypertension increases rapidly in older age groups. More than half of all Americans over age 60 have high blood pressure. Heredity can make some individuals more prone to developing high blood pressure. But the increasing prevalence of overweight children and adults means that more people already have hypertension at even younger ages (McCrindle, 2006). High blood pressure often leads to other conditions, such as heart disease, kidney failure, or stroke (Lloyd-Jones et al., 2007). The NIH (2006) promotes several lifestyle changes to help prevent or control hypertension:

- eating healthy foods that include fruits, vegetables, grains, and low-fat dairy products
- cutting down on salt and sodium in the diet
- maintaining a healthy weight
- staying physically active (e.g., walking for 30 minutes daily)
- limiting alcohol intake
- not smoking, or quitting if you do
- taking prescribed medication as directed

Medications can help reduce high blood pressure. Regular blood pressure screenings several times a year are

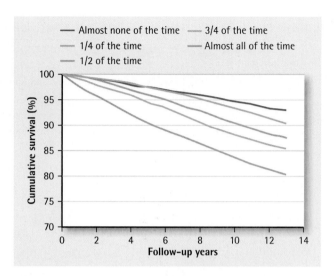

FIGURE 15.3 A Sedentary Lifestyle (Sitting) Is Associated with Serious Health Risks—Get Moving! This graph from a mortality study shows the cumulative survival, or the probability of surviving over time, across different levels of sitting during the day. Note that people who spend nearly all of their day sitting have a much lower chance of being alive after 13 years than people who spend very little time sitting.
Source: Louisiana State University System: Pennington Biomedical Research Center. *Scientific Report 2008–2009.* Katzmarzyk, P. T., p. 82. Retrieved from http://www .pbrc.edu/pdf/PBRC-ScientificReport-2008-2009.pdf

recommended during middle adulthood and are available free in many community settings, such as neighborhood clinics, pharmacies, churches, senior centers, and schools. Adults with a high risk for hypertension can purchase diagnostic instruments to take their blood pressure readings at home. Following the DASH (Dietary Approaches to Stop Hypertension) eating plan, which emphasizes fresh fruits and vegetables, low-fat dairy, whole grains, fish, poultry, and nuts, has been shown to have a positive effect on blood pressure ("Facts About the DASH Eating Plan," 2006). With a doctor's supervision, increasing one's activity level usually improves one's hypertension readings and cardiovascular fitness (see Figure 15.3).

Cholesterol   A white, waxy fat that occurs naturally in the body and is an essential substance used to build the cell walls and make certain hormones is **cholesterol,** which has been the "buzz word" in health for the past 20 years. Too much of it in one's diet can clog arteries and eventually choke off the supply of blood to the heart. High cholesterol is a leading risk factor for heart disease. The National Cholesterol Education Program (NCEP) suggests being tested from age 20 on. Cholesterol level can be determined with a simple, inexpensive blood test. Men 35 and older and women 45 and older should have this test every five years at least. HDL is considered the "good" cholesterol that cleans the blood vessels; LDL is the "bad" cholesterol that builds up and clogs arteries.

TABLE 15.2 Blood Cholesterol Levels
ATP III classification of LDL, total, and HDL cholesterol (mg/dL) (Obtain Complete Lipoprotein Profile After 9- to 12-Hour Fast.)

LDL Cholesterol—Primary Target of Therapy

<100	Optimal
100–129	Near optimal/above optimal
130–159	Borderline high
160–189	High
≥190	Very high

Total Cholesterol

<200	Desirable
200–239	Borderline high
≥240	High

HDL Cholesterol

<40	Low
≥60	Optimal for men and women

Source: National Cholesterol Education Program. (2001, May). NIH Publication No. 01-3305. Bethesda, MD: National Institutes of Health.

See Table 15.2 for recommended blood cholesterol levels (American Heart Association, 2007b). The NCEP has a calculator on its Web site that enables you to assess your risk for having a heart attack (National Cholesterol Education Program, 2005). One can raise beneficial HDL cholesterol by changing one's diet to reduce consumption of saturated fats and increasing one's intake of fruits, vegetables, and whole grains and certain nuts, and by exercising regularly (brisk walking, running, swimming, rowing, cycling, dancing, jumping rope, skating, and aerobics). Reaching the recommended level of HDL helps to lower the damaging effects of LDL cholesterol. Blacks and Hispanics are less informed about hypertension, but they are at greatest risk for high cholesterol levels (Gans et al., 2003).

Triglycerides   **Triglycerides** are the chemical form of fats in food and are major components of very low density lipoprotein (VLDL). When we eat foods containing fats, the body absorbs fat through the lining of the intestines. As one type of energy source, fats play an important role in metabolism and contain more energy than carbohydrates and proteins. Excessive levels of triglycerides in the bloodstream, however, have been linked to an increased risk of stroke, heart disease, and diabetes (American Heart Association, 2008b). At a medical checkup, one can request blood tests to determine cholesterol and triglyceride levels. To reduce triglyceride levels, eat a heart-healthy diet, avoid smoking, exercise regularly, and limit alcohol consumption.

Other Risk Factors   Certain emotions and personality traits can have an impact on cholesterol levels. One study found that women who express anger with verbal and physical hostility have significantly higher overall cholesterol and LDL cholesterol (the "bad" cholesterol). Outbursts of anger were a predictor of cardiovascular disease in this study (Suarez, 2006). Another study has found that men who cope with stress effectively have higher levels of HDL cholesterol (the "good" cholesterol). The amount of stress was not the salient factor for these men; what mattered in reducing the risk of cardiovascular disease was focusing on solving problems instead of reacting emotionally to them (Doheny, 2007).

Race-ethnicity is associated with risk of death from cardiovascular disease. Black men are at higher risk for heart disease than white men. Almost one-third of all black Americans have high blood pressure (American Heart Association, 2010). Mexican Americans also have a higher rate of premature death from heart disease, linked to a higher rate of obesity (Office of Minority Health, 2008).

Smoking, especially long-term, can lead to many health risks. Smoking-related illnesses and diseases cost Americans billions of dollars in medical care every year, along with the emotional devastation associated with the loss of loved ones who would not give up the habit. Thus, laws are passed banning smoking in public places, in private corporations and restaurants, and (in some cities) in parks or on beaches. Many empirical studies have documented that smoking can lead to heart disease, stroke, lung disease, kidney and bladder disease, and many types of cancers. A variety of smoking-reduction programs (and medications in pill or patch form) are available to those who wish to make this lifestyle change to promote better health and well-being, not just for oneself but for one's family as well. A great deal of research has documented that secondhand smoke (SHS) is a risk factor for lung cancer, and about 3,000 people die each year in the United States as a result of exposure to SHS (Asomaning et al., 2008). People who have quit usually state that food tastes better, breathing is easier, endurance for activity improves, and energy level is higher—and, as a boon to people around them, they no longer reek of stale smoke. It is never too late to quit, and quitting can add years to a person's life.

Inflammation, Metabolic Syndrome, and Heart Disease   Recent studies point to inflammation as a factor that may be as important as cholesterol level in causing heart attacks and strokes (LeWine, 2005). Endocrinologists are exploring the links between cellular inflammation and heart attack and diabetes. Research has shown that inflamed monocytes and lymphocytes are present in obese people, who are at greater risk for heart disease and diabetes. These inflamed cells are also linked to atherosclerosis or insulin resistance and can enter the brain ("Cellular Inflammation Precursor to

Heart Disease," 2005). *Metabolic syndrome* (also known as insulin resistance syndrome or *prediabetes syndrome*) is a group of risk factors for heart disease. It includes:

- a triglyceride level of 150 mg/dL or higher
- an HDL lower than 40 mg/dL in men and lower than 50 mg/dL in women
- blood pressure of 130/85 or higher or drug treatment for hypertension
- a fasting plasma glucose level of 100 mg/dL or higher
- a waist measurement of more than 35 inches for women and 40 inches for men (Robbins, Powers, & Burgess, 2008)

A diet that is high in refined grains (versus whole or natural grains), fried foods, and red meat increases the risk of metabolic syndrome. A surprising finding was that consumption of diet soda is also linked to this condition (Bakalar, 2008). Black Americans, Native Americans, and Mexican Americans are more vulnerable to this silent disease than other ethnic-racial groups in the United States (Robbins, Powers, & Burgess, 2008).

Improving one's diet and increasing exercise levels are important ways to reduce the symptoms of metabolic syndrome (Deen, 2004). Metabolic syndrome and cardiovascular risk factors have also been found to have an impact on the development of Alzheimer's disease and vascular dementia (Yaffe et al., 2004). Even borderline levels of risk factors such as blood pressure, cholesterol, glucose intolerance, and smoking should be considered for treatment to prevent heart disease (Vasan & Sullivan, 2005). According to Neighborhood Heart Watch, another risk factor for heart disease is the presence of gum disease (Watch & Update, 2005).

Questions

How do smoking, excessive cholesterol and triglycerides, hypertension, and inflammation contribute to cardiovascular disease, diabetes, and other health risks?

Cancer

Breast cancer is now the most often diagnosed cancer among U.S. women, followed by lung and colorectal cancer—lung cancer in women leads to more deaths. But prostate cancer is the leading cancer among men, followed by lung and colorectal cancer. More than 200,000 U.S. women are diagnosed with breast cancer each year (U.S. Cancer Statistics Working Group, 2010). Overall, the incidence of breast cancer has decreased in all age groups over age 40 in the past several years, after the Women's Health Initiative announced findings about the association of HRT with higher risk of breast cancer (Jemal, Ward, & Thune, 2007). Also, incidence rates for

cervical cancer have declined significantly over the past 40 years (Division of Cancer Prevention and Control, 2006/2007). Annual medical checkups include various cancer-detection screenings, such as mammograms, Pap tests, and PSA tests. Reaching age 50 is a major milestone, but it also should trigger annual exams and signal the advent of higher costs for maintaining health. Early detection and advances in diagnostics and treatment have contributed to more people surviving a cancer diagnosis.

A complex combination of factors predisposes a person to developing cancer (Ries et al., 2007). *Smoking* is the number one controllable cause of cancer, and not smoking is the first rule to follow in one's efforts to avoid cancer. Anyone who has a history of cancer is at a higher risk for developing other cancers. Other risk factors are these:

- *Poverty.* Among persons diagnosed with cancer, those who have financial resources and access to medical insurance live longer than poorer people.
- *Longevity.* Those who live longer have a greater likelihood of getting some type of cancer. Cancer incidence begins to rise at about age 45 for both men and women.
- *Gender and race.* More men than women, and more blacks than whites, die from cancer.
- *Family.* Genetics plays a role in the incidence and types of cancers diagnosed. Inform every healthcare provider you consult of any familial disposition to cancer.

Unlike years ago, when cancer was the whispered "C word," many communities now have support groups available to help cancer patients and their families cope with this serious ordeal; there are also support groups online. Researchers around the world are making scientific breakthroughs daily in the global campaign to understand and cure cancer.

The Brain

As the brain ages, certain brain functions begin to change because of reductions in brain gray matter (volume) in the prefrontal cortex and temporal medial regions. Recently, neuropsychologists studying precursors for dementia also found that the personality trait of conscientiousness was related to larger volumes of gray matter and slower decline with age, whereas the trait of neuroticism was related to lower volumes of gray matter (Jackson, Balota, & Head, 2009). *Reaction time* on intellectual tasks also gets slower in comparison with younger people, for example (Knowlton, 2005). Older adults tend to take longer to generate solutions to new problems that arise in daily life. But in the context of problems that occur in familiar terrain, midlife adults can draw on their storehouse of life experience and often do better than younger people. By midlife, many adults also begin to

FURTHER DEVELOPMENTS

Information for Breast Cancer Survivors

Although breast cancer is the most commonly diagnosed cancer in women, it is the second leading cause of death among U.S. women, after lung cancer. From 2000 to 2006, the incidence rate declined by 2 percent a year, partly as a consequence of the reduced use of hormone replacement therapy (American Cancer Society, 2010). Despite this reduction, the U.S. incidence rate is the second highest in Western countries—but the *highest survival rate* is in the United States (see Table 15.3) (American Cancer Society, 2011). The American Cancer Society projected that more than 200,000 women and about 2,000 men would be diagnosed in 2011. Researchers are exploring a link between genetic hormone levels among different ethnic groups and the incidence of breast cancer. Groups with high levels of estrogen after menopause, including Native Hawaiian and Japanese American women, have higher rates of breast cancer after menopause than white women and Hispanic women (Setiawan et al., 2006).

The vast majority of women in the United States who get breast cancer in midlife survive, but the likelihood of survival depends on a number of social and environmental factors. Male surgeons and those trained outside the United States are less likely to suggest radiation therapy after surgery, even though it is considered the standard of care because it reduces the likelihood of recurrence (HealthDay News, 2008). A woman's race-ethnicity and socioeconomic status affect her care significantly. More white women survive than black women, and white women are more likely to be diagnosed earlier and to have access to care and support resources. Black women, who are more likely to be poor, have less access to health insurance and medical care and are more likely to be diagnosed at a later stage of the disease (American Cancer Society, 2010).

Today, over 2 million women in the United States are breast cancer survivors (American Cancer Society, 2010). These women have waged a battle that has taught them many things. Many survivors emphasize that staying positive is a key to survival. Belonging to a support group is a vital emotional resource, but the group members also share medical knowledge. Women are empowered by becoming active and educated participants in medical decisions. "Take responsibility for your healing" is a statement shared among survivors (Anderson, 2002).

Breast cancer survivors have medical vulnerabilities for the rest of their lives. They need to be proactive to ensure that they get proper care. For example, blood pressure cuffs should never be used on the arm on the side of the body where lymph nodes were dissected. This is because of an elevated risk of *lymphedema,* a blockage in the lymph drainage system that causes swelling and arm discomfort. If left untreated, the swelling becomes hardened and permanent (Kavanah, 2007). Women need to insist that blood pressure, injections, and IVs take place at a different site in the body, even if health-care practitioners downplay the risk. Some breast cancer therapies, including chemotherapy and radiation therapy, increase the risk of cardiovascular disease. One study is examining whether exercise can reduce the damage to the heart that these treatments can cause (Jones et al., 2007).

The side effects of treatment may linger for several years after treatment ends. "Chemobrain," a side effect of chemotherapy, causes memory lapses, confusion, and difficulty concentrating. Researchers found that dexmethylphenidate, or d-MPH, reduces these symptoms in many women (University of Cincinnati, 2005). Fatigue is also a post-treatment symptom that may linger for a long time. It is important for survivors and their families to realize that the end of treatment does not mean that life returns to "normal." A new normal emerges. Many survivors feel that they have been given an opportunity to make different choices about how they balance the various facets of their lives (Shaw, 2006).

TABLE 15.3 Breast Cancer Survival Rates, Females Aged 15 and Older in Selected Countries

Country	Percent
United States (1999–2006)	89
China (1999–2001)	82
Switzerland (1995–1999)	82
Spain (1995–1999)	80.3
Austria (1995–1999)	80
South Korea (1990–2001)	79
Germany (1995–1999)	78.3
Denmark (1995–1999)	77.5
England (1995–1999)	77.3
Belgium (1995–1999)	77.3
Poland (1995–1999)	73.7
Thailand (1990–2001)	63
India (1990–2001)	52
Uganda (1990–2001)	46

Source: American Cancer Society. (2011). *Global Cancer Facts & Figures, 2nd edition.* Atlanta, GA: American Cancer Society. Retrieved from http://www.cancer.org/acs/groups/content/@epidemiologysurveillance/documents/document/acspc-027766.pdf

complain about memory problems, a development that is consistent with changes in the same prefrontal cortex and temporal medial regions (Knowlton, 2005).

However, even though cross-sectional studies suggest that some aspects of age-related cognitive declines begin when adults are in their twenties and thirties, changes in mental processing are highly variable. It is difficult to make generalizations for any person or group (Knowlton, 2005; Salthouse, 2009). No single ability declines for all people in a given age group, but we know that beginning in a person's sixties, the likelihood that at least one cognitive ability will begin to decline is quite high (Salthouse, 2009). In a recent study with several hundred subjects ranging in age from 61 to 96, cognitive decline accelerated mainly in speed of processing and various aspects of memory (Salthouse, 2009).

Recent research suggests that people can slow the process of brain cell loss by staying intellectually active, continuing to problem-solve, and using challenging thought processes. People in midlife should continue the path of active learning: Learn and use new words, play games of Scrabble, compete along with *Jeopardy* and *Who Wants to Be a Millionaire?* contestants, get creative, try a new hobby, take a college course or continue education in some other fashion, mentor someone, join a speakers' group, join an Elderhostel (now called Road Scholar) program—in other words, do things that keep you intellectually engaged with the world.

The incidence of stroke is fairly low in the 40-to-59 age group (about 2 percent of those affected). Between ages 60 and 79, the incidence increases to around 6 percent. After age 80, the figure is around 13 percent of the population (Rosamond et al., 2008). A **stroke** occurs when blood circulation to the brain fails, and hypertension is the leading risk factor. Brain cells can die from decreased blood flow and lack of oxygen, and both blockage and bleeding can be involved. Stroke is the third leading killer of Americans and is the most common cause of disability, but between 1994 and 2004, the stroke death rate fell by nearly 25 percent (Rosamond et al., 2008). Each year about 600,000 Americans have a stroke for the first time (Kung et al., 2008).

In addition to high blood pressure, other risk factors for stroke are cigarette smoking, heart disease, physical inactivity, family history of stroke, and diabetes. Higher rates of hypertension and diabetes in the African American population have been linked to increased risk of stroke. Sickle-cell anemia, a disease that affects blacks, is also linked to risk of stroke (Rosamond et al., 2008). Women are more vulnerable to stroke than men. Although women and men present the same symptoms, such as *sudden* numbness or weakness on one side of the body, confusion or trouble speaking, trouble walking, or severe headache with no known cause, women present unique symptoms. These include the *sudden* appearance of the following: face and limb pain, hiccups, nausea, general weaknesss, chest

pain, shortness of breath, and heart palpitations (National Stroke Association, 2008). Certain lifestyle changes decrease the risk of stroke; these include engaging in more physical activity, abstaining from smoking, lowering one's body mass index (BMI), and eating a healthy diet (American Heart Association, 2008a). The effects of this brain disorder will be discussed in more detail in Chapter 17.

Parkinson's disease belongs to a group of neurological disorders that result from the loss of brain cells that produce the neurotransmitter *dopamine*. About 50,000 Americans are diagnosed with Parkinson's disease each year. Parkinson's affects more men than women, and it knows no social, economic, or geographic boundaries. A small percentage of adults under age 50 are affected, but the average age of onset is about age 60. The primary symptoms are tremors or trembling in hands, arms, legs, jaw, and face; rigidity or stiffness of limbs and trunk; slowness of movement; and impaired balance and coordination. There is no cure at this time for Parkinson's, but a variety of medications can increase dopamine levels and provide some relief (National Institute of Neurological Disorder and Stroke, 2011). We discuss this disorder further in Chapter 17.

The National Institutes of Health reports that it is likely that more than 5 million adults of middle age and older have disabling cognitive impairments, but early-onset *Alzheimer's disease* (*AD*) is the most common dementia disorder diagnosed after age 65. Getting a diagnosis of Alzheimer's at middle age is very difficult, and it is common for a person to lose a job and subsequent income because of this disorder and yet be too young for Social Security or Medicare benefits to cover medical costs or long-term care costs. AD begins slowly, and at first the only symptom may be mild forgetfulness (National Institute on Aging, 2010). Minimal memory loss is also a symptom of the complex hormonal changes that women experience during menopause, and many middle-aged women fear that they are developing Alzheimer's when they find themselves forgetting things. This serious form of dementia, memory loss, and cognitive decline is addressed in more detail in Chapter 17.

Brain activity is also slowed down by long-term *abuse of alcohol* (a depressant), which affects alertness, judgment, coordination, and reaction time. It also weakens the immune system, slows healing, impairs bone formation, and hinders recovery from surgery (Jung et al., 2010). Alcohol consumption increases the risk of accidents, injury, and fatality. Research has shown that it takes less alcohol to affect older people than younger ones. An older body cannot absorb or dispose of alcohol or other medications as easily as a younger body (National Council on the Aging, 2003). Over time, heavy drinking damages the brain and central nervous system, as well as the liver, heart, kidneys, and stomach. Alcohol is especially harmful (and may even be fatal) when mixed with prescription or over-the-counter

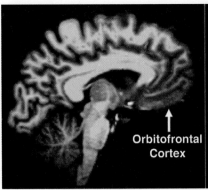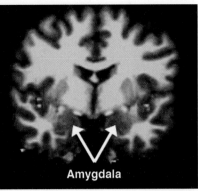

Personality Traits and Changes in Brain Matter Volume in Prefrontal Cortex and Amygdala The orbitofrontal cortex is involved in social-emotional processing, and the amygdala is also involved in social-emotional processing and conscientiousness.
Source: Jackson, J., Balota, D. A., & Head, D. (2009). Exploring the relationship between personality and regional brain volume in healthy aging. *Neurobiology of Aging* (2009, December 23). doi:10.1016/j.neurobiolaging.2009.12.009

Orbitofrontal Cortex

Amygdala

medications. Some people develop an alcohol problem later in life because of situational factors, such as a job layoff, forced retirement, failing health, loss of a spouse, or loss of friends and other loved ones. Signs of alcohol abuse include mood swings and memory lapses, which are often mistakenly attributed to normal aging. Once a person decides to seek help, there are many treatment avenues available to help change this brain-destroying behavior. Interestingly, *The Zutphen Elderly Study* (a longitudinal study begun in 1985 on lifestyle, chronic diseases, and health with aging men from various countries) revealed that "long-term, *light alcohol intake* [(half a glass or 1.5 ounces of red wine)] among middle-aged men was associated not only with lower cardiovascular and all-cause death risk, but also with longer life expectancy at age 50" (Streppel, Ocke, Boshuizen, Kok, & Kromhout, 2009).

> **Question**
>
> What are some cancers, cardiovascular problems, and brain disorders that may be associated with aging, and why are they so life-threatening?

Stress and Depression

Midlife is associated with change, adaptation, and efforts to maintain one's health and well-being. Typically children leave home, elderly parents move in or need more care, divorce or remarriage is possible, as well as a change of jobs, retirement, relocation, adult children returning home with grandchildren, and so on. Midlife is also associated with losses—forced early retirement, traditional retirement, physical changes or health decline, death of a spouse, parents' loss of physical well-being or death, more responsibility for aging parents, sale of a long-term residence to move into a smaller home, and so forth. Samuels (1997) reports in *Midlife Crisis: Helping Patients Cope with Stress, Anxiety, and Depression* that depression and substance abuse are common, but often not recognized and undertreated, in middle-aged adults. Major depression in midlife is common and is associated with increased mortality or suicide, even after controlling for physical illness

and disability. Dr. Samuels recommends that physicians pay attention to change and loss in a person's life, because these may be serious predictors of depression, and suggests using a rating scale (such as the Social Readjustment Rating Scale found in Chapter 13) to assess such patients for depression during a checkup, because of increased suicide risk, particularly in adult males.

Another common factor that can affect memory and can cause mood disorders, falling, fainting, or worse is the misuse or overuse of prescription drugs or failure to follow instructions about the use of prescribed drugs, especially in the case of *polypharmacy,* or the use of multiple drugs (Liu, 2007). People with mood disorders are likely to self-medicate with alcohol or other substances. An analysis of the adult's history, a full physical, and assessment of neurological and mental status can help determine whether a patient is suffering from multiple stressors and depression. An individualized treatment regimen should be established, which might include changes in lifestyle and/or the prescription of antidepressant medications. The goal is to give the patient a renewed sense of control, to eliminate stressors, and to develop coping strategies for those that cannot be eliminated. Depression is a treatable illness, and many organizations provide support and educational materials for midlife patients faced with complex problems (Haber, 2007).

Research suggests a U-shaped curve with respect to rates of depression in adulthood. High rates occur in young adulthood and then again in later life. This distribution is found to hold for black as well as white Americans. It is important to point out, however, that the majority of research on depression in adulthood is cross-sectional in nature. This method is not well suited to explaining age-related or generational differences because it confounds the effects of aging and cohort (Paludi, 2002).

Sexual Functioning

Ground-breaking research on human sexuality by Masters and Johnson (1966) revealed that sexual activity does not end as humans age and that healthy men and women might function sexually into their eighties and beyond. Recent research analysis of two cross-sectional,

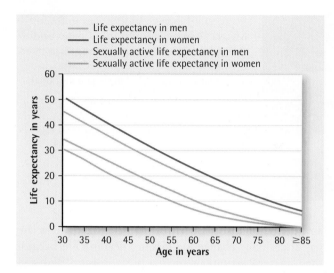

FIGURE 15.4 Life Expectancy and Sexually Active Life Expectancy in U.S. Men and Women Throughout the lifespan, men appear to be more interested in sex than women and have a greater availability of partners. But frequency of sexual activity, a good-quality sex life, and interest in sex are positively associated with health in middle age and late life for both women and men. Based on data from the National Survey of Midlife Development in the United States (MIDUS).
Source: Lindau, S. T., & Gavrilova, N. (2010). Sex, health, and years of sexually active life gained due to good health: Evidence from two U.S. population-based cross sectional surveys of ageing. *BMJ, 340,* 810. doi: 10.1136/bmj.c810

U.S. representative samples of 3,000 adults each (one sample was aged 25 to 74, the other aged 57 to 85) reaffirms that many middle-aged and older adults are sexually active, but they become less active with increasing age, illness, or loss of a spouse (see Figure 15.4) (Lindau & Gavrilova, 2010). The results indicate that men are more interested in sex than women, are more likely to be sexually active, and are more likely to report a good sex life. Middle-aged and older women in these samples were more likely to be widowed or living alone, were less likely to be in an intimate relationship, and reported less sexual activity than men. "Physical health is significantly correlated with sexual activity and many aspects of sexual function" (Lindau & Gavrilova, 2010, p. 1). Although aging takes its toll, it need not eliminate sexual desire or bar its fulfillment. However, less is known about the sexual health of aging homosexual, bisexual, or intersexed aging adults.

In far too many cases, older people accept the social myth of their sexlessness. Believing they will lose their sexual effectiveness becomes a self-fulfilling prophecy. The belief that they are sexless may be reinforced in some men when they are unable to attain or maintain an erection during a number of sexual attempts. This is a common occurrence among men of any age group and can be caused by stress, illness, or overindulgence in alcohol or prescribed medications. Indeed, fear of failure is not uncommon among older men. Often, a woman is unaware of her partner's

fears, and she mistakes his caution for lack of interest. Only a small percentage of males or females ever discuss any sexual difficulties with a physician (Lindau et al., 2007).

Changes nonetheless do occur with age. Generally, men over 60 find that it takes longer for them to achieve an erection, and the erection is generally not as firm or full as when they were younger; maximum erection is achieved only just before orgasm. With advancing age comes a reduction in the production of sperm and seminal fluid, in the number of orgasmic contractions, and in the force of the ejaculation. And the frequency of sexual activity typically declines with advancing age. In a recent large-scale, cross-cultural study of nearly 28,000 men aged 20 to 75 from Europe, North America, and South America, about 16 percent of men self-reported having erectile dysfunction (ED) with advancing age, diabetes, or depression. While more than half with ED had sought medical attention, only a small percentage reported continuing their use of oral therapy (Rosen et al., 2004). Notably, if men have maintained elevated levels of sexual activity from their earlier years, and if ill health does not intervene, they are able to continue some form of active sexual expression into advanced age.

Physicians find that some medical problems in men or women manifest themselves sexually and affect interest, arousal, orgasm, pain, or satisfaction. Some medical problems, such as *Peyronie's disease*, affect male sexual performance; this scarring of the tissue inside the shaft of the penis is more common in men who have diabetes or high blood pressure. Psychological depression is also associated with a decrease in sexual desire. Medications for heart disease, high blood pressure, and coronary artery disease also affect performance by reducing the flow of blood into the pelvic area. In older men the result is often impotence; then medications such as *Viagra* may be prescribed.

Menopause or advancing age should not interfere with a woman's sexual capacity, performance, or drive. Older women tend to lubricate more slowly than they did earlier in life, and the vaginal walls become thinner, but a gentle partner and the use of vaginal lubricants can do much to minimize discomfort. The increase in blood flow to the vagina during arousal diminishes with age (Crooks & Baur, 2008). Midlife women may also need longer stimulation to reach orgasm, but orgasm remains very important to them as part of sex. Like aging men, older women typically have fewer orgasmic contractions.

Freed, after menopause, from worries about becoming pregnant, some women embrace their sexuality enthusiastically, including taking the initiative. The timing of sexual response may be a factor; as men's sexual response slows down, the love-making slows down, giving women a better chance of reaching orgasm. Women who were sexually active at a younger age are more likely to have fulfilling sex lives after menopause (Hunter, Sundel, & Sundel, 2002).

Learning about how prevalence of sexual activity varies with age and other factors helps professionals to understand and combat the epidemic of sexually transmitted infections, including HIV/AIDS, and to understand other quality-of-life issues associated with aging. The *MIDUS Survey* (the longitudinal Mid-Life in the U.S. National Study of Americans sponsored by the National Institute on Aging), asked a number of questions about sexual behavior of more than 6,000 adults aged 25 to 85 from the mid-1990s to the mid-2000s (Lindau & Gavrilova, 2010). The results enable us to understand how sexual behavior changes over time with aging (see Figure 15.4). Results reveal gender differences at midlife and later ages: Men are more likely than women to be sexually active. However, very good to excellent health increased the likelihood of interest in sex, frequency of sexual activity, and a high-quality sex life for both women and men in midlife (Lindau & Gavrilova, 2010).

Various studies report marital infidelity occurring in about 20 to 25 percent of marriages, with infidelity being the main reason cited for divorce. Infidelity is associated with "anguish, depression, fury, and humiliation . . . and with major depression and anxiety" (Brand, Markey, Mills, & Hodges, 2007). Infidelity may occur because of sexual or emotional dissatisfaction in the primary relationship, and men are more likely than women to engage in acts of infidelity. Today's researchers are also investigating romantic (or nonsexual) infidelity in the age of Internet dating (Underwood & Findlay, 2004). Although some such couples eventually arrive at a comfortable level of forgiveness, often after therapy, other couples do not (Hall & Fincham, 2005).

Midlife Men and Women at Risk for HIV/AIDS

New diagnoses of HIV/AIDS continue to rise for adults age 50 and older in the U.S. population. In 2005 they made up 24 percent of those living with HIV/AIDS and 15 percent of new cases. Adults diagnosed with HIV/AIDS are living longer with modern antiretroviral therapies, and by 2015, more than half of HIV-positive Americans will be over 50 (Yale University, 2010). The diagnosis may be missed in an aging adult because HIV/AIDS symptoms are similar to those of normal aging—for example, depression, fatigue, weight loss, and mental confusion. The disease is hitting the black community particularly hard. Although blacks account for about 13 percent of the general population, they account for about half of all new cases (Laurencin, Christensen, & Taylor, 2008). Blacks with HIV/AIDS do not live as long as whites; because of poverty, lack of health insurance, and less access to health care, they often seek treatment later. Members of this group who are unaware of their partners' risk factors, who have other STIs, and who live in

poverty are at higher risk of contracting HIV/AIDS (Laurencin, Christensen, & Taylor, 2008). Homophobia and stigma cause many black men who have sex with men to conceal their sexual behavior from female partners. According to findings in the ROAH study (Research on Older Adults with HIV), adults in middle age or older fear disclosing their HIV status to family and loved ones—thus nondisclosure is common (Karpiak, Shippy, & Cantor, 2006).

Today the group most severely and disproportionately affected by this epidemic continues to be gay and bisexual men of all races (National Center for HIV/AIDS, Viral Hepatitis, STD, and TB Prevention, 2009). But as the disease has spread to the heterosexual population, women have come to account for more than one-fourth of new cases each year. They are now a focus of research and education. For women in all ethnic-racial groups, the disease is transmitted most often through unprotected sex with men, and only a small percentage of midlife women report using condoms. Some women cannot convince male partners to use condoms and are afraid to push the issue for fear that their partner will physically abuse or leave them (Centers for Disease Control, 2010b). The CDC now recommends routine testing for HIV/AIDS for all persons up to age 64 and extensive public education for an aging population.

Risk Factors   An extensive body of research links child sexual abuse and risk for HIV infection. Various studies find that between 30 and 40 percent of American women were sexually abused as children—but most child sex abuse is not reported (Wyatt et al., 2002). For these women, a history of sexual abuse, physical abuse, and/or domestic abuse is highly correlated with engaging in behaviors that put them at high risk for HIV infection: use of intravenous drugs, exchange of sex for drugs, paying money for shelter, multiple sexual partners, and having sex with a person at high risk for HIV. Another risk factor is adolescent or adult sexual assault. A review of 149 studies of child sexual abuse revealed that ethnic-minority boys under age 13 and living in poor circumstances were at highest risk—especially if the father did not reside in the home (Holmes & Slap, 1998). This sad association illustrates one of the many lifetime effects and externalizing behaviors that can result from child sexual abuse.

Living with HIV/AIDS and Aging   In the mid-1990s, highly active antiretroviral therapy (HAART) was introduced for people with HIV/AIDS, and suddenly HIV/AIDS was no longer a quick death sentence. Living longer with HIV/AIDS became the focus. Now the population of people over 50 who have lived with HIV/AIDS for over a decade is growing, and a broad constellation of medical problems is emerging for them and their medical providers (see Figure 15.5). Many in this age group are no longer

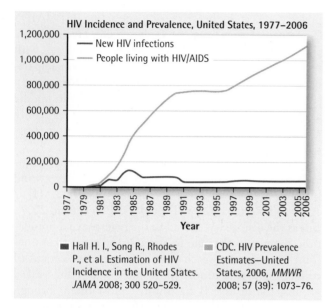

FIGURE 15.5 HIV/AIDS Patients Are Living Longer with HIV The number of people 50 and older living with HIV in the United States increased 77 percent from 2001 to 2006. Members of this age group now represent one-quarter of all people living with HIV/AIDS. The lower line on the graph represents U.S. citizens newly diagnosed with HIV infections.
Source: Centers for Disease Control and Prevention. (2011). HIV and AIDS in the United States. Retrieved from http://www.cdc.gov/hiv/topics/surveillance/resources/factsheets/us_media.htm

working. They are unemployed, on disability, or retired, and many do not have enough income to meet their medical expenses. Many have few people to turn to for emotional support, even though family members are still alive. Many choose not to disclose their condition because they are likely to experience greater stigma than a younger person. The majority suffer depression due to their poor health and financial problems (Karpiak, Shippy, & Cantor, 2006).

Higher rates of arthritis, hepatitis, cognitive decline, and hypertension occur among people who have lived with HIV/AIDS for a long time. Severe osteoporosis is also more common, as is the need for hip replacements among these midlife men. In short, people who live with HIV/AIDS age much more rapidly; they function at lower levels than their own fathers in their eighties. Researchers do not know whether this happens because of the antiretroviral medication or because of HIV/AIDS itself, but as hundreds of thousands of survivors of HIV/AIDS reach middle age, the health-care system, the social services, and funding for Medicaid and Medicare will have to adapt to find ways to meet their needs (Karpiak, Shippy, & Cantor, 2006).

Gay, Lesbian, and Bisexual Health Care at Midlife
Middle-aged gays, lesbians, and bisexuals have known discrimination for most of their lives. Although the social climate and legal context have changed in a positive direction for this population in the past 20 years, there are still gaps in the public's knowledge—and even in that of

professional groups. This issue often emerges when a gay or lesbian adult visits a health-care provider. Health providers may be unaware of the particular psychological and physical needs of homosexual patients and thus fail to discuss issues related to identity and sexuality—especially for patients over age 50 (Brotman, Ryan, & Myer, 2006).

As gays, lesbians, and bisexuals enter middle age and retire, they experience relief that they are no longer at risk of losing a job or pension because of their sexual orientation. The psychological and medical needs of lesbians are not a part of the purview of most medical practices. The lesbian patient may appear isolated to her health-care providers because she seems to have no spouse or family to help her through her illness. In reality, she may have a long-term partner and a large extended "family of choice" that knows and cares for her. That is, she is more likely than heterosexuals in her age group to have a circle of close friends that provide support during any long-term or chronic illness.

Health-care providers might need to know the gender of a patient's partner, but some patients have a compelling need to conceal that information. Confidentiality is paramount in such situations. A lesbian with breast cancer may be reluctant to reveal her sexual orientation to health-care providers (Cantor, Brennan, & Shippy, 2004). This deprives the health-care providers of information they need to offer the most effective medical care. Significantly, gays and lesbians entering middle age want to have their partner with them while they are hospitalized, not only for emotional support but also to be a health-care proxy on their behalf if they are incapacitated. Yet most U.S. hospitals have a standard practice of recognizing only immediate biological or legally married family members for health decisions. As civil unions and same-sex marriages become more widely accepted, health-care providers can legally honor the committed-couple visitation rights and the right to know important medical information (Harris & Kliks Fones, 2008).

Questions

What does research say in general about sexual performance and sexual health among middle-aged adults? Why is HIV/AIDS increasing among the middle-aged? What are some of the factors that prevent same-sex couples from having open, honest communication with health-care professionals about their health issues?

COGNITIVE FUNCTIONING

As noted earlier in this chapter, as people age, they change physically in several different ways. Some physical changes, such as graying hair and facial wrinkles, are obvious and can be quickly verified in a nearby mirror. But what about cognitive abilities and brain functions?

Do parallel changes occur in aging adults' intellectual facilities as well? And if so, how? Research studies designed to answer this question have yielded mixed results: yes, no, and it depends.

Research Findings: A Methodological Problem

Most of the data on age-related cognitive differences are based on IQ scores and have been tabulated using a *cross-sectional research* method. Results of studies that have employed the cross-sectional method indicate that overall composite IQ reaches a peak for most people when they are in their twenties, remains stable for a couple of decades, and then drops more dramatically after age 60 (Schaie, 1996; Salthouse, 2009). Remember from Chapter 1 that cross-sectional studies employ the "snapshot" approach. Researchers administer tests of intelligence to a large group of individuals of different ages at about the same time and compare their performance. Thus, a major weakness of cross-sectional studies is that "uncertainty regarding comparability" is always a problem. That is, we can never be sure that the reported age-related differences between subjects are not the product of other variables or events. For example, people in their fifties might have a lower average score than those in their twenties not because of their age difference, but simply because they have less experience taking standardized tests. Also, many of today's midlife adults are completing college at this stage of life, so they differ greatly from the post–high school cohort that is represented by higher numbers of students in college. And for decades American women were underrepresented in college, but now they constitute the majority. Moreover, women over age 40 make up more than 60 percent of today's nontraditional college students with families (U.S. Department of Education, 2009).

As psychologist Schaie (1996) and Salthouse (2009) have pointed out, cross-sectional studies of adult aging do not allow for generational differences in performance on intelligence tests. Because of increasing educational opportunities and other social changes, successive generations of Americans perform at progressively higher levels. Hence, the measured intelligence (IQ) of the population is increasing. To compare adults from different generations—80-year-olds with 40-year-olds, for instance—is to compare people from vastly different environments. Thus, cross-sectional studies tend to confuse generational differences with differences associated with chronological age.

Using the *longitudinal research method,* researchers study the same individuals over a period of years, as in a case history. When this technique is used, the results are quite different: Overall IQ, or global IQ, tends to rise until the mid-fifties and then gradually declines (Salthouse, 2009). However, the longitudinal method also presents a problem for the researcher. Whereas the cross-sectional method tends to magnify, or overestimate, the decline in

intelligence with age, the longitudinal method tends to minimize, or underestimate, it. One reason is that some people drop out of the study over time; the probability is higher that the eldest will die over the course of a 10-year study. Generally, the more able, healthy, and intelligent subjects remain in the study, and those who perform poorly on intelligence tests tend to be less available for longitudinal retesting. Consequently, the researchers are left with an increasingly smaller, or biased, sample as the subjects are retested at each later period. Furthermore, a recent study of longitudinal analyses found that in adults between 18 and 60 years of age, a period of at least 7 years was needed between cognitive tests to compensate for the effects of retesting—that is, the positive effects of learning from the test itself (Salthouse, 2009).

> ### Questions
>
> What are the problems with cross-sectional and longitudinal research on intelligence conducted with subjects over the life span? What does each type of research tend to reveal?

The Varied Courses of Cognitive Abilities

As we saw in Chapter 7, intelligence is not a unitary concept in the same sense in which a chemical compound is a single entity. People do not have intelligence as such but, rather, *intelligences.* Thus, different abilities can follow quite different courses as a person grows older and learns from experiences in his or her environment (Gardner, 2006b). There are several major theories about what intelligence is and where it comes from: Binet's view of a general intelligence (g) that is inherited from parents and can be measured by IQ testing; Piaget's progressive stages of increasing reasoning from infancy to adult, culminating in formal operational thought; Gardner's information-processing view that individuals vary in several capacities that he calls multiple intelligences (verbal, mathematical, art, music, kinesthetic, etc.); and other theories. Traditional measures of intelligence focus on abilities that are useful in academic environments. For instance, tests that measure *verbal* abilities (defining a series of words, solving arithmetic word problems) tend to show little or no decline after the age of 60, whereas those that measure *performance* (the ability to perform a physical task, such as assembling a puzzle or filling in symbols to correspond to numbers) do seem to show a decline (Schaie, 1996).

Fluid Versus Crystallized Intelligence   Some psychologists distinguish between **fluid intelligence** (the ability to make original adaptations in novel situations) and **crystallized intelligence** (the abilities learned from education, experience, and acculturation) (Cattell, 1943, 1971). Fluid intelligence (Birney & Sternberg, 2006) is generally tested by measuring an individual's facility in abstract reasoning,

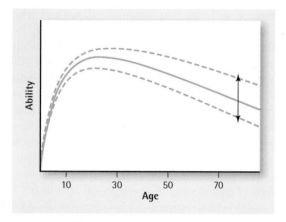

FIGURE 15.6 Cognitive Abilities and Aging Early researchers on intelligence posited that intelligence is fixed early in life. Yet psychometric studies with 1,200 participants across the life span revealed this variation in pattern in the ability-age relationship: Cognitive abilities become increasingly differentiated with age.
Source: Birney, D. P., & Sternberg, R. J. (2006). Intelligence and cognitive abilities as competencies in development. In E. Bialystok & F. I. M. Craik (Eds.), *Lifespan cognition: Mechanisms of change* (pp. 315–330). New York: Oxford University Press.

often by means of nonword materials (matrices, mazes, block designs, and picture arrangements). Presumably, fluid intelligence is "culture-free" and based on the individual's genetic and neurological structures. Crystallized intelligence is commonly measured by achievement testing, which assesses an individual's awareness of concepts and vocabulary terms in areas such as science, mathematics, social studies, and English literature. Crystallized intelligence is acquired in the course of one's formal educational and social experience. Often crystallized intelligence increases with age, and it does not normally decline until one's sixties or seventies, whereas fluid intelligence declines with age (Birney & Sternberg, 2006). However, with age, cognitive abilities become increasingly differentiated (see Figure 15.6).

In the earliest published account of the theory, Cattell (1943) argued that fluid ability is "a purely general ability to discriminate and perceive relations between any fundamentals, new or old." Cattell hypothesized that fluid ability would increase until adolescence and then slowly decline. Further, fluid intelligence was thought to be the cause of the general (*g*) factor found among ability tests administered to children and among the "speeded or adaptation-requiring" tests administered to adults. Crystallized intelligence, on the other hand, was thought to increase with age (the older you get, the more likely you are to know "things" from education and experience) (Cattell, 1987).

So, does intelligence really decline with age, or do certain kinds of abilities decline? When the data are gathered and examined within a framework of fluid versus crystallized intelligence, the answer is yes and no. It depends on how you define intelligence. In the *Seattle*

Longitudinal Study, which tested the mental abilities of more than 5,000 adults over a period of 35 years, results clearly showed no uniform patterns of age-related changes across all intellectual abilities (Schaie, 1996). The majority of participants showed no statistically significant reduction in most abilities until after age 60, and even beyond that time, they showed declines only in certain abilities. The only tests on which ability declined with age were related to *speed of performance.* It was found that fluid intelligence tended to decrease in young adulthood, but these deficits were offset by crystallized abilities, which remained stable or increased into middle age, followed by slight declines (Schaie, 1996). Older students returning to college often do very well academically because of their crystallized intelligence—translating theory into practice by drawing on their life experiences.

Maximizing Cognitive Abilities

Exceptional performance among healthy adults is being studied more extensively by researchers. In the last several years, interest in exceptional achievement and performance has proliferated, and differing approaches are being employed to explore the behavior of expert performers (Birney & Sternberg, 2006). One approach, studying the individual characteristics of exceptional performers, has been spearheaded by Howard Gardner, whose work on multiple intelligences was discussed in Chapter 7. Gardner contends that the importance of multiple intelligences does not decline as a person ages but, rather, that these intelligences become more internalized and less visible (Gardner, 2006b). Gardner proposes that exceptional performance in later life is dependent on early identification of talent and nurturing of that talent through regular practice over long periods of time (Gardner, 2006a). Many of Gardner's research findings are based on advances in brain physiology and on the achievements of savants, prodigies, and geniuses in specific domains. The important aspect of talent, according to Gardner (2006b), is not the innate ability of the individual but the capacity to learn material relevant to one of the nine intelligences. Gardner believes that in order to persist throughout life, innate intellectual abilities must be practiced regularly and over long periods of time. Acquiring expertise takes a great deal of time, but what it takes to be an "expert" is constantly evolving. For example, what an expert such as Piaget knew about cognition in 1950 is very limited compared to what a neuroscientist or geneticist knows about cognition today (Keil, 2006).

Maintaining Expert Performance Many elite or expert performers in most domains are engaged in their domain of expertise essentially full-time from childhood to late adulthood. For example, millions of people are active in sports, music, visual arts, and chess, but only a small number reach the highest levels of performance—these are distinguished by the amount of time they commit to practicing their skill and by the duration of time over which they make this effort.

Performers rarely reach their optimal performance before adulthood, but performance does not necessarily continue to improve in those who keep exercising their skills across the life span. Rather, as Leman (1953) first noted, peak ages for performance seem to fall in the twenties, thirties, and forties. In vigorous sports, such as professional basketball, it is rare for elite athletes to reach their personal best above age 30. Michael Jordan, Cal Ripken, and Lance Armstrong are noted exceptions to this rule. Similar age distributions, centered on age 30, are also found for fine motor skills and some cognitive activities (Buckner, Head, & Lustig, 2006). Typically the probability of producing an outstanding work declines with age. However, in novel writing, history, and philosophy, the optimal ages are in the forties and fifties. One common hypothesis on aging and expertise is that experts generally age more slowly than other performers. Research on expert performance has shown this not to be the case in chess (Charness & Gerchak, 1996), typing (Bosman, 1993), and music (Krampe, 1994). The superior performance of older experts is found to be restricted to relevant tasks in their preferred domains of expertise.

The Role of Deliberate Practice   The most marked age-related decline is generally observed in perceptual-motor performance as displayed in different sports. High levels of practice are necessary to attain the physical readiness found in mature performers, and the effects of practice appear to be particularly large when intense practice overlaps with physical development during childhood and adolescence. Most of these adaptations require that practice be maintained. When older master athletes are compared with young athletes at a similar level, many physiological measurements do not differ between them. However, at least some physiological functions, such as maximum heart rate, show an age-related decline independent of past or current practice. The ability to retain superior performance in some domains appears to depend critically on maintaining practice during adulthood and into old age (Ericsson, 2005). Expert performance continues to improve well into the adult years, typically reaching its peak between the ages of 30 and 50 (Ericsson, 2005). Yet some abilities, such as the acquisition of a second language, especially accents and pronunciation, appear easier to acquire at young rather than adult ages.

The traditional view of talent, which concludes that successful individuals have special innate biological or cognitive abilities, is not consistent with the reviewed evidence. Efforts to specify and measure characteristics of talent that allow early identification and successful prediction of adult performance have failed. Differences between expert and less-accomplished performers reflect acquired knowledge and skills or physiological adaptations developed through training and deliberate practice (Ericsson, 2005). Thus, expertise in human performance is not limited to traditional domains, such as sports. Through systematic practice and training, similar changes can be expected in other domains, such as thinking, problem solving, and communication. As a matter of fact, Gardner (2006a) has proposed that five essential lifetime cognitive abilities can be taught: discipline, creativity, respect, ethics, and synthesis of ideas. What it takes is desire, practice, and commitment, whether in a sport, such as tennis, or in an academic pursuit, such as taking a computer science course in a college continuing-education program. The optimal course of action is achieved, and is maintained longer, when adults continue to stay physically, mentally, and socially active (Knowlton, 2005).

Cognition and Dialectical Thinking

If we look at cognition instead of intelligence, we see that a slightly different debate has emerged over the years concerning the existence of post–formal operations. Recall that Piaget maintained that cognitive development stops during the late teens with what he called formal operations, or abstract reasoning. Critics assert that the thought processes of adults are qualitatively different from the logical problem-solving characteristics upon which Piaget focused. These post–formal operations enable adults to enter the realm of dialectical thought, which does not insist on a single correct answer to any given problem or dilemma but, rather, seeks complex and changing understandings of the processes or elements involved in the problem.

One proponent of **dialectical thinking** sums it up this way: Dialectical thinking is an organized approach to analyzing and making sense of the world one experiences; thus it differs fundamentally from formal analysis. The latter involves the effort to find fundamental fixed realities—basic elements and immutable laws. The former attempts to describe the fundamental process of change and the dynamic relationship through which the change occurs (Basseches, 1980). One example of post–formal thought is understanding that a family quarrel might be nobody's "fault" and that the solution does not involve one of the parties "giving in" or changing her or his view of the situation. Instead, the dialectical approach consists of understanding the merits of different or opposing points of view and looks at the possibility of integrating them into a workable solution. This dialectical approach to problem solving is apparent when you think of situations where you have been on both sides of the same issue—for example, being a child arguing with your parents, and then being a parent arguing with your child. One reason why post–formal operations are attributed to older individuals is that life experience is probably necessary to see the "bigger" picture. Schaie has proposed a four-stage model of cognitive development that is quite different from Piaget's in that it covers the entire life span and is not confined to preadulthood. Schaie's (1994) four stages are as follows:

1. *Acquisitive stage.* What should I know? (childhood-adolescence)
2. *Achieving stage.* How should I use what I know in career and love? (young adult)
3. *Responsible/executive stage.* How should I use my knowledge in social and family responsibilities? (middle adulthood)
4. *Reintegrative stage.* What should I know? (old age)

In Stage 4 the acquisition of information is guided by one's interests, attitudes, and values. An older adult is willing to expend effort on a problem she or he faces in everyday life.

This interest in problem solving might shed light on another aspect of cognition—creativity. J. P. Guilford (1967) distinguished two sorts of thinking—convergent and divergent. **Convergent thinking** is very much like formal operations—the application of logic and reasoning to arrive at a single correct answer to a problem. **Divergent thinking** is more open-ended, and multiple solutions are sought, examined, and probed, thereby leading to what are deemed creative responses on measures of creativity. A creative person not only solves problems but also sees problems that others have not yet recognized. Creativity seems to demand imagination, motivation, and a supportive environment—characteristics that often do not gel for the individual until middle or late adulthood, when the peak period of creative productivity occurs (Lindauer, 2003). The major problem with assessing creativity is the difficulty in defining criteria that capture creativity as well as originality, utility, and productivity. The history of science and art indicates that Michelangelo, Verdi, Goethe, Picasso, and Monet created highly original work throughout the life span. From a positive psychological perspective, creativity results in "flow": "the state in which people are so involved in an activity that nothing else seems to matter: the experience itself is so enjoyable that people will do it at great cost, for the sheer sake of doing it" (Nakamura & Csikszentmihalyi, 2002). During such "flow" experiences, people become so absorbed in an activity that they disregard distracting concerns such as their personal life, material gain, security, or personal advancement. Think of artists working away day and night, going without food or sleep in order to finish a masterpiece. It is almost as if they are possessed by the activity, unable to see beyond or outside of it.

Midlife and Creativity Midlife can be a creative period as a lifetime of knowledge and expertise come together. Artists at midlife are often able to produce pieces that speak to audiences in a universal language. Sculptor Penelope Jencks was middle-aged when she produced the well-known eight-foot bronze sculpture of Eleanor Roosevelt (herself depicted in midlife) that stands at the entrance to Riverside Park in New York City.

Questions

How do cognitive processes commonly change in midlife? How can middle-aged adults maximize their cognitive abilities?

MORAL COMMITMENTS

Moral development in certain individuals leads to something akin to flow: They become committed to doing "good" activities to the extent that, like saints, they have "dedicated the totality of their psychic energy to an all-encompassing goal [which they] follow unto death" (Csikszentmihalyi, 1997). Two of Lawrence Kohlberg's colleagues set out to find individuals dedicated to acts of morality whom they designated as **moral exemplars** (Colby & Damon, 1992). After an extensive search throughout the United States, they found 23 people who demonstrated all of the following characteristics:

- a sustained commitment to moral ideals that include respect for humanity
- consistency between ideals and actions

- a willingness to risk one's self-interest for the sake of one's moral values
- being an inspirational force for others, who then became active in moral work
- humility about one's work and importance, little concern with ego

Most of the moral exemplars were in their forties, fifties, and sixties, and they were a diverse collection of individuals. Five of the exemplars were chosen to be interviewed in depth to discover what motivates a moral exemplar. Of these five, two did not finish high school, one had a bit of college, one finished college, and one had a PhD; all were religious; politically they were conservative, moderate, or liberal; and vocationally they were a minister, a businessperson, an innkeeper, a civil rights advocate, and a charity worker.

While interviewing these exemplars, Colby and Damon found that they showed enormous ability to critically examine old habits and assumptions and adopt new strategies for dealing with problems; and they constantly took up new and interesting challenges while maintaining a lasting dedication to their particular values, goals, and moral projects. This amounted to the ability to remain morally stable without becoming cognitively or behaviorally stagnant. Rugeley and Van Wart (2006) also studied "everyday folks" who fit the description of moral exemplars and found the following traits: reflection, fairness, benevolence, professionalism, humility, and sacrifice.

Colby and Damon (1992) found that the Reverend Charleszetta Waddles was one of the exemplars, and through her activities you can get a hint of how moral acts affect people on a day-to-day basis. Mother Waddles, as she liked to be called, ran the Perpetual Mission for Saving Souls of All Nations in Detroit. The mission served 100,000 people a year by offering food, clothing, legal services, tutoring, and emergency assistance, among other services. Her ultimate goals were to lift the poor out of their condition, help them believe in themselves, and encourage them to take full responsibility for their lives. She did whatever was in her power to help anyone who came to her mission, be it a woman who needed money for an eye operation, a young girl who needed advice about her pregnancy, or a man who had lost everything in a fire and had no place to go. Often she used most of her $900 monthly income to pay for these services herself when she was unable to find resources elsewhere. With an eighth-grade education, Mother Waddles ran her mission for 30 years, during which time she also raised 10 children (Colby & Damon, 1992). She died in 2001 at the age of 88.

Judging on the basis of the experiences of Mother Waddles and other exemplars, such as Nelson Mandela of South Africa and Mother Theresa of Calcutta, Walker and Frimer (2007) suggest that it is moral commitment that develops in adulthood, rather than the moral cognition that Kohlberg theorized. They found that most of the exemplars were between the third and fourth stages in Kohlberg's model of moral development (see Chapter 9). In essence, the development of moral commitment results when adults are motivated by what they observe in the society around them to transform their personal goals, especially when they have a "sense of continued openness to change and growth, an openness that is not the usual expectation in most adult lives" (Colby & Damon, 1992). Following up on his body of research on the sense of purpose demonstrated by moral children and moral exemplars, Damon (2008) proposed that today's young adults appear to be adrift in anxiety, apathy, and disengagement despite experiencing a curriculum of "character education" in schools. In his book *Path to Purpose*, Damon (2008) describes why purpose is crucial for thriving throughout life. We will see in Chapter 19 that the impetus for making moral commitments and finding one's purpose in life often comes from religious or spiritual beliefs and from following healthy adult role models.

SEGUE

Significantly, today's baby boomers are looking, acting, and feeling younger at middle age than prior generations did. Indeed, the defining characteristics of middle age are starting later and lasting longer, so age 50 has taken on the connotations that age 40 had only a few decades ago. T-shirts proclaim "50 Never Looked So Good!" Many prominent persons over age 50 continue to lead, inform, or entertain; consider Oprah Winfrey, Bill Gates, Steve Jobs, John Boehner, Paul McCartney, Diane Sawyer, Barbara Walters, Meryl Streep, Tom Brokaw, Harrison Ford, Al Pacino, Jack Nicholson, and the Rolling Stones. Midlife baby boomers are actively revolutionizing cultural attitudes toward the "middle-aged"—in much the same way that the generation of Americans now over 50 initiated sweeping social, political, and cultural changes in the 1960s. In Chapter 16 we will examine the changing self-concept of adults in midlife, as they reevaluate intimate relationships, reestablish life priorities and cope with loss, become grandparents or great-grandparents, shift occupational ventures, or prepare for retirement.

SUMMARY

Redefining Middle Age

1. The boundaries for the age range of midlife have become more fluid than they were a century ago. Some developmentalists suggest that middle age may range from the early forties through the late sixties.

2. By midlife, the body's organs and systems are functioning less efficiently than they did in early adulthood, although the decline is gradual.

Sensory and Physical Changes

3. Many Americans over age 40 experience presbyopia, a normal condition in which the lens of the eye starts to harden, losing its ability to accommodate as quickly as it did in youth.

4. By age 50, about one in every three men and one in every four women have difficulty hearing a whisper. However, only a small number of the age-50 population can be deemed to have substantial hearing problems.

5. By the forties, one may notice a gradual drop in the ability to taste because taste buds are replaced at a slower rate. Half of those who reach the age of 65 are likely to have a noticeable loss of the sense of smell.

6. One of the major concerns of some midlife adults is body composition, or proportion of muscle to fat. Muscle mass declines an average of 5 to 10 percent each decade, generally resulting in more body fat.

7. Maintaining a healthy body weight becomes increasingly important during midlife. For those who are overweight, exercising regularly and losing weight can lower the risk of many diseases.

8. Millions of Americans, largely women, pay for cosmetic procedures each year. The cosmetic surgery industry is largely unregulated, and these elective surgeries carry risks.

9. Women and men begin to lose bone mass at midlife, which can lead to osteoporosis later in life. Weight-bearing exercise and a healthy diet with adequate calcium are beneficial.

10. Menopause is one of the most readily identifiable signs of the female climacteric, which is characterized by changes in the ovaries and in the various hormonal processes associated with these changes.

11. Hormone replacement therapy (HRT) is linked to an increased risk of breast cancer and stroke, among other diseases. It is no longer the treatment of choice for women undergoing menopause. Alternative medical approaches, such as eating more foods with soy and calcium, exercising regularly, getting adequate sleep, and using stress-reduction exercises are recommended.

12. Men's testosterone levels decline at midlife, causing loss of muscle mass, bone mass, and height. A small percentage of men experience a rapid decline in testosterone levels, which produces symptoms that are similar to the symptoms of female menopause. Testosterone replacement therapy for these men is controversial.

13. By age 40, 10 percent of males experience enlargement of the prostate gland, and by age 60, a majority of males are likely to experience prostate problems. A middle-aged male should have regular physical checkups and a PSA test for diagnostic purposes.

Health and Lifestyle

14. Several risk factors are associated with cardiovascular (heart and blood vessel) fitness or disease. Heart disease is the leading cause of death in the United States—especially for women. Risk factors include high blood pressure (hypertension), smoking, high cholesterol, a family history of heart disease, being male, being diabetic, or being obese. After menopause, women are likely to have high blood pressure at the same rate as men. Black Americans and Hispanic Americans have higher rates of heart disease.

15. For women between the ages of 40 and 60, breast cancer is the second leading cause of death, after lung cancer. Ovarian and cervical cancers are also more prevalent during midlife. Colon cancer and lung cancer are other leading causes of death for midlife males and females. Smoking, environmental factors, poverty, and hereditary factors are associated with a higher risk of cancer. Black adults have higher risks for various diseases in midlife.

16. A stroke occurs when blood circulation to the brain fails. Stroke is the third leading killer of Americans and is the most common cause of disability. Women and African Americans are more vulnerable to stroke than white men. Lifestyle changes can reduce the risk of stroke.

17. Women are much more likely than men to become infected by an HIV-positive heterosexual partner. The rate at which middle-aged men and women are becoming HIV-positive is on the rise. Males who have sex with men are at the highest risk of all groups. Blacks account for almost half of all new cases of HIV/AIDS.

18. Brain changes in middle age include loss of gray matter in the prefrontal cortex and the amygdala, which is associated with some memory changes and slower response time. Some adults experience neurotransmitter changes (dopamine) or more severe brain cell loss that results in early-onset Parkinson's disease (affecting motor control) or early-onset Alzheimer's disease (affecting memory and normal adaptive living). Brain researchers suggest that adults stay intellectually active, continue to problem-solve, and use challenging thought processes.

19. Depression and substance abuse are common in middle-aged adults but are often underrecognized and undertreated. Depression in older life is associated with increased mortality (or suicide), even after controlling for physical illness and disability.

20. Far too many older people accept social stereotypes of themselves as sexless; they can become victims of this myth. Most middle-aged men and women are still sexually active, and healthy men and women are interested for many more years. Women who are single or widowed and unhealthy adults are less likely to have an active sex life.

21. Gays, lesbians, and bisexuals are often reluctant to seek health care or to be open with health-care providers

about their sexual orientation and practices. And physicians are often reluctant to question patients about sexual health. These attitudes create a barrier to proper health care for this population.

Cognitive Functioning

22. Tests that measure verbal abilities tend to show little or no decline after the age of 60, whereas tests that measure performance do show a decline. Longitudinal research studies show that overall IQ tends to rise until the mid-fifties and then gradually declines.

23. Psychologists distinguish between fluid intelligence (the ability to make original adaptations in novel situations) and crystallized intelligence (abilities learned through education and experience).

24. Midlife adults can maximize their cognitive abilities by practicing them regularly over time. Even experts must be committed to practice in their domains of expertise.

Moral Commitments

25. Some people in middle adulthood have been identified as moral exemplars; they consistently demonstrate sustained commitment to moral ideals that include respect for humanity, self-sacrifice, and doing good for others. One investigator has classified exemplars as having a strong sense of purpose in life.

KEY TERMS

audiology testing *(478)*

basal-cell carcinoma *(479)*

cardiovascular *(487)*

cataracts *(477)*

cholesterol *(490)*

climacteric *(484)*

convergent thinking *(502)*

crystallized intelligence *(499)*

DHEA (dehydroepiandrosterone) *(485)*

dialectical thinking *(501)*

diastolic pressure *(490)*

diuretics *(483)*

divergent thinking *(502)*

dry eye *(477)*

endocrinologist *(484)*

erectile dysfunction *(486)*

floaters *(477)*

fluid intelligence *(499)*

glaucoma *(477)*

hormone replacement therapy (HRT) *(484)*

hypertension *(490)*

macular degeneration (AMD) *(477)*

melanoma *(479)*

menopause *(484)*

moral exemplars *(502)*

osteoarthritis *(483)*

osteoporosis *(483)*

perimenopause *(484)*

periodontal disease *(479)*

postmenopause *(484)*

premature menopause *(484)*

presbycusis *(478)*

presbyopia *(476)*

prostate gland *(485)*

prostatitis *(486)*

PSA test *(486)*

rheumatoid arthritis *(483)*

stroke *(494)*

systolic pressure *(490)*

triglycerides *(491)*

FOLLOWING UP ON THE INTERNET

Web sites for this chapter focus on physical and health changes, cognitive functioning, and moral commitments common to those in middle adulthood. Please access the text Web site at www.mhhe.com/crandell10 for up-to-date hot-linked Internet addresses for the following organizations, topics, and resources:

National Institute on Aging
http://www.nia.nih.gov/

National Program on Women & Aging
http://iasp.brandeis.edu/womenandaging/research.htm

Office of Men's Health—CDC
http://www.cdc.gov/men/

Office of Women's Health—CDC
http://www.cdc.gov/women/

Office of Minority Health
http://www.cdc.gov/minorityhealth/index.html

North American Menopause Society
http://www.menopause.org/

Dr. Susan Love's Research Site on Breast Cancer
http://www.dslrf.org/breastcancer/

AIDS Community Initiative of America—*Research on Older Adults with HIV Study*
http://www.acria.org/

AARP Policy and Research
http://www.aarp.org/research/ppi/

International Federation on Aging
http://www.ifa-fiv.org/

16 Middle Adulthood
Emotional and Social Development

Critical Thinking Questions

1. Suppose that each stage of a person's life could be defined in terms of a consuming purpose. That is, suppose that the child's purpose is to play, the adolescent's purpose is to explore, and the young adult's purpose is to settle. What would the middle-aged adult's consuming purpose be?

2. What would you think if your 55-year-old doctor had her or his tongue pierced? Would you judge this person to be acting immaturely?

3. Who do you think is happier in midlife—people who are married with a job and now raising grandchildren, or people who remained single and have the resources and time to do whatever they desire? Why?

4. Suppose that pay were inversely related to job popularity. Would you collect garbage for $150,000 a year or be a surgeon for $47,000 a year? When thinking of a career in this way, which would motivate you more—economic security or job satisfaction?

Transition and adaptation are central features in middle adulthood, perhaps more prominently than in other phases of life. Midlife is a period of looking back and at the same time looking forward. Some of the emotional-social changes of middle age are associated with the family life cycle. Many parents at midlife today enter the "empty nest" period of life, yet some couples at midlife are just beginning their families and are raising young children.

Others are caring for both growing children or grandchildren and elderly parents or grandparents, and we refer to these middle-age adults as the *sandwich generation* (Kohli & Künemund, 2005). There have also been changes in the workplace. Because of advances in technology, international corporate relocations and mergers, and worldwide economic upheaval since 2008, job loss and employment uncertainty confront both white-collar and blue-collar workers. This has had a particularly negative economic impact on black and Hispanic American adults in midlife. Those midlife adults employed in white-collar and professional occupations are reaching the prime time of their careers and are more likely to be engaged in volunteerism and civic activities. Some midlife Americans must summon new inner resources to deal with unemployment, underemployment, forced early retirement, raising grandchildren, declining health, or losing a parent or spouse. In this chapter we examine the changing emotional-social context of middle adulthood from theoretical, individual, social, occupational, and cultural perspectives.

THEORIES OF THE SELF IN TRANSITION

Traditionally, developmental psychologists have focused their attention on the many changes that occur during infancy, childhood, adolescence, and early adulthood. But middle age is now garnering more research attention because the *baby-boom generation* has entered middle age. This huge cohort is commanding many resources from society and is, in turn, changing society itself (Wolff, 2007). Underlying most of this human development research is the notion that each individual has a relatively unique and enduring set of personality traits and reveals them in the course of interacting with others and the environment. Only since the mid-1990s have middle-aged adults been studied to determine how and in what ways they continue to develop, and one of the first and most comprehensive such studies was the MIDUS study (Midlife in the United States) conducted by the Institute on Aging, University of Wisconsin-Madison. Much of the early research on the midlife experience focused on physical-health and cognitive changes in the white, middle-class, male population. It was limited by its use of cross-sectional data across cohorts with different historical contexts and by its focus on clinical populations (those who were experiencing declines in their physical health or having mental-health problems).

Only recently have a few studies investigated the emotional and social development of a diversity of adults in midlife, the period that is often identified as 45 to 65 years old (although some consider midlife to extend from age 40 to age 70). With increasing longevity to the late eighties, nineties, and beyond in the United States, the European Union, Japan, and other nations, many of the life events that used to occur in what was called old age (such as grandparenthood and retirement) now occur during midlife years:

> Now in their fifties, many American men and women are confronted with the fact that there are time limits to their lives. A powerful reminder is the symbolic meaning attached to the number 50. In terms of the life span, age 50 is roughly two-thirds of the way through life, but because 50 marks a half century, the 50th birthday carries a strong symbolic connotation that many men and women see as marking their entry into the "last half of life." . . . They begin counting the number of birthdays left to them rather than how many they have reached. So the fifties become a time for more introspective reflection and stock taking. (Sheehy, 1998)

In recent years a life-span perspective on development has emerged. It views middle adulthood as a period of both continuity and transition in which individuals must adapt to new life situations and make a variety of role transitions—in the family, at work, in the community, and so on. Recent cross-cultural and gender development research shows that individuals take multiple paths during this transitional time before late adulthood (Lachman, 2006). That is why it is more common today to see two 48-year-olds who are at different phases of their life cycle—one a first-time parent and the other a grandparent, or one launching a new career and the other retired. Consequently, Helson (1997, p. 23) says that "middle age has different meanings in different times and places for different individuals." We now examine some multidisciplinary research, some that addresses midlife from a gender perspective, and some that looks at issues of midlife for adults in other cultures. Interestingly enough, we also learn that adults in some societies experience neither a middle adulthood stage nor a midlife crisis (Freund & Ritter, 2009).

Maturity and Self-Concept

Most personality theorists emphasize the importance of individual maturity as people move through life. **Maturity** is our capacity to undergo continual change to adapt successfully and cope flexibly with the demands and responsibilities of life. Maturity is not some sort of plateau or final state but a lifetime process of becoming (Waterman, 1993). It is a never-ending search for a meaningful and comfortable fit between ourselves and the world—a struggle to "get it all together." Gordon W. Allport (1961, p. 307) identifies six criteria that psychologists commonly employ for assessing individual personalities:

> The mature personality will have a widely extended sense of self; be able to relate warmly to others in both intimate and nonintimate contacts; possess a fundamental emotional security and accept himself [or herself]; perceive, think, and act with zest in accordance with outer reality; be capable of self-objectification, of insight and humor; and live in harmony with a unifying philosophy of life.

Underlying these elements of the mature personality is a positive self-concept (Hattie, 2004). **Self-concept** is the view we have of ourselves through time as "the real me" or "I myself as I really am." Self-concept has considerable impact on behavior. Indeed, much of our significant behavior can be understood as an attempt to approach or avoid some of our "possible selves" (Cross & Gore, 2004). For instance, a middle-aged man whose feared self includes being a heart attack victim and who worries about how to avoid becoming that self might undertake an exercise and diet regimen. The human ability to preserve, enhance, promote, defend, and revise notions about the self (our self-schemas) helps us explain how older people, experiencing the changes and, in some cases, frailties of advancing age, nonetheless function so

People View Their Experiences Through Somewhat Different Cognitive Filters

Source: Lynn Johnston Productions. © 2005, *For Better or For Worse.* Lynn Johnston Productions Inc./Distributed by Uclick. Reprinted with permission. All rights reserved.

well, especially on the subjective level. It seems that aging people do not simply react to aging processes but instead make cognitive shifts and behavioral adjustments that preserve their mental health and behavioral functioning despite their losses (Bardi & Ryff, 2007).

Mounting evidence suggests that both sad people and happy people are biased in their basic perceptions of themselves and the world (Sedikides & Gregg, 2003). People bring to the world somewhat different cognitive templates, or filters, through which they view their experiences (Feist, 2006). And the way they structure their experiences determines their mood and behavior. If we see things as negative, we are likely to feel and act depressed. If we see things as positive, we are likely to feel and act happy. That is why some view middle age as a time of feeling secure and settled, whereas others view it as a time of being bored or in a rut. Such perceptions tend to reinforce and even intensify people's feelings about their self-worth and their adequacy in the larger world. It is how individuals take their ideas of self and interact in social situations that interest the theorists we will next encounter.

Stage Models

Erikson posits that the midlife years are devoted to resolving the "crisis" of **generativity versus stagnation.** Erikson (1968b, p. 267) views **generativity** as "primarily the concern in establishing and guiding the next generation." He viewed generativity as a sign of psychological maturity and psychological health, and a body of research validates Erikson's theory. "Measures of generativity are positively correlated with self-reports of life satisfaction, happiness, self-esteem, and sense of coherence in life" (McAdams, 2001). Adults express generativity through nurturing, teaching, mentoring, volunteering, and leading—by promoting the overall interests of the next generation while contributing to the world of politics, art, culture, and

community. As a group, they seek to benefit the larger society and facilitate its continuity across generations. McAdams (2001) also sees generativity as springing from two deeply rooted desires: the communal need to be nurturant and the personal desire to do something or be something that transcends death. You will recognize the two poles of this crisis in stereotypical portrayals of adults. The generative teacher thinks of each pupil as "one of my own children" and tries to generate a love of life in each of the students. The individual whose resolution is weighted toward stagnation is usually depicted as a "humbug" sort; Scrooge is probably the best-known example. Stories that show an "old grump" turning into an avuncular, caring person depict the transition from stagnation to generativity.

Erikson's "crisis" view has been criticized by others, such as Costa and McCrae (2005), who study the stability of personality traits in adulthood. They find no evidence that psychological disturbance is any more common during midlife than during other periods of life. Other critics of Erikson's stage approach say midlife is more accurately characterized as a time of productivity and altruism, not a time of turmoil. Research with midlife women, though, confirms that the concept of generativity predicted "positive personality characteristics, satisfaction with marriage and motherhood, and successful aging" (Peterson & Duncan, 2008, p. 411).

Other psychologists have elaborated on Erikson's formulations. Robert C. Peck (1968) took a closer look at midlife and suggests that it is useful to identify more precisely the tasks confronting midlife individuals. Peck defines these four tasks:

- *Valuing wisdom versus valuing physical powers.* As we saw in Chapter 15, when individuals progress through middle age, they experience a decline in their physical strength. Even more important, in a culture that emphasizes looking youthful, people lose much of their edge in physical attractiveness. But they also enjoy new advantages. The experience of longer living brings with it an increase in accumulated knowledge and greater powers of judgment. Rather than relying primarily on their strength and physical capabilities, they must more often employ their maturity and wisdom in coping with life. This wisdom is highly valued in Japan and China, where it is not uncommon for well-respected public officials to be in their seventies and eighties (Menon, 2001).

- *Socializing versus sexualizing in human relationships.* Allied to midlife physical decline, although in some ways separate from it, is the sexual climacteric. In their interpersonal lives, individuals must now cultivate greater understanding and compassion. They must come to value others as personalities in their own right rather than chiefly as sex objects.
- Achieving *emotional flexibility versus emotional impoverishment.* This task concerns the ability to become emotionally flexible. With this flexibility, people find the capacity to shift emotional investments from one person to another and from one activity to another. Many middle-aged individuals confront the death of, or need to care for, their elderly parents and the departure of their children from the home, and they must widen their circle of acquaintances to embrace new people in the community. They must also "try on" and cultivate new roles to replace those that they are relinquishing. Those who do not are likely to experience a sense of isolation, loneliness, and despair.
- *Maintaining mental flexibility versus mental rigidity.* As they grow older, some people too often become set in their ways or closed-minded. Those who have reached their peak in status and power are tempted to forgo the search for new solutions to problems. But what worked in the past might not work in the future. Hence, they must strive for mental flexibility and cultivate new perspectives as provisional guidelines to tackling problems.

Peck's formulations provide a more positive, dynamic image of middle age than those that portray midlife as a time of turmoil and crisis as people reevaluate their lives. Research findings from the extensive, longitudinal study on *Midlife in the United States* (MIDUS) confirm Peck's view of midlife. Another study found that only one-fourth of midlife adults knew someone who had undergone a midlife crisis. Further, most midlife men and women experience greater psychological well-being in terms of more personal freedom, higher workplace status, and expanding social networks (Freund & Ritter, 2009). Most adult Americans also see middle age as a time

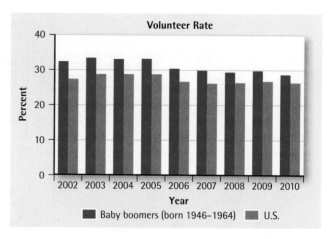

FIGURE 16.1 Baby Boomers' Volunteerism in America: 2002–2010 In 2010, 22.2 million baby boomers dedicated at least 3.1 billion hours of service. Volunteers aged 45 to 64 are most likely to serve in religious, educational, service, and medical settings.
Sources: Bureau of Labor Statistics. (2010, January 26). Volunteering in the United States, 2010. [News Release.] Retrieved from http://www.bls.gov/news.release/pdf/volun.pdf. Corporation for National and Community Service. (2010). *Volunteering in America 2010.* Retrieved from http://www.volunteeringinamerica .gov/assets/resources/ IssueBriefFINALJune15.pdf

when people deepen their relationships and intensify their acts of caring. A variety of studies confirm that people in their fifties become more altruistic and community-oriented than they were at age 25 (see Figure 16.1). Midlife Americans, aged 45 to 64, are volunteering in all types of service and nonprofit organizations at rates that are the highest in the last 30 years (Reingold & Nesbit, 2006). They feel that "giving back to society is what makes this stage rewarding"; indeed, some midlifers suggest calling this stage the "giving stage" (Relin, 2006).

Questions

How is Erikson's stage theory different from Peck's task theory of midlife personality development? Why are midlife adults more likely to volunteer?

Trait Models

Until relatively recently, most psychologists believed that personality patterns are established during childhood and adolescence and then remain relatively stable over the rest of the life span. This view is largely derived from Sigmund Freud's psychoanalytic theory. As described in Chapter 2, Freud traced the roots of behavior to personality components formed in infancy and childhood—needs, defense mechanisms, and so on. He deemed any changes that occur in adulthood simply to be variations on established themes, for he believed that an individual's character structure is relatively fixed by late childhood.

Likewise, clinical psychologists and personality theorists have assumed that an individual gradually forms certain characteristics that become progressively resistant to change with the passage of time. These patterns are usually regarded as reflections of inner traits, cognitive structures, dispositions, habits, or needs. Indeed, almost all forms of personality assessment assume that the individual has stable *traits* (stylistic consistencies in behavior) that the investigator is attempting to describe. For example, developmentalists Costa and McCrae (2005) have found that a few dimensions of personality recur across their many investigations. They propose that the "big five" traits—extraversion, neuroticism, openness, agreeableness, and conscientiousness—constitute the core of personality. Most models concur on the existence of extraversion-introversion and neuroticism (emotional stability/instability), although what lies beyond extraversion and neuroticism is a more perplexing issue. Some neuorpsychologists argue that the regulation of certain brain chemicals, such as noradrenaline, serotonin, and dopamine, is primarily responsible for our personality traits (Williams et al., 2009).

Moreover, we all typically view ourselves as having a measure of consistency, and we anticipate and adapt to many events without appreciably changing our picture of the entirety of our lives. So we see ourselves as essentially stable, even though we assume somewhat different roles in response to changing life circumstances.

Situational Models

The trait approach to personality views a person's behavior in terms of recurring, consistent patterns. In contrast, proponents of situational models view a person's behavior as the outcome of the characteristics of the *situation* in which the person is momentarily involved. Cognitive learning theorist Walter Mischel (1977, 1985, 2007) provides a forthright statement of the person-situation position. Mischel says that behavioral consistency is more illusory than real. He concludes that we are motivated to believe that the world around us is orderly and patterned because only in this manner can we take aspects of our daily lives for granted and view them as predictable. Consequently, we perceive our own behavior and that of other people as having continuity. Mischel notes that the correlation between personality trait test scores and behavior seems to reach a maximum of about +.30, not a particularly high figure for predictability. People's behavior across situations is highly consistent only when the situations in which the behavior is tested are quite similar. When circumstances vary, little similarity is apparent.

It appears that there is an element of truth in what Mischel has posited for 40 years. Using one of Costa and McCrae's seemingly enduring personality traits, ex-

traversion, as an example, is it not possible that most of us would be more outgoing/extraverted when around people who share our own recreational, artistic, or work-related pursuits than when in a situation with total strangers? Mischel (2007) has pursued extensive research on individual differences in behavior—and the findings become even more variable when cross-cultural studies of personality and behavior are conducted.

Interactionist Models

In recent years psychologists have come to recognize the inadequacies of both trait and situational models. Instead, they have come to favor an *interactionist* approach to personality. They claim that behavior is a joint product of the person *and* the situation. Moreover, people seek out congenial environments—selecting settings, activities, and associates that provide a comfortable context and fit—and thereby reinforce their preexisting bents. And through their actions, individuals create as well as select environments. By fashioning their own circumstances, they produce some measure of stability in their behavior (Bardi & Ryff, 2007). In a National Public Radio (2011) interview, baby-boomer writer and scholar Shelby Steele relates how boomers shaped—and continue to shape—the American environment:

. . . we came of age at that moment when America was in deep doubt and there was a void, I think, in authority. And, you know, as young people will do, we assumed a lot of that authority. We said, well, we'll reinvent America. We'll make it good and we'll correct for all of these problems [civil rights, women's rights, rights for ethnic groups]. . . . And so we had this almost kind of license to invent ourselves anew and we would reinvent everything—the family, the sexual revolution, and so forth . . . And, you know, we've done that with every phase of life. We'll probably do that with retirement.

Psychologists have employed a variety of approaches for specifying the form of interaction that transpires between a person and a situation. One approach is to distinguish between those people for whom a given trait predicts behavior across situations and those people for whom that trait is not predictive of behavior. For example, individuals who report that their behavior is consistent across situations with respect to friendliness and conscientiousness do exhibit these traits in their behavior. In contrast, individuals who report that their behavior is inconsistent across situations with respect to these qualities demonstrate little consistency in their behavior. Moreover, people vary in their consistency on different traits (Vogt & Colvin, 2003). Hence, if we are asked to characterize a friend, we select a small number of traits that strike us as pertinent and discard as irrelevant the hundreds of other traits. Usually, the friendship traits—such as trustworthiness, kindness, and acceptance—that we select are those that hold for the person across a variety of situations.

Question

Which personality theory—trait, situational, or interactionist—do you think explains why you might not mind waiting in a slow movie line one day but might become agitated doing so another time?

Gender and Personality at Midlife

In recent years psychologists have moved away from the assumption that masculinity and femininity are opposing characteristics of personality and behavior. A variety of studies have examined the dynamics of gender and personality traits during middle adulthood.

Levinson's Theory of Male Midlife Development

Psychologist Daniel Levinson (1986) and his associates at Yale University studied stages of male adult development and formed their life structure theory (see Chapter 14). Central to this theory are family roles and one's occupation in life. Analysis of their subjects' intensive biographies, described in *The Seasons of a Man's Life,* led them to conclude that men often experience a turning point in their lives between the ages of 35 and 45 (Levinson et al., 1978). More recently, Levinson concluded that men's inner struggles occur with renewed intensity by the mid-fifties (a phenomenon typically called a midlife crisis) (Goleman, 1989). These Yale researchers believe that a man cannot go through his middle adult years unchanged because during this period he encounters the first indisputable signs of aging and reaches a point at which he is compelled to reassess the fantasies and illusions he has held about himself. In the mid-1970s, Levinson identified several substages in the period from 40 to 65 in his initial study with men (and with women in the early 1980s):

- *Midlife transition (age 40 to 45).* This is a developmental bridge between early adulthood and middle adulthood. People come to terms with the end of their youth in the late thirties and try to create a new young-old way of being. Working at individuation at midlife is an especially important task. Initiation into midlife involves making choices.
- *Entry life structure for middle adulthood (age 45 to 50).* People establish an initial place in a new generation and a new season of life. Even if they are in the same job, marriage, or community, they create important differences in these relationships. They try to establish a new place in midlife.
- *Age 50 transition (age 50 to 55).* This is a time to reappraise and explore one's self within this new

Male Midlife Developmental Transition Men typically work on the developmental tasks of midlife with different resources. Two retired men that your authors know toured the United States on motorcycles for a year. Another friend was a cowboy for two weeks at a "dude ranch" in Montana. Another competed in an American road rally in a vintage classic car, and still others sail around the world. These men fulfilled lifelong dreams.

midlife structure. Developmental crises are common in this period, especially for persons who have made few life changes in the previous 10 to 15 years.

- *Culminating life structure for middle adulthood (age 55 to 60).* This is a time for realizing midlife aspirations and goals.
- *Late adult transition (age 60 to 65).* This period requires a profound reappraisal of the past and a readiness for the next era of adulthood. This involves termination of midlife and readiness for late adulthood.

For men, work and career provide the main outlet for identity, self-esteem, productivity, and creativity. The second part of a man's work life, from age 40 to age 65, is often characterized by "higher work satisfaction, positive work motivation, social and professional expertise, mature social relations, and responsibility" (Dittmann-Kohli, 2005, p. 344). Although there have been federal age discrimination laws since 1967 regarding hiring, promoting, compensating, laying off (and providing benefits, assignments, and training), managers in business and industry continue to replace men (and women) in their forties and fifties with younger employees. Sometimes this is done by offering early retirement incentives, but other times workers are abruptly terminated. Many midlife men have legitimate fears about losing their jobs or being replaced in their jobs, as corporations continue to "merge," "outsource" to foreign countries, and "downsize." Levinson did not foresee that some of today's midlife boomer adults, when faced with joblessness or being passed over for promotions given to very young employees, would often become self-employed entrepreneurs (Giandrea, Cahill, & Quinn, 2008). Only recently, some companies have begun to demonstrate an attitudinal shift to valuing their older workers, who often show more loyalty, a stronger work ethic, and greater job satisfaction than younger workers (Kumar & Giri, 2009).

Levinson concluded that there are age-graded periods in adult development for personality development, cognitive development, and family development. He further states that it is a much more complex matter to determine the "satisfactoriness" of individual lives within these stages (Levinson, 1996, p. 29). Levinson concluded before his death in 1994 that even though the genders experience different life circumstances, and even though women work on the developmental tasks of each period with different resources than men have, women and men both go through these life stages. Life-span researchers find that today, the stages of an adult man's life are not as clearly defined as Levinson described, and they are likely to be more extended. Many adult males are staying in college longer to prepare for careers, are delaying marriage, are having children later, are sharing in home and child responsibilities, and are retiring later and living much longer.

Questions

According to Levinson's 1980s findings, what are the stages of a man's life? Since his study was published, what changes have occurred in the middle-adulthood stage of an American man's life?

Levinson's Theory of Women's Midlife Development

A white-male-centered view of adult life has been dominant since the earliest social science studies—and before that in the history and literature of many cultures. Although in his initial study in the late 1970s Levinson chose to study adult male development, he said that one couldn't study one gender without studying the other, for both influence each other in complex ways (e.g., relationships of husbands and wives, fathers and daughters, mothers and sons, and ex-husbands and ex-wives). In the early 1980s, Levinson used the method of intensive biographical interviewing with 45 females aged 35 to 45. The subjects, selected randomly, constituted three equal groups: (1) primarily homemakers (not in a career or employed outside the home); (2) women with careers in the corporate world; and (3) women with careers in the academic world. His research findings indicate that there are apparent gender differences in adult development, particularly in the realms of domestic and public life, within a marriage, in the division of labor in the

home (with women raising children and men working in a career world), and in the male and female psyches.

Because most contemporary women are not stay-at-home mothers and are employed outside the home, as well as being responsible for many of the household tasks and child care, Levinson's stage theory for adult women is not as valid today. Today, a man might decide to stay at home to care for children, and a woman might pursue an advanced degree, launch a career, or start her own business. In Levinson's study of women, midlife homemakers' self-esteem and identity were seriously affected by their "empty nest" experience, which is likely to occur during menopausal years. In the past two decades, the timing and experiences of female midlife have changed markedly. Today's midlife women are more likely to experience the "empty *next*" as a result of divorce or of adult children leaving home. Many of these women are anticipating the long-awaited time to pursue a new career, start their own business, travel, volunteer, care for aging parents, and so forth (Miller, 2008). Critics of Levinson's stage theory also cite the small sample of subjects (45 in each study). They point out that men or women in their fifties and sixties were not interviewed, even though Levinson's life structure theory extends to these ages. Further, Levinson's sample was not representative of women and men across various racial-ethnic and socioeconomic groups.

No Longer Primarily Homemakers   When Levinson's women's study was published in the late 1980s, he argued that while men's lives were usually centered in the broader public sphere, women's lives were not. Women who lived primarily as homemakers in a marriage centered their lives within the home, family, and a narrower social sphere. These women were less involved in the public world, played a limited role as financial providers in the family, and were less prepared to engage in the work world (if they became divorced or widowed).

Since Levinson's study was conducted, millions of women have entered the professions of law, medicine, dentistry, pharmacy, chiropractic, architecture, corporate management, finance and banking, real estate, academic administration, scientific research, engineering, computer science, and so forth (see Figure 16.2). But in many nonindustrial societies of the world, women's lives are still mainly centered in the domestic sphere, raising children and supporting families. The home has been the key source of their identity, meaning, and satisfaction. Nonetheless, as more women in developing countries earn their own income, or join together in cooperatives to sell their art, textiles, jewelry, and the like, they are slowly becoming empowered in some governance roles in their communities (Tripp, 2003).

Marriage   Levinson said that in many societies, love is not the primary motivating factor for marriage. It is, "first of all, about building an enterprise in which the partners

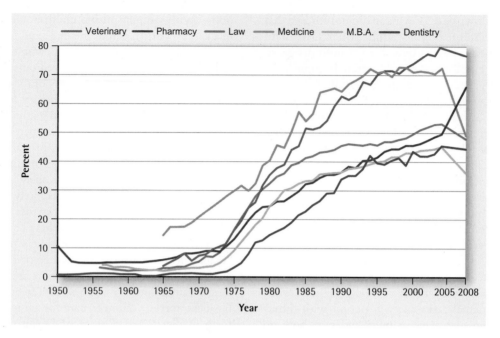

FIGURE 16.2 Percentage of Professional Degrees Earned by American Women, 1950–2008 Baby-boom women broke barriers and entered prestigious, high-paying professions. American women now earn more than half of the associate's, bachelor's, and master's degrees conferred each year, as well as the indicated percentages of the professional degrees shown here. *Sources:* Cox, W. M., & Alm, R. (2007, May). Women at work: A progress report. *Economic Newsletter—Insights from the Federal Reserve Bank of Dallas.* Retrieved from http://www.dallasfed.org/research/eclett/2007/el0705.html. Snyder, T. D., & Dillow, S. A. (2010, April). *Digest of Education Statistics 2009* (NCES 2010-013). Table 280. First-professional degrees conferred by degree-granting institutions, by sex of student, control of institution, and field of study. Washington, DC: U.S. Department of Education, National Center for Education Statistics.

can have a good life" and "take care of each other" in their own fashion (Levinson, 1996). As we noted in Chapter 14, arranged marriages are still common in many countries. In a **traditional marriage,** the women are *homemakers* and the men are *providers* (involving themselves much more in their work world than in their family). Most adults in late adulthood today are of a cohort where such traditional marriages were the norm. But contemporary midlife Americans, the baby-boom cohort, have chosen various lifestyle forms, including remaining single, single parenthood, marriage where both partners are providers, marriage-divorce-remarriage, marriage-divorce-single parenthood, open marriage, cohabitation, same-sex unions, and (in the case of women and men in religious orders) cooperative living arrangements.

However, *patriarchy,* the rule of the father or husband, remains the theme to some degree in most societies of the world. In patriarchal societies, the man is still the dominant authority over the family. A wife in a patriarchal situation might work on the family farm or business and contribute time to the local school, church, or community. In the United States, an example of this can be found in the thousands of hardworking farm wives in the past who were not employed outside the farm, were not able to contribute to Social Security, and consequently are ineligible for their own Social Security

benefits. Also, women who have lived their lives as stay-at-home parents and then become divorced or widowed during midlife are often faced with a major transition as they confront the need to enter the workforce for self-support.

Farm wives, and divorced or widowed wives, may not be eligible for a percentage of their husband's Social Security and health-care coverage if they were not married for at least 10 years. They cannot receive reduced Social Security payments until age 62, unless they are eligible for disability payments. In contrast, women who have raised families and have also been employed and earned their own incomes have amassed a variety of resources and social networks to cope more effectively with the inevitable changes in midlife (Hunter, Sundel, & Sundel, 2002). However, since 2008 as U.S. workers face early retirement or lose pension plans and investments, there has been a dramatic increase in reliance on Social Security benefits, especially for women (Institute for Women's Policy Research, 2010). One 2010 survey estimates that about half of the millions of U.S. working but undocumented migrant women (and men) were not paid Social Security–based wages. They will not be able to draw on the Social Security retirement system in old age unless they make a contribution through legal employment (Burtless & Singer, 2010).

Midlife Career Women   Many midlife women today have transitioned into and out of employment. Sylvia Hewlett (2007) finds that about one-third of professional women leave the paid labor force at some point in their careers. Women experience both "push" and "pull" factors that move them into and out of paid employment. The "push" factors include unreasonable or long hours that do not enable them to balance work and family. The "pull" factors include caring for family members, such as raising children when women are usually younger and caring for aging parents when the women reach midlife (Hewlett, 2007). In Levinson's 1990s study, women in midlife transition recognized that their efforts to combine love and marriage, motherhood, and full-time career had not brought them as much satisfaction as they had hoped.

U.S. women still find it challenging to maintain family life and pursue careers. Women have been pushing against the boundaries of gender discrimination in business, industry, and academia since the 1970s, when they began entering the professions in significant numbers (see Figure 16.2). In the 1990s, the term *glass ceiling* was coined to describe the invisible ceiling on job advancement for women in many professions. In 2010 the U.S. Department of Labor reported that women now hold 49 percent of all jobs and earn over half of all professional degrees. Yet the glass ceiling still exists: "Women comprise 46.4 percent of all employees in Fortune 500 companies, they make up just 15.7 percent of board seats, 14.4 percent of executive officers, 7.6 percent of top earning executive officers, and 2.6 percent of CEOs" (U.S. Congress Joint Economic Committee, 2010). Many who have reached the top of their professions concede that it is still very difficult to balance family life and pursue career goals—echoing the observations of the working women in Levinson's 1980s study of midlife women. Still, many women believe that it is possible to be both mothers and workers and feel that they have important contributions to make. Congresswoman Zoe Lofgren poignantly states this position:

I think making a contribution to the well-being of society in the public and political arena is an important thing. I think that to do that [by foregoing] a wanted motherhood you would be making a terrible mistake. The greatest education I ever had was becoming a mother. It transformed my outlook on life; I understood what is important not just for me but for society. (Mason & Ekman, 2007, p. 98)

American women call for new workplace policies that would enable them to bear and raise children without significant penalties (congressional acts are pending that, if they become law, will reduce such penalties). For example, in the academic world, stopping the coursework or tenure clock for several years while women are caring for infants would enable them to bear children and complete their degrees without jeopardizing their careers. In

other fields, ending the workday at 5 P.M., helping parents find good child care with stipends or on-site child-care facilities, providing the option of a flexible schedule, and not penalizing women for taking extended parental leave are all policies that would make it easier for women to pursue careers and raise families. It is just as important for women as for men to reach high-level positions in all professions because of the point of view they bring. Consider the fact that until women became a significant percentage of researchers in medicine and psychology, all studies were performed with men as the sole subjects—even breast cancer research (Mason & Ekman, 2007).

It is not just midlife women who look for a more accommodating workplace. A majority of the males of the baby-boom generation who were surveyed in 2002 agreed that the optimal family arrangement involves both the husband and the wife being wage earners. Most U.S. workers, male and female, prioritize family life or give equal weight to family life and work; only a small percentage value work over family. At midlife, both male and female workers are typically prime candidates for promotion to positions of greater responsibility. Yet the Families and Work Institute (2004) found that fewer midlife workers were willing to accept promotions, because more work responsibility would make it more difficult for them to maintain a healthy family life. This was especially true among women workers. The concept of "negative spillover," where job stress negatively affects family life, has become a marker that researchers monitor. Those who do not experience negative spillover will consider promotion and advancement at work (Families and Work Institute, 2004). Another factor that addresses the gender pay gap, which is larger for older workers, and promotes change is the "equal pay for equal work" *Lilly Ledbetter Fair Pay Act,* which became federal law in 2009 (see Figure 16.3). It is still reported that

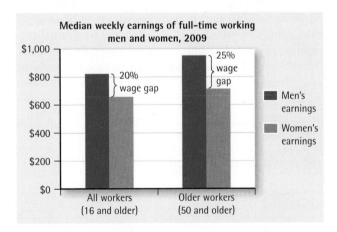

FIGURE 16.3 Gender Pay Gap Is Larger for Older Workers: 2009

Source: U.S. Congress Joint Economic Committee. (2010, December). *Invest in women, invest in America: A comprehensive review of women in the U.S. economy.* Retrieved from http://jec.senate.gov/public/?a=Files.Serve&File_id=57cfaf04-f297-4c61 -964b-6321af47db03

women earn only 77 cents for every dollar that a man earns in the same profession (Institute for Women's Policy Research, 2010). Obviously, there are individual differences, and some women's earnings surpass that of comparable males.

New Beginnings at Midlife   For some people, midlife offers opportunities to explore new career avenues or resume educational goals and avocational pursuits that were deferred due to marriage and child-care responsibilities. Now freed of some of the familial and financial responsibilities of younger adults, middle-aged adults, more than half of whom are women, are returning to college (Philibert, Allen, & Elleven, 2008). Advances in technology have allowed many midlife adults to use experience gained in their homemaking and jobs to forge their own home-based ventures. Dedication to healthy lifestyles enables midlife adults to enjoy sport and adventure activities. Mitchell and Helson (1990) describe women's *prime of life* as being in their early fifties, when a sense of accomplishment from occupational achievement and/or launching of children converges with personality resources and a new, freer lifestyle.

Culture and Middle Age   Perceptions of age are always mediated by cultural models of the life course, and the Western view of middle age differs significantly from the views that prevail in non-Western cultures. For example, in India there is a well-defined extended family structure with a designated role for each family member throughout life. The elders in the home are to be accorded respect, supported by the young, and cared for by them. This is a long-held cultural view, and midlife adults look forward to their later years. Tikoo (1996) says it is difficult to give a definite age at which one is middle-aged in India, because the average life expectancy in India is only 58 years; "middle age" in that context would be younger than American middle age. In Japan, the traditional perception of the ideal life course is age-graded—that is, "the life cycle is predominantly a social process involving community rituals in which people born the same year participate together" (Lock, 1998). Further, the female's life cycle has been shaped more by her biology than a male's. Middle age, referred to as the prime of life (*sônen*), is simply a part of the life cycle that begins with marriage and ends at the ritual of turning 60—old age.

Questions

According to Levinson's findings, what are some of the factors that affect a woman at midlife? How are contemporary women navigating through this stage in Western and non-Western societies?

Continuity and Discontinuity of Characteristics by Gender   Carl Jung (1933, 1960), the influential Swiss psychoanalyst, was one of the first to suggest that gender differences tend to diminish or even "cross over" in later life. Some research confirms that men and women move in *opposite* directions across the life span with respect to assertiveness and aggressiveness, so that patterns of a later-life "unisex" tend to emerge (Hyde, Krajnik, & Skuldt-Niederberger, 1991).

David Gutmann has studied personality and aging in a wide range of cultures (Huyck & Gutmann, 2007). He reports that around age 55, men begin to use passive instead of active techniques in dealing with the demands of their environment. Women, however, appear to move in the opposite direction, from passive to active mastery. They tend to become more forceful, domineering, managerial, and independent. Those who study the effects of lowered levels of estrogen and progesterone—and thus an increasing influence of testosterone—in postmenopausal women are beginning to document similar findings. Sheehy (1992, p. 237) describes women's shift to active mastery as *postmenopausal zest*:

Today's pioneering women in postmenopause in advanced societies eventually give up the futile gallantry of trying to remain the same younger self. Coming through the passage of menopause, they reach a new plateau of contentment and self-acceptance, along with a broader view of the world that not only enriches one's personality but gives one a new perspective on life and humankind. Such women—and there are more and more of them today—find a potent new burst of energy by their mid-fifties.

Grandfathers Often Become More Nurturant Some psychologists have found that by their mid-fifties, men's and women's gender characteristics begin to change direction. This grandfather is very nurturant with his grandchild.

Gutmann's approach to gender behaviors is controversial, and it has been criticized on theoretical and methodological grounds (McGee & Wells, 1982). Even so, it has provided a starting point for research on changes in gender-role orientation across the life span. The findings of Gutmann and other researchers seem to suggest that in later life, people tend toward androgynous responses that are thought to be associated with increased flexibility and adaptability and hence with successful aging (Wink & Helson, 1993). **Androgyny** is the incorporation of both male-typed and female-typed characteristics within a single personality and provides an alternative perspective. Androgynous individuals do not restrict their behavior to that embodied in cultural stereotypes of masculinity and femininity.

Personality Continuity and Discontinuity

As noted earlier, Costa and McCrae (1980, 2005) find considerable continuity in an individual's personality across the adult years. They have tracked individuals' scores over time on standardized self-report personality scales. On such personality dimensions as warmth, impulsiveness, gregariousness, assertiveness, anxiety, and disposition to depression, a high correlation exists from one decade to another. An assertive 19-year-old is typically an assertive 40-year-old and later an assertive 80-year-old. Likewise, "neurotics" are likely to be "complainers" throughout life

(they might complain about their love life in early adulthood and decry their poor health in late adulthood)—although people can "mellow" with age or become less impulsive by the time they are in their sixties.

In sum, for many facets of our personality there is strong evidence of continuity across the adult years (Costa & McCrae, 2005). This element of stability makes us adaptive. We know what we are like and hence can make more intelligent choices regarding our living arrangements, careers, spouses, and friends. If our personality changed continually and erratically, we would have a hard time mapping our future and making wise decisions.

This conclusion is supported by much of the work exploring Erikson's thesis regarding generativity (Peterson & Duncan, 2008). As the Neugartens note (1996), the psychological realities confronting the individual shift with time. Middle age, for instance, often brings with it multiple responsibilities for jobs and careers, as well as caring for one's children, aging parents, and possibly grandchildren or grandparents. Often these duties weigh more heavily on women (Hunter, Sundel, & Sundel, 2002). With these obligations comes the awareness of oneself as the bridge between the generations—the so-called **sandwich generation.** As members of the sandwich generation try to meet the needs of their children and parents, their own needs may become less prominent, yet perhaps more important than ever before (see Table 16.1)

TABLE 16.1 The Sandwich Generation: Caught in the Middle—The Needs of Middle-Aged Adults, Their Children, and Their Aging Parents

What Kids Want and Need	What Middle-Aged Adults Want and Need	What Aging Parents Want and Need
Independence	Help	Acceptance
Respect	Appreciation	Independence
Sounding board	Pressure off	Respect
Separate entity	"My turn"	Control of their own life
Patience	Independence	Sharing
Guidelines	Listening ear	Involvement
Flexibility	Acceptance	Emotional support
Acceptance	Time with their own generation	Interpersonal relationships
Security	Solitude	Interaction
Money	Space	Inclusion
Support	Unconditional love	
Freedom to make choices	Control of their own life	
Unconditional love		
Control of their own life		

Source: Herbert G. Lingren and Jayne Decker, *The Sandwich Generation: A Cluttered Nest.* Cooperative Extension, Institute of Agriculture and Natural Resources, University of Nebraska–Lincoln, December 1992, issued online August 1996, http://ianrpubs.unl.edu/family/g1117.htm

(Kohli & Künemund, 2005). As a perceptive woman observed in Neugarten's study of middle age,

> It is as if there are two mirrors before me, each held at a partial angle. I see part of myself in my mother who is growing old, and part of her in me. In the other mirror, I see part of myself in my daughter. I have had some dramatic insights, just from looking in those mirrors . . . . It is a set of revelations that I suppose can only come when you are in the middle of three generations. (Neugarten, 1968, p. 98)

In a sense, individuals in their forties and fifties are catching up with their own parents, so they might experience increased identification with them and a greater awareness of their own approaching senescence. Some of the issues of middle age are related to increased stocktaking, in which individuals come to restructure their time perspective in terms of time left to live rather than time since birth.

Questions

What do we know about men's and women's transition through middle adulthood? Do studies of midlife development include ethnic minorities and those from all socioeconomic groups?

THE SOCIAL MILIEU

Close and meaningful social relationships play a vital part in human health and happiness. Through our association with others—family, friends, neighbors, acquaintances, and coworkers—we achieve a sense of worth, acceptance, and psychological well-being. This social network is often referred to as a **social convoy**, the company of other people who travel with us from birth to death. Some midlife women have formed local chapters of the national Red Hat Society to forge meaningful social relationships. Middle-aged adults also play a prominent role in other well-known international, national, and local social and service-oriented organizations, including the American Legion, Habitat for Humanity, Kiwanis, the Knights of Columbus, B'nai B'rith, the Lion's Club, the Rotary, YMCA, YWCA, the American Association of University Women, Foster Grandparents, SCORE (Service Corps of Retired Executives), AmeriCorps, and Hospice, among others. A number of studies have found that as we age, we are increasingly motivated to look for emotionally based meaning in life, and friendship networks are an important component of that search (Krause, 2007). Levinson (1996) said,

> To study an individual life, we must include all aspects of living. A life involves significant interpersonal relationships—with friends and lovers, parents and siblings, spouses and children, bosses, colleagues, and mentors. It

also involves significant relationships with groups and institutions of all kinds: family, occupational world, religion, and community.

Familial Relations

As we noted in Chapter 14, the vast majority of adult Americans have a profound wish to be part of a couple, to share their lives, and to make the relationship work. Maintaining a healthy family life continues as a top priority for most adults in middle age (Lachman, 2006).

First-Time Motherhood in Midlife   In recent years, an unprecedented trend has emerged in childbearing, and older motherhood is changing the face of aging (Friese, Becker, & Nachtigall, 2008). Every year, more women in their forties to late fifties and early sixties are becoming first-time mothers (Martin et al., 2010). Some women conceive without medical intervention, but most turn to assisted reproductive technologies, which is more likely to yield multiples. Even if an older woman becomes pregnant with her own or donor eggs, she still has a high risk of miscarriage (American Society for Reproductive Medicine, 2010). However, in 2007 the births to U.S.

New Mothers at Midlife   A growing number of single and married women in middle adulthood are bearing children and becoming first-time parents. Thus, the responsibilities and developmental challenges for some midlife adults have become more expansive.

women 40–44 years old increased to more than 105,000 and for women 45–54 increased to over 7,000 (U.S. Department of Health and Human Services, 2009a).

Why are so many women bearing children at later ages, and who are these mothers? Many are professional women who wanted to establish their careers before they began their families. They felt that first completing their education or professional training and then moving up the career ladder made sense before beginning childbearing. And there is some logic to this strategy. Women in their mid-forties earn significantly more than women in their twenties—from $20,000 to $50,000 or much more annually, depending on the profession. Because of their skills, work experience, and value to their employers, women past 40 may also be in a position to negotiate for increased maternity leave, flexible work time, and better corporate policies regarding child care. Employers who don't want to see considerable experience and skill walk out the door may be more willing to make concessions to older mothers; women in their twenties simply don't have that kind of bargaining leverage in the workplace. Many women are watching this new trend in fertility and are hoping that just as the baby-boom generation of women workers opened new doors, this generation of women giving birth at midlife will be able to pressure corporate America and the federal government to institute flexible work policies like those in other industrialized nations (Gregory, 2007). Couples can store embryos indefinitely by cryogenic methods, and scientists are working on ways to safely store a young woman's unfertilized eggs for a few decades while she establishes her career before deciding to bear a child. Such a scientific advancement may make sense in view of the fact that more women are living well into their eighties and beyond (Dworkin, 2007).

Married Couples   The 2009 census figures revealed that about two-thirds of U.S. women and men in middle adulthood were married (see Figure 16.4). This statistic does not reveal how many were remarriages, but marriage is the main relationship of choice for most middle-aged adults. Many couples still have children living at home, since they started their families later than their parents did (this was the first generation to use the birth control pill to delay childbearing). Most were well educated, were employed full-time and in decent financial shape, and seemed to be happy with their sex lives (Lachman, 2006). As both men and women search for meaning in life, many feel they have a personal responsibility to serve their community and make the world a better place. Service to others and religion now take on significant roles as a source of community, spirituality, and comfort.

As they have grown older, the first of the cohort of baby boomers (born right after World War II and now in their mid-sixties) have found themselves to be more conservative in their views, and many still enjoy material

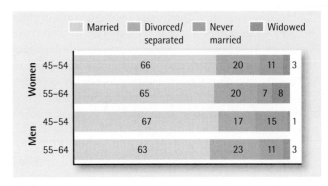

FIGURE 16.4 Marital Status of Middle-Aged Americans, Aged 45 to 64: 2009
Source: U.S. Census Bureau. (2010). *Statistical Abstract of the United States: 2009.* Washington, DC: U.S. Bureau of the Census.

success and comforts. They look forward to spending leisure time with their spouses. Still, the majority are concerned about developing health problems, about the health and economic well-being of their aging parents, about maintaining their lifestyle after retirement and perhaps not having enough savings, and (for a growing number) about staying employed and not being able to retire. Most indicate that they don't feel their age—indeed, they feel much younger (Harris, 2007).

An earlier study of 12,000 U.S. couples was undertaken by sociologists Blumstein and Schwartz (1983). They surveyed a nationally representative sample of adults in four types of couple relationships: married, cohabiting, gay male, and lesbian. Three hundred couples were then selected for in-depth interviews and were re-interviewed later. As with most studies of the early 1980s, this sample was composed of white, well-educated couples. These couples turned out to be more conventional than the researchers had expected. Although 60 percent of the wives worked outside the home, only 30 percent of the men and 39 percent of the women believed that both spouses should work. Wives with full-time jobs still did most of the housework. In several older studies, working women still did much of the household work, but more recent studies indicate that most men are sharing housework chores and have increased their time in child care (Sullivan & Coltrane, 2008). However, if the man does not take on what the woman believes is a more equitable share of the housework, especially if she is working full-time, their relationship may suffer (Sayer & Nicholson, 2006).

Typically, one partner in a marriage expressed a desire for "private time." Early in marriage, husbands were more likely than wives to assert that they needed more time on their own. But in long-standing marriages, it was the wives who more often asserted that they needed more time to themselves. Women in particular report greater marital satisfaction when they retire jointly with their husbands or their husband continues to work after they retire (Price and Joo, 2005).

Heterosexual men apparently took pleasure in their partner's success only if it was not superior to their own. Men, both straight and gay, placed a considerable premium on power and dominance. Gay males likewise tended to be competitive about their career success. In contrast, lesbians did not feel themselves particularly threatened by their partner's achievements, perhaps because women are not socialized to link their self-esteem so closely with success in the workplace (Peplau & Fingerhut, 2007).

Most married couples in this large sample pooled their money, although some wives did not pool their money. Regardless of how much the wife earned, married couples measured their financial success by the husband's income. In contrast, cohabitors and gay couples appraised their economic status individually rather than as a unit. Research shows that married couples are more collectively oriented and emphasize shared goods and benefits, whereas cohabiting couples focus on individual benefits and equality (Hamplova & Le Bourdais, 2008).

A study of midlife nonmarital cohabitors was drawn from about a thousand participants in the *National Survey of Families and Households*. King and Scott (2005) found that older cohabitors viewed living together as an alternative to marriage rather than as a prelude to marriage. Estimates suggest that more than one million adults aged 51 and older are cohabiting, and 90 percent were previously married but have no plans to remarry. Another study by social scientists examining extensive data about older cohabitors found that they appear to be more disadvantaged socioeconomically, physically, and emotionally than adults who have remarried (Brown, Lee, & Bulanda, 2006). In a survey by the Pew Research Center (2007) with more than 2,000 adults from 18 to 70 and older, one-third of the respondents aged 54 to 64 said they had cohabited or were cohabiting, and nearly 10 percent 65 and older said they had cohabited.

Factors Promoting Lifelong Marriage   People who are religious report more marital happiness, more commitment to their marriages, and lower divorce rates than couples who are not religious (Amato, Booth, Johnson, Rogers, 2007). In the 1980s, sociologists Jeanette and Robert Lauer (1985) looked into the question of what makes successful marriages. They surveyed more than 300 happily married couples, asking why their marriages survived. Both husband and wife ranked the top few reasons the same: "My spouse is my best friend," "I like my spouse as a person," and "Marriage is a long-term commitment" (see Figure 16.5 for results of a recent survey).

> **Question**
>
> What are some of the factors associated with long-lasting and satisfying relationships and marriages of middle-aged men and women?

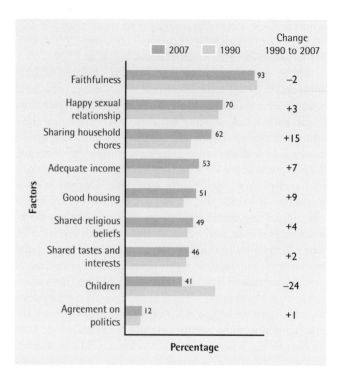

FIGURE 16.5 What Makes a Marriage Work? Percentage saying each is very important for a successful marriage. Note the increased emphasis on sharing chores, good housing, and shared religious beliefs, but less emphasis on children.
Source: Taylor, P., Funk, C., & Clark, A. (2007, July 1). As marriage and parenthood drift apart, public is concerned about social impact. PEW Research Center. Retrieved March 16, 2008, from http://pewresearch.org/assets/social/pdf/Marriage.pdf

Extramarital Sexual Relations   Traditionally, Western society has strongly disapproved of extramarital sexual relations (referred to now as EMS). Opposition has mainly been the result of two beliefs: that marriage provides a sexual outlet and therefore the married person is not sexually deprived, and that extramarital involvement threatens the marriage relationship and therefore imperils the family institution.

In comparison to the initial findings of Kinsey and colleagues (1953), rates of EMS reported in surveys from the 1970s to the 2000s have varied (some studies examined the incidence of EMS over the past year, while others examined the rate of EMS over a lifetime). Individuals with a more permissive view of sex are more likely to have engaged in extramarital sexual relations over a lifetime, although a majority of adults say they disapprove because it is immoral (Blow & Hartnett, 2005). Widmer and colleagues (1998) surveyed nearly 34,000 adults in 24 countries, and a majority disapproved of EMS on moral grounds. Other researchers found that men rationalized a distinction between extramarital sex and love and that men had a natural need for frequent sexual satisfaction. Some adults also made distinctions between different kinds of infidelity (emotional versus sexual)—and some said there were situations that justified infidelity (Blow & Hartnett, 2005). In terms of prevalence, studies find that "married women were the least likely (4 percent), dating women more likely (18 percent), and cohabiting women most likely (20 percent) to have had a secondary sex partner" (Blow & Hartnett, 2005, p. 219). Based on a comprehensive review of the research literature, less than 25 percent of married, heterosexual adults had engaged in EMS in the past year, and more men than women engaged in EMS. There is very limited research on fidelity in same-sex relationships (Blow & Hartnett, 2005).

Studies that examine extramarital relations and the marriage relationship conclude that EMS is both cause and effect in the deterioration of the marriage relationship (Amato et al., 2007). Sex is not the only lure for extramarital affairs. Affairs are often initiated to fill emotional needs. Many people involved in EMS report that they sought a new partner because they craved companionship and someone to make them feel special.

Evolutionary psychologists contend that human beings are designed to fall in love but not to stay in love. According to this view, males are "programmed" to maximize the spread of their genes into the future by copulating with many women. In contrast, women are more given to fidelity because they can have only one offspring a year (Wright, 1994). Lifetime rates of EMS were twice as high among those who had been divorced or legally separated as among those who had never divorced or separated (at a statistically significant level) (Blow & Hartnett, 2005).

Separation and Divorce   One's lifetime chance of experiencing marital separation, divorce, and remarriage has become greater—especially for those in midlife today (see Table 16.2). Women now in their mid-fifties to mid-sixties are a somewhat unique group. Their generation was the trendsetter, attending college and entering careers in the workforce in unprecedented numbers and shaping new gender-role and social standards. These changes had vast consequences for traditional marital relationships. Some research suggests that wives tend to be more critical of their marriage and are more aware of relationship problems than husbands (Amato et al., 2007). According to 2009 census data, men and women in the cohort 45 to 64 have the highest divorce and remarriage rates of any age group, 23 percent (see Table 16.2) (Elliott & Lewis, 2010). However, being in a long-term marriage *and* having a college education are generally associated with lower rates of divorce (Heuveline, 2005).

The first longitudinal empirical study of women at midlife—the *National Longitudinal Survey of Mature Women*—was conducted with several thousand women from the 1960s through the 1980s. Hiedemann and colleagues (1998) examined the data on the two thousand women who remained in a first marriage and were biological

TABLE 16.2 Percentages of U.S. Adults' Married or Remarried, by Age and Times Married: 2008

Age	Total Ever Married	Times Married		
		Once	Twice	Three Times or More
15 to 24	2.1	2.7	0.3	—
25 to 34	13.5	16.2	6.1	1.9
35 to 44	20.5	21.6	18.7	11.9
45 to 54	**23.1**	21.6	27.8	27.9
55 to 64	**18.6**	16.2	24.4	31.8
65+	22.2	21.7	22.7	26.4

Note: Those in middle adulthood today have experienced the highest percentages of divorce and remarriage of all adult cohorts.

Source: Elliott, D. B., & Lewis, J. M. (2010, April 17). Embracing the institution of marriage: The characteristics of remarried Americans. Paper presented at Population Association of America (PAA) Annual Meeting, Dallas, Texas. Retrieved from U.S. Census Bureau. (http://www.census.gov/population/www/socdemo/marr-div/Remarriage.pdf)

mothers and looked at risk factors for separation and divorce. On average, the women had been married for 17 years. Their analysis finds an association between the following factors and the risk of separation or divorce:

- Educational attainment reflects the wife's economic independence and the couple's economic status. College-educated women are more likely to remain married, but those who did not finish high school face higher risks of marital disruption.
- Marriage at young ages increases the risk of marital disruption.
- The longer a marriage survives, the less likely it is to be disrupted.
- Having children and purchasing a home indicate greater emotional investment in a marriage.
- The last child's departure from the home increases marital disruption for those who reach this phase early in their marriage (around 20 years), but it tends to decrease disruption for those who reach this phase later in their marriage (30 years or more).

Many research studies conducted in America and European countries over the past 40 years show the decline in status of marriage in family life. Even so, most young American adults anticipate someday being married (Cherlin, 2009). This view of marriage is unlike that of young adults in most European countries, where a larger percentage choose to live alone or live with parents much longer before marriage, and they call this "partnering with parents." For Europeans aged 35 to 49, the main living arrangement is living as a couple with children, but living arrangements are more diverse for those aged 50 to 64 (Kotowska et al., 2010). U.S. divorce rates have stabilized since the mid-1990s, and cohabitation

The Role of Grandparents With single parenthood, separation, divorce, and remarriage rates high, grandparents provide stability and support in grandchildren's lives. Grandparents also benefit from their relationships with grandchildren. Reliance on extended kinship ties is more common in ethnic-minority families.

rates have increased among people of nearly all adult ages. Statistics from 2009 from the U.S. Bureau of the Census (2011c) show that married household rates vary among racial-ethnic groups: Married households account for 67 percent of Asian households, 60 percent of white households, 56 percent of Hispanic households, and 40 percent of black households (U.S. Bureau of the Census, 2011c). Socioeconomic factors such as lower incomes, higher rates of unemployment, and less education are suspected to be the major sources of these racial-ethnic differences that compromise marital stability.

Some African Americans have long, stable marriages. Historically, cultural values, family practices, and strengths such as special care for children and elders, kinship ties, and collectivism have been a part of African American life (Waites, 2009). These intact families and the strengths of African American families are often overlooked. Extended kinship ties in three-generation African American families are common, and grandparents are very involved in the upbringing of grandchildren. The older generations are an important source of value transmission and have an impact on socialization outcomes of children (McWright, 2002). However, African American grandparents who are raising their grandchildren experience high levels of stress, especially when they are married. The need to devote time and attention to children at a time in a marriage when the couple should be able to devote time to each other creates tensions within

marriages. Similarly, grandparent caregivers who were also employed felt high levels of stress as they sought to balance the demands of their employers with the needs of their grandchildren (Ross & Aday, 2006).

> ### Questions
>
> What is the status of marriage at midlife? What factors are associated with midlife marital stability, infidelity, separation, or divorce?

Life as a Single   The likelihood of adults divorcing at midlife is significantly lower than for younger adults, and Table 16.2 shows that divorce has already occurred for a significant number of adults at younger ages (Schoen & Canudas-Romo, 2006). If it does occur, returning to single life after divorce is a very difficult experience. In many cases divorce exacts a greater emotional and physical toll than almost any other life stressor, including the death of a spouse (Kurdek, 1991).

Divorce affects midlife men and women differently. Men tend to become depressed and to have lower achievement goals. Women tend to become more outgoing and action-oriented (Lachman, 2004). Many women report that they have a more positive self-image and higher self-esteem than they did during their dissatisfying marriage. And nearly two-thirds say that the process helped them gain control for the first time in their lives (in marriage, they report, they had to "knuckle under"). Nor are the women necessarily lonely, because most have supportive female friends. Moreover, many find new activities and careers (Peterson, 1993). However, some become very lonely and distressed and need a great deal of social support from family and friends, or possibly therapeutic counseling.

In contrast, men seem to be unwilling converts to single life (Gross, 1992). Overall, divorced men have much narrower support networks than divorced women. Even when men have ample money, many find it difficult to put together new lives that can sustain them. American men have typically depended on women to create social lives for them. Not only do men suffer from lack of regular companionship, but they also miss the amenities of established domestic life. And some men begin questioning their worth and competence. Although men might find it easier than women to remarry (statistics favor men), they still do not find it easy to find love, comfort, and a feeling of at-homeness. If men do not remarry, their rates of car accidents, drug abuse, alcoholism, and emotional problems tend to rise, especially five to six years after their divorce. Whereas two decades ago many Americans were willing to divorce, in recent years they have become more conservative and more realistic in their marital expectations.

More couples are finding it better to make up than to break up.

As women become better educated and establish occupational and economic independence, the gap of well-being between marrieds and singles is diminishing. For example, the economic strain due to remaining single or returning to single status can become less of an issue. The stigma of being single is decreasing, with more divorced women staying single and unmarried persons engaging in sexual relationships with less negative social stigma (but potential risk to their health). Some women at midlife are single by choice and have never married. However, more midlife women with the resources have adopted children over recent years or have had children by assisted reproduction.

The **displaced homemaker** is a woman whose primary activity has been homemaking and who has lost her main source of income because of divorce or the death of her husband. Most of the displaced homemakers who are 65 and older are widowed, whereas most of the displaced homemakers under age 35 are divorced or separated, and many have young children living with them (for older women, the children might be grandchildren). Some displaced homemakers work part-time or seasonally, and some do not work at all. These women are typically ill-equipped to deal with the financial consequences of divorce. They usually find themselves cut off from their ex-husband's private pension plan, life insurance, and medical insurance, but they might be eligible for some Social Security benefits if their marriage lasted 10 or more years.

Remarriage   Most divorced people do not reject marriage and eventually remarry, but it has become more common for them to cohabit before remarriage (Hamplova & Le Bourdais, 2008; Xu, Hudspeth, & Bartowski, 2006). About five of every six divorced men and three of every four divorced women marry again (see Table 16.2). In fact, in 2002 about one-third of marriages were remarriages for one or both partners, and some of these remarriages were third and fourth marriages. This social pattern is known as *serial marriage*. Men are more likely than women to remarry, for a number of reasons. For one thing, men typically marry younger women, and thus they have a larger pool of potential partners. Moreover, men are more likely to marry someone who was not previously married and often marry women with less education than themselves. The likelihood that a woman will remarry declines with age and with increasing levels of education. However, women who remarry eventually are more likely than men to bring children from a previous union into their new marriage. Thus, stepfather families are more common than stepmother families. Furthermore, remarriages have additional challenges and higher divorce rates than first marriages (Ganong & Coleman, 2004).

Stepfamilies   A stepfamily is formed when one or both of the partners bring children from a previous relationship into a new union. According to the National Stepfamily Resource Center (2008), about 25 percent of current stepfamilies are actually made up of cohabiting couples and children. Various estimates suggest that between one-third and one-half of all new marriages in the United States involve divorced, widowed, or single parents with children from previous relationships. These circumstances with at least one stepparent create what are known as "blended families."

Stepparents are probably the most overlooked group of parents in the United States. This is surprising, considering that the stepparent-stepchild relationship is pivotal in determining the relative success of stepfamily functioning (Schrodt, 2006). Social scientists have by and large studied intact original families, single-parent families, and, more recently, cohabiting families. For their part, a good number of stepparents feel stigmatized. Images of wicked stepmothers, cruel stepbrothers and stepsisters, and victimized stepchildren found in such tales as *Cinderella* still abound. But stepparents, just like biological or adoptive parents, vary widely in terms of their care of and involvement with their stepchildren (Svare, Jay, & Mason, 2004).

Depending on their age at the time of parental divorce, children may already be dealing with profound loss, grief, sadness, anxiety, anger, guilt, and often shame. Stephanie Staal (2000), herself a child of divorce, interviewed 150 adults whose parents divorced and says there is instant realization that "childhood is over." A parent's remarriage or cohabitation compounds a child's emotional turmoil. With remarriage, parents achieve a sense of control in their lives, which bolsters their self-esteem and confidence, but children have no sense of control. Judges, court-appointed attorneys, divorce lawyers, and social workers make the most crucial decisions about the child's well-being. After dealing with separation, divorce, and loss of a biological parent (if he or she was involved), often with loss of home, neighborhood, friends, and teachers, and probably with a time of single parenthood, children are again confronted with new upheaval and adjustment. If both parents remarry, the stress and strain can be overwhelming for the child—who may be hostile with, or withdrawn from, all adults and stepsiblings involved (see Figure 16.6). Remarriage shatters children's fantasy that their parents will get together again. And the new spouse threatens the special bond that often forms between a child and a single parent. Matters are complicated because adults often expect instant respect or love in the new household. Many women assume, "I love my new husband, so I will love his children, and we all will find happiness together." Such notions are invalid because close relationships take time to develop (Zimmerman & Thayer, 2003). Complicated scenarios

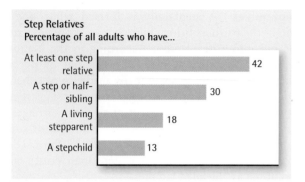

FIGURE 16.6 Percentage of All U.S. Adults Who Have a Step Relative: 2010 More than 4 in 10 adults in the United States have at least one step relative.
Source: Parker, K. (2011, January 18). A portrait of stepfamilies. Pew Research Center, Social and Demographic Trends. Retrieved from http://pewsocialtrends.org/2011/01/13/a-portrait-of-stepfamilies/

arise, such as the following, which would not occur in a traditional family:

My ex-husband has money and he bought our son Ricky a car. That's great! But when my stepson David needs transportation, he is not permitted to borrow Ricky's car because my ex is adamant about not wanting to support someone else's child. Ricky would love to share the car with his stepbrother, but he can't risk angering his father. Besides, David is sensitive about being the "poor" brother and would not drive it anyway. It just burned us up [her and her current husband]. So we scraped together some money we could ill afford and bought an old junker for David. Of course, we fixed it up so it runs safely, and now we've put that problem behind us. (Fishman, 1983)

Most stepparents attempt to re-create an intact-family setting because it is the only model they have. Remarriages with complex social systems (for instance, stepsiblings, stepgrandparents, and in-laws from a previous marriage) are more likely to experience difficulties. One woman in a stepfamily with seven children tells of this experience:

Our first-grader had a hard time explaining to his teacher whether he had two sisters or four, since two of them weren't living in our home. The teacher said, "Justin seems unusually confused about his family situation," and we told her, "He's absolutely right to be confused. That's how it is." (Collins, 1983, p. 21)

With stepfamilies there is yet another dimension—the natural parent who lives elsewhere. A stepparent's existence can pose insecurity and loyalty problems for the children. They wonder, "If I get close to my stepparent, will I betray my real parent?" Children are happier when they can maintain a consistent, easy relationship

with the absent parent. Commonly, however, ex-spouses resent having lost control over raising their children and fail to maintain strong relationships, and some use child-support payments or money for child activities and college as forms of control. In most cases, the child has to continually adjust to different lifestyles, traditions, and discipline in two homes and becomes the intermediary of bad news and jealous inquiries between two hostile ex-spouses. Such conflict between ex-spouses can continue for years and often puts the child in the position of lying or of keeping "secrets" from both parents. The attitudes, emotional insecurities, and dysfunctional patterns of behavior that the child develops to survive can carry over into their own close adult relationships (Marquardt, 2005).

Given these excessive tensions, it is not surprising that stepparents report significantly less satisfaction with their family life than married couples feel with their biological children. Remarriages that bring children from previous relationships into the household have a much higher divorce rate (DeLongis & Preece, 2002). To succeed, the stepfamily must develop workable solutions that leave some of the "old" traditions, rituals, and customs intact while fashioning new ones. Although additional strains are associated with stepfamilies, so is a good deal of positive adaptation. From their clinical experience, Zimmerman and Thayer (2003) are hopeful about children recovering their emotional stability with time. Parents can build healthy relationships with children by demonstrating unconditional love, showing trust and respect, setting reasonable limits and age-appropriate boundaries, valuing accomplishments, helping children make reasonable decisions, and carefully "picking their battles" (carefully considering which arguments are worth winning and which are not) as children develop through their own life stages (Zimmerman & Thayer, 2003). To read more about adjusting to life in a stepfamily, see the *More Information You Can Use* box, "Adaptation in Stepfamilies."

Question

What are some of the additional stressors for adults who remarry into stepfamilies and for their children?

Adult Children and Grandchildren The term **empty nest** refers to a household that had children living at home who now have left home to pursue an education, enter the military, and/or start jobs and their own households. The household now contains only one or both parents. However, as we saw in Chapter 14, more adult children are returning to live with their parents during life transitions, such as while attending college or when establishing their careers. Or they might return home with grandchildren during a separation or divorce or through longer periods of unemployment or mortgage

MORE INFORMATION YOU CAN USE

Adaptation in Stepfamilies

Each stepfamily presents its own set of problems and requires its own unique solutions because of the complex mix of the members of the blended family. Several matters of everyday living are common sources of conflict for stepfamilies, but a little prudence can go a long way.

Food

Food preferences are quite salient, especially to the step-children. Mealtimes are normally times when a family is together, so there are more chances during mealtimes for disruptions to occur. Finding out what family members enjoy eating—and what they don't like—can make for a more pleasant experience when dining. Preparing each child's favorite meal for a birthday or a special occasion is a way of saying to each child, "You are special. I care about you." Table manners and hygiene should be taught carefully over a period of time. A recently popular expression (and the title of a book stepparents might consider reading) is "Don't sweat the small stuff—and it's all small stuff."

Household Chores

To resolve the completion of chores, prepare charts allocating duties. This practice seems to work. Find out each child's abilities, make tasks age-appropriate, and solicit the child's input. Even 2-year-olds enjoy setting the table. Children often resist even biological parents when it comes to chores, so expect friction when a stepparent has expectations. The best advice is to do the chore with the child in the beginning. Tasks should be age-appropriate and need to be broken down into smaller, manageable tasks. Stepchildren who make scheduled visits still need to have responsibilities—it gives them a sense of belonging ("I had to clean *my* room at Dad's"). Even though they may be resistant at first, children develop more confidence and security the more capable they become.

Personal Territory

Changes in living arrangements pose turf problems. The stepparent who moves into the spouse's home finds that areas of the house are already designated for use and that intrusions are deeply resented. This matter is more easily handled by moving to a new house or making personal spaces within the old one. New paint, fresh curtains, and a new rug selected by children can personalize their space. Solicit the children's opinions, and enlist their help. Bring things from the other home to put in their new room. Even new husbands and wives do not like sleeping in the ex-spouse's bed. Biological siblings squabble over what belongs to whom, so expect these types of spats among stepsiblings.

Stepfamilies A growing number of American households are composed of stepfamilies. Because half of all remarried persons are parents, their new partners become stepparents, and the children become stepchildren. Becoming a member of a stepfamily requires adaptation, cooperation, patience, a sense of humor, and a great deal of faith.

In the beginning, it is best if the biological parent manages discipline, but there must be rules about civility in the home. Stepchildren, even young ones, feel that stepparents have no right to tell them what to do (any more than we like a stranger telling us what to do). Expect to hear "You're not my Mom (or Dad)!" Be prepared to acknowledge and discuss the underlying feelings behind sharp remarks. Get feelings into the open for age-appropriate discussions ("I know you're angry that I'm asking you to put your clothes away. It isn't easy having to pack and unpack every weekend, is it? It's a lot of work for you. Let's do this together.")

Financial Matters

The biological parent is probably paying alimony and/or child support to an ex-spouse, so there are often financial strains in supporting the "new" family. Where monies come from and how funds are allocated must be mutually

continued

decided. Stepfamily finances come under close scrutiny by outsiders, such as lawyers, courts, the social services system, and the IRS. Keep track of medical expenses, insurance monies, orthodontia payments, clothing and school-related expenses, and so on. Over time, an ex-spouse is likely to initiate court-ordered audits of a family's income for support readjustment (mainly if there is a raise in pay). Or a tax audit might be required—dependents are often split equally between ex-spouses by the courts for tax purposes. Limited finances require careful management. Using a computer program for managing family finances makes tracking income and expenses easier. You will have an easier time in court, and save money, if your records are organized. The demands of an ex-spouse might seem unfair, but this is up to the courts or a mediator to decide. Make sure separation and divorce documents indicate explicitly who is responsible for what expenses. There are legal consequences if a biological parent does not follow through with court-ordered support payments.

Discipline

This is the area of most disputes between parent and stepparent. Children accustomed to one type of discipline have to adjust to another, often on a weekly basis. Professionals agree that the parents must present a united front. Children must not learn to pit one parent against the other. In natural families, parenting techniques evolve gradually as the parents and children move through the family life cycle. In blended families, there is no time for such evolution. A solid understanding of child and adolescent development helps parents communicate effectively. Discuss whatever forms of discipline are best without the child being present. Assign discipline as promptly after the infraction as possible, especially for young children, and the type and degree of discipline should match the misbehavior. As in any family, fairness

should prevail. The most effective discipline teaches the child what she or he should do rather than focusing on what was done wrong. ("You didn't pick up your room, so you will have to do it now rather than going to your friend's house" instead of "You're grounded!") The stepfamily must reevaluate what is really important in the family over the long run.

Changes over Time

Teenagers want to spend more time with friends. Both sets of parents need to support the adolescent's interests in school and outside activities. Adolescence is a time when teens need to express themselves and have some independence, and parents who force children to adhere to a rigid visitation schedule spend a lot of time with an unhappy teen. Allow teens to make more choices. Do not, however, let the teen get away with less supervision. At this stage, manipulation of both sets of parents is common. A child who has two homes will think, "I can always go to the other home." Try not to dwell on the negative; that type of attention is a reinforcer for some children. Look for and praise the positive. Make children be responsible and learn from the consequences of their actions.

Support Groups

Communities and Web sites have stepparent support groups for adults and children. Experienced stepparents understand the special stresses and emotions that new stepparents are subject to. Schools often have support groups for children of divorced parents or in blended families, such as *Banana Splits* (see http://www.bananasplitsresourcecenter.org). Children in intact families will say, "I love you." It can be years before a stepparent hears this. Recognize that children do not realize the sacrifices any parent makes to raise them (until they themselves become parents).

Adapted, with contributions from Thomas L. Crandell and Corinne Haines Crandell, from Jannette Lofas. (2004). *Stepparenting: Everything You Need to Know to Make It Work*. New York: Kensington Pubishing Corp.

foreclosures, as occurred in 2008. In 2009, more than 6 percent of children under age 18 were reported to be residing in the home of their grandparents—and more than half of these were also with one or both parents (Child Trends Databank, 2011). Social scientists refer to "two skip generations" when grandchildren live with grandparents and no parent is present (see Figure 16.7).

Also, more middle-aged adults (primarily women) are caring for their own elderly parents and/or their in-laws with the assistance of health-care aides and adult day care or are raising grandchildren whose parents are incarcerated, institutionalized, or incapable of parenting. Middle-aged parents of young adults with disabilities (such as severe intellectual disabilities, head injuries and paralysis, and other multiple handicaps) today have difficult, time-consuming decisions to make about the eventual

placement of their children in group homes or supported apartments. They also need to become the legal guardians of their adult child and assist with sheltered employment or supervised employment. These are often complex, heart-wrenching decisions for aging parents. We normally expect that our adult children will be capable of making their own life decisions.

But for some older married couples, the nest stays empty after the children depart. This can be especially stressful for a smaller percentage of women who have been "stay-at-home" mothers raising children, the central ingredient in their life and identity. Clinical psychologists and psychiatrists have emphasized the emotional depression such women face when their children leave home, calling their psychological distress the **empty-nest syndrome** (Willis & Martin, 2005). However, many

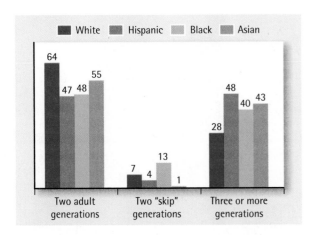

FIGURE 16.7 Living Arrangements Among Those in Multigenerational Family Households, by Ethnicity, United States: 2008 This figure shows the percentages of U.S. families living in each of three different multigenerational arrangements. "Skip" generation is a grandchild living with a grandparent, no parent present.
Source: The Pew Research Center. (2010, March 18). The return of the multigenerational family household. Retrieved from http://pewsocialtrends.org/2010/03/18/the-return-of-the-multi-generational-family-household/

midlife parents have derived their identity and meaning in life both from nurturing children and from pursuing a career, and these parents experience less psychological distress or sense of loss when the children move on with their lives. Adults of immigrant status have more depressive symptoms if left alone when grown children move on with their lives (Wilmoth & Chen, 2003). Community agencies and churches need to promote social integration of these adults for their health and emotional well-being.

Some women object to the overemphasis on physical changes in their midlife maturation. Cross-sectional and longitudinal studies find that many women do not regret the end of fertility, feel happy when their children are successfully launched, and experience satisfaction when their children continue to stay in touch with them (Helson, 1997, p. 29). Couples often view the empty-nest period "as a time of new freedom," and most parents adapt to the empty-nest period quite well. Overall, midlife adults' sense of self-acceptance, purpose in life, and environmental mastery were strongly linked with their assessments of their grown children's adjustment (Brim, Ryff, & Kessler, 2004).

Caring for Elderly Parents Social scientists call middle-aged adults the *sandwich generation* because many have responsibilities both for their own children and for their elderly parents or grandparents (who are living much longer). Three or more generations are often living together (see Figure 16.7). While most are launching their own children and looking forward to having more time for themselves, many encounter new demands from their

parents. Some midlife couples find that after reaching the empty-nest stage for a while, the home is suddenly refilled with either an elderly parent or a grown child who returns home after a divorce or the loss of a job (see Chapter 14). On average, a woman in the United States will spend the same number of years helping elderly parents as she did raising children. Since more American couples are delaying childbirth, more couples will find themselves sandwiched between child care and elder care in the coming decades (Willis & Martin, 2005).

Aging parents increasingly require more time, emotional energy, and financial aid from their adult children. Adult daughters and daughters-in-law are more likely to bear the primary responsibility for their aged parents (Amato et al., 2007). Financial assistance might be supplemented with income for health-care costs through Social Security, Medicare, and Medicaid programs. But changes in reimbursements stipulated by the Balanced Budget Act of 1997 led to significant reductions in Medicare support for home health care. Further, such stress has led to serious strains on the finances, health, and psychosocial well-being of both the patient and familial caregivers (Davitt, 2009). Various federal acts have proposed *paid leave* from work for several weeks to aid caregivers, but none has yet become law (Mintz, 2007). As of 2011, Congress put these on hold and is deliberating more cuts to entitlement programs. It is not clear what the extent of medical-coverage provisions for the elderly will be when (and if) the Patient Protection and Affordable Care Act of 2010 goes into effect in 2014.

The Family and Medical Leave Act (FMLA) of 1993 was amended in 2009 and provides certain employees with up to 12 weeks of unpaid, job-protected leave per year to care for immediate family members upon their birth or adoption or for members (including oneself) with a serious health condition; this act also includes military family leave requirements. Group health benefits must be maintained during the leave (U.S. Department of Labor, 2011).

A meta-analysis of 229 studies on caregiver stresses found that despite the changing roles of women, when it comes to the elderly, the old maxim still holds: "A son's a son till he takes a wife, but a daughter's a daughter the rest of her life." Adult daughters and daughters-in-law provide more caregiving hours, help with more caregiving tasks, and assist with more personal care than adult sons (Pinquart & Sörensen, 2006). They juggle the competing role demands of employee, homemaker, wife, mother, grandmother, and caregiver. More caregivers of elderly parents are working alone (Wolff & Kasper, 2006). When an entire family shares in care for an elderly parent instead of just one sibling, mutual help strategies lessen the burden, and levels of distress may be decreased for all concerned (Mintz, 2007). If midlife children are working full-time, elderly parents are more likely to rely on services such as public transit or medi-vans, Office for Aging adult day care, GROW (for home maintenance, repairs, and yard work), American Red Cross shopper programs, Meals on Wheels, and care from paid home health aides. But seniors are also more vulnerable to problems with provisional services (Scharlach, Gustavson, & Dal Santo, 2007). Mintz (2007, p. 27) cites adult-child caregiver Anna Shank on the common upheaval in family dynamics: "What's the hardest thing about being a family caregiver? Changing roles from being the child to being the one in control."

The motivations and expectations of the middle-aged and the elderly differ to some extent because of their different life-history periods and cohort experiences. Today's middle-aged adults are more familiar with technology than their elderly parents, who may have much difficulty with complex TV remote controls and DVRs, digital home appliances and vehicle panels, cell phones, digital thermostats, ATMs, computers, complex "phone trees," and paying bills online. Such differences are a source of intergenerational strain. Yet resentment or hostility is less when the financial independence of the aging parents enables them to stay in their own home or pay for long-term-care insurance. Both generations seem to prefer intimacy at a distance and opt for residing independently as long as possible. Thus, those elderly parents who call on children for assistance are apt to be frail, quite disabled, gravely ill, or failing in memory or emotional well-being—and even then, some insist on remaining in their homes.

When middle-aged adults express reluctance to take on the primary care of an ailing parent, they are not necessarily being hardhearted. Rather, they recognize that their marriage or emotional health could be endangered by taking on those caretaking responsibilities, but this realization can produce strong feelings of guilt while creating resentment among adult siblings. In fact, the common predictors of emotional strain for adult-child caregivers are a caregiver's perceived overload, family disagreement, and limitations on a caregiver's life (Kang, 2006).

Financial Security and Retirement Risks Midlife women who leave employment to care for ailing parents face other financial security risks. A serious concern is midlife women's lack of awareness and preparedness for their own imminent retirement. Becoming the recipient of Social Security retirement benefits at 62 or older depends on a set of interrelated factors. Presently, two-thirds of older women receive spouse or widow benefits because they did not work outside the home or their husband's income was considerably greater than theirs. "Spouse and widow benefits are distributed on the basis of marital rather than employment status and generally require recipients either to be currently married or to have had a ten-year marriage. The unprecedented retreat from marriage, particularly among black women, means the distributional impact of these benefits changes dramatically for each cohort that enters old age" (Meyer, Wolf, & Himes, 2004). Nonemployed women who have been

The Sandwich Generation Middle age often brings with it responsibilities for one's own children, grandchildren, and aging parents or grandparents. The tasks fall disproportionately upon women, because it is often assumed that they will take primary responsibility for family caregiving.

cohabiting long-term and those who were married for a short time and divorced, or who divorced and then chose to cohabit, may be at risk of not qualifying for these vital financial benefits (see Figure 16.4). Women who plan to retire and receive Social Security benefits based on their ex-husband's income lose that eligibility if they remarry. The benefit distribution model is outdated, but at present Congress shows an unwillingness to alter this policy.

Questions

What is meant by the phrase "the sandwich generation"? How does being in this life stage affect the relationships of middle-aged adults with their parents, grown children, and grandchildren? How might some women be jeopardizing their Social Security benefits for retirement?

Friendship

Most people distinguish friends from relatives and coworkers. But a relative can also be a close friend. Friends are people we socialize with and with whom we can talk and share activities and for whom we have warm feelings (Fingerman & Pitzer, 2007). As noted throughout this text, close and meaningful social relationships play a vital part in human happiness and health (Krause, 2007). In many studies, researchers report that people who have friends to whom they can turn for affirmation, empathy, advice, assistance, and affection are less likely to become ill and are more likely to survive health challenges such as heart attacks, cancer, and major surgery. It is more important to have at least one close friend with whom we can share open and honest thoughts and feelings than it is to have a substantial network of acquaintances (Fingerman & Pitzer, 2007). Krause (2007) reports that for older adults, "more emotional support from family members and friends is associated with a greater sense of meaning in life."

People who have at least one best friend, as well as a happy marriage and close family relationships, do best as they move through middle age and into old age. They have a high level of well-being. Individuals who feel unhappy with their marriage can also do quite well if they have the support of a close friend and a strong family network. The researchers noted that close friends are apt to fulfill everyday emotional needs, while families and spouses are needed for overall well-being (Birditt & Antonucci, 2007).

Adams and Blieszner (1998) have been studying the generation born between 1946 and 1964 and its patterns of friendship. They find that women in midlife are more likely than men to have intimate friendships. Men often have many acquaintances with whom they share experiences, but they often have few or no close friends. The social contacts of many elderly men are restricted to their wives, their children, and their children's families. Male relationships are often limited to group settings involving those who share a hobby or a sports team, occupational colleagues, or fraternal organizations, such as Rotary, VFW, Shriners, and Knights of Columbus. Moreover, women tend to maintain family contacts and emotionally invest themselves in the family to a greater degree than men do throughout the lifetime of a family. Women's friendships often take up where their marriages leave off. A woman's best friends typically compensate her for the deficits of intimacy she encounters within her marriage. Overall, women tend to have more extensive support networks, provide and receive more support, and report being more satisfied with their friendships (Welch & Houser, 2010). Yet as we age, our friendship network is likely to grow smaller as midlife adults retire, relocate, become caregivers with great responsibility, experience illness, or die—but new and variable friendships can be made (Blieszner, 2006). See the *Further Developments* box on page 530, "Baby Boomers and Social Networking."

Friendship, Social Support, and Meaning in Life
Throughout life, our siblings, best friends, and other relatives make up a vital network of social support that helps us cope with life's challenges. Some midlife women develop close friendships through activities and organizations, such as the Red Hat Society, that have a central mission of expanding the bonds of sisterhood.

THE WORKPLACE

Workplace trends in the past two decades (such as corporate downsizing, takeovers, and outsourcing to foreign sites) threaten older adults' sense of work identity and economic security. Such changes include new technologies, new service industries, new markets, immigrant coworkers accepting lower pay, job migration, population shifts, and continuing education. Employees, especially those in their forties and fifties, experience continual demands to retrain, upgrade their job skills, and take on more responsibility at work. Today's midlife employees can no longer rely on the education and training acquired 35-40 years ago. Cross-sectional studies on age and work productivity find that aging accounts for only a small amount of variance in work performance (Czaja, 2001).

Some have been forced into long-term unemployment, underemployment, disability, or early retirement; others are making career changes in order to reenter the

---

Question

How do women's and men's friendships in midlife differ in value, settings, and purpose?

FURTHER DEVELOPMENTS

Baby Boomers and Social Networking

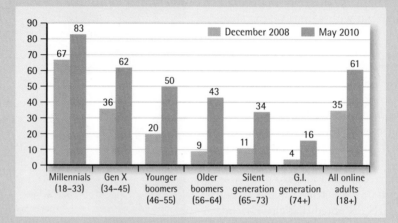

FIGURE 16.8 Changes in the Use of Social Network Sites, by Generation: 2008–2010 This graph shows the percentages of Internet users who use social network sites, in each of six age groups and overall. Note the significant increase in use across all ages.

Source: Zickhur, K. (2010, December 16). Generations: 2010. Pew Research Center's Internet & American Life Project, April 29–May 30, 2010 Tracking Survey. N=2,252 adults 18 and older. Retrieved from http://www.pewinternet.org/~/media//Files/Reports/2010/PIP_Generations_and_Tech10.pdf

More than 16.5 million U.S. adults aged 55 and older engage in social networking; Facebook has seen the most growth among users 50 and older (della Cava, 2009). In just the first year after AARP.org unveiled its social networking platform, about 350,000 users created 1,700 groups for everything from gardening to social activism. Among middle-aged adults, social networking started out as a way to check on kids and grandchildren, but now it is all about their individual connections with peers. Their reasons for connecting with others online vary, but the passion for it is unwavering.

A 52-year-old retired software consultant says that sharing his passion for NASCAR and barbecue with fellow devotees has "made me a lot of great new friends I otherwise wouldn't have." At 45 years old, a family counselor from Park City, Utah, used to get her social fix while traveling to work. She has turned to social networking "to find other women who are raising teens, enjoying good careers and have something to say." Baby boomers using Facebook increased 107 percent between 2008 and 2009. As the word about these social networking sites continues to spread among middle-aged adults, the percentage of users is expected to skyrocket (see Figure 16.8).

Of course, some young Facebookers are annoyed by the older generation's encroachment on their territory (Gates, 2009). For example, a middle-aged mother put in friend requests to her teenage daughters and was promptly rejected. Facebook is not for people her age, they informed her, but the growing trend suggests otherwise. Moreover, there are Facebook-related advantages to age. Finding or being found by old friends, all the way back to grammar school, can be a real kick. How many 14-year-olds have truly long-lost friends? And what teenager can understand the joy of seeing that a once-arrogant young man has gained weight and gone bald (Gates, 2009)?

But for all its wonders, Internet social networking may have a downside. In fact, for some middle-aged users it's the "social" part that is the issue. For example, a Facebook user states, "When I started, it was exciting, but then I was getting friended by people I met once and people I had purely business relationships with, and it made me wonder, 'What's the definition of a friend?'" Further, there are privacy issues that come along with opening up your life to others online. One woman explains, "It's almost voyeuristic. Everyone can see you and you can see them," she says. "Sometimes, I feel like yelling, 'Just pick up the phone and call me!'" (della Cava, 2009). *Time Magazine* tech columnist Josh Quittner, a boomer who can social network with the best of them, offers his advice, "It's not Las Vegas, what happens on Facebook does not stay on Facebook." But for all the pros and cons of social networking, one thing remains certain: Baby boomers' interest in social media is here to stay. So whether it's a member of Congress Twittering during presidential speeches, parents connecting with high school flames on Facebook, or empty-nesters planning group outings on grown-up sites, boomers have made social networks a place of their own.

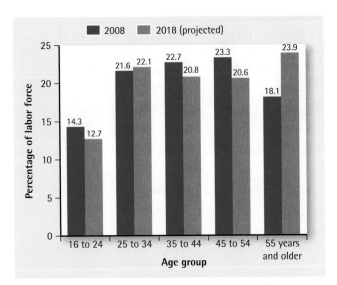

FIGURE 16.9 Percentage of U.S. Workers in the Labor Force, by Age Group: 2008 and Projected to 2018
Adults aged 40 to 64 make up more than half of the U.S. labor force. Thus many in midlife are at the top of their careers, productive, and contributing to society—and not retired.
Source: Bureau of Labor Statistics. (2011a). *Occupational Outlook Handbook, 2010–2011 Edition: Overview of the 2008–18 Projections.* Washington, DC: The U.S. Department of Labor. Retrieved from http://www.bls.gov/oco/oco2003.htm

workforce. A few attempt self-employment. This experience has a significant impact on economic and long-term financial security, marital stability, retirement planning, and self-esteem. But with very careful planning, retraining, or moving into career areas that are in demand, the employment picture need not look so bleak. The U.S. Bureau of Labor predicts that from 2008 to 2018, "workers aged 55 years and older are anticipated to leap from 18.1 percent to 23.9 percent" (see Figure 16.9) (U.S. Bureau of Labor Statistics, 2011b).

Job Satisfaction

French philosopher Albert Camus captured the importance of work in giving meaning and satisfaction to our lives: "Without work, all life goes rotten. But when work is soulless, life stifles and dies." Work that is not fulfilling can erode and undermine much of our humanness. Some social scientists have applied the concept of alienation to such troubles and have sought solutions to these problems in programs designed to decrease alienation. The word **alienation** commonly implies a pervasive sense of powerlessness, meaninglessness, normlessness, isolation, and self-estrangement (Erikson, 1986). Alienation can result in psychological effects called **job burnout.** The problem that confronts most people in occupational life today is that they cannot gain a sense of self-actualization in their work. The most potent factors in job satisfaction are those that relate to workers' self-respect, their chance

to perform well, their opportunities for achievement and growth, and the chance to contribute something personal and quite unique. People want to be appreciated for their contributions at work and are likely to offer to mentor others who are moving up (Sterns & Huyck, 2001). However, not everyone experiences satisfaction in their work, and some take "psychological retirement" (Levinson, 1996, p. 375). Some whose work performance is minimally adequate accept "early retirement."

Work affects an individual's personal and family life in many ways (Perrone, Webb, & Jackson, 2007). Jobs that permit occupational self-direction—initiative, thought, and independent judgment—foster intellectual flexibility. Individuals who enjoy opportunities for self-direction in their work are more likely to become more self-confident, less authoritarian, less conformist in their ideas, and less fatalistic in their nonwork lives than other individuals are. These traits lead, in time, to promotions to more responsible jobs that allow even greater latitude for occupational self-direction. In sum, life satisfaction and overall well-being are linked to work satisfaction (Perrone, Webb, & Jackson, 2007).

The Families and Work Institute has done extensive research on the needs and priorities of U.S. workers for the past three decades. Its research shows that both male and female workers want flexibility so that they can balance family roles and devote enough time to work to do a good job. The researchers thought that they would find that people choose to emphasize either work *or* family. They were surprised to learn that a growing number of workers emphasize work and family equally and try to give their best in both realms. Those who choose this strategy are much more likely to be satisfied at work, and they have lower levels of stress than counterparts who choose a singular focus. They achieved this dual focus by choosing not to take work home and being fully emotionally present when they are with their families (Families and Work Institute, 2004).

It had been thought that job satisfaction increased with age. However, some researchers argue that the relationship between job satisfaction and age is U-shaped, declining from a moderate level in early years of employment and then steadily increasing up to retirement (Clark, Oswald, & Warr, 1996). Workers just beginning their careers and workers nearing the end of their careers report being more satisfied than those at the midpoint. According to one theory, younger workers expect a more casual work environment that allows for more worker input and decision making. Because this expectation has been found to be realistic, new companies have adopted this strategy. For example, the work environment at Google is more casual than the environment at a more traditional company. Proponents of this view cite as key features of the "new values" a willingness to question authority and a demand that work be fulfilling and enriching.

Midlife Career Transition—Women Midlife offers women opportunities to explore new career avenues or resume the pursuit of educational goals that were deferred because of marriage and child-care responsibilities. Some are returning to college, while others forge their own home-based ventures.

Source: Between Friends. © Sandra Bell Lundy. Distributed by King Features Syndicate.

These values contradict those of an older industrial order founded on deference to authority and responsiveness to such traditional rewards as income and promotion.

A second interpretation of age differences in job satisfaction looks to life-cycle effects (Sterns & Huyck, 2001). Proponents of this hypothesis say that older workers are more satisfied with their jobs because, on the whole, they have had better jobs than younger workers do. In the usual career pattern, a person begins at or near the bottom and, where possible, moves up. Young people require little more than a start—a job that is "good enough" for the immediate present, supplies sufficient money to meet short-term needs, and affords some opportunity for advancement. But as workers develop new needs (marry, have children, and grow older), they also accumulate the experience, skills, and seniority that enable them to find positions that are progressively more satisfying.

> **Question**
>
> What are some factors affecting middle-aged workers' job satisfaction?

Midlife Career Change

Surveys on emotional well-being and aging have indicated that those who enter the professions (law, medicine, dentistry, pharmacy, chiropractic, veterinary medicine) are likely to become dissatisfied with the demands of their careers, but many feel they cannot change occupations because the financial rewards, security, and prestige are so great. This serious conflict between changing to more satisfying work and living at a different status or remaining in a career that gives no satisfaction might contribute to the rise in the suicide rate for people, mainly males, in their forties and older. But middle-aged adults who are low-income earners do not have the luxury of such career-change considerations. Earle and Heymann (2004)

found in their study of work, family, and social class that nearly one-fourth of all employed parents lacked paid vacation, paid sick leave, or paid medical, education, or retirement benefits, nor did they have adequate time off. Thus, job changes for this group of adults come out of necessity, because they are looking for more flexible policies and benefits to meet family obligations. In the changing economic times since 2007, it is more common for employers to trim such benefits, terminate older workers, and hire more temporary staff, which increases employee insecurity. As a result, midlife workers often have to work multiple jobs to make ends meet.

The U.S. Bureau of Labor Statistics gathers data on workers who are doing work that is different from what they did one year earlier. Both men and women switch jobs or careers for a variety of reasons. Some find that their career has not provided the fulfillment they had expected or that it no longer challenges them. One professor who left academic life at age 43 for a career in marketing told one of the authors,

> I just got fed up with teaching. It no longer turned me on. I would wake up in the morning and dread the day ahead. When driving over to the university, I would develop waves of nausea. I began thinking to myself, "This is no way to spend the rest of my life." I had always been interested in marketing, and I had done consulting for a number of years before I left the university. It took me about five years before I got the business really rolling but now I'm doing pretty well. I like being my own boss and I like making money—big money. I never could do that as a prof.

At midlife many people take stock of themselves and reassess where they are going and what they are doing with their lives. Some return to college to learn new skills. Others build on contacts, interests, skills, or hobbies. Another reason for midlife adults' changing jobs or becoming self-employed is to allow for a more flexible work schedule to care for aging parents or grandchildren residing in the home. Midlife males who choose self-employment often have had a parent or parents who were self-employed. Executives, administrative workers, and service workers (including child-care workers, building service workers, and home health aides) are expected to become self-employed in increasing numbers (Perrone, Webb, & Jackson, 2007). In 2009, 15 percent of U.S. workers aged 50 to 64 and 25 percent of workers aged 65 and older were self-employed (Morin, 2009).

Unemployment, Underemployment, and Early Retirement

Adults find unemployment to be a very painful experience. U.S. job insecurity is rising as a consequence of corporate downsizing, the demand for continual technological training, the outsourcing of jobs to other countries, and the present U.S. recession. With higher rates of U.S. unemployment, there has been an increase in the number of contingent workers that employment agencies call "contract," "part-time," or "temporary" workers, especially in service industries (8.5 million persons in May 2011) (U.S. Bureau of Labor Statistics, 2011b). These workers are typically not eligible for standard company benefits, such as employee health insurance and pensions; they often earn lower wages; and they lack job security (Connelly & Gallagher, 2004). In fact, a significant and growing percentage of U.S. college faculty members are part-time workers (adjuncts), especially at two-year colleges (Snyder & Dillow, 2010).

Social scientists find that unemployment and underemployment have serious adverse effects on physical and mental health and family life (Paul, 2005). A growing body of research finds that such ill effects can include "depression, hopelessness, apathy, anxiety, psychosomatic symptoms, low self-esteem, low life satisfaction, negative mood, alcoholism, and (para)suicide." The worst psychological effects of job loss, however, can be minimized if opportunities exist for reemployment (Paul, 2005).

Unemployment also increases the financial and role strains of parents, intensifies marital conflict and conflict between parents and their children, and undermines children's school achievement and health. George Clem, a 31-year-old unemployed manufacturing worker in Jackson, Michigan, observed, "I've lost everything I ever had—it's all gone. I've lost my job. I've lost my home. I thought I had my future assured, but now I know I have no future." A woman in the same community said, "Emotionally, you begin to feel worthless. Rationally, you know you're not worthless, but the rational and the emotional don't always meet" (Nelson, 1983, p. 8).

National unemployment figures in 2011 hover between 9 to 10 percent and include people who are currently eligible for unemployment benefits, but the actual unemployment rate of people who are no longer eligible

for unemployment and are unemployed on a long-term basis is estimated to be much higher. Studies of unemployed workers reveal that their behavioral and emotional reactions to unemployment typically pass through several stages (Kaufman, 1982):

- Initially, they undergo a sequence of shock, relief, and relaxation. Some had expected job loss. Upon dismissal, they may feel a sense of relief that at last the stress of suspense has ended. They tend to remain confident and hopeful that they will find a new job soon. For the first few months, they maintain normal relationships with their family and friends.

- The second stage is a concerted effort to find a new job. Typically, they marshal their resources and concentrate their energy on finding a new job. This stage can last for up to several months. Those who do not find another job during this time move into the next stage.

- The third stage lasts several weeks or more. The self-esteem of the unemployed begins to crumble, and they experience high levels of self-doubt and anxiety. Those nearing retirement age find their outlook particularly bleak.

- The fourth stage finds unemployed workers drifting into a state of resignation and withdrawal. They are discouraged and convinced that they are not going to find work, so they either stop looking for work or search for it only intermittently. Some make a conscious decision to change careers or to settle for some other line of work. And they may look for other sources of self-esteem, including helping their family or friends, or through volunteering.

However, families of the unemployed are more likely to experience divorce (Hayhoe, 2006). Health benefits, sick time, vacations, and other benefits end for most Americans when they lose their jobs, and many lose their retirement pensions as well. Financial pressures mount. They are unable to keep up making their mortgage payments or they fall behind in the rent. As they see their cars and furniture repossessed, they feel that they are losing control of their lives. Weekly visits to food pantries become a necessity. Child abuse, family quarreling, alcoholism, and other signs of maladjustment mounts. Many men feel emasculated when confronted by an involuntary change of identity and deprived of the role of provider for the family, and they lash out with destructive reactions (Hayhoe, 2006). The unemployment scenario is more prevalent for teenagers, for black and Hispanic families, and especially for unskilled laborers without an education (U.S. Bureau of Labor Statistics, 2011b).

Many communities now have career centers and offer periodic job fairs. Job hunters can search the Internet to get professional assistance in writing and preparing résumés and letters of application, updating and practicing interviewing skills, and so on. The Labor Department, vocational services, and community colleges also can help persons with long-term unemployment find retraining opportunities.

Questions

Why are many middle-aged American workers unemployed or forced into early retirement? How are they affected, and what can they do to become reemployed?

Choosing Retirement

The recent economic crisis has had a major impact on the work, retirement, and residential arrangements of today's retirees. Losses in the value of homes, pensions, savings, investments, and home equity are taking their toll on workers in their forties to fifties. Baby boomers on the verge of retirement and those already retired are faced with the challenge of uncertain financial security (Pynoos & Liebig, 2009). The traditional definition of *retirement* is "withdrawal from job or career or from active occupation/employment." Within today's cohort of midlife adults, there are multiple paths to retirement: Some have already retired, many are contemplating retirement, some have no wish to retire, and those in their late forties are probably planning to retire within the next 10 to 15 years (Pynoos & Liebig, 2009). For many, one spouse is retired and the other is not, which is an important factor in retirement satisfaction (Smith & Moen, 2004). Judith Sugar, gerontology and life-span expert, sees this cohort of retirees as changing the definition of retirement. Sugar says today's retirees are "a pool of talent and abilities that we as a society cannot afford to lose," especially because

the cohort in the next generation has barely half as many adults (Chamberlin, 2004, p. 82).

In her book *Retire Smart, Retire Happy: Finding Your True Path in Life*, Nancy Schlossberg (2004), psychology professor, author, and consultant on life transitions, says it takes time to get comfortable with a new life. Upon retirement, everything changes: Relations with a spouse and adult children shift, your identity becomes separate from your primary profession, and daily routines must be adjusted. In the past, retirement was conceptualized as a period of decline, and the change of self-concept was often perceived as negative. But many of today's retirees expect their retirement to be a period of growth and development (Brougham & Walsh, 2009). Retirement intentions often include new careers, self-employment, part-time work, and consulting. Schlossberg identifies six types of retirees: (1) *continuers* stay connected with past skills and activities, (2) *adventurers* start new activities or learn new skills, (3) *searchers* are looking for a new niche, (4) *easy gliders* enjoy unscheduled time and "go with the flow," (5) *involved spectators* stay interested in their previous field of work but assume a different role, and (6) *retreaters* become depressed and give up on finding something meaningful to occupy their time and talent (Schlossberg, 2004). Being retired is an evolving state of becoming.

Many in this age group today focus on planning financial portfolios but do not plan or reflect on what it is they are going to do to enjoy this new phase of life. Sterns and Kaplan (2003) have proposed a model for retirement that suggests considering several specific factors before retiring. These include work satisfaction, satisfaction in community involvement, relationship and degree of family responsibilities (i.e., caregiving for older relatives), and possibilities of new friends and activities as part of a "future self" moving into late adulthood.

SEGUE

Perhaps more than at any other life stage, there are evident, dynamic changes for adults in midlife. This is a time of looking back on one's life and of looking forward and making plans for retirement years, possibly without the daily structure of an occupation. Our self-esteem and personality traits affect our family, our occupational choices, and our overall happiness at this stage of life. Those who feel overwhelmed with the responsibilities of work and family will be psychologically distressed. Those who learn to manage their time and adapt to changing family and occupational responsibilities usually have a positive outlook and are often much happier as they go

through these years. Adaptability, flexibility, friendship, and a sense of humor all contribute to successful passage through this stage of life. Fewer women today are displaced homemakers, because many are engaged in meaningful occupational pursuits along with their spouses. Many of those who are dissatisfied with their employment (or unemployment) status are taking charge of their careers, going back to college (in their fifties and sixties), entering new occupations, or becoming self-employed entrepreneurs. Those who are unemployed or are subjected to forced early retirement can experience great distress. They may understandably feel "old before their time."

SUMMARY

Theories of the Self in Transition

1. Maturity is the capacity to undergo continual change in order to adapt successfully and cope flexibly with the demands and responsibilities of life. It is a lifetime process of becoming.

2. Self-concept is the view we have of ourselves through time as "the real me."

3. Erik Erikson posits that the midlife years are devoted to resolving the "crisis" of generativity versus stagnation, where generativity is "primarily the concern in establishing and guiding the next generation."

4. Robert C. Peck suggested that midlife individuals confront four tasks: making the transition from valuing physical powers to valuing wisdom, socializing instead of sexualizing in relationships, becoming emotionally flexible, and becoming open rather than "closed-minded."

5. Trait models are based on the assumption that an individual develops certain personality characteristics that become more resistant to change with the passage of time.

6. Situational models view a person's behavior as the outcome of the characteristics of the situation in which the person is momentarily located.

7. According to interactionist models of personality, behavior is always a joint product of the person and the situation.

8. According to Levinson's male stage theory, a man changes through his middle adult years because he encounters the first signs of aging.

9. Levinson's study of women in midlife found that combining love/marriage, motherhood, and full-time career has not given women as much satisfaction as they had hoped for. He did not foresee that women would explore new ways to achieve satisfaction in middle adulthood.

10. In later life, people's masculinity or femininity moves toward androgyny, which is associated with increased flexibility and adaptability and with more successful aging.

11. On the whole, the greatest consistency in personality appears in various intellectual and cognitive dimensions, such as IQ, cognitive style, and self-concept. The least consistency is in the realm of interpersonal behavior and attitudes.

The Social Milieu

12. Most American adults desire to be or to remain married. Most baby boomers born in 1946 are currently married. Having a positive attitude toward one's spouse is associated with longevity and satisfaction with marriage.

13. Rates of extramarital sexual activity have varied since Kinsey's original self-report surveys of sexual behavior in the early 1950s. EMS rates are higher among men than among women.

14. Although divorce is relatively common, it can exact a greater emotional and physical toll than almost any other life stress. Divorced adults have higher rates of health difficulties.

15. Marital separation, divorce, cohabitation, and remarriage have also become more common for those in midlife and older, but some couples have had long-term marriages.

16. Most divorced people eventually remarry, often after a period of cohabitation.

17. At least one-third of all new marriages in the United States involve divorced or widowed parents with children under the age of 18. Living in a blended family presents many challenges for the adults and children involved.

18. Middle-aged adults constitute a sandwich generation, with responsibilities for their own children and for their aging parents. Typically, daughters and daughters-in-law care for elderly persons.

19. Friendships are very important in middle age. Women are more likely than men to have close friendships in midlife. The quality of friendships for middle-aged adults has implications for their support networks in old age.

20. Middle-aged adults are increasingly using social networking sites, such as Facebook, to connect or reconnect with family, friends, and acquaintances.

The Workplace

21. Work fills many needs beyond income. Midlife adults want satisfying work or want to make a contribution or create a "legacy" for the next generation. Because of job burnout, early retirement, forced early retirement, and contingency work, not everyone experiences job satisfaction.

22. The past four decades have brought considerable economic change in the status of women. A majority of midlife women are employed either full-time or part-time. However, some are not preparing for economic security in their retirement years because their jobs are low-paying or they do not contribute toward a pension. Some women, especially ethnic minorities, are vulnerable to a lack of Social Security coverage for their retirement years.

23 Women and men are switching careers in midlife for a variety of reasons, and more midlife adults are returning to college or becoming self-employed.

24. Unemployment is difficult for many reasons. Serious financial pressures mount, and various psychological and marital maladjustments increase. The divorce rate soars among the long-term unemployed.

25. Today there are multiple paths to retirement, although more seniors are not retiring.

KEY TERMS

alienation *(531)*

androgyny *(517)*

displaced homemaker *(523)*

empty nest *(524)*

empty-nest syndrome *(526)*

generativity *(509)*

generativity versus stagnation *(509)*

job burnout *(531)*

maturity *(508)*

sandwich generation *(517)*

self-concept *(508)*

social convoy *(518)*

traditional marriage *(514)*

FOLLOWING UP ON THE INTERNET

Web sites for this chapter focus on successful midlife transitions of middle-aged adults. Please access the text Web site at www.mhhe.com/crandell10 for up-to-date hot-linked Internet addresses for the following organizations, topics, and resources:

APA Office on Aging
http://www.apa.org/pi/aging/index.aspx

APA Division 20 on Adult Development and Aging
http://www.apa.org/about/division/div20.aspx

The National Institute on Aging
http://www.apa.org/pi/aging/index.aspx

Journals on Aging and Human Development
http://crab.rutgers.edu/~deppen/journals.htm

Gerontological Society of America
http://www.geron.org/

Financial Literacy for the Sandwich Generation
http://www.ficpa.org/Content/CPAResources/
    Professional/360/Kits/Generation.aspx

National Stepfamily Resource Center
http://www.stepfamilies.info/

National Family Caregiver Association
http://www.thefamilycaregiver.org/

What Color Is My Parachute? (for job hunters and career-changers)
http://www.jobhuntersbible.com/

AARP
http://www.aarp.org/

Late adulthood brings a broader range of physical-sensory, cognitive, and social-emotional changes than any other stage in life. In Chapter 17, we will see that there is no consensus about when old age begins and that humans are living longer than ever. Many assume that "old age" starts around retirement or when eligibility for public or private pensions begins. The "beginning of old age" is changing, though, because millions of elderly worldwide are now living into their eighties—and well beyond. Recent research disputes the myths that portray old age as an undesirable time of life characterized mainly by debilitation. As we will see in Chapter 18, although the elderly experience changes in their cognitive functioning, some of the "supercentenarians" continue to care for themselves and remain socially engaged into their nineties and older. Great-great-grandmother Anna Ferris (at left) from Orange County, New York, was 111 years and 85 days old when she died on May 7, 2011. At the time of her passing, she was among the oldest 78 confirmed supercentenarians worldwide. Many of the elderly, like Anna, continue to share their maturity, wit, and wisdom. When asked about her exceptionally long life, she said that the secret to her longevity was to "help others, laugh, marry well—and 'don't just sit there.'" As the elderly experience physical, cognitive, and social changes, most call on their religion and on inner reserves of faith and spirituality for comfort and satisfaction with having lived a meaningful life.

17 Late Adulthood
Physical and Cognitive Development

This chapter looks at the changing physical and cognitive functioning of adults in the final stage of life. *Longevity, biodemographics, stem cell research, regenerative medicine,* and *antiaging medicine* are relatively new areas of study, and we will see where the research stands. Most physical and health changes are due to biological aging, though some 80-year-olds stay active and proclaim they feel like 60-year-olds. Because more people are living longer worldwide, all industrialized countries are experiencing a "graying" of their population and are reexamining social and economic policies for their citizenry. Issues such as when the elderly should retire, where the funding for old-age pensions and health care is going to come from, how many are working to provide for the elderly, and who is going to pay the bill are serious concerns all over the world. Significantly, antiaging specialists predict that in future years, in *your* lifetime, human life will be extended by many more years.

Although most elderly experience a slowing in physical and cognitive functioning, they also experience a newfound sense of inner peace, finding hope and meaning in their faith and religious rituals. We will examine this last stage not as the final chapters of a book, but more as an explorer's tentative steps toward the unknown, pushing boundaries and breaking barriers.

AGING: MYTH AND REALITY

Many of us have a half-conscious, irrational fear that someday we will find ourselves old. It is as if we will suddenly fall off a cliff—as if what we will become in old age has little to do with who we are now. But at no point in life do people stop being themselves and suddenly turn into "old people." Aging does not destroy the continuity of what we have been, what we are, and what we will be. In some cultures, such as Japan, aging is viewed positively as leading to the highest level of wisdom and understanding, but westernized cultures tend to view aging ambivalently, even negatively. The older the old become, especially as they reach quite advanced age, the more likely they are to be unfavorably stereotyped. Take a minute to think about words commonly used to describe people who are in this late stage of life: *lonely, poor, sexless, ill, frail, dependent, incompetent, slow drivers, difficult, senile, demented,* and *disabled,* to mention just a few. People are socialized into believing these labels, and they begin to think about their own aging as though the labels were true (McGuire, Klein, & Chen, 2008).

Ageism consists of stereotyping and judging a group of people solely on the basis of their age. Unfortunately, in some cultures, older adults have been ostracized, hidden away from mainstream society, stripped of power, or made to feel ashamed and unequal to others because of their age, rather than being seen as unique individuals of value (McGuire, Klein, & Chen, 2008). Further, some social scientists believe that ageism might be more prevalent than either sexism or racism in our own society. In fact, it is so deeply ingrained that it may actually be an unintentional, unconscious force. However, it is hoped that these outdated notions will gradually disappear as older people become more visible through their increasing numbers and active participation in, and contributions to, society.

The truth about aging is far more optimistic than myths would have us believe. Many losses of function once thought to be age-related, particularly declines in cognitive ability and mobility, are overgeneralized and exaggerated. New research on successful aging suggests that exercise and maintaining cognitive function and a positive attitude are crucial. This is based on a new paradigm that has shifted away from the static descriptions of memory and cognitive functions declining with age and focuses instead on interventions that maintain or improve cognitive abilities (Verhaeghen & Hoyer, 2007).

We will see in this chapter and the next that aging does eventually affect physical, cognitive, emotional, and social development, but we have all heard many inconsistent views on when these changes occur, how much change occurs, and why these changes occur. Ongoing research in **gerontology,** the study of aging and the special problems associated with it, and **geropsychology,** the study of the behavior and needs of the elderly, can help us separate myths from reality. Since 2004, the National Institute on Aging (NIA) has established several U.S. Centers on the Demography and Economics of Aging at various universities. Federal funding supports the study of a broad range of worldwide aging issues, such as biodemography, neuroeconomics, behavior genetics, disease and disability, medical technology, migration and geographic concentration of American elderly, decision making about retirement, pensions, savings, living arrangements, and health disparities by gender and race (Mjoseth, 2004). Findings are published often at the NIA's *Age Page.*

Aging is not a disease, and the ravages of aging are somewhat of a myth, for the studies of the "oldest old" (centenarians and supercentenarians) and their offspring in the *New England Centenarian Study* (NECS) reveal that these extreme elderly escape getting common diseases of aging until into their 100s, with a relative short decline in health before death. The findings from the NECS study suggest that centenarians and supercentenarians are living longer because of rare combinations of genetic, environmental, and behavioral factors that lead to longevity and good health (Perls et al., 2007). A NECS study of the long-living offspring of centenarians reveals similar personality traits, including low neuroticism and higher rates of extraversion, conscientiousness, openness, and agreeableness (Givens et al., 2009). Nevertheless, ignorance, superstition, and prejudice have surrounded aging for generations. To dispel some of the misperceptions, we will look at the demographics of aging and some myths in the light of current research.

Older Adults: Who Are They?

The time at which old age is said to begin varies according to period, place, and social rank. One researcher reported, for instance, that the Arawak of Guyana (in South America) seldom lived more than 50 years and that between the thirtieth and fortieth years in the case of men, and even earlier in the case of women, "the body, except the stomach, shrinks, and fat disappears, [and] the skin hangs in hideous folds" (Im Thurn, 1883). Life expectancy for the Andaman Islanders of the Bay of Bengal rarely exceeded 60 years (Portman, 1895), and the Arunta women of Australia were regarded as fortunate to reach 50 (Spencer & Gillen, 1927). In addition, the Creek Indians of North America were considered lucky if they lived to see gray hair on the heads of their children (Adair, 1775). Historically, in 1840 the record for life expectancy was held by Swedish women, who lived on average about 45 years.

Today, Dan Buettner (2008) has identified what he calls "blue zones" where people live the longest: Okinawa, Japan, has a large and growing population of centenarians, as do Greeks who live in Icaria, Costa Ricans who live in the Rain Forest, the Seventh Day Adventists of Loma Linda, California, and Italians who live in Sardinia.

Factors Related to Longevity How do people age so successfully? Many of us assume it takes good genes, luck, or a life of ease. One of the longest and most comprehensive longitudinal studies of human development ever undertaken suggests the contrary: We are very much in control of our own aging. The *Study of Adult Development* at Harvard Medical School comprises three projects begun in the 1920s, 1930s, and 1940s. In all, 824 men and women have been followed from their teens into their 80s. The Harvard study found these four attributes vital to successful aging: *orientation toward the future, ability to cope with stress, an active lifestyle,* and *strong social relationships.* Another study found that men who lived over 90 years had adhered to health-promoting behaviors during their early elderly years, including smoking abstinence, weight management, blood pressure control, and regular exercise (Yates et al., 2008). These studies suggest that our lifestyle habits, rather than our genes, have the greatest influence on longevity.

Yet some medical researchers would not agree. In parts of Nova Scotia, centenarians are up to 3 times more common than they are in the United States as a whole, and up to 16 times more common than they are in the world population (Duenwald, 2003). The higher-than-average number of Nova Scotians who live to 100 years and beyond has led researchers to try to determine whether living so long is a result of genetics or lifestyle. Evidence for a genetic cause comes from the Nova Scotians' DNA. Researchers discovered that many of the centenarians had similarities in their DNA along the same stretch of chromosome 4 (Duenwald, 2003). Scientists suspect that there may be a few age-defying genes and hope to develop drugs that mimic their action. Perls (2007) says, "Without the appropriate genetic variations, I think it's extremely difficult to get to 100. Taking better care of yourself might add a decade, but what matters is what you're packin' in your chassis."

Future Growth Since the early 1900s, a gradual transformation has taken place across most of the world. The population has been aging as a result of the ongoing decline in fertility of younger cohorts, coupled with increasing longevity. Biomedical researchers have noticed that *quality* of life has been increasing and has added to the *quantity* of years in the average life (Britton, Shipley, Singh-Manoux, & Marmot, 2008). Eventually the number of older people will exceed the number of

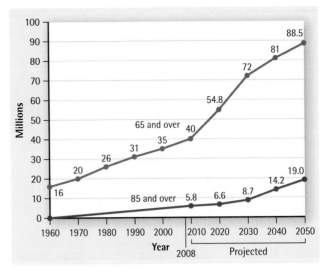

FIGURE 17.1 U.S. Population Aged 65 and Over and Aged 85 and Older, for Selected Years 1960–2008 and Projected for 2010–2050 (in millions) There were 16 million people over age 65 in 1960 and 35 million in 2000. From 2008, the population of people 65 and older could double to more than 72 million by 2030.
Source: Federal Interagency Forum on Aging-Related Statistics. (2010). *Older Americans 2010: Key indicators of well-being.* Washington, DC: U.S. Government Printing Office. Retrieved from http://www.agingstats.gov/agingstatsdotnet/ Main_Site/Data/2010_Documents/Docs/OA_2010.pdf

younger people, and among the older population there will be an increase in the extremely old (those 100 and beyond). The U.S. population of adults 65 and older was about 40 million in 2010, or more than 13 percent of the total population. Over the twentieth century, those Americans living into late adulthood grew from 3 million to 39 million. It is projected that the 85-and-older population could reach 19 million by 2050. On the more immediate horizon, the baby-boom cohort began causing a dramatic rise in the 65-and-older population in 2011, when the first of this cohort reached their sixty-fifth birthdays. It is projected that by 2030, the 65-and-older population will double the number it was in 2000 (see Figure 17.1) (Federal Interagency Forum on Aging-Related Statistics, 2010).

The population of Americans growing into old age also differs from current generations of older adults in important ways (see Figure 17.2). The current older population is predominantly female and white. But it is projected that from 2008 to 2050, the entire white non-Hispanic population age 65 and over will decrease from 80 million in 2008 to 59 million. Over this time, it is projected that the Hispanic population 65 and over will *increase* to 20 million people—an increase of 300 percent. The Asian American population 65 and over is projected to triple from 3 to 9 million. The American black

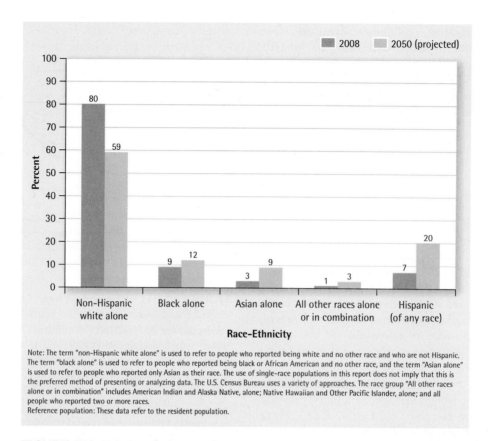

FIGURE 17.2 U.S. Population Aged 65 and Older by Race-Ethnicity: 2008 and Projected for 2050 (in millions)

Source: Federal Interagency Forum on Aging-Related Statistics. (2010). *Older Americans 2010: Key indicators of well-being.* Washington, DC: U.S. Government Printing Office. Retrieved from http://www.agingstats.gov/agingstatsdotnet/Main _Site/Data/2010_Documents/Docs/OA_2010.pdf

population 65 and over is projected to rise to 12 million by 2050 (Federal Interagency Forum on Aging-Related Statistics, 2010).

Such increases in the numbers of elderly Americans will lead to unprecedented increases in health-care costs (medicine, prosthetic devices and medical supplies, physician visits, lab tests, hospitalization, short-term rehabilitation, long-term nursing care, hospice care, home health care, etc.); in the numbers of health-care professionals needed (physicians, nurses, pharmacists, surgeons, dentists, physical therapists, etc.); in the residential facilities required; and in elder-care services (e.g., social workers, psychologists, gerontologists, Meals on Wheels and similar programs, clergy, First Alert safety programs, adult day care, senior transit services, financial planning, legal estate planning, and funeral services) over the next 40 years (Gottschalk, 2009).

The increase in the minority elderly population will be accompanied by significant socioeconomic shifts as well, because current statistics indicate that rates of pov-

erty are much higher for older blacks and Hispanics than for whites. The increased risks for illness and disability associated with lower socioeconomic status (SES) will lead to longer hospitalizations, more home health care and hospice care, and greater per capita health-care expenditures. There will be increases in those subgroups at highest risk for compromised health outcomes, and these populations are least likely to have private health-care insurance and will require public assistance for health care (Doubeni et al., 2010).

Although the United States has a smaller percentage of people over age 65 (13 percent) than other developed countries (15 percent in the European Union and 20 percent in Japan), this will increase as the baby boomers enter late adulthood. Although a majority of the oldest adults report good-to-excellent health and experience little or no functional impairment, the risks for sensory declines, physical impairment, and disability are higher at older ages (Federal Interagency Forum on Aging-Related Statistics, 2010). For those who experience chronic health conditions (long-term illness or disease), the most common ailments are hypertension, arthritis, heart disease, cancer, and diabetes.

Researchers examine demographic characteristics, economic status, lifestyle factors, cognitive ability, personality, family environment, religiosity, and social network structure as predictors of health behaviors. A growing body of evidence suggests that the elderly increase their chances for more successful aging through lifestyle choices that include personal control and efficacy, increasing levels of physical activity, proper nutrition and weight control, a positive attitude, and participation in social activities (Martins, Verissimo, Silva, Cumming, & Telxiera, 2010). According to Crimmins and Seeman (2004), the two biggest challenges are (1) to convince older adults of the value of such behaviors; and (2) to develop programs and policies that not only encourage such lifestyle changes but also promote and facilitate their adoption by all socioeconomic and ethnic segments of the growing numbers of older Americans. Beyond health-care concerns, the effects of these population changes are likely to include

- *An increased dependency ratio in the nation.* As the large baby-boom cohort begins to retire in record numbers, there remains a smaller, younger workforce of adult workers to replace them and contribute, through payroll taxes, to the federal, state, and local budgets and social welfare programs that support those on disability or in retirement. It is estimated that between the years 2030 and 2080, the annual shortfall of benefits paid to retirees, compared to payroll taxes of workers, will increase from 3.5 percent to almost 6 percent (Iams, Reznik, & Tamborini, 2009).
- *An increased demand by the aged for various government entitlement resources* such as Social Security, Medicaid, Medicare, welfare, the Home Energy Assistance Program (HEAP—utility costs for heat), adult day care, public transit, medical and rehabilitative facilities and services, social services, and recreational centers. "Spending on entitlement programs like Social Security, Medicare, and Medicaid is growing faster than we can afford, and there are painful choices ahead if America stays on this path: massive tax increases, sudden and drastic cuts in benefits, or crippling deficits" (Fact Sheet: The President's FY09 Budget, 2008).
- *The emergence of the oldest cohort as a political force and social movement.* The AARP and the National Education Association (NEA) are powerful lobbying groups in Washington, and senior citizens have a history of being politically active. Their influence will command legislative action, giving their interests higher priority than those of younger

citizens. About 70 percent of registered voters 65 and older voted in the presidential election of 2008 (File & Crissey, 2010).
- *The migration of a large number of the U.S. elderly population from the northeastern and north-central states to the southern and western states.* The South and West are more congenial to senior living, with warmer climates and lower taxes. This mass migration will drain the tax base of the northern and eastern states, while burdening the resources of the southern and western states (Frey, 2007).

As a government report states, "With 45 percent of the 2010 federal budget of $3.5 trillion allocated for Medicare, Medicaid, and Social Security, a considerable portion of the budget is used for legislated programs that support the elderly population" (see Figure 17.3) (Congressional Budget Office, 2010). The *Medicare Prescription Drug Improvement and Modernization Act* offers Medicare beneficiaries subsidized prescription drug coverage as of January 1, 2006. Those with incomes below 135 percent of the poverty level pay no monthly premium, no deductible, and a small co-pay. These allocations are rising as the elderly retired population increases. Economic growth in the next few years will probably be stagnant to modest for the 2009–2018 period in the aftermath of the 2008 financial and economic crisis and the multi-trillion-dollar federal debt (Congressional Budget Office, 2010). The retirement of the baby-boom cohort and rising health-care spending per person will cause more outlays for Medicare, Medicaid, and Social Security (Congressional Budget Office, 2010). So there is a growing concern over the so-called graying of the budget. Some are concerned that age divisiveness will appear in U.S. politics. (See the *Further Developments* box on page 544, "Generational Tensions: The Social Security Debate," to take a closer look at such contentious issues.)

Myths

The facts of aging are often obscured by a great many myths that have little to do with the actual process of growing old. Let's examine some of these misconceptions in light of recent findings from research.

Myth: Most persons aged 65 and over live in hospitals, nursing homes, and other elder-care institutions.

Fact: Only recently have many people lived long enough to require long-term care—an outcome that has resulted from significant improvements in the social and physical environments and in health care itself (Rousson & Paccaud, 2010). Genetic research has also contributed to prolonging the life span. Although census data reveal that the chance that one will need nursing-home care increases with

FURTHER DEVELOPMENTS

Generational Tensions:
The Social Security Debate

Note, in Figure 17.3, the striking increase in the spending for senior supports and services (and for disabled persons, widows, and dependents) in the U.S. federal budget for Social Security, Medicare, and Medicaid from 1992 to the present through projections for 2082. U.S. adults are mandated to contribute to Social Security through payroll and self-employment taxes. "Social Security is the most common and the largest source of income for both women and men, and it is a particularly critical source of income for those who are widowed, divorced, separated, or never married" and "women are more than twice as likely to be unmarried—widowed, divorced, separated, or never married" (Hayes, Hartmann, & Lee, 2010). At present, Congress has many proposals to modify yet sustain this essential system as millions more draw from the system that was supposed to grow from their contributions.

The proportion of elderly is growing, and this affects every American and every U.S. institution. In the mid-1900s, various social policies were put in place that have allowed most elderly workers to disengage from employment and to experience an improved standard of living and greater longevity. The Social Security program was created in 1935. In the beginning, it provided low benefit payments—such that in the 1960s one-third of seniors lived below the poverty line (in 1965, "the poverty line" was $3,317; to put this in perspective, in the 1960s a teacher's

annual pay was about $4,950) (Odden & Kelley, 2002). In 1965 the *Older Americans Act,* which supports an array of services intended for older persons, was passed. *Medicare* was enacted to help the elderly pay health-care costs, and *Medicaid* was introduced as a health insurance program to help low-income persons pay for health care. Since 1965, several amendments to the Social Security Act have been passed to provide more services to the elderly, people with disabilities, and widows and orphans (Administration on Aging, 2009).

The U.S. Treasury oversees four trust funds related to Social Security and Medicare, which handle the revenues collected from taxes on people's wages, as well as the outgoing payments and benefits. There is an *income cap* of $106,800 in 2011, above which FICA taxes are not collected. Because it is a trust fund, any monies not needed for the current year are invested in government securities that accumulate interest. These funded programs are intended to provide seniors with a basic income and health care. However, Americans are encouraged to save and invest for their own retirement as well, which most poor adults have been unable to do.

What Is the Issue?

The future funding structure and allocation of Social Security is uncertain. Yet the Trustees of the Social Security and Medicare Programs (2010) say it is Medicare that is in more imminent danger. "The Medicare Hospital Insurance (HI) Trust Fund that pays hospital benefits had negative cash flows in 2010 and annual cash flow deficits are expected to continue and to grow rapidly after 2010 as baby boomers begin to retire." Health-care costs are expected to rise faster than the amount Social Security can pay based on the taxes it collects from workers' wages (Social Security Administration, 2008). As a result, Congress passed the Health Care and Education Reconciliation Act of 2010 (the "Affordable Care Act" or ACT), which is supposed to reduce payments for Medicare goods and services. The plan is to develop a new Medicare Trust Fund that will be funded by increased taxes accrued from the U.S. economy, which is projected to grow over the next 12 years. The government plans to reduce health-care costs by paying health-care providers less, a strategy better known as the "Doc Fix" (Congressional Budget Office, 2010).

Social Security has a $2.5 trillion surplus, but benefit payments are already exceeding revenues in 2011 (this had been projected to occur in 2018). The Social Security trust fund

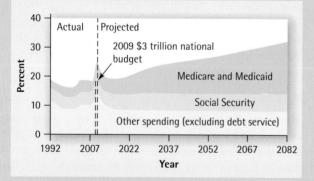

FIGURE 17.3 U.S. Federal Spending for Programs Supporting the Aging Population Are Crowding Other Federal Programs

Source: Office of Management and Budget. (2010, April 26). *Budget of the United States Government, FY 2010, Historical Tables,* Table 3.2, at http://www .whitehouse.gov/omb/budget/Historicals (April 26, 2010). Figures for FY 2010 through 2020 represent current-policy baseline projections calculated using Congressional Budget Office, "The Budget and Economic Outlook: Fiscal Years 2010 to 2020," January 2010, at http://www.cbo.gov/ftpdocs/108xx/ doc10871/BudgetOutlook2010_Jan.cfm

can continue paying scheduled benefits until about 2037 by drawing down its surplus (Congressional Budget Office, 2011). The crisis is attributable in part to the economic downturn since 2008 and to the fact that the ratio of workers supporting beneficiaries is declining. In 1950 there were 16 workers for each beneficiary. Now there are 3 workers for each beneficiary. Thus, for the first time since the enactment of the Social Security Amendments of 1983, there were more funds being released to Social Security recipients than tax revenues being collected in 2010 (Congressional Budget Office, 2010). The reason for this is the large cohort of baby boomers and a much smaller cohort born after 1965. By 2033 the support ratio will become 2 workers per beneficiary. The Social Security trustees predict that the increased costs associated with the large baby-boom cohort will stabilize by 2035, as many baby boomers die (Congressional Budget Office, 2010).

Social Security was never intended to provide for all the needs of Americans when they retired, became widowed, or became disabled. Yet many poor retirees rely solely on Social Security for their income, especially women and ethnic minorities who are more likely to be poor, or widowed, and

do not have pensions and assets (Hayes, Hartmann, & Lee, 2010). Pension planners view Social Security as one leg of a three-legged stool, with private pensions and savings or investments providing the other two kinds of support. Some have suggested that the solution is to allow workers to put their Social Security contributions into a private pension plan. But this argument fails to consider the disability and survivor's benefits that workers or their families might begin drawing at an earlier age. Economists say that Social Security cannot become voluntary. Some would get out because they could get better investment returns elsewhere. The high-cost people would stay in, and the system would collapse.

Many ideas about how to stem the impending Social Security shortfalls are being deliberated. One proposed plan to strengthen Social Security would gradually increase the retirement age to 68 or 69 and broaden the payroll tax base in order to capture 90 percent of wages (Trustees of the Social Security and Medicare Programs, 2010). This proposal is currently under review by federal leaders; its efficacy is largely dependent on the strength of the economy. There is great uncertainty about the best way to preserve this vital system that provides some measure of security for seniors.

age, and the numbers of nursing-home residents will increase because the population of the elderly is increasing, the rates of nursing-home placements are decreasing. From 1985 to 1999, the rate of nursing-home residence among people aged 65 to 74 declined by 15 percent; among 75- to 84-year-olds, the rate declined by 25 percent; and the rate for those 85 and older declined by 17 percent (Federal Interagency Forum on Aging-Related Statistics, 2010).

Myth: Many of the elderly are incapacitated and spend much of their time in bed because of illness.

Fact: About 4 percent of U.S. elderly are bedridden at home, and about 9 percent are housebound. Another 5 percent are seriously incapacitated, while 10 to 16 percent are restricted in mobility. By contrast, a majority function without any limitation; more than one-third of those 85 and older report no incapacitating limitation on their activity. A person who becomes severely ill or disabled in advanced old age is likely not to linger several years but, rather, to experience a short terminal decline of 90 to 120 days. Given the trend toward longevity, demographers believe that the baby-boom generation will spend less time in nursing homes and fewer years being severely disabled than did previous cohorts. In sum, gradual aging may well be replaced with perceptions of vigorous adulthood across the life span, followed

by a brief, precipitous **senescence** (mental decline in old age) or period of physical decline (Federal Interagency Forum on Aging-Related Statistics, 2010).

Myth: Most elderly people are "prisoners of fear" who are "under house arrest" by virtue of their fear of crime.

Fact: Overall, in 2010 Americans 65 and over had the lowest victimization rate of all age groups—only 2.4 per 1,000. By far, the highest rate of victimization is among the 16- to 19-year-old age group (Federal Interagency Forum on Aging-Related Statistics, 2010).

Myth: Most people over 65 find themselves in serious financial straits.

Fact: As a group, Americans over 65 are in better financial shape today than in previous decades (see Table 17.1). The poverty level for those 65 and older dropped to 10 percent in 2007 (Federal Interagency Forum on Aging-Related Statistics, 2010). Social Security and private pensions are the primary sources of income, and the elderly pay a smaller share of their income to taxes. But in 2010, the cost of gasoline, medical care, food, and utilities increased rapidly—and many elderly lived on a small fixed income. A small but growing percentage of adults over 62 are continuing to work. Although many elderly people have lower incomes than most U.S. householders, they have a higher *net worth*—primarily through

TABLE 17.1 Average Annual Income by Age for U.S. Women and Men Aged 65 and Older: 2009

	Women	Men
Aged 65 and older	$20,593	$38,350
Aged 65 to 74	$22,489	$43,910
Aged 75 and older	$18,601	$30,783

Source: Authors' calculations based on 2009 Current Population Survey Annual Social and Economic (ASEC) Supplement Survey. Earnings and income data are for calendar year 2008. Hayes, J., Hartmann, H., & Lee, S. (2010, March). Briefing paper: Social Security: Vital to retirement security for 35 million women and men. (IWPR Publication #D487). Institute for Women's Policy Research. Retrieved from http://www.iwpr.org/publications/pubs/social-security-vital-to-retirement-security-for-35-million-women-and-men

TABLE 17.2 U.S. Social Security Benefits: Full Retirement Ages as of 2011

A worker can choose to retire as early as age 62. But if such early retirement is chosen, the benefit will be reduced by a certain percentage.

Year of Birth*	Full Retirement Age
1937 or earlier	65
1938	65 and 2 months
1939	65 and 4 months
1940	65 and 6 months
1941	65 and 8 months
1942	65 and 10 months
1943–1954	66
1955	66 and 2 months
1956	66 and 4 months
1957	66 and 6 months
1958	66 and 8 months
1959	66 and 10 months
1960 and later	67

If you were born on January 1st of any year, you should refer to the previous year.

Source: U.S. Bureau of the Census. (2005, September 19). Normal retirement age. Social Security Administration. Retrieved from http://www.socialsecurity.gov/retire2/agereduction.htm

home ownership. For 20 years, some elderly have been taking advantage of reverse mortgages that allow Americans age 62 and older to get a monthly payment based on the value of their home; but this type of "loan" lowers one's equity in the home, and there are fees and other charges. Seniors can easily be victimized (Duhigg, 2008). One hospitalization can force some elderly to consider this option. In 2008, Fidelity Investments released a study that concluded that a 65-year-old couple retiring this year will need about $225,000 in savings to cover medical costs in retirement (Hundley, 2008).

The economic gap between men and women widens in retirement. Since the 1970s, more than 80 percent of women have entered the workforce either full-time or part-time, but women's average 2008 annual Social Security benefits were $9,782, compared with $12,669 for men (Hayes, Hartmann, & Lee, 2010). Even though some women also have income from private pension plans, their pensions tend to be lower because women have generally earned less than men, or they might have worked part-time or left the workforce for several years for family reasons. For most women who receive SSI benefits through their husbands, the benefits—equal to half their husbands' monthly check if the women wait until full retirement age before receiving benefits—are more than the amount they would receive on the basis of their own work record. Women account for nearly 60 percent of Social Security beneficiaries after age 62—and for 70 percent of those 85 and older. For nearly half of unmarried women (and widows), SSI constitutes 90 percent of their income (Social Security Administration, 2007). Social security is the *only* source of income for about one of every three women 75 and older, and single older women have high rates of poverty (Hayes, Hartmann, & Lee, 2010). Note in Table 17.2 that the age for receiving full SSI benefits is rising but that a worker can retire as early as age 62 (or is eligible to receive benefits on the basis of her husband's Social Security) with a considerable reduction in benefits.

Myth: Most grown children live away from their elderly parents and basically abandon them.

Fact: Most middle-aged children take care of their elderly parents rather than abandoning them, according to the National Alliance for Caregiving and AARP (2010). In 2009, more than 30 million American adults provided care for an elderly relative or friend, on average 21 hours per week, or helped support their elderly parents financially. AARP estimates that more than one-third of informal family caregivers, mainly women, will quit their jobs to provide care to the elderly (National Alliance for Caregiving and AARP, 2010). As a result, elder-care benefits could become an employment issue.

Additional misperceptions about the elderly will be considered in the course of these two chapters. Although the issues cited above do not affect most elderly adults, they are realities for some smaller segments of the older population. Overall, many of the elderly are resilient and very much alive; they are not hopeless, inert masses teetering on the edge of senility and death. Generalizations that depict the elderly as an economically and socially deprived group do them a disservice, for such stereotypes may tempt some younger people to distance themselves from the elderly and treat them as though they were of inferior status.

TABLE 17.3 Average Life Expectancy at Birth (both sexes) Across Selected Cultures: 2008

Country	Age	Country	Age
Japan	82	Brazil	73
Australia	82	Egypt	73
Italy	82	Philippines	72
Canada	81	Iraq	71
Germany	80	Ukraine	69
Britain/(U.K.)	80	India	67
United States	78	Russia	66
Argentina	77	Cambodia	63
Mexico	76	Kenya	59
China	75	Congo	55
Turkey	73	Angola	39

Source: U.S. Census Bureau. (2010, December 28). International Data Base. Retrieved from http://www.census.gov/ipc/www/idb/informationGateway. php

Growth and longevity in the older population is not unique to the United States (see Table 17.3). In nearly all industrialized societies, the number of elderly people is growing. And the numbers of elders are projected to grow at even higher rates in the developing countries than in the developed countries. In countries such as the People's Republic of China, South Korea, India, Egypt, Cambodia, Congo, Brazil, the Philippines, and Turkey, the size of the population aged 65 and older is expected to double between 2000 and 2025. Mexico's elderly population is projected to more than triple (U.S. Bureau of the Census, 2009b).

As of 2006, the average life expectancy of American women is 80.2 years, whereas men can expect to live to age 75.1 (Federal Interagency Forum on Aging-Related Statistics, 2010). Women outlive men in almost every nation. Life expectancy in the developed countries is comparable to that in the United States, but the figures are different in less developed countries. A large difference in life expectancy for women between the developed and less developed countries is due to higher rates of maternal mortality and disease-specific mortality (Danaei et al., 2010). A child born in the United States in 2007 could expect to live about 78 years—about 30 years longer than a child born in 1900. The major cause of this greater longevity is the fact that the United States has experienced lower death rates for infants, children, and young adults. Longevity statistics are averaged to include stillborn babies or those who die at birth, those who die in infancy and childhood, and all adult deaths.

Generally, adults who are 65 or older are considered to be in the final stage of human development. Yet considering how much these adults vary in their activities, health, and welfare, it is difficult to say when old age begins. Probably the simplest and safest rule is to consider individuals old whenever they become so regarded and treated by their contemporaries (Berg et al., 2009). Indeed, while our society is getting older, the old are getting younger. The activities and attitudes of a 70-year-old today closely approximate those of a 50-year-old two decades ago. Their quality of life, especially for the "youngest old," ages 60 to 75, is much greater than that of their parents. A large number remain physically and mentally active, even continuing to work full- or part-time.

Questions

How will U.S. population demographics change as a consequence of the aging of the population? What effect will these changes have on our society's social, health, and economic policies in the next few decades?

Increase in Health-Care Costs and Concerns The chances of sensory and physical impairments increase in late adulthood, but lifestyle choices and social support improve the chance of successful aging.

For Better or For Worse © 2005 Lynn Johnston Productions. Dist. By Universal Uclick. Reprinted with permission. All rights reserved.

Women Live Longer Than Men

Jeanne Calment, a citizen of France and the world's oldest living person at that time, died in 1997 at the age of 122. She loved wine and candy and smoked until she was 117. She rode her bicycle daily until she was 100 and lived alone until the age of 110, when she entered a nursing home (Neuharth, 1997). She reached an old age that antiaging researchers predict many people will achieve in a few decades—during your lifetime!

In the mid-1980s the National Institute on Aging began a program to research the oldest population—those over 85—of whom the majority (nearly 70 percent in 2008) are women (U.S. Bureau of the Census, 2010b). These older women are extending life to its chronological limit, and they hold the secret of what normal aging is at the extreme of old age. What accounts for their ability to survive so long? Perls (2006) is trying to find the explanation for such remarkable longevity in the *New England Centenarian Study,* because there are between 50,000 and 60,000 Americans 100 and older now, and their numbers are increasing rapidly (at this age 90 percent are women). Genetic differences might play a part in women's greater longevity (Phillips, 2006; Perls et al., 2007). Women seem to have an inherent sex-linked resistance to some types of life-threatening diseases. Apparently, a woman's hormones give her a more efficient immune system. A woman's own estrogen appears to be protective against cardiovascular disease, because premenopausal women have a substantially lower risk of heart disease than men of comparable ages. Most medical experts believe that smoking accounts for about half of the gender difference in longevity, and now only about 20 percent of elderly American men and women smoke (Federal Interagency Forum on Aging-Related Statistics, 2010).

Another longitudinal study on health, lifestyle, and aging is the *Nun Study* that began in 1986. By studying 678 nuns, who have been donating their brains to research after death, biomedical researchers are gaining insights into women's health issues, aging, and factors related to Alzheimer's disease and other cognitive impairments. These women are an excellent resource for medical research because their diet, secluded way of life, and insularity provide the type of research control needed. Tyas and colleagues (Tyas, Salazar, et al., 2007; Tyas, Snowden, Desrosiers, Riley, & Markesbery, 2007), through their ongoing research in the *Nun Study,* define healthy aging as "based on measures of global cognitive function, short-term memory, basic and instrumental activities of daily living, and self-rated function." Early results suggest that both decreasing risk of mild cognitive impairments and positive emotional content in early-life autobiographies are strongly related to longevity (Tyas, Salazar, et al., 2007). Surprisingly, recent autopsy results from some of the oldest participants who met the criteria for healthy aging were found to have some Alzheimer pathology or brain infarcts—but the nuns were functioning as if disease-free (Tyas, Snowden, et al., 2007).

For women who enter the oldest years without severe disability and with adequate financial resources, these years can be a time of independence, personal mastery, and self-assurance. Researchers report that centenarian autonomy is associated with healthy practices as well as overall good physical status (Ozaki, Uchiyama, Tagaya, Ohida, & Ogihara, 2007). However, those without resources are dependent on federal assistance for home health care, nursing care, medical coverage, and so forth. Future research might do well to focus on helping this group of women develop their potential, which should ultimately benefit us all.

> **Question**
>
> Why do more women than men survive into old age, and how are these women in their eighties and nineties—as well as centenarians—faring?

HEALTH

Although the general public may believe that the elderly suffer poor health, in fact the majority of people aged 65 and older report their health status as good to excellent. Only about one-fourth reported their health as fair or poor in 2008, although among people of minority status, about one-third reported fair to poor health (Federal Interagency Forum on Aging Related Statistics, 2010). Indeed, the incidence of self-reported *acute illnesses* (upper respiratory infections, injuries, digestive disorders, varicose veins, and the like) is lower among the elderly than among other segments of the population. However, the incidence of *chronic diseases* (hypertension, heart conditions, arthritis and joint and ligament problems, cancer, diabetes, stroke, respiratory illness, osteoporosis, and so on) rises steadily with advancing years (Federal Interagency Forum on Aging-Related Statistics, 2010).

Despite the higher incidence of chronic health problems among the elderly, most do not consider themselves seriously handicapped in pursuing their ordinary activities, and only 4 percent of people aged 65 and older reside in some care facility (Federal Interagency Forum on Aging-Related Statistics, 2010). Most of the conditions that create chronic disease increase with advanced age. Over time, it is likely that a person will accumulate more risk factors for a variety of illnesses. As the risk factors increase, the efficiency of the body's systems is reduced by primary aging or the irreversible changes that occur over time. An older adult

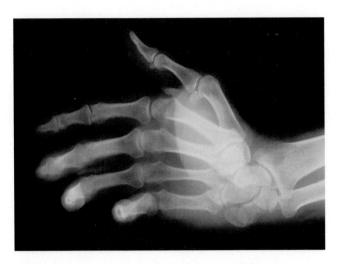

Rheumatoid Arthritis This is an X ray of the hand of someone with rheumatoid arthritis, a chronic joint disease that causes cartilage destruction, bone erosion, and tendon inflammation. This disease causes pain, swelling, and stiffness, although medications can alleviate some of the discomfort.

is more susceptible to disease, requires longer to recuperate from an illness or surgery, and is more likely to develop other complications.

The *Baltimore Longitudinal Study*, which began in 1958, has contributed much to our understanding of the health of older Americans (Gunby, 1998). The study follows nearly 2,500 volunteers ranging in age from the early twenties through the late eighties. Every two years these individuals undergo two and a half days of comprehensive physical tests. The study's recent finding that a growing percentage of people, especially women, over 65 tend to be overweight causes researchers to be quite concerned. Recent research suggests that higher weights are likely to result in higher death rates, particularly from heart disease (Federal Interagency Forum, 2010). Currently, over 450,000 deaths occur each year in the United States as a consequence of heart disease (Capewell et al., 2009).

Also, since it has been found that 60 percent of those over age 60 have high blood sugar levels in glucose tolerance tests, medical authorities are questioning many diagnoses of diabetes in older people. Perhaps a reduction in insulin production in the elderly is a normal occurrence and not a sign of disease. As a result of this research, the American Diabetes Association and the World Health Organization have lowered the statistical range used to diagnose diabetes. In studies across cultures (Canada, Australia, England, Kenya, Germany, United States, etc.), researchers confirm that regular, proper exercise pursued throughout life—even into the eighties and beyond—can significantly deter

the deterioration of bodily functions that traditionally accompany aging (Capewell et al., 2009). Yet only 20 percent of adults over 65 reported engaging in regular leisure-time physical activity (Federal Interagency Forum on Aging-Related Statistics, 2010).

Exercise and Longevity

The percentage of people 65 and over that are obese has increased from 22 percent in 1998 to nearly one-third in 2008 (Federal Interagency Forum, 2010). Researchers predict that obesity will affect longevity, since obesity is highly correlated with cardiovascular disease (CVD), diabetes, kidney disease, various cancers, joint deterioration, and other health problems. Cardiovascular disease is among the leading causes of mortality in the United States, claiming over 450,000 U.S. deaths annually (Capewell et al., 2009). The demonstrated benefits of exercise, both aerobic and resistance training, to maintain proper weight and fitness include increased work capacity, improved heart and respiratory function, lower blood pressure, increased muscle strength, denser bones, greater flexibility, quicker reaction times, clearer thinking, improved sleep, and reduced susceptibility to depression (Bengtson et al., 2009). Furthermore, cardiovascular fitness is associated with healthy brain tissue in aging humans and with enhancing cognitive function in older adults. Exercise and strength training are especially important for women because they have more body fat and less muscle and bone mass than men, which makes them more susceptible to fractures, muscle deterioration, and the risk of fall-induced injuries (Dorgo, Robinson, & Bader, 2009).

Does exercise add years to life? This is still being debated. Medical authorities generally concur that moderate exercise contributes to a healthier life, but recent evidence suggests that exercise must be strenuous to add to the life span. Recent research has found that older adults who participate in moderate exercise for 20 to 30 minutes on most days have better physical function than older persons who are active throughout the day or are more sedentary (Crimmins, Hayward, Hagedorn, Saito, & Brouard, 2009). Harvard researchers followed more than 17,000 healthy male alumni over a 26-year period and found that only vigorous exercise increased longevity (Brody, 1995). The risk of dying for men who expended more than 1,500 calories a week in such activities as running, cycling, and swimming was as much as 25 percent lower than the risk for men who expended fewer than 150 calories a week in such activities. Even so, most exercise physiologists believe there is a point at which too much exercise is detrimental to health. The *Harvard Alumni Health Study* defined as vigorous any activity that raised the metabolic rate in a 10-second interval to six or more times the rate at rest. Activities such as the following would achieve the level of caloric expenditure associated with the lowest death rates:

- Walking for 45 minutes at 4 to 5 mph five times a week
- Playing tennis for 1 hour three times a week
- Swimming laps for 3 hours a week
- Cycling at 10 mph for 1 hour four times a week
- Running for 30 minutes at 6 to 7 mph five to six times a week
- In-line skating for 2½ hours a week

In sum, staying active physically, mentally, and socially contributes to successful aging and, perhaps, to longevity.

Nutrition and Health Risks

Good nutrition is another controllable factor that contributes to health in old age. Although energy requirements decrease with advancing age, elderly people require just as many nutrients as younger adults (Velho, Marques-Vidal, Baptists, & Camilo, 2008). Indeed, they may require more for adequate cognitive function. Recall from Chapter 15 that older adults experience some dental changes, swallowing difficulties, and sensory loss of smell and taste, all of which affect their desire to eat and the foods they eat—and certain medications can affect appetite as well (Bengtson et al., 2009). Research suggests that vitamins and minerals are metabolized differently as people age and that the recommended dietary allowances could be inaccurate for elderly persons (Velho et al., 2008).

Lifestyle differences also contribute to gender differences in life expectancies. The longest-living populations are found in Okinawa, Japan, and in Sardinia, Italy, and among Seventh-Day Adventists in Loma Linda, California. The Adventists are nonsmoking vegetarians with

Regular Exercise Is a Factor in Extending Life

religious beliefs (vegetarians eat more fruit, legumes, nuts, vegetables, and whole-wheat bread). In a longitudinal study from 1974 to 1988, 34,000 Adventists from California participated in the *Adventist Health Study–1* (Fraser, 2005). Findings showed that the Adventists weighed less and had a much lower risk of heart disease, cancer, and prostate problems than did nonvegetarians. *Adventist Health Study–2* began in 2001 and was expected to be finished in 2011; its goal was studying lifestyle and aging with more than 100,000 participants from the United States and Canada. Marge Jetton, a participant in the current study at 101 years old, was asked how she felt. Her reply: "The first 100 years are not bad, after that it commences down on you." Researchers hope the information collected in Adventist Health Study–2 will shed light on heart disease, diabetes, other chronic and deadly diseases, and lifestyle factors (Schwartz, 2006).

Bone Weakness and Fractures   Another silent disease that occurs over time and affects a large percentage of adults is loss of bone mass, which begins by age 25 to 30 (and even earlier for younger persons who have eating disorders or who have had cancer treatments). **Osteoporosis** is a condition associated with a significant loss of calcium and other minerals over time that results in porous bones that can lead to fracture; *osteopenia* is characterized by bone density lower than normal, but not low enough to be classified as osteoporosis. Americans annually suffer more than 275,000 hip fractures, 500,000 vertebral fractures, and 200,000 wrist fractures because of these conditions. A simple bone densitometry scan reveals whether someone has low bone mass density (BMD), and women over 65 should be screened regularly for bone mass density (younger women should ask their doctor whether they should begin this regular screening earlier).

Older women are at greater risk for osteoporosis because they have less bone mass and because they lose bone tissue more rapidly after menopause. Thin and small-boned women are also at greater risk. A woman at 60 years of age has a 50 percent chance of fracturing a bone over her lifetime (Britton et al., 2008). Along with internal bones becoming more "porous" and brittle, the discs between the vertebrae of the spine become less dense, causing vertebrae to form small cracks and become closer to each other. This results in back pain. A person's upper back begins to curve, over a period of years, as he or she loses height. In time it becomes difficult to breathe, because the person can no longer stand up straight.

Hip fractures cost close to $13 billion a year in the United States. Such fractures are associated with higher rates of mortality in 80-year-old and older women. Nearly one-third of affected women must give up their independent status and enter rehab facilities or nursing homes (National Institute on Aging, 2007a). Long-term bedridden elderly are more susceptible to pneumonia, blood clots, muscle loss—and earlier death. Calcium supplements with vitamin D seem to slow or stop bone loss, but they do not increase bone mass. However, bone mass may increase when various prescription drugs are taken in addition to the calcium supplements and the individual gets regular weight-bearing exercise (such as walking). Any therapeutic regimen should be carefully monitored by a physician. If treatment is begun early, the progress of bone loss can be slowed and later fractures prevented. Women who remain physically active, keep their leg and arm muscles strong, and exercise into their seventh and eighth decades seem to have less of a problem. Women who undergo early menopause, are very thin, or lead a sedentary life are more likely to develop the problem. Britton and colleagues (2008) urge older adults to take advantage of periodic screenings and activities that can help prevent osteoporosis at community senior centers.

Medications and Absorption Effects   Some health problems of older Americans result from overmedicating, mixing medications, skipping medications, and taking an incorrect dosage. Elderly persons do not absorb drugs from the intestinal tract as readily as young people

do, their livers are less efficient in metabolizing medications, and their kidneys are 50 percent less efficient in excreting chemicals. Hence, use of medications in the elderly should be kept to a minimum, with safe, nondrug alternatives considered whenever possible (Bengtson et al., 2009).

Although older people might need higher doses of some medications, they need lower doses of others. For instance, the aging brain and nervous system are unusually sensitive to antianxiety drugs such as *Valium* and *Librium,* which can produce confusion and lethargy in the elderly. Sedatives such as *phenobarbital* often have a paradoxical effect on the elderly, inducing excitement and agitation rather than sleep. One U.S. study found that one-fifth of people aged 65 and over received at least one of 33 potentially inappropriate medications (Zhan et al., 2001). These facts are quite dismaying when we realize that people over 65 take more than one out of four of all prescription drugs (the use of several medications is called polypharmacy). Indeed, the average healthy elderly person takes several different prescription medicines in the course of a year. When taken in combination, some of these medications can produce severe secondary reactions (Hajjar, Cafiero, & Hanlon, 2007). Because the elderly go to various doctors for different conditions, each doctor may prescribe some potent medications—often unaware of other medications the patient is taking. Another area of concern is the use of sedative medications in elderly nursing-home residents who are experiencing high levels of stress (American Psychological Association, 2010). Many pharmacy chains now have computerized networks that share information among pharmacies to help prevent harmful mixing of pharmaceuticals, and potential drug effects are now printed out for the patient. Establishing a routine for taking medications as prescribed can be a challenge—some people resist taking medications, and others have memory difficulties. Some inexpensive devices can help those with failing memory to remember to take daily medications.

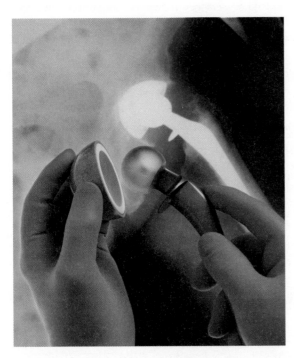

Osteoporosis: Bone Loss and Joint Replacement   A loss of calcium can result in osteoporosis, in which bones become more porous and brittle. A daily regimen of calcium with vitamin D, weight-bearing exercise, and prescription medication can slow bone loss. Artificial hip joint replacements can improve joint flexibility.

Mental Health and Depression   Most older adults adapt well to the changes and losses that confront them in late adulthood and have good mental health—yet those who live with chronic disease or pain are likely to experience mental-health problems. In 2006, for adults 65 and older, about 12 percent of women and 5 percent of men were prescribed antidepressants (National Institute of Mental Health, 2008). Even so, a small percentage of elderly people develop more serious depressive disorders or mental illness if not treated. Symptoms might include loss of energy, fatigue or sleep disorders, loss of appetite, loss of interest in normal activities, and/or loss of interest in sexual activity. Risk factors for depression include diagnosis of health problems, cognitive dysfunction, strained interpersonal relations, stressful life events,

The Elderly with Animal Companions Go to the Doctor Less Psychologist Judith M. Siegel finds that the elderly who have animal companions visit their doctors less often than those without animal companions. Those with dogs have the fewest visits. Pets provide companionship, serve as objects of attachment, and seem to help their owners in times of stress.

and inheritance of depression. Depression can also result from a physical illness or its treatment. Naturally, people living with chronic pain or a fatal diagnosis have much higher rates of depression and higher incidence of alcoholism, use of drugs, and troubled relationships (National Institute of Mental Health, 2008).

Generally, women have more depressive disorders than men, although this difference reverses in very old age. Certain factors are associated with depressive disorders and higher rates of suicide: being a recent elderly immigrant, being an inpatient or institutionalized client, being male, being 75 years of age or older, or having substantial health and mobility problems or cognitive impairment (National Center for Health Statistics, 2011). The suicide rate for adults 75 and over is the highest of all age groups—with a much higher rate for males (see Chapter 19).

Depressed elderly adults often do not seek treatment. The older adult might not see a physician, or the physician might focus on a physical condition and miss the depressive symptoms, especially if the patient does not mention them. Allowing depression to go untreated until it becomes more severe can lead to use of potent medications, electroconvulsive therapy, or suicide. Recent findings from a longitudinal study suggest that a combination of medications and psychotherapy yield the best results for elderly patients suffering from major depression (National Institute of Mental Health, 2008). Social support, coping styles, perceived control of life factors, and cognitive appraisals play a protective role against depression (Ouwehand, de Ridder, & Bensing, 2007). Another protective factor can be found in religious practices and faith (see the *More Information You Can Use* box on page 567, "Faith and Well-Being in Later Life").

Immigrant Seniors and Health Issues   With increasing immigration from many countries, a growing body of cross-cultural research is available to inform medical practitioners, social workers, and other service providers of the health-care practices of seniors by race-ethnicity and culture (Wittenberg et al., 2006). The American health-care and social-service delivery systems have goals and values that differ from the familiar beliefs, values, and customs of many immigrant seniors. The idea of outside intervention with preventive measures to promote well-being or alleviate illness is often viewed as undesirable—as are medications, diagnostic procedures, and therapies. Speaking English increases one's ability to identify and access health-care services in the United States. Consequently, language and culture can be barriers to both the service provider and the family in need of care, creating confusion, embarrassment, frustration, anger, withdrawal, or rejection of services (see Table 17.4) (Garcia & Duckett, 2009). Simple nonverbal gestures have entirely different meanings across cultures; shaking hands may be a forbidden gesture (especially if using the left hand, which is offensive to a Muslim), as may be stroking a person's head.

Seniors who are recent immigrants typically experience "culture shock" for a long time. In some cultures, women do not speak directly to outsiders; communication is done with the senior male in the family or the group. U.S. service providers encounter practices or cures that are difficult to accept, such as using leeches, having a shaman ward off evil spirits, using purification

TABLE 17.4 List of Therapeutic Agents and People Sought by Various Cultural Groups for Help with Psychosocial Disorders and Aging Issues

Mainstream White American	Mexican American
• Counselors	• Curanderos
• Psychiatrists	**Puerto Rican**
• Psychologists	• Espiristas
• Social workers	• Santerios
• Ministers	**Cuban**
African American	• Santerios
• Ministers	**Southeast Asian American**
• Root workers	• Herbalists
• Voodoo priests	• Family/friends
Native American	• Diviners
• Medicine man	**Haitian**
• "Singers"	• Voodoo priests

Source: Randall-David, E. (1989). *Strategies for working with culturally diverse communities and clients* (p. 26). Washington, DC: Association for the Care of Children's Health. From p. 13 in Lynch, E. W., & Hanson, M. J. (2004). *Developing Cross-Cultural Competence: A Guide for Working with Children and Their Families* (3rd ed.). Baltimore, MD: Paul H. Brookes.

or religious rituals or unusual foods for certain illnesses, and coining (scratching the skin). Another major factor is that in many collectivist cultural groups, the family is responsible for the care of an elderly person, even one with severe dementia or Alzheimer's. Accepting any help from "outsiders" represents a loss of face.

Service providers must increase their understanding of cultural beliefs and practices and must also adopt strategies to reduce inequities in health-care delivery with these vulnerable families. For those who want to increase their understanding, a recent compendium of cross-cultural research on physical and mental-health practices can be found in the *Textbook of Cultural Psychiatry* (Bhugra & Bhui, 2007), the *Oxford Textbook of Old Age Psychiatry* (Jacoby, Oppenheimer, Dening, & Thomas, 2008), or *The SAGE Handbook of Social Psychology* (Hogg & Cooper, 2007). In 2008, New Jersey began requiring physicians to have *culturally competent care education* (CCCE) and training to obtain a medical license. The state's directive is that "faculty and students must demonstrate an understanding of the manner in which people of diverse cultures and belief systems perceive health and illness and respond to various symptoms, diseases, and treatments" (White & Hoffman, 2007).

Questions

What is the relationship among activity, exercise, and aging? To what extent are the elderly likely to experience depression, and what approaches might help them cope with this disorder? What are some special considerations for senior immigrants regarding health and wellness?

Biological Aging

Biological aging consists of changes that occur in the structure and functioning of the human organism over time (see Figure 17.4). *Primary aging,* or time-related change, is a continuous process that begins at conception and ceases at death. As humans advance from infancy through young adulthood, biological change typically enables them to make a more efficient and effective adaptation to the environment. Beyond this period, however, biological change generally leads to impairment in the ability to adapt to the environment—ultimately, it jeopardizes survival. Improvements in the conditions of health at birth and early childhood and advances in medicine in childhood and adulthood have facilitated longevity and successful aging (Baltes & Smith, 2003; Crimmins et al., 2009). Those elderly who remain socially involved, mentally stimulated, and physically active increase the likelihood of successful aging (Cartensen, 2007).

Physical Changes   Some of the most visible changes associated with aging are changes in physical characteristics. The hair grows thinner, turns gray, and becomes somewhat coarser. The skin changes texture, loses its elasticity and moistness, and gathers spot pigmentation. By age 40, every man and woman begins losing muscle, which, coupled with the loss of the elasticity of the skin, begins to produce skin folds and wrinkling—a condition called *sarcopenia,* or age-related loss of muscle (Rattan & Kassem, 2006). Exercises such as yoga, weight and resistance training, and *Tai Chi* help to reduce muscle loss, improve balance, and reduce frailty. Tai Chi is a gentle martial art with graceful exercise sequences used to improve coordination, relieve stress, promote overall well-being, and strengthen the immune system. Practicing Tai Chi is reported to have positive effects on various ailments, such as diabetes, arthritis, chronic fatigue, and high blood pressure (Humecky, 2005).

Other changes are noticeable in body height, shape, and weight. The vertebrae begin to settle closer because the "cushioning" material between them becomes thinner, reducing the length of the spine. There are also muscular changes that result in a loss of flexibility, making it harder to stand straight. Changes in body shape result from the redistribution of fat away from the arms, legs, and face and onto the torso (Newell, Vaillancourt, & Sosnoff, 2006). There is also a decline in the capacity for physical work, exercise, and maintaining balance (Costarella, Monteleone, Steindler, & Zuccaro, 2009). By age 70, maximum oxygen intake declines significantly, and maximum ventilatory volume declines during exercise. Because oxygen is needed to combine with nutrients for the release of chemical building blocks and energy, the older person generally has less staying power and lower reserves.

Collagen, a substance that constitutes a very high percentage of the total protein in the body, appears to be implicated in the aging process. Collagen is a basic structural component of connective tissue. Loose connective tissue resembles loose pellet-packing material. It supports and holds in place blood vessels, nerves, and internal organs, while permitting some freedom of movement. It also holds muscle cells together and binds skin to underlying tissue. Over time, collagen fibers become thicker and less elastic, contributing to a loss of elasticity in the skin, hardening of the arteries, and stiffening of the joints. Thus, over time, collagen speeds the destruction of the organism it originally helped to build.

Sensory and Functional Changes   Our sensory abilities—such as hearing, sight, taste, and smell—also become less "sensitive" with age. It is important to understand both the magnitude of the changes and the course of action that can reduce the amount of impairment.

FIGURE 17.4 Tendencies in Rates of Aging The rate of aging varies considerably among individuals—and even among different organs in the same person. Nonetheless, a number of tendencies in aging occur in a predictable fashion. *Source:* © 1992 Reprinted by permission of the *Columbus Dispatch.*

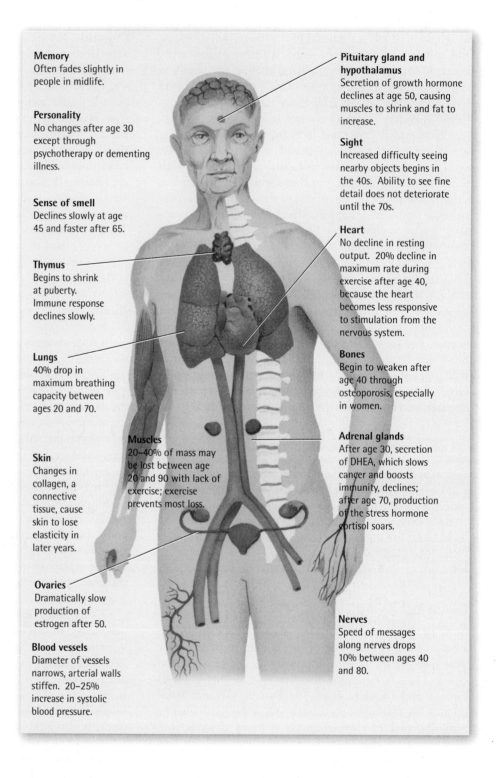

Memory
Often fades slightly in people in midlife.

Personality
No changes after age 30 except through psychotherapy or dementing illness.

Sense of smell
Declines slowly at age 45 and faster after 65.

Thymus
Begins to shrink at puberty. Immune response declines slowly.

Lungs
40% drop in maximum breathing capacity between ages 20 and 70.

Skin
Changes in collagen, a connective tissue, cause skin to lose elasticity in later years.

Ovaries
Dramatically slow production of estrogen after 50.

Blood vessels
Diameter of vessels narrows, arterial walls stiffen. 20–25% increase in systolic blood pressure.

Muscles
20–40% of mass may be lost between age 20 and 90 with lack of exercise; exercise prevents most loss.

Pituitary gland and hypothalamus
Secretion of growth hormone declines at age 50, causing muscles to shrink and fat to increase.

Sight
Increased difficulty seeing nearby objects begins in the 40s. Ability to see fine detail does not deteriorate until the 70s.

Heart
No decline in resting output. 20% decline in maximum rate during exercise after age 40, because the heart becomes less responsive to stimulation from the nervous system.

Bones
Begin to weaken after age 40 through osteoporosis, especially in women.

Adrenal glands
After age 30, secretion of DHEA, which slows cancer and boosts immunity, declines; after age 70, production of the stress hormone cortisol soars.

Nerves
Speed of messages along nerves drops 10% between ages 40 and 80.

Recent studies have shown a strong link between sensory acuity and cognitive functioning in aging. A person with declining memory ability is more likely to have impaired hearing as well (Hoyer & Verhaeghen, 2006). Baltes and Lindenberger (1997) found a comparable relationship among visual acuity, auditory thresholds, and intelligence.

Vision and Hearing   Some of the visual changes associated with aging begin to occur during middle age (see Table 17.5). We saw in Chapter 15 that many adults in their forties need to wear bifocals; some develop "dry" eyes, often requiring drops of "liquid tears." Annual eye exams are recommended to check for pressure buildup in the fluid of the eye, or *glaucoma,* which, when it occurs,

TABLE 17.5 Percentages of U.S. Adults Aged 65 and Older Who Reported Having Trouble Hearing, Trouble Seeing, or No Natural Teeth

Age	Men Trouble Hearing	Women Trouble Hearing
65–74	36%	20.7%
75–84	43.7	31.7
85 and over	66.7	56.6
	Trouble Seeing	Trouble Seeing
65–74	11.3	16.9
75–84	17.2	19.5
85 and over	28.5	28.4
	No Natural Teeth	No Natural Teeth
65–74	19.2	21.4
75–84	30.7	30.8
85 and over	33	34.4

Source: Federal Interagency Forum on Aging-Related Statistics. (2010). Indicator 17, Sensory Impairments and Oral Health. *Older Americans 2010: Key indicators of well-being.* Washington, DC: U.S. Government Printing Office. Retrieved from http://www.agingstats.gov/agingstatsdotnet/Main _Site/Data/2010_Documents/Docs/OA_2010.pdf

must be treated to prevent blindness. Blurred detail vision for most is not a problem until sometime in the seventies or eighties, when it can be a sign of a *cataract,* or hardening of the lens of the eye, so that it cannot accommodate as efficiently. Fortunately, cataract surgery has become routine. The "oldest old" are also more prone to *retinal detachment,* a serious condition in which the retinal layer at the back of the eyeball begins to "peel away." If the condition is caught early enough, laser surgery may be able to reattach the retina. A person with other health complications (such as high blood pressure, diabetes, or stroke) often finds vision difficulties appearing as well.

Hearing loss is a hazard in some activities and occupations, such as working near large engines or motors or working with construction equipment or sound equipment for rock bands. Some hearing loss appears to have a genetic component. Increased hearing loss occurs more with advancing age (National Center for Health Statistics, 2007a). Some seniors cannot afford hearing devices, because they are costly and Medicare provides limited coverage. Severe hearing loss or loss of vision diminishes the person's quality of life, making him or her more dependent on others to meet even basic needs. Loss of vision or hearing can even lead to one of the most upsetting things that can happen to an older person—losing a driver's license and the freedom of choice and mobility that it makes possible.

Taste and Smell   Older people frequently report that they are losing their ability to enjoy food. This problem is related to a decline in the taste buds (the small protuberances on the surface of the tongue). Persons 70 to 85 years old have, on average, about one-third as many taste buds as young adults (Schiffman, 2009). Medications, especially when drug-to-drug interactions occur, are the most significant yet unappreciated contributors to taste disorders in the elderly. Olfactory sensitivity (smell—the ability to distinguish oranges from lemons or chocolate from cheese) also declines among older adults, which helps explain why many complain about their food. Cross-sectional studies reveal that a large number of older individuals have higher detection thresholds for smell, diminished intensities, and an impaired ability to identify and discriminate odors (Schiffman, 2009).

Dental, Swallowing, and Breathing Difficulties Adults who lose teeth and cannot afford dental care are unable to eat a range of foods that provide essential nutrients; in addition, they might isolate themselves because of their appearance (Copeland, Krall, Brown, Garcia, & Streckfus, 2004). Numerous studies have linked deterioration of oral health to subsequent dementia, including Alzheimer's. Participants with the fewest teeth had the highest risk of and incidence of dementia. One suggestion is that oral bacteria may use the branches of the trigeminal nerve to reach the brain (Stein, Desrosiers, Donegan, Yepes, & Kryscio, 2007). Older adults also have an increased risk of swallowing disorders (called *dysphagia*) as aging occurs. Many medical conditions can lead to dysphagia, such as stroke, diabetes, alcoholism, head injury, Alzheimer's, multiple sclerosis, and Parkinson's. Swallowing is a complex process, and dysphagia, if left untreated, can lead to malnutrition, dehydration, respiratory infections, aspiration pneumonia, or even death. One study found that 60 percent of the elderly in long-term care facilities suffer from dysphagia. Assessment includes swallowing tests and other medical diagnostics. Treatment may include swallowing therapy with a speech-language therapist, exercises, medication, or a feeding tube (Prasse & Kikano, 2004). Inability to swallow has a significant impact on a person's health and social-emotional well-being.

Late-onset asthma and other respiratory problems affect some seniors. Another condition that results in breathing difficulties is *chronic obstructive pulmonary disease (COPD),* which often afflicts those who smoke(d) or were exposed to chemicals in a work environment. Allergists and pulmonologists can help to control symptoms (Parkinson, 2005).

Touch and Temperature Sensitivity   Hand dexterity and grip strength are found to diminish in older adults on some measures (Snih, Markides, Ray, Ostir, & Goodwin,

2002). The elderly are also less sensitive to changes in temperature (Smolander, 2002). Elderly individuals can fail to notice a drop of 9 degrees Fahrenheit. Consequently, older people tend to be susceptible to **hypothermia**—a condition in which body temperature falls more than 4 degrees Fahrenheit and persists at that level for a number of hours. Early symptoms of hypothermia include drowsiness and mental confusion, and eventually there is a loss of consciousness. This can be life-threatening, especially because the aging body becomes less able to maintain an even temperature in winter weather. Social services programs such as HEAP provide funds so that the elderly who are too poor to pay for the heat in their apartments do not get hypothermia during the winter. Also, thyroid dysfunction among the elderly is common, and one symptom of *hypothyroidism* is always feeling cold (Sidani, 2001). Have you noticed that an elderly relative's thermostat is set at least 10 degrees higher than your own?

Sleep Changes Complaints of sleep difficulties increase with age, because sleep may be disrupted by illness, medication, the physical changes of aging, or moves to and from hospitals and rehabilitation facilities. Many persons aged 65 and older report problems with the earlier timing and shorter duration of sleep, frequent awakenings, and daytime sleepiness. The two main reasons why the ability to sleep decreases with age are changes in circadian rhythms and the presence of sleep disorders (Zilli, Ficca, & Salzarulo, 2009). Light therapy, melatonin, and psychological interventions for sleep disorders have generally been found effective. They have the potential to provide an alternative treatment without the side effects or long-term negative impact associated with many medications used for sleep (Knight, Kaskie, Shurgot, & Dave, 2006). Another common disorder that often disrupts sleep is *restless legs syndrome* (*RLS*), which causes unpleasant prickling or tingling sensations in the legs and feet and an urge to move them to get relief (Thorpy, 2005).

Obstructive **sleep apnea** is a serious disorder in which the person often stops breathing during sleep. Typically, the person snores loudly, gasps for air, and might jump up to breathe again; she or he may also exhibit chronic daytime sleepiness. The likelihood of this disorder increases with age (Norman & Loredo, 2008). Diagnosis can be determined at a sleep clinic, where treatments are prescribed.

Questions

What are some common physical and sensory changes in late adulthood? How do sleep changes in later years manifest themselves?

Sexuality With the aging of the baby boomers and the development and hugely successful marketing of Viagra and similar drugs to treat erectile dysfunction, the attention of sexologists, pharmaceutical companies, and the public has become focused on the sexuality of aging adults (Chew, Bremner, Stuckey, Earle, & Jamrozik, 2009): "The need for companionship, tenderness, love, intimacy and yes, sex, remains as important as ever, but the rules of the game have changed" (Rimer, 1998, A1). In surveys of older people's attitudes toward sexuality, most respondents felt that sex was important for both physical and emotional health. According to one study, nearly half of all Americans over the age of 60 have sexual relations at least once a month, and 40 percent would like to have it more often (Balon, 2008). So the question is, Why can't a good portion of older adults have sexual relations as desired?

Four major factors are partner availability, difficulty with sexual arousal, the overall health of older adults, and privacy. As we noted earlier, women account for about 70 percent of the 85-and-older population and are likely to be widowed. And older single men tend to choose younger women for companionship. Difficulties with sexual arousal occur in both men and women, but male impotence is the more frequently occurring problem. Women also experience physical changes after the onset of menopause (less vaginal lubrication, thinning of the vaginal walls, smaller size of uterus, cervix, and ovaries), which can make sexual intercourse uncomfortable or

Human Sexuality, Attraction, and Aging Sexuality and intimacy remain important throughout life for most adults. Four major factors are partner availability, level of difficulty with sexual arousal, the overall health of older adults, and privacy.

painful, although medications that are available can help. Other contributing factors include medications that diminish desire or inhibit erection in males, pain from chronic illness, mobility problems, and lack of privacy in nursing homes (Balon, 2008). Recently collected national data indicate that nearly 10 percent of all cases of AIDS were diagnosed in people 50 and older; thus older adults need education programs to be informed about the risk of this disease (Centers for Disease Control and Prevention, 2010c).

Questions

What physical changes are considered a normal part of sexual aging for women and men? What are some factors that might account for a decrease in sexual activity?

Biological Theories of Aging

Now you might be asking, "What drives the changes associated with aging—why do they occur, or how does aging occur?" There are many competing theories that seek to explain the process. We will review several that have received the most attention.

Wear-and-Tear Theory   Although body cells die and are replaced every day (except brain cells and stem cells), the wear-and-tear theory posits that there is a natural limit to the human life expectancy and that little can be done to push the figure upward (Moody, 2006). Rheumatologist James Fries (1997, 2007) is the leading proponent of the notion of inborn limits. He contends that the human body is biologically destined to fall apart after 85 years—frailty rather than disease being the primary killer of people at very old ages. Around age 85, give or take seven years, the tiniest insults—a fall that would be trivial to a 20-year-old, a spell of hot weather, or a mild case of the flu—are sufficient to cause death. Fries likens the process to a sun-rotted curtain: You sew up a tear in one place and it promptly tears somewhere else. In the opposing camp are those who argue that old people do die from such causes as heart disease or osteoporosis, but that these diseases—once deemed to be the inevitable hallmarks of old age—now can be prevented or delayed. Also, aging is not uniform across the body—different parts of the body age at different rates (Moody, 2006).

Error Accumulation Theory   Related to the wear-and-tear theory, the error accumulation theory holds that human life eventually ends because body cells eventually develop errors in duplicating themselves. The new cells formed from old cells are thought to deteriorate in accuracy with the number of recopying events (Ferenac, Polancec, Huzak, Pereira-Smith, & Rubelj, 2005). Think of this as similar to what happens when one copies the same image on a copy machine over and over, using each successive copy as the original—eventually the image becomes flawed and less visible.

Somatic Mutation Theory   Based on another line of evidence related to wear-and-tear theory, the somatic mutation theory suggests that alterations (mutations) occur in the DNA molecules of the cells—that is, errors (such as radiation can cause) creep into the chemical blueprint—and impair cell function and division. Note, however, that although radiation causes cell mutations, it does not necessarily affect aging (Hasty, 2005; Moody, 2006).

Genetic Preprogramming Theory   Also referred to as "mean time to failure," the genetic preprogramming theory is like engineers' contention that every machine has a built-in obsolescence and that its lifetime is limited by the wear and tear on the parts. Most significantly, DNA repair capacity declines with age, and DNA damage accumulates (Warner & Price, 1989). Westendorp and Kirkwood (2007) state, "Animals in nature die young, only rarely do they survive long enough to reveal significant aging." A similar statement could be applied to primitive human populations before the advent of civilization. Consequently, based on the lack of an evolutionary need or opportunity to evolve genes for aging, we must look beyond strict genetic programming for an understanding of the genetic contribution to aging and longevity (Westendorp & Kirkwood, 2007).

Accumulation of Metabolic Waste (or Free-Radical) Theory   Biologists have suggested that organisms age because waste products of metabolism slowly poison cells or prevent normal functioning. Such waste products accumulate, leading to progressive organic malfunctioning (Moody, 2006). For instance, researchers have found changes with age in the amounts and kinds of metals in certain organs, including the lens of the eye. Some waste molecules that are the normal by-products of cells' use of oxygen—called *free radicals*—are toxic to nearly every molecule they encounter, wreaking havoc on vital cellular machinery. Eventually, the injuries are so substantial that cells no longer function properly, organ systems fail, arthritis cripples joints, emphysema undermines lungs, cataracts cloud the eyes, diseases such as cancer and heart disease occur, and finally the organism dies (Moody, 2006).

Daily caloric restriction (eating less) and taking dietary supplements that are known *antioxidants,* such as vitamins C and E and beta-carotene, are believed to be helpful in reducing free radicals. Biologists have identified specific genetic traits associated with the improvement of an organism's defense system against free radicals. This knowledge has enabled them to breed fruit flies that live the human equivalent of 150 years (McDonald & Ruhe, 2003).

Forecasting Life Expectancy As the population becomes generally healthier, people will enter old age in better shape, and so life spans are likely to increase. Biodemographers project that by the year 2070, the average life expectancy for women will be between 92.5 and 101.5 (Rector-Page, 2004). Another demographer, S. Jay Olshansky (Olshansky & Carnes, 2001), argues that it will become harder and harder to maintain the pace, so that any major increase is very unlikely. As in economics, a curve of diminishing returns operates. It is not so much that we are programmed to die, says Olshansky. Rather, we are not programmed to survive very long past the end of our reproductive period. To get an average life expectancy of 85 from today's overall average of about age 78, we would need to reduce death rates by half at each age interval (a feat equivalent to the complete elimination of heart disease and cancer). And once life expectancy reaches age 85, he says, a practical limit is reached because there are too few people over 85 to influence the overall statistics. Yet today's 60,000+ American centenarians, as well as increasing numbers worldwide, seem to support a longer life span.

In evaluating these perspectives, it is useful to examine the more prominent theories that seek to explain the biological process of aging. So far researchers have not reached a consensus. Indeed, the process of aging may be too complex for any one-factor explanation.

Autoimmune Theory Some scientists believe that aging slows the capabilities of the immune system, which produces antibodies to defend against invasion by bacteria, viruses, parasites, and other substances. The immune system is also supposed to remove the body's own damaged or mutant cells (to prevent cancers in the body). Yet in an aging body, the immune system can attack its own healthy cells, as it does with rheumatoid arthritis and other autoimmune diseases (Moody, 2006). For example, it is not uncommon for an elderly person to get shingles, a very painful nerve inflammation caused by reactivation of the chickenpox virus; in a limited area of the body the skin itches, and then a rash erupts, followed by small blisters. The body's natural defenses against infection begin to decline after adolescence and may be induced by some genetic messages to attack healthy cells, or the body's normal cells may be changing in ways that make them appear "foreign" (Schmeck et al., 2004). Vaccinations do not work as well in an aging body, and influenza is especially serious for an elderly person.

Hormone Effects Hormones can promote or inhibit aging, depending on the conditions. Reducing the secretion of some hormones (e.g., pituitary hormones) in rodents depresses their body metabolism and delays the aging of their tissues; we noted earlier that caloric restrictions also seem to slow aging. However, a reduction in the secretion of many hormones also occurs with age in rodents and humans. Increasing these hormones (e.g., growth hormone and DHEA) has been found to enhance metabolism and stimulate organ functioning. One study found that replacing the hormone DHEA can play a role in the prevention and treatment of the metabolic syndrome (insulin resistance, diabetes, and atherosclerosis) associated with abdominal obesity (Villareal & Holloszy, 2004).

Longevity Assurance Theory The theories just outlined focus on cell-destroying mechanisms within the body. In sharp contrast to these approaches, George Sacher (1978) offers what he terms a "positive" theory of aging because he portrays evolution as having prolonged life among some species. Thus, instead of asking why organisms age and die, he asks why they live as long as they do. Sacher observes that the life spans of mammals vary enormously, from about 2 years for some shrews to more than 60 years for great whales, elephants, humans, and some turtles. He says that in long-living species, *natural selection* has favored genes that repair cells, while weeding out genes that impair cell functioning. Individuals who are the bearers of cell repair genes are more likely to survive and thus pass on their favorable genes to their offspring. Sacher notes that the amount of DNA repair that occurs is in direct proportion to the life span of the species.

Slowing the Aging Process Given what we know about physical changes in late adulthood, there appear to be three primary ways of slowing the aging process and living longer: (1) Individuals can make behavior changes in diet and lifestyle that are known to further life expectancy, such as restricting calorie consumption; (2) medical scientists can develop ways to replace the body's growth factors, hormones, and chemical defense systems that diminish over time and affect youthfulness; and (3) medical scientists can change the genetics of aging with drugs, body or stem cells, and gene therapies. Clearly, the first option is the principal one currently and readily available to us, although studies have reported significant improvement in well-being, mood, and sexuality with HGH and DHEA supplements (Genazzani, Lanzoni, & Genazzani, 2007).

Questions

What are the major theories about why biological aging occurs? In what ways might we slow the aging process?

COGNITIVE FUNCTIONING

Sooner or later adults worry about whether they are thinking, remembering, problem solving, and making decisions with the same sharpness as when they were younger. Even as early as 40, we can begin to notice occasional mental lapses. It could be as simple as having difficulty remembering a word or someone's name, where we put our car keys, or why we walked into a certain room of our house. We might wonder whether these are normal consequences of aging or whether they foretell Alzheimer's disease. Attitudes or perceptions about aging appear to be important in determining whether people are honored for their wisdom or cast aside for their incompetence. Not all societies value old age in the same way. The Bible celebrates the wisdom of the elderly King Solomon, and cultures in the Far East have long revered their elders. In the United States a less positive attitude has prevailed, although much depends on the person and the historic period in which she or he lives.

In reality, the cognitive lives of older adults are characterized by stability, decline, and improvement—depending on the area of functioning. However, the literature puts a greater emphasis on the deterioration of cognitive aging (Carstensen, 2007). Conversely, there is less decline—or even little or no decline—for people with favorable lifestyles and good health (Luo & Craik, 2008; Carstensen, 2007). Indeed, a growing body of research suggests that disease, including depression, metabolic disorders, hardening of the arteries, chronic liver and kidney failure, amnesia, and Alzheimer's disease—not age in itself—underlies much of the decline and loss of cognitive and intellectual functioning among the elderly (*polypharmacy*—the use of many drugs—for chronic conditions also plays a role).

Researchers who study the physiology of aging brains are surprised at their flexibility and resilience (Yang, Planck, Krampe, & Baltes, 2006). For instance, contrary to what was established scientific opinion just a few years ago, investigators now find that older folks' brains have remarkable capacities to maintain their professional skills or acquire new learning skills and rewire themselves to compensate for losses. This process is referred to as *cognitive plasticity*. According to Stanley Rapoport, chief of the Brain, Physiology, and Metabolism Section of the National Institute on Aging, as brains age, neighboring brain cells (neurons) help take up the slack; indeed, responsibilities for a task can actually shift from one region to another, a process called *adaptive compensation* (Finch & Zelinski, 2005). Overall, even though a small percentage of aging adults get Alzheimer's disease, and although there is some decline in cognitive functioning for some people in their seventies, many people seem not to be affected. Let's take a closer look at some of these issues.

The Varied Courses of Different Cognitive Abilities

Not only do the declines in cognitive functioning appear later in life than we might have expected, but cognitive abilities vary in how they are affected by aging. The

Seattle Longitudinal Study (see Chapter 15) found that many abilities begin a dramatic downward trend in the twenties—and an even greater one as advanced age is reached. There are important exceptions, however. The cross-sectional data for verbal and numeric abilities indicate a peak in midlife with relatively little change into early old age, but a significant decline in the eighties. Take a minute to review some weaknesses of a cross-sectional design. The major one, of course, is that you don't know whether your groups are comparable. For instance, would your 80-year-olds, if measured at the age of 40, be similar to your current 40-year-olds? In the Seattle study, both longitudinal and cross-sectional data were collected and analyzed.

The only ability that shows profound linear decrement is perceptual speed. This decline is the result of progressive slowing of neural impulses throughout the central nervous system. Another important finding is the extent of individual variation; that is, some very old people are capable of quite quick responses (Hartley, 2006). However, most other abilities show a gain from young adulthood into midlife. Intellectual competence generally peaks in the forties and fifties, because people continue to gain experience—without significant physiological loss to offset the gain. Speed of numeric computation declines significantly with age when followed longitudinally, but in contrast, verbal ability does not peak until the sixties and declines only modestly after that age.

Some researchers believe that cognitive functioning should be assessed in less traditional ways than standard intelligence testing. Critics of traditional intelligence testing suggest that aspects of adult functioning, such as social or professional competence and the ability to deal with one's environment, should also be considered (Berg & Sternberg, 1992). Many psychologists are developing new measures of adult intelligence and revising our notions of what it is. Howard Gardner's (1993a, 1993b, 2000a, 2006a) theories of multiple intelligences also provide insight into adult cognition.

For example, psychologist Gisela Labouvie-Vief is investigating how people approach everyday problems in logic (Kausler, Kausler, & Krupsaw, 2007). Researchers often find that the elderly do poorly on measures of formal reasoning ability. But she contends that this poor performance results from differences in the way younger and older adults approach tasks. Older adults tend to personalize the tasks, to consider alternative ways to answer a question, and to examine affective and psychological components associated with a solution. She says that reasoning by intuition rather than by principles of formal logic is not an inferior mode of problem solving—merely a different one. Consider, for example, a likely age difference in response to information given that a wife has threatened to leave her husband if he comes home drunk one more time—and eventually he does. Young adults typically respond with the seemingly logical conclusion that she will certainly leave her husband. Many elderly adults, however, go beyond the information given and consider situational factors—that is, the context that may be involved. Perhaps the husband heard that day of the death of a close friend, and he had a few drinks to relieve his sorrow (Kausler, Kausler, & Krupsaw, 2007).

Cognitive functioning depends to some extent on whether the elderly use their abilities. You probably have heard the expression "Use it or lose it." For instance, people can perform such complex cognitive tasks as playing chess or the cello well into old age at the same time that they are losing many simpler abilities. Many elderly persons find that what they have been doing, they can keep on doing. John Glenn, in his late seventies, returned to space as an astronaut to conduct research on aging. Jack LaLanne, born in 1914, pioneered the first TV exercise program and was awarded a lifetime achievement award from the President's Council for Physical Fitness and Sports; he was going strong and planned a long swim at age 95 before he died in 2011. Erik Erikson, Jean Piaget, Bernice Neugarten, Dr. Benjamin Spock, Eubie Blake, Martha Graham, George Burns, Bob Hope, Andrés Segovia, Pablo Picasso, George Bernard Shaw, Arthur Miller, James Michener, Bertrand Russell, Supreme Court Justice John Paul Stevens, and artist Georgia O'Keeffe are examples of people who continued to excel, performing up to the same high standards well into advanced age. In fact, the execution of cognitive tasks or everyday cognitive activities can improve cognitive functioning or maintain it at the same level in old age (Marcoen, Coleman, & O'Hanlon, 2007). In brief, much of our fate is in our own hands, and "use it or lose it" is an underlying principle.

Older adults do slow down in their performance of many tasks (Hartley, 2006), and slower reflexes are a disadvantage in tasks such as driving a car. Further, the speed of processing information has been used as a measurement of cognitive decline in old age. Developmentalist K. Warner Schaie (1994, 2005; Schaie, Borghesani, Weaver, & Aylward, 2010), whose pioneering work has done much to shape our understanding of cognitive functioning across the life span, finds that a variety of factors reduce the risk of cognitive decline in old age: (1) good health and the absence of chronic diseases; (2) environmental circumstances characterized by above-average education, a history of stimulating occupational pursuits, above-average income, and the maintenance of an intact family; (3) a complex and stimulating lifestyle, including extensive reading, travel, and a continuing pursuit of educational opportunities; (4) a personality that is flexible and adaptable at midlife; and (5) marriage to a spouse with high cognitive capabilities.

Some aspects of intelligence, such as memory, perceptual speed, and fluid ability, appear to be more affected by biological aging factors than others (Singer,

Learning and Everyday Cognitive Activities Older people continue to learn throughout life but need a little more time than a younger adult might need. They are less motivated to learn irrelevant material. Regularly engaging in mental tasks such as bingo, poker, bridge, chess, Sudoku, crossword puzzles, *Jeopardy,* and the like helps prevent memory decline.

Lindenberger, & Baltes, 2003). But older people can learn to compensate, and they can still learn what they need to, although it may take them a little longer. Other aspects of intelligence, notably crystallized intelligence, might increase, at least until rather advanced age. There are also considerable individual differences; some fare poorly and others quite well. One of the major factors in maintaining or improving mental capabilities is using them. Findings from the *Berlin Aging Study,* the *Kungsholmen Study* (in Sweden), the *Nun Study,* and the *Seattle Longitudinal Study* agree that those who do well in old age remain intellectually involved in the world about them and are socially and physically active (Gerstorf, Smith, & Baltes, 2006; Rovio et al., 2005).

> **Questions**
>
> What factors have been associated with aging with optimal cognitive abilities? What can one do to mitigate the decline in certain intellectual abilities?

Overestimating the Effects of Aging

What happens in psychological aging is complex, and we are only beginning to understand it. It is clear, however, that psychologists have taken too negative a view of the impact of aging on intellectual functioning. One reason for this is that researchers have relied too heavily on cross-sectional studies. As we noted in Chapter 1, cross-sectional studies employ the snapshot approach; they test individuals of different ages and compare their performance. Longitudinal studies are more like case histories; they retest the same individuals over a period of years (Hofer & Sliwinski, 2006). For the more accurate understanding of aging, longitudinal studies offer many advantages relative to cross-sectional studies, because between-person age comparisons cannot provide a basis for disentangling changes due to aging from stable individual characteristics (Hofer & Sliwinski, 2006).

Psychologists such as Baltes and Schaie (1976; Schaie, 1996) have pointed out that cross-sectional studies of adult aging do not account for generational differences in performance on intelligence tests. Because of increasing educational achievement and other social changes, successive generations of Americans (as well as residents of other industrialized countries) perform at progressively higher levels. Hence, the measured intelligence (IQ) of the population is increasing. When individuals who were 50 years old in 1993 are compared with those who were 50 in 1973, the former score higher on almost every kind of cognitive task. Because the people who were 50 years old in 1993 were 30 in 1973, a cross-sectional study undertaken in 1973 would falsely suggest that they were "brighter" than those who were 50 in 1993. This result would lead to the false conclusion that intelligence declines with age. When you compare people from different generations— 80-year-olds with 40-year-olds, for instance—you are comparing people from different environments. Thus, cross-sectional studies tend to confuse generational differences with differences in chronological age.

Other factors have also contributed to an overestimation of the decline in intellectual functioning that occurs with aging. Research suggests that a marked intellectual decline, called the **death drop** or *terminal decline* phenomenon, occurs just a short time before a person dies (Schaie, 2005). Because relatively more people in an older age group can be expected to die within any given span of time, compared with a younger group, the average scores of older age groups are depressed relatively more as a result of the death-drop effect than are the average scores for younger age groups.

Whereas the cross-sectional method tends to magnify or overestimate the decline in intelligence with age, the longitudinal method tends to minimize or underestimate it. One reason is that some people drop out of a longitudinal study over time. Generally it is the more able, healthy, and intelligent subjects who remain available. Those who perform poorly on intelligence tests tend to be less available for longitudinal retesting. Consequently, the researchers are left with an increasingly smaller, biased sample as the subjects are retested at each later period.

Question

What are some reasons for the apparent overestimation of declines in intellectual functioning in old age?

Memory and Aging

Growing older is difficult on a personal level for many people. They might have trouble adjusting to changes in how they look or what they can do; and the limitations in daily life, even if minor, can cause them concern. One concern for nearly all older adults is *memory*. No other criterion is used more often to evaluate how we are doing. And for good reason! If we had no memory, in the broadest sense of the term, we would not be able to function. Memory is essential for all of life's activities (Zacks & Hasher, 2006). One of the common concerns of middle-aged and older adults is that their memory is "not as good as it used to be." Older adults often say that the first sign of cognitive aging they noticed was difficulty remembering people's names. As they age, the pool of names they know also becomes larger, so they might have difficulty remembering, not so much because their memories are not as good as they once were, but because they have more things stored in their memory and searching therefore takes longer. Although the memory for names seems to decline regularly over a lifetime, verbal memory remains stable and can even increase slightly with regular physical activity (Stroth, Hille, Spitzer, & Reinhardt, 2009).

Samples of adults ranging from 40 to 80 years old suggest that as executive cognitive functioning declined with age, participants experienced some deterioration in working memory (Clarys, Bugaiska, Tapia, & Baudouin, 2009). Clearly, large percentages of middle-aged and older adults believe they have some difficulty with their memory. But with sufficient motivation, time, instruction, and a suitable environment, older adults can continue to expand their interests, abilities, and outcomes. Recent research has pointed out the relationship between cardiovascular fitness and positive effects on memory performance in older adults. These investigators suggest that cardiovascular fitness increases blood flow to the brain, which increases neural activation in the memory storage centers of the brain (Stroth et al., 2009).

Moreover, a progressive loss of memory does not always accompany advancing age (see Figure 17.5) (Schaie et al., 2010). Instead, some memory loss is found with each advance in chronological age, but some elderly retain a sound memory. Short-term memory loss affects daily functioning, such as remembering whether you took a prescribed pill this morning, whether you just went to the grocery store, whether an adult child just visited, or whether you just asked a person the same question five times in an hour. Older adults have more difficulty with short-term memory if they are taking medications. Particularly anticholinergic medication prescribed for incontinence in older adults has been implicated in memory decline (Lajiness, 2009). Such memory problems may be diagnosed as a type of dementia, but more serious memory loss, such as not remembering

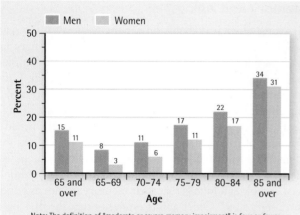

Note: The definition of "moderate or severe memory impairment" is four or fewer words recalled (out of 20) on combined immediate and delayed recall tests among self-respondents. Self-respondents who refused either the immediate or delayed word recall test were excluded from the analysis. Proxy respondents with an overall memory rating of "poor" were included as having moderate or severe memory impairment. Because of some changes in methods from the 2000 edition of *Older Americans*, no inference should be made about longitudinal trends. Reference population: These data refer to the civilian noninstitutionalized population.

FIGURE 17.5 Percentage of People Aged 65 and Older with Moderate or Severe Memory Impairment, by Age Group and Sex: 2002 Note that some memory loss is natural and increases with aging in both men and women, with the oldest adults experiencing the most impairment. The degree of memory loss is most severe for those with Alzheimer's.

your children's names, not knowing how to get dressed, or not remembering how to get home from an activity might be diagnosed as Alzheimer's disease. Younger adults are sometimes amazed by older adults' *long-term memory,* such as their recall of something from their youth 85 years ago, their ability to recite poetry they learned in grade school, or their remembering specific events, places, and names from childhood.

Question

What types of memory is an older adult likely to retain, and with which type of memory is an older adult most likely to have difficulty?

Phases in Information Processing When information is remembered, three things occur: (1) **encoding,** the process by which information is put into the memory system; (2) **storage,** the process by which information is retained in memory until it is needed; and (3) **retrieval,** the process by which information is regathered from memory when it is needed. These components are assumed to operate sequentially. Incoming signals are transformed into a "state" (or "trace"). A *trace* is a set of information; it is the residue of an event that remains in memory after the event has vanished. When encoded, the trace is said to be placed in storage. To remember that

stored information, the individual actively searches for the stored material (see Figure 7.7, page 223).

Information processing has been likened to a filing system (Vander Zanden & Pace, 1984). Suppose you are a secretary and have the task of filing a company's correspondence. You have a letter from a customer criticizing a major product of your firm. Under what category are you going to file the letter? If the contents of the letter involve a defect in a product, will you decide to create a new category—"product defects"—or will you file the letter under the customer's name? The procedure you used for categorizing the letter must be used consistently for categorizing all other correspondence you receive. You cannot file this letter under "product defects" and the next letter like it under the customer's name and hope to have an efficient system.

Encoding involves perceiving information, abstracting from it one or more characteristics needed for classification, and creating corresponding memory traces for it. As in the case of the filing system, the way in which you encode information has an enormous impact on your ability to retrieve it. If you "file" an item of experience haphazardly, you will have difficulty recalling it. But encoding is not simply a passive process whereby you mechanically register environmental events on some sort of trace. Rather, in information processing you tend to abstract general ideas from material. Hence, you are likely to have a good retention of the meaning, or *gist,* of prose material you read—but poor memory for the specific words.

Memory Failure Memory failure can occur at any phase in information processing. For instance, difficulty can occur in the *encoding phase.* Returning to the example of the office filing system, you might receive a letter from a customer and accidentally place the letter with trash and discard it. In this case the letter is never encoded because it is not placed in the filing cabinet. It is unavailable because it was never stored. This difficulty is more likely to be experienced by older than by younger people. Older individuals are not as effective as younger ones are in carrying out the elaborate encoding of information that is essential to long-term retention. That is, older adults find it increasingly difficult to process new information, particularly when the quantity or complexity of the stimuli increases. However, age-related adapted processes, including an increased focus on emotional goals and greater experience, lead to better decision making (Peters, Hess, Vastfjall, & Auman, 2007). Memory failure can also stem from *storage problems.* For instance, when filing, you might place the letter in the filing cabinet but put it in the wrong folder by mistake. The letter is available, but it is not accessible because it was improperly stored. For example, the elderly tend to show more deficits than younger adults in remembering source information, as a consequence of storing the desired recall items in the wrong context (Hoyer & Verhaeghen, 2006).

But other factors are also involved. **Decay theory** posits that forgetting is due to deterioration of the memory traces in the brain (Salthouse, 1991). The process is believed to resemble the gradual fading of a photograph over time or the progressive obliteration of the inscription of a tombstone. **Interference theory** says that retrieval of a cue becomes less effective as more and newer items come to be classed or categorized in terms of it (Kausler, Wiley, & Lieberwitz, 1992). For example, as you file more and more letters in the cabinet, more items compete for your attention, and your ability to find a letter is impaired by all the other folders and letters.

Faulty retrieval of knowledge is a third major cause of memory loss. As John C. Cavanaugh (1998) explains, older persons can suffer a breakdown in the mechanisms and strategies by which stored information is recalled. Attention is an important aspect of information processing (Cavanaugh, 1998). The ability to *focus* on what we need to do (selective attention), *perform more than one task at the same time* (divided attention), and *sustain attention* to accomplish long-term tasks all can result in *cue overload*—a state of being overwhelmed or engulfed by excessive stimuli—and failure to process retrieval information effectively. (For instance, you may file a letter under a customer's name but later lack the proper cue to activate the category under which you filed it.)

Overall, older adults have more difficulty with memory than younger adults do. This fact has practical implications. Older people are more likely to be plagued by doubts about whether or not they have carried out particular activities—"Did I mail that letter this morning?" "Did I close the window earlier this evening?" And they are more likely to have difficulty remembering where they placed an item or where buildings are geographically located (Schaie et al., 2010). On a safety level, they may forget they turned on the stove to cook something and then walk away. Or they might forget to take certain medications, which might cause fainting. Or they might forget where they put their $2,500 hearing aid or their false teeth!

Question

What are some of the theories associated with memory difficulties in old age?

Learning and Aging

Psychologists are finding that the distinctions they once made between learning and memory are becoming blurred. Learning parallels the encoding process whereby individuals put into memory material presented to them. Psychologist Endel Tulving (1968) says that learning

constitutes an improvement in retention. Hence, he contends, the study of learning is the study of memory. Clearly, all processes of memory have consequences for learning. If people do not learn (encode) well, they have little to recall; if their memory is poor, they show few signs of having learned much. Therefore, psychologists find that younger adults do better than older adults on various learning tasks (Schaie, 2005). This fact has given rise to the adage "You can't teach an old dog new tricks." But this adage is clearly false. Both older dogs and older humans can and do learn. They would be incapable of adapting to their environment and coping with new circumstances if they did not.

Research suggests that allowing people ample time gives them more opportunity to rehearse a response and establish a linkage between events, and it increases the probability that they will encode the information in a way that facilitates later search and recall. Older adults benefit even more than younger ones when more time is made available for them to learn something.

Older people often give the impression that they have learned less than younger people have, because they tend to be more reluctant to venture a response. And when tested in a laboratory setting, older adults seem less motivated to learn arbitrary materials that appear irrelevant and useless to them. Complicating matters, more of today's young adults are better educated than their older counterparts. Another hidden bias is that many elderly individuals take medications that can diminish mental functions. We should exercise caution when appraising the learning potential of the elderly, lest we prematurely conclude that they are incapable of learning new things (Fotuhi, 2004).

Decline in Cognitive Functioning

Until recently, most everyone, including physicians, accepted the view that senility is natural for people living longer than the Biblical *three score and ten years,* or age 70. **Senility** is typically characterized by progressive mental deterioration, memory loss, and disorientation regarding time and place. Irritability, confusion, inability to use complete sentences, and other marked personality changes usually accompany the intellectual decline. When those affected no longer remember a spouse or children, terror can set in, with screams, because loved ones become total strangers (Cohen et al., 1993):

> My wife refused to believe I was her husband. Every day we went through the same routine: I would tell her we had been married for thirty years, that we had four children. She listened, but she still thought she lived in her home-town with her parents. Every night when I got into bed she'd say, "Who are you?" (Husband of an Alzheimer's patient)

Yet findings from the longitudinal and cross-sectional *Berlin Aging Study* (with participants aged 70 to 104) dispute common thought. Singer and colleagues (2003) report that perceptual speed, fluency, and memory began to decline with age, but knowledge remained stable up to age 90, with decline thereafter. Rates of decline did not differ between men and women, but women in old age scored higher than men on memory and fluency. Life-history variables, such as higher income, social class, and education, were positively correlated with higher levels of functioning across all four cognitive tasks (Gerstorf, Smith, & Baltes, 2006). Also, adults in their seventies showed less marked decline in the four variables (intelligence, speed, memory, and fluency) than individuals in their eighties and nineties. But declines begin to accelerate among the "old-old" age group (nineties and older), a result consistent with life-span theory (Singer, Lindenberger, & Baltes, 2003).

Senility is one of the most serious conditions that a physician can diagnose in a patient. The prognosis is grim, and the benefit of current treatments is uncertain. Consequently, it is incumbent on professionals who treat the elderly to do a full battery of tests to make certain a treatable cause for a patient's symptoms has not been overlooked (Lajiness, 2009). Often, underlying physical diseases that can make an elderly person seem senile go unnoticed and untreated. Such individuals are simply put into the category of "senile" by families and physicians who have accepted the conventional wisdom that senility is inevitable in the aging process. Common problems mistakenly diagnosed as senility include tumors, vitamin deficiencies (especially B_{12}, or folic acid), anemia, depression, such metabolic disorders as hyperthyroidism and chronic liver or kidney failure, and toxic reactions to prescription or over-the-counter drugs (including tranquilizers, anticoagulants, and medications for heart problems and high blood pressure). Many of these conditions can be reversed if they are identified and treated early in the course of the illness.

Stroke When a blood vessel that carries nutrients and oxygen to the brain is blocked by a clot or when a blood vessel bursts, spilling blood into the brain, a person experiences a *stroke*, which may be life-threatening. If part of the brain cannot get blood and oxygen, then cells in the brain die. Since stroke is the third leading cause of death and the main cause of severe, long-term disability, it is important to recognize the sudden signs: (1) numbness or weakness of the face, arm, or leg, especially on one side of the body; (2) confusion, trouble speaking or understanding; (3) trouble seeing in one or both eyes; (4) trouble walking, dizziness, or loss of balance or coordination; and/or (5) sudden, severe headache with no known cause. Any of these signs is a medical emergency, and the person needs immediate

medical care (National Stroke Association, 2008). If the patient survives, there can be a long period of rehabilitation and recovery in an attempt to regain functioning. Many medical professionals assist in the rehabilitation and recovery process. In persons over 65, about 20 to 25 percent of all senility results from **multi-infarcts** (known as "little strokes"), which destroy a small area of brain cells and often are a precursor to a stroke. The National Stroke Association has a public campaign to educate and recognize symptoms called FAST: Face (Does one side of the face droop?); Arm (Can the person raise both arms?); Speech (Is the speech slurred?); and Time (If any symptom is noticed, called 9-1-1 *fast*) (National Stroke Association, 2008).

Alzheimer's Disease **Alzheimer's disease (AD)** is a progressive, degenerative disorder that involves deterioration of brain cells. Autopsies of victims show microscopic changes in brain structure, mainly in the cerebral cortex. Areas involved in cognition, memory, and emotion are riddled with masses of proteins called "plaques" and tangles of nerve cells. The clumps of degenerating nerve cells disrupt the passage of electrochemical signals across the brain and nervous system. The disease reduces production of the neurotransmitters *acetylcholine, norepinephrine, dopamine,* and *serotonin.* Neuronal loss leads to brain atrophy. Serious effects occur in three stages and include memory loss and other cognitive deficits, anxiety, agitation, disorientation, depression, sleep disturbances, irritability, aggression, delusions, hallucinations, and parkinsonian symptoms. In the severe stage, the person can no longer walk or perform self-care tasks, is incontinent, and is likely to be mute but displays psychotic symptoms (Alzheimer's Association, 2010).

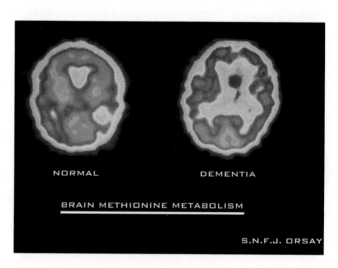

Normal Brain Scan and Brain Scan Typical of Alzheimer's Disease Note the larger areas of blue and green in the cerebral cortex (on the right) of the patient with Alzheimer's dementia, which reveals extensive loss of neuronal activity.

However, the promising field of stem cell research, as it applies to regenerative medicine, may be able to address some of the deficits brought on by Alzheimer's.

The disorder has a devastating impact on patients and families. Eventually those diagnosed need skilled nursing care at home and, in the late stage, in residential facilities (as did President Ronald Reagan). With millions more elderly projected to be affected in the next few decades, families need government insurance programs to pay for care during the prolonged period of deterioration, and there is a great need for more geriatric social workers and nurses and for programs to assist families in coping with the demands of patients (Rapp, Krampe, & Baltes, 2006). Predictably, the patients themselves and family members caring for them are at high risk for tension and profound stress (Hummert, 2007). Families find their loved one regressing, becoming more childlike, and eventually unable to communicate needs, perform simple tasks, or remember a spouse or children. One woman, Marion Roach (1983, p. 22), told of her experiences with her 54-year-old mother, who suffered from the disease:

In the autumn of 1979, my mother killed the cats. We had seven; one morning, she grabbed four, took them to the vet and had them put to sleep. She said she didn't want to feed them anymore. . . . Day by day, she became more disoriented. She would seem surprised at her surroundings, as if she had just appeared there. She stopped cooking and had difficulty remembering the simplest things. . . . Until she recently began to take sedation, she would hallucinate that the television or the toaster was in flames.

The disease typically proceeds through three phases, eventually affecting all areas of the brain (American Psychiatric Association, 2007). At first, in the "forgetfulness phase," individuals forget where things are placed and have difficulty recalling events of the recent past. Later, in the "confusional phase," difficulties in cognitive functioning worsen and can no longer be overlooked. Finally, in the "dementia phase," individuals become severely disoriented. They are likely to confuse a spouse or a close friend with another person. Behavior problems surface: Victims may wander off, roam the house at night or turn on a stove and forget, engage in bizarre actions, hallucinate, and exhibit "rage reactions" of verbal and even physical abuse. In time, they become infantile. The course of the disease varies, but median survival ranges from five to nine years. Patients usually die of infections (*septicemia*) or pneumonia (Alzheimer's Association, 2010).

Alzheimer's researchers resemble the blind men studying the elephant: Each grabs onto a different part of the disease and comes to a different conclusion about its causes. One popular hypothesis relates Alzheimer's

disease to increased levels of oxidative damage brought on by free-radical production (Liu et al., 2007). The current body of knowledge suggests that oxidative damage is a major factor in Alzheimer's disease. Therefore, therapeutic approaches using antioxidants may be effective in the treatment of neurodegenerative disease, such as Alzheimer's (Ancelin, Christen, & Ritchie, 2007; Liu et al., 2007). Also, scientists are looking at neural stem cells that carry the potential for brain repair, by targeting specific genes that have been associated with Alzheimer's disease (Ertekin-Taner, 2010).

Because Alzheimer's disease tends to run in families, researchers are seeking a genetic source. A family history of Parkinson's disease, which also causes dementia, was found more frequently in the families of patients with Alzheimer's disease (Polymeropoulos, Higgins, & Golbe, 1997). Duke University scientists found a connection between certain genes and the risk of contracting Alzheimer's. Additional evidence of genetic or chromosomal factors is found in studies of patients with Down syndrome, showing that many adults with this syndrome eventually succumb to Alzheimer's lesions (National Down Syndrome Society, 2011). Still other researchers have attributed the onset of Alzheimer's disease to the *metabolic syndrome*, which is characterized by the clustering of abdominal obesity, hypertension, and high levels of cholesterol that have reached epidemic proportions (Razay, Vreugdenhil, & Wilcock, 2007).

Alzheimer's disease now affects more than 5.4 million Americans (see Figure 17.6). An estimated one out of every eight people aged 65 and older has Alzheimer's disease. It is estimated that 10 million adults in the baby-boom cohort will be diagnosed with AD at an unprecedented cost to families and society (Alzheimer's Association, 2011a). This disease is more prevalent

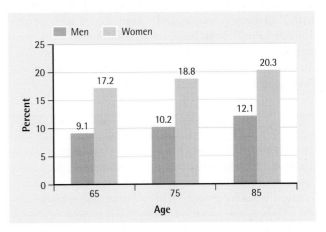

FIGURE 17.6 Estimated Percentages of U.S. Adults Aged 65, 75, and 85 with Alzheimer's Disease, by Gender: 2006
Source: Alzheimer's Association. (2010). Alzheimer's disease: Facts and figures. *Alzheimer's & Dementia, 6*(2), 158–194. Retrieved from http://www.alzheimersanddementia.com/article/PIIS1552526010000142/fulltext#bib111

in blacks and Hispanics than in whites. Earlier onset of Alzheimer's is rare. Alzheimer's is the fourth most common cause of death in the elderly—after cardiovascular disease, cancer, and stroke. As of this writing, there is no specific cure for AD, but pharmaceutical researchers are testing more than 100 compounds that might relieve or delay the symptoms of the disease. The drug *tacrine* (also known as THA or Cognex) alleviates some of the cognitive symptoms during the early and middle stages of the disease. Other medications can help control behavioral symptoms such as sleeplessness, agitation, wandering, anxiety, and depression. The Alzheimer's Association reports all new findings.

Doctors recommend lab tests, neurological exams, and neuroimaging for adults who may have Alzheimer's. They also suggest there might be protective factors in middle age: (1) taking vitamins A, C, and E; (2) exercising regularly; (3) eating a well-balanced diet including teas; fruits and vegetables such as apples, beans, cherries, garlic, tomatoes, broccoli, peppers, spinach, carrots, mangos, blueberries, blackberries, grapes, and others; (4) and, most important, participating in mental activities (such as doing crossword puzzles or playing bridge, poker, or Bingo) and remaining physically active (Jedrziewski, Ewbank, Wang, & Trajanowski, 2010).

Parkinson's Disease A progressive brain disease, *Parkinson's disease* occurs when specific neurons die or are damaged in a part of the brain that produces a neurochemical called *dopamine*. This neurochemical makes possible the smooth, coordinated function of the body's muscles and movement. When dopamine-producing cells are damaged, the symptoms of Parkinson's disease appear; these include shaking, stiffness and slowness of movement, and difficulties with balance (National Parkinson Foundation, 2008). Actor Michael J. Fox is living with Parkinson's disease, and it contributed to the death of Pope John Paul II. Researchers continue to work with stem-cell, gene, viral, deep-brain stimulation, and drug therapies to alleviate symptoms of this disease (National Parkinson Foundation, 2008).

Questions

What does it mean when a person is classified as "senile"? How does Alzheimer's disease affect the person's brain functioning? What are its effects on a person's quality of life? What is Parkinson's disease?

MORAL DEVELOPMENT

In discussing cognitive capacity in late adulthood, we cannot overlook the significant role of organized religion, a personal faith, and a sense of spirituality that shape

the moral foundation of our lives. Azar (2010) and others state that various religions exist in every culture and serve adaptive purposes. Using neuroimaging techniques, neuroscientists have shown that religious thoughts and prayer activate the same area of the brain that interprets emotions and intentions; thus, "we are whole people; the biological, psychological, social, cultural, and spiritual are all connected" (Azar, 2010). And we learn morals, values, and beliefs from a diversity of formal and informal religious influences. The purpose of organized religions—such as Christianity, Judaism, Islam, Buddhism, Hinduism, Confucianism, and Taoism—is to give spiritual meaning to life. (See the *More Information You Can Use* box, "Faith and Well-Being in Later Life.") These beliefs, traditions, and rituals bring people together, offer a source of strength and hope in difficult times, supply healthy behavioral guidelines for living one's life (i.e., foods, abstinence or fasting, moderation), and provide a sense of continuity throughout life.

One of the continuous tasks facing each of us is the need to make sense of our lives and, above all, to give our lives meaning. Each of the major theorists we have reviewed throughout this book is concerned with explaining how our behaviors make sense as we understand the meaning-making system within which they occur. Let us now examine a developmental theory whose locus is faith. It is well documented that the elderly, especially women, are much more likely to be involved in religion and religious activities than are younger adults, and there is a growing body of research that supports the benefits of religiosity, especially as one nears the end of life (Nelson-Becker & Canda, 2008; Pew Forum on Religion & Public Life, 2008).

James Fowler's Theory of Faith Development

James Fowler, an ordained minister and professor, has attempted to combine theology and developmental psychology to explain the different trajectories that faith takes in individuals. A system of faith continually changes in response to cognitive development, maturation, and both religious and life experiences. Although Fowler posits seven stages of faith development, we examine only *Stage 5: Conjunctive Faith and the Interindividual Self* (midlife and beyond), because this stage is most likely to be reached after midlife (see Table 17.6).

As we progress through the different stages of faith, we begin and then continue to ask the fundamental questions regarding existence: What is life all about? Who is the ultimate authority over my life? How do I give meaning to my life? What is the purpose of my life? Is my life really over when I die? The answers to these questions revolve around what Fowler calls our *Master Story*, which contains the crucial ideas we draw on to give meaning to our lives. The Master Story will become increasingly explicit as we mature; in many instances it can be

MORE INFORMATION YOU CAN USE

Faith and Well-Being in Later Life

Some research studies reveal positive effects of spirituality on health, such as the finding that regular attendance at a church, mosque, temple, or synagogue leads to living a longer life. Also, religiosity and faith help people deal with the more frequent personal loss, depression, and disability that occur with aging (Baker & Cruickshank, 2009; Glazer, 2005). A national survey shows that the vast majority of Americans (95 percent) profess a belief in God or a higher power. Nine out of ten people pray—and most pray every day. Religious/spiritual beliefs and practices have always been important in the lives of people across cultures. In the United States the main religions are Christian (Protestant, Catholic, Orthodox, and Mormon), but the diversity of religious groups within Christianity and other religions continues to grow (Nelson-Becker & Canda, 2008; Pew Forum on Religion & Public Life, 2008).

Dale Matthews and Connie Clark (1998) relate findings from hundreds of empirical studies on what they call the catalyst of the "faith factor" and its powerful benefits to overall well-being and attitude for people of all ages. They say that centuries ago, Western cultures separated medicine from religion, but today the medical community recognizes the powerful relationship among mind, body, and spirit. Most American medical schools offer courses on spirituality and healing, and some doctors screen patients about their spiritual beliefs or pray with their patients. More hospitals are offering alternative healing centers for meditation and prayer (Glazer, 2005). Medical practitioners from emergency rooms, oncology, cardiology, and geriatrics, as well as members of the clergy, often help patients cope with spiritual crises. In medical and institutional settings, older adults who are able to follow their religious beliefs and practices experience less depression, anxiety, and distress (Fowler, 2009). People of faith have hopeful and positive expectations that protect them against depressive symptoms (Baker & Cruickshank, 2009). Further, healthy lifestyles (including abstinence from cigarettes, alcohol, tobacco, and meat) followed by practitioners of some religious groups (such as Seventh Day Adventists and the order of nuns in the *Nun Study*) are related to lower incidence of disease and greater longevity (Fraser, 2003).

Morris and McAdie (2009) reviewed the connection between religion or spirituality and health. They examined several hypotheses: church/service attendance protects against death; religion or spirituality protects against cardiovascular disease; religion or spirituality protects against

The Meaning of Religion and Prayer For adults in old age undergoing changes and loss, calling upon their faith and observing religious customs give them strength to live their lives with an attitude of hopefulness and thanksgiving.

cancer mortality; deeply religious people are protected against death; religion or spirituality protects against disability; religion or spirituality slows the progression of cancer; people who use religion to cope with difficulties live longer; religion or spirituality improves recovery from acute illness; and being prayed for improves physical recovery from acute illness. Among their conclusions is that attending services bestows a generalized protection against mortality. Furthermore, a belief in an afterlife "reward expectation" helps act as a coping strategy for people of faith (Morris & McAdie, 2009). They call for further studies on the factors that produce this "protection."

In sum, practicing a faith can positively influence physical and mental health, well-being, and happiness (Oser, Scarlett, & Bucher, 2006). The most controversial of the hypotheses—the effect of being prayed for (called *intercessory prayer*), has not held up to close scientific scrutiny—even though people say anecdotally that it does (Krause, 2007). Although some conclude that there is a relationship between religion or spirituality and health, others see it simply as operation of the *placebo effect* and insist that spirituality cannot be proved scientifically. Nevertheless, a large body of research shows that religious participation is positively associated with good mental-health status and lasting treatment effects (Azar, 2010; Chen, Cheal, Herr, Zubritsky, & Levkoff, 2007).

TABLE 17.6 Fowler's Seven Stages of Faith Development

Stage 0	Primal Faith (birth to age 2)	Really more like a basic trust in caretakers.
Stage 1	Intuitive-Projective Faith (2–8 years)	Beginning to understand cause-and-effect relationships, which are given meaning through the stories and images one gets from caretakers.
Stage 2	Mythic-Literal Faith (childhood and beyond)	Separation of fantasy and real world, but meaning is carried and restricted by the narrative it occurs in.
Stage 3	Synthetic-Conventional Faith (adolescence and beyond)	Belief that everyone has basically the same received beliefs; e.g., that all Catholics understand their religion in the same way. Not yet a personal belief.
Stage 4	Individuative-Reflective Faith (young adulthood and beyond)	A personal faith that can be reflected upon.
Stage 5	Conjunctive Faith and the Interindividual Self (midlife and beyond)	Seeks truth of faith in a dialectical, multidimensional manner. (Few people get to this stage.)
Stage 6	Universalizing Faith	Committed to selfless, universal goals. Gandhi and Mother Teresa are examples.

"Seven Stages of Faith Development" from STAGES OF FAITH: THE PSYCHOLOGY OF HUMAN DEVELOPMENT AND THE QUEST FOR MEANING by James W. Fowler. Copyright 1981 by James W. Fowler. Reprinted by permission of HarperCollins Publishers, Inc.

summed up in a few words, such as "It's all about me," or it might be in the form of a communal ritual such as the Passover *Haggadah* for the devout Jewish community.

Fowler's seven stages are usually called "soft stages" because they do not involve the strict adherence to logical structures associated with a "hard-stage" theory like Piaget's. Furthermore, transitions between stages are usually experienced during developmental milestones such as adolescence, young adulthood, midlife, and old age.

For individuals in mid- and late adulthood (who typically are at Fowler's Stage 5), life's paradoxes are numerous and not easily brushed aside. The capacity for appreciating opposites, polarities, and diverse perspectives because one has experienced these aspects of life firsthand contributes to a higher level of meaning-making for some of those in their "winter" years (or what some researchers call the Fourth Age). Older adults understand that all narratives point to the existence of a "grand narrative," which in turn suggests that every religious perspective is a "vehicle for grasping truth" (Fowler, 1981). In other words, the individual in Stage 5 realizes that religions are much more similar than they are different—they all have the same seed of truth at the core. The moral aspect of faith becomes apparent if we assume, as Fowler does, that we invest faith in an aggregate of ideas, values, attitudes, and behaviors that are significant to us.

Those at the higher stages of faith development are likely to invest in goals focused more on others and less on self, much as Gandhi, Martin Luther King, Jr., and Mother Teresa did. Fowler worked with Kohlberg for a time, and at one point Kohlberg entertained a seventh stage for his model that reflected an element of faith. Additionally, at 93 years of age in 1997, Joan Erikson published the last of Erik Erikson's works. Before Erik died (in his early nineties), they had collaborated on an update of *The Life Cycle Completed* in which they incorporated a ninth psychosocial stage called "Very Old Age." Their ninth stage outlines the critical role that hope and faith play in the lives of those in their eighties, nineties, and beyond.

Many elderly find strength, comfort, and meaning in following religious practices. Those who live into old age often make religion and spirituality an essential part of their lives, attend religious services, and engage in private prayer; and they tend to have better health and to be more optimistic than others (Krause, 2005). The emotional-social support they find in their religious community is responsible for their closer relationship to God or a higher being, which in turn leads to greater optimism. From many years of studying the elderly, Vaillant (2002) suggests that successful aging means "giving to others joyously whenever one is able; receiving from others gratefully, whenever one needs it; and being capable of personal development in between." These findings on successful aging are elements of the doctrine of many religions. Because values are an important component of meaning and they provide a sense of direction, purpose, and legitimacy in daily life, it is not hard to see how they can enhance feelings of psychological well-being and stability among older people who are most likely to experience many changes.

Questions

Why do most elderly adults become more interested in religious and spiritual observances? How would you explain Fowler's fifth stage of faith development?

SEGUE

In many societies around the world, the "oldest old" are a growing population of adults who are living longer with a higher quality of life than past generations had. Philosophical concerns are being raised about extending life and about the allocation of resources to the elderly. Our understanding of biological aging continues to grow, and we now know that longevity is generally associated with healthy genes, a lifestyle of regular exercise, sensible health habits, regular medical checkups, and a network of social support. Recent research on longevity and aging has given rise to the medical field of antiaging and to the development of gene therapies to combat or prevent the chronic diseases of aging.

Concerning intellectual functioning, those elderly who remain engaged in mental activities are less likely to experience declines in cognitive functioning, although certain types of memory decline before other types. Even though it can take longer for older people to remember recent events, they often retain a wealth of information about the past. Furthermore, older adults are typically concerned about staying healthy, remaining independent, and not being left alone in their last years. Eventually, most cope with continual loss—loss of friends and loved ones, loss of health, loss of one's lifelong home, and loss of independence—which can lead to depression and mental illness. For coping with these losses, many find a sense of peace by having or developing a faith in some type of spiritual life after this physical one. And as we shall see in Chapter 18, a network of social relationships, woven through family support, social contacts, and adult day care, can do a great deal to mediate these losses—and thus to improve the elderly person's quality of life.

SUMMARY

Aging: Myth and Reality

1. At no point in life do people stop being themselves and suddenly turn into "old people." Aging does not destroy the continuity between what we have been, what we are, and what we will be.

2. There are a great many myths about aging that have little to do with the actual process of growing old. They inaccurately portray a large proportion of the elderly as abandoned, institutionalized, incapacitated, in serious financial straits, and living in fear of crime.

3. On the average, women live several years longer than men, probably because of an inherent sex-linked resistance to some types of life-threatening disease. Lifestyle differences also contribute to gender differences in longevity.

Health

4. Regular exercise is associated with longevity. Most conditions that create chronic disease increase with advanced age, such as heart conditions, cancer, arthritis, diabetes, osteoporosis, and so on. Some of the health problems experienced by older Americans are the product of side effects associated with medication. Most older adults consider themselves healthy.

5. Some of the most obvious changes associated with aging are related to an individual's physical characteristics. There is a decline in the individual's capacity for physical work and exercise. Sleep patterns also change.

6. The incidence of self-reported acute illnesses (upper respiratory infections, varicose veins, injuries, digestive disorders, and the like) is lower among the elderly than among other segments of the population.

7. The elderly experience physiological changes such as muscle loss, decreases in both size and strength of muscles, a decline in oxygen intake, and reduced heart efficiency.

8. Sensory abilities, such as hearing, vision, taste, smell, and skin sensitivity to temperature decline with age.

9. More than 50 percent of persons aged 65 and older report problems with the timing and duration of sleep. The likelihood of sleep apnea, a disorder in which the person occasionally stops breathing during sleep, increases with age.

10. Some factors that can lead to decreased sexual activity in older adults are difficulty with sexual arousal, a decline in overall health, and the unavailability of a partner.

11. Many theories seek to explain the biological process of aging by focusing on cell-destroying mechanisms. Although the effects of aging are often confounded with the effects of disease, aging is not the same thing as disease.

Cognitive Functioning

12. Some decline in adult intelligence occurs after age 60, mainly with slowing of response time and declines in short-term memory. However, there is much individual variation in aging effects. Aspects of intelligence are measured by tests of fluid and crystallized thinking abilities.

13. Psychologists have traditionally taken too negative a view of the impact of aging, because researchers have relied too heavily on cross-sectional studies instead of longitudinal studies of individuals over time.

14. Memory loss among the elderly is highly individual, from little to extensive, and there are many causes related to the acquisition, retention, and retrieval of knowledge.
15. Senility is typically characterized by progressive mental deterioration, memory loss, and disorientation regarding time and place.
16. Several serious brain disorders are associated with aging but have different causes. They include stroke, Alzheimer's disease, and Parkinson's. Such disorders have life-changing outcomes.

Moral Development

17. Morals, values, beliefs, and standards of behavior and lifestyle are often transmitted to members of society through formal religious organizations. Those involved with religion are comforted throughout the trials of life and aging by their faith and their religious community.
18. Fowler has attempted to combine theology and developmental psychology to explain the different trajectories that an individual's faith takes throughout the life course with a stage model of faith development.

KEY TERMS

ageism *(540)*

Alzheimer's disease (AD) *(564)*

collagen *(553)*

death drop *(561)*

decay theory *(563)*

encoding *(562)*

gerontology *(540)*

geropsychology *(540)*

hypothermia *(556)*

interference theory *(563)*

multi-infarcts *(564)*

osteoporosis *(550)*

retrieval *(562)*

senescence *(545)*

senility *(563)*

sleep apnea *(556)*

storage *(562)*

FOLLOWING UP ON THE INTERNET

Web sites for this chapter focus on the changing health needs, declining cognitive functioning, and growing spiritual needs of those in late adulthood. Please access the text Web site at www.mhhe.com/crandell10 for up-to-date hot-linked Internet addresses for the following organizations, topics, and resources:

Administration on Aging Statistics on the Aging Population
http://www.aoa.gov/AoARoot/Aging_Statistics/index.aspx

National Institute of Aging's Age Page
http://www.nia.nih.gov/HealthInformation/Publications

National Archive of Computerized Data on Aging
http://www.icpsr.umich.edu/NACDA

Social Security Administration Statistical Information
http://www.ssa.gov/policy

American Geriatrics Society
http://www.americangeriatrics.org/

Journal of Cross-Cultural Gerontology
http://www.springer.com/social+sciences/
    population+studies/journal/10823

Gerontological Society of America
http://www.geron.org/

Adventist Health Studies
http://www.llu.edu/public-health/health/index.page

The New England Centenarian Study
http://www.bumc.bu.edu/centenarian/

Alzheimer's Association
http://www.alz.org/index.asp

APA Division 36 Psychology of Religion
http://www.division36.org/

Late Adulthood
Emotional and Social Development

Critical Thinking Questions

1. Do you think that a 75-year-old and a 25-year-old could fall in love with each other and have a high-quality life together? Why or why not?

2. If U.S. society painted an exciting or respectful picture of old age, do you think most elderly individuals would view their own lives differently? How does the media's portrayal of old age affect people's self-perceptions?

3. Nursing homes exist largely because most adults work and cannot take care of those in need on a full-time basis. If the time came when your elderly parent(s) needed help, do you think you would bring them into your home and support those who sacrificed for you? Why or why not?

4. If, starting tomorrow, you could no longer work or attend school, had no family or close friends, and did not know how many more years you had to live—what would you do or think about? How do you think you might feel about living "in limbo," away from the mainstream of life?

5. Wisdom is defined sometimes as (1) knowing the truth and acting justly and sometimes as (2) questioning assumed truths as well as one's own actions. Which of these two approaches seems wiser to you?

As we move more than a decade into the new century, the rapid paradigm shift from the Industrial Age to the Digital Age continues to significantly affect individuals, societies, and nations. In 2008 over 39 million Americans aged 65 and older made up more than 13 percent of the U.S. population; projections indicate a doubling of their numbers, to about 72 million, by 2030 (Federal Interagency Forum on Aging-Related Statistics, 2010). Six of the eight Hurlburt siblings (on page 571) are reflective of the oldest healthy seniors who are under study in the Long Life Family Study—but seniors worldwide are living much longer, too. The high number of elderly foretells a need for major changes in government programs that support them and more options for affordable elder-care housing and living arrangements, as well as an increase in products, services, and trained professionals to enable this population to grow older with dignity and vitality (Radwan & Morgan, 2010). Advances in medicine, technology, education, and social services have ushered in the fields of *telehealth* and *telemedicine*—networks of professionals who will provide preventive health education and a range of health services to an aging population. These innovations are allowing more people to reach old age with fewer ailments and to live independently longer with a higher-quality life.

Significantly, as the number of American minority elderly is increasing rapidly, many of these elderly hold positions of respect within their ethnic communities and are taken care of by family members. Only about 5 percent of elderly Americans enter institutional care facilities to live out their later years if they develop a serious physical illness or serious dementia. Today, home health-care and alternative living arrangements are available for elderly persons who need special assistance to maintain independent living and for persons caring for an elderly relative in their home. According to the social model of living, the elderly will have a higher quality of life, and greater satisfaction with life, if they can maintain independence, control, and social engagement.

SOCIAL RESPONSES TO AGING

Given our culture's preoccupation with youthfulness, many Americans disregard late adulthood entirely or have distorted notions about it (such as that the elderly are suffering or are frail and living in pain or have dementia). Recall that worldwide, the fastest-growing segment of the population is the oldest adult population over 80, and the populations of *centenarians* (those reaching 100) and *supercentarians* (those reaching 110) are also growing. It is estimated that by the year 2030, nearly 20 percent of the U.S. population will be over age 65. And while the population of those aged 65 and older is expected to double by 2030, the population of those aged 85 and older could reach about 19 million by 2050 (Federal Interagency Forum on Aging-Related Statistics, 2010). Also, female and Hispanic attitudes about age and aging will become a larger determining factor in American perceptions (Achenbaum, 2007; Ruppel, Jenkins, Griffin, & Kizer, 2010).

False Stereotypes

You have heard people speak of "the graying of America," or "the golden years," or "the silent revolution." But specifically to whom do these phrases refer? Gerontologists tend to divide late adulthood into the periods of "young old" (65 to 75 or 80) and "old old" (80 and above) (Gerstorf, Smith, & Baltes, 2006). W. Andrew Achenbaum (1998), gerontologist and chair of the National Council on Aging, reminds us why we historically have held more negative views of late adulthood:

1. Old age has always been considered to be the last stage of existence before death, and no one wants to be reminded about mortality.
2. Old age is undefined: There are few rites of passage comparable to those celebrated in youth. Not all elderly are married to celebrate golden anniversaries, nor are all grandparents, nor do all elderly retire.
3. There is a growing, diverse composition of elders with varied physical, cognitive, behavioral, and socioeconomic characteristics. Discussion about a "typical" older adult is difficult, yet many are dependent on government entitlements and family support.

These stereotypical views weigh heavily on older adults' self-esteem: Some—but certainly not a majority—of our elderly have illnesses or impairments associated with physiological aging and are likely to be overmedicated (medications for various chronic conditions can cause polypharmacy effects and adverse reactions). A common stereotype is that most adults in old age are unhappy, but a growing body of research disputes this myth. Indeed, some do suffer from depression and loneliness, and suicide rates are highest among American elderly males. Yet emerging empirical research on our elderly population reveals that growing into late adulthood is not necessarily an unhealthy burden. The "oldest old" are more likely to live an active, disease-free life with a short decline at the end of life (Perls, 2010).

Baltes (2006) suggests that industrialized societies have achieved remarkable efficacy and flexibility in extending longevity for many people and in providing the economic and social resources for them to lead a more satisfying life in old age. Many who are living longer are also staying physically active, mentally engaged, and socially and economically involved longer. Even now, the sight of vigorous people in their eighth and ninth decades is not unusual. Given present trends in mortality, a larger segment of the population is expected to live well into their eighties and beyond, with a high rate of mortality in their mid-eighties. Recent reviews of research results from the *Berlin Aging Study* (BASE) report that the "oldest old" are at the limits of functional capacity and that at present, science and social policy cannot meet their increasing needs (Gerstorf, Smith, & Baltes, 2006). A few research efforts have focused on the cognitive functioning of the "youngest old," those aged 60 to 75. There is a growing body of research worldwide with those 80 and older, particularly in the areas of health and genetics, cognitive functioning, emotional well-being, and social functioning (Chen, Murayama, & Kamibeppu, 2010; Dorgo, Robinson, & Bader, 2009; Perls, 2006).

It has become clear that social-emotional and behavioral factors influence the quality of aging, as do the physical, health, cognitive, religious, and economic factors discussed in Chapter 17. Because we know that physical and intellectual declines eventually become common in old age, can we predict a constricted range of emotions in elderly adults? If so, what emotional states can we expect most elderly to experience? If not, what life circumstances help some elderly maintain a rich range of emotions, especially the positive ones that promote constructive coping?

Questions

Why has little empirical research been done with the elderly until recently? Why are behavioral scientists now studying more issues related to late adulthood and what are those issues?

Positive and Negative Attitudes

As part of the *Kungsholmen Project,* researchers in Stockholm, Sweden, reported finding both positive and negative affect (emotional components of subjective well-being) in 105 people, 90 to 99 years of age, who were not cognitively impaired (Hilleras, Herlitz, Jorm, & Winblad, 1998). *Positive affect* was defined as the extent to which a person feels active, alert, and enthusiastic. *Negative affect* was defined as the extent to which a person feels guilt, anger, and fear. One recent study found that certain personality traits, health status, and personal relationships were the strongest predictors of positive and negative affect in very old age (Fry & Keyes, 2010). For example, it is well known that depression, anxiety, hostility, and anger are associated with illness and disease (Ruppel et al., 2010).

Yet only recently, psychologists have formed a new branch of the study of human behavior, called *positive psychology,* that focuses on human strengths and resilience. Greater happiness and emotional well-being derive from such positive attitudes as "courage, future mindedness, optimism, interpersonal skill, faith, a work ethic, hope, honesty, perseverance, and the capacity for flow and insight" in daily life (Seligman & Csikszentmihalyi, 2000, p. 7). Some American elderly who exhibit such traits continue to experience much satisfaction in their later years. For example, "people high in optimism tend to have better moods, to be more persevering and successful, and to experience better physical health" (in Seligman & Csikszentmihalyi, 2000, p. 9).

In the research literature, an individual's overall cognitive assessment of his or her well-being is one component of life satisfaction (it is called subjective well-being, or SWB), whereas the affective component (emotions or feelings) consists of a person's pleasant and unpleasant experiences (Schimmack, 2007). Lachman (2006) reveals that future-oriented planning enhances life satisfaction and the perception of control. These effects were most helpful for older adults, which suggests that future-oriented planning is an important life management strategy. Transition planning to retirement has become a new career focus in *geropsychology* and *gerontology.* Positive affect is related to favorable life events, positive health status and functional ability, and the availability of social contacts (Fry & Keyes, 2010). However, correlates of positive and negative affect in the very elderly have only recently become the focus of research.

Using the *Positive and Negative Affect Schedule* (PANAS), Hilleras and colleagues (1998) surveyed their elderly subjects to examine whether similar patterns of positive and negative affect were correlated with personality traits. Factors associated with affect in this study were grouped into categories of personality, social relationship, subjective health, activities, life events, religiousness, and sociodemographic variables. Some of the results follow.

Factors Associated with Positive Affect

- social relationships, such as contact with friends, attending religious services, and participating in clubs/society/organizations
- reading and following news
- an extraverted personality
- definite beliefs and definite disbeliefs
- living with other persons

Volunteerism in Late Adulthood Staying socially active through volunteerism is associated with health benefits and emotional satisfaction.

Factors Associated with Negative Affect

- neuroticism
- having a major illness
- money problems
- living alone or feeling lonely

The Stockholm study also demonstrated that positive affect and negative affect were not correlated with each other. That is, the very elderly who scored high on positive affect (active, alert, and enthusiastic) did not necessarily score low on negative affect (guilt, anger, and fear). This means these elderly subjects responded with a full range of emotions on this scale, not unlike younger adults. One observation, though, was that subjects took a long time to answer each question during the interview process. Findings from this study also underscore that the emotional health of the "oldest old" is quite diverse and that further research is needed on the affective well-being of this population of adults.

SELF-CONCEPT AND PERSONALITY DEVELOPMENT

Recall from Chapter 17 that genetics, biochemistry, and lifestyle factors are variables that play a large role in physical health and longevity. In this chapter, we continue to examine research findings from social and emotional perspectives: Is there such a thing as an ideal personality type that promotes a high quality of life and longevity? Is there continuity in personality across the life span, or are there dramatic changes along the way? Once a person is retired or has less of a family role, what factors promote a positive identity and psychological well-being?

Psychosocial Theories

Alas, many of the theories proposed on social-emotional development in the earlier years of life did not extend very far into adulthood, especially not into late adulthood. At the height of Freud's career, the average human life span was half of what it is today. However, because societies around the world are experiencing a similar demographic shift to a much older population, many gerontologists, geropsychologists, and sociologists are studying the concepts of "antiaging," "successful aging," "satisfaction with aging," "productive aging," and "optimal aging." Several psychosocial theories of late adulthood have been proposed.

Erikson: Integrity Versus Despair   A recurrent theme in Erikson's work is that psychosocial development occurs in stages across the life span. According to him, the elderly confront the issue of **integrity versus despair.** In this eighth stage, Erikson says, individuals recognize that they are reaching the end of life. If they have successfully navigated the previous stages of development, they are capable of facing their later years with optimism and enthusiasm. With retrospection, they can take satisfaction in having led an active, full, and complete life. This recognition produces contentment, compensates for decreased physical potency and performance, and unifies their personality, producing a sense of integrity.

For a person in late adulthood, conducting a life review is another way to promote a sense of integrity. A **life review** is reminiscence and sharing of family history from one generation to another (see the *More Information You Can Use* box on page 576, "Reminiscence: Conducting a Life Review"). This is difficult today, because more families are geographically separated from one another or have such busy schedules that they see each other infrequently. The older person gains feelings of self-worth, continuity in personality, and happiness about preserving family history (Cappeliez & O'Rourke, 2006). During this connection among the generations, individuals discover interesting life experiences and memories about each other, too. Life reviews affirm the importance of life experiences and achievements and give new meaning to life. Further, reminiscing serves a healing purpose by resolving, reorganizing, and reintegrating past events and feelings (Binder, Mastel-Smith, Hersch, & Symes, 2009). As Erikson has indicated, adults in this stage of life strive to integrate past psychological themes into a new level of meaning, and they have an individual and wiser perspective on the world, and on life itself, that is different from the perspective they had when they were younger (Baumeister & Vohs, 2002).

Erikson himself exemplified a life of ego integrity at age 87 when he wrote and published *Vital Involvements in Old Age,* reporting the results of his personal interviews with American men and women in their eighties and nineties. His last works examined why some elderly live hopeful, productive lives despite failing health and alertness, and why others, though relatively robust, succumb to loneliness, narcissism, and despair (Blackburn & Dulmus, 2007). At 92 he was formulating and personally experiencing a last stage of personality development in which each individual confronts his life in relation to existence itself (Woodward, 1994). Joan Erikson (in her nineties) published an update of Erikson's *The Life Cycle Completed,* incorporating his ninth stage of psychosocial development. She writes of the challenges that confront elderly adults facing lost autonomy and more limited life choices. At the end of his life, Erikson viewed *hope* and *faith* as playing critical roles in developing *wisdom* in this life stage.

Those who appraise their lives as having been wasted, believing that they missed opportunities they should have taken years ago (following a different career path, marrying a different person, retiring later or sooner, having children) experience a sense of despair. They realize that time is running out and that it is too late to make up for past mistakes. They view their lives with a feeling of disappointment, loss, and purposelessness. Consequently, Erikson says, they approach death with regrets and fear.

> **Question**
>
> According to Erikson, what psychosocial tasks confront those in late adulthood, and what does he consider the successful resolution of this life stage?

Peck's Psychosocial Tasks of Later Adulthood
Psychologist Robert C. Peck (1968) offers a view of personality development during the later years that is related to Erikson's but more focused. Peck says that old age confronts men and women with three challenges, or tasks, which we will examine here.

Ego Differentiation Versus Work-Role Preoccupation   The central issue here is presented by retirement from the workforce. Men and women must redefine their worth in terms of something other than their work roles. They confront this question: "Am I a worthwhile person only insofar as I can do a full-time job; or can I be worthwhile in other, different ways—as a performer of several other roles and also because of the kind of person I am?" (Peck, 1968, p. 90). The ability to see themselves as having multiple dimensions allows individuals to pursue new avenues for finding a sense of satisfaction and being worthwhile.

Body Transcendence Versus Body Preoccupation   As people age, they might develop a chronic illness, daily aches

MORE INFORMATION YOU CAN USE

Reminiscence: Conducting a Life Review

For a person in late adulthood, conducting a life review is a significant experience. A *life review* consists of reminiscence and the sharing of family history from one generation to another. This is especially difficult today, because more families are geographically separated or have such busy schedules that they rarely see each other. The older person gains feelings of self-worth, continuity, and happiness about preserving family history. During this connection among the generations, individuals discover interesting life experiences and memories about each other, too. "The therapeutic life review involves not only a recollection of stories to revive interest, self-esteem, and personal relationships, but an evaluative method for the reconciliation of past events and feelings" (Binder et al., 2009). As Erikson has indicated, adults in this stage of life strive to integrate past psychological themes into a new level of meaning, and they have an individual and wiser perspective on the world—and on life itself—that is different from the perspective they had when they were younger. A life review enables the older adult to take a look at her or his lifetime as a whole and promotes a sense of integrity.

Sometimes natural reminiscence occurs at family reunions or funerals. However, as people age and significant people in their lives move, become disabled, or die, they have fewer contacts that promote natural reminiscence. Reminiscence can be incorporated into private or group settings and sometimes into therapeutic settings. Kunz and Soltys (2007) suggest that practitioners who conduct intake interviews at nursing homes, group homes, or adult day-care facilities should be attentive to their elderly interviewees and should expect the interview to take some time, because an elderly person can have more history to tell, and relating that history can be therapeutic. When reminiscence is done in a group, such as an adult day-care setting, those of the same age often benefit from each other, as long as no one or two people dominate the reminiscence.

Taking the time to listen to others lets them know they are important. Here are some suggestions that might spark reminiscence with someone you love or know.

Items That Prompt Sharing

- Photographs (from childhood, or from family reunions, birthdays, and anniversaries)
- Family scrapbooks, journals, books, family genealogy, and favorite music
- Newspaper clippings and old magazines
- Mementos from life accomplishments (trophies, badges, ribbons, plaques, etc.)
- Special personal belongings (keepsakes, jewelry, etc.)

Reminiscence: Sharing a Life A life review is a normative process engaged in by anyone, regardless of age, who is aware that time is growing short. The person looks back at his or her entire life, tries to resolve issues that were unresolved, tries to accept negative experiences, celebrates the good experiences, and gains a sense of accomplishment in life and closure.

Some Good Communication Skills

- Be an active listener.
- Maintain eye contact.
- Ask questions that encourage the person to explain or expand on things that seem important.
- Watch nonverbal cues (such as posture, eye contact, and expressions) for comfort or discomfort.
- Accept what is said, and allow the person to continue talking without jumping in with your own life experiences.
- Realize there may be times of silence or tears (this is normal; give the person time to gather his or her thoughts and continue).

There are many ways to preserve a life review, including preparing a scrapbook; compiling an audiocassette or videotape/DVD; or writing a newspaper article, a letter, or a book for family members or as a contribution to a local museum, historical society, or library. These are forms of remembrance of this special person. The American Association of Retired Persons has an interactive bulletin board on the Internet called "Through the Years," where people can tell the world about their memories of the twentieth century and be a part of history.

Source: Adapted from Kunz, J. A., & Soltys, F. G. (2007). *Transformational reminiscence: Life story work.* New York: Springer.

and pains, or a substantial decline in their physical capabilities. Those who equate pleasure and comfort with physical well-being can feel that this decrease in health and strength is the gravest of insults. Further, some may have to rely more heavily on their family or on other social support groups that may or may not be willing to help. Consequently, they either become preoccupied with their bodily health or find new sources of happiness and comfort in life. Many elderly persons suffer considerable pain and physical unease and yet manage to enjoy life greatly. They do not succumb to their physical aches, pains, and disabilities but, rather, find fulfillment in human relationships and creative mental activities. This process of transcendence may prove more difficult for males, who have identified with being strong and placed more reliance on their physical well-being. It is well documented that older males have the highest rates of suicide of all groups in the life span (Xu et al., 2010).

> From age 55 on, you have to focus on what is on the inside, not just what is on the outside. People need to do an internal audit to see what they can improve and what they can throw away. (C. Kermit Phelps, 91, of Kansas City, Missouri, in Volz [2000])

Ego Transcendence Versus Ego Preoccupation   Younger individuals typically define death as a distant possibility, but this privilege is not accorded the elderly. They must come to terms with their own mortality, and their adaptation need not be one of passive resignation. Rather, the elderly can come to see themselves as living on after death through their children, their work, their contributions to culture or community, and their friendships. Thus, they perceive themselves as transcending a mere earthly presence. Note the high number of college scholarships and community foundations established to give an elderly person or couple the opportunity to have their good fortune "transcend" time and space, in perpetuity, for the benefit of others. An ironic example is Alfred Nobel. This Swedish chemist and engineer, who had earlier invented dynamite and other munitions, included contributions to world peace among the five categories in which he arranged for the Nobel Prize to be conferred. (Nobel established the Nobel Prize in his will in 1895.)

Common to the approaches that Erikson, Peck, and many other psychologists take to psychosocial development is the notion that life is never static and seldom allows a prolonged respite (Bengtson et al., 2009). Both the individual and the environment constantly change, necessitating new adaptations and new life structures.

Question

What are Robert Peck's views about personality development during late adulthood?

Vaillant's Theory of Emotional Health   As noted earlier regarding findings from the Stockholm study, and from Perl's *New England Centenarian Study,* an individual's personality makes a difference in promoting or detracting from emotional health and happiness. These recent results support findings from ongoing longitudinal research. At five-year intervals, researchers have followed several hundred men who graduated from Harvard University from 1939 to 1945 (Goleman, 1990). Psychiatrist George Vaillant and colleagues conducted an extensive follow-up study of the 173 of these men at age 65 who participated in the *Grant Study of Adult Development* (Vaillant & Milofsky, 1980). Over time, Vaillant added two other pools of diverse adult cohorts to the study of aging: the *Inner City Cohort Study* of poor adults in Boston and the *Terman Women Sample* (from Terman's study of gifted children, begun at Stanford University in 1921). This continuing and expanded project provides insights into which personality factors matter, for better or worse, in later life.

At age 65 the subjects who developed a *sense of resilience* to absorb the shocks and changes of life were best able to enjoy life (although recovering from a job loss or death of a spouse certainly takes much longer than recovering from some other life stressors). An ability to handle life's blows without passivity, blame, or bitterness proved especially important. These subjects developed mature adaptive mechanisms instead of lashing out in anger or blame—a response that promoted their own emotional satisfaction and well-being.

Men who in college were rated as being good practical organizers of coursework were among those who made the best emotional adjustment in their later years. So were those who in college had been described as "steady, stable, dependable, thorough, sincere, and trustworthy." These two traits—*pragmatism* and *dependability*—seemed to matter more than traits such as spontaneity and the ability to make friends easily. Even a difficult childhood (being poor, orphaned, or a child of divorce) had little effect on well-being at age 65. Being close to one's siblings while in college was strongly linked to later emotional health. Most recently, Vaillant (2002) summed up several protective factors related to healthy aging that are under our personal control:

- a good marriage before age 50
- ingenuity to cope with difficult situations
- altruistic behaviors (forgiveness, gratitude, helping others)
- not smoking—or having stopped
- not using alcohol to the point where one's behavior is shameful to oneself or one's family
- staying physically active—walking, running, swimming, mowing the grass, playing tennis or golf
- keeping one's weight down

- pursuing education as far as native intelligence permits
- after retirement, staying engaged with life, doing new things, learning how to play again

The Harvard study continues to reveal how extraordinarily resilient some adults are. After six decades of study, most surviving participants retained the capacity to recover from adversity and get on with their lives.

A Trait Theory of Aging

Most of us go about our daily lives "typing" or "pigeonholing" people on the basis of a number of traits that seem particularly prominent in their behavior. They reveal these traits in the course of interacting with others and with their environment. On the basis of this observation, a number of psychologists, including Bernice L. Neugarten, R. J. Havighurst, and S. Tobin (1968), were pioneers in attempting to identify major personality patterns, or traits, that have relevance for the aging process. They studied several hundred persons aged 50 to 80 in the Kansas City area over a six-year period. From their ground-breaking research, they identified four major patterns of aging (considering personality, social engagement, and life satisfaction):

- integrated
- armored-defended
- passive-dependent
- unintegrated

The *integrated* elderly are functioning well and reveal a complex inner life, intact cognitive abilities, and competent egos. They are flexible, mellow, and mature. However, they differ from one another in their activity levels, and the researchers identified three subgroups of integrated elderly. Findings from the longitudinal *Okinawa Centenarian Study* suggest that the "oldest old" Japanese are optimistic, are easygoing, and adapt to life situations (Willcox, Willcox, & Suzuki, 2000). The *reorganizers* are capable people who place a premium on staying young, remaining active, and refusing to "grow old." As they lose one role in life, they find another, continually reorganizing their patterns of activity. The *focused* elderly display medium levels of activity. They are selective in what they choose to do and invest their energy in one or two roles. The *disengaged* elderly also show integrated personalities and high life satisfaction. But they are self-directed people who pursue their own interests in a calm, withdrawn, and contented fashion, with little need for networks of social interaction.

The *armored-defended* elderly are striving, ambitious, achievement-oriented individuals with high defenses against anxiety and with the need to retain tight control over events. Here, too, there are differences: The *holders-on* view aging as a threat and relentlessly cling to the patterns of middle age as long as possible. They take the approach "I'll work until I drop dead." They are successful in their adaptation as long as they can continue their old patterns. The *constricted* elderly structure their world to ward off what they regard as an imminent collapse of their rigid defenses. They tend to be preoccupied with "taking care of themselves," but in their preoccupation they close themselves off from other people and experiences.

Passive-dependent elderly form a third group: The *succorance-seeking* have strong dependency needs and elicit responsiveness from others. They appear to do well as long as they have one or two people on whom they can lean and who meet their emotional needs. The *apathetic* elderly are "rocking chair" people who have disengaged from life. They seem to "survive" but have medium to low levels of life satisfaction.

Finally, there are those elderly who show an *unintegrated* pattern of aging. They reveal gross defects in psychological functions and an overall deterioration in their thought processes. Television shows about hoarders exemplify this pattern of aging. Their activity levels and life satisfaction are low. Neugarten, Havighurst, and Tobin (1968) concluded that personality is an important influence on how people adapt to aging. It has major consequences for their relationships with other people, their level of activity, and their satisfaction with life.

Other Theories of Aging

How successfully people age depends on a complex interaction of variables, including physical and mental health, educational achievement, financial security, and individual and cultural perceptions about aging. Most significantly, people also need social settings to develop and express their humanness throughout life. Accordingly, geropsychologists, gerontologists, and sociologists have advanced several theories that describe changes in the elderly in the United States in terms of the changes in their self-perception and social environments. A few of these theories are described here.

- **Disengagement theory of aging:** the first (early 1970s) formal attempt to explain aging and a view of aging as a progressive process of physical, psychological, and social withdrawal from the wider world. As a consequence of this process, the elderly can face death peacefully, knowing that their social ties are minimal, that they have said all their good-byes, and that nothing more remains for them to do. However, many elderly today do not necessarily want to "step aside" and prefer to be engaged in work and life.

Differing Cultural Responses to Aging In China and in many other countries, being able to engage in favorite activities helps the "oldest old" maintain a zest for life. There are differing cultural views toward aging in U.S. and Chinese societies. *Source:* Sushu Xia. *China Comics.* Used by permission.

- **Activity theory of aging:** the view that the healthiest older persons maintain fairly stable levels of activity as long as possible and then find substitutes for the activities they must relinquish. The amount and types of activity that occur appear to be more a function of past life patterns, socioeconomic status, ability to use the English language, and health than of anything inherent in the aging process.

- **Role exit theory of aging:** the view that retirement and widowhood terminate the participation of the elderly in the main institutions of society—the workforce and the family—which reduces opportunities for the elderly to remain socially useful. The loss of occupational status and marital status is particularly devastating, because these positions are master statuses and anchoring points for adult identity. It is also demoralizing if one is forced to retire prematurely. Furthermore, today's elderly are not motivated to conform to a socially devalued status.

- **Social exchange theory of aging:** the theory that people enter into social relationships because these provide rewards—economic sustenance, recognition, a sense of security, love, social approval, gratitude, and the like. In the process of seeking such rewards, they also incur costs—they have negative, unpleasant experiences (effort, fatigue, embarrassment, etc.), or they are forced to abandon other pleasant experiences in order to pursue the rewarding activity. A relationship tends to persist only as long as both parties glean profit from it (total reward minus total cost). As applied to old age, social exchange theory suggests that the elderly find themselves in a situation of increasing vulnerability because of the deterioration in their bargaining position (Heckhausen & Heckhausen, 2008). In industrial societies, skills become increasingly outmoded through technological change; and as a consequence of the decline in power for the elderly, older workers exchange their position in the labor force for the promise of Social Security and Medicare. In other words, they "retire."

- **Modernization theory:** the view that the status of the aged tends to be high in traditional societies and lower in urbanized, industrialized societies (Cowgill, 1986; Moody, 2006). This theory assumes that the position of the aged in nonindustrial, traditional societies is high because the aged tend to gain knowledge and control through their years of experience. It is widely believed that *elder respect* continues to be an important element of collectivist cultures in Africa, Asia, India, and South America, but less so in individualistic cultures such as Canada, Australia, and the United States (Gal, 2009). Respect is shown by *filial responsibility;* that is, adult children care for the elderly. In Singapore, laws of compulsory filial responsibility have been passed, whereas in the United States, filial responsibility is more a matter of custom and personal ethics (Moody, 2006). As industrialization and urbanization have affected most countries in the past century, the multigenerational family has become more fragmented, loosening strong familial bonds. A further complication is the number of reconstituted or blended families made up of individuals from two or more previous marriages. From the children's point of view, their "parents" include biological parent(s) and stepparent(s). Whom will they support? Concurrently, age peers have become central to social life outside the family and have largely displaced older family members as the principal social group. The generation gap raises serious questions about the desire of younger family members to support family elders. Further, ineffective government policies and a weak economy have economically strained families that would otherwise have been willing and able to support family elders.

Perhaps, if elders could take a larger part in caring for and bringing up their grandchildren, in doing housework, in adding to household income, and in contributing in other ways, they would feel that they were an integral part of the family instead of feeling estranged. The family support system will become vitally important if the social welfare system cannot solve the health and welfare problems plaguing the elderly population. The question still remains: Who among the younger generation will accept filial obligations toward elderly family members? Resolving this issue often occasions great emotional conflict among American adult offspring, whereas support of parents is more widely accepted, and even expected, in other cultures.

Although social exchange theory and modernization theory draw attention to elements of exchange that

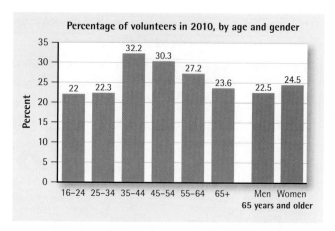

FIGURE 18.1 Percentage of U.S. Adults Volunteering, by Age and Gender: 2010 About one out of four U.S. adults aged 65 and older were volunteers in 2010. More elderly women than elderly men volunteer in religious and secular settings. Common volunteer tasks for the elderly include collecting and distributing food for food banks, performing managerial tasks, and assisting with general office works.
Source: Bureau of Labor Statistics. (2011, January 26). Volunteering in the United States—2010. [News release.] Retrieved from http://www.bls.gov/news.release/pdf/volun.pdf

affect the position of the elderly in a society, they fall short of providing a complete explanation (Heckhausen & Heckhausen, 2008). Van Willigen (2000) studied the perception of physical well-being and the psychological impact of volunteering on elderly persons. Older volunteers experienced greater increases in life satisfaction than young adults did, as well as greater positive changes in perceived health. A national survey revealed that in 2009 over 26 percent of adults aged 65 and older were actively volunteering, and nearly half of those volunteers did so through their religious affiliations (U.S. Bureau of Labor Statistics, 2010a). Also, more women volunteer than men, and there was an increase among black women volunteers in 2009 (see Figure 18.1). Volunteering gives the elderly an opportunity to stay actively engaged in a social community and to have meaning in their lives. Older people in other cultures, where there is no official "retirement" date or age, often remain engaged in life into old adulthood.

> *Questions*
>
> Which models of aging deal with internal aspects and which deal with external aspects? What factors do all of these theories recognize as promoting life satisfaction?

Selective Optimization with Compensation

Paul and Margret Baltes endorse the life-span model they call **selective optimization with compensation.** At all stages, and especially in old age, we are adjusting our standards of expectation. A great deal depends on how each elderly person perceives old age. The aging adult who views late adulthood as a time of gaining knowledge and wisdom will have a healthier, more positive self-concept; the aging adult who views old age as a time of physical debilitation and loss of control will form a more negative self-concept. We will enjoy more successful aging if we recognize our capabilities and compensate for losses and limitations. Late adulthood brings many changes in life. That is, we demonstrate "the ability to adjust and to transform reality so that the self continues to operate well if not better than in earlier years. Because of this remarkable power of the self, older adults on average are not at all more depressed or anxious than younger ones" (Baltes & Baltes, 1998). Findings from the recent *Berlin Aging Study* (BASE) suggest that people aged 70 to 100 continue to have a purpose in life, and for the most part they live in the present with much engagement, mastering the tasks of everyday life (Baltes, 2006).

The Third Age The idea that later stages of the life span are most suitable for developing wisdom was set forth clearly in medieval Christian writings and also appears in Eastern teachings, religions, and philosophies (Bond, Peace, Dittmann-Kohli, & Westerhof, 2007). It is the stage of life when men and women become free to pursue a more contemplative lifestyle, after having been released from many societal duties. Some research indicates that certain aspects of personality actually improve during what the Balteses call the *Third Age*. These aspects include emotional intelligence and wisdom. Emotional intelligence includes the ability to understand the causes of emotions (their expression, underlying feelings, and the associated nonverbal cues). **Wisdom** is "expert knowledge about life in general and good judgment and advice about how to conduct oneself in the face of complex, uncertain circumstances" (Baltes & Baltes, 1998; Kleyman, 2008). The Balteses suggest that "our store of wisdom benefits from the ability to engage ourselves with others in discussions of life dilemmas and from having a personality that is open to new experiences and strives toward excellence in matters of human lives" (Baltes & Baltes, 1998, p. 14). Further, wisdom goes beyond what we define as intelligence. Perhaps the most salient difference between intelligence and wisdom is that wisdom is applied toward the achievement of ends that are perceived as yielding a common good, whereas the various kinds of intelligences may be applied deliberately toward achieving either good ends or bad ones (Bornstein & Lamb, 2005).

The Balteses propose that on a sociocultural level, the elderly have potential that is inactivated. Can we take the adult focus on productivity and transform it into other forms of productivity for society? Are there better ways to prepare for old age? What are the emerging biomedical and genetic interventions that may make it possible to repair body systems, prevent diseases, and allow for longer productivity?

The Fourth Age Paul and Margret Baltes advance the theory that as people move into the *Fourth Age* (the late eighties and older), they face increasingly difficult obstacles and become more vulnerable. People of these advanced ages normally require more cultural, technical, and behavioral resources to maintain high levels of functioning because they have biological deficits. Baltes and Baltes (1998) point to the findings of the *Berlin Aging Study,* which focuses on the functioning of those aged 70 to 100 and older. The results indicate that the oldest old do experience more demands and stressors and that they have fewer mental, emotional, and social reserves to cope with and compensate for these conditions. For example, in the Berlin study the prevalence of Alzheimer's disease was found to be 3 percent in those aged 70 to 80, 10 to 15 percent in those 80 to 90, and about 50 percent in those over 90. But Smith and Baltes (2007) suggest that in old age, people can still find effective strategies for life management. By carefully selecting, optimizing, and compensating, they are able to minimize the negative consequences of old age. They remind us that the indomitable human spirit, when confronted with the challenges of living, comes up with many adaptations and solutions (Lachman, 2006).

Aging and Wisdom Some older adults exhibit wisdom. Josephine Zaharis (a retired schoolteacher, mother, and grandmother, and a lifelong volunteer at her church, the Red Cross, and a Retired Senior Volunteer Program) celebrates her 95th birthday reading stories to preschool children at the Child Development Center. She maintains a large network of relatives and friends and radiates an optimistic philosophy: "I try to find something every day that will make me happy."
Source: Bob Ellis/*Cortland Standard.* Laubenstein, Christine. (2008, March 11). Zaharis still teaching at age 95. *The Cortland Standard.* Retrieved April 9, 2008, from http://www.cortlandstandard.net/articles/03112008n.html

A Life-Span Model of Developmental Regulation

Schulz and Heckhausen (1996) propose a life-span theory with the construct of *control* as the central theme for characterizing human development from infancy to old age, a view that now seems to hold true across cultures (Adams, 2006). Implicit in their view is the idea that successful aging includes the development of primary control throughout the life course. Schulz and Heckhausen (1996, p. 708) explain, "Primary control targets the external world and attempts to achieve the effects in the immediate environment external to the individual, whereas secondary control targets the self and attempts to achieve changes directly within the individual." Both types of control involve thought, emotions, and action. Because primary control is directed outward, it enables individuals to explore and shape their environment to fit their particular needs and optimize their developmental potential. Their life-span theory is that primary control follows an *inverted* U-shaped life trajectory like this ∩, increasing from infancy through childhood and adolescence, then peaking in middle adulthood but declining gradually throughout late adulthood.

Control is associated with a person's multiple social roles in life (as son or daughter, stepchild, sibling, friend, colleague, spouse or partner, parent and grandparent, employee, volunteer, and so forth). As people get older, they expend effort and time on the roles that are most important to them, but they begin to relinquish roles that start to lose value or that they can no longer perform. They exert *primary control* in the domains of family, finances, and friendship by making decisions about a social role. For example, once adult children move from home, parents devote less effort to parenting but might decide to spend more time together and with friends. If primary control efforts are not available, then *secondary control* takes charge, and one modifies one's goals and standards or engages in self-protective attributions (Blackburn & Dulmus, 2007). Let's say an aging woman has great difficulty walking and can no longer do her grocery shopping. She might ask a son or daughter to carry out that role, or she might contact the American Red Cross (which has a volunteer shopper program for the elderly), and she subsequently feels that her grocery needs are under control.

Increasing age-related biological and social challenges to primary control put a premium on secondary (self-directed) control strategies. The older person's own competencies and motivation will lead to experiences of either failure or positive outcomes. Failures have the potential to undermine one's self-concept, and therefore the elderly develop various strategies of *compensation,* such as moving from a two-story home to a residence on one floor and using hearing aids, pill containers, walkers, grab bars in the bathroom, stair lifts, canes, medical alert services, Meals on Wheels, and other adaptive devices and services. Those

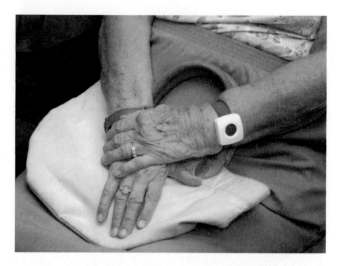

Compensatory Measures Help Seniors to Be Independent Longer Most elderly adults adapt to physical and health changes and use compensatory strategies to be able to stay safely in their homes and maintain their independence longer. For those who live alone, medical alert services are standing by 24 hours a day to respond to the call button, which can be worn on the wrist or as a necklace.

elderly who are able to engage and affect their environments for the longest time would be judged most successful.

A review of research from evolutionary, comparative, developmental, and cross-cultural psychology finds that *primary control* does hold functional primacy throughout the life span and across cultures—with some variability on the basis of gender, race-ethnicity, socioeconomic status, and cultural beliefs and values throughout historical time periods (Skaff & Gardiner, 2003).

The Impact of Personal Control and Choice

As psychologists since Alfred Adler (1870–1937) have noted, a sense of control over one's fate makes a substantial contribution to most people's mental health. On the one hand, it seems that most individuals prefer and benefit from control most of the time. On the other hand, psychoanalyst Erich Fromm (1941) argued that a good many people do not wish to be masters of their own fate and hence are attracted to totalitarian leaders and movements. Witness the large number of people (in any culture) who voluntarily sign up for a life in the military, for instance. Perceived control and the desire for control can also decrease with age, as a result of motivational decline (Stephan, Fouquereau, & Fernandez, 2008). Heckhausen and Heckhausen (2008) studied the relationship between perceived control over development and subjective well-being. They found that for older adults, their perceptions of control are more adaptive when they can be adjusted to different situations and when they reflect a positive evaluation of their abilities. As we shall see, generally those elderly who are forced into institutionalized living arrangements have serious health conditions and lose their sense of control and purpose as others make their daily decisions for them, including when to bathe, when to eat, when to sleep, what to eat, and what to wear.

A Sense of Purpose   The important contribution that a sense of responsibility, usefulness, and purpose makes to successful aging is highlighted by the research of social psychologists today. Earlier, Langer and Rodin (1976) investigated the impact that feelings of control and personal choice had among residents of a high-quality nursing home in Connecticut. Forty-seven residents of the home heard a talk by the nursing-home administrator in which he stressed the residents' responsibility for caring for themselves and shaping the home's policies and programs. After his talk, he gave each resident a plant "to keep and take care of as you'd like." He also told them that a movie would be shown on two nights, saying, "You should decide which night you'd like to go, if you choose to see it at all." The administrator also spoke to 45 residents on another floor. This time he emphasized the staff's responsibility for the residents. He gave them plants with the comment, "The nurses will water and care for them for you." Finally, he told them that they would be seeing a movie the following week and would be notified later about which day they were scheduled to see it.

A trained researcher interviewed each resident one week before and again three weeks after the administrator's talk. To prevent bias, the researcher was not told the purpose of the experiment. The questions she asked the residents dealt with how much control they felt they had over their lives and how happy and active they believed themselves to be. She also rated residents for alertness. On each occasion, the nursing staff filled out a questionnaire. Each resident was evaluated in terms of overall activity, happiness, alertness, sociability, and dependence. The nurses also were not aware of the nature and purpose of the study. Prior to the administrator's talks, the two groups of residents were quite similar in their feelings of control, alertness, and satisfaction. Three weeks after the talks, the differences were marked.

Despite the high-quality care given them, nearly three-fourths of those in the second group (where the staff retained control and took primary responsibility) were rated as having become more debilitated—over a mere three-week period. In contrast, 93 percent of those in the first group (the residents who were encouraged to make their own decisions) showed overall improvement. Langer and Rodin (1976, p. 197) conclude that their findings support the view that "some of the negative consequences of aging may be retarded, reversed, or possibly prevented by returning to the aged the right to make decisions and a feeling of competence." Langer and Rodin (1976) found that the residents who were given responsibilities during

the experimental period were healthier than comparable residents who had been treated in a conventional manner. The two treatment groups also showed different death rates. By the time of the follow-up, twice as many members of the conventional-treatment group, compared with the responsibility-induced group, had died. In sum, medical practitioners, nursing home administrators, home health aides, and family caregivers would be well advised to incorporate patient choice into their caregiving.

Questions

In what ways do aging adults maintain a sense of control in their lives as long as possible? How do elderly individuals benefit from personal control and choice?

FAMILIAL ROLES: CONTINUITY AND DISCONTINUITY

Although the majority of older persons live in a family setting today, the social support of old age differs significantly from that of early and middle adulthood when occupational, economic, functional, and health challenges increase (Bond et al., 2007; Merz & Consedine, 2009). Changes in physical vigor, health, and cognitive functioning have social consequences. And shifts in marital and work roles profoundly affect the lives of elderly people. Hence, the "social life space" of aging adults provides the context in which elderly men and women, like their younger counterparts, define reality, formulate their self-images, realize their self-worth, and generate their interaction with other individuals.

Throughout history, there has been obvious continuity in intergenerational relations in families: Parents cared for and nurtured children, launched them into independent lives, and typically transferred resources to children and grandchildren upon death. But Bond and colleagues (2007) suggest that the contemporary baby-boom generation is experiencing unique issues and challenges, unlike previous generations, as a consequence of the many different family forms that result from divorce, remarriage, single parenting, stepparenting, the single lifestyle, cohabitation, same-sex civil unions and marriages, and alternative family forms that create a wide range of kinship bonds. Also, in general, younger adults today are more dependent on the labor market than on family resources for their livelihood, so intergenerational support is more a choice than an obligation. For elderly adults who require assistance, past cultural experience demonstrates that sustained, stable support requires very close kin with time to devote to care. But some of today's seniors have fewer offspring, and their adult children are likely to live at a distance. Moreover, a majority of younger U.S. women (who will provide filial care and support) are in the workforce

(Gal, 2009). Thus, there is serious concern—even ambivalent feelings—about who is going to provide care for a growing number of frail and aging elderly relatives. As the baby-boom cohort becomes more elderly and requires assistance, public policy analysts predict a labor shortage among workers prepared to assist those elderly.

Two possible ways to ease that shortage have attracted some interest. First, family members might be paid to provide care for their aging relatives and would thus leave their jobs to do so. Second, legislation might be passed mandating that adult children provide care for aging parents (Caputo, 2005). Support takes many forms: assistance with tasks, help getting to medical appointments, financial aid, affection and emotional support, and information—and support might come from siblings or other relatives, best friends, neighbors, community and church groups, and/or hired aides, depending on the resources available (Birditt & Antonucci, 2007). Clearly, participating in a support network should be seen by health professionals as an effective health-promoting and illness prevention strategy for older adults (McDonald & Brown, 2008). And as we noted earlier, telehealth and telemedicine can also provide some assistance.

Virtual Medical Checkups Filial caregivers and home health aides are already in short supply for some seniors. The fields of telehealth and telemedicine are changing the nature of preventive care. Home monitoring should reduce the number of doctors' appointments, ensure that adults who need medical care receive it, reduce the cost of medical services for seniors, and provide greater peace of mind.

Love and Marriage

The parents of the baby-boom generation are more likely still to be married, because they had lower rates of divorce than any other cohort of the twentieth century (Tamborini, 2007). Caregiving research indicates that the spouse is the first person that married elders turn to when they need care. Until age 75, most American householders are part of a married couple. Accordingly, social scientists have asked, "What is the nature of marriage in older age?" It seems that most Americans believe that marriages that do not end in divorce begin with passionate love and evolve into cooler but closer companionship. Yet marital satisfaction and adjustment begin declining quite early in marriage, as children arrive. The speed and intensity of this decline vary from one couple to another. Usually, they report a U-shaped curve, with a decline in satisfaction during the early years, a leveling off during the middle years, and an increase in satisfaction during the later years (Kamp Dush, Taylor, & Kroeger, 2008).

Sexual activity continues to play an important role in healthy relationships in elderly couples (see Figure 18.2) (Lindau et al., 2007). Researchers have found a correlation between elderly sexual satisfaction and increased self-esteem and marital happiness (Choi, Jang, Lee, & Kim, 2010). However, several issues regarding the sexuality of older adults arise, including physical changes

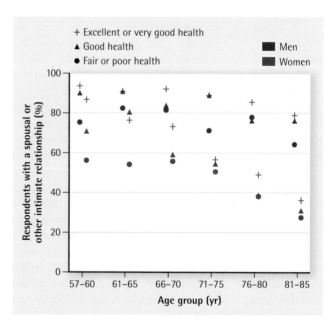

FIGURE 18.2 Sexual Activity Within a Marital or Intimate Relationship for Adults Aged 57 to 85 More than 3,000 U.S. men and women, aged 57 to 85, were surveyed about sexual activity, behavior, and problems. Sexual activity declined with age and with health problems; women reported less sexual activity than men; and about half of the sample reported at least one type of sexual problem.

Source: Lindau, S. T., Schumm, L. P., Laumann, E. O., Levinson, W., O'Muircheartaigh, C. A., & Waite, L. J. (2007). A study of sexuality and health among older adults in the United States. *New England Journal of Medicine, 357,* 762-774.

related to aging and compensatory strategies, patterns of change in sexual behavior, psychosocial and cultural aspects of sexuality, sexual dysfunction, and issues of special concern to cognitively impaired and physically disabled older adults. Consequently, there is an increasing demand among elderly couples for help with sexual dysfunction (Bitzer, Platano, Tschudin, & Alder, 2008).

Grusec and Hastings (2007) found that older couples expressed more affection toward each other and resolved marital conflicts with less anger than middle-aged couples. Although marital quality varies among couples, most elderly husbands and wives—especially those with a more egalitarian relationship—report greater happiness and satisfaction during their later years (Kaufman & Taniguchi, 2006). Several factors contribute to marital improvement in the later years. For one thing, children are launched, which reduces financial costs, strain, and conflict in marital relations. Notably, marital happiness is generally highest during the "empty nest" stage. The parents can now refocus on the relationship and spend more time together as a couple (Mitchell, 2010). In later life, problems with such issues as in-laws, money, and sex have often been resolved, or the stresses associated with them have dissipated; but retirement can create new strains for a couple. One retiree points out the following:

> A husband and wife may each have a dream of what retirement would be, but those dreams don't necessarily mesh. They've got to sit down and talk—outline their activities, restructure their time, and define their territories. I discovered that my wife was very afraid that after I retired she'd have to wait on me hand and foot and would lose all her freedom. (Brody, 1981, p. 13)

Women who are nonemployed, traditional housewives report that they feel "smothered" having their retired husbands around so much of the time. Such wives might view husbands who increase their involvement in household tasks as intruders, whereas other wives welcome their husbands' sharing responsibilities. The loss of privacy and independence is often offset by opportunities for nurturing and companionship. And wives mention having the "time available to do what you want" and the greater flexibility in schedules as advantages of retirement. Yet perhaps the most important factors influencing a wife's satisfaction with her husband's retirement are her own and her husband's good health and adequate finances (Donald & Montgomery, 2009).

Over the past four decades, as women have entered the labor force in growing numbers, more couples have had to confront the issue of whether the husband and wife will retire about the same time (Mitchell, 2010). In fact, retired husbands viewed their wives as having more influence on their retirement decision than the wives thought they had. By contrast, women were more satisfied with retirement when they felt their husbands had not been overly influential in their decision to retire (Grusec & Hastings,

Satisfaction with Marriage Among the Elderly Marital satisfaction can be high among the elderly, despite developmental changes. Amelia (100) and John (101) Rocchio from Rhode Island were married 82 years as of 2005 and attributed their long, happy marriage to a great sex life and compromise. They were actually married 83 years—the longest recorded marriage in the history of the world—and both passed away in 2006.

2007). Overall, men report being happier when working part-time after retirement, whereas retired women often find satisfaction in volunteer activities and being with family and close friends. When both have been retired for a few years, marital quality tends to improve (Fingerman & Pitzer, 2007). Because retirees are living much longer, researchers suggest that there will be new ideas in policies and practices such as preretirement planning, transitional or phased-in retirement, part-time retirement, part-year employment/retirement, and so forth.

Marriage also seems to protect people from chronic health issues that lead to premature death (Ellis, 2008). Married individuals are healthier than unmarried ones, and death rates are consistently higher among single and socially isolated people (even after adjustments are made for age, initial health status, smoking, physical activity, and obesity). Although popular folklore depicts marriage as a blessed state for women and a burdensome trap for men, it is men, not women, who receive marriage's greatest emotional and physical benefits (Donald & Montgomery, 2009). Further, women are more likely to be named as confidants by their husbands than women are to name their husbands as confidants. Women are more likely to select as confidants adult daughters and female friends (Fingerman & Pitzer, 2007).

Questions

Why does the happiness of couples who have been married for many years typically follow a U-shaped curve? What has been discovered about the well-being of elderly singles and elderly couples?

Widows and Widowers   A majority of elderly men—about three-quarters of them—live with their spouses. But because women tend to outlive their husbands, there are far more widows than there are widowers. Fewer than half of elderly women still reside with their husbands. This statistic demonstrates particular gender issues that are of great concern worldwide: (1) Elderly women are at much higher risk of living in poverty, especially in nonindustrialized countries where they did not earn an income or pension; (2) most are not able to afford adequate healthcare services; (3) they are likely to reside with older children; and (4) they are at higher risk for neglect and elder abuse. American women 65 and older were three times as likely as men 65 and older to be widowed (Federal Interagency Forum on Aging-Related Statistics, 2010).

Remarriage in Late Adulthood   Remarriage in later life is another recent trend, and research findings reveal that this event has profound consequences for the entire family, especially the adult children, if it follows a divorce in midlife or later (Brown & Kawamura, 2010). Family rituals get lost and family gatherings become more complex to arrange—and relationships with children and grandchildren change. Divorce or widowhood in late adulthood often results in coresidence with an adult child—more likely with mothers who are of minority status or have less education. However, divorced fathers have lower rates of contact or coresidence with adult children. Widowed women often experience financial insecurity, and remarriage or cohabitation might improve their economic circumstances.

On the other hand, remarriage may improve an older adult's self-esteem and improve his or her relations with adult children, who relinquish being in a support role for parents (Brimhall, Wampler, & Kimball, 2008). With many more people in late adulthood now, more remarriages are occurring. According to Brown, Lee, and Bulanda (2006), more than half of older men, but only one out of four older women, remarry. With increasing longevity and more later-life remarriages, middle-aged adults could conceivably have several groups to whom they feel obligated: grandparents, parents, children, adopted children, grandchildren, in-laws, stepchildren, stepparents, step-grandchildren, and/or children from cohabiting relationships. Whereas intergenerational studies have demonstrated that adult children (often women) sense a filial obligation toward biological elderly parents, such obligation does not extend to stepparents or stepsiblings acquired through remarriage. In fact, when stepchildren are adults, they often are not perceived as having any responsibility to help their stepparents (Ganong & Coleman, 2004).

Statistics on remarriage for this population of aging adults are somewhat misleading, since the number of elderly adults who choose to cohabit rather than remarry has nearly doubled since 2000 (Brown & Kawamura,

2010). Recent research has found that cohabitation offers some of the benefits of marriage in older adulthood—namely, comparable relationship quality and enduring union. Further, the growing practice of cohabitation for this age group is due to several factors: prior experience with the stress and costs of divorce; concerns for adult children and grandchildren's inheritance; concerns about being the beneficiary of a deceased spouse's private pension; eligibility stipulations of being the widow(er) of a deceased Social Security and Medicare recipient, such as not remarrying; retaining a deceased spouse's medical benefit eligibility; being the guardian of a disabled adult child's or grandchildren's SSI benefits; and avoidance of family disputes that might arise if a remarriage were to occur (Brown & Kawamura, 2010).

Singles

Over half of U.S. women aged 75 and older are single and lived alone in 2008 (see Figure 18.3) (Federal Interagency Forum on Aging-Related Statistics, 2010). The

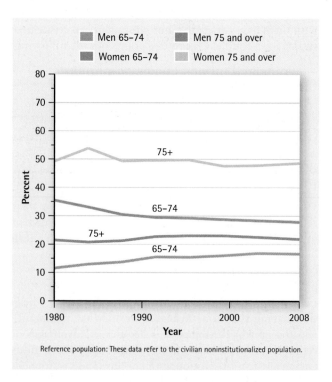

FIGURE 18.3   U.S. Population Aged 65 and Older Living Alone, by Age and Gender: 1980–2008   With advancing age, rates of widowhood rise, and more elderly women live alone, especially those 75 and over. Note that the percentage of elderly men who live alone is much lower. Older adults who live alone are more likely to live in poverty, and some are at risk for self-neglect.

Source: Federal Interagency Forum on Aging-Related Statistics. (2010). *Older Americans 2010: Key indicators of well-being.* Washington, DC: U.S. Government Printing Office. Retrieved from http://www.agingstats.gov/agingstatsdotnet/Main_Site/Data/2010_Documents/Docs/OA_2010.pdf

FURTHER DEVELOPMENTS

Older Adults and Their Online Romantic Relationships

It is clear that online romantic relationships are rapidly becoming the "norm" for most segments of the population, but what about the elderly? The Web is serving millions as an electronic matchmaker, and a recent AOL study found that nearly 40 percent of wired seniors had used the Web to find a friend or lover. A *New York Times* article described seniors seeking seniors online by saying that "romance in old age has come in from the cold." Recent research on older adults' intimate/romantic Internet relationships counteracts two prevailing stereotypes: the misconception that older adults don't do computers (and certainly not the Internet), and the misconception that older adults don't do sex (that is, that they are asexual).

However, current evidence indicates that older adults are making the digital conversion in increasing numbers. For instance, the Australian Bureau of Statistics reported that whereas most age groups are experiencing small declines or a plateau in computer usage, the proportion of adults aged 65 years and over using computers was continuing to grow. Comparable results were seen in the United States, where 22 percent of seniors reported that they use the Internet regularly. As for older adults being asexual, research again suggests otherwise. For example, a survey on older adults' sexual activity when meeting their online romantic partners face-to-face found that 85 percent of them engaged in sexual behavior. These results clearly demonstrate that the desire for love, romance, and intimacy is of fundamental importance, regardless of age. In addition, for older adults, finding a companion via the Internet is often a comfortable and secure experience. The following quotations are typical of many older adults' online experiences:

> I had no luck offline. First, I have no idea how to meet single men because I had been married for a long time. Second, I'm not gorgeous, and hate being rejected out of hand. Using *Match.com* was amazingly easy and good for my ego.

Another senior online participant states,

> I do not like the pub and club scene. Plus, using dating sites gives me a sense of confidentiality, security, and privacy.

Some older adults have reported that once trust and rapport were established, online relationships were often closer than offline ones. Moreover, the phenomenon of older adults engaging in romantic Internet connections doesn't seem to be going away anytime soon. Given the anticipated future size of the older-adult population and their increasing use of the Internet, it can only be expected that finding a partner online will become the "norm" for much of this generation, as it is for countless others. However, older adults are vulnerable to loneliness and can easily be victimized, so the old caveat "Let the buyer beware" still applies.

Adapted from Sue Malta, Love Actually! Older Adults and their Romantic Internet Relationships. (2007). *Australian Journal of Emerging Technologies and Society, 5*(2), 84–102. Retrieved from http://www.swinburne.edu.au/hosting/ijets/journal/V5N2/pdf/Article2-MALTA.pdf

elderly who remain single and those who become single by divorce or widowhood tend to have more emotional and physical pathology than the married elderly. The married have continuous companionship with a spouse, and spouses normally provide interpersonal closeness, nurturing, emotional gratification, and support in dealing with life's hassles and stress (Manzoli, Villari, Pirone, & Boccia, 2007). A 17-nation study that examined marital status and happiness found that being married is associated with higher levels of personal well-being, financial support, physical health, and social connectedness (Stack & Eshleman, 1998).

Studies of intergenerational social supports demonstrate that the people most likely to be listed as key network members at all times are parents and children. If singles who have never married have no children, they are lacking a main component of a key social network in their later years—especially males (Dykstra & Hagestad, 2007). If singles have been married and then divorced or widowed, their social and support networks can be unstable and unreliable. As mentioned earlier, death rates are consistently higher among single and socially isolated people—even after adjustments are made for age, gender, hypertension, smoking, physical activity, and obesity (Molloy, Stamatakis, Randall, & Hamer, 2009). Males are particularly vulnerable to being socially isolated, which probably contributes to their higher rate of suicide. But older women typically establish a social support network with other females and with family members. Senior men and women also use social network sites to find companionship. See the *Further Developments* box, "Older Adults and Their Online Romantic Relationships." With greater numbers of divorced or widowed singles in late life, there are more remarriages and cohabiting relationships, which create elderly stepparent-stepchild-stepgrandchildren relationships. These new family structures create strains on adult children and make it less likely that stable intergenerational support will be available when needed.

> **Questions**
>
> Who are more likely to be widowed or alone and to need more filial support in late adulthood, men or women? Do widowed adults tend to remarry or remain single?

Lesbian, Gay, Bisexual, and Transgender Elderly

According to the best estimates, there are about 2 to 3 million lesbian, gay, bisexual, and transgender (LGBT) adults now 65 and older in the United States (Masini & Barrett, 2008). Older LGBT adults have been stereotyped as being lonely, isolated, and frustrated. Yet this group is quite diverse. Some were married in heterosexual relationships and had children in their younger years; others did not marry and do not have children; and some have adopted children. In self-report surveys of older gay men and lesbians, they say they are well adjusted and have established social networks. Although they are more likely than heterosexuals to live alone and without a partner, they may have stronger social networks of friends outside the family. Further, support from friends rather than family may have led to a higher mental quality of life and lower depression and anxiety (Masini & Barrett, 2008). Friends and acquaintances provide socializing support, whereas partners, siblings, and other relatives provide emotional support. Those who live with domestic partners are not only less lonely than those who live alone but also rate their physical and mental health more positively.

Both lesbians and gay men who are in civil unions seem to get more support from families, but lesbians in civil unions are more likely to be "out" than men in civil unions (Phillips & Marks, 2008). Koch and Mansfield (2002) studied older gay men and lesbians and found reports of closer intimacy in their long-term relationships than in male-female relationships. One lesbian participant stated, "Many straight women in 20- to 25-year marriages are distant and emotionally separate from their husbands. I think this is a time when lesbian women and their partners come into their own—their best time together." History-graded influences on development have affected different cohorts of lesbians, gay men, and bisexuals (Kimmel, Rose, & David, 2006).

Members of the LGBT community continue to organize and lobby for civil rights protections under the law to secure equal housing, employment, and civil unions. They lobby for the right to marry in all states with all the legal benefits of marriage, including pensions, medical insurance, Social Security, hospital visitation and next-of-kin decision making, and inheritance benefits. Many psychological and economic disadvantages result from not having legal status when the partner of a gay, lesbian, or bisexual dies. For example, the surviving partner is not entitled to Social Security benefits, is required to pay taxes as a beneficiary on retirement plans such as 401K or IRAs (legally married spouses do not pay such taxes), and is charged estate taxes on inherited property even if it is jointly owned (Services and Advocacy for GLBT Elders, 2010).

Programs like Senior Action in a Gay Environment (SAGE) are working with LGBT elders to overcome the challenges of discrimination in the community. Only recently, a few retirement communities have been established for older lesbians. Social scientists continue to study many aspects of health care and economic policies that affect aging LGBT adults (Phillips & Marks, 2008).

> **Questions**
>
> Overall, how do gay and lesbian elderly rate their life satisfaction? What factors contribute to their well-being in late adulthood?

Children or Childlessness

The stereotype that most elderly people are lonely and isolated from their families and have no other meaningful social ties is false (Gal, 2009). Moreover, the elderly are often involved in exchanges of mutual intergenerational aid with their grown children or grandchildren as both providers and receivers. Many times, the elderly parent helps the adult child by performing child care and other home-related roles, whereas the adult child helps the parent with heavy housework or yard work, shopping, bureaucratic mediation, and transportation. Some divorced adults with children move in with their elderly parent(s). Among the American middle class, gifts from living parents play a substantial role in bolstering the living standards of their adult children.

Also, in most cases, care for the elderly is provided by their families. This is especially true for ethnic-minority elders, who are likely to live in a multigenerational home. Despite substantial social change (increased geographic mobility, divorce, and women's participation in the labor force), which has been thought by many to weaken intergenerational family cohesion, adult children, particularly daughters, remain major sources of instrumental support to their parents (Gal, 2009). Significantly, older

Americans are less likely than their adult children to believe that when elderly parents can no longer take care of themselves, the best solution is for them to move in with their children. The elderly value their privacy and independence (Clark, 2005). Those with adult children prefer to live near but not with them—what psychologists term "intimate distance." In sum, most elderly are not so isolated from kin and friendship networks as is commonly believed.

Grandparenting and Great-Grandparenting

Child psychologists emphasize that both children and their grandparents are physically and emotionally better off when they spend a good deal of time in each other's company (Longoria, 2009). In the early 1900s, surviving grandparents were rare. A century later, with the increase in adult life expectancies, more children and adults have living grandparents, step-grandparents, great-grandparents, and great-great-grandparents. Presently in the United States, grandparents are likely to have five or six grandchildren, on average. Today's grandparents are healthier, live longer, are more active, and are better educated than they used to be, and many have more money and leisure time (Crimmins et al., 2009).

Grandparenthood, for most, is now a sequential phase of life rather than an overlapping phase. In the past, people often became grandparents while still raising their own youngest children, whereas today the youngest has usually left home before people become grandparents (Goodman & Silverstein, 2006). Grandmothers outnumber grandfathers because women's life expectancy is about five years longer than that of men at age 65 (Xu et al., 2010). However, many middle-aged and older women are working and are unlikely to be available to baby-sit full-time for their grandchildren. Great-grandparents are also much more common.

A majority of grandparents are closely involved with their grandchildren (Longoria, 2009). In contemporary society, the most common kind of relationship between grandparents and grandchildren is companionate, where the grandparent and grandchild are essentially good pals. Grandparents might play, joke, teach the children hobbies or skills, and watch television with their grandchildren, but they are less inclined to discipline them. By the same token, grandparents also want freedom and fulfillment; they want to spend their leisure time as they please and expect to have close but not constant association with their children and grandchildren (Crimmins et al., 2009).

More than 1.9 million U.S. children under 18 lived with their grandparents in a formal custody arrangement in 2010 (U.S. Bureau of the Census, 2010c). In actuality, there are many more grandchildren living with grandparents in informal arrangements. A majority of

custodial grandparents have custody because of parental drug addiction, abuse and neglect, mental illness, incarceration, illness due to AIDS, absence due to employment or military service, or death (Conway, Magai, Springer, & Jones, 2008). Of the children who live with their grandparents, about half also live with their mothers in the same household, but another 35 percent have little or no contact with their parents (U.S. Bureau of the Census, 2010c). Custodial grandmothers usually assume most of the care of grandchildren, and they have greater life satisfaction when a grandchild has a healthy relationship with at least one of the parents, who assumes some of the responsibility (grandparents typically invest efforts in family unity) (Conway et al., 2008). Sometimes, grandparents are caught in bitter custody disputes with their own adult child, which creates great tension within the family system.

Custodial grandparents are more likely than others to be poor and lack health insurance. Generally they become eligible for child welfare benefits when their grandchildren reside with them, but navigating this bureaucratic system is stressful and time-consuming (Hayslip & Kaminski, 2005; Patrick & Tomczewiski, 2007). Studies on African American grandparents raising grandchildren found that African American grandmothers in particular were economically vulnerable (Attar-Schwartz, Tan, & Buchanan, 2009). Patrick & Tomczewiski (2007) found that custodial grandparenting can increase anxiety, hypertension, and sleep disorders and that it is associated with depressive symptoms in grandparents. Although the grandparenting role has different meanings for different people, some themes recur: For most, grandparenting is a source of biological renewal or continuity.

Grandparents Are Raising an Increasing Number of Grandchildren In many American homes, grandparents play a substantial role in rearing their grandchildren, both on a formal and an informal basis. For about 6 percent of American children, grandparents assume the role of custodial parents.

Being a grandparent instills a sense of extension of self and family into the future and is often a source of emotional self-fulfillment. It generates feelings of companionship and satisfaction between the grandparent and a child. AARP has special resources on its Web site for grandparents who have custodial responsibility for grandchildren (see "Following Up on the Internet" at the end of this chapter).

Siblings

The longest-lasting, and arguably the most pervasive, of all close relationships that people have are with siblings, and siblings generally play a significant role in the lives of the elderly (Rocca, Martin, & Dunleavy, 2010). Today, sibling relationships are complex: There are biological siblings, half-siblings, stepsiblings, adoptive siblings, and unrelated siblings residing in a home with cohabiting or same-sex adults. Siblings within each family may also differ in birth order, gender, race-ethnicity, and age-cohort influences. And adult siblings usually bring in-laws into the kin network. Five types of sibling interactions have been identified, ranging from extremely close to distant: congenial, loyal, intimate, apathetic, and hostile (Gold, Woodbury, & George, 1990).

But what can social psychologists tell us about the strength of sibling relationships? Much depends on the family's cultural background of values and beliefs, socioeconomic status, length of coresidence in the parental home, and the way parents treated each sibling differently through life (in reality, "equal treatment" as the norm is a myth). Parents may be compelled to help adult children through difficult life circumstances that vary from sibling to sibling (such as disability, military duty overseas, job loss, divorce, serious accident or illness, addiction, etc.). Some adult siblings continue to compete for parental concern and resources (Matthews, 2005). Some adult siblings do not have a sense of filial care, which can result in resentment and conflict for those who provide care for an aging parent (Myers & Goodboy, 2010). Yet the majority of elderly report congenial and loyal relationships with siblings. The sister-sister relationship tends to be the most potent sibling relationship, followed by the sister-brother and brother-brother relationships (Cicirelli, 2001).

Siblings provide continuity in family history that is uncommon in most other family relationships—they eventually are the only members of the family of origin that remain. A shared family history frequently affords a foundation for interaction that supplies companionship and a support network, as well as validation for an older person's reminiscences of family events. As they advance into old age, many siblings report that they think more often about one another and find that their acceptance, companionship, closeness, and caring for each other increases. Siblings are especially important kin for those

Siblings and Social Support The longest-lasting relationships we normally have are with our siblings, who provide continuity in family history that is uncommon in most other family relationships. A shared family history often gives siblings a foundation for interaction that supplies companionship, closeness, and a support network, as well as validation for an older person's memories of family events.

with few or no children. Close relationships with siblings can contribute to fewer depressive symptoms, greater life satisfaction, and a greater sense of emotional security in later years (Rocca et al., 2010).

Questions

In what ways has the role of grandparent been redefined over the past few decades? How do grandparents and grandchildren benefit from their relationship with each other? How does the presence or absence of children, grandchildren, and siblings affect the elderly adult's emotional well-being?

SOCIAL AND CULTURAL SUPPORT

Numerous findings from scientific research support the notion that frequent social contact is associated with good health, ability to cope with stress, decreased mortality, and greater life satisfaction (Cagley, 2009). A functioning network of social ties is necessary in times of stress, illness, and aging; it can provide both emotional support and practical assistance. Indeed, in order to grow old gracefully and have a good life, it is important to know how to build and maintain satisfactory social relations (Cavallero, Morino-Abbelle, & Bertocci, 2007).

Friendships

Overall, in terms of companionship, friends are more important and satisfying to older people than their

Friendship Older adults are usually retired, establish new routines, and engage in new activities. Having more time provides opportunities to reestablish old friendships or make new friends, who are often more important and satisfying to older people than their offspring. Developmental decline, however, can reduce interaction with friends.

offspring are. In fact, friendship plays a major role in the health and well-being of the elderly (Moremen, 2008). An elderly widow who lives with her daughter's family can be quite lonely if she has little contact with close friends her own age. Individuals differ greatly in what they view as adequate socialization. Older adults typically have to conserve their physical and emotional energies and concentrate their efforts on a smaller number of close friendships. Frail, older adults with physical impairments have fewer opportunities for contact with friends, which results in more social isolation, loneliness, and possibly suicide (Hawthorne, 2008).

Solitude need not be experienced as loneliness, whereas loneliness can be felt in the presence of other people. For instance, people who live in nursing homes often complain of loneliness, even though they are surrounded by others and, at a superficial level, are interacting with them. **Loneliness** is the "awareness of an absence of meaningful integration with other individuals or groups of individuals, a consciousness of being excluded from the system of opportunities and rewards in which other people participate" (Busse & Pfeiffer, 1969, p. 188).

The quality of a relationship is more important than mere frequency of contact. Overall, maintaining a few meaningful close relationships is more closely associated with good mental health and high morale among the elderly than is a high level of social interaction—even for married adults (Birditt & Antonucci, 2007). A close friend serves as a buffer against the losses associated with

declining health, widowhood or divorce, and retirement (Moremen, 2008). Most communities have senior centers, which are excellent settings where new supportive friendships can easily be formed—especially if seniors live alone (Hawthorne, 2008).

Retirement/Employment

Retirement did not exist in preindustrial American society—nor does it exist in some societies today. Older people formerly were not sidelined from employment, but life expectancies were much shorter. In 1900 an American male had a life expectancy of 47 years and spent only about 3 percent of his lifetime in retirement. Today the average life expectancy of Americans is about 78 years, and retirement averages more than 10 years, or at least 13 percent of one's lifetime. In 1940, the proportion of males aged 65 and over who were gainfully employed was 42 percent; in 2008 it had dropped to about 26 percent. Yet in 2008, more than 6 million workers over the age of 65 were working (see Figure 18.4). The labor force participation rate for men over 70 is also higher now and has reached 15 percent.

"Retirement," however, has become a somewhat ambiguous term because it is often a transitional process in which a person leaves a "career" job and engages in other paid activities or becomes self-employed before fully retiring (Karoly & Zissimopoulos, 2004). About one-fourth of self-employed U.S. workers are aged 65 and older, with more men than women choosing self-employment (Federal Interagency Forum on Aging-Related Statistics, 2010). Recently, labor force participation rates for men and women over the age of 55 have been gradually increasing; they are staying at their jobs longer or reentering the workforce in response to the poor economic times. In 2008, fewer than half of U.S. working women had a pension plan or 401K plan at work, and women generally earn lower wages and save little for their retirement years. Because their financial security is in doubt for their retirement years, many will have to work long after they become eligible for Social Security retirement benefits (Irwin & Cardenas, 2008). For example, your authors recently have noted the very elderly female workers at fast-food establishments.

Retirement is a complex decision of mounting significance in the lives of American men and women. At present, three-fourths of men and more than four-fifths of women who retire on Social Security currently leave their jobs before they are 65 years old. In government settings, nearly two-thirds of civil service employees retire before the age of 62. Workers who retire at age 60 or 62 can expect to live 15 to 20 years longer. Women often leave the workforce or work part-time while raising children and have to reenter the labor force later and continue to work in late adulthood to make up for lost

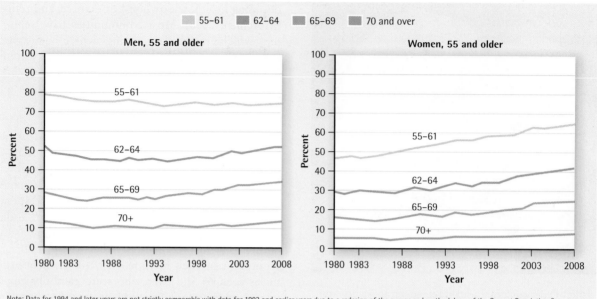

FIGURE 18.4 Older Americans Continue in the Labor Force: 1980–2008 Americans 55 and older continue to be in the labor market. Higher education rates are associated with greater labor force participation. For those 65 to 74, 24 percent work full-time; it is projected that 30 percent will do so by 2014. Many adults transition to part-time work, or self-employment, before full retirement.

Source: Federal Interagency Forum on Aging-Related Statistics. (2010). *Older Americans 2010: Key indicators of well-being.* Washington, DC: U.S. Government Printing Office. Retrieved from http://www.agingstats.gov/agingstatsdotnet/Main_Site/Data/2010_Documents/Docs/OA_2010.pdf

income and build a pension; some women must retire earlier than they planned in order to care for aging or ailing parents (Robinson, Demetre, & Corney, 2010).

A survey of workers' intentions after retirement found that nearly 40 percent of retirees planned to work for pay after retiring (Rappaport, 2008). Also, self-employment rates begin to rise in middle and late adulthood (Federal Interagency Forum on Aging-Related Statistics, 2010). Increased longevity and better health also incline workers to continue working past traditional retirement age in their current jobs, whereas some attempt to launch new careers. Studies have found that survival probabilities are much higher for men and women employed where there are no mandatory retirements (Brockmann, Müller, & Helmert, 2009). Of men aged 55 or older who retire, about one-third return to the workforce. Although a majority of retirees who resume work do so in the first year, another 20 percent join them in the next few years. At older ages, self-employment may be a form of partial retirement, offering greater satisfaction, flexibility in hours, and earnings in accordance with Social Security stipulations (Rappaport, 2008).

Involuntary Retirement   Prior to 1978, about half of the nation's employers had policies requiring employees to step down at 65. Congress in 1978 passed legislation banning compulsory retirement for most workers before age 70 and in 1986 largely abolished mandatory retirement at any age. Many Americans view the practice of compelling workers to retire as a curtailment of basic rights. Baby boomers who are now reaching retirement age may be needed to fill jobs that the much smaller age cohorts that follow them cannot. Although baby boomers number about 78 million, Generation X includes only about 44 million.

Nevertheless, high unemployment in many industries (especially in mining, construction, and manufacturing), coupled with the prospect of an extended layoff or a difficult job search, has led many older workers to opt for early retirement. A majority believe that older workers are the first to go when employers make cuts, although many companies realize that their older employees are a valuable asset—especially given projections of future labor shortages. To accommodate the need for retaining or recruiting these experienced workers, work design and management models are changing to reflect the value of older workers in the workplace. Corporations are offering variable exit strategies in order to meet these needs, such as gradual or phased retirement, job sharing, temporary work, and consulting

(Hanel, 2010). A survey of baby boomers conducted by AARP revealed that two out of five workers were interested in a gradual, "phased" retirement instead of an abrupt cessation of work, and nearly 80 percent of those said that the availability of phased-retirement programs at work would encourage them to keep working longer (Coy, 2005).

Retirement Satisfaction   By Western norms, people are integrated into the larger society by their work roles. Work is seen as a main aspect of identity and self-esteem and as providing people with personal gratification, meaningful peer relationships, and opportunities for creativity—in sum, the foundation for life satisfaction. For those adults whose work identity is central to their self-concept and gives them the greatest satisfaction, retirement represents somewhat of a crisis as a major life transition (Wong & Earl, 2009).

In recent years a more positive view of retirement has emerged. A recent study found that most Americans see retirement not as a stressful event but, rather, as a natural transition or life stage. Only individuals high in neuroticism perceived retirement as a negative event (Robinson et al., 2010). With the trend toward staying in the workforce longer (perhaps working part-time or from the home) and the increased ability to launch new ventures, aging workers can feel useful and stimulated on the job (Smyer & Pitt-Catsouphes, 2007). One longitudinal survey of 5,000 men found that most men who retire for reasons other than poor health are "very happy" in retirement and would, if they had to do it over again, retire at the same age. Only about one out of five said they would have chosen to retire later. Some older workers decide to stay in the labor force for reasons of good physical health and personal fulfillment (Brougham & Walsh, 2009).

Several studies have looked at the effect of retirement on marriage. Older married couples tend to plan their retirement transition to occur at about the same time (Johnson, 2004). Another study that examined the retirement behavior of married couples found that men were more likely to retire if their wife was also retired. However, women were less affected by the labor force status of their husbands (Brockmann et al., 2009). Women who felt that their retirement was too early or had been forced felt more depressed, whereas the same effect was not found in men (Grusec & Hastings, 2007).

Increasing numbers of retirees are also going back to college. Senior citizens who wish to keep mentally engaged often attend college and audit courses, and tuition is often free or reduced after a certain age. In 2008, twice as many students were auditing college classes as had done so during the previous five years. Some colleges and universities do not permit auditors of undergraduate classes or have imposed caps on the number of auditors; other universities have embraced auditors,

Nola Ochs Graduates with a Master's Degree at Age 98
In 2007, at age 95, Ochs completed her bachelor's degree in history and was briefly the world's oldest college graduate. Then, in May 2010, she regained her place in the *Guinness World Records* when she earned her master's degree at age 98.

seeing this policy as bolstering their image in the community and in the eyes of potential funders. Nola Ochs was 95 in 2007 when she graduated from Fort Hays State University in Kansas—and she was 98 when she earned her master's degree in 2010 (Bauer, 2010). Some campuses offer special retirement learning institutes or *Roads Scholar* (formerly Elderhostel) programs for seniors. Positive anticipation of retirement and concrete and realistic planning for this stage in life are related to adjustment in retirement. On the whole, voluntary retirees are more likely to have positive attitudes and higher satisfaction in retirement than those who are forced into early retirement. However, other factors (such as poor health) are not always controllable and influence retirement satisfaction. In sum, those with better health, positive and openness traits, and higher socioeconomic status seem to make a better adjustment to retirement (Robinson et al., 2010).

> *Questions*
>
> Who is most likely to retire early? In what different ways do U.S. retirees find life satisfaction after retirement? Which elderly adults are most likely to take another job or attempt self-employment after retirement?

A Change in Living Arrangements

A change in living (housing) arrangements represents a major life event for an older person. And living arrangements for older adults also differ by race-ethnicity and

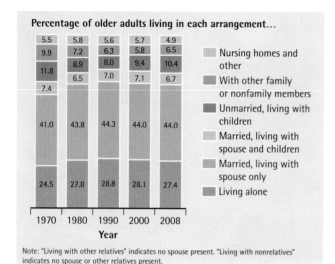

Percentage of older adults living in each arrangement...

1970	1980	1990	2000	2008
5.5	5.8	5.6	5.7	4.9
9.9	7.2	6.3	5.8	6.5
11.8	8.9	8.0	9.4	10.4
7.4	6.5	7.0	7.1	6.7
41.0	43.8	44.3	44.0	44.0
24.5	27.8	28.8	28.1	27.4

Legend:
- Nursing homes and other
- With other family or nonfamily members
- Unmarried, living with children
- Married, living with spouse and children
- Married, living with spouse only
- Living alone

Year

Note: "Living with other relatives" indicates no spouse present. "Living with nonrelatives" indicates no spouse or other relatives present.
Reference population: These data refer to the civilian noninstitutionalized population.

FIGURE 18.5 Living Arrangements of U.S. Adults 65 and Older: 1970 to 2008 The largest percentage of older adults is likely to be married, followed by those who are single and live alone. Note the growing percentage of elderly adults who are unmarried and live with their children, as the percentage of adults reside in nursing homes or adult care facilities declines.
Source: Pew Research Center. (2010, March 8). *The return of the multi-generational family household.* Retrieved from http://pewsocialtrends.org/files/2010/10/752-multi-generational-families.pdf

gender (see Figure 18.5) (Federal Interagency Forum on Aging-Related Statistics, 2010). Older widowed Asian and Hispanic women and men are much more likely to reside with family members. Older men are more likely to reside with a spouse than are older women, who are more likely to be widowed and living alone. Older black men who are single are much more likely to live alone. Note the small percentage of older adults who reside with nonrelatives, in some form of institutional care.

Several factors are likely to initiate a change (or changes) in living arrangements for U.S. elderly; these include retirement, low socioeconomic status, a change in economic conditions from divorce, death of a spouse, remarriage, or declining physical and/or mental capacities. Potential living arrangements include living at home alone; moving to a new location in the case of remarriage; living at home with assisted-living services; living with adult children with adult day-care options; and living in long-term-care facilities (includes nursing homes and prisons), retirement communities, small adult group homes, community shelters, and adult foster care—or homelessness. Most elderly adults prefer to remain independent in their own homes, where they believe they have more autonomy, a greater sense of security, and a higher quality of life (Bilsen, Hamers, Groot, & Spreeuwenberg, 2008).

Living Alone at Home and Assisted-Living Services
Over 50 percent of Americans over the age of 65 live alone (see Figures 18.3 and 18.5). Of those living at home, 80 percent are women (Federal Interagency Forum on Aging-Related Statistics, 2010). Large numbers of the elderly are now cared for more suitably, as well as more economically, in their homes—with the help of adult children and grandchildren, older siblings and friends, visiting nurses, social workers, and Meals on Wheels volunteers. But some elderly lack any caregivers: "Elders neglecting themselves usually live alone. They display behaviors such as piling garbage inside the home, allowing food to spoil, failing to maintain utilities in the home, [and] ignoring serious medical issues" (Dyer, Pickens, & Burnett, 2007, p. 1448). At present, there is a shortage of home health aides, and the U.S. Department of Labor lists this job among the most rapidly growing for the future. In addition, the demand for assisted-living services has increased because of the unfortunate incompetent care and lack of compassion that have come to light in some nursing homes (Hasson & Arnetz, 2008). Depending on the state, home-care assistance may be available under the following programs: Medicare, Medicaid, the *Older Americans Act,* and Title 20 of Social Security. The crises with federal, state, and local budgets will affect the quality of life for millions of elderly as more social programs are inevitably reduced in scope or cut entirely (Eckholm, 2009).

Most elderly fear being forced to leave their home because of frailty, illness, widowhood, a decaying neighborhood and crime, or rural isolation and fear of becoming dependent on others. One of your authors had a very distant aunt, aged 99, who rarely left her home, and the only person who checked on her daily was the mail carrier ("Mail Carrier Saves Elderly Woman's Life, 2008). With rural post offices being closed, more elderly will be left vulnerable. One report on American centenarians suggests that these "oldest old" fear losing their independence and avoid census takers and medical practitioners. Although the philosophy today within the field of aging is to promote independence, many elderly eventually develop physical impairments or cognitive problems that make them unable to remain in their homes safely. An electronic monitoring system that can be installed in the home has been considered a way to oversee the well-being of the elderly from afar. This current technology would enable seniors to lead independent lives within their homes, while having a sense of security (Prince & Butler, 2007). Also, families can now use video-chat Web sites such as *Skype* to check on and communicate with aging relatives who live out of town or in remote areas (Komando, 2009).

Living with Children and Adult Day Care For the elderly who are living with relatives, senior day-care centers give busy family members a break from caregiving

and a chance to work or catch up on tasks. **Adult day care** involves daily care and support to adults who live in the community, providing transportation, health, social, and support services in a supervised, protective setting during the day. Socialization, recreation, nutrition, and professional supervision are provided for a few hours or on a daily basis, as needed. Some ethnic-minority elderly with debilitating illness or dementia expect to live with their adult children, who are then expected to care for their parent or grandparent without seeking assistance from the greater community. To seek help outside of the family would be interpreted as shameful or as indicating failure on the part of the adult child to meet filial obligations. This inflicts a great emotional, psychological, and economic burden on the adult children or grandchildren.

Institutional Care   The most recent *National Nursing Home Survey* was conducted in 2004. The updated survey of nursing homes revealed that there were 1.7 million U.S. residents in 15,900 nursing homes (U.S. National Center for Health Statistics, 2007a). By 2004, the age of nursing-home residents was likely to be 85 and older, with fewer residents between 75 and 84 or younger (see Figure 18.5). Alternative residential care settings, senior centers, and community adult day care are also available in most cities. As the baby-boom cohort reaches these advancing years, the number needing both home and institutional care will grow substantially. Expenditures for good nursing-home care are already significant but are expected to triple by 2030, when the oldest of the baby-boom cohort will reach their mid-eighties (Schade & Brehm, 2010).

Each caregiving environment has its own distinct social climate. Some communal settings are friendlier, more oriented toward independence, and better organized than others, and they provide a range of services within a religious and spiritual context. Certainly many facilities do their best to provide the elderly with decent care. U.S. ethnic minorities are significantly underrepresented in nursing homes. Further, elder minorities are much more likely than white elders to use informal home care and less likely to use formal care (Kirby & Lau, 2010). Language, monetary, and bureaucratic barriers are often cited as reasons, as well as collectivist cultural norms that enforce intergenerational responsibility in certain ethnic groups.

Even so, nursing homes are hardly "homes." Becoming a resident of a nursing home shifts control of one's life from the individual to the "total institution" and is often regarded as a last resort (Lim, 2009). Once in a nursing home, the elderly typically become physically, emotionally, and economically dependent on the facility for the rest of their lives. Further, depending so heavily on staff care often leads to cognitive and physical decline (Lim, 2009). Indeed, some of the characteristics

frequently encountered among the institutionalized aged, including depression, feelings of helplessness, and accelerated decline, are partly attributable to the loss of control over their lives. Consequently, the prevalence of depression is much higher among elderly people living in nursing homes than among their peers living in the community (Schade & Brehm, 2010). Under circumstances of forced dependency, the elderly come to see themselves as powerless—as passive objects manipulated and buffeted by the environment. In many nursing homes, the majority of residents share a small bedroom with others; eat mass-prepared, high-carbohydrate meals in a large, linoleum-floored dining hall; and watch television in a central "common room."

Many of the nation's skilled-care nursing homes fail to meet federal standards for clean food and do not administer drugs properly or on a timely basis. Inspection reports on code violations in nursing homes can be difficult to locate, and the decision to place a relative in a nursing home is usually made in a few days under emergency circumstances through recommendations of hospital staff or a social worker. Having limited time to get the facts they need to make the best placement decision, most people select a home nearby so they can visit their loved one readily. The elderly poor, especially minorities, are often placed in public facilities that generally provide inferior care. As the U.S. nursing-home industry has evolved, nursing homes have become a place of last resort for a variety of reasons. They are used by terminally ill patients who require intensive nursing care, by recuperating individuals who need brief convalescence, and by infirm aged who lack the social and financial resources to manage in their homes and community. Thus, nursing-home residents differ greatly in degree of physical impairment and mental disorientation. Increasingly, the elderly and their children are considering the option of assisted-living apartments as an alternative to nursing homes (Hasson & Arnetz, 2007). Assisted living provides a greater measure of privacy with individual apartments, but it also provides as-needed care through its staff. Brown Wilson (2007) noted that over 800,000 people were served through assisted-living arrangements in the United States at the time he wrote.

Retirement Communities   More retirement communities are being developed for middle-class and well-to-do elderly, particularly in the warm southern coastal states and the golf resort communities of the Southwest. Of concern to politicians in many northern states is the mass migration of their newly retired elderly, who have been productive citizens and provided a stable tax base in many communities. Some retirement communities are known as "trailer" communities, where the elderly can live comfortably with fewer home-care responsibilities and continue to lead active lives with senior citizens like themselves. Some communities offer townhouses and condos that border lush golf courses and other prime real estate. Such communities, however, are unlike a typical community where people of all ages live side by side. Some elderly especially miss being with grandchildren, children, and younger adults daily.

Adult Group Homes   More communities are experimenting with newer alternatives such as sheltered housing, assisted-living facilities, and continuing-care retirement communities (CCRCs)—protected communities arranged in apartment complexes and/or detached cottages—that provide such supportive services as centrally prepared meals, housekeeping, laundry, transportation, recreational options, and health care. This is projected to become a more common living arrangement over the next decade, because it enables the elderly to maintain much of their self-reliance, while providing a sense of security and support (Bilsen et al., 2008).

Questions

What are some alternatives for assisted-living arrangements for elderly adults who need supervision or care? When helping an elderly relative consider whether to enter a nursing home, what are some advantages and disadvantages that one should take into account?

Elder Abuse

Elder abuse and neglect can be defined as a single or repeated act or lack of appropriate action, occurring within any relationship where there is an expectation of trust, which causes harm or distress to an older person (Action on Elder Abuse, 2008). Elder abuse is now internationally recognized as a pervasive and growing problem. It is not known how many older Americans have been abused because there is no uniform reporting system, which makes it difficult to collect national data. Further, because most cases go unreported, the full scope of the problem isn't known (Poythress, Burnett, Nailk, Pickens, & Dyer, 2007). The need for a national study of elder abuse and neglect is supported by the growing number of older people, increasing public awareness of the problem, and new legal requirements for reporting abuse (Federal Interagency Forum on Aging-Related Statistics, 2010).

The old stereotype of a younger male abusing a frail elderly female victim is inaccurate. Pillemer and Finkelhor (1988) found that spousal abuse was more prevalent than abuse by adult children—and that finding was confirmed by Teaster's (2002) national study. But a significant percentage of women 60 years or older report that they have experienced abuse by a relative (Fisher & Regan, 2006). A spouse with a disability or dementia who is socially isolated is more at risk for such abuse or

neglect. Adult protective services are the first responders to vulnerable adults who are being mistreated, neglected, or exploited and are unable to protect themselves. Also, "the most common report to adult protective service agencies in the United States is self-neglect, a syndrome that afflicts vulnerable older adults who are not able to meet basic needs . . . and is actually an independent risk factor for early death" (Dyer, Pickens, & Burnett, 2007).

Unfortunately, institutional care often involves frail and the disabled elderly being pushed into passive roles; some patients are tied to their beds or wheelchairs or given powerful tranquilizing drugs on the premise that "a quiet patient is a good patient." Research suggests that it is rarely necessary to restrain nursing-home patients suffering from mental confusion or extreme physical weakness. Furthermore, laws have been passed that state that patients have the right to be free from physical and chemical restraints, except if these are being used for treating a medical condition (for example, to ensure that a person does not fall out of bed) (Carlson, 2006). The federal *Nursing Home Reform Law* outlines patient rights. Inadequate, unskilled staffing is a major problem in many nursing homes. People with little education and minimal skills (and even people with a criminal record) are often hired as aides, orderlies, janitors, and kitchen help because the jobs are viewed as unattractive, low-paying, and rather stressful. Because they must assist many who

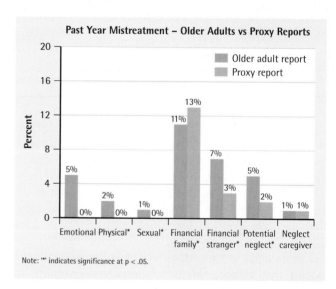

FIGURE 18.6 Substantiated Reports of Elder Abuse, Adults Aged 60 and Older, by Category and by Person Reporting Such Mistreatment: 2008 Note that financial mistreatment by family and others (often caregivers) is the most commonly reported and substantiated by police or Adult Protective Services (proxy), followed by emotional mistreatment or neglect (often by an older spouse, partner, or other relative).
Source: Acierno, R., Hernandez-Tejada, M., Muzzy, W., & Steve, K. (2009, March). *National Elder Mistreatment Study.* National Institute of Justice. Retrieved from http://www.ncjrs.gov/pdffiles1/nij/grants/226456.pdf

have dementia or multiple care needs, some personnel may not develop a strong commitment to their jobs or to the nursing home and, in extreme cases, may abuse the patients (Ferrini & Ferrini, 2008).

In most states, health-care professionals, dentists, lawyers, social workers, clergy, and bankers are mandated to report any elder abuse or exploitation that they observe or suspect. Elder abuse is the form of family violence about which we know the least—for it often goes unreported. The legal definitions of abuse include the following:

- *Abuse.* Physical abuse typically means intentionally inflicting, or allowing someone else to intentionally inflict, bodily injury or pain and includes such harmful behaviors as slapping, kicking, biting, pinching, and burning, as well as sexual abuse. It might also include inappropriate use of drugs and physical restraints.
- *Psychological abuse.* This includes verbal harassment, intimidation, denigration, and isolation. It might include repeated threats of abandonment or of physical harm.
- *Neglect.* This includes failure of a caretaker to provide the goods, services, or care necessary to maintain the health or safety of a vulnerable adult. Neglect can be repeated conduct or a single incident that endangers the person's physical or psychological well-being (Action on Elder Abuse, 2008).
- *Exploitation.* Although not physical, this form of abuse involves taking advantage of an older adult for monetary gain or profit. One of the most heart-wrenching things one of your authors ever witnessed was a very elderly woman crying, in a bank, because her adult son had completely cleaned out her accounts and left her nothing.
- *Self-harm and neglect.* This occurs when an elderly person who lives alone has mental impairments and cannot attend to his or her own nutritional, hygiene, or daily-living needs.

Laws related to elder abuse and neglect, and the reporting of such crimes, are inconsistent in many states (Action on Elder Abuse, 2008). Lachs and colleagues reported findings from a 13-year study (1998). They analyzed risk factors for both reported and verified elder abuse and neglect in a Connecticut cohort of nearly 3,000 adults aged 65 and older from diverse ethnic, racial, and social backgrounds. They discovered an association between the following risk factors and elder mistreatment: poverty, minority status, functional and cognitive impairment, worsening cognitive impairment, and living with someone (spouse or family member). Living alone was significantly associated with protecting older adults from abuse, because most mistreated subjects (80 percent) lived with someone else (Lachs & Pillemer, 2004).

Elder Abuse in the Long-Term-Care Community

Federal reports reveal that nursing-home abuse is on the rise. Providers recognize that elder abuse and neglect must be prevented—for these crimes have a devastating impact on the victim, on the trust of other residents, on their families, and on staff morale (see Figure 18.6 on page 596). They also arouse the outrage of the public and of law enforcement officials. But each state establishes different laws and regulatory procedures for the investigation of complaints about nursing homes (Daly & Jogerst, 2007). Massachusetts has instituted a program of video training, conferences, and workshops to educate staff in recognizing and preventing elder abuse. The American Health Care Association (AHCA), which represents 11,000 long-term-care facilities nationwide, is distributing this training video and lobbying Congress for a federal database for CORE (criminal offenders record information) investigations to screen out employment candidates with prior convictions or pending charges of elder abuse, theft, or other serious crimes.

In 1997, in a significant victory for patient rights, the Arizona Supreme Court upheld a lower-court ruling that families of elderly persons who are abused by their caretakers may recover damages for the victims' pain and suffering—even after their deaths (*Denton v. American Family Care Corp.*) (Cassens, 1998). In 2008, the U.S. Senate Special Committee on Aging introduced the *Patient Safety and Abuse Prevention Act* to protect the elderly from abuse; the Senate budget attempts to "set aside $160 million over three years to protect America's vulnerable seniors from predators through the creation of a comprehensive nationwide system of background checks for long-term care workers" (Glacel, 2008). Also, the *Nursing Home Transparency and Improvement Act of 2008* was introduced to improve the quality of care in nursing homes by providing more and better information for consumers through the Nursing Home Compare Web site. It also recognized the pivotal role that nurses play within a multiagency approach to identifying and preventing elder abuse in the practice setting. More important, nurses need to be proactive in setting the agenda in terms of prevention and health education (McGarry & Simpson, 2007).

Caregiver Burnout Caregivers of elderly adults with cognitive and functional impairments—even those who are loving and dedicated—are at high risk of experiencing "caregiver burnout." It is most likely that women will become the underappreciated caretakers of disabled elders (Choi & Marks, 2006). In one study, 20 percent of caregivers said their tasks were so frustrating and difficult that they were afraid they might hurt the patient (Lachs & Pillemer, 2004). Pillemer says caregivers must first recognize that there is a problem and that they should not feel guilty but *must* seek help. Caretakers should address these questions: "Am I depressed?" "Do I fly off the handle?" "Do I resent my relative?" "Am I denying my relative social activity?" "Do I threaten nursing-home placement?" Pillemer recommends the following strategies to cope with elder caregiving:

- Join a support group made up of people who experience the same problems.
- Continue activities you enjoy.
- Seek professional help for parents' physical needs.
- Get more information about caregiver burnout from area agencies on aging.
- Investigate adult day care or adult respite options in your community.

Questions

In what ways are the elderly victimized by abuse, and who is most likely to perpetrate that abuse? What can be done to prevent elder abuse in nursing homes and in home care?

Policy Issues and Advocacy in an Aging Society

The original *Older Americans Act* was passed in 1965 in response to the growing numbers of older people, and it was reauthorized by Congress in 2000 and 2006. This legislation established the *Administration on Aging* (AOA), an agency of the U.S. Department of Health and Human Services. This agency advocates and administers programs for senior citizens across the country. It also sponsors research and training programs on aging and, through its regional, state, and area offices, seeks to educate older people and the public about the benefits and services available. Nationwide there are 650 Area Agencies on Aging. AOA programs are collaborating with local health departments to help the elderly remain independent in their homes longer and to offer opportunities for older Americans to enhance their health and/or remain active in their communities through volunteer and employment programs. Supportive services include:

- information and referral, outreach, case management, escort and transportation
- in-home services, such as personal care, chores, home-delivered meals, and home repair
- community services, such as senior centers, adult day care, elder-abuse prevention, congregate meals, health promotion, employment counseling and referral, and fitness
- caregiver services, such as counseling, education, and respite

In the 1990s, nearly 70 U.S. behavioral science organizations and federal agencies formulated a national research agenda called the *Human Capital Initiative* to address the serious challenges and opportunities that increasing numbers of diverse elderly present to our society. The *Vitality for Life* proposal calls for ongoing research in four major aspects of aging: (1) behavior change to prevent damage to body systems and maintain health; (2) promoting the psychological health of the oldest old; (3) maximizing and maintaining productivity; and (4) assessing mental health and treating mental disorders. Research, training, and consulting in these areas improve our understanding of the needs of this large group of adults and enhance their quality of life (see the *Implications for Practice* box "Professor and Gerontologist"). Another goal is improving life for elderly immigrants who are becoming accustomed to an "American" way of life. A greater respect and caring for the elderly of all ethnic and cultural backgrounds is surfacing in American society.

In 2003 Congress passed the *Medicare Modernization Act and Prescription Drug Reform* to ease some of the burden of costs to the elderly. In 2006, Congress reauthorized the *Older Americans Act* that supports such programs as Meals on Wheels and jobs in elder care. The reauthorization continues to fund community service job programs that channel funds to organizations including AARP, Green Thumb, and the National Council of Senior Citizens, but it has set higher performance standards for these organizations. The bill also created a new $125 million National Family Caregiver Support Program that helps families care for the elderly at home by subsidizing respite care, providing counseling and support groups, and disseminating information on obtaining services (Nather, 2000). One major area that needs improvement is a federal system for reporting elder abuse and neglect (Action on Elder Abuse, 2008).

Americans face complex decisions in the near future, because the first of the baby-boom "tidal wave" began turning 65 in 2011. Public policymakers are going to alter public policy and legislation to plan for the collective needs of society. Special challenges include financing or restructuring the government insurance programs—Social Security, Medicare, and Medicaid—with soaring numbers of recipients who are living decades longer (Crimmins et al., 2009). An aging, longer-living population will increase both private and public costs, although the baby-boom cohort has more education, better private pension plans, and greater personal wealth than any previous cohort. To motivate older workers to continue working, the *Pension Protection Act of 2006* contains a provision that gives private pension plans the option of providing some benefits to participants who remain in the workforce at age 62 and beyond (Walker, 2007).

Three emerging fields that can serve the rising numbers of elderly are *telehealth, telemedicine,* and *Smart Homes.* "**Telehealth** is defined as the use of electronic information and communication technology to

IMPLICATIONS FOR PRACTICE

Professor and Gerontologist, William C. Lane, PhD

I am a professor emeritus of sociology at SUNY Cortland and vice president of Golden-Lane Associates, Inc., a gerontological consulting firm located in Glenmont, New York. At SUNY Cortland, I taught undergraduates from many majors. I created an Introduction to Social Gerontology course for sophomores, and I also designed and taught the senior seminar in human services. I started my consulting firm several years ago with a former student. Together, we work with several counties to establish programs to support caregivers of older people, as well as grandparents raising grandchildren. We do training and strategic planning, develop materials and marketing plans, and work on aging policy issues.

As a college professor, I taught students, did academic advisement, and conducted college service programs. I also took gerontology students to professional meetings and into settings where they work with older people. Now, I write manuals and training materials, conduct training seminars, do research, conduct marketing focus groups, and work on strategic planning for agencies and service providers. I am the past president of both the New York State Society on Aging (formerly SAGE) and Sigma Phi Omega, the national honor society in gerontology, and past treasurer of the Association for Gerontology in Higher Education.

I received a bachelor's degree in sociology, with a minor in psychology, from Pittsburgh State University (Kansas). I earned my master's in sociology and was supported by a grant to develop special educational programs for adults 55 and older, working with 27 school districts and 6 community colleges in southeast Kansas. That is how I got *hooked*

on gerontology. I earned a PhD in sociology at Kansas State University, where I was supported by a grant from the Midwest Council for Social Research in Aging, a training program for sociologists. As a professor, I did not have to complete a certification exam, but social workers, nurses, and other professionals complete certification exams for working with older people. My previous careers were as a professional jazz musician and an accountant.

To teach in a college setting, you have to like working with all kinds of students. Some students have difficulty getting started in their college careers but go on to do exceptionally well in graduate school and excel as professionals. You also have to pay attention to details. As a consultant in gerontology, you need a range of professional experiences.

Internships are essential, for both undergraduate and master's students. Internships, clinical experience, and volunteer experiences help individuals confirm their career direction. Such work demonstrates a commitment to the field and allows a person to learn the "language of the field" by working with professionals. I have become a better professor, researcher, and consultant from every research project, every board I have served on, and every group of older people I have encountered. I enjoy working with college students, but I really like working with older people and with professionals who serve this population. I find that service providers of the aging are among the most committed professionals I have encountered. They are sincerely interested in improving the quality of life for older people and their families. And, with the aging of the baby-boom cohort upon us, there will be no shortage of older people to work with over the next 50 years.

deliver medical information and services over distances through a standard telephone line. In most cases, an interactive monitor is placed in an individual's home—often accompanied by devices such as blood pressure machines or pulse oximeters—and daily information on health status, symptoms, and activities can be transmitted to and monitored by health care personnel" (Orr, Rogers, & Scott, 2006, p. 876). "**Telemedicine** is defined as the incorporation of telehealth technologies into a physician, hospital, clinic, medical institution, or other health-care organization's practice of medicine. The use

of telecommunications technology assists such entities in transmitting images, such as X rays or other diagnostic images, for examination at another site. Home health-care providers are already using telemedicine to monitor blood pressure, heart rate, and other vital information" (Orr et al., 2006, p. 876). Because of the rising demand, construction contractors are starting to build *Smart Homes,* "a residence equipped with technology that enhances safety of residents and monitors their health conditions" (Demiris, Hensel, Skubic, & Rantz, 2008). Private research companies are also contributing to monitoring the health care of the elderly, through inventions such as the "smart" pillbox: "About the size of a coffee-maker, [it] not only dispenses medications, but also has an audio feature that reminds patients when it's time to take their medication. If they don't retrieve the medicine from the dispenser, the machine beeps for 45 minutes, then calls a service center. . . . For patients with hearing loss, there's also a flashing light" (Quirk, 2007).

Economists predict that issues regarding the American economy will affect decisions about tax code configurations, specific regulations, the ability to purchase goods and services, the ability to provide a range of services for the "graying" population, and alterations to the customary lifestyle of all Americans. Policymakers believe that older workers will have to work longer. Indeed, age limits have risen for full eligibility for Social Security and other

public assistance programs, and at present Congress is considering raising these age limits again. Also, this demographic shift means an increased need for a skilled workforce (physicians, surgeons, nurses, therapists, pharmacists, social workers, gerontology professors, and geropsychologists) to provide services that are important to the elderly. And more facilities and providers will be needed for long-term care (day care, home health care, homemaker services, respite care, rehab care, and hospice) (Crimmins et al., 2009). It is also likely that future scientific, pharmaceutical, and medical breakthroughs (in such areas as stem cell research and nanotechnology) will improve health care and extend life expectancy even further. In 2007, Harvard University released a clinical study suggesting that a compound found in red wine called *resveratrol* may extend the human life span—with estimates ranging up to 150 years!

SEGUE

Now that you have read the research findings about the overall status of an increasing number of elderly, note the remarkable progress that has occurred in improving the longevity and quality of life for our senior citizens. The United States is third after China and India in its numbers of senior citizens. Many of our elderly are reaping the benefits of recent years of research in the physical and social sciences. It seems that it was only a few years ago when we heard the words *geriatric* and *gerontology* for the first time, yet now countless researchers worldwide are studying longevity, aging, and the quality of life

for everyone who reaches late adulthood. In 1998, John Glenn reentered the world of space exploration at the age of 77 to provide American scientists with never-before-gathered data on the effects of aging. To be selected, he passed rigorous physical and cognitive tests. His research in space aptly demonstrates that the study of aging is still in its infancy—and "the sky's the limit" for seniors living worldwide. In our concluding chapter, we shall examine several end-of-life scenarios for people of all ages and the range of coping strategies employed by the loved ones who remain.

SUMMARY

Social Responses to Aging

1. Industrialized societies have extended longevity for many older adults and have provided economic and social resources to enable them to lead more satisfying lives.
2. Most Americans want to ignore late adulthood or harbor distorted perceptions of it. These stereotypic views have negative effects on older adults' self-esteem.
3. Among the elderly, positive emotions have been found to be related to favorable life events, positive health status and functional ability, availability of social contacts, and higher levels of educational attainment.

Self-Concept and Personality Development

4. The elderly confront the issue of integrity versus despair. If they have successfully navigated middle adulthood, many are capable of facing their later years with optimism

and enthusiasm; but some appraise their lives as having been wasted and live with despair.
5. Peck stresses the changes people go through, from their reflections on retirement to recurring illness and mortality.
6. Emotional health among the elderly is described as the "clear ability to play and work and to love." An ability to handle life's blows without passivity, blame, or bitterness leads to greater satisfaction with life.
7. Neugarten and colleagues identified four major personality types, or traits, related to the aging process: integrated, armored-defended, passive-dependent, and unintegrated.
8. Other theories of aging focus on disengagement, activity levels, social usefulness, social exchange, and the modernization of society.
9. Some research indicates that a few aspects of personality, including emotional intelligence and wisdom, actually

improve during what is called the "Third Age," although developmental decline is evident in the "Fourth Age."

Familial Roles: Continuity and Discontinuity

10. The quality of marriage varies among older couples. Some elderly husbands and wives report greater happiness and satisfaction with marriage during their later years.
11. Fewer than half of elderly women still reside with their husbands, as a consequence of widowhood, divorce, or never having married. This statistic is of great concern worldwide: Elderly women are at much higher risk than elderly men of living in poverty.
12. A majority of elderly have living children, and many have kin and friendship networks and sources of mutual aid and support.
13. Both children and their grandparents are generally better off when they spend time together.
14. Siblings usually play a significant role in the lives of the elderly, providing continuity in family history and a source of filial support.

Social and Cultural Support

15. Some single elderly who live with relatives are lonelier than those who live alone, especially if they have little contact with close friends their own age.

16. Retirement is a recently evolved practice that does not exist in some societies today. Many of today's workers are living much longer, are working longer, and can expect to have 15 to 20 years of life remaining after they retire.
17. Nearly 10 million Americans over the age of 65 live alone, but 2 million indicate that they have no one to turn to when they need help. Several other types of living arrangements provide care and support for such persons.
18. It is estimated that about 1 to 2 million Americans age 65 and older are abused or neglected in domestic settings annually, and the perpetrator is often a spouse or an adult child. Most of the cases are not reported to Adult Protective Services. A common type of elder abuse is self-neglect.
19. The quality of life for American elderly has been improved by public policy mandates, the Older Americans Act, AARP, the Office for Aging services, and other community supports. However, some significant policy changes loom ahead as Social Security and Medicare are revamped to meet the collective needs of an aging society.
20. Telehealth and telemedicine will ease some of the burden of increasing costs, while providing preventive care.

KEY TERMS

activity theory of aging *(579)*

adult day care *(595)*

disengagement theory of aging *(578)*

elder abuse *(596)*

integrity versus despair *(575)*

life review *(575)*

loneliness *(591)*

modernization theory *(580)*

role exit theory of aging *(579)*

selective optimization with compensation *(580)*

social exchange theory of aging *(579)*

telehealth *(598)*

telemedicine *(599)*

wisdom *(581)*

FOLLOWING UP ON THE INTERNET

Web sites for this chapter focus on the changing demographics and quality of life for those in late adulthood. Please access the text Web site at www.mhhe.com/crandell10 for up-to-date hot-linked Internet addresses for the following organizations, topics, and resources:

AARP Sources on Aging
http://www.aarp.org/research/internet_resources/

APA Division 20: Adult Development and Aging
http://apadiv20.phhp.ufl.edu/

National Institute on Aging
http://www.nia.nih.gov

Gerontological Society of America
http://www.geron.org/

International Federation on Ageing
http://www.ifa-fiv.org/

The Okinawa Centenarian Study
http://www.okicent.org/

Grandparents Raising Grandchildren
http://www.usa.gov/Topics/Grandparents.shtml

National Academy on an Aging Society
http://www.agingsociety.org/agingsociety/

National Family Caregiver Support Program
http://www.aoa.gov/aoaroot/aoa_programs/hcltc/caregiver/index.aspx

National Center on Elder Abuse
http://www.ncea.aoa.gov/NCEAroot/Main_Site/Index.aspx

PART
10 THE END OF LIFE

Across the world, evolutionary psychologists, medical researchers, and artificial-intelligence scientists in the new field of "transhumanism" are working toward the goal of extending human life—perhaps even hundreds of years—and defying death. But life as we know it today as human mortals comes to a conclusion. An outpouring of scholarly (and not so scholarly) works in sociology, psychology, thanatology, and medicine; television documentaries; best-selling books; feature articles in newspapers and magazines; and Web sites have drawn attention to every aspect of the topic. Simultaneously, controversy has swirled in the mass media, in the political arena, in legislative and judicial chambers, in courtrooms across the country, and in our own homes about such matters as abortion, assisted suicide, clinical death, homicides and suicides, the death penalty, mass suicide, tragic deaths from causes such as SIDS, and life after death. Today people are more willing to discuss dying and death than in the past, and such discussions have paved the way for families to experience more meaningful closure to life for loved ones. Our gradual cultural embracing of death as a natural stage of development is leading toward a deeper understanding of the meaning of life.

19 Dying and Death

Critical Thinking Questions

1. If death is a natural part of life—if the natural progression of life is birth, growth, maturity, aging, and death—then why do so many people regard death as bad?

2. If you could transplant organs and have stem cell therapy or computer chip implants to maintain cognitive functioning, do you think you would like to live 500 or 1,000 years? Why?

3. If you had a life-threatening illness, would you want the physician to tell you? Why or why not?

4. Would you fill out a do-not-resuscitate order or living will for yourself? Why or why not?

5. Why is it so difficult for us to console someone who is grieving after the loss of a loved one?

6. Does consciousness end when a person dies?

All the world's a stage,
And all the men and women merely players;
They have their exits and their entrances,
And one man in his time plays many parts,
His acts being seven ages.
—**Shakespeare,** *As You Like It*

In the cycle of life, as Shakespeare reminds us, each person is born into this world and then—typically many years later—dies. During the time in between, called a *lifetime,* each of us ponders this mystery of mortality many times: when witnessing the birth of a child, when falling in love, when suffering the loss of a loved one, when viewing media portrayals of dying and death, or perhaps when conducting one's daily life as a soldier or police officer, firefighter, medical professional, member of the clergy, social worker, or hospice volunteer.

Throughout the ages, people from every culture have tried to probe this great mystery by taking risks and "teasing" death (illusionist David Blaine comes to mind, as does Alain Robert, who climbs tall buildings without safety gear), by wrestling with or writing about their fears, by creating tales and movies that "scare us to death," by devising elaborate rituals to prepare for "passing on," and by building monuments and memorials to honor a loved one after death. Some even welcome or promote their own "final exit." We conclude our final chapter on human development by discussing cultural awareness of issues in thanatology, cross-cultural views of death and grief, the role of religious beliefs, the stages of dying, and adjusting to the death of a loved one. At best, it can be said that facing death is as individual as our own personal philosophies about how we have lived our lives.

THE QUEST FOR "HEALTHY DYING"

Until the late 1800s, in American homes, families typically sat with and cared for their loved one who was dying, prepared the body when the person died, and then "laid out" the deceased in his or her best clothing (or wedding apparel) for a viewing in the parlor of the home. (In other cultures, women still wash and perfume the body and wrap it in cloths for burial or cremation.) A local carpenter or furniture maker (called an "undertaker") made a wooden casket and brought it to the home for the viewing and in readiness for burial. Often, some of the deceased person's hair was cut and braided into a bracelet to be saved and worn. There were no morticians to embalm the body, no funeral homes, and no corporations that made expensive caskets. Other family, friends, and community members would come to the parlor of the house to pay their respects and bring all kinds of food for the "wake." They would "call on" the family (thus funeral "homes" have "calling hours" today).

There were many superstitions about the spiritual state of the deceased—people believed the spirit lingered, and they made sure to compliment the deceased to avoid bad luck or revenge. To allow the spirit to leave, a window was opened and the doorway kept clear. Often family and friends would sit and talk all night with the deceased and celebrate his or her life. Dying and death were a natural part of life, and children grew up learning about death. The surviving family performed these mourning rituals to demonstrate their love and respect for the deceased, to ease their grief, and to allay their fear of any spirits that might harm them (Kastenbaum, 2004). A widow or widower was expected to mourn in black apparel for two years (a common custom across many cultures even today). A family's personal preparation, conversation, and celebration are still phases of the ritual in many parts of the world.

By the early 1900s, dying and death gradually were removed from the responsibility of families in Western society. Typically the gravely ill were whisked away to a hospital, and senile relatives and the "oldest old" were sent to "nursing homes" to live out their remaining days—or at least those who could afford this luxury were. Funeral parlors opened, and morticians retrieved the deceased from homes and hospitals for embalming and viewings. Families were no longer part of the personal care, cleaning, and dressing of the deceased. Funeral preparations, now conducted by professionals in the funeral industry, became more impersonal—and costly—and dying, death, and preparation of the body became something to be kept out of sight and out of mind. Over time, family "parlors" in homes became "living rooms," to reflect that the deceased no longer lingered there. Even medical schools avoided the topic of dying and death, and physicians focused as little as possible on dealing with dying patients and their families, for their professional oath was (and is) to maintain and prolong life. A review of 50 top-selling medical texts across various specialties found that medical students were provided with little helpful information on end-of-life care for patients (Rabow, Hardie, Fair, & McPhee, 2000). Here is the general medical view:

> We live in a society that chooses to hope that death can somehow be averted. As physicians, we suffer from the same death phobia, often offering dying patients therapies we know to be ineffective. Our medical education and texts include little information about the skills needed to treat symptoms common at the end of life, and few residency programs require hospice rotations. We are also taught throughout our training that no matter how dire the circumstance, we cannot take away a patient's hope. As a result, the psychologic and spiritual suffering that patients experience, often expressed as intractable physical pain, remains untreated. We are not taught that, for most patients who are in the final phase of an incurable disease, hope for cure or even for increased longevity will be proven tragically false. Dying patients and their families need our help in redirecting hope toward living without undue suffering, having time with loved ones, and preserving some sense of control and dignity. These are things we can help patients achieve. (Gazelle, 2003)

Some social scientists also claim that the United States continues to be a "death-denying culture." American culture stresses youth, beauty, power, physical fitness and health, cosmetic surgery, and other antiaging practices. Only about half of Americans surveyed in 2007 have wills, and many people are uncomfortable with discussions of death (Allebrand, 2007). Other social scientists claim the United States is a death-obsessed culture; over 50 million abortions have been performed to date, prosecutors can seek to impose the death penalty in federal courts and in many states, we have higher murder rates than any other industrialized country, and the states of Oregon and Washington allow physician-assisted suicide (Jones & Kooistra, 2011; Yardley, 2009).

Death confronts us both subtly and blatantly in diseases such as Alzheimer's, cancer, and cardiovascular failure, and in devastating epidemics such as AIDS and severe acute respiratory syndrome (SARS). On a nationwide scale, it tore at our hearts and prompted us to action when we witnessed the September 11, 2001, attacks; the Oklahoma City bombing; Columbine, and Virginia Tech; the senseless murders at the American Civic Association in upstate New York in 2009, the Fort Hood massacre in 2010, and the shooting rampage in 2011 at a Tucson shopping center; the more than 6,100 American military deaths suffered by 2011 during the U.S. campaign against terrorism; the incredible devastation caused by the 2005 tsunami in Southeast Asia and by Hurricanes Katrina and Rita; the aftermath of the earthquake in Haiti in 2010 that left over 250,000 dead, and other such disasters (Department of Defense, 2011). We conceal death under a variety of names—selective reduction, stillbirth, SIDS, mortality, homicide, suicide, suicide bombings, natural disasters, drive-by shootings, schoolyard shootings, occupational fatalities, auto fatalities, terrorism, casualties, collateral damage, friendly fire, and so forth. We routinely use such euphemisms to express our discomfort with the raw visceral facts that lie beneath the surface of our language and, thus, our consciousness.

We are reminded of its inevitability in rituals invoking collective memories, such as memorials commemorating the deaths of famous persons—Pope John Paul II, Princess Diana, Mother Teresa, President Ronald Reagan, Martin Luther King, Jr., and President John Kennedy, for example. As the traveling AIDS quilt and the traveling Vietnam Memorial, respectively, make their way around the country, whole communities come together in deep sorrow for the thousands of lives lost. And most of us experience some forms of preliminary finality in our lives in the "endings" of marriages by divorce or widowhood; the end of jobs or careers by termination, retirement, or resignation; and the end of family traditions when a couple divorces or adult children move away or marry and start their own family traditions.

Even our everyday conversations are sprinkled with expressions about death: "My back is killing me!" "I was so embarrassed I could have died!" "You scared me to death!" and "I'm bored to death." Some people risk death on a daily basis: those in police and fire departments, soldiers, the construction crew on a superhighway, stunt people who allow themselves to be set afire or make death-defying leaps out of buildings, those who abuse drugs, those who have unprotected sex with multiple partners, gang members, women who endure spousal abuse, and others. Television movies, popular action films, assassin video games, the evening news, and both national tabloids and mainstream newspapers sensationalize death, making it seem less than real. Yet we also trivialize or flout death by referring to it obliquely or glibly (bought the farm, kicked the bucket, ate his gun, eighty-sixed); by resorting to euphemisms to describe killing animals (put the dog to sleep, harvested the deer, culled the aged ewes); by naming products "Death by Chocolate," and by approaching the edge of mortality in such thrill-seeking activities as bungee jumping and skydiving, extreme skiing and other sports, amusement park rides, and even dining on the Japanese delicacy *fugu*, when too much of the poison has been left in the flesh of the blow (or puffer) fish. Death and the true meaning of life have been themes in great literature from its origins in the oral tradition to modern graphic novels. And they are central to the stories of the Bible, the *Iliad*

and the *Odyssey,* Shakespeare's *Romeo and Juliet,* and Tolstoy's "The Death of Ivan Ilych," among countless others. We personify death by giving it names like "the Grim Reaper," "the Gentle Comforter," "the long goodbye," "shuffl[ing] off this mortal coil," "the last dance," "eternal rest," "the sacred passage," "the ultimate sacrifice," "the elephant in the room," or "going home to God" (Kastenbaum, 1977, 2007).

In 2004, an A&E reality television show called *Family Plots* documented the routines of the staff, the preparation of the deceased, and the grieving families served at a mortuary. *Six Feet Under* was an award-winning HBO drama about a family that owned a funeral home. Other recent death themes in literature and the media include the ideas of near-death experiences, past lives, life after death, communicating with the dead, and the presence of angels (the television series *Medium, Touched by an Angel,* and *Ghost Whisperer* are examples). Some published books on this theme have become bestsellers, such as *Life After Life* by Ray Moody, Jr., *Embraced by the Light* by Betty J. Eadie, *Conversations with God* (Books 1, 2, and 3) by Neale Donald Walsch, and *Talking to Heaven: A Medium's Message of Life After Death* by James Van Praagh. Although they are not grounded empirically, these works prick our consciousness and urge us to confront what we think about life and death.

With today's sophisticated life-saving medical technology, many people report coming back from the brink of death. The highly reputable *Canadian Medical Association Journal* included a piece titled "Cardiac Arrest Remembered," in which a patient offered a detailed

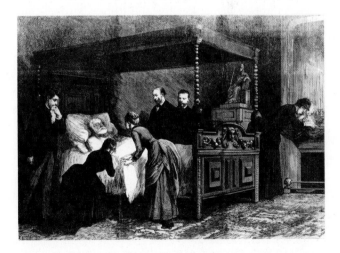

Traditional Western Rituals of Dying and Death A century ago in Western societies, death was a natural part of everyday life, and families cared for dying members and personally attended to the deceased in the home. A widow or widower sat for calling hours, when visitors brought food, drink, and their respects prior to the decedent's burial in a simple wooden coffin. Mourning in black for two years was the custom. Family preparation and mourning rituals are still common across cultures.

narrative of his near-death experience: "I saw myself leave my body, coming out through my head and shoulders. . . . I thought 'So this is what happens when you die' [and my] next sensation was of floating in a bright, pale yellow light . . . a very delightful feeling" (Gilbert, 2006). Many people in most societies throughout the centuries have believed in some form of survival after death. However, doubt and questioning have also persisted since the emergence of science (Kastenbaum, 2007). Brian L. Weiss—psychiatrist, experimental psychologist, distinguished university chairperson, and author of *Many Lives, Many Masters*—says that after decades of being immersed in the traditional, conservative aspects of his profession, scientists still have much to learn about the human mind that now seems to be beyond our comprehension.

Questions

How have the supervision and rituals surrounding death varied throughout American history? In contemporary American society, what events and media are promoting a more open discussion of death and dying?

Thanatology: The Study of Death and Dying

Over the past 30 years, public and professional awareness of the dying person's experience has increased dramatically. "Death with dignity!" has become a major rallying cry. Interest in the field of **thanatology**—the study of death (*thanatos* is the Greek word for "death")—has grown. In recent years university centers have been established to study dying, death, grief, and bereavement across cultures. Daniel Leviton and Robert Kastenbaum established one of the first such centers (Strack & Feifel, 2003). In 2006, Kastenbaum released the newest edition of *The Psychology of Death*, which he first authored four decades ago. Death awareness advocates assert that the power to control one's own dying process is a basic human right. They point out that in the United States, the majority of those who die spend part of their final year in a nursing home or hospital, often alone and in pain. Allowing someone to die naturally often involves a team of professionals who must make a conscious decision whether to continue medical treatment. Some professionals draw a distinction between ordinary and extraordinary treatment, contending that ordinary measures such as supplying nutrition and hydration should be continued, whereas extraordinary treatment such as dialysis with a kidney machine and artificial maintenance of blood circulation may be halted if the case is hopeless. Death-with-dignity advocates insist that aggressive medical care—the norm that life must be maintained at all costs—prevents people from dying quickly and naturally.

The "healthy dying" quest has led some *thanatologists* to expound on the good, acceptable, or self-actualized

death (Kastenbaum, 2007). According to this view, it is not enough for death to be reasonably free of pain and trauma. Instead, it is argued, individuals suffering from a terminal illness should be able to select the particular type of death that they believe is consistent with their total lifestyle, such as a romantic death, a brave death, or a death that integrates and confirms the person's unique identity (Berger, 2006).

Overall, it seems that more people are trying to take back control of the time, place, and circumstances of their death (*cryopreservation* is an extreme example of this tendency). We are granting *powers of attorney* and making *advance directives;* purchasing cemetery plots, customized caskets, and gravestones; executing wills and *living wills;* and so on. Some choose to leave the hospital to die at home. Many are giving family members, same-sex partners, or close friends the power to terminate medical treatment when they themselves can no longer make such decisions. An **advance directive** is a legal document that allows a person to state explicit instructions about end-of-life care ahead of time. In a number of states, death-with-dignity advocates have secured the passage of laws that provide for the drawing up of a **living will**—a legal document that expresses an individual's wishes regarding medical care (such as refusal of "heroic measures" to prolong his or her life in the event of terminal illness) in case the person becomes incapacitated and unable to participate in decisions about his or her medical care (see the *More Information You Can Use* box, "An Example of a Living Will").

The 1994 deaths of Jacqueline Kennedy Onassis and Richard Nixon, both of whom rejected medical treatment that could have prolonged their lives, have accelerated changes in Americans' approach to death (Scott, 1994). Dr. Phillip Nitschke, a long-time activist and campaigner for assisted suicide, has developed a "peaceful pill" made from common household products for those who want to end their lives without a medical professional present. Dr. Nitschke states, "At a certain age you become old enough to understand about death, and if your life is no longer worth living according to your estimation, you have the right to give it away" (International Task Force, 2005). These people and events draw a great deal of attention to the right-to-die movement. But as with every great moral issue, there is another side: Other activists and thinkers oppose taking one's own life or assisting others to do so, and that perspective is supported by a majority of the clergy, who pose questions such as "Is this method one of killing or caring?" (Sheldon, 2005).

Questions

How would you describe the study of thanatology? Do you believe firmly in prolonging life or not? Why?

MORE INFORMATION YOU CAN USE

An Example of a Living Will

To my family, my physician, my lawyer and all others whom it may concern: Death is as much a reality as birth, growth, maturity, and old age. It is the one certainty of life. If the time comes when I can no longer take part in decisions for my own future, let this statement stand as an expression of my wishes and directions, while I am still of sound mind.

If at such a time the situation should arise in which there is no reasonable expectation of my recovery from extreme physical or mental disability, I direct that I be allowed to die and not be kept alive by medications, artificial means, or "heroic measures." I do, however, ask that medication be mercifully administered to me to alleviate suffering even though this may shorten my remaining life.

This statement is made after careful consideration and is in accordance with my strong convictions and beliefs. I want the wishes and directions here expressed carried out to the extent permitted by law. Insofar as they are not legally enforceable, I hope that those to whom this Will is addressed will regard themselves morally bound by these provisions.

Signed _____

Date _____

Witness _____

Witness _____

Copies of this request have been given to _____

_____

Source: From Judy Oaks & Gene Ezell, *Dying and Death: Coping, Caring, Understanding* (Scottsdale, AZ: Gorsuch Scarisbrick, 1993), p. 197. Reprinted by permission of Judy Oaks Davidson.

The Right-to-Die Movement

"Healthy dying" has become a more controversial issue in the United States, especially after the *New York Times* published an article about Jo Roman, a 62-year-old artist with terminal cancer who took her own life with an overdose of medication after gathering close friends around her for a celebration before she died (Johnston, 1979). Then Dr. Jack Kevorkian began to help people with terminal illness end their lives, although his efforts were curtailed by a prison sentence. The disputes in the Terri Schindler-Schiavo case became national news in 2005. Gallup polls in 2007 indicated that more than half of those surveyed agreed that physician-assisted suicide should be allowed when a person has an incurable disease and is in great pain. (Perhaps at the heart of the Schiavo controversy was the fact that although she had brain damage and needed a feeding tube to survive, she was not terminally ill—and had not completed a living will expressing her wishes.) As Dr. Jack Kevorkian was released from prison in 2007 after serving eight years for second-degree murder in the assisted death of a man with Lou Gehrig's disease, new polls suggested that his cause retains strong support (Padgett, 2007). In a 2005 Pew Research Center Survey, "84 percent said they approved of laws which say medical treatment that is keeping a terminally ill patient alive can be stopped, if that is what the patient desires" (Parker, 2009).

Much criticism is currently leveled at how modern technology is applied to the aged with dementia and to the terminally ill. Critics contend that too much is done for too long a time at too high a cost, all at the expense of basic human considerations and sensitivities, and that the terminally ill become the property of health-care institutions, which override individual autonomy, endurance, and dignity. Additionally, the argument is often made that ending "futile" medical care for dying patients could be an important cost-saving step in overhauling the nation's health-care system. *Futile care* is sometimes defined as "any clinical circumstance in which the doctor and consultants conclude that further treatment cannot,

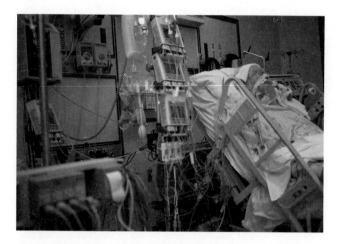

Extending Life by Extraordinary Treatment Although many people claim they would not want their lives extended by extraordinary technological means, others have not declared their wishes should such circumstances arise. Intensive care units (ICUs) and cardiac care units (CCUs) offer extraordinary means of survival. Family members often experience conflict among themselves—and even in their own minds—about making such decisions for a loved one.

within a reasonable possibility, cure, palliate, ameliorate, or restore a quality of life that would be satisfactory to the patient" (Snider & Hasson, 1993, p. 1A).

This concept of *futile care* is a serious bioethics issue because there are some proponents, such as Ezekiel Emanuel, MD, PhD, and head of the Department of Bioethics at The Clinical Center of the National Institutes of Health, warns about overutilization of health care in the United States, and who supports rationing for those who are costing the U.S. medical system too much. His proposal to allocate resources to younger adults and prioritize their needs is the "complete lives system," and at this time, his theory is limited to the demand for organs and influenza vaccines in a pandemic (Persad, Wertheimer, & Emanuel, 2009b).

> The complete lives system lets us consider the morally relevant factors at work in the choice between providing three 60-year-olds with a treatment that would save their lives for 15 years each or providing it to a 30-year-old and extending her life by 45 years. Youngest-first and providing individuals a complete life counsels saving the one. (Persad, Wertheimer, & Emanuel, 2009a)

In a somewhat related way, under the *Patient Protection and Affordable Care Act* (national health-care plan) passed in 2010, any American turning age 65 is eligible for an annual physical paid for by Medicare, at which time the physician and patient are encouraged to discuss end-of-life care (confidentially) as a component of retirement planning (Phipps, 2011).

Physician-Assisted Suicide (PAS) Requests for physician-assisted suicide are not new, and most physi-

cians are likely to face this challenge. Physicians say they have a problem deciding what medical measures they should undertake. At times, patients and their families are so distraught, frightened, and conflicted that they will not or cannot say what they want done. The decision the family must make often presents an avoidance-avoidance conflict in which people's emotionally charged thoughts tend to freeze: Do we attempt to save our loved one at all costs, even though this person may never regain consciousness or be the person he or she used to be? How can we let this person die whom we love so dearly?

Physicians often withhold antibiotics from terminally ill and senile patients who develop respiratory infections. It is often the nurses who shoulder much of the responsibility for carrying out such decisions. The nurses might decide not to call the physician after the onset of fever, or they might influence the physician to opt for nontreatment. Significantly, the decisions on end-of-life care fall to the physician, family, or a court-appointed guardian (Ferrini & Ferrini, 2008). Results vary, but surveys reveal that about half of the physicians in the United States support assisted-suicide legislation, and about one-third would be willing to participate in hastening the death of a terminally ill patient. One survey of almost 2,000 physicians found that more than one in six of the respondents had received requests for physician-assisted suicide. About 6 percent had helped a patient commit suicide, either by pills or by lethal injection (Ferrini & Ferrini, 2008).

Some of the most painful decisions physicians confront concern newborns. With today's neonatal technology, about half of the infants born weighing 750 grams (1 pound 10 ounces) can be saved. However, there is a high risk that they will have serious physical and/or mental handicaps. Another dilemma concerns infants born with life-threatening complications, such as a blockage of the intestinal tract or a heart defect, that require surgical correction. A somewhat similar issue is posed by newborns with *meningomyelocele*, a defect in which the spinal cord protrudes outside the body. If untreated by surgery, such infants develop a spinal infection and die; if treated, they often suffer paralysis and incontinence. All these cases entail complex bioethical decisions about whether severely handicapped infants should be treated so they can survive.

In 1986, the American Medical Association (AMA) said that doctors could ethically withhold all means of life-prolonging medical treatment from patients in irreversible comas, even if death was not imminent (Malcolm, 1986; Zimmerman et al., 1986). Withholding such therapy is permitted only when a patient's coma is beyond doubt irreversible and there are adequate safeguards to confirm the accuracy of the diagnosis. Although the opinion of the 271,000-member association did not make such an action mandatory for doctors, it opened the way for them to withdraw life-prolonging treatment with less fear of being taken to court and to use the opinion as a defense if they are challenged. Two doctors hired by Terri Schiavo's husband agreed that she was in an irreversible coma, but other doctors hired by her parents said she was not. Such a diagnosis, then, is complex and not clear-cut. The debate on these issues has spread to the treatment of patients with other terminal illnesses, as well.

Probably most controversial of all is the issue of **euthanasia,** or "good death," which is sometimes referred to as mercy killing. The practice of euthanasia goes back to ancient history. *Passive euthanasia* allows death to occur by withholding or removing treatments that would prolong life. In *involuntary euthanasia,* someone in the family or a legally empowered person decides to withhold or remove medical treatments when the patient is medically considered brain dead. In *voluntary euthanasia,* the patient grants permission to remove treatments that would prolong life. Some people have prepared and signed a living will that states the person's wishes about medical treatment in case she or he becomes unable to participate in decisions regarding medical care (see the *More Information You Can Use* box on page 609, "An Example of a Living Will").

In Australia, the Northern Territory became the first state in the world to legalize voluntary active euthanasia under the *Rights of the Terminally Ill Act of 1995,* yet in 1997 the Federal Parliament overturned this legislation. In the Netherlands, euthanasia has been widely practiced since 1973 and was legalized by the Dutch Parliament in 2000 (International Task Force, 2005). As of 2011, active euthanasia is also legal in Belgium and Luxembourg (Deliens & van der Wal, 2003). In North Korea, babies of mixed races and those born with disabilities are euthanized, and pregnant women in prison are forced to undergo abortion (Muntarbhorn, 2005). In the United States, Oregon (1998) and Washington (2008) residents passed *Death with Dignity* laws that allow adult residents who are terminally ill to use prescriptions from their physicians for self-administered, lethal doses of medications (Euthanasia Research & Guidance Organization, 2011; Oregon Department of Human Services, 2008). In *Gonzales v. Oregon,* the U.S. Supreme Court allowed Oregon's PAS law to stand (Greenhouse, 2006). From 1997 through 2010, official reports state, 572 residents took lethal medications to end their lives. In both states, more patients requested and were provided with lethal medications but did not use them (Oregon Public Health Division, 2011; Washington State Department of Health, 2010). The majority who chose PAS tended to be white, married or widowed, between 55 and 84, with a college education, and diagnosed with cancer or amyotrophic lateral sclerosis (ALS, or Lou Gehrig's disease). Most patients chose to die at home and were under hospice care.

Although Oregonians passed this legislation by 51 percent, many people still oppose physician-assisted suicide. Californians, for example, did not pass a third proposed physician-assisted suicide bill. The PAS proponents in California attribute their latest defeat to the opposition of the Catholic Church and of the disabled and those advocating for them (Ertelt, 2007). Most religious groups maintain their right-to-life position. The Roman Catholic Church regularly reaffirms its condemnation of euthanasia, while stating that individuals in certain circumstances have the right to renounce extraordinary and burdensome life-support systems (Ertelt, 2007). One quality-of-care result of the assisted-suicide law in Oregon is that doctors report that they are more attentive to patient pain and depressive symptoms, and they are more likely to refer terminal patients to hospice care (Niemeyer, 2005).

As we have seen, over the next few decades there will be far greater numbers of increasingly disabled and frail elderly citizens in countries worldwide who will need government-sponsored health care, long-term residential care, and hospice services. The "mercy killing" of a man in the early stages of Alzheimer's and of another with dementia was approved in Holland. In addition, the "mercy killing" of newborns and infants with severe medical conditions has been reported in Holland, France, Great Britain, Italy, Spain, Germany, Sweden, Switzerland, and North Korea (Verhagen & Sauer, 2005). In 2005, a Dutch "assessment committee" decided that the nation's euthanasia law should apply to those "suffering with living" (Sheldon, 2005). Doctors in the Netherlands proposed the *Groningen Protocol,* whereby a committee of doctors and lawyers is charged with making decisions about life or death for seriously ill newborns and other severely handicapped or disabled people (Hewitt, 2004). Under this protocol, physicians must follow specific criteria when they and the patients' families consider ending the lives of critically ill newborns and severely disabled children and teens (Verhagen, van der Hoeven, van Meerveld, & Sauer, 2007). Some pediatric physicians and neonatologists are highly critical of this form of active euthanasia (Jotkowitz & Glick, 2006).

One wonders where this slippery slope might lead. A number of opposing concerns and attitudes have converged in the right-to-die/right-to-life dialog. Americans tend to favor a quick transition between life and death. Many people also have a profound fear of being held captive as "vegetables" sustained entirely by life-support equipment. There is a pervasive fear and intolerance of pain and a growing expectation that one should be without pain in the ordinary course of life. Medical staff regularly use pain scales to help patients convey the intensity of their pain so that it can be properly alleviated (see Figure 19.1) (Leleszi & Lewandowski, 2005). Some physicians have cautioned that focusing on patient autonomy

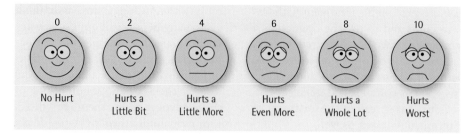

FIGURE 19.1 Wong-Baker FACES Pain Rating Scale In the hospital, and especially in hospice and palliative care, nursing staff and trained volunteers pay close attention to the discomfort level of seriously ill patients. This pain rating scale is often on display so that a patient of nearly any age can easily choose the face that best describes his or her own pain, whereupon suitable medications can be dispensed to ease pain.
Source: Hockenberry M. J., Wilson D., Winkelstein M. L.: *Wong's Essentials of Pediatric Nursing,* ed. 7, St. Louis, 2005, p. 1259. Used with permission. Copyright, Mosby.

and death with dignity can lead doctors and patients to make clinically inappropriate decisions. They warn of the perils of taking patients at their word. Like patients in great pain, depressed patients are particularly likely to ask that they be allowed to die. Psychiatric illness, including symptoms of deep despair and hopelessness, can severely distort rational decision making.

Concern has also been expressed that legalizing physician-assisted suicide for the terminally ill opens the door to widespread abuse. Studies conducted in Oregon and the Netherlands found that among patients suffering from HIV/AIDS, there was an increased percentage of euthanized individuals (Battin, van der Heide, Ganzini, van der Wal, & Onwuteaka-Philipsen, 2007; Vastag, 2007). Carlo Giovanardi, the Italian Parliamentary minister, stated his concern for the growing acceptance of euthanasia in Europe (Smith, W. J., 2006). Some ethicists fear that the patients most at risk will be those who are unable to speak for themselves—the millions of elderly people suffering from dementia, Alzheimer's, Parkinson's, and other diseases in nursing homes and the severely disabled of all ages.

In 1983 a U.S. presidential commission reached a consensus that decisions on whether to continue life-sustaining medical treatment should generally be left to mentally competent patients. Family members could make similar decisions for mentally incompetent patients. The commission said that ending a patient's life intentionally could not be sanctioned on moral grounds. Even so, doctors would be allowed to administer a pain-relieving drug that hastens death, provided that the sole reason for giving the drug was to relieve pain (Cosgrove, Nesbitt, & Bartley, 2006). Related developments include "living will" laws that afford protection against dehumanized dying and confer immunity on physicians and hospital personnel who comply with a patient's wishes. Linda Emanuel (1998) proposed a model of response to the patient who requests

physician-assisted suicide (PAS) (see Table 19.1). She describes a series of steps to assess a patient's competency to make such a decision; these steps include evaluation for depression and other psychiatric conditions, listing goals of care, providing full information to the patient, physician consultation with professional colleagues, following care plans, removing all unwanted life-support interventions, and securing maximum relief of suffering. The patient would ultimately have the right to decline nutrition and hydration and any regular oral intake (Blackburn & Dulmus, 2007).

Questions

What is our nation's stance on the issues of euthanasia and physician-assisted suicide? What are some other nations' perspectives and practices on these crucial issues?

Suicide In many countries, suicide is one of the leading causes of death, and the number of annual U.S. suicides increased nearly 18 percent from 2000 (29,350) to 2007 (34,598), increasing mainly among people aged 45 to 64 (American Foundation for Suicide Prevention, 2011). Suicide is the second leading cause of death among American college students, and it is the third leading cause of death among all youth aged 15 to 24 (only accidents and homicide claim more young lives) (American Foundation for Suicide Prevention, 2008). *Suicidologists* report that in many societies, because of the stigma associated with suicide, many cases are reported as accidents or as deaths from an undetermined cause. (Tragically, we have also become accustomed to hearing about "suicide bombers" in Israel, Afghanistan, Iraq, and other parts of the world—such as bus and subway "suicide bombers" in Spain and Great Britain—whose intent is to kill many innocent persons while committing suicide.) In addition to the

TABLE 19.1 Emanuel's Eight-Step Approach to the Patient Who Requests Physician-Assisted Suicide

Step	Suggested Procedure
1	**Assess for depression:** If Yes, then treat for depression. If No, then see Step 2.
2	**Assess for decision-making capacity:** If No, then assess for treatable causes; if none, seek proxy. If Yes, continue with Step 3.
3	**Engage in structural deliberation including advance care planning. Affirm other form of comfort and control:** Request for PAS may be dropped. Provide care as discussed in patient/proxy. Request for PAS may continue. See Step 4.
4	**Establish and treat root cause(s) of request: physical, personal, or social. Hospice philosophy, palliative care skills, as appropriate:** Request dropped. Provide care as discussed in patient/proxy. Request continues. See Step 5.
5	**Ensure full information on consequences, risk, and responsibilities; attempt to dissuade from PAS:** Request dropped. Provide care as discussed with patient/proxy. Request continues. See Step 6.
6	**Involve consultants or institutional committee as appropriate:** Request dropped. Provide care as discussed with patient/proxy. Request continues. See Step 7.
7	**Review adherence to goals and care plan, supporting removal of unwanted intervention and providing full-comfort care:** Request dropped. Provide care as discussed with patient/proxy. Request continues. See Step 8.
8	**Decline PAS (all states except Oregon and Washington) explaining why and affirming alternatives.** Provide care as discussed with patient/proxy.

Source: Linda Emanuel (1998). "Facing Requests for Physician-Assisted Suicide: Toward a Practical and Principled Clinical Skill Set." *Journal of the American Medical Association* (JAMA), Vol. 280, No. 7. Copyright © 1998 American Medical Association. All Rights Reserved.

emotional burden for those whom a suicide leaves behind, there is an economic burden because most life insurance policies do not cover those who take their own lives. The social isolation of survivors is also greater than that experienced with any other cause of death, as was expressed by the bereaved mother of a child who died from a self-inflicted gunshot wound:

> People I had known for years stopped speaking to me. They couldn't even look me in the eyes in the grocery store. All of a sudden we had no friends. People didn't call, visit, or invite us over. They treated us like we had some dreaded disease. (Oaks & Ezell, 1993, p. 209)

To commit suicide is to intentionally kill oneself. The National Institute of Mental Health (NIMH) has defined three concepts pertaining to suicide (Oaks & Ezell, 1993, p. 209):

- *Suicide ideas.* This pertains to the observation or inference that someone might be moving in the direction of taking his or her life. The person might seem to be suggesting it, writing about it, talking about it—but does not carry it out.
- *Suicide attempts.* This pertains to the situation in which a person performs an overt life-threatening behavior with the intent of taking his or her own life (e.g., cutting wrists, jumping off a bridge, overdosing on pills). This may become a repetitive behavior with the intent of communicating a message to a loved one and may represent a call for help rather than true intent to end her or his life.
- *Completed suicide.* This pertains to all persons who were successful in taking their own lives.

Cultural attitudes toward suicide vary. They range from the early Christian view that only God can take a life, to viewing the victim as insane or weak, to considering suicide the honorable choice when confronted with capture, defeat, or disgrace (this was the attitude of Japanese *kamikaze* pilots in World War II). Criminologists, on the other hand, are likely to take the position that the person who commits suicide is mentally ill and has a flawed, deviant mind, as when an ex-spouse murders his own family and then takes his own life or when terrorists are bent on destroying themselves as well as others.

Who Commits Suicide and Why?   How do we classify the thousands of suicides committed every year (see Figure 19.2)? Although many more females *attempt* suicide, more males actually *succeed* at taking their own lives (National Institute of Mental Health, 2008). Suicide is the eleventh leading cause of death in the United States. Males 75 and older are at higher risk than others; they may feel depressed over the loss of physical strength, may be recently widowed or realize that fewer and fewer of their loved ones are still alive, may recently have been diagnosed with a terminal illness or Alzheimer's disease, or may be overmedicated. For young males, common causes include the pressures associated with peer acceptance (reported to have been a factor in the shootings at

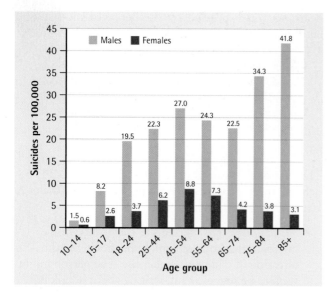

FIGURE 19.2 U.S. Suicide Rates by Age and Gender: 2007 Older males are disproportionately likely to die by suicide. Individuals aged 65 and older accounted for almost 13 percent of all suicide deaths in 2007. White males aged 65 and older have the highest rates of suicide. In all age groups, rates of suicide among males far exceed rates among females. Each suicide affects many survivors.

Source: Centers for Disease Control and Prevention. (2010, February 24). National Center for Health Statistics: Health Data Interactive. Mortality by underlying cause among children: US/State, 1990–2007 (Source: NVSS); Mortality by underlying and multiple cause, ages 18+: US, 1981–2007 (Source: NVSS). Retrieved from http://www.cdc.gov/nchs/hdi.htm

Columbine High School), job goals, loneliness, and/or poor health. In one case,

> His parents were moving to Houston because the father had been transferred by his employer. He said he was not going with them. He was an honor student, involved in sports and extracurricular activities. He showed his friends his gun, but no one took him seriously enough to tell school personnel. He walked to the front of the classroom, put the gun in his mouth, and pulled the trigger. Postvention assistance included individual counseling for some students and teachers, participation in support groups led by professional counselors, and a memorial service held at the school. The event was so traumatic, it was weeks before the school atmosphere returned to normal. (Martin & Dixon, 1986, p. 265)

People of Native American heritage (including Alaska Natives) have the highest age-adjusted rates of suicide in the United States. Non-Hispanic whites had the second highest rates of suicide. The rates for African American, Hispanic, and Asian people are about half the rates for whites and Native Americans (Kung et al., 2008). However, the rate of suicide among young Hispanics is of great concern, because Hispanic youth are the fastest-growing segment of the population in the United States.

Suicide is the third leading cause of death among Hispanics aged 10 to 24 (Eaton et al., 2006).

One study in particular looked at suicide rates within various occupations. Among the 32 occupational groups studied, the results revealed that occupations with higher than average suicide rates included dentists, artists, machinists, auto mechanics, and carpenters (Stack, 2001). It is generally believed that Christmastime and springtime have the highest rates of suicide. Yet one study of 678 cases found no correlation between time of year and number of suicides (Bennett & Collins, 2000). The most vulnerable times are during "rites of passage," such as graduation, anniversaries, birthdays, retirement, major family holidays, or the death of a spouse or child. Those who are divorced, widowed, and separated commit suicide more than those who remain married and have children. White males during their postretirement years commit suicide at much higher rates than any other group. Since the early 1980s, the rates of teenage suicide have increased significantly. Teens are at most risk of committing suicide after a "crisis" of rejection or humiliation. Youth with nonheterosexual orientation are also at higher risk for suicide (Bridge, Goldstein, & Brent, 2006). Consider the case of Tyler Clementi, an 18-year-old violinist in his first year at Rutgers University, who committed suicide in 2010 by jumping off a bridge after he had been secretly filmed in his dorm room during an intimate encounter, which was circulated live-stream on the Internet (Foderaro, 2010; Schwartz, 2010).

Kastenbaum (1991, 2007) argues that suicide victims view suicide as a reunion with God or a loved one, as a rest or refuge, as getting back at or hurting someone, as a penalty for failure, as a way to get attention, or as the loss of a life-sustaining drive. Each year over 800,000 people in the United States attempt suicide. Some estimate that there are 25 suicide attempts for each death by suicide (American Association of Suicidology, 2010). Those who succeed leave unbelievable shock and grief behind. If someone exhibits several of the signs listed in Table 19.2, it is time to talk to the person, demonstrate love and concern, convince the person to get counseling, and make sure that any weapons in the home are locked up or removed.

Questions

Who is most likely to attempt suicide, and what behavioral changes are often noted prior to suicide? What life events are potential triggers to suicide attempts?

The Hospice Movement

Some have called death the "undiscovered country." At its border, hospice programs provide an affordable

TABLE 19.2 Warning Signs of Suicide

Signs Among Elderly	Behavioral Signs Typical for Teens	Environmental Signs	Verbal Cues
Severe physical illness	Lack of energy or increased fatigue	Previous suicide attempts by a family member or friend	Direct statements that may need immediate attention:
Chronic pain	Acting bored or disinterested	Problems at school	"I want to die."
Marked change in body image	Tearful sadness	Family violence	"I don't want to live anymore."
Loss of significant emotional ties	Difficulty concentrating or making decisions, confusion	Sexual abuse	"Life sucks and I want to get out."
Decrease in level of socialization	Silent or withdrawn	Major family change	"I won't be a problem much longer."
Lack of a religious faith	Angry and destructive behaviors		"Nothing matters anymore."
Physical disability	Less interest in usual activities		
Cognitive deficiencies	Giving away prized possessions		
Change in or loss of familiar surroundings	Poor school performance		
Isolation	Dwelling on death in creative activities, such as music, poetry, and artwork		
Loss of functional capacities	Difficulty sleeping or change in sleeping patterns		
Reduction of responsibilities	Increased thrill-seeking and risky behaviors		
	Increased use of drugs and alcohol		
	Change in appearance or cleanliness		
	Change in appetite or eating habits		
	Suddenly cheerful after a depression		

Source: Gary J. Kennedy, ed., *Suicide and Depression in Late Life*, p. 88. Copyright © 1996 by John Wiley & Sons, Inc. Reprinted by permission of John Wiley & Sons, Inc.

alternative for dealing with pain and the end of life in a dignified, graceful fashion. In medieval times, a hospice was a place where sick and weary travelers could seek comfort and care before continuing on their journey. The **hospice** of today likewise provides comfort and care, but with the knowledge that the recipients are nearing the end of their life's journey—that they are dying. The approach is modeled after St. Christopher's Hospice in England, which has been in operation since 1967. It entails a variety of programs designed to afford an alternative to conventional hospital care for the terminally ill, especially cancer patients:

Hospice neither hastens nor postpones death. It affirms life, recognizes dying as a part of the normal process of living, and focuses on maintaining the quality of remaining life. (P. North, 1998)

Polls show that most people are less terrified of dying at home than they are of dying an agonizing, painful, impersonal, and undignified death among machines and strangers. Although few people can be accorded a "perfect death," most can be free of pain; and the fear of terror, isolation, and chaos can be replaced by calm and control. Many hospice proponents believe that rather than debating the merits and drawbacks of euthanasia and assisted suicide, the nation should be more concerned

about care for the dying (Marx, 2005). There were an estimated 5,000 hospice programs in the United States in 2009 (National Hospice and Palliative Care Organization [NHPCO], 2010) (see Figure 19.3). It should be noted that hospice is a concept of care, not a place (Hospice Foundation of America, 2005). (This is why we speak of someone as being "in hospice," rather than being "in a hospice.") A typical hospice staff includes nurses, members of the clergy, social workers, physicians, home health aides, and a host of volunteers.

The hospice program takes a positive attitude toward dying, but the emphasis falls on "comfort-care" rather than on prolonging life. Comfort-care involves the aggressive treatment of symptoms, both physical and emotional, through the use of psychological, religious, and nutritional counseling, antidepressant medications, and high-dose morphine preparations (designed to free patients from the severe and recurrent pain that frequently accompanies terminal cancer). Significantly, a study of patients at major cancer centers reveals that nearly half are reluctant to report their pain. Others are reluctant to take pain medication for fear that when their pain becomes truly intolerable, it will then be ineffective. And others fear that narcotic painkillers will result in addiction. Many physicians share these misconceptions. Yet much can be done to ease the pain and suffering of patients (and their families) with cancer, AIDS,

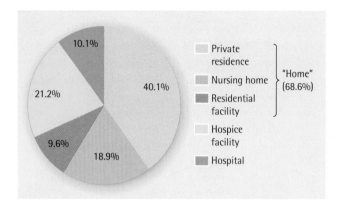

FIGURE 19.3 Hospice Care in America: 2009 Over two-thirds of hospice patients chose to die in a private residence, nursing home, or other residential facility, whereas about 58 percent of the general population die in a traditional hospital setting (ICU, CCU, etc.). More than one million Americans died in hospice care in 2009.
Source: National Hospice and Palliative Care Organization (NHPCO). (2010, October). NHPCO Facts and figures: Hospice care in America. Retrieved from www.nhpco.org/research

and degenerative neuromuscular disorders (NHPCO, 2010). Children, too, can be well served by hospice care (Himelstein, Hilden, Morstad Boldt, & Weissman, 2004).

Most hospice programs are centered on caring for the dying person at home. Reportedly, most people say that if they were terminally ill and had only six months to live, they would prefer to receive care and die in their own home or in that of a family member (see Figure 19.3). In 2009, of all Americans who died, about one-third died at home. For patients under hospice care, about two-thirds died at home (NHPCO, 2010). More hospice services are offered now through hospitals as well. In a hospital hospice setting, families are included as part of the treatment, visiting hours are unlimited, and day beds are available in the patient's room so that family members can stay overnight to be with a loved one as desired. Physicians, nurses, social workers, clergy, and volunteers provide emotional and spiritual assistance as well as medical care.

But the concept of hospice is not so much a place as it is a program or mode of care. It seeks to give dying patients personalized care and greater independence and control over their lives so that they do not have to surrender themselves to the care of impersonal bureaucratic organizations. One hospice had a client whose one wish was to walk again, so the hospice arranged the services of a physical therapist who helped the man regain his ability to walk. In sum, the hospice movement undertakes to restore dignity to death. The focus on death does not ignore life:

One of those values is that, as death approaches, life is equally precious to what it was in more active days. These values affirm that even in dying there can be

healing and [palliative care] strives for that. The end of life is the time when the patient can come to closure with this life and bring completion to relationships, reconciliation with problems of the past, and a feeling of spiritual peace. Allowing for these activities contributes to a truly "good death." (Dunlop, 2007)

Advocates of the hospice approach say that it is difficult for medical professionals taking care of patients in hospital settings to accept the inevitability of death. Hospitals are geared to curing illness and prolonging life. An incurable case is evidence of medical failure. Hospice proponents say an alternative-care arrangement is required—one that accepts the inevitability of death and provides for the needs of the dying and their families. Hospice programs hope to make dying less emotionally traumatic for both patient and loved ones. Much effort is directed toward helping family members face the problems that surround terminal illness.

The visiting home-care staff also assists the family with bathing, changing bedding, securing all necessary medical equipment, informing the hospice nurse or physician when the patient is in great discomfort and may need a medication change, sitting for hours with the patient or family members during reminiscence, or discussing many spiritual questions about what to expect during the stages of dying and death. With hospice assistance, the patient and family have time to notify family members, organize finances, come to terms with spiritual beliefs, and make funeral and burial or cremation arrangements. Staff members give the immediate family members time for a brief respite, as needed. Each patient and family is treated with dignity and warmth. After the patient dies, staffers make arrangements to return any borrowed medical equipment. A bereavement follow-up service maintains contact with the family in the period following the loved one's death. Most major health insurance plans, including Medicare, now cover virtually the entire cost of treatment in hospices that meet standards set by the U.S. Department of Health and Human Services. Even so, there are some patients (and families) who feel anxious about death and dying and choose to be in a typical hospital setting getting aggressive medical treatment for their last days of life.

The newest model of end-of-life care is *perinatal hospice*—for expectant parents of a fetus with a life-threatening condition. Prenatal testing has become routine, and it is known that newborns with certain diagnoses survive only hours, days, or weeks (Ramer-Chrastek & Thygeson, 2005). Some pregnant women do not choose partial-birth abortion in such circumstances and deliver the baby. These families are in urgent need of extensive comfort-care; information through birth, delivery, and after; and emotional support, as well as pertinent medical support. Profound grief surrounds the loss of a baby.

Perinatal Hospice Programs   Recently hospice has become available to pregnant women who are giving birth to a child with a severe chromosomal disorder or other fatal diagnosis. For those who choose to give birth, trained volunteers and medical staff prepare them for coping with this profound loss. Some babies are stillborn, and others might live for weeks before dying; but relatives get to see and hold the child as a member of their family.

With perinatal hospice, the family is encouraged to see and name the baby, cherish the baby, sing to the baby, include the baby as part of the family, and begin the process of grieving and healing (Dahlstrom, 2008).

Questions

What is the philosophy of the hospice approach to dying from a terminal illness? Who is most likely to be eligible for these services, and what services are provided?

THE DYING PROCESS

Throughout history, human societies seem to have given death their most elaborate and reverent attention (Ariès, 1978, 1981; Robben, 2006). Some of the world's most gigantic constructions, its most splendid works of art, and its most elaborate rituals have been associated with death. The elaborate funeral mass and burial of Pope John Paul II at the Vatican in Rome was witnessed by at least 1 billion people via TV, with hundreds of thousands from around the world making the pilgrimage in his honor. More than 500,000 years ago, ceremonial rituals for burying the dead were being employed by Peking Man. And we still are awed by the Egyptian pyramids (and fascinated by King Tut), the huge European burial mound of Silbury Hill, the towering Pyramid Tomb of the High Priest in the Central American Yucatán forest, the beehive tombs at Mycenae, the Taj Mahal, more than 40,000 megalithic burial mounds of northwestern Europe, and areas of Stonehenge in England (once a ritual burial ground for chieftains and leaders) ("English Heritage," 2005).

Monotheistic world religions—Judaism, Christianity, and Islam—put an end to the practice of burying or cremating the elite dead with wives, concubines, slaves, horses, jewels, armor, and other luxuries in hopes of guaranteeing their enjoyment and comfort on their journey to the next world (Ashenburg, 2002). However, in a paradigm shift in thinking, Christianity changed the elaborate rituals surrounding the act of dying, mourning, and funerals, infusing them with new conviction that all people are equal in the eyes of God and that death is a release into a better life with God. The same Mass of Christian Burial is said for everyone, rich or poor (Ashenburg, 2002; Robben, 2006). Such rituals, including many prayers, serve to honor the deceased, usher the deceased's soul through a transitional realm of purgatory to heaven, and reintegrate a family or community after a crisis. The American funeral industry emerged after the Civil War when it became acceptable to embalm bodies in order that loved ones could travel and view the body for final farewells (Laderman, 2003). One of the greatest illustrations of such devotion occurred in 1865 after the assassination of Abraham Lincoln. While the funeral train bearing the embalmed body of the slain President made its steady, 1,700-mile journey through more than a dozen American cities, some 30 million mourners paused to pay their respects as the train made its way toward a final resting place in Springfield, Illinois (The Lincoln Institute, 2011). Today in industrialized societies, we rarely have personal contact with the deceased because the funeral industry has become a ubiquitous presence that exerts subtle (and not-so-subtle) influence. Local funeral directors and clergy typically offer loved ones comfort and guidance with burial plans, specific rituals, and religious ceremonies, but in 2010 the cost of a funeral and burial averaged $6,500, which is unaffordable for many families (National Funeral Directors Association, 2010).

Defining Death

To leaven a somber subject with a little wit, comic George Carlin said, "Death is caused by swallowing small amounts of saliva over a long period of time." For centuries, using only sheer observation, some just might have thought of that as a plausible cause of death. The earliest biblical sources, as well as English common law, considered a person's ability to breathe independently to be the prime index of life. This view coincided with the physiological state of the organism. In the past, the absence of spontaneous breathing or of a heartbeat resulted in the prompt death of the brain. Conversely, destruction of the brain produced prompt cessation of respiration and circulation.

Over the past 50 years, technological advances have rendered these traditional definitions of death obsolete. In 1962, Johns Hopkins University physicians developed a coordinated method of resuscitation by artificial ventilation, heart compression (CPR), and electric shock (defibrillation) by which many victims of cardiac arrest can be saved. Another advance has been the invention of the mechanical respirator, which sustains breathing when the brain is no longer sending out the proper signals to the lungs. Still another innovation has been the use of an artificial pacemaker to induce regular heartbeat after failure of the heart's own electrical conduction system. And dialysis machines prolong the lives of patients suffering kidney failure. Successful organ transplants have prolonged life, usually because a person diagnosed as "brain dead" had earlier stipulated that in the event of his or her death, organs could be transplanted to prolong the life of others (or because the family has agreed, absent such documentation). As medical procedures are invented that can prolong life, determining when death has occurred becomes more complex (Blackburn & Dulmus, 2007; Truog, 2004). (See the *Further Developments* box, "End of Life: Who Decides?")

These life-extending technologies have compelled courts and legislatures to grapple with new definitions of death. The need to accept brain death as one standard has now been acknowledged in most states and endorsed by the American Medical Association, by the American Bar Association, and, in 1981, by the President's Commission for the Study of Ethical Problems in Medicine and the *Uniform Determination of Death Act*. **Brain death** occurs when there is no activity in the brain. When the thinking part of the brain (cortex) and the thalamus (which connects the brain stem to the cortex) no longer function, the patient is considered brain dead ("When Does the Brain Go Blank," 2005). The first stage of total brain death is *cerebral death* (the cerebral cortex is no longer functioning). However, the patient might still have a functioning lower brain stem (which regulates breathing, pulse, blood pressure, and other vital functions). A series of landmark court decisions have upheld the validity of the brain-death criterion. Many of these cases involved *transplantation of organs* (such as cornea, kidney, lung, liver, or heart). With organ extraction, the patient's heart is still beating so that the organs still have blood circulating, and it has been found that the patient's body reacts to the extraction (which is done without anesthesia because the patient is "brain dead").

As one might expect, efforts to define what constitutes death have fueled a continuing debate among medical professionals, bioethicists, and legal scholars (Truog, 2004). This is especially true for the estimated 15,000 individuals who exist in a **persistent vegetative state,** where the functions of the brain stem, such as breathing and circulation, remain intact, but the person has lost the higher functioning of the cerebral cortex (Ferrini & Ferrini, 2008). The patient in a persistent vegetative state has periods of sleep and wakefulness and responds to some stimuli, such as light and noise. The patient may have gag and swallowing reflexes. Some in the medical field believe that the patient does not have the capability of emotional response, cognition, or willful activity (Quill, 2004). In cases such as those of Nancy Cruzan, Karen Ann Quinlan, and Terri Schiavo, who were deemed legally alive, the courts ruled that families can allow persistent vegetative patients to die by withholding life support. The case of Terri Schiavo elicited unprecedented public attention. The general public, right-to-die groups, right-to-life groups, the legal community, the medical community, and the political community hotly expressed divergent views. The legal battles related to the Schiavo case were brought to public attention by the media and the woman's biological family, spawning further controversy and debate (Annas, 2005). In the end, a judicial decision authorizing Schiavo's husband to allow her to die by withholding life support was upheld and was enforced by the criminal justice system. The patient in this case, being rather young at the time of her collapse, had not prepared any legal documents detailing her own wishes concerning the manner of death. Consequently, if there is one positive thing to come out of Terri Schiavo's ordeal, it is that attention has been focused on the need for people to make their health-care directives known (Perry, Churchill, & Kirshner, 2005).

Confronting One's Own Death

People differ considerably in the degree to which they are consciously aware of death (Wanzer & Glenmullen, 2007). Some individuals erect formidable defenses to shield themselves from facing the reality that they too will die. In Tolstoy's story "The Death of Ivan Ilych," for example, the main character, a judge faced with his own imminent death, cannot accept the certain fact of his own end. Considering a syllogism from a book of logic, that Caius is a man, men are mortal, and therefore Caius is mortal, Ivan Ilych believes it applied to Caius, but certainly not to himself. Similarly, throughout the story other characters deny their own mortality. Worldwide, many individuals and research societies are striving to defy death. **Transhumanism** researchers are making efforts to conquer diseases, to extend the abilities of the human body by transplanting organs, using stem cells, and implanting

FURTHER DEVELOPMENTS

End of Life: Who Decides?

Most people wish for a death free of pain and suffering. Yet death is inevitable, and the best one can hope for is a "good death." Precisely what this entails varies among individuals. Although some might wish to slip away peacefully in their sleep, others might wish to be conscious and surrounded by loved ones. Yet others may wish to die a heroic death in a blaze of glory or heroic self-sacrifice. Notwithstanding our wishes, nobody knows precisely when or how she or he will die. We must all face death in our own way.

Death, however, is the end point of life. It is dying—the final process between life and death—that raises ethical, religious, medical, legal, social, and cultural questions (Searight & Gafford, 2005). How one dies and who makes that decision are issues that arise when a person faces a terminal illness, is not competent to make his or her own medical decisions, or has not prepared legal documentation of any final wishes.

Having a clear, written statement of one's final wishes can bring a measure of comfort. One might wish to draw up what are called "advance directives," such as a *living will*, an organ donor certificate, a *DNR* (Do Not Resuscitate) order or a durable **power of attorney** (a legal document designating someone to make medical decisions if the patient is unable to do so). The ethical decision one comes to is extremely important and can have a great impact on loved ones, medical staff, clergy, and the legal system. For clarity, it might be helpful to pose some hypothetical situations.

Let us suppose that a person facing a terminal illness is mentally competent and able to express his wishes. The person is facing real or anticipated suffering as the illness progresses, through physical pain and/or incapacitation. The first decision might center on the person's moral/religious beliefs about euthanasia and suicide. The suffering might be a small price to pay compared to committing a sin. A study found that older adults' end-of-life decisions were greatly influenced by their religiosity and commitment to the preservation of life, as well as by their quality of life, their fear of death, and their locus-of-control belief (Cicirelli & MacLean, 2000).

After considering the religious/moral perspective, the person might ask, "How would this affect my family?" The legal aspects of insurance and other death benefits might be taken into account—in order to provide security for one's family. What medical options are available if palliative care should become ineffective? *Palliative care* is the attempt to relieve uncomfortable symptoms and is given along with treatment for the disease.

Slightly more than half of those surveyed in a 2007 Gallup poll agreed that a doctor should be permitted to assist a patient in suicide when the person has an incurable disease and is in pain (Padgett, 2007). Physician-assisted suicide

Preparing for the End of Life Openly discussing end-of-life plans is very difficult in most families.
Source: Walt Handelsman, Copyright 2005. Tribune Media Services. Reprinted with permission.

(PAS) is legal in the states of Oregon and Washington at this writing (legislation is pending in other states). The law allows doctors to prescribe lethal doses of specific medications—but the patient must self-administer them. After more than a decade, it seems that well-educated white adults 55 and older and married or widowed persons are more likely than others to use PAS. Between 1998 and 2010, 525 Oregonians used PAS methods (Oregon Public Health Division, 2011).

Voluntarily refusing food and fluid is a legal way to end one's life. Nurses who had witnessed the deaths of patients by self-starvation were surveyed, and they rated the quality of this method of death on a scale from 0 (very bad) to 9 (very good), reporting a median score of 8 (Ganzini et al., 2003). In younger patients this method takes several days before death occurs, and for some, it was a gruesome way to die (Jacobs, 2003). *Terminal sedation* involves having a physician administer medication to induce a coma, while withholding hydration and nutrition. In 1997 the U.S. Supreme Court decided that terminal sedation is legal, but this practice raises many issues. Physicians, who take an oath to uphold life and do no harm, often find that it poses a moral dilemma. Another legal practice is the withholding of life-sustaining treatment. This practice precedes 80 percent of hospital deaths (Ferrini & Ferrini, 2008).

Most of the decisions involved in end-of-life care are very difficult. But with knowledge and forethought, one can make informed decisions. Then, it is important to share one's wishes with family members, in writing, to reduce any confusion or family conflict should such a situation arise.

microscopic computer chips, to extend life indefinitely, and to change the meaning of being human:

> Transhumanism, transcending human limitations, is a philosophy that humanity can, and should, strive to higher levels, both physically, mentally and socially. It encourages research into such areas as life extension, cryonics, nanotechnology, physical and mental enhancements, uploading human consciousness into computers and megascale engineering. (Bostrum, 2005)

Under this philosophy of human evolution and life extension, many lives have already been extended through *gerotechnology* and *regenerative medicine*. Organ transplants have become more routine and successful for prolonging life. With organ creation from a person's own stem cells, the shortage of human organs may soon be overcome. Stem-cell and gene-therapy researchers worldwide are working to prolong human lives or to enable humans to live forever—to become *posthuman*. Three American companies offer human life "preservation" in a suspended state through cryonic life-support technology; for example, the body of the famous baseball player Ted Williams has been cryogenically frozen (Sandomir, 2005). Using *cryopreservation*, a person's body is kept in a state that might be viable and treatable by future medicine. Researchers in *biostasis medicine* expect that in the future, *molecular nanotechnology* methods will be able to heal at the cellular and molecular levels.

Yet at present, in one way or another, everyone must accept the fact of their own dying and death. Indeed, a realistic acceptance of death may well be the hallmark of emotional maturity. Its meaning tends to vary from individual to individual. Some elderly visualize death as the dissolution of bodily life and the doorway to a new life—a passing into another world. Those with Western religious convictions express the belief that in death they will be reunited with loved ones who have died. Such individuals see death as transcendence to a better state of being; few say that death will entail punishment. One study using regression analysis found that self-efficacy variables (factors pertaining to a person's perception of being able to achieve desired outcomes in life) were predictors of fear of dying and fear of the unknown after death in older adults. Spiritual health efficacy variables were important predictors for women, and instrumental efficacy variables were important for men (Fry, 2003). Although individuals vary in the extent of their fear of death, it is perhaps quite normal to fear the process of dying:

> No, I'm not afraid to die—it seems to me to be a perfectly normal process. But you never know how you will feel when it comes to a showdown. I might get panicky. (Jeffers & Verwoerdt, 1969, p. 170)

And a 90-year-old man put it this way: "I'm afraid of the unknown, and if I had my druthers, I'd rather not do it" (quoted by Chase, 1995, p. B1). One of the questions most frequently asked of health practitioners about dying (incidentally, mothers about to have a baby also ask it about giving birth) is "How long is it going to take, and is it going to hurt?" Generally, younger people show greater fear of death than those 65 and over (Wanzer & Glenmullen, 2007). In one study, 96 terminally ill elders were asked how they felt about dying. One out of four indicated that they were not ready to die but that they had accepted the fact that they were dying. One-third spoke strongly about not being ready to die or willing to accept that death was imminent, and only one out of six indicated readiness and acceptance (Schroepfer, 2006). Interestingly, those who reported acceptance of their impending death believed that one's time of death was God's decision and not one's own, had no fear of death, and believed that dying may be better than living (Schroepfer, 2006).

A Life Review   Psychologist Robert N. Butler (1971) suggests that the elderly tend to take stock of their lives, to reflect and reminisce about it—a process he calls the **life review.** Often the review proceeds silently without obvious manifestations and provides a positive force

Preparing for the End of Life   Openly discussing end-of-life plans is very difficult in most families.
Source: For Better or For Worse © 2006. Lynn Johnston Productions Inc./Distributed by United Uclick. Reprinted with permission. All rights reserved.

in personality reorganization. In some cases, this process finds pathological expression in intense guilt, self-deprecation, despair, and depression. Reviewing one's life can be a response to crises of various types—such as retirement, the death of one's spouse, the death of one's elderly parents, or one's own imminent death. In Butler's opinion, the life review is an important element in an individual's overall adjustment to death, a continuation of personality development right to the very end of life. Butler's notions of life review have generally held sway for many years, although some skepticism exists (Merriam, 1993).

Nevertheless, some people engage meaningfully in the life-review process if they write autobiographical accounts of their lives, if a close family member (often a grandchild) does a videotaped interview, or if any person simply sits and listens. Life reviews can give new meaning to people's present lives by helping them understand the past more fully (Haight & Haight, 2007). The life-review process contributes to their successful aging by increasing their self-understanding, personal meaning, self-esteem, and life satisfaction (Cappeliez & O'Rourke, 2006). (*Reminiscence* and conducting *a life review* are discussed in detail in Chapter 18, and a little book called *The Handbook of Structured Life Review* [Haight & Haight, 2007], is an excellent resource.)

Changes Before Death Various investigators report that systematic psychological changes occur before death, even several months ahead of the event, in what is sometimes called the *death drop* or *terminal drop*. These changes do not appear to be a simple result of physical illness. Individuals who become seriously ill and recover apparently do not exhibit similar changes. Lieberman and Coplan (1970) report, for instance, that individuals whom they later found to be a year or less away from death showed poorer cognitive performance, lower introspective orientation, and a less aggressive and more docile self-image on personality tests than those who were three or more years away from death. Cognitive researchers also report a decline in measured intelligence and in the complexity of information processing for those who die within a year, compared with those who die several years later (Sliwinski et al., 2006). Psychomotor performance tests, depression scales, and self-report health ratings likewise have predictive value and can alert the physician to the patient's decline (American Geriatrics Society, 1996). Also, the *Berlin Aging Study* reveals that those who live into their "Fourth Age" typically experience a critical loss in intellectual functioning, higher incidence of depression, and dementia that is predictive of needing help with survival (Gerstorf et al., 2006).

Not all dying people panic when they realize their death is near. Some become nostalgic, want to see people they have not seen for a long time, want to patch up differences with loved ones, and become more sensitive to those who will be left behind. Some take the opportunity to enhance relationships and forgive long-held grudges and misunderstandings. Social workers, hospice volunteers, thanatologists, and family members report that dying patients have "other-worldly" conversations with and visitations from loved ones who have passed on. Here's what one nurse and one well-known thanatologist who collaborated with Elisabeth Kübler-Ross said:

> We had an inservice on end-of-life issues yesterday sponsored by Hospice and it's very common. Many of them also "talk" to deceased friends/relatives. I've also witnessed this many times in my career. (allnurses.com, 2008)

> My father . . . told me that my mother, his wife, *had come to him the night before*. "I was looking at all I was losing, and I'd forgotten that I was going to be with her again. I'm going to see her soon," he said. . . . "We'll be there waiting for you." (Kessler, 2010)

Questions

Is there a universal experience of dying, or is it highly individual? What is transhumanism? How does a life review benefit a dying person? Besides observing (or experiencing) physical decline, how do we know death is imminent?

Dying

Social scientists observe that modern societies attempt to control death by turning over its management to large, bureaucratic organizations (Robben, 2006). As we noted earlier, only a few generations ago, most people in the United States died at home surrounded by family and close friends. Before the twentieth century, doors on homes were built wide enough to allow a coffin to pass through them, and home parlors were designed to hold mourners. The family assumed the responsibility of laying out the corpse and otherwise preparing for the funeral. Today, in general, the nursing home, hospital, or hospice volunteers typically care for the terminally ill and manage the crisis of dying. A mortuary establishment—euphemistically called a "home"—prepares the body and makes the funeral arrangements or undertakes the cremation. There are exceptions to this among pockets of immigrants who are unaware that they are required by law to notify various authorities of any death—and some of these families still attempt to manage death and burial according to their cultural customs.

This bureaucratization of death minimizes exposure to it. The dying and the dead are segregated from others and entrusted to specialists for whom contact with death has become a routine and impersonal matter (Kamerman,

" WELCOME TO THE NEIGHBORHOOD, MR. ROGERS..."

Mr. Rogers's New Neighborhood Writers and artists often depict an afterlife in biblical images of pearly gates, a vast setting of white clouds, and throngs of saints and angels gathered around a deity. How fitting it is to imagine America's beloved favorite neighbor for over 30 years (and Presbyterian minister) being greeted so warmly to his new neighborhood.
Source: Bill Schorr. © United Features Syndicate, Inc.

1988). Being less exposed to death, we have less opportunity to learn how to cope adequately with it. Often neither the person who is dying nor family and friends understand how to deal with death. These trends concern many thanatologists, who point out that people are often ill-equipped to do the "grief work" so essential to coming to terms with the death of a loved one. Sometimes grief seems to be even more prolonged, on a massive scale, when a prominent person such as President John Kennedy or a celebrity dies an early or tragic death, as did Elvis, Marilyn Monroe, John Lennon, the Mexican American pop singer Selena, and Princess Diana. Witness the proliferation of Web sites and philanthropic foundations set up to memorialize such prominent people. But as thanatologists point out, funerals, memorial services, and other grieving rites give continuity to both family and community life.

Stages of Dying Since the 1960s, Elisabeth Kübler-Ross (1969, 1981), a Swiss-born psychiatrist who moved to the United States, contributed a good deal to the movement to restore dignity and humanity to death and to restore the process of dying to the full course of human life. She noted that when medical personnel and the family attempt to hide the fact that a patient is dying, they create a barrier that prevents everyone from preparing for death. Furthermore, the dying patient generally sees through the make-believe. Kübler-Ross found that it is better for all parties if their genuine emotions are respected and allowed expression. In this way, dying can afford a new opportunity for personal growth. Indeed, surveys reveal that four out of five individuals would want to be told if they had an incurable disease. And today, physicians are sharing with patients and their

families medical information about the probable outcome of an illness.

> If you can begin to see death as an invisible, but friendly, companion on your life's journey—gently reminding you not to wait until tomorrow to do what you mean to do—then you can live your life rather than simply passing through it. (Elisabeth Kübler-Ross, 1993, p. 47)

Thanatologists are finding that dying, like living, is a process. Even though there are different styles of dying, just as there are different styles of living, some elements seem to typically occur in the death experience. Kübler-Ross (1969) observed that dying persons usually pass through five stages. Not everyone goes through all the stages, some slip back and forth between stages, and some experience several stages at the same time. Kübler-Ross (who had a series of strokes and died in 2004) described the five stages of dying as follows:

1. *Denial.* Individuals resist acknowledging the reality of impending death. In effect, they say "No!" to it.
2. *Anger.* Dying people ask the question "Why me?" They might look at the persons around them and feel envy, jealousy, and rage over their health and vigor. During this phase a dying person often makes life difficult for others, criticizing friends, family, and medical personnel with little justification.
3. *Bargaining.* Dying individuals often begin to bargain with God, fate, or the illness itself, hoping to arrange a temporary truce. For instance, a dying person might say, "Just let me live long enough to attend my son's marriage" or "Allow me to get my business in order." In turn the patient promises to be "good" or to do something constructive during his or her remaining time alive. The "bargain" generally is successful for only a short period, because the advance of the illness itself invalidates the "agreement."
4. *Depression.* Dying people begin to mourn their own approaching death, the loss of all the people and things they have found meaningful, and the plans and dreams never to be fulfilled—they experience what Kübler-Ross terms "preparatory grief."
5. *Acceptance.* The dying have by this time mourned their impending loss, and they begin to contemplate the coming of the end with a degree of quiet expectation. In most cases they are tired and quite weak. They no longer struggle against death but make their peace with it.

Says Kübler-Ross about the fifth stage:

> Acceptance should not be mistaken for a happy stage. It is almost void of feelings. It is as if the pain had gone, the struggle is over, and there comes a time for "the final rest before the long journey," as one patient phrased it. (Kübler-Ross, 1969, p. 113)

Although noting the many important contributions of Kübler-Ross's pioneering work on death and dying, which was conducted over many years with thousands of patients, some believe that the linear stage model of grief and bereavement is too confining and requires further study (Corr, 2001).

Kastenbaum's Trajectories of Death Psychologist Robert Kastenbaum (1975) points out that although Kübler-Ross's theory has merit, it neglects certain aspects of the dying process. One of the most important is the nature of the disease itself, which generally determines pain, mobility, the length of the terminal period, and the like:

> Within the realm of cancer alone, for example, the person with head or neck cancer looks and feels different from the person with leukemia. The person with emphysema, subject to terrifying attacks in which each breath of air requires a struggle, experiences his situation differently from the person with advanced renal failure, or with a cardiovascular trajectory [condition]. Although Kübler-Ross's theory directs welcome attention to the universal psychosocial aspects of terminal illness, we also lose much sensitivity if the disease process itself is not fully respected. (Kastenbaum, 1975, p. 43)

Other factors that must be considered are differences in sex, ethnic-group membership, personality, religiosity, developmental level, and the death environment (a private home or a hospital). Kastenbaum believes that Kübler-Ross's stages are very narrow and subjective interpretations of the dying experience. He claims that her stages are exaggerated and are isolated from the total context of the individual's previous life and current circumstances. And he is concerned lest this stage approach encourage an attitude in which, for instance, medical personnel or the family are able to say, "He is just going through the anger stage," when there may be concrete, realistic factors that are arousing the patient's ire (Kastenbaum & Costa, 1977).

Questions

According to Elisabeth Kübler-Ross, what are the five stages of dying? Why is Kastenbaum critical of Kübler-Ross's stages, and what does he mean by the "trajectories" of death?

Causes of Death

The most recent comprehensive national statistics on circumstances of American deaths available at the time of publication of this text come from the *1993 National Mortality Followback Survey* (NMFS)—the first study since the 1980s to examine detailed patterns of mortality by supplementing the information provided by birth certificates with interviews of next of kin. The updated survey, published by the Centers for Disease Control and Prevention (1998), allowed for the examination of trends in mortality, differences by income and education, risk factors and causes of death, and health-care utilization in the last year of life. This survey was based on examination of nearly 23,000 records of individuals aged 15 years and older who died in 1993. This sample of subjects was drawn from all states except South Dakota (a state law restricts the use of death certificate information). It is likely that today more people are dying at home, because more people have been using hospice care. Here is a summary of the major findings:

Where does death occur?

- 56 percent of deaths occurred in a hospital, clinic, or medical center.
- 21 percent of people died at home.
- 19 percent died in a nursing home.

What diseases did people have?

- 25 percent had a heart attack and about an equal number had angina; more than 40 percent had hypertension.
- Other frequent conditions were cancer and arthritis, each reported for about one-third of decedents.
- 15 percent suffered from memory impairment.

How many smoked or used drugs or alcohol?

- 50+ percent of all decedents smoked cigarettes at some point in their lives.
- About 25 percent of all decedents used alcohol during the last year of their life.
- 29 percent of drinkers used alcohol every day.
- About 2 percent used marijuana during their last year of life.
- Less than 1 percent were reported to have used other types of illicit drugs.

How was their last year of life?

- 58 percent of those with functional limitations received help at home from a spouse.
- 50 percent reported functional limitations due to physical or mental conditions the last year.
- 46 percent had daughters who provided care.
- 39 percent of the decedents took pain medication in the last year of life.
- 31 percent received help from visiting nurses.
- 10 percent were in bed most of their last year of life due to illness or injury.

For those who died of homicide, suicide, or fatal motor vehicle accident:

- 33 percent of decedents involved in fatal vehicle crashes were not wearing seat belts.
- 19 percent had an alcoholic beverage within 4 hours of death.

- 17 percent had taken drugs or medication within 24 hours of death.
- Of the 36,000 firearm-related deaths, 72 percent involved handguns.

Who gets and pays for health care?

- 75 percent of decedents were covered by Medicare.
- 50+ percent were covered by private insurance or HMOs.
- For 46 percent, Medicare was the principal source of medical payments.
- 20 percent had private medical insurance.
- 10 percent paid for their own medical care.
- 10 percent relied on Medicaid as the source of payment.
- 10 percent of decedents were reported never to have visited a doctor during the last year of life.
- Nearly 10 percent had made 50 or more visits for health care during the previous year.

Questions

Where do most Americans die? Do you think the decedents' families would give honest answers to the survey questions about drug and alcohol use and who actually cared for a dying relative? Would you give honest answers to this type of survey?

The Centers for Disease Control (CDC) reports that in 2007, heart disease became the leading cause of death for Americans 75 and older (Xu et al., 2010). The second leading cause is cancer, and rates increased significantly among adults over 75: Lung, lymphoid, colorectal, prostate, and breast cancers are main causes of death. Alzheimer's deaths are also rising significantly with the growing elderly population. Cancer is the leading cause of death for those in middle adulthood, ages 45 to 64. Accidents (mainly auto accidents) are the leading cause of death for adolescents and young adults (Xu et al., 2010). HIV/AIDS death rates are highest in states on the East and West Coasts and in nearly every urban area of the United States, and the numbers of men and women diagnosed at age 45 and older continue to rise (National Center for Health Statistics, 2011).

Homicide, suicide, and motor vehicle–related deaths (often alcohol-related) are also major public health problems in well-defined geographic patterns. Homicide rates are high for young black adults in urban areas, but for young white men the high rates are in southern and southwestern states (National Center for Health Statistics, 2011). Among young American children, the primary causes of death are in the understudied areas of accidents and injuries suffered because of traffic accidents, intentional harm, drowning, falling, fire, and poisoning, which are now classified as "behavior-related" injuries and under closer research scrutiny (Xu et al., 2010). In developing countries, over half of deaths under age 5 are caused by pneumonia, diarrhea, or newborn anomalies—conditions for which there are simple treatments, though too costly in poor countries (Save the Children, 2007). Table 19.3 lists the major causes of death or disability for various age groups.

TABLE 19.3 Ten Leading Causes of Death in the United States, by Developmental Stage: 2007

Causes are rank ordered, with the most frequent cause listed first.

Adolescence (ages 15–24)	Early Adulthood (ages 25–44)	Mid-Adulthood (ages 45–64)	Late Adulthood (ages 65 and older)
Accidents/Unintentional injuries	Accidents/Unintentional injuries	Cancer (malignant neoplasms)[1]	Heart diseases[2]
Assaults (homicide)	Cardiovascular diseases	Heart diseases	Cancer (malignant neoplasms)
Suicide (self-harm)	Cancer (malignant neoplasms)	Accidents/Unintentional injuries	Cerebrovascular diseases
Cancer (malignant neoplasms)	Suicide	Diabetes	Chronic lower respiratory disease
Major cardiovascular diseases	Homicide	Chronic lower respiratory disease	Alzheimer's disease
Birth defects	HIV/AIDS disease	Cerebrovascular diseases	Diabetes
Cerebrovascular diseases	Chronic liver disease	Chronic liver disease	Influenza and pneumonia
Diabetes	Cerebrovascular diseases	Suicide	Nephritis (kidney disease)
Influenza and pneumonia	Diabetes	Nephritis (kidney disease)	Accidents/Unintentional injuries
HIV/AIDS	Influenza and pneumonia	Septicemia	Septicemia

[1]Note that in 2007 the Centers for Disease Control and Prevention reported that cancer (malignant neoplasms) is now the leading cause of death in middle adulthood and the second leading cause in late adulthood.
[2]Heart disease is still the leading cause of death for the oldest adults, but Alzheimer's disease is rising rapidly.

Source: Xu, J., Kochanek, K., Murphy, S. L., & Tejada-Vera, T. (2010). Deaths: Final data for 2007. *National Vital Statistics Reports*, 58(19), 27–31. Retrieved from http://www.cdc.gov/NCHS/data/nvsr/nvsr58/nvsr58_19.pdf

Questions

What are the major causes of death of individuals in the United States, and do the major causes of death change across the life span? What are the major causes of death of children?

GRIEF, BEREAVEMENT, AND MOURNING

We know for certain that there is life after death—for the relatives and friends who survive. As they go on with their lives, they must come to terms with the death of the loved one and make many types of adjustment. First, there is psychological coping, often termed "grief work" (mourning, talking about, and acknowledging the loss). Second, there are numerous procedural details that must be attended to, including funeral arrangements and legal routines (securing several copies of the death certificate with cause of death; dealing with attorneys; settling the estate; and filing for any insurance, pension, medical, or Social Security benefits). Third, there is the social void produced by the death of a family member, which requires revising life patterns and family roles (for instance, housekeeping, marketing, or securing a livelihood). Where the death of a loved one is anticipated, individuals frequently experience **anticipatory grief**—a "state of emotional limbo, [where one is] unable to resolve the loss because it has not yet occurred, and unable to avoid the authoritative diagnosis that death will occur" (Stephenson, 1985, p. 163). Life after the death of a loved one is still difficult, even when one feels somewhat "prepared" for the inevitable.

Adjusting to the Death of a Loved One

Bereavement is a state in which a person has been deprived of a relative or friend by death. **Grief** involves keen mental anguish and sorrow over the death of a loved one. A person in initial grief is often said to be "numb" or in "shock" and is likely to want to withdraw from social contact (Ashenburg, 2002). **Mourning** is the socially established manner of displaying signs of sorrow over a person's death (for instance, wailing, chanting, wearing black, sitting *shivah* for one week, draping windows and doorways in black, flying flags at half-mast, writing obituaries, going to a cemetery daily, and the like).

Expressing Anguished Feelings   In *Macbeth* Shakespeare proclaims, "Give sorrow words. The grief that does not speak / Whispers the o'er-fraught heart and bids it break." And a Turkish proverb declares, "He that conceals his grief finds no remedy for it." Contemporary

Bereavement Ceremonies   Throughout the world, societies have evolved funeral rituals to assist their members in coming to grips with the death of a loved one. The ceremonies highlight the finality of death. Here Hindu mourners prepare a body for their traditional sacred custom of cremation, followed by disposal of ashes into a sacred river.

clinicians, psychologists, social workers, home health aides, and hospice volunteers agree with these statements. Sympathetic assistance can be all-important in the process of expressing anguished feelings. Rather than uttering platitudes ("She lived a full life"), psychologists suggest, well-meaning individuals can offer emotional support and a ready ear. Today in most communities there are support groups associated with nearly every cause of death to help other people go through their grief work. Bereavement is less an intellectual process than one of coming to terms with one's feelings. A social worker who found herself "on the fringe of madness" when her husband died of a heart attack eight years earlier, leaving her with three young children, said: "Being strong and bucking up is a lot of baloney. You don't feel like bucking up. It is a real process that you must be allowed to go through" (Gelman, 1983, p. 120). People who receive the support and comfort of family and friends typically have a lower incidence of mental and physical disorders following bereavement. And for most people, the expression of grief following the death of a loved one is an important component in recovery. But there are exceptions. Those whose grief includes an intense yearning for and a high degree of dependency on the deceased person tend to have a harder time recovering from their loss (Ashenburg, 2002).

Culture and Grief Work   Sometimes cultural expectations, social values, and community practices interfere with necessary grief work. Dying is often left to medical technology and often takes place in a clinical facility outside the home. Funeral rituals are often brief and simplified, and mourning may be viewed as a form of mental pathology (the cultural ideal is the self-controlled widow who keeps a "stiff upper lip"). Yet thanatologists believe that expressions of grief and mourning rituals are therapeutic for survivors. Such traditions as the Irish wake and the Jewish *shivah* help the bereaved come to terms with the loss and reconstruct new life patterns with family and friends. For those with a religious affiliation, church-, synagogue-, temple-, and mosque-related organizations can provide significant support systems (Koenig, 2002).

In Japan, however, the bereaved are not expected to sever their relationship with the dead by the grief work that is promoted in the West. Japanese culture encourages the survivors to maintain a relationship with the deceased in the form of a family shrine, with cremated remains present. The family altar can be used to make direct contact with the spirit of the deceased as though one were calling them on a spiritual "telephone." In this way all family members can access ancestors, so they can continue to have a relationship with those who remain on earth (Robben, 2006). Native Americans are also raised with a strong spiritual connection through honoring and communicating with ancestors.

Consequences of Grief   Bereavement and grief often have a much greater impact than is evident in the period immediately following the death. The survivor is more vulnerable to physical illness and mental illness and even to death, especially if the loss of the loved one was sudden and unexpected. Bereaved people have a higher than average incidence of illness, accidents, mortality, unemployment, and other indices of a damaged life (Kastenbaum, 2007). For most people, the passage of time lessens their grief for departed love ones. If time does not lessen the pain, if there is no improvement in coping over a period of months, or even if there is an absence of grief, the individual may be experiencing *complicated grief* (Ferrini & Ferrini, 2008). Depression, anxiety, substance abuse, and even post-traumatic stress disorder are common symptoms of complicated grief. In addition, significant clinical depression at the time of a spouse's death substantially increases the risk of psychological complications during the bereavement process, and survivors of spouses who committed suicide are at even greater risk (Ferrini & Ferrini, 2008). An authority on bereavement has this to say about grief:

> It isn't a problem or an illness that can be solved or cured. That's why it is really inappropriate for someone to say: "You can get over this. You can recover." In fact, people can't recover in the sense of going back to the way things were. You must make changes in your life in order to go on. The death and the bereavement wizen you, weather you and make you look at life differently. (Silverman, 1983, p. 65)

Adjusting to Violent and Premature Death   Violent and premature deaths often result in the most severe grief reactions. Senseless tragedies such as the violent mass murders committed by mentally ill gunmen at Virginia Tech in 2007, at Fort Hood in Texas in 2009, and in Tucson, Arizona, in 2011 prompt national grief and pervasive apprehension. Also, suicide is one of the most difficult types of death for survivors to handle. They may have difficulty acknowledging that the death was a suicide, and even when they do grasp the truth, they can feel guilt and shame that prevent normal mourning. Suicide survivors frequently feel that they are somehow to blame—for not seeing the signs and for not fulfilling the stated or unstated needs of the person who died. They also must bear the thought that the dead person did not believe they were worth living for. And survivors' guilt can be intensified if they experience a sense of relief after an ordeal of mental illness or of suicide threats and attempts (Murphy et al., 1999).

Adjusting to the Death of a Parent   The bereavement experienced by adult children following the death of an elderly parent has until recently been largely ignored by the media and the academic community. One recent study explores the impact of the death of a grandparent on the surviving children and on the family as a whole (Abeles, Victor, & Delano-Wood, 2004). As noted in prior chapters, ties between a parent and an adult child often remain strong across the life span. The bereavement associated with a parent's death is a complex emotional, cognitive, and behavioral process. Most men and women experience their mother's death as a profound loss. Women seem to be more emotionally affected than men are by the death of

A Nation in Grief A fellow college student committed America's worst carnage by firearm on April 16, 2007, at Virginia Polytechnic Institute. Thirty-two students and faculty were killed, and many others were wounded. This epic tragedy caused deep nationwide grief and sparked debate about college policies, campus security, gun laws, mental-health privacy issues, and prevention issues.

their fathers (Douglas, 1990–1991) and by the loss of the last surviving parent (Moss, Rubenstein, & Moss, 1997). Bereavement can be especially difficult for adult children who provided care before the parent's death—particularly those who experienced an intensification of their bonds during caregiving (Pratt, Walker, & Wood, 1992).

For middle-aged adults, a parental death is often an important personal and symbolic event that heightens the survivor's awareness of her or his own mortality, and bereavement can stimulate personal growth and development by fostering a greater sense of personal identity and stronger ties to family members (Bass & Bowman, 1990). Even elderly adults lose parents. Robert Kastenbaum (2007) shares his experience: "I have stood at the side of a 74-year-old man as tears ran down his cheeks because his 97-year-old father was dead." An outsider might rush to the conclusion that the death of a very old parent should not mean so much to a child also advanced in years. Consider, however, how long this relationship had to develop and flourish and what a blow it now was for this survivor to go on without the father he had known for three-quarters of a century.

Bereavement seems to unfold in a three-step progression for healthy adults who have lost a parent, according to a study by Petersen and Rafuls (1998). Based on their study of six adults who had recently lost a parent, they suggest that a transition in family values occurs, which they call a model for "receiving the scepter" of family values. Each new generation takes over the responsibility, role, and authority of the previous generation in this three-step transformation (Petersen & Rafuls, 1998):

Step 1. *Going back to the origins.* Duty and obligation become the most important response the first few days after death, along with an unconscious emotional "moving away" from one's own family.

Step 2. *Reevaluation phase.* A period of preoccupation permeated with a formal sadness, with release in one or two intense periods of crying and very different from depression found with other grief. Participants dealt with this stage quietly, internally, without sharing, yet thought about the deepest meanings of life. Also, within relationships, the most evident consequence during this stage was reduced lovemaking by a couple.

Step 3. *Assuming leadership.* Partners brought the second phase to a conclusion by reminding spouses that they were needed by their own families. These phases seemed to bring about a sense of strength never experienced by these subjects before; they reordered their priorities and began to appreciate the richness of life around them.

Phases in the Bereavement Process In standard bereavement by adults, the individual typically passes through a number of phases (Malinak, Hoyt, & Patterson, 1979). The *first phase* is characterized by shock, numbness, denial, disbelief, and often a need to withdraw (Ashenburg, 2002). The most intense feelings of shock and numbness usually last several days, although the process of struggling with denial and disbelief can persist for many days, even for months—especially if the death was sudden and unexpected.

The *second phase* involves pining, yearning, and depression. It usually reaches its peak within 5 to 14 days but can continue longer. Weeping, feelings of hopelessness, a sense of unreality, feelings of emptiness, distance from people, lack of vigor and interest, and preoccupation with the image of the deceased are quite common during this stage. Other symptoms might include anger, irritability, fear, sleeplessness, episodes of impaired recall or concentration, lack of appetite, and weight loss. Not uncommonly, the bereaved idealizes the dead person, maintaining an element of "reverence" despite recognition of the deceased's human faults and failings. In fact, survivors of a bad marriage can become hopelessly stuck in grief. They mourn not only for the marriage that was but also for the marriage that might have been and was not. In cases of pathological grief following the death of a spouse, three factors are typically present: an unexpected death, ambivalence regarding the marriage, and over-dependence on the spouse (Rees, 1997). Recovery from grief seems to take less time and to be more complete when the marriage was happy.

The *third phase* of bereavement involves emancipation from the loved one and an adjustment to the new circumstances. In this period the individual mobilizes his or her resources, attempts to become reconnected with people and activities, and seeks to establish a new equilibrium that will permit some element of satisfaction and comfort. Some people may complete the psychological and emotional work of this stage in about six to eight weeks, others in a matter of months; but for still others the process may continue for years.

The *fourth phase* is characterized by identity reconstruction. The person crystallizes new relationships and assumes new roles without the loved one. At this stage approximately half of the survivors report realizing some benefit or experiencing some growth from bereavement. These gains include an increased sense of self-reliance and strength, a greater caring for friends and loved ones, and a more general quickening to life and deepening appreciation of existence.

Individual Variations in the Bereavement Process
People differ greatly in how they handle the death of a loved one, in their specific symptoms of grief, and in the intensity and duration of the symptoms (Costello & Kendrick, 2000). Recent criticism of the literature on bereavement points out that there is no consensus on the

definition of normal grief reactions (Bonanno & Kaltman, 2001). These reactions cannot be neatly plotted in a series of well-defined stages, nor is the progression from the time of death to the resolution of bereavement necessarily a straight line. And although shock, anger, and depression are common reactions to loss, not everyone experiences them, no matter how deeply they cared about the person they lost. For instance, a man who lost his wife six months earlier might say he is ready to remarry, and a young mother might laugh with her friends only days after losing her child. Some who lose a loved one do not show great distress. However, a few aspects of grief work do not end for a significant proportion of bereaved individuals. They still feel themselves strongly affected by the deceased person, say they are upset on the yearly anniversary of the person's death, and experience an emotional void in their lives. Their sense of loss may overshadow other experiences, changing the way they interpret even positive events because the events remind them of their loss and their inability to share the experiences with the loved one (Zautra, Reich, & Guarnaccia, 1990). At unguarded moments people can stumble into "little ambushes" of grief. One widower tells of being out driving and spotting a woman with a hairstyle similar to his wife's:

> I said to myself, "There's Nola." Then I laughed out loud and told myself, "How silly of me. Nola is dead." Then my next thought was, "I must go home and tell Nola how silly I just was." It all happened in a fraction of a second. (Gelman, 1983, p. 120)

In sum, we are increasingly coming to realize that there is no universal prescription for how best to grieve and that people handle grief in a great many different ways (Costello & Kendrick, 2000).

Questions

Why do so many people think that the one-year anniversary of the death of a loved one is the time to be "over it"? What would your advice be to a grieving person who has been told by someone that it's time to "get over it"?

Widows and Widowers

"Until death do us part." This traditional phrase in Christian marriage vows continues to be meaningful. The U.S. Census Bureau in 2006 estimated that about 45 percent of women and 14 percent of men who had been married were now widows or widowers at age 65 and older. At age 85 and older, spousal bereavement rises to 80 percent for women and about 40 percent for men. This situation results from the fact that the life expectancy of women tends to be five or more years longer than that of

men and from the tradition that has ordained that women marry men older than themselves. (Of interest: Women married to men younger than themselves tend to live longer than would otherwise be expected, whereas women married to older men tend to die sooner than would be expected) (Klinger-Vartabedian & Wispe, 1989). Consequently, remarriage tends to be a male prerogative.

Of the more than 800,000 Americans widowed each year, about one-fourth still suffer serious depression a year or more later. Their eating habits frequently are altered, resulting in poorer health and nutrition (Kastenbaum, 2007). Their use of alcohol, drugs, and cigarettes rises. Health problems in survivors tend to be worse among those who were already in poor physical or mental health, those who are alcohol or drug abusers, and those who lack a social support network. Survivors with a strong social support network and those who remarry seem to suffer fewer health problems. Varying responses to widowhood can include chronic grief, chronic depression, relentless responsibilities of doing the job of two parents as a single parent, depression followed by improvement, and resilience, according to one study (Bonanno, Wortma, & Nesse, 2004).

The death of a spouse is a most traumatic event in a person's life. One problem confronted by widowers is the cultural dictate that men are not supposed to feel emotion and pain or to say, "I need help." Traditionally,

Losing a Life Partner When a person's life partner dies, the surviving spouse or partner usually experiences major life changes. Those without a support network are likely to suffer severe depression for a long period of time.

men have had difficulty expressing emotion. Further, many widowers have trouble cooking and caring for themselves. They develop poor eating habits, which, together with other poor health practices and feelings of loneliness and emptiness, often lead to heavy drinking, sleeplessness, and chronic ailments. Overall, in the United States, middle-aged and older men seem to have a more difficult time living alone than do women, they are far less likely to receive help from others, and they have the highest rates of suicide in the life span (National Center for Health Statistics, 2011). In fact, elderly white widowers have the highest rates of suicide in the nation.

We know quite a bit more about widows than about widowers, largely because of research by sociologist Helena Lopata (1981). The women Lopata interviewed and studied lived in metropolitan Chicago. Lopata was able to distinguish three categories of widows on the basis of the extent of their involvement in different types of social relationships. At one extreme were women, primarily better educated and belonging to the middle class, who were strongly involved in the role of wife when their husbands were alive. They built many other roles on the husband's presence as a person, a father, and a partner in leisure-time activities. There was a strong tendency for these women to idealize the late husband (Futterman, Gallagher, Thompson, Lovett, & Gilewski, 1990). (Former First Lady Nancy Reagan has been quoted as saying, "Everything was about Ronnie . . . it was always about him.")

At the other extreme were women, primarily lower-SES or working-class women living in black or ethnic neighborhoods, who belonged to sex-segregated worlds and were immersed in kin, neighboring, or friendship relationships with other women. Between these two extremes were women who led multidimensional lives in which the husband was involved in only part of the total set of relations. The adjustments confronting the women tended to vary with the degree to which their social relationships revolved about or were integrated with those of their husbands.

The main conclusion Lopata drew from her data was that the higher the woman's education and socioeconomic class, the more disorganized her self-identity and life became with her husband's death—but by the same token, the more resources she had to form a new lifestyle once her grief work was accomplished. Other research has suggested that the negative long-term consequences of widowhood seem to derive from socioeconomic loss rather than from widowhood itself (Bound, Duncan, Laren, & Oleinick, 1991).

Of considerable interest, Lopata found that about half of the widows lived entirely alone, and most of these women said they much preferred to do so. Only 10 percent had moved in with their married children. One reason this figure was so low is that the widows cherished their independence, which they did not wish to jeopardize by giving up their own homes and moving

into an unfamiliar network of relations (Mahoney, 2006). Furthermore, the widows anticipated problems in their role as mothers of grown-up children. They said that if they could not criticize or speak up, they would feel inhibited, but that if they did speak up, their children would become upset. They regarded their relationships with grandchildren as presenting similar problems.

> **Question**
>
> What are the differences in the ways in which widows and widowers are likely to cope with the loss of a spouse?

The Death of a Child

The loss of a child is also associated with deep depression, anger, guilt, and despair. The death of a child is not the natural order of life. Hence, recovery can take a very long time. In addition to the child's birthdays and the anniversary of the death, there are continual reminders of developmental milestones experienced by a dead child's peers: year of graduation from high school, year of graduation from college, probable years of marriage and parenthood, and so forth. Parents must come to recognize the limits of their protective powers. Women who find their primary satisfactions in the role of mother may feel useless without someone to care for. Guilt can be especially intense after a death from sudden infant death syndrome (SIDS). Parents of children who die from cancer might find that their grief intensifies during the second year. Parents who feel they did all they could do to care for a child during the final illness seem to recover sooner (Murphy et al., 1999).

Wheeler's (2001) qualitative study showed that parents search for meaning and for a renewed sense of purpose after the death of a child. The parents often report feeling irritable and are more likely to direct anger at each other. This can become particularly destructive when one parent blames the other, either for the death or for past actions related to the lost child. The parents may withdraw into their own grief and therefore away from each other. Nevertheless, most couples do not divorce or even seriously consider this possibility after the death of a child. Instead, there will be many years of trying to integrate the continuing absence of the child with the challenges and opportunities that arise in their ongoing lives (Kastenbaum, 2007).

Loss by Miscarriage   Parents who have lost a child by miscarriage often receive no recognition of their loss from others, yet their grief work might continue for a lifetime. Support groups may provide comfort to some grieving partners. However, results of a study evaluating perinatal loss support groups do not show any statistically significant differences in parents' grief reactions between those who do and those who do not attend such groups (DiMarco, Menke, & McNamara, 2001). Statements such

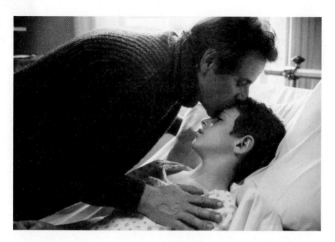

Loss of a Child It is hard to imagine any greater trauma than the fatal illness or sudden loss of a child. Mourning and grief last for years, and life goes on but is never the same.

as "At least you can have another one" or "This child wasn't meant to be" do not comfort people experiencing this loss. Every anniversary of the loss is a reminder of the child, who often has been named and placed in a gravesite but didn't have the opportunity for life. The mother is likely to feel a great deal of guilt, thinking that if only she had done something differently, the child would still be there. Most fathers suffer in silence and make efforts to go on with their lives. Repetitive miscarriages can bring about deep depression and feelings of failure in the mother. There are Internet sites devoted to loss by miscarriage or still-birth that provide a forum for parents to commemorate the short life of a child and to share feelings and thoughts with other parents who are coping with such a deep loss.

Loss by Murder or Violence Nicholas Green was a 7-year-old American boy on vacation in Italy in 1994 with his parents, Reg and Maggie Green, when he was fatally shot by highway robbers during a nighttime drive toward their destination. Within hours, his parents made the difficult decision to donate his organs to seven Italian citizens, who survived because of this gift. To this day, Reg Green says he thinks of his son a hundred times a day, and though it does not take away the pain of the loss of his son, he does have a sense of peace knowing that his son helped people in life-threatening situations. John Walsh and his wife lost their son Adam to a vicious child killer, and their lives have never been the same. The loss of a child is one of life's greatest agonies, even when parents know it is inevitable because of illness or disease, but when someone senselessly takes the life of a child, the bereavement process goes on indefinitely.

Another study examined the coping strategies of parents who lost their children to accident, suicide, or homicide (Murphy, Johnson, & Weber, 2002). Some parents start a crusade in honor of their child, such as the campaign for laws establishing victims' rights, the National

Center for Missing and Exploited Children, and the show *America's Most Wanted.* (John and Revé Walsh started this television show to honor their 6-year-old son Adam, who was abducted and brutally murdered.) President Bush signed the *Adam Walsh Child Protection and Safety Act* in 2006. This federal statute organizes sex offenders into three tiers and mandates that the most serious offenders comply with lifetime residency registration requirements (Bush, 2006). *Megan's Law* requires that community residents be notified whenever a released child molester moves into the community. Since 2003, most media outlets issue national *Amber Alerts* to quickly notify the public of child abductions; such alerts were named for 9-year-old Amber Hagerman, who was abducted and murdered in Texas in 1996 (Zgoba, 2004). In 2011, a national movement was launched to pass "Caylee's Law" after the acquittal in Orlando of Casey Anthony, who had been charged with the murder of her daughter. The proposed legislation "would make it a felony for parents [or a guardian] not to report the death of a child to law enforcement within an hour of discovering that death, or within 24 hours in the case of child disappearance" (Lee, 2011).

No parents want their child to have lived in vain, and humanitarian efforts help these parents keep the memories of their child alive. Often as the result of a tragic event, researchers call for further investigation or expansion of their field of study. The massive deaths that resulted from the events of September 11, 2001, were part of the impetus for a type of study called *macrothanatology.* This study focuses on large-scale death and on death resulting from complex and multidomain processes (Kastenbaum, 2007).

> **Question**
>
> The loss of a child is so tragic, but what might parents and loved ones do to cope with such a profound life-changing experience?

TOWARD AN UNDERSTANDING OF THE AFTERLIFE

The theme of "a beautiful death" has been linked by some with belief in a life hereafter. The "life after life" movement—supported and researched by Elisabeth Kübler-Ross, Ray Moody, Brian L. Weiss, Bruce Greyson, Betty Eadie, Pim van Lommel, Trudy Harris, and others—claims that there is evidence of a spiritual existence beyond death.

Near-Death Experiences

Holden, Greyson, & James (2009) present criteria for defining near-death experiences (NDEs). Some individuals who have been pronounced clinically dead but then have been resuscitated (by medical measures, through some miraculous intervention, or simply in a way we do not yet understand) have told of having left their bodies and undergone otherworldly experiences before they were resuscitated. Plato wrote about such an event centuries ago in the *Republic,* says Greyson, psychiatrist and NDE researcher, and such reports seem to occur across all cultures (Kastenbaum, 2007). A **near-death experience (NDE)** commonly is precipitated by medical illness, traumatic accident, surgical operation, childbirth, or drug ingestion. An estimated 7 million people have reported near-death experiences ("Brushes with Death," 2002).

The "typical" report runs along the following lines (Morse, 1992; Rees, 1997): The dying individuals feel themselves leave their bodies and watch, as spectators, from a few yards above their bodies, the resuscitation efforts being made to save them. "I had a floating sensation . . . and I looked back and I could see myself on the bed below" (Moody, 1976). After coming back to life (or being told by a supernatural being that it is not their time and they are to return), individuals often report in detail who attended them, what occurred, what went wrong, what was said by rescuers, and so forth. About a third of them report passing through a tunnel and entering some unearthly realm: "I went through this dark black vacuum at super speed" (Moody, 1976). Half say they see guides or the spirits of departed relatives, a religious figure, or a being of brilliant, yet not blinding, light. "From the moment the light spoke to me, I felt really good—secure, and loved" (Moody, 1976). Many individuals report having approached a sort of border, seemingly representing the divide between earthly life and the next world, through some type of "telepathic" communication. But they are told they cannot cross the divide now. They are told they must go back to earth, for the time of their death has not yet arrived. They resist turning back to life, for they are overwhelmed by intense feelings of love, joy, and peace. In some metaphysical manner, they are then reunited with their physical body, and they live.

A near-death experience can be a catalyst for spiritual awakening and a change in personality and attitude. Many individuals develop firmer beliefs in God and an afterlife, become less materialistic and more spiritual, no longer fear death, feel a greater love for other people, become more sensitive or prophetic, and spend more time searching for the meaning of life (Rees, 1997). The more NDEs are openly discussed or written about, the more people claim to have had such an otherworldly experience themselves. However, a neuroscientist in a research setting at Laurentian University in Sudbury, Ontario, has induced many of the characteristics of an NDE by stimulating the brain's right temporal lobe, the area of the brain above the right ear that is responsible for perception (Koerner, 1997). A recent study found that the temporal lobe may have an effect on near-death experiences and that having

such an experience may be associated with particular physiological characteristics and positive coping styles (Britton & Bootzin, 2004).

Cardiologist Bruce Greyson studied cardiac patients who reported near-death experiences and found that they tend to be younger than other patients and more likely to have lost consciousness, but they did not differ from other patients in socio-demographic variables (Greyson, 2003). Psychologist Ronald K. Siegel (1981) notes that the visions reported by dying people are virtually identical to the descriptions given by individuals experiencing drug-induced hallucinations, who often report hearing voices and seeing bright lights and tunnel imagery. Siegel suggests that the episodes derive from intense arousal of the central nervous system and disorganization of the brain's normal information-processing procedures. Another major skeptic is Daniel Alkon (Koerner, 1997), former chief of the Neural Systems Laboratory at the National Institutes of Health, who says that *anoxia* (the brain being deprived of oxygen) can induce such mental states. An anesthesiologist attributed reports of bright lights and tunnels to the effect of lack of oxygen on the retina of the eye. He also attributes the sensation of floating or flying to the tensing and relaxing of muscle spindles (the portion of the muscle fiber that transmits these sensations to the brain) (Woerlee, 2004).

In England, Karl Jansen has zeroed in on the shifting levels of a brain neurotransmitter called *ketamine* (Koerner, 1997). A related interpretation holds that at death, various forces combine to sever the connections between consciousness and somatic processes while the brain remains active. Dying people who are aware that they are dying may turn their thoughts to the possibility of reuniting with loved ones and the broader meaning of life. And experiences of intense joy, profound insight, and love may be produced by *endorphins* (molecules that act as both neurotransmitters and hormones), which arose in the course of our evolution and persisted because they blot out overwhelming pain (Irwin, 1985).

Psychologist Robert Kastenbaum (1977) suggests that the current fascination with "life after life" is simply another "mind trip." He cites cases of some heart attack victims who, when pronounced clinically dead and then resuscitated, have no recollection of an out-of-body experience. And he tells of people in respiratory failure (choking on a bone or undergoing an acute episode of emphysema) who later report feeling as though they had been in direct hand-to-hand combat with death. Kastenbaum (1977, p. 33) expresses concern lest death be "romanticized" and cautions,

> Death seems to be less demanding, perhaps more friendly, than life. . . . I do not believe the frustrated adolescent, the unemployed worker, the grieving widow or the ailing old person needs to be offered the invitation to suicide on quite so glittering a silver platter.

Hence, there is considerable controversy about near-death experiences, and researchers on both sides of this issue continue to investigate NDEs in as scientific a manner as possible. Despite skepticism, the field of near-death experiences continues to grow, attracting rigorous scrutiny that examines what happens to consciousness after physical death. Since 1975 the field has drawn many scientists, doctors, and writers engaged in studying the phenomenon, investigating the possibility of the afterlife and what happens after life as we know it ends. They pose questions such as whether or not consciousness transcends death. And even in the face of continuing skepticism, growing evidence suggests that it does.

In *Glimpses of Heaven: True Stories of Hope and Peace at the End of Life's Journey*, Trudy Harris, a hospice nurse for many years, reveals to readers her skepticism at what those in her care were telling her at the end of their lives:

> When patients and friends who were dying would say to me, "Today is my day" . . . or "I heard them call my name" or "My son is here with me now; he said it's time to go," at first I simply did not understand. When many others told me about seeing angels in their rooms, being visited by loved ones who had died before them, or hearing beautiful choirs or smelling fragrant flowers when there were none around, I assumed it was the result of medications they were taking or possibly dehydration. Surely the visions could not be real. But when others who were not dying and not on medication and not dehydrated were saying the same things, I started to listen, really listen. (Harris, 2008, p. 19)

What follows in *Glimpses of Heaven* is a collection of true stories about what Harris witnessed among those in her care who were terminally ill or dying. These poignant end-of-life stories relate their final thoughts, words and visions—stories that she tells with compassion and honesty as she searches for understanding. What the dying were able to teach her about the last moments of life and the transition to the afterlife through death is instructive and profoundly moving. Her book "offers a portrait of what we might expect when our time inevitably comes and demystifies death as only first-person accounts can do" (Harris, 2008). "I have the feeling that people do not die at the exact minute or hour that we say they do. In some inexplicable way that we do not yet understand, they seem to travel back and forth from this world to the next" (Harris, 2008). She writes, "there are so many important lessons people are trying to teach us moments before they die. We had better listen. We are standing on holy ground during these moments, and we dare not miss one of them" (Harris, 2008). She concludes, from her three decades of witnessing the deaths of many persons in her care, that the dying have what she calls "spiritual eyes and ears and [they] seem to see and understand things in a way [the living] cannot" (Harris, 2008). Those who undergo a near-death experience, and then return

to life, come back to tell of an unconditional love that awaits them. Often they emphatically tell us that we have nothing to be afraid of. Though skeptics disagree, perhaps these glimpses Harris speaks of throughout the book are the patients' glimpses of God or heaven.

Harris writes that "People who are about to die are very generous in sharing their experiences if they feel you will be open to hearing them. They tell you about their experiences as they are living them and seem to want to help you understand the simplicity of it all" (Harris, 2008, p. 18).

More recently, a comprehensive examination of the field of NDEs was published, providing a survey of the literature of the field as it now exists. Drawing together empirical, philosophical, religious, and first-hand experiences, *The Handbook of Near-Death Experiences: Thirty Years of Investigation* is intended for scholars, teachers, doctors and nurses, researchers, and clergy, the wider public, and certainly those who have survived a near-death experience. In his foreword, Kenneth Ring says of his three decades of investigation of NDEs, "What we wished to do was to subject the near-death experience to critical scientific scrutiny. We were out neither to prove it nor debunk it; our aim instead was only to try to understand it and to encourage other scientists and scholars to do likewise" (Holden, Greyson, & James, 2009).

Further adding to this growing body of work, the Dutch cardiologist Pim van Lommel (2010), in studying his patients, considers the important question "What happens to consciousness after death?" His recent book, *Consciousness Beyond Life: The Science of the Near-Death Experience,* is based on more than 25 years of studying the near-death experiences of a number of patients who survived cardiac arrest. He presents scientific evidence that near-death phenomena are indeed authentic experiences that cannot be brushed aside simply as the product of imagination, psychosis, or oxygen deprivation. In his introduction to the book, van Lommel writes that "An NDE is a special state of consciousness that occurs during an imminent or actual period of physical, psychological, or emotional death." Yet the enigmatic nature of the NDE, he confides, raises many unanswered questions, such as how and why does an NDE occur, and why does an NDE bring about such profound changes in someone's life? He reveals that after an NDE, most patients' personalities undergo a permanent change. "Evidence has shown that most people lose all fear of death. . . . Their experience tells them that death is not the end of everything and that life goes on in one way or another" (van Lommel, 2010, p. xii). Significantly changed by his experience, one of van Lommel's patients wrote to him after his NDE, trying to explain what had happened to him:

> "I'm not qualified to discuss something that can only be proven by death. However, for me personally this experience was decisive in convincing me that consciousness

endures beyond the grave. Dead turned out to be not dead, but another form of life." (van Lommel, 2010, p. xiii)

Van Lommel adds that for those who have undergone a near-death experience, "death is nothing other than a different way of being with an enhanced and broadened consciousness, which is everywhere at once because it is no longer tied to a body" (van Lommel, 2010, p. xiii). He continues, "There is no beginning and there will never be an end to our consciousness. For this reason we ought to seriously consider that death, like birth, may be a mere passing from one state of consciousness into another" (van Lommel, 2010, p. 318). "Following an NDE, people realize that everything and everybody are connected, that every thought has an impact on oneself and others, and that our consciousness survives physical death. People realize that death is not the end" (van Lommel, 2010, p. xix).

The journalist Lisa Miller, in her book *Heaven: Our Enduring Fascination with the Afterlife,* writes, "Certain people throughout history—prophets, visionaries, those who have had near-death experiences—have claimed to have seen heaven and I treat these testimonials as important or even inspired stories, not factual accounts. I do not believe we know, in any empirical way, anything real about heaven. Without such evidence, the story of heaven is as much about believers as it is about belief—for how people imagine heaven changes with who they are and how they live" (Miller, 2010, p. xviii). Miller's book surveys belief and skepticism about heaven and the afterlife. People from many nations report similar experiences in numerous articles in the *Journal of Near Death Studies.* Written centuries ago, but translated into English only recently, the *Tibetan Book of the Dead* describes Tibetan Buddhist beliefs in liberation through several stages of consciousness through death, including visions of white light, life review, and eventual rebirth (Coleman, Jinpa, & Dorje, 2006).

Van Lommel (2010, p. 9) says, "Regrettably, people with an NDE are still too often dismissed as dreamers, fantasists, attention seekers, or confused patients." He adds, "Many thousands of people are known to have had a near-death experience, but estimates put the number of people who have had one in the past fifty years at more than 25 million worldwide. Fairly recent studies in the United States and in Germany suggest that approximately 4 percent of the population has reported an NDE." The actual number is probably much higher, however, because some may be reluctant to discuss the experience for fear of being disbelieved or even shunned.

Questions

What elements are common in descriptions of near-death experiences? How do scientists explain such supernatural sensations? What do you think happens to consciousness when human life ends?

Religious Beliefs

Notions of life after death have old roots. Ancient Greek philosophy frequently mentioned Hades, the Bible speaks of the "kingdom of Heaven," and Eastern religions speak of realms of life we'll inhabit after this one. Eastern religions, such as Hinduism, posit an afterlife and reincarnation of the souls of animals and people—and so teach their followers not to harm animals or people. Native Americans and the Aborigines of Australia also believe in an afterlife and also believe they can communicate with ancestors who have passed on.

Christian theologians traditionally have viewed the book of Revelation as providing the most vivid and familiar biblical images of a mystical heaven: images of "pearly gates and streets of gold, of a vast white throne, and of throngs of saints and angels gathered around God at the culmination of history" (Sheler, 1997). Now that the new millennium has begun, writings about being "born again," the signs of the Apocalypse, the second coming of Christ, and the "Rapture" have proliferated. These books have a powerful influence on the way some Christians, and others, view an afterlife. Strikingly, "nearly 80 percent of Americans—of various religious faiths and of none—say they believe in life after death, and two thirds are certain there is a heaven" (Sheler, 1997; Koenig, 2002). In his book *Teaching Your Children About God,* Rabbi David Wolpe reminds us of the experience of birth into the unknown world of joyous waiting arms, which so much resembles the classic view of death and the afterlife—a birth into a place that we humans can only try to imagine (Sheler, 1997, p. 66). In contrast, *agnostics* are unsure about the existence of an afterlife, whereas *atheists* believe that death is the end of their existence.

The Jewish position has been that no one knows the nature of life after death, and therefore speculation is pointless and to be discouraged. Judaism rejects the concept of hell, but Orthodox Jews do believe that in a Messianic era there will be a resurrection—a time when the souls and bodies of the dead will be reunited.

Most Buddhists believe that the body retains "life" for 8 to 12 hours after death, and so it is possible to speak and act in a meaningful way with the deceased. That the person still exists after death has implications for Buddhists because their idea of rebirth hinges on the fact that people experience changes in consciousness every moment. For the Buddhist, every instant involves the several stages of death and rebirth of consciousness (refer to the *Tibetan Book of the Dead*). In the moment just before death, people recollect parts of their past lives and have glimpses of the future. Then the mind drops into a non-aware state, only to reawaken into one of the six realms of the universe: Hell, Hungry Ghost, Animal, Human, Jealous Gods, or Gods. None of these realms is very desirable, and Buddhism teaches a doctrine of liberation from *karma* into a state of *nirvana*. This detailed picture of the after-death state is very different from the uncertain picture in the West about the nature of afterlife and after-death experience.

In the New Testament, Jesus spoke in the Gospels about the kingdom of Heaven as a place of eternal reward: "I go to prepare a place for you, and if I go to prepare a place for you I will come again, and receive you to myself; that where I am you may be also" (John 14:2–3). Because the majority of U.S. citizens profess to be of some Christian denomination, this belief is likely to be the one you encounter most often. However, for those of you who enter the human services and medical professions—especially those of you who serve clients in an end-of-life situation or their families—it will be especially important for

you to provide culturally competent care. And you can do this most effectively if you are aware of your clients' and patients' religious or spiritual beliefs and traditions.

Final Thoughts About Life and Death

This book has been written in the fervent hope that with better understanding of human life stages—through the study of human development from conception to death and beyond—and of the contexts in which we live together, we can all continue to affirm the meaning of our lives, to enjoy our lives, and to improve the lives of those we care about and meet on our life's journey.

SEGUE

Perhaps the most difficult transition anyone has to make after the death of a loved one is the journey from grief and sorrow to remembrance and honoring. Our loss seems to overwhelm us and, fearing that we will dishonor the one we love by forgetting, we nurture grief, clinging to it with a desperation that comforts us. But in time, this grieving must give way to honoring and remembering. So often are the words "get on with your life" spoken to the one who

is left behind, alone. To move on is *not* to forget. It is to remember. It is to remember all that your loved one gave you and all that you shared with your loved one. To move on is to celebrate those gifts and to know your loved one lives on in your memories. It is to realize how deeply he or she touched your life.

Ted Menten, *Gentle Closings: How to Say Goodbye to Someone You Love*, 1991, p. 136

SUMMARY

The Quest for "Healthy Dying"

1. Until very recently, death was a taboo topic in Western society. Today, considerable controversy swirls about such matters as the right to die, clinical death, the death penalty, life after death, and life extension methods, such as cryonics.
2. Thanatology is the study of death and dying, and interest in this field has grown markedly.
3. Over the past 30 years, public and professional awareness of the dying person's experience has increased dramatically. Many activists assert that the power to control one's own dying process is a basic human right. Much criticism is currently leveled at the way modern technology is applied to the terminally ill.
4. Cultural attitudes toward suicide are still widely polarized. Some people consider suicide a sin; others view suicide victims as insane or weak. Others consider suicide an honorable choice when an individual is faced with capture, defeat, disgrace, severe and prolonged pain, or the possibility of disfigurement or dementia.
5. The hospice approach involves a variety of programs designed to provide an alternative to conventional hospital care for anyone who is terminally ill. The emphasis of the movement falls on "comfort-care" and support, rather than on attempts to prolong life. Most hospice programs are centered on caring for the dying person at home,

although there are also independent hospice programs and hospice programs set up as hospital units.

The Dying Process

6. The earliest biblical sources, as well as English common law, considered a person's ability to breathe independently to be the prime index of life. Over the past few decades, technological advances have rendered this traditional definition of death obsolete. A growing acceptance in medical and legal circles of the need for a more specific criterion for death has resulted in a legal definition that includes the absence of spontaneous brain function.
7. A realistic acceptance of death is considered to be the hallmark of emotional maturity. Yet transhumanist researchers are making progress toward extending life. The meaning of death varies from individual to individual.
8. Elisabeth Kübler-Ross identifies five stages through which dying persons typically pass: denial, anger, bargaining, depression, and acceptance.

Grief, Bereavement, and Mourning

9. Bereavement and grief have a considerably greater impact than is evident in the period immediately following the death of a loved one. The bereaved adult typically passes

through a number of phases—from shock, numbness, denial, and disbelief to pining, yearning, and depression. Then an adjustment to the new circumstances occurs and identity reconstruction begins. The timing of grief varies among individuals.

10. Cultures differ in how they perceive death and dying. Every culture has a unique approach to dealing with death, but every approach entails an understanding of death, spiritual beliefs, rituals, expectations, and taboos.

11. The major causes of death vary from country to country. Heart disease and cancer are major causes of adult deaths in the United States. Accidental injuries are the leading cause of child deaths.

12. Women 65 and over are much more likely to be widowed than married. But older men seem to have a more difficult time adjusting to widowhood. Even though they are also more likely to remarry (since there are many more older women than men), some are at a higher risk for ending their lives.

13. Loss of a parent, loss of a spouse, and loss of a child all have a significant impact on a person. Typically parents and adult children retain strong ties throughout life. The loss of a child is one of life's most agonizing experiences, one that most people never quite get over.

Toward an Understanding of the Afterlife

14. In some cases, persons who have been pronounced clinically dead but then have been revived have told of leaving their bodies and undergoing otherworldly experiences. Some have interpreted such near-death experiences as evidence of a spiritual existence beyond death. Skeptics rejoin that the visions reported by dying people are hallucinations associated with the intense arousal of the central nervous system and with disorganized brain functioning. Yet some who have studied the phenomenon for many years conclude that near-death experiences cannot be fully explained by hallucinations, psychosis, or oxygen deprivation.

15. Most religions of the world promote a belief in some form of transcendence to a spiritual state or rebirth after leaving the human body. Some believe communication is possible with deceased ancestors—thus honoring one's deceased relatives is common in certain faiths. Knowledge about any such specific cultural beliefs is very useful to those entering medical and human services professions.

KEY TERMS

advance directive *(608)*

anticipatory grief *(625)*

bereavement *(625)*

brain death *(618)*

euthanasia *(611)*

grief *(625)*

hospice *(615)*

life review *(620)*

living will *(608)*

mourning *(625)*

near-death experience (NDE) *(631)*

persistent vegetative state *(618)*

power of attorney *(619)*

thanatology *(608)*

transhumanism *(618)*

FOLLOWING UP ON THE INTERNET

Web sites for this chapter focus on controversies about "healthy" dying, the dying process, and ways for survivors to cope. Please access the text Web site at www.mhhe.com/crandell10 for up-to-date hot-linked Internet addresses for the following organizations, topics, and resources:

Center for Thanatology Research and Education
http://www.thanatology.org/home.html

End-of-Life Issues—National Institute of Health
http://www.nlm.nih.gov/medlineplus/endoflifeissues.html

Omega—Journal of Death and Dying
http://www.baywood.com/Journals/PreviewJournals.asp?Id=0030-2228

Death Studies
http://www.informaworld.com/smpp/title~content=t713657620~db=all

Death with Dignity National Center
http://www.deathwithdignity.org/

American Hospice Foundation
http://www.americanhospice.org/

American Foundation for Suicide Prevention
http://www.afsp.org/

Near-Death Experience Research Foundation
http://www.nderf.org/

The Compassionate Friends—Grief Support
http://www.compassionatefriends.org/home.aspx

The American Academy of Hospice and Palliative Medicine
http://www.aahpm.org/

The Hospice and Palliative Nurses Association
http://www.hpna.org/

Journal of Hospice & Palliative Nursing
http://journals.lww.com/jhpn/pages/default.aspx

Transhumanism
http://www.fightaging.org/archives/2001/11/transhumanism-and-healthy-life-extension-1.ph

GLOSSARY

A

abortion Spontaneous or induced expulsion of the fetus prior to the time of viability, occurring most often during the first 20 weeks of the human gestation period.

accommodation In Piaget's cognitive theory, the process of changing a schema to make it a better match to reality.

activity theory of aging The theory that as an elderly person's level of activity declines, so do that person's feelings of satisfaction, contentment, and happiness.

adaptation Begins with the single reflexes at birth and continues as a child gradually modifies behaviors to meet environmental demands.

adolescent growth spurt Rapid increase in height and weight during the early adolescent years.

adult day care A program of long-term care and support to adults who live in the community, providing health, social, and support services in a protective setting during any part of the day.

advance directive A legal document that allows a person to state decisions about end-of-life care ahead of time.

afterbirth Placenta and the remaining umbilical cord expelled from the uterus through the vagina after childbirth.

age cohort (also called *cohort* or *birth cohort*) A group of persons born in the same time interval.

age grading Arranging people in social layers based on place in the life cycle.

age norms Social standards that define what is appropriate for people to be and to do at various ages over the life span.

age strata Social layers within societies that are based on chronological age and serve to differentiate people as superior or inferior, higher or lower.

ageism Stereotyping and judging a group of people solely on the basis of their age.

aggression Behavior that is socially defined as injurious or destructive to people, animals, and objects.

aging The process of biological and social change across the life span.

alienation A pervasive sense of powerlessness, meaninglessness, isolation, and estrangement from others.

allele A pair of genes found on corresponding chromosomes that affect the expression of one or more hereditary traits.

Alzheimer's disease A progressive, degenerative neurological disorder that involves deterioration of brain cells and can occur in late adulthood.

amniocentesis A commonly used invasive procedure conducted between the 14th and the 20th weeks of gestation to determine the genetic status of the fetus; it involves withdrawing and analyzing amniotic fluid.

amnion Structure that forms a closed sac around the embryo and is filled with a watery amniotic fluid to keep the embryo moist and protect it against shock or adhesions.

anaphylaxis A severe allergic reaction that is life threatening, usually caused by certain foods.

androgyny The presence of both male-typed and female-typed characteristics.

anorexia nervosa A potentially life-threatening eating disorder that affects primarily females and a smaller percentage of males, in which the person becomes obsessed with looking thin and seriously alters her or his eating behaviors in order to lose weight. Excessive exercise is also associated with anorexia.

anoxia Oxygen deprivation; in childbirth, caused when the umbilical cord becomes squeezed or wrapped around the baby's neck during labor and delivery.

anticipatory grief A state of emotional limbo wherein the death of a loved one is anticipated and individuals feel unable to resolve the loss because it has not yet occurred and are unable to avoid the diagnosis that death will occur.

antisocial behavior A type of behavior that is persistent in violating the socially prescribed patterns of behavior.

anxiety A state of uneasiness, apprehension, or worry about future uncertainties.

Apgar scoring system A standard scoring system developed by anesthesiologist Virginia Apgar to objectively appraise the normalcy of a baby's condition at birth, based on five criteria.

Asperger's syndrome One of the disorders closely related to autism, classified as a PDD (pervasive developmental disorder).

assimilation In Piaget's cognitive theory, the process of taking in new information and interpreting it in such a way that it conforms to a currently held model of the world.

assisted reproductive technologies (ARTs) Scientific technological options used to increase a woman's chance of becoming pregnant when conception does not occur through heterosexual intercourse.

asthma A chronic lung disease characterized by inflammation and constriction of the lower airways.

asynchrony Dissimilarity in the growth rates of different parts of the body. For example, during adolescence the hands, feet, and legs grow before the trunk of the body.

attachment An affectional bond that one individual forms for another and that endures across time and space.

attention-deficit hyperactivity disorder (ADHD) A disorder characterized by impulsivity and the inability to follow instructions, remain seated, and stick with a task. Those with the disorder can be characterized as hyperactive-impulsive, inattentive, or combined hyperactive and inattentive.

audiology testing Assessment to determine the extent of hearing loss.

authoritarian parenting A parenting style distinguished by attempts to shape, control, and evaluate a child's behavior in accordance with traditional and absolute values and standards of conduct.

authoritative parenting A parenting style distinguished by firmly directing a child's overall activities but allowing the child freedom to make some decisions within reasonable limits and supervision.

autism A lifelong developmental disability characterized by impaired attachment and social interaction, sensory-perceptual differences, speech difficulties, and unusual, repetitive patterns of behavior.

autism spectrum disorders A classification of neurological disorders characterized by impairment in social and cognitive functioning, ranging in severity from mild to disabling. Some affected also have medical issues such as seizures, sleep problems, and gastrointestinal, metabolic, and immunological challenges.

autonomous morality The second stage of Piaget's two-stage theory of moral development, which arises from the interaction among peers.

autosomes The 22 pairs of chromosomes similar in size and shape that each human being normally possesses in addition to the pair of sex chromosomes.

B

basal-cell carcinoma The most common form of skin cancer.

behavior modification The application of learning theory and experimental psychology to alter behavior.

behavioral genetics The study of genes that cause individuals within a species to exhibit different behaviors.

behavioral theory A psychological theory that focuses on observable behavior—what people do and say—and on how their environment shapes their development across the life span.

bereavement Being deprived of a relative or friend by death.

bilingualism Instruction in both first and second languages by teachers proficient in both; proficiency in two or more languages.

binge drinking Downing five or more alcoholic drinks in a row for men, or four or more in a row for women, over a 2-hour period.

binge-eating disorder An established eating disorder characterized by regular binge eating, and those affected are likely to be overweight or obese.

biological aging Changes in the structure and functioning of the human organism over time.

birth The fetus's transition from dependent existence inside the woman's uterus to life as a separate organism.

birthing centers Primary care facilities, other than hospitals, typically located in urban centers, that are used for low-risk childbirth.

birthing rooms A homelike environment in a hospital or other setting where labor and delivery can occur.

blastocyst The gel-like fluid-filled ball of cells produced after the zygote goes through early meiotic cell division. The blastocyst gradually moves into the uterus, implants itself in the uterine wall to nourish itself, and becomes the embryo.

body mass index (BMI) An index used to calculate a person's body fat percentage.

brain death Cessation of neural activity when the brain receives insufficient oxygen to function.

bulimia Also called *binge-purge syndrome*. A serious eating disorder characterized by repeated episodes of bingeing—particularly on high-calorie foods like candy bars, cakes, pies, and ice cream—and afterwards purging by forced vomiting; taking laxatives, enemas, or diuretics; or fasting.

bullying A deliberate, repeated aggressive behavior that involves an imbalance of power and strength toward another person perceived as weaker.

C

cardiovascular Pertaining to the heart and circulatory system.

caregiver speech The simplified form of language used by adults when they are talking to infants and young children.

case-study method A special type of longitudinal study that focuses on a single individual rather than on a group of subjects.

cataracts A clouding of the lens of the eye that impairs vision, typically seen in older adults; in rarer cases can be found in infants or young people.

causality A cause-and-effect relationship between two paired events that occur in succession. Piaget concluded that children younger than 7 or 8 fail to grasp cause-and-effect relationships.

centration (centering) The process whereby preoperational children, ages 2 to 7, concentrate on only one feature of a situation and neglect other aspects. It is characteristic of preoperational thought.

cephalocaudal development (cephalocaudal principle) Development that proceeds from the head to the feet.

child abuse Intentional neglect, physical attack, or sexual abuse or injury to a child.

child maltreatment Any recent act or failure to act on the part of a parent or caretaker, which results in death, serious physical or emotional harm, sexual abuse, or exploitation.

cholesterol A white, waxy substance found naturally in the body that builds the cell walls and makes certain hormones. Certain foods can cause cholesterol buildup in the bloodstream, which can result in cardiovascular problems.

chorion A membrane that surrounds the amnion and links the embryo to the placenta.

chromosomes Found in the nuclei of all cells, the long threadlike structures made up of protein and nucleic acid that contain the genes, which transmit hereditary materials.

chronosystem In Bronfenbrenner's ecological theory, the changes within the individual and changes in the environment across time, as well as the relationship between these two processes.

classical conditioning A type of learning in which a new, previously neutral stimulus, such as a bell, comes to elicit a response, such as salivation, by repeated pairings with an unconditioned stimulus, such as food.

climacteric A time in a woman's life characterized by changes in the ovaries and in the various biological processes over two to five years prior to complete cessation of menstruation.

cloning A form of asexual reproduction, which creates an embryo by a process called somatic cell nuclear transfer (SCNT).

cognition The act or process of knowing, including understanding and reasoning.

cognitive development A major domain of development that involves changes in mental activity, including sensation, perception, memory, thought, reasoning, and language.

cognitive learning The process of observing other people and learning new responses or behaviors without first having had the opportunity to make the responses oneself.

cognitive stages Sequential periods in the growth or maturation of an individual's ability to think, to gain knowledge, and to be aware of the self and the environment.

cognitive styles Consistent individual differences in how a person perceives, organizes, processes, recalls, and uses information.

cognitive theory A theory that attempts to explain how we go about representing, organizing, treating, and transforming information as we modify our behavior.

cohabitation Living together outside of marriage.

colic An uncomfortable condition of unknown origin that can cause a baby to cry for at least an hour or more (typically every day about the same time). Colic typically disappears after the first several months of development.

collagen A basic structural component of connective tissue in body cells that appears to be implicated in the aging process. During late adulthood the body has less collagen; thus a person's skin appears more wrinkled.

collective self-esteem How individuals evaluate their social group and how they feel their social group is evaluated by the public.

collectivism A cultural view that fosters in children a strong emotional bonding and feeling of oneness with parents and respect for authority.

colostrum A substance in mother's milk that provides antibodies that build up the newborn's immune system, protecting the infant from a variety of infectious and noninfectious diseases.

communication The processes by which people transmit information, ideas, attitudes, and emotions to one another.

companionate love According to Sternberg, the kind of love a person has for a very close friend.

conceptualization A grouping of perceptions into classes or categories on the basis of certain similarities. Related ideas can come together to create a concept.

confluence theory The view that the intellectual development of a family is like a river, with the inputs of each family member flowing into it.

confounding A variable that may occur in research when the elements under study are mingled in such a way that they cannot be distinguished or separated.

consciousness of oneness A sympathetic identification in which group members come to feel that their inner experiences and emotional reactions are similar.

conservation Understanding that the quantity or amount of something stays the same regardless of changes in its shape or position. According to Piaget, preoperational children (2 to 7 years old) do not have the concept of conservation. Children are typically in elementary school before they learn this concept.

consummate love According to Sternberg, the kind of love present when all three aspects of his triangular theory of love exist in a relationship.

continuum of indirectness The notion that the role played by hereditary factors is more central in some aspects of development than in others.

control group In an experiment, a group of participants who are similar to the participants in the experimental group but do not receive the independent variable (treatment). The results obtained with the control group are compared with the results of the experimental group.

convergent thinking The application of logic and reasoning to arrive at a single, correct answer to a problem.

coping The responses, behaviors, and actions one takes in order to master, tolerate, or reduce stress.

correlation analysis (r) A statistical analysis that does not prove causation but can be used for predictive purposes.

correlation coefficient The numerical expression of the degree or extent of relationship between two or more variables or conditions.

Couvade syndrome A prospective father's complaints of uncomfortable physical symptoms, dietary changes, and weight gain because of his partner's pregnancy.

craniosacral system A closed system involving the pumping or inflow and outflow of cerebrospinal fluid within the membranes around the brain and spinal cord that affects the functioning of the nervous system.

creativity Characterized by originality of useful responses and creations.

critical period For the developing embryo, the time of development when each organ and structure is most vulnerable to damaging influences. Also a relatively short period of time in which specific development or imprinting normally takes place.

cross-cultural method A study in which researchers compare data from two or more societies and cultures. Culture, rather than individuals, is the subject of analysis.

cross-sectional design Investigation of development by simultaneously comparing people from different age groups.

crowning The stage during childbirth when the widest diameter of the baby's head is at the mother's vulva.

crystallized intelligence The abilities learned from education, experience, and acculturation. Crystallized intelligence often shows an increase with age.

cultural dislocation A sense of homelessness and alienation from a previous way of life.

culture The social heritage of a people—those learned patterns of thinking, feeling, and acting that are transmitted from one generation to the next.

D

death drop A marked intellectual decline that occurs shortly before a person dies.

decay theory The theory of cognitive decline that holds that forgetting occurs because of deterioration in the memory traces in the brain.

delivery (childbirth) The process that begins when the infant's head passes through the mother's cervix and ends when the baby has completed its passage through the birth canal.

deoxyribonucleic acid (DNA) The active biochemical substance of genes that programs the cells to manufacture vital protein substances.

dependent variable In an experiment, an objective measure of the subject's behavior—the variable that is affected by the independent variable.

depression A state of mind characterized by prolonged feelings of gloom, despair, and futility, profound pessimism, and a tendency toward excessive guilt and self-reproach.

development The orderly and sequential changes that occur with the passage of time as an organism moves from conception to maturation to death.

developmental psychology The branch of psychology that investigates how individuals change over time, while remaining in some respects the same.

deviant identity A lifestyle that is at odds with, or at least is not supported by, the values and expectations of society.

DHEA (dehydroepiandrosterone) A hormone produced by the body that is used to treat depression, improve memory, and block the decline of the body's immune system.

dialectical thinking An organized approach to analyzing and making sense of the world one experiences that differs fundamentally from formal analysis.

diastolic pressure Blood pressure when the heart is at rest, in between beats.

disengagement theory of aging A view of aging as a progressive process of physical, psychological, and social withdrawal from the wider world.

disorganized/disoriented infants Those who lack coherent coping strategies during separation episodes and indicate confusion and apprehension toward their mothers.

displaced homemaker A woman whose primary life activity has been homemaking and who has lost her main source of income because of divorce or widowhood.

diuretics Liquids that cause water loss and also loss of calcium and zinc in the urine.

divergent thinking Open-ended thought in which multiple solutions are sought, examined, and probed, thereby leading to what are deemed creative responses on measures of creativity.

dizygotic (fraternal) twins Multiple, nonidentical siblings.

dominant character In genetics, the property of an allele (gene) that produces the same visible trait (phenotype) whether its paired allele is identical (AA) or different (Aa).

drug abuse Excessive or compulsive use of chemical agents to an extent that interferes with an individual's health and social or vocational functioning, or with the functioning of the rest of society.

dry eye Diminished tear production that can be uncomfortable and can usually be eased with eyedrops; typically a condition in late adulthood.

dyslexia A type of brain dysfunction that causes extreme difficulty in learning to read in an otherwise normally intelligent, healthy child or adult.

E

eclectic approach An approach to studying behavior in which psychologists select, from the various theories and models, those aspects that provide the best fit for the descriptive and analytical task at hand.

ecological approach/ecological theory Bronfenbrenner's system of understanding development, according to which the study of developmental influences must include the person's interaction with the environment, the person's changing physical and social settings, the relationship among those settings, and how the entire process is affected by the society in which the settings are embedded.

ectoderm The cells of the embryo that form the nervous system, the sensory organs, the skin, and the lower part of the rectum.

ectogenesis The process by which the fetus gestates in an environment external to the mother.

educational self-fulfilling prophecies Teacher expectation effects whereby some children fail to learn because those who are charged with teaching them do not believe that they will learn, do not expect that they can learn, and do not act toward them in ways that motivate them to learn.

effortful control A child's ability to regulate his or her impulse to respond or act on a given emotion.

egocentric Characterized by lack of awareness that there are viewpoints other than one's own.

egocentrism A lack of awareness that there are viewpoints other than one's own. There are two characteristic forms of egocentric thinking in adolescents: the personal fable and the imaginary audience.

elder abuse A single or repeated act or lack of appropriate action occurring within any relationship where there is an expectation of trust, which causes harm or distress to an older person.

embryo The developing organism from the time the blastocyst implants itself in the uterine wall until the organism becomes a recognizable human fetus.

embryonic period The second stage of prenatal development, the period from the end of the second week to the end of the eighth week of gestation.

emerging adulthood A stage between adolescence and adulthood, a time allowing for greater exploration of life's possibilities in work, love, and worldviews.

emotional intelligence (EI) A concept proposed by Goleman that includes such abilities as being able to motivate oneself, persisting in the face of frustrations, controlling impulses and delaying gratification, empathizing, hoping, and regulating one's moods to keep distress from overwhelming one's ability to think.

emotional-social development (also called *psychosocial development*) A major domain of development that includes changes in an individual's personality, emotions, and relationships with others.

emotions The physiological changes, subjective experiences, and expressive behaviors that are involved in such feelings as love, joy, grief, and anger.

empathy Feelings of emotional arousal that lead an individual to take another person's perspective and to experience an event as the other person experiences it.

empty nest That period of the family life cycle when children have grown up and left home.

empty-nest syndrome A variety of emotions parents can experience associated with their children growing up and leaving home.

encoding A cognitive process that involves perceiving information, abstracting from it one or more characteristics needed for classification, and creating corresponding memory traces for it.

endocrinologist Physician who specializes in treating patients with hormonal disorders.

endoderm The cells of the embryo that develop into the digestive tract, the respiratory system, the bladder, and portions of the reproductive organs.

English as a second language (ESL) approach Instructional methods focused on teaching English to children with limited English proficiency.

English language learners (ELLs) Students whose native language is not English and who cannot participate effectively in school because they have difficulty speaking, understanding, reading, and writing English.

entelechy A particular type of motivation, need for self-determination, and an inner strength and vital force directing life and growth to become all one is capable of being.

entrainment A kind of biological feedback system across two organisms in which the movement of one influences the other.

epidural narcotics The administration of certain drugs to manage the mother's pain during labor.

epigenetic principle According to Erikson, the principle that each part of the personality has a particular range of time in the life span when it must develop if it is going to develop at all.

equilibrium In Piaget's theory, the result of balance between the processes of assimilation and accommodation.

erectile dysfunction A male's inability to have or sustain an erection.

ethology The study of the behavior patterns of organisms from a biological perspective.

euthanasia The act of terminating an ill or injured person's life for reasons of mercy. Also called *assisted suicide* and *mercy killing*.

event sampling A research technique of recording a class of behaviors observed at specific time intervals.

evolutionary psychology A newer discipline that investigates what mental functions, behaviors, and traits are innate, or instinctive. Researchers study how human's physical body, organs, and mind and cognition have been shaped, or have adapted, over time from biological and environmental/cultural influences.

exosystem Bronfenbrenner's third level of environmental influence, consisting of the social structures that directly or indirectly affect a person's life.

experiment A rigorous study in which the investigator manipulates one or more variables and measures the resulting changes in the other variables in an attempt to determine the cause of a specific behavior or event.

experimental design A rigorously objective scientific technique that enables a researcher to attempt to determine the cause of a behavior or event.

experimental group In an experiment, the group that receives the independent variable (treatment) and is compared with the control group.

expressive tie A social link formed when we invest ourselves in and commit ourselves to another person.

expressive vocabulary Words used by children to effectively convey meaning, feeling, or mood.

extraneous variables Factors that can confound the outcome of an experiment, such as the age and gender of the subjects, the time of day the study is conducted, the educational levels of the subjects, the setting for the experiment, and so on.

extrinsic motivation The kind of motivation at work when an activity is undertaken for some reason other than its own sake. Rewards such as school grades, wages, and promotions are examples of extrinsic motivation.

F

failure to thrive (FTT) An infant or child being severely underweight for its age and sex.

fallopian tubes Passages from the two ovaries to the uterus that carry the ova from the ovary to the uterus. Fertilization, if it occurs, typically occurs in the fallopian tubes.

family life cycle The sequential changes and realignments that occur in the structure and relationships of family life between the time of marriage and the death of one or both spouses.

fear An unpleasant emotion aroused by impending danger, loss, pain, or misfortune.

fertilization/fusion The union (or fusion) of an ovum and a sperm that usually occurs in the upper end of the fallopian tube and that results in a new structure called the zygote.

fetal alcohol spectrum disorder (FASD) The range of fetal birth defects caused by drinking alcohol during pregnancy.

fetal period The third stage of prenatal development, extending from the end of the eighth week until birth.

fetus The developing organism during the fetal period while in the mother's womb.

fixation According to psychoanalytic theory, the tendency to stay at a particular psychosexual stage of development.

floaters Floating spots that actually are particles suspended in the gel-like fluid that fills the eyeball but generally do not impair vision.

fluid intelligence A cognitive ability to make original adaptations in novel situations. Fluid intelligence is generally tested by measuring an individual's facility in reasoning; it usually declines with age in later life.

food security Having access at all times to enough food to support a healthy, active life.

G

gametes Reproductive cells (sperm and ova).

gender The state of being male or female.

gender cleavage The tendency for boys to associate with boys, and girls with girls.

gender identity The conception that people have of themselves as being female or male.

gender roles A set of cultural expectations that define the ways males and females should behave.

gender stereotypes Exaggerated generalizations about female or male behaviors.

generation gap Mutual antagonism, misunderstanding, and separation between youth and adults.

generativity The concern of an older generation in establishing and guiding the next generation.

generativity versus stagnation The crisis that, according to Erikson, the midlife years are devoted to resolving. Generativity involves guiding the next generation through nurturing and mentoring. Failure to do so is to become self-centered, which results in psychological invalidism.

genes Small units of heredity located on chromosomes that transmit inherited characteristics from biological parents to children.

genetic counseling A process whereby physicians and specialists counsel couples about concerns they may have about inherited diseases in their family history.

genetic counselor A professional who has a graduate degree, training, and experience in medical genetics and counseling and provides information and support to those who may be at risk for an inherited condition.

genetics The scientific study of biological inheritance.

genotype The genetic makeup of an organism.

germinal period The first stage of prenatal development, which extends from conception to the end of the second week.

gerontology The study of aging and the special problems associated with it.

geropsychology The study of the changing behaviors and psychological needs of the elderly.

glaucoma A condition of vision impairment characterized by increased pressure caused by fluid buildup within the eye that can damage the optic nerve and lead to blindness if left untreated.

goodness of fit The opportunities, expectations, and demands of the environment are in accord with the child's temperament.

grief An experience involving keen mental anguish and sorrow over the death of a loved one.

group Two or more people who share a feeling of unity and are bound together in relatively stable patterns of social interaction.

growth The increase in size that occurs with age.

gynecologist A physician who specializes in women's reproductive health.

H

harmonious parenting A parenting style distinguished by an unwillingness to exert direct control over children, in an attempt to cultivate an egalitarian relationship.

heredity The genes we inherit from our biological parents, which help shape our physical, intellectual, social, and emotional development.

heteronomous morality The first stage of Piaget's two-stage theory on moral development, which arises from the unequal interaction between children and adults.

heterozygous In biological inheritance, the arrangement in which two paired alleles (genes) are different.

hierarchy of needs A key concept of Abraham Maslow's humanistic theory, which indicates that basic needs must be met before self-development and self-esteem needs can be fulfilled.

holistic approach The humanistic approach according to which the human condition must be viewed in its totality, and each person is seen as a whole rather than as a mere collection of physical, social, and psychological components.

holophrase A single word used to convey complete thoughts or sentences; characteristic of the early stages of language acquisition in young children.

homozygous In biological inheritance, the arrangement in which the two paired alleles (genes) are the same.

horizontal décalage According to Piaget, a type of sequential development in which the development of each skill is dependent on the acquisition of earlier skills.

hormone replacement therapy (HRT) A medical regimen of estrogen and progestin, administered to slow bone loss, maintain cardiovascular fitness, slow memory loss, and maintain sexual desire.

hospice A program or mode of providing comfort, care, and pain relief to persons dying of cancer or other terminal illness and of offering comfort to the relatives of the patient. Care may be provided in a hospice center or in the patient's home.

human genome A map of the genetic makeup of all the genes on their appropriate chromosomes, created through extensive study by researchers in the Human Genome Project.

humanistic psychology A psychological theory, deriving from Abraham Maslow, Carl Rogers, and others, proposing that humans are different from all other organisms in that they actively intervene in the course of events to control their destinies and shape the world around them.

hypertension High blood pressure.

hypothermia A condition in which body temperature falls more than 4 degrees Fahrenheit below normal and remains at this low level for a number of hours.

hypothesis A tentative proposition that can be tested in a research study; forming a hypothesis is one of the initial steps in the scientific method.

I

identity According to Erikson, identity is defined as a sense of well-being achieved by being comfortable in one's body, by knowing where one is going, and by being recognized by significant others.

identity achievement One of James Marcia's four identity types. Identity achievement is characterized by the adolescent's ability to achieve inner stability that corresponds to how others perceive that person.

identity diffusion One of James Marcia's four identity types. Identity diffusion is characterized by the adolescent's inability to commit to an occupational or ideological position or to assume a recognizable station in life.

identity foreclosure One of James Marcia's four identity types. Identity foreclosure is characterized by the adolescent's avoidance of autonomous choice.

identity moratorium One of James Marcia's four identity types. Identity moratorium occurs when the adolescent experiments with various roles, ideologies, and commitments.

imaginary audience An adolescent's belief that everyone in the local environment is primarily concerned with her or his appearance and behavior.

imaginary friend An invisible character whom a young child names, refers to in conversations, and plays with.

implantation The process in which the blastocyst completely buries itself in the wall of the uterus.

imprinting A process of attachment that occurs only during a relatively short period and is so resistant to change that the behavior appears to be innate.

in vitro fertilization (IVF) Fertilization that occurs outside the body, typically in a petri dish in a medical lab, followed by implantation of a fertilized egg into a woman's uterus in an attempt to bring about pregnancy.

inclusion The integration of students with special needs within the regular classroom programs of the school.

independent variable The variable that is manipulated by the researcher during an experiment in order to observe its effects on the dependent variable. It is often referred to as the treatment variable.

individualism A cultural view that individual autonomy is paramount.

individualized education plan (IEP) A plan developed in a collaborative effort by the school psychologist, the child's teachers, an independent child advocate, and the parent(s) or guardian. The IEP is a legal document ensuring that the child with special learning needs will be provided with educational support services in the least restrictive learning environment possible.

Individuals with Disabilities Education Act (IDEA) Legislation providing early intervention services that seek to enhance the development of infants and toddlers with disabilities and their families' ability to meet their needs.

industry versus inferiority The fourth stage of Erikson's psychosocial model of development, in which children either work industriously and are rewarded or fail and develop a sense of inferiority.

infancy The period of child development during the first two years of life.

infant mortality The death of an infant within the first year of life.

information-processing theory Bandura's cognitive learning theory that discrete mental operations based on rules and strategies become more sophisticated as a child develops.

informed consent An ethical standard, established by the American Psychological Association, that requires the researcher to inform all subjects about the research study they are engaging in and to obtain from each subject his or her voluntary, written consent to participate in a research study.

initiative versus guilt According to Erikson, the psychosocial stage in early childhood (about ages 3 to 6) when children strive exuberantly to do things and to test their developing abilities, sometimes reaching beyond their competence.

inner cell mass The internal disc or cluster of cells that compose the blastocyst, which produces the embryo.

insecure/avoidant infants (pattern A attachments) In the Strange Situation, infants who ignored or avoided their mother when she returned.

insecure/resistant infants (pattern C attachments) In the Strange Situation, infants who were reluctant to explore a new setting and would cling to their mothers and hide from a stranger.

instrumental tie A social link that is formed when people cooperate with others to achieve a limited specific goal.

integrity versus despair Erikson's psychosocial stage of late adulthood in which individuals recognize that they are reaching the end of life. People either take satisfaction in having led a full and complete life, or view their lives with feelings of loss, disappointment, and purposelessness—depending on how they navigated the previous stages of development.

intellectual disabilities The classification of having below-average mental functioning and limitations in adaptive skills; such a diagnosis must occur before the age of 18; formerly classified as mental retardation.

intelligence According to Wechsler, a global capacity to learn exhibited by an understanding of the world, rational thought, and resourceful coping with the challenges of life.

intelligence quotient (IQ) A single number derived from tests of intelligence.

interference theory The theory that retrieval of a cue becomes less effective as more and newer items come to be classed or categorized in terms of it.

intimacy The ability to experience a trusting, supportive, and tender relationship with another person.

intimacy versus isolation Erikson's stage of psychosocial development in which young adults reach out and attempt to make close connections with other people. Failure to do so can lead to more isolated lives devoid of meaningful bonds.

intrinsic motivation The motivation at work when activity is undertaken for its own sake.

in vitro fertilization Fertilization of an egg with sperm outside a woman's body to create a zygote, which will be grown into an embryo and then transplanted into the woman's uterus.

J

job burnout Feelings of dissatisfaction and lack of fulfillment regarding work that once was fulfilling and satisfying.

joint custody A legal custody arrangement where both parents share equally in significant child-rearing decisions and share in regular child-care responsibilities.

K

kinesics Communication by body language.

kinship care An arrangement in which a relative or someone else emotionally close to the child takes primary responsibility for rearing a child.

L

labor In childbirth, the stage when the strong muscle fibers of the mother's uterus rhythmically contract and push the infant downward toward the birth canal.

language A structured system of sound patterns (words and sentences) that have socially standardized meanings that enable people to categorize objects, events, and processes in their environment and communicate with each other about them.

language acquisition device (LAD) An inborn language-generating mechanism in humans, hypothesized by Chomsky. Central to Chomsky's theory of language development is the idea that young children, just from having heard words and sentences spoken, can produce speech.

language reception The quality of receiving or taking in communication.

learning The more or less permanent change in behavior that results from the individual's experience in the environment across the entire life span.

learning disabilities (LDs) The classification used for children, adolescents, and college students who encounter difficulty with school-related material, despite the fact that they appear to have normal intelligence and lack a demonstrable physical, emotional, or social impairment.

life events Turning points at which individuals change direction in the course of their lives.

life review A reminiscence and sharing of family history from one generation to another.

lifestyle The overall pattern of living whereby one attempts to meet biological, social, and emotional needs.

lightening The repositioning of the infant that occurs a few weeks prior to birth, shifting the infant downward and forward in the uterus. The effect is to lighten the mother's discomfort and ensure that the baby will be born head first.

limited English proficiency (LEP) The legal educational term used to describe students who were not born in the United States and/or whose native language is not English and who cannot participate effectively in the regular school curriculum because they have difficulty speaking, understanding, reading, and writing English.

living will A legal document that states the individual's wishes regarding medical care in case the individual becomes incapacitated and unable to participate in decisions about medical care (such as a refusal of heroic measures to prolong her or his life in the event of terminal illness).

locomotion The infant's ability to walk, which typically evolves between 11 and 15 months of age. Preceded by crawling and creeping, it is the culmination of a long series of stages in early motor development.

locus of control An individual's perception regarding who or what is responsible for the outcomes of events and behaviors in her or his life. An important moderator of an individual's experience of stress.

loneliness Awareness of an absence of meaningful integration with other individuals or groups of individuals, a consciousness of being excluded from the system of opportunities and rewards in which other people participate.

long-term English language learners (LTELs) Those students who are arriving in secondary schools seven or more years later and still lack proficient English and academic skills.

long-term memory Information retained in memory over an extended period of time.

longitudinal design A research approach in which scientists study the same individuals at different points in their lives to assess developmental changes that occur with age.

low birth weight By common standards, a baby weighing less than 5 pounds 5 ounces at birth.

M

macrosystem Bronfenbrenner's fourth level of environmental influence, consisting of the overarching cultural patterns of a society that find expression in family, educational, economic, political, and religious institutions.

macular degeneration (AMD) A thinning of the layers of the retina and/or a rupturing of tiny blood vessels in the eye, producing faded, distorted, or blurred central vision; more common in late adulthood.

marriage A legally, socially, and/or religiously sanctioned union traditionally between one woman and one man with the expectation that they will perform mutually supportive roles. A few U.S. states have judicial or legislative decisions that allow for same-sex couples to marry, and a few U.S. states allow for civil unions of same-sex couples.

maturation A component of development that involves the more or less automatic unfolding of biological potential in a sequence of physical changes and behavior patterns.

maturity In human beings, the capacity to undergo continual change in order to adapt successfully and cope flexibly with the demands and responsibilities of life.

meiosis The process of cell division in reproductive cells that produces gametes with half of the organism's normal number of chromosomes.

melanoma A serious skin cancer that can be life threatening.

memory The cognitive capacity to retain information that has been experienced.

menarche The first menstrual period.

menopause The normal aging process that culminates in the cessation of female menstrual activity. In Western countries, women typically experience menopause between the ages of 45 and 55 years.

menstrual cycle A series of hormonal changes within a woman, beginning with menstruation and ovulation, typically about 28 days per cycle.

menstruation The maturing of an ovum and the process of ovulation and eventual shedding of the uterine lining and expulsion of an unfertilized ovum from the body through the vagina.

mental health Involves people's ability to function effectively in their social roles and to carry out the requirements of group living.

mentor A wise older counselor, experienced coworker, boss, or the like who shares expertise and guides someone in new learning.

mesoderm The cells of the embryo, which give rise to the skeletal, muscular, and circulatory systems and to the kidneys.

mesosystem Bronfenbrenner's second level of environmental influences, consisting of the interrelationships among the various settings in which the developing person is immersed.

metacognition An individual's awareness and understanding of his or her own mental processes.

metamemory An individual's awareness and understanding of her or his memory processes.

methylphenidate A mild stimulant of the central nervous system used to treat the behavior disorders ADD and ADHD (brand name Ritalin).

microsystem Bronfenbrenner's first level of environmental influence, which consists of the network of social relationships and the physical settings in which a person is involved each day.

midwifery The legalized provision of prenatal care and delivery by midwives.

miscarriage Expulsion of the zygote, embryo, or fetus from the uterus before it can survive outside the mother's womb.

mitosis The process of ordinary cell division, which results in two new cells identical to the parent cell.

modernization theory The theory that the status of the elderly tends to be high in traditional societies and lower in urbanized, industrialized societies.

monozygotic (identical) twins Multiple, identical siblings from one fertilized egg.

moral development The process by which children adopt principles and values that lead them to evaluate behaviors as "right" or "wrong" and to govern their own actions in terms of these principles.

moral exemplars Individuals dedicated to acts of morality.

moral relativism The theory that there are no set moral principles or guidelines by which everyone is obligated to live.

morphology The study of word formation and changes, as when a child learns to say "Jim's and mine" instead of "Jim's and mine's."

motherese (parentese) The speech adults tend to use with infants and young children; language that characteristically is simplified, redundant, and highly grammatical.

motivation The inner emotional or cognitive states and processes that prompt, direct, and sustain a person's activity.

mourning The culturally or socially established manner of expressing sorrow over a person's death.

multifactorial transmission The interaction of environmental factors with genetic factors to produce traits. For example, a child's inborn predisposition to musical talent can be nurtured or deterred by environmental forces, such as parents or teachers.

multi-infarcts "Little strokes" that destroy small areas of brain tissue.

multiple intelligences (MIs) Nine distinctive intelligences that interact: verbal-linguistic, logical-mathematical, visual-spatial, musical, bodily-kinesthetic, interpersonal, naturalist, intrapersonal, and existentialist (philosophical).

multiple mothering An arrangement in which responsibility for a child's care is dispersed among several caregivers.

N

natural childbirth A form of childbirth in which the woman is awake, aware, and unmedicated during labor and delivery.

naturalistic observation A research method that involves carefully watching and recording behavior as it occurs in natural settings. The researchers must be careful not to disturb or affect the events under investigation.

near-death experience (NDE) An experience such as having spiritually left one's body, having undergone otherworldly experiences, and having been "told to come back"—commonly reported by people experiencing a medical illness, a traumatic accident, a surgical operation, childbirth, or drug ingestion.

negative identity A diminished self-image, often associated with a diminished social role.

neglect A type of abuse committed by a caretaker in failing to provide adequate social, emotional, and physical care to maintain the health or safety of a vulnerable person.

neonatal intensive care unit (NICU) A special medical unit staffed with perinatologists and neonatologists who specialize in managing complicated, high-risk pregnancies, birth, and postbirth experience.

neonate A newborn baby in the first month of life.

nonnormative life events In the timing-of-events model, a set of unique turning points at which people change some direction in their life.

normative age-graded influences In the timing-of-events model, a set of influences that include physical, cognitive, and psychosocial changes at predictable ages.

normative history-graded influences In the timing-of-events model, historical events (such as wars, epidemics, and economic depressions) that affect large numbers of individuals at about the same time.

norms In child development, standards used for evaluating a child's developmental progress relative to the average for the child's age group.

nuclear family A family arrangement consisting of a mother, a father, and their biological or adopted children.

O

obesity For women, having at least 30 percent of body weight being fat; for men, having at least 25 percent body fat.

object permanence The understanding that objects continue to exist when they are out of sight; Piaget said this cognitive capacity is mastered by the end of infancy.

obstetrician Physician who specializes in reproduction, prenatal development, birth, and the woman's postbirth care.

occupational therapist A therapist who helps people improve basic motor function and reasoning abilities and also learn to compensate for permanent loss of function.

operant conditioning A type of learning in which the consequences of a behavior alter the strength of that behavior.

oral-sensory stage Erikson's first stage of psychosocial development in which an infant develops trust in others if a caregiver is responsive and consistent in feeding, comforting, and caring for the infant.

osteoarthritis Joint inflammation that results from cartilage degeneration; the most common form of arthritis; related to aging.

osteoporosis A serious bone-thinning disorder that is a "silent" disease but is most evident in late adulthood. An adult's bones typically begin thinning during the mid-thirties, but weight-bearing exercise and calcium in the diet can prevent or slow the progression of osteoporosis.

otitis media A painful ear infection in young children that causes fluid buildup in the middle ear with the potential for hearing loss if left untreated.

ovaries A pair of almond-shaped structures in the pelvis that are the primary female reproductive organs. The ovaries produce mature ova and the female sex hormones, estrogen and progesterone.

overweight Having a body mass index (BMI) at or above 25; the proportion of overweight children has quadrupled since the 1970s to nearly one-third of children ages 6 to 11.

ovulation The discharge of a mature ovum from a follicle in the ovary into the fallopian tube.

ovum The female gamete (sex cell), or egg.

P

paralanguage The stress, pitch, and volume of vocalizations by which we communicate expressive meaning.

parentese (motherese) A simplified, redundant, highly grammatical type of language that caretakers use with infants.

parent-infant bonding A process of interaction and mutual attention that occurs over time and builds an emotional bond between parent and infant.

peers Individuals of approximately the same age.

penis A man's external reproductive organ, and the role in reproduction is to deliver the sperm to the female's body.

perimenopause The period of two to four years before the cessation of menstruation, with sometimes heavy flow and the extension of intervals between periods.

period of concrete operations Piaget's cognitive stage of middle childhood during which children demonstrate a qualitative change in cognitive functioning and develop a set of rules or strategies for examining the world.

period of formal operations Piaget's highest stage in the development of cognitive functioning, characterized by the ability to think abstractly and plan for the future. This stage is generally reached during adolescence, but adults with cognitive disabilities may never reach the stage of formal operations.

periodontal disease Condition in which the gums of the teeth begin to recede.

permissive parenting A style of parenting distinguished by a nonpunitive, accepting, and affirmative environment in which the child regulates her or his own behavior as much as possible.

persistent vegetative state The state in which the functions of the brain stem, such as breathing and circulation, remain intact, but the person loses the higher functioning of the cerebral cortex.

person permanence The notion that an individual exists independently of immediate visibility.

personal fable Romantic imagery in which adolescents tend to view themselves as somehow unique and even heroic—as destined for unusual fame and fortune.

phenotype The observable (expressed) characteristics of an organism.

phobia An excessive, persistent, and maladaptive fear response—usually to benign or ill-defined stimuli.

phonemes The smallest units of language, such as the long *a* in *bake*.

phonology The study of the sounds involved in a given language.

physical development Changes that occur in a person's body, including changes in weight and height; in the brain, heart, and other organ structures and processes; and in skeletal, muscular, and neurological features that affect motor, sensory, and coordination skills.

placenta A structure formed from uterine tissue and the trophoblast of the blastocyst. It functions as an exchange terminal, permitting entry of food materials, oxygen, and hormones into the fetus and allowing exit of carbon dioxide and metabolic wastes.

placenta praevia A condition in which the placenta is lower in the uterus than the fetus's head, partially or fully covering the cervix. This condition may lead to hemorrhaging of the placenta or prevent vaginal delivery—thus necessitating a cesarean delivery. Such a serious condition can be detected by ultrasound.

play Enjoyable voluntary activities that are performed for their own sake.

polygenic inheritance The determination of traits by a large number of genes in combination, rather than by a single gene. Examples include personality, intelligences, aptitudes, and abilities.

post-formal operational thought A fifth stage of cognitive development proposed by neo-Piagetians that is characterized by three features: Adults come to realize that knowledge is not absolute but relativistic, that contradiction is inherent in life, and that they must find some encompassing whole by which to organize their experience.

postmature infant A baby delivered more than 2 weeks after the usual 40 weeks of gestation in the womb.

postmenopause Time period in a woman's life after she has not menstruated for one year.

postpartum major depression (PMD) Symptoms of depression experienced by some new mothers, such as feeling unable to cope, thoughts of not wanting to take care of the baby, or thoughts of wanting to harm the baby. Also called *postpartum blues.*

post-traumatic stress disorder (PTSD) A person's delayed response to severe or prolonged stress. Symptoms may include numbing and helplessness, increased irritability and aggressiveness, extreme anxiety, panic and fears, an exaggerated startle response, sleep disturbances, and bed-wetting.

power of attorney A legal document designating someone to make medical (or other) decisions if a patient is unable to do so.

pragmatics Rules governing the use of language in different social contexts.

prejudice A system of negative conceptions, feelings, and actions regarding the members of a particular religious, racial, or ethnic group.

premature infant By common standards, a baby weighing less than 5 pounds 8 ounces at birth or having a gestational age of less than 37 weeks.

premature menopause Early menopause (before age 40) often brought about by a hysterectomy.

prenatal diagnosis A determination of the health and condition of an unborn fetus.

prenatal period The period of development from conception to birth.

preoperational period Piaget's stage of cognitive development of children aged 2 to 7. The principal achievement of this stage is the developing capacity to represent the external world internally through the use of symbols.

presbycusis The inability to hear high-pitched sounds, which is more common in elderly adults.

presbyopia A normal condition in which the lens of the eye starts to harden with age, losing its ability to accommodate as quickly as it did in younger years.

preterm infant A baby having a gestational age less than 37 weeks.

primary relationship A social interaction based on significant expressive ties, such as with parents, spouse, siblings, and children.

primary sex characteristics The anatomical parts of the body specific to human reproduction.

private speech Speech commonly used by toddlers and older children that is directed toward oneself or toward nobody in particular.

prosocial behavior Being sympathetic, cooperative, helpful, rescuing, comforting, and generous; learning such behavior is considered to be an aspect of moral development.

prostate gland A small gland in males at the base of the urethra that produces prostate fluid for semen. It generally enlarges as males reach their fifties or sixties, creating urinary difficulties.

prostatitis An inflammation of the prostate gland.

proximodistal development (proximodistal principle) Development that proceeds outward from the central axis of the body toward the extremities.

PSA test Medical test that measures a substance called prostate-specific antigen, which is made by the prostate.

psychoanalytic theory Theory based on Freud's view that personality is fashioned progressively as the individual passes through various psychosexual stages of development.

psychoprophylactic method A preparatory technique in childbirth used to encourage women to relax and concentrate on their breathing when a contraction occurs during labor.

psychosexual stages The stages of personality development that Freud believed all human beings pass through: oral, anal, phallic, latency, and genital.

psychosocial development An individual's development within a social context over the life course.

puberty The period during early adolescence when sexual and reproductive maturation becomes evident.

puberty rites Cultural initiation ceremonies that socially symbolize an adolescent's transition from childhood to adulthood.

R

random sampling A sample for which each member of the population has an equally likely probability of being chosen; a technique to ensure that the sample under study represents the larger population.

reactive attachment disorder (RAD) A clinical diagnosis that includes disturbed and developmentally inappropriate social relatedness with peers (autistic-like behaviors, hyperactivity).

recall Act of remembering something previously learned.

receptive vocabulary An understanding of spoken words, exhibited by infants before they have developed an expressive vocabulary (speaking their first words).

recessive character A gene that can determine a trait in an individual only if the other member of that gene pair is also recessive, as in *aa*.

reciprocity A process that leads to a child's valuing another person in a way that allows the child to remember the values that their interactions bring about. Piaget asserts that reciprocity of attitudes and values is the foundation of social interchange in children.

recognition A perception, with the assistance of cues, of something that we have previously encountered.

recreational therapist A physical therapist who works with patients to help restore function, improve mobility, relieve pain, and prevent or limit permanent physical disabilities.

reflex A simple, involuntary, and unlearned response to a stimulus.

rehearsal A type of memory process in which we repeat information to ourselves to retain information.

reinforcement One event's strengthening the probability of another event's occurrence. A concept of behavioral theory popularized by B. F. Skinner.

releasing stimuli Biologically preadapted behaviors and features in infants that activate parenting.

reproduction The process by which organisms create more organisms of their own kind.

resource dilution hypothesis The theory that in large families, resources get spread thin, to the detriment of all the offspring.

response A term that behavioral theorists use to break down behavior into units.

retrieval The cognitive process by which information is gathered from memory when it is required for recall or recognition.

reversibility of operations The recognition that operations can be done in reverse to regain an earlier state. According to Piaget, the child's failure to grasp the reversibility of operations is the most distinguishing characteristic of preoperational thought.

rheumatoid arthritis An inflammatory disease common in the elderly that causes pain, swelling, stiffness, and loss of function of the joint.

right to privacy An ethical standard established by the American Psychological Association requiring that researchers keep confidential all their records of information about and behaviors of research participants.

role conflict A type of stress that occurs when people experience pressures within one role that are incompatible with the pressures that arise within another role (for example, having to be at work and also having to take care of a sick child).

role exit theory of aging A theory that views retirement and widowhood as life events that terminate the participation of the elderly in the principal institutional structures of society—the job and the family.

role overload A type of stress that occurs when people have too many role demands and too little time to fulfill them.

romantic love What we typically think of as being "in love" with someone.

rooming in An arrangement in a hospital whereby the newborn stays in a bassinet beside the mother's bed, allowing the mother, father, and other family members to care for and become acquainted with the newborn.

S

sandwich generation People in middle adulthood who are caring for growing children at the same time as they are helping elderly parents and relatives.

scaffolding Helping the child to learn through intervention and tutoring that is geared to the child's current level of functioning.

schemas Piaget's term for mental structures that people construct to deal with events in their environment.

scientific method A systematic and formal process for conducting research, including selecting a researchable problem, formulating a hypothesis, testing the hypothesis, arriving at conclusions, and making the findings public.

secondary relationship A social interaction based on instrumental ties, such as a relationship with a mechanic, or a teacher in a classroom, or a clerk at a store.

secondary sex characteristics The initial visible physical changes that occur in the development of males and females.

securely attached infants (pattern B attachments) In the Strange Situation, infants who greet their mothers warmly, show little anger, or indicate a desire to be picked up and comforted.

selective attrition The theory that individuals who drop out of a study tend to be different from those who remain in a study.

selective optimization with compensation The life-span model endorsed by Paul and Margret Baltes. Older people cope with aging through a strategy that involves focusing on the skills most needed, practicing those skills, and developing ways to compensate for the loss of other skills.

self The system of concepts we use in defining ourselves; the awareness of ourselves as separate entities who think and initiate action. The self provides us with the capacity to observe, respond to, and direct our behavior.

self-actualization Maslow's concept from humanistic psychology that each person needs to fulfill his or her unique potential to the greatest extent possible.

self-concept (self-image) The image a person has of herself or himself.

self-esteem An overall dimension of one's sense of self-worth or self-image.

self-image The overall view people have of themselves, which can be positive or negative.

self-regulation The infant's growing ability to control negative emotions and integrate his or her emotions adaptively into daily social interactions.

semantics The rules of meaning in a language, by which words have meaning and are combined to express thoughts and ideas.

senescence The process of growing old, which affects a person both physically and cognitively.

senility A deterioration in cognitive functioning in late adulthood characterized by a lack of consistency in personality and/or behavior.

sensorimotor period Piaget's first stage of cognitive development, lasting from birth to about two years. Infants use actions—looking, grasping, and so on—to learn about their world. The major tasks of the period revolve around coordinating motor activities with sensory inputs.

sensory information storage The preservation of sensory information in the sensory register just long enough to permit the stimuli to be scanned for processing, generally less than 2 seconds.

sensory integration A normal developmental process that enables one to take in, process, and organize sensations received from one's body and the environment.

separation anxiety An infant's fear of being separated from the caregiver, demonstrated by distress behaviors.

sequential design A combination of the longitudinal and cross-sectional methods of research.

sex chromosomes The 23rd pair of chromosomes, either XX or XY, which determine the baby's sex.

sex-linked traits Traits other than gender that are affected by genes found on the sex chromosomes. For example, hemophilia is a sex-linked characteristic carried on the X chromosome.

sexual abuse of children A type of maltreatment that consists of the coercive involvement of the child in sexual activity to provide sexual gratification or financial benefits to the perpetrator.

sexually transmitted infections (STIs) Infections that are transmitted during sexual activity and cause symptoms that, if left untreated, can cause disease and infertility.

shaken baby syndrome (SBS) Serious brain damage or death that occurs when a baby's head is violently shaken back and forth or strikes something, resulting in bruising or bleeding of the brain, spinal cord injury, and eye damage.

short-term memory The retention of information in memory for a very brief period, usually no more than 30 seconds.

sleep apnea A sleep disorder in which the person occasionally stops breathing during sleep.

small-for-term infant A low-birth-weight infant that has developed over the usual 40 weeks of gestation in the womb but is born weighing less than is expected.

social aging Changes in an individual's assumptions and roles as she or he ages.

social clock A set of social concepts regarding the appropriate ages for reaching milestones of the adult years.

social competence The ability to understand causes of emotions, predict the emotional reactions of others, know when emotional display is appropriate, and successfully participate in social groups.

social convoy The company of other people who travel with us from birth to death.

social exchange theory of aging The theory that people enter into social relationships in order to derive rewards (economic, social, emotional). People also incur costs in social relationships. Relationships persist as long as both parties "profit."

social norms Standards and expectations that specify what constitutes appropriate and inappropriate behavior for individuals at various periods in the life span.

social referencing The practice whereby an inexperienced person relies on a more experienced person's interpretation of an event to regulate his or her own behavior.

social relationships Bonds forged with other people in relatively stable social circumstances.

social smile An infant's smile that emerges at around 6 to 10 weeks of age in response to adult smiles and interactions.

social survey method A research method used to study the incidence of specific behaviors, attitudes, or beliefs in a large population of people.

social understanding The capacity to predict the intention of another person, manage conflict, and talk about feelings.

socialization The process of transmitting culture to children in order to transform them into well-functioning members of society.

sociocultural theory The theory that such psychological functions as thinking, reasoning, and remembering are facilitated through language and anchored in the child's interpersonal relationships.

spatial ability The ability to form mental images, visualize graphic representations, and recognize interrelationships among objects.

sperm The male gamete (sex cell).

spontaneous abortion The medical term for miscarriage, which is usually preceded by cramping or bleeding.

states In child development, an infant's continuum of alertness, which ranges from sleep to vigorous activity and includes such behaviors as crying, sleeping, eating, and eliminating. By regulating their internal states, infants shut out certain stimuli or set the stage to actively respond to their environment.

stem cells Cells that have the capacity to reproduce themselves and to produce distinct differentiated tissues.

stereotypes Exaggerated cultural understandings that guide us in identifying the mutual set of expectations that will govern the social exchange.

stimuli A term used by behavioral theorists to break down the environment into units.

stimulus-rich environment An environment in which a child has many opportunities to learn about and try new things.

storage The phase of information processing in which information is retained in memory until it is needed.

storm and stress Hall's notion that adolescence is a stage of inevitable turmoil, maladjustment, tension, rebellion, dependency conflicts, and exaggerated peer-group conformity.

Strange Situation A research technique consisting of a series of eight episodes in which researchers observe infants in an unfamiliar playroom in order to study their attachment to a mother.

stranger anxiety A wariness or fear of strangers first exhibited by infants at about 8 months, peaking around 13 to 15 months, and decreasing thereafter.

stress A body's involuntary reaction involving the recognition of and response to a threat or danger, but stress can also accompany positive experiences as well.

stroke A life-threatening blockage of blood flow to the brain.

substance abuse The regular use of drugs or alcohol, lasting over a prolonged period, that can result in harm to the user or to others.

sudden infant death syndrome (SIDS) Sudden death of an infant during sleep, due to unknown causes; also called *crib death*. One of the leading causes of infant death during the first several months of life. Babies should sleep on their backs to reduce the risk of SIDS.

syntax Rules governing the proper ordering of words to form sentences.

systolic pressure Blood pressure when the heart contracts and is pumping blood.

T

telegraphic speech The use of two- or three-word utterances to express complete thoughts; characteristic of young children's speech.

telehealth The use of electronic information and communication technology to deliver medical information and services over distances through a standard telephone line.

telemedicine The incorporation of telehealth technologies into a physician's office, hospital, clinic, medical institution, or other health care organization's practice of medicine, using telecommunications technology to transmit diagnostic images and monitor blood pressure, heart rate, and other vital information.

temperament The relatively consistent, basic dispositions inherent in people that underlie and modulate much of their behavior.

teratogen Any agent that contributes to birth defects or anomalies.

teratology The study of teratogens and birth defects.

testes A pair of primary male reproductive organs, normally lying outside the body in a pouchlike structure called a scrotum.

testosterone Male sex hormone.

thanatology The study of death and dying.

theory A set of interrelated statements intended to explain a class of events.

theory of mind In child development, research that probes children's developing conceptions of major components of mental activity.

time sampling An observational technique that involves counting the occurrences of a specific behavior over systematically spaced intervals of time.

total immersion programs The instructional approach of placing children of all language backgrounds together in regular classrooms and using English for all instruction (with or without support in their first language).

traditional marriage The style of marriage in which women are homemakers and men are providers.

transhumanism A philosophy that humanity can, and should, strive to reach higher levels physically, mentally, and socially. It encourages research into such areas as life extension, cryonics, nanotechnology, physical and mental enhancements, uploading human consciousness into computers, and megascale engineering.

transition points Periods in development when the individual relinquishes familiar roles and assumes new ones.

triangular theory of love Sternberg's theory that different stages and types of love can be explained as combinations of the three elements of intimacy, passion, and commitment.

triglycerides The chemical form of fats in food; triglycerides are major components of low-density lipoprotein.

trophoblast Outer layer of cells of the blastocyst; this layer is responsible for embedding the embryo in the uterine wall.

two-factor theory of intelligence Spearman's view that intelligence is a general intellectual ability employed for abstract reasoning and problem solving.

two-way bilingual programs The instructional approach in which both native-speaking students and nonnative speakers receive instruction in English and in another language; participation is voluntary, and instruction is equally divided between the two languages.

U

ultrasound A noninvasive diagnostic procedure that allows physicians to see inside the body—for instance, to determine the size and shape of the fetus and placenta, the amount of amniotic fluid, and the appearance of fetal anatomy.

umbilical cord A connecting lifeline carrying two arteries and one vein linking the embryo to the placenta.

uterus A hollow, thick-walled, muscular organ in a female that can house and nourish a developing embryo and fetus.

V

vagina A muscular passageway in the female reproductive system that is capable of considerable dilation, allowing for intercourse and the birth of a baby.

values The criteria individuals use in deciding the relative merit and desirability of things (such as themselves, other people, objects, events, ideas, acts, and feelings).

W

wisdom Expert knowledge about life in general and good judgment and advice about how to conduct oneself in complex, uncertain circumstances.

Y

youth culture Characteristics of a large body of young people that become standardized ways of thinking, feeling, and behaving.

Z

zone of proximal development (ZPD) Vygotsky's concept that children develop through participation in activities slightly beyond their competence when helped by a more skilled partner.

zygote A single fertilized ovum (egg).

REFERENCES

Abe, J. A., & Izard, C. E. (1999). A longitudinal study of emotion expression and personality relations in early development. *Journal of Personality and Social Psychology, 77,* 566–577.

Abeles, N., Victor, T. L., & Delano-Wood, L. (2004). The impact of an older adult's death on the family. *Professional Psychology: Research and Practice, 35*(3), 234–239.

Aboim, S. (2010). Family and gender values in contemporary Europe: The attitudinal gender gap from a cross-national perspective. *Portuguese Journal of Social Science, 9*(1), 33–58. doi:10.1386/pjss.9.1.33_1

Aboud, F. E. (2003, January). The formation of in-group favoritism and out-group prejudice in young children: Are they distinct attitudes? *Developmental Psychology, 39,* 48–60.

AbouZahr, C., & Wardlaw, T. (2001). Maternal mortality at the end of the decade: Signs of progress? *Bulletin of the World Health Organization, 79*(6), 561–573.

Abu-Saad, K., & Frasar, D. (2010). Maternal nutrition and birth outcomes. *Epidemiologic Reviews, 32*(1), 5–25. doi:10.1093/epirev/mxq001

Academic statistics on homeschooling. (2004, October 22). Home School Legal Defense Association. Retrieved from http://nche.hslda.org/

Accornero, V. H., Anthony, J. C., Bandstra, E. S., Culberston, J. L., Morrow, C. E., & Xue, L. (2006). Learning disabilities and intellectual functioning in school-aged children with prenatal cocaine exposure. *Developmental Neuropsychology, 30*(3), 905–931.

Achenbaum, W. (1998). Perceptions of aging in America. *National Forum: Phi Kappa Phi Journal, 78,* 30–33.

Achenbaum, W. A. (2007). A history of old age. *Journal of Social History, 40*(4), 1059–1061.

Acredolo, L. P., & Goodwyn, S. (2009). *Baby signs: How to talk with your baby before your baby can talk* (3rd ed.). New York: McGraw-Hill.

Acredolo, L. P., & Hake, J. K. (1982). Infant perception. In B. B. Wolman (Ed.), *Handbook of developmental psychology.* Englewood Cliffs, NJ: Prentice Hall.

Acs, G., & Nelson, S. (2002, July). *The kids are alright? Children's well-being and the rise in cohabitation.* Discussion paper B–48, New Federalism: National Survey of America's Families. Washington, DC: The Urban Institute. Retrieved from http://www.urban.org/UploadedPDF/310544_B48.pdf

Action on Elder Abuse. (2008). *Fact sheet.* Retrieved from http://www.elderabuse.org.uk/com

Adair, J. (1775). *The history of the American Indians.* London: E. D. Dilly.

Adams, R. G., & Blieszner, R. (1998, Spring). Baby boomer friendships. *Generations, 22,* 70–75.

Adamson, L. (1996). *Communication development during infancy.* Boulder, CO: Westview Press.

Adamczyk, A. (2009, April). Socialization and selection in the link between friends' religiosity and the transition to sexual intercourse. *Sociology of Religion, 70*(1), 5–27. doi:10.1093/socrel/srp010

Adams Hillard, P. J. (2008). Menstruation in adolescence: What's normal, what's not. *Annals of the New York Academy of Sciences, 11*(35), 29–35. doi: 0.1196/annals.1429.022

Adams, C. (2010). Cyberbullying. *Instructor, 120*(2), 44. Retrieved from *MasterFILE* Premier database.

Adams, M. (2006). Towards an existential phenomenological model of life span human development. *Existential Analysis, 17*(2), 261–280.

Adamy, J. (2010, December 17). Judge leery of health mandate. *Wall Street Journal, 256*(143), p. A2. Retrieved from EBSCOhost.

Addison, S. (2004). Understanding early intervention services. *The Exceptional Parent, 34*(8), 63–65.

Adelson, J. (1972). The political imagination of the young adolescent. In J. Kagan & R. Coles (Eds.), *Twelve to sixteen: Early adolescence* (pp. 106–143). New York: Norton.

Adelson, J. (1975). The development of ideology in adolescence. In S. E. Dragastin & G. H. Elder, Jr. (Eds.), *Adolescence in the life cycle: Psychological change and social context* (pp. 27–34). New York: Wiley.

Adler, A. (1964). *Problems of neurosis.* New York: Harper & Row.

Administration for Children and Families. (2006). *Findings from the survey of Early Head Start Programs: Communities, programs, and families.* Washington, DC: Office of Planning, Research and Evaluation.

Administration on Aging. (2009, July 16). Historical evolution of programs for older Americans. Retrieved from http://www.aoa.gov/aoaroot/aoa_programs/oaa/resources/History.aspx

Adolphs, R., & Damasio, A. (2001). The interaction of affect and cognition: A neurobiological perspective. In J. P. Forgas (Ed.), *The handbook of affect and social cognition* (pp. 27–49). Mahwah, NJ: Erlbaum.

Advisory Committee for Immunization Practices. (2010). Recommendations and guidelines. Retrieved from http://www.cdc.gov/vaccines/recs/default.htm

Ahmad, I., & Szpara, M. Y. (2003). Muslim children in urban America: The New York City schools experience. *Journal of Muslim Minority Affairs, 23*(2), 295–301.

Ahmadi, K., & Hossein-abadi, F. H. (2009). Religiosity, marital satisfaction and child rearing. *Pastoral Psychology, 57,* 211–221. doi:10.1007/s11089-008-0176-4

Ahnert, L., & Lamb, M. (2001). The East German child care system: Associations with caretaking and caretaking beliefs, and children's early attachment and adjustment. *American Behavioral Scientist, 44*(11), 1843–1863.

Ahrons, C. (2007). Family ties after divorce: Long-term implications for children. *Family Process, 46*(1), 53–65.

Ainsworth, M. D. S. (1967). *Infancy in Uganda: Infant care and the growth of attachment.* Baltimore: Johns Hopkins University Press.

Ainsworth, M. D. S. (1983). Patterns of infant-mother attachment as related to maternal care. In D. Magnusson & V. Allen (Eds.), *Human development: An interactional perspective.* New York: Academic Press.

Ainsworth, M. D. S. (1992). A consideration of social referencing in the context of attachment theory and research. In S. Feinman (Ed.), *Social referencing and the social construction of reality in infancy.* New York: Plenum.

Ainsworth, M. D. S. (1993). Attachment as related to mother-infant interaction. *Advances in Infancy Research, 8,* 1–50.

Ainsworth, M. D. S. (1995). On the shaping of attachment theory and research: An interview with Mary Ainsworth (Fall 1994). *Monographs of the Society for Research in Child Development, 60,* 3–21.

Ainsworth, M. D. S., Bell, S. M., & Stayton, D. J. (1974). Infant-mother attachment and social development. In M. P. M. Richards (Ed.), *The integration of a child into a social world.* New York: Cambridge University Press.

Ainsworth, M. D. S., & Wittig, B. A. (1969). Attachment and the exploratory behavior of one-year-olds in a strange situation. In B. M. Foss (Ed.), *Determinants of infant behavior* (Vol. 4). London: Methuen.

Aitchison, J. (2006). Whassup? Slang and swearing among school children. *Education Review, 19*(2), 18–24.

Akinbami, L. J. (2006). The state of childhood asthma, United States, 1980–2005. *Advance Data from Vital and Health Statistics, 381,* 1–23.

Akos, P., & Levitt, D. H. (2002). Promoting healthy body image in middle school. *Professional School Counseling, 6*(2), 138–145.

Albert, B. (2007, February). *With one voice: America's adults and teens sound off about teen pregnancy.* Washington, DC: The National Campaign to Prevent Teen Pregnancy.

Albert, W. (2003, December 16). *Teens continue to express cautious attitudes toward sex.* Washington, DC: The National Campaign to Prevent Teen Pregnancy.

Aldhous, P., & Coghlan, A. (2006). Ten years on, has the cloning dream died? *New Scientist, 191*(2558), 8–10.

Alexander, K. L., Entwisle, D. R., & Olson, L. S. (2001). Schools, achievement, and inequality: A seasonal perspective. *Educational Evaluation and Policy Analysis, 23*(2), 171–191.

Alink, L. R. A., Mesman, J., Van Zeijl, J., Stolk, M. N., Juffer, F., Koot, H. M., . . . van IJzendoorn, M. H. (2006). The early childhood aggression curve: Development of physical aggression in 10- to 50-month-old children. *Child Development, 77*(4), 954–966.

All About Depression. (2004). *Causes of depression.* Retrieved from http://allaboutdepression.com/cau_01.html

Allebrand, C. (2007, November 19). *57 percent of Americans do not have a will.* Bankrate.com. Retrieved from http://investor.bankrate.com/releasedetail.cfm?ReleaseID=276290

Allen, E. S., & Baucom, D. H. (2006). Dating, marital, and hypothetical extradyadic involvements: How do they compare? *The Journal of Sex Research, 43*(4), 307–317.

Allen, J. D., Kennedy, M., Wilson-Glover, A., & Gilligan, T. D. (2007). African-American men's perceptions about prostate cancer: Implications for designing educational interventions. *Social Science & Medicine, 64*(11), 2189–2200.

Alley, T. R. (1983). Growth-produced changes in body shape and size as determinants of perceived age and adult caretaking. *Child Development, 54*, 241–248.

Alliance for Excellent Education. (2009, February). *Fact sheet: High school dropouts in America.* Washington, DC: Alliance for Excellent Education.

Allison, B. N., & Schultz, J. B. (2004). Parent-adolescent conflict in early adolescence. *Adolescence, 39*(153), 101–120.

Allman, W. F. (1991, August 19). The clues in the idle chatter. *U.S. News & World Report,* 61–62.

allnurses.com. (2008, June 26). "Why do dying people reach upward?" (2008). Retrieved from http://allnurses.com/general-nursing-discussion/why-do-dying-312997.html

Allport, G. W. (1961). *Pattern and growth in personality.* New York: Holt, Rinehart & Winston.

Alsop, R. (2008). *The trophy kids grow up: How the Millennial Generation is shaking up the workplace.* San Francisco: Jossey-Bass.

Alternatives to Abortion. (2010). National-Right-to-Life Committee. Retrieved from http://www.nrlc.org/abortion/ASMF/asmf15.html

Altman, L. K. (2008, January 15). New bacteria strain is striking gay men. *New York Times,* p. F7(L).

Alzheimer's Association. (2010). Alzheimer's disease: Facts and figures. *Alzheimer's & Dementia, 6*(2), 158–194. Retrieved from http://www.alzheimersanddementia.com/article/PIIS1552526010000142/fulltext#bib111

Alzheimer's Association. (2011a). Alzheimer's disease: Facts and figures. *Alzheimer's & Dementia, 7*(2), 1–68. Retrieved from http://www.alz.org/downloads/Facts_Figures_2011.pdf

Alzheimer's Association. (2011b). *Generation Alzheimer's: The defining disease of the baby boomers.* Retrieved from http://www.alz.org/news_and_events_generation_alz.asp

Alvik, A., Haldorsen, T., Groholt, B., & Lindemann, R. (2006). Alcohol consumption before and during pregnancy comparing concurrent and retrospective reports. *Alcoholism Clinical and Experimental Research, 30*(3), 510–515.

Amato, P. R. (2000). The consequences of divorce for adults and children. *Journal of Marriage and the Family, 62*, 1269–1287.

Amato, P. R. (2005). The impact of family formation change on the cognitive, social, and emotional well-being of the next generation. *The Future of Children, 15*(2), 75–96.

Amato, P. R., Booth, A., Johnson, D. R., & Rogers, S. J. (2007). *Alone together: How marriage in America is changing.* Cambridge, MA: Harvard University Press.

Amato, P. R., & Cheadle, J. E. (2008). Parental divorce, marital conflict and children's behavior problems: A comparison of adopted and biological children. *Social Forces, 86*(3), 1139–1161. doi:10.1353/sof.0.0025

Amato, P. R., & Dorius, C. (2010). Fathers, children, and divorce. In M. E. Lamb (Ed.), *The role of the father in child development* (pp. 177–200). Hoboken, NJ: Wiley.

American Academy of Dermatology. (2007). *Consumer alert: Questions to ask for safe and successful cosmetic surgery.* Retrieved from http://www.aad.org/media/background/news/cosmetic_2007_07_25_consumer.html

American Academy of Dermatology. (2010, March 6). Dermatologists can help women win the fight against common forms of hair loss. *ScienceDaily.* Retrieved from http://www.sciencedaily.com/releases/2010/03/100306143329.htm

American Academy of Pediatric Dentistry. (2005). *April is national facial protection month.* Retrieved from http://www.aapd.org/upload/news/2004/528.pdf

American Academy of Pediatrics. (1996). *Puberty: Information for boys.* Retrieved from http://www.aap.org/pubserv/patedcd/demo/pdffiles/papers/HE020802.pdf

American Academy of Pediatrics. (2009). Policy statement—Media violence. *Pediatrics, 124*(5), 1495–1503. doi:10.1542/peds.2009-2146

American Academy of Pediatrics. (2010a). AAP updates guidance to help families make positive media choices. Healthy Children. Retrieved from http://www.healthychildren.org/English/news/Pages/AAP-Updates-Guidance-to-Help-Families-Make-Positive-Media-Choices

American Academy of Pediatrics. (2010b, June 8). Your preschooler's physical appearance and growth. Retrieved from http://www.healthychildren.org/English/ages-stages/preschool/pages/Your-Preschoolers-Physical-Appearance-and-Growth.aspx

American Association of Suicidology. (2010). *Fact sheet: Suicide in the U.S.A.* Retrieved February 1, 2011 from http://www.suicidology.org/c/document_library/get_file?folderid=232&name=DLFE-244.pdf

American Association of University Women (AAUW). (2001b). *Hostile hallways: Bullying, teasing, and sexual harassment in school.* Washington, DC: AAUW Educational Foundation.

American Association of University Women Educational Foundation (AAUW). (1992). *How schools shortchange girls: The AAUW report.* Washington, DC: AAUW.

American Cancer Society. (2010). *Cancer facts & figures 2010.* 1–68. Atlanta, GA: American Cancer Society. Retrieved from http://www.cancer.org/acs/groups/content/@epidemiologysurveilance/documents/document/acspc-026238.pdf

American Cancer Society. (2011). *Global cancer facts & figures 2nd edition.* 1–60. Atlanta, GA: American Cancer Society. Retrieved from http://www.cancer.org/acs/groups/content/@epidemiologysurveilance/documents/document/acspc-027766.pdf

American College of Nurse-Midwives. (2007). *Midwifery in 2007: Evidence-based practice.* Silver Spring, MD: American College of Nurse-Midwives.

American Foundation for Suicide Prevention. (2008). *Facts and figures: National statistics.* Retrieved from http://www.afsp.org/

American Foundation for Suicide Prevention, (2011). *Facts and figures.* Retrieved from http://www.afsp.org/index.cfm?page_id=04ea1254-bd31-1fa3-c549d77e6ca6aa37

American Geriatrics Society. (1996). *Measuring quality of care at the end of life: A statement of principles.* Retrieved from http://www.americangeriatrics.org

American Heart Association. (2007a). Physical activity and public health: Updated recommendation for adults from the American College of Sports Medicine and the American Heart Association. *Circulation, 116*, 1081–1093.

American Heart Association (2007b). What does my cholesterol mean? Retrieved from http://www.americanheart.org/statistics/html

American Heart Association. (2008a). *Heart disease and stroke statistics.* Dallas, TX: American Heart Association.

American Heart Association. (2008b). *Triglycerides.* Retrieved from http://www.americanheart.org/presenter.jhtml?identifier=4778

American Heart Association. (2010). Heart disease and stroke statistics: 2010 Update at a glance. Dallas, TX: American Heart Association. Retrieved from http://www.americanheart.org/downloadable/heart/1265665152970DS-3241%20Heart StrokeUpdate_2010.pdf

American Psychiatric Association. (2007). *DSM-IV-TR 2007: Diagnostic criteria for Alzheimer's disease.* Washington, DC: Author.

American Psychological Association (APA). (2003). *Ethical principles of psychologists and code of conduct.* Retrieved from http://www.apa.org/ethics/code2002.html

American Psychological Association (APA). (2008a). *Briefing sheet: Women & depression.* Retrieved from http://www.apa.org/ppo/issues/pwomenanddepress.html

American Psychological Association (APA). (2008b). *New report on women and depression: Latest research findings and recommendations.* Retrieved from http://www.apa.org/releases/depressionreport.html

American Psychological Association (APA). (2010, November 9). *Stress in America: Mind/body health: For a healthy mind and body, talk to a psychologist.* 1–68. Washington, DC: APA Printing Office. Retrieved from http://www.apa.org/news/press/releases/stress/national-report.pdf

American SIDS Institute. (2004). *Reducing the risk of SIDS.* Retrieved from http://www.sids.org/nprevent.htm

American Society for Aesthetic Plastic Surgery. (2009). *ASPAPS 2009 statistics on cosmetic surgery.* Retrieved from http://www.surgery.org

American Society of Plastic Surgeons. (2010). 2009 cosmetic surgery age distribution. Retrieved from http://www.plasticsurgery.org/Media/Statistics.html

American Society of Plastic Surgeons. (2010). Plastic surgery for teenagers briefing paper. Retrieved from http://www.plasticsurgery.org/Media/Briefing_Papers/Plastic_Surgery_for_Teenagers.html

American Society for Reproductive Medicine, Society for Assisted Reproductive Technology. (2010). 2008 Assisted Reproductive Technology Success Rates: National Summary and Fertility Clinic Reports. Atlanta: U.S. Department of Health and Human Services. Retrieved from http://www.cdc.gov/art/ART2008/PDF/ART_2008_Full.pdf

American Speech-Language-Hearing Association. (2007). *Acquiring English as a second language: What's normal and what's not.* Retrieved from http://www.asha.org/public/speech/development/easl.htm

Anastasi, A. (1986). Intelligence as a quality of behavior. In R. J. Sternberg & D. K. Detterman (Eds.), *What is intelligence? Contemporary viewpoints on its nature and definition* (pp. 19–21). Norwood, NJ: Ablex.

Ancelin, M. L., Christen, Y., & Ritchie, K. (2007). Is antioxidant therapy a viable alternative for mild cognitive impairment? Examination of the evidence. *Dementia and Geriatric Cognitive Disorders, 24,* 1–19. doi:10.1159/00010256

Anderson, B. J. (2002). *Life after breast cancer: Surviving and thriving.* Retrieved from http://www.giftfromwithin.org/html/lifeaftr.html

Anderson, C. A., Gentile, D. A., & Buckley, K. E. (2007). *Violent video game effects on children and adolescents.* New York: Oxford University Press.

Anderson, P., de Bruijn, A., Angus, K., Gordon, R., & Hastings, G. (2009). Impact of Alcohol Advertising and Media Exposure on Adolescent Alcohol Use: A Systematic Review of Longitudinal Studies. *Alcohol & Alcoholism, 44*(3), 229–243. doi:10.1093/alcalc/agn115

Anderson, R. J. (2011, March). Dynamics of economic well-being: Poverty, 2004–2006. *Current Population Reports* (P70–123). 1–32. Retrieved from http://www.census.gov/prod/2011pubs/p70-123.pdf

Andersson, G., Noack, T., Seierstad, A., & Weedon-Fekjaer, H. (2006). The demographics of same-sex "marriages" in Norway and Sweden. *Demography, 43*(1), 79–98.

Andrade, C. & Radhakrishnan, R. (2009). Prayer and healing: A medical and scientific perspective on randomized controlled trials. *Indian Journal of Psychiatry, 51*(4), 247–253. doi:10.4103/0019-5545.58288

Annas, G. J. (2005). "Culture of life" politics at the bedside—The case of Terri Schiavo. *New England Journal of Medicine, 352,* 1710–1715.

Antonucci, T., Akiyama, H., & Takahashi, K. (2004). Attachment and close relationships across the life span. *Attachment and Human Development, 6*(4), 353–370.

Apgar, V. (1953). Proposal for a new method of evaluation of the newborn infant. *Anesthesia and Analgesia, 32,* 260–267.

Appell, A. R. (2008). The endurance or biological connection: Heteronormativity, same-sex parenting and the lessons of adoption. *BYU Journal of Public Law, 22,* 289–325.

Apple, D. (1956). The social structure of grandparenthood. *American Anthropologist, 58,* 656–663.

Apple, M. W. (Ed.). (2004). *Ideology and curriculum* (3rd ed.). New York: Routledge.

Aquilino, W. S. (2005). Impact of family structure on parental attitudes toward the economic support of adult children over the transition to adulthood. *Journal of Family Issues, 26*(2), 143–167.

Arabin, B. (2004). Two-dimensional real-time ultrasound in the assessment of fetal activity in single and multiple pregnancy. *Ultrasound Review of Obstetrics and Gynecology, 4,* 37–45.

Arcelus, J., Bouman, W. P., & Morgan, J. F. (2008). Treating young people with eating disorders: Transition from child mental health to specialist adult eating disorder services. *European Eating Disorders Review, 16*(1), 30–36. doi:10.1002/erv.830

Ariès, P. (1962). *Centuries of childhood* (R. Baldick, Trans.). New York: Random House.

Ariès, P. (1978). *Western attitudes toward death: From the Middle Ages to the present.* Baltimore: Johns Hopkins University Press.

Ariès, P. (1981). *The hour of our death.* New York: Knopf.

Armstrong, M. L., Roberts, A. E., Owen, D. C., & Koch, J. R. (2004). Toward building a composite of college student influences with body art. *Issues in Comprehensive Pediatric Nursing, 27,* 277–295.

Armstrong, S. (2004, March 8). A rights revolution. *Maclean's, 117,* 38–40.

Arnett, J. J. (2000). Emerging adulthood: A theory of development from the late teens through the twenties. *American Psychologist, 55,* 469–480.

Arnett, J. J. (2001). *Adolescence and emerging adulthood: A cultural approach.* Upper Saddle River, NJ: Pearson Education.

Arnett, J. J. (2006a). Emerging adulthood: Understanding the new way of coming of age. In J. J. Arnett and J. L. Tanner (Eds.), *Emerging adults in America: Coming of age in the 21st century* (pp. 3–20). Washington, DC: American Psychological Association.

Arnett, J. J. (2006b). G. Stanley Hall's *Adolescence*: Brilliance and nonsense. *History of Psychology, 9*(3), 186–197.

Arnett, J. J. (2007a). The long and leisurely route: Coming of age in Europe today. *Current History, 130–136.*

Arnett, J. J. (2007b). Suffering, selfish, slackers? Myths and reality about emerging adults. *Journal of Youth Adolescence, 36,* 23–29.

Arnett, J. J., & Tanner, J. L. (2006). *Emerging adults in America: Coming of age in the 21st century.* Washington, DC: American Psychological Association.

Aronson, E., Brewer, M., & Carlsmith, J. M. (1985). Experimentation in social psychology. In G. Lindzey & E. Aronson (Ed.), *Handbook of social psychology* (3rd ed., Vol. 2). New York: Random House.

Arria, A. M., Derauf, C., Lagasse, L. L., Grant, P., Shah, R., Smith, L., . . ., Lester, B. (2006, May). Methamphetamine and other substance use during pregnancy: Preliminary estimates from the infant development, environment, and lifestyle (IDEAL) study. *Maternal & Child Health Journal, 10*(3), 293–302.

Artis, J. E. (2007). Maternal cohabitation and child well-being among kindergarten children. *Journal of Marriage and Family, 69*(1), 222–236.

Artistico, D., Cervone, D., & Pezzuti, L. (2003). Perceived self-efficacy and everyday problem solving among young and older adults. *Psychology and Aging, 18*(1), 68–79.

Arvey, R. D., Harpaz, I., & Liao, H. (2004). Work centrality and post-award behavior of lottery winners. *The Journal of Psychology: Interdisciplinary and Applied, 138*(5), 404–420.

Asberg, K. K., Bowers, C., Renk, K., & McKinney, C. (2008). A structural equation modeling approach to the study of stress and psychological adjustment in emerging adults. *Child Psychiatry & Human Development, 39*(4), 481–501. doi:10.1007/s10578 -008-0102-0

Ashenburg, K. (2002). *The mourner's dance: What we do when people die.* New York: Farrar, Strauss & Giroux.

Ashmead, D. H., McCarty, M. E., Lucas, L. S., & Belvedere, M. C. (1993). Visual guidance in infants' reaching toward suddenly displaced targets. *Child Development, 64,* 1111–1127.

Ashton, P. T. (1975). Cross-cultural Piagetian research: An experimental perspective. *Harvard Educational Review, 45,* 475–506.

Asomaning, K., Miller, D. P., Liu, G., Wain, J. C., Lynch, T. J., Su, L., & Christiani, D. C. (2008). Second hand smoke, age of exposure and lung cancer risk. *Journal of Lung Cancer, 61*(1), 13–20. doi:10.1016/ j.lungcan.2007.11.013

Associated Press. (2009, December 3). Poll finds sexting common among young people. Retrieved from http://abclocal.go.com/ ktrk/story?section=news/technology&id =7150752

Astley, S. J. (2010) Profile of the first 1400 patients receiving diagnostic evaluations for FASD at the Washington State Fetal Alcohol Syndrome Diagnostic & Prevention Network. *Canadian Journal of Clinical Pharmacology, 17*(1), e132–e164.

Attar-Schwartz, S., Tan, J., & Buchanan, A. (2009). Adolescents' perspective on relationships with grandparents: The contribution of adolescent, grandparent, and parent-grandparent relationship variables. *Children and Youth Services Review, 31*(1), 1057–1066. doi:10.1016/j.childyouth.2009.05.007

Aucoin, K. J., Frick, P. J., & Bodin, S. D. (2006). Corporal punishment and child adjustment. *Journal of Applied Developmental Psychology, 27,* 527–541.

Aud, S., Fox, M., and KewalRamani, A. (2010). *Status and trends in the education of racial and ethnic groups* (NCES 2010-015). U.S. Department of Education,

National Center for Education Statistics. Washington, DC: U.S. Government Printing Office.

Aud, S., Hussar, W., Planty, M., Snyder, T., Bianco, K., Fox, M., . . . , Drake, L. (2010). *The Condition of Education 2010* (NCES 2010-028). National Center for Education Statistics, Institute of Education Sciences. Washington, DC: U.S. Department of Education.

Austad, S. N. (2006). Why women live longer than men: Sex differences in longevity. *Gender Medicine, 3*(2), 79–92. doi:10.1016/ S1550-8579(06)80198-1

Ausubel, D. P., & Sullivan, E. V. (1970). *Theory and problems of child development* (2nd ed.). New York: Grune & Stratton.

Autism and Developmental Disabilities Monitoring Network. (2009, December 18). Prevalence of the autism spectrum disorders (ASDs) in multiple areas of the United States, 2004 and 2006. *MMWR Weekly, 58*(SS10), 1–32.

Autism Society of America. (ASA). (2008). About autism. Retrieved from http://www .autism-society.org/site/PageServer ?pagename=about_home

Auwarter, A. E., & Aruguete, M. S. (2008). Effects of student gender and socioeconomic status on teacher perception. *The Journal of Educational Research, 101*(4), 243–246. doi:10.3200/JOER.101.4.243-246

Aviezer, O., Van IJzendoorn, M. H., Sagi, A., & Schuengel, C. (1994). "Children of the Dream" revisited: 70 years of collective early child care in Israeli kibbutzim. *Psychological Bulletin, 116,* 99–116.

Avis, N. E., Ory, M., Matthews, K. A., Schocken, M., Bromberger, J., & Colvin, A. (2003). Health-related quality of life in a multiethnic sample of middle-aged women: Study of Women's Health Across the Nation (SWAN). *Medical Care, 41*(11), 1262–1276.

Ayala, G. X., Mickens, L., Galindo, P., & Elder, J. P. (2007). Acculturation and body image perception among Latino youth. *Ethnicity and Health, 12*(1), 21–41.

Ayres, A. J. (1972). *Sensory integration and learning disorders.* Los Angeles: Western Psychological Services.

Azar, B. (2010). A reason to believe. *Monitor on Psychology, 41*(11), 52. Retrieved from http://www.apa.org/monitor/2010/12/ believe.aspx

Azrin, N. H., Ehle, C. T., & Beaumont, A. L. (2006). Physical exercise as a reinforcer to promote calmness of an ADHD child. *Behavior Modification, 30*(5), 564–570.

Bach, P. B., Schrag, D., Brawley, O. W., Galaznik, A., Yakren, S., & Begg, C. B. (2002). Survival of blacks and whites after a cancer diagnosis. *JAMA, 287*(16), 2106–2113.

Bachman, J. G., O'Malley, P. M., Schulenberg, J. E., Johnston, L. D., Bryant, A. L.,

& Merline, A. C. (2007). *The decline of substance use in young adulthood* (Vol. 1). Hillsdale, NJ: Erlbaum.

Bacon, C. G., Mittleman, M. A., Kawachi, I., Giovannucci, E., Glasser, D. B., & Rimm, E. G. (2003). Sexual function in men over 50 years of age: Results from the Health Professionals Follow-Up Study. *Annals of Internal Medicine, 139*(3), 161–168. Retrieved from http://www.annals.org/ content/139/3/161.short

Bainbridge, J., Meyers, M. K., Tanaka, S., & Waldfogel, J. (2005). Who gets an early education? Family income and the enrollment of three- to five-year-olds from 1968–2000. *Social Science Quarterly, 86*(3), 724–745. doi:10.1111/j.0038-4941.2005.00326.x

Baines, E., & Blatchford, P. (2009). Sex differences in the structure and stability of children's playground social networks and their overlap with friendship relations. *British Journal of Developmental Psychology, 27,* 743–760. doi:10.1348/026151008X371114

Bakalar, N. (2008, February 5). Symptoms: Metabolic syndrome is tied to diet soda. *New York Times.* Retrieved from http:// www.nytimes.com /2008/02/05/health/ nutrition/05symp.html.

Baker, J. L., Olsen, L. W., & Sorensen, T. I. (2007). Childhood body-mass index and the risk of coronary heart disease in adulthood. *New England Journal of Medicine, 357*(23), 2329–2337.

Baker, P., & Cruickshank, J. (2009). I am happy in my faith: The Influence of religious affiliation, saliency, and practice on depressive symptoms and treatment preference. *Mental Health, Religion & Culture, 12*(4), 339–357. doi:10.1080/13674670902725108

Baker, W., Trofimovich, P., Flege, J. E., Mack, M., & Halter, R. (2008). Child-adult differences in second-language phonological learning: The role of cross-language similarity. *Language and Speech, 51*(4), 317–342. doi:10.1177/0023830908099068

Bakken, J. P., & Obiakor, F. E. (2008). *Transition planning for students with disabilities: What educators and service providers can do.* Springfield, IL: Charles C Thomas.

Ball, H. (2007). Positive attitudes toward condom use do not equal safer sex among teenagers. *Perspectives on Sexual and Reproductive Health, 2,* 61–62.

Balon, R. (2008). Introduction: New developments in the area of sexual dysfunction(s). In R. Balon (Ed.), *Advances in Psychosomatic Medicine: Vol. 29. Sexual dysfunction: The brain-body connection* (pp. 1–26). New York: Karger.

Balter, L., & Tamis-LeMonda, C. S. (Eds.). (2006). *Child psychology: A handbook of contemporary issues* (2nd ed.). New York: Taylor & Francis.

Baltes, P. B. (2006). Facing our limits: Human dignity in the very old. *American Academy of Arts & Sciences, 135*(1), 32–39.

Baltes, P. B., & Baltes, M. M. (1998). Savoir vivre in old age: How to master the shifting balance between gains and losses. *National Forum: Phi Kappa Phi Journal, 78,* 13–18.

Baltes, P. B., & Lindenberger, U. (1997). Emergence of a powerful connection between sensory and cognitive functions across the adult life span: A new window to the study of cognitive aging? *Psychology and Aging, 12,* 12–21.

Baltes, P. B., Lindenberger, U., & Staudinger, U. M. (2006). Lifespan theory in developmental psychology. In W. Damon & R. M. Lerner (Eds.), *Handbook of child psychology: Vol. 1. Theoretical models of human development* (6th ed., pp. 569–664). New York: Wiley.

Baltes, P. B., Reuter-Lorenz, P. A., & Rösler, F. (2006). *Lifespan development and the brain: The perspective of biocultural coconstructivism.* New York: Cambridge University Press.

Baltes, P. B., & Schaie, K. W. (1976). On the plasticity of intelligence in adulthood and old age. *American Psychologist, 31,* 720–725.

Baltes, P. B., & Smith, J. (2003). New frontiers in the future of aging: From successful aging of the young old to the dilemmas of the fourth age. *Gerontology, 49*(2), 123–135.

Balz, D. (2005, February 27). Microsoft's Gates urges governors to restructure U.S. high schools. *Washington Post,* p. A10. Retrieved from http://www.washington post.com/wp-dyn/articles/A56466 -2005Feb26.html

Banchero, S. (2010, September 14). Students' SAT scores stay in rut. *Wall Street Journal,* p. A4.

Bancroft, J. (2003). *Sexual development in childhood.* Indiana University Press.

Bandura, A. (1973). *Aggression: A social learning analysis.* Englewood Cliffs, NJ: Prentice Hall.

Bandura, A. (1977). *Social learning theory.* Englewood Cliffs, NJ: Prentice Hall.

Bandura, A. (1986). *Social foundations of thought and action: A social cognitive theory.* Englewood Cliffs, NJ: Prentice Hall.

Bandura, A. (1997). *Self-efficacy: The exercise of control.* New York: Freeman.

Bandura, A. (1999). Moral disengagement in the perpetration of inhumanities. *Personality and Social Psychology Review, 3*(3), 193–209.

Bandura, A. (2006). Toward a psychology human agency. *Perspectives on Psychological Science, 1*(2), 164–180.

Bandura, A. (2007). Self-efficacy. In S. Clegg & J. Bailey (Eds.), *International encyclopedia of organization studies.* Thousand Oaks, CA: Sage.

Bandura, A., & Locke, E. A. (2003). Negative self-efficacy and goal effects revisited. *Journal of Applied Psychology, 88*(1), 87–98.

Bandura, A., Ross, D., & Ross, S. (1963). Imitation of film-mediated aggressive

models. *Journal of Abnormal and Social Psychology, 66,* 3–11.

Banerjee, I., & Clayton, P. (2007). The genetic basis for the timing of human puberty. *Journal of Neuroendocrinology, 19*(11), 831–838. doi:10.1111/j.1365-2826 .2007.01598.x

Banet-Weiser, S. & Portwood-Stacer, L. (2006). "I just want to be me again!" Beauty pageants, reality television and post-feminism. *Feminist Theory, 7*(2), 255–272.

Baney, C. (1998). Wired for sound: The essential connection between music and development. *Early Childhood News.* Retrieved from http://www.early-childhoodnews .com/wiredfor.htm

Bangerter, A., Grob, A., & Krings, F. (2001). Personal goals at age 25 in three generations of the twentieth century: Young adulthood in historical context. *Swiss Journal of Psychology, 60*(2), 59–64. doi:10.1024//1421 -0185.60.2.59

Bank, S. P., & Kahn, M. D. (1997). *The sibling bond.* New York: HarperCollins.

Barber, B. L., & Demo, D. H. (2006). The kids are alright (at least, most of them): Links between divorce and dissolution and child well-being. In M. A. Fine & J. H. Harvey (Eds.), *Handbook of divorce and relationship dissolution* (pp. 289–312). New York: Routledge.

Barber, G. (2010). Female genital mutilation: A review. *Practice Nursing, 21*(2), 62. Retrieved from CINAHL Plus with Full Text database.

Barclay, L., & Murata, P. (2008). Bone density evaluation in teens prevents future osteoporosis. Medscape Medical News. Retrieved from http://cme.medscape.com/ viewarticle/545997

Bardi, A., & Ryff, C. D. (2007). Interactive effects of traits on adjustment to a life transition. *Journal of Personality, 75*(5), 955–984.

Barkley, R. (2001). *The statistics of AD/HD.* AdditudeMag.Com. Retrieved from http:// www.additudemag.com

Barkow, J., Cosmides, L., & Tooby, J., (Eds.). (1992). *The adapted mind: Evolutionary psychology and the generation of culture.* New York: Oxford University Press.

Barnes, P. M., Adams, P. F., & Schiller, J. S. (2003). Summary health statistics for the U.S. Population: National Health Survey, 2001. *Vital Health Statistics, 10*(217). 1–90. Retrieved from http://www.cdc.gov/nchs/ data/series/ sr_10/sr10_217.pdf

Barnes, S. B. (2009). Relationship networking: Society and education. *Journal of Computer-Mediated Communication, 14*(3), 735–742. doi:10.1111/j.1083-6101.2009.01464.x

Barnes, S. K. (2010). Sign language with babies: What difference does it make? *Dimensions of Early Childhood, 38*(1), 21–29.

Baron-Cohen, S. (2005, Winter/Spring). The essential difference: The male and female brain. *Phi Kappa Phi Forum. 85*(1), 23–26.

Retrieved from http://www.phikappaphi .org/Web/Files/Win-Spr_05.pdf

Barr, J. J., & Higgins-D'Alessandro, A. (2009). How adolescent empathy and prosocial behavior change in the context of school culture: A two-year longitudinal study. *Adolescence, 44*(176), 751–772.

Barr, R., Lauricella, A., Zack, E., & Calvert, S. L. (2010). Infant and early childhood exposure to adult-directed and child-directed television programming. *Merrill-Palmer Quarterly, 56*(1), 21-48. doi: 10.1353/mpq.0.0038

Barrett, D. (2010). *Secrecy and strained relationships: Moving to a same-sex family* (Doctoral dissertation, Institute for Clinical Social Work). Retrieved from http://www.icsw .edu/_dissertations/Barrett,%20Debbie %20[2010]%20-%20Secrecy%20& %20Strained%20Relationships— Moving%20to%20a%20Same-Sex %20Stepfamily.pdf

Barrios Marcelo, K. (2007, July). Volunteering among high school students. *Circle: Fact sheet.* The Center for Information & Research on Civic Learning & Engagement. School of Public Policy. College Park, MD: University of Maryland.

Barth, R. P. (2009). Preventing child abuse and neglect with parent training: Evidence and opportunities. *The Future of Children, 19*(2), 95–118.

Bartocci, M., Winberg, J., Ruggiero, C., Bergqvist, L., Serra, G., & Lagercrantz, H. (2000). Activation of olfactory cortex in newborn infants after odor stimulation: A functional near-infrared spectroscopy study. *Pediatric Research, 48*(1), 18–23.

Basham, P., Merrifield, J., & Hepburn, C. R. (2007). *Home schooling: From the extreme to the mainstream.* Studies in Education Policy. Vancouver, BC: Frasier Institute.

Bass, D., & Bowman, K. (1990). The impact of an aged relative's death on the family. In K. F. Ferraro (Ed.), *Gerontology: Perspectives and issues.* New York: Springer.

Basseches, M. (1980). Dialectical schemata: A framework for the empirical study of the development of dialectical thinking. *Human Development, 23,* 400–421.

Bates, E., Bretherton, I., & Snyder, L. (1988). *From first words to grammar: Individual differences and dissociable mechanisms.* New York: Cambridge University Press.

Batlan, F., & Gordon, L. (2011, January 29). Major acts of Congress: Aid to Dependent Children (1935). Retrieved from Enotes, http://www.enotes.com/major-acts -congress/aid-dependent-children/print

Battin, M. P., van der Heide, A., Ganzini, L., van der Wal, G., & Onwuteaka-Philipsen, B. D. (2007). Legal physician-assisted dying in Oregon and the Netherlands: Evidence concerning the impact on patients in "vulnerable" groups. *Journal of Medical Ethics, 33*(10), 591–597.

Bauer, I. (2001, Spring). *The gentle wisdom of natural infant hygiene.* Retrieved from http://www.natural-wisdom.com/

Bauer, P. J. (2006). Event memory. In W. Damon, R. M. Lerner, D. Kuhn, & R. S. Siegler (Eds.), *Handbook of child psychology: Cognition, perception, and language* (6th ed., Vol. 2, pp. 373–425). New York: Wiley.

Bauer, P. J. (2007). *Remembering the times of our lives: Memory in infancy and beyond.* Mahwah, NJ: Erlbaum.

Bauer, L. (2010, May 19). Once-oldest college grad earns her master's at 98. *The Columbus Dispatch.* Retrieved from http://www.dispatch.com/live/content/life/stories/2010/05/19/once-oldest-college-grad-earns-her-masters-at-98.html

Bauermeister, J. J., Shrout, P. E., Chávez, L., Rubio-Stipec, M., Ramírez, R, Padilla, L., . . . , Canino, G. (2007). ADHD and gender: Are risks and sequela of ADHD the same for boys and girls? *Journal of Child Psychology and Psychiatry, 48*(8), 831–839. doi:10.1111/j.1469-7610.2007.01750.x

Baumeister, R. F., & Vohs, K. D. (2002). The pursuit of meaningfulness in life. In C. R. Snyder & S. J. Lopez (Eds.), *Handbook of positive psychology* (pp. 608–618). New York: Oxford University Press.

Baumeister, R. F., Vohs, K. D., & Tice, D. T. (2007). The strength model of self-control. *Current Directions in Psychological Science, 16*(6), 351–355.

Baugh, E., Mullis, R., Mullis, A., Hicks, M., & Peterson, G. (2010). Ethnic identity and body image among black and white college females. *Journal of American College Health, 59*(2), 105–109. doi:10.1080/07448481.2010.483713

Baum, N. (2004). Coping with "absence-presence": Noncustodial fathers' parenting behaviors. *American Journal of Orthopsychiatry, 74*(3), 316–324.

Baum, S., Ma, J., & Payea, K. (2010). Education pays 2010: The benefits of higher education for individuals and society. The College Board Advocacy & Policy Center. Retrieved from http://trends.collegeboard.org/downloads/Education_Pays_2010.pdf

Baumeister, R. F., & Vohs, K. D. (2002). The pursuit of meaningfulness in life. In C. R. Snyder & S. J. Lopez (Eds.), *Handbook of positive psychology* (pp. 608–618). New York: Oxford University Press.

Baumeister, R. F., Vohs, K. D., & Tice, D. T. (2007). The strength model of self-control. *Current Directions in Psychological Science, 16*(6), 351–355.

Baumrind, D. (1967). Child care practices anteceding three patterns of preschool behavior. *Genetic Psychology Monographs, 75,* 43–88.

Baumrind, D. (1971). Current patterns of parental authority. *Developmental Psychology Monographs, 4,* 1.

Baumrind, D. (1980). New directions in socialization research. *American Psychologist, 35,* 639–652.

Baumrind, D. (1996). The discipline controversy revisited. *Family Relations, 45,* 405–414.

Baumwell, L., Tamis-LeMonda, C. S., & Bornstein, M. H. (1997). Maternal verbal sensitivity and child language comprehension. *Infant Behavior and Development, 20,* 247.

Bauserman, R. (2002). Child adjustment in joint-custody versus sole-custody arrangements: A meta-analytic review. *Journal of Family Psychology, 16*(1), 91–102.

Bayley, N. (1936). *The California infant scale of motor development: Birth to three years.* Berkeley: University of California Press.

Bayley, N. (1956). Individual patterns of development. *Child Development, 27,* 45–74.

Bayley, N. (1965). Research in child development: A longitudinal perspective. *Merrill-Palmer Quarterly, 11,* 184–190.

Beard, R. M. (1969). *An outline of Piaget's developmental psychology for students and teachers.* New York: New American Library.

Beauchamp, G. K., & Manella, J. A. (2009). Early flavor learning and its impact on later feeding behavior. *Journal of Pediatric Gastroenterology and Nutrition,* 48S, S25–30. doi:10.1097/MPG.0b013e31819774a5

Bech, B. H., Henriksen, T. B., Obel, C., & Olsen, J. (2007). Effect of reducing caffeine intake on birth weight and length of gestation: Randomised controlled trial. *British Medical Journal, 334*(7590), 409.

Becker, W. C. (1964). Consequences of different kinds of parental discipline. In M. L. Hoffman & L. W. Hoffman (Eds.), *Review of child development research* (pp. 169–208). New York: Russell Sage Foundation.

Beckett, C., Maughan, B., Rutter, M., Castle, J., Colvert, E., Groothues, C., . . . , Sonuga-Barke, J. S. (2006). Do the effects of early severe deprivation on cognition persist into early adolescence? Findings from the English and Romanian adoptees study. *Child Development, 77*(3), 696–711.

Beckmann, C. A. (2003, April). The effects of asthma on pregnancy and perinatal outcomes. *Journal of Asthma, 40*(2), 171–180.

Bedrova, F., & Leong, D. J. (2007). *Tools of the mind: The Vygotskian approach to early childhood education* (2nd ed.). Upper Saddle River, NJ: Merrill/Prentice Hall.

Beilin, H. (1992). Piaget's enduring contribution to developmental psychology. *Developmental Psychology, 28,* 191–204.

Belluck, P. (2007, April 12). Massachusetts agency proposes health coverage that most can afford. *New York Times,* p. A14(L).

Belsky, J. (1990). Parental and nonparental child care and children's socioemotional development: A decade in review. *Journal of Marriage and the Family, 52,* 885–903.

Belsky, J. (1997). Attachment, mating, and parenting: An evolutionary interpretation. *Human Nature, 8*(4), 361–381.

Belsky, J. (1999). Modern evolutionary theory and patterns of attachment. In J. Cassidy & P. R. Shaver (Eds.), *Handbook of attachment: Theory, research, and clinical applications* (pp. 141–161). University Park, PA: Guilford Press.

Belsky, J. (2001). Marital violence in evolutionary perspective. In A. Booth and A. Crouter (Eds.), *Couples in conflict* (pp. 27–36). Mahwah, NJ: Earlbaum.

Belsky, J., & Barends, N. (2002). Personality and parenting. In M. Bornstein, *Handbook of parenting: Vol. 3. Being and becoming a parent* (2nd ed., pp. 415–438). Mahwah, NJ: Erlbaum.

Belsky, J., Crnic, K., & Gable, S. (1995). The determinants of coparenting in families with toddler boys: Spousal differences and daily hassles. *Child Development, 66,* 629–642.

Belsky, J., Booth-Laforce, C., Bradley, R., Brownell, C. A., Burchinal, M., Campbell, S. B., et al. (2008). Mothers' and fathers' support for child autonomy and early school achievement. *Developmental Psychology, 44*(4), 895–907. doi:10.1037/0012-1649.44.4.895

Bem, S. L. (1993). *The lenses of gender: Transforming the debate on sexual inequality.* New Haven, CT: Yale University Press.

Bender, W. N. (2008). *Learning disabilities: Characteristics, identification, and teaching strategies* (6th ed.). Boston: Pearson Education.

Bengtson, V. L., Gans, D., Putney, N. M., & Silverstein, M. (2009). *Handbook of theories of aging* (2nd ed.). New York: Springer.

Bennett, A. T., & Collins, K. A. (2000). Suicide: A ten-year retrospective study. *Journal of Forensic Sciences, 45*(6), 1256–1258.

Benninghoven, D., Tetsch, N., Kunzendorf, S., & Jantschek, G. (2007). Body image in patients with eating disorders and their mothers, and the role of family functioning. *Comprehensive Psychiatry, 48,* 118–123.

Benson, P. L., Scales, P. C., Hamilton, S. F., & Sesma, A., Jr. (2006). Positive youth development: Theory, research, and applications. In W. Damon & R. M. Lerner (Eds.), *Handbook of child psychology* (6th ed., Vol. 4, pp. 894–941). New York: Wiley.

Benzies, K., Keown, L., & Magill-Evans, J. (2009). Immediate and sustained effects of parenting on physical aggression in Canadian children aged 6 years and younger. *The Canadian Journal of Psychiatry, 54*(1), 55–64.

Bérard, A., Azoulay, L., Koren, G., Blais, L. Perreault, S., & Oraichi, D. (2007). Isotretinoin, pregnancies, abortions and birth defects: A population-based perspective. *British Journal of Clinical Pharmacology, 63*(2), 196–205.

Berg, A. I., Hoffman, L., Hassing, L. B., McClearn, G. E., & Johansson, B. (2009).

What matters, and what matters most, for change in life satisfaction in the oldest-old? A study over 6 years among individuals 80+. *Aging & Mental Health, 13*(2), 191–201. doi:10.1080/13607860802342227

Berg, C. A., & Sternberg, R. J. (1992). Adults' conceptions of intelligence across the adult life span. *Psychology and Aging, 7,* 221–231.

Berger, A. (2006). How to have a good death. *British Medical Journal, 332*(7544), 799–805.

Berk, L. E., & Winsler, A. (1995). *NAEYC research into practice series: Vol. 7. Scaffolding children's learning: Vygotsky and early childhood education* Washington, DC: National Book Association for Young Children.

Berko Gleason, J. (2005). The development of language: An overview and a preview. In J. Berko Gleason (Ed.), *The development of language* (6th ed., pp. 1–38). Boston: Pearson Education.

Berkowitz, D., & Marsiglio, W. (2007, May). Gay men: Negotiating procreative, father, and family identities. *Journal of Marriage and Family, 69,* 366–381.

Bernstein, I. L. (1990). Salt preference and development. *Developmental Psychology, 26,* 552–554.

Berry, J. W., Phinney, J. S., Sam, D. L., & Vedder, P. (2006). Immigrant youth: Acculturation, identity, and adaptation. *Applied Psychology, 55*(3), 303–332.

Bersamin, M. M., Walker, S., Waiters, E. D., Fisher, D. A., & Grube, J. W. (2005). Promising to wait: Virginity pledges and adolescent sexual behavior. *Journal of Adolescent Health, 36*(5), 428–436.

Bertenthal, B. I., & Longo, M. R. (2007). Is there evidence of a mirror system from birth? *Developmental Science. 10*(5), 526–529. doi:10.1111/j.1467-7687.2007.00633.x

Besser, A., & Blatt, S. J. (2007). Identity consolidation and internalizing and externalizing problem behaviors in early adolescence. *Psychoanalytic Psychology, 24*(1), 126–149.

Bessey, P. Q., Arons, R. R., DiMagio, C. J., & Yurt, R. W. (2006). The vulnerabilities of age: Burns in children and older adults. *Surgery, 140*(4), 705–717.

Best, D. L. (1993). Inducing children to generate mnemonic organizational strategies: An examination of long-term retention and materials. *Developmental Psychology, 29,* 324–336.

Betancourt, J. R. (2003). Cross-cultural medical education: Conceptual approaches and frameworks for evaluation. *Academic Medicine, 78*(6), 560–569.

Bettes, B. A. (1988). Maternal depression and motherese: Temporal and intonational features. *Child Development, 59,* 1089–1096.

Beveridge, R. M., & Berg, C. A. (2007). Parent–adolescent collaboration: An interpersonal model for understanding optimal interactions. *Clinical Child and Family Psychology Review, 10*(1), 25–52.

Bhugra, D., & Bhui, K. (2007). *Textbook of cultural psychiatry.* New York: Cambridge University Press.

Bialystok, E., & Craik, F. I. (Eds.). (2006). *Lifespan cognition: Mechanisms of change.* New York: Oxford University Press.

Bianchi, S. M., Robinson, J. P., & Milkie, M. A. (2006). *Changing rhythms of American family life.* New York: Russell Sage Foundation.

Bierman, K. L., & Erath, S. A. (2006). Promoting social competence in early childhood: Classroom curricula and social skills coaching programs. In *Blackwell handbook of early childhood development* (pp. 594–615). Malden, MA: Blackwell.

Bijou, S. W., & Baer, D. M. (1965). A social learning model of attachment: Socialization—The development of behavior to social stimuli. In *Child development II.* New York: Appleton-Century-Crofts.

Bilsen, M. A., Hamers, J., Groot, W., & Spreeuwenberg, C. (2008). Sheltered housing compared to independent housing in the community. *Scandinavian Journal Caring Science, 22*(2), 265–274. doi:10.1111/j.1471-6712.2007.00529.x

Bilszta, J., Ericksen, J., Buist, A., & Milgrom, J. (2010). Women's experience of postnatal depression—Beliefs and attitudes as barriers to care. *Australian Journal of Advanced Nursing, 27*(3), 44–54. Retrieved from http://www.ajan.com.au/Vol27/27-3_Bilszta.pdf

Bina, R. (2008). The impact of cultural factors upon postpartum depression: A literature review. *Health Care for Women International, 29*(6), 568–592. doi:10.1080/07399330802089149

Binder, B. K., Mastel-Smith, B., Hersch, G., & Symes, L. (2009). Community-dwelling, older women's perspectives on therapeutic life review: A qualitative analysis. *Issues in Mental Health Nursing, 30*(5), 288–294. doi:10.1080/01612840902753885

Birditt, K. S., & Antonucci, T. C. (2007). Relationship quality profiles and well-being among married adults. *Journal of Family Psychology, 21*(4), 595–604.

Biringen, Z., Fidler, D., Barrett, K., & Kubicek, L. (2005). Applying the Emotional Availability Scales to children with disabilities. *Infant Mental Health Journal, 26*(4), 369–391. doi:10.1002/imhj.20058

Birney, D. P., Citron-Pousty, J. H., Lutz, D. L., & Sternberg, R. J. (2005). The development of cognitive and intellectual abilities. In M. H. Bornstein & M. E. Lamb (Eds.), *Developmental science: An advanced textbook* (5th ed., pp. 327–358). Mahwah, NJ: Erlbaum.

Birney, D. P., & Sternberg, R. J. (2006). Intelligence and cognitive abilities as competencies in development. In E. Bialystok & F. I. M. Craik (Eds.), *Lifespan cognition: Mechanisms of change* (pp. 315–330). New York: Oxford University Press.

Biro, F. M., Striegel-Moore, R. H., Franko, D. L., Padgett, J., & Bean, J. A. (2006). Self-esteem in adolescent females. *Journal of Adolescent Health, 39*(4), 501–507. doi:10.1016/j.jadohealth.2006.03.010

Bischof, L. J. (1976). *Adult psychology* (2nd ed.). New York: Harper & Row.

Bishop, D. V. M., Price, T. S., Dale, P. S., & Plomin, R. (2003, June). Outcomes of early language delay: Etiology of transient and persistent language difficulties. *Journal of Speech, Language, & Hearing Research, 46*(3), 561–575.

Bishop, D. V. M., Whitehouse, A. J. O., Watt, H. J., & Line, E. A. (2008). Autism and diagnostic substitution: Evidence from a study of adults with a history of developmental language disorder. *Developmental Medicine & Child Neurology, 50*(5), 341–345. doi:10.1111/j.1469-8749.2008.02057.x

Bisping, R., Steingrueber, H. J., Oltmann, M., & Wenk, C. (1990). Adults' tolerance of cries: An experimental investigation of acoustic features. *Child Development, 61,* 1218–1229.

Bitzer, J., Platano, G., Tschudin, S., & Alder, J. (2008). Sexual counseling in elderly couples. *Journal of Sexual Medicine, 5*(1), 2027–2043. doi:10.1111/j.1743-6109.2008.00926.x

Bjorklund, D. F., & Green, B. L. (1992). The adaptive nature of cognitive maturity. *American Psychologist, 47,* 46–54.

Black, M. M., Dubowitz, H., Krishnakumar, A., & Starr, R. H. (2007). Early intervention and recovery among children with failure to thrive: Follow-up at age 8. *Pediatrics, 120*(1), 59–69. doi:10.1542/peds.2006-1657

Blackburn, J. A., & Dulmus, C. A. (Eds.). (2007). *Handbook of gerontology.* New York: Wiley.

Blackson, T. C., Butler, T., Belsky, J., Ammerman, R. T., Shaw, D. S., & Tarter, R. E. (1999). Individual traits and family contexts predict sons' externalizing behavior and preliminary relative risk ratios for conduct disorder and substance use disorder outcomes. *Drug and Alcohol Dependence, 56*(2), 115–131.

Blake, S., Simkin, L., Ledsky, R., Perkins, C., & Calabrese, J. M. (2001). Effects of a parent-child communications intervention on young adolescents' risk for early onset of sexual intercourse. *Family Planning Perspectives, 33*(2), 52–61.

Blankenhorn, D. (2007). *The future of marriage.* New York: Encounter Books.

Blass, E. M., & Ciaramitaro, V. (1994). A new look at some old mechanisms in human newborns: Taste and tactile determinants of state, affect, and action. *Monographs of the Society for Research in Child Development, 59* (Serial No. 239).

Blieszner, R. (2006). A lifetime of caring: Dimensions and dynamics in late-life close relationships. *Personal Relationships, 13*(1), 1–18. doi:10.1111/j.1475-6811.2006.00101.x

Block, J. (2007). *Pushed: The painful truth about childbirth and modern maternity care.* Cambridge, MA: Da Capo Press.

Bloom, L. (1970). *Language development: Form and function in emerging grammar.* Cambridge, MA: MIT Press.

Bloom, B., & Cohen, R. A. (2007). Summary health statistics for U.S. children: National Health Interview Survey, 2006. *Vital and Health Statistics, 10*(234). Hyattsville, MD: National Center for Health Statistics.

Blos, P. (1962). *On adolescence: A psychoanalytic interpretation.* New York: Free Press.

Blow, A. J., & Hartnett, K. (2005). Infidelity in committed relationships I: A methodological review. *Journal of Marital and Family Therapy, 31*(2), 183–216. Mahwah, NJ: Erlbaum.

Blumenthal, K. J. (2004). *A valuable aspect of college and university life.* Recreation Management. National Intramural-Recreational Sports Association. Retrieved from http://www.recmanagement.com

Blumstein, P., & Schwartz, P. (1983). *American couples.* New York: Morrow.

Bodenmann, G., Ledermann, T., & Bradbury, T. N. (2007). Stress, sex, and satisfaction in marriage. *Personal Relationships, 14*, 551–569. doi:10.1111/j.1475-6811.2007.00171.x

Bodrova, E., & Leong, D. J. (2007). *Tools of the mind: The Vygotskian approach to early childhood education* (2nd ed.). Upper Saddle River, NJ: Pearson Education.

Bogaert, A. F. (2004). Asexuality: Prevalence and associated factors in a national probability sample. *Journal of Sex Research, 41*, 279–287.

Bogdashina, O. (2003). *Sensory perceptual issues in autism and Asperger syndrome: Different sensory experiences, different perceptual worlds.* London: Jessica Kingsley Publishers.

Bohannon, J. N., & Bonvillian, J. D. (2009). Theoretical approaches to language acquisition. In J. B. Gleason & B. Ratner (Eds.), *The development of language* (7th ed., pp. 227–284). Boston: Allyn & Bacon.

Bokhorst, C. L., Bakermans–Kranenburg, M., Pasco Fearon, R., van IJzendoorn, M., Fonagy, P., & Schuengel, C. (2003). The importance of shared environment in mother-infant attachment security: A behavioral genetic study. *Child Development, 74*, 1769–1782.

Boles, R. E., Roberts, M. C., Brown, K. J., & Mayes, S. (2005, February 23). Children's risk-taking behaviors: The role of child-based perceptions of vulnerability and temperament. *Journal of Pediatric Psychology.* Retrieved from http://jpepsy.oupjournals.org

Bonanno, G. A., & Kaltman, S. (2001). The varieties of grief experience. *Clinical Psychology Review, 21*(5), 705–734.

Bonanno, G. A., & Mancini, A. D. (2008). The human capacity to thrive in the face of potential trauma. *Pediatrics, 121*(2), 369–375. doi:10.1542/peds.2007-1648

Bonanno, G. A., Wortman, C. B., & Nesse, R. M. (2004). Prospective patterns of resilience and maladjustment during widowhood. *Psychology and Aging, 19*(2), 260–271.

Bond, B., Peace, S., Dittmann-Kohli, F., & Westerhof, G. J. (Eds.). (2007). *Ageing in society: European perspectives on gerontology* (3rd ed.). New York: Sage.

Bond, M. A., & Wasik, B. A. (2009). Conversation stations: Promoting language development in young children. *Early Childhood Education Journal, 36*, 467–473. doi:10.1007/s10643-009-0310-7

Bone, J. (2006, July 4). 59-year-old mother has twins to join her toddler. *TimesOnline.* Retrieved from http:// www.timesonline.co.uk/tol/news/world/ us_and_americas/article682551.ece

Bonnet, M. H., & Arand, D. L. (2010). How much sleep do adults need? *National Sleep Foundation.* Retrieved from http://www.sleepfoundation.org/article/white-papers/how-much-sleep-do-adults-need

Boonsong, S. (1968). *The development of concentration of mass, weight, and volume in Thai children.* Unpublished master's thesis, College of Education, Bangkok, Thailand.

Bornstein, M. H. (1989). Sensitive periods in development: Structural characteristics and causal interpretations. *Psychological Bulletin, 105*, 179–197.

Bornstein, M. H. (2006). Parenting science and practice. In W. Damon & R. M. Lerner (Eds.), *Handbook of child psychology* (6th ed., Vol. 4, pp. 893–949). New York: Wiley.

Bornstein, M. H., & Cote, L. R. (2007). Mother-infant interaction and acculturation: I. Behavioural comparisons in Japanese American and South American families. *International Journal of Behavioral Development, 25*(6), 549–563.

Bornstein, M. H., Deater-Deckard, K., & Lansford, J. E. (2007). Introduction: Immigrant families in contemporary society. In M. H. Bornstein, K. Deater-Deckard, & J. E. Lansford (Eds.), *Immigrant families in contemporary society* (pp. 1–6). New York: Guilford Press.

Bornstein, M. H., & Lamb, M. E. (Eds.). (2005). *Developmental science: An advanced textbook* (5th ed.). Mahwah, NJ: Erlbaum.

Bornstein, M. H., & Marks, L. E. (1982, January). Color revisionism. *Psychology Today,* 64–73.

Bos, H. M. W., van Balen, F., & van den Boom, D. (2007). Child adjustment and parenting in lesbian-planned families. *American Journal of Orthopsychiatry, 77*(1), 38–48.

Bos, H. M. W., van Balen, F., Gartrell, N. K., Peyser, H., Sandfort, T. G. M. (2008). Children in planned lesbian families: A cross-cultural comparison between the United States and the Netherlands. *American Journal of Orthopsychiatry, 78*(2), 211–219. doi:10.1037/a0012711

Bosello, R., Favaro, A., Zanetti, T., Soave, M., Vidotto, G., Huon, G., & Santonastaso, P. (2010, March-April). Tattoos and piercings in adolescents: Family conflicts and temperament. [Abstract], *45*(2), *Rivista di psichiatria,* 102–106.

Bosman, E. A. (1993). Age-related differences in motoric aspects of transcription typing skills. *Psychology and Aging, 8*, 88–102.

Bostrum, N. (2005, April). A history of transhumanist thought. *Journal of Evolution & Technology, 14*, 1–25. Retrieved from http://jetpress.org/volume14/bostrom.pdf

Bouchard, T. J., Jr., Lykken, D. T., McGue, M., Segal, N. L., & Tellegen, A. (1990). Sources of human psychological differences: The Minnesota study of twins reared apart. *Science, 250*, 223–228.

Boudreaux, E. D., Emond, S. D., Clark, S., & Camargo, C. A. (2003, May). Race/ethnicity and asthma among children presenting to the emergency department: Differences in disease severity and management. *Pediatrics, 111*, 615–621.

Bound, J., Duncan, G. J., Laren, D. S., & Oleinick, L. (1991). Poverty dynamics in widowhood. *Journal of Gerontology, 46*, S115–S124.

Bowen, C. (1998). *Developmental phonological disorders.* Retrieved from http://www.speech-language-therapy.com/ parentinfo.html

Bowen, C. (2001). *Stuttering: What can be done about it?* Retrieved from http://www.speech-language-therapy.com/ stuttering.htm

Bower, T. G. R. (1976, November). Repetitive processes in child development. *Scientific American, 235*, 38–47.

Bowlby, J. (1969). *Attachment.* New York: Basic Books.

Bowlby, J. (1988). *A secure base: Clinical application of attachment theory.* London: Routledge.

Boyles, S. (2008, February 14). *Overweight, obesity linked to cancers.* WebMD, Retrieved from http://www.webmd.com/cancer/news/20080214/overweight-obesity-linked-to-cancers

Bracey, G. W., & Stellar, A. (2003). Long-term studies of preschool: Lasting benefits far outweigh costs. *Phi Delta Kappan, 84*(10), 780–783.

Bradley, R. G., Binder, E. B., Epstein, M. P., Tang, Y., Nair, H. P., Liu, W., . . . , Ressler, K. J. (2008). Influence of child abuse on adult depression: Moderation by the corticotropin-releasing hormone receptor gene. *Archives of General Psychiatry, 65*(2), 190–200.

Bradley, R. H. (1993). Children's home environments, health, behavior, and intervention efforts: A review using the HOME inventory as a marker measure. *Genetic, Social and General Psychology Monographs, 119*(4), 437–490.

Bradley, R. H., & Corwyn, R. F. (2005). Productive activity and the prevention of behavior problems. *Developmental Psychology, 41*(1), 89–98.

Brady, S. S., & Halpern-Felsher, B. L. (2007). Adolescents' reported consequences of having oral sex versus vaginal sex. *Pediatrics, 119*(2), 229–236. doi:10.1542/peds.2006-1727

Brain facts: A parent's guide to early brain development. (2009.) *I Am Your Child.* Retrieved from http://www.burchschool.com/brainfax.html

Bramlett, M. D., & Mosher, W. D. (2002, July). Cohabitation, marriage, divorce, and remarriage in the United States. *Vital Health Statistics, 23*(22), 1–93.

Brand, S., Luethi, M., von Planta, A., Hatzinger, M., & Holsboer-Trachsler, E. (2007). Romantic love, hypomania, and sleep pattern in adolescents. *Journal of Adolescent Health, 41*(1), 69–76.

Brand, R., Markey, C., Mills, A., & Hodges, S. (2007). Sex differences in self-reported infidelity and its correlates. *Sex Roles, 57*(1/2), 101. Retrieved from EBSCOhost.

Bray, J. H., & Hetherington, E. M. (1993). Families in transition: Introduction and overview. *Journal of Family Psychology, 7,* 3.

Brazelton, T. B. (1978). Introduction. In A. J. Sameroff (Ed.), Organization and stability of newborn behavior: A commentary on the Brazelton Neonatal Behavior Assessment Scale [Monograph]. *Monographs of the Society for Research in Child Development, 43*(177), 1–13.

Brazelton, T. B. (1998, December 6). Early bonding is important to parents, infants. *Houston Chronicle,* p. 9.

Brazelton, T. B. (2001). *The Clinical Neonatal Behavioral Assessment Scale: What Is It?* The Brazelton Institute. Harvard Medical School. Retrieved from http://www.childrenshospital.org/brazelton/clnbas.html

Brazelton, T. B., & Nugent, J. K. (1995). *The Neonatal Behavioral Assessment Scale.* Cambridge: MacKeith Press.

Bremner, J. G., Johnson, S. P., Slater, A., Mason, U., Cheshire, A., & Spring, J. (2007). Conditions for young infants' failure to perceive trajectory continuity. *Developmental Science, 10*(5), 613–624.

Brennan, A., Marshall-Lucette, S., Ayers, A., & Ahmed, H. (2010). A qualitative exploration of the Couvade syndrome in expectant fathers. *Journal of Reproductive and Infant Psychology, 25*(1), 18–39. doi:10.1080/02646830601117142

Brewster, K. L., & Tillman, K. H. (2008). Who's doing it? Patterns and predictors of youths' oral sexual experiences. *Journal of Adolescent Health, 42*(1), 73–80.

Brewaeys, A. (2010). Men not included: A review of single and lesbian mother D I families: Mother-child relationships in child development. *Facts, Views, and Vision in ObGyn,* 74–79. Retrieved from http://www.fvvo.be/assets/105/24-Brewaeys.pdf

Bricker, D. (2000). Inclusion: How the scene has changed. *Topics in Early Childhood Special Education, 20*(1), 14–20.

Bridge, J. A., Goldstein, T. R., & Brent, D. A. (2006). Adolescent suicide and suicidal behavior. *Journal of Child Psychology and Psychiatry,* (47)3/4, 372–394. doi:10.1111/j.1469-7610.2006.01615.x

Briggs, G. G., & Wan, S. R. (2006). Drug therapy during labor and delivery, part 1. *American Journal of Health-System Pharmacy, 63*(11), 1038–1047.

Brim, O. G., Ryff, C. D., & Kessler, R. C. (Eds.). (2004). *How healthy are we: A national study of well-being at midlife.* Chicago: University of Chicago Press.

Brimhall, W., Wampler, K., & Kimball, T. (2008). Learning from the past, altering the future: A tentative theory of the effect of past relationships on couples who remarry. *Family Process, 47*(3), 373–387. doi:10.1111/j.1545-5300.2008.00259.x

Brittingham, S. (2005, March 1). Leading high-achieving schools. *No Child Left Behind: The Achiever.* Retrieved from http://www.ed.gov/news/ newsletters/achiever/2005/030105.html#2

Britton, A., Shipley, M., Singh-Manoux, A., & Marmot, M. G. (2008). Successful aging: The contribution of early-life and mid-life risk factors. *Journal of American Geriatrics, 56*(6), 1098–1105. doi:10.1111/j.1532-5415.2008.01740.x

Britton, W., & Bootzin, R. R. (2004). Near-death experiences and the temporal lobe. *Psychological Science, 15*(4), 254–258.

Brock, R. L., & Lawrence, E. (2008). A longitudinal investigation of stress spillover in marriage: Does spousal support adequacy buffer the effects? *Journal of Family Psychology, 22*(1), 11–20.

Brockmann, H., Müller, R., & Helmert, U. (2009). Time to retire: Time to die? *Social Science & Medicine, 69*(1), 160–164. doi:10.1016/j.socscimed.2009.04.009

Brody, E. M., Litvin, S. J., Albert, S. M., & Hoffman, C. J. (1994). Marital status of daughters and patterns of parent care. *Journal of Gerontology: Social Sciences, 49,* S95–S103.

Brody, J. E. (1981, May 27). Planning to prevent retirement "shock." *New York Times,* p. 13.

Brody, J. E. (1995, April 19). Study says exercise must be strenuous to add to lifespan. *New York Times,* pp. A1, B7.

Brody, N. (1992). *Intelligence* (2nd ed.). New York: Academic Press.

Bronfenbrenner, U. (1979). *The ecology of human development: Experiments by nature and design.* Cambridge, MA: Harvard University Press.

Bronfenbrenner, U. (1986, February). Alienation and the four worlds of childhood. *Phi Delta Kappan, 67,* 430–436.

Bronfenbrenner, U. (1997). Systems vs. associations: It's not either/or. *Families in Society, 78,* 124.

Bronfenbrenner, U. (Ed.). (2005). *Making human beings human.* Thousand Oaks, CA: Sage.

Bronfenbrenner, U., & Crouter, A. C. (1983). Evolution of environmental models of developmental research. In P. Mussen and W. Kessen (Eds.), *Handbook of child psychology.* New York: Wiley.

Bronson, G. W. (1972). Infants' reactions to unfamiliar persons and novel objects. *Monographs of the Society for Research in Child Development, 37*(3), 1–46.

Bronson, W. (1974). Mother-toddler interaction: A perspective on studying the development of competence. *Merrill-Palmer Quarterly, 20,* 275–301.

Brooker, R. J., Widmaier, E. P., Graham, L. E., & Stiling, P. D. (2008). *Biology.* New York: McGraw-Hill.

Brookfield, S. D. (2005). Overcoming impostership, cultural suicide, and lost innocence: Implications for teaching critical thinking in the community college. *New Directions for Community Colleges, 130,* 49–57. doi:10.1002/cc.195

Brooks-Gunn, J., Phelps, E., & Elder, G. H., Jr. (1991). Studying lives through time: Secondary data analysis in developmental psychology. *Developmental Psychology, 27,* 899–910.

Brophy, J. E. (2004). *Motivating students to learn.* Mahwah, NJ: Erlbaum.

Brotman, S., Ryan, B., & Meyer. (2006). *The health and social service needs of gay and lesbian seniors and their families in Canada.* Montreal: McGill School of Social Work.

Brougham, R. R., & Walsh, D. A. (2009). Early and late retirement exits. *International Journal of Aging and Human Development, 69*(4), 267–286.

Brougham, R. R., Zail, C. M., Mendoza, C. M., & Miller, J. R. (2009). Stress, sex differences, and coping strategies among college students. *Current Psychology, 28*(2), 85–97. doi:10.1007/s12144-009-9047-0

Brown, B. B., & Huang, B. H. (1995). Examining parenting practices in different peer contexts: Implications for adolescent trajectories. In L. Crockett & A. C. Crouter (Eds.), *Pathways through adolescence: Individual development in relation to social contexts* (pp. 151–174). Hillsdale, NJ: Erlbaum.

Brown, J. D., Halpern, C. T., & L'Engle, K. L. (2005). Mass media as a sexual super peer for early maturing girls. *Journal of Adolescent Health, 36*(5), 420–427.

Brown, J. D., L'Engle, K. L., Pardun, C. J., Guo, G., Kenneavy, K., & Jackson, C. (2006). Sexy media matter: Exposure to sexual content in music, movies, television, and magazines predicts black and white adolescents' sexual behavior. *Pediatrics, 117*(4), 1018–1027.

Brown, L. M., & Gilligan, C. (1992). *Meeting at the crossroads: Women's psychology and girls' development.* Cambridge, MA: Harvard University Press.

Brown, R. (1973). *A first language.* Cambridge, MA: Harvard University Press.

Brown, S. L., Lee, G. R., & Bulanda, J. R. (2006). Cohabitation among older adults: A national portrait. *Journal of Gerontology, 61*(2), S71–S79.

Brown, S. L., & Kawamura, S. (2010). Relationship quality among cohabitors and marrieds in older adulthood. *Social Science Research, 39*(5), 777–786. doi:10.1016/j.ssresearch.2010.04.010

Brown, T. (1996). Values, knowledge, and Piaget. In E. Reed, E. Turiel, & T. Brown (Eds.), *Values and knowledge.* Mahwah, NJ: Erlbaum.

Brown Wilson, K. (2007). Historical evolution of assisted living in the United States, 1979 to the present. *Gerontologist, 47*, 8–22.

Brownell, C. A., Zerwas, S., & Ramani, G. B. (2007). "So Big": The development of body self-awareness in toddlers. *Child Development, 78*(5), 1426–1440.

Bruggemann, O. M., Parpinelli, M. A., Osis, M., Cecatti, J. G., Carvalhinho-Neto, A. S. (2007). Support to woman by a companion of her choice during childbirth: A randomized controlled trial. *Reproductive Health, 4*(5), 1–7. doi:10.1186/1742-4755-4-5

Bruner, J. S. (1970, December). A conversation with Jerome Bruner. *Psychology Today, 4*, 51–74.

Bruner, J. S. (1983). *Child's talk: Learning to use language.* New York: Norton.

Bruner, J. S. (1990). *Acts of meaning.* Cambridge, MA: Harvard University Press.

Brunner, R., & Resch, F. (2006). Eating disorders—An increasing problem in children and adolescents? *Therapeutische Umschau, 63*(8), 545–549. doi: 10.1024/0040-5930.63.8.545

Brushes with death: Scientists validate near death experiences. (2002). ABCNews.Com. Retrieved January 8, 2002, from http://abcnews.go.comsections/GMA/DrJohnson/SMA020108Near_death_experiences.html

Bryant-Waugh, R. (2006). Recent developments in anorexia nervosa. *Child and Adolescent Mental Health, 11*(2), 76–81.

Buckner, R. L., Head, D., & Lustig, C. (2006). Brain changes in aging: A lifespan perspective. In E. Bialystok & F. I. M. Craik (Eds.), *Lifespan cognition: Mechanisms of change* (pp. 27–42). Oxford: Oxford University Press.

Buddeberg-Fischer, B., Stamm, M., Buddeberg, C., Bauer, G., Haemmig, O., Knecht, M., & Klaghofer, R. (2010). The impact of gender and parenthood on physicians' careers—Professional and personal situation seven years after graduation. *BMC Health Services Research, 10*(40), 1–10.

Buehner, M. J., & May, J. (2009). Causal induction from continuous event streams: Evidence for delay-induced attribution shifts. *Journal of Problem Solving, 2*(2), 42–80. Retrieved from EBSCO*host.*

Buettner, D. (2008). *The Blue Zones: Lessons for living longer from the people who've lived the longest.* Washington, DC: National Geographic Books.

Bugental, D. B., & Grusec, J. E. (2006). Socialization processes. In W. Damon & R. M. Lerner (Eds.), *Handbook of child psychology* (6th ed., Vol. 1, pp. 366–428). New York: Wiley.

Buhrmester, D., & Furman, W. (1990). Perceptions of sibling relationships during middle childhood and adolescence. *Child Development, 61*, 1387–1398.

Bulanda, R. E., & Majumdar, D. (2009). Perceived parent-child relations and adolescent self-esteem. *Journal of Child and Family Studies, 18*, 203–212. doi:10.1007/s10826-008-9220-3

Bulik, C. M., Slof-Op't Landt, M. C., van Furth, E. F., & Sullivan, P. F. (2007). The genetics of anorexia nervosa. *Annual Review of Nutrition, 27*, 263–275. doi: 10.1146/annurev.nutr.27.061406.093713

Bull, R. (2004). Legal psychology in the twenty-first century. *Criminal Behaviour in Mental Health, 4*(3), 167–181.

Bundy, A., Lane, S., & Murray, E. (2002). *Sensory integration theory and practice* (2nd ed.). Philadelphia: F. A. Davis.

Buntaine, R. L., & Costenbader, V. K. (1997). Self-reported differences in the experience and expression of anger between girls and boys. *Sex Roles: A Journal of Research, 36*(9), 625–638.

Burdette, H. L., & Whitaker, R. C. (2005). A national study of neighborhood safety, outdoor play, television viewing, and obesity in preschool children. *Pediatrics, 116*(3), 657–662.

Bureau of Labor Statistics. (2010, August). Employment and unemployment among youth: Summer 2010. [Press release]. Retrieved from http://www.bls.gov/news.release/youth.nr0.htm

Bureau of Labor Statistics. (2011a). EPP Table 1.3 Fastest growing occupations. Employment Projections Program. Retrieved from http://www.bls.gov/emp/

Bureau of Labor Statistics. (2011b). Teachers—Kindergarten, elementary, middle, and secondary. *Occupational Outlook Handbook 2010–11 Edition.* Retrieved from http://www.bls.gov/oco/pdf/ocos318.pdf

Bureau of Labor Statistics. (Winter 2010–11). Hiring outlook looking up for Class of '11. *Occupational Outlook Quarterly Online, 54*(4), 1–36. Retrieved from http://www.bls.gov/opub/ooq/2010/winter/winter2010ooq.pdf

Burke, K., & Sutherland, C. (2004, Winter). Attitudes toward inclusion: Knowledge vs. experience. *Education, 125*(2), 163–173.

Bursuck, W. D., & Damer, M. (2007). *Reading instruction: For students who are at risk or have disabilities.* Boston: Pearson Education.

Burtless, G., & Singer, A. (2010, December 7). The earnings and Social Security contributions of documented and undocumented Mexican immigrants. Washington, DC: The Brookings Institution. Retrieved from http://www.brookings.edu/~/media/Files/rc/papers/2010/1207_immigrant_earnings_burtless_singer/1207_immigrant_earnings_summary_burtless_singer.pdf

Burton, R. V. (1976). Honesty and dishonesty. In T. Lickona (Ed.), *Moral development and behavior: Theory, research, and social issues.* New York: Holt, Rinehart & Winston.

Bush, G. W. (2006). Remarks on signing the Adam Walsh Child Protection and Safety Act of 2006. *Weekly Compilation of Presidential Documents, 42*(30), 1395–1396. Retrieved from EBSCO*host.*

Bushnell, E. W. (1985). The decline of visually guided reaching during infancy. *Infant Behavior and Development, 8*, 139–155.

Buss, D. (2008). *Evolutionary psychology: The new science of the mind* (3rd ed.). Boston: Pearson Education.

Busse, E. W., & Pfeiffer, E. (Eds.). (1969). *Behavior and adaptation in late life.* Boston: Little, Brown.

Bussey, K. (1992). Lying and truthfulness: Children's definitions, standards, and evaluative reactions. *Child Development, 63*, 129–137.

Bussey, K., & Bandura, A. (1984). Influence of gender constancy and social power on sex-linked modeling. *Journal of Personality and Social Psychology, 47*, 1292–1302.

Butler, R. N. (1971, December). The life review. *Psychology Today, 5*, 49–51ff.

Buttenschøn, H. N., Lauritsen, M. B., Daoud, A. E., Hollegaard, M., Jorgensen, M., Tvedegaard, K., . . . Mors, O. (2009). A population-based association study of glutamate decarboxylase 1 as a candidate gene for autism. *Journal of Neural Transmission, 116*(3), 381–388. doi:10.1007/s00702-008-0142-4

Byely, L., Archibald, A. B., Graber, J., & Brooks-Gunn, J. (2000). A prospective study of familial and social influences on girls' body image and dieting. *International Journal of Eating Disorders, 28*, 155–164.

C. D. Publications. (2010). V.A. launches $50 million homeless prevention to include children. *Children and Youth Funding Report*, 4–5.

Cabrera, N. J., & Garcia Coll, C. G. (2004). Latino fathers: Uncharted territory in need of much exploration. In M. E. Lamb (Ed.), *The role of the father in child development* (4th ed., pp. 98–120). New York: Wiley.

Cacciatore, J. (2007). Effects of support groups on post traumatic stress responses in women experiencing stillbirth. *Omega, 55*(1), 71–90.

Cagley, M. (2009, June). Social support, networks, and happiness. Today's Research on Aging: Program and Policy Implications. 17, 1–6. Washington, DC: Population Reference Bureau. Retrieved from http://www.prb .org/pdf09/TodaysResearchAging17.pdf

Cahill, S. E. (1990). Childhood and public life: Reaffirming biographical divisions. *Social Problems, 37,* 390–402.

Calkins, S. D. (2007). The emergence of self-regulation: Biological and behavioral control mechanisms supporting toddler competencies. In C. A. Brownell, & C. B. Kopp (Eds.), *Socioemotional development in the toddler years: Transitions and transformations* (pp. 261–282). New York: Guilford Press.

Calkins, S. D., & Howse, R. B. (2004). Individual differences in self-regulation: Implications for childhood adjustment. In P. Phillipot & R. S. Feldman (Eds.), *The regulation of emotion* (pp. 307–332). Mahwah, NJ: Erlbaum.

Camarata, S. (1996). On the importance of integrating naturalistic language, social intervention, and speech-intelligibility training. In L. Koegel, R. Koegel, & G. Dunlap (Eds.), *Positive behavior support* (pp. 333–351). Baltimore, MD: Brookes.

Campbell, D., Scott, K. D., Klaus, M. H., & Falk, M. (2007). Female relatives or friends trained as labor doulas: Outcomes at 6 to 8 weeks postpartum. *Birth, 34*(3), 220–227.

Campbell, S. S., & Murphy, P. J. (2007). The nature of spontaneous sleep across adulthood. *Journal of Sleep Research, 16,* 24–32.

Campos, J. J., Mumme, D. L., Kermoian, R., & Campos, R. G. (1993). A functionalist perspective on the nature of emotion. *Monographs of the Society for Research in Child Development, 5*(2–3, Serial No. 240).

Camras, L. A., & Fatani, S. S. (2008). The development of facial expressions: Current perspectives on infant emotions. In M. Lewis & J. M. Haviland-Jones (Eds.), *Handbook of emotions* (pp. 291–303). New York: Guilford Press.

Canfield, R. L., Henderson, C. R., Cory Slechta, D. A., Cox, C., Jusko, T. A., & Lanphera, B. P. (2003, April 17). Intellectual impairment in children with blood lead concentrations below 10 mg per deciliter. *New England Journal of Medicine, 348,* 1517–1526.

Cannon, T. D., Cadenhead, K., Cornblatt, B., Woods, S. W., Addington, J., Walker, E., . . . , Heinssen, R. (2008). Prediction of psychosis in youth at high clinical risk: A multisite longitudinal study in North America. *Archives of General Psychiatry, 65*(1), 28–37.

Cantor, M. H., Brennan, M., & Shippy, R. A. (2004). *Caregiving among older lesbian, gay, bisexual, and transgender New Yorkers.* New York: National Gay and Lesbian Task Force Policy Institute.

Capella, E. (2006). The prevention of social aggression among girls. *Social Development, 15*(3), 434–462.

Capewell, S., Ford, E. S., Croft, J. B., Critchley, J. A., Greenlund, K. J., & Labarthe, D. R. (2009). Cardiovascular risk factor trends and potential for reducing coronary heart disease mortality in the United States of America. *Bulletin of the World Health Organization, 88*(1), 120–130.

Cappeliez, P., & O'Rourke, N. (2006). Empirical validation of a model of reminiscence and health in later life. *Journal of Gerontology, 61*(4), 237–244.

Caputo, R. K. (2005). *Challenges of aging on U.S. families: Policy and practice implications.* Binghamton, NY: Haworth Press.

Card, N., Stucky, B., Sawalani, G., & Little, T. (2008). Direct and indirect aggression during childhood and adolescence: A meta-analytic review of gender differences, intercorrelations, and relations to maladjustment. *Child Development, 79*(5), 1185–1229. doi:10.1111/j.1467-8624.2008.01184.x

Carlson, E. (2006). Twenty common nursing home problems and the laws to resolve them. *Clearinghouse Review Journal of Poverty Law and Policy, 39*(9–10), 519–533.

Carlson, M. J., & McLanahan, S. S. (2010). Fathers in fragile families. In M. E. Lamb (Ed.) *The role of the father in child development* (pp. 241–269). Hoboken, NJ: Wiley.

Carlson, V. J., & Harwood, R. L. (2003). Attachment, culture, and the caregiving system: The cultural patterning of everyday experiences among Anglo and Puerto Rican mother-infant pairs. *Infant Mental Health Journal, 24*(1), 53–73.

Carpendale, J. M. (2009). Piaget's theory of moral development. In U. Müller, J. M. Carpendale, L. Smith (Eds.), *The Cambridge companion to Piaget* (pp. 270–286). New York: Cambridge University Press.

Carpenter, M. (2001, June 10). The IQ factor: Despite advances in defining gifted children, intelligence testing still plays a large role. *Pittsburgh Post-Gazette.* Retrieved from http://www.post-gazette.com/regionstate/ 20010610giftediqsidereg8.asp

Carstensen, L. L. (2007). Growing old or living long: Take your pick; research to understand the psychological and emotional processes of aging is essential to creating a society in which the elderly can thrive. *Science and Technology, 23*(2), 41–54.

Carver, L. J., & Vaccaro, B. G. (2007). 12-month-old infants allocate increased neural resources to stimuli associated with negative adult emotion. *Developmental Psychology, 43*(1), 54–69. doi:10.1037/0012 -1649.43.1.54

Carver, P. R., Egan, S. K., & Perry, D. G. (2004). Children who question their heterosexuality. *Developmental Psychology, 40*(1), 43–53.

Casamassimo, P. S. (2004, December 1). Oral health in primary care medicine: Practice and policy challenges. [Editorial]. *American Family Physician, 70*(11), 2074–2076.

Case, R. (Ed.). (1991). *The mind's staircase: Exploring the conceptual underpinnings of children's thought and knowledge.* Hillsdale, NJ: Erlbaum.

Caspe, M. (2005). *Family literacy: A review of programs and critical perspectives.* Cambridge, MA: Harvard Family Research Project.

Caspi, A., & Shiner, R. L. (2006). Personality development. In W. Damon & R. Lerner (Eds.). *Handbook of child psychology* (6th ed.). New York: Wiley.

Cassens, D. (1998). Expanded damages in elder abuse cases. *ABA Journal, 84,* 39.

Cast, A. D., & Burke, P. J. (2002). A theory of self-esteem. *Social Forces, 80*(3), 1041–1068.

Cattell, R. B. (1943). The measurement of adult intelligence. *Psychological Bulletin, 40,* 153–193.

Cattell, R. B. (1971). *Abilities: Their structure, growth, and action.* Boston: Houghton Mifflin.

Cattell, R. B. (1987). *Intelligence: Its structure, growth and action.* Amsterdam: Elsevier Science.

Cavallero, P., Morino-Abbele, F., & Bertocci, B. (2007). The social relations of the elderly. *Archives of Gerontology, 1,* 97–100.

Cavanaugh, J. C. (1998). Memory and aging. *National Forum: Phi Kappa Phi Journal, 78,* 34–37.

Cavell, T. A., Hymel, S., Malcolm, K. T., & Seay, A. (2007). Socialization and interventions for antisocial youth. In J. E. Grusec & P. D. Hastings (Eds.), *Handbook of socialization: Theory and research* (pp. 42–67). New York: Guilford Press.

Ceci, S. J. (2006). Urie Bronfenbrenner. *American Psychologist, 61*(2), 173–174.

Cellular inflammation precursor to heart disease. (2005, February 2005). *USA Today Magazine, 133,* 8–9.

Center for Applied Linguistics. (2010). Two-way immersion: Directory of two-way bilingual immersion programs in the U.S. Retrieved from http://www.cal.org/twi/ directory/index.html

Center for Biology Evaluation and Research. (2004, June 29). *Xenotransplantation action plan* (FDA Approach to the Regulation of Xenotransplantation). Washington, DC: U.S. Food & Drug Administration.

Center for Public Education. (2010). Cutting to the bone: How the economic crisis affects schools. Alexandria, VA: The National School Boards Association. Retrieved from http://www.centerforpubliceducation.org/

Centers for Disease Control and Prevention. (1998). *National Mortality Followback Survey (NMFS).* National Center for Health Statistics. Retrieved from http://www.cdc.gov/ nchswww/about/major/nmfs /nmfs.htm

Centers for Disease Control and Prevention. (2003c). HIV/STD risks in young men who have sex with men who do not disclose their sexual orientation—Six U.S. cities, 1994–2000. *MMWR Weekly, 52*(5), 81–85.

Centers for Disease Control and Prevention. (2004). Blood mercury levels in young children and childbearing-aged women—United States: 1999–2002. *MMWR Weekly, 53*(43), 1018–1020.

Centers for Disease Control and Prevention. (2005). Health disparities experienced by black or African Americans—United States. *MMWR Weekly, 54*(1), 1–3.

Centers for Disease Control and Prevention. (2006). Improved national prevalence estimates for 18 selected major birth defects—United States, 1999–2001. *MMWR Weekly, 54*(51&52), 1301–1305.

Centers for Disease Control and Prevention. (2007a). *HIV/AIDS surveillance report: 2005.* Retrieved from http://www.cdc.gov/hiv/topics/surveillance/resources/reports/

Centers for Disease Control and Prevention. (2007b). *Human papillomavirus: HPV information for clinicians.* Retrieved from http://www.cdc.gov/std/HPV/common-clinicians/ClinicianBro-br.pdf

Centers for Disease Control and Prevention. (2007c). *Sexually transmitted disease surveillance 2006 supplement, Chlamydia prevalence monitoring project: Annual Report 2006.* Atlanta, GA: U.S. Department of Health & Human Services.

Centers for Disease Control and Prevention. (2007d). *Teen birth rate rises for first time in 15 years.* [News Release]. Retrieved on from http://www.cdc.gov/nchs/pressroom/07newsreleases/teenbirth.htm

Centers for Disease Control and Prevention. (2007e). *Impaired driving.* Retrieved from http://www.cdc.gov/ncipc/factsheets/drving.htm

Centers for Disease Control and Prevention. (2008a). *HIV/AIDS among Youth.* Atlanta, GA: U.S. Department of Health and Human Services. Retrieved from http://www.cdc.gov/hiv/resources/factsheets/PDF/youth.pdf

Centers for Disease Control and Prevention. (2008b). HIV/AIDS among persons aged 50 and older: CDC HIV/AIDS Facts. Retrieved from www.cdc.gov/ hiv/topics/over50/resources/factsheets/pdf/ over50.pdf

Centers for Disease Control and Prevention. (2009a). *Assisted reproductive technology success rates 2007: National summary and fertility clinic reports.* U.S. Department of Health and Human Services. Retrieved from http://ftp.cdc.gov/pub/publications/art/2007/ART.pdf

Centers for Disease Control and Prevention. (2009b). *Autism spectrum disorders: Data and statistics.* Retrieved from http://www.cdc.gov/ncbddd/autism/data.html

Centers for Disease Control and Prevention. (2009c). *Sexually transmitted disease surveillance, 2008.* Atlanta, GA: U.S. Department of Health and Human Services. Retrieved from http://www.cdc.gov/std/stats08/surv2008-Intro.pdf

Centers for Disease Control and Prevention. (2010a). *Condoms and STDs: Fact sheet for public health personnel.* Retrieved from http://www.cdc.gov/condomeffectiveness/latex.htm

Centers for Disease Control and Prevention. (2010b). *HIV in the United States.* U.S. Department of Health and Human Services. Retrieved from http://www.cdc.gov/hiv/html

Centers for Disease Control and Prevention. (2010c). *HIV/AIDS statistics and surveillance report: 2010.* Retrieved from http://www.cdc.gov/hiv/topics/surveillance/basic.html

Centers for Disease Control and Prevention. (2010d, August 3). Vital signs: State-specific prevalence of obesity among adults—United States, 2009. *MMWR Weekly, 59,* 765–768.

Centers for Disease Control and Prevention. (2010e). *Breastfeeding Report Card: United States, 2010.* Retrieved from http://www.cdc.gov/breastfeeding/data/

Centers for Disease Control and Prevention. (2010f). *National Birth Defects Prevention Study examines potential risk factors.* Retrieved from http://www.cdc.gov/Features/BirthDefectsStudy/

Centers for Disease Control and Prevention. (2010g). *Pertussis (whooping cough)—What you need to know.* Retrieved from http://www.cdc.gov/features/pertussis/

Centers for Disease Control and Prevention. (2010h). Youth risk behavior surveillance—United States, 2009. *MMWR Weekly, 59*(SS-5), 1–142.

Centers for Disease Control and Prevention. (2011). *Frequently asked questions about Thimerosal-free vaccines.* Retrieved from http://www.cdc.gov/vaccinesafety/concerns/thimerosal/thimerosal_faqs_availfree.html#3

Cesario, S. K., & Hughes, L. A. (2007). Precocious puberty: A comprehensive review of literature. *Journal of Obstetric, Gynecologic, & Neonatal Nursing, 36*(3), 263–274. doi:10.1111/j.1552-6909.2007.00145.x

Chadefaux-Vekemans, B., Rabier, D., Cadoudal, N., Lescoat, A., Chabli, A., Aupetit, . . . , Oury, J. F. (2006). Prenatal diagnosis of some metabolic diseases using early amniotic fluid samples: Report of a 15 years experience. *Prenatal Diagnosis, 26*(9), 814–818.

Chamberlin, J. (2004, November). No desire to fully retire. *Monitor on Psychology, 35*(10), 82–83.

Chamberlain, J., Miller, M., & Bornstein, B. H. (2008). The rights and responsibilities of gay and lesbian parents: Legal developments, psychological research, and policy implications. *Social Issues and Policy Review, 2*(1), 103–126. doi:10.1111/j.1751-2409.2008.00012.x

Chambers, W. C. (2007). Oral sex: Varied behaviors and perceptions in a college population. *Journal of Sex Research, 44*(1), 28–42.

Chance, P., & Fischman, J. (1987, May). The magic of childhood. *Psychology Today, 21,* 48–58.

Chao, Y. M., Pisetsky, E. M., Dierker, L. C., Dohm, F. A., Rosselli, F., May, A. M., . . . , Striegel-Moore, A. H. (2008). Ethnic differences in weight control practices among U.S. adolescents from 1995 to 2005. *International Journal of Eating Disorders, 41*(2), 124–133. doi:10.1002/eat.20479

Chapman, C., Laird, J., & Kewalramani, A. (2010). *Trends in High School Dropout and Completion Rates in the United States: 1972–2008* (NCES 2011-012). National Center for Education Statistics, Institute of Education Sciences, U.S. Department of Education. Washington, DC. Retrieved from http://nces.ed.gov/pubsearch

Charles, S. T., & Pasupathi, M. (2003). Age-related patterns of variability in self-descriptions: Implications for everyday affective experience. *Psychology and Aging, 18,* 524–536.

Charness, N., & Gerchak, Y. (1996). Participation rates and maximal performance: A log-linear explanation for group differences, such as Russian and male dominance in chess. *Psychological Science, 7,* 46–51.

Charsky, D., Kish, M. L., Briskin, J., Hathaway, S., Walsh, K., & Barajas, N. (2009, November/December). Millennials need training too: Using communication technology to facilitate teamwork. *TechTrends, 53*(6), 42–48.

Charsley, K. (2007). Risk, trust, gender and transnational cousin marriage among British Pakistanis. *Ethnic and Racial Studies, 30*(6), 1117–1131.

Chase, M. (1995, February 27). Gently guiding the gravely ill to the end of life. *Wall Street Journal,* p. B1.

Chase-Lansdale, P. L., Cherlin, A. J., & Kiernan, K. E. (1995). The long-term effects of parental divorce on the mental health of young adults: A developmental perspective. *Child Development, 66,* 1614–1634.

Chelli, D., & Chanoufi, B. (2008). Fetal audition: Myth or reality. *Journal of Gynecology, Obstetrics & Biology of Reproduction, 37*(6), 554–558.

Chen, H., Cheal, K., Herr, E. M., Zubritsky, C., & Levkoff, S. E. (2007). Religious participation as a predictor of mental health status and treatment outcomes in older persons. *International Journal of Geriatric Psychiatry, 22,* 144–153.

Chen, J., Murayama, S., & Kamibeppu, K. (2010). Factors related to well-being among the elderly in urban China focusing on multiple roles. *BioScience Trends, 4*(2), 61–71.

Chen, X., French, D. C., & Schneider, B. H. (Eds.). (2006). *Peer relationships in cultural context*. New York: Cambridge University Press.

Cherbuin, N., & Brinkman, C. (2006). Hemispheric interactions are different in left-handed individuals. *Neuropsychology, 20*(6), 700–707.

Cherlin, A. (2004). The deinstitutionalization of American marriage. *Journal of Marriage and Family, 66*, 848–861.

Cherlin, A. J. (2009). *The marriage-go-round: The state of marriage and the family in America today*. New York: Knopf.

Cheung, A. & Slavin, R. E. (2005). Effective reading programs for English language learners and other language-minority students. *Bilingual Research Journal, 29*(2), 241–267. Retrieved from http://www.bestevidence.org/word/ell_read_2005_BRJ.pdf

Chew, K., Bremner, A., Stuckey, B., Earle, C., & Jamrozik, K. (2009). Sex life after 65: How does erectile dysfunction affect ageing and elderly men? *The Ageing Male, 12*(2/3), 41–46. doi:10.1080/13685530802273400

Chia, R. C., & Poe, E. (2004, Spring). Innovations in international education. *International Psychology Reporter, 8*, 7.

Child Trends Databank. (2002). *Charting parenthood: A statistical portrait of fathers and mothers in America*. Washington, DC: Child Trends. Retrieved from http://www.childtrends.org/files/Parent-hoodRpt2002.pdf

Child Trends Databank. (2007d). *Juvenile detention: Adolescents in residential placements*. Retrieved from http://www.childtrendsdatabank.org/indicators/88JuvenileDetention.cfm

Child Trends Databank. (2008a). Calculations of U.S. Census Bureau, *Current Population Survey, 2006*. America's Families and Living Arrangements: 2006. Table C-2. Retrieved from http://www.census.gov/population/www/socdemo/hh-fam/cps2006.html

Child Trends DataBank. (2008b). *Percentage of births to mothers receiving late or no prenatal care, selected years, 1970–2006*. Retrieved from http://www.childtrendsdatabank.org/indicators/25PrenatalCare.cfrh

Child Trends DataBank. (2010a). *Infants and young children: Health and well-being status, alphabetical indicators*. Retrieved from http://childtrendsdatabank.org/alphalist

Child Trends Databank. (2010b, September). Educational attainment (youth). Retrieved from www.childtrendsdatabank.org/?q=node/163.

Child Trends Databank. (2010c, October). Youth neither enrolled in school nor working. Retrieved from Child Trends Databank:www.childtrendsdatabank.org/?q=node/181

Child Trends Databank. (2010d). Binge drinking. Retrieved from Child Trends Databank: www.childtrendsdatabank.org/alphalist?q=node/140

Child Trends Databank. (2010e). Illicit drug use. Retrieved from Child Trends Databank: www.childtrendsdatabank.org/?q=node/281

Child Trends Databank. (2010f). Individualized education plans. Retrieved from http://www.childtrendsdatabank.org/?q=node/260

Child Trends Databank. (2010g). *Team homicide, suicide and firearm deaths*. Retrieved from http://www.childtrendsdatabank.org/?q=node/319 <http://www.childtrendsdatabank.org/?q=node/319>

Child Trends Databank. (2011). Family structure. Table 2 Percent of Children Living in the Home of their Grandparents: 1970–2009. Retrieved from http://www.childtrendsdatabank.org/?q=node/334

Child Welfare Information Gateway. (2007). *What is child abuse and neglect?* Retrieved from http://www.childwelfare.gov/pubs/can_info_packet.pdf

Children's Defense Fund. (2003). *Defining poverty and why it matters to children*. Retrieved from http://www.childrensdefense.org/

Children's Defense Fund. (2008). *The state of America's children*. Washington, DC.

Choi, H., & Marks, N. F. (2006). Transition to caregiving, marital disagreement, and psychological well-being. *Journal of Family Issues, 27*(12), 1701–1722.

Choi, K., Jang, S., Lee, M., & Kim, K. (2010). Sexual life and self-esteem in married elderly. *Archives of Gerontology and Geriatrics, 1*, 1–4. doi:10.1016/j.archger.2010.08.011

Chomsky, N. (1957). *Syntactic structures*. The Hague: Mouton.

Chomsky, N. (1965). *Aspects of a theory of syntax*. Cambridge, MA: MIT Press.

Chomsky, N. (1975). *Reflections on language*. New York: Pantheon Books.

Chomsky, N. (1980). *Rules and representations*. New York: Columbia University Press.

Chomsky, N. (1995). *Language and thought*. Wakefield, RI: Moyer Bell.

Choy, N. L. L., Brauer, S. G., & Nitz, J. C. (2007, October). Age-related changes in strength and somatosensation during midlife: Rationale for targeted preventive intervention programs. *Annals of the New York Academy of Science, 1114*, 180–193.

Chozick, A. (2010, November 5). The turf war for tots: In TV's battle for the hearts and minds of preschoolers, it's Mandarin and math vs. stories and sparkle. *Wall Street Journal*, pp. D1, D2.

Christakis, D. A., & Zimmerman, F. J. (2007). Violent television viewing during preschool is associated with antisocial behavior during school age. *Pediatrics, 120*(5), 993–999.

Christensen, R. D., Havranek, T., Gerstmann, D. R., & Calhoun, D. A. (2005). Enteral administration of a simulated amniotic fluid to very low birth weight neonates. *Journal of Perinatology, 25*(6), 380–385. doi:10.1038/sj.jp.7211306

Chua, A. (2011, January 8). Why Chinese mothers are superior. Can a regimen of no playdates, no TV, no computer games and hours of music practice create happy kids? And what happens when they fight back? *Wall Street Journal*. Retrieved from http://online.wsj.com/article/SB10001424052748704111504576059713528698754.html

Chugani, H. T., & Phelps, M. E. (1986). Maturational changes in cerebral functions in infants determined by FDG positron emission tomography. *Science, 231*, 840–843.

Cicirelli, V. G. (1994). Sibling relationships in cross-cultural perspective. *Journal of Marriage and the Family, 56*, 7–20.

Cicirelli, V. G. (2001). Sibling relationships. In G. Maddux (Ed.), *Encyclopedia of Aging* (3rd ed., pp. 928–930). New York: Springer.

Cicirelli, V. G., MacLean, A. P., & Cox, L. S. (2000). Hastening death: A comparison of two end-of-life decisions. *Death Studies, 24*(5), 401–419.

Clark, A., Oswald, A., & Warr, P. (1996). Is job satisfaction U-shaped in age? *Journal of Occupational and Organizational Psychology, 69*(1), 57–82.

Clark, E. V., Gelman, S. A., & Lane, N. M. (1985). Compound nouns and category structure in young children. *Child Development, 56*, 84–94.

Clark, J. B. (2005, May). A home for the rest of your life. *Kiplinger*, 3–5.

Clark, L., & Tiggemann, M. (2006). Appearance culture in nine- to 12-year-old girls: Media and peer influences on body dissatisfaction. *Social Development, 15*(4), 628–643.

Clarys, D., Bugaiska, A., Tapia, G., & Baudouin, A. (2009). Ageing, remembering, and executive function. *Memory, 17*(2), 158–168. doi:10.1080/09658210802188301

Cleveland, J. N., & Lim, A. S. (2007). Employee age and performance in organizations. In K. S. Shultz & G. A. Adams (Eds.), *Aging and work in the 21st century* (pp. 112–138). Mahwah, NJ: Routledge.

Closson, L. M. (2009). Aggressive and prosocial behaviors within early adolescent friendship cliques: What's status got to do with it? *Merrill-Palmer Quarterly, 55*(4), 406–435. doi:10.1353/mpq.0.0035

Coch, D., Fischer, K. W., & Dawson, G. (Eds.). (2007). *Human behavior, learning, and the developing brain*. New York: Guilford Press.

Cochran, G., & Lekies, K. (2008). *Skills for success in the knowledge economy*. Retrieved from http://www.ohio4h.org/workforceprep/documents/SkillsforSuccess-ActionBriefMay2008.pdf

Cochran, G. R., & Ferrari, T. M. (2009). Preparing youth for the 21st century knowledge economy: Youth programs and workforce preparation. *Afterschool Matters, 8,* 11–25. Retrieved from http://www.robertbowne foundation.org/pdf_files/2009_asm_spring.pdf

Cochran, M., & Niego, S. (1995). Parenting and social networks. In M. H. Bornstein (Ed.), *Handbook of parenting* (Vol. 3, pp. 123–148). Hillsdale, NJ: Erlbaum.

Cocke, A. (2002, January–February). Brain may also pump up from workout. *Brain-Work—The Neuroscience Newsletter, 12*(1).

Cogan, M. F. (2010, Summer). Exploring academic outcomes of homeschooled students. *Journal of College Admission,* (208), 18–25.

Cohen, D., Eisdorfer, C., Gorelick, P., Paveza, G., Luchins, D. J., Freels, S., . . . , Hirschman, R. (1993). Psychopathology associated with Alzheimer's disease and related disorders. *Journal of Gerontology: Medical Sciences, 48,* M2555–M260.

Cohen, J. (2007). Venter's genome sheds new light on human variation. *Science, 317*(5843), 1311.

Cohen, L. B., & Cashon, C. H. (2006). Infant cognition. In W. Damon & R. M. Lerner (Eds.), *Handbook of child psychology* (6th ed., Vol. 2, pp. 214–251). New York: Wiley.

Cohen, S. A. (2004, October). Promoting the "B" in ABC: Its value and limitations in fostering reproductive health. *The Guttmacher Report on Public Policy, 7*(4). Retrieved from http://www.guttmacher.org/pubs/tgr/07/4/ gr070411.html

Cohen-Kettenis, P. T. (2002). Adolescents who are eligible for sex reassignment surgery: Parental reports of emotional and behavioural problems. *Clinical Child Psychology and Psychiatry, 7*(3), 412–422.

Colby, A., & Damon, W. (1992). *Some do care.* New York: Free Press.

Coldren, J. T., & Colombo, J. (1994). The nature and processes of preverbal learning. *Monographs of the Society for Research in Child Development, 59*(4, Serial No. 241).

Cole, A. (2006, July 8). Complacency over sexually transmitted infections leads to rise in cases. *British Medical Journal, 333*(7558), 63.

Cole, P. M., & Tan, P. Z. (2007a). Children's development of cultural repertoires through participation in everyday routines and practices. In J. E. Grusec & P. D. Hastings (Eds.), *Handbook of socialization: Theory and research* (pp. 490–515). New York: Guilford Press.

Cole, P. M., & Tan, P. Z. (2007b). Emotion socialization from a cultural perspective. In J. E. Grusec & P. D. Hastings (Eds.), *Handbook of socialization: Theory and research* (pp. 516–542). New York: Guilford Press.

Cole, P. M., Bruschi, C. J., & Tamang, B. L. (2002). Cultural differences in children's emotional reactions to difficult situations. *Child Development, 73*(3), 983–996. doi:10.2307/3696263\

Cole, R. A. (1979, April). Navigating the slippery stream of speech. *Psychology Today, 12,* 77–87.

Coleman, E. E., & Miller, M. K. (2006–2007). Assessing legal responses to prenatal drug use: Can therapeutic responses produce more positive outcomes than punitive responses results? *Journal of Law and Health, 20*(1), 35–67.

Coleman, G., Jinpa, T., & Dorje, G. (2006). *The Tibetan Book of the Dead: First complete translation.* New York: The Penguin Group.

Colgrove, J. (2006, December 7). The ethics and politics of compulsory HPV vaccination. *New England Journal of Medicine, 355,* 2389–2391.

Colledge, E., Bishop, D. V. M., Koeppen-Schomerus, G., Price, T. S., Happe, F. G. E., Eley, . . . , Plomin, R. (2002, September). The structure of language abilities at 4 years: A twin study. *Developmental Psychology, 38,* 749–757.

Colletti, C. (2007). Athlete, scholar, leader. *Independent School, 66*(4), 58–64.

Collins, G. (1983, October 24). Stepfamilies share their joys and woes. *New York Times,* p. 21.

Collins, W. A., & van Dulmen, M. (2006). Friendships and romance in emerging adulthood. In J. J. Arnett & J. L.Tanner (Eds.), *Emerging adults in America: Coming of age in the 21st century* (pp. 219–234). Washington, DC: American Psychological Association.

Collins, W. A., Maccoby, E. E., Steinberg, L., Hetherington, E. M., & Bornstein, M. H. (2000). Contemporary research on parenting: The case for nature and nurture. *American Psychologist, 55*(2), 218–232.

Coloma, R. S. (2006). Disorienting race and education: Changing paradigms on the schooling of Asian Americans and Pacific Islanders. *Race, Ethnicity, and Education 9*(1), 1–5. doi:10.1080/13613320500490606

Coltrane, B. (2003, May). *Working with young English language learners: Some considerations.* Center for Applied Linguistics. Retrieved from http://www.cal.org/resources/ digest/digest_ pdfs/0301coltrane.pdf

Commission of the European Communities. (2008, March 10). Report from the Commission to the European Parliament, the Council, the European Economic and Social Committee and the Committee of the Regions: Implementation of the Barcelona objectives concerning childcare facilities for pre-school-age children. SEC(2008)2597, 1–9.

Condon, W. S., & Sander, L. W. (1974a). Neonate movement is synchronized with adult speech: Interactional participation and language acquisition. *Science, 183,* 99–101.

Condon, W. S., & Sander, L. W. (1974b). Synchrony demonstrated between movements of the neonate and adult speech. *Child Development, 45,* 456–462.

Condrasky, M., Ledikwe, J. H., Flood, J. E., & Rolls, B. J. (2007). Chefs' opinions of restaurant portion sizes. *Obesity, 15*(8), 2086–2094.

Cong, R., Zhou, B., Sun, Q., Gu, H., Tang, N., & Wang, B. (2008). Smoking and the risk of age-related macular degeneration: A meta-analysis. *Elsevier, 18*(8), 647–656. doi:10.1016/j.annepidem.2008.04.002

Congressional Budget Office. (2010, January). *The budget and economic outlook: Fiscal years 2010 to 2020.* Retrieved from http://www.cbo.gov/ftpdocs/108xx/ doc10871/01-26-Outlook.pdf

Congressional Budget Office. (2011, January). *The budget and economic Outlook: Fiscal years 2011 to 2021.* Retrieved from http://www.cbo.gov/ftpdocs/120xx/ doc12039/01-26_FY2011Outlook.pdf

Connelly, C. E., & Gallagher, D. G. (2004). Emerging trends in contingent work research. *Journal of Management, 30*(6), 959–983. doi:10.1016/j.jm.2004.06.008

Conners, N. A., Tripathi, S. P., Clubb, R., Bradley, R. H. (2007). Maternal characteristics associated with television viewing habits of low-income preschool children. *Journal of Child and Family Studies, 16,* 415–425. doi:10.1007/s10826-006-9095-0

Connolly, M. P., Hoorens, S., & Chambers, G. M. (2010). The cost and consequences of assisted reproductive technology: An economic perspective. *Human Reproduction Update, 16*(6), 603–613. doi:10.1093/ humupd/dmq013

Conrad, M. M., & Pacquiao, D. F. (2005). Manifestation, attribution, and coping with depression among Asian Indians from the perspectives of health care practitioners *Journal of Transcultural Nursing, 16*(1), 32–40.

The Convention on the Rights of the Child. (2001). The United Nations Convention on the Rights of the Child: Article 31. Retrieved from http://www.unicef.org/ CRCpamphlet/pamphlet.htm

Conway, F., Magai, C., Springer, C., & Jones, S. C. (2008). Optimism and pessimism as predictors of physical and psychological health among grandmothers raising their grandchildren. *Journal of Research in Personality, 42*(1), 1352–1357. doi:10.1016/ j.jrp.2008.03.011

Cook-Cottone, C. (2004). Childhood post-traumatic stress disorder: Diagnosis, treatment, and school reintegration. *School Psychology Review, 33*(1), 127–140.

Cooley, C. H. (1909). *Social organization.* New York: Scribner's.

Coontz, S. (2005). *Marriage, a history: From obedience to intimacy, or how love conquered marriage.* New York: Penguin.

Coontz, S. (2006). How to stay married. *The Times of London,* November 30. Retrieved from http://www.stephaniecoontz.com/ articles/article34.htm

Coontz, S. (2007). Feminism has not made women unhappy: Expectations have risen, says Stephanie Coontz. *First Post, October 8.* Retrieved from http:// stephaniecoontz .com/articles/article37.htm

Cooper, M., Rowland, N., McArthur, K., Pattison, S., Cromarty, K., & Richards, K. (2010). Randomised controlled trial of school-based humanistic counselling for emotional distress in young people: Feasibility study and preliminary indications of efficacy. *Child and Adolescent Psychiatry and Mental Health, 4*(12), 1–12. doi:10.1186/1753-2000-4-12

Coopersmith, S. (1967). *Antecedents of self-esteem.* San Francisco: Freeman.

Copeland, L. B., Krall, E. A., Brown, L. J., Garcia, R. I., & Streckfus, C. F. (2004, Winter). Predictors of tooth loss in two U.S. adult populations. *Journal of Public Health Dentistry, 64*(1), 31–37.

Corcoran, S. P. (2007). Long-run trends in the quality of teachers: Evidence and implications for policy. *Education Finance and Policy, 2*(4), 395–407.

Cord blood banking industry flourishes amid controversy. (2004). *Blood Weekly,* 58–60.

Corr, C. A. (2001). Stage theory of dying. In G. Howarth & O. Leaman (Eds.), *Encyclopedia of death and dying* (pp. 433–434). London: Routledge.

Cosgrove, J. F., Nesbitt, I. D., & Bartley, C. (2006). Palliative care on the intensive care unit. *Current Anaesthesia & Critical Care, 17*(5), 283–288.

Cosman, M. P. (2005). Illegal aliens and American medicine. *Journal of American Physicians and Surgeons, 10*(1), 6–10.

Cosmetic surgery: Are tougher safety regulations needed? (2005). *CQ Researcher, 15*(14), 317–344.

Costa, P. T., Jr., & McCrae, R. R. (1980). Influence of extraversion and neuroticism on subjective well-being: Happy and unhappy people. *Journal of Personality and Social Psychology, 38*(4), 668–678.

Costa, P. T., Jr., & McCrae, R. R. (2005). A five-factor model perspective on personality disorders. In Strack, S. (Ed.), *Handbook of personology and psychopathology* (pp. 257–270). New York: Wiley.

Costarella, M., Monteleone, L., Steindler, R., & Zuccaro, S. (2009). Decline of physical and cognitive conditions in the elderly measured through the functional reach test and the mini-mental state examination. *Archives of Gerontology and Geriatrics, 50*(3), 332–337. doi:10.1016/j.archger.2009.05.013

Costello, J., & Kendrick, K. (2000). Grief and older people: The making or breaking of emotional bonds following partner loss in later life. *Journal of Advanced Nursing, 32*(6), 1374–1382.

Costin, C. (2007). *The eating disorders sourcebook: A comprehensive guide to the causes, treatments, and prevention of eating disorders.* New York: McGraw-Hill.

Cote, L. R., & Bornstein, M. H. (2005). Child and mother play in culture of origin, acculturating cultures, and cultures of destination. *International Journal of Behavioral Development, 29*(6), 479–488. doi:10.1177/01650250500147006

Coulter, D. J. (1995). Music and the making of the mind. *Early Childhood Connections: The Journal of Music and Movement-Based Learning.* Cited in *Early Childhood News.* Retrieved from http://earlychildhoodnews.com/wiredfor.htm

Cowan, P. A., & Cowan, C. P. (2003). Normative family transitions, normal family process, and healthy child development. In F. Walsh (Ed.), *Normal family processes: Growing diversity and complexity* (3rd ed., pp. 424–459). New York: Guilford Press.

Cowgill, D. O. (1986). *Aging around the world.* Belmont, CA: Wadsworth.

Coy, P. (2005, June). Old. Smart. Productive. *Business Week,* pp. 80–84.

Coyle, J. T. (2000). Psychotropic drug use in very young children. *JAMA, 283*(8), 1059.

Cozolino, L. (2006). *The neuroscience of human relationships: Attachment and the developing social brain.* New York: Norton.

Cozza, S. J., Chun, R. S., & Polo, J. A. (2005). Military families and children during Operation Iraqi Freedom. *Psychiatric Quarterly, 76*(4), 371–378.

Craddock, H. L., Yorke, V. C., & Chan, M. F. (2007). Cosmetic rehabilitation following successful treatment of aggressive periodontitis. *Dental Update, 34*(2), 91–96.

Crain, W. C. (1985). *Theories of development.* New York: Prentice Hall.

Cramer, K., & Rosenfield, S. (2008). Effect of degree of challenge on reading performance. *Reading & Writing Quarterly: Overcoming Learning Difficulties, 24*(1), 119–137. doi:10.1080/10573560701501586

Crandell, T. L. (1979). The effects of educational cognitive style and media format on reading procedural instructions in picture-text amalgams. *Dissertation Abstracts.* Ann Arbor, MI: University Microfilms International.

Crandell, T. L. (1982, June). Integration of illustrations and text in reading. In B. A. Hutson (Ed.), *Advances in reading language research* (Vol. 1). Greenwich, CT: JAI Press.

Crano, W. D. (1998). The leniency contract and persistence of majority and minority influence. *Journal of Personality and Social Psychology, 74,* 1437–1450.

Crary, D. (2004, June 4). *Spanking and aggression—Survey tracks parent, child conduct.* WTOC.com. Retrieved from http://www.nospank.net/n-m35r.htm

Cratty, B. J. (1970). *Perceptual and motor development in infants and children.* New York: Macmillan.

Crawford, J. (2007). *Issues in U.S. language policy: Language legislation in the U.S.A.* Retrieved from http://ourworld.compuserve.com/homepages/JWCRAWFORD/langleg.htm#State

Cray, L., Woods, N. F., & Mitchell, E. S. (2010). Symptom clusters during the late menopausal symptom stage: Observations from the Seattle Midlife Women's Health Study. *Menopause, 17*(5), 972–977. doi:10.1097/gme.0b013e3181dd1f95

Crespi, B., Summers, K., & Dorus, S. (2007). Adaptive evolution of genes underlying schizophrenia. *Proceedings of The Royal Society, 274*(1627), 2801–2810. doi:10.1098/rspb.2007.0876

Crews, F. C. (1998). *Unauthorized Freud: Doubters confront a legend.* New York: Viking.

Crider, K. S., Cleves, M., Berry, R. J., & Hobbs, C. (2009). Antibacterial medication use during pregnancy and risk of birth defects. *Archives of Pediatrics & Adolescent Medicine, 163*(11), 978–985. Retrieved from http://archpedi.ama-assn.org/cgi/reprint/163/11/978

Crimmins, E. M., & Seeman, T. E. (2004). Integrating biology into the study of health disparities. *Population and Development Review: Aging, Health, and Public Policy, 30*(Suppl.), 89–107.

Crimmins, E. M., Hayward, M. D., Hagedorn, A., Saito, Y., & Brouard, N. (2009). Change in disability-free life expectancy for Americans 70 years old and older. *Demography, 46*(3), 627–646.

Crnic, K., & Low, C. (2002). *Everyday stresses and parenting.* Mahwah, NJ: Erlbaum.

Crockenberg, S., & Litman, C. (1990). Autonomy as competence in 2-year-olds: Maternal correlates of child defiance, compliance, and self-assertion. *Developmental Psychology, 26,* 961–971.

Crocker, J., & Park, L. E. (2004). The costly pursuit of self-esteem. *Psychological Bulletin, 130*(3), 392–414.

Cronin, A., & Mandich, M. (2005). *Human development and performance: Throughout the lifespan.* Clifton Park, NY: Thomson Delmar Learning.

Crook, C. K., & Lipsitt, L. P. (1976). Neonatal nutritive sucking: Effects of taste stimulation upon sucking rhythm and heart rate. *Child Development, 47,* 518–522.

Crooks, R., & Baur, K. (2008). *Our sexuality* (10th ed.) Belmont, CA: Thomson Wadsworth.

Cross, S. E., & Gore, J. S. (2004). The relational self-construal and closeness. In D. J. Mashek & A. A. Mashek (Eds.), *Handbook of closeness and intimacy* (pp. 229–246). Mahwah, NJ: Erlbaum.

Crothers, L. M., Kehle, T. J., Bray, M. A., & Theodore, L. A. (2009). Correlates and suspected causes of obesity in children. *Psychology in the Schools, 46*(8), 787–796. doi:10.1002/pits.20417

Crump, W. J. (2001, July). The patient with no prenatal care: Managing an infant whose mother used cocaine. *Family Practice Recertification, 23*(9), 48–50, 53–54.

Csikszentmihalyi, M. (1997). *Creativity: Flow and the psychology of discovery and invention.* New York: HarperPerennial.

Cummings, E. M., Goeke-Morey, M. C., & Raymond, J. (2004). Fathers in family context: Effects of marital quality and marital conflict. In M. E. Lamb (Ed.), *The role of the father in child development* (4th ed., pp. 196–221). New York: Wiley.

Cunningham, M. (2007). Influences of women's employment on the gendered division of household labor over the life course: Evidence from a 31-year panel study. *Journal of Family Issues, 28*(3), 422–444.

Cunningham, M. (2008). Changing attitudes toward the male breadwinner, female homemaker family model: Influences of women's employment and education over the life-course. *Social Forces, 87*(1), 299–323. doi:10.1353/sof.0.0097

Curhan, S. G., Eavey, R., Shargorodsky, J., & Curhan, G. C. (2010). Analgesic use and the risk of hearing loss in men. *The American Journal of Medicine, 123*(3), 231–237. doi:10.1016/j.amjmed.2009.08.006

Custers, C., & Van den Bulck, J. (2009). Viewership of pro-anorexia websites in seventh, ninth, and eleventh graders. *European Eating Disorders Review, 17*(3), 214–219. doi:10.1002/erv.910

Czaja, S. J. (2001). Technological change and the older worker. In J. E. Birren & K. W. Schaie (Eds.), *Handbook of the psychology of aging* (5th ed., pp. 547–568). New York: Academic Press.

D'Augelli, A. R., Grossman, A. H., Salter, N. P., Vasey, J. J., Starks, M. T., & Sinclair, K. O. (2005). Predicting the suicide attempts of lesbian, gay, and bisexual youth. *Suicide and Life-Threatening Behavior, 35*, 646–660.

Dahlstrom, L. (2008, March 24). *When a baby is destined to die. Perinatal hospices support families with a terminal prenatal diagnosis.* Retrieved from http://www.msnbc.msn.com/id/23682263/

Dailard, C. (2003). Understanding "abstinence": Implications for individuals, programs and policies. *The Guttmacher Report on Public Policy,* December. Retrieved from http:// www.guttmacher.org/pubs/tgr/06/5/gr060504.html

Daly, B. P., Creed, T., Xanthopoulos, M., & Brown, R. T. (2007). Psychosocial treatments for children with attention deficit/hyperactivity disorder. *Neuropsychology Review, 17*, 73–89.

Daly, J. M., & Jogerst, G. J. (2007). Nursing home abuse report and investigation legislation, *Journal of Elder Abuse & Neglect, 19*(3/4), 119–131.

D'Amato, R., & Snyder, J. (2000). *Macular degeneration: The latest scientific discoveries and treatments for preserving your sight.* Birmingham, AL: Walker Publishing.

Damon, W. (2008). *The path to purpose: How young people find their calling in life.* New York: The Free Press.

Damon, W., & Hart, D. (1982). The development of self-understanding from infancy through adolescence. *Child Development, 53*, 841–864.

Damon, W., & Lerner, R. M. (Eds.). (2006). *Handbook of child psychology.* New York: Wiley.

Dandeneau, S. D., Baldwin, M. W., Baccus, J. R., Sakellaropoulo, M., & Pruessner, J. C. (2007). Cutting stress off at the pass: Reducing vigilance and responsiveness to social threat by manipulating attention. *Journal of Personality and Social Psychology, 93*(4), 651–666.

Danaei, G., Rimm, E. B., Oza, S., Kulkarni, S. C., Murray, C., & Ezzati, M. (2010). The promise of prevention: The effects of four preventable risk factors on national life expectancy. *Journal of Preventable Medicine, 7*(3), 1–13.

Daniel, M. (1997). Intelligence testing: Status and trends. *Journal of the American Psychological Association, 52*, 1038–1045.

Daniels, D. (1986). Differential experiences of siblings in the same family as predictors of adolescent sibling personality differences. *Journal of Personality and Social Psychology, 51*, 339–346.

Daniels, H., Wertsch, J., & Cole, M. (Eds.). (2007). *The Cambridge companion to Vygotsky.* New York: Cambridge University Press.

David, M., & Daum, R. (2010). Community-associated methicillin-resistant *Staphylococcus aureus:* Epidemiology and clinical consequences of an emerging epidemic. *Clinical Microbiology Reviews, 23*(3), 616–687. Retrieved from EBSCO*host.*

Davidson, M., & Lickona, T. (2007). Smart & good. *Independent School, 66*(2), 24–30.

Davidson, P., Digiacomo, M., Zecchin, R., Clarke, M., Paul, G., Lamb, K., . . ., Daly, J. (2008). A cardiac rehabilitation program to improve psychosocial outcomes of women with heart disease. *Journal of Women's Health, 17*(1), 123–134.

Davies, R. D. (2009). Adolescent substance abuse: Psychiatric comorbidity and high-risk behaviors. *The American Journal of Psychiatry, 166*, 117. doi: 10.1176/appi.ajp.2008.08071017

Davis, M. M., Gance-Cleveland, B., Hassink, S., Johnson, R. L., Paradis, G., & Resnicow, K. (2007). Recommendations for prevention of childhood obesity, *Pediatrics, 120*(4), S229–S253.

Davitt, J. K. (2009). Policy changes in Medicare home health care: Challenges to providing family-centered, community-based care for older adults. *Journal of Family Social Work, 12*(4), 291–308. doi:10.1080/10522150903321264

Dawe, H. C. (1934). An analysis of two hundred quarrels of preschool children. *Child Development, 5*, 139–157.

Dawson, G., Ashman, S. B., & Carver, L. J. (2000, Autumn). The role of early experience in shaping behavioral and brain development and its implications for social policy. *Development and Psychopathology, 12*(4), 695–712.

DeAngelis, T. (2001). Welfare reform and women, five years later. *Monitor on Psychology, 32*(9), 70–81.

de Bruyn, E. H., & Cillessen, A. H. N. (2008). Leisure activity preferences and perceived popularity in early adolescence. *Journal of Leisure Studies, 40*(3), 442–457. Retrieved from EBSCO*host.*

DeCasper, A. J., Lecanuet, J. P., Busnel, M. C., Granier-Deferre, C., & Maugeais, R. (1994). Fetal reactions to recurrent maternal speech. *Infant Behavior and Development, 17*, 159–164.

Deen, D. (2004, June 15). Metabolic syndrome: Time for action. *American Academy of Family Physicians, 69*(12), 2875–2882.

DeFrances, C. J., & Hall, M. J. (2007, July 12). 2005 National Hospital Discharge Survey. *Advance Data from Vital and Health Statistics, 385*, 1–20.

DeFries, J. C. (1999). *Colorado twin study and reading disability.* Institute for Behavioral Genetics, Boulder, Colorado. Retrieved from http://ibgwww.colorado.edu/learning.html

DeHart, T., Pelham, B. W., & Tennen, H. (2006). What lies beneath: Parenting style and implicit self-esteem. *Journal of Experimental Social Psychology, 42*, 1–17. doi:10.1016/j.jesp.2004.12.005

de Jong, E. J. (2008). Contextualizing policy appropriation: Teachers' perspectives, local responses, and English-only ballot initiatives. *Urban Review, 40*(4), 350–370. doi:10.1007/s11256-008-0085-y

DeKlyen, M., Brooks-Gunn, J., McLanahan, S., & Knab, J. (2006). The mental health of married, cohabiting, and non-coresident parents with infants. *American Journal of Public Health, 96*(10), 1836–1841.

DeLaguna, G. (1929). Perception and language. *Human Biology, 1*, 555–558.

deLemos, M. M. (1969). The development of conservation in Aboriginal children. *International Journal of Psychology, 4*, 255–269.

Deliens, L., & van der Wal, G. (2003). The euthanasia law in Belgium and the Netherlands. *The Lancet, 362*(9391), 1239–1240. doi:10.1016/S0140-6736(03)14520-5

della Cava, M. R. (2009, March 27). Boomers make social networks a place of their own. *USA Today,* p. 01A.

DeLongis, A., & Preece, M. (2002). Emotional and relational consequences of coping in stepfamilies. *Marriage and Family Review, 34*(1), 115–138. doi:10.1300/J002v34n01_06

Delpeuch, F., Maire, B., Monnier, E., & Holdsworth, M. (2009). *Globesity: A planet out of control?* London: Earthscan.

Dement, W. C. (2000). *The promise of sleep: A pioneer in sleep medicine explores the vital connection between health, happiness, and a good night's sleep.* New York: Random House.

Demetriou, A. (Ed.). (1988). *The NeoPiagetian theories of cognitive development: Toward an integration.* Amsterdam: North-Holland.

Demetriou, A., Efklides, A., & Platsidou, M. (1993). The architecture and dynamics of developing mind: Experiential structuralism as a frame for unifying cognitive developmental theories. *Monographs of the Society for Research in Child Development, 58*(5–6, Serial No. 234).

Demiris, G., Hensel, B. K., Skubic, M., & Rantz, M. (2008). Senior residents' perceived need of and preferences for *"smart home"* sensor technologies. *International Journal of Technology Assessment in Health Care, 24*(1), 120–124.

Demo, D., & Cox, M. (2000). Families with young children: A review of research in the 1990s. *Journal of Marriage and Family, 62,* 876–895.

Denham, S. A. (2006). The emotional basis of learning and development in early childhood education. In B. Spodek & O. N. Saracho (Eds.), *Handbook of research on the education of young children* (2nd ed., pp. 85–104). Mahwah, NJ: Erlbaum.

Denizet-Lewis, B. (2004, May 30). Friends, friends with benefits and the benefits of the local mall. *New York Times Magazine,* p. 30. InfoTrac Newsstand.

Denmark, F. L. (2004, Spring). Psychologists working with depression across the life cycle. *International Psychology Reporter, 8,* 14.

Denmark, F., Rabinowitz, V. C., & Sechzer, J. A. (2005). *Engendering psychology: Women and gender revisited.* Boston: Pearson Education.

Denney, N. (1985). A review of lifespan research with the twenty questions task (TQT). *International Journal of Aging and Human Development, 21,* 161–173.

Denny, C. H., Tsai, J., Floyd, R. L., & Green, P. P. (2009). Alcohol use among pregnant and nonpregnant women of childbearing age: United States, 1991–2005. *MMWR Weekly, 58*(19), 529–532.

DeNoon, D. J. (2004, July 13). HIV's bisexual bridge to women: Risk posed by "down low" men still unknown. *WebMD Medical News,* Retrieved from http://www.webmd.com/sexual-conditions/guide/20061101/hiv-bisexual-bridge-to-women

D'Entremont, B., & Seamans, E. (2007, May/June). Do infants need social cognition to act socially? An alternative look at infant pointing. *Child Development, 78*(3), 723–728.

Department of Defense. (2011, February 20). Operation Iraqi Freedom U.S. casualty status as of February 18, 2011. Retrieved from http://www.defense.gov/news/casualty.pdf

DePaulo, B. M. (2006). Singled out: How singles are stereotyped, stigmatized, and ignored and still live happily ever after.

Current Directions in Psychological Science, 15(5), 251–254.

De Rosa, C. J., Ethier, K. A., Kim, D. H., Cumberland, W. G., Afifi, A. A., Kotleman, J., . . . , Kerndt, P. R. (2010). Sexual intercourse and oral sex among public middle school students: Prevalence and correlates. *Perspectives on Sexual and Reproductive Health, 42* (3), 197–205.

Despete, A. (2001). Metacognition and mathematical problem solving in grade 3. *Journal of Learning Disabilities, 34*(5), 435–449.

Determinants of health in children. (1996). National Crime Prevention Council of Canada. Retrieved from http://www.crimeprevention.org/ncpc

DeVito, J. A. (1970). *The psychology of speech and language.* New York: Random House.

De Vries, B., & Walker, L. J. (1981). Moral reasoning and attitudes toward capital mental sequelae of maltreatment in infancy. In R. Rizley & D. Cicchetti (Eds.), *Developmental perspectives on child maltreatment.* San Francisco: Jossey-Bass.

DeWeerdt, S. E. (2001). *What's a genome?* Retrieved from http://www.celera.com/genomics/news/whats_a_ genome/Chp1_1_1.cfm

DeWitt, P. M. (1993). The birth business. *American Demographics, 15,* 44–49.

Dick-Read, G. (1944/1994). *Childbirth without fear.* New York: Harper.

Diehl, M., & Hay, E. L. (2010). Risk and resilience factors in coping with daily stress in adulthood: The role of age, self-concept incoherence, and personal control. *Developmental Psychology, 46*(5), 1132–1146. doi:10.1037/a0019937

Dietary Guidelines Advisory Committee. (2005, January). *Dietary guidelines for Americans, 2005.* U.S. Department of Health and Human Services and U.S. Department of Agriculture. Retrieved from http://www.health.gov/dietaryguidelines/

Dill, P. L., & Henley, T. B. (1998). Stressors of college: A comparison of traditional and nontraditional students. *Journal of Psychology, 132,* 25–32.

Diller, L. H. (2002). Lessons from three-year-olds. *Journal of Developmental and Behavioral Pediatrics, 23,* S10–S12. Retrieved from http:// www.jrnldbp.com

Dilmaç, B. (2009, Summer). Psychological needs as a predictor of cyber bullying: A preliminary report on college students. *Educational Sciences: Theory & Practice, 9*(3), 1307–1325. Retrieved from http://eric.ed.gov/PDFS/EJ858926.pdf

Dilmaç, B., & Aydoğan, D. (2010). Values as a predictor of cyber-bullying among secondary school students. *International Journal of Social Sciences, 5*(3), 185–188. Retrieved from http://www.waset.org/journals/ijhss/v5/v5-3-27.pdf

DiMarco, M. A., Menke, E. M., & McNamara, T. (May–June 2001). Evaluating a support

group for perinatal loss. *American Journal of Maternal/Child Nursing, 26*(3), 135–140.

Dittmann-Kohli, F. (2005). Middle age and identity in a cultural and lifespan perspective. In S. L. Willis & M. Martin (Eds.), *Middle adulthood: A lifespan perspective* (pp. 319–354). Thousand Oaks, CA: Sage.

DiVall, S. A., & Radovick, S. (2008). Pubertal development and menarche. *Annals of the New York Academy of Sciences, 1135,* 19–28. doi:10.1196/annals.1429.026

Division of Cancer Prevention and Control. (2006/2007). *The burden of cancer.* Atlanta, GA: Centers for Disease Control and Prevention. Retrieved from http://www.cdc.gov/cancer/ 00_pdf/0607_dcpc_fs.pdf

Dix, T., Ruble, D. N., & Zambarano, R. J. (1989). Mothers' implicit theories of discipline: Child effects, parent effects, and the attribution process. *Child Development, 60,* 1373–1391.

Division of STD Prevention. (2009, November). Sexually transmitted disease surveillance, 2008. Atlanta, GA: U.S. Department of Health and Human Services. Retrieved from http://www.cdc.gov/std/stats08/surv2008-Intro.pdf

Dobson, V., Candy, T. R., Hartmann, E. E., Mayer, D. L., Miller, J. M., & Quinn, G. E. (2009). Infant and child vision research: Present status and future directions. *Optometry and Vision Science, 86*(6), 559–560.

Dodge, K. A., & Putallaz, M. (2007). Series editors' notes. In Lansford, E. L., Deater-Deckard, K., & Bornstein, M. H. (Eds.), *Immigrant families in contemporary society* (pp. xi–xii), New York: Guilford Press.

Dodge, K. A., Coie, J. D., & Lynam, D. (2006). Aggression and antisocial behavior in youth. In W. Damon & R. M. Lerner (Eds.), *Handbook of child psychology* (6th ed., Vol. 4, pp. 719–788). New York: Wiley.

Doheny, K. (2007, August 20). Coping with stress helps cholesterol: Good coping skills may raise "good" cholesterol levels. *WebMD Health News* [News Release]. Retrieved from http://www.ghi.com/Article.aspx?page=091e9c5e800fc7c9

Donate-Bartfield, E., & Passman, R. H. (1985). Attentiveness of mothers and fathers to their baby's cries. *Infant Behavior and Development, 8,* 385–393.

Donnelly, D., & Finkelhor, D. (1992). Does equality in custody arrangement improve the parent-child relationship? *Journal of Marriage and the Family, 54,* 837–845.

Donald, P., & Montgomery, P. R. (2009). Marital status, partner satisfaction, and depressive symptoms in older men and women. *The Canadian Journal of Psychiatry, 54*(7), 487–492.

Donze, P. L. (2006, August). *Labor force status, work and family attitude change, and the time bind; General Social Survey 1994–2002.* Paper presented at the annual meeting of the American Sociological Association, Montreal Convention Center, Montreal, Quebec. Retrieved from http://www .allacademic.com/meta/ p104862_index .html

Dopheide, J. A., & Pliszka, S. R. (2009). Attention-deficit-hyperactivity disorder: An update. *Pharmacotherapy, 29*(6), 656–679.

Dorgo, S., Robinson, K. M., & Bader, J. (2009). The effectiveness of a peer-mentored older fitness program on perceived physical, mental, and social function. *Journal of the American Academy of Nursing Practitioners, 21*(2), 116–122. doi:10.1111/j.1745-7599 .2008.00393.x

Dorn, L. D., Dahl, R. E., Woodward, H. R., & Biro, F. (2006). Defining the boundaries of early adolescence: A user's guide to assessing pubertal status and pubertal timing in research with adolescents. *Applied Developmental Science, 10*(1), 30–56.

Doubeni, C. A., Laiyemo, A. O., Klabunde, C. N., Young, A. C., Field, T. S., & Fletcher, R. H. (2010). Racial and ethnic trends of colorectal cancer screening among medicare enrollees. *American Journal of Preventive Medicine, 38*(2), 184–191. doi:10.1016/j.amepre.2009.10.037

Douglas, J. (1990–1991). Patterns of change following parent death in midlife adults. *Omega: Journal of Death and Dying, 22,* 123–138.

Douglass, R. L., McGadney-Douglass, B. F., Antwi, P., & Apt, N. A. (2007). Filial factors of kwashiorkor survival in urban Ghana: Rediscovering the roles of the extended family. *African Journal of Food Agriculture, Nutrition, and Development, 7*(1). Retrieved from http://www.ajfand .net/Issue-XII-files/PDFs/DOUGLAS _1885.pdf

Dowda, M., Pate, R. R., Gelton, G. M., Saunders, R., Ward, D. S., Dishman, R. K., . . . , Trost, S. G. (2004, December). Physical activities and sedentary pursuits in African American and Caucasian girls. *Research Quarterly for Exercise and Sport, 75*(4), 352–360.

Dowker, A. (2006). What can functional brain imaging studies tell us about typical and atypical development in children? *Journal of Physiology, 99,* 333–341. doi:10.1016/ j.jphysparis.2006.03.010

Downie, M., Mageau, G. A., Koestner, R., & Liodden, T. (2006). On the risk of being a cultural chameleon: Variations in collective self-esteem across social interactions. *Cultural Diversity and Ethnic Minority Psychology, 12*(3), 527–540.

Doyle, M. E., & Smith, M. K. (2002). Friendship: Theory and experience. *The Encyclopaedia of Informal Education.* Last update: September 3, 2009.

Dracic, S. (2009). Bullying and peer victimization. *Materia Socio Medica, 21*(4), 216–219.

Draper, B., Pfaff, J. J., Pirkis, J., Snowdon, J., Lautenschlager, N. T., Wilson, I., & Almeida, O. P. (2008). Long-term effects of childhood abuse on the quality of life and health of older people: Results from the Depression and Early Prevention of Suicide in General Practice Project. *Journal of the American Geriatrics Society, 56*(2), 262–271. doi:10.1111/j.1532 -5415.2007.01537.x

Driver, J. L, & Gottman, J. M. (2004). Daily marital interactions and positive affect during marital conflict among newlywed couples. *Family Process, 43*(3), 301–314.

Dube, S. R., Felitti, V. J., Dong, M., Chapman, D. P., Giles, W. H., & Anda, R. F. (2003). Childhood abuse, neglect, and household dysfunction and the risk of illicit drug use: The adverse childhood experiences study. *Pediatrics, 111*(3), 564–572.

Dubow, E. F., Huesmann, L. R., & Greenwood, D. (2007). Media and youth socialization. In J. E. Grusec & P. D. Hastings (Eds.), *Handbook of socialization: Theory and research* (pp. 404–430). New York: Guilford Press.

Duenwald, M. (2003, January). Puzzle of the century. *Smithsonian, 3.* Retrieved from http://www.smithsonian-mag.com/smithso nian/issues03/jan03/ centenarians.html

Duffy, A. L., & Nesdale, D. (2008). Peer groups, social identity, and children's bullying behavior. *Social Development, 17*(4), 131–139. doi:10.1111/j.1467-9507 .2008.00484.x

Duhaime, A. C., Christian, C. W., Rorke, L. B., & Zimmerman, R. A. (1998). Nonaccidental head injury in infants—The "shaken-baby syndrome." *New England Journal of Medicine, 338,* 1822–1829.

Duhigg, C. (2008, March 2). Tapping into homes can be pitfall for the elderly. *New York Times,* p. A1(L).

DuMont, K. A., Widom, C. S., & Czaja, S. J. (2007). Predictors of resilience in abused and neglected children grown-up: The role of individual and neighborhood characteristics. *Child Abuse and Neglect, 31*(3), 205–209. doi:10.1016/j.chiabu.2005.11.015

Dundek, L. H. (2006). Establishment of a Somali doula program at a large metropolitan hospital. *Journal of Perinatal & Neonatal Nursing, 20*(2), 128–137.

Dunlop, J. (2007, July 20). A good death. *Ethics and Medicine: An International Journal of Bioethics, 23*(2), 69–75. Center for Bioethics and Human Dignity. Retrieved from http://www.cbhd.org/resources/endoflife/ dunlop_2007-07-20_print.htm

Dunn, J. (1986). Growing up in a family world: Issues in the study of social development of young children. In M. Richards & P. Light (Eds.), *Children of social worlds: Development in a social context.* Cambridge, MA: Harvard University Press.

Dunn, J. (2007). Siblings and socialization. In J. E. Grusec & P. D. Hastings (Eds.), *Handbook of socialization: Theory and research* (pp. 309–327). New York: Guilford Press.

Dunn, J., Slomkowski, C., & Beardsall, L. (1994). Sibling relationships from the preschool period through middle childhood and early adolescence. *Developmental Psychology, 30,* 315–324.

Dunn, R., Beaudry, J. S., & Klavas, A. (1989). Survey of research on learning styles. *Educational Leadership, 46,* 50–58.

Dunne, E. F., Unger, E. R., Sternberg, M., McQuillan, G., Swan, D. C., Patel, S. S., & Markowitz, L. E. (2007). Prevalence of HPV infection among females in the United States. *JAMA, 297*(8), 813–819. doi:10.1001/ jama.297.8.813

Dunning, D., Heath, C., & Suls, J. (2004). Flawed self-assessment. *Psychological Science in the Public Interest, 5*(3), 69–106.

Durkheim, E. (1964). *The division of labor in society.* New York: Free Press. (Original work published 1893.)

Durston, S., Davidson, M. C., Tottenham, N., Galvan, A., Spicer, J., Fossella, J. A., . . . , Casey, B. J. (2006). A shift from diffuse to focal cortical activity with development. *Developmental Neuroscience, 9*(1), 1–20.

Durston, S., & Casey, B. J. (2006). What have we learned about cognitive development from neuroimaging? *Neuropsychologia, 44,* 2149–2157.

Dworkin, R. W. (2007, December 17). The next sexual revolution. *Wall Street Journal,* p. A21.

Dye, B. A., Tan, S., Smith, V., Lewis, B. G., Barker, L. K., Thornton-Evans, G., . . . , Chien-Hsun, L. (2007). Trends in oral health status: United States, 1988–1994 and 1999–2004. National Center for Health Statistics, *Vital Health Statistics, 11*(28), 1–104.

Dyer, C. B., Pickens, S., & Burnett, J. (2007). Vulnerable elders: When it is no longer safe to live alone. *JAMA, 298,* 1448–1450.

Dyer, S., Lombard, C., & Spuy, Z. (2009). Psychological stress among men suffering from couple infertility in South Africa: A quantitative assessment. *Human Reproduction, 24*(11), 2821–2826. doi:10.1093/ humrep/dep278

Dykstra, P. A., & Hagestad, G. O. (2007). Childlessness and parenthood in two centuries. *Journal of Family Issues, 28*(11), 1518–1532.

Earle, A., & Heymann, J. (2004). Work, family, and social class. In O. G. Brim, C. D. Ryff, & R. C. Kessler (Eds.), *How healthy are we? A national study of well-being at midlife* (pp. 485–513). Chicago, IL: University of Chicago Press.

Early Childhood Learning and Knowledge Center. (2010) *Head Start Program fact sheet fiscal year 2010.* Retrieved from http://eclkc. ohs.acf.hhs.gov/hslc/Head%20Start%20 Program/Head%20Start%20Program%20 Factsheets/fHeadStartProgr.htm

East, L., Jackson, D., & O'Brien, L. (2006). Father absence and adolescent development: A review of the literature. *Journal of Child Health Care, 10*(4), 283–295.

Eaton, D. K., Kann, L., Kinchen, S., Ross, J., Hawkins, J., Harris, W. A., . . . Wechsler, H. (2006, June 9). Youth Risk Behavior Surveillance—United States, 2005. *MMWR Weekly, 55*(SS05), 1–108.

Eaton, D. K., Kann, L., Kinchen, S., Shanklin, S., Ross, J., Hawkins, J., . . ., Wechsler, H. (2010, June 4). Youth risk behavior surveillance—United States, 2009. *MMWR Weekly, 59*(SS-5), 1–142. Retrieved from http://www.cdc.gov/mmwr/preview/mmwrhtml/ss5905a1.htm

Eaton, W. W., Addington, A. M., Bass, J., Forman, V., Gilbert, S., Hayden, K., & Mielke, M. (2004, June). *Risk factors for major mental disorders: A review of the epidemiologic literature.* Departments of Society, Human Development, and Health and Epidemiology. Cambridge, MA: Harvard School of Public Health.

Eberwine, D. (2002). Globesity: The crisis of growing proportions. *Perspectives in Health Magazine, 7*(3). Retrieved from http://www.paho.org/English/DPI/Number15_article2_5.htm <http://www.paho.org/English/DPI/Number15_article2_5.htm>

Ebner, N. C., Freund, A. M., & Baltes, P. B. (2006). Developmental changes in personal goal orientation from young to late adulthood: From striving for gains to maintenance and prevention of losses. *Psychology and Aging, 21*(4), 664–678.

Eccles, J. S. (2007). Where are all the women? Gender differences in participation in physical science and engineering. In S. J. Ceci & W. M. Williams (Eds.), *Why aren't more women in science?* (pp. 199–210). Washington, DC: American Psychological Association.

Eccles, J. S., & Wigfield, A. (2002, February). Motivational beliefs, values, and goals. *Annual Review of Psychology, 53*, 109–132.

Eccles, J. S., Roeser, R., Vida, M., Fredricks, J., & Wigfield, A. (2006). Motivational and achievement pathways through middle childhood. In L. Balter & C. S. Tamis-LeMonda, *Child psychology: A handbook of contemporary issues* (2nd ed., pp. 325–356). New York: Psychology Press.

Eckerman, C. O., & Didow, S. M. (1988). Lessons drawn from observing young peers together. *Acta Paediatrica Scandinavica, 77*, 55–70.

Eckholm, E. (2009, April 12). States slashing social programs for vulnerable. *New York Times*, p.1

Edelstein, B. L., & Chinn, C. H. (2009). Update on disparities in oral health and access to dental care for America's children. *Academic Pediatrics, 9*(6), 415–419. doi:10.1016/j.acap.2009.09.010

Eder, D., & Hallinan, M. T. (1978). Sex differences in children's friendships. *American Sociological Review, 43*, 237–250.

Edmonds, M. H. (1976). New directions in theories of language acquisition. *Harvard Educational Review, 46*, 175–198.

Egan, J. (2006, April 2). Wanted: A few good sperm. *New York Times Magazine*, p. 46L.

Egeland, B. (2007). Understanding developmental processes of resilience and psychology: Implications for policy and practice. In A. S. Masten (Ed.), *Multilevel dynamics in developmental psychopathology: Pathways to the future* (Vol. 34, pp. 83–117). Mahwah, NJ: Erlbaum.

Eimas, P. D. (1985, January). The perception of speech in early infancy. *Scientific American, 252*, 46–52.

Einstein, A. (1949). Autobiography. In P. Schilpp (Ed.), *Albert Einstein: Philosopher-scientist.* Evanston, IL: Library of Living Philosophers.

Eisen, A. R. (Ed.) (2007). *Treating childhood behavioral and emotional problems: A step-by-step evidence-based approach.* New York: Guilford Press.

Eisenberg, N. (Ed.). (2006). *Handbook of child psychology* (6th ed., Vol. 3). New York: Wiley.

Eisenberg, N. (2007). Empathy-related responding and prosocial behaviour. *Novartis Foundation Symposium. 278*, 71–80.

Eisenberg, N., Fabes, R. A., & Spinrad, T. L. (2006). Prosocial development. In W. Damon & R. J. Lerner (Eds.), *Handbook of child psychology* (6th ed., Vol. 3, pp. 646–718). New York: Wiley.

Eisenberg, N., Gershoff, E. T., Fabes, R. A., Shepard, S. A., Cumberland, A. J., Losoya, S. H., . . ., Murphy, B. C. (2001). Mothers' emotional expressivity and children's behavior problems and social competence medication through children's regulation. *Developmental Psychology, 37*, 475–490.

Eisenberg, N., Zhou, Q., Spinrad, T. L., Valiente, C., Fabes, R. A., & Liew, J. (2005). Relations among positive parenting, children's effortful control, and externalizing problems: A three-wave longitudinal study. *Child Development, 76*(5), 1055–1071.

Ekman, P. (1980). *The face of man: Expressions of universal emotions in a New Guinea village.* New York: Garland STPM Press.

Ekman, P. (1994). Strong evidence for universals in facial expressions: A reply to Russell's mistaken critique. *Psychological Bulletin, 115*, 268–287.

Ekman, P. (2003). *Emotions revealed: Recognizing faces and feelings to improve communication and emotional life.* New York: Henry Holt.

Ekman, P., & Friesen, W. V. (2003). *Unmasking the face: A guide to recognizing emotions from facial expressions.* Los Altos, CA: Institute for the Study of Human Knowledge.

Elias, C. L., & Berk, L. E. (2002). Self-regulation in young children: Is there a role for sociodramatic play? *Early Childhood Research Quarterly, 17*(2), 216–238.

Elias, M. (1989, August 9). Inborn traits outweigh environment. *USA Today*, pp. 1D, 2D.

Elkind, D. (1970, April). Eric Erikson's eight stages of man. *New York Times Magazine*, p. 24.

Elkind, D. (1974). *A sympathetic understanding of the child from birth to sixteen.* Boston: Allyn & Bacon.

Elkind, D. (1987, May). Superkids and super problems. *Psychology Today, 21*, 60–61.

Elkind, D. (1998). *All grown up and no place to go: Teenagers in crisis.* Cambridge, MA: Da Capo Press.

Elkind, D. (2001). *The hurried child: Growing up too fast too soon* (3rd ed.) Cambridge, MA: Perseus.

Elkins, D. (2009). Whatever happened to Carl Rogers? An examination of the politics of clinical psychology. Humanistic Psychology: A clinical manifesto. In L. Hoffman (Ed.) *Humanistic Psychology: A clinical manifesto. A critique of clinical psychology and the need for progressive alternatives.* (pp. 7–20). Colorado Springs, CO: University of the Rockies Press.

Elliot, A. J., & Dweck, C. S. (Eds.). (2005). *Handbook of competence and motivation.* New York: Guilford Press.

Elliott, D. B., & Lewis, J. M. (2010, April 17). Embracing the institution of marriage: The characteristics of remarried Americans. Paper presented at Population Association of America (PAA) Annual Meeting, Dallas, Texas. Retrieved from U.S. Census Bureau.

Ellis, A. A., Nixon, R. D. V., & Williamson, P. (2009). The effects of social support and negative appraisals on acute stress symptoms and depression in children and adolescents. *British Journal of Clinical Psychology, 48*, 347–361. doi:10.1348/014466508X401894

Ellis, B. J., Figueredo, A. J., Brumbach, B. H., & Schlomer, G. L. (2009). Fundamental dimensions of environmental risk: The impact of harsh versus unpredictable environments on the evolution and development of life history strategies. *Human Nature, 20*(2), 204–268. doi:10.1007/s12110-009-9063-7

Ellis, W. L. (2008). Well-being of marital groups in later life: Are divorced elders disadvantaged? *Marriage and Family Review, 44*(1), 125–139. (http://www.census.gov/population/www/socdemo/marr-div/Remarriage.pdf)

El Nasser, H., & Overberg, P. (2011, March 25). Ethnicity shifts in youngest classes: Kindergarten, more Hispanics, Asians. *USA Today.* p. 1A.

Else-Quest, N. M., Hyde, J. S., Goldsmith, H. H., & Van Hulle, C. A. (2006). Gender differences in temperament: A meta-analysis. *Psychological Bulletin, 132*(1), 33–72. doi:10.1037/0033-2909.132.1.33

Emanuel, L. (1998). Facing requests for physician-assisted suicide: Toward a practical and principled clinical skill set. *Journal of the American Medical Association, 280,* 643–647.

Emery, D. W., & Vandenberg, B. (2010). Special education teacher burnout and act. *International Journal of Special Education, 25*(3), 119–131.

Emig, C., Moore, A., & Scarupa, H. J. (2001, October). *School readiness: Helping communities get children ready for school and schools ready for children.* Child Trends research brief. Washington, DC: ChildTrends.Org

Engen, T. (1991). *Odor sensation and memory.* New York: Praeger.

Engen, T., Lipsitt, L. P., & Kaye, H. (1963). Olfactory responses and adaptation in the human neonate. *Journal of Physiology and Psychology, 56,* 73–77.

Engen, T., Lipsitt, L. P., & Peck, M. B. (1974). Ability of newborn infants to discriminate sapid substances. *Developmental Psychology, 10,* 741–744.

Engle, P. L., & Black, M. M. (2008). The effect of poverty on child development and educational outcomes. *Annals of the New York Academy of Sciences, 1136,* 243–256. doi:10.1196/annals.1425.023

English heritage. (2005). *Stonehenge.* Retrieved from http://www.english-heritage.org.uk/server/show/ConProperty.313/chosenImageId/2

Epperson, C. N. (1999). Postpartum major depression: Detection and treatment. *American Family Physician, 59*(8), 2247–2262.

Erdley, C. A., & Dweck, C. S. (1993). Children's implicit personality theories as predictors of their social judgments. *Child Development, 64,* 863–878.

Ericsson, K. A. (2005). Recent advances in expertise research: A commentary on the contributions to the special issue. *Applied Cognitive Psychology, 19*(2), 233–241.

Erikson, E. H. (1959). Identity and the life cycle. *Monograph, Psychological Issues* (Vol. 1). New York: International Universities Press.

Erikson, E. H. (1963). *Childhood and society.* New York: Norton.

Erikson, E. H. (1964). Inner and outer space: Reflections on womanhood. *Daedalus, 93,* 582–606.

Erikson, E. H. (1968a). *Identity: Youth and crisis.* New York: Norton.

Erikson, E. H. (1968b). Life cycle. In D. L. Sills (Ed.), *International encyclopedia of the social sciences* (Vol. 9). New York: Free Press and Macmillan.

Erikson, E. H. (1977). *Toys and reasons: Stages in the ritualization of experience.* New York: Norton.

Erikson, E. H. (1982). *The life cycle completed: A review.* New York: Norton.

Erikson, E. H., & Erikson, J. M. (1997). *The life cycle completed* (Ext. Version). New York: Norton.

Erikson, E. H., Erikson, J. M., & Kivnick, H. Q. (1986). *Vital involvement in old age.* New York: Norton.

Erikson, K. (1986). On work and alienation. *American Sociological Review, 51,* 1–8.

Erlandsson, K., Dsilna, A., Fagerberg, I., & Christensson, K. (2007). Skin-to-skin care with the father after cesarean birth and its effect on newborn crying and prefeeding behavior. *Birth, 34*(1), 105–114.

Ertekin-Taner, N. (2010). Genetics of Alzheimer's disease in the pre- and post-GWAS era. *Alzheimer's Research & Therapy, 2*(3), 1–12. doi:10.1186/alzrt26

Ertelt, S. (2007). *California pro-life advocates protest lawmaker's assisted suicide bill.* Life-News.com. Retrieved from http://www.christianliferesources.com/

Escamilla, K., Shannon, S., Carlos, S., & Garcia, J. (2003). Breaking the code: Colorado's defeat of the anti-bilingual Education Initiative (Amendment 31). *Bilingual Research Journal, 27*(3), 357–372.

Eskin, M., Ertekin, K., & Demir, H. (2008) Efficacy of a problem-solving therapy for depression and suicide potential in adolescents and young adults. *Cognitive Therapy and Research, 32*(2), 227–245. doi:10.1007/s10608-007-9172-8

Euling, S. Y., Herman-Giddens, M. E., Lee, P. A., Selevan, S. G., Juul, A., Sorensen, T. I., . . ., Swan, S. H. (2008). Examination of U.S. puberty-timing data from 1940 to 1994 for secular trends: Panel findings. *Pediatrics, 121,* S172–S191. doi: 10.1542/peds.2007-1813D

European Commission. (2010). *Taxation: Country Chapters.* Retrieved from http://ec.europa.eu/taxation_customs/taxation/gen_info/economic_analysis/tax_structures/article_6047_en.htm

Eurostat Press Office. (2010). Young adults in the EU27 in 2008: One in three men and one in five women aged 25 to 34 live with their parents. [News Release]. Retrieved from http://epp.eurostat.ec.europa.eu/

Euthanasia Research & Guidance Organization. (2011). Frequently asked questions. Retrieved from http://www.finalexit.org/ergo_faq.html

Evans, J. L. (2007). The emergence of language: A dynamical systems account. In E. Hoff & M. Shatz (Eds.), *Blackwell handbook of language development* (pp. 129–147). Malden, MA: Blackwell.

Evans, J. R., Fletcher, A. E., & Wormald, R. P. (2005, May). 28,000 cases of age-related macular degeneration causing visual loss in people aged 75 years and above in the United Kingdom may be attributable to smoking. *British Journal of Ophthalmology, 89*(5), 550–553.

Evenson, R. J., & Simon, R. W. (2005). Clarifying the relationship between parenthood and depression. *Journal of Health and Science Behavior, 46*(4), 341–358.

Eyer, D. E. (1992, November 24). Infant bonding: A bogus notion. *Wall Street Journal,* A14.

FAAN. (2006). *Annual report 2006.* Fairfax, VA: FAAN.

FAAN. (2007). *Food allergy basics.* Retrieved from http://www.foodallergy.org/downloads/FABasics.pdf

Fabes, R. A., Gaertner, B. M., & Popp, T. K. (2006). Getting along with others: Social competence in early childhood. In K. McCartney & D. Phillips (Eds.), *Blackwell handbook of early childhood development* (pp. 297–316). Malden, MA.

Fabricius, W. V., & Wellman, H. M. (1983). Children's understanding of retrieval cue utilization. *Developmental Psychology, 19,* 15–21.

Fact sheet: The President's FY09 Budget. (2008, February 4). Retrieved from http://www.whitehouse.gov/news/releases/2008/02/print/20080204.html

Facts about the DASH eating plan. (2003). National Heart, Lung, and Blood Institute (NHLBI). NIH Publication No. 03-4082. U.S. Retrieved from http://www.nhlbi.nih.gov/health/public/heart/hbp/dash/new_dash.pdf

Fadiman, A. (1998). *The spirit catches you and you fall down.* New York: Farrar, Straus and Giroux.

Fadjukoff, P., Pulkkinen, L., & Kokko, K. (2005). Identity processes in adulthood: Diverging domains. *Identity, 5*(1), 1–20.

Fagan, J., Bernd, E., & Whiteman, V. (2007). Adolescent fathers' parenting stress, social support, and involvement with infants. *Journal of Research on Adolescence, 17*(1), 1–22. doi:10.1111/j.1532-7795.2007.00510.x

Fagot, B. I., & Kavanagh, K. (1993). Parenting during the second year: Effects of children's age, sex, and attachment classification. *Child Development, 64,* 258–271.

Fahrenthold, D. M. (2006, April 5). Massachusetts bill requires health coverage: State set to use auto insurance as a model. Retrieved from http://www.washingtonpost.com/wpdyn/content/article/2006/04/04/AR2006040401937.html

Fairtlough, A. (2008). Growing up with a lesbian or gay parent: Young people's perspectives. *Health and Social Care in the Community, 16*(5), 521–528. doi:10.1111/j.1365-2524.2008.00774.x

Families and Work Institute. (2004). *Generation & gender in the workplace.* New York: American Business Collaboration.

Farel, A. M. (2005). Children and youth with special health care needs. In J. B. Kotch, (Ed.), *Maternal and child health* (2nd ed., pp. 385–415). Sudbury, MA: Jones & Bartlett.

Farias, M. M., Cuevas, A. M., & Rodriguez, F. (2010, November 30). Set-point theory and obesity. *Metabolic Syndrome and Related Disorders.* Epub. doi:10.1089/met.2010.0090

Farner, S. M., & Brown, E. E. (2008). College students and the work world. *Journal of Employment Counseling, 45*(3), 106–114.

Farooqi, M. (2003, September 30). A scientific compromise: Ectogenesis may satisfy a long debate. *The Battalion*, Texas A&M. Retrieved from http://www.thebatt.com/

Farrar, M. J., & Goodman, G. S. (1992). Developmental changes in event memory. *Child Development, 63,* 173–187.

Farrar, M. J., Raney, G. E., & Boyer, M. E. (1992). Knowledge, concepts, and inferences in childhood. *Child Development, 63,* 673–691.

Farrell, M., Rich, S., Turner, L., Seith, D., & Bloom, D. (2008). Welfare time limits: An update on state policies, implementation, and effects on families. *MDRC*. Retrieved from http://eric.ed.gov/PDFS/ED502532.pdf

Fass, S. (2009, March). *Paid leave in the States: A critical support for low-wage workers and their families.* National Center for Children in Poverty. Retrieved from http://www.paidfamilyleave.org/pdf/PaidLeaveinStates.pdf

Fass, S., & Cauthen, N. K. (2007). *Who are America's poor children? The official story.* New York: National Center for Children in Poverty. Retrieved from http://www.nccp.org/publications/pub_787.html

Fassino, S., Daga, G., Piero, A., & Delsedime, N. (2007). Psychological factors affecting eating disorders: A new classification for DSM-V. *Advances in Psychosomatic Medicine, 28,* 141–168.

Fauble, M. A. (2009). How maternal childhood maltreatment negatively impacts children's mental health outcomes among polysubstance exposed children. *Dissertation Abstracts International Section A, 70* (4-A). Retrieved from EBSCO*host*.

Favazza, P. C. (1998). Preparing for children with disabilities in early childhood. *Early Childhood Education Journal, 25*(4), 255–258. doi: 10.1023/A:1025650922587

Favazza, P. C., & Odom, S. L. (1996). Use of acceptance scale to measure attitudes of kindergarten-age children. *Journal of Early Intervention, 20,* 232.

Federal Interagency Forum on Aging-Related Statistics. (2010). *Older Americans 2010: Key indicators of well-being.* Washington, DC: U.S. Government Printing Office. Retrieved from http://www.agingstats.gov/agingstatsdotnet/Main_Site/Data/2010_Documents/Docs/OA_2010.pdf

Federal Interagency Forum on Child and Family Statistics. (2007). *America's children in brief: Key national indicators of well-being, 2007.* Washington, DC: U.S. Government Printing Office.

Federal Interagency Forum on Child and Family Statistics. (2010). *America's children: Key national indicators of well-being, 2010.* Washington, DC: U.S. Government Printing Office.

Federal Interagency Forum on Child and Family Statistics. (2011). *America's children in brief: Key national indicators of well-being, 2010.* Forum on Child and Family Statistics. Retrieved from http://www.childstats.gov/pdf/ac2010/ac_10.pdf

Feist, G. J. (2006). How development and personality influence scientific thought, interest, and achievement. *Review of General Psychology, 10(2),* 163–182.

Feldhusen, J. F., Proctor, T. B., & Black, K. N. (1986). Guidelines for grade advancement of precocious children. *Roeper Review, 9,* 25–27.

Feng, J. (1994). *Asian-American children: What teachers should know.* Urbana, IL: ERIC Clearinghouse on Elementary and Early Childhood Education. Retrieved from http://www.ed.gov/databases/ERIC_Digests/ed369577.html

Fennell, C. T., Byers-Heinlein, K., & Werker, J. (2007, September–October) Using speech sounds to guide word learning: The case of bilingual infants. *Child Development, 78*(5), 1510–1525.

Fenson, L., Dale, P. S., Reznick, J. S., Bates, E., Thal, D. J., & Pethick, S. J. (1994). Variability in early communicative development. *Society for Research in Child Development Monograph, 59*(5), 1–173.

Ferber, S. G., & Makhoul, I. R. (2004). The effect of skin-to-skin contact (kangaroo care) shortly after birth on the neurobehavioral responses of the term newborn: A randomized, controlled trial. *Pediatrics, 113*(4), 858–865.

Ferenac, M., Polancec, D., Huzak, M., Pereira-Smith, O. M., & Rubelj, I. (2005, July). Early-senescing skin fibroblasts do not demonstrate accelerated telomere shortening. *Journals of Gerontology: Series A. Psychological Sciences and Social Sciences, 60*(7), 820–829.

Fergusson, D. M., Boden, J. M., & Horwood, L. J. (2006). Circumcision status and risk of sexually transmitted infection in young adult males: An analysis of a longitudinal birth cohort. *Pediatrics, 118*(5), 1971–1977.

Fernald, A. (1985). Four-month-old infants prefer to listen to motherese. *Infant Behavior and Development, 8,* 181–195.

Fernald, A. (1990). Intonation and communicative intent in mothers' speech to infants: Is the melody the message? *Child Development, 60,* 1497–1510.

Fernald, A., & Morikawa, H. (1993). Common themes and cultural variations in Japanese and American mothers' speech to infants. *Child Development, 64,* 637–656.

Ferrara, L., Gandhi, M., Litton, C., McClung, E. C., Moshier, E., Eddleman, K., & Stone, J. (2008). Chorionic villus sampling and the risk of adverse outcome in patients undergoing multifetal pregnancy reduction. *American Journal of Obstetrics and Gynecology, 199*(4), 1-4.

Ferraro, G. P. (2006). *Cultural anthropology: An applied perspective.* Belmont, CA: Thomson Wadsworth.

Ferrini, A. F., & Ferrini, R. L. (2008). *Health in the later years* (4th ed.). New York: McGraw-Hill.

Field, T. (1998). *Depressed mothers and their newborns.* Miami: University of Miami School of Medicine.

Field, T. (2006). *The amazing infant.* New York: Wiley.

Field, T., Diego, M., & Hernandez-Reif, M. (2007). Massage therapy research. *Developmental Review, 27,* 75–89.

Field, T., Diego, M., & Hernandez-Reif, M. (2010). Preterm infant massage therapy research: A review. *Infant Behavior & Development, 33*(2), 115–124. doi:10.1016/j.infbeh.2009.12.004

Fiese, B. H., & Spagnola, M. (2007). The interior life of the family: Looking from the inside out and the outside in. In A. S. Masten (Ed.), *Multilevel dynamics in developmental psychology* (Vol. 34, 285–299). Mahwah, NJ: Erlbaum.

File, T., & Crissey, S. (2010, May). Voting and registration in the election of November 2008: Population characteristics. (P20-562). U.S. Department of Commerce. Retrieved from http://www.census.gov/prod/2010pubs/p20-562.pdf

Finch, C. E., & Zelinski, E. M. (2005). Normal aging of brain structure and cognition: Evolutionary perspectives. *Research in Human Development, 2*(1 & 2), 69–82.

Fincham, F. C., Beach, S. R. H., & Davila, J. (2007). Longitudinal relations between forgiveness and conflict resolution in marriage. *Journal of Family Psychology, 21*(3), 542–545.

Fine, M. A., & Harvey, J. H. (2006). *Handbook of divorce and relationship dissolution.* New York: Routledge.

Fingerman, K. L., & Pitzer, L. (2007). Socialization in old age. In J. E. Grusec & P. D. Hastings (Eds.), *Handbook of socialization theory and research* (pp. 232–255). New York: Guilford Press.

Finkelhor, D., & Jones, L. M. (2004, January). *Explanations for the decline in child sexual abuse cases.* Juvenile Justice Bulletin. Washington, DC: Office of Juvenile Justice and Delinquency Prevention. Retrieved from http://www.ncjrs.org/pdffiles1/ojjdp/199298.pdf

Finkelhor, D., Ormond, R., Turner, H., & Hamby, S. L. (2005). The victimization of children and youth: A comprehensive national survey. *Child Maltreatment, 10*(1), 5–25.

Fisher, B. S., & Regan, S. L. (2006). The extent and frequency of abuse in the lives of older women and their relationship with health outcomes. *Gerontologist, 46*(2), 200–209.

Fisher, H. E. (2004). *Why we love: The nature and chemistry of romantic love.* New York: Macmillan.

Fisher, M. O., Nager, R. G., & Monaghan, P. (2006). Compensatory growth impairs adult cognitive performance [Electronic version]. *PLoS Biology, 4*(8), e251.

Fisher, S. E., & Marcus, G. (2006). The eloquent ape: Genes, brains and the evolution of language. *Nature Reviews Genetics, 7*(1), 9–20.

Fishman, B. (1983). The economic behavior of step-families. *Family Relations, 32,* 359–366.

Fitton, T., Farrell, C. J., & Millspaw, T. N. (2008, June 30). Examining the FDA's HPV vaccine records: Detailing the approval process, side-effects, safety concerns, and marketing practices of a large-scale public health experiment. Washington, DC: Judicial Watch, Inc. Retrieved from http://www .judicialwatch.org/documents/2008/ JWReportFDAhpvVaccineRecords.pdf

Fitzpatrick, K. M., Piko, D. R., Wright, B. F., & LaGory, M. (2005). Depressive symptomatology, exposure to violence, and the role of social capital among African American adolescents. *American Journal of Orthopsychiatry, 75*(2), 262–274.

Fitzpatrick, L. (2010, July 12). How we fail our female vets. *Time, 176*(2), 42–45.

Flavell, J., Freidrichs, A., & Hoyt, J. (1970). Developmental changes in memorization processes. *Cognitive Psychology, 1,* 324–340.

Flavell, J. H. (1992). Cognitive development: Past, present, and future. *Developmental Psychology, 28,* 998–1005.

Flavell, J. H., Green, F. L., & Flavell, E. R. (2000). Development of children's awareness of their own thoughts. *Journal of Cognition and Development, 1,* 97–112.

Flegal, K. M., Carroll, M. D., Ogden, C. L., & Curtin, L. R. (2010). Prevalence and trends in obesity among U.S. adults, 1999–2008. *JAMA, 303*(3), 235–241. doi:10.1001/ jama.2009.2014

Fletcher, J. K., Jordan, J. V., & Miller, J. B. (2000). Women and the workplace applications of a psychodynamic theory. *American Journal of Psychoanalysis, 60*(3), 243–261.

Florsheim, P., Sumida, E., McCann, C., Winstanley, M., Fukui, R., Seefeldt, T., & Moore, D. (2003). The transition to parenthood among young African American and Latino couples: Relational predictors of risk for parental dysfunction. *Journal of Family Psychology, 17*(1), 65–79.

Foderaro, L. W. (2010, September 30). Private moment made public, then a fatal jump. *New York Times.* p. 1. Retrieved from EBSCO*host*.

Fogel, A., & Thelen, E. (1987). Development of early expressive and communicative action: Reinterpreting the evidence from a dynamic systems perspective. *Developmental Psychology, 23,* 747–761.

Folkman, S., & Lazarus, R. S. (1985). If it changes it must be a process: Study of emotion and coping during three stages of a college examination. *Journal of Personality and Social Psychology, 48,* 150–170.

Folven, R. J., & Bonvillian, J. D. (1991). The transition from nonreferential to referential language in children acquiring American Sign Language. *Developmental Psychology, 27,* 806–816.

Foner, A., & Kertzer, D. (1978). Transitions over the life course: Lessons from age-set societies. *American Journal of Sociology, 83,* 1081–1104.

Forgas, J. P., Baumeister, R. H., & Tice, D. M. (Eds.). (2009). *Psychology of self-regulation: Cognitive, affective and motivational processes.* New York: Psychology Press.

Forgione, P. D. (1998). *Pursuing excellence: A study of U.S. twelfth-grade mathematics and science achievement in international context.* National Center for Education Statistics (NCES). Retrieved from http://www.nces .edu/gov/timss/

Fotuhi, M. (2004). *The memory cure: How to protect your brain against memory loss and Alzheimer's disease.* New York: McGraw-Hill.

Fowler, J. W. (1981). *Stages of faith: The psychology of human development and the quest for meaning.* San Francisco: Harper Collins.

Fowler, J. W. (2001). Faith development theory and the postmodern challenges. *International Journal for the Psychology of Religion, 11*(3), 159–172.

Fowler, J. W., & Dell, M. L. (2004). Stages of faith and identity: Birth to teens. *Child and Adolescent Psychiatric Clinics of North America, 13*(1), 17–33.

Fowler, M. D. (2009). Religion, bioethics, and nursing practice. *Nursing Ethics 2009, 16*(4), 393–405. doi: 10.1177/0969733009104604

Fowler, T., Harold, G., Hay, D., Rice, F., Scourfield, J., Thaper, A., et al. (2003). Maternal smoking during pregnancy and attention deficit hyperactivity disorder symptoms in offspring. *American Journal of Psychiatry, 160*(11), 1985–1989.

Fragoso, M. (2007, October 19). China's surplus of sons: A geopolitical time bomb. *Christian Science Monitor.* Retrieved from http://www.csmonitor.com/2007/1019/ p09s02-coop.html

Fraleigh, J. (2009). Vaccination: Compliance controversy. *RN, 72*(5), 36–40. Retrieved from CINAHL Plus with Full Text database.

Frank, D. A., Augustyn, M., Knight, W. G., Pell, T., & Zuckerman, B. (2001, March 28). Growth, development, and behavior in early childhood following prenatal cocaine exposure. *Journal of the American Medical Association, 285,* 1613–1625.

Frank, S., Dahler, L., Santurri, L. E., & Knight, K. (2010, November 9). Hyper-texting and hyper-networking: A new health-risk category for teens? American Public Health Association 138th Annual Meeting November 6–10, 2010. Denver, Colorado. Retrieved from http://apha

.confex.com/apha/138am/webprogram/ Paper224927.html

Frankel, N. R. (2004, September). Editorial: Ask your gynecologist. *Sexuality, Reproduction, and Menopause, 2*(3), 131–132.

Franks, A. L., Kelder, S. H., Dino, G. A., Horn, K. A., Gortmaker, S. L., Wiecha, J. L., . . . , Simoes, E. J. (2007). School-based programs: Lessons learned from CATCH, Planet Health, and Not-on-Tobacco. *Preventing Chronic Disease, 4*(2), 1–7.

Fraser, G. E. (2003). *Diet, life expectancy and chronic disease: Studies of Seventh-Day Adventists and other vegetarians.* New York: Oxford University Press.

Fraser, G. E. (2005, March 31). Studies of Adventist health: Does our health message really make a difference in people's lives? *Adventist Review, 182*(13), 36–41.

Fraser, J. (2001). *New research on children who stutter—Situation should not be ignored.* Stuttering Foundation of America. Retrieved from http://www.stutteringhelp .org/pressrm/newresrc.htm

Free Press Release. (2010, February 2). Liposuction death rate—the shocking truth you never knew. Retrieved from http://www .prlog.org/10516025-liposuction-death-rate -the-shocking-truth-youve-never-knew.html

French, S. E., Seidman, E., Allen, L., & Aber, J. L. (2006). The development of ethnic identity during adolescence. *Developmental Psychology, 42*(1), 1–10.

Freud, A. (1936). *The ego and the mechanisms of defense.* New York: International Universities Press.

Freud, A. (1958). Adolescence. *Psychoanalytic Study of the Child, 13,* 255–278.

Freud, S. (1930/1961). *Civilization and its discontents.* London: Hogarth Press.

Freud, S. (1940). An outline of psychoanalysis. In J. Strachey (Ed. and Trans.), *The standard edition of the complete psychological works of Sigmund Freud.* London: Hogarth.

Freund, A. M., & Ritter, J. O. (2009). Midlife crisis: A debate. *Journal of Gerontology, 55*(5), 582–591. doi:10.1159/000227322

Frey, W. H. (2007, May). *Mapping the growth of older America: Seniors and boomers in the early 21st century.* The Brookings Institution Living Cities Census Series.

Friedlmeier, W., & Trommsdorff, G. (1999). Emotional regulation in early childhood: A cross-cultural comparison between German and Japanese toddlers. *Journal of Cross-Cultural Psychology, 30*(6), 684–711.

Friedman, M. A., & Brownell, K. D. (1995). Psychological correlates of obesity: Moving to the next research generation. *Psychological Bulletin, 117,* 3–20.

Friedman, R. (1998). *Body love—Learning to like our looks and ourselves.* New York: Harper & Row.

Friel, B., Smallen, J., & Dick, J. (2007, November 11). Head Start bill is completed. *National Journal, 39*(46/47), 54.

Fries, J. F. (1997). Can preventive gerontology be on the way? *American Journal of Public Health, 87,* 1591–1593.

Fries, J. F. (2007). The irreversible component of the disability index of the health assessment questionnaire: Comment on the article by Aletaha et al. *Arthritis Rheumatology, 56*(4), 1368–1369.

Friese, C., Becker, G., & Nachtigall, R. D. (2008). Older motherhood and the changing life course in the era of assisted reproductive technologies. *Journal of Aging Stud*ies, *22*(1), 65–73.

Frisch, R. E. (1978, June 30). Menarche and fatness. *Science, 200,* 1509–1513.

Fromm, E. (1941). *Escape from freedom.* New York: Avon.

Fromm, E. (1980). *Greatness and limitations of Freud's thought.* New York: Harper & Row.

Frost, J. L. (2009). *A history of children's play and play environments: Toward a contemporary child saving movement.* New York: Routledge.

Frost, J., & McKelvie, S. (2004, July). Self-esteem and body satisfaction in male and female elementary school, high school, and university students. *Sex Roles, 51*(1/2), 45–54.

Fry, D. P. (1993). The intergenerational transmission of disciplinary practices to conflict. *Human Organization, 52,* 176–185.

Fry, D. P. (2006). Reciprocity: The foundation stone of moral development. In M. Killen & J. G. Smetana (Eds.), *Handbook of moral development* (pp. 399–422). Mahwah, NJ: Erlbaum.

Fry, P. S. (2003). Perceived self-efficacy domains as predictors of fear of the unknown and fear of dying among older adults. *Psychology and Aging, 18*(3), 474–486.

Fry, P. S., & Keyes, C. L. (2010). *New frontiers in resilient aging.* Cambridge: Cambridge University Press.

Frye, B. J., & Vogt, H. A. (2010). The causes of underrepresentation of African American children in gifted programs and the need to address this problem through more culturally responsive teaching practices in teacher education programs. *Black History Bulletin, 73*(1), 11–17. doi:10.1260/0028-2529.73.1.11

Fuchs, D., Fuchs, L. S., & Stecker, P. M. (2010). The "blurring" of special education in a new continuum of general education placements and services. *Exceptional Children, 76*(3), 301–323. Retrieved from EBSCO*host*.

Fulkerson, J. A., & Strauss, J. (2007). Correlates of psychosocial well-being among overweight adolescents: The role of the family. *Journal of Consulting and Clinical Psychology, 75*(1), 181–186.

Furman, E. (2005). *Boomerang generation: How to survive living with your parents . . . the second time around.* New York: Simon & Schuster.

Futterman, A., Gallagher, D., Thompson, L. W., Lovett, S., & Gilewski, M. (1990). Retrospective assessment of marital adjustment and depression during the first 2 years of spousal bereavement. *Psychology and Aging, 5,* 277–283.

Gable, S., Chang, Y., & Krull, J. L. (2007). Television watching and frequency of family meals are predictive of overweight onset and persistence in a national sample of school-aged children. *Journal of the American Dietetic Association, 107,* 53–61.

Gaffney, M., Eichwald, J., Grosse, S. D., & Mason, C. A. (2010, March 5). Identifying infants with hearing loss—United States, 1999–2007. *MMWR Weekly, 59*(8), 220–223.

Gaines, R., & Missiuna, C. (2006). Early identification: Are speech/language-impaired toddlers at increased risk for Developmental Coordination Disorder? *Child Care, Health and Development, 33*(3), 325–332. doi:10.1111/j.1365-2214.2006.00677.x

Gal, A. (2009). Social protection of the elderly. *Ploiesti Bulletin, 31*(2), 61–66.

Gallahue, D. L., & Ozmun, J. C. (2006). Motor development in young children. In B. Spodek & O. N. Saracho (Eds.), *Handbook of research on the education of young children* (2nd ed., pp. 105–117). Mahwah, NJ: Erlbaum.

Gallegly, E. (2001, July 31). *Gallegly Persian Gulf veterans' legislation approved by House.* [News Release]. From U.S. House of Representatives. Retrieved from http://www.house.gov/gallegly/073101gulf.htm

Ganong, L. H., & Coleman, M. (2004). *Stepfamily relationships: Development, dynamics, and interventions.* New York: Kluwer Academic.

Gans, K. M., Burkholder, G. J., Risica, P. M., & Lasater, T. M. (2003). Baseline fat-related dietary behaviors of white, Hispanic, and black participants in a cholesterol screening and education project in New England. *Journal of the American Dietetic Association, 103*(6), 699–706. doi:10.1053/jada.2003.50135

Ganzini, L., Goy, E. R., Miller, L. L., Harvath, T. A., Jackson, A., & Delorit, M. A. (2003). Nurses' experiences with hospice patients who refuse food and fluids to hasten death. *New England Journal of Medicine, 349,* 359–365.

Gao, G. (2001). Intimacy, passion, and commitment in Chinese and U.S. American romantic relationships. *International Journal of Intercultural Relations, 25*(3), 329–342.

Garbarino, J. (1999). *Lost boys: Why our sons turn violent and how we can save them.* New York: Free Press.

Garces, E., Thomas, D., & Currie, J. (2000, December). Longer-term effects of Head Start: Working mothers and child well-being. *Joint Center for Policy Research Newsletter,* 1–27. Retrieved from http://www.jcpr.org/newsletters/ VOL6_NO2/articles.html#story_1

Garcia, C. M., & Duckett, L. J. (2009). Language barriers among Latinos seeking health care. *Journal of Cultural Diversity, 16*(3), 120–126.

Gardner, H. (1983). *Frames of mind: The theory of multiple intelligences.* New York: Basic Books.

Gardner, H. (1993a). Lessons in life from creative geniuses: Freud, Einstein, Picasso, Stravinsky, Eliot, Graham and Gandhi. *Boardroom Reports, 22,* 13.

Gardner, H. (1993b). *Multiple intelligences: The theory in practice.* New York: Basic Books.

Gardner, H. (2000a). *Intelligence reframed: Multiple intelligences for the 21st century.* New York: Basic Books.

Gardner, H. (2000b). *The disciplined mind.* New York: Penguin Books.

Gardner, H. (2006a). *Five minds for the future.* Cambridge, MA: Harvard Business School Press.

Gardner, H. (2006b). *Multiple intelligences: New horizons.* Basic Books.

Gardner, H. (2008). The five minds for the future. *Schools: Studies in Education, 5*(1–2), 17–24.

Gardner, M., & Steinberg, L. (2005). Peer influence on risk taking, risk preference, and risky decision making in adolescence and adulthood: An experimental study. *Developmental Psychology, 41*(4), 625–635.

Garrison, M. M., & Christakis, D. A. (2005, December). *A teacher in the living room? Educational media for babies, toddlers, and preschoolers.* Menlo Park, CA: Henry J. Kaiser Family Foundation

Garvey, C., & Hogan, R. (1973). Social speech and social interaction: Egocentrism revisited. *Child Development, 44,* 562–568.

Gass, K., Jenkins, J., & Dunn, J. (2007). Are sibling relationships protective? A longitudinal study. *Journal of Child Psychology and Psychiatry, 48*(2), 167–175. doi:10.1111/j.1469-7610.2006.01699.x

Gates, A. (2009, March 22). For Baby Boomers, the joys of Facebook. *New York Times,* p. 7. Retrieved from EBSCO*host*.

Gathercole, R. (2007). *The well-adjusted child: The social benefits of homeschooling.* New York: Midpoint Trade Books.

Gaudiosi, J. A. (2010). *Child maltreatment 2008.* U.S. Department of Health and Human Services, Administration on Children, Youth and Families. Retrieved from http://www.acf.hhs.gov/programs/cb/pubs/cm08/cm08.pdf

Gauvain, M., & Perez, S. M. (2007). The socialization of cognition. In J. E. Grusec & P. D. Hastings (Eds.), *Handbook of socialization: Theory and research* (pp. 538–613). New York: Guilford Press.

Gazelle, G. (2003). A good death: Not just an abstract concept. *Journal of Clinical Oncology, 21*(9S), 95s–96s.

Ge, X., Natsuaki, M. N., Neiderhiser, J. M., & Reiss, D. (2007). Genetic and environmental influences on pubertal timing: Results from two national sibling studies. *Journal of Research on Adolescence, 17*(4), 767–788. doi:10.1111/j.1532-7795.2007.00546.x

Gearing, R. E., & Mian, I. (2009, January). The role of gender in early and very early onset of psychotic disorders. *Clinical Schizophrenia & Related Psychoses,* 298–306. doi:10.3371/CSRP.2.4.3

Geber, M., & Dean, R. (1957a). Gesell tests on African children. *Pediatrics, 20,* 1055–1065.

Geber, M., & Dean, R. (1957b). The state of development of newborn African children. *Lancet, 1,* 1216–1219.

Gee, C. B., & Rhodes, J. E. (2003). Adolescent mothers' relationship with their children's fathers: Social support, social strain, and relationship continuity. *Journal of Family Psychology, 17*(3), 370–383.

Gehring, J. (2000). Survey: Teens want job security. *Education Week, 19*(28), 10.

Gelman, D. (1983, November 7). A great emptiness. *Newsweek,* 120–126.

Gelman, R., & Meck, E. (1986). The notion of principle: The case of counting. In J. Hiebert (Ed.), *Conceptual and procedural knowledge: The case of mathematics.* Hillsdale, NJ: Erlbaum.

Gelman, S. A. (2003). *The essential child: Origins of essentialism in everyday thought.* New York: Oxford University Press.

Gelman, S. A., & Kremer, K. E. (1991). Understanding natural cause: Children's explanations of how objects and their properties originate. *Child Development, 62,* 396–414.

Gelman, S. A., & Raman, L. (2007). This cat has nine lives? Children's memory for genericity in language. *Developmental Psychology, 43*(5), 1256–1268.

Genazzani, A. D., Lanzoni, C., & Genazzani, A. R. (2007). Might DHEA be considered a beneficial replacement therapy in the elderly? *Drugs Aging, 24*(3), 173–185.

Gender Identity. (1998). *Encyclopedia of Childhood and Adolescence.* Retrieved from FindArticles.com

Georgas, J., Berry, J. W., van de Vijver, F. J. R., Kağitçibaşi, C., & Poortinga, Y. H. (2006). *Families across cultures: A 30-nation psychological study.* New York: Cambridge University Press.

Gerstorf, D., Smith, J., & Baltes, P. B. (2006). A systemic-wholistic approach to differential aging: Longitudinal findings from the Berlin Aging Study. *Psychology and Aging, 21,* 645–663.

Gerwitz, J. L. (1972). *Attachment and dependency.* Washington, DC: Winston.

Gesell, A. (1928). *Infancy and human growth.* New York: Macmillan.

Giandrea, M. D., Cahill, K. E., & Quinn, J. F. (2008, April 10). *Self-employment transitions among older American workers with career jobs.* BLS Working Paper 418, U.S. Department of Labor Statistics. Retrieved from http://www.bls.gov/ore/pdf/ec080040.pdf

Giannarelli, L., Sonenstein, F. L., & Stagner, M. W. (2006). Child-care arrangements and help for low-income families with young children: Evidence from the national survey of America's families. In N. J. Cabrera, R. Hutchens, & H. E. Peters (Eds.), *From welfare to child care: What happens to young children when single mothers exchange welfare for work?* (pp. 3–18). Mahwah, NJ: Erlbaum.

Gibb, S. J., Fergusson, D. M., & Horwood, L. (2008). Effects of single-sex and coeducational schooling on the gender gap in educational achievement. *Australian Journal of Education, 52*(3), 301–317. Retrieved from EBSCOhost.

Gibbs, J. C. (2003). *Moral development and reality: Beyond the theories of Kohlberg and Hoffman.* Thousand Oaks, CA: Sage.

Gibbs, J. C., Basinger, K. S., Fuller, D., & Fuller, R. L. (1992). *Moral maturity: Measuring the development of sociomoral reflection.* New York: Routledge.

Gibbs, J. T. (1997). African-American suicide: A cultural paradox. *Suicide and Life-Threatening Behavior, 27,* 68–79.

Gibbs, N. (2007, October 18). Birth control for kids? *Time.* Retrieved from http://www.time.com/time/printout/0,8816,1673227,00.html

Gibson, E. J., & Walk, R. D. (1960, April). The "visual cliff." *Scientific American, 202,* 64–71.

Gibson, M. J., & Houser, A. (2007, June). Valuing the invaluable: A new look at the economic value of family caregiving. Washington, DC: AARP Public Policy Institute.

Gibson-Davis, C. M. (2008). Family structure effects on maternal and paternal parenting in low-income families. *Journal of Marriage and Family, 70*(2), 452–465. doi:10.1111/j.1741-3737.2008.00493.x

Gifford-Smith, M. E., & Brownell, C. A. (2003, July/August). Childhood peer relationships: Social acceptance, friendships, and peer networks. *Journal of School Psychology, 41*(4), 235–284.

Gilbert, S. M. (2006). *Death's door: Modern dying and the ways we grieve.* New York: Norton.

Gilgun, J. F. (1995). We shared something special: The moral discourse of incest perpetrators. *Journal of Marriage and the Family, 57,* 265–281.

Gilliard, J. L., Moore, R. A., & Lemieux, J. J. (2007, Fall). In Hispanic culture, the children are the jewels of the family: An investigation of home and community culture in a bilingual early care and education center serving migrant and seasonal farm worker families. *Early Childhood Research and Practice, 9*(2). Retrieved from http://ecrp.uiuc.edu/v9n2/gilliard.html

Gilligan, C. (1982a). *In a different voice: Psychological theory and women's development.* Cambridge, MA: Harvard University Press.

Gilligan, C. (1982b, June). Why should a woman be more like a man? *Psychology Today, 16,* 68–77.

Gilligan, C., Sullivan, A., & Taylor, J. M. (1995). *Between voice and silence: Women and girls, race and relationship.* Cambridge, MA: Harvard University Press.

Gillis, B., Mobley, C., Stadler, D. D., Hartstein, J., Virus, A., Volpe, S. L., . . ., McCormick, S. (2009). Rational, design and methods of the HEALTHY Study nutrition intervention component. *International Journal of Obesity, 33,* S29–S36. doi:10.1038/ijo.2009.114

Ginsburg, K. R., Committee on Communications, & the Committee on Psychosocial Aspects of Child and Family Health. (2007). The importance of play in promoting healthy child development and maintaining strong parent-child bonds. *Pediatrics, 119*(1), 182–191.

Ginty, M. M. (2007, February 17). *Silicone breast implants face hearings in Congress.* Women's eNews. Retrieved from http://www.alternet.org/story/47700/

Girdler, S. S., Leserman, J., Bunevicius, R., Klatzkin, R., Petersen, C. A., & Light, K. C. (2007). Persistent alterations in biological profiles in women with abuse histories: Influence of premenstrual dysphoric disorder. *Health Psychology, 26*(2), 201–213.

Givens, J., Frederick, M., Silverman, L., Anderson, S., Senville, J., Silver, M., & . . ., Perls, T. (2009). Personality traits of centenarians' offspring. *Journal of the American Geriatrics Society, 57*(4), 683–685. Retrieved from EBSCOhost.

Gjerde, P. (2004). Culture, power and experience: Toward a person-centered cultural psychology. *Human Development, 47,* 138–147.

Glacel, A. (2008, March 14). *Kohl, Domenici amendment to protect elderly from abuse included in Senate budget.* Washington, DC: United States Senate Special Committee on Aging. Retrieved from http://aging.senate.gov/hearing_detail.cfm?id=295576&.

Glassbrenner, D., & Ye, J. (2007). *Traffic Safety Facts* (Research Note DOT HS 810 796). Washington, DC: National Highway Traffic Safety Administration, NHTSA's National Center for Statistics and Analysis.

Glazer, S. (2005, January 14). Prayer and healing: Can spirituality influence health? *The CQ Researcher, 15*(2), 1–51.

Gleason, J. B. (1993). *The development of language.* New York: Macmillan.

Gleason, J. B., & Ely, R. (2002). Gender differences in language development. In McGillicuddy-De Lisi & R. De Lisi (Eds.), *Biology, society and behavior: The* development of sex differences in cognition (pp. 127–154). Westport, CT: Greenwood.

Gleason, T. R., & Hohmann, L. M. (2006). Concepts of real and imaginary friendships in early childhood. *Social Development, 15*(1), 128–144.

Gleeson, J. P., Wesley, J. M., Ellis, R., Seryak, C., Talley, G., & Robinson, J. (2009). Becoming involved in raising a relative's child: Reasons, caregiver motivations and pathways to informal kinship care. *Child and Family Social Work, 14*(3), 300–310. doi:10.1111/j.1365-2206.2008.00596.x

Glenn, J. (2000, September 27). *Before it's too late: A report to the nation from the National Commission on Mathematics and Science Teaching for the 21st Century.* Washington, DC: U.S. Department of Education, National Commission on Mathematics and Science.

GLSEN (Gay, Lesbian, and Straight Education Network). (2005). *From teasing to torment: School climate in America.* New York: GLSEN and Harris Interactive.

Glynn, M., & Rhodes, P. (2005). *Estimated prevalence of HIV in the United States at the end of 2003.* National HIV Prevention Conference, 2005. Retrieved from http://www.aegis.com/ conferences/nhivpc/2005/T1-B1101.pdf

Gobert, F., Freudenthal, D., & Pine, J. M. (2004). Modelling syntactic development in a cross-linguistic context. In W. G. Sadas (Ed.), *Proceedings of the First COLING Workshop on Psycho-computational Models of Human Language Acquisition.* Retrieved from http://www.aclweb.org/anthology-new/W/W04/W04-1300.pdf

Goddard, S. (2005). *Reflexes, learning and behavior: A window into the child's mind.* Eugene, OR: Fern Ridge Press.

Goethe, J. W. V. (1809/1872). Elective affinities, with an introduction by Victoria C. Woodhull. Boston: D. W. Niles and Ithaca, NY: Cornell University Library Digital Collections, Historical Mongraph Collections. Retrieved from http://www.amazon.com/dp/1429740647?tag=corneunivelib-20#reader_1429740647

Gogate, L. L., & Bahrick, L. E. (2000). A study of multimodal motherese: The role of temporal synchrony between verbal labels and gestures. *Child Development, 71,* 878–895.

Gohm, C. L., Oishi, O., & Darlington, J. (1998). Culture, parental conflict, parental marital status, and the subjective well-being of young adults. *Journal of Marriage and the Family, 60,* 319–334.

Gold, D., Woodbury, M., & George, L. (1990). Relationship classification using grade of membership analysis: A typology of sibling relationships in later life. *Journal of Gerontology: Social Sciences, 45,* S43–S51.

Gold, E. B., Bromberger, J., Crawford, S., Samuels, S., Greendale, G. A., Harlow,

S. D., & Skurnick, J. (2001). Factors associated with age at natural menopause in a multiethnic sample of midlife women. *American Journal of Epidemiology, 153*(9), 865–874.

Goldfield, G. S., Moore, C., Henderson, K., Buchholz, A., Obeid, N., & Flament, M. F. (2010). Body dissatisfaction, dietary restraint, depression, and weight status in adolescents. *Journal of School Health, 80*(4), 186–192. doi:10.1111/j.1746-1561.2009.00485.x

Goldfinch, M. (2009). 'Putting Humpty together again': Working with parents to help children who have experienced early trauma. *The Australian and New Zealand Journal of Family Therapy, 30*(4), 284–299. doi: 10.1375/anft.30.4.284

Goldin-Meadow, S. (2000, Jan–Feb). Beyond words: The importance of gesture to researchers and learners. *Child Development, 71,* 231–239.

Golding, L. H. (2005). *YMCA Fitness Testing and Assessment Manual.* Chicago, IL: YMCA of the USA.

Goldscheider, F., & Kaufman, G. (2006). Single parenthood and the double standard. *Fathering: A Journal of Theory, Research, & Practice about Men as Fathers, 4*(2), 191–208.

Goldscheider, F., Hofferth, S., Spearin, C., & Curtin, S. (2009). Fatherhood across two generations: Factors affecting early family roles. *Journal of Family Issues, 30*(5), 586–604. Retrieved from EBSCO*host.*

Goldscheider, F. K., Thornton, A., & Yang, L. (2001). Helping out the kids: Expectations about parental support in young adulthood. *Journal of Marriage and Family, 63,* 727–740.

Goleman, D. (1985, May 28). Spacing of siblings strongly linked to success in life. *New York Times,* pp. 17, 18.

Goleman, D. (1989, February 7). For many, turmoil of aging erupts in the 50's, studies find. *New York Times,* pp. 17, 21.

Goleman, D. (1990, January 16). Men at 65: New findings on well-being. *New York Times,* pp. 19, 23.

Goleman, D. (1995). *Emotional intelligence: Why it can matter more than IQ.* New York: Bantam Books.

Goleman, D. (2007). *Social intelligence: The new science of human relationships.* New York: Bantam/Dell.

Golombok, S., & Tasker, F. (2010). Gay fathers. In M. E. Lamb (Ed.), *The role of the father in child development* (pp. 319–340). Hoboken, NJ: Wiley.

Golub, M. S. (2000). Adolescent health and the environment. *Environmental health perspectives, 108,* 355–362.

Goncy, E. A., & van Dulmen, M. H. M. (2010, Winter). Fathers do make a difference: Parental involvement and adolescent alcohol use. *Men's Studies Press, 8*(1), 93–108. doi:10.3149/fth.0801.93

Gonzales, P., Williams, T., Jocelyn, L., Roey, S., Kastberg, D., & Brenwald, S. (2009).

Highlights from TIMSS 2007: Mathematics and Science Achievement of U.S. Fourth- and Eighth-Grade Students in International Context (NCES 2009–2001 Revised). Washington, DC: National Center for Education Statistics, Institute of Education Sciences, U.S. Department of Education.

Gonzalez, A., Kohn, M., & Clarke, S. (2007). Eating disorders in adolescents. *Australian Family Physician, 36*(8), 614–619.

Goodman, C. C., & Silverstein, M. (2006). Grandmothers raising grandchildren: Ethnic and racial differences in well-being among custodial and coparenting families. *Journal of Family Issues, 27*(11), 1605–1626.

Goodvin, R., Meyer, S., Thompson, R. A., & Hayes, R. (2008). Self-understanding in early childhood: Associations with child attachment security and maternal negative affect. *Attachment & Human Development, 10*(4), 433–450. doi:10.1080/14616730802461466

Goran, M. I., Nagy, T. R., Gower, B. A., Mazariegos, M., Solomons, N., & Johnson, R. (1998). Influence of sex, seasonality, ethnicity, and geographic location on the components of total energy expenditure in young children: Implications for energy requirements. *American Journal of Clinical Nutrition, 68,* 675–682.

Gordon, C. M., DePeter, K. C., Feldman, H. A., Grace, E., & Emans, S. J. (2004). Prevalence of vitamin D deficiency among healthy adolescents. *Archives of Pediatrics & Adolescent Medicine, 158,* 531–537.

Gore, S., & Aseltine, R. H. (2003). Race and ethnic differences in depressed mood following the transition from high school. *Journal of Health and Social Behavior, 44*(3), 370–389. doi:10.2307/1519785

Gormley, W. T., Phillips, D., Adelstein, S., & Shaw, J. (2010). Head Start's comparative advantage: Myth or reality? *Policy Studies Journal, 38*(3), 397–418. doi:10.1111/j.1541-0072.2010.00367.x

Gorospe, E. C., & Gerstenberger, S. L. (2008). Atypical sources of childhood lead poisoning in the United States: A systematic review from 1966–2006. *Clinical Toxicology, 46*(8), 728–737. doi:10.1080/15563650701481862

Gostin, L. O., & DeAngelis, C. D. (2007). Mandatory HPV vaccination: Public Health vs private wealth. *JAMA, 297*(17), 1921–1923.

Goswami, U. (2008). The development of reading across languages. *Annals of the New York Academy of Sciences, 1145,* 1–12. doi:10.1196/annals.1416.018

Gottlieb, G. (2007). Probabilistic epigenesis. *Developmental Science, 10*(1), 1–11.

Gottschalk, M. (2009). Sick on arrival: Health care reform in the age of Obama. *New Labor Forum, 18*(3), 28–36.

Gould, C. G. (1983, April). Out of the mouths of beasts. *Science, 83,* 4, 69–72.

Goulet, L., Fall, A., D'Amour, D., & Pineault, R. (2007). Preparation for discharge, maternal satisfaction, and newborn readmission for jaundice: Comparing postpartum models of care. *Birth, 34*(2), 131–139.

Goyal, S. (2009). Inside the house of learning: The relative performance of public and private schools in Orissa. *Education Economics, 17*(3), 315–327. doi:10.1080/09645290903142577

Grady, S., Bielick, S., & Aud, S. (2010). *Trends in the use of school choice: 1993 to 2007* (NCES 2010-004). National Center for Education Statistics, Institute of Education Sciences, U.S. Department of Education. Washington, DC. Retrieved from http://nces.ed.gov/pubs2010/2010004.pdf

Graf, D. L., Pratt, L. V., Hester, C. N., & Short, K. E. (2009). Playing active video games increases energy expenditure in children. *Pediatrics, 124*(2), 534–540. doi:10.1542/peds.2008-2851

Graf Estes, K. G., Evans, J. L., Alibali, M. W., & Saffran, J. R. (2007). Can infants map meaning to newly segmented words? Statistical segmentation and word learning. *Psychological Science, 18*(3), 254–260.

Gralinski, J. H., & Kopp, C. B. (1993). Everyday rules for behavior: Mothers' requests to young children. *Developmental Psychology, 29*, 573–584.

Grall, T. S. (2009, November). Custodial mothers and fathers and their child support: 2007. *Current Population Reports* (P60-237). 1–12. Washington, DC: U.S. Department of Commerce.

Grandin, T. (2008). *The way I see it: A personal look at autism and Asperger's.* Arlington, TX: Future Horizons.

Graziano, A. M., & Rualin, M. L. (2007). *Research methods* (6th ed.). Boston: Allyn & Bacon.

Greenberg, J. (2006). The road less traveled: The problem with binary sex categories. In P. Currah, R. M. Juang, & S. P. Minter (Eds.), *Transgender rights* (pp. 51–73). Minneapolis: University of Minnesota Press.

Greene, J. P., & Winters, M. A. (2005, February). *Public high school graduation and college-readiness rates: 1991–2002.* Education Working Paper No. 8. Manhattan Institute for Policy Research. Retrieved from http://www.manhattan-institute.org/html/ewp_08.htm

Greene, M. F., & Ecker, J. L. (2004, January 8). Abortion, health and the law. *New England Journal of Medicine, 350,* 184–187.

Greenfield, P. M. (1966). On culture and conservation. In J. Bruner, R. R. Olver, & P. M. Greenfield (Eds.), *Studies in cognitive growth.* New York: Wiley.

Greenhouse, L. (2006, January 18). Justices reject U.S. bid to block assisted suicide; Court, 6–3, says attorney general was wrong in Oregon case. *New York Times,* pp. A1, A16.

Greenspan, S., & Greenspan, N. T. (1985). *First feelings.* New York: Viking Press.

Greenspan, S. I., DeGangi, G., & Wieder, S. (2001) *Functional Emotional Assessment Scale: Clinical and research applications.* Bethesda, MD: Interdisciplinary Council on Developmental and Learning Disorders.

Greenwald, J. L., Burstein, G. R., Pincus, J., & Branson, B. (2006). A rapid review of rapid HIV antibody tests. *Current Infectious Disease Reports, 8,* 125–131.

Gregory, A. M., Light-Häusermann, J. H., Rijskijk, F., & Eley, T. C. (2009). Behavioral genetic analyses of prosocial behavior in adolescents. *Developmental Science, 12*(1), 165–174. doi:10.1111/j.1467-7687.2008.00739.x

Gregory, E. (2007). *Ready: Why women are embracing the new later motherhood.* New York: Basic Books.

Greyson, B. (2003). Incidence and correlates of near-death experiences in a cardiac care unit. *General Hospital Psychiatry, 25*(4), 269–276B.

Grolnick, W. S. (2003). *The psychology of parental control: How well-meant parenting backfires.* Mahwah, NJ: Erlbaum.

Grolnick, W. S., McMenamy, J. M., & Kurowski, C. O. (2006). Emotional self-regulation in infancy and toddlerhood. In L. Balter & C. S. Tamis-LeMonda (Eds.), *Child psychology: A handbook of contemporary issues* (pp. 3–25). New York: Psychology Press.

Gross, J. (1992, December 7). Divorced, middle-aged and happy: Women, especially, adjust to the 90's. *New York Times,* p. A8.

Grossman, K., Grossman, K. E., & Kindler, H. (2005). Early care and the roots of attachment and partnership representations: The Bielefield and Regensburg longitudinal studies. In K. E. Grossman, K. Grossman, & E. Waters (Eds.), *Attachment from infancy to adulthood: The major longitudinal studies* (pp. 98–136). New York: Guilford Press.

Growing up healthy: An overview of the National Children's Study. (2010). *The National Children's Study.* Washington, DC: U.S. Department of Health and Human Services.

Grumbach, M. M., & Styne, D. M. (2003). Puberty: Ontogeny, neuroendocrinology, physiology, and disorders. In H. M. Kronenberg, P. R. Larsen, S. Melmed, & K. S. Plonsky (Eds.), *Williams textbook of endocrinology* (10th ed., 1115–1286). Philadelphia: Saunders.

Grusec, J. E., & Davidov, M. (2007). Socialization in the family: The roles of parents. In J. E. Grusec & P. D. Hastings (Eds.). *Handbook of socialization.* New York: Guilford Press.

Grusec, J. E., & Hastings, P. D. (Eds.). (2007) *Handbook of socialization: Theory and research.* New York: Guilford Press.

Guajardo, N. R., Snyder, G., & Petersen, R. (2009). Relationships among parenting practices, parental stress, child behaviour, and children's social-cognitive development. *Infant and Child Development, 18*, 37–60. doi:10.1002/icd.578

Guilford, J. P. (1967). *The nature of human intelligence.* New York: McGraw-Hill.

Guillemin, R. (1982). Growth hormone-releasing factor from a human pancreatic tumor that caused acromegaly. *Science, 218,* 583–587.

Gullone, E. (2000). The development of normal fear: A century of research. *Clinical Psychology Review, 20*(4), 429–451.

Gunby, P. (1998). "Life begins" for Baltimore longitudinal study of aging—Research group has 40th birthday. (Medical News & Perspectives). *Journal of the American Medical Association, 279*(13), 982–983.

Gurian, M. (1996). *The wonder of boys: What parents, mentors, and educators can do to shape boys into exceptional men.* New York: Putnam.

Gurian, M., & Stevens, K. (2005). *The minds of boys: Saving our sons from falling behind in school and life.* New York: Wiley.

Gutman, L. M., & Eccles, J. S. (2007). Stage-environment fit during adolescence: Trajectories of family relations and adolescent outcomes. *Developmental Psychology, 43*(2), 522–537.

Guttmacher Institute. (2006). *U.S. teenage pregnancy statistics: National and state trends and trends by race and ethnicity.* New York: Guttmacher Institute. Retrieved from http://www.guttmacher.org/ pubs/2006/09/12/USTPstats.pdf

Guttmacher Institute. (2008, January). *Facts on induced abortion in the United States.* Retrieved from http:// www.guttmacher.org/pubs/fb_induced_ abortion.pdf

Guttmacher Institute. (2009, June). Facts on sexually transmitted infections in the United States. *In Brief.* New York: Guttmacher Institute.

Guttmacher Institute. (2010a). The impact of medication abortion 10 years after FDA approval. Retrieved from http://www.guttmacher.org/media/inthenews/2010/09/27/index.html

Guttmacher Institute. (2010b, June). Facts on contraceptive use in the United States. Retrieved from http://www.guttmacher.org/pubs/fb_contr_use.html

Haber, D. (Ed.) (2007). *Health promotion and aging: Practical applications for health professionals.* New York: Springer.

Hacker, K. A., Williams, S., Myagmarjav, E., Cabral, H., & Murphy, M. (2009). Persistence and change in Pediatric Symptom Checklist scores over 10 to 18 months. *Academic Pediatrics, 9*(4), 270–277. doi:10.1016/j.acap.2009.03.004

Haggerty, J. J. (2009). Gender disparity: Boys v. girls in special education. Retrieved from http://works.bepress.com/jennifer_haggerty/1

Haight, B. K., & Haight, B. S. (2007). *The handbook of structured life review.* Baltimore, MD: Health Professions Press.

Hair, E., Halle, T., Terry-Humen, E., Lavelle, B., & Calkins, J. (2006). Children's school readiness in the ECLS-K: Predictions to academic, health, and social outcomes in first grade. *Early Childhood Research Quarterly, 21*, 431–454. doi:10.1016/j.ecresq.2006 .09.005

Hajjar, E. R., Cafiero, A. C., & Hanlon, J. T. (2007). Polypharmacy in elderly patients. *The American Journal of Geriatric Pharmacotherapy, 5*(4), 345–351.

Halford, G. S., Maybery, M. T., O'Hare, A. W., & Grant, P. (1994). The development of memory and processing capacity. *Child Development, 65*, 1338–1356.

Hall, G. S. (1904). *Adolescence: Its psychology, and its relations to physiology, anthropology, sociology, sex, crime, religion, and education.* New York: Appleton.

Hall, H. I., Espinoza, L., Benbow, N., Hu, Y. W., & the Urban Areas HIV Surveillance Workgroup. (2010). Epidemiology of HIV infection in large urban areas in the United States. *PLoS One, 5*(9), e12756. doi:10.1371/journal.pone.0012756.

Hall, H. R., Song, R., Rhodes, P., Prejean, J., An, Q., Lee, L., . . . , Janssen, R. S. (2008). Estimation of HIV incidence in the United States. *JAMA, 300*(5), 520–529. Retrieved from CINAHL Plus with Full Text database.

Hall, J. (2006). Spirituality at the beginning of life. *Journal of Clinical Nursing, 15*(7), 804–810.

Hall, J. H., & Fincham, F. D. (2005). Relationship dissolution following infidelity. In M. A. Fine & J. H. Harvey (Eds.), *Handbook of divorce and relationship dissolution* (pp. 153–168). Mahwah, NJ: Routledge.

Hallmayer, J., Glasson, E. J., Bower. C., Petterson, B., Croen, L., Grether, J., . . . , Risch, N. (2002) On the twin risk in autism. *American Journal of Human Genetics, 71*, 941–946.

Halpern, C. J. T., Udry, J. R, Suchindran, C., & Campbell, B. (2000). Adolescent males' willingness to report masturbation. *Journal of Sex Research, 37*(4), 327–332.

Halpern, D. F. (1997). Sex differences in intelligence: Implications for education. *American Psychologist, 52*(10), 1091–1102.

Halpern, D. F. (2000). *Sex differences in cognitive abilities.* Mahwah, NJ: Erlbaum.

Halpert, S., & Warren, M. P. (2004). Exercise and female adolescents: Effects on the reproductive and musculoskeletal systems. *International SportMed Journal, 5*(1), 78–88.

Haltiwanger, J., & Harter, S. (1988). *A behavioral measure of young children's presented self-esteem.* Unpublished manuscript, University of Denver.

Hamer, R. D., & Skoczenski, A. M. (2001). *Milestones in visual development. Infant Vision Lab.* The Eunice Kennedy Shriver Center. Waltham, MA: University of Massachusetts Medical School. Retrieved from http://www.shriver.org/research/ psychological/infantvision/milestones.htm

Hamarus, P., & Kaikkonen, P. (2008). School bullying as a creator of pupil peer pressure. *Educational Research, 50*(4), 333–345. doi:10.1080/00131880802499779

Hamilton, B. E., Martin, J. A., & Ventura, S. J. (2010a, April 6). Births: Preliminary data for 2008. *National Vital Statistics Reports, 58*(16), 1–18. Hyattsville, MD: National Center for Health Statistics. Retrieved from http://www.cdc.gov/nchs/ data/nvsr/nvsr58/nvsr58_16.pdf

Hamilton, B. E., Martin, J. A., & Ventura, S. J. (2010b, December 21). Births: Preliminary data for 2009. *National Vital Statistics Reports, 59*(3), 1–29. Retrieved from http:// www.cdc.gov/nchs/data/nvsr/nvsr59/ nvsr59_03.pdf

Hamilton, N. A., Catley, D., & Karlson, C. (2007). Sleep and the affective response to stress and pain. *Health Psychology, 26*(3), 288–295.

Hamilton, S. F., & Hamilton, M. A. (2006). School, work, and emerging adulthood. In J. J. Arnett & J. L. Tanner (Eds.), *Emerging adults in America: Coming of age in the 21st century* (pp. 257–277). Washington, DC: American Psychological Association.

Hammer, C. S., Farkas, G., & Maczuga, S. (2010). The language and literacy development of Head Start children: A study using the Family and Child Experiences Survey database. *Language, Speech, and Hearing Services in Schools, 41*(1), 70–83. doi:10.1044/ 0161-1461(2009/08-0050)

Hamplova, D., & Le Bourdais, C. (2008). One pot or two strategies? *Journal of Comparative Family Studies, 62*(1), 355–385.

Hamre, B. K., & Pianta, R. C. (2005). Can instructional and emotional support in the first-grade classroom make a difference for children at risk of school failure? *Child Development, 76*(5), 949–967.

Hanel, B. (2010). Financial incentives to postpone retirement and future effects on employment: Evidence from a natural experiment. *Labor Economics, 17*(1), 474–486. doi:10.1016/j.labeco.2009.10.001

Hansen, B. (2004, October 22). Cloning debate: Should all forms of human cloning be banned? *CQ Researcher, 14*(37), 877–900.

Hanson, M. J., Horn, E., Sandall, S., Beckman, P., Morgan, M., Marquart, J., . . . Chou, H. Y. (2001). After preschool inclusion: Children's educational pathways over the early school years. *Exceptional Children, 68*(1), 65–83.

Harawa, N. T., Greenland, S., Bingham, T. A., Johnson, D. F., Cochran, S. D., Cunningham, W. E., . . . , Valleroy, L. A. (2004, March 15). Associations of race/ethnicity with HIV prevalence and HIV-related behaviors among young men who have sex with men in 7 urban centers in the United States. *Journal of Acquired Immune Deficiency Syndrome, 35*(5), 526–536.

Hardcastle, M. (2008). Teen fatherhood FAQ: A closer look at your rights and responsibilities. Retrieved from http:// teenadvice.about.com/od/ teenfathers/a/ teenfathersFAQ.htm

Hardman, M. L., Drew, C. J., & Egan, M. W. (2008). *Human exceptionality: School, community, family* (9th ed.). Boston: Houghton Mifflin.

Hardman, M. L., Drew, C. J., & Egan, M. W. (2011). *Human exceptionality: School, community, and family* (10th ed.). Belmont, CA: Wadsworth.

Hardy, L. T. (2007). Attachment theory and reactive attachment disorder: Theoretical perspectives and treatment implications. *Journal of Child and Adolescent Psychiatric Nursing, 20*(1), 27–39. doi:10.1111/j.1744 -6171.2007.00077.x

Hargreaves, D. A., & Tiggemann, M. (2009). Muscular ideal media images and men's body image: Social comparison processing and individual vulnerability. *Psychology of Men and Masculinity, 10*(2), 109–119. doi: 10.1037/a0014691

Harkness, S., & Super, C. M. (1996). *Parents' cultural belief systems: Their origins, expressions, and consequences.* New York: Guilford Press.

Harlow, H. F. (1971). *Learning to love.* San Francisco: Albion.

Harold, G. T., Aitken, J. J., Shelton, K. H. (2007). Inter-parental conflict and children's academic attainment: A longitudinal analysis. *Journal of Child Psychology and Psychiatry, 48*(12), 1223–1232. doi:10.1111/j.1469 -7610.2007.01793.x

Harper, B. (2005). *Gentle birth choices.* Rochester, VT: Healing Arts Press.

Harris, K. M., Gordon-Larsen, P., Chantala, K., & Udry, J. R. (2006). Longitudinal trends in race/ethnic disparities in leading health indicators from adolescence to young adulthood. *Archives of Pediatric & Adolescent Medicine, 160*, 74–81.

Harris, L. J., & Kliks Fones, D. (2008). *Same-sex unions around the world: Marriage, civil unions, registered partnerships: What are the differences and why do they matter?* Retrieved from http://works .bepress.com/cgi/viewcontent.cgi ?article=1007&context=leslie_harris

Harris, M. (2007, October). Forever young. *Money, 36*(10), 84–88.

Harris, S. M. (2004). The effect of health value and ethnicity on the relationship between hardiness and health behaviors. *Journal of Personality, 72*(2), 379–412.

Harris, T. (2008). *Glimpses of heaven: True stories of hope & peace at the end of life's journey.* Grand Rapids, MI: Revell.

Harrison, W. C., & Hood-Williams, J. (2002). *Beyond sex and gender.* London: Sage.

Harter, S. (1983). Developmental perspectives on the self-system. In W. Damon & N. Eisenberg (Eds.), *Handbook of child psychology* (pp. 276–385). New York: Wiley.

Harter, S. (1999). *The construction of the self: A developmental perspective.* New York: Guilford Press.

Harter, S., & Pike, R. (1984). The pictorial scale of perceived competence and social acceptance for young children. *Child Development, 55,* 1969–1982.

Hartley, A. A. (2006). The changing role of the speed of processing construct in the cognitive psychology of human aging. In J. E. Birren & K. W. Schaie (Eds.), *Handbook of the psychology of aging* (pp. 183–207). New York: Academic Press.

Hartmann, E. E., Bradford, G. E., Nottingham Chaplin, P. K., Johnson, T., Kemper, A. R., Kim, S., . . . , Marsh-Tootle, K. (2006). Project universal preschool vision screening: A demonstration project. *Pediatrics, 117*(2), 226–237.

Hartshorne, H., & May, M. A. (1928). *Studies in the nature of character: Vol. 1. Studies in deceit.* New York: Macmillan.

Hartwell, L. H., Hood, L., Goldberg, M. L., Reynolds, A. E., Silver, L. M., & Veres, R. C. (2008). *Genetics: From genes to genomes* (3rd ed.). New York: McGraw-Hill.

Harvey, G. (2006). *Animism: Respecting the living world.* New York: Columbia University Press.

Harvey, J., & Berry, J. A. (2009). Andropause in the aging male. *Journal for Nurse Practitioners, 5*(3), 207–212. doi:10.1016/j.nurpra.2008.09.019

Harvey, J. H., & Weber, A. L. (2002). *Odyssey of the heart: Close relationships in the 21st century.* Mahwah, NJ: Erlbaum.

Harwood, K., McLean, N., & Durkin, K. (2007). First-time mothers' expectations of parenthood: What happens when optimistic expectations are not matched by later experiences? *Developmental Psychology, 43*(1), 1–12. doi:10.1037/0012-1649.43.1.1

Harwood, R. L. (1992). The influence of culturally derived values on Anglo and Puerto Rican mothers' perceptions of attachment behavior. *Child Development, 63,* 822–839.

Hasson, H., & Arnetz, J. E. (2007). Nursing staff competence, work strain, stress and satisfaction in elderly care: A comparison of home-based care and nursing homes. *Journal of Clinical Nursing, 10*(11), 468–481. doi:10.1111/j.1365-2702.2006.01803.x

Hasson, H., & Arnetz, J. (2008). The impact of an educational intervention for elderly care nurses on care recipients' and family relatives' ratings of quality of care: A prospective, controlled intervention study. *International Journal of Nursing Studies, 45*(2), 166–179. Retrieved from EBSCOhost.

Hastings, P. D., Zahn-Waxler, C., Robinson, J., Usher, B., & Bridges, D. (2000). The development of concern for others in children with behavior problems. *Developmental Psychology, 36*(5), 531–546.

Hasty, P. (2005, January). The impact of DNA damage, genetic mutation and cellular responses on cancer prevention, longevity and aging: Observations in humans and mice. *Mechanisms of Aging and Development, 126*(1), 71–77.

Hattie, J. (2004, July). Models of self-concept that are neither top-down nor bottom up: The rope model of self-concept. Paper presented at the Third International Self Conference, Max Planck Institute, Berlin.

Hawke, J. L., Olson, R. K., Willcut, E. G., Wadsworth, S. J., & DeFries, J. C. (2009). Gender ratios for reading difficulties. *Dyslexia, 15*(3), 239–242. doi:10.1002/dys.389

Hawkins, S. M., & Matzuk, M. M. (2008). The menstrual cycle: Basic biology. *Annals of the New York Academy of Sciences, 1135,* 10–18. doi:10.1196/annals.1429.018

Hawley, T. L., & Disney, E. R. (1992, Winter). Crack's children: The consequences of maternal cocaine abuse. *Social Policy Report: Society for Research in Child Development, 4,* 1–23.

Haworth-Hoeppner, S. (2000, February). The critical shapes of body image: The role of culture and family in the production of eating disorders. *Journal of Marriage and the Family, 62,* 212–228.

Hawthorne, G. (2008). Perceived social isolation in a community sample: Its prevalence and correlates with aspects of people's lives. *Social Psychiatry and Psychiatric Epidemiology, 43*(2), 140–150. doi:10.1007/s00127-007-0279-8

Hayes, J., Hartmann, H., & Lee, S. (2010, March). Briefing paper: *Social Security: Vital to retirement security for 35 million women and men.* (IWPR Publication #D487). Institute for Women's Policy Research. Retrieved from http://www.iwpr.org/publications/pubs/social-security-vital-to-retirement-security-for-35-million-women-and-men

Hayes, J. E., & Duffy, V. B. (2008). Oral sensory phenotype identifies level of sugar and fat required for maximal liking. *Physiology & Behavior, 95*(1–2), 77–87. doi:10.1016/j.physbeh.2008.04.023

Hayes, J. E., Sullivan, B. S., & Duffy, V. B. (2010). Explaining variability in sodium intake through oral sensory phenotype, salt sensation and liking. *Physiology & Behavior, 100*(4), 369–380. doi:10.1016/j.physbeh.2010.03.017

Hayhoe, C. R. (2006). Helping families in transition due to unemployment. *Journal of Human Behavior in the Social Environment, 13*(1), 63–73. doi:10.1300/J137v13n01_04

Hays, D. G., Forman, J., & Sikes, A. (2009). Using artwork and photography to explore adolescent females' perceptions of dating relationships. *Journal of Creativity in Mental Health, 4*(4), 295–307. doi: 10.1080/15401380903385960

Hays, S. M., Chushing, C. A., Leung, H. W., Pyatt, D. W., Holicky, K. C., & Paustenbach, D. J. (2003). Exposure of infants and children in the U.S. to the flame retardant decabromodiphenyl oxide (DBDPO). *Journal of Children's Health, 1*(4), 449–475.

Hayslip, B., & Kaminski, P. (2005). Grandparents raising their grandchildren: A review of the literature and suggestions for practice. *Gerontologist, 45*(2), 262–269.

Hayward, C., Killen, J. D., Wilson, D. M., Hammer, L. D., Litt, I. F., Kraemer, H. C., . . . , Taylor, C. B. (1997). Psychiatric risk associated with early puberty in adolescent girls. *Journal of the American Academy of Child and Adolescent Psychiatry, 36*(2), 255–262.

HealthDay News. (2008). Surgeons' characteristics influence breast cancer care. Retrieved from http:// www.healthcentral.com/breast-cancer/news-201450-31_pf.html

HealthNewsDigest. (2007, January 22). States differ on treatment or incarceration program for women who abuse alcohol. In *Health NewsDigest.com.* Retrieved from http://www.healthnewsdigest.com/news/Women_s_Health_shtml

Healthy Families Act, H.R.2460. (2009). 111th Congress, 1st Session. Retrieved from http://www.govtrack.us/congress/bill.xpd?bill=h111-2460&tab=summary

Healthy People 2020. (2010, November). U.S. Department of Health and Human Services. Office of Disease Prevention and Health Promotion (Publication No. B0132). Retrieved from http://healthypeople.gov/2020/TopicsObjectives2020/pdfs/HP2020_brochure.pdf

Heath, S., & Cleaver, E. (2003). *Young, free and single? Twenty-somethings and household change.* New York: Palgrave Macmillan.

Heckhausen, J., & Heckhausen, H. (2008). *Motivation and action.* New York: Cambridge University Press.

Heid, I. M., Jackson, A. U., Randall, J. C., Winkler, T. W., Qi, L., Steinthorsdottie, V., & Thorleifsson, G. (2010). Meta-analysis identifies 13 new loci associated with waist-hip ratio and reveals sexual dimorphism in the genetic basis of fat distribution. *Nature Genetic, 42*(11), 949–960. doi:10.1038/ng.685

Heimann, M., Strid, K., Smith, L., Tjus, T., Ulvund, S. E., & Meltzoff, A. N. (2006). Exploring the relation between memory, gestural communication, and the emergence of language in infancy: A longitudinal study. *Infant and Child Development, 15,* 233–249.

Hellmich, N. (2010, August 16). Families: Wii can do it. *USA Today,* p. 5D.

Helms, H. M., Walls, J. K., Crouter, A. C., & McHale, S. M. (2010). Provider role attitudes, marital satisfaction, role overload, and housework: A dyadic approach. *Journal of Family Psychology, 24*(5), 568–577. doi:10.1037/a0020637

Helson, R. (1997). The self in middle age. In M. E. Lachman & J. B. James (Eds.), *Multiple paths of midlife development* (pp. 21–43). Chicago: University of Chicago Press.

Helwig, C. C. (1995). Adolescents' and young adults' conceptions of civil liberties: Freedom of speech and religion. *Child Development, 66,* 152–166.

Henry, L. (2001, August). What's going on in your baby's mind? *Baby Talk, 66*(6), 46–50.

Hepper, P. (2006). Prenatal development. In A. Slater and M. Lewis (Eds.), *Introduction to infant development* (2nd ed.). New York: Oxford University Press.

Herman-Giddens, M. E. (2007). The decline in the age of menarche in the United States: Should we be concerned? *Journal of Adolescent Health, 40*(1), 201–203.

Herman-Giddens, M. E., Wang, L., & Koch, G. (2001). Secondary sexual characteristics in boys: Estimates from the national health and nutrition examination survey III, 1988–1994. *Archives of Pediatric and Adolescent Medicine, 155*(9), 1022–1028.

Herodotus. (1964). *The histories* (A. de Selincourt, Trans.). London: Penguin Books.

Herrnstein, R. J., & Murray, C. (1994). *The bell curve: Intelligence and class structure in American life.* New York: Free Press.

Hershatter, A., & Epstein, M. (2010). Millennials and the world of work: An organization and management perspective. *Journal of Business and Psychology, 25*(2), 211–233. doi:10.1007/s10869-010-9160-y

Hershey, J. C., Niederdeppe, J., Evans, W. D., Nonnemaker, J., Blahut, S., Holden, D., . . . , Haviland, M. L. (2005). The theory of "truth": How counterindustry campaigns affect smoking behavior among teens. *Health Psychology, 24*(1), 22–31.

Hetherington, E. M., & Kelly, J. (2003). *For better or for worse: Divorce reconsidered.* New York: Norton.

Hetherington, E. M., & Stanley-Hagan, M. (2002). Parenting in divorced and remarried families. In M. Bornstein (Ed.), *Handbook of parenting: Vol. 3. Being and becoming a parent* (2nd ed., pp. 287–315). Mahwah, NJ: Erlbaum.

Hetherington, E. M., Cox, M., & Cox, R. (1976). Divorced fathers. *Family Coordinator, 25,* 417–427.

Heuveline, P. (2005, November 15). *How do they do that? Estimating the proportion of marriages that end in divorce.* A Research Brief prepared for the Council on Contemporary Families. Chicago, IL: University of Chicago.

Hewitt, H. (2004, December 2). Death by committee: What the Groningen Protocol says about our world, and where it might lead next. *Daily Standard.* Retrieved from http://www.weeklystandard.com

Hewlett, S. A. (2007). Off-ramps and on-ramps: Women's nonlinear career paths. In B. Kellerman & D. L. Rhodes (Eds.), *Women and leadership: The state of play and strategies for change* (pp. 407–430). San Francisco, CA: Jossey-Bass.

Heyge, L. L. (1996). Music makes a difference. *Early Childhood Connections: The Journal of Music and Movement-Based Learning.* Cited in *Early Childhood News.* Retrieved from http:// www .earlychildhoodnews.com/wiredfor.htm

Heymann, J., Earle, A., Simmons, S., Breslow, S., & Kuehnhoff, A. (2007). *The work, family and equity index: Where does the United States stand globally?* The Project on Global Working Families, Boston, MA: Harvard School of Public Health.

Heyneman, S. P. (2005). Student background and student achievement: What is the right question? *American Journal of Education, 112*(1), 1–9. doi:10.1086/444512

Hiedemann, B., Suhomlinova, O., & O'Rand, A. (1998). Economic independence, economic status, and empty nest in midlife marital disruption. *Journal of Marriage and the Family, 60,* 219–231.

Hill, M. A. (2007). Early human development. *Clinical Obstetrics and Gynecology, 50*(1), 2–9.

Hill, R. (1964). Methodological issues in family development research. *Family Process, 3,* 186–206.

Hilleras, P., Herlitz, A., Jorm, A., & Winblad, B. (1998). Negative and positive affect among the very old: A survey on a sample age 90 years or older. *Research on Aging, 20,* 593–610.

Himelstein, B. P., Hilden, J. M., Morstad Boldt, A., & Weissman, D. (2004). Pediatric palliative care. *New England Journal of Medicine, 250,* 1752–1762.

Himes, J. H., Park, K., & Styne, D. (2009). Menarche and assessment of body mass index in adolescent girls. *The Journal of Pediatrics, 155*(3), 393–397.

Hinchliff, G. (2008, Winter). Toddling toward technology: Computer use by very young children. *Children and Libraries,* 47–49.

Hines, M. (2004). Androgen, estrogen, and gender: Contributions of the early hormone environment to gender-related behavior. In A. H. Eagly, A. E. Beall, & R. J. Sternberg (Eds.), *The psychology of gender* (2nd ed., pp. 9–37). New York: Guilford Press.

Hingson, R. W., Zha, W., & Weitzman, E. R. (2009). Magnitude of and trends in alcohol-related mortality and morbidity among U.S. college students ages 18–24, 1998–2005. *Journal of Studies on Alcohol and Drugs, Supplement 16,* 12.

Hiott, A., Grzywacz, J. G., Arcury, T. A., & Quandt, S. A. (2006). Gender differences in anxiety and depression among immigrant Latinos. *Families, Systems, & Health, 24*(2), 137–146.

Hoeft, F., McCandliss, B. D., Black, J. M., Gantman, A., Zakerani, N., Hulme, C., . . . , Gabrieli, J. D. E. (2011). Neural systems predicting long-term outcome in dyslexia. *Proceedings of the National Academy of Sciences (PNAS), 108*(1), 361–366. doi:10.1073/pnas.1008950108

Hofer, S. M., & Sliwinski, M. J. (2006). Design and analysis of longitudinal studies on aging. In J. E. Birren & K. W. Schaie (Eds.), *Handbook of the psychology of aging* (6th ed., pp. 15–37). Boston: Elsevier.

Hoff, E., & Shatz, M. (Eds.). (2007). *Blackwell handbook of language development.* Oxford: Blackwell.

Hofferth, S. L. (1998, November). *Healthy environments, healthy children: Children in families.* Ann Arbor, MI: Institute for Social Research.

Hofferth, S. L. (2010). Home media and children's achievement and behavior. *Child Development, 81*(5), 1598–1619. doi:10.1111/j.1467-8624.2010.01494.x

Hofferth, S. L., & Anderson, K. G. (2003, February). Are all dads equal? Biology versus marriage as a basis for paternal involvement. *Journal of Marriage and Family, 65,* 213–232.

Hoff-Ginsberg, E., & Shatz, M. (1982). Linguistic input and the child's acquisition of language. *Psychological Bulletin, 92,* 3–26.

Hoffman, S. (2006). *By the numbers: The public cost of teen childbearing. National Campaign to Prevent Teen Pregnancy Report.* Milwaukee, WI: National Association of Health Education Centers.

Hofman, A., Jaddoe, V. W., Mackenbach, J. P., Roza, S. J., Steegers, E. A., . . . , Tiemeier, H. (2007). Effects of maternal smoking in pregnancy on prenatal brain development: The generation R study. *European Journal of Neuroscience, 25,* 611–617.

Hogg, M. A., & Cooper, J. (Eds.). (2007). *The SAGE handbook of social psychology.* Thousand Oaks, CA: Sage.

Hojat, M., Shapurian, R., Nayerahmadi, H., Farzaneh, M., Foroughi, D., Parsi, M., & Azizi, M. (1999). Premarital sexual, child rearing, and family attitudes of Iranian men and women in the United States and in Iran. *The Journal of Psychology, 133*(1), 19–31.

Holahan, C. K., & Suzuki, R. (2004). Adulthood predictors of health promoting behavior in later aging. *International Journal of Aging and Human Development, 58*(4), 289–313.

Holmes, E. (2010). The ERA Project: The English and Romanian Adoptee Study: Effects of early deprivation on long-term adjustment. Retrieved from http://www.iop.kcl.ac.uk/departments/?locator=750

Holmes, E. K., & Huston, A. C. (2010). Understanding positive father-child interaction: Children's, fathers', and mothers' contributions. *Fathering, 8*(2), 203–225. doi:10.3149/fth.1802.203

Holden, J. M., Greyson, B., & James, D. (2009). *The handbook of near-death experiences: Thirty years of investigation.* Santa Barbara, CA: Praeger.

Holmes, W. C., & Slap, G. B. (1998). Sexual abuse of boys: Definition, prevalence, correlates, sequelae, and management. *JAMA, 280*(21), 1855–1862.

Holzer, H. J., Schanzenbach, D. W., Duncan, G. J., & Ludwig, J. (2008). The economic costs of childhood poverty in the United States. *Journal of Children and Poverty 14*(1), 41–61. doi:10.1080/10796120701871280

Hong, E., & Perkins, G. (1997). Children's responses to self-concept questionnaire administered in different contexts. *Child Study Journal, 27,* 111.

Hood, L. (2004). *High school students at risk: The challenge of dropouts and push-outs.* New York: Carnegie Corporation of New York. Retrieved from http://www.carnegie .org/pdf/ challenge_dropouts.pdf

Hook, J. (2006). Care in context: Men's unpaid work in 20 countries, 1965–2003. *American Sociological Review, 71*(August), 639–660.

Hooker, S., & Brand, B. (2009, December). *Success at every step: How 23 programs support youth on the path to college and beyond.* Washington, DC: American Youth Policy Forum.

Hopson, J. L. (1998). Fetal psychology: Research shows that a 32-week-old fetus can feel and dream. *Psychology Today, 31*(5), 44–49.

Horn, W. F., & Sylvester, T. (Eds.). (2004). *Father facts* (4th ed.). Gaithersburg, MD: National Fatherhood Initiative. Retrieved from http://www.father-hood.org/father -facts/late.htm

Horneman, G., & Emanuelson, I. (2009). Cognitive outcome in children and young adults who sustained severe and moderate traumatic brain injury 10 years earlier. *Brain Injury, 23*(11), 907–914. doi:10.1080/ 02699050903283239

Hosken, F. P. (1998). *Female genital mutilation: Strategies for eradication.* Retrieved from http://www.nocirc.org/symposia/first/ hosken.html

Hospice Foundation of America (2005). *What is hospice?* Retrieved from http:// www.hospicehoundation.org/hospiceInfo/

Hough, L. (2007). A Head Start they deserve. *Harvard Graduate School of Education.* Retrieved from http://www.gse.harvard .edu/news_events/ed/2007/spring/features/ headstart.html

House of Lords, Select Committee on the Assisted Dying for the Terminally Ill Bill. (2005, April 5). Assisted Dying for the Terminally Ill Bill [HL Paper 86–II]. Retrieved from http://www.publications.parliament .uk/pa/ld200405/ldselect/ldasdy/86/86ii.pdf

Houston, D., Jusczyk, P. W., & Jusczyk, A. M. (2003). Memory for bisyllables in 2-month-olds. In D. Houston, A. Seidl, G. Hollich, E. Johnson, & A. Jusczyk (Eds.), *Jusczyk Lab Final Report.* Retrieved from http://hincapie.psych.purdue.edu/Jusczyk

Howard, B. J., Broughton, D. D., & Committee on Psychosocial Aspects of Child and Family Health. (2004). The pediatrician's role in the prevention of missing children. *Pediatrics, 114*(4), 1100–1105. doi:10 .1542/peds.2004-1397

Howard, E. R., Sugarman, J., Christian, D., Lindholm-Leary, K. J., & Rogers, D. (2007). *Guiding principles for dual language education* (2nd ed.). Washington, DC: Center for Applied Linguistics.

Howard, K. S., Lefever, J. E. B., Borkowski, J. G., & Whitman, T. L. (2006). Fathers' influence in the lives of children with adolescent mothers. *Journal of Family Psychology, 20*(3), 468–476.

Howe, M. L., & Courage, M. L. (1993). On resolving the enigma of infantile amnesia. *Psychological Bulletin, 113,* 305–326.

Hoyer, W. J., & Verhaeghen, P. (2006). Memory aging. In J. E. Birren, K. W. Schaie, R. P. Abeles, M. Gatz, & T. A. Salthouse (Eds.), *Handbook of the psychology of aging* (pp. 209–232). Burlington, MA: Elsevier.

HSLDA. (2009). *Homeschool progress report 2009: Academic achievement and demographics.* Retrieved from http://www.hslda .org/docs/study/ray2009/2009_Ray_Study -FINAL.pdf

Hsu, F. L. K. (1943). Incentives to work in primitive communities. *American Sociological Review, 8,* 638–642.

Hudson, J. I., Hiripi, E., Pope, H. G., & Kessler, R. C. (2007). The prevalence and correlates of eating disorders in the National Comorbidity Survey Replication. *Biological Psychiatry, 61,* 348–358.

Hughes, C., Fujisawa, K. K., Ensor, R., Lecce, S., & Marfleet, R. (2006a). Cooperation and conversations about the mind: A study of individual differences in 2-year-olds and their siblings. *British Journal of Developmental Psychology, 24,* 53–72. doi:10.1348/026151005X82893

Hughes, C., Jaffee, S. E., Happé, F., Taylor, A., Caspi, A., & Moffitt, T. (2005). Origins of individual difference in theory of mind: From nature to nurture? *Child Development, 76*(2), 356–370. doi:10.1111/ j.1467-8624.2005.00850.x

Hughes, D., Bachman, M. A., Ruble, D. N., & Fuligni, A. (2006b). Tuned in or tuned out: Parents' and children's interpretation of parental racial/ethnic socialization practices. In L. Balter (Ed.), *Child psychology: A handbook of contemporary issues* (2nd ed., pp. 591–610). New York: Psychology Press.

Hughes, D., Rodriguez, J., Smith, E. P., Johnson, D. J., Stevenson, H. C., & Spicer, P. (2006c). Parents' ethnic-racial socialization practices: A review of research and directions for future study. *Developmental Psychology, 42*(5), 747–770.

Hull, L., May, J., Farrell-Moore, D., & Svikis, D. S. (2010). Treatment of cocaine abuse during pregnancy: Translating

research to clinical practice. *Current Psychiatry Report 12*(5), 454–461. doi:10.1007/ s11920-010-0138-2

Humecky, J. (2005, April 28). Tai Chi, a healthy practice for life. *Mendocino Beacon.* Retrieved from http://www.mendocinobea con.com

Hummert, M. L. (2007). As family members age: A research agenda for family communication. *The Journal of Family Communication, 7*(1), 3–21.

Humphrey, T. (1978). Function of the nervous system during prenatal life. In U. Stave (Ed.), *Perinatal physiology.* Hillsdale, NJ: Erlbaum.

Hundley, G. (2006). Family background and the propensity for self-employment. *Industrial Relations, 45*(3), 377–392.

Hunter, S., Sundel, S. S., & Sundel, M. (2002). *Women at midlife: Life experiences and implications for the helping professions.* Washington, DC: NASW Press.

Huston, A. C., & Wright, J. C. (1998, May). Television & the informational & educational needs of children. *Annals of the American Academy of Political and Social Science, Children and Television, 557,* 9–23.

Huston, A. C., Wright, J. C., Rice, M. L., Kerkman, D., & St. Peters, M. (1990). Development of television viewing patterns in early childhood: A longitudinal investigation. *Developmental Psychology, 26,* 409–420.

Huston, T. L., Caughlin, J. P., Houts, R. M., Smith, S. E., & George, L. J. (2001). The connubial crucible: Newlywed years as predictors of marital delight, distress, and divorce. *Journal of Personality and Social Psychology, 80*(2), 237–252.

Hutson, S. (2009). NIH draft seen as "working compromise." *Nature Medicine, 15*(6), 589–601. doi:10.1038/nm0609-585

Huttenlocher, J., Vasilyeva, M. Waterfall, H. R., Vevea, J. L., & Hedges, L. V. (2007). The varieties of speech to young children. *Developmental Psychology, 43*(5), 1062–1083.

Huyck, M. H., & Gutmann, D. L. (2007). Men and their wives: Why are some married men vulnerable at midlife? In V. H. Bedord & B. F. Turner (Eds.), *Men in relationships: A new look from a life course perspective* (pp. 27–50). New York: Springer.

Hwang, Y. S., & Vrongistinos, K. (2010). Hispanic parents' perceptions of children's education. *Education, 130*(4), 595–602. Retrieved from http://theresadehoyos.com/ ruiz_summer/Hwang.pdf

Hyde, D. M. (1959). *An investigation of Piaget's theories of the development of number.* Unpublished doctoral dissertation, University of London.

Hyde, J. S. (2005). The gender similarity hypothesis. *American Psychologist, 60*(6), 581–592. doi:10.1037/0003-066X.60.6.581

Hyde, J. S., Krajnik, M., & Skuldt-Niederberger, K. (1991). Androgyny across the life span: A replication and longitudinal follow-up. *Developmental Psychology, 27,* 516–519.

Hymowitz, K. S. (2003). *Liberation's children: Parents and kids in a postmodern age.* Chicago: Ivan R. Dee.

Hymowitz, K. S. (2007a). Father's Day without fathers: A melancholy occasion for millions of American kids. *City Journal, 17*(2). Retrieved from http:// www.city-journal .org/html/eon2007-06-15kh.html

Hymowitz, K. S. (2007b). The incredible shrinking father. *City Journal, 17*(2). Retrieved from http://www.city-journal.org/ html/issue_17_2.html

Hyson, M. C. (1994). *The emotional development of young children: Building an emotion-centered curriculum.* New York: Teachers College Press.

Hyson, M. C. (2004). *The emotional development of young children: Building an emotion-centered curriculum* (2nd ed.) New York: Teachers College Press.

Iams, H. M., Reznik G. L., & Tamborini, C. R. (2009). Earning sharing in Social Security: Projected impacts of alternative proposals using the MINT model. *Social Security Bulletin, 69*(1), 1–17.

Ickovics, J. R., Kershaw, T. S., Westdahl, C., Magriples, U., Massey, Z., Reynolds, H., . . . , Schindler Rising, S. (2007). Group prenatal care and perinatal outcomes. *Obstetrics & Gynecology, 110*(2), 330–339.

Iglehart, J. K. (2010, August 5). Health reform, primary care, and graduate medical education. *New England Journal of Medicine, 363*(6), 584–590.

Ilies, R., Schwind, K. M., Wagner, D. T., Johnson, M. D., DeRue, D. S., & Ilgen, D. R. (2007). When can employees have a family life? The effects of daily workload and affect on work–family conflict and social behaviors at home. *Journal of Applied Psychology, 92*(5), 1368–1379.

Im Thurn, E. F. (1883). *Among the Indians of Guiana.* London: Kegan Paul, Trench & Trubner.

Inagaki, K., & Hatano, G. (1993). Young children's understanding of the mind-body distinction. *Child Development, 64,* 1534–1549.

Information about anaphylaxis. (2005). The Food Allergy and Anaphylaxis Network. Retrieved from http:// www.foodallergy .org/anaphylaxis.html

Inhelder, B., & Piaget, J. (1964). *The early growth of logic in the child.* New York: Norton.

Insel, P., Turner, R. E., & Ross, D. (2010). *Discovering nutrition.* Sudbury, MA: Jones and Bartlett.

Insel, P. M., & Roth, W. T. (2008). *Core concepts in health* (10th ed., updated). New York: McGraw-Hill.

Institute for Women's Policy Research. (2007). *Fact sheet: Maternity leave in the United States.* [News release.] Retrieved from http://www.iwpr.org/pdf/parental leaveA131.pdf

Institute for Women's Policy Research. (2010). *Fact sheet: The gender wage gap, 2009.* [News release.] Retrieved from http:// www.iwpr.org/pdf/C350.pdf

International Society for Clinical Densitometry. (2007). Osteoporosis statistics. Retrieved from www.vocusgr.com/gr/Newsroom/ ViewAttachment.aspx?SiteName=ISCD& Entity=PRAsset&AttachmentType=F& EntityID= 355&AttachmentID=4dbbc86f -f2f7-4a94-8a79-e096d29e3c20.

International Task Force. (2005). *Assisted suicide & death with dignity.* Retrieved from www.international-taskforce.org/ rpt2005_3html.

Intersex Society of North America. (2010). What is intersex? Retrieved from http:// www.isna.org/faq/what_is_intersex

Ireland, J. L., & Culpin, V. (2006). The relationship between sleeping problems and aggression, anger, and impulsivity in a population of juvenile and young offenders. *Journal of Adolescent Health, 38,* 649–655.

Irwin, D., & Cardenas, G. (2008). *Most working women will struggle to retire: Groups highlight problems and solutions.* AARP [News release]. Retrieved from http://www.dol.gov/wb/media/ pressAARP .htm

Irwin, H. J. (1985). *Flight of mind: A psychological study of the out-of-body experience.* Metuchen, NJ: Scarecrow Press.

Ivey, P. (2000). Cooperative reproduction in Ituri Forest hunter-gatherers: Who cares for Efé infants? *Current Anthropology, 41*(5), 856–866.

Izard, C. E. (2001). Emotional intelligence or adaptive emotions? *Emotion, 1,* 249–257.

Izard, C. E. (2004). *The psychology of emotions.* New York: Plenum Press.

Izard, C. E. (2007). Levels of emotion and levels of consciousness. *Behavioral and Brain Sciences, 30,* 96–98.

Izard, C. E., Fine, S. E., Mostow, A. J., Trentacosta, C. J., & Campbell, J. (2002). Emotion processes in normal and abnormal development and preventive intervention. *Development and Psychopathology, 14*(4), 761–787.

Izard, C. E., & King, K. A. (2009). Differential emotions theory. In K. Scherer (Ed.), *Oxford Companion to the Affective Sciences* (pp. 117–119). New York: Oxford University Press.

Izard, C. E., & Malatesta, C. Z. (1987). Perspectives on emotional development: Differential emotions theory of early emotional development. In J. D. Osofsky (Ed.), *Handbook of infant development* (2nd ed., pp. 494–554). New York: Wiley.

Izard, C. E., Hembree, E. A., & Huebner, R. R. (1987). Infants' emotion expressions to acute pain: Developmental change and stability of individual differences. *Developmental Psychology, 23,* 105–113.

Jacklin, C. N., & Reynolds, C. (1993). Gender and childhood socialization. In A. E. Beall & R. J. Sternberg (Eds.), *The psychology of gender* (pp. 197–214). New York: Guilford Press.

Jackson, A., Brooks-Gunn, J., Huang, C., & Glassman, M. (2000). Single mothers in low-wage jobs: Financial strain, parenting, and preschoolers' outcomes. *Child Development, 71*(5), 1409–1423.

Jackson, J., Balota, D. A., & Head, D. (2009). Exploring the relationship between personality and regional brain volume in healthy aging. *Neurobiology of Aging.* doi:10.1016/j .neurobiolaging.2009.12.009

Jackson, J. F. (1993). Multiple caregiving among African Americans and infant attachment. The need for an emic approach. *Human Development, 36,* 87–102.

Jackson, S. A., & Savaiano, D. A. (2001). Lactose maldigestion, calcium intake and osteoporosis in African-, Asian-, and Hispanic-Americans. *Journal of the American College of Nutrition, 20*(2 Suppl), 198S–207S.

Jacobs, J. E., Vernon, M. K., & Eccles, J. (2005). Activity choices in middle childhood: The role of gender, self-belief, and parents' influence. In J. L. Mahoney, R. Larson, & J. S. Eccles (Eds.), *Organized activities as contexts of development: Extracurricular activities, after school, and community programs* (pp. 245–254). Mahwah, NJ: Erlbaum.

Jacobs, S. (2003). Death by voluntary dehydration—What the caregivers say. *New England Journal of Medicine, 349,* 325–326.

Jacobsen, T., Edelstein, W., & Hofmann, V. (1994). A longitudinal study of the relation between representations of attachment in childhood and cognitive functioning in childhood and adolescence. *Developmental Psychology, 30,* 112–124.

Jacoby, R., Oppenheimer, C., Dening, T., & Thomas, A. (2008). *Oxford textbook of old-age psychiatry.* New York: Oxford University Press.

Jaffe, J., Beebe, B., Feldstein, S., Crown, C. J., & Jasnow, M. D. (2001). Rhythms of dialogue in infancy. *Monographs of the Society for Research in Child Development, 66,* 1–132. doi:10.2307/3181589

Jago, R., Fox, K. R., Page, A. S., Brockman, R., & Thompson, J. L. (2010). Parent and child physical activity and sedentary time: Do active parents foster active children? *BMC Public Health, 10*(194), 1–9. doi:10 .1186/1471-2458-10-194

James, S. L. (1990). *Normal language acquisition.* Boston: Allyn & Bacon.

Jamra, R. A., Fuerst, R., Kaneva, R., Diaz, G. O., Rivas, F., Mayoral, F., . . . , Schumacher, J. (2007). The first genomewide interaction and locus-heterogeneity linkage scan in bipolar affective disorder: Strong evidence of epistatic effects between loci on chromosomes 2q and 6q. *American Journal of Human Genetics, 81*(5), 974–986.

Jang, K. L., Dick, D. M., Wolfe, H., Livesley, W. J., & Paris, J. (2005). Psychosocial adversity and emotional instability: An application of gene-environment interaction model. *European Journal of Personality, 19,* 359–372.

Jaswal, V. K., & Fernald, A. (2007). Learning to communicate. In A. Slater & M. Lewis (Eds.), *Introduction to infant development.* New York: Oxford University Press

Jayson, S. (2006, October 23). Generation Y gets involved. *USA Today,* p. 1D.

Jedrziewski, K. M., Ewbank, D. C., Wang, H., & Trajanowski, J. Q. (2010). Exercise and cognition: Results from the national long term care survey. *Alzheimer's & Dementia, 6*(1), 448–455.

Jeffers, F. C., & Verwoerdt, A. (1969). How the old face death. In E. W. Busse & E. Pfeiffer (Eds.), *Behavior and adaptation in late life.* Boston: Little, Brown.

Jemal, A., Ward, E., & Thune, M. (2007). Recent trends in breast cancer incidence rates by age and tumor characteristics among U.S. women. *Breast Cancer Research, 9*(3), 1–6.

Jemmott, J., Jemmott, L., & Fong, G. (2010). Efficacy of a theory-based abstinence-only intervention over 24 months: A randomized controlled trial with young adolescents. *Archives of Pediatrics & Adolescent Medicine, 164*(2), 152–159. Retrieved from EBSCO*host.*

Jencks, C. (1972). *Inequality: A reassessment of the effect of family and schooling in America.* New York: Basic Books.

Jenkins, A. (2007). Binge eating: The hidden disease. *Primary Health Care, 17*(4), 19–21.

Jenkins, R., Fitch, C., Hurlston, M., & Walker, M. (2009). Recession, debt, and mental health: Challenges and solutions. *Mental Health in Family Medicine, 6*(2), 85–90.

Jensen, A. R. (1972, Summer). The heritability of intelligence. *Saturday Evening Post,* 149.

Jensen, A. R. (1984, March). Political ideologies and educational research. *Phi Delta Kappan, 65,* 460–462.

Jensen, K. (1932). Differential reactions to taste and temperature stimuli in newborn infants. *Genetic Psychological Monographs, 12,* 363–479.

Jessor, R., Turbin, M. S., & Costa, F. M. (1998). Protective factors in adolescent health behavior. *Journal of Personality and Social Psychology, 75,* 788–800.

Jiménez-Cruz, A., Castellón-Zaragoza, A. M., García-Gallardo, J. L., Bacardí-Gascon, M., & Hovell, M. F. (2008). Strong beliefs on personal responsibilities and negative attitudes towards the child with obesity among teachers and parents. *Revista Biomédica, 19*(2), 84–91.

Johansson, U. (1998). The transformation of gendered work: Dualistic stereotypes and paradoxical reality. *Gender, Work and Organization, 5*(1), 43–58. doi:10.1111/1468-0432.00045

John-Steiner, V. (1986). *Notebooks of the mind: Explorations of thinking.* Albuquerque: University of New Mexico Press.

Johnson, A. S., Heitgerd, J., Koenig, L. J., VanHandel, M., Branson, B. M., Connelly, E., . . . , Valleroy, L. A. (2010, December 3). Vital signs: HIV testing and diagnosis among adults—United States, 2001–2009. *MMWR Weekly, 59*(47), 1550–1555.

Johnson, C. N. (1990). If you had my brain, where would I be? Children's understanding of the brain and identity. *Child Development, 61,* 962–972.

Johnson, C. P., & Myers, S. M. (2007). Identification and evaluation of children with autism spectrum disorders. *Pediatrics, 120*(5), 1183–1215.

Johnson, D. (1994, September 21). Study says small schools are key to learning. *New York Times,* p. B12.

Johnson, G., & Losos, J. (2008). *The living world* (5th ed.). New York: McGraw-Hill.

Johnson, R. W. (2004, July). Do spouses coordinate their retirement decisions? *Issue in Brief,* No. 19. Boston, MA: Center for Retirement Research at Boston College.

Johnson, S., Slemmer, J., & Amso, D. (2004). Where infants look determines how they see: Eye movements and object perception performance in 3-month-olds. *Infancy 6*(2), 185–201. doi:10.1207/s15327078in0602_3

Johnson, W., & Bouchard, T. J. (2005). The structure of human intelligence: It is verbal, perceptual, and image rotation (VPR), not fluid and crystallized. *Intelligence, 33*(4), 393–416.

Johnston, L. (1979, June 17). Artist ends her life after ritual citing "self-termination" right. *New York Times, 1,* 10.

Johnston, L. D., O'Malley, P. M., Bachman, J. G., & Schulenberg, J. E. (2006, December 21). *Teen drug use continues down in 2006, particularly among older teens; but use of prescription-type drugs remains high.* Ann Arbor, MI: University of Michigan News and Information Services.

Johnston, L. D., O'Malley, P. M., Bachman, J. G., & Schulenberg, J. E. (2010). *Monitoring the Future national survey results on drug use, 1975–2009.* Volume I: Secondary school students (NIH Publication No. 10-7584). Bethesda, MD: National Institute on Drug Abuse.

Joint United Nations Programme on HIV/AIDS. (2010). *Global report: UNAIDS report on the global AIDS epidemic 2010.* Retrieved from http://www.unaids.org/documents/20101123_GlobalReport_em.pdf

Jolliffe, C. J., & Janssen, I. (2006). Vascular risks and management of obesity in children and adolescents. *Vascular Health and Risk Management, 2*(2), 171–187.

Jones, L. W., Haykowsky, M. J., Swartz, J. J., Douglas, P. S., & Mackey, J. R. (2007). Early breast cancer therapy and cardiovascular injury. *Journal of the American College of Cardiology, 50*(15), 1435–1441.

Jones, M. C. (1957). The later careers of boys who were early- or late-maturing. *Child Development, 28,* 113–128.

Jones, M. C., & Bayley, N. (1950). Physical maturing among boys as related to behavior. *Journal of Educational Psychology, 41,* 129–148.

Jones, R. K., & Kooistra, K. (2011). Abortion incidence and access to services in the United States, 2008. *Perspectives on Sexual and Reproductive Health, 43*(1), 41–50. Retrieved from http://www.guttmacher.org/pubs/journals/4304111.pdf

Jónsdóttir, V. (2001). *Early intervention as a framework for music therapy with caretakers and their special-needs infants.* Unpublished thesis. Sognog Fjordane University College, Sandane, Norway. Retrieved from http://www.voices.no/ mainissues/mi40004000140.html

Josselson, R. (1988). *Finding herself: Pathways to identity development in women.* New York: Jossey-Bass.

Josselson, R., Lieblich, A., & McAdams, D. P. (2007). *The meaning of others: Narrative studies of relationships.* Washington, DC: APA Books.

Jotkowitz, A. B., & Glick, S. (2006). The Groningen protocol: Another perspective. *Journal of Medical Ethics, 32*(3), 157–158. doi:10.1136/jme.2005.012476

Joyner, A. (2003, September). No strings attached: Wireless networks provide students with anytime, anywhere access. *American School Board Journal,* Special Report. Retrieved from http://www.asbj.com/specialreports/ 0903SpecialReports/S5.html

Juby, H., Billette, J. M., Laplante, B., & Le Bourdais, C. (2007). Nonresident fathers and children: Parents' new unions and frequency of contact. *Journal of Family Issues, 28*(9), 1220–1245.

Jung, C. G. (1933). *Modern man in search of a soul.* New York: Harcourt, Brace & World.

Jung, C. G. (1960). The stages of life. In H. Reed, M. Fordham, & G. Adler (Eds.), *Collected works* (Vol. 8). Princeton, NJ: Princeton University Press. (Original work published 1931.)

Jung, M. K., Callaci, J. J., Lauing, K. L., Otis, J. S., Radek, K. A., Jones, M. K., & Kovacs, E. J. (2010). Alcohol exposure and mechanisms of tissue injury and repair. *Alcoholism, Clinical and Experimental Research, 35*(3), 392–399. doi: 10.1111/j.1530-0277.2010.01356.x.

Jung, S., & Stone, S. (2008). Sociodemographic and programmatic moderators of Early Head Start: Evidence from the National Early Head Start Research and Evaluation Project. *Children & Schools, 30*(3), 149–157.

Jusko, T. A., Henderson, C. R., Lanphear, B. P., Cory-Slechta, D. A., Parsons, P. J., & Canfield, R. L. (2008). Blood lead concentrations < 10 μg/dL and child intelligence at 6 years of age. *Environmental Health Perspectives, 116*(2), 243–248. doi:10.1289/ehp.10424

Juster, F. T., Ono, H., & Stafford, F. P. (2004, November). Changing times of American youth: 1981–2003. Ann Arbor, MI: Institute for Social Research, University of Michigan. [News Release.] Retrieved from http://www.umich.edu/news/releases/2004/Nov04/teen-time_report.pdf

Kagan, J. (1972). A conception of early adolescence. In J. Kagan & R. Coles (Eds.), *Twelve to sixteen: Early adolescence.* New York: Norton.

Kagan, J. (1983). Stress and coping in early development. In N. Garmezy & M. Rutter (Eds.), *Stress, coping, and development.* New York: McGraw-Hill.

Kagan, J. (1993). On the nature of emotion. *Monographs of the Society for Research in Child Development, 59*(2–3, Serial No. 240).

Kagan, J. (1997). Temperament and the reactions to unfamiliarity. *Child Development, 68*(1), 139–143.

Kagan, J., & Fox, N. A. (2006). Biology, culture, and temperamental biases. In W. Damon, R. M. Lerner, & N. Eisenberg (Eds.), *Handbook of child psychology* (6th ed., Vol. 3, pp. 167–225). New York: Wiley.

Kagan, J., & Herschkowitz, N. (2005). *A young mind in a growing brain.* New York: Routledge.

Kagan, J., & Snidman, N. (1991). Temperamental factors in human development. *American Psychologist, 46,* 856–862.

Kağitçibaşi, C. (2007). *Family, self, and human development across cultures.* Mahwah, NJ: Erlbaum.

Kaiser Family Foundation. (2005). *U.S. teen sexual activity.* Retrieved from http://www.douglascountyaidsproject.org/LetsTalk.files/Info.US-Teen-Sexual-Activity.pdf

Kaiser Family Foundation. (2007, December). *Women's health insurance coverage.* Retrieved from http://www.kff.org/womenshealth/upload/6000_06.pdf.

Kaiser Family Foundation. (2009). *States moving toward comprehensive healthcare reform.* Retrieved from http://www.kff.org/uninsured/kcmu_statehealthreform.cfm

Kalter, H. (2004, January–February). Teratology in the 20th century: Environmental causes of congenital malformations in humans and how they were established. *Neurotoxicology and Teratology, 26*(1), 1–12.

Kamerman, J. B. (1988). *Death in the midst of life: Social and cultural influences on death, grief, and mourning.* Englewood Cliffs, NJ: Prentice Hall.

Kamin, L. J. (1974). *The science and politics of IQ.* Hillsdale, NJ: Erlbaum.

Kamin, L. J. (1981). Commentary. In S. Scarr (Ed.), *IQ: Race, social class, and individual differences.* Hillsdale, NJ: Erlbaum.

Kamin, L. J. (1994, November 23). Intelligence, IQ tests, and race. *Chronicle of Higher Education,* p. B5.

Kamp Dush, C. M., Taylor, M. G., & Kroeger, R. A. (2008). Marital happiness and psychological well-being across the life course. *Family Relations, 57*(2), 211–226.

Kang, S. Y. (2006). Predictors of emotional strain among spouse and adult child caregivers. *Journal of Gerontological Social Work, 47*(1–2), 107–131. doi:10.1300/J083v47n01_08

Kanner, L. (1943). Autistic disturbances of affective contact. *Nervous Child, 2,* 217–250. Retrieved from http://affect.media.mit.edu/Rgrads/Articles/pdfs/Kanner-1943-OrigPaper.pdf

Kaplan, P. S., Bachorowski, J. & Zarlengo-Strouse, P. (1999, June). Child-directed speech produced by mothers with symptoms of depression fails to promote associative learning in 4-month-old infants. *Child Development, 70,* 560–570.

Kaplowitz, P. B. (2008). Link between body fat and the timing of puberty. *Pediatrics, 121,* S208–S217. doi:10.1542/peds.2007-1813F

Karasik, S. (2000, April 14). *Experts: More latchkey kids means more trouble—High risk behavior increases when parents are gone.* APB News. Retrieved from http://www.apbnews.com/safetycenter/family/2000/04/14/sitter0414_01.html

Karoly, L. A., & Zissimopoulos, J. (2003, December). Self-employment trends and patterns among older U.S. workers. Working paper for the RAND Labor and Population. Retrieved from http:// rand.org/pubs/working_papers/WR136/WR136.pdf

Karpiak, S. E., Shippy, R. A., & Cantor, M. H. (2006). *Research on older adults with HIV.* New York: AIDS Community Research Initiative of America.

Kasen, S., Chen, H., Sneed, J., Crawford, T., & Cohen, P. (2006). Social role and birth cohort influences on gender-linked personality traits in women: A 20-year longitudinal analysis. *Journal of Personality and Social Psychology, 91*(5), 944–958.

Kasland, K. (2008, October). Power play: Gamers get up and get moving. *Current Health 2, a Weekly Reader Publication,* p. 16. Retrieved from http://www.highbeam.com/doc/1G1-193406262.html

Kastenbaum, R. (1975). Is death a life crisis? On the confrontation with death in theory and practice. In N. Datan & L. H. Ginsbuerg (Eds.), *Lifespan developmental psychology: Normative life crisis.* New York: Academic Press.

Kastenbaum, R. (1977, September). Temptations from the ever after. *Human Behavior, 6,* 28–33.

Kastenbaum, R. (1991). Where do we come from? What are we? Where are we going?

An annotated bibliography of aging and humanities by Donna Polisar, Larry Wygant, Thomas Cole, and Cielo Perdomo. *International Journal of Aging and Human Development, 33,* 247.

Kastenbaum, R. (2004). Death writ large. *Death Studies, 28*(4), 375–392.

Kastenbaum, R. (2007). *Death, society, and human experience* (9th ed.). Boston: Pearson Education.

Kastenbaum, R., & Costa, P. T., Jr. (1977). Psychological perspectives on death. In M. R. Rosenzweig & L. W. Porter (Eds.), *Annual review of psychology* (Vol. 28). Palo Alto, CA: Annual Reviews.

Katchadourian, H. A. (1985). *Fundamentals of human sexuality.* New York: Holt, Rinehart & Winston.

Katz, E. (2007). A family therapy perspective on mediation. *Family Process, 46*(1), 93–107.

Katz, I., Kaplan, A., & Gueta, G. (2010). Students' needs, teachers' support, and motivation for doing homework: A cross-sectional study. *The Journal of Experimental Education, 78,* 246–267. doi:10.1080/00220970903292868

Katzmarzyk, P. T., Bray, G. A., Greenway, F. L., Johnson, W. D., Newton, R. L. Jr., Ravussin, E., . . . , Bouchard, C. (2011). Ethnic-specific BMI and waist circumference thresholds. *Obesity,* doi:10.1038/oby.2010.319

Katz, P. A. (2003, November). Racists or tolerant multiculturalists? How do they begin? *American Psychologist, 58,* 897–909.

Kaufman, G., & Taniguchi, H. (2006). Gender and marital happiness in later life. *Journal of Family Issues, 27*(6), 735–757.

Kaufman, H. G. (1982). *Professionals in search of work: Coping with the stress of job loss and underemployment.* New York: Wiley.

Kaufman, J., & Zigler, E. (1993). The intergenerational transmission of abuse is overstated. In R. J. Gelles and D. R. Loseke (Eds.), *Current controversies on family violence* (pp. 209–221). Newbury Park, CA: Sage.

Kausler, D. H., Kausler, B. C., & Krupsaw, J. A. (2007). *The essential guide to aging in the twenty-first century: An everyday guide to mind, body, and behavior.* Columbia: University of Missouri Press.

Kausler, D. H., Wiley, J. G., & Lieberwitz, K. J. (1992). Adult age differences in short-term memory and subsequent long-term memory for actions. *Psychology and Aging, 7,* 309–316.

Kavanah, M. (2007). *Patient information: Lymphedema after breast cancer surgery.* Retrieved from http://patients.uptodate.com/topic.asp?file=cancer/6211

Kavanaugh, R. D. (2006). Pretend play. In B. Spodek & O. N. Saracho (Eds.), *Handbook of research on the education of young children* (2nd ed., pp. 269–276). Mahwah, NJ: Erlbaum.

Kazdin, A. E. (Ed.). (2000). *Encyclopedia of psychology* (Vol. 4). New York: Oxford University Press.

Kazdin, A. E., Marciano, P. L., & Whitley, M. (2005). The therapeutic alliance in cognitive-behavioral treatment of children referred for oppositional, aggressive, and antisocial behavior. *Journal of Consulting and Clinical Psychology, 73,* 726–730.

Keefer, C. H., Tronick, E., Dixon, S., & Brazelton, T. B. (1982). Special differences in motor performance between Gusii and American newborns and a modification of the neonatal behavioral assessment scale. *Child Development, 53,* 754–759.

Keenan, T. A. (2006). Physical activity survey, 2006. Washington, DC: AARP. Retrieved from http://www.aarp.org/research/health/ healthquality/ fitness_06.html.

Keener, D., Goodman, K., Lowry, A., Zaro, S., & Kettel Khan, L. (2009). Recommended community strategies and measurements to prevent obesity in the United States: Implementation and measurement guide. Atlanta, GA: U.S. Department of Health and Human Services, Centers for Disease Control and Prevention.

Kegan, R. (1988). *In over our head.* Boston: Harvard University Press.

Keil, F. (2006). Cognitive science and cognitive development. In D. Kuhn, R. Siegler, W. Damon, & R. M. Lerner (Eds.), *Handbook of child psychology* (6th ed., pp. 609–635). New York: Wiley.

Keller, B. (2001). Schools seen as out of sync with teens. *Education Week, 20*(33), 17–18.

Keller, H. (2007). *Cultures of infancy.* Mahwah, NJ: Erlbaum.

Kellogg, N. (2005). The evaluation of sexual abuse in children. *Pediatrics, 116*(2), 506–512.

Kellogg, N. D., & Committee on Child Abuse and Neglect. (2007). Evaluation of suspected child physical abuse. *Pediatrics, 119*(6), 1232–1241.

Kelly, G. A. (1955). *The psychology of personal constructs.* New York: Norton.

Kelly, J. B. (2007). Children's living arrangements following separation and divorce: Insights from empirical and clinical research. *Family Process, 46*(1), 35–52.

Kemper, A. R. (2006). Preschool vision screening in pediatric practices. *Clinical Pediatrics, 45*(3), 263–266.

Kennedy, H. P., Erickson-Owens, D., & Davis, J. P. (2006). Voices of diversity in midwifery: A qualitative research study. *Journal of Midwifery & Women's Health, 51*(2), 85–90.

Kenney, C. T., & McLanahan, S. S. (2006). Why are cohabiting relationships more violent than marriage? *Demography, 43*(1), 127–140.

Kenrick, D. T., Griskevicius, V., Neuberg, S. L., & Schaller, M. (2010). Renovating the Pyramid of Needs: Contemporary extensions built upon ancient foundations.

Perspectives on Psychological Science, 5(3), 292–314. doi:10.1177/1745691610369469

Kerig, P. K., Cowan, P. A., & Cowan, C. P. (1993). Marital quality and gender differences in parent-child interaction. *Developmental Psychology, 29,* 931–939.

Kessler, D. (2010). *Visions, trips, and crowded rooms. Who and what you see before you die.* Carlsbad, CA: Hay House.

Kessler, S. (2010). 4 effective tools for monitoring your child's online safety. Retrieved from http://mashable.com/2010/12/07/ child-online-safety/#

Khan, D. A., Qayyum, S., Saleem, S., Ansari, W. M., & Khan, F. A. (2010). Lead exposure and its adverse health effects among occupational workers' children. *Toxicology and Industrial Health, 26*(8), 497–504. doi:10.1177/0748233710373085

Kilbride, H. W., Thorstad, K., & Daily, D. (2004, April). Preschool outcome of less than 801-gram preterm infants compared with full-term siblings. *Pediatrics, 113,* 742–747.

Kileny, P. R., Zwolan, T. A., & Ashbaugh, C. (2001). The influence of age at implantation on performance with a cochlear implant in children. *Otology and Neurotology, 22,* 42–46.

Killen, M., & Smetana, J. (Eds.). (2006). *Handbook of moral development.* Mahwah, NJ: Erlbaum.

Kim, C. C., & Rector, R. (2010, February 19). Evidence on the effectiveness of abstinence education: An update. *Executive Summary: Backgrounder, 2372.* Washington, DC: The Heritage Foundation.

Kim, H. H., & Barrs, D. M. (2006). Hearing aids: A review of what's new. *American Academy of Otolaryngology, 134*(6), 1043–1050. doi:10.1016/j.otohns.2006.03.010

Kim, J. Y., McHale, S. M., Crouter, A. C., & Osgood, D. W. (2007). Longitudinal linkages between sibling relationships and adjustment from middle childhood through adolescence. *Developmental Psychology, 43*(4), 960–973.

Kim, S. A., Stein, A. D., & Martorell, R. (2007). Country development and the association between parity and overweight. *International Journal of Obesity, 31*(5), 805–812. doi:10.1038/sj.ijo.0803478

Kimble, G. A. (1984). Psychology's two cultures. *American Psychologist, 39*(8), 833–839.

Kimmel, D., Rose, T., & David, S. (Eds.). (2006). *Lesbian, gay, bisexual, and transgender aging: Research and clinical perspectives* (2nd ed). Irvington, NY: Columbia University Press.

Kincheloe, J. L., & Steinberg, S. R. (1993). A tentative description of post-formal thinking: The critical confrontation with cognitive theory. *Harvard Educational Review, 63,* 296–320.

King, M. A., Sims, A., & Osher, D. (2001). *How is cultural competence integrated in education?* Center for Effective

Collaboration and Practice. Washington, DC. Retrieved from http:// www.air.org/ cecp/cultural/Q_integrated.htm#top

King, N. J., Muris, P., Ollendick, T. H., & Gullone, E. (2005). Childhood fears and phobias: Advances in assessment and treatment. *Behaviour Change, 4,* 99–211.

King, P. E., & Furrow, J. L. (2008). Religion as a resource for positive youth development: Religion, social capital, and moral outcomes. *Psychology of Religion and Spirituality, S*(1), 34–49. doi:10.1037/ 1941-1022.S.1.34

King, R. (2005, April 13). More teens say smoking is a drag, survey says. *The Indianapolis Star.* Retrieved from http://www .indystar.com/

King, R. A., & Apter, A. (2003). *Suicide in children and adolescents.* New York: Cambridge University Press.

King, V., & Scott, M. E. (2005). A comparison of cohabiting relationships among older and younger adults. *Journal of Marriage and Family, 67*(2), 271–185.

Kinnish, K. K., Strassberg, D. S., Turner, C. W. (2005). Sex differences in the flexibility of sexual orientation: A multidimensional retrospective assessment. *Archives of Sexual Behavior, 34*(2), 173–183.

Kins, E., Beyers, W., Soenens, B., & Vansteenkiste, M. (2009). Patterns of home leaving and subjective well-being in emerging adulthood: The role of motivational processes and parental autonomy support. *Developmental Psychology, 45*(5), 1416–1429.

Kinsey, A. C., Pomeroy, W. B., Martin, C. E., & Gebhard, P. H. (1953). *Sexual behavior in the human female.* Philadelphia: Saunders.

Kinsey Institute. (2007). *Infidelity.* Retrieved from http:// www.kinseyinstitute.org/ resources/FAQ.html#Infidelity.

Kinsey Institute. (2010). *Infidelity.* Retrieved from http://www.iub.edu/~kinsey/ resources/FAQ.html#Infidelity

Kinsman, S. B., Romer, D., Furstenberg, F. F., & Schwarz, D. F. (1998). Early sexual initiation: The role of peer norms. *Pediatrics, 102,* 1185–1192.

Kirby, D. B. (2008). The impact of abstinence and comprehensive sex and STD/HIV education programs on adolescent sexual behavior. *Sexuality Research and Social Policy, 5*(3), 18–27. doi:10.1525/srsp.2008.5.3.18

Kirby, J. B., & Lau, D. T. (2010). Community and individual race/ethnicity and home health care use among elderly persons in the United States. *Health Services Research, 45*(5), 1251–1267. doi:10.1111/j.1475-6773 .2010.01135.x

Kirkendoll, S. (2010, March 13). Children who eat school lunches more likely to be overweight: Findings by University of Michigan Cardiovascular Center show need for initiatives such as Project Healthy Schools, which teaches sixth-graders heart-healthy lifestyles. [News Release]. Retrieved from http://www2.med.umich.edu/prmc/media/newsroom/details.cfm?ID=1514

Kirkorian, H. L., Wartella, E. A., & Anderson, D. R. (2008). Media and young children's learning. *The Future of Children, 18*(1), 39–61.

Kirp, D. L. (2004, November 21). Life way after Head Start. *New York Times Magazine.* Retrieved from http://www.nytimes.com/2004/11/21/magazine/21IDEA.html

Kirsh, G., McVey, G., Tweed, S., & Katzman, D. K. (2007). Psychosocial profiles of young adolescent females seeking treatment for an eating disorder. *Journal of Adolescent Health, 40,* 351–356.

Kisilevsky, B. S., Hains, S. M. J., Jacquet, A. Y., Granier-Deferre, C., & Lecanuet, J. P. (2004). Maturation of fetal responses to music. *Developmental Science, 7*(5), 550–559.

Kisilevsky, B. S., Hains, S. M. J., Lee, K., Xie, X., Huang, H., Ye, H. H., . . . , Wang, Z. (2003, May). Effects of experience on fetal voice recognition. *Psychological Science, 14*(3), 220–224.

Kitchener, K. S., Lynch, C. L., Fischer, K. W., & Wood, P. K. (1993). Developmental range of reflective judgment: The effect of contextual support and practice on developmental stage. *Developmental Psychology, 29,* 893–906.

Kite, M. E., Stockdale, G. D., Whitley, B. E., & Johnson, B. T. (2005). Attitudes toward younger and older adults: An updated meta-analytic review. *Journal of Social Issues, 61*(2), 241–266. doi:10.1111/j.1540-4560.2005.00404.x

Kivipelto, M., Ngandu, T., Fratiglioni, L., Viitanen, M., Kareholt, I., Winblad, B., . . . , Nissinen, A. (2005). Obesity at midlife may raise your Alzheimer's risk. *Archives of Neurology, 62,* 1556–1560.

Klaus, M. H., & Klaus, P. H. (1998). *Your amazing newborn.* Cambridge, MA: Perseus.

Klein, R., Chou, C. F., Klein, B. E. K., Zhang, X., Meuer, S. M., & Saaddine, J. B. (2011). Prevalence of age-related macular degeneration in the U.S. population. *Archives of Ophthalmology, 129*(1), 75. doi:10.1001/archophthalmol.2010.318

Kleinman, R. E. (2004). *Pediatric nutrition handbook.* (5th ed.) Elk Grove Village, IL: American Academy of Pediatrics.

Kleyman, P. (2008). Old masters, young geniuses and the wisdom of elders. *Aging Today, 24*(1), 4, 12.

Kliewer, W., & Sandler, I. N. (1992). Locus of control and self-esteem as moderators of stressor-symptom relations in children and adolescents. *Journal of Abnormal Psychology, 20*(4), 393–413.

Kliff, S. (2007, July 30). A stem-cell surprise. *Newsweek, 150*(5), 46–47.

Klima, T., & Repetti, R. L. (2008). Children's peer relations and their psychological

adjustment: Differences between close friendships and the larger peer group. *Merrill-Palmer Quarterly, 54*(2), 151–178. doi:10.1353/mpq.2008.0016

Klinger-Vartabedian, L., & Wispe, L. (1989). Age differences in marriage and female longevity. *Journal of Marriage and the Family, 51,* 195–202.

Klingman, A. (2006). Children and war trauma. In W. Damon & R. M. Lerner (Eds.), *Handbook of child psychology* (6th ed., Vol. 4, pp. 619–652). New York: Wiley.

Klonsky, E. D., & Moyer, A. (2008). Childhood sexual abuse and non-suicidal self-injury: Meta-analysis. *The British Journal of Psychiatry, 192,* 166–170. doi:10.1192/bjp.bp.106.030650

Kluckhohn, C. (1960). *Mirror for man.* Greenwich, CT: Fawcett.

Knefelkamp, L. L. (1984). *A workbook for the practice-to-theory-to-practice model.* Unpublished manuscript. University of Maryland, College Park.

Knight, B. G., Kaskie, B., Shurgot, G. R., & Dave, J. (2006). Improving the mental health of older adults. In J. E. Birren, K. W. Schaie, R. P. Abeles, M. Gatz, & T. A. Salthouse (Eds.), *Handbook of the psychology of aging* (pp. 408–424). New York: Academic Press.

Knitzer, J., Theberg, S., & Johnson, K. (2008). *Reducing maternal depression and its effect on young children: Toward a responsive early childhood policy framework.* National Center for Children in Poverty. Retrieved from http://www.nccp.org/publications/pdf/text_791.pdf

Knopf, M., Kraus, U., & Kressley-Mba, R. A. (2006). Relational information processing of novel unrelated actions by infants. *Infant Behavior and Development, 29,* 44–53. doi:10.1016/j.infbeh.2005.07.005

Knowlton, B. J. (2005). Cognitive neuropsychology of learning and memory. In K. Lamberts & R. L. Goldstone (Eds.), *The handbook of cognition* (pp. 365–404). Thousand Oaks, CA: Sage.

Knox, D., & Zusman, M. E. (2009). Become involved with someone who is on the rebound? How fast should you run? *College Student Journal, 43*(1), 99–104.

Koch, P. B., & Mansfield, P. K. (2002). *Women's sexuality as they age: The more things change, the more they stay the same* (SIECUS Report). Sex Information & Education Council of the United States.

Kochanek, K. D., Xu, J., Murphy, S. L., Miniño, A. M., & Kung, H. C. (2011, March 16). Deaths: Preliminary data for 2009. *National Vital Statistics Reports, 59*(4), 1–69.

Kochanska, G. (1995). Children's temperament, mothers' discipline, and security of attachment: Multiple pathways to emerging internalization. *Child Development, 66,* 597–615.

Kochanska, G., & Aksan, N. (1995). Mother-child mutually positive affect, the quality of child compliance to requests and prohibitions, and maternal control as correlates of early internalization. *Child Development, 66,* 236–254.

Kochenderfer-Ladd, B., & Skinner, K. (2002). Children's coping strategies: Moderators of the effects of peer victimization? *Developmental Psychology, 38*(2), 267–278. doi:10.1037//0012.1649.38.2.267

Koenig, H. G. (2002). A commentary: The role of religion and spirituality at the end of life. *Gerontologist, 42,* 20–23.

Koerner, B. I. (1997). Is there life after death? *U.S. News & World Report, 122,* 58–64.

Kohlberg, L. (1966). A cognitive-developmental analysis of children's sex-role concepts and attitudes. In E. E. Maccoby (Ed.), *The development of sex differences.* Stanford, CA: Stanford University Press.

Kohlberg, L., & Colby, A. (1990). *Measurement of moral judgment.* New York: Cambridge University Press.

Kohlberg, L., & Gilligan, C. F. (1971). The adolescent as philosopher: The discovery of the self in a postconventional world. *Daedalus, 100,* 1051–1086.

Kohlberg, L., & Ullian, D. Z. (1974). Stages in the development of psychosexual concepts and attitudes. In R. C. Friedman, R. N. Richart & R. L. Vande Wiele (Eds.), *Sex differences in behavior.* New York: Wiley.

Kohli, M., & Künemund, H. (2005). The midlife generation in the family: Patterns of exchange and support. In S. L. Willis & M. Martin (Eds.), *Middle adulthood: A lifespan perspective* (pp. 35–61). Thousand Oaks, CA: Sage.

Kohut, A., & Doherty, C. (2004, February 27). *Gay marriage a voting issue, but mostly for opponents; constitutional amendment rates as low priority.* Washington, DC: The Pew Research Center for the People and the Press. Retrieved from http://people-press.org/reports/display.php3?ReportID=204

Komando, K. (2009, March 26). Technology can now help keep the elderly safe. *USA Today,* Retrieved from http://www.usatoday.com/tech/columnist/kimkomando/2009-03-26-tech-elderly_N.htm

Komisaruk, B. R., Beyer-Flores, C., & Whipple, B. (2006). *The science of orgasm.* Baltimore, MD: Johns Hopkins University Press.

Koppel, N., & Jones, A. (2010, August 25). Are "Sext" messages a teenage felony or folly? *Wall Street Journal,* D1–D2.

Korner, A. F., Brown, B. W., Jr., Reade, E. P., Stevenson, D. K., Fernbach, S. A., & Thom, V. A. (1988). State behavior of preterm infants as a function of development, individual and sex differences. *Infant Behavior and Development, 11,* 111–124.

Kornreich, J. L., Hearn, K. D., Rodriguez, G., & O'Sullivan, L. F. (2003, February). Sibling influence, gender roles, and the sexual socialization of urban early adolescent girls. *The Journal of Sex Research, 40*(1), 101–110. doi:10.2307/3813774

Kost, K., Henshaw, S., & Carlin, L. (2010). *U.S. teenage pregnancies, births and abortions: National and state trends and trends by race and ethnicity.* Retrieved from http://www.guttmacher.org/pubs/USTPtrends.pdf

Kotch, J. B. (Ed.). (2005). *Maternal and child health* (2nd ed.). Sudbury, MA: Jones & Bartlett.

Kotowska, I. E, Matysiak, A., Styrc, M., Pailhé, A., Solaz, A., & Vignoli, D. (2010, March*). Second European Quality of Life Survey: Family life and work.* Dublin, Ireland: European Foundation for the Improvement of Living and Working Conditions. Retrieved from http://www.eurofound.europa.eu/publications/htmlfiles/ef1002.htm

Kottak, C. P. (2008). *Cultural anthropology* (12th ed.). New York: McGraw-Hill.

Kotter-Gruhn, D., Kleinspehn-Ammerlahn, A., Gerstorf, D., & Smith, J. (2009). Self-perceptions of aging predict mortality and change with approaching death: 16-year longitudinal results from the Berlin aging study. *Psychology and Aging, 24*(3), 654–667. doi:10.1037/a0016510

Krampe, R. T. (1994). *Maintaining excellence: Cognitive-motor performance in pianists differing in age and skill level.* Berlin, Germany: Edition Sigma.

Krause, N. (2005, March). God-mediated control and psychological well-being in late life. *Research on Aging, 27*(2), 136–165.

Krause, N. (2007). Longitudinal study of social support and meaning in life. *Psychology and Aging, 22*(3), 456–469.

Krebs, D. L., & Denton, K. (2005). Toward a more pragmatic approach to morality: A critical evaluation of Kohlberg's model. *Psychological Review, 112*(3), 629–649. doi:10.1037/0033-295X.112.3.629

Kreppner, J. M., Rutter, M., Beckett, C., Castle, J., Colvert, J., S. Groothnes, C., . . . , Sonuga-Barke, E. J. S. (2007). Normality and impairment following profound early institutional deprivation: A longitudinal follow-up into early adolescence. *Developmental Psychology, 43(4),* 931–946. doi:10.1037/0012-1649.43.4.93

Krishnakumar, A., & Black, M. B. (2003). Family processes within three-generation households and adolescent mothers' satisfaction with father involvement. *Journal of Family Psychology, 17*(4), 488–498.

Kronholz, J. (2001, December 18). Dropout rate? Getting one depends on whom is asked. *Wall Street Journal,* p. A18.

Kubik, M., Wall, M., Shen, L., Nanney, M., Nelson, T., Laska, M., & Story, M. (2010). State but not district nutrition policies are associated with less junk food in vending machines and school stores in U.S. public schools. *Journal of the American Dietetic Association, 110*(7), 1043–1048. doi:10.1016/j.jada.2010.04.008.

Kübler-Ross, E. (1969). *On death and dying: What the dying have to teach doctors nurses, clergy and their own families.* New York: Macmillan.

Kübler-Ross, E. (1981). *Living with dying.* New York: Macmillan.

Kübler-Ross, E. (1993). *On death and dying.* New York: Collier.

Kuczynski, L., & Kochanska, G. (1995). Function and content of maternal demands: Developmental significance of early demands for competent action. *Child Development, 66,* 616–628.

Kuehn, B. M. (2006). CDC panel backs routine HPV vaccination. *JAMA, 296*(6), 640–641.

Kuehn, B. M. (2007). Scientists examine benefits, risks of treating preschoolers with ADHD drugs. *JAMA, 298*(15), 1747–1749.

Kuehn, B. M. (2008). Birth control patch. *JAMA, 299*(8), 890. doi:10.1001/jama.299.8.890-d

Kuehn, B. M. (2010). Increased risk of ADHD associated with early exposure to pesticides, PCBs. *JAMA, 304*(1), 27–28. doi:10.1001/jama.2010.860

Kuhl, P. K., Stevens, E., Hayashi, A., Deguchi, T., Kiritani, S., & Iverson, P. (2006). Infants show a facilitation effect for native language phonetic perception between 6 and 12 months. *Developmental Science, 9*(2), F13–F21.

Kuhl, P. K., Williams, K. A., Lacerda, F., Stevens, K. N., & Lindblom, B. (1992). Linguistic experience alters phonetic perception in infants by 6 months of age. *Science, 255,* 606–608.

Kuhn, D., & Siegler, R. (Eds.). (2006). *Handbook of child psychology* (6th ed., Vol. 2). New York: Wiley.

Kumar, P., & Giri, V. N. (2009). Effect of age and experience on job satisfaction and organizational commitment. *Journal of Organizational Behavior, 8*(1), 28–36.

Kung, H. C., Hoyert, D. L., Xu, J., & Murphy, S. L. (2008). Deaths: Final data for 2005. *National Vital Statistics Reports, 56*(10), 1–66.

Kunz, J. A., & Soltys, F. G. (2007). *Transformational reminiscence: Life story work.* New York: Springer.

Kurdek, L. A. (1991). The relations between reported well-being and divorce history, availability of a proximate adult, and gender. *Journal of Marriage and the Family, 53,* 71–78.

Kurdek, L. A. (2005). What do we know about gay and lesbian couples? *Current Directions in Psychological Science, 14*(5), 251–254.

Kurdek, L. A. (2008). Change in relationship quality for partners from lesbian, gay male, and heterosexual couples. *Journal of Family Psychology, 22*(5), 701–711. doi:10.1037/0893-3200.22.5.701

Kutner, L. (1990, February 8). It isn't unusual when the father-to-be wakes up feeling sick. *New York Times,* p. B8.

Kyle, J., McEntee, L., & Ackerman, J. (1998). *Deaf children developing sign: A guide for parents and teachers.* Bristol, UK: Centre for Deaf Studies.

Labouvie-Vief, G. (1986). Modes of knowledge and the organization of development. In M. L. Commons, L. Kohlberg, F. A. Richards, & J. Sinnot (Eds.), *Models and methods in the study of adult and adolescent thought: Vol. 3. Beyond formal operations.* New York: Praeger.

Labouvie-Vief, G., DeVoe, M., & Bulka, D. (1989). Speaking about feelings: Conceptions of emotion across the life span. *Psychology and Aging, 4,* 425–437.

Lachman, M. E. (2004). Development in midlife. *Annual Review of Psychology, 55,* 305–332.

Lachman, M. E. (2006). Perceived control over aging-related declines: Adaptive beliefs and behaviors. *Current Directions in Psychological Science, 15*(6), 282–286.

Lachs, M. S., & Pillemer, K. (2004). Elder abuse. *The Lancet, 364*(6), 1192–1263.

Lachs, M. S., Williams, C. S., O'Brien, S., Pillemer, K. A., & Charlson, M. E. (1998). The mortality of elder mistreatment. *JAMA, 280,* 428–432.

Ladd, G. W., Buhs, E. S., & Seid, M. (2000). Children's initial sentiments about kindergarten: Is school liking an antecedent of early classroom participation and achievement? *Merrill-Palmer Quarterly, 46*(2), 255–279.

Laderman, G. M. (2003). Funeral industry. In R. Kastenbaum (Ed.), *Macmillan Encyclopedia of Death and Dying* (Vol. 1). New York: Macmillan Reference Books.

LaFontaine, T. (2008). Physical activity: The epidemic of obesity and overweight among youth: Trends, consequences, and interventions. *American Journal of Lifestyle Medicine, 2*(1), 30–36.

LaForett, D. R., Murray, D. W., & Kollins, S. H. (2008). Psychosocial treatments for preschool-aged children with attention-deficit hyperactivity disorder. *Developmental Disabilities Research Reviews, 14*(4), 300–310. doi:10.1002/ddrr.36

Lagattuta, K. H. (2005). When you shouldn't do what you want to do: Young children's understanding of desires, rules, and emotions. *Child Development, 76*(3), 713–733. doi:10.1111/j.1467-8624.2005.00873.x

Lagercrantz, H., & Slotkin, T. A. (1986, April). The "stress" of being born. *Scientific American, 254,* 100–107.

Lai, C. S. L., Fisher, S. E., Hurst, J. A., Vargha-Khadem, F., & Monaco, A. P. (2001). A forkhead-domain gene is mutated in a severe speech and language disorder. *Nature, 413,* 519–523.

Laible, D., & Thompson, R. A. (2007). Early socialization: A relationship perspective. In J. E. Grusec & P. D. Hastings (Eds.), *Handbook of socialization: Theory and research* (pp. 181–207). New York: Guilford Press.

Lajiness, M. J. (2009). Overactive bladder medications: Do they cause bladder loss? *Urologic Nursing, 29*(4), 261–263.

Lamaze, F. (1958). *Painless childbirth: Psychoprophylactic method.* London: Burke.

Lamb, M. E. (Ed.). (2010a). How do fathers influence children's development? Let me count the ways. In M. E. Lamb (Ed.) *The role of the father in child development* (pp. 1–26). Hoboken, NJ: Wiley.

Lamb, M. E. (Ed.). (2010b). *The role of the father in child development* (5th ed.). Hoboken, NJ: Wiley.

Lamb, M. E., & Ahnert, L. (2006). Nonparental child care: Context, concepts, correlates, and consequences. In K. A. Renninger & I. E. Sigel (Eds.), *Handbook of child psychology* (6th ed., Vol. 4, pp. 950–1016). New York: Wiley.

Lamb, M. E., & Lewis, C. (2004). The development and significance of father-child relationships in two-parent families. In M. E. Lamb (Ed.), *The role of the father in child development* (4th ed., pp. 272–306). New York: Wiley.

Lamb, M. E., & Lewis, C. (2010). The development and significance of father-child relationships in two-parent families. In M. E. Lamb (Ed.) *The role of the father in child development* (pp. 94–153). Hoboken, NJ: Wiley.

Lamont, R. F., & Jaggat, A. N. (2007). Emerging drug therapies for preventing spontaneous preterm labor and birth. *Expert Opinion on Investigational Drugs, 16*(3), 337–345.

Lampl, M., Cameron, N., Veldhuis, J. D., & Johnson, M. L. (1995). Patterns of human growth. *Science, 268*, 445–447.

Landau, M. (2007). Exogenous factors in skin aging. *Current Problems in Dermatology, 35*, 1–13.

Lane, J. M., & Addis, M. E. (2007). Male gender role conflict and patterns of help seeking in Costa Rica and the United States. *Psychology of Men & Masculinity, 6*(3), 135–168.

Langer, E. J., & Rodin, J. (1976). The effects of choice and enhanced personal responsibility for the aged: A field experiment in an institutional setting. *Journal of Personality and Social Psychology, 34*, 191–198.

Lansford, J. E. (2009). Parental divorce and children's adjustment. *Perspectives on Psychological Science, 4*(2), 140–152. doi:10.1111/j.1745-6924.2009.01114.x

Lansford, J. E., Ceballo, R., Abbey, A., & Stewart, A. J. (2001). Does family structure matter? A comparison of adoptive, two-parent biological, single-mother, stepfather, and stepmother households. *Journal of Marriage and Family, 63*, 840–841.

Lansford, J. E., Chang, L., Dodge, K. A., Malone, P. S., Oburu, P., Palmerus, K., . . . , Quinn, N. (2005). Physical discipline and children's adjustment: Cultural normativeness as a moderator. *Child Development, 76*(6), 1234–1246. doi:10.1111/j.1467-8624.2005.00847.x

Lanzi, R. G., Ramey, C. T., & Ramey, S. L. (2007). Early intervention research, services, and policies. In A. Slater & M. Lewis (Eds.), *Introduction to infant development* (2nd ed., pp. 291–302). New York: Oxford University Press.

Lapierre, M., Piotrowski, J. T., & Linebarger, D. L. (2010). *Measuring the home media environment of young children: Results from a nationally representative sample of American families.* Philadelphia, PA: Annenberg School for Communication, University of Pennsylvania.

Larson, R. W., & Wilson, S. (2004). Adolescence across place and time: Globalization and the changing pathways to adulthood. In R. Lerner & L. Steinberg (Eds.), *Handbook of adolescent psychology* (pp. 299–330). New York: Wiley.

LaRue, D. E., & Herrmann, J. W. (2008). Adolescent stress through the eyes of high-risk teens. *Pediatric Nursing, 34*(5), 375–380.

Lasky, R. E., Klein, R. E., Yarbrough, C., Engle, P. L., Lechtig, A., & Martorell, R. (1981). The relationship between physical growth and infant behavior development in rural Guatemala. *Child Development, 52*, 219–226.

Lathe, R. (2008). Environmental factors and limbic vulnerability in childhood autism. *American Journal of Biochemistry and Biotechnology. 4*(2), 183–197.

Lauer, J. C., & Lauer, R. H. (1985, June). Marriages made to last. *Psychology Today, 19*, 22–26.

Laughlin, P. R., Hatch, E. C., Silver, J. S., & Boh, L. (2006). Groups perform better than the best individuals on letters-to-numbers problems: Effects of group size. *Journal of Personality and Social Psychology, 90*(4), 644–651.

Laurencin, C. T., Christensen, D. M., Taylor, E. D. (2008). HIV/AIDS and the African-American community: A state of emergency. *Journal of the National Medical Association, 100*(1), 35–43.

Lawrence, E., Rothman, A. D., Cobb, R. J., Rothman, M. T., & Bradbury, T. N. (2008). Marital satisfaction across the transition to parenthood. *Journal of Family Psychology, 22*(1), 41–50.

Lazovich, D., Vogel, R. I., Berwick, M., Weinstock, M. A., Anderson, K. E., & Warshaw, E. M. (2010). Indoor tanning and risk of melanoma: A case-control study in a highly exposed population. *Cancer Epidemiology, Biomarkers and Prevention, 19*(6), 1557–1568. doi:10.1158/1055-9965.EPI-09-1249

Le Grange, D., Crosby, R. D., Rathouz, P. J., & Leventhal, B. L. (2007). A randomized controlled comparison of family-based treatment and supportive psychotherapy for adolescent bulimia nervosa. *Archives of General Psychiatry, 64*(9), 1049–1056.

Leach, P. (1998). *Your baby and child from birth to age five.* New York: Knopf.

Lead poisoning. (2005). California Poison Control System. Retrieved from http://www.calpoison.org/ public/lead.html

Leaper, C., & Friedman, C. K. (2007). The socialization of gender. In J. E. Grusec & P. D. Hastings (Eds.), *Handbook of socialization: Theory and research* (pp. 561–587). New York: Guilford Press.

Learning Disabilities Roundtable. (2005, February). *Comments and recommendations on regulatory issues under the Individuals with Disabilities Education Improvement Act of 2004: Public Law 108–446.* 1–21. Retrieved from http:// www.cec.sped.org/pdfs/APPENDIX2004 LDRoundtable Recs.pdf

LeBeauf, I. (2008). Racial disparities in new millennium schools: Implications for school counselors. *Journal of School Counseling, 6*(10), 1–24. Retrieved from http://www.jsc.montana.edu/articles/v6n10.pdf

Leboyer, F. (1975). *Birth without violence.* New York: Knopf.

Lecca, P. J., Quervalu, I., Nunes, J. V., & Gonzales, H. F. (Eds.). (1998). *Cultural competency in health, social, and human services: Directions for the twenty-first century.* New York: Garland.

Lee, J., Grigg, W. S., & Donahue, P. L. (2007). *The nation's report card* (NCES 2007-496). National Center For Educational Statistics. Retrieved from http://nces.ed.gov/pubsearch/ pubsinfo.asp?pubid=2007496

Lee, J. M., Appugliese, D., Kaciroti, N., Corwyn, R. G., Bradley, R. H., & Lumeng, J. C. (2007). Weight status in young girls and the onset of puberty. *Pediatrics, 119*(3), 624–630.

Lee, J. M., Lim, S., Zoellner, J., Burt, B. A., Sandretto, A. M., Sohn, W., & Ismail, A. I. (2010). Don't children grow out of their obesity? Weight transitions in early childhood. *Clinical Pediatrics, 49*(5), 466–469. doi:10.11770009922809356466

Lee, P. G. (2011, July 6). Proposed "Caylee's Law" generates virtual frenzy. *Wall Street Journal.* Retrieved from http://blogs.wsj.com/law/2011/07/06/proposed-caylees-law-generates-virtual-frenzy/

Lee, S. M., Burgeson, C. R., Fulton, J. E., & Spain, C. G. (2007). Physical education and physical activity: Results from the School Health Policies and Programs Study 2006. *Journal of School Health, 77*(8), 435–463.

Lefkowitz, E. S., & Gillen, M. M. (2006). "Sex is just a normal part of life": Sexuality in emerging adulthood. In J. J. Arnett and J. L. Tanner (Eds.), *Emerging adults in America: Coming of age in the 21st century* (pp. 235–255). Washington, DC: American Psychological Association.

Lehren, A., & Leland, J. (2006). Scant drop seen in abortion rate if parents are told. *New York Times,* March 6, p. A1.

Leininger, L. J., & Ziol-Guest, K. M. (2008). Reexamining the effects of family structure on children's access to care: The single-father family. *Health Services Research, 43*(1), 117–133. doi:10.1111/j.1475-6773 .2007.00758.x

Leis, J. A., Mendelson, T., Tandon, S. D., & Perry, D. F. (2009). A systematic review of home-based interventions to prevent and treat postpartum depression. *Archives of Women's Mental Health, 12*(1), 3–13. doi:10 .1007/s00737-008-0039-0

Leistikow, B. N., & Tsodikov, A. (2005). Cancer death epidemics in United States black males: Evaluating courses, causation, and cures. *Preventive Medicine, 41*(2), 380–385.

Leleszi, J. P., & Lewandowski, J. G. (2005, March). Pain management in end-of-life care. *Journal of the American Osteopathic Association, 105*(3), S6–S11.

Leman, H. C. (1953). *Age and achievement.* Princeton, NJ: Princeton University Press.

Leman, K. (2004). *The birth order book: Why you are the way you are.* Grand Rapids, MI: Baker.

Leman, K. (2009). *The birth order book.* Grand Rapids, MI: Revell.

Lemonick, M. D. (1997, December 1). The new revolution in making babies. *Time, 150,* 40–46.

Lenhart, A., Madden, M., Macgill, A. R., & Smith, A. (2007, December). *Teens and social media: The use of social media gains a greater foothold in teen life as they embrace the conversational nature of interactive online media.* Washington, DC: PEW Internet & American Life Project.

Lenneberg, E. H. (1967). *Biological foundations of language.* New York: Wiley.

Lenneberg, E. H. (1969). On explaining language. *Science, 164,* 635–643.

Lepper, M. R., & Greene, D. (1975). Turning play into work: Effects of adult surveillance and extrinsic rewards on children's intrinsic motivation. *Journal of Personality and Social Psychology, 31,* 479–486.

Lester, B. M., Kotelchuck, M., Spelke, E., Sellers, M. J., & Klein, R. E. (1974). Separation protest in Guatemalan infants: Cross-cultural and cognitive findings. *Developmental Psychology, 10,* 79–85.

Lester, P., Peterson, K., Reeves, J., Knauss, L., Glover, D., Mogil, C., . . . , Beardslee, W. (2010). The long war and parental combat deployment: Effects on military children and at-home spouses. *Journal of the American Academy of Child & Adolescent Psychiatry. 49*(4), 310–320. doi:10.1097/00004583 -201004000-00006

Levant, R. F. (2001). Men and masculinity. In J. Worell (Ed.), *Encyclopedia of women and gender: Sex similarities and differences and the impact of society on gender* (Vol. 2, pp. 717–727). San Diego, CA: Academic Press.

Levendosky, A. A., Leahy, K. L, Bogat, G. A., Davidson, W. S., & von Eye, A. (2006). Domestic violence, maternal parenting, maternal mental health, and infant externalizing behavior. *Journal of Family Psychology, 20*(4), 544–542.

Levin, I., & Druyan, S. (1993). When socio-cognitive transaction among peers fails: The case of misconceptions in science. *Child Development, 64,* 157.

Levinson, D. J. (1986). A conception of adult development. *American Psychologist, 41*(1), 3–13.

Levinson, D. J. (1996). *The seasons of a woman's life.* New York: Knopf.

Levinson, D. J., Darrow, C. M., Klein, E. B., Levinson, M. H., & McKee, B. (1978). *The seasons of a man's life.* New York: Knopf.

Levinson, H. (1964, March 9). Money aside, why spend life working? *National Observer,* 20.

Levy, S. R., & Hughes-Milligan, J. (2009). Development of racial and ethnic prejudice among children. In Todd D. Nelson (Ed.), *Handbook of Prejudice, Stereotyping, and Discrimination* (pp. 23–40). New York: Taylor & Francis.

Lewin, T., & Dillon, S. (2010, April 20). Districts warn of deeper teacher cuts. *New York Times.* Retrieved from http://www.nytimes .com/2010/04/21/education/21teachers .html?_r=1

LeWine, H. (2005). Another culprit to watch. *Newsweek, 145*(3), 48.

Lewis, A. (2007). Looking beyond NCLB. *Phi Delta Kappan, 88*(7), 483–484.

Lewis, C., & Lamb, M. E. (2003). Fathers' influence on children's development: The evidence from two-parent families. *European Journal of Psychology of Education, 18*(2), 212–230.

Lewis, B. H., Legato, M., & Fisch, H. (2006). Medical implications of the male biological clock. *JAMA, 296*(19), 2369–2371. doi:10 .1001/jama.296.19.2369

Lewis, J. S. (1985, April 3). Fathers-to-be show signs of pregnancy. *New York Times,* p. 13.

Lewis, M. (2001). Issues in the study of personality development. *Psychological Inquiry, 12*(2), 67–83.

Lewis, M. (2007). Early emotional development. In A. Slater & M. Lewis (Eds.), *Introduction to infant development* (2nd ed., pp. 216–232). New York: Oxford University Press.

Lewis, M., & Starr, M. D. (1979). Developmental continuity. In J. D. Osofsky (Ed.), *Handbook of infant development.* New York: Wiley.

Lewis, M. M. (1936/1951). *Infant speech: A study of the beginnings of language.* Boston: Routledge & Kegan Paul.

Li, C. (2000). Instruction effect and developmental levels: A study on water-level task with Chinese children ages 9–17. *Contemporary Educational Psychology, 25*(4), 488–498.

Li, D. K., Daling, J. R., Mueller, B. A., Hickok, D. E., Fantel, A. G., & Weiss, N. S. (1995). Oral contraceptive use after conception in relation to the risk of congenital urinary tract anomalies. *Teratology, 51*(1), 30–36.

Lieberman, M. A., & Coplan, A. S. (1970). Distance from death as a variable in the study of aging. *Developmental Psychology, 2,* 71–84.

Lieberson, S. (1992). Einstein, Renoir, and Greeley: Some thoughts above evidence in sociology. *American Sociological Review, 57,* 1–15.

Liebow, E. (1967). *Tally's corner: A study of Negro streetcorner men.* Boston: Little, Brown.

Lieven, E., Behrens, H., Speares, J., & Tomasello, M. (2003). Early syntactic creativity: A usage-based approach. *Journal of Child Language, 30,* 333–370.

Lightfoot, C., Cole, M., & Cole, S. R. (2009). *The development of children.* New York: Worth.

Lillo-Martin, D. (1997). In support of the language acquisition device. In M. Marschark and P. Siple (Eds.), *Relations of language and thought: The view from sign language and deaf children.* New York: Oxford University Press.

Lim, E. S. (2009). Predictors of nursing home admission: A social work perspective. *Australian Social Work, 62*(1), 90–98. doi:10 .1080/03124070802626901

Limber, S. P. (2002). *Bullying among children and youth.* Proceedings of the Educational Forum on Adolescent Health: Youth bullying. Chicago, IL: American Medical Association.

The Lincoln Institute. (2011). *The funeral train of Abraham Lincoln.* Retrieved from http://www.abrahamlincolnsclassroom .org/Library/newsletter.asp?ID=116& CRLI=164

Lindau, S. T., & Gavrilova, N. (2010). Sex, health, and years of sexually active life gained due to good health: Evidence from two U.S. population-based cross sectional surveys of ageing. *BMJ, 340,* 810. doi: 10.1136/bmj.c810

Lindau, S. T., Schumm, L. P., Laumann, E. O., Levinson, W., C. A. O'Muircheartaigh, C. A., & Waite, L. J. (2007). A study of sexuality and health among older adults in the United States. *New England Journal of Medicine, 357*(8), 762–774.

Lindauer M. S. (2003). *Aging, creativity, and art: A positive perspective on late-life development.* New York: Springer.

Lindelow, M. (2008). Health as a family matter: Do intra-household education externalities matter for maternal and child health? *Journal of Development*

Studies, 44(4), 562–585. doi:10.1080/00220380801980905

Linebarger, D. L., & Walker, D. (2005). Infants' and toddlers' television viewing and language outcomes. *American Behavioral Scientist, 48*(5), 624–645.

Lippman, L., Vandivere, S., Keith, J., & Atienza, A. (2008). Child care use by low-income families: Variations across states. *Child Trends.* Retrieved from http://www.childtrends.org/Files//Child_Trends-2008_07_02_RB_ChildCareLowIncome.pdf

Lipset, S. M. (1989, May 24). Why youth revolt. *New York Times,* p. 27.

Liu, J. H. (2006, May 2). The WHI and the postmenopausal woman: No magic bullet. *Journal Watch Women's Health.* Retrieved from http://womens-health.jwatch.org/cgi/content/ full/2006/502/1

Liu, Q., Xie, F., Rolston, R., Moreira, P. I., Nunomura, A., Zhu, X., . . . , Perry, G. (2007). Prevention and treatment of Alzheimer disease and aging: Antioxidants. *Mini Reviews in Medicinal Chemistry, 7*(2), 171–180.

Liu, W. P. (2007). Medication misuse: A growing concern for aging population. *Aging Today, 28*(6), 10.

Liu, X., Liu, L., Owens, J. A., & Kaplan, D. L. (2005). Sleep patterns and sleep problems among schoolchildren in the United States and China. *Pediatrics, 115,* 241–249.

Livesley, W. J., & Bromley, D. B. (1973). *Person perception in childhood and adolescence.* New York: Wiley.

Livingston, B. A., & Judge, T. A. (2008). Emotional responses to work-family conflict: An examination of gender-role orientation among working men and women. *Journal of Applied Psychology, 93*(1), 207–216.

Livingston, G., & Cohn, D. (2010a, April 6). U.S. birth rate decline linked to recession. *Pew Research Center's Social and Demographic Trends Project.* Retrieved from http://pewsocialtrends.org

Livingston, G., & Cohn, D. (2010b, August 19). The new demography of American motherhood. Pew Research Center. Retrieved from http://pewsocialtrends.org/files/2010/10/754-new-demography-of-motherhood.pdf

Livingstone, S. (2008). Taking risky opportunities in youthful content creation: Teenagers' use of social networking sites for intimacy, privacy, and self-expression. *New Media & Society, 19*(3), 393–411.

Lloyd-Jones, D. M., Dyer, A. R., Wang, R., Daviglus, M. L., & Greenland, P. (2007). Risk factor burden in middle age and lifetime risks for cardiovascular and non-cardiovascular death. *The American Journal of Cardiology, 99*(4), 535–540.

Lock, J., & Fitzpatrick, K. K. (2009). Advances in psychotherapy for children and adolescents with eating disorders. *American Journal of Psychotherapy, 63*(4), 287–303.

Lock, M. (1998). Deconstructing the change: Female maturation in Japan and North America. In R. A. Shweder (Ed.), *Welcome to middle age! And other cultural fictions* (pp. 45–74). Chicago: University of Chicago Press.

Loeber, R., & Farrington, D. P. (2000). Young children who commit crime: Epidemiology, developmental origins, risk factors, early interventions, and policy implications. *Development and Psychopathology, 12,* 737–762.

Loehlin, J. C., Lindzey, G., & Spuhler, J. N. (1975). *Race differences in intelligence.* San Francisco: Freeman.

Loehr, D. (2007). Aspects of rhythm in gesture and speech. *Gesture, 7*(2), 179–214.

Loewy, J. (2004, March 1). *Integrating music, language and the voice in music therapy.* Voices: A World Forum for Music Therapy. Retrieved from http://www.voices.no/mainissues/mi40004000140.html

Loftus, M. (2001). The lost children of Rockdale County: Teenage syphilis outbreak revisited. *SIECUS Report, 30*(1), 24–27.

Lok, I. H., Yip, A., Lee, D. T., Sahota, D., & Chung, T. (2010). A 1-year longitudinal study of psychological morbidity after miscarriage. *Fertility and Sterility, 93*(6), 1966–1975.

Longoria, R. A. (2009). Grandparents raising grandchildren: Perceived neighborhood risk as a predictor of emotional well-being. *Journal of Human Behavior in the Social Environment, 19*(5), 483–511. doi:10.1080/10911350902987292

Lopata, H. Z. (1981). Widowhood and husband satisfaction. *Journal of Marriage and the Family, 43,* 439–450.

Lord, C., & Bishop, S. L. (2010). Autism spectrum disorders: Diagnosis, prevalence, and services for children and families. *SRCD Social Policy Report, 24*(2), 1–27. Retrieved from http://www.inaap.org/uploads/pdf.pdf

Lord, H., & Mahoney, J. L. (2007). Neighborhood crime and self-care: Risks for aggression and lower academic performance. *Developmental Psychology, 43*(6), 1321–1333.

Lorenz, K. Z. (1935). Imprinting. In R. C. Birney & R. C. Teevan (Eds.), *Instinct.* London: Van Nostrand, 1961.

Lorion, R. P., & Sokoloff, H. (2003). Building assets in real-world communities. In R. M. Lerner & P. L. Benson (Eds.), *Developmental assets and asset-building communities* (pp. 121–156). New York: Kluwer Academic.

Lotfabadi, H. (2008). Criticism on moral development theories of Piaget, Kohlbert, and Bandura and providing a new model for research in Iranian students' moral development. *Quarterly Journal of Educational Innovations, 24,* 31–46. Retrieved from http://www.sid.ir/en/VEWSSID/J_pdf/97420082403.pdf

Lothian, J., & De Vries, C. (2010). *The official Lamaze guide: Giving birth with confidence.* Minnetonka, MN: Meadowbrook Press.

Loutzenhiser, L., & Sevigny, P. R. (2008). Infant sleep and the quality of family life for first-time parents of three-month-old infants. *Fathering: A Journal of Theory, Research, & Practice about Men as Fathers, 6*(1), 2–19.

Lovecky, D. V. (1994). Exceptionally different children: Different minds. *Roeper Review, 17,* 116–120.

Lovern, E. (2001, January 29). New kids on the block: Here comes the next generation of workers. *Modern Healthcare, 31,* 28–29.

Lower, J., & Schwarz, T. (2008). Brace yourself here comes Generation Y. *Critical Care Nurse, 28*(5), 80–85.

Lucas-Thompson, R., & Clarke-Stewart, K. A. (2007). Forecasting friendship: How marital quality, maternal mood, and attachment security are linked to children's peer relationships. *Journal of Applied Developmental Psychology, 28,* 499–514. doi:10.1016/j.appdev.2007.06.004

Ludwig, J., & Phillips, D. A. (2008). Long-term effects of Head Start on low-income children. *Annals of the New York Academy of Sciences, 1136,* 257–268. doi:10.1196/annals.1425.005

Luo, L., & Craik, F. I. (2008). Aging and memory: A cognitive approach. *Canadienne de Psychiatrie, 53*(6), 346–352.

Luthar, S. S., & Latendresse, S. J. (2005). Children of the affluent: Challenges to well-being. *Current Directions in Psychological Science, 14*(1), 49–53. doi:10.1111/j.0963-7214.2005.00333.x

Lutman, E., Hunt, J., & Waterhouse, S. (2009). Placement stability for children in kinship care. *Adoption & Fostering, 33*(3), 28–39. Retrieved from CINAHL Plus with Full Text database.

Lynch, E. W., & Hanson, M. J. (2004). *Developing cross-cultural competence: A guide for working with children and their families* (3rd ed.). Baltimore, MD: Paul H. Brookes.

Lyndon-Rochelle, M. T. (2004). Minimal intervention nurse-midwives in the United States. *New England Journal of Medicine, 351,* 1929–1931.

Lynne, S. D., Graber, J. A., Nichols, T. R., Brooks-Gunn, J., & Botvin, G. J. (2007). Links between pubertal timing, peer influences, and externalizing behaviors among urban students followed through middle school. *Journal of Adolescent Health, 40*(1), 7–13.

Lyon, T. D., & Flavell, J. H. (1994). Young children's understanding of "remember" and "forget." *Child Development, 65,* 1357–1371.

Maccoby, E. E. (1961). The taking of adult roles in middle childhood. *Journal of Abnormal and Social Psychology, 63,* 493–503.

Maccoby, E. E. (1980). *Social development: Psychological growth and the parent-child relationship.* New York: Harcourt Brace Jovanovich.

Maccoby, E. E. (1990). Gender and relationships: A developmental account. *American Psychologist, 45,* 513–520.

Maccoby, E. E. (1991). Different reproductive strategies in males and females. *Child Development, 62,* 676–681.

Maccoby, E. E. (1999). The uniqueness of the parent-child relationship. In W. A. Collins and B. Laursen (Eds.), *Minnesota Symposium on Child Psychology: Vol. 30. Relationships as Developmental Contexts* (pp. 157–176). Mahwah, NJ: Erlbaum.

Maccoby, E. E. (2002). Gender and group process: A developmental perspective. *Current Directions in Psychological Science, 11,* 54–58. doi:10.1111/1467-8721.00167

Maccoby, E. E., & Jacklin, C. N. (1974). *The psychology of sex differences.* Stanford, CA: Stanford University Press.

Maccoby, E. E., & Jacklin, C. N. (1987). Gender segregation in childhood. In H. W. Reese (Ed.), *Advances in child development and behavior* (Vol. 20). New York: Academic Press.

Maccoby, E. E., & Masters, J. C. (1970). Attachment and dependency. In P. H. Mussen (Ed.), *Carmichael's manual of child psychology* (3rd ed.). New York: Wiley.

MacDonald, E. E., & Hastings, R. P. (2010). Fathers of children with developmental disabilities. In M. E. Lamb (Ed.), *The role of the father in child development.* (pp. 486–516). Hoboken, NJ: Wiley.

MacDorman, M. F., Munson, M. L., & Kirmeyer, S. (2007, October 11). Fetal and perinatal mortality, United States, 2004. *National Vital Statistics Reports, 56*(3), 1–20.

Macmillan, R., & Eliason, S. (2003). *Social differentiation in the structure of the life course: A latent life path analysis of the transition to adulthood in the United States.* Paper prepared for the 2003 Annual Meeting of the American Sociological Association, Atlanta, Georgia.

MacNeilage, P. F., & Davis, B. L. (2000, April 21). On the origin of the internal structure of word forms. *Science, 288,* 527–531.

Macunovich, D. J. (2010, November 2). Reversals in the patterns of women's labor supply in the United States, 1977–2009. *Monthly Labor Review, 133*(11), 16–36. Retrieved from http://www.bls.gov/opub/mlr/2010/11/art2full.pdf

MacWhinney, B. (2005). Language development. In M. H. Bornstein & M. E. Lamb (Eds.), *Developmental science: An advanced textbook* (5th ed., pp. 359–390). Mahwah, NJ: Erlbaum.

Madden, D. J., Whiting, W. L., & Huettel, S. A. (2005). Age-related changes in neural activity during visual perception and attention. In R. Cabeza, L. Nyberg, & D. Park (Eds.), *Cognitive neuroscience of aging: Linking cognitive and cerebral aging* (pp. 157–185). New York: Oxford University Press.

Madkour, A. S., Farhat, T., Halpern, C., Godeau, E., & Gabhainn, S. N. (2010). Early adolescent sexual initiation as a problem behavior: A comparative study of five nations. *Journal of Adolescent Healt, 39*(10), 1211–1225. doi:10.1007/s10964-010-9521-x

Magnuson, K. A., & Waldfogel, J. (2005). Early childhood care and education: Effects on ethnic and racial gaps in school readiness. *The Future of Children, 15*(1), 169–196.

Maguen, S., & Armistead, L. (2006). Abstinence among female adolescents: Do parents matter above and beyond the influence of peers? *American Journal of Orthopsychiatry, 76*(20), 260–264.

Mahalik, J. R., Burns, S. M., & Syzdek, M. (2007). Masculinity and perceived health behaviors as predictors of men's health behaviors. *Social Science and Medicine, 64*(11), 2201–2209.

Mahoney, S. (2006, June). The secret lives of single women. *AARP Magazine,* pp. 64–66.

Mail Carrier Saves Elderly Woman's Life. (2008, July 7). *Aging Parents' Authority.* Retrieved from http://agingparentsauthority.com/social/mail-carrier-saves-elderly-womans-life/

Main, M., & Solomon, J. (1986). Discovery of an insecure-disorganized/disoriented attachment pattern. In T. B. Brazelton & M. Yogman (Eds.), *Affective development in infancy* (pp. 95–124). Norwood, NJ: Ablex.

Maine, M. (2000). *Body wars: Making peace with women's bodies.* Carlsbad, CA: Gurze Books.

Makarenko, A. S. (1967). *The collective family: A handbook for Russian parents.* Garden City, NY: Doubleday.

Maki, P. L. (2004). *Assessing for learning: Building a sustainable commitment across the institution.* Sterling, VA: Stylus.

Makros J., & McCabe, M. P. (2001). Relationships between identity and self-representations during adolescence. *Journal of Youth and Adolescence, 30*(5), 623–639.

Malcolm, A. H. (1986, March 23). The dialysis dilemma: Extending life or prolonging death? *New York Times, 135,* p. E24(L).

Maldonado, S. (2009). Taking account of children's emotions: Anger and forgiveness in "renegotiated families." *Virginia Journal of Social Policy and the Law, 16*(2), 443–470.

Malinak, D. P., Hoyt, M. F., & Patterson, V. (1979). Adults' reactions to the death of a parent: A preliminary study. *American Journal of Psychiatry, 136,* 1152–1156.

Malt, B. C., Sloman, S. A., & Gennari, S. P. (2003). *Language in mind: Advances in the study of language and thought.* Cambridge, MA: MIT Press.

Malta, S. (2007). Love actually! Older adults and their romantic Internet relationships. *Australian Journal of Emerging Technologies and Society, 5*(2), 84–102.

Malti, T., Gummerum, M., Keller, M., & Buchmann, M. (2009). Children's moral motivation, sympathy, and prosocial behavior. *Child Development, 80*(2), 442–460. doi:10.1111/j.1467-8624.2009.01271.x

Mandler, J. M. (2004). *The foundations of mind: Origins of conceptual thought.* New York: Oxford University Press.

Manlove, J., & Terry-Humen, E. (2007). Contraceptive use patterns within females' first sexual relationships: The role of relationships, partners, and methods. *The Journal of Sex Research, 44*(1), 3–16.

Manning, S., & Bestnoy, K. D. (2008). Special Population. In F. A. Karnes & K. R. Stephens (Eds.), *Achieving excellence in gifted and talented* (pp. 116–134). Upper Saddle River, NJ: Pearson Education.

Manning, W. D., & Brown, S. (2006). Children's economic well-being in married and cohabiting parent families. *Journal of Marriage and Family, 68*(2), 345–362.

Manzoli, L., Villari, P., Pirone, G. M., & Boccia, A. (2007). Marital status and mortality in the elderly: A systematic review and meta-analysis. *Social Science & Medicine, 64*(2), 77–94.

March of Dimes. (2004). PeriStats. *Born too soon and too small in the United States.* Retrieved from http://www.marchofdimes.com/peristats/prematurity

March of Dimes. (2007a). Premature birth: #1 cause of newborn death. Retrieved from http://www.marchofdimes.com/prematurity/21198_10734.asp_69

March of Dimes. (2007b). PeriStats. Retrieved from http://marchofdimes.com/peristats/

March of Dimes. (2010). PeriStats. *Quick facts.* Retrieved from http://www.marchofdimes.com/peristats/

Marcia, J. E. (1991). Identity and self-development. In R. M. Lerner, A. C. Peterson, & J. Brooks-Gunn (Eds.), *Encyclopedia of adolescence* (Vol. 1). New York: Garland.

Marcia, J. E. (2007). Theory and measure: The identity status interview. In M. Watzlawik & A. Born (Eds.), *Capturing identity: Quantitative and qualitative methods* (pp. 1–15). Lanham, MD: University Press of America.

Marcoen, A., Coleman, P. G., & O'Hanlon, A. (2007). Psychological ageing. In J. Bond, S. Peace, F. Dittmann-Kohli, & G. Westerhof (Eds.), *Ageing in society* (3rd ed., pp. 38–67). New York: Sage.

Marder, D. (2007, November 23). Tainted toys: Recalls keep parents wrapped up in worries about lead paint from China. *Philadelphia Inquirer.* Retrieved from http://www.philly.com/inquirer/business/

Maree, C. L., Daum, R. S., Boyle-Vavra, S., Matayoshi, K., & Miller, L. G. (2007). Community-associated methicillin-resistant *Staphylococcus aureus* isolates causing healthcare-associated infections. *Emerging Infectious Diseases, 13*(2), 236. Retrieved from EBSCO*host.*

Marini, Z., & Case, R. (1994). The development of abstract reasoning about the physical and social world. *Child Development, 65,* 147–159.

Marlow, N., Wolke, D., Bracewell, M. A., & Samara, M. (2005). Neurologic and developmental disability at six years of age after extremely preterm birth. *New England Journal of Medicine, 352*(1), 9–19.

Marquardt, E. (2005). *Between two worlds: The inner lives of children of divorce.* New York: Random House.

Marsh, H. W., & Kleitman, S. (2005). Consequences of employment during high school: Character building, subversion of academic goals, or a threshold? *American Educational Research Journal, 42,* 331–369.

Marshall, W., & Tanner, J. M. (1970, February). Variations in pattern of pubertal changes in boys. *Archives of Disease in Childhood, 45*(239), 13–23.

Martin, A., Ryan, R. M., & Brooks-Gunn, J. (2010). When fathers' supportiveness matters most: Maternal and paternal parenting and children's school readiness. *Journal of Family Psychology, 24*(2), 145–155. doi:10.1037/a0018073

Martin, C. L., & Ruble, D. (2004). Children's search for gender cues: Cognitive perspectives on gender development. *Current Directions in Psychological Science, 13*(2), 67–70.

Martin, J. A., Hamilton, B. E., Sutton, P. D., Ventura, S. J., Mathews, T. J., Kirmeyer, S., & Osterman, M. J. K. (2010, August 9). Births: Final data for 2007. *National Vital Statistics Reports, 58*(24), 1–125. Retrieved from http://www.cdc.gov/nchs/data/nvsr/nvsr58/nvsr58_24.pdf

Martin, J. A., Hamilton, B. E., Sutton, P. D., Ventura, S. J., Mathews, T. J., & Osterman, M. J. K. (2010, December 8). Births: Final data for 2008. *National Vital Statistics Reports, 59*(1), 1–72. Retrieved from http://www.cdc.gov/nchs/data/nvsr/nvsr59/nvsr59_01.pdf

Martin, J. A., Hamilton, B. E., Sutton, P. D., Ventura, S. J., Menacker, F., & Kirmeyer, S. (2006, September 29). Births: Final data for 2004. *National Vital Statistics Reports, 55*(1), 1–102.

Martin, J. N., & Fox, N. A. (2006). Temperament. In K. McCartney & D. Phillips (Eds.), *Blackwell handbook of early childhood development* (pp. 127–146). Malden, MA: Blackwell.

Martin, L. R., & Friedman, H. S. (2000). Comparing personality scales across time: An illustrative study of validity and consistency in life-span archival data. *Journal of Personality, 68,* 85–110.

Martin, M. O., Mullis, I. V .S., & Foy, P. (with Olson, J. F., Erberber, E., Preuschoff, C., & Galia, J). (2009). *TIMSS 2007 International Science Report: Findings from IEA's Trends in International Mathematics and Science Study at the fourth and eighth grades.*

Chestnut Hill, MA: TIMSS & PIRLS International Study Center, Boston College.

Martin, N. K., & Dixon, P. N. (1986). Adolescent suicide: Myths, recognition, and evaluation. *School Counselor, 33,* 265–271.

Martinez, S., Hand, M., Da Pra, M., Pollack, S., Ralston, K., Smith, . . . , Newman, C. (2010, May). *Local food systems: Concepts, impacts, and issues.* ERR97. U.S. Department of Agriculture, Economic Research Service.

Martínez, R. W., & Semrud-Clikeman, M. (2004). Emotional adjustment and school functioning of young adolescents with multiple versus single learning disabilities. *Journal of Learning Disabilities, 37*(5), 411–420. doi:10.1177/00222194040370050401

Martins, R. A., Verissimo, M. T., Silva, M. C., Cumming, S. P., & Telxiera, A. M. (2010). Effects of aerobic and strength-based training on metabolic health indicators in older adults. *Lipids in Health and Disease, 9*(76), 1–6.

Marx, T. L. (2005). Partnering with hospice to improve pain management in the nursing home setting. *Journal of the American Osteopathic Association, 105*(3), 22–26.

Masci, D., Lozano-Bielat, H., Ralston, M., & Podrebarac, E. (2009, July 9). Gay marriage around the world. *Pew Research Center's Forum on Religion & Public Life.* Retrieved from http://pewforum.org/Gay-Marriage-and-Homosexuality/Gay-Marriage-Around-the-World.aspx#allow

Masini, B. E., & Barrett, H. A. (2008). Social support as a predictor of psychological and physical well-being and lifestyle in lesbian, gay, and bisexual adults aged 50 and over. *Journal of Gay and Lesbian Social Services, 20*(1), 91-110. doi:10.1080/10538720802179013

Maslow, A. H. (1968). *Toward a psychology of being* (2nd ed.). New York: Van Nostrand.

Maslow, A. H. (1970). *Motivation and personality* (2nd ed.). New York: Harper & Row.

Mason, K. L. (2008). Cyberbullying: A preliminary assessment for school personnel. *Psychology in the Schools, 45*(4), 323–348. doi:10.1002/pits.20301

Mason, M. A., & Ekman, E. M. (2007). *Mothers on the fast track: How a new generation can balance family and careers.* New York: Oxford University Press.

Masters, E.T., Jedrychowski, W., Schleicher, R. L., Tsai, W. Y., Tu, Y. H., Camann, D., Tang, D., . . . , Perera, P. (2007). Relation between prenatal lipid-soluble micronutrient status, environmental pollutant exposure, and birth outcomes. *American Journal of Clinical Nutrition, 86*(4), 1139–1145.

Masters, W. H., & Johnson, V. E. (1966). *Human sexual response.* Boston: Little, Brown.

Matchcock, R., & Susman, E. J. (2006). Family composition and menarcheal age: Antiinbreeding strategies. *American Journal of Human Biology, 18,* 481–491.

Matlin, M. W. (2008). *The psychology of women* (6th ed.). Belmont: Thomson Wadsworth.

Matthews, D. A, & Clark, C. (1998). *The faith factor: Proof of the healing power of prayer.* New York: Penguin Putnam.

Matthews, S. H. (2005). Reaching beyond the dyad: Research on adult siblings. In V. L. Bengtson (Ed.), *Sourcebook of family theory & research* (pp. 181–183). New York: Sage.

Matud, M. P. (2004). Gender differences in stress and coping styles. *Personality and Individual Differences, 37*(7), 1401–1415.

Mau, W. C., & Kopischke, A. (2001). Job search methods, job search outcomes, and job satisfaction of college graduates: A comparison of race and sex. *Journal of Employment Counseling, 38*(3), 141–149.

Maume, D. (2006). Gender differences in restricting work efforts because of family responsibilities. *Journal of Marriage and the Family, 68*(November), 859–869.

Mauther, N. S. (1999). "Feeling low and feeling really bad about feeling low." Women's experiences of motherhood and postpartum depression. *Canadian Psychology, 40*(2), 143–161.

Maxwell, E. (1998). Exceptionally gifted children. *Gifted Child Quarterly, 39,* 245.

Mayer, S. J. (2005). The early evolution of Jean Piaget's clinical method. *History of Psychology, 8*(4), 362–382. doi:10.1037/1093-4510.8.4.362

Mayer, J. D., Ciarrochi, J., & Forgas, J. P. (2001). Emotional intelligence and everyday life: An introduction. In J. Ciarrochi, J. P. Forgas, & J. D. Mayer (Eds.), *Emotional intelligence and everyday life* (pp. xi–xviii). New York: Psychology Press.

Maynard, A. E. (2008). What we thought we knew and how we came to know it: Four decades of cross-cultural research from a Piagetian point of view. *Human Development, 51,* 56–65. doi:10.1159/000113156

Maynard, A. E., & Greenfield, P. M. (2003). Implicit cognitive development in cultural tools and children: Lessons from Maya Mexico. *Cognitive Development, 18,* 489–510.

McAdams, D. P. (2001). Generativity in midlife. In M. E. Lachman (ed.), *Handbook of midlife development* (pp. 395–443). New York: Wiley.

McAuliffe, G. (2006). The evolution of professional competence. In C. Hoare (Ed.). *The handbook of adult development and learning* (pp. 476–496). Oxford: Oxford University Press.

McCabe, M. P., Ricciardelli, L. A., & Holt, K. (2010, January 14). Are there different sociocultural influences on body image and body change strategies for overweight adolescent boys and girls? *Eating Behaviors, 11*(3), 156–163. doi:10.1016/j.eatbeh.2010.01.005

McCandless, B. R. (1970). *Adolescents: Behavior and development.* New York: Holt, Rinehart & Winston.

McCarter-Spaulding, D., & Horowitz, J. A. (2007). How does postpartum depression affect breastfeeding? *American Journal of Maternal Child Nursing, 32*(1), 10–17.

McClelland, D. C., Constantian, C. A., Regalado, D., & Stone, C. (1978, June). Making it to maturity. *Psychology Today, 12,* 42.

McClelland, D. E., & Katz, L. G. (2001). *Assessing young children's social competence.* ERIC Clearinghouse on Elementary and Early Childhood Education, University of Illinois, Champaign, IL.

McClure, A. C., Tanski, S. E., Kingsbury, J., Gerrard, M., & Sargent, J. D. (2010). Characteristics associated with low self-esteem among U.S. adolescents. *Academic Pediatrics, 10*(4), 238–244. doi:10.1016/j.acap .2010.03.007

McCoy, E. (1982, May 6). Children of single parents. *New York Times,* pp. 19, 21.

McCoy, K. (2003). *Fitness helps protect young adults from developing cardiovascular risk factors.* NYU Medical Center Web site. Retrieved from http://www.med.nyu.edu/ patientcare/library/article.html?ChunkIID =46909

McCoy, K., Cummings, E. M., & Davies, P. T. (2009). Constructive and destructive marital conflict, emotional security and children's prosocial behavior. *Journal of Child Psychology and Psychiatry, 50*(3), 270–279. doi:10.1111/j.1469-7610.2008.01945.x

McCracken, M., Jiles, R., Blanck, H. M. (2007). Health behaviors of the young adult U.S. population: Behavioral risk factor surveillance system. *Preventing Chronic Disease, 4*(2), 1–15.

McCrindle, B. W. (2006). Will childhood obesity lead to an epidemic of premature cardiovascular disease? *Evidence-Based Cardiovascular Medicine, 10*(2), 71–74.

McDonald, R. B., & Ruhe, R. C. (2003). The progression from physiological aging to disease: The impact of nutrition. In C. A. Bales & C. S. Ritchie (Eds.), *Handbook of clinical nutrition and aging,* (pp. 49–62). Totowa, NJ: Humana Press.

McDonald, R. M., & Brown, P. J. (2008). Exploration of social support systems for older adults: A preliminary study. *Contemporary Nurse, 29*(2), 184–194.

McDowell, M. A., Brody, D. J., & Hughes, J. P. (2007). Has age at menarche changed? Results from the National Health and Nutrition Examination Survey (NHANES) 1999–2004. *Journal of Adolescent Health, 40*(1), 227–231.

McFarlane, J. M., Groff, J. Y., O'Brien, J. A., & Watson, K. (2003). Behaviors of children who are exposed and not exposed to intimate partner violence: An analysis of 330 black, white, and Hispanic children. *Pediatrics, 112*(3), 202–207.

McGarry, J., & Simpson, C. (2007). Nursing students and elder abuse: Developing a learning resource. *Gerontological Care and Practice, 19*(2), 27–30.

McGee, J., & Wells, K. (1982). Gender typing and androgyny in later life: New directions for theory and research. *Human Development, 25,* 116–139.

McGoldrick, M., & Carter, B. (2003). The family life cycle. In F. Walsh (Ed.), *Normal family processes: Growing diversity and complexity* (3rd ed.) (pp. 375–398). New York: Guilford Press.

McGovern, V. (2005). Metal toxicity: Safe symbols? *Environmental Health Perspectives, 113*(9), 590.

McGraw, M. B. (1935). *Growth: A study of Johnny and Jimmy.* New York: Appleton-Century.

McGuire, S. L., Klein, D. A., & Chen, S. (2008). Ageism revisited: A study measuring ageism in East Tennessee, USA. *Nursing and Health Sciences, 10*(1), 11–16. doi:10.1111/ j.1442-2018.2007.00336.x

McHale, S. M., Whiteman, S. D., Kim, J. Y., & Crouter, A. C. (2007). Characteristics and correlates of sibling relationships in two-parent African American families. *Journal of Family Psychology, 21*(2), 227–235.

McIntosh, W. A., Dean, W., Jan, J., Torres, C., Nayga, R., Kubena, K., & Anding, J. (2008, July 28). Parental work and time children spend in eating and non-sedentary activities. *Paper presented at the annual meeting of the Rural Sociological Society, Radisson Hotel-Manchester, Manchester, New Hampshire.* Retrieved from http://www.allacademic .com/meta/p254988_index.html

McIntyre, C. L., Sheetz, A. H., Carroll, C. R., & Young, M. C. (2005). Administration of epinephrine for life-threatening allergic reactions in school settings. *Pediatrics, 116*(5), 1134–1140.

McKenna, J. J., & McDade, T. (2005). Why babies should never sleep alone: A review of the co-sleeping controversy in relation to SIDS, bedsharing and breast feeding. *Paediatric Respiratory Reviews, 6*(2), 134–152.

McKenzie, B. E., Skouteris, H., Day, R. H., Hartman, B., & Yonas, A. (1993). Effective action by infants to contact objects by reaching and leaning. *Child Development, 64,* 415–429.

McLeod, B. D., Wood, J. J., & Weisz, J. R. (2007). Examining the association between parenting and childhood anxiety: A meta-analysis. *Clinical Psychology Review, 27,* 155–172.

McLeod, V. C. (2004). Linking race and ethnicity to culture: Steps along the road from inference to hypothesis testing. *Human Development, 47,* 185–191.

McLoyd, V. C., Aikens, N. L., & Burton, L. M. (2006). Childhood poverty, policy, and practice. In K. A. Renninger & I. E. Sigel (Eds.), *Handbook of child psychology* (6th ed., Vol. 4, pp. 700–775). New York: Wiley.

McLoyd, V. C., Kaplan, R., Purtell, K. M., Bagley, E., Hardaway, C. R., & Smalls, C. (2009). Poverty and socioeconomic disadvantage in adolescence. In R. M. Lerner & R. Steinberg (Eds.), *Handbook of adolescent psychology* (3rd ed., pp. 444–491). New York: Wiley.

McNall, L. A., Masuda, A. D., & Nicklin, J. M. (2010). Flexible work arrangements, job satisfaction, and turnover intentions: The mediating role of work-to-family enrichment. *The Journal of Psychology, 144*(1), 61–81. doi:10.1080/00223980903356073

McNeely, C., Shew, M. L., Beuhring, T., Sieving, R., Miller, B. C., & Blum, R. W. (2002). Mothers' influence on the timing of first sex among 14- and 15-year-olds. *Journal of Adolescent Health, 31,* 256–265.

McTaggart, J. (2009). Single-gender education. *Briarpatch, 38*(5), 16–19. Retrieved from EBSCO*host.*

McWright, D. (2002). African American grandmothers' and grandfathers' influence in the values socialization of grandchildren. In H. P. McAdoo (Ed.), *Black children: Social, educational, and parental environments* (2nd ed., pp. 27–46). Thousand Oaks, CA: Sage.

Mead, G. H. (1934). *Mind, self, and other.* Chicago: University of Chicago Press.

Meier, B. (1987, February 5). Companies wrestle with threats to workers' reproductive health. *Wall Street Journal,* p. 21.

Meier, J. A., McNaughton-Cassill, M., & Lynch, M. (2006). The management of household and childcare tasks and relationship satisfaction in dual-earner families. *Marriage & Family Review, 40*(2/3), 61–88.

Melby, M. K., Lock, M., & Kaufert, P. (2005). Culture and symptom reporting at menopause. *Human Reproduction Update, 11*(5), 495–512.

Melov, S., Tarnopolsky, M. A., Beckman, K., Felkey, K., & Hubbard, A. (2007). Resistance exercise reverses aging in human skeletal muscle. PLoS *ONE, 2*(5), e465.

Melrose, S. (2010). Paternal postpartum depression: How can nurses begin to help? *Contemporary Nurse, 34*(2), 199–207. doi: 10.5172/conu.2010.34.2.199

Meltzoff, A. N., & Moore, M. K. (1983). Newborn infants imitate adult facial gestures. *Child Development, 54,* 702–709.

Meltzoff, A. N., & Moore, M. K. (1997). Explaining facial imitation: A theoretical model. *Early Development and Parenting, 6,* 179–192.

Meltzoff, A. N., & Prinz, W. (2002). *The imitative mind: Development, evolution, and brain bases.* New York: Cambridge University Press.

Menacker, F., Martin, J. A., MacDorman, M. F., & Ventura, S. J. (2006, September 29). Births to 10–14 year-old mothers, 1990–2004: Trends and health outcomes. *National Vital Statistics Reports, 55*(1), 1–19.

Menella, J. A., Pepino, M. Y., & Reed, D. R. (2005). Genetic and environmental determinants of bitter perception and sweet preferences. *Pediatrics, 115*(2), 216–222.

Menon, U. (2001). Middle adulthood in cultural perspective: The imagined and the experienced in three cultures. In M. E. Lachman (Ed.), *Handbook of midlife development* (pp. 40–76). New York: Wiley.

Mental Health America. (2008). *Depression in women*. Retrieved from http://www.nmha.org/go/information/ get-info/depression/depression-in-women

Menten, T. (1991). *Gentle closings: How to say goodbye to someone you love*. Philadelphia: Running Press.

Meredith, H. V. (1973). Somatological development. In B. B. Wolman (Ed.), *Handbook of general psychology*. Englewood Cliffs, NJ: Prentice Hall.

Merikangas, K. R. (2009, December 1). NIMH report: Half of children with MH disorders go untreated. *Mental Health Weekly, 19*(48), 5–7. doi:10.1002/mhw

Merriam, S. B. (1993). Butler's life review: How universal is it? *International Journal of Aging and Human Development, 37*(3), 163–175.

Merz, E., & Consedine, N. S. (2009). The association of family support and well-being in later life depends on adult attachment style. *Attachment & Human Development, 11*(2), 203–221. doi:10.1080/14616730802625185

Messick, S. (1984). The nature of cognitive styles: Problems and promises in educational practice. *Educational Psychologist, 19*, 59–74.

Meyer, E. J. (2008). A feminist reframing of bullying and harassment: Transforming schools through critical pedagogy. *McGill Journal of Education, 43*(1), 33–48.

Meyer, M. H., Wolf, D. A., & Himes, C. L. (2004). *Linking benefits to marital status: Race and diminishing access to Social Security spouse and widow benefits in the U.S.* Chestnut Hill, MA: Center for Retirement Research at Boston College.

Meyer, P. (2007, Spring). Can Catholic schools be saved? Lacking nuns and often students, a shrinking system looks for answers. *Education Next, 7*(2), 12–20. Retrieved from http://www.hoover.org/publications/ednext/6010606.html

Migration Policy Institute. (2008). *Children Age 17 and Under in Immigrant and Native Families: The United States, New York, and Nevada, 1990 to 2008*. Retrieved from http://www.migrationinformation.org/datahub/charts/children1.shtml

Milan, S., Ickovics, J. R., Kershaw, T., Lewis, J., Meade, C., & Ethier, K. (2004). Prevalence, course, and predictors of emotional distress in pregnant and parenting adolescents. *Journal of Counseling and Clinical Psychology, 72*(2), 328–340.

Miles, B. W., & Okamoto, S. K. (2008). The social construction of deviant behavior in homeless and runaway youth: Implications for practice. *Child & Adolescent Social Work Journal, 25*(5), 4. doi:10.1007/s10560-008-0131-3

Miller, B. (2008). *Empty nest does not mean "empty life."* Retrieved from http://www.helium.com/ items/832066-write-article-empty-syndrome

Miller, C., & Golden, N. (2010). An introduction to eating disorders: Clinical presentation, epidemiology, and prognosis. *Nutrition in clinical practice, 25*(2), 110–115. doi:10.1177/0884533609357566

Miller, L. (2010). *Heaven: Our enduring fascination with the afterlife*. New York: Harper.

Miller-Perrin, C. L., & Perrin, R. D. (2007). *Child maltreatment: An introduction* (2nd ed.). Thousand Oaks, CA: Sage.

Millstein, R. A., Carlson, S. A., Fulton, J. E., Galuska, D. A., Zhang, J., Blanck, H. M., & Ainsworth, B. E. (2008). Relationships between body size satisfaction and weight control practices among U.S. adults. *The Medscape Journal of Medicine, 10*(5), 119.

Milner, J. S., Thomsen, C. J., Crouch, J. L., Rabenhorst, M. M., Martens, P. M., Dyslin, C. W., . . . , Merrill, L. L. (2010). Do trauma symptoms mediate the relationship between childhood physical abuse and adult child abuse risk? *Child Abuse and Neglect, 34*(5), 332–344. doi:10.1016/j.chiabu.2009.09.017

Milodragovich, J. (2011, March 31). *Back To basics: What is the ADEA and how does it apply to Washington employers?* Washington Workplace Law. Retrieved from http://www.washingtonworkplacelaw.com

Miniño, A. M., Heron, M. P., Murphy, S. L., & Kochanek, K. D. (2007, August 21). Deaths: Final data for 2004. *National Vital Statistics Reports, 55*(19), 1–120.

Miniño, A. M., Xu, J. Q., & Kochanek, K. D. (2010, December 9). Deaths: Preliminary data for 2008. *National Vital Statistics Reports, 59*(2). 1–72. Retrieved from http://www.cdc.gov/nchs/data/nvsr/nvsr59/nvsr59_02.pdf

Mintz, S. G. (2007). *A family caregiver speaks up: "It doesn't have to be this hard."* Herndon, VA: Capital Press.

Mirowsky, J., & Ross, C. E. (2003). *Education, social status, and health*. New York: Aldine de Gruyter.

Mischel, W. (1977). On the future of personality measurement. *American Psychologist, 32*, 246–254.

Mischel, W. (1985). *Diagnosticity of situations*. Paper presented at the October meeting of the Society for Experimental Social Psychology, Evanston, IL.

Mischel, W. (2007). Toward a cognitive social learning reconceptualization of personality. In Y. Shoda (Ed.), *Persons in context: Building a science of the individual* (pp. 278–326). New York: Guilford Press.

Mishna, F., Cook, C., Gadalla, T., Daciuk, J., & Solomon, S. (2010). Cyber bullying behaviors among middle and high school students, *American Journal of Orthopsychiatry, 80*(3), 362–374. doi:10.1111/j.1939-0025.2010.01040.x

Misra, A., & Khurana, L. (2008). Obesity and the metabolic syndrome in developing countries. *The Journal of Clinical Endocrinology and Metabolism, 93*(11), S9–S30. doi:10.1210/jc.2008-1595

Missouri Physical Assessment Manual. (2000). Jefferson City, MO: Missouri Department of Elementary and Secondary Education.

Mitalipov, S. (2007). Monkey clones lead the way. *New Scientist, 194*(2610), 32.

Mitchell, B. A. (2010). Midlife marital happiness and ethnic culture: A life course perspective. *Journal of Comparative Family Studies, 1*, 167–184.

Mitchell, C. E. (1992). Waiver of rights under the Age Discrimination In Employment Act: Implications of the Older Workers Benefit Protection Act of 1990. *Labor Law Journal, 43*(11), 735–744. Retrieved from EBSCOhost.

Mitchell, V., & Helson, R. (1990). Women's prime of life. *Psychology of Women Quarterly, 14*, 451–470.

Mjoseth, J. (2004, October 26). *NIA establishes new demography centers to enhance knowledge about older Americans*. National Institute on Aging (NIA), National Institutes of Health. Retrieved from http://www.nia.nih.gov/

Mo, Y., & Singh, K. (2008). Parents' relationships and involvement: Effects on students' school engagement and performance. *Research in Middle Level Education Online, 31*(10), 1–11.

Moen, P. (2003). *It's about time: Couples and careers*. Ithaca, NY: Cornell University Press.

Moen, P., & Roehling, P. (2005). *The career mystique*. Boulder, CO: Rowman & Littlefield.

Molfese, V. J., Modglin, A., & Molfese, D. L. (2003). The role of environment in the development of reading skills: A longitudinal study of preschool and school-age measures. *Journal of Learning Disabilities, 36*(1), 59–67. doi:10.1177/00222194030360010701

Molloy, G. J., Stamatakis, E., Randall, G., & Hamer, M. (2009). Marital status, gender, cardiovascular mortality: Behavioral, psychological distress, and metabolic explanations. *Social Science & Medicine, 69*(1), 223–228.

Monteiro, M. B., de França, D. X., & Rodrigues, R., (2009). The development of intergroup bias in childhood: How social norms can shape children's racial behaviours. *International Journal of Psychology, 44*(1), 29–39. doi:10.1080/00207590802057910

Montgomery, D. (2009). Special educational needs and dual exceptionality. In T. Balchin, B. Hymer, & D. J. Matthews (Eds.), *The Routledge international companion to gifted education* (pp. 218–225). New York: Routledge.

Montgomery, R. (2008, February 9). In the Internet's alternate universes, avatars can be liberating. *Kansas City Star*. Retrieved from http://www.kansascity.com/105/story/483342.html

Moody, H. (2006). *Aging: Concepts and controversies*. Thousand Oaks, CA: Sage.

Moody, R. (1976). *Life after life*. New York: Bantam Books.

Moody-Ayers, S., Lindquist, K., Sen, S., & Covinsky, K. E. (2007). Childhood social and economic well-being and health in older age. *American Journal of Epidemiology, 166*(9), 1059–1067.

Mooney, C. G. (2006). *Theories of childhood*. Saddle River, NJ: Prentice Hall.

Moore, C., Bryant, D., & Furrow, D. (1989). Mental terms and the development of certainty. *Child Development, 60*, 167–171.

Moran, S., & Gardner, H. (2006). Extraordinary achievements: A developmental and systems analysis. In W. Damon & R. M. Lerner (Eds.), *Handbook of child psychology* (6th ed., Vol. 3, pp. 905–949). New York: Wiley.

Moreau, R., & Yousafzai, S. (2004, October 11). "Living dead" no more. *Newsweek, 144*(15), 37–38.

Moremen, R. D. (2008). Best friends: The role of confidantes in older women's health. *Journal of Women & Aging, 20*(1), 149–167. doi:10.1300/J074v20n01_11

Moren-Cross, J. L., & Lin, N. (2006). Social networks and health. In R. H. Binstock & R. L. George (Eds.), *Handbook of aging and the social sciences* (6th ed., pp. 111–124). Burlington, MA: Academic Press.

Morin, R. (2009, September 17). Take this job and love it. The Pew Research Center: Social & Demographic Trends. Retrieved from http://pewsocialtrends.org/2009/09/17/take-this-job-and-love-it/

Morris, G. J., & McAdie, T. (2009). Are personality, well-being and death anxiety related to religious affiliation? *Mental Health, Religion & Culture, 12*(2), 115–120.

Morrow, G., & Malin, N. (2004). Parents and professionals working together: Turning the rhetoric into reality. *Early Years, 24*(2), 163–177. doi:10.1080/0957514032000733019

Morse, M. (1992). *Transformed by the light*. New York: Villard.

Morsünbül, Ü. (2009). Attachment and risk taking: Are they interrelated? *International Journal of Social Sciences, 4*(4), 233–238. Retrieved from http://www.waset.org/journals/ijhss/v4/v4-4-32.pdf

Mortimer, J. (2010). The benefits and risks of adolescent employment. *Prevention Researcher, 17*(2), 8–11. Retrieved from EBSCO*host*.

Mosher, W. D., & Jones, J. (2010, August). Use of contraception in the United States: 1982–2008. *Vital and Health Statistics, 23*(29), 1–84. Retrieved from http://www.cdc.gov/nchs/pressroom/data/Contraception_Series_Report.pdf

Mosier, C., & Rogoff, B. (2003, November). Privileged treatment of toddlers: Cultural aspects of individual choice and responsibility. *Developmental Psychology, 39*(6), 1047–1060.

Moskowitz, B. A. (1978, November). The acquisition of language. *Scientific American, 239*, 92–108.

Moss, L. (2007, September 6). Final go-ahead is given for human-animal embryos. *The Scotsman*. Retrieved from http://news.scotsman.com/topics.cfm?tid=10&id=1420572007

Moss, S. Z., Rubinstein, R. L., & Moss, M. S. (1997). Middle-aged son's reactions to father's death. *Omega: Journal of Death and Dying, 34*(4), 259–277.

Mueller Gathercole, V. C., & Hoff, E. (2007). Input and the acquisition of language: Three questions. In E. Hoff & M. Shatz (Eds.), *Blackwell handbook of language development* (pp. 107–127). Malden, MA: Blackwell.

Mullis, I. V. S., Martin, M. O., & Foy, P. (with Olson, J. F., Preuschoff, C., Erberber, E., Arora, A., & Galia, J.). (2008). TIMSS *2007 International Mathematics Report: Findings from IEA's Trends in International Mathematics and Science Study at the Fourth and Eighth Grades*. Chestnut Hill, MA: TIMSS & PIRLS International Study Center, Boston College.

Munro, N. (2007). Two roads on stem-cell policy. *National Journal, 39*(31), 44–45.

Muntarbhorn, V. (2005, January 10). *Question of the violation of human rights and fundamental freedom in any part of the world. Situation of human rights in the Democratic People's Republic of Korea*. United Nations High Commission for Human Rights. Retrieved from http://daccessdds.un.org/

Munton, A. G., Blackburn, T., & Barreau, S. (2002). Good practice in out of school care provision. *Early Child Development and Care, 172*(3), 223–230. doi:10.1080/0300443029030750

Murdock, G. P. (1935). Comparative data on the division of labor by sex. *Social Forces, 15*, 551–553.

Murdock, G. P. (1949). *Social structure*. New York: Macmillan.

Murdock, G. P. (1957). Anthropology as a comparative science. *Behavioral Science, 2*, 249–254.

Murdock, S., Zey, M., Cline, M. E., & Klineberg, S. (2010). Poverty, educational attainment, and health among America's children: Current and future effects of population diversification and associated socioeconomic change. *Journal of Applied Research on Children: Informing Policy for Children at Risk, 1*(1), 1–34. Retrieved from http://digitalcommons.library.tmc.edu/childrenatrisk/vol1/iss1/2

Muris, P., & Broeren, S. (2009). Twenty-five years of research on childhood anxiety

disorders: Publication trends between 1982 and 2006 and a selective review of the literature. *Journal of Child and Family Studies, 18*, 388–395. doi:10.1007/s10826-008-9242-x

Murphey, P., Yamazaki, Y., M., McMahan, C. A., Walter, C. A., Yanagimachi, R., & McCarrey, J. R. (2009). Epigenetic regulation of genetic integrity is reprogrammed during cloning. *Proceedings of the National Academy of Sciences, 106*(12), 1–5. doi:10.1073/pnas.0900687106

Murphy, S. A., Das Gupta, A., Cain, K. C., Johnson, L. C., Wu, L., & Mekwa, J. (1999). Changes in parents' mental distress after the violent death of an adolescent or young adult child: A longitudinal prospective analysis. *Death Studies, 23*, 129–159.

Murphy, S. A., Johnson, L. C., & Weber, N. A. (2002). Coping strategies following a child's violent death: How parents differ in their responses. *Omega: Journal of Death and Dying, 45*(2), 99–118.

Murphy, S. A, Johnson, L. C, Wu, L., Fan, J. J., & Lohan, J. (2003). Bereaved parents' outcomes 4 to 60 months after their children's deaths by accident, suicide, or homicide: A comparative study demonstrating differences. *Death Studies, 27*(1), 39–61.

Mussen, P. H., & Jones, M. C. (1957). Self-conceptions, motivations, and interpersonal attitudes of late- and early-maturing boys. *Child Development, 28*, 243–256.

Mutter, J., Naumann, J., Schneider, R., Walach, H., & Haley, B. (2005). Mercury and autism: Accelerating evidence? *Neuro Endocrinology Letters, 26*(5), 439–446.

Myers, S. A., & Goodboy, A. K. (2010). Relational maintenance behaviors and communication channel use among adult siblings. *North American Journal of Psychology, 12*(1), 103–116.

Myers, S. M., Johnson, C. P., & the Council on Children with Disabilities. (2007). Management of children with autism spectrum disorders. *Pediatrics, 120*(5), 1162–1182.

Naglieri, J. A., Drasgow, F., Schmit, M., Handler, L., Prifitera, A., Margolis, A., & Velasquez, R. (2004, April). Psychological testing on the Internet: New problems, old issues. *American Psychologist, 59*(3), 150–162.

Nakamura, J., & Csikszentmihalyi, M. (2002). The concept of flow. In C. R. Snyder & S. J. Lopez (Eds.), *Handbook of positive psychology* (pp. 89–105). New York: Oxford University Press.

Namboodiri, V., Sanju, G., Sylvie, B., & Fair, M. (2010). Pregnant heroin addict: What about the baby? *British Medical Journal Case Reports, 24*(11), 36–47. doi:10.1136/bcr.09.2009.2246

Nandutu, A. (2008, January 20). *UGANDA: We escaped female circumcision*. The Female Genital Cutting Education and Networking Project. Retrieved from http://www.fgmnetwork.org

Nano, S. (2004, March 3). Harvard's new stem cells offered to other researchers. *The Arizona Daily Star*. Retrieved from http://www.azstarnet.com/sn/health/12372.php

Nansel, T. R., Overpeck, M. D., Haynie, D. L., Ruan, W. J., & Scheidt, P. C. (2003). Relationships between bullying and violence among U.S. youth. *Archives of Pediatric Adolescent Medicine, 157*, 348–353.

Nansel, T. R., Overpeck, M., Pilla, R. S., Ruan, J., Simons-Morton, B., & Scheidt, P. (2001). Bullying behaviors among U.S. youth: Prevalence and association with psychosocial adjustment. *Journal of the American Medical Association, 285*, 2094–2100.

Nather, D. (2000). Senate clears reauthorization of 1965 Older Americans Act in states-vs.-nonprofits compromise. *CQ Weekly, 58*(42), 2537.

National Abstinence Education Association. (2010, September 30). HHS awards evidence-based teen pregnancy prevention grants. Retrieved from http://www.abstinenceassociation.org/newsroom/093010_TPP_Announcement.html

National Alliance for Caregiving and AARP. (2010, June). *Caregiving in the U.S.* Retrieved from http://www.caregiving.org/data/2010finalreport.pdf

National Association of School Psychologists. (2009). *Position statement on inclusive programs for students with disabilities.* Retrieved from www.nasponline.org/about_nasp/pospaper_ipsd.aspx

The National Campaign to Prevent Teen and Unplanned Pregnancy. (2007). *What works: Curriculum-based programs that prevent teen pregnancy.* Washington, DC: Author.

National Cancer Institute. (2008). *Cancer of the prostate.* Retrieved from http://seer.cancer.gov/statfacts/html/prost.html

National Cancer Institute. (2010). A snapshot of melanoma. Retrieved from http://www.cancer.gov/aboutnci/servingpeople/snapshots/melanoma.pdf

National Cancer Institute. (2011). Prostate cancer. Retrieved from http://www.cancer.gov/cancertopics/types/prostate

National Center for Education Statistics. (2005a). *The Nation's Report Card: NAEP 2004 Trends in Academic Progress: Three decades of student performance in reading and mathematics* (NCES 2005-463). Washington, DC: U.S. Department of Education.

National Center for Education Statistics. (2007c). *The Nation's Report Card: Reading 2007: NAEP Progress at Grades 4 and 8.* (NCES 2007-4960. Washington, DC: U.S. Department of Education.

National Center for Education Statistics. (2009). Average reading scale score, by age, sex, and race/ethnicity: Selected years, 1971 to 2008. Retrieved from http://nces.ed.gov/fastfacts/display.asp?id=147

National Center for Education Statistics. (2010). *The Condition of Education 2010* (NCES 2010-028. Retrieved from http://nces.ed.gov/programs/coe/

National Center for Health Statistics. (2007a). *Health, United States 2007 with Chartbook on Trends in the Health of Americans.* Hyattsville, MD: National Center for Health Statistics. Retrieved from http://www.cdc.gov/nchs/data/hus/hus10.pdf

National Center for Health Statistics. (2007b). Prevalence of overweight among children and adolescents: United States, 2003–2004. In *Health E-Stats.* Retrieved from http://www.cdc.gov/nchs/products/pubs/pubd/hestats/overwght99.htm

National Center for Health Statistics. (2010a). *Health, United States, 2009: With special feature on medical technology.* Hyattsville, MD: Centers for Disease Control and Prevention. Retrieved from http://www.cdc.gov/nchs/data/hus/hus09.pdf

National Center for Health Statistics. (2010b, August 27). Births, marriages, divorces, and deaths: Provisional data for 2009. *National Vital Statistics Report. 58*(25). Retrieved from http://www.cdc.gov/nchs/data/nvsr/nvsr58/nvsr58_25.pdf

National Center for Health Statistics. (2011). *Health, United States, 2010: With special feature on death and dying.* Hyattsville, MD: U.S. Department of Health and Human Services. Retrieved from http://www.cdc.gov/nchs/data/hus/hus10.pdf#specialfeature

National Center for HIV/AIDS, Viral Hepatitis, STD, and TB Prevention. (2009). *HIV prevention in the United States: At a critical crossroads.* Atlanta, GA: Centers for Disease Control and Prevention.

National Center for Injury Prevention and Control. (2010). 2007, United States suicide injury deaths and rates per 100,000: All races, both sexes, ages 20 to 44. Retrieved from http://webappa.cdc.gov/cgi-bin/broker.exe

National Cholesterol Education Program. (2005, June). *High blood cholesterol: What you need to know.* Retrieved from www.nhlbi.nih.gov/health/public/heart/chol/wyntk.pdf

National Coalition on Health Care. (2008). *Health insurance coverage.* Retrieved from http://www.nchc.org/facts/coverage.shtml

National Conference of State Legislatures. (2010b, October). HPV vaccine: State legislation and statutes. Retrieved from http://www.ncsl.org/default.aspx?tabid=14381

National Conference of State Legislatures. (2011, May). Same-sex marriage, civil unions and domestic partnerships. Retrieved from http://www.ncsl.org/default.aspx?tabid=16430

National Council on the Aging. (2003). Get connected! Linking older Americans with medication, alcohol, and mental health resources. DHHS Pub. No. (SMA) 03-3824. Retrieved from http://store.samhsa.gov/shin/content/SMA03-3824/SMA03-3824.pdf

National Down Syndrome Congress. (2010). Facts about Down syndrome. Retrieved from http://www.ndsccenter.org/?page_id=614

National Down Syndrome Society. (2011). Alzheimer's and Down Syndrome—Alzheimer's Disease and Down Syndrome. Retrieved from http://www.ndss.org/index.php?option=com_content&view=article&id=180&limitstart=1

National Down Syndrome Society (NDSS). (2007). *Parent and professional information.* Retrieved from http://www.ndss.org/information/general_info.html

National Eating Disorders Screening Program. (2001). *Fact sheet on eating disorders.* Retrieved from http://www.mentalhealthscreening.org/eat/eatfact.htm

National Funeral Directors Association. (2010, October 6). NFDA Releases Results of 2010 General Price List Survey. [News Release.] http://www.nfda.org/news-a-events/all-press-releases/2192-nfda-releases-results-of-2010-general-price-list-survey.html

National Highway Traffic Safety Administration. (2010, September). Distracted driving 2009. Retrieved from http://www-nrd.nhtsa.dot.gov/Pubs/811379.pdf

National Hospice and Palliative Care Organization. (2010, September). NHPCO Facts and Figures: Hospice Care in America. 1–15. Alexandria, VA: National Hospice and Palliative Care Organization. Retrieved from http://www.nhpco.org/files/public/Statistics_Research/Hospice_Facts_Figures_Oct-2010.pdf

National Human Genome Research Institute. (2007a). *A brief guide to genomics.* Retrieved from http://www.genome.gov/pfv.cfm?

National Human Genome Research Institute. (2007b). *About the institute: A history and timeline.* Retrieved from http://www.genome.gov/pfv.cfm?/10001763

National Human Genome Research Institute. (2007c). *What's next? Turning genomics vision into reality.* Retrieved from http://www.genome.gov/pvf.cfm?/11006944

National Institute for Literacy. (2007). *National Even Start Family Literacy Program.* Retrieved from http://www.nifl.gov/nifl/facts/EVEN.html

National Institute of Allergy and Infectious Disease. (2006). *HIV infection in women.* Retrieved October 1, 2007 from http://www.niaid.nih.gov/factsheets/womenhiv.html

National Institute of Allergy and Infectious Diseases. (2010). *Facts and figures: HIV/AIDS statistics.* Retrieved from http://www.niaid.nih.gov/facts-sheets/aidsstat.htm

National Institute of Child Health & Human Development. (2006). *The NICHD Study of Early Child Care and Youth Development.* Rockville, MD: NICHD.

National Institute of Child Health & Human Development. (2007). *Research on miscarriage and stillbirth.* National Institutes of Health. Retrieved from http://www.nichd .nih.gov/health/ topics/Miscarriage.cfm

National Institute of Child Health and Human Development Early Child Care Research Network. (2004). Are child developmental outcomes related to before- and after-school care arrangements? Results from the NICHD study of early child care. *Child Development, 75*(1), 280–295.

National Institute of Mental Health. (2008). *Suicide in the U.S.: Statistics and prevention.* Retrieved from http://www.nimh.nih.gov/ health/publications/suicide-in-the-us-statistics -and-prevention-html

National Institute of Neurological Disorder and Stroke. (2011). Parkinson's disease: Hope through research. Retrieved from http://www.ninds.nih.gov/disorders/parkin sons_disease/detail_parkinsons_disease .htm?css=print

National Institute on Aging. (2007a). *Growing Older in America: The Health and Retirement Study.* The University of Michigan. Retrieved from http://hrsonline.isr .umich.edu/index.php?p=dbook

National Institute on Aging. (2010). Alzheimer's disease fact sheet. Retrieved from http://www.nia.nih.gov/NR/ rdonlyres/7DCA00DB-1362-4755-9E87- 96DF669EAE20/13991/ADFactSheet FINAL2510.pdf

National Institute on Alcohol Abuse and Alcoholism. (2006). Young adult drinking. *Alcohol Alert* (No. 68). Rockville, MD: U.S. Department of Health & Human Services.

National Institute on Alcohol Abuse and Alcoholism. (2010). Statistical snapshot of college drinking. Retrieved from http:// www.niaaa.nih.gov/AboutNIAAA/ NIAAASponsoredPrograms/Documents/ StatisticalSnapshotofCollegeDrinking.pdf

National Institute on Out-of-School Time. (2009). *Fact sheet on school age children's out-of-school time.* Center for Research on Women, Wellesley College. Retrieved from http://www.niost.org/pdf/factsheet2009.pdf

National Institutes of Health. (2006). *Your guide to lowering your blood pressure with DASH.* Retrieved from http://www.nhlbi .nih.gov/health/dci/index/html

National Institutes of Health. (2009). *Guidelines for human stem cell research.* Retrieved from http://edocket.access.gpo.gov/2009/ pdf/E9-15954.pdf

National Institutes of Health. (2010). *Pregnancy loss.* Retrieved from http://www.nim .nih.gov/medlineplus/pregnancyloss.html

National Kidney and Urologic Diseases Information Clearinghouse. (2006, June).

Prostate enlargement: Benign prostatic hyperplasia (NIH Publication No. 07–3012). Retrieved from http://www.kidney.niddk .nih.gov

National Marriage Project. (2009). *The state of our unions: 2009.* Retrieved from http:// www.stateofourunions.org/2009/marriage _and_the_recession.php

National Marriage Project. (2010). *When marriage disappears: The New Middle America.* Charlottesville, VA: University of Virginia.

National Mental Health Association. (2008). *Bullying in schools: Harassment puts gay teens at risk.* Retrieved from http://www .nmha.org/pbedu/ backtoschool/bullying -GayYouth.cfm

National Organization on Fetal Alcohol Syndrome. (2010). *Frequently asked questions at NOFAS.* In FAQs. Retrieved from http://www.nofas.org/faqs

National Parkinson Foundation. (2008, January 1). Developments on the horizon for PD. Retrieved from http://www.parkinson .org/

National Public Radio. (2011, January 3). First baby boomer turns 65. Retrieved from http://www.npr.org/2011/01/03/132628267/ First-Baby-Boomers-Turn-65

National Safety Council. (2010). Licensed drivers and number in accidents by age: 2007. *Injury Facts, 2009.* Retrieved from http://www.nsc.org

National SIDS/Infant Death Resource Center. (2007). *SIDS deaths by race and ethnicity, 1995–2001.* Retrieved from http:// www.sidscenter.org/

National Sleep Foundation. (2010). *How much sleep do we really need?* Retrieved from http://www.sleepfoundation.org/ article/how-sleep-works/how-much-sleep -do-we-really-need

National Stepfamily Resource Center. (2008). *Stepfamily fact sheet.* Retrieved from http:// www.stepfamilies.info/faqs/factsheet.php

National Stroke Association. (2008). *What is a stroke?* Retrieved from http://www.stroke .org/site/PageServer?pagename=STROKE

National Youth Employment Coalition. (2008). *Some key youth statistics.* Retrieved from http://www.nyec.org/page.cfm?page ID=245

Nauck, B., & Suckow, J. (2006). Intergenerational relationships in cross-cultural comparison: How social networks frame intergenerational relations between mother and grandmothers in Japan, Korea, China, Indonesia, Israel, Germany, and Turkey. *Journal of Family Issues, 27*(8), 1159–1185.

Nawrot, E., Mayo, S. L., & Nawrot, M. (2009). The development of depth perception from motion parallax in infancy. *Attention, Perception, & Psychophysics, 71*(1), 194–199.

Nee-Benham, M. K. P. A., & Cooper, J. E. (2000). *Indigenous educational models for*

contemporary practice: In our mother's voice. Mahwah, NJ: Erlbaum.

Needham, A., & Baillargeon, R. (1998). Effects of prior experience on 4.5-month-old infants' object segregation. *Infant Behavior and Development, 21*, 1–24.

Neff, K. D., & Harter, S. (2003). Relationship styles of self-focused autonomy, other-focused connectedness, and mutuality across multiple relationship contexts. *Journal of Social and Personal Relationships, 20*(1), 81–99.

Neisser, U. (1967). *Cognitive psychology.* New York: Appleton-Century-Crofts.

Neisser, U. (2004). Memory development: New questions and old. *Developmental Review, 24*, 154–158.

Nelms, L. W., Hutchins, E., Hutchins, D., & Pursley, R. J. (2007). Spirituality and the health of college students. *Journal of Religion and Health, 46*(2), 249–265. doi:10 .1007/s10943-006-9075-0

Nelson, B. (1982, December 7). Early memory: Why is it so elusive? *New York Times,* p. 17.

Nelson, B. (1983, April 2). Despair among jobless is on rise, studies find. *New York Times,* p. 8.

Nelson, K. (1973). Structure and strategy in learning to talk. *Monographs of the Society for Research in Child Development, 38*(149), 1–135.

Nelson, K., Rescorla, L., Gruendel, J., & Benedict, H. (1978). Early lexicons: What do they mean? *Child Development, 49,* 960–968.

Nelson, K. E., Aksu-Ko, A., & Johnson, C. E. (2001). *Children's language: Developing narrative and discourse competence* (Vol. 10). Mahwah, NJ: Erlbaum.

Nelson, T. F., Naimi, T. S., Brewer, R. D., & Wechsler, H. (2005, March). The state sets the rate: The relationship among state-specific college binge drinking, state binge drinking rates, and selected state alcohol control policies. *American Journal of Public Health, 95*(3), 441–446.

Nelson, V. (2006, August 24). *Single mothers by choice.* Retrieved from http://single -parenting.families.com/blog/single -mothers-by-choice

Nelson-Becker, H., & Canda, E. R. (2008). Spirituality, religion, and aging research in social work: State of the art and future possibilities. *Journal of Religion, Spirituality & Aging, 20*(3), 177–193. doi:10.1080/15528 030801988849

Nesdale, D., Maass, A., Kiesner, J., Durkin, K., Griffiths, J., & James, B. (2009). Effects of peer group rejection and a new group's norms on children's intergroup attitudes. *British Journal of Developmental Psychology, 27*, 799-814. doi:10.1348/026151008X381690

Network on Transitions to Adulthood. (2006). *Demographics.* Retrieved from http://www.transad.pop.upenn.edu/trends/ index.html

Neugarten, B. L. (1982a). Age or need? *National Forum: Phi Kappa Phi Journal, 42,* 25–27.

Neugarten, B. L. (1982b). The aging society. *National Forum: Phi Kappa Phi Journal, 42,* 3.

Neugarten, B. L., Havighurst, R. J., & Tobin, S. S. (1968). Personality and patterns of aging. In B. L. Neugarten (Ed.), *Middle age and aging.* Chicago: University of Chicago Press.

Neugarten, B. L., & Neugarten, D. A. (1987, May). The changing meanings of age. *Psychology Today, 21,* 29–33.

Neugarten, B. L., & Neugarten, D. A. (1996). *The meanings of age: Selected papers of Bernice L. Neugarten.* Chicago, IL: University of Chicago Press.

Neuharth, A. (1997, August 8). What did she prove by living to be 122? *USA Today,* p. A15.

Neumark-Sztainer, D., Wall, M., Guo, J., Story, M., Haines, J., & Eisenberg, M. (2006, April). Obesity, disordered eating, and eating disorders in a longitudinal study of adolescents: How do dieters fare 5 years later? *Journal of American Dietetic Association, 106*(4), 559–568. doi:10.1016/j.jada.2006.01.003

New York Society for the Prevention of Cruelty to Children. (2010). Identifying child abuse and neglect: Possible behavioral and environmental characteristics of abusive adults. Retrieved from http://www.nyspcc .org/nyspcc/

Newbury, D. F., Bonora, E., Lamb, J. A. Fisher, S. E., Lai, C. S. L., Baird, G., . . . , Monaco, A. P. (2002). FOXP2 is not a major susceptibility gene for autism or specific language impairment. *American Journal of Human Genetics 70*(5), 1318–1327.

Newcomb, A. F., & Bagwell, C. L. (1995). Children's friendship relations: A meta-analytic review. *Psychological Bulletin, 117,* 306–347.

Newcomb, A. F., Bukowski, W. M., & Pattee, L. (1993). Children's peer relations: A meta-analytic review of popular, rejected, neglected, controversial, and average sociometric status. *Psychological Bulletin, 113,* 99–128.

Newcombe, N., & Fox, N. A. (1994). Infantile amnesia: Through a glass darkly. *Child Development, 65,* 31–40.

Newcombe, N., & Huttenlocher, J. (1992). Children's ability to solve perspective-taking problems. *Developmental Psychology, 28,* 635–643.

Newell, K. M., Vaillancourt, D. E., & Sosnoff, J. J. (2006). Aging, complexity, and motor performance. In J. E. Birren, K. W. Schaie, R. P. Abeles, M. Gatz, & T. A. Salthouse (Eds.), *Handbook of the psychology of aging* (pp. 163–182). Burlington, MA: Elsevier.

Newman, B. M., Lohman, B. J., & Newman, P. R. (2007). Peer group membership and a sense of belonging: Their relationship to adolescent behavior problems. *Adolescence, 42*(166), 241–263.

Ni Mhurchu, C., Maddison, R., Jiang, Y., Jull, A., Prapavessis, H., & Rodgers, A. (2008). Couch potatoes to jumping beans: A pilot study of the effect of active video games on physical activity in children. *International Journal of Behavioral Nutrition and Physical Activity, 5,* 8. doi:10.1186/1479

Nicholas, J. G., & Geers, A. E. (2007). Will they catch up? The role of age at cochlear implantation in the spoken language development of children with severe to profound hearing loss. *Journal of Speech, Language, and Hearing Research, 50*(4), 1048–1062.

Nickerson, A. B., & Nagle, R. J. (2004). The influence of parent and peer attachments on life satisfaction in middle childhood and early adolescence. In A. Dannerbeck, F. Casas, M. Sadurni, & G. Coenders (Eds.), *Quality-of-life research on children and adolescents* (pp. 35–60). Boston, MA: Kluwer.

Nicpon, M., Allmon, A., Sieck, B., & Stinson, R. D. (2011). Empirical investigation of twice-exceptionality: Where have we been and where are we going? *Gifted Child Quarterly, 55*(1), 3–17. Retrieved from EBSCO*host.*

Nielsen. (2009). Television audience 2008. Retrieved from http://blog.nielsen.com/ nielsenwire/wp-content/uploads/2009/07/ tva_2008_071709.pdf

Nielsen, S. S., McKean-Cowdin, R., Farin, F. M., Holly, E. A., Preston-Martin, S., & Mueller, B. A. (2010). Childhood brain tumors, residential insecticide exposure, and pesticide metabolism genes. *Environmental Health Perspectives, 118*(1), 144–149. doi:10 .1289/ehp.0901226.S1

Niemeyer, D. (2005, March 10). Seventh annual report on Oregon's Death with Dignity Act. Portland, OR: Department of Human Services. Retrieved from http://egov. oregon.gov/DHS/ph/pas/docs/year7.pdf

NIH News. (2007, April 18). Decrease in breast cancer rates related to reduction in use of hormone replacement therapy. *NIH News* [News Release]. Retrieved from http://www.nih.gov/news/pr/apr2007/ nci-18a.htm

Nilsson, L., & Hamberger, L. (2004). *A child is born* (4th ed.). New York: Random House.

Nishida, T. K., & Lillard, A. S. (2007). The informative value of emotional expressions: "Social referencing" in mother-child pretense. *Developmental Science, 10*(2), 205–121.

Nishina, A., Ammon, N. Y., Bellmore, A. D., & Graham, S. (2006). Body dissatisfaction and physical development among ethnic minority adolescents. *Journal of Youth and Adolescence, 35*(2), 189–201.

Nora, J. J., & Nora, A. H. (1975). A syndrome of multiple congenital anomalies associated with teratogenic exposure. *Archives of Environmental Health, 30,* 17–21.

Nord, M. (2009, September). Food insecurity in households with children: Prevalence, severity, and household characteristics. *Economic Information Bulletin No.* (EIB-56).

1–49. Retrieved from http://www.ers.usda .gov/Publications/EIB56/

Norman, D., & Loredo, J. S. (2008). Obstructive sleep apnea in older adults. *Clinics in Geriatric Medicine, 24*(1), 151–165.

North, P. (1998). *Hospice care ring.* Retrieved from http://www.cp-tel.net/pamnorth/hos -ring.htm

Nosich, G. M. (2005). Problems with two standard models for teaching critical thinking. *New Directions for Community Colleges, 130,* 59–67. doi: 0.1002/cc.196

Novak, J., & Gowin, D. (1989). *Learning to learn.* New York: Cambridge University Press.

Novosad, C., & Thoman, E. B. (2003). The Breathing Bear: An intervention for crying babies and their mothers. *Journal of Developmental Behavior and Pediatrics, 24*(April), 89–95.

Nsamenang, A. B. (2010). Fathers, families, and children's well-becoming in Africa. In M. E. Lamb (Ed.). *The role of the father in child development* (pp. 341–387). Hoboken, NJ: Wiley.

Nucci, L. (1998). *Moral development and moral education: An overview.* Retrieved from http://tigger.uic.edu/lnucci/MoralEd/ overview.html

Oaks, J., & Ezell, G. (1993). *Death and dying: Coping, caring and understanding* (2nd ed.) Scottsdale, AZ: Gorsuch Scarisbrick.

O'Brien, I., Duffy, A., & Nicholl, H. (2009). Impact of childhood chronic illnesses on siblings: A literature review. *British Journal of Nursing (BJN), 18*(22), 1358. Retrieved from EBSCO*host.*

O'Brien, M., & Moss, P. (2010). Fathers, work, and family policies in Europe. In M. E. Lamb (Ed.), *The role of the father in child development* (pp. 551–577). Hoboken, NJ: Wiley.

O'Brien, M., Nader, P. R., Houts, R. M., Bradley, R., Friedman, S. L., Belsky, J., & Susman, E. (2007, April). The ecology of childhood overweight: A 12-year longitudinal analysis. *International Journal of Obesity, 31,* 1469–1478.

O'Callaghan, T. (2010, May 24). Cancer, cancer everywhere. *Time, 175*(20), 18.

O'Connor, M. J., & Whaley, S. E. (2007). Brief intervention for alcohol use by pregnant women. *American Journal of Public Health, 97*(2), 252–258.

O'Connor, T. G., & Rutter, M. (2000). Attachment disorder behavior following early severe deprivation: Extension and longitudinal follow-up. *Journal of the American Academy of Child & Adolescent Psychiatry, 39*(6), 703–712.

O'Donovan, E. (2010). Sexting and student discipline. *District Administration, 46*(3), 60. Retrieved from MasterFILE Premier database.

Oberst, U. (2009). Educating for social responsibility. *The Journal of Individual Psychology, 65*(4), 397–411.

Odden, A., & Kelley, C. (2002). *Paying teachers for what they know and do: New and smarter compensation strategies to improve schools.* Thousand Oaks, CA: Corwin Press.

Office of Applied Studies. (2007). *Results from the 2006 National Survey on Drug Use and Health: National Findings* (DHHS Publication No. SMA 07-4293, NSDUH Series H-32). Rockville, MD: Substance Abuse and Mental Health Services Administration.

Office of Applied Studies. (2010, April 29). A day in the life of American adolescents: Substance use facts update. *The OAS Report.* 1–5. Rockville, MD: Substance Abuse and Mental Health Services Administration. Retrieved from https://dawninfo.samhsa .gov/files/SpecTopics/OAS2010_SR185.pdf

Office of Management and Budget. (2011). Department of Education: Federal Budget Fiscal Year 2011. Retrieved from http:// www.whitehouse.gov/omb/factsheet _department_education/

Office of Minority Health. (2008). *Heart disease data/statistics.* Retrieved from http:// www.omhrc.gov/ templates/browse.aspx ?lvl=2&lvlID=9

Office of Population Research. (2010). The emergency contraception website. Princeton, NJ: Princeton University. Retrieved from http://ec.princeton.edu/questions/ dose.html

Ogden C. L., Carroll, M. D., Curtin, L. R., McDowell, M. A., Tabak, C. J., & Flegal, K. M. (2006). Prevalence of overweight and obesity in the United States, 1999–2004. *JAMA, 295*(13), 1549–1555.

Ogden, C. L., & Flegal, K. M. (2010, June 25). Changes in terminology for childhood overweight and obesity. *National Health Statistics Reports,* pp. 1–8.

Ogden, C. L., Lamb, M. M, Carroll, M. D., & Flegal, K. M. (2010). Obesity and socioeconomic status in adults: United States, 2005–2008. *NCHS Data Brief, 50,* 1–8. Retrieved from EBSCO*host.*

Ogden, J. (2010). *The psychology of eating: From healthy to disordered behavior.* Malden, MA: Wiley-Blackwell.

Ojanen, T., & Perry, D. G. (2007). Relational schemas and the developing self: Perceptions of mother and of self as joint predictors of early adolescents' self-esteem. *Developmental Psychology, 43*(6), 1474–1483.

Oldehinkel, A. J., Verhulst, F. C., & Ormel, J. (2011). Mental health problems during puberty: Tanner stage-related differences in specific symptoms. The TRAILS Study. *Journal of Adolescence, 34*(1), 73–85. doi:10 .1016/j.adolescence.2010.01.010

Olfson, M., Crystal, S., Huang, C., & Gerhard, T. (2010). Trends in antipsychotic drug use by very young, privately insured children. *Journal of the American Academy of Child and Adolescent Psychiatry, 49*(1), 13–23. doi:10.1016/j.jaac.2009.09.003

O'Laughlin, M. J., & Malle, B. F. (2002). How people explain actions performed by groups and individuals. *Journal of Personality and Social Psychology, 82*(1), 33–48.

Oller, D. K. (2005). Vocal language development in deaf infants: New challenges. In P. E. Spencer & M. Marschark (Eds.), *Advances in the spoken language development of deaf and hard-of-hearing children* (pp. 22–41). New York: Oxford University Press.

Olmstead, D. (2007, February 28). Mercury rising: A possible link between chemical exposure and autism may have been overlooked in the very earliest cases at Johns Hopkins. *Baltimore City Paper.* Retrieved from http://www2.citypaper.com/news/ story.asp?id=13317

Olsen, L. (2010). Reparable harm: Fulfilling the unkept promise of educational opportunity for California's long term English learners. Long Beach, CA: Californians Together. Retrieved from http://www .calfund.org/pub_documents/reparable _harm_full_final_lo.pdf

Olshansky, S. J., & Carnes, B. A. (2001). *The quest for immortality: Science at the frontiers of aging.* New York: Norton.

Olson, R. J., Werner, L., Mamalis, N., & Cionni, R. (2005). New intraocular lens technology. *American Journal of Ophthalmology, 140*(4), 709–716.

Olstad, D. L., & McCargar, L. (2009). Prevention of overweight and obesity in children under the age of 6 years. *Applied Physiology, Nutrition, and Metabolism, 34,* 551–571. doi:10.1139/H09-016

Oppenheimer, J. R. (1955). *The open mind.* New York: Simon & Schuster.

Oppo, A., Mauri, M., Ramacciotti, D., Camilleri, V., Banti, S., Borri, C., . . . , Casano, G. B. (2009). Risk factors for postpartum depression: The role of the Postpartum Depression Predictors Inventory-Revised (PDPI-R). *Archives of Women's Mental Health, 12*(4), 239–249. doi:10.1007/ s00737-009-0071-8

Oregon Department of Human Services. (2008, March). Summary of Oregon's Death with Dignity Act–2007. Retrieved from http:// oregon.gov/DHS/ph/pas/ docs/year10.pdf

Oregon Public Health Division. (2011). Oregon's Death with Dignity Act–2010. Retrieved from http://oregon.gov/DHS/ph/ pas/docs/year13.pdf

Orr, A. L., Rogers, P., & Scott, J. (2006). The complexities and connectedness of the public health and aging networks. *Journal of Vision Impairment and Blindness, 100*(Suppl.), 874–877.

Osborne, C., Manning, W. D., & Smock, P. (2007). Married and cohabiting parents' relationship stability: A focus on race and ethnicity. *Journal of Marriage and Family, 69*(5), 1345–1366.

Oser, F. K., Scarlett, W. G., & Bucher, A. (2006). Religious and spiritual development

throughout the lifespan. In W. Damon & Richard M. Lerner (Series Eds.) & R. M. Lerner (Volume Ed.), *Handbook of child psychology* (6th ed.), vol. 1: *Theoretical models of human development* (pp. 942–998). Hoboken, NJ: Wiley.

Ouwehand, C., de Ridder, D. T., & Bensing, J. M. (2007). A review of successful aging models: Proposing proactive coping as an important additional strategy. *Clinical Psychology Review, 27*(8), 873–884.

Owen, J. J., Rhoades, G. K., Stanley, S. M., & Fincham, F. D. (2010). "Hooking up" among college students: Demographic and psychosocial correlates. *Archives of Sexual Behavior, 39*(3), 653–663. doi:10.1007/ s10508-008-9414-1

Owen, P. R. (1998). Fears of Hispanic and Anglo children: Real-world fears in the 1990s. *Hispanic Journal of Behavioral Sciences, 20,* 483–491.

Ozaki, A., Uchiyama, M., Tagaya, H., Ohida, T., & Ogihara, R. (2007). The Japanese centenarian study: Autonomy was associated with healthy practices as well as physical status. *The American Geriatric Society, 55*(1), 95-101. doi:10.1111/j.1532 -5415.2006.01019.x

Ozakinci, G., Hallman, W. K., & Kipen, H. M. (2006). Persistence of symptoms in veterans of the first Gulf War: 5-year follow-up. *Environmental Health Perspectives, 114*(10), 1553–1557.

Pacey, S. (2005). Step change: The interplay of sexual and parenting problems when couples form stepfamilies. *Sexual & Relationship Therapy, 20*(3), 359–369. Retrieved from EBSCO*host.*

Padgett, R. (2007). Assisted suicide has national support as Kevorkian leaves jail. *Christian Century, 124*(13), 16–19.

Palferman, S., Matthew, N., & Turner, M. (2001). A genome wide screen for autism: Strong evidence for linkage to chromosomes 2q, 7q and 16p. *The American Journal of Human Genetics, 69,* 570–581.

Paludi, M. A. (Ed.). (2002). *Human development in multicultural contexts: A book of readings.* Englewood Cliffs, NJ: Prentice Hall.

Paniagua, F. A. (2005). *Assessing and treating culturally diverse clients: A practical guide.* Thousand Oaks, CA: Sage.

Papathanasiou, A., & Hadjiathanasiou, C. (2006). Precocious puberty. *Pediatric Endocrinology Reviews 3*(Suppl. 1), 182–187.

Parenting Empowerment Project: African American Culture. (2001). National Black Child Development Institute. Washington, DC. Retrieved from http://www.nbcdi.org/ PEP_CULTURE.htm

Paris, R., Bolton, R. E., & Weinberg, M. K. (2009). Postpartum depression, suicidality, and mother-infant interactions. *Archives of Women's Mental Health, 12*(5), 309–321. doi: 10.1007/s00737-009-0105-2

Park, M. J., Mulye, T. P., Adams, S. H., Brindis, C. D., & Irwin, C. E., Jr. (2006). The health status of young adults in the United States. *Journal of Adolescent Health, 39,* 305–317.

Parke, R. D. (1979). Perspectives on father-infant interaction. In J. D. Osofsky (Ed.), *Handbook of infant development* (pp. 549–590). New York: Wiley.

Parke, R. D. (1995). Fathers and families. In M. H. Bornstein (Ed.), *Handbook of parenting* (Vol. 3, pp. 27–63). Hillsdale, NJ: Erlbaum.

Parke, R. D. (1996). *Fatherhood.* Cambridge, MA: Harvard University Press.

Parke, R. D., & Deur, J. L. (1972). Schedule of punishment and inhibition of aggression in children. *Developmental Psychology, 7,* 266–269.

Parker, K. (2009, August 20). End-of-life decisions: How Americans cope. Pew Research Center: Pew Social & Demographic Trends. Retrieved from http://pewsocialtrends.org/pubs/740/public-views-end-of-life-care

Parker, S. (1987, June 25). Mom's troubles affect the kids. *USA Today,* p. D1.

Parkinson, G. (2005). What to do about allergies. In J. P. Arm & K. C. Allison (Eds.), *Special Health Reports* (SR81000, pp. 19–26). Boston, MA: Harvard Medical School.

Parsad, B., & Lewis, L. (2009). After-school programs in public elementary schools. (NCES2009-043). National Center for Education Statistics. Washington, DC: U.S. Department of Education. Retrieved from http://nces.ed.gov/pubs2009/2009043.pdf

Parsons, T. (1955). Family structure and the socialization of the child. In T. Parsons & R. Bales (Eds.), *Family, socialization and interaction process.* New York: Free Press.

Parten, M. B. (1933). Social play among preschool children. *Journal of Abnormal and Social Psychology, 28,* 136–137.

Patrick, J. H., & Tomczewski, D. K. (2007). Grandparents raising grandchildren: Benefits and drawbacks? *Journal of Intergenerational Relationships, 5*(4), 113–116.

Patrick, M. E., Wray-Lake, L., Finlay, A. K, & Maggs, J. L. (2010). The long arm of expectancies: Adolescent alcohol expectancies predict adult alcohol use. *Alcohol & Alcoholism, 45*(1), 17–24. doi:10.1093/alcalc/agp066

Paternoster, R., Bushway, S., Brame, R., & Apel, R. (2003). The effect of teenage employment on delinquency and problem behaviors. *Social Forces, 82*(1), 297–335.

Patterson, C. J., & Hastings, P. D. (2007). Socialization in the context of family diversity. In J. E. Grusec & P. D. Hastings (Eds.), *Handbook of socialization: Theory and research.* New York: Guilford Press.

Paul, K. I. (2005). *The negative mental health effect of unemployment: Meta-analyses of cross-sectional and longitudinal data.* Unpub-

lished doctoral dissertation, Friedrich-Alexander-Universität ErlangenNürnberg.

Pazol, K., Gamble, S. B., Parker, W. Y., Cook, D. A., Zane, S. B., & Hamdan, S. (2009, November 27). Abortion Surveillance—United States: 2006. *MMWR Weekly, 58*(SS8), 1–35. Retrieved from http://www.cdc.gov/mmwr/PDF/ss/ss5808.pdf

Pear, R. (2010, December 3). Congress approves Child Nutrition Bill. *New York Times,* p. A16. Retrieved from http://www.nytimes.com/2010/12/03/us/politics/03child.html

Pearson, Q. M. (2008). Role overload, job satisfaction, leisure satisfaction, and psychological health among employed women. *Journal of Counseling & Development, 86*(1), 57–63.

Peck, R. C. (1968). Psychological developments in the second half of life. In B. L. Neugarten (Ed.), *Middle age and aging.* Chicago: University of Chicago Press.

Pedersen, S., Vitaro, F., Barker, E. D., & Borge, A. I. H. (2007). The timing of middle-childhood peer rejection and friendship: Linking early behavior to early-adolescent adjustment. *Child Development, 78*(4), 1037–1051.

Pennisi, E. (2007). Working the (gene count) numbers: Finally, a firm answer? *Science, 316*(5828), 1113.

Peplau, L. A., & Fingerhut, A. W. (2007). The close relationships of lesbians and gay men. *Annual Review of Psychology, 58,* 405–424.

Perani, D., Paulesu, E., Galles, N. S., Dupoux, E., Dehaene, S., Bettinardi, V., . . . , Mehler, J. (1998, October). The bilingual brain. Proficiency and the age of acquistion of the second language. *Brain, 121*(10), 1841–1852. doi:10.1093/brain/121.10.1841

Perlmutter, M., & Myers, N. A. (1976). Recognition memory in preschool children. *Developmental Psychology, 12,* 271–272.

Perls, T. (2010). Health and disease in people over 85: Despite disease, disability is low. *BMJ, 340,* 59–60. doi: 10.1136/bmj.b4715

Perls, T., Kohler, I. V., Anderson, S., Schoenhofen, E., Pennington, J., Young, R., . . . , Elo, I. T. (2007). Survival of parents and siblings of Supercentenarians. *Journal of Gerontology, 62*(9), 1028–1034.

Perls, T. T. (2007). The different paths to 100. *The American Journal of Clinical Nutrition, 83*(2), 484–487.

Pernice-Duca, F., & Onaga, E. (2009). Examining the contribution of social network support to the recovery process among clubhouse members. *American Journal of Psychiatric Rehabilitation, 12,* 1–30.

Perrino, T., Fernández, M. I., Bowen, G. S., & Arheart, K. (2006). Main partner's resistance to condoms and HIV protection among disadvantaged, minority women. *Women and Health, 42*(3), 37–56.

Perrone, K. M., Webb, K. L., & Jackson, Z. V. (2007). Relationships between parental attachment, work and family roles, and life satisfaction. *Career Development Quarterly, 55*(3), 237–248. Retrieved from EBSCO*host.*

Perry, J. E., Churchill, L. R., & Kirshner, H. S. (2005). The Terri Schiavo case: Legal, ethical, and medical perspectives. *Annals of Internal Medicine, 143*(10), 744–748.

Perry, W. G., Jr. (1968). *Forms of intellectual and ethical development in the college years: A scheme.* New York: Holt, Rinehart & Winston.

Perry, W. G., Jr. (1981). Cognitive and ethical growth: The making of meaning. In A. W. Chickering & Associates (Eds.), *The modern American college: Responding to the new realities of diverse students and a changing society* (pp. 76–116). San Francisco: Jossey-Bass.

Persad, G., Wertheimer, A., & Emanuel, E. J. (2009a). Ethical criteria for allocating health-care resources. *The Lancet, 373*(9673), 1425–1426. doi:10.1016/S0140-6736(09)60818-7

Persad, G., Wertheimer, A., & Emanuel, E. J. (2009b). Principles for allocation of scarce medical interventions. *The Lancet, 373*(9661), 423–431. doi:10.1016/S0140-6736(09)60137-9

Perske, R. (1981). *Hope for the families: New directions for parents of persons with retardation or other disabilities.* Nashville: Abingdon Press.

Pescitelli, D. (1998). Women's identity development: Out of the inner space and into new territory. *Psybernetika, 3* (Spring). Retrieved from http://www.sfu.ca/wwwpsyb/98spring/pescitel.htm

Peters, E., Hess, T. M., Vastfjall, D., & Auman, C. (2007). Adult age differences in dual information processes. *Perspectives on Psychological Science, 2*(1), 1–23. doi:10.1111/j.1745-6916.2007.00025.x

Petersen, S., & Rafuls, S. E. (1998). Receiving the scepter: The generational transition and impact of parent death on adults. *Death Studies, 22,* 493–524.

Peterson, B. E., & Duncan, L. E. (2008). Midlife women's generativity and authoritarianism: Marriage, motherhood, and 10 years of aging. *Psychology and Aging, 22*(3), 411–419.

Peterson, J. L., & Zill, N. (1986). Marital disruption, parent-child relationships, and behavior problems in children. *Journal of Marriage and the Family, 48*(2), 295–307.

Peterson, K. S. (1993, April 23). Divorce needn't leave midlife women adrift. *USA Today,* p. 7D.

Petitto, L. A., Holowka, S., Sergio, L. & Ostry, D. (2001, September 6). Language rhythms in babies' hand movements. *Nature, 413,* 35–36.

Pew Forum on Religion & Public Life. (2008, February). U.S. Religious Landscape

Survey: Religious affiliation, diverse and dynamic. Retrieved from http://religions .pewforum.org/pdf/report2-religious -landscape-study-full.pdf

Pew Forum on Religion & Public Life. (2010, February 17). Religion among the Millennials: Less religiously active than older Americans, but fairly traditional in other ways. *Millennials: A portrait of Generation Next.* Retrieved from http:// pewforum.org/uploadedFiles/Topics/ Demographics/Age/millennials-report.pdf

Pew Research Center. (2007). *From 1997 to 2007: Fewer mothers prefer full-time work.* Retrieved from http:// pewresearch.org/ assets/social/pdf/ WomenWorking.pdf

Pew Research Center. (2010a). Social media & mobile Internet use among teens and young adults. *Pew Internet and American Life Project.* Retrieved from http://pewin ternet.org/Reports/2010/Social-Media-and -Young-Adults.aspx

Pew Research Center. (2010b, February 17). *Millennials, A portrait of Generation Next: Confident. Connected. Open to change.* Retrieved from http://pewsocialtrends .org/files/2010/10/millennials-confident- connected-open-to-change.pdf

Pew Research Center. (2010c, November 18). The decline of marriage and rise of new fam- ilies. *Social & Demographic Trends Project.* Retrieved from http://pewsocialtrends.org/ files/2010/11/pew-social-trends-2010 -families.pdf

Phares, V., Steinberg, A. R., & Thompson, J. K. (2004, October). Gender differences in peer and parental influences: Body image dis- turbance, self-worth, and psychological func- tioning in preadolescent children. *Journal of Youth and Adolescence, 33*(5), 421–429.

Philibert, N., Allen, J., & Elleven, R. (2008). Nontraditional students in community col- leges and the model of college outcomes for adults. *Community College Journal of Re- search and Practice, 32*(8), 582–596. doi:10 .1080/10668920600859913

Phillips, D., & Adams, G. (2001, Spring/Sum- mer). Child care and our youngest children. *The Future of Children.* The David and Lucile Packard Foundation. Retrieved from http://www.futureofchildren.org

Phillips, J., & Marks, G. (2008). Ageing lesbi- ans: Marginalizing discourses and social exclusion in the aged care industry. *Journal of Gay and Lesbian Social Services, 20*(1/), 187-202. doi:10.1080/10538720802179237

Phillips, S. D., Gleeson, J. P., & Waites- Garrett, M. (2009). Substance-abusing par- ents in the criminal justice system: Does substance abuse treatment improve their children's outcomes? *Journal of Offender Rehabilitation, 48,* 120–138. doi:10.1080/ 10509670802640925

Phillips, S. P. (2006). Risky business: Explain- ing the gender gap in longevity. *Journal of Men's Health & Gender, 3*(1), 43–44.

Phinney, J. S. (2006). Ethnic identity explora- tion. In J. J. Arnett & J. L.Tanner (Eds.), *Emerging adults in America: Coming of age in the 21st century* (pp. 117–134). Washington, DC: American Psychological Association.

Phinney, J. S., & Ong, A. (2007). Ethnic iden- tity development in immigrant families. In J. Landsford, K. Deater-Deckard, & M. Born- stein (Eds.), *Immigrant families in America* (pp. 51–68). New York: Guilford Press.

Phipps, J. L. (2011, January 3). Post- retirement—a plan to die. BankRate.com. Retrieved from http://www.bankrate.com/ financing/retirement/post-retirement -a-plan-to-die/?ec_id=m1078090

Piaget, J. (1932). *The moral judgment of the child* (M. Gaban, Trans.). London: Kegan Paul, Trench, & Trubner.

Piaget, J. (1952). *The origins of intelligence in children* (M. Cook, Trans.). New York: International Universities Press.

Piaget, J. (1954). *The construction of reality in the child.* New York: Basic Books.

Piaget, J. (1962). *Play, dreams and imitation in childhood.* New York: Norton.

Piaget, J. (1963). *The child's conception of the world.* Patterson: Littlefield.

Piaget, J. (1965). *The child's conception of number.* New York: Norton. (Original work published 1941.)

Piaget, J. (1967). *Six psychological studies.* New York: Random House.

Piaget, J. (1970, May). Conversations. *Psy- chology Today, 3,* 25–32.

Piaget, J. (1999). *The moral judgment of the child.* New York: Routledge. (Original work published 1932.)

Picard, A. (1993, July 1). Women unprepared for labour pain, psychologist says. *Globe and Mail,* p. A4.

Pickett, K. E., Kelly, S., Brunner, E., Lob- stein, T., & Wilkinson, R. G. (2005). Wider income gaps, wider waistbands? An ecologi- cal study of obesity and income inequality. *Journal of Epidemiology and Community Health, 59*(8), 670–674.

Piemont, L. (2009). The epigenesis of psycho- pathology in children of divorce. *Modern Psychoanalysis, 34*(2), 98–116.

Pierceall, E. A., & Keim, M. C. (2007). Stress and coping strategies among community college students. *Community College Jour- nal of Research and Practice, 31*(9), 703–712. doi:10.1080/10668920600866579

Pike, A., Coldwell, J., & Dunn, J. F. (2005). Sibling relationships in early/middle child- hood: Links with individual adjustment. *Journal of Family Psychiatry, 19*(4), 523–532.

Pillemer, K., & Finkelhor, D. (1988). The prevalence of elder abuse: A random sample survey. *Gerontologist, 28,* 51–57.

Pines, M. (1983, November). Can a rock walk? *Psychology Today, 17,* 46–54.

Pinker, S. (1994). *The language instinct: How the mind creates language.* New York: William Morrow.

Pinker, S. (2001, October). Talk of genetics and vice versa. *Nature, 413,* 465–466.

Pinquart, M., & Sörensen, S. (2006). Gender differences in caregiver stressors, social re- sources, and health: An updated meta- analysis. *The Journals of Gerontology Series B: Psychological Sciences and Social Sciences, 61,* P33–P45.

Pinto, D., Pagnamenta, A. T., Klei, L., Anney, R., Merico, D., Regan, R., . . . , Betancur, C. (2010). Functional impact of global rare copy number variation in autism spectrum disorders. *Nature, 466,* 368–372. doi:10.1038/nature09146

Pipher, M. (1994). *Reviving Ophelia: Saving the selves of adolescent girls.* New York: Putnam.

Player, C. L. (2006). *Loving firmness: Success- fully raising teenagers without losing your mind.* Denver, CO: Maple Tree Publishing.

Pleck, J. H. (2010). Fatherhood and masculin- ity. In M.E. Lamb (Ed.) *The role of the father in child development* (5th ed., pp. 27–57). Hoboken, NJ: Wiley.

Pleck, J. H., & Masciadrelli, B. P. (2004). Intervention: Changing the nature and extent of father involvement. In M. E. Lamb (Ed.), *The role of the father in child development* (4th ed., pp. 222–271). New York: Wiley.

Pliszka, S. R. (2007). Pharmacologic treat- ment of attention-deficit/hyperactivity dis- order: Efficacy, safety and mechanisms of action. *Neuropsychology Review, 17,* 61–72.

Plomin, R., & Dale, P. S. (2000). Genetics and early language development: A UK study of twins. In D. V. M. Bishop & B. E. Leonard (Eds.), *Speech and language impairments in children: Causes, characteristics, intervention and outcome* (pp. 35–51). Hove, Sussex: Psychology Press.

Plomin, R., Asbury, K., Dip, P. G., & Dunn, J. (2001). Why are children in the same fam- ily so different? Nonshared environment a decade later. *Canadian Journal of Psychia- try, 46,* 2001.

Plomin, R., DeFries, J. C., & Fulker, D. W. (2006). *Nature and nurture during infancy and early childhood.* Mahwah, NJ: Erlbaum.

Plomin, R., & Schalkwyk, L. C. (2007). Microarrays. *Developmental Science, 10*(1), 19–23.

Poehlmann, J., Park, J., Bouffiou, L., Abra- hams, J., Shlafer, R., & Hahn, E. (2008). Representations of family relationships in children living with custodial grandparents. *Attachment and Human Development, 10*(2), 165–188. doi:10.1080/ 14616730802113695

Polan, E., & Taylor, D. (2003). *Journey across the life span: Human development and health promotion.* Philadelphia, PA: F. A. Davis.

Pole, N., Neylan, T. C., Otte, C., Metzler, T. J., Best, S. R., Hen-Haase, C., & Mar- mar, C. R. (2007). Associations between childhood trauma and emotion-modulated psychophysiological responses to startling sounds: A study of police cadets. *Journal of Abnormal Psychology, 116*(2), 352–361.

Polka, L., Rvachew, S., & Mattock, K. (2007). Experiential influences on speech perception and speech production in infancy. In E. Hoff & M. Shatz (Eds.), *Blackwell handbook of language development* (pp. 153–172). Malden, MA: Blackwell.

Pollack, W. S. (2006). The "*war*" for boys: Hearing "real boys'" voices, healing their pain. *Professional Psychology: Research and Practice, 37*(2), 190–195.

Pollard, I. (2007). Neuropharmacology of drugs and alcohol in mother and fetus. *Seminars in Fetal & Neonatal Medicine, 12,* 106–113.

Pollet, S. L. (2009). A nationwide survey of programs for children of divorcing and separating parents. *Family Court Review, 47*(3), 523–543. doi:10.1111/j.1744-1617 .2009.01271.x

Polymeropoulos, M. H., Higgins, J. J., Golbe, L. I. (1997). Mapping of a gene for Parkinson's disease to chromosome 4q21–q23. *Science, 274,* 1197–1199.

Pons, F., & Harris, P. L. (2005). Longitudinal change and longitudinal stability of individual differences in children's emotion understanding. *Cognition and Emotion, 19*(8), 1158–1174. doi:10.1080/02699930500282108

Poortinga, W. (2006). Social relations or social capital? Individual and community health effects of bonding social capital. *Social Science & Medicine, 63*(1), 255–270.

Popenoe, D. (2007). Cohabitation, marriage, and child well-being: A cross-national perspective. Piscataway, NJ: The National Marriage Project. Retrieved from http:// marriage.rutgers.edu/ Publications/ NMP2008Cohabitation Report.pdf

Popenoe, D. (2009). Cohabitation, marriage, and child well-being: A cross-national perspective. *Society, 46*(5), 429-436. doi:10.1007/ s12115-009-9242-5

Popenoe, D., & Whitehead, B. D. (2004, November). From the National Marriage Project's *Ten Things to Know* Series. Piscataway, NJ: Rutgers University. Retrieved from http://marriage.rutgers.edu/

Popkin, B. M., & Udry, R. (1998, April). Adolescent obesity increases significantly in second and third generation U.S. immigrants. *Journal of Nutrition, 128,* 701–706.

Population Reference Bureau. (2010). Analysis of data from the U.S. Census Bureau, 2009 American Community Survey. Retrieved from http://datacenter.kidscount .org/data/acrossstates/Rankings.aspx?ind=35

Porath, M. (2006). The conceptual underpinnings of giftedness: Developmental and educational implications. *High Ability Studies, 17*(2), 145–158.

Portman, M. V. (1895). Notes on the Andamanese. *Anthropological Institute of Great Britain and Ireland, 25,* 361–371.

Posada, G., Carbonell, O. A., Alzate, G., & Plata, S. J. (2004). Through Colombian lenses: Ethnographic and conventional analyses of maternal care and their associations with secure base behavior. *Developmental Psychology, 40*(4), 508–518.

Posthuma, D., De Geus, E. J. C., Baare, W. F. C., Hulshoff Pol, H. E., Kahn, R. S., & Boomsma, D. I. (2002). The association between brain volume and intelligence is of genetic origin. *Nature Neuroscience, 5,* 83–88.

Potoczniak, D. J., Aldea, M. A., & DeBlaere, C. (2007). Ego identity, social anxiety, social support, and self-concealment in lesbian, gay, and bisexual individuals. *Journal of Counseling Psychology, 54*(4), 447–457. doi: 10.1037/0022-0167.54.4.447

Potts, A., Grace, V., Gavey, N., & Vares, T. (2004). Viagra stories: Challenging "erectile dysfunction." *Social Science and Medicine, 59*(3), 489–499.

Powell, L. M., Szczypka, G., Chaloupka, F. J., & Braunschweig, C. L. (2007). Nutritional content of television food advertisements seen by children and adolescents in the United States. *Pediatrics, 120*(3), 576–583.

Power, J. J., Perlesz, A., Schofield, M. J., Pitts, M. K., Brown, R., McNair, R., ... Bickerdike, A. (2010). Understanding resilience in same-sex parented families: The Work, Love, Play study. *BMC Public Health, 10,* 115–125.

Poythress, E. L., Burnett, J., Nailk, A. D., Pickens, S., & Dyer, C. B. (2007). Severe self-neglect: An epidemiological and historical perspective. *Journal of Elder Abuse & Neglect, 18*(4), 1–3.

Prasse, J. E., & Kikano, G. E. (2004, November/December). An overview of dysphagia in the elderly. *Advanced Studies in Medicine, 4*(10), 527–533.

Pratt, C. C., Walker, A. J., & Wood, B. L. (1992). Bereavement among former caregivers to elderly mothers. *Family Relations, 41,* 278–283.

Pratt, M. W., Diessner, R., Hunsberger, B., Pancer, S. M., & Savoy, K. (1991). Four pathways in the analysis of adult development and aging: Comparing analyses of reasoning about personal-life dilemmas. *Psychology and Aging, 4,* 666–675.

President's Council on Physical Fitness and Sports. (2007). *A report of the surgeon general: Physical activity and health: Adolescents and young adults.* Retrieved from http://www.fitness.gov/ adoles.htm

Pressley, J. C., Barlow, B., Kendig, T., & Paneth-Pollak, R. (2007). Twenty-year trends in fatal injuries to very young children: The persistence of racial disparities. *Pediatrics, 119*(4), 875–884.

Preti, A., Pinna, C., Nocco, S., Mulliri, E., Pilia, S., Petretto, R., ..., Masala, C. (2006). Body evidence: Tattoos, body piercing, and eating disorder symptoms among adolescents. *Journal of Psychosomatic Research, 61,* 561–566.

Preventing Domestic Violence. *Peacework, 36*(393), 14–15.

Price, C. A., & Joo, E. (2005). Exploring the relative relationship between marital status and women's retirement satisfaction. *International Journal of Aging and Human Development, 61*(1), 37–55.

Price, C. S., Thompson, W. W., Goodson, B., Weintraub, E. S., Croen, L. A., Hinrichsen, V. L., ... Destefano, F. (2010). Prenatal and infant exposure to thimerosal from vaccines and immunoglobulins and risk of autism. *Pediatrics, 126*(4), 656–664. doi:10.1542/ peds.2010-0309

Prince, D., & Butler, D. (2007, August 20). *Attitudes of seniors and baby boomers on aging in place.* Clarity 2007 Aging in Place Study (Seniors and Baby Boomers). Retrieved from http://www.clarityproducts .com/research/Clarity_Aging_in_Place _2007.pdf

Provencio-Vasquez, E., & Rodriguez, A. (2009). Circumcision revisited. *Journal for Specialists in Pediatric Nursing, 14*(4), 295–297. doi:10.1111/j.1744-6155.2010.00234.x

Project on Student Debt. (2010). *Student debt and the class of 2009.* Retrieved from www.projectonstudentdebt.org/files/pub/ classof2009.pdf

PSA Rising. (2007, October 11). Human genome search helps African American men fight prostate cancer. Retrieved from http:// www.psa-rising.com/prostatecancer/african -american-genome06.htm

Public Affairs Committee. (2000). Teratology Society Public Affairs Committee position paper: Thalidomide. *Teratology, 62,* 172–173.

Pugliesi, K. (1995). Work and well-being: Gender differences in the psychological consequences of employment. *Journal of Health and Social Behavior, 36,* 57–71.

Pulkkinen, L., & Caspi, A. (Eds.). (2002). *Paths to successful development.* New York: Cambridge University Press.

Purnell, A. (2009). Providing creativity through origami instruction. New York City Writing Project, Lehman College, CUNY. Retrieved from http://www.lehman .edu/deanedu/litstudies/ELP/PDF/ AnnettePurnell_Origami%5B1%5D.pdf

Puzzanchera, C. (2009, December). Juvenile arrests 2008. *Juvenile Justice Bulletin.* Washington, DC: U.S. Department of Justice. Retrieved from http://www.ncjrs .gov/pdffiles1/ojjdp/228479.pdf

Pynoos, J., & Liebig, P. (2009). Changing work, retirement, and housing patterns. *Journal of American Society on Aging, 33*(3), 20–27.

Quill, T. E. (2004). Dying and decision making—Evolution of end-of-life options. *New England Journal of Medicine, 350,* 2029–2032.

Quirk, K. (2007). *"Smart" pillbox could help seniors live at home longer.* University of Wisconsin at Milwaukee. Retrieved from http://www.uwm.edu/News/Features/06.05/Smart_Pillbox.html

Rabow, M. W., Hardie, G. E., Fair, J. M., & McPhee, S. J. (2000). End-of-life care content in 50 textbooks from multiple specialties. JAMA, 283(6), 771–778.

Radcliffe-Brown, A. R. (1940). On joking relationships. Africa, 13, 195–210.

Radwan, T. J., & Morgan, R. C. (2010). Today's elderly in bankruptcy and predictions for the elderly of tomorrow. National Academy of Elder Law Attorneys Journal, 6(1), 1–24.

Rahman, A., & Toubia, N. (2000). Female genital mutilation: A guide to laws and policies worldwide. New York: Zed Books.

Räikkönen, K., Pesonen, A. K., Heinonen, K., Komsi, N., Järvenpää, A. L., & Strandberg, T. E. (2006). Stressed parents: A dyadic perspective on perceived infant temperament. Infant and Child Development, 15, 75–87.

Rajkumar, S. V. (2004, July). Thalidomide: Tragic past and promising future. Mayo Clinic Proceedings, 79(7), 899–904.

Ramakrishnan, K. (2008). Evaluation and treatment of enuresis. American Family Physician, 78(4), 489–496. PMID: 18756657

Ramer-Chrastek, J., & Thygeson, M. V. (2005). A perinatal hospice for an unborn child with a life-limiting condition. International Journal of Palliative Nursing, 11(6), 274–276.

Ramstetter, C. L., Murray, R., & Garner, A. S. (2010). The crucial role of recess in schools. Journal of School Health, 80(11), 517–525. doi:10.1111/j.1746-1561.2010.00537.x

Ramus, F. (2002). Language discrimination by newborns: Teasing apart phonotactic, rhythmic, and intonational cues. Annual Review of Language Acquisition, 2, 85–115.

Rando, T. A. (2006). Stem cells, ageing and the quest for immortality. Nature, 441(7097), 1080–1086.

Raneri, L. G., & Constance, W. M. (2007). Social ecological predictors of repeat adolescent pregnancy. Perspectives on Sexual and Reproductive Health, 39(1), 39–47.

Rapp, M. A., Krampe, R. T., & Baltes, P. B. (2006). Adaptive task prioritization in aging: Selective resource allocation to postural control is preserved in Alzheimer disease. The American Journal of Geriatric Psychiatry, 14(1), 52–61.

Rappaport, A. (2008). The future of retirement: An exploration and comparison of different scenarios. Benefits Quarterly, 3, 40–62.

Rathunde, K., & Csikszentmihalyi, M. (2005). The social context of middle school: Teachers, friends, and activities in Montessori and traditional school environments. The Elementary School Journal, 106(1), 59–79. doi:10.1086/496907

Rathunde, K., & Csikszentmihalyi, M. (2006). The developing person: An experiential perspective. In W. Damon & R. M. Lerner (Eds.), Handbook of child psychology: Vol. 1. Theoretical models of human development (6th ed.). New York: Wiley.

Rattan, S. I. S., & Kassem, M. (Eds.). (2006). Prevention and treatment of age-related disease. The Netherlands: Springer.

Rauscher, F. (1996). The power of music. Early Childhood News. Retrieved from http://www.earlychildhood.com/music.htm

Ray, B. D. (2010). Academic achievement and demographic traits of homeschool students: A nationwide study. Academic Leadership: The Online Journal, 8(1), 1–26. Retrieved from http://www.academicleadership.org/pdf/ALJ_ISSN1533-7812_8_1_392.pdf

Ray, B. D. (2011, January 3). 2.04 million homeschool students in the United States in 2010. National Home Education Research Institute. Retrieved from http://www.nheri.org/HomeschoolPopulationReport2010.pdf

Raymo, J. M., & Ono, H. (2007). Coresidence with parents, women's economic resources, and the transition to marriage in Japan. Journal of Family Issues, 28(5), 653–681.

Razay, G., Vreugdenhil, A., & Wilcock, G. (2007). The metabolic syndrome and Alzheimer disease. Arch Neurology, 64, 93–96.

Reaction time studies of lexical production in young second language learners. (2005). Center for Research in Language. Retrieved from http://crl.ucsd.edu/bilingual/children/html

Reardon, L. E., Leen-Feldner, E. W., & Hayward, C. (2009). A critical review of the empirical literature on the relation between anxiety and puberty. Clinical Psychology Review, 29(1), 1–23. doi: 10.1016/j.cpr.2008.09.005

Reber, A. S. (1993). Implicit learning and tacit knowledge: An essay on the cognitive unconscious. New York: Oxford University Press.

Recchia, H. E., & Howe, N. (2009). Associations between social understanding, sibling relationship quality, and siblings' conflict strategies and outcomes. Child Development, 80(5), 1564–1578. doi:10.1111/j.1467-8624.2009.01351.x

Recognizing and screening for postpartum depression in mothers of NICU infants. (2003, March 24). Advances in Neonatal Care, 3(1). 37–46. Retrieved from http://www.medscape.com/ viewarticle/450938

Recommended childhood and adolescent immunization schedule. (2005, January 7). MMWR Weekly, 53(51), Q1–Q3. Retrieved from http://www.cdc.gov/mmwr/preview/mmwrhtml/mm5351-Immunizationa1.htm

Rector-Page, L. (2004). Healthy healing: A guide to self-healing for everyone (12th ed.). Healthy Healing, Inc.

Rees, D. (1997). Death and bereavement: The psychological, religious, and cultural interfaces. London: Whurr.

Rees, N. S. (1998, January). The self-esteem fraud. USA Today Magazine, pp. 66–68.

Reeve, J. (2009). Why teachers adopt a controlling motivating style toward students and how they can become more autonomy supportive. Educational Psychologist, 44(3), 159–175. doi:10.1080/00461520903028990

Regalado, M., Sareen, H., Inkelas, M., Wissow, L. S., & Halfon, N. (2004). Parents' discipline of young children: Results from the National Survey of Early Childhood Health. Pediatrics, 113(6), 1952–1958.

Reichman, J. (1996). I'm too young to get old: Health care for women over forty. New York: Random House.

Reingold, D., & Nesbit, R. (2006, December). Volunteer growth in America: A review of trends since 1974. Washington, DC: Corporation for National and Community Service.

Relin, D. O. (2006, March). Don't call them old, call them . . . Parade Magazine. Retrieved from http://www.hsph.harvard.edu/chc/reinventingaging/ press/parade2.html

Repetti, R., Taylor, S. E., & Saxbe, D. (2007). The influence of early socialization experiences on the development of biological systems. In J. E. Grusec & P. D. Hastings (Eds.), Handbook of socialization: Theory and research (pp. 124–152). New York: Guilford Press.

Resendes, B. L., Williamson, R. E., & Morton, C. C. (2001, September 27). At the speed of sound: Gene discovery in the auditory system. American Journal of Human Genetics, 69, 923–935.

Resnick, S. M., Espeland, M. A., Jaramillo, S. A., Hirsch, C., Stefanick, M. L., Murray, A. M., . . . , Davatzikos, C. (2009). Postmenopausal hormone therapy and regional brain volumes. Journal of Neurology, 72(2), 135–142. doi:10.1212/01.wnl.0000339037.76336.cf

Restak, R. (1984). The brain. New York: Bantam.

Reynolds, A. J., Temple, J. A., Suh-Ruu, O., Robertson, D. L., Mersky, J. P., Topitzes, J. W., & Niles, M. D. (2007). Effects of a school-based, early childhood intervention on adult health and well-being: A 19-year follow-up of low-income families. Archives of Pediatric & Adolescent Medicine, 161(8), 730–739.

Reynolds, C. (2004). Gen X: The unbeholden. American Demographics, 26(4), 8–9.

Rheingold, H. L. (1969a). The effect of a strange environment on the behavior of infants. In B. M. Foss (Ed.), Determinants of infant behavior (Vol. 4). New York: Wiley.

Rheingold, H. L. (1969b). The social and socializing infant. In D. A. Goslin (Ed.), Handbook of socialization theory and research. Chicago: Rand McNally.

Rheingold, H. L. (1985). Development as the acquisition of familiarity. Annual Review of Psychology, 36, 105–130.

Rheingold, H. L., & Adams, J. L. (1980). The significance of speech to newborns. Developmental Psychology, 16, 397–403.

Rheingold, H. L., Hay, D. F., & West, M. J. (1976). Sharing in the second year of life. *Child Development, 47,* 1148–1158.

Rice, M. (2007, July 3). *Danish clinics achieve 70 per cent success rates in fertility treatment.* European Society of Human Reproduction & Embryology. Retrieved from http://www.eshre.com/emc.asp?pageId=948

Richard, J. F., & Schneider, B. H. (2005). Assessing friendship motivation during preadolescence and early adolescence. *Journal of Early Adolescence, 367–385.* doi:10.1177/0272431605276930

Rideout, V. J., Foehr, U. G., & Roberts, D. F. (2010). Generation M2: Media in the lives of 8- to 18-year-olds. Menlo Park, CA: Kaiser Family Foundation. Retrieved from http://www.kff.org/entmedia/upload/8010.pdf

Riediger, M., Freund, A. M., & Baltes, P. B. (2005). Managing life through personal goals: Intergoal facilitation and intensity of goal pursuit in younger and older adults. *Journal of Gerontology, 60B*(2), 84–91.

Ries, L. A. G., Eisner, M. P., Kosary, C. L., Hankey, B. F., Miller, B. A., Clegg, L., . . . , Edwards, B. K. (Eds.). (2007). *SEER Cancer Statistics Review, 1975–2004,* Bethesda, MD: National Cancer Institute.

Riggle, E. D. B., Whitman, J. S., Olson, A., Rostosky, S. S., & Strong, S. (2008). The positive aspects of being a lesbian or a gay man. *Professional Psychology: Research and Practice, 39*(2), 210–217. doi:10.1037/0735-7028.39.2.210

Riley, L. (2006). *You & your baby: Pregnancy.* Des Moines, IA: Meredith Books.

Rimer, S. (1998, December 23). For aged, dating game is numbers game. *New York Times,* Late Edition, p. A1.

Rimsza, M. E., & Kirk, G. M. (2005). Common medical problems of the college student. *Pediatric Clinics of North America, 52,* 9–24.

Rischitelli, G., Nygren, P., Bougatsos, C., Freeman, M., & Helfand, M. (2006). Screening for elevated lead levels in childhood and pregnancy: An updated summary of evidence for the U.S. Preventive Services Task Force. *Pediatrics, 118*(6), 1867–1895.

Riskind, R. G., & Patterson, C. J. (2010). Parenting intentions and desires among childless lesbian, gay, and heterosexual individuals. *Journal of Family Psychology, 24*(1), 78–81. doi:10.1037/a0017941

Roach, L. T. (2010, October 6). Letter to President's Committee for People with Intellectual Disabilities (PCPID). Washington, DC: U.S. Department of Health and Human Services.

Roach, M. (1983, January 16). Another name for madness. *New York Times Magazine,* pp. 22–31.

Roazen, P. (1992). *Freud and his followers.* New York: Knopf.

Robben, A. C. (Ed.). (2006). *Death, mourning, and burial.* Malden: Blackwell.

Robbins, G., Powers, D., & Burgess, S. (2008). *A fit & well way of life.* New York: McGraw-Hill.

Robers, S., J. Zhang, J., & Truman, J. (2010). *Indicators of school crime and safety: 2010.* Washington, DC: U.S. Department of Education, U.S. Department of Justice.

Roberts, K. (1988). Retrieval of a basic-level category in prelinguistic infants. *Developmental Psychology, 24,* 21–27.

Robinson, C. W., & Sloutsky, V. M. (2007). Linguistic labels and categorization in infancy: Do labels facilitate or hinder? *Infancy, 11*(3), 233–253.

Robinson, O. C., Demetre, J. D., & Corney, R. (2010). Personality and retirement: Exploring the links between the Big Five personality traits, reasons for retirement and the experience of being retired. *Personality and Individual Differences, 48*(1), 792–797.

Robinson, P. (1993). *Freud and his critics.* Berkeley, CA: University of California Press.

Rocca, K. A., Martin, M. M., & Dunleavy, K. N. (2010). Siblings' motives for talking to each other. *The Journal of Psychology, 144*(2), 205–219.

Rochat, P., & Striano, T. (1998). Primary action in early ontogeny. *Human Development, 41,* 112–115.

Rodgers, B., & Rodgers, T. A. (2006). *The singlehood phenomenon: 10 brutally honest reasons why people aren't getting married.* Colorado Springs, CO: NavPress.

Rodkin, P. C., Farmer, T. W., Pearl, R. & Van Acker, R. (2006). They're cool: Social status and peer group supports for aggressive boys and girls. *Social Development, 15*(2), 175–204. doi:10.1046/j.1467-9507.2006.00336.x

Rodriguez, B. (1998). "It lets the sad out": Using children's art to express emotions. *Early Childhood News.* Retrieved from http://www.earlychildhoodnews.com/sad.htm

Rogers, C. R. (1970). *On becoming a person: A therapist's view of psychotherapy.* Boston: Houghton Mifflin.

Rogoff, B. (2003). *The cultural nature of human development.* New York: Oxford University Press.

Rogoff, B., Moore, L. Najafi, B., Dexter, A., Correa-Chavez, M., & Solis, J. (2007). Children's development of cultural repertoires through participation in everyday routines and practices. In J. E. Grusec & P. D. Hastings (Eds.), *Handbook of socialization: Theory and research* (pp. 490–515). New York: Guilford Press.

Rohner, R. P., & Rohner, E. C. (1981). Parental acceptance-rejection and parental control: Cross-cultural codes abstract. *Ethnology, 20,* 245–260.

Rohner, R. P., & Veniziano, R. A. (2001). The importance of father love: History and contemporary evidence. *Review of General Psychology, 5*(4), 382–405.

Rokach, A. (1999). Cultural background and coping with loneliness. *Journal of Psychology, 133*(2), 217–229.

Rollins, N. K., Vachha, B., Srinivasan, P., Chia, J., Pickering, J., Hughes, C. W., & Gimi, B. (2009). Simple developmental dyslexia in children: Alterations in diffusion-tensor metrics of white matter tracts at 3 T. *Radiology, 251,* 882–891.

Rooks, J. (2007). Use of nitrous oxide in midwifery practice—complementary, synergistic, and needed in the United States. *Journal of Midwifery & Women's Health, 52*(3), 186–189.

Rosales, F. J., Reznick, J. S., & Zeisel, S. H. (2009). Understanding the role of nutrition in the brain and behavioral development of toddlers and preschool children: Identifying and addressing methodological barriers. *Nutritional Neuroscience, 12*(5), 190–202. doi:10.1179/147683009X423454

Rosales-Ruiz, J., & Baer, D. M. (1997). Behavioral cusps: A developmental and pragmatic concept for behavior analysis. *Journal of Applied Behavior Analysis, 30,* 533–544.

Rosamond, W., Flegal, K., Furie, K., Go, A., Greenlund, K., Haase, N., . . . , Hong, Y. (2008). Heart disease and stroke statistics 2008 update: A report from the American Heart Association Statistics Committee and Stroke Statistics Subcommittee. *Circulation, 117*(4), e25–e146.

Rosen, R. C., Fisher, W. A., Eardley, I., Niederberger, C., Nadel, A., & Sand, M. (2004). The multinational Men's Attitudes to Life Events and Sexuality (MALES) study: *Current Medical Research and Opinion, 20*(5), 607–617.

Rosenfeld, R. L., Lipton, R. B., & Drum, M. L. (2010). Therlarche, pubarche, and menarche attainment in children with normal and elevated body mass index. *Pediatrics, 123,* 84–88. doi:10.1542/peds.2008-0146

Rosenthal, E. (1992, August 18). Troubled marriage? Sibling relations may be at fault. *New York Times,* pp. C-1, C-9.

Rosenwaks, Z., Goldstein, M., & Fuerst, M. L. (2010). *A baby at last: The couple's complete guide to getting pregnant—from cutting-edge treatments to commonsense wisdom.* New York: Simon & Schuster.

Rosick, E. R. (2003, August). Protecting muscle mass as you age. *Life Extension Magazine.* Retrieved from http://www.lef.org/magazine/mag2003/aug2003_report_muscle_01.html

Rosinski, R. R., Pellegrino, J. W., & Siegel, A. W. (1977). Developmental changes in the semantic processing of pictures and words. *Journal of Experimental Child Psychology, 23,* 282–291.

Rosman, K. (2010, October 14). Y U Luv Texts, H8 Calls: We want to reach others but not to be interrupted. *Wall Street Journal,* D1–D2.

Rosner, M. (2000). *Future trends of the kibbutz—An assessment of recent changes.* University of Haifa: Institute for Study and Research of the Kibbutz. Publication No. 83.

Ross, P., & Cuskelly, M. (2006). Adjustment, sibling problems and coping strategies of brothers and sisters of children with autistic spectrum disorder. *Journal of Intellectual & Developmental Disability, 31*(2), 77–86. Retrieved from EBSCOhost.

Ross, M. E. T., & Aday, L. A. (2006). Stress and coping in African American grandparents who are raising their grandchildren. *Journal of Family Issues, 27*(7), 912–932.

Rossi, A. S. (1968). Transition to parenthood. *Journal of Marriage and the Family, 30,* 26–39.

Rossi, S., & Wittrock, M. C. (1971). Developmental shifts in verbal recall between mental ages two and five. *Child Development, 42,* 333–338.

Rothbart, M. K. (2004). Temperament and the pursuit of an integrated developmental psychology, *Merrill-Palmer Quarterly, 50*(4), 492–505.

Rothbart, M. K., & Bates, J. E. (2006). Temperament. In W. Damon & R. M. Lerner (Eds.), *Handbook of child psychology* (6th ed., Vol. 3, pp. 99–166). New York: Wiley.

Rothbart, M. K., Posner, M. I., & Kieras, J. (2006). Temperament, attention, and the development of self-regulation. In K. McCartney & D. Phillips (Eds.), *Blackwell handbook of early childhood development* (pp. 338–357). Malden, MA: Blackwell.

Rothbart, M. K., Sheese, B. E., & Posner, M. I. (2007). Executive attention and effortful control: Linking temperament, brain networks, and genes. *Child Development Perspectives, 1*(1), 2–7.

Rothbaum, F., & Trommsdorff, G. (2007). Do roots and wings complement or oppose one another? The socialization of relatedness and autonomy in cultural context. In J. E. Grusec & P. D. Hastings (Eds.), *Handbook of socialization: Theory and research* (pp. 461–489). New York: Guilford Press.

Rothbaum, F., Weisz, J., Pott, M., Miyake, K., & Morelli, G. (2000). Attachment and culture: Security in the United States and Japan. *American Psychologist, 55*(10), 1093–1104.

Rousson, V., & Paccaud, F. (2010). A set of indicators for decomposing the secular increase of life expectancy. *Population Health Metrics, 8*(18), 1–9.

Rovee-Collier, C. (1987). Learning and memory in infancy. In J. D. Osofsky (Ed.), *Handbook of infant development* (2nd ed.). New York: Wiley.

Rovee-Collier, C., Lipsitt, L. P., & Hayne, H. (Eds.). (2000). *Progress in infancy research* (Vol. 1). Mahwah, NJ: Erlbaum.

Rovio, S., Kåreholt, I., Helkala, E. L., Viitanen, M., Winblad, B., Tuomilehto, J., ...

Kivipelto, M. (2005). Leisure-time physical activity at midlife and the risk of dementia and Alzheimer's disease. *The Lancet Neurology, 4*(11), 705–711.

Ruble, D. N., Martin, C. L., & Berenbaum, S. A. (2006). Gender development. In W. Damon & R. M. Lerner (Eds.), *Handbook of child psychology* (6th ed., Vol. 3, pp. 858–932). New York: Wiley.

Rue, V. M., Coleman, P. K., Rue, J. J., & Reardon, D. C. (2004). Induced abortion and traumatic stress: A preliminary comparison of American and Russian women. *Medical Science Monitor, 10*(10), 5–16.

Rugeley, C., & Van Wart, M. (2006). Everyday moral exemplars: The case of Judge Sam Medina. *Public Integrity, 8*(4), 381–394. doi:10.2753/PIN1099-9922080405

Ruppel, S. E., Jenkins, W. J., Griffin, J. L., & Kizer, J. B. (2010). Are they depressed or just old? A study of perceptions about the elderly suffering from depression. *North American Journal of Psychology, 12*(1), 31–42.

Russell, S. T., & Joyner, K. (2001, August). Adolescent sexual orientation and suicide risk: Evidence from a national study. *American Journal of Public Health, 91,* 1276–1281.

Rust, P. C. (2003). Monogamy and polyamory: Relationship issues for bisexuals. In L. D. Garnets & D. C. Kimmel (Eds.), *Psychological perspectives on lesbian, gay, and bisexual experiences* (pp. 475–496). New York: Columbia University Press.

Rutherford, M. (2001, March). What did you say? More folks are losing their hearing—and many don't even realize how much they're missing. *Time Bonus Section: Generations,* G7–G10.

Rutland, A. (2005). The development and self-regulation of intergroup attitudes in children. In M. Bennett & F. Sani (Eds.), *The development of the social self* (pp. 247–266). Hove, Sussex: Psychology Press.

Rutter, D. R., & Kurkin, K. (1987). Turn-taking in mother-infant interaction: An examination of vocalizations and gaze. *Developmental Psychology, 23,* 54–61.

Ryan, M., & Berkowitz, D. (2009). Constructing gay and lesbian parent families "beyond the closet." *Qualitative Sociology, 32*(2), 153–172. doi:10.1007/s11133-009-9124-6

Rutter, M. (2007). Gene-environment interdependence. *Developmental Science, 10*(1), 12–18.

Ryan, A. M. (2001). The peer group as a context for the development of young adolescent motivation and achievement. *Child Development, 72,* 1135–1150.

Sable, J., & Plotts, C. (2010). *Public elementary and secondary school student enrollment and staff counts from the Common Core of Data: School Year 2008–09* (NCES 2010-347). U.S. Department of Education. Washington, DC: National Center for

Education Statistics. Retrieved from http://nces.ed.gov/pubsearch

Sacher, G. A. (1978). Longevity, aging, and death: An evolutionary perspective. *Gerontologist, 18,* 112–119.

Sachs, J. (1987). Preschool boys' and girls' language use in pretend play. In S. U. Phillips, S. Steele, & C. Tanz (Eds.), *Language, gender and sex in comparative perspective.* New York: Cambridge University Press.

Sachs, J., Bard, B., & Johnson, M. (1981). Language learning with restricted input: Case studies of two hearing children of deaf parents. *Applied Psycholinguistics, 2,* 33–54.

Sacker, I., & Zimmer, M. (1987). *Dying to be thin.* New York: Warner Books.

Sadler, W. A. (1978). Dimensions in the problem of loneliness: A phenomenological approach in social psychology. *Journal of Phenomenological Psychology, 9,* 157–187.

Safdar, S., Friedlmeier, W., Matsumoto, D., Yoo, S. H., Kwantes, C. T., Kakai, H., & Shigemasu, E. (2009). Variations of emotional display rules within and across cultures: A comparison between Canada, USA, and Japan. *Canadian Journal of Behavioural Science, 41*(1), 1–10. doi:10.1037/a0014387

Saffran, J. R., Werker, J. F., & Werner, L. A. (2006).The infant's auditory world: Hearing, speech, and the beginnings of language. In W. Damon & R. M. Lerner (Eds.), *Handbook of child psychology* (6th ed., Vol. 2, pp. 58–108). New York: Wiley.

Sallie Mae. (2009). *How undergraduate students use credit cards: Sallie Mae's national study of usage rates and trends, 2009.* Retrieved from https://www.salliemae.com/about/news_info/newsreleases/041309.htm

Salthouse, T. A. (1991). *Theoretical perspectives on cognitive aging.* Hillsdale, NJ: Erlbaum.

Salthouse, T. A. (2009). When does age-related cognitive decline begin? *Neurobiology of Aging, 30*(4), 507–514. doi:10.1016/j.neurobiolaging.2008.09.023

Samanci, O. (2010). Teacher views on social skills development in primary school students. *Education, 131*(1), 147–157.

Same-Sex Marriage, Civil Unions, and Domestic Partnerships. (2011, June 27). *New York Times* [online]. Retrieved from http://topics.nytimes.com/top/reference/timestopics/subjects/s/same_sex_marriage/index.html

Sameroff, A. J. (1968). The components of sucking in the human newborn. *Journal of Experimental Child Psychology, 6,* 607–623.

Sampaio, R. C., & Truwit, C. L. (2001). Myelination in the developing brain. In C. A. Nelson & M. Luciana (Eds.), *Handbook of developmental cognitive neuroscience* (p. 35–44). Cambridge, MA: MIT Press.

Samuels, S. C. (1997). Midlife crisis: Helping patients cope with stress, anxiety, and depression. *Geriatrics, 52,* 55–63.

Sanchez, A., Norman, G. J., Sallis, J. F., Calfas, K. J., & Cella, J. (2007). Patterns and correlates of physical activity and nutrition behaviors in adolescents. *American Journal of Preventive Medicine, 32*(2), 124–130.

Sanderson, S. K. (2001). Explaining monogamy and polygyny in human societies: Comment on Kanazawa and Still. *Social Forces, 80*(1), 329–336.

Sanderson, S. L. (2004). Could your food be hurting you? *Exceptional Parent, 3*(2), 20–21.

Sandfort, T. G. M., Melendez, R. M., & Diaz, R. M. (2007). Gender nonconformity, homophobia, and mental distress in Latino gay and bisexual men. *Journal of Sex Research, 44*(2), 181–189.

Sandler, I., Miles, J., Cookston, J., & Braver, S. (2008). Effects of father and mother parenting on children's mental health in high- and low-conflict divorces. *Family Court Review, 46*(2), 282–296.

Sandomir, R. (2005, February 13). Please don't call the customers dead. *New York Times,* p. BU1.

Sanford, K. (2006). Communication during marital conflict: When couples alter their appraisal, they change their behavior. *Journal of Family Psychology, 20*(2), 256–265.

Sanford, K. (2007). Attributions and anger in early marriage: Wives are event-dependent and husbands are schematic. *Journal of Family Psychology, 19*(2), 180–188.

Sani, F., & Bennett, M. (2004). Developmental aspects of social identity. In M. Bennett & F. Sani (Eds.), *The development of the social self* (pp. 77–102). Hove, Sussex: Psychology Press.

Sanson, A., & Rothbart, M. K. (1995). Child temperament and parenting. In M. H. Bornstein (Ed.), *Handbook of parenting* (Vol. 4, pp. 299–321). Hillsdale, NJ: Erlbaum.

Santen, R. J., Allred, D. C., Ardoin, S. P, Archer, D. F., Boyd, N., Braunstein, G. D., . . . , Utian, W. H. (2010). Postmenopausal hormone therapy: An Endocrine Society Statement. *The Journal of Clinical Endocrinology & Metabolism, 95*(S1-7), 1–71. doi:10.1210/jc.2009-2509

Santoro, E. (2008). Breast implants and mammography: What we know and what we don't know. Retrieved from http://www.breastimplantinfo.org/ what_know/ bimammo.html

Sartin, J. S. (2006). Gulf War syndrome: The final chapter? *Mayo Clinic Proceedings, 81*(11), 1425–1426.

Satter, E. M. (1998). *Secrets of raising a healthy eater.* Chelsea, MI: Kelcy Press.

Savage-Rumbaugh, E. S., Murphy, J., Sevcik, R. A., Brakke, K. E., Williams, S. L., & Rumbaugh, D. M. (1993). Language comprehension in ape and child. *Monographs of the Society for Research in Child Development, 58*(3–4, Serial No. 233).

Save the Children. (2007, May). *State of the world's mothers: Saving the lives of children under 5.* Retrieved from http://www.savethechildren.org/publications/mothers/2007/SOWM-2007-final.pdf

Savin-Williams, R. C., & Ream, G. (2003). Suicide attempts among sexual-minority male youth. *Journal of Clinical Child and Adolescent Psychology, 32*(4), 509–522.

Savitsky, L., Illingworth, M., & DuLaney, M. (2009). Civilian social work: Serving the military and veteran populations. *Social Work, 54*(4), 327–339.

Sayer, L. C., & Nicholson, L. L. (2006). Economic resources, marital bargains, and marital quality. Paper presented at the Annual Meeting of the Population Association of America. Retrieved from http://paa2006.princeton.edu/

Scarlett, W. G., Naudeau, S., Ponte, I., Salonius-Pasternak, D., & Ponte, I. (2004). *Children's play.* Thousand Oaks, CA: Sage.

Scarr, S. (1997). Why child care has little impact on most children's development. *Current Directions in Psychological Science, 6,* 143–148.

Schacter, D. L., & Tulving, E. (Eds.). (1994). *Memory systems.* Cambridge, MA: MIT Press.

Schade, C. P., & Brehm, J. G. (2010). Improving the home health acute-care hospitalization quality measure. *Health Services Research, 45*(3), 712–727. doi:10.1111/j.1475-6773.2010.01106.x

Schafer, G., & Plunkett, K. (1998). Rapid word learning by 15-month-olds under tightly controlled conditions. *Child Development, 69,* 309–320.

Schaffer, H. R. (1971). *The growth of sociability.* Baltimore: Penguin Books.

Schaffer, H. R. (1996). *Social development.* Cambridge, MA: Blackwell.

Schaffer, H. R., & Emerson, P. E. (1964). The development of social attachments in infancy. *Monographs of the Society for Research in Child Development, 29*(3, Series No. 94).

Schaie, K. W. (1994). The course of adult intellectual development. *American Psychologist, 49,* 304–313.

Schaie, K. W. (1996). *Intellectual development in adulthood: The Seattle Longitudinal Study.* New York: Cambridge University Press.

Schaie, K. W. (2005). *Developmental influences on adult intelligence: The Seattle Longitudinal Study.* New York: Oxford University Press.

Schaie, K. W. (2007). Generational differences: The age-period cohort model. In J. E. Birren (Ed.), *Encyclopedia of gerontology* (2nd ed., pp. 601–610). Oxford: Elsevier.

Schanzenbach, D. W. (2009). Do school lunches contribute to childhood obesity? *The Journal of Human Resources, 44*(3), 684–709.

Scharlach, A. E., Gustavson, K., & Dal Santo, T. S. (2007). Assistance received by employed caregivers and their care recipients: Who helps care recipients when caregivers work full time? *Gerontologist, 47,* 752–762.

Scheffler, R. M., Hinshaw, S. P., Modrek, S., & Levine, P. (2007, March/April). The global market for ADHD medications. *Health Affairs, 2,* 450–457.

Scheib, J. E., Riordan, M., & Rubin, S. (2005). Adolescents with open-identity sperm donors: Reports from 12–17 year olds. *Human Reproduction, 20*(1), 239–252.

Scheibe, S., Freund, A. M., & Baltes, P. B. (2007). Toward a developmental psychology of longings: The optimal (utopian) life. *Developmental Psychology, 43*(3), 778–795.

Schempf, A. H., Branum, A. M., Lukacs, S. L., & Schoendorf, K. C. (2007). Contribution of preterm birth to the black-white infant mortality gap, 1990 and 2000. *American Journal of Public Health, 97*(7), 1255–1260.

Scherer, K. R. (1979). Nonlinguistic vocal indicators of emotion and psychopathology. In C. E. Izard (Ed.), *Emotions in personality and psychopathology* (pp. 495–529). New York: Plenum.

Schiffman, S. (2009). Effects of aging on the human taste system. *International Symposium on Olfaction and Taste, 1170,* 725–729. doi:10.1111/j.1749-6632.2009.03924.x

Schimmack, U. (2007). Methodological issues in the assessment of the affective component of subjective well-being. In A. D. Ong & M. H. M. van Dulmen, *Oxford handbook of methods in positive psychology* (pp. 96–110). London: Oxford University Press.

Schlesinger, B. (1998). Separating together: How divorce transforms families. *Family Relations, 47,* 308.

Schlossberg, N. (2004). *Retire smart, retire happy: Finding your true path in life.* Washington, DC: American Psychological Association.

Schmeck, B., Gross, R., Dje N'Guessan, P., Hocke, A. C., Hammerschmidt, S., Mitchell, T., . . . , Hippenstiel, S. (2004, September). *Streptococcus pneumoniae*–induced caspase 6–dependent apoptosis in lung epithelium. *Infection and Immunity, 72*(9), 4940–4947.

Schmidt, C. W. (2008), Face to face with toy safety: Understanding an unexpected threat. *Environmental Health Perspectives, 116*(2), A71–A76. doi:10.1289/ehp.116-a70

Schmidt, M. E., Pempek, T. A., Kirkorian, H. L., Lund, A. F., & Anderson, D. R. (2008). The effects of background television on the toy play behavior of very young children. *Child Development, 79*(4), 1137–1151. doi:10.1111/j.1467-8624.2008.01180.x

Schneider, K., Bugental, J. F. T., & J. F. Pierson. (Eds.). (2002). *Handbook of humanistic psychology: Leading edges in theory, research, and practice.* Thousand Oaks, CA: Sage.

Schnitzer, P. G., & Ewigman, B. G. (2005). Child deaths resulting from inflicted injuries: Household risk factors and perpetrator characteristics. *Pediatrics, 116*(5), e687–e693.

Schoen, R., & Canudas-Romo, V. (2006). Timing effects: 20th century experience in the United States. *Journal of Marriage and Family, 68*(3), 749–758.

Schöner, G., & Thelen, E. (2006). Using dynamic field theory to rethink infant habituation. *Psychological Review, 113*(2), 273–299.

Schonwald, A., Horan, K., & Huntington, N. (2009). Developmental screening: Is there enough time? *Clinical Pediatrics, 48*(6), 648–655. doi:10.1177/0009922809334350

Schrader, D. (1988). *Exploring metacognition: A description of levels of metacognition and their relation to moral judgment.* Unpublished doctoral dissertation, Harvard University.

Schrodt, P. (2006). The stepparent relationship index: Development, validation, and associations with stepchildren's perceptions of stepparent communication competence and closeness. *Personal Relationships, 13*(2), 167–182. doi:10.1111/j.1475-6811.2006 .00111.x

Schroepfer, T. A. (2006). Mind frames towards dying and factors motivating their adoption by terminally ill elders. *The Journals of Gerontology Series B: Psychological Sciences and Social Sciences, 61*(3), S129–S139.

Schulenberg, J., Wadsworth, K. N., O'Malley, P. M., Bachman, J. G., & Johnston, L. D. (1997). Adolescent risk factors for binge drinking during the transition to young adulthood: Variable-and pattern-centered approaches to change. In G. A. Marlatt and G. R. VandenBox (Eds.), *Addictive behaviors: Readings on etiology, prevention, and treatment* (pp. 129–165). Washington, DC: American Psychological Association.

Schulz, R., & Heckhausen, J. (1996). A life span model of successful aging. *American Psychologist, 51*, 702–714.

Schunk, D. (2008). *Learning theories: An educational perspective* (5th ed.). Upper Saddle River, NJ: Pearson Education.

Schwalb, D. W., Nakazawa, J., Yamamoto, T., & Hyun, J. H. (2004). Fathering in Japanese, Chinese, and Korean cultures: A review of the research literature. In M. E. Lamb (Ed.), *The role of the father in child development* (4th ed., pp. 146–181). New York: Wiley.

Schwartz, J. (2010, October 2). Bullying, suicide, punishment. *New York Times.* Retrieved from www.nytimes.com/2010/ 10/03/weekinreview/03schwartz.html?_r= 1&ref=tylerclementi

Schwartz, M. (2006). Live long, and proper. *Personal Health, 23*(5), 21–24.

Schweinhart, L. J., Montie, J., Xiang, Z., Barnett, W. S., Belfield, C. R., & Nores, M. (2005). *Lifetime effects: The High/Scope Perry Preschool Study through age 40.* Ypsilanti, MI: High/Scope Press.

ScienceDaily. (2007, March 21). Physical activity reduces hypertension risk in young adults. *ScienceDaily.* Retrieved from http://www.sciencedaily.com/releases/2007/03/ 070320110911.htm

Scott, J. (1994, June 4). Another legacy of Onassis: Facing death on own terms. *New York Times,* pp. 1, 8.

Searight, H. R., & Gafford, J. (2005). Cultural diversity at the end of life: Issues and guidelines for family physicians. *American Family Physician, 71*(3), 518–525.

Sears, R. R. (1972). Attachment, dependency, and frustration. In J. L. Gewirtz (Ed.), *Attachment and dependency.* Washington, DC: Winston.

Sears, R. R., Maccoby, E. E., & Levin, H. (1957). *Patterns of child rearing.* New York: Harper & Row.

Sebanc, A. M. (2003). The friendship features of preschool children: Links with prosocial behavior and aggression. *Social Development, 12*(2), 249–268.

Sedikides, C., & Gregg, A. P. (2003). Portraits of the self. In M. Hogg & J. Cooper (Eds.), *The Sage handbook of social psychology* (pp. 110–138). London: Sage.

Sedlak, A. J., & Bruce, C. (2010, December). Youth's characteristics and backgrounds: Findings from the survey of youth in residential placement. *Juvenile Justice Bulletin.* Washington, DC: U.S. Department of Justice. Retrieved from http://www.ncjrs.gov/ pdffiles1/ojjdp/227730.pdf

Sedlak, A. J., Finkelhor, D., Hammer, H., & Schultz, D. J. (2002, October). National estimates of missing children: An overview. *National Incidence Studies of Missing, Abducted, Runaway, and Thrownaway Children.* Washington, DC: Office of Juvenile Justice and Delinquency Prevention, Office of Justice Programs, U.S. Department of Justice.

Seefeldt, K. S., & Smock, P. J. (2004). *Marriage on the public policy agenda: What do policy makers need to know from research?* University of Michigan: Population Studies Center. Retrieved from http://www .psc.isr.umich.edu/pubs/pdf/ rr04-554 .pdf

Segal, N. L. (1993). Twin, sibling, and adoption methods: Tests of evolutionary hypotheses. *American Psychologist, 48,* 943–956.

Segal, S. J., & Mastroianni, L. (2003). *Hormone use in menopause and male andropause: A choice for women and men.* New York: Oxford University Press.

Seger, C. A. (1994). Implicit learning. *Psychological Bulletin, 115,* 163–196.

Seifert, K. L. (2007). Cognitive development and the education of young children. In J. E. Grusec & P. D. Hastings (Eds.), *Handbook of socialization: Theory and research* (pp. 9–19). New York: Guilford Press.

Seligman, M., & Darling, R. B. (2007). *Ordinary families, special children: A systems approach to childhood disability.* New York: Guilford Press.

Seligman, M. E. P., & Csikszentmihalyi, M. (2000). Positive psychology: An introduction. *American Psychologist, 55*(1), 5–14.

Selman, R. L. (1980). *The youth of interpersonal understanding: Developmental and clinical analyses.* New York: Academic Press.

Selye, H. (1956). *The stress of life.* New York: McGraw-Hill.

Senn, T. E., Carey, M. P., Vanable, P. A., Coury-Doniger, P., & Urban, M. A. (2007). Characteristics of sexual abuse in childhood and adolescence influence sexual risk behavior in adulthood. *Archives of Sexual Behavior, 36*(5), 637–745.

Serbin, L. A., Poulin-Dubois, D., Colburne, K. A., Sen, M. G., & Eichstedt, J. A. (2001). Gender stereotyping in infancy: Visual preferences for and knowledge of gender-stereotyped toys in the second year. *International Journal of Behavioral Development, 25*(1), 7–15. doi:10.1080/ 01650250042000078

Services & Advocacy for GLBT Elders. (2010). *Why LGBT older people turn to SAGE for help.* Retrieved from http://www .sageusa.org

Sessler, D. I., & Badgwell, J. M. (1998, November). Exposure of postoperative nurses to exhaled anesthetic gases. *Anesthesia and Analgesia, 87*(5), 1083–1088.

Setiawan, V. W., Haiman, C. A., Stanczyk, F. Z., Le Marchand, L. L., & Henderson, B. E. (2006). Racial/ethnic differences in postmenopausal endogenous hormones: The multiethnic cohort study. *Cancer Epidemiology Biomarkers & Prevention, 15*(10), 1849–1855.

Setlik, J., Bond, G. R., & Ho, M. (2009). Adolescent prescription ADHD medication abuse is rising along with prescriptions for these medications. *Pediatrics, 124*(3), 875–880. doi: 10.1542/peds.2008-0931

Settersten, R. A. (2006, March). *Becoming an adult: Meanings and markers for young Americans.* Network on Transitions to Adulthood Research Working Paper. Chicago, IL: MacArthur Foundation. Retrieved from http:// www.transad.pop.upenn.edu/ downloads/ Settersten%20Becoming%20 Adult%20 final%203-06).pdf

Settersten, R. A., Jr., Furstenberg, F. F., Jr., & Rumbaut, R. G. (Eds.). (2005). *On the frontier of adulthood: Theory, research, and public policy.* Chicago: University of Chicago Press.

Sewell, W. H., & Mussen, P. H. (1952). The effects of feeding, weaning, and scheduling procedures on childhood adjustment and the formation of oral symptoms. *Child Development, 23,* 185–191.

Shapiro, L. (1990, May 28). Guns and dolls. *Newsweek,* 56–65.

Shapiro, M. (2009, September 15). Study gives high marks to retailers' clinics: Walk-in sites are thrifty for routine ills. The *Washington Post,* E1.

Shapiro-Mendoza, C. K., Kimball, M., Tomashek, K. M., Anderson, R. N., & Blanding, S. (2009, February). U.S. infant mortality trends attributable to accidental suffocation and strangulation in bed from 1984 through 2004: Are rates increasing? *Pediatrics, 123*(2), 533–539.

Shargorodsky, J., Curhan, S. G., Curhan, G. C., & Eavey, R. (2010). Change in prevalence of hearing loss in U.S. adolescents. *JAMA, 304*(7), 772–778. doi: 10.1001/jama .2010.1124

Sharp, E., & Ganong, L. (2007). Living in the gray: Women's experiences of missing the marital transition. *Journal of Marriage and the Family, 69*(3), 831–844.

Shaw, D. S., Dishion, T. J., Supplee, L., Gardner, F., & Arnds, K. (2006). Randomized trial of a family-centered approach to the prevention of early conduct problems. *Journal of Consulting and Clinical Psychology, 74*(1), 1–9.

Shaw, G. (2006). Breast cancer survivors: Life after the treatments end. *WebMD.* Retrieved from http://www.webmd.com/breast-cancer/ guide/life-after-breast-cancer-treatment

Shaywitz, B. A., Lyon, R. G., & Shaywitz, S. E. (2006). The role of functional magnetic resonance imaging in understanding reading and dyslexia. *Developmental Neuropsychology, 30*(1), 613–632.

Shaywitz, S. (2003). Overcoming dyslexia: A new and complete science-based program for reading problems at any level. New York: Knopf.

Shechory, M., & Ziv, R. (2007). Relationships between gender role attitudes, role division, and perception of equity among heterosexual, gay and lesbian couples. *Sex Roles, 56*(9–10), 629–638.

Sheehan, G., Darlington, Y., Noller, P., & Feeney, J. (2004). Children's perceptions of their sibling relationships during parental separation and divorce. *Journal of Divorce and Remarriage, 41*(1/2), 69–94.

Sheehy, G. (1976). *Passages.* New York: Dutton.

Sheehy, G. (1992). *The silent passage: Menopause.* New York: Random House.

Sheehy, G. (1995). *New passages: Mapping your life across time.* New York: Random House.

Sheehy, G. (1998). *Understanding men's passages: Discovering the new map of men's lives.* New York: Random House.

Sheldon, T. (2005). Dutch committee approves euthanasia for a patient with Alzheimer's disease. *British Medical Journal, 330,* 1041.

Sheler, J. L. (1997, March 31). Heaven in the age of reason. *U.S. News & World Report, 122,* 65–66.

Shen, C. (2005). How American middle schools differ from schools of five Asian countries: Based on cross-national data from TIMSS 1999. *Educational Research & Evaluation, 11*(2), 179–199.

Sheridan, C., Draganova, R., Ware, M., Murphy, P, Govindan, R., Siegel, E. R., . . . , Preissl, H. (2010). Early development of brain responses to rapidly presented auditory stimulation: A magnetoencephalographic study. *Brain & Development, 32,* 642–657. doi:10.1016/j.braindev.2009 .10.002

Sherman, M. (2010, April 18). Supreme Court OKs abortion procedure ban. Retrieved from http://www.breitbart.com/article.php ?id=d8oj5jlg1&show_article=1

Sherrod, R. (2006, October 18). U.S. medical school enrollment continues to climb: Class sizes increase in all regions for second straight year. Washington, DC: Association of American Medical Colleges. Retrieved from http://www.aamc.org/newsroom/ pressrel/2006/061018.htm

Shiel, W. C. (2008). *Osteoarthritis: Degenerative arthritis.* Retrieved from http://www .medicinenet.com/osteoarthritis/article.htm

Shiraev, E., & Levy, D. (2007). *Cross-cultural psychology: Critical thinking and contemporary applications* (3rd ed.). Boston: Pearson Education.

Shonkoff, J. P., & Phillips, D. A. (Eds.) (2000). *From neurons to neighborhoods: The science of early childhood development.* Washington, DC: National Academy Press.

Shore, C. (1986). Combinatorial play, conceptual development, and early multiword speech. *Developmental Psychology, 22,* 184–190.

Short, M. B., & Rosenthal, S. L. (2008). Psychosocial development and puberty. *Annals of the New York Academy of Sciences,* 36–42. doi:10.1196/annals.1429.011

Shwalb, D. W., Nakazawa, J., Yamamoto, T., & Hyun, J. H. (2010). Fathering in Japan, China, and Korea: Changing contexts, images, and roles. In M. E. Lamb (Ed.). *The role of the father in child development* (pp. 341–387). Hoboken, NJ: Wiley.

Shweder, R. A., Goodnow, J. J., Hatano, G., LeVine, R. A., Markus, H. R., & Miller, P. J. (2006). The cultural psychology of development: One mind, many mentalities. In W. Damon & R. J. Lerner (Eds.), *Handbook of child psychology* (6th ed., Vol. 1, pp. 716–792). New York: Wiley.

Sicherer, S. H. (2006). *Understanding and managing your child's food allergies.* Baltimore, MD: Johns Hopkins University Press.

Sickels, A. K. (2007). Teen dad. Retrieved from http://www.teenwire.com/education/ activity-014.php

Sidani, M. (2001, February). Thyroid disorders in the elderly. *The Female Patient, 26*(2), 52–57.

Siegel, R. K. (1981, January). Accounting for "afterlife" experiences. *Psychology Today, 15,* 65–75.

Silk, J. S., Morris, A. S., Kanaya, T., & Steinberg, L. (2003). Psychological

control and autonomy granting: Opposite ends of a continuum or distinct constructs? *Journal of Research on Adolescence, 13,* 113–128. doi:10.1111/1532 -7795.1301004

Silverman, P. (1983, November 14). Coping with grief—It can't be rushed. *U.S. News & World Report,* 65–68.

Simon, C. (2008). Testosterone deficiency: The male menopause? *Oxford Journals, 1*(9), 625–630. doi:10.1093/innovait/inn103

Simon, E., & Bögels, S. M. (2009). Screening for anxiety disorders in children. *European Child and Adolescent Psychiatry, 18*(10), 625–634. doi:10.1007/s00787-009-0023-x

Simonds, J., Kieras, J. E., Rueda, M. R., & Rothbard, M. K. (2007). Effortful control, executive attention, and emotional regulation in 7–10-year-old children. *Cognitive Development, 22*(4), 474–488.

Simonstein, F. (2009). Artificial reproductive technologies and the advent of the artificial womb. *International Library of Ethics, Law, and the New Medicine, 40.* Retrieved from http://www.springer.com/ series/6224

Simonton, D. K. (1991). Emergence and realization of genius: The lives and works of 120 classical composers. *Journal of Personality and Social Psychology, 61,* 829–840.

Sims, M., Sims, T., L., & Bruce, M. A. (2007). Urban poverty and mortality rate disparities. *Journal of the National Medical Association, 99*(5), 349–356.

Singer, L. T., Fulton, S., Kirchner, L. H., Lewis, B., & Baley, J. E. (2010). Longitudinal predictors of maternal stress and coping after very low-birth-weight birth. *Archives of Pediatrics & Adolescent Medicine, 164*(6), 518–524.

Singer, T., Lindenberger, U., & Baltes, P. B. (2003). Plasticity of memory for new learning in very old age: A story of major loss? *Psychology and Aging, 18*(2), 306–317.

Singer, T., Verhaeghen, P., Ghisletta, P., Lindenberger, U., & Baltes, P. B. (2003). The fate of cognition in very old age: Six-year longitudinal findings in the Berlin Aging Study (BASE). *Psychology and Aging, 18*(2), 318–331.

Sinno, S. M., & Killen, M. (2009). Moms at work and dads at home: Children's evaluations of parental roles. *Applied Developmental Science, 13*(1), 16–29. doi:10.1080/ 10888690802606735

Sirois, S., & Mareschal, D. (2004). An interacting systems model of infant habituation. *Journal of Cognitive Neuroscience, 16*(8), 1352–1362.

Sisk, C. L., & Foster, D. L. (2004). The neural basis of puberty and adolescence. *Nature Neuroscience, 7*(10), 1040–1047.

Sisk, C. L., & Zehr, J. L. (2005). Pubertal hormones organize the adolescent brain and behavior. *Frontiers in Neuroendocrinology, 26*(3–4), 163–174.

Skaff, M. M., & Gardiner, P. (2003). Cultural variations in meaning of control. In S. H. Zarit, L. I. Pearlin, & K. W. Schaie (Eds.), *Personal control in social and life course contexts* (pp. 83–105). New York: Springer.

Skinner, B. F. (1957). *Verbal behavior.* New York: Appleton-Century-Crofts.

Skolnick, A. S., & Skolnick, J. H. (2011). *Family in transition.* Boston, MA: Allyn & Bacon.

Slater, A., & Lewis, M. (Eds.) (2007). *Introduction to infant development* (2nd ed.). New York: Oxford University Press.

Slatter, I. (2011, January 4). Over two million children are homeschooled. [News Release.] Purcellville, VA: Home School Legal Defense Association. Retrieved from http://www.hslda.org/docs/media/2011/201101140.asp

Sleep problems: Nightmares. (2001). National Sleep Foundation. Retrieved from http://www.sleepfoundation.org/nightmares.html

Slep, A. M., & O'Leary, S. G. (2007). Multivariate models of mothers' and fathers' aggression toward their children. *Journal of Counseling and Clinical Psychology, 75*(5), 739–751.

Sliwinski, M. J., Stawski, R. S., Hall, C. B., Katz, M., Verghese, J., & Lipton, R. (2006). Distinguishing preterminal and terminal cognitive decline. *European Psychologist, 11*(3), 172–181.

Slobin, D. I. (1972, July). They learn the same way all around the world. *Psychology Today, 6,* 71–82.

Small, M. (1998). *Our babies, ourselves: How biology and culture shape the way we parent.* New York: Doubleday/Anchor.

Smart Plastic Surgery.com. (2008). *Cosmetic plastic surgery basics.* Retrieved from http://www.smartplasticsurgery.com/surgery/costs.html

Smetana, J. G. (1986). Preschool children's conceptions of sex-role transgressions. *Child Development, 57*(4), 862–871.

Smetana, J. G. (2006). Social-cognitive domain theory: Consistencies and variations in children's moral and social judgments. In M. Killen & J. G. Smetana (Eds.), *Handbook of moral development* (pp. 119–153). Mahwah, NJ: Erlbaum.

Smidt, S. (2011). *Playing to learn: The role of play in the early years.* New York: Routledge.

Smith, D. (2003, January). What you need to know about the new code. *Monitor on Psychology.* Retrieved from http://www.apa.org/monitor/Jan03/newcode.html

Smith, D. B., & Moen, P. H. (2004, March). Retirement satisfaction for retirees and their spouses: Do gender and the retirement decision-making process matter? *Journal of Family Issues, 25*(2), 262–285.

Smith, J., & Baltes, P. B. (2007). Healthy aging from seventy to over one hundred in Germany: Lessons from the Berlin Aging Study. In M. Robinson, W. Novelli, C. Pearson, & L. Norris (Eds.), *Global health and global aging* (pp. 118–127). San Francisco: Jossey-Bass.

Smith, L. (Ed.) (1992). *Jean Piaget: Critical assessments.* New York: Routledge.

Smith, L. B., & Thelen, E. (2000). *A dynamic systems approach to development of cognition and action.* Cambridge, MA: MIT Press.

Smith, L. B., & Thelen, E. (2003). Development as a dynamic system: *Trends in Cognitive Sciences, 7*(8), 343–348.

Smith, L. M., LaGasse, L. L., Derauf, C., Grant, P., Shah, R., Arria, A., . . ., Lester, B. M. (2006). The Infant Development, Environment, and Lifestyle Study: Effects of prenatal methamphetamine exposure, polydrug exposure, and poverty on intrauterine growth. *Pediatrics, 118*(3), 1149–1156.

Smith, P. H., White, J. W., & Moracco, K. E. (2009). Becoming who we are: A theoretical explanation of gendered social structures and social networks that shape adolescent interpersonal aggression. *Psychology of Women Quarterly, 33*(1), 25–29. doi:10.1111/j.1471-6402.2008.01470.x

Smith, R. P. (1957). *"Where did you go?" "Out." "What did you do?" "Nothing."* New York: Norton.

Smith, T. W. (2006). *Altruism and empathy in America: Trends and correlates.* National Opinion Research Center, University of Chicago. Retrieved from http://www.norc.org/publications/altruism+and+empathy+in+america+trends+and+correlates.htm

Smith, W. J. (2006, May 1). Right to die movement is really about euthanasia, not compassion. *LifeNews.*, Retrieved from http://www.discovery.org/scripts/viewDB/index.html

Smith, Y. L. S., Van Goozen, S. H. M., Kuiper, A. J., & Cohen-Kettenis, P. T. (2005). Sex reassignment: Outcomes and predictors of treatment for adolescent and adult transsexuals. *Psychological Medicine, 35*(1), 89–99.

Smolander, J. (2002). Effect of cold exposure on older humans. *International Journal of Sports Medicine, 23*(2), 86–92.

Smyer, M. A., & Pitt-Catsouphes, M. (2007). The meanings of work for older workers. *Generations, 31,* 23–30. Retrieved from EBSCOhost.

Snapp-Childs, W., & Corbetta, D. (2009). Evidence of early strategies in learning to walk. *Infancy, 14*(1), 101–16. doi:10.1080/15250000802569835

Snider, M., & Hasson, J. (1993, May 19). Halt urged to "futile" health care. *USA Today,* p. 1A.

Snih, S. A., Markides, K. S., Ray, L., Ostir, G. V., & Goodwin, J. S. (2002). Handgrip strength and mortality in older Mexican Americans. *Journal of the American Geriatrics Society, 50*(7), 1250–1256.

Snow, C. E. (1977). The development of conversation between mothers and babies. *Journal of Child Language, 4,* 1–22.

Snyder, H. N., & Sickmund, M. (2006, March). *Juvenile offenders and victims: 2006 national report.* National Center for Juvenile Justice. Retrieved from http://ojjdp.ncjrs.gov/ojstatbb/nr2006/ downloads/NR2006.pdf

Snyder, T. D., & Dillow, S. A. (2010, April). *Digest of Education Statistics, 2009* (NCES2010-013).Washington, DC: National Center for Education Statistics. Retrieved from http://nces.ed.gov/pubs2010/2010013.pdf

Snyder, T. D., & Dillow, S. A. (2011). *Digest of Education Statistics 2010* (NCES 2011-015). National Center for Education Statistics, Institute of Education Sciences, U.S. Department of Education. Washington, DC. Retrieved from http://nces.ed.gov/pubs2011/2011015.pdf

Sobotka, T. (2004, June). Is lowest-low fertility in Europe explained by the postponement of childbearing? *Population and Development Review, 30*(2), 195–220.

Social Security Administration. (2007, October). Social Security is important to women. *Fact sheet: Social Security.* Retrieved from http://www.socialsecurity.gov/pressoffice/factsheets/women-alt.pdf

Social Security Administration. (2008, March 25). 2008 Annual Report of the Board of Trustees of the Federal Old-Age and Survivors Insurance and Disability Insurance Trust Funds. Retrieved from http://www.ssa.gov/OACT/TR/TR08/tr08.pdf

Soenens, B., Vansteenkiste, M., Luyckx, K., & Goossens, L. (2006). Parenting and adolescent problem behavior: An integrated model with adolescent self-disclosure and perceived parental knowledge as intervening variables. *Developmental Psychology, 42*(2), 305–318.

Sohr-Preston, S. L., & Scaramella, L. V. (2006). Implications of timing of maternal depressive symptoms for early cognitive and language development. *Clinical Child and Family Psychology Review, 9*(1), 65–83.

Soja, N. N. (1994). Young children's concept of color and its relation to the acquisition of color words. *Child Development, 65*(3), 918–937.

Sokol, R. J. (2003). Fetal alcohol spectrum disorder. *JAMA, 290*(2), 2996–2999.

Solecki, S., & Goldschmidt, K. (2011). Adolescents texting and twittering: The flash mob phenomena. *Journal of Pediatric Nursing, 26*(2), 167–169. Retrieved from Science Direct.

Solis, H. L., & Hall, K. (2010, December). *Women in the labor force: A databook.* U.S. Department of Labor and U.S. Bureau of

Labor Statistics. Retrieved from http://www.bls.gov/cps/wlf-databook-2010.pdf

Sonfield, A., Benson-Gold, R. B., Frost, J. J. & Darroch, J. E. (2004). U.S. insurance coverage of contraceptives and the impact of contraceptive coverage mandates, 2002. *Perspectives on Sexual and Reproductive Health, 36*(2), 72–79.

Song, A. V., & Halpern-Felsher, B. L. (2011). Predictive relationship between adolescent oral and vaginal sex: Results from a prospective, longitudinal study. *Archives of Pediatrics & Adolescent Medicine, 165*(3), 243–249. doi:10.1001/archpediatrics.2010.214

Song, J., Chang, H. J., Tirodkar, M., Chang, R. W., Manheim, L. M., & Dunlop, D. D. (2007). Racial/ethnic differences in activities of daily living disability in older adults with arthritis: A longitudinal study. *Arthritis Care & Research, 57*(6), 1058–1066.

Sorensen, E. S. (1993). *Children's stress and coping: A family perspective.* New York: Guilford Press.

Sosinsky, L. S., Lord, H., & Zigler, E. (2007). For-profit/nonprofit differences in center-based child care quality: Results from the National Institute of Child Health and Human Development study of early child care and youth development. *Journal of Applied Developmental Psychology, 28,* 390–410. doi:10.1016/j.appdev.2007.06.003

Southerland, J. N. (2006, November 3). *Formulating a new model of college choice and persistence.* Paper presented at the ASHE Annual Conference. Retrieved from http://www.eric.ed.gov/

Spearman, C. (1904). "General intelligence" objectively determined and measured. *American Journal of Psychology, 15*(2), 201–293.

Spearman, C. (1927). *The abilities of man.* New York: Macmillan.

Speicher, B. (1994). Family patterns of moral judgment during adolescence and early adulthood. *Developmental Psychology, 30,* 624–632.

Spelke, E. S., von Hofsten, C., & Kestenbaum, R. (1989). Object perception in infancy: Interaction of spatial and kinetic information for object boundaries. *Developmental Psychology, 25*(2), 185–196.

Spencer, B., & Gillen, F. J. (1927). *The Arunta* (Vol. 1). London: Macmillan.

Spencer, M. B. (2006) Phenomenology and ecological systems theory: Development of diverse groups. In W. Damon and R. Lerner (Eds.), *Handbook of child psychology* (6th ed., Vol. 1, pp. 829–893). New York: Wiley.

Spencer, R. (2007). "I just feel safe with him": Emotional closeness in male youth mentoring relationships. *Psychology of Men and Masculinity, 8*(3), 185–198.

Sperling, D. (1990, July 5). Summer cools off sperm. *USA Today,* p. 1A.

Sperry, R. W. (1993). The impact and promise of the cognitive revolution. *American Psychologist, 48,* 878–885.

Spilton, D., & Lee, L. C. (1977). Some determinants of effective communication in four-year-olds. *Child Development, 48*(3), 968–977.

Spinath, F. B., Price, T. S., Dale, P. S., & Plomin, R. (2004, March/April). The genetic and environmental origins of language disability and ability. *Child Development, 75,* 445–454.

Spinillo, A. G., & Bryant, P. (1991). Children's proportional judgments: The importance of "half." *Child Development, 62,* 427–440.

Spiro, M. E. (1947). *Ifaluk: A South Sea culture.* Unpublished manuscripts, Coordinated Investigation of Micronesian Anthropology, Pacific Science Board, National Research Council, Washington, DC.

Spitz, R. A. (1957). *No and yes: On the genesis of human communication.* Madison, CT: International Universities Press.

Spodek, B., & Saracho, O. N. (Eds.). (2006). *Handbook of research on the education of young children* (2nd ed.). Mahwah, NJ: Erlbaum.

Spotlight on the baby milk industry. (1998). McSpotlight Organization. Retrieved from http://www.mcspotlight.org/beyond/nestle.html

Sprecher, S., & Chandak, R. (1992). Attitude about arranged marriages and dating among men and women from India. *Free Inquiry in Creative Sociology, 20,* 1–11.

Spring, J. (2007). *Deculturalization and the struggle for equality: A brief history of the education of dominated cultures in the United States.* New York: McGraw-Hill.

Sroufe, L. A. (2007). Commentary: The place of development in developmental psychology. In A. S. Masten (Ed.), *Multilevel dynamics in developmental psychology.* Mahwah, NJ: Erlbaum.

Staal, S. (2000). *The love they lost: Living with the legacy of our parents' divorce.* New York: Dell.

Stack, S. (2001). Occupation and suicide. *Social Science Quarterly, 82*(2), 384–396.

Stack, S., & Eshleman, J. R. (1998). Marital status and happiness: A 17-nation study. *Journal of Marriage and Family, 60*(2), 527–536.

Staff, J., & Mortimer, J. T. (2007). Educational and work strategies from adolescence to early adulthood: Consequences for educational attainment. *Social Forces, 85*(3), 1169–1194.

Stamler, B. (2004, June 21). Now that there are choices, how to choose? *New York Times,* p. F10.

Stanley, B., & Sieber, J. E. (Eds.). (1992). *Social research on children and adolescents: Ethical issues.* Newbury Park, CA: Sage.

Stark, A., & Bardi, J. (2008, March 14). Researchers use light to detect Alzheimer's: New technique may help identify ways to predict and prevent deadly disease. Optical

Society of America. [News Release].Retrieved from http://www.osa.org/about_osa/newsroom/news_releases/releases/03.2008/alzheimersdetection.aspx

Steele, H. (2002). State of the art: Attachment. *The Psychologist, 15*(10), 518–522.

Stein, D. J., Fan, J., Fossella, J., & Russell, V. A. (2007). Inattention and hyperactivity-impulsivity: Psychobiological and evolutionary underpinnings of ADHD. *The International Journal of neuropsychiatric Medicine, 12*(3), 190–196.

Stein, P. S., Desrosiers, M., Donegan, S. J., Yepes, J. F., & Kryscio, R. J. (2007). Tooth loss, dementia and neuropathology in the nun study. *Journal of the American Dental Association, 138*(10), 1314–1322.

Stein, R. (2010, February 2). Abstinence programs might work, report says; Classes focused on delaying sex were more effective than mixed programs in U.S. study. *Washington Post,* A1.

Stein, R. (2010, October 28). Obama administration's sex-ed program criticized by both sides of abstinence debate. *The Washington Post.* Retrieved from http://www.washingtonpost.com

Stein, Z., & Dawson-Tunik, T. L. (2004). *"It's all good": Moral relativism and the millennial mind.* Lectica. Paper presented at the Annual Meeting of the Jean Piaget Society, Vancouver.

Steinberg, L., & Monahan, K. C. (2007). Age differences in resistance to peer influence. *Developmental Psychology, 43*(6), 1531–1543.

Steinberg, L., Elmen, J. D., & Mounts, N. S. (1989). Authoritative parenting, psychosocial maturity, and academic success among adolescents. *Child Development, 60,* 1424–1436.

Steinberg, L., Lamborn, S. D., Darling, N., Mounts, N. S., & Dornbusch, S. M. (1994). Over-time changes in adjustment and competence among adolescents from authoritative, authoritarian, indulgent, and neglectful families. *Child Development, 65*(3), 754–770.

Steingraber, S. (2007). *The falling age of puberty in U.S. girls: What we know, what we need to know.* San Francisco, CA: Breast Cancer Fund.

Stephan, Y., Fouquereau, E., & Fernandez, A. (2008). The relation between self-determination and retirement satisfaction among active retired individuals. *International Journal of Aging and Human Development, 66*(4), 329–345.

Stephenson, J. (1985). *Death, grief, and mourning: Individual and social realities.* New York: Free Press.

Stern, L. (2007). When baby comes back. *Newsweek, 149*(23), 70–71.

Sternberg, R. J. (1986, March/April). Inside intelligence. *American Scientist, 74,* 137–143.

Sternberg, R. J. (1988). *The triangle of love: Intimacy, passion, commitment.* New York: Basic Books.

Sternberg, R. J. (1990). *Metaphors of mind: Conceptions of the nature of intelligence.* New York: Cambridge University Press.

Sternberg, R. J. (1997). Educating intelligence. In R. Sternberg (Ed.), *Intelligence, heredity, and environment.* Cambridge: University of Cambridge.

Sternberg, R. J. (1998). Principles of teaching for successful intelligence. *Educational Psychologist, 33,* 65–72.

Sternberg, R. J. (2006a). A duplex theory of love. In R. J. Sternberg & K. Weis (Eds.). *The new psychology of love* (pp. 184–199). New Haven, CT: Yale University Press.

Sternberg, R. J. (2006b). Creating a vision of creativity: The first 25 years. *Psychology of Aesthetics, Creativity, and the Arts, S*(1), 2–12.

Sternberg, R. J. (2009). Wisdom, intelligence, creativity, synthesized: A model of giftedness. In T. Balchin, B. Hymer, & D. J. Matthews (Eds.), *The Routledge International Companion to Gifted Education* (pp. 255–264). New York: Routledge.

Sternberg, R. J., & Grigorenko, E. L. (1997). Are cognitive styles still in style? *American Psychologist, 52,* 700–712.

Sternberg, R. J., & Hojjat, M. (Eds.). (1997). *Satisfaction in close relationships.* New York: Guilford Press.

Sternfeld, B., Bhat A. K., Wang, H., Sharp, T., & Quesenberry, C. P., Jr. (2005). Menopause, physical activity and body composition/fat distribution in midlife women. *Medicine and Science in Sports and Exercise, 37*(7), 1195–1202.

Sterns, H., & Kaplan, J. (2003). Self-management of career and retirement. In G. A. Adams & T. A. Beehr (Eds.), *Retirement: Reasons, processes and results.* (pp. 188–233). New York: Springer.

Sterns, H. L., & Huyck, M. H. (2001). The role of work in midlife. In M. E. Lachman (Ed.), *Handbook of midlife development* (pp. 447–486). New York: Wiley.

Stevens, S. B., & Morris, T. L. (2007). College dating and social anxiety: Using the Internet as a means of connecting to others. *Cyberpsychology & Behavior, 10*(5), 680–688.

Stevenson-Hinde, J., & Shouldice, A. (1995). Maternal interactions and self-reports related to attachment classifications at 4.5 years. *Child Development, 66,* 583–596.

Steward, D. K., Moser, D., K., & Ryan-Wenger, N. A. (2001, June). Biobehavioral characteristics of infants with failure to thrive. *Journal of Pediatric Nursing, 16*(3), 162–171.

Stewart, K. (2009, Spring). Lessons from teaching Millennials. *College Teaching, 57*(2), 111–117. doi:10.3200/CTCH.57.2.111-118

Stewart, R. C. (2007). Maternal depression and infant growth: A review of recent evidence. *Maternal & Child Nutrition, 3*(2), 94–107.

Stice, E., Presnell, K., Gau, J., & Shaw, H. (2007). Testing mediators of intervention effects in randomized controlled trials: An evaluation of two eating disorder prevention programs. *Journal of Consulting and Clinical Psychology, 75*(1), 20–32.

Stillwell, R. (2010, June). *Public school graduates and dropouts from the Common Core of Data: School year 2007–08* (NCES 2010-341). National Center for Education Statistics, Institute for Education Sciences. Washington, DC: U.S. Department of Education.

Stipek, D., Recchia, S., & McClintic, S. (1992). Self-evaluation in young children. *Monographs of the Society for Research in Child Development, 57*(1, Serial No. 226).

Stocco, C., Telleria, C., & Gibori, G. (2007). The molecular control of corpus luteum formation, function, and regression. *Endocrine Reviews, 28*(1), 117–149. doi:10.1210/er.2006-0022

Stoff, D. M., & Susmann, E. J. (2005). *Developmental psychobiology of aggression.* New York: Cambridge University Press.

Stoneman, B. (1998). Beyond rocking the ages. *Demographics, 20,* 44–49.

Storm, D. S., Boland, M. G., Gortmaker, S. L., He, Y., Skurnick, J., Howland, L., & Oleske, J. M. (2005, January 3). Protease inhibitor combination therapy, severity of illness, and quality of life among children with perinatally acquired HIV-1 infection. *Pediatrics* (epub, ahead of print). Retrieved from http://pediatrics.aappublications.org

Storms, M. (2010). Circumcision revisited: Why informed parents just say no. *Pediatrics for Parents. 26*(5 & 6), 18. Retrieved from EBSCOhost.

Strack, S., & Feifel, H. (Eds.). (2003). *Death and the quest for meaning: Essays in honor of Herman Feifel.* Northvale, NJ: Jason Aronson.

Strasburger, V. C. (2007). Go ahead punk, make my day: It's time for pediatricians to take action against media violence. *Pediatrics, 119*(6), e1398–e1399.

Strasburger, V. C., Jordan, A. B., & Donnerstein, E. (2010). Health effects of media on children and adolescents. *Pediatrics, 125*(4), 756–767. doi:10.1542/peds.2009-2563

Strauss, W., & Howe, N. (2000). *Millennials rising: The next great generation.* New York: Random House.

Streppel, M. T., Ocke, M. C., Boshuizen, H. C., Kok, F. J., & Kromhout, D. (2009). Long-term wine consumption is related to cardiovascular mortality and life expectancy independently of moderate alcohol intake: The Zutphen Study. *Journal of Epidemiology and Community Health, 63*(7), 534–540. doi:10.1136/jech.2008.082198

Strier, R., & Roer-Strier, D. (2010). Fatherhood in the context of immigration. In M. E. Lamb (Ed.), *The role of the father in child development* (pp. 435–458). Hoboken, NJ: Wiley.

Stroth, S., Hille, K., Spitzer, M., & Reinhardt, R. (2009). Aerobic endurance benefits memory and affect in young adults. *Neuropsychological Rehabilitation, 19*(2), 223–243. doi:10.1080/09602010802091183

Stubbs, M. L. (2008). Cultural perceptions and practices around menarche and adolescent menstruation in the United States. *Annals of the New York Academy of Sciences, 1135,* 58–66. doi:10.1196/annals.1429.008

Suarez, E. C. (2006). The relation of free plasma tryptophan to anger, hostility, and aggression in a nonpatient sample of adult men and women. *Annals of Behavioral Medicine, 31*(3), 254–260.

Suárez-Orozco, C. (2007). Afterword: Reflections on research with immigrant families. In M. H. Bornstein, K. DeaterDeckard, & J. E. Lansford (Eds.), *Immigrant families in contemporary society* (pp. 311–326). New York: Guilford Press.

Substance Abuse and Mental Health Services Administration. (2007). *A day in the life of American adolescents: Substance use facts.* Rockville, MD: U.S. Department of Health & Human Services.

Substance Abuse and Mental Health Services Administration. (2008). *The NSDUH Report: Misuse of Over-the-Counter Cough and Cold Medications among Persons Aged 12 to 25.* Rockville, MD: Author.

Substance Abuse and Mental Health Services Administration. (2010). *Results from the 2009 National Survey on Drug Use and Health: Mental Health Findings* (Office of Applied Studies, NSDUH Series H-39, HHS Publication No. SMA 10-4609). Rockville, MD. Retrieved from http://www.oas.samhsa.gov/NSDUH/2k9NSDUH/MH/2K9MHResults.pdf

Sudden infant death syndrome. (2004). SHANDS Health Care. Retrieved from http://shands.org/ health/Health%20Illustrated%20Encyclopedia/1/001566.htm

Sugarman, S. (1987). *Piaget's construction of the child's reality.* New York: Cambridge University.

Sugden, D., & Chambers, M. (Eds.). (2005). *Children with developmental coordination disorder.* New York: Wiley.

Sugiyama, Y. (2001, November). On students' mathematics achievement in Japan. *Mathematics Education Dialogues.* National Council of Teachers of Mathematics. Retrieved from http://www.nctm.org/dialogues/2001-11/20011103.htm

Sullivan, H. S. (1953). *The interpersonal theory of psychiatry.* New York: Norton.

Sullivan, M. E. (2010). Urging Congress to oppose legislation that would create a federal law of child custody controlling state custody cases involving military service member parents. *American Journal of Family Law, 23*(4), 232–238.

Sullivan, M. G. (2005). Abstinence pledges don't protect against STDs. *Pediatric News, 39*(5), 13.

Sullivan, O., & Coltrane, S. (2008). *Men's changing contribution to housework and child care.* Discussion Paper on Changing Family Roles. Prepared for the 11th Annual Conference of the Council on Contemporary Families, April 25–26, 2008, University of Illinois, Chicago.

Sulloway, F. J. (1997). *Born to rebel: Birth order, family dynamics, and creative lives.* New York: Pantheon Books.

Svare, G. M., Jay, S., & Mason, M. A. (2004). *Stepparents on stepparenting: An exploratory study of stepparenting approaches.* New York: Haworth.

Syed, I. B. (2007). Education of Muslim children: Challenges and opportunities. *Islam for Today.* Retrieved from http://www.islamfortoday.com/syed07.htm

Taddio, A., Goldbach, M., Ipp, M., Stevens, B., & Koren, G. (1995). Effect of neonatal circumcision on pain responses during vaccination in boys. *Lancet, 345*(8945), 291–292. doi:10.1016/S0140-6736(95)90278-3

Takanishi, R. (2004). Leveling the playing field: Supporting immigrant children from birth to eight. *The Future of Children, 14*(2), 60–79.

Talaro, K. P. (2008). *Foundations in microbiology* (6th ed.). New York: McGraw-Hill.

Talbot, M. (2001, February 4). A desire to duplicate. *New York Times Magazine,* pp. 40–45, 67–68.

Talbot, N. L., Chapman, B., Conwell, Y., McCollumn, K., Franus, N., Cotescu, S., & Duberstein, P. R. (2009). Childhood sexual abuse is associated with physical illness burden and functioning in psychiatric patients 50 years of age and older. *Psychosomatic Medicine, 71*(4), 417–422. doi:10.1097/PSY.0b013e318199d31b

Taliaferro, L. A., Rienzo, B. A., & Donovan, K. A. (2010). Relationships between youth sport participation and selected health risk behaviors from 1999 to 2007. *Journal of School Health, 80*(8), 399–410. doi:10.1111/j.1746-1561.2010.00520.x

Tallack, P., & Murkoff, H. (2006). *In the womb.* Washington: National Geographic Society.

Tallandini, A. M., & Scalembra, C. (2006). Kangaroo mother care and mother-premature infant dyadic interaction. *Infant Mental Health Journal, 27*(3), 251–275.

Tamborini, C. R. (2007). The never married in old age: Projections and concerns for the near future. *Social Security Bulletin, 67*(2), 25–40.

Tamis-LeMonda, C. S., Cristofaro, T. N., Rodriguez, E. T., & Bornstein, M. H. (2006). Early language development: Social influences in the first years of life. *Child psychology: A handbook of contemporary issues* (2nd ed.). New York: Psychology Press.

Tamis-LeMonda, C. S., & McFadden, K. E. (2010). Fathers from low-income backgrounds: Myths and evidence. In M. E. Lamb (Ed.), *The role of the father in child development* (pp. 296–318). Hoboken, NJ: Wiley.

Tamis-LeMonda, C. S., Shannon, J. D., Cabrera, N. J., & Lamb, M. E. (2004). Fathers and mothers at play with their 2- and 3-year-olds: Contributions to language and cognitive development. *Child Development, 75*(6), 1806–1820. doi:10.1111/j.1467-8624.2004.00818.x

Tan, T. X., & Yang, Y. (2005, February 1). Language development of Chinese adoptees 18–35 months old. *Early Childhood Research Quarterly, 20*(1), 57–68.

Tang, C. S., Yeung, D. Y., & Lee, A. M. (2003). Psychosocial correlates of emotional response to menarche among Chinese adolescent girls. *Journal of Adolescent Health, 33,* 193–201.

Tanne, J. H. (2000). Body art: Marks of identity. *British Medical Journal, 320,* 64.

Tannen, D. (2007). *Talking voices: Repetition, dialogue, and imagery in conversational discourse.* New York: Cambridge University Press.

Tanner, J. L. (2006). Recentering during emerging adulthood: A critical turning point in life span human development. In J. J. Arnett & J. L. Tanner (Eds.), *Emerging adults in America: Coming of age in the 21st century* (pp. 21–55). Washington, DC: American Psychological Association.

Tanner, J. M. (1972). Sequence, tempo, and individual variation in growth and development of boys and girls aged twelve to sixteen. In J. Kagan & R. Coles (Eds.), *Twelve to sixteen: Early adolescence.* New York: Norton.

Tanner, J. M. (1973, September). Growing up. *Scientific American, 229,* 34–43.

Taylor, A. Z., & Graham, S. (2007). An examination of the relationship between achievement values and perceptions of barriers among low-SES African American and Latino students. *Journal of Educational Psychology, 99*(1), 52–64.

Taylor, J. M., Gilligan, C., & Sullivan, A. M. (1999). *Between voice and silence: Women and girls, race and relationships.* Cambridge, MA: Harvard University Press.

Taylor, L., Davis-Kean, P., & Malanchuk, O. (2007). Self-esteem, academic self-concept, and aggression at school. *Aggressive Behavior, 33*(2), 130–136. Retrieved from EBSCO*host.*

Taylor, M., Carlson, S. M., Maring, B. L., Gerow, L., & Charley, C. M. (2004). The characteristics and correlates of fantasy in school-age children: Imaginary companions, impersonation, and social understanding. *Developmental Psychology, 40*(6), 1173–1187.

Taylor, P., & Keeter, S. (Eds.). (2010, February). Millennials: A Portrait of Generation Next. Pew Research Center. Retrieved from http://pewsocialtrends.org/files/2010/10/millennials-confident-connected-open-to-change.pdf.

Taylor, S. E. (2002). *The tending instinct: Women, men, and the biology of our relationships.* New York: Henry Holt.

Taylor, S. E. (2008). *Health psychology* (7th ed.). New York: McGraw-Hill.

Taylor, S. S. (2001, January 12). Educators urge end to classroom "gender wars." *Women's eNews.* Retrieved from http://www.womensenews.org/article.cfm?aid=502&mode=today

Taylor, Z. E., Conger, R. D., Widaman, K. F., Larsen-Rife, D., & Cutrona, C. E. (2010). Life stress, maternal optimism, and adolescent competence in single mother, African American families. *Journal of Family Psychology, 24*(4), 468–477. doi:10.1037/a0019870

Teaster, P. B. (2002). *A response to the abuse of vulnerable adults: The 2000 Survey of Adult Protective Services.* The National Center on Elder Abuse, National Committee for the Prevention of Elder Abuse, and The National Association of Adult Protective Services Administrators. Retrieved from http://www.elderabusecenter.org/pdf/research/apsreport030703.pdf

Teixeira, L. R., Fischer, F. M., Nagai, R., & Turte, S. L. (2004). Teen at work: The burden of a double shift on daily activities. *Chronobiology International, 21*(6), 845–858.

Telingator, C. J., & Patterson, C. (2008). Children and adolescents of lesbian and gay parents. *Journal of the American Academy of Child and Adolescent Psychiatry, 47*(12), 1364–1368. doi:10.1097/CHI.0b013e31818960bc

Tenenbaum, H. R., & Ruck, M. D. (2007). Are teachers' expectations different for racial minority than European American students? A meta-analysis. *Journal of Educational Psychology, 99*(2), 253–273.

Tenore, F. B., Dunn, A. C., Laughter, J. C., & Milner, H. R. (2010). Teacher candidate selection, recruitment, and induction: A critical analysis with implications for transformation. In V. Hill-Jackson & C. W. Lewis (Eds.), *Transforming Teacher Education* (pp. 93–118). Sterling, VA: Stylus Publishing.

Terkel, S. (1987, April 5). Hero of the life cycle. *New York Times Book Review,* 36–37. Reflections on death, rebirth, and hunger for a faith. New York: New Press.

Terman, L. M., & Merrill, M. A. (1937). *Measuring intelligence.* Boston: Houghton Mifflin.

Teti, D. M., & Ablard, K. E. (1989). Security of attachment and infant-sibling relationships: A laboratory study. *Child Development, 60,* 1519–1528.

Than, K. (2010). Human genome at ten: 5 breakthroughs, 5 predictions. *National*

Geographic News. Retrieved from http://news.nationalgeographic.com/news/human-genome-project-tenth-anniversary.html

Thapar, A., Fowler, T., Rice, F., Scourfield, J., van den Bree, M., Thomas, H., . . . , Hay, D. (2003). Maternal smoking during pregnancy and attention deficit hyperactivity disorder symptoms in offspring. *American Journal of Psychiatry, 160*(11), 1985–1989.

Tharenou, P. (2005). Does mentor support increase women's career advancement more than men's? The differential effects of career and psychosocial support. *Australian Journal of Management, 30*(1), 77–108.

Thelen, E. (1986). Treadmill-elicited stepping in seven-month-old infants. *Child Development, 57*, 1498–1506.

Thelen, E. (1995). Motor development: A new synthesis. *American Psychologist, 50*, 79–95.

Thiedke, C. C. (2001, January 15). Sleep disorders and sleep problems in childhood. *American Family Physician, 63*(2), 277–284.

Thiedke, C. C. (2003, April 1). Nocturnal enuresis. *American Family Physician, 67*(7), 1499–1506. Retrieved from http://www.aafp.org/afp/20030401/1499.pdf

Thielfoldt, D., & Scheef, D. (2004). *Generation X and the Millennials: What you need to know about mentoring the new generations.* Retrieved from http://www.abanet.org/lpm/lpt/articles/mgt08044.html

Thiessen, E. D., Hill, E. A., & Saffran, J. R. (2005). Infant-directed speech facilitates word segmentation. *Infancy, 7*, 53–71.

Thomas, A., & Chess, S. (1987). Roundtable: What is temperament? *Child Development, 58*, 505–529.

Thomas, A., Chess, S., & Birch, H. G. (1970, August). The origin of personality. *Scientific American, 223*, 102–109.

Thomas, A., Chess, S., Birch, H. G., Hertaig, M. E., & Korn, S. (1963). *Behavioral individuality in early childhood.* New York: New York University Press.

Thomas, F., Renaud, F., Benefice, E., De Meeüs, T., & Guegan, J. F. (2001). International variability of ages at menarche and menopause: Patterns and main determinants. *Human Biology, 73*(2), 271–290.

Thomas, J. N. (2007). Evidence-based practice can reduce child abuse in low-income communities. *Journal for Specialists in Pediatric Nursing, 12*(4), 294–296. doi:10.1111/j.1744-6155.2007.00125.x

Thomas, M. S. C., & Johnson, M. H. (2008). New advances in understanding sensitive periods in brain development. *Current Directions in Psychological Science, 17*(1), 1–5. doi: 10.1111/j.1467-8721.2008.00537.x

Thomas, S., & Hall, J. M. (2008). Life trajectories of female child abuse survivors thriving in adulthood. *Qualitative Health Research, 18*, 149–166. doi:10.1177/1049732307312201

Thompson, D. A., & Christakis, D. A. (2005). The association between television viewing and irregular sleep schedules among children less than 3 years of age. *Pediatrics, 116*(4), 851–856.

Thompson, D. R., Obarzanek, E., Franko, D. L., Barton, B. A., Morrison, J., Biro, F. M., . . . , Striegel-Moore, R. H. (2007). Childhood overweight and cardiovascular disease risk factors: The National Heart, Lung, and Blood Institute Growth and Health Study. *Journal of Pediatrics, 150*(1), 18–25.

Thompson, G. (1998, December 14). With obesity in children rising, more get adult type of diabetes. *New York Times*, p. A1.

Thompson, J. A., & Halberstadt, A. G. (2008). Children's accounts of sibling jealousy and their implicit theories about relationships. *Social Development, 17*(3), 488–511. doi:10.1111/j.1467-9507.2007.00435.x

Thompson, K. J., & Cafri, G. (2007). *The muscular ideal: Psychological, social, and medical perspectives.* Washington, D.C.: American Psychological Association.

Thompson, M., & Barker, T. (2008). *It's a boy: Understanding your son's development from birth to age 18.* New York: Random House.

Thompson, R., & Tabone, J. K. (2010). The impact of early alleged maltreatment on behavioral trajectories. *Child Abuse & Neglect, 34*(12), 907–916. doi:10.1016/j.chiabu.2010.06.006

Thompson, R. A. (2001). Development in the first years of life. Caring for Infants and Toddlers. The Future of Children. *The David and Lucile Packard Foundation, 11*(1). Spring-Summer 2001. Retrieved from http://www.future-ofchildren.org/pubs-info2825/pubs-info.htm?doc_id=79324

Thompson, R. A., & Goodvin, R. (2007). Taming the tempest in the teapot. In C. A. Brownell & C. B. Kopp (Eds.), *Socioemotional development in the toddler years: Transitions and transformations* (pp. 320–341). New York: Guilford Press.

Thompson, R. A., & Lagattuta, K. H. (2006). Feeling and understanding: Early emotional development. In K. McCartney & D. Phillips (Eds.), *Blackwell handbook of early childhood development* (pp. 317–337). Malden, MA: Blackwell.

Thorpy, M. J. (2005). New paradigms in the treatment of restless legs syndrome. *Neurology, 64*(12), S28–S33.

Thurston, R. C., Blumenthal, J. A., Babyak, M. A., & Sherwood, A. (2006). Association between hot flashes, sleep complaints, and psychological functioning among healthy menopausal women. *International Journal of Behavioral Medicine, 13*(2), 163–172. doi:10.1207/s15327558ijbm1302_8

Tikoo, M. (1996). An exploratory study of differences in developmental concerns of middle-aged men and women in India. *Psychological Reports, 78*, 883–887.

Tikotzky, L., Sharabany, R., Hirsch, I., & Sadeh, A. (2010). Ghosts in the nursery: Infant sleep and sleep-related cognitions of parents raised under communal sleeping arrangements. *Infant Mental Health Journal, 31*(3), 312–334. doi:10.1002/imhj.20258

TIMSS & PIRLS International Study Center. (2007, November 28). Students in Russian Federation, Hong Kong SAR, and Singapore top global assessment of reading literacy. [News Release.] Chestnut Hill, MA: Lynch School of Education, Boston College.

Tisak, M. S., Tisak, J., & Goldstein, S. E. (2006). Aggression, delinquency, and morality: A social-cognitive perspective. In M. Killen & J. G. Smetana (Eds.), *Handbook of moral development* (pp. 611–629). Mahwah, NJ: Erlbaum.

Tolan, P. H., Gorman-Smith, D., & Henry, D. B. (2003). The developmental ecology of urban males' youth violence. *Developmental Psychology, 32*, 274–291.

Tolin, D. F., & Foa, E. B. (2006). Sex differences in trauma and posttraumatic stress disorder: A quantitative review of 25 years of research. *Psychological Bulletin, 132*(6), 959–992.

Tomasello, M. (2006). Acquiring linguistic constructions. In D. Kuhn & R. Siegler (Eds.), *Handbook of child psychology.* New York: Wiley.

Tomasello, M., & Bates, E. (2001). *Language development: The essential readings.* Malden, MA: Blackwell.

Tomasello, M., Carpenter, M., & Lizskowski, U. (2007). A new look at infant pointing. *Child Development, 78*, 705–722.

Tomison, A. M. (1996, Winter). *Intergenerational transmission of maltreatment.* Issues in Child Abuse Prevention. Melbourne, Australia: National Child Protection Clearinghouse.

Tomlinson, C., & Hockett, J. (2007). Instructional strategies and programming models for gifted learners. In F. Karnes and K. Stephens (Eds.). *Achieving excellence: Educating the gifted and talented* (pp. 154–169). Upper Saddle River, NJ: Pearson Education.

Torrey, E. F. (1992). *Freudian fraud: The malignant effect of Freud's theory on American thought and culture.* New York: Harper Collins.

Tortolero, S., Markham, C., Peskin, M., Shegog, R., Addy, R., Escobar-Chaves, S., & Baumler, E. (2010). It's your game: Keep it real: Delaying sexual behavior with an effective middle school program. *Journal of Adolescent Health, 46*(2), 169–179. doi:10.1016/j.jadohealth.2009.06.008

Torvaldsen, S., Roberts, C. L., Simpson, J. M., Thompson, J. F., & Ellwood, D. A. (2006). Intrapartum epidural analgesia and breast-feeding: A prospective cohort study. *International Breastfeeding Journal, 1*, 24.

Toscano, M. G., Romero, Z., Muñoz, P., Cobo, M., Benabdellalh, K., & Martin. F. (2011). Physiological and tissue-specific vectors for treatment of inherited diseases.

Gene Therapy, 18, 117–127. doi:10.1038/gt.2010.138

Trachtenberg, S., & Viken, R. J. (1994). Aggressive boys in the classroom: Biased attributions or shared perceptions? *Child Development, 65*, 829–835.

Treffert, D. A. (2001). *The savant syndrome: Islands of genius.* State Medical Society of Wisconsin. Retrieved from http://www.wismed.org/foundation/islands.htm

Tremblay, L., & Limbos, M. (2009). Body image disturbance and psychopathology in children: Research evidence and implications for prevention and treatment. *Current Psychiatry Reviews, 5*(1), 62–72. doi:10.2174/157340009787315307

Tremblay, R. E., Nagin, D. S., Séguin, J. R., Zoccolillo, M., Zelazo, P. D., Boivin, M., . . ., Japel, C. (2004). Physical aggression during early childhood: Trajectories and predictors. *Pediatrics, 114*(1), e43–e50.

Trinder, L., Kellet, J., & Swift, L. (2008). The relationship between contact and child adjustment in high conflict cases after divorce or separation. *Child and Adolescent Mental Health, 13*(4), 181–187. doi:10.1111/j.1475-3588.2008.00484.x

Tripp, A. M. (2003). Non-formal institutions, informal economies, and the politics of inclusion. In S. Kayizzi-Mugerwa (Ed.), *Reforming Africa's institutions: Ownership, incentives, and capabilities* (pp. 301–321). New York: United Nations University Press.

Trotter, R. J. (1987, May). You've come a long way, baby. *Psychology Today, 21*, 34–45.

Truog, R. D. (2004, August). Brain death: At once "Well Settled" and "Persistently Unresolved." *Policy Forum of American Medical Association, 6*(8). Retrieved from http://www.ama-assn.org/ama/pub/category/print/12715.html

Trustees of the Social Security and Medicare Programs. (2010). *Status of the Social Security and Medicare Programs.* Retrieved from http://www.ssa.gov/OACT/TRSUM/trsummary.html

Tucker-Drob, E. M., & Salthouse, T. A. (2008). Adult age trends in the relations among cognitive abilities. *Psychology of Aging, 23*(2), 453–460.

Tulving, E. (1968). Theoretical issues in free recall. In T. R. Dixon & D. L. Horton (Eds.), *Verbal behavior and general behavior theory.* Englewood Cliffs, NJ: Prentice Hall.

Tulving, E., & Craik, F. (2000). *Oxford handbook of memory.* New York: Oxford University Press.

Turbin, M. S., Jessor, R., Costa, F. M., Dong, Q., Zhang, H., & Wang, C. (2006). Protective and risk factors in health-enhancing behavior among adolescents in China and the United States: Does social context matter? *Health Psychology, 25*(4), 445–454.

Turiel, E. (2006a). The development of morality. In W. Damon & R. J. Lerner (Eds.),

Handbook of child psychology (6th ed., Vol. 3, pp. 789–857). New York: Wiley.

Turiel, E. (2006b). Thought, emotions, and social interactional processes in moral development. In M. Killen & J. G. Smetana (Eds.), *Handbook of moral development* (pp. 7–36). Mahwah, NJ: Erlbaum.

Turkle, S. (2003). Sociable technologies: Enhancing human performance when the computer is not a tool but a companion. In M. C. Roco & W. S. Bainbridge (Eds.), *Converging technologies for improving human performance* (pp. 150–158). The Netherlands: Kluwer Academic.

Tyas, S. L., Salazar, J. C., Snowdon, D. A., Desrosiers, M. F., Riley, K. P., Mendiondo, M. S., . . . , Kryscio, R. J. (2007). Transitions to mild cognitive impairments, dementia, and death: Findings from the Nun Study. *American Journal of Epidemiology, 165*(11), 1231–1238.

Tyas, S. L., Snowdon, D. A., Desrosiers, M. F., Riley, K. P., & Markesbery, W. R. (2007). Healthy ageing in the nun study: Definition and neuropathologic correlates. *Age and Ageing, 36*, 650–655.

U.S. Bureau of Labor Statistics. (2006). *Class of worker by sex and selected characteristics: 2005* [Data file]. Available from National Technical Information Service Web site, http://www.bls.gov/cps/home.htm

U.S. Bureau of Labor Statistics. (2007). *Preliminary multifactor productivity trends, 2006.* Retrieved from http://www.bls.gov/mfp.release/pdf/hsgec.pdf

U.S. Bureau of Labor Statistics. (2009). Occupational employment of workers without disabilities and workers with disabilities, April 2009. *Occupational Outlook Quarterly Online, 53*(2), 1–32. Retrieved from http://www.bls.gov/opub/ooq/2009/summer/oochart.pdf

U.S. Bureau of Labor Statistics. (2010a). *Volunteering in the United States, 2010.* [News Release.] Retrieved from http://www.bls.gov/news.release/volun.nr0.htm

U.S. Bureau of Labor Statistics. (2010b, October). Issues in labor statistics. Retrieved from http://www.bls.gov/opub/ils/pdf/opbils87.pdf

U.S. Bureau of Labor Statistics. (2011a). Table 4. Families with own children: Employment status of parents by age of youngest child and family type, 2008–09 annual averages. Retrieved from http://www.bls.gov/emp/

U.S. Bureau of Labor Statistics. (2011b, February 4). Employment situation summary. [Economic News Release]. Retrieved from http://www.bls.gov/news.release/empsit.nr0.htm

U.S. Bureau of the Census. (1960). *Historical statistics of the United States: Colonial times to 1957.* Washington, DC: Author.

U.S. Bureau of the Census. (2004, March 18). U.S. interim projections by age, sex, race,

and Hispanic origin. Retrieved from http://www.census.gov/ipc/www/usinterimproj

U.S. Bureau of the Census. (2007a). *American families and living arrangements: 2006.* Retrieved from http://www.census.gov/population/www/socdemo/hh-fam/cps2006.html.

U.S. Bureau of the Census. (2007b). Household relationship and family status of children under 18 years, by age, sex, race, Hispanic origin: 2006. *Population Survey, 2006 Annual Social and Economic Supplement.* Retrieved from http://www.census.gov/population/socdemo/hh-fam/cps2006/tabC1-all.xls

U.S. Bureau of the Census. (2009a). America's families and living arrangements: 2009. *Current Population Survey, 2009.* Retrieved from http://www.census.gov/population/www/socdemo/hh-fam/cps2009.html

U.S. Bureau of the Census. (2009b). *Births, deaths, and life expectancy by country or area: 2009 and 2010.* Retrieved from http://www.census.gov/ipc/www/idb.html.

U.S. Bureau of the Census. (2009c). Children living with married parents: 2009. *Current Population Survey, 2009.* Retrieved from http://www.census.gov/population/www/socdemo/hh-fam/cps2009.html

U.S. Bureau of the Census. (2010a). *Annual estimates of the resident population by sex and five-year age groups for the United States: April 1, 2000, to July 1, 2009* (NC-EST2009-01). Washington, DC: U.S. Census Bureau, Population Division.

U.S. Bureau of the Census. (2010b). Current population survey, 1970–2010 annual social and economic supplements. *Income, Poverty, and Health Insurance Coverage in the United States: 2009.* Washington, DC. Retrieved from http://www.census.gov/hhes/www/poverty/data/incpovhlth/2009/table5.pdf

U.S. Bureau of the Census. (2010c). *Children living with grandparents by race and sex: 2010.* Retrieved from http://www.census.gov/apsd/techdoc/cps/cpsmar10.pdf

U.S. Bureau of the Census. (2010d). Estimated median age at first marriage, by sex: 1890–the present. *Current Population Survey, March and Annual Social and Economic Supplements, 2010 and Earlier.* Retrieved from www.census.gov/population/socdemo/hh-fam/ms2.xls

U.S. Bureau of the Census. (2010e). Family status and household relationship of people 15 years and older, by marital status, age, and sex: 2010. *Current Population Survey, 2010 Annual Social and Economic Supplement.* Retrieved from http://www.census.gov/population/www/socdemo/hh-fam/cps2010.html

U.S. Bureau of the Census. (2010f). Health insurance coverage status and type of coverage by selected characteristics: 2009. *Current Population Survey, Annual Social and*

Economic Supplement. Retrieved from http://www.census.gov/hhes/www/cpsta bles/032010/health/h01_001.htm

U.S. Bureau of the Census. (2010g). Income and earnings summary measures by selected characteristics: 2008 and 2009. *Current Population Reports: Income, Poverty, and Health Insurance Coverage in the United States: 2009.* Retrieved from http://www.census.gov/prod/2010pubs/p60-238.pdf

U.S. Bureau of the Census. (2010h). Income, poverty, and health insurance coverage in the United States: 2009. *Current Population Reports: Consumer Income.* Retrieved from http://www.census.gov/prod/2010pubs/p60-238.pdf

U.S. Bureau of the Census. (2010i). Marital status of people 15 years and over, by age, sex, personal earnings, race, and Hispanic origin, 2010. *Current Population Survey, 2010 Annual Social and Economic Supplement.* Retrieved from http://www.census.gov/population/www/socdemo/hh-fam/cps2010.html

U.S. Bureau of the Census. (2010j). People without health insurance coverage by selected characteristics: 2008–2009. *Current Population Survey, 2009 and 2010 Annual Social and Economic Supplements.* Retrieved from http://www.census.gov/hhes/www/hlthins/data/incpovhlth/2009/tab8.pdf

U.S. Bureau of the Census. (2010k). Population by sex, age, nativity, and U. S. citizenship: 2008. *Current Population Survey, Projections of the Population by Selected Age Groups for the United States: 2008 to 2050.* Retrieved from http://www.census.gov/population/www/projections/tables andcharts.html

U.S. Bureau of the Census. (2010l). *Statistical Abstract of the United States: 2009.* Washington, DC: U.S. Bureau of the Census.

U.S. Bureau of the Census. (2010m). *The nation has nearly 350,000 fewer nonemployer business locations, 2010.* Retrieved from http://www.census.gov/econ/nonemployer/methodology.htm

U.S. Bureau of the Census. (2010n). *Voting and registration in the election of November 2008.* Retrieved from http://www.census.gov/population/www/socdemo/voting.html.

U.S. Bureau of the Census. (2010o). America's Families and Living Arrangements: *Population Profile of the United States.* Retrieved from http://www.census.gov/population/www/socdemo/hh-fam/cps2010.html <http://www.census.gov/population/www/socdemo/hh-fam/cps2010.html>

U.S. Bureau of the Census. (2011a). *America's families and living arrangements: 2009.* Table C5: Nativity status of children under 18 years by presence of parents by race, and Hispanic origin by selected characteristics. Retrieved from http://www.census.gov/population/www/socdemo/hh-fam/cps2009.html

U.S. Bureau of the Census. (2011b). Households, families, subfamilies, and married couples: 1980 to 2009. *Statistical Abstract of the United States: 2011.* Retrieved from http://www.census.gov/compendia/statab/2011/tables/11s0059.pdf

U.S. Bureau of the Census. (2011c). Table 56. Marital status of the population by sex, race, and Hispanic origin: 1990–2009. *Statistical Abstract of the United States: 2011.* Retrieved from http://www.census.gov/compendia/statab/2011/tables/11s0060.pdf

U.S. Bureau of the Census. (2011d). *The 2011 Statistical Abstract of the United States.* Retrieved from http://www.census.gov/compendia/statab/2011edition.html

U.S. Cancer Statistics Working Group. (2010). *United States Cancer Statistics: 1999–2007 Incidence and Mortality Web-based Report.* Atlanta (GA): Department of Health and Human Services, Centers for Disease Control and Prevention, and National Cancer Institute. Retrieved from http://www.cdc.gov/uscs.

U.S. Census Bureau News. (2010, July 19). Unmarried and single Americans week, September 19–25, 2010: Single life. [News release]. *Facts for Features.* Washington, DC: U.S. Department of Commerce. Retrieved from http://www.census.gov/newsroom/releases/pdf/cb10ff-18_single.pdf

U.S. Congress Joint Economic Committee. (2010, December). Invest in women, invest in America: A comprehensive review of women in the U.S. economy. Retrieved from http://jec.senate.gov/public/?a=Files.Serve&File_id=57cfaf04-f297-4c61-964b-6321af47db03

U.S. Department of Commerce. (1998). *Cohabitation. Current population reports.* (October). Washington, DC: U.S. Government Printing Office.

U.S. Department of Education. (2001). *No Child Left Behind: Executive summary.* Retrieved from http://www.ed.gov/inits/nclb/part2.html

U.S. Department of Education. (2005, March 15). *Biennial evaluation report to Congress on the implementation of the state formula grant program, 2002–2004: English Language Acquisition, Language Enhancement and Academic Achievement Act (ESEA, Title III, Part A).* Washington, DC: Office of English Language Acquisition, Language Enhancement and Academic Achievement for Limited English Proficient Students. Retrieved from http://www.ncela.gwu.edu/oela/biennial05/full_report.pdf

U.S. Department of Education. (2007). Even Start. Retrieved from http://www.ed.gov/programs/evenstartformula/index.html

U.S. Department of Education. (2009). Fast facts. *Digest of Education Statistics, 2008* (NCES 2009-020). National Center for Education Statistics, Table 190. Retrieved from http://www.nces.ed.gov/fastfacts/display/html

U.S. Department of Education. (2010). *Meeting the needs of English learners and other diverse learners.* Washington, DC: U.S. Government Printing Office.

U.S. Department of Education. (2011). National Assessment of Education Progress (NAEP), 1990–2009. National Center for Education Statistics. Retrieved from http://nces.ed.gov/nationsreportcard/

U.S. Department of Education, Office of Planning, Evaluation, and Policy Development. (2010). *A blueprint for reform: The reauthorization of the Elementary and Secondary Education Act.* Washington, DC: U.S. Government Printing Office.

U.S. Department of Health and Human Services. (2006). *Child health USA 2006.* Rockville, MD: Maternal and Child Health Bureau.

U.S. Department of Health and Human Services. (2007). *Child maltreatment 2005.* Administration on Children, Youth and Families. Washington, DC: U.S. Government Printing Office. Retrieved from http://www.acf.hhs.gov/programs/cb/pubs/cm05/cm05.pdf

U.S. Department of Health and Human Services. (2009a). Births: Preliminary data for 2007. *National Vital Statistics Report, 57*(12), 1–23.

U.S. Department of Health and Human Services. (2009b). Pregnancy and alcohol: Civil commitment: Policy description. *National Institute on Alcohol Abuse and Alcoholism.* Retrieved from http://www.alcoholpolicy.niaaa.nih.gov/Alcohol_and_Pregnancy_Civil_Commitment.html

U.S. Department of Health and Human Services. (2010a). 2009/2010 HHS Poverty Guidelines. Retrieved from http://liheap.ncat.org/profiles/povertytables/FY2010/popstate.htm

U.S. Department of Health and Human Services. (2010b). About *the Affordable Health Care Act.* Retrieved from http://www.healthcare.gov/law/about/index.html

U.S. Department of Health and Human Services. (2010c). *Child Health USA 2010.* Health Resources and Services Administration, Maternal and Child Health Bureau. Retrieved from http://www.mchb.hrsa.gov/chusa10/pdfs/c10.pdf

U.S. Department of Health and Human Services. (2010d). *Child Maltreatment 2008.* Administration for Children and Families, Administration on Children, Youth and Families, Children's Bureau. Retrieved from http://www.acf.hhs.gov/programs/cb/pubs/cm08/cm08.pdf

U.S. Department of Health and Human Services. (2010e). *Child Maltreatment 2009.* Administration for Children and Families, Administration on Children, Youth and Families, Children's Bureau. Retrieved from http://www.acf.hhs.gov/programs/cb/stats _research/index.htm#can.

U.S. Department of Health and Human Services. (2010f). *Menstruation and the menstrual cycle.* Office of Women's Health. Retrieved from http://www.womenshealth .gov/faq/menstruation.pdf

U.S. Department of Health and Human Services. (2010g). *2010 Strategic plan for autism spectrum disorder research.* Interagency Autism Coordinating Committee. Retrieved from http://www.iacc.hhs.gov

U.S. Department of Health and Human Services. (2010h). *Fact sheet: Benefits for women and children of new Affordable Care Act rules on expanding prevention coverage.* Retrieved from http://www.healthcare .gov/

U.S. Department of Housing and Urban Development. (2003, June). *Protect your family from lead in your home.* Washington, DC: Environmental Protection Agency.

U.S. Department of Justice. (2010, May). *The crime of family abduction: A child's and parent's perspective.* Washington, DC: Office of Juvenile Justice and Delinquency Prevention. Retrieved from http://www .ncjrs.gov/pdffiles1/ojjdp/229933.pdf

U.S. Department of Labor. (2010a). Economic and employment projections: 2008–2018. Table 6. The 30 occupations with the largest employment growth, 2008–18. Retrieved from http://www.bls.gov/news .release/ecopro.toc.htm

U.S. Department of Labor. (2010b). *Employment characteristics of families in 2009.* [News Release.] Retrieved from http:// www.bls.gov/news.release/famee.nr0.htm

U.S. Department of Labor. (2010c). *Fact Sheet #28: The Family and Medical Leave Act of 1973.* Wage and Hour Division. Retrieved from http://www.dol.gov/whd/regs/ compliance/whdfs28.pdf

U.S. Department of Labor. (2010d). *Labor force participation rates among mothers: 2008.* Retrieved from http://data.bls.gov/ cgi-bin/print.pl/opup/ted_20100507.htm

U.S. Department of Labor. (2011). The Family Medical Leave Act (FMLA). Retrieved from http://www.dol.gov/compliance/laws/ comp-fmla.htm

U.S. Food and Drug Administration. (2008). *Liposuction information.* Retrieved from http:// www.fda.gov/cdrh/ liposuction/complete.html

U.S. Food and Drug Administration. (2010). Medicines in my home: Caffeine and your body. Retrieved from http://www.fda.gov/ Consumers/BuyingUsingMedicalSafely/ UnderstandingOver0the-CounterMedicines/ UCM205286.pdf

U.S. Government Accountability Office (GAO). (2010). National Health Care Workforce Commission. *Patient Protection and Affordable Care Act*: Subtitle B. Retrieved from http://www.gao.gov/hcac/nwcsec5101_ hr_3590.pdf

U.S. Maternal and Child Health Bureau. (2006). *Child health USA 2006.* Rockville, MD: U.S. Department of Health and Human Services.

U.S. Maternal and Child Health Bureau. (2010). *Child health USA 2010.* Rockville, MD: U.S. Department of Health and Human Services.

U.S. National Center for Health Statistics. (2007). Deaths and death rates by leading causes of death and age: 2004. *National Vital Statistics Reports, 55*(19), 1–96.

U.S. Public Health Service Task Force. (2002, November 22). U.S. Public Health Service Task Force recommendations for use of antiretroviral drugs in pregnant HIV-1 infected women for maternal health and interventions to reduce perinatal HIV-1 transmission in the United States. *MMWR Weekly, 51*(RR18), 1–38.

U.S. Surgeon General rolls out 2005 agenda: The Year of the Healthy Child. (2005, January 24). U.S. Department of Health and Human Services. [News Release]. Retrieved from http://www.surgeongeneral.gov/ pressreleases/sg01242005.html

Udry, J. R. (1988). Biological predispositions and social control in adolescent sexual behavior. *American Sociological Review, 53,* 709–722.

UNAIDS/WHO. (2009, November). *2009 AIDS epidemic update.* Retrieved from http://data.unaids.org/pub/Report/2009/ JC1700_Epi_Update_2009_en.pdf

UNAIDS/WHO. (2010). *AIDS epidemic update: December 2009.* Retrieved from http://data.unaids.org/pub/Report/2009/ JC1700_Epi_Update_2009_en.pdf

Underage Drinking. (2005, April). *SADD statistics.* Retrieved from http://www .saddonline.com

Underwood, H., & Findlay, B. (2004). Internet relationships and their impact on primary relationships. *Behavior Change, 21*(2), 127–140. doi:10.1375/bech.21.2.127.55422

Underwood, M. K., Mayeux, L., & Galperin, M. (2006). Peer relationships during middle childhood: Gender, emotions, and aggression. In L. Balter & C. S. Tamis-LeMonda, *Child psychology: A handbook of contemporary issues* (2nd ed., pp. 241–262). New York: Psychology Press.

United Nations. Department of Economic and Social Affairs. (2007). *Demographic yearbook 2004.* New York: United Nations. Retrieved from http://unstats.un.org/unsd/ demographic/products/dyb/dybsets/2004 %20DYB.pdf

University of Cincinnati. (2005, June 8). Possible treatment found for "Chemo-brain." *ScienceDaily.* Retrieved from http://www .sciencedaily.com/releases/2005/06/ 050608052704.htm

Updegraff, K. A., Helms, H. M., McHale, S. M., Crouter, A. C., Thayer, S. M., & Sales, L. H. (2004, October). Who's the

boss? Patterns of perceived control in adolescents' friendships. *Journal of Youth and Adolescence, 33*(5), 403–420.

Updegraff, K. A., McHale, S. M., Crouter, A. C., & Kupanoff, K. (2001). Parents' involvement in adolescents' peer relationships: A comparison of mothers' and fathers' roles. *Journal of Marriage and Family, 63*(3), 655–668.

Upledger, J. E. (2004, August). A look inside the craniosacral system and how CST helps. *Massage Today, 4*(8). Retrieved from http:// www.massagetoday.com/

Utrecht, T. S. (2002, June 8). Reported euthanasia cases in Holland fall for second year. *British Medical Journal, 324,* 1354.

Vaillant, G. (2002). *Aging well: Surprising guideposts to a happier life from the Landmark Harvard Study of Adult Development.* Boston: Little, Brown.

Vaillant, G. E., & Milofsky, E. (1980). Natural history of male psychological health. IX: Empirical evidence for Erikson's model of the life cycle. *American Journal of Psychiatry, 37,* 1348–1359.

Valenti, C. A. (2006). Infant vision guidance: Fundamental vision development in infancy. *Optometry & Vision Development, 37*(3), 147–155. Retrieved from http://drsamberne .com/articles/Infant_Vision_Guidance.pdf

Valkenburg, P. M., & Peter, J. (2007). Who visits online dating sites? Exploring some characteristics of online daters. *CyberPsychology & Behavior, 10*(6), 849–852.

Van Asselt, K. M., Kok, H. S., Pearson, P. L., Dubas, J. S., Peeters, P. H. M., te Velde, E. R., . . . , Van Noord, A. H. (2004, November). Heritability of menopausal age in mothers and daughters. *Fertility and Sterility, 82*(5), 1348–1351.

Van Bockern, S. (2006). Soul-filled teaching and learning. *Reclaiming Children and Youth, 14*(4), 218–222.

van den Boom, D. (2001). First attachments: Theory and research. In G. Bremner & A. Fogel (Eds.), *Blackwell handbook of infant development* (pp. 296–325). Malden, MA: Blackwell.

Vander Zanden, J. W. (1987). *Social psychology* (4th ed.). New York: Random House.

Vander Zanden, J. W., & Pace, A. (1984). *Educational psychology* (2nd ed.). New York: Random House.

Vandewater, E. A., Bickham, D. S., Lee, J. H., Cummings, H. M., Wartella, E. A., & Rideout, V. J. (2005). When the television is always on: Heavy television exposure and young children's development. *American Behavioral Scientist, 48*(5), 562–577.

Vandewater, E. A., Rideout, V. J., Wartella, E. A., Huang, X., Lee, J. H., & Shim, M. S. (2007). Digital childhood: Electronic media and technology use among infants, toddlers, and preschoolers. *Pediatrics, 119*(5), 1006–1015. doi:10.1542/peds.2006 -1804

van Gelder, M., Reefhuis, J., Caton, A. R., Werler, M. M., Druschel, C. M., & Roeleveld, N. (2010). Characteristics of pregnant illicit drug users and associations between cannabis use and perinatal outcome in a population-based study. *Drug and Alcohol Dependence, 109*(1–3), 243–247.

Van IJzendoorn, M. H., & Kroonenberg, P. M. (1988). Cross-cultural patterns of attachment: A meta-analysis of the strange situation. *Child Development, 59*, 147–156.

Van IJzendoorn, M. H., & Sagi, A. (1999). Cross-cultural patterns of attachment. In J. Cassidy and P. H. Shaver, (Eds.), *Handbook of attachment theory, research, and clinical applications.* (pp. 713–734). New York: Guilford Press.

Van Kleef, G. A. (2009). How emotions regulate social life: The emotions as social information (EASI) model. *Current Directions in Psychological Science, 18*(3), 184–188. doi:10.1111/j.1467-8721.2009.01633.x

van Lommel, P. (2010). *Consciousness beyond life: The science of the near-death experience.* New York: HarperOne.

Van Mechelen, W., Twisk, J., Molendijk, A., Blom, B., Snel, J., & Kemper, H. C. (1996). Subject-related risk factors for sports injuries: A one-year prospective study in young adults. *Medicine and Science in Sports and Exercise, 28* (9), 1171–1178.

Van Voorhees, B. W., Paunesku, D., Kuwabara, S. A., Basu, A., Gollan, J., Hankin, B. L., Melkonian, S., & Reinecke, M. (2008). Protective and vulnerability factors predicting new-onset depressive episode in a representative of U.S. adolescents. *Journal of Adolescent Health, 42*(6), 605–616. doi:10.1016/j.jadohealth.2007.11.135

Van Willigen, M. (2000). Differential benefits of volunteering across the life course. *The Journals of Gerontology. Series B, Psychological Sciences and Social Sciences, 55*(5), S308–318.

Vasan, R., & Sullivan, L. M. (2005). Relative importance of borderline and elevated levels of coronary heart disease risk factors. *Annals of Internal Medicine, 142*(6), 393–406.

Vasquez, J. A. (1998). Distinctive traits of Hispanic students. *Prevention Researcher, 5*, 1.

Vastag, B. (2007). No slippery slope. *Science News, 172*(14), 212.

Vaughan, B. S., Wetzel, M. W., & Kratochvil, C. J. (2008). Beyond the 'typical' patient: Treating attention-deficit/hyperactivity disorder in preschoolers and adults. *International Review of Psychiatry, 20*(2), 143–149. doi:10.1080/09540260801887751

Vaught, S. E., & Castagno, A. E. (2008). "I don't think I'm a racist": Critical Race Theory, teacher attitudes, and structural racism. *Race Ethnicity and Education, 11*(2), 95–113. doi:10.1080/13613320802110217

Vecchio, M. S., Sasco, A. J., & Cann, C. I. (2003). Occupational risk in health care and research. *American Journal of Industrial Medicine, 43*(4), 369–397.

Veitch, J., Salmon, J., & Ball, K. (2010). Individual, social and physical environmental correlates of children's active free-play: A cross-sectional study. *International Journal of Behavioral Nutrition and Physical Activity, 7*(11). doi:10.1186/1479-5868-7-11

Velde, S. J., Bourdeaudhuij, I. D., Thorsdottir, I., Rasmussen, M., Hagstromer, . . . , Brug, J. (2007). Patterns in sedentary and exercise behaviors and associations with overweight in 9–14-year-old boys and girls: A cross-sectional study. *BMC Public Health, 7*(16), 1–9.

Velho, S., Marques-Vidal, P., Baptists, F., & Camilo, M. (2008). Dietary intake adequacy and cognitive function in free-living active elderly: A cross-sectional and short-term prospective study. *Clinical Nutrition, 27*(1), 77–86.

Ventura, S. J., & Hamilton B. E. (2011, February). U.S. teen birth rate resumes decline. *National Vital Statistics Reports, 58.* Hyattsville, MD: National Center for Health Statistics.

Verba, M. (1994). The beginnings of collaboration in peer interaction. *Human Development, 37*, 125–139.

Verhaeghen, P., & Hoyer, W. J., (2007). Aging, focus switching, and task switching in a continuous calculation task: Evidence toward a new working memory control process. *Aging, Neuropsychology, and Cognition, 14*, 22–39. doi:10.1080/13825580969357

Verhagen, A. A. E., van der Hoeven, M. A. H., van Meerveld, C., & Sauer, P. J. J. (2007). Physician medical decision-making at the end of life in newborns: Insight into implementation at 2 Dutch centers. *Pediatrics, 120*(1), e20–e28.

Verhagen, E., & Sauer, P. J. (2005, March 10). The *Groningen* protocol—Euthanasia in severely ill newborns. *New England Journal of Medicine, 352*, 959–962.

Viding, E., Spinath, F. M., Price, T. S., Bishop, D. V. M., Dale, P. S., & Plomin, R. (2004). Genetic and environmental influence on language impairment in 4-year-old same-sex and opposite-sex twins. *Journal of Child Psychology and Psychiatry and Applied Disciplines 45*(2), 315–325.

Vietze, D. L., & Hildebrandt, E. J. (2009). Multiculturally conscious parenting: Promoting peace and teaching tolerance to young children. *ENCOUNTER: Education for Meaning and Social Justice, 22*(4), 33–37.

Villalonga-Olives, E., Rojas-Farreras, S., Vilagut, G., Palacio-Vieira, J. A., Valderas, J. M., Herdman, M., . . . , Alonso, J. (2010). Impact of recent life events on the health related quality of life of adolescents and youths: The role of gender and life events typologies in a follow-up study. *Health and Quality of Life Outcomes, 8*(71), 1–9. doi:10.1186/1477-7525-8-71

Villareal, D. T., & Holloszy, J. O. (2004). Effect of DHEA on abdominal fat and insulin action in elderly women and men. *Journal of the American Medical Association, 292*(18), 2243–2248.

Virick, M., Lilly, J. D., & Casper, W. J. (2007). Doing more with less: An analysis of work life balance among layoff survivors. *Career Development International, 12*(5), 463–480.

Vogt, D. S., & Colvin, C. R. (2003). Interpersonal orientation and the accuracy of personality judgements. *Journal of Personality, 71*, 267–295.

Volbrecht, M. M., Lemery-Chalfant, K., Aksan, N., Zahn-Waxler, C., & Goldsmith, H. H. (2007). Examining the familial link between positive affect and empathy development in the second year. *Journal of Genetic Psychology, 168*(2), 105–130.

Volling, B. L., & Belsky, J. (1992). The contribution of mother-child and father-child relationships to the quality of sibling interaction: A longitudinal study. *Child Development, 63*, 1209–1222.

Volterra, V., Iverson, J. M., & Castrataro, M. (2006). The development of gesture in hearing and deaf children. In B. Schick, M. Marschark, & P. E. Spencer (Eds.), *Advances in the sign language development of deaf children* (pp. 46–70). New York: Oxford University Press.

Volz, J. (2000). Successful aging: The second 50: Psychologists' research is changing attitudes about what it takes to live the good— and longer—life. *Monitor on Psychology, 31*(1), 24–28.

von Hofsten, C. (1982). Eye-hand coordination in the newborn. *Developmental Psychology, 18*, 450–461.

Vondra, J. I., Shaw, D. S., Swearingen, L., Cohen, M., & Owens, E. B. (2001). Attachment stability and emotional and behavioral regulation from infancy to pre-school age. *Development and Psychopathology, 13*(1), 13–33.

Voorpostel, M., & van der Lippe, T. (2007). Support between siblings and friends: Two worlds apart? *Journal of Marriage and Family, 69*(5), 1271–1282.

Votipka, J. (1997). Misoprostol for cervical ripening and labor induction. *Journal of Family Practice, 45*(1), 20.

Vuchinich, S., Bank, L., & Patterson, G. R. (1992). Parenting, peers, and the stability of antisocial behavior in preadolescent boys. *Developmental Psychology, 28*, 510–521.

Vygotsky, L. S. (1962). *Thought and language.* Cambridge, MA: MIT Press.

Vygotsky, L. S. (1978). *Mind in society.* Cambridge, MA: Harvard University.

Waanders, C., Mendez, J. L., & Downer, J. T. (2007). Parent characteristics, economic stress and neighborhood context as predictors of parent involvement in preschool children's education. *Journal of School Psychology, 45*(6), 619–636.

Wagner, M. (2006). *Born in the USA: How a broken maternity system must be fixed to put women and children first.* Los Angeles: University of California Press.

Wainright, J. L., & Patterson, C. J. (2008). Peer relations among adolescents with female same-sex parents. *Developmental Psychology, 44*(1), 117–126. doi:10.1037/0012 -1649.44.1.117

Waites, C. (2009). Building strengths: Intergenerational practice with African American families. *Social Work, 54*(3), 278–287.

Waldman, I. D., & Gizer, I. R. (2006). The genetics of attention deficit hyperactivity disorder. *Clinical Psychology Review, 26,* 396–432.

Walker, D. M. (2007, February 28). *Older workers: Some best practices and strategies for engaging and retaining older workers* (GAO-07-438SP). Washington, DC: United States Government Accountability Office.

Walker, L., & Hill, A. J. (2009). Obesity: The role of child mental health services. *Child and Adolescent Mental Health, 14*(3), 114–120. doi:10.1111/j.1475-3588.2008.00522.x

Walker, L. J., de Vries, B., & Bichard, S. L. (1984). The hierarchical nature of stages of moral development. *Developmental Psychology, 20,* 960–966.

Walker, L. J., & Frimer, J. A. (2007). Moral personality of brave and caring exemplars. *Journal of Personality and Social Psychology, 93*(5), 845–860.

Walker, L. J., & Hennig, K. H. (2004). Differing conceptions of moral exemplarity: Just, brave, and caring. *Journal of Personality and Social Psychology, 86*(4), 629–647. doi:10.1037/0022-3514.86.4.629

Wallace, D. B., Franklin, M. B., & Keegan, R. T. (1994). The observing eye: A century of baby diaries. *Human Development, 37,* 1–29.

Waller, K., Kaprio, J., & Kujala, U. M. (2008). Associations between long-term physical activity, waist circumference and weight gain: A 30-year longitudinal twin study. *International Journal of Obesity, 32*(2), 353–361. doi:10.1038/sj.ijo.0803692

Wallerstein, J., Lewis, J., & Blakeslee, S. (2000). *The unexpected legacy of divorce: A 25-year landmark study.* New York: Hyperion.

Wallerstein, J. S., & Kelly, J. B. (1980). *Surviving the breakup: How children actually cope with divorce.* New York: Basic Books.

Walsh, E. & Eggert, L. L. (2007). Suicide risk and protective factors among youth experiencing school difficulties. *International Journal of Mental Health Nursing, 16*(5), 349–359. doi:10.1111/j.1447-0349 .2007.00483.x

Walsh, F. (2006). *Strengthening family resistance.* New York: Guilford Press.

Walters, R. H., Leat, M., & Mezei, L. (1963). Inhibition and disinhibition of responses through empathetic learning. *Canadian Journal of Psychology, 17,* 235–243.

Walton, G. E., Bower, N. J. A., & Bower, T. G. R. (1992). Recognition of familiar faces by newborns. *Infant Behavior and Development, 15,* 265–269.

Walvoord, E. (2010). The timing of puberty: Is it changing? Does it matter? *Journal of Adolescent Health, 47*(5), 433–439. Retrieved from CINAHL Plus with Full Text database. doi:10.1016/j.jadohealth .2010.05.018

Wang, Q. (2006). Relations of maternal style and child self-concept to autobiographical memories in Chinese, Chinese immigrant, and European American 3-year-olds. *Child Development, 77*(6), 1794–1809.

Wang, Q., Pomerantz, E. M., & Chen, H. (2007). The role of parents' control in early adolescents' psychological functioning: A longitudinal investigation in the United States and China. *Child Development, 78*(5), 1592–1610. doi:10.1111/j.1467-8624 .2007.01085.x

Wang, S. (2010, May, 25). Scanning babies for autism. *Wall Street Journal,* p. D2.

Wang, S. S., Brownell, K. D., & Wadden, T. A. (2004, October). The influence of the stigma of obesity on over-weight individuals. *International Journal of Obesity Related Metabolism Disorders. 28*(10), 1333–1337.

Wann, J. (2007). Current approaches to intervention in children with developmental coordination disorder. *Developmental Medicine & Child Neurology, 49*(6), 405.

Wanzer, S. H., & Glenmullen, J. (2007). *To die well.* Cambridge: Da Capo Press.

Ward, M. H., Colt, J. S., Metayer, C., Gunier, R. B., Lubin, J., Crouse, V., . . . , Buffler, P. A. (2009). Residential exposure to polychorinated biphenyls and organochloride pesticides and risk of childhood leukemia. *Environmental Health Perspectives, 117*(6), 1007–1013. doi:10.1289/ehp.0900583

Wardlaw, G. M., & Smith, A. M. (Eds.). (2007). *Contemporary nutrition* (6th ed.). New York: McGraw-Hill.

Warner, H. R., & Price, A. R. (1989). Involvement of DNA repair in cancer and aging. *Journal of Gerontology, 44,* 45–54.

Washington State Department of Health. (2010). Washington State 2009 Death with Dignity Act Report: Executive Summary. Retrieved from http://www.doh.wa.gov/ dwda/forms/DWDA_2009.pdf

Watch, N. H., & Update, M. (2005, February). *Gum disease further linked to heart disease.* Retrieved from http://www.neigh borhood-heart-watch. org/newsletter/ article_278.shtml

Waterfield, B. (2008, March 26). Teens need right to "medically assisted suicide." *Telegraph.* Retrieved from http://www .telegraph.co.uk/news/

Waterman, A. S. (1993). Two conceptions of happiness: Contrasts of personal expressiveness (eudaimonia) and hedonic enjoyment. *Journal of Personality and Social Psychology, 64,* 678–691.

Waters, E., Matas, L., & Sroufe, L. A. (1975). Infants' reactions to an approaching stranger: Description, validation, and functional significance of wariness. *Child Development, 46,* 348–356.

Watson, D. L., & Tharp, R. G. (2007). *Self-directed behavior* (9th ed.). Belmont, CA: Thomson Wadsworth.

Watson, T. J. (2003). *Sociology, work and industry* (4th ed.). New York: Routledge.

Webber, G., & Williams, C. (2008). Part-time work and the gender division of labor. *Qualitative Sociology, 31*(1), 15–36. doi:10 .1007/s11133-007-9088-3

Webber, R. & Boromeo, D. (2005). The sole parent family: Family and support networks. *Australian Journal of Social Issues, 40*(2), 269–283.

Wechsler, D. (1975). Intelligence defined and undefined. *American Psychologist, 30,* 135–139.

Wechsler, H., & Nelson, T. F. (2008). What we have learned from the Harvard School of Public Health College Alcohol Study: Focusing attention on college student alcohol consumption and the environmental conditions that promote it. *Journal on Studies on Alcohol and Drugs, 69*(4), 481–490.

Weiner, B. (1993). On sin versus sickness: A theory of perceived responsibility and social motivation. *American Psychologist, 48,* 957–965.

Weismer, S. E., Lord, C., & Esler, A. (2010). Early language patterns of toddlers on the autism spectrum compared to toddlers with developmental delay. *Journal of Autism and Developmental Disorders, 40,* 1259.

Weiss, L. H., & Schwarz, J. C. (1996). The relationship between parenting types and older adolescents' personality, academic achievement, adjustment, and substance use. *Child Development, 67*(5), 2101–2114. doi: 10.1111/j.1467-8624.1996.tb01846.x

Weitzman, E. R. (2004). Poor mental health, depression, and associations with alcohol consumption, harm, and abuse in a national sample of young adults in college. *The Journal of Nervous and Mental Disease, 192*(4), 269–277. doi:10.1007/s10803-010-0983-1

Welch, R. D., & Houser, M. E. (2010). Extending the four-category model of adult attachment: An interpersonal model of friendship attachment. *Journal of Social and Personal Relationships, 27*(3), 351–366. doi: 10.1177/0265407509349632

Wellman, H. M. (1990). *The child's theory of mind.* Cambridge, MA: MIT Press.

Wellman, H. M., Ritter, K., & Flavell, J. H. (1975). Deliberate memory behavior in the delayed reactions of very young children. *Developmental Psychology, 11,* 780–787.

Werker, J. F., & Stager, C. L. (1997, July 24). Infants listen for more phonetic detail in speech perception than in word-learning tasks. *Nature, 388,* 381–382.

Werner, E. E. (1990). Protective factors and individual resilience. In S. J. Meisel & J. Shonkoff (Eds.), *Handbook of early childhood intervention.* New York: Cambridge University Press.

Westendorp, R. G. J., & Kirkwood, T. B. L. (2007). The biology of ageing. In J. Bond, S. Peace, F. Dittmann-Kohli, & G. Westerhof (Eds.), *Ageing in society* (3rd ed., pp. 17–36). London: Sage.

Wheeler, I. (2001). Parental bereavement: The crisis of meaning. *Death Studies, 25*(1), 51–66.

When does the brain go blank? (2005, April 4). *Time, 165*(14), 26–27.

Whisman, M. A., & Kwon, P. (1993). Life stress and dysphoria: The role of self-esteem and hopelessness. *Journal of Personality and Social Psychology, 65,* 1054–1060.

Whitbeck, L. B., Hoyt, D. R., Simons, R. L., Conger, R. D., Elder, G. H., Jr., Lorenz, F. O., . . . , Huck, S. (1992). Intergenerational continuity of parental rejection and depressed affect. *Journal of Personality and Social Psychology, 63,* 1036–1045.

White, A. W., & Hoffman, H. L. (2007). Culturally competent care education: Overview and perspectives. *Journal of the American Academy of Orthopedic Surgeons, 15*(1), S80–S85.

White, J. (2006). Multiple invalidities. In J. A. Schaler (Ed.), *Howard Gardner under fire: The rebel psychologist faces his critics* (pp. 45–71). Chicago: Open Court.

White, L., & Rogers, S. J. (2000). Economic circumstances and family outcomes: A review of the 1990s. *Journal of Marriage and Family, 62,* 1035–1051.

White, L. A. (1949). *The science of culture: A study of man and civilization.* New York: Farrar, Straus.

Whiting, B. B., & Edwards, C. P. (1988). *Children of different worlds: The formation of social behavior.* Cambridge, MA: Harvard University Press.

WHO (World Health Organization). (2003). *The World Health Report 2003.* Geneva: World Health Organization.

WHO (World Health Organization). (2008). Gender and women's mental health. Retrieved from http:// www.who.int/mental _health/prevention/genderwomen/en/

WHO (World Health Organization). (2010). Obesity and overweight. *Global Strategy on Diet, Physical Activity, and Health.* Retrieved from http://www.who.int/dietphysicalactivity/publications/facts/obesity/en/

WHO/UNICEF/UNFPA/World Bank. (2010) *Trends in maternal mortality: 1990–2008.* Estimates developed by WHO, UNICEF, UNFPA, and the World Bank. Retrieved from http://whqlibdoc.who.int/publications/2010/9789241500265_eng.pdf

Whorf, B. L. (1956). *Language, thought, and reality.* Cambridge, MA: MIT Press.

Widmer, E. D., Treas, J., & Newcomb, R. (1998). Attitudes toward nonmarital sex in 24 countries. *Journal of Sex Research, 35*(4), 349–357.

Wiese, A. M., & Garcia, E. E. (2006). Educational policy in the United States regarding bilinguals in early childhood education. In B. Spodek & O. N. Saracho (Eds.), *Handbook of research on the education of young children* (2nd ed., pp. 361–387). Mahwah, NJ: Erlbaum.

Wifley, D. E., Tibbs, T. L., Van Buren, D. J., Reach, K. P., Walker, M. S., & Epstein, L. H. (2007). Lifestyle interventions in the treatment of childhood overweight: A meta-analytic review of randomized controlled trials. *Health Psychology, 26*(5), 521–532.

Wight, V. R., Raley, S. B., & Bianchi, S. M. (2008). Time for children, one's spouse and oneself among parents who work nonstandard hours. *Social Forces, 87*(1), 243–271. doi:10.1353/sof.0.0092

Wilcox, W. B. (Ed.). (2010). *The state of our unions, 2010.* Charlottesville, VA: National Marriage Project, University of Virginia. Retrieved from http://www.stateoffour unions.org

Wildsmith, E., Schelar, E., Peterson, K., & Manlove, J. (2010, May). Sexually transmitted diseases among young adults: Prevalence, perceived risk, and risk-taking behaviors. *Child Trends Research Brief.* Washington, DC: ChildTrendsOrg.

Wilke, M., Krägeloh-Mann, I., & Holland, S. K. (2007). Global and local development of gray and white matter volume in normal children and adolescents. *Experimental Brain Research, 178*(3), 296–307. doi:10.1007/s00221-006-0732-z

Willard, N. E. (2007). *Cyberbullying and cyberthreats: Responding to the challenge of online social aggression, threats, and distress.* Champaign, IL: Research Press.

Willcox, B. J., Willcox, D. C., & Suzuki, M. (2000). *Evidence-based extreme longevity: The case of Okinawa, Japan.* Okinawa Centenarian Study. Retrieved from http://okinawaprogram.com/ evidence.html

Willett, J. A. (2008). "A father's touch": Negotiating masculinity and sexual subjectivity in child care. *Sexuality & Culture, 12,* 275–290. doi:10.1007/s12119-008-9033-y

Willett, J. B., Singer, J. D., & Martin, N. C. (1998). The design and analysis of longitudinal studies of development and psychopathology in context: Statistical models and methodological recommendations. *Development and Psychopathology, 10,* 395–426.

Willi, J. (1997). The significance of romantic love for marriage. *Family Process, 36,* 171–182.

Williams, C. L., & Pleil, K. E. (2008). Toy story: Why do monkey and human males prefer trucks? Comment on "Sex differences in rhesus monkey toy preferences parallel those of children" by Hassett, Siebert, and Wallen. *Hormones and Behavior, 54,* 355–358. doi:10.1016/j.yhbeh.2008.05.003

Williams, D., Ishikawa-Brush, Y., Cleak, J., & Monaco, A. P. (2001). *The genetics of specific language impairment.* The Cambridge Language and Speech Project. Retrieved from http://www.well.ox.ac.uk/monaco/slidianne.html

Williams, J. C., & Cooper, H. C. (2004). The public policy of motherhood. *Journal of Social Issues, 60*(4), 849–865.

Williams, L. M., Gatt, J. M., Kuan, S. A., Dobson-Stone, C., Palmer, D. M., Paul, R. H., . . . , Gordon, E. (2009). A polymorphism of the MAOA gene is associated with emotional brain markers and personality traits on an antisocial index. *Neuropsychopharmacology, 34,* 1797–1809.

Willis, S. L., & Martin, M. (2005). *Middle adulthood: A lifespan perspective.* Thousand Oaks, CA: Sage.

Wilmoth, J. M., & Chen, P. C. (2003). Immigrant status, living arrangements, and depressive symptoms among middle-aged and older adults. *The Journals of Gerontology Series B: Psychological Sciences and Social Sciences 58,* S305–S313.

Wilson, J. Q. (1993). *The moral sense.* New York: Free Press.

Wilson, J. Q. (2002). *The marriage problem: How our culture has weakened its families.* New York: HarperCollins.

Wilson, M., & Daly, M. (1997). Life expectancy, economic inequality, homicide, and reproductive timing in Chicago neighborhoods. *British Medical Journal, 314,* 1271–1274.

Wilson, S. (2001). Attachment disorders: Review and current status. *Journal of Psychology, 135*(1), 37–52.

Wilson-Costello, D. (2007). Is there evidence that long-term outcomes have improved with intensive care? *Seminars in Fetal and Neonatal Medicine, 12*(5), 344–354.

Wimmer, J. S., Vonk, M. E., & Bordnick, P. (2009). A preliminary investigation of the effectiveness of attachment therapy for adopted children with reactive attachment disorder. *Child and Adolescent Social Work Journal, 26*(4), 351–360. doi:10.1007/s10560-009-0179-8

Wincze, J. P., & Carey, M. P. (2001). *Sexual dysfunction: A guide for assessment and treatment.* New York: Guilford Press.

Wingfield, N., Hobson, K., & Wakabayshi, D. (2010, December 31). Nintendo warns on 3D for children. *Wall Street Journal, 256*(154), A1–A4.

Wingo, P., Smith, R., Tevendale, H., & Ferré, C. (2010). Recent changes in the trends of teen birth rates, 1981–2006. *Journal of Adolescent Health, 48*(3), 281–288. doi:10.1016/j.jadohealth.2010.07.007

Winik, M. (2004). The time of my life. *Health, 18*(3), 98–100.

Wink, P., & Helson, R. (1993). Personality change in women and their partners. *Journal of Personality and Social Psychology, 65,* 597–605.

Winterich, J. A. (2007). Aging, femininity, and the body: What appearance changes mean to women with age. *Gender Issues, 24*(3), 51–69. doi:10.1007/s12147-007-9045-1

Witte, A. D., & Queralt, M. (2006). Infant and toddler care after welfare reform: A cross-state comparison. In N. J. Cabrera, R. Hutchens, & H. E. Peters (Eds.), *From welfare to child care: What happens to young children when single mothers exchange welfare for work?* (pp. 51–73). Mahwah, NJ: Erlbaum.

Wittenberg, E., Halpern, E., Divi, N., Prosser, L. A., Araki, S. S., & Weeks, J. C. (2006). The effect of age, race and gender on preference scores for hypothetical health states. *Quality of Life Research, 15*(4), 645–653. doi:10.1007/s11136-005-3514-3

Woerlee, G. M. (2004). Darkness, tunnels, and light. *Skeptical Inquirer, 28*(3), 28–32.

Wojcicki, J. M., & Heyman, M. B. (2010). Let's move—childhood obesity prevention from pregnancy and infancy onward. *The New England Journal of Medicine, 362*(16), 1457–1459. doi:10.1056/NEJMp1001857

Wolf, M. A. (2005). Life span well-being. In M. A. Wolf (Ed.), *Adulthood: New terrain* (pp. 53–59). New York: Wiley.

Wolfe, E. L., Davis, T., Guydish, J., & Delucchi, K. L. (2004, October 21). Mortality risk associated with perinatal drug and alcohol use in California. *Journal of Perinatology, 24,* 93–100.

Wolff, E. N. (2007). The retirement wealth of the baby boom generation. *Journal of Monetary Economics, 54*(1), 1–40. doi:10.1016/j.jmoneco.2006.12.009

Wolff, J. L., & Kasper, J. D. (2006). Caregivers of frail elders: Updating a national profile. *Gerontologist, 46*(3), 344–356.

Wolff, P. F. (1966). *The development of behavioral states and expression of emotions in early infancy: New proposals for investigation.* Chicago: University of Chicago Press.

Wolfson, A. R., & Carskadon, M. A. (2008). Sleep schedules and daytime functioning in adolescents. *Child Development, 69*(4), 875–867. doi: 10.2307/1132351

Womenaid International. (2003). *The Green Belt movement: Reforestation in Kenya.* Retrieved from http://www.womenaid.org/press/info/ development/greenbelt project .html

Wong, J. Y., & Earl, J. K. (2009). Towards an integrated model of individual, psychosocial, and organizational predictors of retirement adjustment. *Journal of Vocational Behavior, 75,* 1–13.

Wong, P. T. P., & Wong, L. C. J. (Eds.). (2006). *Handbook of multicultural perspectives on stress and coping.* New York: Springer.

Wood, J. J., & Repetti, R. L. (2004). What gets Dad involved? A longitudinal study of change in parental child caregiving involvement. *Journal of Family Psychology, 18*(1), 237–249.

Wood, R. B., Goesling, B., & Avellar, S. (2007, June 19). *The effects of marriage on health: A synthesis on recent research evidence.* Washington, DC: U.S. Department of Health & Human Services. Retrieved from http://www.healthymarriageinfo.org/docs/marriagehealth.pdf

Woodward, K. L. (1994). Erik Erikson: Teaching others how to see. *America, 171,* 6–8.

Woon, T., Masuda, M., Wagner, N., & Holmes, T. H. (1971). The Social Readjustment Rating Scale: A cross-cultural study of Malaysians and Americans. *Journal of Cross-Cultural Psychology, 2*(4), 373–386. doi:10.1177/002202217100200407

Woosley, J., Dennis, C., Robertson, K., & Goldstein, J. (2009). Perceived psychological well-being of children from divorced and nondivorced families. *Psi Chi Journal of Undergraduate Research, 14*(1), 34–39.

Workman, L., & Reader, W. (2008). *Evolutionary psychology* (2nd ed.). New York: Cambridge University Press.

World Bank. (2010). Life expectancy. *World Development Indicators.* Retrieved from http://data.worldbank.org/data-catalog/world-development-indicators

World Health Organization. (2007). *HIV surveillance, estimations and monitoring and evaluation.* Retrieved from http://www.who.int/hiv/topics/me/ en/index.html

World Health Organization. (2010). *Breastfeeding.* Retrieved from http://www.who.int/child_adolescent_health/topics/prevention_care/child/nutrition/breastfeeding/en/index.html

World Health Organization. (2010). Global strategy to stop health-care providers from performing female genital mutilation: UNAIDS, UNDP, UNFPA, UNICEF, UNHCR, UNIFEM, WHO, FIGO, ICN, IOM, WCPT, WMA, MWIA. Retrieved from http://whqlibdoc.who.int/hq/2010/WHO_RHR_10.9_eng.pdf

Wright, H. (1967). *Recording and analyzing child behavior.* New York: Harper & Row.

Wright, H., & Barker, R. C. (1950). *Methods in psychological ecology, a progress report.* New York: Oxford University Press.

Wright, J. C., & Huston, A. C. (1995). *Effects of educational TV viewing of lower income preschoolers on academic skills, school readiness, and school adjustment one to three years later.* Lawrence, KS: University of Kansas, Center for Research on the Influences of Television on Children.

Wright, M., & Lo, C. (2007, October). Infant formulas: A practical guide. *Family Practice Recertification, 29*(10), 33–39.

Wright, M. A. (1998). *I'm chocolate, you're vanilla: Raising healthy black and biracial children in a race-conscious world.* San Francisco: Jossey-Bass.

Wright, R. (1994). *The moral animal: Evolutionary psychology and everyday life.* New York: Pantheon.

Wu, Z., Costigan, C. L., Hou, F., Kampen, R., & Schimmele, C. M. (2010). Change and stability in cohabitation and children's educational adjustment. *Journal of Comparative Family Studies, 41*(4), 557–579.

Wyatt, G. E., Carmona, J. V., Loeb, T. B., Ayala, A., & Chin, D. (2002). In G. M. Wingwood & R. J. DiClemente (Eds.) *Handbook of women's sexual and reproductive health* (pp. 195–216). New York: Plenum.

Wyman, L. C. (1970). *Blessingway.* Tucson: University of Arizona Press.

Xu, H., Kotak, V. C., & Sanes, D. H. (2007). Conductive hearing loss disrupts synaptic and spike adaptation in developing auditory cortex. *Journal of Neuroscience, 27*(35), 9417–9426.

Xu, J., Kochanek, M. A., Murphy, S. L., & Tejada-Vera, B. (2010, May 20). Deaths: Final data for 2007. *National Vital Statistics Reports, 58*(19), 1–135. Retrieved from http://www.cdc.gov/nchs/data/nvsr/nvsr58/nvsr58_19.pdf

Xu, X., Hudspeth, C. D., & Bartkowski, J. P. (2006). The role of cohabitation in remarriage. *Journal of Marriage and Family, 68*(2), 261–274.

Yaffe, K., Kanaya, A., Lindquist, K., Simonsick, E., Harris, T., Shorr, R. I., . . . , Newman, A. B. (2004). The metabolic syndrome, inflammation and risk of cognitive decline. *Journal of the American Medical Association, 292*(18), 2237–2242.

Yale University. (2010, October 27). Yale professor speaks at White House on HIV and aging. [News Release]. Retrieved from http://dailybulletin.yale.edu/aricle.aspx?id=7932#

Yang, C. C., Wan, C. S., & Chiou, W. B. (2010). Dialectical thinking and creativity among young adults: A postformal operations perspective. *Psychological Reports, 106*(1), 79–92.

Yang, L., Planck, M., Krampe, R. T., & Baltes, P. B. (2006). Basic forms of cognitive plasticity extended into the oldest-old: Retest learning, age, and cognitive functioning. *Psychology and Aging, 21*(2), 372–378.

Yaratan, H., & Yucesoylu, R. (2010). Self-esteem, self-concept, self-talk and significant others' statements in fifth grade students: Differences according to gender and school type. *Procedia Social and Behavioral Sciences, 2,* 3506–3518. doi:10.1016/j.sbspro.2010.03.543

Yardley, W. (2009, May 23). First death for Washington assisted-suicide law. *New York Times,* A10. Retrieved from http://www.nytimes.com/2009/05/23/us/23suicide.html

Yarrow, L. J., MacTurk, R. H., Vietze, P. M., McCarthy, M. E., Klein, R. P., & McQuiston, S. (1984). Developmental course of parental stimulation and its relationship to mastery motivation during infancy. *Developmental Psychology, 20,* 492–503.

Yates, B. L., Djousse, L., Kurth, T., Buring, J. E., & Gaziano, M. J. (2008). Exceptional longevity in men: Modifiable factors associated with survival and function to age 90 years. *Archives of Internal Medicine, 168*(3), 284–290.

Yerbury, H. (2010). Who to be: Generations X and Y in civil society online. *Youth Studies Australia, 29*(2), 25–32.

"The young and jobless." (2010, July 24). New evidence that the minimum wage has hurt teenage workers. *Wall Street Journal, 256*(20), A12. Retrieved from EBSCO*host.*

Young, D. A., Lyon, L., & Acevedo, S. (2010). The role of dental hygiene caries management: A new paradigm. *The Journal of Dental Hygiene, 84*(3), 121–129. Retrieved from EBSCO*host.*

Younger, B. (1992). Developmental change in infant categorization: The perception of correlations among facial features. *Child Development, 63,* 1526–1535.

Youngstrom, E., Wolpaw, J. M., Kogos, J. L., Schoff, K., Ackerman, B., & Izard, C. (2000). Interpersonal problem-solving in preschool and first grade: Developmental change and ecological validity. *Journal of Clinical Child Psychology, 29*(4), 589–602.

Yu, T., Pettit, G.S., Lansford, J. E., Dodge, K. A., Bates, J. E. (2010). The interactive effects of marital conflict and divorce on parent-adult children's relationships. *Journal of Marriage and Family, 72*(2), 282–292. doi:10.1111/j.1741-3737.2010.00699.x

Zachry, W. (1978). Ordinality and interdependence of representation and language development in infancy. *Child Development, 49,* 681–687.

Zacks, R. T., & Hasher, L. (2006). Aging and long-term memory: Deficits are not inevitable. In E. Bialystok & F. I. M. Craik (Eds.), *Lifespan cognition: Mechanisms of change* (pp. 162–177). New York: Oxford University Press.

Zaidi, A., & Shuraydi, M. (2002). Perceptions of arranged marriages by young Pakistani Muslim women living in a Western society. *Journal of Comparative Family Studies, 33*(4), 495–514.

Zajonc, R. B., & Mullally, P. R. (1997). Birth order: Reconciling conflicting effects. *American Psychologist, 52*(7), 685–699. doi:10.1037/0003-066X.52.7.685

Zangl, R., & Mills, D. L. (2007). Increased brain activity to infant-directed speech in 6- and 13-month-old infants. *Infancy, 11*(1), 31–62.

Zautra, A. J., Reich, J. W., & Guarnaccia, C. A. (1990). Some everyday life consequences of disability and bereavement for older adults. *Journal of Personality and Social Psychology, 59,* 550–561.

Zeanah, C. H., & Gleason, M. M. (2010). Reactive attachment disorder: A review for DSM-V. American Psychiatric Association.

Zeanah, C. H., Smyke, A. T., Koga, S. F., & Carlson, E. (2005). Attachment in institutionalized and community children in Romania. *Child Development, 76*(5), 1015–1028. doi:10.1111/j.1467-8624.2005.00894.x

Zentall, S. S. (2006). *ADHD and education: Foundations, characteristics, methods, and collaboration.* Upper Saddle River, NJ: Pearson Education.

Zgoba, K. (2004). The Amber Alert: The appropriate solution to preventing child abduction? *Journal of Psychiatry & Law, 32*(1), 71–88. Retrieved from EBSCO*host.*

Zhan, C., Sangl, J., Bierman, A. S., Miller, M. R., Friedman, B., Wickizer, S., . . . , Meyer, G. S. (2001). Potentially inappropriate medication use in the community-dwelling elderly: Findings from the 1996 medical expenditure panel survey. *Journal of the American Medical Society, 286*(22), 2823–2830.

Zhang, S. Y. (1995). *Chinese parents' influence on academic performance.* New York State Association for Bilingual Education, 10, 46–53.

Zhao, X., Tang, R., Gao, G., Shi, Y., Zhou, J., Gou, S., . . . , He, L. (2007). Functional variants in the promoter region of Chitenase 3-Like 1 (CHI3L1) and susceptibility to schizophrenia. *American Journal of Human Genetics, 80*(1), 12–18.

Zigler, E., & Finn-Stevenson, M. (2010). A new role for schools: Providing child care and family support services. In David D. Preiss & Robert J. Sternberg (Eds.), *Innovations in educational psychology: Perspectives on learning, teaching, and human development* (pp. 359–379). New York: Springer.

Zigler, E. F. (1970). The environmental mystique: Training the intellect versus development of the child. *Childhood Education, 46,* 402–412.

Zigler, E. F. (1994). Foreword. In M. Hyson, *The emotional development of young children: Building an emotion-centered curriculum.* New York: Teachers College Press.

Zilli, I., Ficca, G., & Salzarulo, P. (2009). Factors involved in sleep satisfaction in the elderly. *Sleep Medicine, 10*(2), 233–239. doi:10.1016/j.sleep.2008.01.004

Zimmer-Gembeck, M. J., & Mortimer, J. T. (2006). Adolescent work, vocational development, and education. *Review of Educational Resources, 76*(4), 537–566.

Zimmerman, F. J., Christakis, D. A., & Meltzoff, A. (2007). Television and DVD viewing in children younger than 2 years. *Archives of Pediatric Adolescent Medicine, 161,* 473–479.

Zimmerman, J., & Thayer, E. S. (2003). *Adult children of divorce: How to overcome your parents' breakup and enjoy love, trust, and intimacy.* Oakland, CA: New Harbinger.

Zimmerman, J. E., Knaus, W. A., Sharpe, S. M., Anderson, A. S., Draper, E. A., & Wagner, D. P. (1986). The use and implications of do not resuscitate orders in intensive care units. *JAMA, 255*(3), 351–356.

Zimmerman, T. S., Aberle, J. T., Krafchick, J. L., & Harvey, A. M. (2008). Deconstructing the "Mommy Wars:" The battle over the best mom. *Journal of Feminist Family Therapy, 20*(3), 203–219. Retrieved from http://www.workandfamily.cahs.colostate.edu/articles/files/Mommy_Wars%5B1%5D.pdf

Zinn, M. (2009). (Th)ink Culture: Motivation and meaning making in modern tattoos. (Master's thesis, Queen's University, 2009). Queen's Theses and Dissertations. Retrieved from https://qspace.library.queensu.ca/bitstream/1974/5221/1/Zinn_Michael_J_200909_MEd.pdf

Zito, J. M., Safer, D. J., de Jong-van den Berg, L. T., Jahnsen, K., Fegert, J. M., Gardner, J. F., . . . , Valluri, S. C. (2008). A three-country comparison of psychotropic medication prevalence in youth. *Child and Adolescent Psychiatry and Mental Health, 2*(1), 26. doi:10.1186/1753-2000-2-26

Zito, J. M., Safer, D. J., Valluri, S., Gardner, J. F., Korelitz, J. J., & Mattison, D. R. (2007). Psychotherapeutic medication prevalence in Medicaid-insured preschoolers. *Journal of Child and Adolescent Psychopharmacology, 17*(2), 195–203.

Zoba, W. (1999). *Generation 2K: What parents and others need to know about the Millennials.* Downers Grove, IL: InterVarsity Press.

Zoccolillo, M., Paquette, D., & Tremblay, R. (2005). Maternal conduct disorder and the risk for the next generation. In D. J. Peppler, K. C. Madsen, C. Webster, & K. S. Levene (Eds.), *The development and treatment of girlhood aggression* (pp. 225–252). New York: Routledge.

Zolotor, A. J., Theodore, A. D., Coyne Beasley, T., & Runyan, D. K. (2007). Intimate partner violence and child maltreatment: Overlapping risk. *Brief Treatment and Crisis Intervention, 7*(4), 305–321.

Zucker, A. N., Ostrove, J. M., & Stewart, A. J. (2002). College-educated women's personality development in adulthood. Perceptions and age differences. *Psychology and Aging, 17*(2), 236–244.

CREDITS

PHOTOGRAPHS

Part 1

Opener: © Jupiter Images/BananaStock/Alamy; **Chapter 1** Opener: © Bob Daemmrich/The Image Works; p. 6: Courtesy of the Wellesley Public Library; p. 7: © Comstock Images; p. 12 (line): © Bettmann/Corbis; p. 12 (Elvis): Library of Congress Prints and Photographs Division [LC-USZ6-2067]; p. 12 (astronaut): © Digital Vision/Getty Images; p. 12 (buildings): © Sean Adair/Reuters/Corbis; p. 13: AP Photo/Akron Beacon Journal, Bob Demay; p. 24: © Jeffrey Greenberg/Photo Researchers, Inc.; p. 26: © Farooq Naeem/AFP/Getty Images;

Chapter 2 Opener: © Amy Snyder/Exploratorium; p. 34: Library of Congress Prints and Photographs Division [LC-USZ62-72266]; p. 36: © Sarah Putnam/The Picture Cube/Index Stock; p. 37: Robert Caplin/eyevine/Redux; p. 38: © David De Lossy/Getty Images; p. 41: © Joe McNally; p. 42: © Fotosmurf03/iStock; p. 45: © Bill Anderson/Photo Researchers Inc.; p. 47: © C Squared Studios/Getty Images; p. 53: © Matt Campbell/AFP/Newscom; p. 55: © Thomas McAvoy/TIME-Life Pictures/Getty Images.

Part 2

Opener: © Adrian Neal/Getty Images; **Chapter 3** Opener: © Photographer's Choice/Getty Images; p. 65: © David M. Phillips/The Population Council/Photo Researchers, Inc.; p. 72: © The McGraw-Hill Companies, Inc/Christopher Kerrigan, photographer; p. 76: The National Human Genome Research Institute; p. 80: Courtesy of Luba Djurdjinovic; p. 81: Courtesy of Corinne Crandell; p. 84: © Lennart Nilsson; p. 85: © Lennart Nilsson.

Part 3

Opener: © Barbara Brown/Shutterpoint; **Chapter 4** Opener: © Penny Gentieu/Babystock.com; p. 99: © PhotoDisc/Getty Images; p. 109: © Paige King/Shutterpoint; p. 112: © Claudia Daut/Reuters/Corbis; p. 114: © Janine Wiedel Photolibrary/Alamy; p. 117: © Bill Bachmann/The Image Works; p. 118 (sucking): © Laura Dwight; p. 118 (tonic neck): © MediaFocus.com; p. 118 (stepping): © Elizabeth Crews/The Image Works; p. 118 (grasping): © Losevsky Pavel/Shutterstock; p. 123: © 2004 image100 ltd.; p. 126: © Douglas M. Bovitt/AP Images

Chapter 5 Opener: © Bronwyn Kidd/Getty Images; p. 134: The McGraw-Hill Companies, Inc./Jill Braaten, photographer; p. 137: © Jeff Miller/University of Wisconsin-Madison;

p. 138 (top): © Ryan McVay/Getty Images; p. 138 (bottom): © Brand X Pictures/PunchStock; p. 139: © Stockbyte/Getty Images; p. 142: © Scientifica/ADEAR/Visuals Unlimited, Inc.; p. 148: © Ariel Skelley/Blend Image/Getty Images; p. 150: © Nicole Hill/Rubberball Productions/Getty; p. 152: © Michael Newman/PhotoEdit Inc.; p. 154: © Christina Kennedy/Alamy Images

Chapter 6 Opener: © Adam Crowley/Getty Images; p. 163: © Penny Gentieu/Babystock; p. 164: From: A. N. Meltzoff & M. K. Moore, "Imitation of facial and manual gestures by human neonates." Science, 1977, 198, 75–78.; p. 166: © Shehzad Noorani/The Image Works; p. 167: © Royalty-Free/Corbis; p. 169: © Kevin Peterson/Getty Images; p. 170: Courtesy of Carole Rosen; p. 180: © Ryan McVay/Getty Images; p. 183: © Jean-Philippe Soule.

Part 4

Opener: © BananaStock/age footstock; **Chapter 7** Opener: © Ariel Skelly/Getty Images; p. 196: © RubberBall Productions/Getty Images; p. 197: © Guy Cali/Corbis; p. 198: © Keith Eng; p. 199: © Royalty-Free/Corbis; p. 202: © Vicky Kasala Productions/The Image Bank/Getty Images; p. 204: © Amy Etra/PhotoEdit, Inc.; p. 206: © Peter Essick/Aurora Photos; p. 209: © Ellen B. Senisi/The Image Works; p. 212: © Kerstin Geier/Gallo Images/Getty Images; p. 215: © Royalty-Free/Corbis; p. 218: © Purestock/Getty Images; p. 219: Courtesy of Aleshia Larson; p. 220: © BananaStock/PunchStock

Chapter 8 Opener: © Brand X Pictures/PunchStock; p. 232: © Sean Justice/Corbis; p. 233: Courtesy of Corinne Crandell; p. 236 (top): Courtesy of Corinne Crandell; p. 236 (middle): © LWA/Sharie Kennedy/Getty Images; p. 236 (bottom): © MedioImages; p. 237 (top): © White Rock/Getty Images; p. 337 (bottom): © Royalty-Free/Corbis; p. 242: © Jose Luis Pelaez Inc/Blend Images/Corbis; p. 256: © BananaStock/PunchStock; p. 258: © Realistic Reflections/Getty Images; p. 261: © Rob Van Petten/Digital Vision/Getty Images.

Part 5

Opener: © Bananastock **Chapter 9** Opener: © Rebecca Emery/Getty Images; p. 272: Courtesy of Dr. Fumiko Hoeft, Stanford University School of Medicine; p. 275 (right): © SW Productions/Getty Images; p. 275 (left): © American Images, Inc/Getty; p. 276: © Fancy/Veer; p. 279: © Jonathan Alcorn/Zuma Press; p. 283: © Gabe Palmer; p. 286: © Rhoda Sidney/The Image Works; p. 290: Courtesy of Dr Ross Cunnington; p. 293: Courtesy of James Crandell; p. 298: ©PhotoAlto

p. 138 (top): © Ryan McVay/Getty Images;

Part 10 / Chapter 10 section
Chapter 10 Opener: Courtesy of Corinne Crandell; p. 304: © Stockbyte/Punchstock; p. 306: © Blend Images/Getty Images; p. 309: © Nomad/SuperStock; p. 315: Courtesy of Corinne Crandell; p. 321: © Image Source/PunchStock; p. 322: © BrandXPictures.com; p. 324: © Peter Dazeley/Photographer's Choice/Getty; p. 325: © Bananastock/AGE Fotostock.

Part 6

Opener: © Photodisc/Getty Images; **Chapter 11** Opener: © Tim Pannell/Corbis; p. 342: © Ellen B. Senisi/The Image Works; p. 344: © Kent Tompkins, www.kentart.com; p. 345: © Per-Anders Pettersson/Getty Images; p. 351: © Jack Star/Photolink/Gettyimages; p. 356: © Roger L. Wollenberg/UPI/Landov

Chapter 12 Opener: © Image Source/PunchStock; p. 374: © Corbis; p. 375: Courtesy of Corinne Crandell; p. 377: USDA; p. 380: © The McGraw-Hill Companies, Inc/John Flournoy, photographer; p. 382: © Blend Images/Alamy; p. 385: © Vicky Kasala/Getty Images; p. 395: © BananaStock/PunchStock.

Part 7

Opener: © Corbis/Punchstock; **Chapter 13** Opener: © Yuri Arcurs/Cutcaster; p. 409: © Daniel R. Patmore/AP Images; p. 412: © Courtesy of Ronald Dingwell; p. 418: Courtesy of Corinne Crandell; p. 423: © Spencer Grant/Photo Researchers, Inc; p. 427: © Thinkstock

Chapter 14 Opener: Courtesy of Corinne Crandell; p. 439: Courtesy of Corinne Crandell; p. 444: © Flying Colours Ltd.; p. 450: © Plush Studios/Brand X/Corbis; p. 453: AP Photo/Mike Hutchings; p. 465: © Jupiter Images; p. 469: © Left Lane Productions/Left Lane Productions/Corbis.

Part 8

Opener: © Robert Michael/Corbis; **Chapter 15** Opener: Courtesy of Corinne Crandell; p. 477: © Courtesy of Merida R. Radro; p. 478: © Cordelia Molloy/Photo Researchers, Inc.; p. 479: © Dr. p. Marazzi/Photo Researchers, Inc.; p. 483: © Science Photo Library RF/Getty Images; p. 495 (both): Courtesy of Drs Denise Head and David Balota; p. 502: © Brooks Kraft/Sygma/Corbis

Chapter 16 Opener: © Royalty-Free/Corbis; p. 512: © Comstock/Punchstock; p. 516: Courtesy of Corinne Crandell; p. 519: © Mark Andersen/Getty Images; p. 522: Courtesy of Corinne Crandell; p. 525: Courtesy of Corinne Crandell; p. 528: © Jose Luis Pelaez Inc/Blend Images LLC; p. 529: © Courtesy of Kevin Farrington and the Red Hat Society.

Part 9

Opener: Courtesy of Laurie Begendorf;
Chapter 17 Opener: © AFP/Getty Images;
p. 548: © Jim Wehtje/Getty Images; p. 550:
© Toru Hanai/Reuters/Landov; p. 551:
© Photodisc/Getty Images; p. 552: © Creatas/
PictureQuest; p. 556: © Michael Krasowitz/
Getty Images; p. 560: ©Big Cheese Photo/
PunchStock; p. 564: © Phototake Inc./Alamy;
p. 567: © Peter Turnley/Corbis
Chapter 18 Opener: © Jason Grow
Photography; p. 574: © Jupiter Images/Brand
X/Alamy; p. 576: © ColorBlind Images/Blend
Images/Corbis; p. 581: © Bob Ellis/Cortland
Standard; p. 582: © Enigma/Alamy; p. 584:
American Telecare's combined interactive
video and remote patient monitor,
LifeView™.; p. 585: AP Photo/Stew Milne;
p. 589: © Kraig Scarbinsky/Getty Images;
p. 590: Courtesy of Corinne Crandell; p. 591:
Courtesy of Corinne Crandell; p. 593: AP
Photo/Charlie Riedel; p. 599: Courtesy of
Dr. William C. Lane.

Part 10

Opener: © Skip Nall/Getty Images;
Chapter 19 Opener: © Ingram Publishing;
p. 607: © Archives Charmet/Bridgeman Art
Library; p. 610: © Grafton Marshall Smith/
Corbis; p. 617: © Ruth Fremson/The New
York Times/Redux; p. 265: © Devendra M.
Singh/AFP/Getty Images; p. 627: © Charles
Dharapak/Associated Press; p. 629 (left):
© Royalty-Free/Corbis; p. 629 (right):
© Deborah Roundtree/Getty Images.

TEXT

Chapter 1 p. 23 *Calvin and Hobbes*
© Watterson. Dist. By Universal Uclick.
Reprinted with permission. All rights reserved.
Chapter 2 Figure 2.5 Bronfenbrenner's
Ecological Theory of Development. From
Claire B. Kopp & Joseph B. Krakow, 1982,
Child Development in the Social Context,
p. 648. Used with permission from Addison-
Wesley/Pearson Education; Figure 2.6 Source:
From *Mankind Evolving: The Evolution
of the Human Species* by Theodosius
Dobzhansky. Copyright © 1962 by
Yale University. Reprinted by permission
of Yale University Press.
Chapter 3 Fig. 3.6 From Stephanie Nano,
"Scientists Give Free Access to Stem Cell
Lines," *Associated Press,* March 3, 2004.
Copyright 2004 Associated Press. Reprinted
by permission.
Chapter 4 p. 102 Permission granted by
Jennifer Vanderlaan, Colonie, New York from
www.birthingnaturally.net; Fig 4.3 MyDoctor
.com.au *Epidural: What You Need to Know;*
Fig 4.5 Adapted from V. A. Apgar, "A
proposal for a new method of evaluation of
the newborn infant," *Current Researches in
Anesthesia and Analgesia,* Vol. 32 (1953),
pp. 260–267. Reprinted by permission of

Lippincott Williams & Wilkins; p. 116 *For
Better or For Worse* © 1997 Lynn Johnston
Productions. Dist. By Universal Uclick.
Reprinted with permission. All rights
reserved.
Chapter 5 p. 147 *Hi & Lois* © King Features
Syndicate; Fig. 5.1 Vandewater, E. A., Rideout,
V. J., Wartella, E. A., Xuan, H., Lee, J. H., Shim,
M. (2007) Digital childhood: Electronic media
and technology use among infants, toddlers,
and preschoolers. *Pediatrics,* 119 (5), 1006–1015.
Used with permission; Table 5.1 Professor
Saffran's Infant Learning Lab, Psychology
Department, University of Wisconsin, Madison.
Reprinted by permission; Fig. 5.4 MacNeilage,
P. F. and Davis, B. L. (2000). Origin of the
internal structure of words. *Science.* 288,
527–531. http://www.utexas.edu/features/
archive/2005/babble.html; Figure 5.5 Used by
permission of babysigns.com.
Chapter 6 Figure 6.2 Source: From
Psychosocial Problems, Screening and the
Pediatric Symptom Checklist, Michael Jellnik,
M. D., and J. Michael Murphy, Ed. D.,
Boston, MA. 1999 depeds.org. Used by
permission.
Chapter 7 Fig 7.2 Adapted with permission
of Simon & Schuster Adult Publishing Group,
from *Solve Your Child's Sleep Problems* by
Richard Ferber. Copyright © 1985; Table 7.3
From: Lisa Feder-Feitel, "Does She Have a
Learning Problem?" *Child,* February 1997.
Copyright © 1997 by Lisa Feder-Feitel.
Originally published by Gruner & Jahr USA
Publishing in the February 1997 issue of
Child Magazine. Used with permission.
Chapter 8 Figure 8.3 Adapted from E. S.
Schaefer, "A Circumplex Model for Maternal
Behavior," *Journal of Abnormal and Social
Psychology,* Vol. 59 (1959), p. 232; and M. L.
Hoffman and L. W. Hoffman, *Review of
Child Development Research,* 1964; p. 248 *For
Better or For Worse* © 2007 Lynn Johnston
Productions. Dist. By Universal Uclick.
Reprinted with permission. All rights
reserved; Figure 8.5 "Little Ones" by
Alejandro Gonzalez. Copyright © 2010, USA
Today. Reprinted with permission.
Chapter 9 p. 295 *Dennis the Menace.*
Reprinted with permission of King Features/
North American Syndicate.
Chapter 10 Figure 10.2 Copyright © 2010 by
the American Psychological Association.
Reproduced with permission. American
Psychological Association. 2010. Stress in
America™ Findings. Released November 9,
2010. Washington, DC: Author. No further
reproduction or distribution is permitted
without written permission from the
American Psychological Association; Fig. 10.5
Zigler, E. F., Finn-Stevenson, M., and
Marsland, K. W. Child day care in the schools:
The school of the 21st century, *Child Welfare,*
74(6), 1303. Copyright © 1995 by Child
Welfare League of America, Inc. Reproduced
with permission of the Child Welfare League

of America, Inc. via Copyright Clearance
Center; p. 331 Drawing by Baloo, from *The
Wall Street Journal.* Used with permission,
Cartoon Features Syndicate.
Chapter 11 Figure 11.2 Lenroot, R. K.,
Giedd, J. J. N. (2006). Brain development in
children and adolescents: Insights from
anatomical magnetic resonance imaging.
Neuroscience and Biobehavioral Reviews, 30,
718–729. Used by permission from Elsevier;
Fig. 11.10 Susan Harter. (1999). *The
Construction of the Self: A Developmental
Perspective.* New York: Guilford Press, p. 70.
Reprinted by permission; Table 11.3 J., Foehr,
U. G., & Roberts, D. F. (2010). *Generation
M2: Media in the lives of 8- to 18-year-olds.*
Menlo Park, CA: Kaiser Family Foundation.
Retrieved November 23, 2010, from http://
www.kff.org/entmedia/upload/8010.pdf. This
information was reprinted with permission of
The Henry J. Kaiser Family Foundation. The
Kaiser Family Foundation, based in Menlo
Park, California, is a nonprofit, independent
national health care philanthropy and is not
associated with Kaiser Permanente or Kaiser
Industries; p. 359 ZITS © Zits Partnership,
King Features Syndicate.
Chapter 12 p. 371 *For Better or for Worse*
© 2005 Lynn Johnston Productions. Dist. By
Universal Uclick. Reprinted with permission.
All rights reserved; p. 383 ZITS © Zits
Partnership, King Features Syndicate.
Chapter 13 Table 13.2 Arnett, J. J. (2006).
What does it mean to be an adult? Young
people's conceptions of adulthood. In L.
Balter & C. S. Tamis-LeMonda (Eds.) *Child
Psychology: A Handbook of Contemporary
Issues* (p. 48). New York: Psychology Press.
Used by permission; Figure 13.1 Pew
Research Center. (2010, February 17).
*Millennials, A portrait of Generation Next:
Confident. Connected. Open to change.*
Retrieved December 28, 2010. http://
pewsocialtrends.org/files/2010/10/millennials-
confident-connected-open-to-change.pdf,
page 1 of report. Used by permission of Pew
Research Center; Figure 13.3 Pew Research
Center. (2010, February 17). *Millennials, A
portrait of Generation Next: Confident.
Connected. Open to change.* Retrieved
December 28, 2010. http://pewsocialtrends.
org/files/2010/10/millennials-confident-
connected-open-to-change.pdf, page 1 of
report. Used by permission of Pew Research
Center; Figure 13.6 Copyright © 2010 by the
American Psychological Association.
Reproduced with permission. American
Psychological Association. (2010). Stress in
America™ Findings. Released November 9,
2010. Washington, DC: Author. No further
reproduction or distribution is permitted
without written permission from the
American Psychological Association; p. 433
CALVIN AND HOBBES © 1995 Watterson.
Dist. By Universal Uclick. Reprinted with
permission. All rights reserved; Table 13.4

Holmes, T. H., & Rahe, R. H. (1967, August). The Social Readjustment Rating Scale. *Journal of Psychosomatic Research, 11,* 213–218. Copyright 1967 Published by Elsevier Science, Inc. All rights reserved. Permission to reproduce granted by the publisher.
Chapter 14 Figure 14.1 Adapted from Janet Shibley Hyde and John D. DeLamater, *Understanding Human Sexuality,* 6th edition. Copyright © 1997 by The McGraw-Hill Companies, Inc. Used with permission; Figure 14.6 Wilcox, W. B. (Ed.) (2010). *The state of our unions, 2010.* Charlottesville, VA: National Marriage Project, University of Virginia. Retrieved from http://www .stateofourunions.org. Used by permission.
Chapter 15 Fig 15.2 Source: From Geoffrey Cowley, "Attention: Aging Men", *Newsweek,* September 16, 1996, p. 68. Copyright © 1996 Newsweek, Inc. All rights reserved. Reprinted by permission; Figure 15.3 From "The Physical Activity Transition: A New Paradigm: 383: 1:05 PM–1:40 PM" by Peter Katzmarzyk from *Medicine & Science in Sports & Exercise,* January 1, 2008. Used by permission of Wolters Kluwer Health; Figure 15.4 Lindau, S. T., & Gavrilova, N. (2010). Sex, health, and years of sexually active life gained due to good health: evidence from two U.S. population-based cross sectional surveys of ageing. *BMJ, 340,* 810. doi: 10.1136/bmj.c810. Used by permission.
Chapter 16 Figure 16.5 Taylor, P., Funk, C., & Clark, A. (2007, July 1). As marriage and parenthood drift apart, public is concerned about social impact. PEW Research Center. Retrieved March 16, 2008, from http:// pewresearch.org/assets/social/pdf/Marriage. pdf, report p 2. Used by permission of Pew Research Center; Figure 16.6 *Source:* Parker,

K. (2011, January 18). A portrait of stepfamilies. Pew Research Center, Social and Demographic Trends. Retrieved from http:// pewsocialtrends.org/2011/01/13/a-portrait-of-stepfamilies. Used by permission of Pew Research Center; Figure 16.7 The Pew Research Center. (2010, March 18). The return of the multigenerational family household. Retrieved from http://pewsocialtrends. org/2010/03/18/the-return-of-the-multi-generational-family-household/. Used by permission of Pew Research Center; Figure 16.9 Zickhur, K. (2010, December 16). Generations: 2010. Pew Research Center's Internet & American Life Project, April 29– May 30, 2010 Tracking Survey. N=2,252 adults 18 and older. Retrieved from http:// www.pewinternet.org/~/media//Files/ Reports/2010/PIP_Generations_and_Tech10 .pdf. Used by permission of Pew Research Center; Table 16.1 Figure 1 from Herbert G. Lingren and Jayne Decker, *The Sandwich Generation: A Cluttered Nest.* Cooperative Extension, Institute of Agriculture and Natural Resources, University of Nebraska-Lincoln, December 1992, issued online August 1996, http://ianrpubs.unl.edu/family/ g1117.htm.
Chapter 17 Figure 17.4 Reprinted, with permission, from *The Columbus Dispatch;* Table 17.6 "Seven Stages of Faith Development" from *Stages of Faith: The Psychology of Human Development and the Quest for Meaning* by James W. Fowler. Copyright © 1981 by James W. Fowler. Reprinted by permission of HarperCollins Publishers; Figure 17.6 Alzheimer's Association. (2010). Alzheimer's disease: Facts and figures. *Alzheimer's & Dementia, 6*(2), 158–194. Retrieved from http://www

.alzheimersanddementia.com/article/ PIIS1552526010000142/fulltext#bib111. Used by permission of Alzheimer's Association.
Chapter 18 Figure 18.2 Lindau, S. T., Schumm, L. P., Laumann, E. O., Levinson, W., O'Muircheartaigh, C. A., & Waite, L. J. (2007). A study of sexuality and health among older adults in the United States. *New England Journal of Medicine, 357,* 762–774. Used with permission; Figure 18.5 Pew Research Center. (2010, March 8). *The return of the multi-generational family household.* Retrieved from http://pewsocialtrends.org/ files/2010/10/752-multi-generational-families. pdf. Used by permission of Pew Research Center; p. 599 Dr. William C. Lane.
Chapter 19 p. 609 Living Will: From Judy Oaks & Gene Ezell, *Dying and Death: Coping, Caring, Understanding* (Scottsdale, AZ: Gorsuch Scarisbrick, 1993), p. 197. Reprinted by permission of Judy Oaks Davidson; Figure 19.1 Hockenberry, J. J., Wilson, D., Winkelstein, M. L.: Wong's *Essentials of Pediatric Nursing,* ed. 7, St. Louis, 2005, p. 1259. Used with permission; Table 19.1 From Linda Emanuel (1998). "Facing Requests for Physician-Assisted Suicide: Toward a Practical and Principled Clinical Skill Set," *Journal of the American Medical Association,* Vol. 280, No. 7, pp. 643– 647. Copyright © 1998, American Medical Association. All rights reserved. Used with permission; Table 19.2 From Gary J. Kennedy, ed., *Suicide and Depression in Late Life,* p. 88. Copyright © 1996 by John Wiley & Sons, Inc. Reprinted by permission of John Wiley & Sons, Inc.; p. 632 From *Glimpses of Heaven* by Trudy Harris, pp. 18–20. Used by permission of Revell, a division of Baker Publishing Group.

NAME INDEX

Page references with a *t* indicate a table; figures and captions are indicated with *f*.

A

Achenbaum, W. Andrew, 573
Acredolo, Linda, 153
Adams, R. G., 529
Adelson, Joseph, 365, 366
Adler, Alfred, 257, 582
Affleck, Ben, 38
Ahmad, I., 235
Ainsworth, Mary, 108, 166, 167, 168, 171
Alkon, Daniel, 631
Allport, Gordon W., 508
Alsop, Ron, 440
American Academy of Pediatric
    Dentistry, 270
American Academy of Pediatrics (AAP),
    121, 135, 197, 203, 262
American Association of University
    Women (AAUW), 324, 375, 376, 385
American Cancer Society, 486
American Heart Association, 414
American Psychological Association
    (APA), 25, 27–28, 32, 172, 310, 425
American Society for Reproductive
    Medicine, 73
Anastasi, Anne, 52
Andersen, Hans Christian, 289
Anderson, K. G., 315, 316
Angelou, Maya, 43
Anthony, Casey, 630
Ariès, Philippe, 14
Aristotle, 38, 82, 364
Armstrong, Lance, 411
Arnett, Jeffrey, 404, 405, 439, 440
Ausubel, David P., 245
Autism Society of America (ASA), 173
Ayres, A. Jean, 171
Azar, B., 566

B

Bachorowski, J., 140
Baldwin, James, 360
Baltes, Margret, 11, 580–581
Baltes, Paul, 11, 554, 561, 573, 580–581, 581
Banchero, S., 362
Bandura, Albert, 46–48, 243, 294,
    374–375
Banerjee, I., 339
Bard, B., 136
Barker, T., 374
Barkow, Jerome, 54
Baum, Nehami, 316
Baumrind, Diana, 250, 251*f*, 252, 383
Bayley, Nancy, 346
Bell, Sylvia M., 166

Belsky, Jay, 245, 246, 340
Bettleheim, Bruno, 35
Binet, Alfred, 211, 499
Bishop, D. V. M., 218
Blaine, David, 605
Blake, Eubie, 560
Blieszner, R., 529
Bloom, Lois, 155
Blumstein, P., 519
Bond, B., 583
Bouchard, T. J., Jr., 213
Bower, T. G. R., 127
Bowlby, John, 54, 108, 166, 167
Brazelton, T. Berry, 105, 117
Brinkman, C., 200
Britton, A., 551
Brock, R. L., 458
Bromley, D. B., 280
Bronfenbrenner, Urie, 8, 10, 48–49, 178
Brown, Louise, 66
Brown, Roger, 150, 155
Brown, S. L., 586
Bruner, Jerome S., 140–141, 278
Buettner, Dan, 541
Bulanda, J. R., 586
Buntaine, R. L., 307
Bureau of Labor Statistics, 391
Burns, George, 560
Bush, George W., 73, 114, 630
Butler, Robert N., 620–621

C

Calkins, Mary Whiton, 6*f*
Calment, Jeanne, 548
Campos, Joseph, 163, 164
Camus, Albert, 531
Carlin, George, 617
Carlson, M. J., 388
Carlson, V. J., 171
Carroll, Lewis, 217
Cattell, R. B., 500
Cavanaugh, John C., 563
Centers for Disease Control and
    Prevention (CDC), 172, 173, 203,
    206, 273, 320, 347, 349*f*, 351, 386,
    417*f*, 427, 497
Cherbuin, N., 200
Cherlin, A., 462
Chess, S., 171, 174
Cheung, A., 218
Cho, Seung-Hui, 372
Chomsky, Noam, 54, 144–145, 218
Chua, Amy, 286–287
Churchill, Winston, 289
Clark, Connie, 567
Clayton, P., 339
Cleaver, E., 441, 444
Cleckley, Hervey M., 21
Clem, George, 533

Clementi, Tyler, 614
Clinton, Bill, 73
Colby, A., 502–503
Condon, W. S., 126–127
Cooney, Martin, 108
Coontz, Stephanie, 454, 455
Coopersmith, Stanley, 305
Cosby, Bill, 465
Cosmides, Leda, 54
Costa, P. T., Jr., 509, 511, 517
Costenbader, V. K., 307
Coulter, Dee Joy, 212
Courage, Mary, 222
Cox, M., 231
Coyle, Joseph, 200
Crandell, James, 292
Crockenberg, S., 252
Cruise, Tom, 289
Cruzan, Nancy, 618

D

Daly, M., 462
Damon, Matt, 38
Damon, W., 502–503, 503
Darlington, J., 462
Darwin, Charles, 21, 38, 163, 296
Davis, B. L., 152
Dawe, Helen, 24
Dawson-Tunik, T. L., 433
De Rosa, C. J., 355
Dean, R., 124
DeCasper, Anthony, 133, 134
DeLaguna, G., 154
Delpeuch, F., 416
Dement, William, 487
Demo, D., 231
Denton, K., 296
DePaulo, B. M., 447
Descartes, René, 38
Deur, J. L., 248
Dewey, John, 39
Diana, Princess, 607, 622
Diaz, Cameron, 38
Dick-Read, Grantly, 98
Dill, P. L., 423
Dingwell, Ronald, 412
Djurdjinovic, Luba, 80
Dowda, M., 275

E

Eadie, Betty J., 607, 630
Earle, A., 532
Edison, Thomas, 240, 289
Edmonds, Marilyn H., 155
Eimas, Peter D., 144
Einstein, Albert, 15, 43, 279, 289

SUBJECT INDEX

Boldface page locators indicate defined terms; tables are noted with a *t*; figures and captions are noted with *f*.

A

AARP, 182, 590, 593
AAUW. *See* American Association of University Women (AAUW)
Abortion, **72**
  China's one-child policy, 76
  crisis pregnancy centers (U.S.), 73
  decline in teen sexual activity rates, 389*t*
  emergency contraceptive pills and, 72
  ethical concerns, 72–73
  selective reduction procedures, 65–66
  spontaneous (miscarriage), 86, 518, 629–630
  teenage, 389
Absentee fathers, 317–318
Abstinence, 72
Abstinence and abstinence-plus programs, 371
Abstinence education, 388–389
Abuse (*see also drug abuse, substance abuse*)
  adolescent abuse of prescription drugs, 353, 394–396
  adolescent relationships, 385
  child abuse, 188–190, **189**, 189*f*, 249–250, 448, 460
  child abuse and neglect, 188–190, 189*f*, 248–250, 249*f*, 448, 460
  Child Abuse Prevention and Treatment Act, 249
  child neglect and abuse fatalities, 189*f*
  elder abuse, **596**, 596*f*, 596–598
  in cohabiting relationships, 448
  in remarried families, 462
  intergenerational transmission of, 190
  Patient Safety and Abuse Prevention Act, 597
  sexual abuse, **249**, 249–250, 410, 497
  sexual abuse victims, 410*f*
  signs of child abuse and maltreatment, 189–190
Acceptance stage of dying, 622
Accepting-demanding parents, 251
Accepting-permissive parents, 251
Accident vs. intentionality, 225
Accommodation, **45**
Accumulation of metabolic waste theory, 557
Acetylcholine, 564
Achieving stage, 502
Acquisitive stage, 502
Active relationship to environment, 52
Activity theory of aging, **579**
Acute illness, reduced with aging, 548–549
Adaptation, **44**, 44–45

Adapted Mind, The (Barkow, Cosmides, & Tooby), 54
ADD/ADHD. *See* Attention-deficit hyperactivity disorder (ADHD)
Administration on Aging (AOA), 598
  Area Agencies on Aging (AOA), 598
Adolescence. *See also* Chapters 11 and 12
  causes of death, 624*t*
  cognitive development, 6, 358–364
  emotional-social development, 6, 370–398
  growth spurt, 341, 341*f*
  health issues, 347–358
  historical changes and notion of, 5–6
  moral development, 364–366
  physical development, 338–347
  suicide warning signs, 615*t*
  surge in current population of, 337
Adolescence (Hall), 370
Adoption, 169–170, 185, 213, 274, 468
  heritability traits, 290,
  mothers-by-choice and, 320
  nature versus nurture controversy, 51–52
  Reactive attachment disorder (RAD), **169**, 169–170
  same-sex parents, 460–461, 465
Adolescent growth spurt, **341**, 341*f*
Adrenal glands, 339
  aging and changes, 485, 554*f*
Adrenaline, 105
Adult day care, **595**
Adult group homes, 596
Adulthood, 404, 406–407, 407*t*, 411. *See also* Early adulthood; Late adulthood; Middle adulthood
Advance directive, **608**, 619
Adventist Health Study–1 and –2, 550
Africa
  age-grade systems, 408–409
  children and age of walking, 124
  female genital mutilation (FGM), 344–345
  HIV/AIDS, 88, 112, 417
  polygyny, 452
African Americans or blacks
  age of menarche, 73, 342
  arthritis rates, 483
  attention-deficit hyperactivity disorder medications, 200
  bulimia in females, 348
  cardiovascular disease risk, 491
  childbirth beliefs and practices, 101*t*
  circumcision at puberty, 107
  conceptions of adulthood, 407*t*
  cultural beliefs of labor and delivery, 101
  cultural expectations for, 235, 236*t*
  diabetes rates, 494
  early menopause, 484
  family ties in adolescence and, 382, 382*f*

HIV risk and, 417
infant and caregiver attachment, 108
infant prematurity death rates, 111
kinship ties extended, 522
lactose maldigestion, 483
marriage rates, 522
menarche timing in girls, 342, 343–344
obesity rates and, 73
physical development of, 270
psychotropic medications and, 200
schools and, 329–330
self-esteem of girls, 306
sickle-cell anemia and, 79, 494
SIDS rates and, 118, 119*f*
single-parent mothers, 462
stable marriages among, 522
stroke risk and, 494
suicide rates of, 614
teenage parents, 387
therapeutic agents sought, 548*f*
Afterbirth, **104**
Age
  birthrates for teens by, 357*f*
  civilian labor force by, 466*f*
  depression and, 495
  direct and indirect operation of, 13
  for full Social Security benefits, 546*t*
  job satisfaction and, 531–532
  marriage and remarriage by, 521*t*
  as master status, 13
  maternal, 90–91, 98*f*
  moral development and, 297
  norms and the social clock, 407–408
  self-esteem and, 306
  sexual abuse victims by, 410*f*
  social norms and, 13–14
  suicide rates by, 614*f*
Age cohorts, **11**, 12*t*. *See also specific generations*
Age grading, **408**, 408–409, 513
Ageism, **540**
Age norms, **408**, 408–409
Age-related macular degeneration (AMD), **477**, 477–478
Age strata, **13**
Aggression, **258**
  bullying, 324–325
  cyberbullying, 363, 380
  in early childhood, 258–259
  youth violence, 397–398
Aging, **407**. *See also* Late adulthood; Longevity; Middle adulthood
  beginning of old age, 537
  biological, 553–557
  biological theories of, 557–558
  care for the elderly, 527–528, 583–584, 588–589
  caregiver burnout, 597–598
  changing conceptions of, 14–15
  decline in cognitive functioning and, 563–566